The Columbia University
College of Physicians
and Surgeons

COMPLETE
HOME
MEDICAL
GUIDE

The Columbia University COLLEGE OF PHYSICIANS AND SURGEONS

MEDICAL EDITORS

DONALD F. TAPLEY, M.D.
*Senior Deputy Vice-President for Health Sciences
and Alumni Professor of Medicine, Columbia University*

ROBERT J. WEISS, M.D.
*DeLamar Professor and Dean Emeritus,
Columbia University School of Public Health*

THOMAS Q. MORRIS, M.D.
*President
Presbyterian Hospital in the City of New York*

GENELL J. SUBAK-SHARPE, M.S.
EDITORIAL DIRECTOR

DIANE M. GOETZ
ASSOCIATE EDITOR

COMPLETE HOME MEDICAL GUIDE

Crown Publishers, Inc.

NEW YORK

CROWN is a trademark of Crown Publishers, Inc.

Published by Crown Publishers, Inc., 225 Park Avenue South, New York, New York 10003 and represented in Canada by the Canadian MANDA Group

Manufactured in the United States of America

Library of Congress Cataloging-in-Publication Data
Main entry under title:

Complete home medical guide.

   Includes index.
   1. Medicine, Popular.   I. Columbia University.
College of Physicians and Surgeons.
RC81.C716 1985   613   85-4150
ISBN 0-517-55842-4
0-517-56892-6 (paper)

Book design by Anita Karl and Jim Kemp

10 9 8 7 6

This edition printed in 1988.

Contents

Acknowledgments

OVER THE LAST THREE YEARS, scores of people have been involved in creating *The Columbia University College of Physicians and Surgeons Complete Home Medical Guide*. While it is impossible to cite all of the many dedicated physicians, consultants, writers, editors, illustrators, and others who have contributed so much to this book, there are some whose dedication and efforts deserve special mention.

First and foremost, we acknowledge the support and efforts of the entire College of Physicians and Surgeons community. Almost 60 physician/specialists at P&S have worked with the editors on this volume. In addition to their myriad other duties, they have drafted manuscripts during vacations and at other free moments, without hesitation or complaint.

A team of skilled medical writers and editors has also been involved in creating this book. They include Victoria Chesler, Larry Frederick, Connie Grzelka, Judith Hoffmann, Christopher Hallowell, Maxine Karpen, Cynthia Keyworth, Susan Lowe, Helene MacLean, Joy Nowlin, Emily Paulsen, Caroline Tapley, Roberta Thumin, Timothy Wetmore, and Lois Wingerson.

We have also worked with a team of leading medical artists, headed by Robert Demarest, John W. Karapelou, and Lauren Keswick from the P&S Audio Visual Service. Illustrations have also been provided by Douglas Cramer, Leonard Dank, Glenna Deutsch, Marsha Dohrmann, Carol Donner, Douglas Dunn, Neil O. Hardy, Kittie Herman, and Beth Willert. In addition, illustrations have been provided by the American Heart Association, the American Cancer Society, and Biomedical Information Corporation. John Bernhartsen of the U.S. Coast Guard and Roger Miller of the Food and Drug Administration have provided valuable help and expertise. Stanley C. Stevens, Sr., of Personal Health Profile designed the medical record charts.

Desiree Cooper; Yolanda Lipari; Mary McLean; David, Sarah, and Hope Subak-Sharpe; Russell Wotman, and Nina Zarnett all have pitched in to help type the manuscript. Diane Goetz, Emily Paulsen, and Josephine Mannino have served above and beyond the call of duty in seeing to the many details involved in preparing a manuscript of this magnitude.

The staff at Crown including Rusty Porter and Teresa Nicholas (production), Jim Davis and Peggy Goddard (design), Jean Thompson Davis and Amy Boorstein (production editors), and particularly our editors, Betty Prashker, Laurie Stark, and David Groff, deserve special thanks for their patience, guidance, and invaluable insight. Finally, the many spouses who have done everything from babysit and keep dinners waiting to reviewing manuscripts and offering practical suggestions deserve an extra tribute.

List of Editors and Contributors

MEDICAL EDITORS

DONALD F. TAPLEY, M.D.
Alumni Professor of Medicine
Senior Deputy Vice-President of the Health
Sciences

THOMAS Q. MORRIS, M.D.
Professor of Clinical Medicine
President of Presbyterian Hospital

ROBERT J. WEISS, M.D.
DeLamar Professor
and Dean Emeritus, Columbia University
School of Public Health

EDITORIAL DIRECTOR

GENELL J. SUBAK-SHARPE, M.S.

ASSOCIATE EDITOR

DIANE M. GOETZ

CONTRIBUTORS

KENNETH ATTSCHULER, M.D.
Lecturer in Psychiatry

STEPHEN J. ATWOOD, M.D.
Associate Professor of Clinical Pediatrics

ARTHUR BANK, M.D.
Professor of Medicine

A. L. LOOMIS BELL, JR., M.D.
Professor of Clinical Medicine

J. THOMAS BIGGER, JR., M.D.
Professor of Medicine

ANN BREUER, M.D.
Assistant Professor of Rehabilitation

PETER J. BUCHIN, M.D.
Assistant Professor of Clinical Medicine

PAUL F. CALIFANO
Assistant Clinical Professor of Psychiatry

RITA A. CHARON, M.D.
Assistant Professor of Medicine

WILLIAM J. DAVIS, M.D.
Associate Professor of Clinical Pediatrics

HAROLD M. DICK, M.D.
Frank E. Stinchfield Professor and Chairman of
Orthopaedic Surgery

ANTHONY DONN, M.D.
Clinical Professor of Ophthalmology

KENNETH C. FINE, M.D.
Assistant Professor of Clinical Medicine

KENNETH A. FRANK, PH.D.
Associate Clinical Professor of Psychology

RICHARD A. GARDNER, M.D.
Clinical Professor of Psychiatry

S. RAYMOND GAMBINO, M.D.
Adjunct Professor of Pathology

RICHARD J. GLAVIN
Assistant Clinical Professor of Psychiatry

HENRY GREENBERG, M.D.
Associate Clinical Professor of Medicine

BARRY J. GURLAND, M.D.
Professor of Clinical Psychiatry

KAREN HEIN, M.D.
Associate Professor of Pediatrics
Albert Einstein College of Medicine

STANLEY S. HELLER, M.D.
Associate Clinical Professor of Psychiatry

DONALD A. HOLUB, M.D.
Professor of Clinical Medicine

ISRAELI JAFFE, M.D.
Professor of Clinical Medicine

RAPHAEL JEWELEWICZ, M.D.
Associate Professor of Clinical Obstetrics and Gynecology

ERIC JOSEPHSON, PH.D.
Lecturer, School of Public Health

NORMAN KAHN, D.D.S., PH.D.
Professor of Pharmacology and Professor of Dentistry

NEIL KAVEY, M.D.
Associate Clinical Professor of Psychiatry

DONALD KORNFELD, M.D.
Professor of Clinical Psychiatry

PHYLLIS LEPPERT, M.D.
Assistant Professor of Obstetrics and Gynecology and Pediatrics

ROBERT LEWY, M.D.
Associate in Clinical Medicine

ALEXANDER N. LEVAY, M.D.
Clinical Professor of Psychiatry

IRWIN MANDEL, D.D.S.
*Professor of Dentistry
Director of the Center for Clinical Research in Dentistry*

ROBERT B. MELLINS, M.D.
Professor of Pediatrics

JAY I. MELTZER, M.D.
Clinical Professor of Medicine

MICHAEL R. MILANO, M.D.
Associate Clinical Professor of Psychiatry

PHILIP R. MUSKIN, M.D.
Assistant Clinical Professor of Psychiatry

HARRIS M. NAGLER, M.D.
Assistant Professor of Urology

HAROLD C. NEU, M.D.
*Professor of Medicine
Head, Infectious Diseases*

CARL A. OLSSON, M.D.
John K. Lattimer Professor and Chairman of Urology

TIMOTHY A. PEDLEY, M.D.
Professor and Vice Chairman, Department of Neurology

JOHN R. ROGLIERI. M.D.
Assistant Professor of Clinical Medicine

STEPHEN N. ROSENBERG, M.D.
Associate Professor of Clinical Public Health

LEWIS P. SCHNEIDER, M.D.
Assistant Professor of Clinical Medicine

MALCOLM H. SCHVEY, M.D.
Associate Clinical Professor of Otolaryngology

LAWRENCE SHARPE, M.D.
Assistant Professor of Clinical Psychiatry

HAMILTON SOUTHWORTH, M.D.
Special Lecturer in Medicine

JOSEPH G. SWEETING, M.D.
Professor of Clinical Medicine

FRANCIS C. SYMONDS, JR., M.D.
Associate Professor of Clinical Surgery

ROBERT N. TAUB, M.D.
Professor of Clinical Medicine

W. DUANE TODD, M.D.
Professor of Clinical Obstetrics and Gynecology

ROBERT R. WALTHER, M.D.
Associate Clinical Professor of Dermatology

RALPH WHARTON, M.D.
Clinical Professor of Psychiatry

RICHARD WORTMAN, M.D.
*Assistant Professor of Psychiatry
Mount Sinai School of Medicine*

STUART YUDOFSKY, M.D.
Associate Professor of Clinical Psychiatry

The Editors

DONALD F. TAPLEY, M.D., Alumni Professor of Medicine and Senior Deputy Vice-President for the Health Sciences, has spent most of his medical career at the College of Physicians and Surgeons. After completing a fellowship at Oxford University, he joined the P&S faculty as an assistant professor of medicine in 1956, rising to dean in 1974. During his ten-year tenure as dean, Dr. Tapley presided over the tremendous growth of the institution and is widely acknowledged as one of the most notable medical-school deans in the nation. His medical specialty is endocrinology, and over the years he has published a number of papers in this field, with special emphasis on the role of the thyroid hormones.

ROBERT J. WEISS, M.D., is deeply involved in the socioeconomic aspects of medicine. A psychiatrist by training, his academic appointments have included professor and chairman of the department of psychiatry at Dartmouth Medical School and associate dean for health planning at Harvard Medical School. He returned to P&S, his alma mater, in 1975 as director of the Centers for Community Health and professor of psychiatry and social medicine. He became dean of the School of Public Health in 1980, and in a short time, reestablished it as one of the nation's leaders in the field. He is now dean emeritus and DeLamar Professor of Public Health. Throughout his medical career, Dr. Weiss has worked to bring health education to the general public, a mission he is continuing as editor of the new *Health & Nutrition* newsletter from the Columbia School of Public Health.

THOMAS Q. MORRIS, M.D., has also spent most of his medical career at P&S—first as a student and trainee and then as a physician, educator, and administrator. His positions have included director of the student health service, acting chairman of the department of medicine, associate dean for Academic Affairs, and Vice-Dean of the Faculty of Medicine. He is now president of Presbyterian Hospital. His many honors include the Dean's Award for Outstanding Contributions to Teaching. He is also a highly regarded medical scientist, particularly recognized for his work in liver disease.

GENELL J. SUBAK-SHARPE is a medical writer and editor who began her journalism career on the metropolitan staff of the *New York Times*. Since then, she has served as vice-president of Biomedical Information Company and as editor of a number of magazines for both physicians and consumers and is the author, coauthor, or editor of twelve books in health and medicine. She is now president of her own medical communications company and editorial director of the *Health & Nutrition* newsletter.

FOREWORD:
How to Use This Book

The Columbia University College of Physicians and Surgeons Complete Home Medical Guide is a unique reference book that teaches you about your body in both sickness and health. Each organ system and its function is described in depth and there are anatomically correct medical illustrations for each.

The book is divided into eight parts, each one devoted to a particular facet of medicine and health. In Part One, you have a guide to the American medical system and how to use it. Questions discussed in this section include: How do you find a doctor who is right for you and your family? When do you seek a second opinion? How can you help control mushrooming medical costs? How can you help meet the medical needs of aging parents and other elderly people? There is also a comprehensive guide to common medical tests which helps you determine whether a test is needed, what it involves, and what you and your doctor should learn from it.

Part Two deals with medical emergencies and what you should do until the doctor comes. Life-saving techniques like cardiopulmonary resuscitation and the Heimlich maneuver for choking victims are illustrated. There is also a directory of hundreds of common first-aid procedures, covering everything from broken bones and cuts to electrocution, drownings, and animal bites. The chapter on poisoning lists common household poisons and also includes a nationwide directory of poison information centers and telephone numbers.

Part Three is devoted to your body and how it works. There is a full-color atlas showing the major organ systems and a chapter on how they work in concert. Sexual and reproductive health and pregnancy and childbirth are discussed in detail, as are the major life stages from infancy through aging.

Part Four is devoted to health maintenance. There are self-tests to help determine your own health quotient and discussions of lifestyle factors, such as smoking, alcohol and substance abuse, nutrition, exercise, and stress management and their impact on your health.

The largest section of the book—Part Five—is devoted to the diagnosis, treatment, and prevention of disease. Each of the twenty chapters in this section covers a category of disease, ranging from cancer and heart disease to allergies and mental and emotional disorders. Each chapter presents an overview of the particular class of disease and organ system(s) involved, followed by discussions of specific disorders and their diagnosis and treatment.

The proper use of drugs is the focus of Part Six. The major categories of drugs are included, along with a listing of what you should include in your home medicine chest.

Part Seven is a directory of resources, with listings of major health agencies, organizations, and sources of information. There is special emphasis on resources available to the disabled and people with chronic disease.

Although every effort has been made to avoid medical jargon and to explain the meaning of technical terms throughout the book, Part Eight is intended to be of further use by presenting a dictionary of common medical terms. There is also a listing of prefixes, word roots, and suffixes to help you determine the meaning of medical terms that may not be in this dictionary.

In keeping with the overall goal of this home medical guide, the appendix offers the basics of a personal medical record system for you and your family. The forms should be used to keep track of things such as major and minor illnesses, medications used, and visits to physicians, dentists, and other health-care professionals.

Keeping your own medical records is becoming increasingly important in our highly mobile society and era of medical specialization. Very few of us go through life with a single family physician. It is important that you be able to give each doctor you see a detailed medical history regarding past illnesses and treatments, but very few of us can accurately remember what tests we have had done, what medications we have taken, or the details of past treatments. Whenever you visit a doctor or clinic, ask your physician to summarize any diagnosis, tests, or treatment for your own medical records. By keeping such records, you can save time and money by avoiding unnecessary duplication, and you become a more informed partner in your own health care.

In buying *The Complete Home Medical Guide*, you have made a major investment in taking charge of your own health. This book should be the most-used volume in your home health library.

How to Keep Your Book Up to Date

Although we have made every effort to provide the latest medical information in this book, there are important new developments occurring almost daily. To keep your *Complete Home Medical Guide* as current as a monthly magazine, Columbia University's School of Public Health has created the *Health and Nutrition* newsletter. This monthly publication is filled with practical, up-to-the-minute information designed specifically to keep the *Complete Home Medical Guide* up to date. To obtain a free sample copy, with no obligation, simply send a stamped, self-addressed, business-size envelope to:

Health and Nutrition Newsletter
G. S. Sharpe Communications, Inc.
606 West 116th Street, #71
New York, New York 10027

Part One

THE NATURE
OF HEALTH
AND MEDICINE

1 An Overview of Medicine Today

Stephen N. Rosenberg, M.D.

AMERICAN MEDICINE has entered a period of profound and healthy reassessment. Advances since World War II have been breathtaking; but, after decades of unqualified enthusiasm, practitioners, educators, and—most of all—the public have begun to question the perfection of the modern medical miracle.

This is to be expected. Rapid progress in any field is rarely uniform or even orderly, and periodic evaluation and adjustment are necessary parts of long-term growth.

In medicine, enormous changes have occurred in the postwar period. A multitude of new diagnostic and therapeutic techniques—and even a few preventive strategies—have emerged from an intensive national biomedical research effort and from the adaptation of "space age" technological breakthroughs, particularly in the area of microelectronics.

We should not be alarmed by the recent realizations that these advances have been somewhat uneven, that changes in the content of medicine have been accompanied by changes in its structure, or even that the positive benefits of progress are mixed with some negative results. These realizations can be healthy if they result in constructive corrections.

The uneven growth of medical science is most striking when we consider the balance between the "hard," or laboratory, sciences and the so-called "soft" social sciences. In the excitement of technological conquest, the interpersonal communication skills that once formed the bulk of a physician's armamentarium have been allowed to lie dormant, perhaps even to atrophy.

With amazing speed, the structure of American medicine—once focused on the office-based solo general practitioner, paid in cash—has evolved into a system in which specialization, partnerships, third-party payments, and hospital facilities now play pivotal roles.

The results of technological progress, which have undeniably brought benefits to millions, include increasingly common problems of iatrogenic or man-made disease, as well as problems of skyrocketing costs.

In addressing these issues, the public, medical administrators, and clinicians need not ignore or deprecate the real benefits of technological progress. An understanding of the shortcomings as well as the triumphs of modern medicine can assist the individual patient and the public at large. Improved technology can be of even greater benefit when it is applied in an individual patient–physician relationship and a health-care system brought into a new balance.

TECHNOLOGICAL ADVANCES

THE METHODS USED to diagnose and treat disease have changed so rapidly and extensively in the past 40 years that the *majority* of the diagnostic tests, medications, and surgical techniques in use in the 1980s were unavailable to patients in the 1940s. This astounding rate of change has been the result of a worldwide explosion of knowledge in which the United States played a leading role.

Wars have always been times of medical progress, and World War II was no exception to this historical irony. Military and civilian injuries on an unprecedented global scale spurred on efforts to improve surgical techniques and to make whole blood transfusion a practical procedure. Even more momentous were the breakthroughs in antimicrobial therapy. For as long as human beings have inhabited the earth, they have been almost helpless when invaded by parasites and bacteria. This millennia-long relationship began to change in 1935, when sulfanilamide was discovered; it was the first substance that was nontoxic to man but could defeat a bacterial infection. Then, during and immediately after World War II, antimalarial drugs and an entire armamentarium of antibiotics were developed, including penicillin, streptomycin, chloramphenicol, and the tetracyclines.

In the period after the Second World War, this momentum was not allowed to die. Instead, medicine embarked on a golden age of technological mastery. In 1910, the Carnegie Foundation for the Advancement of Teaching had issued the report of a committee chaired by Abraham Flexner. The famous Flexner Report called for a restructuring of medical education based on solid scientific principles. In the late 1940s, the federal government committed itself to the full realization of this idea through massive funding of biomedical research. In 1947, only $85 million was spent nationally on such research efforts. By the 1970s, several billions of dollars would be devoted to biomedical research annually, primarily through the funding, by the National Institutes of Health, of medical school faculty research efforts. In the 1950s, the pharmaceutical industry became a major participant in this massive undertaking.

Large-scale biomedical research led quickly to a veritable explosion of knowledge which has totally transformed modern medicine. The extent of these changes, and the rapidity of their occurrence, have led to major problems which will be discussed shortly. But the truly scientific foundation that has been built is a strong one which must be appreciated. The current situation in medicine is an excellent example of the interplay between basic research and applied technology.

Basic scientists, studying the molecular chemistry of enzymes, the genetic transmission of immunity, or the epidemiology of nutritional factors in cancer, add to our understanding of some fundamental biological process. Applied research follows in an attempt to utilize this basic knowledge in practical prevention, diagnosis, and treatment. A number of researchers studied skin grafts during the 1940s and early 1950s. By 1954, Medawar learned enough from skin grafting to describe how the body rejects foreign tissue. Within 4 years, Schwartz and Dameshek found a drug that would suppress this rejection, and within another 4 years, in 1962, the first successful transplantation of a "foreign" kidney (one that had not come from an identical twin) was carried out.

The rate at which basic biomedical discoveries are made has been accelerating rapidly, as has the speed with which they are transformed into practical technology.

One additional historical factor must be added to complete the background for today's technological advances in medicine. Reacting to the Soviet Union's launch of Sputnik in 1957, this country embarked on a prodigious expansion of training in mathematics and scientific and engineering fields, such as electronics and metallurgy. The results were the "space age" technologies best exemplified by ever-smaller, yet more powerful, computers. In the last 2 decades, these spin-offs of the space race have been increasingly important in medical technology, contributing to laboratory diagnosis (automated analysis of microsamples of blood), radiology and associated fields (computerized axial tomography or "CT" scans, nuclear medicine, ultrasound), surgery (artificial blood vessels, heart valves, and joints), and the intensive care of medical, obstetrical, surgical, and pediatric conditions.

A comprehensive catalogue of the medical advances which have resulted from biomedical research and space age technology would require an entire volume, and indeed, much of this book is devoted to describing them. Representative examples from several medical fields are cited here to illustrate their impact and they are discussed in detail in the following chapters.

Bacterial diseases such as pneumonia in adults, ear infections in children, and wound infections in surgical patients of all ages can now be treated with a much wider range of antibiotics. These are often safer than early antibiotics such as chloramphenicol (which has been limited to use in special situations) and effectively combat a much broader spectrum of bacteria.

We are just beginning to develop treatments for viral diseases, but have succeeded in decreasing many viral illnesses dramatically through immunization. Measles, mumps, and rubella (German measles), once almost universal among children and, in the case of rubella, responsible for numerous birth defects, are becoming uncommon. One viral disease, smallpox, which was a leading cause of death internationally, has actually been eradicated from the face of the earth. Polio, at least in industrialized nations, may soon face a similar fate.

Thousands of people with inflammatory diseases such as arthritis have benefited from the development of steroids (such as cortisone) and then nonsteroidal anti-inflammatory drugs. In the case of one specific kind of arthritis—gout—a precise understanding of body chemistry has yielded a drug (allopurinol) which specifically counteracts the responsible genetic defect.

Another set of biomedical discoveries led recently to a medication (cimetidine) which acts on the surface of acid-producing cells in the stomach to control peptic ulcer disease.

The intensive care now provided routinely after heart attacks includes, when needed, electronic monitoring of cardiac function, drugs to correct faulty rhythms and to control blood pressure, potent diuretics to rid the body of extra fluids, and the insertion of artificial pacemakers.

The field of psychiatry has been revolutionized by antipsychotic, antianxiety (tranquilizing), and antidepressive drugs, so that patients once hospitalized for years are now back home within weeks, and the total number of American psychiatric hospital beds is a fraction of the number in 1950.

Maternal and infant complications in obstetrics have declined with better prenatal care, including the careful control of high blood pressure and diabetes during pregnancy, fetal monitoring to detect early distress, and safer cesarean sections. Full understanding of Rh blood type incompatibilities between mother and fetus has led to a drug that can prevent this potentially fatal disorder.

Much of surgery has been transformed by a basic understanding of the healing process, the development of better anesthetics and techniques for their administration, intravenous feeding, and modern blood banking. The invention of pump-oxygenator "bypass" equipment has permitted surgeons to stop a patient's heart, open it, and repair it as never before. Microsurgical techniques now make it possible to reattach severed limbs, to repair the tiny bones of the middle ear, and to bypass clogged arteries in the heart or limbs with natural or synthetic substitutes.

In the most impressive advance of recent decades, organ transplantation—most successful so far for kidneys—has been made possible by combined efforts in surgery and the medical fields of dialysis and immunology.

The biomedical revolution outlined above has had a great impact on the health of Americans and citizens of other industrialized nations. Some of its benefits are reflected in improvements in traditional measures of population health: decreased infant mortality, a modest decrease in death rates for adults and a slight increase in adult life expectancy, and moderate decreases in the prevalence of certain diseases. But much of the benefit remains uncounted. Even the most successful new drug for arthritis will have no impact at all on death rates or life expectancy. Nor will the prevalence of arthritis be affected. What *will* change is the amount of pain and the degree of function experienced by arthritis sufferers, and these are very difficult to measure. I cannot agree with some of modern medicine's critics who totally discount the value of diagnostic and therapeutic progress.

At the same time, it must be admitted that the rapid advances in postwar medicine have been flawed in several significant ways, so that their full potential has been blunted by negative impacts. Uncritical acclaim for technological progress would be just as nearsighted as total rejection.

CURING VERSUS CARING

HIPPOCRATES PRACTICED MEDICINE 400 years before the birth of Christ. In the 2,300 years between his time and the start of this century, there was little that physicians could do technologically to help their patients. Why, then, were doctors respected and sought after during these 23 centuries? Primarily because they exercised interpersonal skills valued by their patients. They knew which disorders were usually minor and provided reassurance and hope to patients who suffered from them. They knew which disorders were often long-lasting, disabling, or fatal, and—to such patients and their families—

they provided understanding and support. They helped their patients to cope, to suffer and endure, to grieve. They listened.

Now that physicians *do* have the tools to cure many patients, the interpersonal skills are almost entirely ignored in medical education and underutilized by many in practice. Compassionate physicians still exist but they are rarely seen by medical students, whose only role models are biomedical researchers and subspecialty clinicians in referral practice.

The unbalanced emphasis on technology and the inattention to interpersonal communication skills are due in part to the massive funding of the former in medical schools and by insurance companies. Private insurance, Medicaid, and Medicare will all pay handsomely for operations, x-rays, and other technological interventions which may require relatively little time on the part of physicians. They pay less—and sometimes do not pay at all—for time spent counseling and listening.

Factors that go beyond the health-care system also play a role. In our society as a whole, a high level of prestige is attached to fast, dramatic actions based on technological solutions, as opposed to prolonged, gradual progress based on relationships. In such a society, it is not surprising that doctors want to quickly diagnose and cure, and are less enthusiastic about patient problems that require gradual education and counseling.

Many patients reinforce this unbalanced emphasis. Critics of the current system have objected to the "medicalization" of society, in which the public expects a pill to "cure" every ache, anxiety, and stress. Ivan Illich points out that this trend has made us less able to cope, to resolve our own problems, and to bear suffering when no pill will work.

A frequent way of expressing these concerns is to state that we emphasize the *science* of medicine and ignore the *art*, an equally essential component.

To some extent this is a valid analysis. On the other hand, in the long run it is dangerous to label—and dismiss—interpersonal skills as an "art." In fact there are social *sciences* which deal with this area rather effectively.

A doctor who successfully treats your heart attack is a good doctor. A doctor who helps you to avoid having the heart attack in the first place is a better doctor. At the present time, we say that this superior physician knows the "art" of medicine. He or she was never taught it in medical school, but somehow "picked it up" or had an "innate ability" all along.

This is an unfortunate attitude. Physicians can learn more effective ways to educate and motivate patients concerning risk factors such as smoking, exercise, and diet so that they are less likely to have heart attacks. There is a great deal of real science required: It just does not happen to be "bench science" involving test tubes.

In the prevention of disease and in the management, especially, of chronic disease, the physician can be an important part of care. And it is possible to learn, "scientifically," to do this well. On a societal level, what is needed is more research in the sociomedical as well as the biomedical sciences, so that interpersonal skills in the patient–physician relationship can be further heightened. In the meanwhile, medical students need a broader range of role models, which will only come about through reforms in the funding of medical schools. Payments for care must also be revised so that practicing physicians have incentives to spend time with patients.

On a personal level, patients must seek out those physicians who will listen and who are willing to develop therapeutic relationships. Such doctors do exist, but are too often bypassed by patients who are overly impressed by academic, research-based credentials.

THE CHANGING STRUCTURE OF HEALTH CARE

IN THE 1940s, the vast majority of American medical care was provided by general practitioners in non-hospital-based solo offices. Their patients paid them directly. Forty years later, the majority of our doctors are specialists, sometimes practicing in groups or clinics and more often in formal or informal partnerships. Their offices are often within or immediately adjacent to hospitals, and their bills go increasingly to insurance companies or governmental agencies, not to their patients.

Two of these changes have fostered the decline in the patient–physician communication that we have discussed. "Third-party payments"—payments by anyone other than the patient—now account for over 40 percent of all health-care reimbursements. To the extent that insurance frees patients from financial burdens and removes barriers to needed care, this is a blessing. Unfortunately, physicians who need not worry about their patients' ability to pay are less likely to give careful consideration to the necessity for every test, medication, or operation they prescribe or perform. This is not only inefficient, it also leads to sloppy thinking and procedures that may be unnecessarily uncomfortable or even dangerous. On a less direct but more pervasive level, the tendency of physicians to think of themselves as mere numbers in a computer payment system does not foster interpersonal relationships.

Specialization, more than any other trend, has changed the doctor–patient interaction. Specialization has been an unavoidable outgrowth of the biomedical information explosion. The prewar general practitioner could keep up with the steady but slow growth of medical knowledge in a fairly adequate way, so that one physician could realistically treat children and adults medically, surgically, and obstetrically with only infrequent referrals to specialists in an unusual or complex situation.

With the vast increase in biomedical knowledge, no single doctor can now cope simultaneously with advances in all of these fields. More than anything else, it is a fear of being second rate that forces modern physicians to choose smaller and smaller areas of expertise. The financial rewards of specialization add a second strong incentive. This results in physicians who can each treat one problem superbly but lack the interest and ability to relate to patients as whole human beings. Many of us, particularly among the growing ranks of the elderly, have several medical problems at once, and most of us have a variety of problems over time.

The solution which is emerging is called "primary care." Under this concept, one practitioner or a small team of professionals provides most of the health care required by a patient or family over an extended period of time. Primary-care practitioners can meet the great majority of ambulatory care needs in an office or clinic, and provide routine in-hospital care. Continuous interpersonal relationships and a stress on education and prevention are possible under this model. When the services of a specialist are required, the primary-care provider arranges for the referral, receives the results of tests and consultations, and helps the patient to integrate the specialist's contribution into the overall picture.

Thus, while providing most of the patient's care personally, the primary-care provider can coordinate *all* of the patient's care, avoiding confusion, fragmentation, and gaps.

Primary care for adults is provided by general internists (as opposed to internal medicine subspecialists such as cardiologists and endocrinologists). Children can receive primary care from general pediatricians. Entire families can receive coordinated primary care from a growing number of family practitioners or from a team consisting, for instance, of a general internist, a general pediatrician, and a part-time obstetrician. Within the past decade, nurse practitioners and physician assistants have also been trained in increasing numbers to help meet the demand for services in each of these primary-care models.

Recent studies indicate that enlarged training programs for physician assistants, nurse practitioners, and primary-care physicians will correct the current shortage nationwide by 1990. Increased efforts are needed to bring this goal closer, and to ensure that national totals do not obscure geographic areas of continuing shortage—particularly in rural and urban poverty areas.

There is a need not only for more primary-care emphasis in professional education, but also for reform of the health-care financing system so that primary care will not be discouraged by fiscal inequities. One emerging model is the Health Maintenance Organization (HMO), a large group practice that can hire a balanced mix of primary-care and subspecialty professionals, and in which families enroll for a total coordinated "package" of care (including hospital coverage) for a fixed yearly price to the family, employer, or insurance company.

At the present time it is certainly possible for individuals and families to find primary-care doctors or teams. While this is not easy in all areas of the country, it is one of the most important steps that a family can take to safeguard future health. Finding an ongoing source of primary care will often satisfy our earlier recommendation to seek out a practitioner willing and able to build a lasting relationship.

THE MISUSE AND OVERUSE OF TECHNOLOGY

THE VERY EXISTENCE of sophisticated medical technology leads to its intensive use in at least two ways—sometimes called the financial and technological imperatives.

Once a doctor, group, or hospital has purchased an expensive piece of diagnostic or therapeutic equipment, there is a great deal of pressure to *use* it, bill for its use, and pay off the investment as soon as possible. This is the financial imperative.

The technological imperative refers to an attitude that pervades our society, not just our health-care system. If we are technologically *capable* of doing something new, you can bet we *will* do it fairly soon, whether or not there is any benefit. Do we all really need digital watches that are accurate to within one second per week but never give us a sense of "half past" or "a quarter of"? Do we need a constant barrage of new food additives, hair dyes, and petrochemical products, some of which are routinely discovered to be cancer-producing after they have been on the market for years?

The American public rebelled in at least one recent instance. We were technologically capable of building a supersonic transport plane, so the aviation industry and governmental funding agencies set out to build one. For once, thousands of citizens began to ask some basic questions: How many people really need to fly from coast to coast two hours faster? How many people will be awakened each night by sonic booms? Should I be paying taxes to finance this? Perhaps some similar questions need to be asked in medicine.

The technological imperative in health care operates in the areas of diagnosis and therapy. Most people with mild or moderate high blood pressure have "essential hypertension." This means that we currently can't find the cause, but we can correct the problem with diet and medication. A few people have specific causes for their hypertension, but many of them respond well to the same diet and medicines. A rational approach would be to start people on weight reduction, a low-salt diet and mild medication, and reserve extensive testing for those who do not respond. But the technological imperative comes into play. Doctors have been taught that they are capable of making a precise diagnosis with modern tests. So many of them will order hundreds of dollars worth of tests—some involving modest risks—for *all* their hypertensive patients. Then most patients can be told "precisely" that they have essential hypertension and be given the same diet and medication they would have gotten without the tests.

Similar things happen in therapeutic situations, although there has been gradual improvement lately. Doctors *can* remove a mildly troublesome tonsil or uterus, so many still do, regardless of the balance between benefit and risk. The most dramatic and ethically complex situations arise in the care of terminally ill patients. We *can* maintain the breathing of patients whose brains are no longer functioning, and revive the hearts of patients with widespread, agonizing cancer. We have only recently begun to ask if we *should* do all we *can* do in these situations. The implications for cost control and humane care are enormous.

Again, long-range improvement in this area requires changes in medical education and the funding of health-care services. A physician trained in careful, sensitive decision making is less likely to order unnecessary tests. A gynecologist salaried by a health maintenance organization is less likely to remove a basically healthy uterus.

If a family is successful in following the earlier suggestions, and has care coordinated by a primary-care doctor or team skilled in the interpersonal as well as technological aspects of medicine, its members are less likely to face the overuse and misuse of technology.

A few additional precautions are helpful. Whenever a physician orders a laboratory test, x-ray, or other diagnostic procedure, a patient or family member should ask, "Why? Will this test provide any information that will change the diagnosis or the treatment? What are the risks involved, and are they worth the gain in information?" When a surgical operation is suggested, or another major and risky therapy such as long-term medication with serious side effects, a second opinion is called for. This needn't be a secretive or adversarial procedure. One can say, "I'm very happy with your care, doctor, but this is such an important decision that I'd be more comfortable with it if I could get a second opinion." Any physician who reacts negatively to such a suggestion is probably not the best doctor to continue with.

SUMMING UP

AMERICAN MEDICINE has made enormous technological advances in recent decades. In the 1980s we are entering a period of healthy adjustment. It is hoped that the near future will see a resurgence of interpersonal communication skills, as the sociomedical sciences catch up with biomedical progress. New models are emerging to provide adequate coordination of specialized services for patients and families.

The excesses of technology, in terms of cost, side effects, and ethical issues, will be controlled once coordinated care in an interpersonal framework is restored as the basis for patient–physician interaction. In the meanwhile, there is much that the individual can do to ensure that the benefits of technology are maximized—not compromised—in his or her own health care.

2 The American Health-Care System and How to Use it

Robert J. Weiss, M.D.

INTRODUCTION

SEVEN MILLION PEOPLE work in the American health-care system, among them half a million physicians. They work in a wide variety of settings: small, rural clinics equipped with little more than an examining table, a scale, and a blood pressure cuff; private offices; community agencies and health centers; long-term care facilities; high-technology urban medical centers with thousands of beds and the most sophisticated modern diagnostic machinery. The list could go on and on, for this is a complex, highly specialized system.

It is a system that presents many alternatives to the consumer—the patient. Understanding something about the various settings and the type of care they offer may minimize the stress of dealing with the system. It can make for better use of health-care resources and may help stabilize the increase of health-care costs, which are currently rising at an annual average rate of 10 percent and fast approaching the point where good health care is out of reach for the poor and middle class.

LEVELS OF CARE WITHIN THE SYSTEM

AMERICAN MEDICINE is organized into a complex structure in which there are three broadly defined levels for the delivery of care.

Primary Care

Primary, or "first contact," care is provided in such settings as doctors' offices, hospital emergency rooms and outpatient clinics, free-standing clinics, and emergency rooms (sometimes called urgicenters). It is care that may be obtained by individuals on their own initiative, without referral by a doctor, and includes health maintenance in infants and children, immunizations, screening for infectious and communicable diseases, the monitoring of normal pregnancies, treating minor injuries and common complaints, and managing chronic diseases. Referrals from the primary level of care provide access to more specialized levels.

Secondary Care

Care at the secondary level is provided by a specialist or subspecialist, often in a community hospital or other similar setting. Specialties that are usually considered secondary-level include obstetrics and gynecology, dermatology, otolaryngology, rheumatology, and cardiology. Access to this level of care may require a doctor's referral. Many people, however, refer themselves.

Tertiary Care

Tertiary care is highly specialized, high-technology care, oriented toward complex programs and out-of-the-ordinary procedures such as neurological surgery, open heart surgery, and heart or kidney transplantation. Care of this kind requires extended training on the part of physicians, sophisticated equipment for diagnosis and treatment, specialized facilities and, in the great majority of cases, hospitalization for the patient. Tertiary-level care is found at hospitals associated with medical schools, at large regional referral centers, and at hospitals specializing in a particular disease or group of diseases. Physicians practicing at this level of the system are almost always subspecialists, with intensive training and experience in a narrowly defined field.

Diagnostic tests such as cardiac catherization, CT-scanning, and nuclear magnetic resonance are considered third-level care. They require highly refined (and extremely expensive) equipment and highly trained technicians.

The distinctions among the different levels of care are far from rigid and there is frequently some overlapping. Many specialists routinely provide primary care, while primary-care doctors may assist at major surgery. From the patient's point of view, the important distinctions among the three levels of care may lie in the fact that referral is necessary at some levels within the system, and not at others.

MEDICAL DOCTORS

Training

To obtain the Doctor of Medicine (M.D.) or Doctor of Osteopathy (D.O.) degree, a student must complete a course of instruction in an approved medical school or college of osteopathy in the United States or abroad. The usual course is 4 years. The first 2 years are given over largely to classroom and laboratory study of the sciences basic to medicine: anatomy, biochemistry, genetics, physiology, pharmacology, and microbiology. The third and fourth years place increasing emphasis on clinical experience, with students being exposed to all the major medical specialties—internal medicine, surgery, pediatrics, obstetrics and gynecology, and psychiatry—in a patient-care setting.

The new M.D. must complete 1 year of approved postgraduate training before he or she can be licensed to practice. This postgraduate year (formerly called "internship" and now called "PGY-1") emphasizes one of the major specialties and provides supervised clinical experience on various hospital services—wards, clinics, emergency room, and, for surgical postgraduates, the operating room.

At the end of this year, the doctor takes the state board examination for medical licensure. Students in U.S. medical schools may take the National Board Examinations, which are given in 3 parts: Part I at the end of the basic science years; Part II at the end of the clinical or fourth year of medical school; and Part III after PGY-1. All states except Texas and Arizona now recognize the National Board Examination for state medical licensure, but may have some additional requirements. (Doctors must hold a license from each state in which they practice; different states have somewhat differing standards.)

Formerly, many doctors began practice as general practitioners after this first year of postgraduate training. Today, most specialize, completing 3 to 6 years of additional in-hospital training ("residency" or PGY-2, etc.) in preparation for certifying examinations administered by one of the 23 national specialty boards, for example, the American Board of Internal Medicine and the American Board of Surgery. Most of today's family practitioners are in fact specialists, certified by the American Board of Family Practice. Specialization is the almost inevitable response on the part of doctors to a field of knowledge that has become extremely broad and complex. It provides the opportunity to master with competence a more limited body of material, and to feel confident in the application of that material to patients' needs.

Continuing Education

Continuing education is an important part of doctors' training, keeping them in touch with new research and techniques in their fields. Many of the specialty boards require periodic recertification of their members, following an examination, evidence of continuing medical education, and at least a brief review of patient records. More than 20 states require that doctors participate in accredited continuing education courses to maintain their medical-practice licenses. In addition, many of the specialty societies (almost all specialists belong to one or more of these professional organizations) require their members to spend a minimum number of hours on continuing education annually. However, the most effective way for a physician to keep up to date is to be on the staff of a hospital with an active teaching program.

Medical School Admissions

A career in medicine is attractive to young people who are looking for challenging and interesting work, who value status and a high income, who enjoy working with people and exercising judgment, and who seek to do good. Students from higher-income backgrounds are not the only ones desiring such a career but, because of the preparation necessary for medical school and the length and expense of a medical education, they are disproportionately selected into the profession. There have been efforts (on the whole, successful) to increase the numbers of minority group and rural students, and the number of women, but the profession remains predominately white, urban, upper-middle class, and male.

Medical school admission committees are responsible for selection of tomorrow's doctors and admission is highly competitive. These committees place great emphasis on students' performance in their college science or premedical courses. As a result, medical students as a group are better developed in scientific ability than in interpersonal skills. In addition, their training demands the mastery of enormous quantities of scientific and technological material, stressing the "science" as opposed to the "art" of medicine, "cure" rather than "care." Thus, a criticism frequently leveled at doctors is that, while they are technically proficient, knowledgeable, and up to date, they are lacking in warmth and personal responsiveness.

To meet such criticisms, most medical schools now include in their curricula courses that focus on the doctor–patient relationship and on ethical issues. Ethics courses aim to make students sensitive to some of the major quandaries in medicine, for example, the question of when life support should be terminated. At the same time, and even more important, they are concerned with the qualities of compassion and mercy, which cannot be "taught." Thus, a major responsibility in selecting those who have the potential to become competent *and* caring doctors still rests with the admissions committee.

Distribution

In 1980, there were almost 200 doctors for every 100,000 people in the United States. It is projected that, in 1990, there will be 242 for every 100,000, that is, 1 doctor for every 400 people. Many experts consider this an oversupply, but others think that the increasing number of elderly as a percentage of the population will keep the increasing number of physicians busy. It is certain to add considerably to the already astronomical cost of health care: Studies indicate that each doctor generates health-care expenditures approximately 4 times greater than his or her own annual income.

Nor is it by any means certain that increasing numbers of doctors will mean better health care for the population as a whole. Doctors tend to locate in wealthier urban areas, often in the shadow of a large medical center and, increasingly, to enter specialties not related to primary care. The present disparity between the doctor:patient ratios of large urban areas and suburban areas and those of sparsely populated rural areas, as well as a similar disparity between wealthy and poor sections of large cities, seems likely to persist unless ways are found to force geographic distribution of physicians.

DOCTORS OF OSTEOPATHY

DOCTORS OF OSTEOPATHY (D.O.s) are generally equivalent to doctors of medicine (M.D.s) in training, licensure, and scope of practice, although M.D.s have 23 specialties from which to choose, whereas D.O.s have 16. The major difference between them is philosophical. Osteopathic physicians place a great emphasis on the body's natural ability to defend itself against disease and infections, and to heal itself if it is intact physically and physiologically. When necessary, osteopathic physicians correct disorders of the system through manipulation of the body. These physicians practice in traditional hospitals and in those devoted solely to osteopathy.

NURSES

THE GREATEST NUMBER of health professionals are nurses. There are 1.7 million licensed registered nurses (R.N.s), more than 3 for every physician. Nursing remains a female occupation (only 2 percent of nurses are men) despite a shift from the traditional "caring" role to more technological functions.

There are 3 educational routes to becoming a registered nurse: associate-degree programs (2-year community college programs), diploma programs (3-year hospital-affiliated programs), and baccalaureate programs (4-year university-affiliated programs). The number of nurses graduating from diploma programs is falling rapidly, largely as the result of professional pressure to upgrade nursing education by placing it within an academic setting. Clearly, the knowledge, expertise, and skill of graduates of the different types of programs differ widely, but all are professional nurses, licensed by the state in which they work. On the whole, nurses are generalists and work as ancillaries to doctors. However, in the past few years there has been a rapid increase in formalized programs for the development of specialized nurses who can function as "physician extenders," taking over much routine treatment and screening and providing a partial solution to rising health-care costs. In hospitals, clinical nurse specialists (mostly with master's degrees and advanced clinical training) work under a doctor's supervision in high-technology areas such as coronary care and organ transplantation. Ambulatory-care nurse specialists, with advanced postgraduate training, include nurse practitioners and nurse midwives.

Nurse practitioners provide preventive care, conduct examinations, monitor chronic conditions, and provide health counseling—much of the general medical care traditionally provided by doctors. Many of the 20,000 nurse practitioners work in underserved areas which doctors generally do not find attractive, and provide services that are more accessible and less expensive than those provided by physicians. Nurse practitioners, however, are not licensed to prescribe medication and therefore always work in some kind of partnership, however informal, with a doctor.

Nurse midwives are trained in the management of essentially normal pregnancies and deliveries, in postpartum care, and continuing gynecological care. There are currently some 1,500 practicing nurse midwives in the United States, most of them working under a doctor's supervision. By definition, the care given by nurse midwives is low-intervention care, with high priority placed on the preferences of patients, many of whom deliver at home. Care is therefore less expensive than a doctor's care.

An emerging role in hospital nursing is that of the primary nurse, a nonspecialist R.N. who is responsible for the total nursing care of a small number of patients, usually 8 to 10. A primary nurse works with 1 associate and is responsible for all nursing orders and hands-on care, as well as for arrangements after discharge from the hospital. There are currently 128 hospitals with all-R.N. staffs doing primary nursing, a departure from the typically fragmented pattern of care.

Nursing is primarily a salaried and institution-based profession. Of R.N.s, 66 percent are employed in hospitals, with only 12 percent working in such noninstitutional settings as doctors' offices and health agencies.

While hospitals remain the principal employers of nurses, a recent change is the expansion of temporary personnel agencies which provide both hospitals and nursing homes with nurses on a per diem basis to make up staff shortages. About 40 percent of hospitals employ agency nurses. For nurses, agency employment offers freedom to control basic working conditions, such as when and where they work. In addition, agencies offer wages that may, in areas where there is a shortage of nurses, be up to 300 percent higher than those offered by hospitals.

THE PRIMARY-CARE PHYSICIAN

THE INCREASING SPECIALIZATION that has characterized American medicine over the past 25 years has resulted in greatly improved health care, especially where serious illness is concerned. However, it has also resulted in a marked diminution in broad, long-term contact between individual doctors and patients. Fragmentation of care among specialists—one doctor for this complaint, another for that operation—too often means that routine preventive care and health maintenance are neglected.

While specialists' services may be needed on occasion (and, when they are needed, may prove invaluable), each individual should have his or her primary-care doctor. This doctor is the one who oversees general health, both mental and physical, over a period of time, who knows the complete medical history, and who is aware of the individual's family situation, living environment, and occupation, together with any accompanying stresses. This doctor is the one who should refer an individual to an appropriate specialist, when necessary. He or she should also, when a patient is hospitalized, act as case manager, coordinating the actions and recommendations of specialists.

The choice of a primary-care doctor should be made when an individual is healthy and has the time to consider alternatives and evaluate impressions—not, as is so often the case, under conditions of pain and pressure. It should be made in advance of need, if only because a physician is under no obligation, legal or otherwise, to treat anyone who is not registered as a patient, no matter how sick.

Until recently, the doctor selected as the primary-care physician was usually a general practitioner (GP). Such nonspecialists are now few and far between; their place at the primary or first-contact level of care has been filled by internists (specialists in internal medicine) and family practitioners. Family practitioners, also specialists, treat people of all ages, not necessarily families as such.

Both internists and family practitioners are qualified to provide comprehensive health care and to diagnose physical and mental disease, but their training differs to some degree. Family practitioners have postgraduate training in such fields as internal medicine, minor surgery, gynecology, pediatrics, orthopedics, and preventive medicine. The postgraduate training of internists places more emphasis on more serious disorders of the heart and lungs, the gastrointestinal and genitourinary tracts, and the endocrine glands—and on chronic diseases such as arthritis and diabetes.

While it is useful for a doctor to have some knowledge of the family constellation, a given family may well require more than one primary-care physician. Different members have different needs and the notion of a "family doctor" should not be a shibboleth, as it unfortunately has become in some circles.

Sources of Names

A reliable source of doctors' names is a good hospital—a teaching hospital or a large medical center or the local community hospital. Any of these can provide the names of internists and family practitioners on their staff who practice in the community. A medical school is another good source: Many faculty

ALLIED HEALTH WORKERS

(A partial listing of health-care professionals, excluding doctors and nurses.)

Dental Hygienists provide services for the maintenance of oral health, including cleaning and scaling the teeth.

Emergency Medical Technicians (EMTs) are licensed to provide immediate care in emergency situations (see *Paramedics)*

Home Health Aides provide personal-care services and some nursing to homebound sick and disabled. Homemakers provide household services under similar circumstances.

Licensed Practical Nurses (LPNs) are trained and licensed to provide hands-on nursing care under the supervision of registered nurses or doctors.

Medical Records Personnel are responsible for keeping patients' records complete, accurate, up-to-date, and confidential.

Medical Technologists perform laboratory tests to help in the diagnosis of disease and to determine its extent and possible causes.

Nurses' Aides, Orderlies, and Attendants assist nurses in hospitals, nursing homes, and other settings.

Occupational Therapists work with disabled patients to help them adapt to their disabilities. This may involve relearning skills needed for daily activities and modifying the physical environment.

Opticians fit corrective glasses and manufacture lenses.

Optometrists measure vision for corrective lenses and prescribe glasses.

Orthotists and Prosthetists prepare and fit braces and artificial limbs.

Paramedics provide care in emergency situations. They are more highly trained than emergency medical technicians.

Pharmacists are trained and licensed to dispense medications in accordance with a doctor's prescription.

Physical Therapists provide services designed to prevent loss of function and to restore function in the disabled. Exercise, heat, cold, and water are among the agents they use.

Physician Assistants (PAs) perform physical examinations, provide counseling, and prescribe certain medications under a doctor's supervision.

Podiatrists prevent, diagnose, and treat diseases, injuries, and abnormalities of the feet. They are the only health-care practitioners other than physicians who may use drugs and surgery to treat human illness.

Psychologists are trained in the study of human behavior. They provide counseling and testing in areas related to mental health. They also do individual and group therapy.

Radiologic Technicians prepare patients for x-ray and take and develop x-ray photographs.

Recreational Therapists provide services to improve patients' well-being through music, dance, and other artistic activities.

Registered Dietitians (RDs) are licensed to apply dietary principles to the maintenance of health and the treatment of disease.

Respiratory Therapists treat breathing disorders, according to the doctor's directions; assist in postoperative rehabilitation.

Social Workers help patients with finances, insurance, discharge plans, placement, housing, and other social and family programs arising out of illness or disability. They also do individual and group counseling and therapy.

Speech Pathologists and Audiologists measure hearing ability and treat disorders of verbal communications.

members, in addition to their teaching responsibilities, practice privately.

A further source of names is the local medical society, which can provide a list of licensed practitioners in the area (the same list may be available at the local library). In some communities, public-interest groups provide lists of doctors' names and addresses together with information on office hours and other practical considerations. Friends and relatives, usually consulted first about a new doctor, are, in fact, the least reliable of the possible sources of names. They may, however, be able to give useful information about doctors' personalities.

Checking a Doctor's Qualifications

The next step is to find some assurance that the doctors under consideration have been well trained. Good training is a *sine qua non*, the basis of future competence. Medical directories, including the *Directory of Medical Specialists* published for the American Board of Medical Specialties, are available at most local libraries. (A list of specialties and sub-specialties covered in this directory appears on page 15.) From these reference works, you can learn which medical school a doctor attended (it should be fully accredited), and where he or she did postgraduate training or residency (large, well-known teaching hospitals usually have the best postgraduate training programs). The directory will also tell whether a doctor is board-certified (has passed the examination given by the appropriate American specialty board) or is board-eligible (has finished postgraduate training, but has not yet been in practice for 2 years, the minimum required before taking the certifying examination, or has not passed the board examination). An older physician may not have gone through the formal certification process; most younger ones have done so, although not all pass the certification examination.

A doctor's hospital appointments, also listed in the medical directories, are an important indicator of qualification and reputation. Most hospitals screen doctors carefully before appointment to the staff; most also periodically reevaluate their staffs' performance. In general, the better the hospital, the better qualified the doctor. Preferably, the doctor's appointment should be with a teaching hospital (one affiliated with a medical school or having a specialty training program), since such hospitals have highly qualified specialists on their staff and are familiar with sophisticated current techniques and equipment. However, many community hospitals enjoy a deservedly high reputation and provide excellent care.

In addition to being initially well-trained, a doctor should be up to date in knowledge of the field. The American Board of Family Practice, among others, recognizes the importance of this in requiring periodic recertification of its members; for internists, and some other specialists, recertification (with the American Board of Internal Medicine) is on a voluntary basis. Signs that a doctor is keeping abreast of medical progress include attendance at approved continuing education courses, attention to current journals and publications, and participation in weekly hospital rounds. A teaching position at a hospital or medical school is a further and highly reliable indicator that a doctor is up to date, and recognized as being so by peers.

Practical Considerations

Practical considerations play an important part in the choice of a doctor. The doctor's office should be conveniently located, near public transportation, or with easy parking; the hours should be compatible with the patient's schedule. The hospital with which the doctor is affiliated (which is the hospital to which the patient will be admitted if he or she becomes seriously ill) should not be too distant. The basic cost of health maintenance—the fee for a regular office visit—should be comfortably affordable.

If there is a family member who is housebound, the doctor chosen should be willing to make essential housecalls. The patient should also find out who covers when the doctor is not available and how emergencies are handled. A doctor should be willing to go to the hospital emergency room if a patient is admitted there.

Other indications of a well-run practice are the efficiency of the doctor's answering service, good record-keeping, the cleanliness and orderliness of the office, and the attitudes displayed by the doctor's nurse and secretary.

Personal Considerations

Personal considerations include the doctor's sex and age. Some people have a strong preference for a doctor of the same sex; for them, this should be a major factor in the decision. Regarding age, a younger doctor is more likely to be up to date than an older one. An older doctor has more clinical experience, and if he or she participates in continuing education courses and reads widely in the professional literature, should also be knowledgeable about current techniques.

Finally, there is the all-important factor of the doctor's personality. Once it has been established that the doctor is well trained and competent, and that the practice is well run, individual reaction to the doctor as a person should be the decisive factor in the choice. It is usually possible to tell in a brief initial interview whether or not a particular doctor is someone with whom the patient can be comfortable.

The Doctor–Patient Relationship

A good relationship between patient and doctor demands input from both individuals. When evaluating a new doctor, or reevaluating a current one, the following points should be considered:

- *Communication*—The doctor should give his or her undivided attention, treating the patient courteously and unhurriedly. He or she should communicate in a language that the patient can understand, avoiding jargon, and answering questions willingly and clearly. The doctor should be responsive to any anxieties expressed by the patient.

- *Emphasis on prevention*—Questions about smoking, drinking, sleep, and exercise, when accompanied by

MEDICAL SPECIALTIES AND SUBSPECIALTIES

Allergy and Immunology
Anesthesiology
Colon and Rectal Surgery
Dermatology
Emergency Medicine
Family Practice
Internal Medicine
  Cardiology
  Endocrinology and Metabolism
  Gastroenterology
  Hematology
  Infectious Diseases
  Medical Oncology
  Nephrology
  Pulmonary Disease
  Rheumatology
Neurological Surgery
Nuclear Medicine
Obstetrics and Gynecology
Ophthalmology
Orthopedic Surgery

Otolaryngology
Pathology
  Blood Banking
Pediatrics
  Pediatric Cardiology
  Pediatric Endocrinology
  Pediatric Hematology–Oncology
  Neonatal–Perinatal Medicine
  Nephrology
Physical Medicine and Rehabilitation
Plastic Surgery
Preventive Medicine
Psychiatry and Neurology
  Psychiatry
  Neurology/Special Competence in Child Neurology
  Psychiatry and Neurology
  Child Psychiatry
Radiology
Surgery
Thoracic Surgery
Urology

recommendations for promoting health, indicate that a doctor places due emphasis on the prevention of disease.

- *Presentation of alternatives*—When recommending a procedure or course of treatment, the doctor should present the alternatives, with a clear explanation of the risks and benefits involved.

- *Explanation of tests*—The doctor should be willing to explain the purpose of any tests that are ordered, and should report back promptly on test results. If a battery of tests is ordered to satisfy the doctor's need for a "complete picture," this should be explained. Tests should complement physical examination and counseling, not supplant it.

- *Habits of referral*—If the patient's condition is one that is beyond the doctor's competence, he or she should willingly refer the patient to a specialist. The patient should not, however, be referred to a specialist for routine or minor complaints. Under-referral could endanger the patient's health; over-referral means unnecessary expense. For major surgical procedures, the doctor should be willing, if necessary, to refer out of the community, to a large medical center.

- *Provision for follow-up*—The doctor should explain clearly what to expect, as far as can be predicted, and should alert the patient to signs or symptoms that indicate a return visit. When a prescription is given, the doctor should explain about possible side effects and should provide for follow-up if necessary. The patient should never be made to feel hesitant about telephoning a doctor.

- *Scheduling checkups*—The scheduling of routine checkups should reflect the now-solid evidence that the optimum frequency, *in the absence of symptoms*, is every 5 years before age 60, every 2 years between ages 60 and 65, and annually thereafter. Prior to age 65, annual physical examinations are unnecessary.

- *Tolerance of differences*—The patient's priorities and lifestyle may well differ from those of the doctor; the doctor should respect these differences. If the patient makes an informed choice about medical treatment, fully understanding the risks and benefits, the doctor should accept the choice—or suggest another physician.

The patient also has responsibilities. Patients who claim a share in the decision making about their health are obligated to be knowledgeable and responsible. They should educate themselves by reading and by asking appropriate questions. They should be accurate and prompt in reporting symptoms and adverse drug reactions. They should follow their doctors' instructions and take medications as directed (a large percentage of patients do not). If they do not understand what the doctor is saying, they should make this clear. Finally, they must take the important preventive measures that only they can take: eating a proper diet, avoiding excessive alcohol and all tobacco, dealing with stress, and seeing to it that their social lives and their work provide as much pleasure and fulfillment as possible.

The Office Visit

A first-time visit to a doctor, or a "complete work-up," has 2 distinct parts: the medical history and the physical examination. These, together with any tests that may be ordered subsequently, provide the doctor with baseline information about the patient and his or her physical condition.

The medical history is the single most important communication from the patient to the doctor and is the only part of an office visit that is under the patient's direct control. Frankness is the best guarantee of good care.

The information elicited from the patient is organized under 5 headings:

1. *Chief complaint*—The doctor will probably lead off with some such question as, "What brings you here today?" The answer given establishes priorities for the rest of the medical history process. A brief, straightforward description of the problem or problems (there may be more than one chief complaint) is what is required of the patient at this point.

2. *Present illness*—This covers the story behind the chief complaint: how long the problem has existed, whether this is a first-time occurrence, and similar points. Here the patient should give the sequence of events in chronological order. (It may help to make a written summary before going to the doctor's office.) Relevant supporting information about drugs, tests, and visits to other doctors should be given, in documentary form if at all possible.

3. *Past medical history*—Questions here are designed to provide the doctor with background information about the patient's general health. The doctor will ask about the health status of parents and siblings, and about the patient's own health in the past, including surgery, pregnancies, and any allergies. He or she will also ask what medications the patient is taking; the answer should include over-the-counter preparations such as laxatives, vitamins, and mild pain-killers.

4. *Review of body systems*—Here the doctor will ask a series of questions about symptoms related to all the body systems (skin, glands, sexual function, lungs, heart, etc.), usually beginning at the head and working down the torso. He or she is looking for information that may have been missed earlier, and for additional factors that may influence treatment.

5. *Social history*—Questions here are intended to elicit information about the patient's lifestyle. The doctor will ask about the family, living conditions, and any interpersonal stresses. There will be questions about occupation, satisfaction with work, and any possible exposure to environmental hazards. In addition, the doctor will ask about smoking and drinking habits, sleep patterns, and the amount and kind of exercise taken.

The physical examination follows the medical history. A good doctor will respect the patient's modesty, but not at the expense of thoroughness: The breasts, genitals, and anal area should be examined as carefully as other parts of the body.

On the basis of the medical history and the physical examination, the doctor may order tests, make recommendations, write prescriptions, or perhaps refer the patient to a specialist. If the patient does not understand what is being said, or what is proposed, or what to expect, he or she should ask for a clear explanation. Studies show that patients are more dissatisfied about the information they receive from their doctors than about any other aspect of medical care; this can be rectified with appropriate questioning. The patient may want to take notes on the answers.

Avoiding Medical Fraud

Today's medical charlatan is less easy to spot than the stereotypical purveyor of snake oil. He usually makes liberal use of scientific terms and references in promoting the remedy or treatment or service offered. The press may label him "a scientist ahead of his time." He may claim research experience or a doctorate in the field (on investigation, the "doctorate" may turn out to be from an institution that is entirely fictional or that does not grant such degrees). The number of adherents is not a reliable guide: Some products whose health claims are scientifically quite unproven have the backing of large and vociferous lobbies.

However, there are a few key questions that may help determine whether a service or product is fraudulent:

● Who, if anyone, endorses it? An endorsement by "millions of satisfied users" is of no value; the endorsement of a national professional organization or a recognized voluntary health agency is conclusive.

● Do experts in the field use or recommend the service or product? If it is worthwhile, they will do so.

● Is the service or product guaranteed? No worthwhile medical service is ever guaranteed—a guarantee of success is not possible in medicine.

● Does the remedy or treatment make sense? By definition, a fraudulent remedy has a false rationale. Common sense—supplemented by some research in the local library—will usually reveal the weak links.

The Second Opinion

Getting a second opinion is a common practice among doctors. The guidelines are stated in the American Medical Association's principles of medical ethics: "A physician should seek consultation upon request; in doubtful or difficult cases; or whenever it appears that the quality of medical care may be enhanced thereby." Under these circumstances, and with their patients' permission, primary-care physicians consult with colleagues in appropriate fields, or refer their patients to these specialists. Similarly, specialists consult other specialists and consult with subspecialists.

In hospitals, consultation is often automatic and mandatory. However, there may be overuse. Mutual back-scratching exists in medicine as in other professions. Therefore, a hospitalized patient should ask the primary-care physician acting as case manager to check on the situation if the number of specialists involved seems excessive.

Patients have a *right* to a second opinion. There are many circumstances in which it is appropriate for a patient to exercise this right and ask for a referral to a second or even a third doctor for consultation. In doing so, a patient is not casting aspersions on a doctor's competence or judgment, but rather is taking a responsible attitude toward his or her own health and well-being.

A second opinion should always be sought if:

- *Surgery is proposed as the treatment for an ailment, or as an aid to diagnosis.*

  About 80 percent of all surgery done in this country is elective, that is, nonemergency. One in 5 of these operations is not indicated by either symptoms or test results. Even when symptoms and tests do indicate intervention, there may be serious questions as to whether the benefits of the surgery—the quality of life, perhaps length of life—outweigh its costs and risks. The risks include the possibility, remote but real, of disability or even death.

  There is a growing feeling among doctors that, for the elderly in particular, many elective procedures do *not* enhance the quality of life. Thus, if surgery is recommended, the patient should get valid statistics both on the probable success of the operation and on the quality of life if the surgery is not done. The patient should also ask about alternative medical treatments; if surgery is proposed for diagnostic purposes, he or she should ask about alternative methods and whether the results will make a difference in treatment or life expectancy. In some cases, it is advisable to get a second opinion from a subspecialist in an appropriate medical field, rather than from another surgeon. However, a second opinion from another qualified surgeon is strongly indicated when the operation proposed is one of several that are commonly done unnecessarily: hysterectomy, cholecystectomy (removal of the gallbladder), hernia repair, tonsillectomy, or an operation to relieve varicose veins, hemorrhoids, or low back pain. It may be difficult to get an unbiased opinion from a second doctor on the same

hospital staff. If at all possible, go to a doctor in another hospital for a second opinion. In cases of disagreement among specialists, a third opinion may be helpful. Most insurance policies that cover consultation fees allow for this.

- *The diagnosis is of a rare or potentially fatal or disabling disease.*

  The original diagnosis may have been incorrect. Or, if it is correct, there may be new or even experimental treatments available at an institution specializing in the disease.

- *Symptoms persist unrelieved and the doctor can provide no explanation for them.*

  Some diseases are incurable; the only treatment is palliative. Studies show that most people with a fatal disease are aware of their condition; most doctors will answer a direct question frankly, if asked. In other cases, however, involving both acute and chronic disease, correct diagnosis and treatment should provide some relief of symptoms within a few months.

- *Risks and benefits of proposed procedures are not satisfactorily explained.*

  The patient has a right to know the risks (including the dollar cost) and the potential benefits of any procedure that is proposed, including any expensive or hazardous tests.

- *Diagnostic procedures seem unnecessarily complex or very expensive or both.*

  Some doctors make excessive use of technology in borderline situations, either out of insecurity or a wish to cover themselves against malpractice actions.

- *The patient lacks confidence in the doctor's ability to do all that can reasonably be done.*

  Effective treatment demands trust. This is as valid a reason as any other for getting a second opinion.

How to Get a Second Opinion. In the great majority of cases, once the patient has openly expressed concern, the doctor should willingly supply the name of a specialist for consultation. There are many advantages to this approach. The primary-care doctor can give the specialist the necessary background information, is in a good position to receive a speedy report from the specialist, and knows what tests and treatments have been done, thus saving repetition. In addition, the doctor is likely to have a good rapport with a specialist of his or her choice; this has important implications for the patient's future care.

If patients must find a specialist on their own (perhaps because the doctor refuses to refer them, or because they choose not to ask for help), a good source of names is a hospital, preferably a teaching hospital, or a medical center or a medical school. A telephone call to the office of the head of the appropriate service or department should yield the names of specialists or subspecialists who have a local practice. The specialists' qualifications (board certification, hospital affiliations, and years of experience) can easily be checked by consulting the medical directories in the local library.

Choosing a Surgeon

The question of experience is particularly important when choosing a surgeon. A surgeon must "practice" to maintain his or her skills and should be thoroughly experienced in the operation. Another important factor is the hospital where the operation will be done, and its experience with the procedure. Necessary equipment and skilled anesthesiologists or technologists will not be found in a hospital where the procedure is done infrequently. Major procedures demand the facilities of a major medical center; less complex surgery can safely be performed in a good community hospital. Finally, in choosing a surgeon, look for one with a good reputation, and one who will operate only if the consequences of surgery are less threatening than the condition that suggests that the procedure should be done.

Choosing a Psychiatrist

While there are a wide variety of settings in which psychiatric care is given and a number of different theoretical approaches to the treatment of mental and emotional illness, for most people choosing a psychiatrist means finding a doctor who will provide individual treatment for what are sometimes called "problems of living."

One of the best sources of names is a trusted family doctor. The department of psychiatry at a medical center or medical school can also provide names of psychiatrists with private practices. Members of the clergy, social workers, and, for children, school guidance counselors are other professionals who may be knowledgeable about the psychiatrists working in the area.

The "match" between doctor and patient is more important in psychiatry than anywhere else in medicine. Therefore, the first few visits should take place with the understanding that there is no stigma attached to changing therapists if little or no rapport develops. At an early visit, the psychiatrist should take a medical and psychiatric history. He or she should check with the family doctor if it appears

possible that there is a complicating or causative physical condition. (Few psychiatrists have the facilities to do a physical examination.)

Patients should be wary of a psychiatrist who resorts immediately to medications, who "blames the victim," or who is reluctant to have them get a second opinion. If visits are scheduled more often than once weekly, they should ask why. As a general rule, an hour a week is sufficient for treatment, unless the patient feels a need for more time.

Changing Doctors

Among the reasons patients commonly give for changing doctors are that the fees are too high, that the doctor is not available when needed, and that the doctor fails to give them enough time. With complaints of this type, it is only fair to give the doctor the benefit of the doubt and discuss the problem; it may be that misinformation or a remediable lack of communication is at the root of the trouble. On the other hand, if the problem is a clash of personalities, discussion is fruitless and the patient should change doctors. If the patient is not comfortable with the doctor—for whatever reasons, or for no obvious reason—the partnership is unworkable.

Patients should also change doctors if the doctor abuses power and attempts to tyrannize or bully them. Women should be aware that sexual harassment, while uncommon, does occur and is unacceptable.

Doctors are human and make mistakes; however, incompetence is an obvious reason for changing physicians. Incompetence is hard to define, but some common signs are prescribing over the telephone for new symptoms, acceding to all the patient's demands (no matter how unreasonable), and overtreating, for example, prescribing antibiotics for a cold. A genuinely incompetent doctor should be reported to the state medical society, which has the power to revoke a doctor's license to practice.

When the patient decides to change, he or she should discuss this with the doctor, if the relationship has not deteriorated too far to do so. While the patient should be sensitive to the fact that the relationship with patients is one of the doctor's "rewards," the patient's first responsibility is to his or her own health. Patients who want records transferred to another doctor must give written authorization for this to be done.

OFFICE AND CLINIC CARE

ACCORDING TO AN ANNUAL SURVEY conducted by the U.S. Public Health Service, the average American

has 5 visits a year with a doctor. The survey defines a visit as an encounter with a physician (or another health professional under the doctor's supervision) in the doctor's office, the patient's home (even by telephone), or in another ambulatory-care setting such as a clinic. Half of these visits are initiated by the doctor, as part of follow-up care.

Between the ages of 17 and 75, women tend to see doctors more often than men; before 17 and after 75 the rate is about equal. The number of visits rises steadily with age.

Today, the poor, who are sick more, logically tend to see doctors more; quite the opposite was true 50 years ago, when the higher the income, the greater the number of doctor visits.

Office-Based Practice

Solo Practice. Although the majority of doctors are in practice by themselves, solo practice is decreasing, except in isolated areas, partly because of the heavy workload and responsibility. While many doctors find solo practice less complicated than sharing, they may be expected by their patients to be on call 24 hours a day. The obvious advantages to the patient of a solo practice is a more personal relationship with a doctor and less fragmented care. On the other hand, if the doctor is not available, it may mean going to a total stranger for a serious illness.

Partnerships. This legal agreement between 2 or more doctors to share space, equipment, and office staff has a number of advantages. By lowering the workload and spreading responsibility for patients, partnership may allow the doctor to spend more time with each patient. It is generally more economical to the doctor, a savings that may be passed on in lower fees. Finally, it affords the opportunity for consultation and education among partners.

The patient has the advantage of having a backup doctor who is known to him or her. This is especially important in specialties like obstetrics, where one doctor may not always be available at patients' delivery time, or in cardiology, where emergencies are common.

Groups. A group is a voluntary association of 3 or more doctors and is generally less formal and more flexible than a partnership. It may be a single-specialty group, such as 3 obstetrician/gynecologists, or it may be a multispecialty group including an internist, an obstetrician/gynecologist, and a pediatrician.

Since the reputation of the group depends on overall performance, the doctors have an interest not only in their own performance but in the standards of their colleagues, an internal control that benefits the patient.

The doctors in the group will probably be more familiar with the medical problems of each other's patients than the patients' doctors who do not practice together. As with partnerships, the availability of other physicians for education and consultation is an important advantage.

The economics of a group practice often allow better equipped offices and may support ancillary services such as laboratories.

Health Maintenance Organizations. A special type of group practice, one that is gaining in popularity, is the Health Maintenance Organization (HMO). HMOs represent a marked departure from the traditional U.S. system of third-party insurance with fee-for-service payments. Instead, for a fixed monthly or annual fee, they provide all necessary health services (either directly or through specialists under contract), including hospitalization. Because they offer preventive medicine at no extra cost to the consumer and because there is a markedly lower use of hospital days per thousand people served, they are seen by many as a potential solution to rising costs of health care.

Prepaid medical service plans are not new to America. A number were in existence in the nineteenth century, under the sponsorship of fraternal lodges, benevolent societies, and the railroad and mining industries, among others. There has, however, been a steady growth in the number of such plans since the 1920s. In 1980, 4 percent of the population was enrolled in prepaid medical plans—more than 9 million people in 234 plans in 39 states and the District of Columbia.

The label health maintenance organization covers a variety of groups, which may have been organized by an employer, union, consumer group, medical society, or insurance company. Many HMOs conform to federal standards, others to varying state regulations.

Generally speaking, an HMO is an organization that:

● Assumes a contractual obligation to provide or assure the delivery of a stated range of health services, including at least physician and hospital services (the comprehensiveness of the guaranteed services varies widely).

● Has a voluntarily enrolled, defined population (which may range from a few thousand to more than 1 million, the average size being 42,000).

● Requires a fixed periodic payment, independent of the use of services.

● Assumes at least part of the financial risk or gain in the provision of services. Some HMOs own their own hospitals outright; others contract for a specific number of beds in a local hospital, or negotiate a per diem room rate.

Two major plans come under the HMO umbrella. The first is prepaid group practice (PGP), in which the member doctors are salaried. The second is the individual (or independent) practice association (IPA), comprising private physicians in private offices who generally bill the HMO on a fee-for-service basis.

HMOs save money for their enrollees. Although the annual premium is generally higher than for conventional medical insurance, and there are sometimes out-of-pocket expenses for services not covered, the total expenditure is lower—in some plans as much as 40 percent—than the expenditure of comparable people with conventional insurance coverage. Lower health-care costs are largely due to a lower hospital admission rate and the fact that more tests are done on an outpatient basis. The lower rate of hospitalization may be the result of a number of factors: careful case management, with improved access to ambulatory care; preventive care that reduces the occurrence of problems requiring hospitalization; or self-selection—the preference for HMOs by those who put a premium on preventive care or earlier hospital discharge.

Studies have shown that HMOs do not reduce hospitalization and achieve savings by lowering the quality of care. If anything, the quality of care provided by HMOs is better than average. One drawback to such prepaid plans is that they offer less continuity of care, in terms of a relationship between a patient and an individual physician, than does traditional fee-for-service practice.

Preferred Provider Organizations. Backed by many health-care providers and consumer groups, Preferred Provider Organizations (PPOs) are another reaction to spiraling health-care costs. A relatively new concept, a PPO is a group of independent physicians who individually contract with an employer or insurance company to offer health services at prices that often are less than the prevailing local rate.

Employees who make use of the service save money by avoiding the standard deductible and co-payments of conventional insurance plans. Doctors who participate are assured of a stable pool of employed patients, a situation many find attractive. The employer or insurance company gains by being able to negotiate with the physicians for lower fees, a practice that may grow as the oversupply of physicians becomes more widespread. Currently, major PPOs are providing health-care services in California, Florida, and Colorado. Unlike HMOs, PPOs charge on a fee-for-service basis. There is less experience with the quality of care offered by a PPO.

Hospital Outpatient Departments

Almost a third of all hospitals offer outpatient departments (OPDs) or clinics for ambulatory care, and 90 percent of community hospitals provide care to outpatients in their emergency departments. OPDs were once free in many cases because they offered a way to train medical students and residents or because doctors volunteered their services. With Medicaid and Medicare to pay for the health care of those who can't, this is no longer true. Nevertheless, hospital clinics retain an unfortunate reputation for offering substandard care. Quite the opposite can be true, especially in teaching hospitals, although the amenities of care may not be as pleasant as in a doctor's private office.

Although it is less true than in the past, OPDs have been known to be less than considerate of patients, requiring them all to come at the same time, rather than offering appointments, or requiring clinic visits to hear the results of normal laboratory reports. Clinic practices have been improved in many communities through citizen action and representation on the hospital board. Patients and community residents should remember that even private voluntary hospitals have public support. In some cities, 50 percent of doctors' income comes from federal sources. Community action sometimes includes legal measures like roadblocking certifications of need for hospital expansion.

Ambulatory Surgical Centers

Also called surgicenters, these facilities may be independent or hospital-related. For minor surgery, such as D&Cs (dilatation and curettage), abortion, hernia repairs, tissue biopsies, and some forms of cosmetic surgery, they may be a good alternative to a traditional hospital. Because they limit the type of surgery they perform to lower risk procedures that do not require sophisticated backup equipment or long hospital stays, they can keep costs down. Most procedures are performed under local anesthesia and the patient is released to go home on the same day.

Freestanding Emergency Centers

These urgicenters, as these facilities are often called, are generally set up by private, for-profit groups and operate something like hospital emergency departments. They provide 12- to 24-hour care on a drop-in basis and can fill several needs in the community. They provide quick access in an emergency when the nearest hospital is far away; they are usually open longer hours than most doctors' offices; and they can keep costs down because they don't have hospital beds to support. Typically, they treat cuts that require stitches, sprains and bruises, and upper respiratory infections.

Urgicenters are usually a little more expensive than an office visit to a physician, but considerably less than a traditional emergency room. On the other hand, since they make their money on the number of individual medical procedures they perform, they may tend to overuse them. Patients should evaluate an urgicenter on the qualifications of the doctors affiliated with them, on whether they have a good hospital to which to transfer patients if necessary, and on whether they are careful about overuse of income-producing procedures and whether they provide adequate follow-up.

COMMUNITY HEALTH FACILITIES

School and College Health

Traditionally, school health programs have been concerned with the control of communicable diseases and periodic screening for dental, hearing, and vision problems. They are usually coordinated by a school nurse who, in addition to administering minor first aid, may also help with health and sex education programs, keep track of vaccinations, and provide consultation and follow-up with parents. In some cities, school nurses are employed by the local health department, but more commonly they work for the board of education. The comprehensiveness of health services varies as a function of what the community is willing to appropriate in the school budget. Some programs provide help in identifying learning disabilities as well as psychological counseling for children.

Most colleges and universities with a large proportion of students living away from home provide some sort of health services, minimally "infirmary" services—inpatient care of acute illness. Larger schools have organized ambulatory health services which in recent years have begun to deal with problems of contraception and pregnancy, drug dependence, alcoholism, and neuroses.

Industrial Health Programs

Although recognition of the hazards of work can be traced to ancient Egypt, it was not until 1910, when states began enacting worker's compensation laws, that employers began to offer health programs on any significant level. Today, employers are not only the major "third-party payers" of health-care costs, but they offer direct services on the job, ranging from treatment of work-related injuries and minor illnesses to periodic physical exams and general medical and dental care. Virtually all the major unions, beginning with the International Ladies Garment Workers in 1913, offer comprehensive health services to workers and their families.

More recently, employers have recognized the value of preventive medicine and many are now offering not only comprehensive worksite education and screening programs, but also services like alcohol abuse counseling, stop smoking clinics, and aerobic fitness classes. In some companies, fitness programs in fully equipped gymnasiums run by exercise physiologists are executive perks; in others they are open to all employees. Some companies have even developed their own health-care delivery systems.

Health Screening

Local health departments and voluntary health agencies provide health screening, which varies considerably from community to community, both in availability and reliability. They may screen for infectious or parasitic diseases or for chronic disorders such as high blood pressure, sickle cell anemia, or diabetes. A key to the value of screening programs is whether they offer, or make referrals to, follow-up medical care for those found through screening to have, or be at risk for, major diseases.

Neighborhood and Primary Health-Care Centers

These programs, including migrant health care, date from the 1960s and were established to provide ambulatory care in underserved communities, mainly rural areas and inner city neighborhoods where medical care was scarce. Many were staffed by nurses and doctors who were part of the U.S. Public Health Service or by nurse practitioners, who played a more expanded role than they might in areas where there are more physicians. Some programs were limited to the poor by income requirements; others served all of the community if there were no other resources available. Much of the funding for these programs came from the Office of Economic Opportunity and has been cut, meaning many of them are being phased out without any substitute form of health care taking their place.

Women, Infant, and Child Care

This is also a federally funded program that is being cut, which is unfortunate, since it has been estimated that for every dollar spent, 3 are saved in future health-care costs. The emphasis in these programs, which are sometimes the only ones available to low-income families, is on providing well-baby care, nutritious food, and nutrition education for pregnant women, infants, and children under 5.

Disease Prevention and Control

These programs are usually undertaken by county or city health departments to help control the spread of communicable diseases through immunization, screening, and follow-up. Typically they are concerned with immunization for childhood diseases such as diphtheria, measles, and polio; with care for tuberculosis and sexually transmitted diseases; and with influenza immunization for the elderly.

The programs vary widely from community to community and depend on the direction of the local health department and its budget. This in turn is influenced by the degree of homogeneity in the community and the willingness to take on responsibility for others' health—a major problem faced by community-based health care. (For information on community-based programs for people with mental, physical, or emotional disabilities, see The Directory of Resources, page 792.)

HOME CARE

CARE AT HOME may be appropriate when a patient has an acute illness or is recovering from an episode of acute illness (as, for example, after hospitalization for a heart attack) or when a person is suffering from a chronic illness. It is also the most common setting for care of the elderly. For that reason, community programs designed to help augment home care, such as day hospitals, medical day care, and mental health day care, are discussed in Chapter 3, Meeting the Needs of the Aged, pages 36–46.

HOSPICES

HOSPICE CARE for the terminally ill is available in a growing number of communities. A hospice may be an independent, freestanding institution, or a special wing in a hospital, or simply a few hospital beds that can be made available to the program as needed. Hospice is a philosophy, an approach to dying, rather than a physical facility as such. Some hospice programs are carried on at home.

Basic to the hospice approach is total care of both patient and family to minimize the two greatest fears associated with dying: fear of isolation and fear of pain. Care is palliative, with emphasis placed on the careful control of pain and the management of other symptoms of terminal illness. Patients remain at home as long as possible; many die there. While the patient is at home, families typically provide much of the care, receiving assistance and support from a team consisting of a physician, nurses, counselors, home health aides, and other workers as needed. When the patient must be admitted to the hospice facility, care by the same team provides continuity. Support of the family continues through the period of bereavement. There are also bereavement counseling and self-help groups, but these are generally not reimbursable.

A patient is accepted into the program at his or her own request, with a doctor's referral. A stipulation is that the prognosis be no more than six months of life. This may create difficulties for patients whose illness is terminal but unpredictable in duration—as, for example, heart disease, the leading cause of death. Hospice care, both at home and in the hospice facility (if this becomes necessary), is now partially reimbursable under Medicare.

HOSPITALS

UNTIL ABOUT A CENTURY AGO, American hospitals had a deservedly bad reputation. The upper and middle classes saw the hospitals as institutions for the poor, who could not afford to pay for care at home. The poor, to whom hospitals traditionally provided free care, saw hospitalization as a sign of economic failure and the humiliating breakdown of the family network. Rich and poor alike saw the hospital as a death-house—and with reason.

The image changed dramatically in the late nineteenth century, with the advent of general anesthesia and the new understanding of antisepsis and asepsis. With these technological improvements, the hospital became the only place where complex surgery could be done safely, and where adequate postoperative care could be provided. The introduction of x-ray and EKG machines at the turn of the century—invaluable diagnostic tools that were far too big and expensive for a doctor's private office—solidified the hospital's new reputation. Among patients of all classes, and their doctors, the hospital had become the place to go for sophisticated, technologically up-to-date care. The shift to hospital care may have been too great.

Other changes took place in parallel. At the time when most patients were charity cases, little provision was made for their comfort: The patient was in the hospital for illness' sake, nothing else. When, however, the rich began to use the hospitals as places for sickness, rather than remaining at home, they demanded "home comforts." Private pavilions were built to meet this need, often by wealthy philanthropists. A "hotel" function was thus added to the "healing" function of the hospital. The two were, and still are, frequently at odds. Where there is a conflict, hospital personnel usually place the hotel function in second place; patients are often inclined to see things differently.

Is Hospitalization Necessary?

This is a question that should be asked more often than it is. The United States has the highest per capita hospitalization rate in the world. (The rate in the United Kingdom is only 40 percent that of the United States.) Studies suggest that up to 50 percent of hospital admissions are not medically necessary. When there are alternatives—home care, outpatient care, ambulatory surgery—the question should be raised. It should also be remembered that hospitalization may be for the doctor's rather than for the patient's convenience.

Hospital care is the most expensive of all care, accounting for $80 of every $100 spent on health care. Conventional insurance policies implicitly encourage hospitalization: Their coverage is much better for inpatient than for outpatient procedures. It should be noted that the hospitalization rate among enrollees in HMOs, where a single payment covers all services, both inpatient and outpatient, is 30 per-

cent that of the population as a whole, depending on the mix of enrollees in the HMO.

Hospitalization is not only expensive, it can be dangerous. In one of seven hospitalized patients, some problem arises *as a result* of the hospitalization. Among these problems are infections, falls and other accidents, adverse reactions to medications, complications of surgery, and problems traceable to mistakes on the part of hospital workers.

The expense of hospitalization, together with greatly improved drug therapies that enable many patients to be treated at the doctor's office, has, in fact, led to a recent drop in hospital use. Another contribution to the decline appears to be a general unwillingness to repeat the hospital experience. Patients complain that they are treated as objects, or as examples of disease, rather than as human beings—and as dependent children rather than as adults. It is in order to avoid what they see as the depersonalization and infantilization of being hospitalized that many women with normal pregnancies decide to deliver at home or in a childbirth center. For similar reasons, many terminally ill patients choose to forgo technology and spend their last days at home.

One broad way of classifying hospitals is by length of stay, the amount of time the average patient spends in the hospital before being discharged. Hospitals can then be described as short-term or long-term or as providing extended care. Short-term care facilities include community, teaching, and public hospitals.

Community Hospitals

The most common type of hospital in the United States, and the one where the majority of people receive their care, is the community (or general) hospital. These hospitals are usually quite small, with 50 to 500 beds. Size is often a hallmark of the quality of services provided: Communities that can support a larger hospital can also support a fuller complement of medical and surgical specialists and appropriate facilities and equipment. Community hospitals usually provide good, personalized care and have facilities adequate for the level of care they undertake to provide: secondary-level care, concerned with everyday medical and surgical problems.

Traditionally, community hospitals have been nonprofit corporations, with a lay board of trustees, using government funds for expanding the plant, and with a constant need for community support. Today, the community hospital is increasingly likely to be proprietary, owned, and run for profit by investor-owned corporations. It has been predicted that by 1990 over 90 percent of the country's hospitals will have some association, whether formal or informal, with one of the investor-owned health-care chains.

Costs at a for-profit community hospital may not differ greatly from those at a similar nonprofit (voluntary) hospital. Savings achieved through modern management techniques, bulk expenditures and sophisticated computer systems are likely to be offset by dividend payments to the investors and the excessive use of procedures and technology.

Teaching Hospitals

A teaching hospital is any hospital where there are students in training—undergraduate medical students, postgraduate students, or fellows. Teaching hospitals range in size from a few hundred to a few thousand beds; virtually all have major medical-school ties.

A university's primary teaching hospitals provide the clinical training program for the university's medical school. Most of the staff have full- or part-time academic appointments at the university; they give classroom instruction and do research in addition to teaching at the bedside. University-affiliated hospitals are those that have one or more specialty-board-approved postgraduate training programs, run in cooperation with the medical school.

Patients in teaching hospitals, by virtue of their being there, have implicitly given permission to be used as "teaching patients." They can expect to be examined by undergraduate and graduate students, to give their medical history several times over, and to have their cases discussed by numerous doctors who are strangers to them. All this may be irritating, but it is an assurance of good care (with so many people involved, it is unlikely that an important fact will be missed or a tender spot remain unexamined) and an active contribution to medical education.

Patients who find this situation intolerable can ask their doctors to speak to the attending physician about it. This may be sufficient. They should remember, however, that a teaching hospital is within its rights in transferring to another institution a patient who refuses to cooperate with teaching procedures.

Teaching hospitals provide care at all three levels: primary care in the clinics and the emergency room, and secondary- and tertiary-level care in the wards and private rooms. They have superb technical resources and highly qualified, up-to-date physicians on the staff. Despite their reputation for only being interested in "interesting diseases," that is, unusual or challenging diseases, teaching hospitals have a broad range of medical capabilities and treat run-of-the-mill illnesses as competently as rare ones. Such hospitals, however, are sometimes chillingly impersonal—even the medical school faculty may remark that the hospital is no place to be sick, unless seriously so. But if your condition is complex or technically difficult, there is no question that a teaching hospital is the best place to be.

Many of the short-term hospitals that are used by state medical schools for teaching purposes are government-owned. Other teaching hospitals may be owned by the university itself, or may be funded and overseen by a nonprofit corporation. Regardless of ownership, however, much of the bill is footed by the government through Medicare and Medicaid, as is the case with many community hospitals.

Public Hospitals

Among public hospitals—those owned by the federal, state, or city governments, and operated by the state, city, or county department of health—are the municipal short-term-stay hospitals. Many of these—dilapidated, very large, and located in run-down neighborhoods—have a reputation for substandard care. This is often undeserved. Such hospitals have a long tradition of providing care for the medically indigent and continue to do so today. Many are teaching hospitals, with the benefits—carefully supervised care, familiarity with current knowledge and techniques—of a teaching hospital. Others have associated rehabilitation units and nursing homes.

Other hospitals wholly supported by public funds are county hospitals, public health service hospitals, and the hospitals run by the Veterans Administration (VA). The VA hospitals treat veterans whose illness is service-related—and also those whose illness is not service-related, if there are beds available and the veteran is without funds or medical insurance. There is no means test for veterans over 65 years of age. Most VA hospitals are associated with medical schools.

The Hospital Hierarchies

Because hospitals have both a "healing" function and a "hotel" function, they have 2 co-existing power structures. The 2 are mutually dependent and often overlap each other. Nevertheless, their focus of interest is different, and clashes are not unknown.

In a community hospital, the head of the medical hierarchy is a physician, whose title may be medical director, chief of staff, or physician-in-chief. This position may be rotated on an annual basis among the physicians on the staff. Alternatively, the medical director may be elected by the other physicians or may be appointed by the hospital's governing body, usually a board of trustees.

In small hospitals, the medical director is directly responsible for the care given in all the various medical departments—surgery, medicine, or pediatrics, for example. In larger hospitals, each of these departments has its own elected or appointed chief of service, who is responsible in turn to the medical director.

The medical director receives a salary from the hospital during his or her tenure in the position. Other doctors usually are not salaried, nor do they pay the hospital for the use of its facilities.

In university hospitals, the hierarchical structure is complicated by the superimposition of an academic structure. The chief of staff for surgery, for example, will also be a professor of surgery at the medical school and (usually) chairman of the school's department of surgery.

Doctors practicing at university hospitals are either "full-time" or "part-time." Full-time doctors are employees of the university and spend their time in research and teaching, including bedside teaching and, thus, patient care. Part-timers have some university responsibilities but also see private patients. Postgraduate trainees in university and other teaching hospitals provide the exception to the general rule that hospitals do not pay the doctors who work there.

At the top of the "hotel" hierarchy of the hospital is the chief administrator (often called the chief executive officer). Increasingly, hospital administrators hold advanced degrees in the administrative rather than the medical field, as was the case in the past. For the hospital administration, the hospital is a complicated business enterprise which must function in an efficient and solvent fashion while still serving as a center for patient care—and often also as a locus for medical education and clinical research.

The hospital's nursing department, focused toward the healing function, is nevertheless responsible to the hospital administration. Nurses are hired and paid by the hospital. Where a hospital is affiliated with a school of nursing, some of the nurses will be students working under the supervision of the nursing school faculty. However, because of the size of the nursing staff (nurses are needed for 3 shifts a day, 7 days a week), the great majority of nurses in *any* hospital are hospital employees.

Nurses' aides and orderlies are also hired and paid by the hospital administration, as are laboratory technicians, members of the housekeeping department, and the business and clerical staff. Clinical support services, for example, physical therapy, occupational therapy, the pharmacy, the blood bank, and diagnostic testing centers such as electrocardiography and electroencephalography, are within the purview of the hospital administration, rather than that of the medical staff.

Special Facilities

Emergency Departments. Most hospitals have an emergency room, although it may not be open around the clock, or may not have a team of physicians (or even one physician) present day and night. As emergency services are, by definition, needed in sudden and serious situations, it is wise to check the staffing and hours of the emergency departments of nearby hospitals before the need arises.

Emergency departments have the equipment (including resuscitative machinery) necessary for treating common emergency conditions, and they have immediate access to the full range of hospital services. In descending order of priority, emergency departments act: first, to save lives immediately endangered; second, to treat illnesses or injuries that might become life-threatening; third, to deal with emergency or urgent problems that are not dangerous but require treatment; fourth, to evaluate and treat minor complaints; and fifth, to treat chronic complaints. (The fourth and fifth categories do not constitute emergencies, but many patients in many emergency rooms fall within them.)

In recent years, the hospital emergency department has become a primary-care facility for everyday ailments. Large city hospitals often have a "triage" nurse on duty at the door to divide urgent cases from those that can be cared for in an outpatient clinic. Unless a patient's condition is immediately life-threatening, a wait is to be expected. How long the wait is will depend on the urgency of the complaint relative to the urgency of the complaints of other patients.

Emergency rooms may not legally refuse to treat a person in need of true emergency care, even if that person cannot demonstrate an ability to pay. It should be remembered that care in an emergency room is much more expensive than that given in a doctor's office and that, unless the situation is demonstrably an emergency, most insurance policies do not cover the hospital bill.

Intensive Care Units. Almost all large community hospitals, and many smaller ones, have an intensive care unit (ICU); the quality of care provided is variable.

ICUs provide close monitoring, observation, and quickly responsive treatment to patients who need this kind of supervision, among them patients with heart failure, recent stroke victims, and, in hospitals that do not have a shock–trauma center (see below), victims of serious accidents. Certain surgical cases go routinely from the operating room to the ICU; others go routinely if the patient is in a particular age group. The nurse:patient ratio is usually 1:2 (as opposed to 1:8 on regular floors).

With its sophisticated and noisy medical machinery, an ICU can be an alarming place. Patients are often heavily sedated. There is no privacy because of the necessity of constant observation, and patients are allowed no personal possessions except dentures and essential toilet articles. Visits are usually limited to the closest relatives (no children) and restricted to short timespans as, for example, 5 minutes every 2 hours.

Many patients in special care units experience transient psychiatric difficulties (the "ICU syndrome"). Distortions of reality, psychiatric difficulties sometimes progressing to auditory or visual hallucinations and then to frank paranoia, may evolve after the first 3 to 5 days in an ICU or coronary care unit (CCU). The syndrome appears to be related to sensory deprivation, lack of human contact, and an environment in which night and day are indistinguishable. Some units have added psychiatric social workers to the team to counteract this emotional deterioration. Families can help by making their brief visits as substantive as possible.

Coronary Care Units (or Coronary Observation Units).
Only the smallest of the U.S. hospitals now lack a coronary care unit (CCU). These units, offshoots of the ICU, have grown enormously in popularity in the past 15 years—past the point, some experts maintain, of cost-effectiveness.

CCUs provide constant monitoring for people who have had a heart attack or who need observation for a variety of cardiac conditions. Emphasis is placed on rest and the gradual reduction of stress; caffeine and tobacco are banned. Visiting is geared to the needs of the patient.

Neonatal Intensive Care Units.
Neonatal intensive care units (NICUs) are found in major medical centers. They specialize in the problems of the newborn, whose fluid requirements, oxygen management, temperature control, and drug dosages are unique. The infants are housed in "isolettes," which both reduce the risk of infection and provide for individualized temperature and oxygen needs. Premature babies weighing as little as 2 pounds have a good chance of survival, given ideal care, in an NICU. How much physical contact parents may have with their newborn will depend on the infant's condition and the policies of the unit.

Shock–Trauma or Critical Care Centers.
These centers, which are few and generally located in major metropolitan areas, provide specialized care for the victims of serious accidents. An ancillary but vital part of the system is a mechanism for transporting the injured to the center, with life-support equipment and trained personnel available en route. Several centers have established "helivac" units, using helicopters.

Shock–trauma centers have a full complement of life-support equipment, immediate access to laboratories, and on-call specialists in every medical field, including the newly recognized field of intensive care.

Other special units that are generally available only in large medical centers include burn units, geared to the special needs of those who have suffered extensive burns; renal dialysis units for the treatment of hospitalized patients and outpatients with chronic kidney disease; neurological injury units that specialize in injuries involving the brain or the spinal cord, or both; cardiac rehabilitation units for those who have had coronary artery bypass surgery.

Elective Surgical Admissions—What to Expect.
An elective procedure is a nonemergency procedure and will therefore be scheduled with several days' or even months' notice. Although this is becoming less true as hospitals face financial penalties by not rendering acute care daily, in general the patient should try to avoid a Friday admission: hospital laboratories operate with a skeleton staff on weekends and the necessary preoperative tests will not be done until Monday.

Before admission, patients should check with the hospital's business office about financial obligations. In all likelihood, their health insurance will cover much of the hospital expense; how much, of course, depends on the policy. No insurance policy, however, will cover a private room, which may be as little as $10 or as much as $300 more a day than a semiprivate room. Insurance usually covers only the cost of a semiprivate room. It may not cover such personal expenses as a bedside telephone, or private-duty nursing, if this is required. The insurance policy will also probably cover most of the expense of medication and laboratory work (these are billed separately from the hospital room) and at least some part of the physicians' fees. The patient should ask whether the choice of room will be reflected in the bill: Some doctors charge more when the patient elects a private rather than a semiprivate room.

Also before admission, the patient should contact the admitting office about room preference and be prepared to give the diagnosis, doctor's name, date for which surgery is scheduled, age, and whether he or she smokes. Patients should ask what time they are expected to check in at the admitting office and whether they are expected to make pre-payment for private rooms.

Admission Procedures. These can be time-consuming. Their basic purpose is to ensure that the admission is voluntary, legal, and financially sound. The patient will be asked to sign several financial forms and the hospital's Conditions of Admission (or Consent to Treatment) form. In signing this latter form, the patient voluntarily consents to treatment; this is the valid consent that precludes the hospital's liability for assault and battery in the event the treatment is unsatisfactory.

The patient should bring the following to the admissions office: insurance card (or a check for partial prepayment of the hospital bill); name, address, and telephone number of employer; social security card; and the name, address, and telephone number of someone who should be informed of any changes in the patient's condition.

Packing should be limited to toilet articles, a bathrobe and slippers, reading materials, letter-writing materials, a note pad and pencil, and no more than $10 in cash. Jewelry and valuable watches should be left home. The patient should bring a list of the medications taken routinely with details as to strength and dosage, but should leave the medications themselves at home.

Preoperative Routines. Preoperative routines include a medical history and physical examination for the hospital records. In a teaching hospital, the history and physical will probably be done by a postgraduate trainee and may be repeated by a medical student. The patient has a right to refuse more than one history and physical. However, one doctor (or student) may see or feel something that another overlooks and it is therefore advisable to agree.

A nurse will repeat many of the questions included in the medical history in order to make a "nursing assessment." Questions about medications, home situation, and the support systems available to patients help provide comprehensive care and give information that will be helpful in discharge-planning.

Routine preoperative tests include a complete blood analysis, electrocardiogram, urine analysis, blood pressure, and chest x-ray. Depending on the patient's condition and the surgery that is planned, a variety of other tests may be done preoperatively. The basic purpose of preoperative tests is to ensure that the patient can undergo surgery safely and to provide the hospital with the information that may be needed if complications arise—if, for example, it is necessary to give a blood transfusion.

The patient will be asked to sign a form consent-ing to surgery. This form states that the "nature of the operation" has been explained. Before signing the form, the patient should be sure that this is so: that he or she has a good understanding of what will be done and what the risks and anticipated benefits of the procedure are. Patients should be certain that the procedure described is the one wanted and that body parts (including "left" or "right") are specified. The surgical consent form may cover a surgeon's options—for example, "left breast biopsy; possible left radical mastectomy." All such options should be explained *before* surgery.

Consent forms similar to those for surgery are required for invasive tests (for example, cardiac catheterization, angiography, percutaneous liver biopsy). The same type of information should be given to the patient, before signing, as is given before surgery.

"Prepping." Prepping for surgery is done the night before the operation if the operation is scheduled early; otherwise it will be done first thing in the morning. Since hair harbors bacteria, the site of the operation and a large area around it will be shaved and painted with antiseptic. If it is anticipated that a skin graft may be needed, that site will also be prepared.

An anesthesiologist (chosen by the surgeon) should see the patient the night before the surgery to inquire about previous experiences with anesthesia and any drug allergies. If there is an option as to the type of anesthesia to be used (local, spinal, or general), this should be explained and the pros and cons of the different types explored. A patient should discuss the various types of anesthesia that may be used with the anesthesiologist, since many factors—comfort, safety, side effects and surgeon's preference—should be taken into account.

The Operation. The patient will be allowed nothing to eat or drink for 12 or more hours before the operation. The stomach must be empty when a general anesthetic is given because of the risk of vomiting and aspirating the vomit while anesthetized. Even if the operation is to be done under local anesthetic, the empty-stomach precaution will be observed, as unforeseen circumstances may arise, making a general anesthetic necessary.

About 1 hour before the operation, the patient may be given a sedative and will then have to remain in bed. Some 20 minutes later, he or she will be moved onto a gurney (a stretcher on wheels), asked to remove eyeglasses and dentures, and taken to the operating suite.

The patient is more likely to feel less human in the operating room than anywhere else in the hospital. The surgical team—the surgeon, the anesthesiologist, the operating room nurse, and their assistants—is technologically oriented and works with speed. Patients will be closely observed but should not expect much "tender loving care." With a general anesthetic, the patient will be completely unaware of what is going on; even with a spinal or local anesthetic, the patient will be less alert because of the preoperative sedation.

After any operation that requires a general anesthetic, patients are taken from the operating room to a special recovery room. Here, "vital signs" (pulse, temperature, respiration, and blood pressure) will be checked every few minutes for an hour or so, to ensure that the patient is recovering satisfactorily from the anesthetic. In addition, a nurse will call the patient's name and ask him or her to respond, testing the extent to which the anesthesia has "worn off."

Recovery. The patient will be taken back to his or her room once the vital signs have stabilized and the patient has begun to emerge from the anesthesia. Pain at the site of the operation is to be expected and there may also be nausea and vomiting. Medications are available for the relief of these postoperative symptoms, and patients should make their needs known.

One aftereffect of general anesthesia is an increase in lung secretions and a consequent risk of pneumonia. Turning in bed and breathing deeply will help the patient mobilize these secretions; coughing brings them up. Turning, coughing, and deep breathing (TCDB in nurses' shorthand) may be painful but are essential to keep the lungs clear. Early ambulation has much the same effect and the additional benefit of preventing muscle deterioration, which can begin after only a few days' immobility.

A spinal anesthetic alters the pressure of fluids within the spinal column. It is important for the patient to follow postoperative instructions carefully so as to avoid the headaches that may accompany pressure changes as the spinal fluid readjusts. Usually it is recommended that a patient who has had a spinal anesthetic lie completely flat (on the back, and without a pillow) for 12 hours or more.

If the patient has had an abdominal operation, a nasogastric tube (running from the stomach up through the esophagus and exiting at the nose) will have been put in place at the end of the operation, to remain for several days. This tube carries out stomach gases that might otherwise accumulate and cause great discomfort. Even so, the patient is likely to have some gas pain on the third day after the operation when the gastric juices become active again.

Depending on the operation, the patient may have other tubes that drain excess fluid from the site of the surgery. There may also be an intravenous tube that delivers fluid and possibly nutrients to a vein in the arm. It may lessen the patient's anxiety to know, before the operation, what measures of this kind to expect.

Patients' Rights

In 1973, following years of bad publicity and pressure from consumer groups, the American Hospital Association formalized a list of the rights of hospitalized patients. This list can be found posted in hospital corridors (in accredited hospitals, it is mandatory to post it) and it is often printed in patient information handbooks. (See the box on page 29.)

Points 5, 6, and 7 concern the concept of "informed consent," which cannot be separated from that of "necessary information." Together, these rights mean that:

- A patient has the right to understand what is medically the matter, and what the doctor intends to do. This explanation does not have to be highly detailed or technical; the patient, however, should understand in a general way what is involved in his condition and in the procedures planned.

- A patient should know what the potential risks of the proposed treatment or procedure are. The doctor is required to provide this information. (In addition, there are statistical probability tables on the frequency of death and serious complications for almost every disease treated in a hospital; the data for the local hospital are usually available, as well as regional and national figures.)

- A patient also has the right to know what measures other than the one proposed by the doctor are available, and what their risks are. (It should be noted that a surgeon's list of alternative measures may differ from an internist's.) He or she has the further right to know the probable outcome if only the most conservative treatment—"do nothing" procedures—is undertaken.

- A patient should understand that he or she is not being coerced into complying with the doctor's plans, is choosing freely, and can reject treatment if he or she changes his or her mind.

- A patient should be aware that any treatment of body or mind without voluntary, fully informed consent is a wrongful act.

Points 8 and 9 concern privacy of information. A patient's chart is not his or her property. (It is, in fact, a legal document, the property of the hospital. Only that information that would be salient in the courtroom must be included; much is therefore

THE PATIENT'S BILL OF RIGHTS

(as established by the American Hospital Association)

The hospital shall establish written policies regarding the rights of patients upon admission for treatment as an inpatient, outpatient, or emergency room patient, and shall develop procedures implementing such policies. These rights, policies, and procedures shall afford patients the right to:

1. receive emergency medical care, as indicated by the patient's medical condition, upon arrival at a hospital for the purpose of obtaining emergency medical treatment;

2. considerate and respectful care;

3. obtain the name of the physician assigned the responsibility for coordinating his or her care and the right to consult with a private physician and/or a specialist for the type of care being rendered, provided such physician has been accorded hospital staff privileges;

4. the name and function of any person providing treatment to the patient;

5. obtain from his or her physician complete current information concerning diagnosis, treatment and prognosis in terms the patient can reasonably be expected to understand;

6. receive from his or her physician information necessary to give informed consent prior to the start of any nonemergency procedure or treatment or both. An informed consent shall include, as a minimum, the specific procedure or treatment or both, the reasonably foreseeable risks involved, and alternatives for care or treatment, if any, as a reasonable medical practitioner under similar circumstances would disclose;

7. refuse treatment to the extent permitted by law, and to be informed of the medical consequences of his or her action.

8. privacy to the extent consistent with providing adequate medical care to the patient. This shall not preclude discreet discussion of a patient's case or examination of a patient by appropriate health-care personnel;

9. privacy and confidentiality of all records pertaining to the patient's treatment, except as otherwise provided by law or third-party payment contract;

10. a response by the hospital, in a reasonable manner, to the patient's request for services customarily rendered by the hospital consistent with the patient's treatment;

11. be informed by his or her physician, or designee of the physician, of the patient's continuing health-care requirement following discharge, and that before transferring a patient to another facility the hospital first informs the patient of the need for and alternatives to such a transfer;

12. the identity, upon request, of other health care and educational institutions that the hospital has authorized to participate in the patient's treatment;

13. refuse to participate in research and that human experimentation affecting care or treatment shall be performed only with the patient's informed effective consent;

14. examine and receive an explanation of his or her bill, regardless of source of payment;

15. know the hospital rules and regulations that apply to his or her conduct as a patient.

16. treatment without discrimination as to race, color, religion, sex, national origin or source of payment, except for fiscal capability thereof;

17. designate any private accommodation to which admitted as a nonsmoking area. In the event that private accommodations are not available, a patient shall have a right to be admitted to accommodations which have been designated by the governing authority as a nonsmoking area. It shall be the duty of the governing authority of the hospital to afford priority to the rights of nonsmokers in all semiprivate, ward, and pediatric common patient areas; and

18. voice grievances and recommend changes in policies and services to the facility's staff, the governing authority and the state department of health without fear of reprisal.

A copy of the provisions of this section shall be made available to each patient or patient's representatives upon admission for treatment as an inpatient, outpatient, and/or emergency room patient, and posted in conspicuous places within the hospital.

---

omitted.) Nevertheless, a patient is within rights in asking to see the chart. Much has been made of the possibility that a patient may not be able to cope with the information found there. In fact, however, hospital charts—written by doctors and nurses in medical shorthand as a record for other health professionals—are seldom helpful to patients who are curious about their conditions.

While hospitals acknowledge the patient's right to privacy concerning program and records, in practice this is difficult to achieve. Details of the patient's condition will inevitably be known, not only to doctors, nurses, and aides, but also to technicians in many different areas—and to the billing department.

The Patient's Bill of Rights was adopted by the American Hospital Association in an attempt to improve relations between patients and hospitals. It has been promoted by many as a legal document, or as a document that has the potential of being legally binding. However, enforcement of any of these rights would be difficult: They deal to a large extent with intangible factors—consideration, respect, confidentiality, reasonableness—that affect the relationship between patients and those who treat them. Nevertheless, patients who feel that their rights have been violated should *always* raise the issue with their doctors and the hospital staff (see Remedying Deficient Hospital Care, page 32).

The Patient's Role in the Hospital

Patients who understand the goals of their medical programs, and cooperate actively with those who are treating them, can make a great difference in the speed of their recovery. Their rights as patients include the right to a full disclosure, in lay language, about their condition and the procedures that are planned (see The Patient's Bill of Rights, page 29). It is their responsibility to exercise this right by asking questions about anything that is not clear to them. (It may be helpful for them to have written notes about questions to ask and also to make notes on the answers.) A patient has a right to read his or her own medical record.

A patient should ask the doctor in advance for details about recovery—whether there will be discomfort or pain and for how long, when is a reasonable time to expect discharge, and how long activities may be limited afterward. Knowing what to expect lessens anxiety and speeds recovery.

Discharge of the patient as soon as it is medically advisable, with continued convalescence at home, in an extended-care facility, or in a nursing home, is in everyone's best interest, and the patient should be willing to leave as soon as the doctor gives an okay. A hospital stay prolonged unnecessarily may deprive another patient of a needed bed. In addition, inefficient use of hospital facilities is an important cause of the spiraling cost of medical care.

Although the patient may be ready to do "anything to get well," he or she should be alert to the fact that the "anything" may be merely a fossilized hospital routine. Questions about routines that seem inappropriate may earn him or her the label of a "difficult" patient, that is, an assertive rather than

a passive one. But the staff's expectation of unquestioning compliance on the part of patients is not legitimate, and a healthy assertiveness is an important step toward recovery.

In Case of Death

If the patient's illness is serious, and there is a possibility of death while in the hospital, there are certain things that should be taken into consideration. The patient may, for example, want to consider donating tissues or body organs (the corneas of the eye, skin, bone, pancreas, or kidneys, among others), or the whole body. In many states, patients 18 or older can authorize that all or any parts of their body be used for specified purposes after death, under the Anatomical Gift Act. Alternatively, the patient can let the immediate family know of his wishes; they can then give the necessary permission. Those wishing to donate their bodies to medical education (dissection of the human body is an essential part of students' training) should contact the department of anatomy, or the dean's office, at any medical school. Usually, bodies used for these purposes are later cremated.

If a member of the family dies while in the hospital, the question of an autopsy may arise. In some hospitals, autopsy is mandatory under certain circumstances—for example, a sudden or unexpected death, or a death during surgery. Usually, however, an autopsy is done at the hospital's request and with the family's permission. (Permission is requested in priority order, from the surviving spouse to more remote relatives.)

For many people, giving permission for an autopsy is not an easy decision to make. However, there are at least two good reasons for doing so. First, since several diseases are known to have hereditary risk factors, families who know the cause of death of one of their members may be able to take steps to avoid succumbing to the same disease.

Although the cause of death may seem to be clear, this is not always the case. There is a reported 40 to 50 percent difference between diagnoses made before death and the findings at autopsy. Second, an autopsy may contribute indirectly to the health of future generations of the country as a whole. Mortality figures often influence decisions as to the allocation of money for research. For example, the research focus on heart disease is in large part due to the fact that mortality figures have established this as the leading cause of death in this country. It is therefore of long-range importance that mortality figures are based to the greatest degree possible on fact rather than on guesswork.

Autopsies are performed by pathologists, who

have a specialized knowledge of the changes that occur in body tissues as the result of disease. Following an autopsy, the body is returned to the family for disposition.

Hospitals and Children

Hospitalization is a traumatic experience for any child, but especially for a child under five. Fear of abandonment by the mother—normal at this stage of development—will be exaggerated by the event. Studies have shown that trauma can be markedly reduced through play. A doll and some of the hospital supplies used in the child's care (or their play-equivalents) provide the child with a vehicle for dealing with inevitable anxiety.

Sick children regress, going back to wetting their beds, or to depending on a favorite blanket or toy. They may become extremely fussy about food and need the reassurance of the familiar. Parents should ask the nurse if they may bring the child food from home.

If possible, parents should stay with a very young child around the clock; some hospitals provide a bed for a parent in the child's room. A child who is old enough to have a bedside phone and use it properly can be left alone more.

In many hospitals, all children under 16 are accommodated in the same pediatric unit. For an adolescent, this may present a problem. It is common for adolescents in the hospital to behave in an intractable, sullen, and generally obnoxious way. The surliness masks fear of losing control, fear of being dependent, or humiliation at the lack of privacy in a room full of younger children. Noncooperation may extend to a refusal to speak to doctors and nurses, which puts the parent in the difficult position of being the conduit for information and "doctor's orders."

The Quality of Hospital Care

Formal Assurances. Of the approximately 7,000 acute-care hospitals in the United States, about 4,800—with approximately 85 percent of the beds—are accredited (approved) by the Joint Commission on Accreditation of Hospitals (JCAH). The accreditation process of JCAH is the major voluntary mechanism for hospital review and assurance of quality. The Commission sets optimal rather than minimal standards in numerous areas, including: the hospital's compliance with patients' rights; the quality of medical, nursing, dietetic, and other services; pathology reports; drug use; record-keeping; the management of the hospital and its long-range planning; the relationship of the hospital to its neighboring community; and the safety and maintenance of buildings and grounds.

Accreditation is usually given for a period of 2 years, after which the hospital is inspected again. A hospital that fails inspection in significant areas, or that fails to take corrective action for problems that have been found, will have its accreditation revoked. While accreditation is an assurance that certain standards have been met, it is no guarantee of quality. However, lack of accreditation, or a recent loss of accreditation, should raise serious questions.

The federal government, acting through Professional Standards Review Organizations (PSROs), also regularly audits the quality of hospital care. PSROs were set up in 1972 to monitor the appropriateness and quality of services provided to patients whose health care is federally financed. This function is carried out by reviewing admissions, certifying the need for continuing treatment, conducting medical care review, and reviewing extended or extremely costly treatment. Hospitals that fail to correct deficiencies identified by PSRO audit lose their ability to collect Medicare and Medicaid payments—a financial catastrophe for most hospitals today.

Hospitals also have their own internal review mechanisms. Quality assurance review committees meet regularly and are concerned with such questions as the appropriateness and length of patients' hospitalizations, patients' complaints, and reports on surgical specimens. Many of the questions that concern these internal reviewers also concern JCAH, thus providing a double-check.

The caliber of the physicians on a community hospital's staff is very largely determined by the staff's medical credentials committee (in teaching hospitals, this function is performed by *ad hoc* appointments committees). Credentials committees review the qualifications of new applicants for a position on the hospital's staff and deal with requests for hospital privileges. Although doctors are legally permitted to perform the full range of medical and surgical services once they have been licensed, in point of fact their practice will be largely determined by their hospital privileges, which are in turn determined by the credentials committee. Doctors' hospital privileges limit what types of patients they may treat in the hospital, what procedures they may do, and under what circumstances they must consult with a colleague. An obstetrician, for example, might have privileges to do manual but not forceps deliveries, or might be required to get a consultation before performing a cesarean section.

Informal Evaluation. As with choosing a doctor, it is wise to investigate local hospitals ahead of need.

Patients have less control here, however, as admission to one hospital rather than another may depend on such factors as their doctors' admitting privileges, the type of disease they have and the kind of treatment it requires, or whether it is an emergency admission. Many doctors, moreover, prefer to limit their practice to one hospital, gathering all their patients under one roof not only for convenience sake, but because such an arrangement often gives them a better chance of getting a bed when one is needed.

If a patient's doctor has admitting privileges at several hospitals, he or she may be able to give an appraisal of the quality of care at the different institutions. In addition, a local nursing association or nursing agency may provide valuable comparative information about the hospitals in the area—which has the lowest nurse–patient ratio, the lowest turnover of nurses, the highest RN:LPN ratio, and the highest proportion of staff to agency nurses. A hospital's ability to attract and keep good nurses is an excellent indication of quality, and good nursing care is an important factor both in a satisfactory outcome and in comfort while in the hospital.

The patient should look also for the presence of volunteers as an indication of community support and involvement. Good hospitals have good relationships with their neighbors.

A smart patient may "shop around," asking about room-rate charges and charges for "ancillary" services such as tests, lab, x-ray, and the pharmacy. There is often a wide difference among hospitals in the same geographic area. A teaching hospital, with its up-to-date equipment and highly trained personnel (including postgraduate trainees, whose salaries are partly paid out of the room rate), is invariably more expensive than a smaller, more limited community hospital.

Remedying Deficient Hospital Care.
It is necessary, first, to distinguish substandard care from the kind of annoyance that is an unavoidable part of being a patient in the hospital. Being awakened in the middle of the night to be given an optional sleeping pill, for example, is quite unnecessary, and a patient should rightfully complain. But being awakened at night for a check on vital signs may be part of the careful, close monitoring that is vital to recovery.

It is also necessary to distinguish between minor and major deficiencies in care. Minor problems are those that interfere with comfort but do not constitute a threat to physical welfare. Some examples are lukewarm food, a longer than anticipated wait for pain-killing medication, extra minutes

spent on the bedpan. Such grievances can usually be resolved by discussing them (calmly and rationally) with the patient representative or ombudsman, or a member of the social services department. (The ombudsman is a relatively recent addition to hospital staffs, a response to increased patient demand for participation in care; most complaints can be handled effectively through that office.)

Alternatively, a discussion with the staff nurse—or, if that fails, with the head nurse, who has a personal interest in keeping her floor comfortable for patients and employees alike—will usually solve such problems. If that, too, fails it may be necessary to complain to the head of the appropriate department: nursing, nutrition, or housekeeping, for example. The complaint should be written, rather than telephoned, since a written complaint will remain on record while a telephone conversation will not.

Deficiencies of care that are in effect denials of a patient's right to "considerate and respectful care" are also minor, in the sense that they seldom threaten physical welfare. They have, however, important implications for the quality of care as a whole and every effort should be made to correct them. Since hospitals are community facilities with public support, a public responsibility exists to prevent repetition of mistreatment.

It is also important to note that the recovery of a patient from an illness may well be influenced by the patient's state of mind. What seem like trivial complaints may be sufficiently upsetting to a patient to delay recovery from illness.

Major deficiencies in care are those that seriously threaten well-being. They usually involve potentially dangerous shortcomings on the part of the nursing staff. There are some basic principles of good nursing care: attentiveness to changes in the patient's condition, promptness in answering calls, taking time to ask questions and listen for the answers, calling the doctor if the patient's condition changes or if the patient requests it, and possessing the training and skills appropriate to the patient's illness and condition. If these principles are not being met, the patient's well-being may be jeopardized and he or she should notify the doctor, who should then intervene vigorously on the patient's behalf. A move to another section of the hospital may afford better care, since the quality of nursing often differs greatly between one floor and another.

If serious deficiencies in care remain—or if you have reason to think that the doctor's care is deficient—a complaint should be made (again, in writing) to the medical director of the hospital, who has the ultimate responsibility for all care given in the institution. In extreme cases of negligent care, the patient may have grounds for suing the doctor or the hospital, or both, for malpractice.

Malpractice. The American Society of Internal Medicine has stated that "a malpractice action is justified when a patient suffers injury, disability or death as a result of an act of negligence by a physician." However, the Society also states that "unanticipated therapeutic outcome which follows appropriate medical care is not malpractice. . . ."

The distinction that is made here between a bad result, on one hand, and negligence, on the other, is an important one. Opinions differ in medicine as to what is the best course to pursue, and even the best treatment may have an unpredictable result. Decisions must be made in medical treatment in the face of uncertainty, but negligence is negligence.

There are four standards of care that, in effect, constitute a doctor's legal obligations toward his patient; violation of any one could be grounds for a lawsuit.

1. The doctor must obtain the patient's informed consent before treatment. This means that a patient must understand the risks involved in a procedure before consenting to it; it does *not* mean that a doctor must detail every remote possibility, nor that he must get a signed consent form every time he treats a patient. A signed consent form, however, is required by law before surgery or an invasive diagnostic test is done. If informed consent is not obtained properly—if, for example, a patient is asked to agree to "any or all" procedures, or the consent is obtained when the patient is sedated just prior to surgery—the doctor is technically open to a charge of assault and battery.

2. In treating a patient, the doctor must use reasonable skill and care in accordance with accepted medical practice, and within the limits of his competence. The key words here are "reasonable" and "accepted." Both are extremely difficult to define, and it has proved to be extremely difficult to establish in court that this standard has been violated, except in cases of extreme negligence.

3. A doctor must adequately supervise those aspects of a patient's care that he or she delegates to others. Doctors customarily delegate to nurses and other health-care personnel; this is acceptable legally as long as the doctor assumes responsibility for supervising those who are helping. (Under certain circumstances, hospital nurses and aides, although not in the doctor's employ, are considered to be under the doctor's supervision.)

4. A patient, once accepted by a doctor, cannot be abandoned by the doctor. A doctor is not under any obligation to accept a patient, but once treatment has begun, he or she must continue to care for that patient until treatment is no longer needed, or until the patient voluntarily leaves the doctor, or until the doctor has properly notified the patient that he or she is no longer responsible for the patient's care.

In an emergency, such as an automobile accident, a doctor is expected to give reasonable care as best he can, given the circumstances. A doctor who initiates treatment has the responsibility to see to it that another doctor takes over the care of the victim. Because many doctors have been wary of lawsuits stemming from roadside treatment, most states have enacted "Good Samaritan" laws that exempt physicians from civil liability when emergency care has been given in good faith.

A patient with a legitimate grievance against the doctor should first talk the matter over with the doctor. This may clarify what is perhaps a genuine misunderstanding. If such a discussion proves fruitless, the patient can contact the grievance committee of the county or state medical society (responsible members of the medical profession take questions of possible professional incompetence seriously), or seek a lawyer.

It should be remembered that no doctors *willfully* engage in negligent conduct, although there are some who are careless or ignorant, and some for whom "winning" the fight with disease is more important than the quality of life remaining to their patients. It should also be remembered that patients enter into contracts with doctors of their own free will and are free to leave at any time. For the most part, the unpleasantness of taking a doctor to court can be avoided by using good judgment (getting a second opinion, seeking another doctor) and by being certain that all questions have been answered and doubts resolved before giving consent to a procedure.

Arbitration. Many states have laws providing for arbitration in malpractice claims, and some HMOs require their enrollees to sign an arbitration agreement before treatment is begun. Cases are heard by a panel of three arbitrators whose decision is binding and not subject to appeal.

Generally, one arbitrator is chosen by the patient and one by the doctor, with the third being a lawyer; where the claim is for less than $1,500, however, the patient has no choice of arbitrator. The advantages of arbitration are that it is speedy (there is no wait for a court date) and that the costs of administering justice are considerably reduced. Also, with relaxed rules of evidence and simplified procedures, it is easier for the patient or the family to present their case.

EXTENDED-CARE FACILITIES

EXTENDED-CARE FACILITIES are a relatively recent innovation, providing care that is intermediate between that given in an acute-care hospital and that provided in a skilled nursing facility (nursing home). These facilities provide short-term, comprehensive inpatient care, usually following hospitalization, for patients who no longer need the full range of hospital services but still require continuous professional nursing and medical supervision. They may also serve people who are not acutely ill, but who have medical conditions that require skilled care. Many extended-care facilities were established to free acute-care beds.

Most extended-care facilities are physically attached to hospitals so that patients simply move from one wing of the building to another. Others are nursing homes that have met standards set for qualification by JCAH or Medicare. The cost of care in such units may be one-third or one-half of that of a hospital bed.

Long-Term Care Facilities and Nursing Homes

Long-term care facilities begin where hospitals leave off—providing extended care for patients with conditions that cannot be accommodated in a general hospital. Among these facilities are hospitals for the treatment of tuberculosis, chronic disease hospitals, rehabilitation hospitals, mental retardation facilities, and psychiatric hospitals for both children and adults. In addition, nursing homes of all types provide long-term care. They generally fall into 3 categories—residential care facilities, intermediate care facilities, and skilled nursing facilities—and range from providing primarily sheltered living to providing around-the-clock nursing care.

WHO PAYS FOR MEDICAL CARE?

SOARING MEDICAL COSTS have become a major factor in health-care delivery, not only in the United States but in virtually every industrialized country. In the last decade, health-care costs have more than tripled in this country. In 1982, health-care expenditures totaled $322.4 billion, an average of $1,365 per person. If costs continue to rise at the present rate, by the year 2000 the total direct and indirect economic costs of health care in the United States will exceed $2 trillion. It is little wonder that even upper income people are alarmed at the prospect of who will pay the bills for a serious or prolonged illness.

Obviously, costs cannot continue to rise in the present fashion, and over the next few years we can expect major changes in the way health care is financed in this country. Even now, major changes

ALTERNATIVE HEALTH CARE

● Acupuncture

An ancient Chinese form of medicine, acupuncture is based on the philosophy that a cycle of energy flowing through the body controls health and that pain and disease develop when there is a disturbance in the flow. To remedy this, acupuncturists insert long, thin needles at specific points along meridians, or longitudinal lines flowing through the body. Each point controls a different corresponding part of the body. Once the needles are inserted, they are rotated gently back and forth or charged with a small electric current for a short time.

Because acupuncture can control pain, it is also used as a method of anesthesia, a practice that is gaining some credence with Western anesthesiologists. No one understands exactly why acupuncture works, but some doctors have postulated that inserting the needles may alter the balance between the sympathetic and parasympathetic nervous systems.

● Chiropractic

Chiropractic is concerned with the skeletal and muscular integrity of the body. Chiropractors attempt to alleviate pain and problems of alignment by manipulating the body, especially the spinal column and joints. These so-called adjustments are sometimes accompanied by other physical therapy methods, including heat and exercise prescription. No drugs or surgery are used.

are being made in Medicare, Medicaid, prepaid health plans, employee health benefits, medical and hospital insurance, and other health benefits. For your own protection, you should have an expert review your present health-care coverage. If you are covered by a group employee insurance plan, you might consult its administrator. If you have your own private insurance, ask to have a counsellor review your policies. If you are covered by Medicare or Medicaid, ask to make an appointment with an administrator. Your objective is to determine exactly what is and is not covered. If physician charges are covered, ask your doctor if he or she will accept payment from your third-party carrier, or if you are expected to pay in advance and then seek reimbursement from your insurance company.

Since benefit programs are undergoing constant change, you should have an insurance or benefit-program checkup at least annually. When changing jobs or preparing to retire, setting up your own business, or making some other major change, make sure that you have a clear picture of health-care benefits. Many people make the mistake of assuming they are fully covered, only to find this is not the case after the need arises.

BEFORE YOU LEAVE THE DOCTOR'S OFFICE: A CHECKLIST

- Do you understand the doctor's diagnosis?
- If you have been given a prescription, do you:*

  Know the name of the drug?
  Understand the directions for taking it: how often, how long, etc.?
  Know what side effects it might produce?
  What, if any, precautions you should take while on the drug?

- Do you need a follow-up appointment?
- Has the doctor told you when you might expect your condition to improve, and what to do if it doesn't?

*For additional information, see Chapter 40 on Proper Use of Drugs, page 772.

● Holistic Health

Holistic (or wholistic) health care is not an alternative in the sense that it is at odds with traditional health care, but in the fact that it stresses treatment of the whole person—medically, emotionally, and spiritually. It has evolved in reaction to the growth of medical specialization that has sometimes led to fractionated health care and the loss of the sense of treating a patient in the context of his environment.

● Homeopathy

Rather than counteracting the symptoms of disease with drugs or remedies designed to have an opposite effect on the disorder, homeopathists prescribe a minute quantity of a drug or agent similar to, but not identical to the causative agent of the disease. The classic example, practiced by the sixteenth-century physician Paracelsus, involved giving plague victims a pill containing minute amounts of the patient's own excreta. A more modern one would be to give a small amount of laxative to treat diarrhea.

● Naturopathy

Naturopathy in this country dates to before the turn of the century when natural remedies—sun, water, heat, and air—were thought by some to be the best treatment for disease. Naturopathists still place emphasis on sunbathing, diet (including emphasis on vegetables and prohibitions against salt and stimulants), steambaths, and exercise.

3 Meeting the Health-Care Needs of the Aged

Barry J. Gurland, M.D.

INTRODUCTION

THE HEALTH-CARE PROFESSIONS have made tremendous strides in the past decade in improving services to the elderly with health problems. Prior to that, there was little experience to guide the development of an appropriate geriatric service: The elderly represented a relatively small proportion of the population; they had inadequate access to medical care; and their symptoms were often ascribed to the natural processes of aging. Thus, health professionals were relatively unaware and unfamiliar with the diagnosis and management of disorders which tend to occur predominantly among the aged.

Matters are very different now. The proportion of the population who are elderly has increased dramatically in recent decades, while absolute numbers of the aged have also risen. Moreover, the old-old (those over 75), who have the most medical problems, have outstripped all other age groups in both actual and relative growth. The introduction of Medicare and Medicaid have made it possible for this growing cohort of elderly persons to pay for a variety of medical services, particularly the very expensive costs of hospital and other institutional services.

Health-care professionals have responded to this increasing contact with elderly patients by acquiring better understanding of the distinctions between normal aging and changes related to diseases which are common to old age. The average physician who sees adult patients, regardless of specialty, spends 45 percent of his or her time treating the elderly. Much of what was previously thought to be an inevitable accompaniment of aging has been found to be amenable to treatment.

The high public (and personal) costs of care for the elderly, especially when delivered in institutional settings, have engaged the attention of policymakers. There is a heightened awareness of the need for prevention, early intervention, and intensive rehabilitation to reduce the declines of aging and promote independent living. Concomitant with the increasing life expectancy of the aging population has come a new concept of what is normal functioning in old age and what might be achieved in retaining good health until an advanced age.

Two major health-care disciplines have developed which focus on the elderly. Geriatrics is the field that deals with the art and science of caring for the health problems of the elderly; gerontology is the study of the aging process itself, from the biological, mental, and social perspectives. Although they have distinct emphases, they are overlapping.

SPECIAL HEALTH PROBLEMS OF THE ELDERLY

THE HEALTH PROBLEMS of the elderly are diverse and complex, cutting across the disciplines of medicine, psychiatry, social work, and nursing. These problems may overwhelm the time and attention available to them from the physician or other health-care professional. In these situations it is likely that insufficient time will be devoted to gaining the understanding and cooperation of the patient and his or her family in the treatment regime. Moreover, the less urgent, but still important, secondary problems are likely to be overshadowed by treatments directed at the main health problem.

The multiple and interdisciplinary health problems of the elderly require help from many different health-care sectors. Often, these multiple sources are uncoordinated and duplicate or conflict with each other in the management plans that they develop and the services they offer the patient.

Adding to the problems of organizing health services is the fact that many elderly are not able to come to traditional sites such as consulting rooms or outpatient clinics. They may be housebound, have difficulty with transportation, reside in a long-term care facility, or simply be unwilling to attempt an excursion beyond their accustomed orbit.

Patients with physical problems may also have mental problems and be attending a community mental health center where medical services are not necessarily available. Similarly, patients with a mixture of problems may only be receiving services at social service agencies, nutrition sites, or ambulatory medical care clinics.

It is not uncommon for the health and related services needed by the elderly person to be ineligible for reimbursement. Health insurance coverage tends to be directed at acute rather than chronic conditions, medical rather than psychiatric problems, and institutional rather than community-based services. Social care and home care are severely restricted.

Elderly persons are not less vulnerable than younger adults to acute conditions, but these are more likely to occur in the context of a chronic disor-

der. The chronic disorder may follow or be aggravated by the acute condition and often comes to be the most important health problem. The treatment of chronic conditions is no less rewarding than that of acute conditions, but does require a different approach. The major goals of treating acute conditions are rapid cure, prevention of complications or residual effects, and avoidance of relapse: These measures require a highly selective diagnosis, concentration on medical factors, introduction of vigorous treatments, and often bed rest or hospitalization.

The management of chronic conditions is a matter of long-term care, with an emphasis on slowing declines or achieving relatively small gains. There must be a comprehensive patient evaluation, including psychosocial factors as well as medical disorders, and coordination of a number of disciplines and agencies. Health-care professionals must help the patient maintain as high an activity level and a quality of life as possible, highlighting progress in functional capacity.

Recognizing Signs and Symptoms

As a general rule, the elderly need to see a physician, even in the absence of a troubling symptom, more often than younger people. Beyond age 65, annual physical exams are recommended. Chapter 14 on The Middle Years and Aging describes normal changes to expect with advancing age. However, new symptoms should not be dismissed on the grounds that they are probably due to the effects of old age. Any change in a person's usual physical or mental state, particularly if the change is relatively rapid, has not been previously experienced, and affects ability to carry out daily activities, should be evaluated by a physician.

A wide variety of new symptoms might alert the older person to the need to seek professional diagnosis and advice. These include, but are not limited to:

- fatigue, sleeplessness, poor appetite, rapid loss or increase of weight, constipation or diarrhea

- headaches, dizziness

- vague aches and pains, swellings around the joints

- problems with the feet—ingrown toenails, ulcers, fungus infections, sepsis, undue coldness, unusual color, pain or inability to walk

- failing vision or hearing, pain in the eyes

- persistent rash, growths on the skin or changes in the color of moles, ulcers that won't heal, blood in the stool or blackness of stools

- a tendency to fall, shaking of the hands or head, weakness of a limb

- sexual problems

- depression, apathy and loss of interest, slowness of movement or thoughts, forgetfulness and confusion

- breathlessness, chest pain (especially on effort)

Medication Problems

Because they have multiple problems, the aged are likely to be on multiple medications, which may interact with each other and potentiate side effects or neutralize one or the other medication. Furthermore, elderly patients react to medications somewhat differently than do younger patients. At the same dosage level, elderly patients will end up with higher levels of active ingredients in their bloodstream than younger ones, making the risk of side effects greater.

Sometimes, the elderly patient will be using medications prescribed by physicians who are not in communication with each other and are thus unaware of the potential for drug interactions. Or the elderly patient may add medications obtained over-the-counter on his or her own initiative, or borrowed from relatives or friends, or drawn from a stock of medications previously acquired.

There is quite often an incomplete understanding between the patient and the physician about the correct procedure for managing the patient's health problem. In particular, the patient needs to understand the importance of:

- maintaining medications in proper dosage for a sufficient length of time to be effective

- continuing medication in some instances even where symptoms have abated

- stopping treatment at the point indicated by the safety limits of the medication

- reporting all other medications to the physician

- being alert to specific side effects that indicate drug toxicity, but trying to tolerate other, perhaps discomforting but harmless, side effects that accompany certain medications (and which may recede on continuation of treatment)

- checking with the physician before reinstituting treatment for a relapse

Inadequate compliance with treatment may also occur where a patient's eyesight is weak and he or she is unable to read directions, where treatment regimes are very complex, where frailty makes it difficult to open bottles or otherwise dispense medication, or where memory lapses occur. These problems are likely to be aggravated when the patient has no one available at home to assist him or her with the treatment requirements.

Involving the Elderly in Their Own Health Care

It is very important, when planning health care, to include the patient in the decision making. It must be "planning with," rather than "planning for." Elderly patients need to maintain a sense of responsibility for their health care as long as possible as well as a sense that they have some control over their fate in the health-care system. Whereas a passive role might be warranted in an acute illness, when conditions tend to be chronic they become inextricably intertwined with the quality and direction of life. In this situation, it is not desirable for either the patient's morale or welfare to remain passive.

Patients should be involved in decisions on where they will reside, how vigorously a condition will be investigated and treated, who will render the treatment, when the treatment is being helpful and should be continued, or when side effects or lack of response suggest a change of treatment. Involvement also means that elderly patients should understand the rationale and plan for the management of their illness and thus be able to cooperate. Such active participation reduces the feeling of helplessness that can undermine the resistance to disease and the resilience required for recovery.

One key decision the patient should participate in is the choice of a primary physician. Because the need to see specialists for various disorders often increases with age, it becomes even more important to have one primary physician who is not only aware of all of the aspects of a patient's health and able to coordinate care among several physicians if necessary, but who is also aware of the patient's family situation, living conditions, and financial resources. It is not necessary that this physician specialize in seeing elderly patients as long as he or she demonstrates an interest in treating the elderly and a willingness to take the time necessary to see that the patient and family fully understand the patient's condition and the course of treatment proposed.

COST REIMBURSEMENT

ATTEMPTS TO REDUCE the high cost of health care for the elderly have involved restriction of reimbursement eligibility for individuals, for the range of health services, and for their site of delivery; the imposition of ceilings on the duration of hospital stay; a ceiling on total expenditures for an institution; and restrictive criteria for admission to long-term care facilities. Particular emphasis has been placed on preventing unnecessary admissions to hospitals and nursing homes, but this restructuring of reimbursement has not yet led to a sufficient expansion of alternative home-care services.

Since Medicare coverage is more liberal for hospital care than for community-based services, some elderly are forced into institutions mainly for financial reasons. Medicare (parts A and B) pays for medical costs and hospital services, but, as of early 1985, has a $400 deductible on hospitalization (part A) and a $75 deductible on the part B medical insurance. The payments are based on predetermined allowable charges of which Medicare will pay 80 percent. The beneficiary is responsible for the other 20 percent, either through direct payment or private medical insurance. Medicare also limits the duration of outpatient psychiatry and the delivery of services other than medical and nursing.

Medicaid has broader coverage than Medicare and will, for example, pay for more than 90 days of long-term care, although this may vary from state to state. Both Medicaid and Medicare cover certain health appliances and aids, and certain nonmedically related home-care services; however, a means test is required for Medicaid, so that patients have to spend down their assets in order to qualify. Many elderly who do not qualify for Medicaid are nevertheless too poor to pay for private services.

Even using Medicare and Medicaid to the full, the average elderly person has out-of-pocket expenses of more than $1,000 per year for health care; and much more if medically debilitated. Private third-party payers tend to concentrate on medical expenses while excluding health-related social services and long-term care in institutions. These exclusions may change as the actuarial costs of chronic illness become better specified. (More specific information about Medicare and Medicaid reimbursement is given under Home Care, Community Care, and Nursing Homes in this chapter.)

Religious philanthropies, such as the Jewish Association of Social Agencies, Catholic Charities, and the Federation of Protestant Welfare Agencies, sometimes provide services for those who require them but who do not have appropriate coverage.

HEALTH-CARE OPTIONS—NEGOTIATING THE SYSTEM

THERE ARE A NUMBER of options for health care of the elderly, ranging from living alone in traditional housing, to living with relatives, to living in special retirement communities or other facilities specifically for the elderly, to institutional care, including various types of nursing homes.

How well older citizens are able to make use of these options often depends on how well they or their family members learn to ferret out information and negotiate the system. They may find it well worth the investment to use the services of a case manager—a private social worker who specializes in obtaining and coordinating services. These managers can often be invaluable in not only providing information about what's available, but also in cutting through red tape in obtaining services and in getting reimbursement where it is offered. They are especially helpful in arranging care long distance for a family member who lives in another city or state.

Case managers generally charge about $50 per hour for their services and, since there is no special certification required for or regulation of the specialty, it is wise to look for a case manager who is a certified social worker. They can often be located through hospital social workers, religious organizations, or state and regional government offices of the aging.

The Directory of Resources, page 792, lists a number of local and regional case management organizations. The 662 area agencies on aging are listed in "A Directory of State and Area Agencies on Aging," available from the U.S. Government Printing Office or at libraries. Family Service America, located in New York, can provide referrals to its more than 265 member agencies in 40 states. Requests for information should be sent to 44 East 23rd Street, New York, NY 10010, along with a stamped, self-addressed envelope.

LIVING ARRANGEMENTS

A SUBSTANTIAL NUMBER of the elderly live alone, preferring independence and familiar surroundings to living with a relative or in a nursing home or other special facility. Whether and how long they are able to maintain a household on their own depends a great deal on planning by other members of the family. Whether a hospital patient—and 12 percent of the elderly enter the hospital each year—returns home or enters a nursing home often depends not only on the patient's health, but on how soon and how carefully predischarge plans are made.

In addition to help from relatives and neighbors, the elderly can take advantage of a number of resources available in the community to make living alone easier—home health workers, services such as Meals-on-Wheels, and attendance at various daycare programs. But, again, these services must be planned for in advance of hospital discharge.

Modifying the home for safe and comfortable living by the elderly is something that cannot be overlooked. Outside ramps, railings, and bright lighting in hallways, grab bars in bathrooms, and low-pile carpeting and nonskid rugs, are all important in helping to prevent accidental falls, a major problem with age. Weatherstripping, storm or thermal windows, and insulation will cut down on drafts and keep the inside temperature more even.

Two considerations that can bring peace of mind to families of elderly who live alone are emergency alerting devices that automatically dial police or ambulance service, and various formal or informal systems for checking for emergency needs. For example, in some communities, postal workers have agreed to alert a designated person if an elderly resident does not pick up mail for a specified period of time. Informal arrangements can be as simple as a daily phone call from a relative or a window shade raised every morning to signal a neighbor that all is well.

There are a growing number of retirement communities that offer continuing care for elderly residents who pay an entry fee and a maintenance fee for accommodation and various amenities. In some arrangements, the entry fee is returnable should the resident leave or die. Some of the early experiments in this direction were disappointing because the rising costs of care were not correctly anticipated and sufficient funds were not available in certain continuing care communities when the elderly residents eventually grew ill and in need of services. However, the financing of such communities has become more sophisticated with experience and there are now more than 400 operating in the United States.

For those elderly who require some assistance or who wish to know that this is immediately available if necessary, but who do not need the intensity of care provided by an institution, there are several arrangements for accommodations. These include shared dwellings, often in close proximity to a nursing home, and sheltered or enriched housing where the elderly residents occupy their own apartments specially designed for the frail or handicapped, and where a staff member is on the premises to provide emergency help, occasional assistance, and advice. Sometimes, sheltered housing is made part of a multilevel campus in which health-related facilities and skilled nursing facilities coexist.

HOME CARE

EVEN TODAY, when families are typically far more scattered than in the past, most of the home care of the elderly is provided by relatives. Caring for an elderly person at home requires teamwork on the part of the family, so that no one person is overwhelmed with the added work and responsibility, and all can have the satisfaction of meeting the needs of one of their own.

With the growth in numbers of the elderly population, most families can now expect that, sooner or later, they will count an older, sick, or disabled person among their members. Families undertaking the long-term care of elderly members should carefully evaluate the commitment they are making, and should reevaluate it periodically. It is important to consider the needs of all members of a family, from children to great-grandparents. Often, families exhaust themselves emotionally, physically, and financially to provide care at home long past the point that such care has ceased to be appropriate.

Families need to consider having unskilled companions and temporary help available, whether for part of each day or for respite on weekends or vacations. In addition to the skilled home health care discussed below, bright and useful part-time help may often be obtained from college and university placement offices. Students will often fill in gaps, and may read to patients and provide companionship as well as help.

Home care remains one of the large gaps in the health-care system, despite a recent resurgence of interest on the part of providers and reimbursers. This interest is generated largely by economic factors, because the public cost of home care is considerably cheaper than institutional care. If the needed services can be provided in the home, an expensive acute-care bed is freed, a nursing home bed not taken. For the patient, especially the chronically ill or disabled elderly patient, however, home care may be more costly, if payment is out-of-pocket and not covered by third-party payers. But it has advantages: continuity of care, independence, and the maintenance of ties with a familiar place, a family, a community. Current efforts to increase reimbursement to families for home care may change this inequity.

Intelligent use of medical services available to elderly people at home, and of supportive services in the community, can make excellent home care possible. Unfortunately, it is often easier to place an elderly person in a hospital or nursing home than it is to negotiate the fragmented and unorganized system available to maintain that person at home, and it is easier to get third-party reimbursement for skilled medical care than for less technical and less expensive supportive care.

Home Health Services

Home health services are provided by some 2,500 home health agencies in this country, either directly or indirectly, under a physician's general direction. These home health agencies may be private, either profit-making or nonprofit; hospital-based home-care services; public health agencies, such as neighborhood health centers, or by local or county health department or community and church programs. Perhaps the most familiar is the voluntary Visiting Nurses Association.

The services provided fall into two general categories: skilled and supportive. Skilled services include nursing, physical therapy, occupational therapy, and speech and hearing therapy. Supportive services are those that enable a person to continue to live independently at home: personal care (bathing, dressing, grooming), homemaker–home health aide (light housekeeping, shopping, meal preparation, nonskilled nursing), chore services, transportation, and so on.

Other services that may be available through a home health agency include dental care, lab services, and nutritional counseling. Larger agencies have social workers on the staff who generally act as case managers, coordinating the services given and providing referrals for any additional ones that may be needed. Smaller agencies may not provide the full range of services needed, but can usually contract for them.

Most home health agencies provide services to anyone who asks for them. The services may be paid for privately, or may be reimbursed, at least partially, under government or individual insurance plans. Sources for information on home health agencies include the discharge-planners at local hospitals, city or county public health and welfare departments, the Area Agency on Aging, the local office of the Social Security Administration, day-care centers, and synagogues and churches. The United Way can provide a list of nonprofit voluntary agencies. Yellow Pages listings under "Home Health Services" and "Nurses" may also be sources of names.

It is important to choose an agency that can provide all the services that are needed, and those that may be needed in the future. And it should be noted that a patient who is being discharged from the hospital has no obligation to choose the hospital-based agency: Selection should always be based on needs and personal preference.

There may be only one home health agency in a given area. But, where there is a choice, the elderly person or the family, or both, should try to make an evaluation of the quality of the services offered and the suitability of a particular agency in meeting particular needs, before selecting one. Among the questions that should be asked are:

- What services are available and do they meet the person's present and anticipated needs?

- What is the cost per visit for each service, and what is the type and rate of reimbursement?

- What medical supplies and equipment are available?

- How many hours per day and days per week can services be provided?

- Who is available in an emergency?

- What kind of supervision is there?

- Is backup service available if the home health worker is unable to come?

Voluntary Health Agencies

Organizations like the American Cancer Society and the Easter Seal Society have volunteer "friendly visitor" services that can be of help to the disabled elderly and can provide needed respite for family members. These agencies may also be able to provide specialized equipment and listings of resources available in the community.

Drugstores and Medical Supply Houses

These are another source of specialized equipment, and of the more usual sickroom supplies. In many cases, wheelchairs, walkers, portable oxygen equipment, and hospital beds may be rented rather than purchased. This may be more economical for families, especially if the need is temporary and the equipment is expensive.

Reimbursement for Home Health Services

Expenses for skilled services may be reimbursable through Medicare, Medicaid, and private insurance plans. Some agencies that provide supportive services receive federal or state funding; the agency or the social services department should be contacted to see if the individual meets state-specified need and eligibility requirements.

Medicare. People eligible for Medicare benefits (that is, those aged 65 or older) may receive coverage for home health care under this program if the following conditions are met:

> 1. A physician must certify (and periodically recertify) that there is a need for home health services for the treatment of a medical condition, and must set up a treatment plan.
>
> 2. The care needed must be part-time skilled nursing care, physical therapy, occupational therapy, or speech therapy.
>
> 3. The patient must be confined to the house.
>
> 4. The home health agency must be certified by Medicare.

If these conditions are met, Medicare will pay the "reasonable cost" (rates of reimbursement are fixed by Medicare and the providers) for an unlimited number of covered home health visits for 1 year following the patient's most recent discharge from the hospital or skilled nursing facility. In addition, Medicare may pay for some supportive services, but only if skilled services are also needed. Medicare does not pay for full-time nursing care at home, drugs, meals delivered to the house, or other services that are designed primarily to help people with their personal or domestic needs. Therefore, it is important to find out how much of the bill will be the patient's responsibility.

Many people assume that Medicare will cover their health needs, both in and out of the hospital, when they reach the age of eligibility, but this is not always so. Most elderly people have chronic health and social problems, but Medicare emphasizes reimbursement for acute care. Many who need help in the home for daily living do not need skilled nursing, but provision of supportive services is contingent on the need for skilled services. Many need assistance with personal care and homemaking but are not homebound—and being homebound is one of the criteria for Medicare benefits.

Medicaid. States are required to provide home health care services in their Medicaid programs. Those eligible to receive these services are people on public assistance and Supplemental Security Income, as well as others who qualify under state means tests (which vary widely from one state to another). Not all home health agencies, however, will accept Medicaid patients, since the reimbursement is often less than the actual cost of care. If an agency *does* accept Medicaid patients, more services, especially personal care services, may be available than under Medicare.

Private Insurance. Until recently, no private insurance plans included coverage for home health services. Some companies now provide partial coverage and some major medical policies cover some home health services in full. However, not all home health agencies will accept private insurance payments; this should be checked before choosing an agency.

COMMUNITY FACILITIES

FOR THE ELDERLY living at home who are not housebound, there are a number of services available in the community and listed below that provide care during the day.

Adult Day Care

Adult day-care programs for the elderly are conducted in a variety of community-based centers and are seen as an alternative to institutionalization. The services provided in the different types of programs are tailored to meet specific needs and each type has a different therapeutic objective.

Day Hospitals

These are usually located at an extended-care facility or hospital and they provide medical care and supervision to people recovering from an acute illness. Where they deal primarily with patients recently discharged from an institution, they are sometimes called after-care clinics. Referral is by a physician; reimbursement is generally the same as for other hospital services.

Medical Day Care

This service is generally located in a long-term institution or freestanding center and provides health-care services such as nursing and other supports to the chronically ill or disabled who do not need frequent medical intervention. Rehabilitation and maintenance are the therapeutic goals. Referral is by a physician and reimbursement is by third-party payment on a sliding scale. In some states, Medicaid pays for care of this kind.

Mental Health Day Care

This service is usually located in a psychiatric institution or freestanding center and provides a supervised environment, together with mental health services, to adults with organic or functional mental illness. The therapeutic goal is supervision, safety, and assistance with coping skills. Referral is by a psychiatrist and reimbursement is by third-party payment on a sliding scale.

Social Adult Day Care

Usually located in a freestanding center, this service caters to adults whose social functioning has regressed and who are not able to function independently. Referral is by families and health facilities, but a physician's examination is required prior to admission. Reimbursement is by third-party payment on a sliding scale; many centers are funded through Title XX of the Social Security Act.

Although the Department of Health and Human Services reported in 1980 that there were more than 600 adult-care programs in operation, serving almost 13,500 people daily, adult day care is a relatively new service alternative in this country. Program objectives and services provided are largely dependent on the philosophy of the sponsoring organization and on negotiation with the funding source. Common to most day-care programs is attendance from several hours to a full day up to 5 days per week, a midday meal, and transportation within a specified area. Services provided vary from state to state and from provider to provider. Selection of a program should therefore be approached with great care to be certain that it is suitable to individual needs.

Nutrition Services

Meals-on-Wheels is a community service, offered under voluntary auspices but supported in part by public funds. The program provides at least 1 hot meal per day, at a reasonable charge, to homebound people aged 60 and older. Specifics vary from state to state; the state agency administering programs for the elderly should be contacted for additional information.

For the elderly attending senior centers, hot meals provided through the Area Agency on Aging (sometimes situated in the mayor's office) provide not only adequate nutrition, but a chance to socialize. This program gives the Agency an opportunity to keep in touch with clients' physical and social situations and therefore has an important element of outreach and prevention. Referral is open-ended, meaning the elderly can refer themselves. In this case, it is important that the center be made aware of any special dietary needs.

NURSING HOMES

A NURSING HOME is a residential facility that provides some degree of nursing service, over and above room and board, personal care, and custodial services. There are about 18,000 nursing homes in the United States, with between 1.3 and 1.5 million beds. These facilities outnumber community hospitals 3 to 1; on any given day, there are twice as many people in nursing homes as in hospitals. About three-quarters of them, with two-thirds of all the beds, are proprietary, that is, they are run for profit by individuals, partnerships, or corporations. Fifteen percent, with 20 percent of all beds, are oper-

ated by voluntary, nonprofit organizations. The remainder are under government auspices.

While nursing homes accommodate some patients with serious congenital illnesses or disorders, as well as patients recently discharged from the hospital after an episode of acute illness, or recovering from strokes or recent surgery, the great majority of residents are the chronically ill elderly. The "typical" current nursing home resident is in her eighties (three-quarters of all residents are women), single or widowed, with 3 or more significant chronic illnesses and considerable mental impairment. Usually her only source of income is her monthly social security check; other assets have long since been exhausted. On average, her stay in the nursing home will last for 2½ years, though for more than one-quarter of the residents, the facility is "home" for 3 years or more. Discharge comes with death, or with referral to a hospital for a terminal illness.

Types of Nursing Homes

Federal regulations provide broad standards for the physical environment, medical and nursing requirements, and staffing patterns for three different types of nursing homes. State interpretations of these standards, however, vary widely.

Residential-Care Facilities (RCFs). They provide meals, sheltered living, and some medical monitoring—supervision of medications and keeping track of signs and symptoms, for example. An RCF is appropriate for someone who can no longer manage household chores but does not need a great deal of medical attention.

Intermediate-Care Facilities (ICFs). They provide room and board and regular, but not round-the-clock, nursing care for people who are unable to live independently. They may also provide social and recreational activities and rehabilitation programs: physical therapy, occupational therapy, speech therapy, and social work services.

Skilled Nursing Facilities (SNFs). They provide 24-hour nursing care by registered nurses, licensed practical nurses, and nurses' aides. An SNF is appropriate for someone who needs intensive nursing care and rehabilitation. Most ICFs and SNFs are state-certified and therefore eligible for public funds in reimbursement for care provided. Certification is not a guarantee of quality care, but lack of it is usually a sign that a nursing home has grave deficiencies.

Reimbursement

Although nursing homes are less expensive than hospitals—a nursing home bed costs an average of $12,000 to $15,000 a year—they consume more than $20 billion annually. While 40 percent of all payments to nursing homes are private, few individuals or families can pay out of pocket for nursing home care for a long period of time, and private insurance for long-term care is minimal. Much of the burden, therefore, falls on federal, state, and local government programs, mainly Medicaid, which takes over when an individual "spends down" to the point that the cost of services exceeds his or her income.

Most state Medicare programs reimburse for care in an ICF and, in some circumstances, in an SNF. However, they may place limitations on the benefits, including the need for prior authorization for care, length of stay, the number of visits by physicians, or the type of setting. These limitations vary widely from state to state—for example, 4 states limit physicians to 1 visit per month to a nursing home patient. Nevertheless, Medicaid remains the main source of government funding for long-term nursing home care.

Medicare, which was designed to reimburse for acute episodic care, will reimburse for needed care in an SNF for 100 days after discharge from a hospital (with the patient paying coinsurance after the first 20 days). Although 90 percent of nursing home residents are Medicare beneficiaries, Medicare pays less than 3 percent of nursing home expenses. But nursing home residents, although they make up only 4 percent of the Medicaid-eligible population, account for 30 percent of total Medicaid expenditures.

Considering Placement

Most referrals to nursing homes are made by families: More than half of the residents come to long-term facilities directly from their own or their family's home. Selection of a facility—even admission—is not generally arranged or controlled by a doctor. In fact, the certification of need for care that has to be made to comply with Medicaid reimbursement regulations is often completed only *after* it has been decided to place an elderly family member in an institution.

Although the rate of use has doubled in the last three decades, it is very important to stress that nursing homes serve only a minority of the elderly who require regular or continuous nursing care. Two-thirds of such elderly people are cared for at home by their families, often using resources available through home health agencies and the community. (See Home Care, page 40.)

It is simply not the case that families are escaping their responsibilities by "dumping" their elderly members in institutions, and that there is a general failure to care. On the contrary, studies show that families most often have tried to avoid placing an elderly person in a nursing home for as long as they could, and at great personal, economic, and physical cost. The large number of people in nursing homes reflects the fact that never before in history have there been so many very old people in need of care.

Families who are considering placing an elderly member in a nursing home should be aware of the alternatives to institutional care that may be available. Frequently a social worker or other professional with knowledge of community resources can make arrangements that will either avoid or postpone placement. Family service agencies, some voluntary nursing homes, senior citizens' centers or, if the elderly person is in the hospital, the hospital social service department, can provide counseling on the various options.

The older person should be included in planning: He or she is an adult with a right to autonomy to the fullest extent possible. It is a mistaken "kindness" to pretend that a nursing home is anything other than a nursing home. Such misinformation is always discovered, with damaging effects on the elderly person's well-being and on family relation-

---

CHECKLIST FOR CHOOSING A NURSING HOME

Initial Considerations

Location—A location near family and friends will make frequent visits easier. If the patient is still ambulatory, it will probably be less disruptive and disorienting to remain in a familiar community, and may open the possibility that his or her personal physician can continue care.

Size—There are both pros and cons to size. A smaller home, with less than 50 beds, may be more "homey," and allow for more individuality. A home with 200 or more beds may seem more institutional, but may be able to offer more activities, more permanent staff, and more specialized care.

Current Residents—Residents of the same religious or ethnic background may provide more commonality of interest. The home may cater to ethnic food preferences or the staff may speak a foreign language common to the residents. For some residents, the opportunity to mix with people with varied backgrounds may be more appealing.

Medical Services—This is especially important if the new resident has a chronic condition that needs considerable care. Some homes have a physician on salary, others contract for services and charge on a fee basis. Although all patients have the right to a doctor of their own choice, they may have to pay extra for this if a staff physician's services are included in the overall price.

Policy Checklist

Admissions—Is there a waiting list? What forms are required? Is a medical exam necessary for admission and who performs it?

Financial Arrangement—Are the home and the patient eligible for Medicaid and Medicare? Is any prepayment required? If so, is it refunded if the resident leaves? What services are included and what costs are extra?

Medical—Is a registered nurse present at all times? Is a doctor on staff, present or on call? What is the procedure for an emergency? What is the backup hospital? What arrangements are made for therapy and rehabilitative services, if needed?

Observation Checklist

Physical Plant—Is it clean, relatively odor-free, well-lit, in good repair, and pleasant looking?

Safety—Are there nonskid floor surfaces, grab rails in halls and bathrooms, fire extinguishers, a sprinkler system, clearly marked exits? When was the last fire drill and state or local inspection? Are there ramps and passageways and doors wide enough to accommodate wheelchairs?

Staff—Do they demonstrate care and respect for the patients? Do they interact with residents? Do they respect privacy? Do they respond promptly to calls for assistance? If patients are kept in bed or restrained in wheelchairs, is this for their benefit or for the convenience of the staff?

Residents—Do they look clean and well-groomed? Are most of them out of bed and dressed? Are they occupied or do they seem isolated, staring vacantly or always watching television? Are they sedated?

Food—Is it plentiful, nutritious, attractive, and tasty? Is it served at the proper temperature and are those who need help eating given it promptly? Are menus prepared by a dietitian? Are menus posted and does the food actually served match up? Is there a dining room and are residents encouraged to use it or do they eat in their rooms?

Activities—Do the activities provided keep patients interested and occupied (as well as meeting licensing requirements)? Is there an activity room and is it well equipped and staffed? Are patients taken on outings or otherwise involved in community activities? Do community residents volunteer time at the home?

Resident Rooms—Are there no more than four to a room? Can residents bring favorite furniture, plants, and other personal possessions? Do they each have a closet and chest of drawers? If husband and wife are both residents, can they share a room? Is there privacy for dressing, phone calls, and visits?

Amenities—Does a barber or beautician visit periodically? Can residents wear their own clothing and is it kept clean? Do they have spending money and how is it handled?

ships. Moreover, studies have shown that participation in decision making is a critical predictor of subsequent physical and mental adjustment.

Choosing a Nursing Home

Lists of nursing homes can be obtained from a social services counselor, from the local Social Security office, or from the state or county public Social Services Agency. Some counties publish consumers' handbooks, which give information on the nursing homes in the area. The home chosen should be licensed, meet appropriate safety regulations, provide the necessary medical and nursing care, and have arrangements for emergencies and transfer to a hospital if necessary. It should provide a religious and cultural environment similar to that to which the patient is accustomed. It should be close enough for the family to visit conveniently. And it should provide the highest possible quality of care.

As a result of recent scandals in the nursing home "industry" and government response to the abuses that were shown to exist, extreme cases of neglect of patients are now rare. Many homes, especially the voluntary ones, have high standards, but others provide care that is not adequate. Unfortunately, standards for licensing vary from state to state, and homes must be chosen carefully. For example, although all licensed ICFs and SNFs are required to employ at least one full-time registered nurse, it is important to look for one where nursing is more than just minimal. Even the best homes, in the states with the strictest requirements, may have only one registered nurse on duty in a unit that may contain as many as 60 beds. Hands-on care in nursing homes is usually provided by aides with little training and a high rate of turnover. The work can be frustrating, discouraging, and seldom more than minimum-wage.

First-hand observation and interviews with residents, staff, and administrators provide the best way to evaluate the quality of care. There is no substitute for a personal visit. Two relatively distinct aspects should be considered: first, the question of skill with which professional (or professionally supervised) services are given; and second, the quality of life in what is, after all, a living arrangement.

Financial arrangements should be discussed in detail before placement is decided. It must be established whether the patient is eligible for Medicare or Medicaid coverage and how such benefits relate to any private medical or hospitalization insurance policies that the patient may have. If the patient has personal funds initially, it should be established whether the home will keep the patient on at the Medicaid rate should these funds run out. It is also important to find out whether the cost quoted is inclusive, since many homes charge separately for laundry service, medications, dressings, special nursing procedures, and other "extras."

The move itself is extremely important. Families should spend as much time with the patient during the settling-in period as good judgment indicates. So that the person entering a nursing home does not feel abandoned by the family, every effort should be made to continue with familiar routines— a weekly shopping expedition, visits from grandchildren—as much as possible. Families need to be aware of the magnitude of the sense of loss that may be felt by the elderly person: loss of home, of continuity with the past, of familiar faces and places. On the other hand, a nursing home may offer welcome companionship to an elderly person who has been living isolated at home, as well as the reassurance of having help within call at all times. For many elderly and disabled people, the specially designed environment of a nursing home offers a new freedom in living.

SUMMING UP

THE HEALTH CARE of the elderly should be broad and complex, integrating and coordinating the efforts of multiple disciplines at multiple sites over long periods of time. Given the opportunity for proper care, the elderly person should be able to expect not only a much longer life expectancy than previous generations experienced, but also a longer active life, and consequently a better quality of life. For adequate health care, the role of the elderly themselves is just as important as that of health-care professionals, allied health workers, family, and friends.

4 Diagnostic Tests and Procedures

S. Raymond Gambino, M.D.

INTRODUCTION

DIAGNOSTIC TESTS are an extension of a physical examination and history. They allow the doctor to see things that are not yet visible or to confirm what the doctor, or the patient, already suspects.

In earliest times, women knew they were pregnant when their bellies grew and they felt their babies move. They soon realized that missing a menstrual period meant the possibility of pregnancy. Then doctors learned that by examining the cervix, they could see changes in the color of the cervix and character of the mucus which signaled pregnancy before the more obvious physical signs.

The famous rabbit test took them one step further, faster. It grew out of the observation that, not long after the fertilized egg is implanted in the uterus, the placenta begins to manufacture a hormone called human chorionic gonadotropin. Although the hormone is present in increasing quantities in the pregnant woman's urine, it can't be seen. However, if the urine is injected into the female rabbit, the rabbit's ovaries enlarge and redden. But, the test takes 4 or 5 days, won't show results unless the woman is at least 4 weeks pregnant, and means sacrificing the rabbit.

Further research produced an antibody to gonadotropin which, when mixed with the pregnant woman's blood in a test tube, can detect small amounts of the hormone. It will do this with 99 percent accuracy as early as 9 days after conception, even before the first missed period. Another test soon to be available will produce the same answers using urine—without taking blood and without rabbits.

The second major reason for testing, in fact, the one that accounts for the greatest volume of tests, is therapeutic drug monitoring, that is, keeping track of exactly how a prescribed drug is acting on the patient's system. Is the patient getting too much of the drug? Too little? Is it causing other body chemicals to be out of balance? A familiar example is insulin monitoring in diabetes by measuring blood sugar, a test usually performed daily by diabetics themselves. Many diabetics now test their blood sugar levels before each meal, allowing them to make small insulin adjustments that keep their disease under much better control than ever before possible. One of the goals of scientists in refining test procedures is to develop more tests that patients can do themselves, so they can be done more often at less expense and with better therapeutic results.

Another goal is to be able to do more with what we have, and we seem to be making progress. A study over a 10-year period at Columbia-Presbyterian Medical Center showed that while the number of new blood tests went up dramatically, the number of blood samples drawn remained constant. Eventually we may be able to test for hundreds of different diseases or conditions from the blood in one small vial.

A third goal is to make the tests more simple and less "invasive" for the patient. In this vein, a whole new area of simple testing is opening up as scientists realize that saliva—a very easy specimen to collect—can tell a number of things that blood and urine may not about the level in the body of, for example, hormones in a free state.

At the other end of the technology scale from saliva testing is another new noninvasive technique—nuclear magnetic resonance (NMR), or magnetic reasonance imaging. Still primarily experimental, NMR may by the end of the decade surpass even CT scanning in sophistication and usefulness. Not only does NMR, like CT, produce high-resolution pictures of the structure of various body organs, but it also provides a look at the biochemistry of living cells—all this without even the small risk of x-ray exposure that CT scanning carries.

NMR uses two simple elements, a magnet and radiowaves, to do its very sophisticated analysis. It works like this: A nucleus is the positively charged central core of an atom. Some nuclei behave like magnetic spinning tops. NMR uses a magnetic field to orient the spinning nuclei of the atoms being studied. Then it temporarily disturbs that orientation with a burst of energy from a radio-frequency transmitter. By measuring the amount of energy released as the spinning tops reorient themselves, scientists can determine the number and chemical form of the nuclei.

The more researchers learn about basic science and how the body works, the more sophisticated and accurate laboratory tests become. As we strive to find tests that are more definitive, show results earlier, and create less discomfort for the patient, the number of tests will probably continue to increase. Yet a major consideration in developing new tests is not only what they can tell the doctor about a patient, but what can be done with the knowledge. If there is no treatment for the condition, there is little solace in knowing exactly what the condition is. For this reason, test development will always follow, not lead, basic science, and this is one reason why support for basic science is so important.

BASIC TYPES OF DIAGNOSTIC TESTS

ALMOST ALL DIAGNOSTIC TESTS fall into four basic categories: those that measure performance (exercise, heart rate, lung function, visual acuity), those that take something out of the body (a specimen) to study, those that look at the body through film or sound (x-ray, scans, ultrasound), and those that use hollow tubes and fiber optics to look inside the body directly (endoscopy).

Specimen Tests

Specimens range from the relatively easy to collect urine, stool, and blood samples, to body fluids that are collected through a hollow needle in a procedure known as centesis, to tissue samples collected with a similar needle through biopsy.

They all work on the same principle. In healthy people, the composition of body tissue, fluids, and waste remains relatively constant or within a normal range. When an organ of the body is not "normal" or when there is a change for any reason, from pregnancy to aging to disease, there is certain to be evidence in the body tissue or in one of the body's secretions. Besides the diseases of blood itself, such as anemia or leukemia, which result in changes in the composition or amount of various types of blood cells, there are many other conditions that can be diagnosed by examining blood samples. The same is true of urine and saliva.

Radiography

X-ray tests range from simple still pictures, like dental x-rays and those used to tell if a bone has been broken, to moving images of the body at work, called fluoroscopy. These images may be recorded on moving film or videotape (cineradiography), or in a series of stills taken in rapid succession. Radiography is used to show abnormalities in size, shape, position, or functioning of various parts of the body.

While some x-rays are noninvasive, meaning nothing is swallowed or injected into the body, many more sophisticated ones depend on the use of a dye or contrast medium to outline or fill parts of the body that would not ordinarily show up on an x-ray. This contrast medium may be swallowed, injected directly into an artery or vein, or fed in through a thin tube called a catheter, which may enter the body through one of its normal openings or through a small incision.

Radioisotope Scans

Radioisotope scanning, also called nuclear scanning or radionuclide imaging, is used to obtain information about the condition and functioning of various organs. Although the equipment used and the views of the body shown are similar to a CT scan, radioisotope scanning involves the use of a small amount of radioactive material. It is based on the fact that various organs absorb or concentrate specific minerals or hormones, but these substances do not show up on a regular x-ray. However, if they are made radioactive by the addition of a radioisotope, they can be seen. And if the organ is not functioning properly, too little or too much of the substance will be taken up or it will be concentrated in some parts of the organ but not in others. The organ will look different on the screen. If a portion of the organ does not show up, it may indicate the presence of a tumor. A rectilinear scanner, gamma camera, or scintoscope is used to read or detect the isotope within the organ. The amount of radiation is very low and the isotope disappears within a day or so.

Computerized Axial Tomography Scans (CT)

Computerized axial tomography, called CAT or, preferably, CT scan for short, was introduced in 1972 and has grown considerably in use because it can detect so many conditions that do not show up on less sophisticated, albeit less expensive, tests. It is 100 times more sensitive than conventional x-rays and (some brain scans being the only exception) does not expose patients to radioactive contrast media as radioisotope scanning does.

Tomography is the focusing of an x-ray on a specific plane of the body, such as a very thin cross section of an organ or the chest cavity. With computerized tomography, the x-ray beam that passes through the cross section is picked up by a detector and fed into the computer, which analyzes the information on tissue density and constructs a picture on a cathode ray tube (CRT) screen. (See figure 4.1.) Tissues of various density show up as different shades of gray, bone (the most dense) as white, and air and liquid as black.

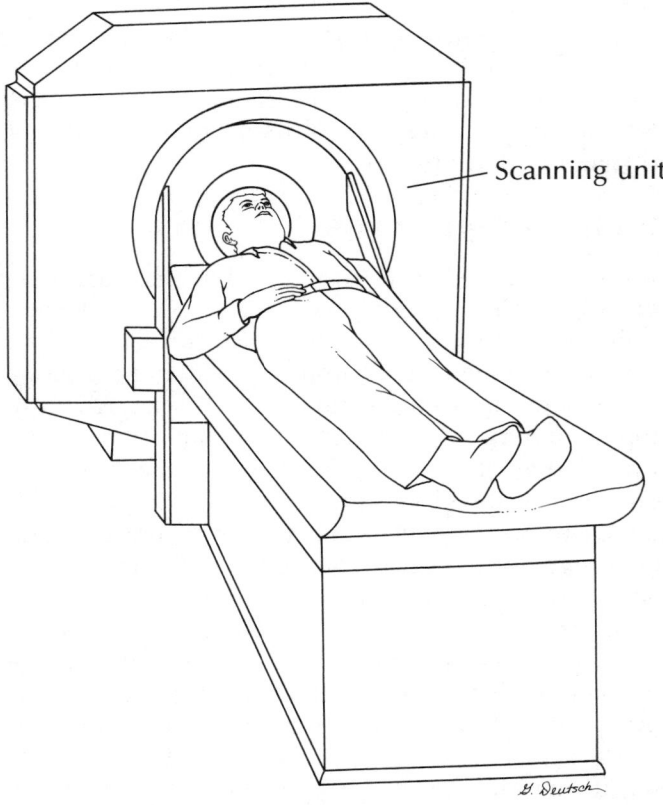

Figure 4.1. **Drawing of a patient positioned in a CT scanner for a brain study. The scanning unit can be moved to make CT scans of any part of the body.**

Conventional x-ray films are not used in CT scanning. Instead, the scanner, which both emits and detects rays, is rotated 360 degrees around the patient as he or she lies on the special table that is part of the machine. The procedure is completely painless and carries only the risk of x-ray exposure, which is minimal.

CT scanning can be used to see inside any of the body's organs, including the brain, and is an outpatient procedure that generally takes about 20 minutes. It easily detects calcium deposits often missed by simple radiography and it is more accurate than ultrasound in obese patients, when fat deposits hinder ultrasound waves. Not only can CT scans detect tumors, cysts, and abscesses but, because of their sensitivity to variations in tissue density, they can even at times distinguish between benign and malignant tumors.

Positron Emission Transaxial Tomography (PETT)

Positron emission transaxial tomography (PETT) is similar to CT scanning, but uses substances such as glucose tagged with a radioisotope to measure some body functions.

Ultrasonography

Ultrasound is a painless and riskless technique that, much like the sonar systems used by ships, uses sound waves and their echos to locate and visualize internal organs. It is particularly useful in looking at soft tissue that does not x-ray well. The area to be examined is first covered with a lubricant such as mineral oil. Then a transducer, a microphone-type machine that both emits sound waves and receives their echos back again, is passed over the body in contact with the skin.

An oscilloscope or computer is used to translate the sound waves into a picture on a television screen. Although ultrasound costs considerably less and involves less risk than CT scans, it is not always as accurate and is being replaced by CT scans in some cases. But it still has many uses, such as in pregnancy, where unnecessary x-ray exposure to the fetus should be avoided. It is also very useful in examining the heart (echocardiography) because it can show the heart at work, particularly the opening and closing of the valves.

Endoscopy

Endoscopy is a general name for a number of test procedures that allow the physician to look inside the body through a hollow tube or a fiberoptic device and see internal organs directly. The tube may be inserted through a surgical incision to view joints, or organs in the chest or abdominal cavity. More commonly, the tube is passed through the body's natural openings—the nose, mouth, anus, bladder, or vagina—to view various organs from the inside.

The endoscope, which has various names depending on its length and use, can be used to inflate a body cavity with air in order to see it better, to take samples for a slide culture or biopsy, or even to perform delicate surgery, such as a tubal ligation or repair of the ligaments in a joint. The tube may be metal and rigid, but more and more, it is likely to be made of threads of fiberglass, bunched together like a cable, which transmit light and allow the doctor to see into the body and even around corners. In some hospitals, a mild dose of tranquilizer, such as Valium, lasting about 15 to 20 minutes, is being given intravenously during endoscopy to help allay patients' anxiety.

WHAT TO ASK THE DOCTOR BEFORE A TEST

NO ONE SHOULD have any medical test without being fully informed about what it entails and why the doctor is recommending it. Here are some questions a patient should ask the doctor before undergoing a test:

- *Why is the test being ordered?* Is it to screen for a disease that has no symptoms, such as high blood pressure? Is it because the doctor is pretty certain about a diagnosis but needs the test to confirm it? Is it because the doctor is really puzzled about the diagnosis and is trying to rule out as much as possible? Or is it even, perhaps, to placate the patient?

- *How definitive is the test?* Will it tell for sure that a condition is or isn't present, or must it be repeated or followed by more sophisticated tests?

- *How accurate is the test?* What might cause a false positive or false negative or other inaccurate result?

- *How much will it cost?* Some tests are included as part of a doctor's office fee, others are not. Sometimes a doctor may not charge the patient extra for performing a test, a Pap smear for example, but the patient will receive a bill from the laboratory that does the analysis. Which tests are covered by medical insurance, and to what degree, may vary from policy to policy.

- *Is hospitalization required?* Sometimes one hospital will require that a patient check in, while another hospital will do the same test on an outpatient basis.

While the former may cost more, it also affords the opportunity to monitor the patient more closely for any side effects afterward. Although the doctor's decision will ultimately be based on what is best for the patient's health, finances should be taken into consideration and alternatives discussed.

- *Is there any pain?* What are the side effects? Most common tests are painless or cause only brief discomfort, such as a pinprick or needle puncture. Others can cause cramps, nausea, headache, or serious discomfort. In these cases, part of the test may involve administering a sedative, or local or general anesthesia. Side effects may last hours or longer, or may only be felt by some patients and not by others.

- *What are the risks?* This is the most important question. Many common tests have no risks at all. Others have risks that may range from transitory side effects to more serious problems. Invasive tests, that is, those that involve introducing instruments or substances, such as barium, into the body, generally have some risks. These may include infection, allergic reaction, or injury to the body, either at the site of the incision or to an internal organ. The "normal risk" for some tests may mean 1 in 100 patients will have a problem; other tests may have a long list of very rare risks that affect only 1 in 1,000 or fewer.

- *What is the risk of not having the test, and what are the alternatives?* This will help the patient to decide whether the risk is one that must be borne because the consequences of an undiagnosed illness may be worse.

CAUSES OF INACCURATE TEST RESULTS

HUNDREDS OF THOUSANDS of diagnostic tests are performed each year, accurately and without problems, but laboratories occasionally make mistakes that lead to inaccurate results. The errors may be technical ones, such as allowing too long a delay from the time a blood sample is collected until it is tested, or unwittingly using equipment that is improperly calibrated. Occasionally, too, there are human failures.

Some errors cannot be controlled. Even a change in the weather can have an effect on test results in some patients. Other patients have genetic traits that cause abnormal results when there is actually nothing wrong.

Another cause of inaccuracy, however unwitting, may be the medicines a patient takes. There are literally thousands of medications, from aspirin and antacids to birth control pills and other prescription drugs that, taken by patients undergoing tests, can affect the results. Patients should report to their doctors any medication they take regularly and ask if there are any other medications they should avoid (and if so, for how long) before the test.

Instructions about eating and drinking before the test must also be followed very carefully. Results can be affected by ordinary foods like milk, coffee, and table salt. The physician may want the patient to eat specific foods for several days prior to a test, or not to eat anything at all for 6 to 12 hours before the exam.

A patient's mood and physical condition can also affect test results. A patient who is nervous about a test or has not had adequate rest should mention this to the doctor, since either can distort certain measurements. Even environmental exposure to certain chemicals can have an effect.

RISKS OF RADIATION

MEDICINE HAS COME A LONG WAY from the time when fluoroscope machines could be found in every good children's shoe store so mothers could see how their children's feet looked inside new shoes. We now realize that such unnecessary exposure to x-rays is a risk that no one should take.

On the other hand, tremendous advances have been made in early and accurate diagnosis as a result of sophisticated use of radiation technology. X-rays can be lifesaving and, under the right circumstance, a patient should not hesitate to have an x-ray or a radioisotope scan. Nevertheless, there are a number of precautions that the patient and the doctor or radiation technician can take. Parents of children to be x-rayed should be especially vigilant, asking that the x-ray film cassette used be the appropriate size for the child, so that no more of the body is exposed than necessary.

Dental x-rays are probably the most common x-ray and perhaps the most overused. According to the American Dental Association, they should not be a routine part of a dental exam, but their use should be at the discretion of the dentist. The patient should wear a lead apron covering the torso.

Pregnant women should not have x-rays unless there is an absolutely medically valid reason for them. (See Chapter 11 on Pregnancy and Childbirth.) In fact, to guard against exposure to the fetus in an as yet undiagnosed pregnancy, a woman of childbearing age should have elective x-rays of her abdomen or pelvis only during her menstrual period or for a few days afterward. For necessary x-rays of other parts of the body, a pregnant woman should wear a lead apron.

All patients, especially those of reproductive age or younger, should have their genitals protected by a lead shield during any x-rays of the abdomen or intestines.

Since the training and experience of x-ray technicians can vary, patients should ask whether the technician is accredited (in large hospitals or laboratories, this is usually the case). Properly trained technicians will practice the technique of "collimation"—limiting the x-ray to the specific area to be diagnosed and not including surrounding parts of the body. This is facilitated if the size of the x-ray film cassette is approximately the size of the area to be x-rayed, and not larger.

Finally, patients should keep track of when and where their x-rays were taken, to avoid possible duplication in the future. Since x-ray films and other medical records are routinely destroyed after 7 to 10 years, depending on hospital practice or state law, patients may want to request that the films, or the reports regarding them, be sent to them before that time.

DIRECTORY OF DIAGNOSTIC TESTS

THE FOLLOWING TESTS are listed according to body systems or major disease groups, and are described as they are carried out at many hospitals or laboratories. Since the procedure may vary somewhat from location to location, the patient should check with the doctor about exactly how the test will be performed.

BLOOD TESTS

Venipuncture

Purpose. This routine procedure is used to obtain one or more small vials of blood for numerous tests involved in diagnosing many conditions other than blood diseases themselves. The most common ones are listed below.

What Is Involved? Venipuncture, which takes about 5 minutes, can be done in a doctor's office or laboratory. Usually an arm vein is used, either the right or the left, depending on which one is larger or closer to the surface. After the skin is cleaned with antiseptic, a rubber tourniquet is used above the elbow to force blood into the vein and make it even more prominent. The patient may also be asked to repeatedly make a fist and open it, for the same reason. The needle is inserted near the crook of the elbow and 1 or more vials of blood withdrawn.

What Is the Risk? Although the patient may develop a hematoma (black and blue mark), there is virtually no risk involved in this procedure.

COMMON BLOOD ANALYSES

THE FOLLOWING are tests commonly done using the blood specimens obtained by venipuncture:

- *Complete blood count (CBC)*—This series analyzes the various elements within the blood, including hemoglobin concentration, hematocrit, and red and white blood counts. It can diagnose anemia and point the way to other, more specialized tests that may need to be done.

- *CBC with differential*—Whereas the CBC merely counts white cells, the differential analyzes the type of white cells present to help identify specific infections or diseases.

- *Thyroid-stimulating hormone, T_4, T_3*—These are common tests of thyroid function, especially hypothyroidism and hyperthyroidism.

- *Blood chemistry group*—This has various commercial names, depending on the testing laboratory, but generally consists of 12 to 25 analyses, including those listed below.

- *Blood culture*—In this test, used when septicemia (blood poisoning) is suspected, the blood sample is cultured for bacteria in a laboratory and then tested to see how the bacteria respond to antibiotics.

- *Thrombin time*—This test, done on the blood plasma, is used primarily to aid in diagnosing liver disease and blood clotting deficiencies. Thrombin, a clotting factor normally found in blood, is added to a sample of the patient's plasma, and the time that it takes a clot to form is measured against a control sample.

- *Prothrombin time*—This test also gives an indication of blood clotting time, although the clotting factors measured are different from those in the Thrombin test. "Pro Time" is the more common of the two assays and is used primarily to monitor the effects of anticoagulant drugs like Coumadin, which decrease blood clotting and are used in the treatment of cardiovascular and other diseases.

Substance	Test for	Substance	Test for
Blood urea nitrogen	Kidney function	**Alkaline phosphatase**	Liver, bone, and gall bladder diseases
Creatinine	Kidney function		
Glucose	Insulin action for the presence of diabetes	**Gamma glutamyl transpeptadise** *(GGTP)*	Liver disease, excess use of alcohol
Calcium and phosphorus	Kidney function and the patient's nutritional condition	**Total protein and albumin**	Water balance, nutrition, liver disease
		Uric acid	Gout, kidney disease
Bilirubin *(conjugated and unconjugated)*	Liver function	**Electrolytes:** *including sodium, potassium, chloride, bicarbonate*	Electrolyte balance—for monitoring patients on IV or diuretics
Transaminase enzymes	Injury to liver, muscles, heart, presence of hepatitis		

CANCER TESTS

Biopsy

Purpose. This procedure is used to obtain a tissue specimen for microscopic examination to determine malignancy.

What Is Involved? Depending on the type of tissue and its location, this procedure may be done with a scalpel, needle, or other instrument. Since biopsies are often done as part of endoscopic exams, they are included in those sections of this chapter and generally not listed separately. (See Bronchoscopy, Colonoscopy, Colposcopy, Cystourethroscopy, Gastroscopy.)

What Is the Risk? The risk, which is generally small, varies with the procedure for obtaining the specimen, and may include bleeding and infection.

Renal Biopsy. This procedure, which takes about 15 minutes, is usually done in a hospital with a local anesthetic and sometimes a sedative. The patient lies prone, with pillows or sandbags under the abdomen, while a long aspirating needle is injected into one or both kidneys and tissue is withdrawn. There is a possibility of bleeding or even the formation and painful passing of blood clots following this procedure.

Liver Biopsy. This procedure is similar to the renal biopsy, but the patient lies on his or her back and the needle is injected between the ribs or under the ribs into the liver.

Bone Marrow Aspiration

Purpose. This procedure, also called sternal tap, provides a small amount of bone marrow for analysis and is used to diagnose leukemia and other cancers, to determine whether various cancers have metastasized, and to evaluate the effectiveness of chemotherapy. Although it is primarily used in cancer diagnosis, it can also be used to diagnose several types of anemia and infections.

What Is Involved? A bone marrow aspiration, which requires no special preparation, can be done in 5 to 10 minutes in a doctor's office or hospital outpatient clinic. (See figure 4.2.) Some patients may be given a tranquilizer. A local anesthetic is given at the site of the puncture, which may be a bone in the pelvis, a rib, the breastbone, or other bone. A thin aspirating needle is then inserted and a small amount of the marrow fluid withdrawn, which may cause a sharp, but brief, pain, followed by some ten-

derness at the puncture site. The specimen is then placed on a slide for microscopic examination.

What Is the Risk? Although there may occasionally be some bleeding at the puncture site, more serious risks, such as infection or air embolism, are rare.

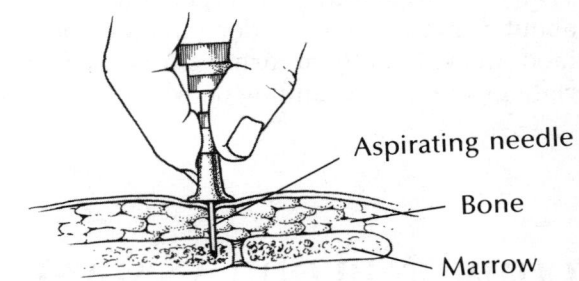

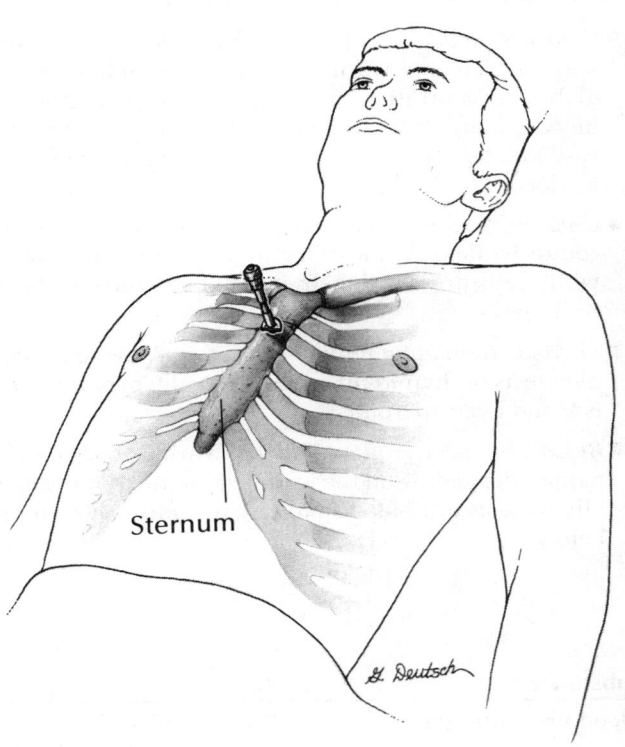

Figure 4.2. **The large drawing shows what is involved in a bone marrow aspiration, in this instance, a sternal tap.**

Mammography

Purpose. This simple procedure provides an x-ray picture of the breast and is used to detect tumors and cysts and to differentiate between benign and malignant tumors.

What Is Involved?   There is no special preparation for this 30-minute procedure, but the patient should not use any powder or lotions on the breasts, which may create false-positive x-rays. The breasts are rested, one at a time, on the film cassette, and x-rays are taken from several angles. The breasts may be compressed against the cassette to get a clear picture, and the patient may be asked to wait until the film is developed to be sure the pictures are readable.

What Is the Risk?   The level of radiation is low, but care should be exercised so that this procedure is not overused. Approximately 90 to 95 percent of malignancies can be detected with this test, but as many as 75 percent of the tests reported as positive may in fact be false positives.

CIRCULATORY SYSTEM TESTS

Angiography

Purpose.   This x-ray visualization of the arteries and veins is used to detect abnormalities, such as aneurysms, in the blood vessels themselves, as well as in the organs they serve. They can be used to locate sites of internal bleeding and blood clots.

What Is Involved?   The procedure generally involves passing a catheter through a vein or artery in the arm or leg to the site to be studied and injecting a contrast medium to make x-ray visualization easier. (For a more specific description of the procedure and risks, see Cardiac Catheterization, below, and Phlebography, page 57.)

Bone Marrow Aspiration

(See page 54.)

Cardiac Catheterization

Purpose.   Cardiac catheterization (venous and arterial) allows the visualization of the heart and the coronary arteries that supply blood to the heart muscle. Venous, or right heart catheterization, is used to assess the functioning of the tricuspid and pulmonary valves, and can determine blood pressure and flow in the chambers of the heart and the pulmonary artery. Arterial, or left side catheterization, is used to assess the coronary arteries and the

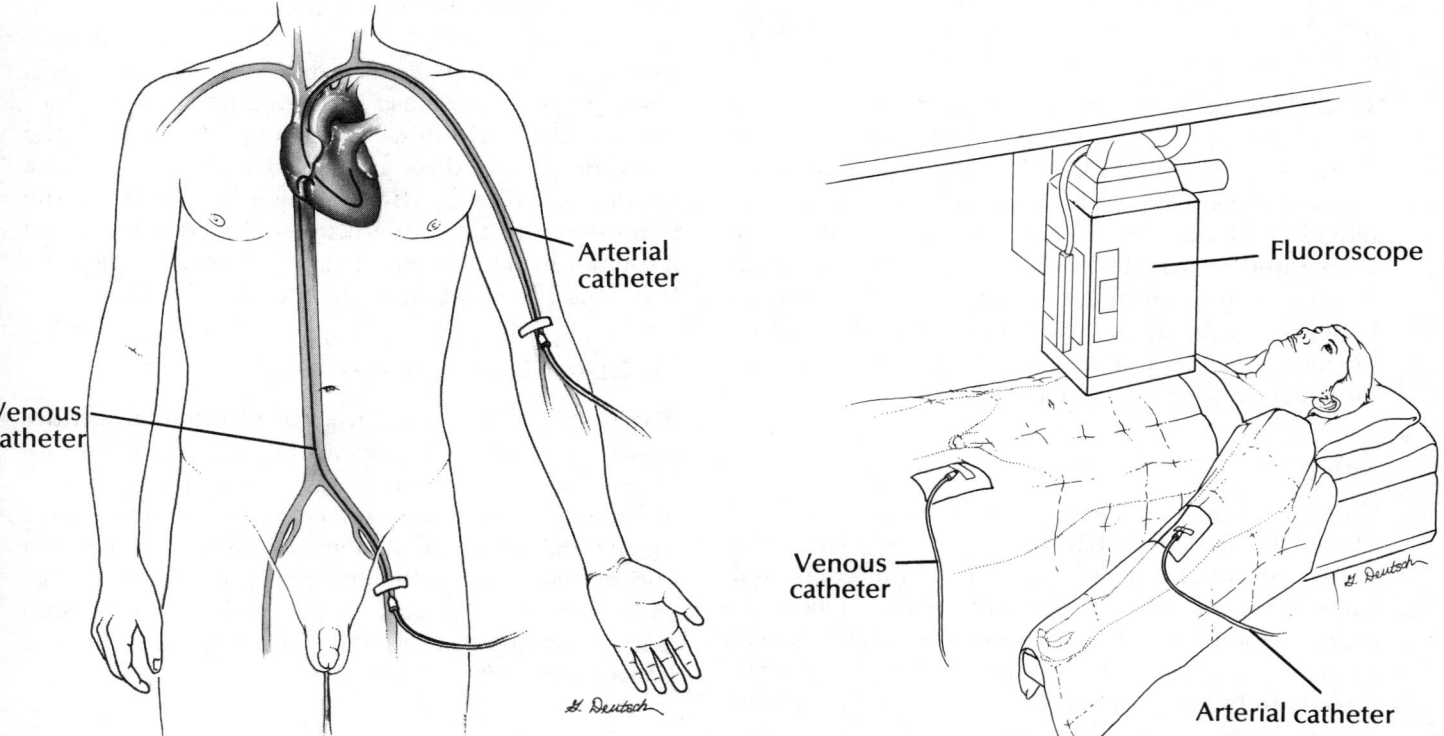

Figures 4.3A and 4.3B.   **These drawings show catheters being threaded through a vein from an incision in the groin into the right side of the heart and through an artery in the arm into the aorta. A fluoroscope is used to guide the doctor inserting the catheter.**

functioning of the mitral and aortic valves and the left ventricle. Since it can show if the arteries are occluded, a major cause of heart attacks, it is often used to determine if bypass surgery is necessary.

What Is Involved?   The patient is hospitalized and is not given anything to eat for at least 6 hours prior to the test. A mild sedative is given, but the patient remains awake throughout the procedure, which usually lasts 2 to 3 hours. An IV is started in order to administer medication if it is needed during the test. After an injection of local anesthetic, a catheter—a long, very thin, flexible tube—is inserted through a small incision in the arm or groin. For a right heart catheterization, the doctor, using a fluoroscope to help guide the catheter, passes the tube through a vein into the heart through the right atrium and then out again through the pulmonary artery. For a left heart catheterization, the catheter is passed through an artery into the aorta and then the coronary arteries or the left atrium, or both. (See figures 4.3A and 4.3B.)

Once the catheter is in place, dye is injected through it into the heart or arteries, at which point the patient may feel a hot flash or burning sensation or nausea. The dye, or contrast medium, filters into all parts of the heart or the arteries and gives a clear indication of any abnormalities or obstructions. The procedure, especially the discomfort of having to lie still in awkward positions for long periods of time, may be very tiring for the patient, who is usually kept in the hospital for at least 24 hours afterward.

What Is the Risk?   Although the risk decreases as this procedure becomes more and more common, there are some risks. The most serious is a heart attack or stroke, which may happen if the catheter dislodges a blood clot or cholesterol deposit in the artery and it travels to the heart, lungs, or brain. Other possible complications include damage to the walls of the heart or blood vessel (rare), swelling, bleeding, or infection at the incision site, and allergic reaction to the contrast medium.

Cardiac Scans

There are 3 major types of scans that can tell doctors about the heart: technetium pyrophosphate (also called infarct or hot spot myocardial imaging), thallium imaging (also called cold spot myocardial imaging), and cardiac blood pool scanning. They can be done on an outpatient basis and all involve approximately the same procedure (intravenous administration of the isotope followed by a scan or series of scans), and the same rare risk of radioisotope overdose. (See below and Radioisotope Scans, page 49, for more information.)

Technetium Pyrophosphate.   This scan can confirm a recent heart attack (myocardial infarction) and determine the extent and exact location of damage to the heart muscle. The technetium pyrophosphate isotope is bound to a substance that seeks out injured muscle and shows up on the scanner as areas of accumulated radioactivity (called "hot spots"). The isotope is injected 2 to 3 hours before the scan and the scan itself takes 30 to 60 minutes.

Thallium.   In some ways, this is the opposite of a technetium scan, in that the thallium isotope accumulates in normal heart muscle, rather than damaged regions, and produces "cold spots" on the screen. The cold spots indicate areas where the coronary arteries are clogged, reducing blood flow to the heart, or where the tissue has been damaged by a heart attack. The patient may be asked to exercise briefly on a treadmill or stationary bicycle to help distinguish between the two conditions. The procedure, which is often used before and after bypass surgery, takes 45 to 90 minutes. If exercise (also called stress) imaging is planned, the patient will be asked not to smoke, drink alcohol, or take nonprescription drugs for 24 hours before the test and not to eat for 3 hours before.

Blood Pool Scanning.   This scan, which looks at the motion of the heart wall, requires only 5 to 10 minutes. It can evaluate how well the heart is pumping and can detect abnormalities such as aneurysms, holes in the heart, valve problems, or damage caused by coronary artery disease or heart attack. The isotope in this case is carried in the blood, not the muscle, and allows the doctor to see how the blood progresses through the heart. This is done by a technique called "gating," which synchronizes the functioning of the camera to the functioning of the patient's heart, so that it takes a series of pictures fractions of seconds apart as the heart beats.

Doppler Ultrasonography

Purpose.   This is another ultrasound procedure which is similar to echocardiography, but studies blood flow in the major veins and arteries of the arms, legs, and head, rather than the heart. It aids in the diagnosis of various conditions, including chronic venous insufficiency, peripheral artery disease and arterial occlusion, aortic stenosis, and arterial trauma. (See the following section and Ultrasonography, page 50.)

Echocardiography

Purpose.   This procedure uses sound waves to examine the size, shape, and motion of the heart, and is useful to diagnose abnormalities of the heart valves and to assess cardiac function.

What Is Involved? There is no special preparation for this test, which is done as an outpatient procedure and takes about 15 to 30 minutes. As with all ultrasonography procedures, there is no pain or risk. (See Ultrasonography, page 50.)

Electrocardiograms

There are 3 major types of electrocardiograms (also called ECG or EKG)—resting, exercise (also called stress), and ambulatory (also called Holter monitoring). They all involve the recording of the electrical impulses of the heart through electrodes attached to the chest and, in the case of a resting ECG, to the arms and legs. The impulses cause special needles to move over a strip of continuous paper and record the heartbeat as a wavy line. The configuration of the line tells the doctor various things about the heart, including unusual rhythms, electrolyte imbalance, enlargement of the chambers, and evidence that the patient has had a heart attack. There is no pain or risk with the resting and ambulatory ECG. The exercise ECG can cause fatigue and, in extreme cases, may lead to cardiac arrthymia or arrest.

Resting ECG. This is a common diagnostic test, often performed as part of a routine physical, and can be done in a doctor's office in about 30 minutes. Although it can detect what has happened and what is happening to the heart, it is not a good predictor of what may happen.

Exercise ECG (Stress Test). This test provides more information than a resting ECG by monitoring what happens to the heart when the patient exercises, either on a treadmill or on a stationary bicycle (called an ergometer). It is used to help diagnose chest pain, to determine the functional capacity of the heart after surgery or a heart attack, and to set limits for a person beginning an exercise program. At various intervals during the test, the patient is asked to pedal faster, or the speed or incline of the treadmill is increased. The patient's blood pressure and pulse are monitored, and oxygen intake may also be measured.

Ambulatory ECG (Holter Monitoring). For this test, the patient wears a small portable reel-to-reel or cassette tape recorder attached to electrodes on the chest for a period of 24 hours while he or she goes about normal daily activities. In some cases, the patient may wear a monitor for 5 or 7 days, activating it only at certain times, for example, when symptoms such as chest pain occur. The monitor, which is worn under clothing, can pick up transient symptoms such as arrthymias, which may not be caught by a resting ECG done for a much shorter period.

Lymphoangiography

Purpose. This contrast x-ray procedure is used to diagnose causes of intractible edema (swelling) in the legs and feet, and the presence or spread of cancer in the lymphatic system.

What Is Involved? This procedure, which may be done on an inpatient or outpatient basis, takes about 2 to 3 hours the first day and, 24 hours later, another 30 minutes. First, a blue dye is injected between the toes, from where it spreads into the lymphatic system in 15 to 30 minutes and outlines the lymphatic vessels in the feet. Once these vessels can be seen, a local anesthetic is given and a small incision is made in the foot, through which a tube is inserted for injection of the oil-based contrast medium. The lymphatic system is monitored on a fluoroscope as it fills with the contrast dye, a process that can take 1½ to 2 hours. After the tube is removed, the incision is sutured and bandaged. A set of x-rays is taken, followed by a second set the next day.

The patient's skin, feces, and urine may have a bluish color for 2 or 3 days until the marker dye disappears. The contrast medium may remain in the body for 6 months, during which time other x-rays may be taken. The sutures are removed in 7 to 10 days.

What Is the Risk? Besides the usual risk of infection or allergy to the contrast medium, there is a small risk of oil embolism. The contrast medium eventually seeps from the lymphatic channels into the general circulation, where it may travel to and lodge in the lungs.

Phlebography

Purpose. Phlebography (also known as venography) allows x-ray visualization of the veins in the legs and the feet and is used to diagnose deep vein thrombosis (which can lead to pulmonary embolism), to distinguish between blood clots and other obstructions (such as tumors), to evaluate congenital abnormalities in the veins, and to locate a suitable vein for a coronary bypass graft.

What Is Involved? This procedure, which may be done on an inpatient or outpatient basis, takes about 30 to 45 minutes and involves no special preparation, although the patient may be asked to fast for 4 hours before the test. A local anesthetic is given and the contrast medium is injected into a large vein in the leg or foot. The contrast dye may cause a burning sensation in the leg and a general flushing sensation or a feeling of nausea. Headache and nausea may continue for several hours after the test. During the procedure the patient may be asked to blow against a closed fist or push his or her foot against the technician's hand, both of which force blood into the veins, making them more visible.

What Is the Risk? Because the contrast medium dilates the veins, there is the possibility of the patient feeling weak and fainting, and there is a less common risk of the procedure actually causing phlebitis or deep venous thrombosis.

CT Scans

(See page 50.)

DIGESTIVE SYSTEM TESTS

Cholangiography (Intravenous)

Purpose. Intravenous cholangiography is a contrast x-ray used to detect gallstones, obstructions, or other abnormalities of the gallbladder and bile ducts. The same procedure may be done using a CT scan rather than conventional x-ray.

What Is Involved? The test, which is almost always done in a hospital, usually lasts about 2 to 2½ hours, if the bile ducts are not obstructed. If they are, it may take 4 to 24 hours for the contrast medium to concentrate in the gallbladder. The patient will have a high-fat meal the evening before the test, followed by nothing but water or fat-free liquids. A laxative may be given since a full bowel can create shadows on the x-ray. After preliminary x-rays are taken with the patient lying down on a tilting x-ray table, the contrast medium is administered intravenously and more pictures are taken at different angles.

What Is the Risk? The only real risk is possible allergic reaction to the contrast medium. To help minimize this, a small amount is administered first, and reaction checked, before the full dose is given. There may, however, be side effects, including nausea, vomiting, hives, or flushing.

Cholangiography (Percutaneous Transhepatic)

Purpose. This is a contrast x-ray study of the bile duct, often used to diagnose causes of jaundice, in which the contrast medium is administered through a needle directly into the liver. It is especially useful with patients who have had their gallbladders removed because it doesn't depend on the gallbladder to concentrate and excrete the contrast medium.

What Is Involved? This procedure, which lasts about 30 minutes, is almost always performed in the hospital since there may be complications and since it is often followed immediately by surgery. No food is given for about 8 hours before the test.

The patient lies on a tilting x-ray table and a local anesthetic is injected into the skin covering the liver and the capsule surrounding it. A long, flexible needle, guided by a fluoroscope, is inserted into the liver in an attempt to find a dilated bile duct, and the contrast medium administered through it. Then a series of x-rays is taken as the table is rotated to different angles. The patient will feel some sting from the needle used for the anesthetic, but will not feel the needle being inserted into the liver. When the dye is injected, there may be a feeling of fullness or pressure. Side effects of the contrast dye sometimes include nausea, vomiting, excessive salivation, hives, and sweating.

What Is the Risk? A number of complications can result from this procedure, including bleeding, septicemia (a bacterial infection of the blood), and bile peritonitis caused by bile leaking from the punctured duct, but they are rare. Although the radiation exposure from a single cholangiography is small, there is a risk if the procedure is repeated several times.

Cholecystography

Purpose. Cholecystography (also called oral gallbladder test) is a contrast x-ray study of the gallbladder used to detect gallstones or to diagnose inflammatory disease and tumors.

What Is Involved? Hospitalization is not required for this test, which usually takes about 30 to 45 minutes. At noon on the day before the test, the patient eats a meal that contains normal amounts of fat, which stimulates release of bile from the gallbladder, emptying it of normal bile and preparing it to accept bile containing a contrast medium. This is followed by a fat-free dinner, which causes the contrast-containing bile to collect in the gallbladder. After dinner, at 5-minute intervals, the patient takes a series of pills containing the contrast dye.

The test itself is simply a series of x-ray pictures taken with the patient in different positions. After the initial pictures, the patient may be given a high-fat meal or a pill to produce the same effect, and asked to wait 15 to 20 minutes, after which another set of pictures is taken.

What Is the Risk? Except for possible allergic reaction to the contrast medium, there is no risk involved in this test. Some people suffer temporary side effects caused by the pills, most commonly diarrhea, and occasionally nausea, vomiting, or difficulty in urinating.

Colonoscopy

Purpose. Colonoscopy is the direct examination of the large intestine using a flexible fiberoptic tube inserted through the anus. (See figure 4.4.) It is used to detect inflammatory or ulcerative bowel disease, to check for polyps or tumors, or to locate the site of gastrointestinal bleeding.

What Is Involved? This procedure, which takes

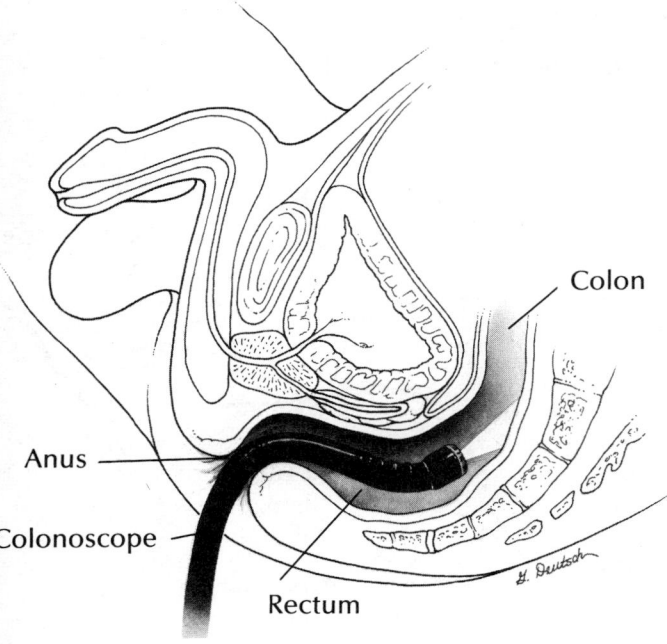

Figure 4.4. **This drawing shows an examination of the colon, or large intestine, with the fiberoptic scope being inserted through the anus and rectum and threaded into the colon.**

30 to 60 minutes, can be done as an outpatient procedure, but is usually done in the hospital. The patient is given a liquid diet for 1 to 2 days before the exam, followed by a laxative and one or more enemas to completely empty the bowels. A sedative or tranquilizer may also be given.

With the patient lying on his or her side, knees flexed, the doctor first inserts a gloved finger into the anus and then passes the colonoscope through the intestine. Air may be injected to expand the folds of the colon, enabling the doctor to see the entire surface area. When the tube has reached the entire length of the colon, it is slowly withdrawn as the doctor examines the mucous lining for any lesions or polyps. Special attachments allow the removal of some small polyps or the collection of a biopsy sample. Many patients feel embarrassment and discomfort during this procedure, especially when air is injected and expelled.

What Is the Risk? There is very little risk of bowel perforation, but the patient should report any bleeding, dark stool, or abdominal pain.

Duodenography

Purpose. Duodenography (also called hypotonic duodenography) provides x-ray pictures of the duodenum and the pancreas and is used to diagnose tumors or lesions that may be causes of upper abdominal pain.

What Is Involved? This test, which takes about 30 minutes, can be done on an inpatient or outpatient basis. After fasting for 6 to 12 hours, the patient is seated, and a long, flexible tube called a catheter is passed through the nose into the stomach. The patient then lies down and the doctor, guided by a fluoroscope screen, continues to pass the catheter into the duodenum. A hormone or drug to relax the duodenum is given by injection or IV, and then the contrast medium is administered through the catheter and x-rays are taken from a number of angles. Some of the barium is then withdrawn and air injected through the catheter, which may cause the patient to have cramps. More x-rays are taken before the catheter is removed.

What Is the Risk? Risks, which include allergy to the contrast medium or possible internal damage from the introduction of the catheter, are rare. More common are side effects, such as reactions to the hormone or drug, which may include nausea, vomiting, hives, flushing, blurred vision, dry mouth, thirst, irregular heart rhythms and, especially in patients with prostate problems, urine retention.

Endoscopic Retrograde Cholangiopancreatography

Purpose.   Also known as ERCP, this x-ray visualization of the ducts leading from the pancreas and the gallbladder is used to diagnose the presence in these ducts of stones or tumors.

What Is Involved?   ERCP, which takes about 60 minutes, can be done on an outpatient basis, but is usually done on an inpatient basis. The patient is asked to fast for 12 hours before the test and is usually given a sedative or tranquilizer. A local anesthetic (generally unpleasant tasting) is used in either spray or gargle form to suppress gagging, and it causes the patient to lose some control of saliva. A mouthguard may be inserted to protect the teeth. The endoscope is inserted into the mouth and down the throat and the patient is instructed to swallow to help pass it down into the esophagus. Guided by a fluoroscope, the doctor then continues to pass it down into the stomach and duodenum, and then injects a drug into the duodenum to relax it. Next the contrast medium is injected through the endoscope and a series of x-rays is taken. Another set may be taken in different positions after the scope is removed. The patient may feel side effects from the drug or hormone used to relax the duodenum and from the contrast medium. These include nausea, hives, blurred vision, dry mouth, urinary retention, and a feeling of burning or flushing. The throat may be sore for 3 or 4 days afterward.

What Is the Risk?   Besides the slight risk of infection or perforation of internal organs that accompanies any invasive procedure, there is also the problem of urine retention, especially in men with prostate problems. This can usually be avoided by voiding completely before the exam.

Esophagography

Although this test is occasionally done alone, when the doctor is reasonably sure that the problem is confined to the esophagus, it is usually done as part of the upper GI Series. (See page 62.)

Gastric Secretion Studies

Purpose.   This procedure allows the physician to collect and study samples of the gastric juices secreted by the stomach in order to diagnose causes of epigastric pain or learn more about suspected ulcers before surgery.

What Is Involved?   Although the secretions are all collected in the same manner, the test can last anywhere from 2 to 12 hours, depending on the objective of the test. The longer test requires hospitalization, but the shorter ones may be done on an outpatient basis.

The patient is usually fed a liquid meal and then asked to fast for 12 hours and to restrict liquids and smoking for 8 hours prior to the test. Part of the test may involve eating, drinking, or chewing to stimulate production of gastric juices. The doctor passes a long, flexible tube through a nostril down the patient's throat into the stomach. Once the tube has been started, the patient is asked to swallow until the tube enters the stomach. The gastric juices are then aspirated and collected through the tube over a period of hours.

What Is the Risk?   The test is uncomfortable and may cause gagging when the tube is initially passed and some irritation in the nostril or throat afterward. Other risks, which are rare, include lung collapse or ulceration of the larynx if the tube is passed into the trachea instead of the esophagus.

Gastroscopy

Purpose.   Gastroscopy (also called esophagogastroduodenoscopy) allows the doctor a direct view of the lining of the esophagus, stomach, and duodenum through an endoscopic tube. It is used to determine the cause of bleeding, perform a biopsy, or diagnose inflammatory disease, tumors, ulcers, and structural abnormalities.

What Is Involved?   The procedure takes about 30 minutes and may be done on an inpatient or outpa-

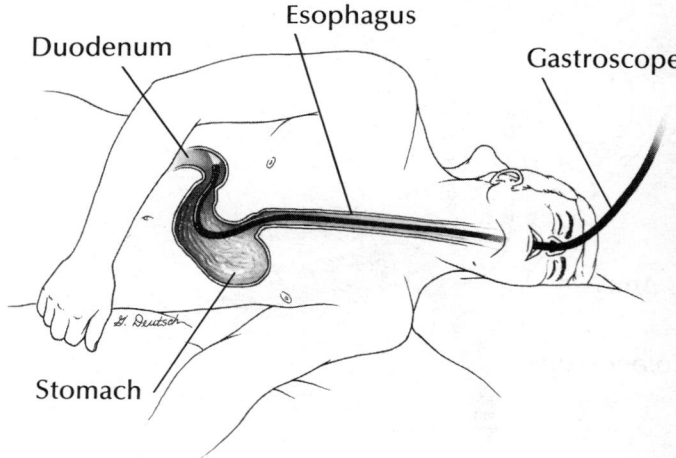

Figure 4.5. **During gastroscopy, a flexible fiberoptic tube is inserted into the mouth and threaded through the esophagus, into the stomach and the upper part of the small intestine (duodenum).**

tient basis. The patient will be asked to fast for 6 to 12 hours beforehand and may be given a sedative or tranquilizer. A local anesthetic is sprayed into the mouth and throat and a flexible fiberoptic tube is passed through the mouth down the esophagus and into the stomach and duodenum. (See figure 4.5.) The tube, which transmits light and allows the doctor to see the internal structure of various organs, also has attachments that allow the suctioning off of secretions, taking of biopsy samples, and introduction of air, which expands the organs and makes examination easier.

The patient may feel some gagging, cramps, or fullness as the tube is passed through various organs or when air is introduced, and will probably have a sore throat afterward.

What Is the Risk? As with all invasive procedures, there is some risk of internal damage to organs or structures, such as perforation, but this is relatively rare.

Liver Scan

Purpose. This isotope study provides information on the structure and functioning of the liver and is used to detect cirrhosis, abscesses, or growths.

What Is Involved? The procedure, which may be done on an outpatient basis, takes about 45 to 60 minutes for a structure scan and 30 minutes for each function scan, which are done in a series with the final one after 24 hours. The isotope is injected and a blocking agent may be used. (See Radioisotope Scans, page 49.)

What Is the Risk? There is no risk, other than the remote possibility of isotope overdose.

Lower GI Series

Purpose. Like the upper GI Series, this x-ray exam (also called barium enema) uses barium as a contrast medium to provide fluoroscopic views, in this case of the large intestine. The procedure is used to detect polyps, tumors, gastroenteritis, telescopic bowel, irritable colon or other causes of lower abdominal pain, or blood, mucus, or pus in the stool.

What Is Involved? The test, which takes 30 to 45 minutes, can be done in the hospital or on an outpatient basis. Before the exam, the patient may be asked to fast or go on a liquid diet, and then laxatives or one or more enemas will be used to empty the bowels. This is followed by the barium enema itself, administered through a tube inserted into the rectum while the patient lies on his or her side on a tilting x-ray table. The table will be rotated to allow

the barium to completely coat the large intestine and x-ray pictures will be taken.

The patient will then be helped to a bathroom or given a bedpan and told to expel as much of the barium as possible. More pictures will be taken of the thin film that remains on the mucous lining of the intestine. In some cases, this will be followed by a double contrast study, meaning air will be carefully injected into the colon to provide further contrast on the film in order to detect possible polyps.

The procedure causes some discomfort, including a strong urge to defecate and mild or, especially with the air contrast study, moderate to severe cramps. The stool will be white or light colored for a few days following the exam, and the barium may be constipating. For this reason, the test is sometimes followed by another laxative or enema.

What Is the Risk? Although this procedure is unpleasant and often uncomfortable, there are no serious complications. Risks, such as perforation of the bowel, are rare.

Pancreas Scan

Purpose. This radioisotope scan provides information on the structure and functioning of the pancreas to help detect cancer, cysts, or infection.

What Is Involved? A pancreas scan, which takes 1 to 2 hours, may be done on an inpatient or outpatient basis. The patient follows a high-protein diet for several days before the test, then fasts for 8 to 12 hours, with the exception of a glass of skim milk a few hours before the test. Another high-protein liquid is given at the time of the test. The isotope is given by IV and sometimes causes nausea or vomiting. (See Radioisotope Scans, page 49.)

What Is the Risk? There is a rare risk of radioisotope overdose.

Proctosigmoidoscopy

Purpose. A proctoscope exam (also called proctoscopy) allows the doctor to see the rectum and the lower part of the large intestine. It may be used to detect hemorrhoids, polyps, and abscesses or to determine the cause of bleeding. It is routinely used to screen for cancer after age 40, even if no symptoms are present.

What Is Involved? This procedure, which takes 10 to 20 minutes, may be carried out in a doctor's office or in a clinic. The patient may be instructed to have a liquid diet or to fast for a few hours, followed by an enema or suppository. With the patient in the knee-chest position, the doctor will do a digital exam, using a gloved finger, and then insert the proctoscope, which may be a rigid or a flexible tube. The procedure is similar to the colonoscopy (see page 59), but not as extensive. The patient may feel some discomfort and the urge to defecate.

What Is the Risk? Although the patient may feel some irritation around the anus afterward, this is a routine, safe procedure, with the risk of injury to the large intestine being very rare.

Sialography

Purpose. This procedure (also called ptyalography) allows x-ray visualization of the salivary glands to diagnose stones in the salivary ducts or other causes of an enlarged or painful salivary gland.

What Is Involved? This procedure, which takes about 45 to 60 minutes and is usually performed on an outpatient basis, requires no special preparation, except possibly fasting for a few hours beforehand. The patient may be given a sedative. A catheter is inserted through the mouth into the duct of the salivary gland to be studied and a contrast medium is injected through the catheter. The doctor examines the gland using a fluoroscope and may take x-rays. There is some discomfort when the catheter is introduced and pain when the dye reaches the salivary gland. The patient will continue to taste the contrast dye (which is somewhat unpleasant) and experience some soreness in the mouth after the procedure.

What Is the Risk? As with all invasive procedures, there is a rare risk of internal damage or infection.

Small Bowel Examination

This exam is usually done in conjunction with an upper GI Series. (See the following description.)

Upper GI and Small Bowel Series

Purpose. This fluoroscopic examination (also called barium milkshake or barium swallow) of the esophagus, stomach, and small intestine is used to diagnose cases of hiatal hernia, ulcers, tumors, obstruction, or enteritis, when there are symptoms such as difficulty in swallowing, regurgitation, burning or gnawing pain, diarrhea, weight loss, or bleeding.

What Is Involved? This test may be done in a hospital on an inpatient or outpatient basis. It may take anywhere from 30 minutes (for just the esophagus) to 60 minutes (for the esophagus and stomach) to 6 or more hours (if the small intestine is also included).

The patient may be asked to eat a low residue diet for 2 or 3 days before the test and will be asked not to eat or smoke for 6 to 12 hours prior to the exam. The test begins with the patient swallowing a "barium milkshake," a sweetened, flavored, but nonetheless chalky-tasting substance containing barium sulfate, a contrast medium that will outline the upper digestive tract. Sometimes a more liquid radiopaque material is used. The patient is strapped securely to a tilting x-ray table, which starts in a vertical position with the patient standing, and is tilted at various angles throughout the test to help spread the contrast medium and to get different views on the fluoroscope. Pressure may be applied to the patient's abdomen to spread the medium further.

If the test is to include a small bowel exam, the patient will have to wait several hours until the barium filters down into the intestine, and may be able to leave and come back, or to spend the time reading.

What Is the Risk? Although the barium is unpleasant tasting and will make the patient's stool white for several days (unless a laxative is given to speed its passing), there is no pain, little discomfort, and virtually no risk with this test, unless it is repeated several times, when radiation becomes a risk.

NEUROMUSCULAR SYSTEM TESTS

Brain Scan

Purpose. This radioisotope study of the brain is used to detect or diagnose tumors, hemmorhage, stroke, or blood vessel abnormalities.

What Is Involved? A brain scan, which is usually done on an outpatient basis, takes about 30 to 60 minutes. A blocking agent is used and the isotope is generally given by IV, but may be given orally, and the scan may be done from one or more positions. (See Radioisotope Scans, page 49.)

Cerebral Angiography

Purpose. Cerebral angiography allows the doctor

to see blood circulating through the brain and is used in locating tumors, blood clots, aneurysms, or other abnormalities and in diagnosing stroke.

What Is Involved? This procedure is virtually the same as angiography of the heart, but the catheter is extended up through the neck into the arteries of the brain. (See Arterial Cardiac Catheterization, page 55.)

What Is the Risk? The risk is the same as for arterial cardiac catheterization.

Cisternal Puncture

This procedure, which provides a small amount of cerebrospinal fluid from the base of the brain, is used to diagnose viral or bacterial infections, brain hemorrhage, and tumors. It is done in place of, or in conjunction with, a lumbar puncture (see page 64). The only difference is the puncture site of the needle. With a cisternal tap, the patient's chin is tucked in as far as possible and the needle is inserted in the back of the neck at the base of the brain. Although the risks are about the same for the two procedures, there is a little less likelihood of headache following a cisternal puncture.

Electroencephalography

Purpose. This test (also known as EEG) records the electrical activity of the brain and is used to diagnose epilepsy, tumors, brain damage, mental retardation, and psychological disorders.

What Is Involved? This procedure, which is done on an outpatient basis, usually takes about 1 hour unless a sleep EEG, which takes about 3 hours, is done. The patient may be asked not to take any medications that have an effect on the nervous system for 1 or 2 days before the test. Electrodes are attached to the patient's scalp, either with electrode paste or by tiny, virtually painless needles. Very weak electrical current is passed through the electrodes, which produces a mild tingling sensation, and the brain's electrical activity is recorded.

After the baseline study is made, the patient is exposed to various stimuli, such as bright or flashing (strobe) lights, noise, or drugs. The patient may be asked to breathe deeply and quickly for 3 minutes or to stare at a black-and-white checkerboard pattern. All of these techniques produce changes in the brain waves.

With a sleep EEG, the patient may be kept awake for many hours and then given a sleep-inducing drug or encouraged to sleep during the test.

What Is the Risk? There is virtually no risk.

Electromyography

Purpose. Electromyography (also called EMG), which studies the electrical activity of muscles at rest and during contraction, is used to diagnose diseases that affect the muscles, peripheral nerves, and spinal cord.

What Is Involved? The study is usually carried out in a hospital and takes 1 hour or longer, depending on how many muscles are being studied. The patient may be asked not to smoke or take caffeine drinks for 2 or 3 hours before the test. For the first part of the test, to study the nerves, electrodes are placed on the skin and a weak electric current is passed through them while the electrical activity of the nerves and muscles is recorded. For the second part of the test, thin needles are inserted into the muscles and the electrical activity is again studied and recorded as photographs or tracings on special recording paper.

What Is the Risk? Although there may be some pain during and after needle insertion, there is no risk associated with this procedure other than infection, which is rare.

Fluorescein Retinal Angiography

Purpose. This test (also called eye angiography), which allows x-ray visualization of the blood circulation in the retina and the choroid of the eye, is used to diagnose retinopathy, tumors, and circulatory or inflammatory disorders.

What Is Involved? Fluorescein angiography, which takes about 1 hour, is usually done as an outpatient procedure and may be done in an ophthalmologist's office. No special preparation is needed. The patient's pupils are dilated with eyedrops, much as for a visual acuity test, to prevent the pupils from closing up when the lighted ophthalmoscope is used to examine the eyes. Then the fluorescein dye is injected through a vein in the arm, at which time the patient may feel some nausea or flushing. The patient sits very still with his or her head resting in a special frame to keep it from moving, and a series of x-rays is taken. The patient may be asked to wait 20 or 30 minutes before another set is taken. The effects of the dilating drops, light sensitivity, and blurred vision will linger for several hours and the patient's skin and urine may have a yellowish tinge for a day or so.

What Is the Risk? On rare occasions, patients may experience an allergic reaction to the dilating drops (elderly patients may develop acute glaucoma) or to the fluorescein.

Intrathecal Scan

Purpose. This radioisotope study (also called cisternography) allows the doctor to see the flow of cerebrospinal fluid to check for changes, abnormalities, or leaks.

What Is Involved? An intrathecal study is done on an inpatient basis and may take as long as 72 hours, including waiting time between scans. The isotope is injected by way of a lumbar puncture (see below). Some of the cerebrospinal fluid is withdrawn, mixed with the radioisotope, and reinjected. It takes about 3 hours to fill the subarachnoid space between the brain and the membrane that covers it before the scan can begin. If the doctor is looking for a leak, cotton may be placed in the patient's nose and ears and later checked to see if it has absorbed any of the isotope.

What Is the Risk? There is some risk and discomfort associated with the lumbar puncture and there is always the remote risk of radioisotope overdose. (See Radioisotope Scans, page 49.)

Lumbar Puncture

Purpose. The lumbar puncture (also known as spinal tap) provides a small amount of cerebrospinal

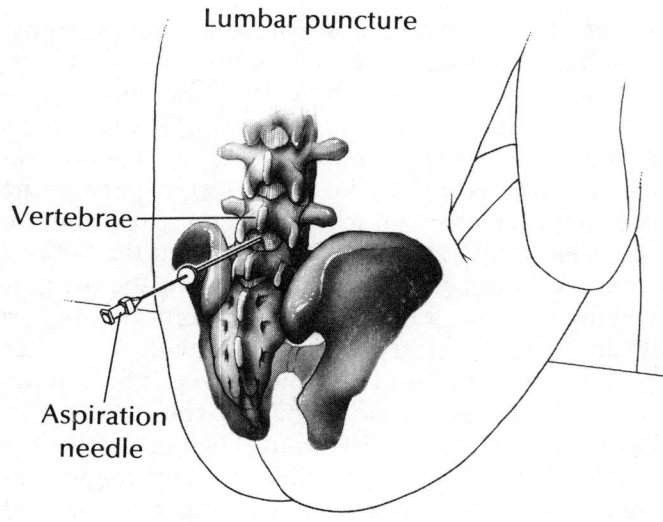

Lumbar puncture

Vertebrae

Aspiration needle

Figure 4.6. **A lumbar puncture, in which a hollow needle is inserted between 2 vertebrae and a small amount of spinal fluid is withdrawn for analysis.**

fluid for laboratory analysis and is used to diagnose viral or bacterial infections, brain hemorrhage, and tumors or other obstructions.

What Is Involved? This procedure, which takes about 30 minutes, may be done on an outpatient basis, but is usually done on an inpatient basis. The patient lies on his or her side, with knees drawn up and chin tucked into the chest in order to provide as much room as possible for the insertion of the needle. (See figure 4.6) A local anesthetic is injected, the needle inserted, and a small amount of fluid withdrawn. There may be a feeling of pressure when this is done.

What Is the Risk? Although a common after-effect is a moderate to severe headache (which usually can be relieved by lying flat), there are very few risks associated with this procedure. There is a rare risk of infection from the needle or of leakage of the fluid through a tear in the membranes that surround the spinal cord.

Myelography

Purpose. This procedure allows x-ray visualization of the spinal subarachnoid space—the area between the spinal cord and the arachnoid membrane that covers it—in order to diagnose herniated disks, spinal nerve injury, and tumors.

What Is Involved? Myelography is usually performed on an inpatient basis and takes from 30 to 90 minutes. The patient will not be allowed to eat or drink for several hours before the procedure and may be given an enema and a tranquilizer or sedative. With the patient lying on a tilting x-ray table, a lumbar or cisternal puncture (see above) is performed, a small amount of spinal fluid is removed, and the contrast medium is injected at the same site. A series of x-rays is taken with the table in various positions, and all or part of the contrast medium may be removed by aspiration afterward. The patient may find the procedure uncomfortable for several reasons: having to lie still for long periods of time in awkward positions; a feeling of pressure, flushing, and nausea and vomiting when the contrast is injected; possibly some pain when it is removed; and the headache that usually accompanies a spinal tap.

What Is the Risk? Although this procedure is uncomfortable, the risk involved is remote. There is always the possibility of infection or allergy to the contrast medium, or the leakage of the dye into the head, but these are rare.

REPRODUCTIVE SYSTEM TESTS

Amniocentesis

Purpose. Amniocentesis, the withdrawal of a small amount of amniotic fluid from the uterus during pregnancy, is used to test for birth defects and other potential problems. The fluid contains waste materials and skin cells normally sloughed off by the fetus, which can tell a number of things about the fetus's chromosomal makeup.

Since there are occasional complications with this test, it is not used routinely unless the mother is over 35 or has a family history of genetic disorders, chromosomal defects, or mental retardation, or when an Rh factor problem is anticipated.

What Is Involved? The test is usually performed after the fifteenth week of pregnancy, when sufficient amniotic fluid has accumulated for a sample to be taken. It takes only about 15 minutes in the doctor's office or in an outpatient clinic. No special preparation is needed, except that the mother may be asked to void prior to the test. A local anesthetic is injected into the abdomen, and the small sting from the needle is the only sensation felt. Using ultrasonography (see page 50) as a guide, the doctor inserts a thin, hollow needle into the abdomen and withdraws a small amount of fluid, less than an ounce. (See figures 4.7A and 4.7B.) The cells from the fluid are cultured in a laboratory; it usually takes about 3 to 4 weeks for test results. An alternative procedure is to take a sample of the placental villus cells that are also representative of the fetus.

Although the test cannot guarantee that the child will be born without birth defects, there are certain conditions that it can rule out, including Down's syndrome (mongoloidism), Tay-Sachs disease, amino acid disorders, and neural tube disorders such as spina bifida. It can also determine sex, fetal age and maturity, and give some indications of general health.

What Is the Risk? Adverse effects are rare. The only serious risk is accidentally puncturing the placenta with the needle, but the use of ultrasound virtually eliminates this. There is a slight risk of spontaneous abortion and, as with all invasive procedures, there is a risk of infection.

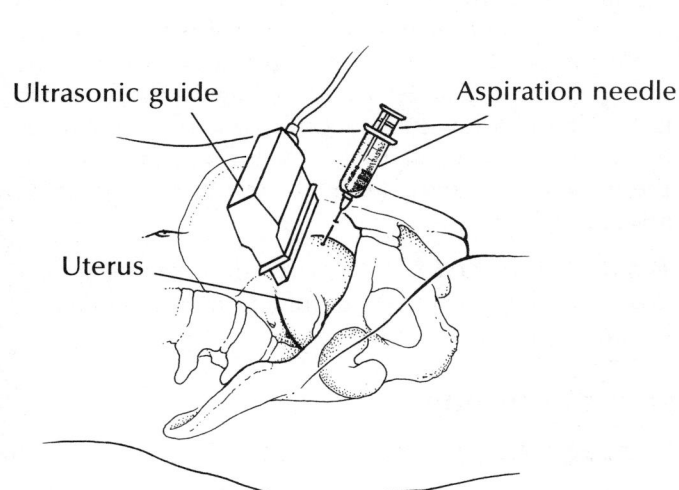
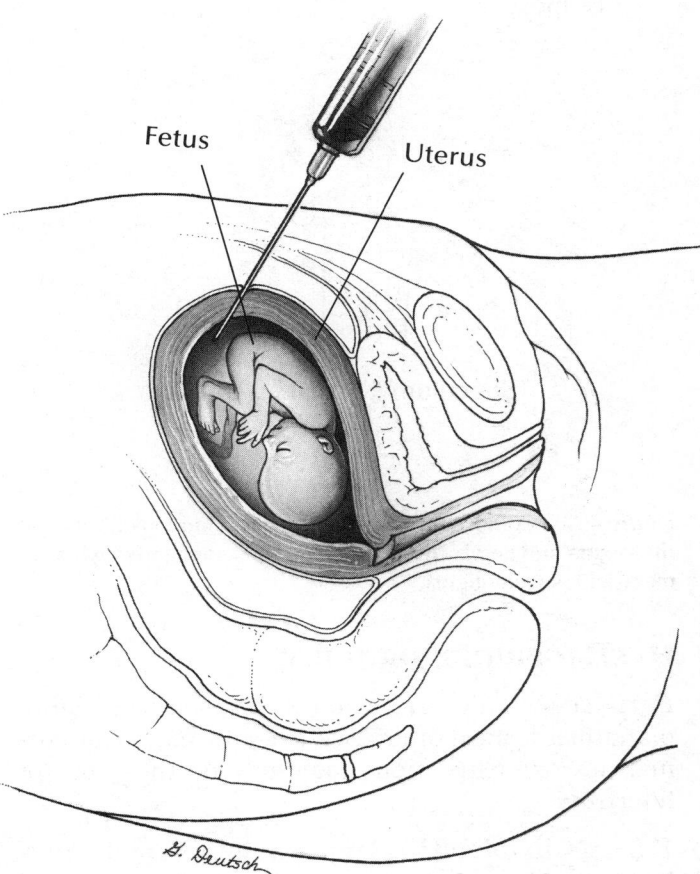

Figures 4.7A and 4.7B. **The large drawing (4.7A) shows amniocentesis in process, with the aspiration needle inserted into the uterus and amnionic sac to withdraw a small amount of the fluid surrounding the fetus. Ultrasonography (4.7B) is used to guide the procedure to ensure that the fetus is not harmed.**

Colposcopy

Purpose. Colposcopy, which allows the doctor direct visualization of the vagina and cervix, is most often used to confirm cervical cancer (after a positive Pap test) or to perform a biopsy. It is also used to monitor patients whose mothers were given DES during pregnancy.

What Is Involved? This procedure, which takes about 15 minutes, can be performed in a doctor's office. With the patient lying on her back, her feet in stirrups, a speculum is inserted into the vagina to spread the vaginal walls and allow insertion of a colposcope, a tube equipped with a light that allows the doctor to examine the cervix and to do a biopsy. (See figure 4.8.) There may be some easily controllable bleeding if a biopsy is done, but there is generally no pain.

What Is the Risk? There is very slight risk of infection or moderately heavy bleeding.

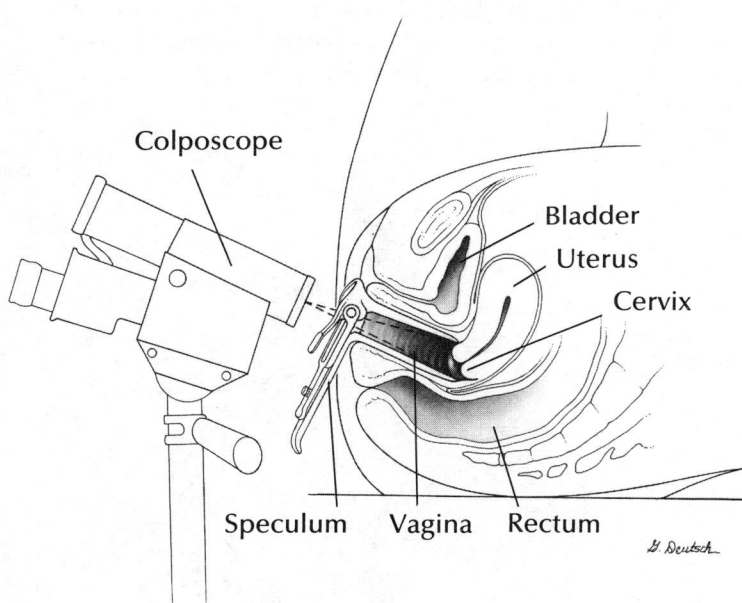

Figure 4.8. **Colposcopy enables a physician to look directly at the vagina and cervix, using a colposcope, a magnifying instrument with special lights.**

Hysterosalpingography

Purpose. This x-ray exam of the uterus and Fallopian tubes is most often used to confirm tubal abnormalities or obstructions that may be the cause of infertility.

What Is Involved? Hysterosalpingography may last from 15 to 45 minutes, and is usually performed on an outpatient basis. The patient may be asked not to eat for several hours before the exam, and may be given a laxative and a sedative. With the patient lying on her back with knees flexed and feet in stirrups, a tube is inserted into the vagina and used to inject contrast medium into the uterus. If the Fallopian tubes are not blocked, the medium will flow from the uterus through the tubes and out into the peritoneal cavity. If they are blocked, the point of obstruction will be visible on the fluoroscope. The patient may feel some cramping from this procedure and more severe pain if the tubes are blocked. There may be a stinging sensation when the contrast medium reaches the peritoneal cavity.

What Is the Risk? Besides the risk of internal injury associated with any endoscopic procedure, there is a rare risk of intravascular injection of the contrast medium.

Laparoscopy

Purpose. Laparoscopy, which allows the doctor to look directly at the uterus, Fallopian tubes, and ovaries, is used to detect endometriosis, ectopic pregnancy, pelvic inflammatory disease or other causes of pelvic pain, or to determine the extent of cancer. It may also be used to perform a tubal ligation (sterilization).

What Is Involved? This procedure, done under local or general anesthesia, is usually performed in a hospital, but may be done on an outpatient basis. The patient is asked to fast for at least 8 hours beforehand. A catheter is inserted into the bladder and a small incision is made to allow insertion of the laparoscope. (See figure 4.9.) Carbon dioxide may be injected into the body cavity to distend the abdominal wall and allow more room to see and maneuver. A dye may be used to check for obstructions in the Fallopian tubes. (See Hysterosalpingography, above.)

What Is the Risk? As with all invasive procedures, there is a rare risk of infection and damage to internal organs.

Mammography

(See page 54.)

Placental Scan

Purpose. This test is performed during pregnancy to determine the cause of vaginal bleeding if problems with the placenta are suspected.

What Is Involved? A placental scan, which is usually done on an outpatient basis, requires about one-half hour. No special preparation is necessary

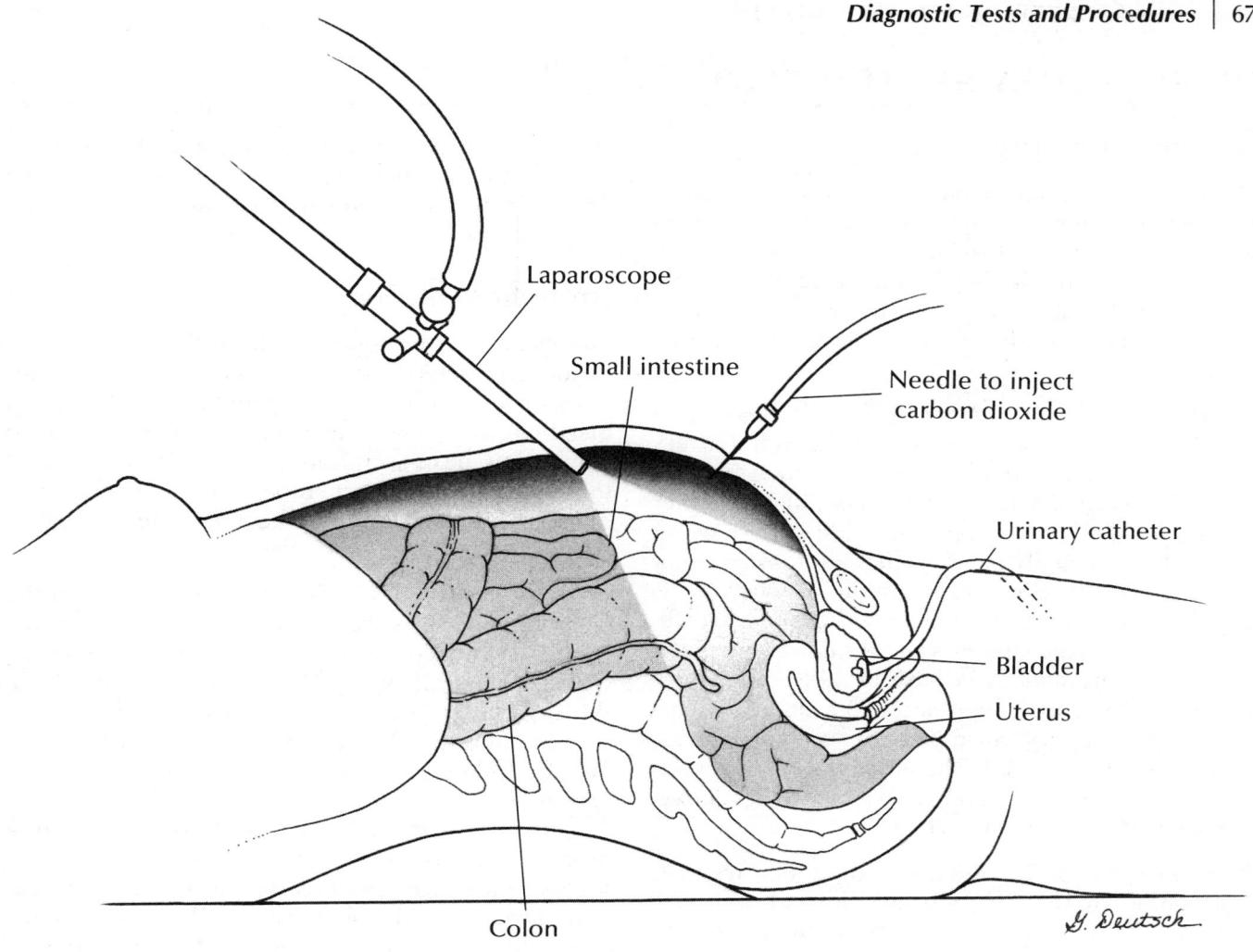

Laparoscope

Small intestine

Needle to inject
carbon dioxide

Urinary catheter

Bladder

Uterus

Colon

G. Deutsch

Figure 4.9. **Laparoscopy is used to view the pelvic or other abdominal organs through a small incision in the abdominal wall.**

other than having the patient void, and there is no serious risk to either the mother or fetus. (See Radioisotope Scans, page 49, for more information.)

Pregnancy Test

This test for determining pregnancy is described in the introduction, page 48.

Semen Analysis

Purpose. Semen analysis (also called sperm count) is primarily used to determine male fertility, but it can also be used in suspected rape cases. Although a number of substances are present in the semen and analyzed, the sperm count is the best known.

What Is Involved? The patient will be asked to abstain from intercourse for a specified period, usually 2 to 6 days, and then to obtain a specimen by masturbation, which is usually done at the laboratory, but may also be done at home into a sterile container provided by the lab. Although masturbation

is the preferred method, coitus interruptus may be used. In rape cases, a semen sample will be drawn from the vagina using an aspirating syringe. There is no risk in this procedure.

Sonogram

Purpose. This procedure (also called ultrasound or sonography) allows the doctor to see the fetus inside the uterus without the risk of exposure to x-ray. It is used to determine the stage of fetal development when there is a discrepancy between apparent size and due date, to confirm the presence of more than one fetus, to determine the position of the fetus or placenta, to diagnose causes of vaginal bleeding, and to guide the needle for an amniocentesis.

What Is Involved? The procedure, which takes about 15 minutes, is simple and painless. There is no preparation needed, but the patient may be asked to drink liquids before the test in order to fill her bladder and create a clearer picture. (See Ultrasonography, page 50.) There is virtually no risk involved.

RESPIRATORY SYSTEM TESTS

Arterial Puncture

Purpose. Arterial blood gas sampling measures how well the lungs are functioning in delivering oxygen to the blood and clearing carbon dioxide from it, and how efficient the heart is as a pump. (On the other hand, venous blood—usually taken from a vein in the crook of the elbow—reflects cell metabolism.)

What Is Involved? After the skin is cleansed, a small needle is inserted, usually in the radial artery at the wrist, and a small amount of blood is withdrawn. The radial artery is chosen because the ulner artery, located on the opposite side of the wrist, serves the same body parts, so that circulation is not interrupted. Since the pressure in the arteries is greater than that in the veins, pressure must be applied to the needle site for several minutes after the needle is withdrawn to be sure that bleeding stops. When frequent sampling is necessary, such as in cardiovascular surgery, an indwelling catheter, or arterial line, may be used. The blood sample is placed in a blood gas analyzer and checked for levels of oxygen, carbon dioxide, and pH.

What Is the Risk? Assuming the ulner artery is functioning, there is virtually no risk involved in this procedure using the radial artery. With an indwelling catheter, there may be a rare risk of infection or of injury to the artery.

Bronchography

Purpose. Bronchography is an x-ray of the trachea and the bronchial tree used to help locate obstructions, tumors, or cysts in the bronchial tube, or to help guide a bronchoscope during bronchoscopy.

What Is Involved? The test, which is usually done in a hospital but may be done on an outpatient basis, takes about 1 hour. To minimize nausea, the patient will be asked not to eat for 6 to 12 hours beforehand. A local anesthetic will be first sprayed and later dripped through a long, thin tube called a catheter, which is passed through the nose or mouth into the throat and down the windpipe. The catheter is then used to administer the contrast medium.

What Is the Risk? Complications are generally rare but, as with all invasive procedures involving contrast dye, there are risks of infection, damage to the trachea or windpipe from the catheter, and the possibility of allergic reaction to either the anesthetic or dye. The contrast medium will usually dissipate over several hours, but if some of it remains blocked in the ends of the small branches of the bronchial tubes, it can cause irritation and, rarely, lung collapse.

Bronchoscopy

Purpose. Bronchoscopy allows the doctor to see inside the trachea and bronchial tree to check for tumors or foreign bodies, to locate the site of internal bleeding, to remove mucus or a foreign body, or to obtain a tissue or secretion specimen. It may be used to help diagnose cancer, tuberculosis, or other pulmonary diseases caused by bacteria, fungi, or parasites.

What Is Involved? The procedure is done in the hospital and may involve either general anesthesia, which is inhaled or injected, or local anesthesia, which is generally sprayed into the nose and mouth. With the latter, a sedative may also be used to help the patient relax. The patient will be asked not to eat for 6 to 12 hours before the test, and to remove any dentures.

For most procedures, the flexible fiberoptic bronchoscope is used, since it allows the doctor to see more and presents less risk of injury to the patient. But the rigid, hollow tube will be used if a foreign body must be removed or if a large biopsy sample is necessary. Various attachments to the bronchoscope allow the suctioning off of excess mucus, the injecting of saline to wash the inner surfaces, and gentle brushing to take samples of cells from the mucous lining. There may be some soreness following the test, especially if a biopsy is taken.

What Is the Risk? As with all invasive procedures, there is a risk of injury to the test site, including the teeth, gums, throat, or bronchial tube, although these are relatively rare and less apt to happen with a flexible tube. There is also a risk of allergic reaction to the anesthesia.

Laryngoscopy

Purpose. This procedure, which allows the doctor to see directly into the larynx to detect foreign bodies, tumors, or other abnormalities, is very similar to a bronchoscopy, except that the endoscope does not enter as far into the body. The preparation and risks are generally the same. The patient may experience a sore throat and may cough up blood afterward, but this is generally not serious. (See preceding description.)

Lung Capacity Test

Purpose. This test (also known as a pulmonary function test) is used to determine the cause of shortness of breath and to detect the presence of diseases or injury. It is often used before surgery or to evaluate disability for insurance purposes.

What Is Involved? The test, which is usually performed in a doctor's office or a laboratory, takes about 45 to 60 minutes. The patient will be told not to eat a heavy meal or smoke for 6 hours before the test and to avoid wearing constricting clothing or taking analgesics. During the test, the patient wears nose clips (to prevent air from escaping through the nostrils) and breathes into a flexible tube called a spirometer. Various breathing patterns are tested, such as breathing normally, exhaling as fast as possible after inhaling normally, or inhaling and exhaling deeply. The patient may also breathe specific quantities of helium, nitrogen, or pure oxygen.

What Is the Risk? Although some patients may find the test tiring, there is no pain or risk associated with it.

Lung Scan

Purpose. There are two types of lung scans, ventilation and perfusion, which can be used to detect infection, pulmonary embolism, and tumors, and to evaluate emphysema and other breathing problems.

What Is Involved? The test, which is usually done on an outpatient basis, takes about 30 minutes. For a perfusion scan, the isotope is given intravenously; for a ventilation scan, it is mixed with a gas and inhaled. (See Radioisotope Scans, page 49, for more information.)

Mediastinoscopy

Purpose. This procedure allows direct visualization of the tissues and organs in the chest cavity behind the breastbone (sternum) and is used to detect or evaluate infections and various types of cancers.

What Is Involved? Mediastinoscopy, which lasts about 1 hour, is performed in the hospital with the patient under general anesthesia. After an endotracheal tube is inserted, the surgeon makes a small incision in the chest and inserts the mediastinoscope, which is used to collect tissue specimens for analysis.

What Is the Risk? After the procedure, the patient will probably experience chest pain, soreness at the incision site, and a sore throat from the endotracheal tube. There is the usual risk that accompanies the use of general anesthesia. Although rare, there are also risks of damage to internal organs, infection, hemorrhage, and laryngeal nerve damage.

Thoracentesis

Purpose. Thoracentesis (also called pleural tap or pleural fluid analysis) is used to obtain a sample of fluid from the cavity between the lungs and the chest wall in order to diagnose cancer, tuberculosis, blood and lymphatic disorders, or to relieve pressure caused by excess fluid in this area.

What Is Involved? This procedure, which is usually performed in the hospital, is very similar to amniocentesis (see page 65), but rather than lying down, the patient is usually seated, leaning forward, and bent over in order to provide as much room as possible between the ribs for insertion of the needle.

What Is the Risk? Occasionally a lung is accidentally punctured, which may cause it to collapse, a condition that is not serious and can be readily treated.

SKELETAL SYSTEM

Arthrography

Purpose. This procedure (also called arthrogram) provides x-ray visualization of a joint, especially the knee or shoulder, used to diagnose abnormalities or injuries to the cartilage, tendons, and ligaments.

What Is Involved? Arthrography is usually performed on an outpatient basis, takes about 1 hour, and requires no special preparation. A local anesthetic is injected first and then the contrast medium—either dye or air, or both—is injected into the joint. If the knee is being examined, the patient may be asked to walk a few steps in order to spread the contrast medium. The joint is examined using fluoroscopy and x-rays may be taken. For a day or so afterward, there may be some pain and swelling and the patient may be able to hear the liquid moving within the joint when the joint is exercised. The patient will generally be advised to rest and not put any strain on the joint.

What Is the Risk? There is little risk in this procedure, other than the slight possibility of infection or allergy to the contrast dye.

Arthroscopy

Purpose. This procedure, which uses a fiberoptic endoscope to see the interior of a joint, is used to diagnose various joint diseases or to perform surgery on the joint.

What Is Involved? Arthroscopy, which takes

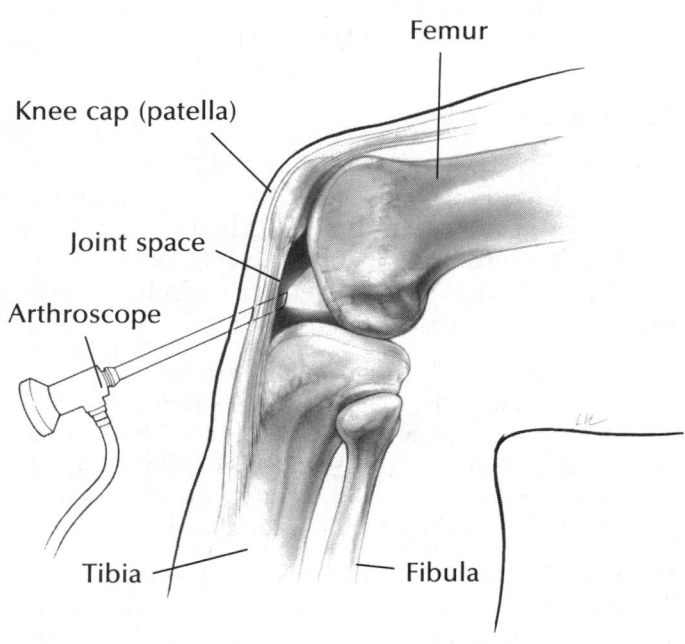

Femur

Knee cap (patella)

Joint space

Arthroscope

Tibia

Fibula

Figure 4.10. **Arthroscopy of the knee, in which the arthroscope is inserted directly into the joint space to allow the doctor to see its interior.**

about 1 hour, can be done on an inpatient or outpatient basis. There is no special preparation, but the patient may be asked to fast for 8 to 12 hours beforehand. The joint, particularly the knee, may be wrapped in an elastic bandage, or a tourniquet may be used to keep as much blood as possible away from the joint. A local anesthetic is injected and a small incision made through which an endoscope—in this instance, an arthroscope—is inserted. (See figure 4.10.) The joint may be rotated to several positions of extension and flexion during the procedure. Various attachments to the endoscope may be used to irrigate the joint or take a biopsy specimen. There may be some pressure or discomfort from the tourniquet or the procedure. The incision will be sutured and bandaged and, although the patient may walk or use the joint afterward, excessive use should be avoided for several days.

What Is the Risk? As with all invasive procedures, there is always the risk of infection or damage to internal structures, but this is rare.

Bone Scan

Purpose. This radioisotope test provides a view of the bone useful in diagnosing cancer, bone trauma, and degenerative disorders.

What Is Involved? A bone scan is usually done on an outpatient basis and requires no special preparation. The isotope is injected and takes about 3 hours to reach the bone, during which time the patient can usually leave. The scan itself takes another hour, with the patient lying in various positions. The patient may be asked to drink several glasses of water or tea before the scan begins. (See Radioisotope Scans, page 49.)

What Is the Risk? Other than the remote possibility of isotope overdose, there is no real risk involved.

THYROID TESTS

Thyroid Scan and Iodine Uptake Test

Purpose. These two radioisotope procedures, often done together, provide information on the size, structure, position, and functioning of the thyroid and are used to aid diagnosis of hyper- and hypothyroidism.

What Is Involved? In preparation for these tests, which are normally done on an outpatient basis, the

patient is required to discontinue for 2 or 3 days any thyroid hormones and medications and food containing iodine (a list is usually provided by the doctor), and to fast for 8 to 12 hours beforehand. The thyroid scan takes only about 10 minutes and the uptake procedure involves 3 separate short scans at 2, 6, and 24 hours, with the patient allowed to leave between scans. The radioisotope-containing iodine is administered orally. (See Radioisotope Scans, page 49.)

What Is the Risk? There is no real risk, other than the remote possibility of a radioisotope overdose.

Thyroid Ultrasonography

Purpose. This noninvasive procedure allows the doctor to see the thyroid gland in order to evaluate its structure, monitor its size during therapy, and differentiate between a cyst and a tumor. Ultrasonography is often done in conjunction with thyroid scans.

What Is Involved? Ultrasonography requires about 30 minutes and is done on an outpatient basis. It is riskless, painless, and requires no special preparation. (See Ultrasonography, page 50, for more information.)

TSH, T_4, T_3
(See the section on Common Blood Analyses, page 53.)

URINARY SYSTEM TESTS

Cystometry

Purpose. This test is used to assess the neuromuscular function of the bladder when there are problems of bladder control.

What Is Involved? Cystometry, which takes about 45 minutes and is usually done on an outpatient basis, requires no special preparation, but the patient may be asked to void beforehand. It consists of several measures of the patient's ability to feel sensations, such as hot and cold and urgency to void, and the ability to suppress voiding. A catheter is inserted into the bladder and a predetermined amount of sterile water or gas (usually carbon dioxide) is injected into the bladder. The patient is asked to report all sensations, such as when the need to void is first felt; when the feeling can no longer be controlled; whether there is any feeling of fullness, nausea, or flushing; and whether the fluid feels warm or cold. The patient is then asked to urinate and the volume is measured. Any urine that remains in the bladder is drained.

What Is the Risk? Although there is always the possibility of infection with catheterization, there is little risk involved in this procedure.

Cystourethroscopy

Purpose. This procedure (also called cystoscopy) is used to diagnose urinary tract disorders and provides a direct view of the urethra, bladder, and sometimes the ureters.

What Is Involved? Cystourethroscopy can be an inpatient or an outpatient procedure using general or local anesthesia, and takes about 30 minutes. If general anesthesia is used, the patient will be asked to fast for at least eight hours beforehand. The patient lies on his or her back with knees drawn up while the instrument, which consists of two tubes used separately, the cystoscope and the urethroscope, is inserted into the urethra and then into the bladder. (See figures 4.11A and 4.11B.) Fluid may be injected into the bladder to distend the walls and provide a better view, and urine and biopsy specimens may be taken during the examination. If local anesthesia is used, the patient may feel some burning or discomfort when the endoscopes are passed and when the bladder is filled.

What Is the Risk? As with all invasive procedures, there is always the possibility of damage to internal structures, but this is rare.

Voiding Cystourethrography

Purpose. Voiding cystourethrography (also called voiding urethrogram) provides an x-ray picture of the bladder and urethra during urination and is used to diagnose abnormalities, infection, or other disorders of the urinary tract.

What Is Involved? The test, which is usually performed on an outpatient basis, takes about 30 minutes and requires no special preparation. A catheter is inserted into the urethra and into the bladder which, after it is drained of any urine, is filled with contrast dye until the patient has the urge to void. Still or moving x-ray pictures are taken of the urinary tract as the patient voids. There may be some discomfort as the catheter is passed.

What Is the Risk? There are no aftereffects and very little risk associated with this procedure, unless it is repeated several times, in which case there is a risk of excess radiation exposure.

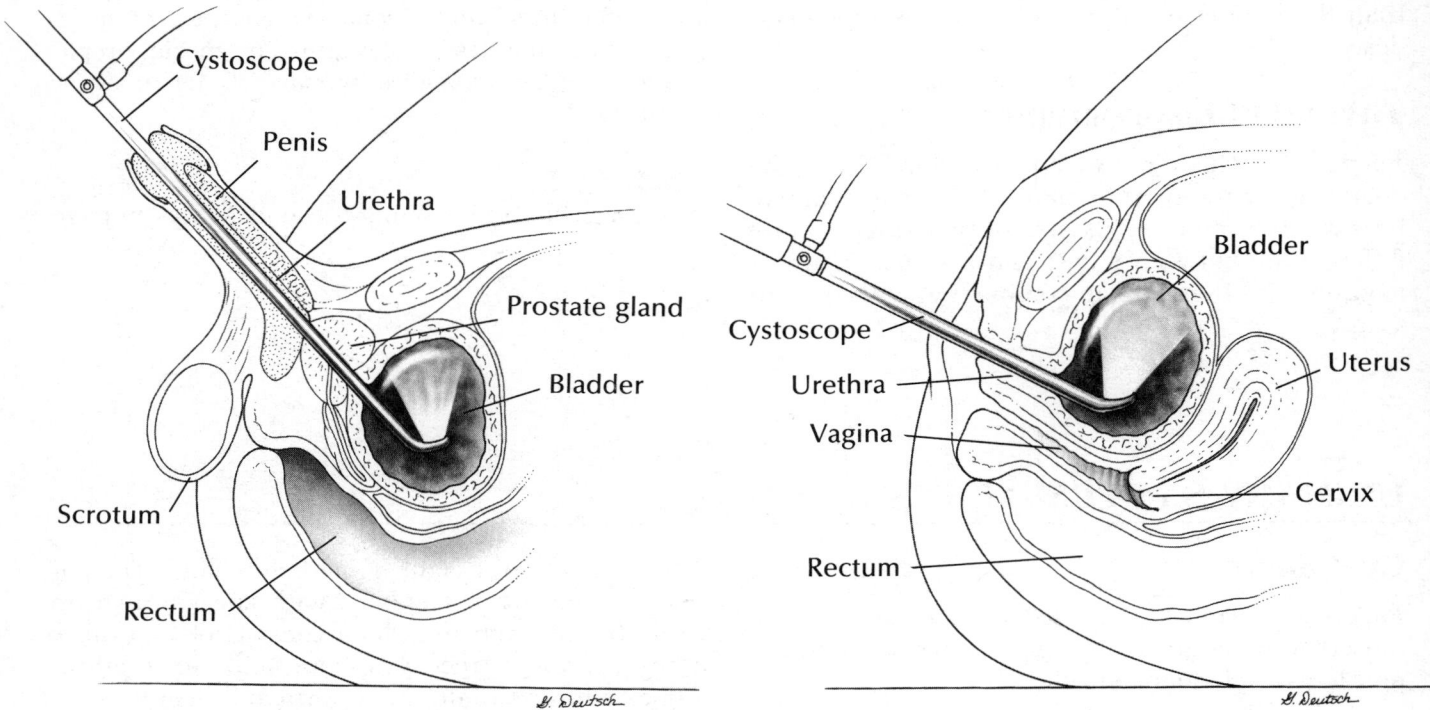

Figures 4.11A and 4.11B. **Drawings of cystourethroscopy in both male (4.11A) and female (4.11B). The cystoscope is threaded through the urethra and into the bladder.**

Pyelography, Intravenous

Purpose. This contrast x-ray procedure (also called excretory urography or IVP) allows the doctor to see inside the kidneys, ureters, and bladder to evaluate the functioning of the kidneys and urinary tract.

What Is Involved? IVP, which can be done on an inpatient or outpatient basis, takes about 60 minutes. The patient is usually given a laxative or enema and asked to fast for 8 hours beforehand. While the patient lies on his or her back on the x-ray table, the contrast medium is injected intravenously and x-rays are taken at regular intervals (5, 10, 15, and 20 minutes) as the dye travels from the kidneys through the urinary tract. The abdomen may be compressed to restrict the dye to the upper urinary tract for the first part of the study. The patient is then asked to void and another x-ray is taken. The contrast medium may produce a burning sensation and a fishy or metallic taste in the mouth (even though nothing is swallowed).

What Is the Risk? There is some risk of allergic reaction to the contrast medium, and the patient should report any unusual sensations to the doctor during the test and afterward. There is also a radiation risk if the procedure is repeated several times.

Renal Scan and Renogram

Purpose. These 2 types of kidney scans, which are often done together, provide information on the size, shape, and position of the kidneys (renal scan) and the flow of blood and production of urine within the kidneys (renogram).

What Is Involved? With the renogram, the patient sits while the scanner is placed against the back over the kidneys. The isotope is administered by IV. With the renal scan, the isotope is injected with the patient lying down. The procedures, which can be done on an outpatient basis, take about 60 to 90 minutes. The patient may feel some flushing or nausea when the radioisotope is administered. (See Radioisotope Scans, page 49.)

What Is the Risk? There is a rare risk of isotope overdose.

Retrograde Urethrography

Purpose. This contrast x-ray visualization of the

front part of the urethra is used to diagnose abnormalities or injuries.

What Is Involved? Retrograde urethrography is usually done on an outpatient basis and takes about 30 minutes, and is done almost exclusively on males. No special preparation is required, but the patient may be given a tranquilizer. The penis is held in an extended position using a special clamp and a catheter is inserted into the urethra, through which the contrast medium is injected. X-rays are taken of the patient in several positions. There may be some dis-

comfort when the contrast dye is injected. If the procedure is done on a woman, a special catheter with a small balloon on each end is inserted into the urethra and the balloons used to keep the contrast medium from running out.

What Is the Risk? There is a risk of allergic reaction to the contrast medium and, as with all invasive procedures, a risk of internal injury or infection. There will probably be some soreness or irritation at the opening of the urethra.

URINE TESTS

MANY OF THE SAME SUBSTANCES that are tested for in the blood are also tested for in the urine.

Routine Urine Analysis

This simple collection of one urine specimen is used to test for the following:

Substance	Test for
Blood	Stones, infection, tumors
White blood cells	Infection
Glucose	Diabetes
Ketones	Diabetes
Bile	Liver disease
Protein	Injured glomeruli (blood vessels in the kidneys)
Protein casts	Kidney disease

Timed Urine Specimens

Some of the substances produced by the body, such as hormones, are excreted in short bursts, rather than continuously. They may show up in the urine, but their presence and quantity will vary throughout the day, and thus one urine sample will not be a reliable indicator. In this case a timed specimen collection is used, with the patient saving all of the urine produced in a 12- or 24-hour period. For exam-

ple, if the test is to begin at 8 A.M., the patient empties his or her bladder at that hour, but does collect that urine. All of the rest of the urine produced in the next 24 hours is collected in a clean container and at 8 A.M. the next day, the patient urinates and collects the final sample.

Calcium, an indication of kidney stones or gallstones, is one of the substances tested for in this way. Timed collection is also used when a case of high blood pressure is not responding to therapy and the doctor suspects that the condition may be caused by the presence of a tumor known as a pheochromocytoma.

Other Collection Methods

First Void. This is the first urine passed in the morning, sometimes used in testing because, since the patient presumably has not urinated in many hours, the sample will be very concentrated, and may show substances that will not be present later.

Clean Catch, Midstream. This is a method used when an infection is suspected and the doctor is looking for evidence of bacteria. Since the first bit of urine may be contaminated with bacteria that has migrated into the urethra from the outside, it is not a reliable indicator. The patient urinates a little into a toilet or bedpan and then, without interrupting the flow, urinates about an ounce more in the collection vial (finishing urinating into the toilet, if necessary).

Part Two

WHAT TO DO UNTIL THE DOCTOR COMES

5 An Overview of First Aid and Safety

Kenneth C. Fine, M.D.

INTRODUCTION

ACCIDENTS ARE NOW our fourth leading cause of death, claiming more than 150,000 lives a year. In some age groups, most notably children and young men, accidents are the leading cause of death. In addition, more than 70 million Americans a year are injured seriously enough to require medical care.

The National Safety Council estimates that more than one-half of these accidents could be prevented by following simple, commonsense precautions: Always wearing seat belts in an automobile, making sure proper maintenance is done and that the car is in good repair, and teaching children proper safety habits are but a few examples. Simple preventive techniques for the entire family are outlined in this chapter. Still, no matter how careful we are, there are some emergency situations that simply cannot be prevented. And, of course, not all medical emergencies result from accidents; heart attacks, diabetic coma, febrile seizures, and other such emergencies are often unpredictable events of illness. Very often, prompt action within minutes is needed to prevent death or further injury. Clearly, knowing what to do in such situations and applying that knowledge in a coolheaded, competent manner can be life-saving. A handbook of the more common first-aid procedures is included in this chapter.

Although the principles of first aid can be understood by following printed instructions and illustrations, certain first-aid or lifesaving techniques, such as cardiopulmonary resuscitation (CPR), must be learned through qualified instructors. Attempting to provide advanced first aid or resuscitation without this training is fraught with uncertainty and hazard to both the provider and the recipient. Everyone over the age of 12 should consider taking a first-aid training course that includes such procedures as CPR and the Heimlich maneuver (for choking victims). Such courses are offered by many schools, police or fire departments, health organizations, community hospitals, or under the auspices of the American Red Cross. Local chapters of the Red Cross or the American Heart Association usually can direct people to first-aid courses. If such courses are not readily available, it is possible to organize a group and then contact the Red Cross for information on starting a formal first-aid course taught by a qualified instructor.

First-aid and CPR courses not only provide the necessary skills for handling a medical emergency, but they also teach participants how to assess illness and accidental situations to determine which are true emergencies requiring immediate action and medical follow-up and which are not. The time to take these courses is now, before being faced with an emergency situation.

SUMMONING HELP

It is also important to know where and how to summon help should an emergency arise. Often, people waste time by trying to call a family doctor, whose response will likely be to summon an ambulance or rescue squad. Emergency phone numbers should be clearly posted on or near all phones and each family member should know who to call. In most areas, this will be an emergency rescue squad. Some operate from a hospital or medical center, others from a fire or police station. In either event, the emergency medical technicians who staff these squads have the proper training and equipment to handle medical emergencies. In most areas, the emergency squad can be summoned by telephoning the police emergency number, 911, or by asking the telephone operator to summon an ambulance or rescue squad.

Other important numbers are the local or regional poison control center (see list on page 838) and the closest major hospital with a well-equipped and staffed emergency department. If you are in doubt about which hospital to choose, ask your family doctor for a recommendation—before you need it.

In calling for an ambulance or emergency squad, make sure that you give the precise location or address, the telephone number from which you are calling, the nature of the emergency, and the number of people involved. For example: "I am calling from the corner of Main Street and Second Avenue. My number here is 555-6385. There has been a car accident and 2 people are badly injured . . ." or "I am at 236 First Avenue South, in apartment 24. My telephone number is 555-4545. My husband is having chest pains and I think he may be having a heart attack."

Don't hang up until you are certain that the person on the line has all the necessary information and your telephone number should it be necessary to call back. Be prepared to give instructions on how to reach you. If it is night, try to have outdoor lights on or someone posted at the driveway or building entrance to give further instructions.

Whenever recommendations are given in this text to transport seriously ill or injured victims, it should be assumed that the best way to do so is by ambulance/rescue vehicle equipped and staffed with personnel trained in stabilization and transport of these victims.

BASIC PRINCIPLES OF FIRST AID

The effective application of first-aid techniques depends primarily on the ability of the rescuer to assess the situation and to make the proper decisions without delay. These situations can be divided into 3 types: life-threatening emergencies that require immediate action on the part of the rescuer as well as complex medical follow-up; potentially serious situations that are not life-threatening but that require medical care; and those that require simple first-aid or self-care. It is the second type of situation that is most difficult for the lay person to judge without first-aid training.

The goals of first aid are:

1. To restore and maintain vital functions (respiration and circulation).

2. To prevent further injury or deterioration.

3. To reassure the victim and make him or her as comfortable as possible.

The order in which first aid should be administered is:

FIRST: Restore respiration if breathing has stopped. (See Rescue Breathing, page 91; and Obstructed Airway and Choking, page 93.)

SECOND: Restore heart action if there is no discernible heartbeat or pulse. (See section on Circulation, page 91.)

THIRD: Stop bleeding. (See section on Hemorrhaging, page 101.)

FOURTH: Treat for shock. (See section on Shock, page 104.)

After seeing to these basics, help should be summoned. If there are other bystanders, one should summon help while emergency first aid is being administered. After help has been called, other first-aid measures can then be initiated, depending upon the circumstances.

TRANSPORTING THE VICTIM

ONE OF THE FUNDAMENTAL RULES of first aid dictates that the victim should not be moved, and instead, treated where he or she lies. But there are circumstances in which a severely injured person must be moved to prevent further injury. If the person is in danger of fire, an explosion, fumes, or other potentially life-threatening hazards, obviously movement is mandatory. If possible, short-distance transport should be accomplished on a firm surface such as a stretcher, or a board that will provide even support for the entire body. (See figure 5.1.) If the victim must be dragged to a safe place, pull him lengthwise, not sideways. If possible, try to place a blanket under the person so that the edge of the blanket can be pulled carrying his or her weight. In any situation where spinal injury is suspected and the patient must be moved, the spine and the neck must be kept in alignment.

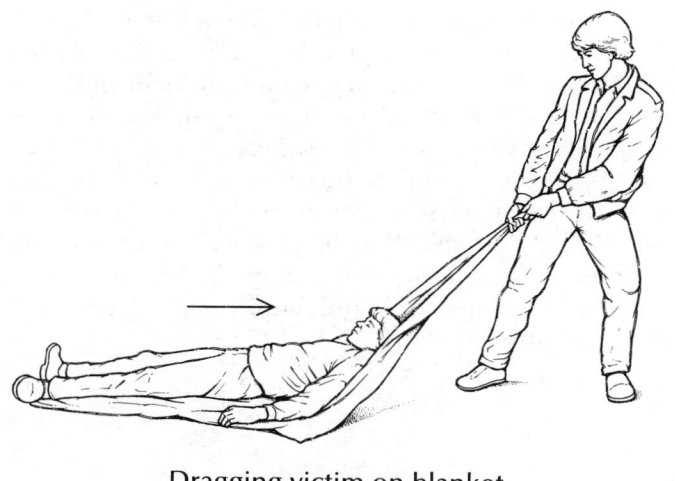

Dragging victim on blanket

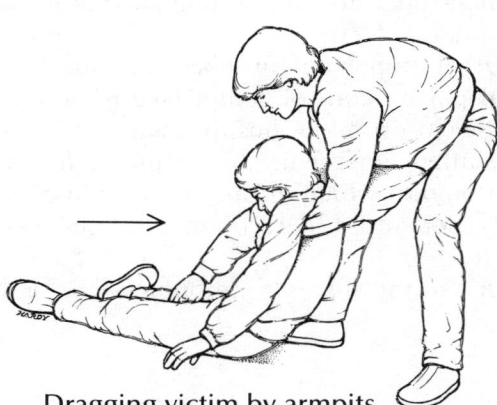

Dragging victim by armpits

Figure 5.1. **Transporting the victim. If it is absolutely necessary to remove a victim from an accident scene, try to place the patient on a blanket, and then drag the blanket instead of bodily pulling the injured person.**

FIRST-AID SUPPLIES

Basic first-aid supplies should be readily available. It is wise to carry a set in the car and to have another at home in your medical supply cabinet or shelf. A portable first-aid kit should be carried in the backpack of campers, hikers, bikers, and anyone who expects to spend time in a remote and unpopulated area. A first-aid kit wrapped in a waterproof cover also should be carried on all boats. These supplies should be checked periodically and replenished promptly. Specific items that should be on hand include:

Sterile gauze pads

Adhesive bandages in assorted sizes, including 4-inch-square compress pads

Two rolls of gauze, 1 inch and 2 inches wide

A roll of adhesive bandage tape, 1 inch wide

A roll of absorbent cotton

Elastic bandages 2 and 3 inches wide

Paper tissues

Cotton-tipped applicators

Precut triangular bandages of various sizes for slings, splints, bandages

Airtight packages of hand-cleansing disposable towels (optional)

Tongue depressors

Several medium-sized boards to use as splints for an arm or leg

Sharp scissors

A pair of tweezers

Fever thermometer

Safety pins

Aspirin or acetaminophen

A tightly covered bottle of hydrogen peroxide

An antiseptic spray or cream

Antihistamine tablets

Antidiarrheal medication

Containers of ipecac syrup and activated charcoal

In addition, these items should be carried at all times in a car or boat:

A folded lightweight blanket (sometimes called a "space" blanket)

A clean, folded sheet

A large waterproof cover (tarpaulin)

A tightly capped plastic bottle of water

A flashlight with fresh batteries

Flares

If a person is hypersensitive to bee or insect stings, he or she also should have a kit containing a syringe of adrenaline, an antihistamine, and a hypodermic needle. These insect-sting kits must be prescribed by and used under the instruction and direction of a physician. Other emergency supplies may be dictated by individual circumstances. Diabetics should always have a reserve of insulin and a handy supply of simple sugar, which can be used to treat insulin shock. Heart patients should carry a supply of nitroglycerin or other needed medication. People with medical conditions that may not be easily recognized and that may involve acute emergencies, such as diabetes, serious allergies, or heart disease, also should wear a Medic Alert bracelet, which immediately tells a rescuer that special precautions may be needed.

ACCIDENT PREVENTION AND SAFETY PRECAUTIONS

MOST ACCIDENTS can be prevented. The first step in securing safety for oneself and family is to have a clear understanding of what is dangerous and what can be done to minimize the hazard. Most hazardous conditions in the home, workplace, and elsewhere can be eliminated or reduced; others can be minimized by taking suitable precautions and developing good safety habits. This discussion is not meant to be an all-inclusive checklist; instead, some of the major considerations for safety at home and for other circumstances are outlined in the hope that they will make you more aware of potential hazards and to start you thinking in terms of commonsense prevention.

Safety at Home

More than 4 million disabling accidents occur each year in the home, resulting in 27,000 avoidable deaths. One of the most effective procedures to ensure safety in the home is a routine room-by-room check for potential dangers. Such examinations are particularly important when there are small children or older people in the household.

Fire Prevention

Fire is one of the major hazards and a leading cause of death among children. More than 70,000 Americans require hospitalization each year because of burns, and about 10,000 per year die. Each family member should know what to do in case of a fire. Periodic family fire drills should be held. In case of a fire, the first priority is to get all family members out of the house safely. Then summon help. Never go back into a burning building to rescue possessions or pets. These specific fire safety rules should be followed:

- Fire extinguishers should be kept in crucial areas—the kitchen, workroom, near stairways—and family members should know how to use them.
- Smoke detectors should be installed—at least one per floor—and kept in good working order. If smoke detectors are sold without specific instructions for where to install them, check with your local fire department.
- Fire ladders or other means of escaping from upper-story windows should be kept in each bedroom.
- Fire exits should never be blocked. City dwellers should be particularly cautious about installing bars and other guards over windows that lead to fire escapes.
- Only flame-resistant materials should be used for clothing and curtains. This is particularly important for children's sleepwear, clothing, cloth dolls, and toys.
- No one should smoke in bed or when sleepy, such as when watching TV and sitting on a couch or upholstered chair. Make sure that all cigarettes are completely extinguished.
- Working fireplaces should have a protective screen in front of them. Chimneys and flues should be inspected and cleaned periodically. Never leave a fire unattended; if you have to leave the house, extinguish the fire beforehand.
- Candles should be used with caution. They can set curtains, table linen, clothing and other objects on fire. Always use a proper candleholder, and extinguish the candles before you leave the dining room.
- Matches should be kept out of the reach of children; children should be taught, at an early age, not to play with matches or fire of any kind.
- Coal and wood stoves should be used with caution and a fire extinguisher should be nearby. Make sure that the stoves are properly installed and vented and that chimneys are cleaned periodically. Portable heaters should be used with great caution and never left unattended.
- When cooking, be particularly careful that grease and drippings do not come in contact with flames or sources of heat.

- Electrical wiring should be checked periodically. Avoid using extension cords as a permanent feature. Check all cords on electrical appliances periodically for any signs of fraying or worn spots. Electrical circuits should be properly fused. For most households, 15-ampere fuses with a time-delay to allow brief surges for appliances are adequate. Twenty-ampere fuses should be used only on special heavy-duty circuits, and 30-ampere fuses are only for main lines.
- The home heating system should be checked annually for safe pressure, venting, and wiring.
- Use protective outlet covers if children are in the household.
- Use flammable chemicals with caution. Cleaning fluids, glue, and certain sprays all present fire hazards. Read and follow labels.

The Kitchen

The kitchen is one of the most dangerous rooms in any household, with falls, fires, poisoning, cuts, and electrical shocks leading the list of potential accidents. Specific kitchen safety rules include:

- Always use a stepstool or ladder when reaching into high cabinets. Never stand on a chair or counter.
- Don't wear long, loose garments when on a ladder.
- Check ladders and stepstools periodically and repair or discard if they are loose, wobbly, or have a missing rung.
- Make sure that the floor has no slippery spots and mop up all the spills promptly.
- Make sure that no curtains can come into contact with the stove or other potential sources of fire.
- Don't wear garments with loose-flowing sleeves when cooking.
- Turn pot handles away from traffic and always use a potholder (not a towel or napkin) to remove a pot from the stove or oven.
- Use salt or baking soda to quench a small stove fire; don't douse it with water.
- Keep a fire extinguisher handy in the kitchen and make sure you and other family members know how to use it.
- Have a smoke alarm installed in or near the kitchen.
- Check the safety features of all appliances when you buy them and use them only according to instructions.
- Unplug all appliances, especially irons and high-speed food processors, immediately after use.
- Unplug the toaster and make sure that it has cooled off if you are going to poke anything into it.
- Keep knives sharp and always cut away from the body.
- Use a cutting board or other appropriate hard surface for cutting and chopping.
- Store sharp knives, including steak knives, in a wall rack or separate case; don't mingle them with other table cutlery or kitchen utensils.
- Keep kitchen (and all other) matches out of the reach of children. Buy only safety matches.
- Check pilot lights periodically and make sure that any

gas appliances are properly installed, vented, and in good working order.
- Store all cleaning materials and compounds in a cabinet with a childproof lock.
- All poisonous materials should be clearly marked; do not transfer poisonous substances to milk bottles or other containers normally used for food.
- Use only skidproof scatter rugs in the kitchen and other high-traffic areas.
- Keep pesticides and other hazardous materials away from areas where they may come in contact with food or dishes.

The Bathroom

The bathroom is the second most dangerous room in the house, the site of about 200,000 injuries a year. Burns, falls, and electric shocks lead the list of accidents in this room. Specific safety precautions include:

- Never turn on an electric switch or an electrical appliance while standing in the bathtub, shower, or on a damp floor.
- Don't use a portable electric heater in the bathroom.
- Don't use a hair dryer in or near the bathtub.
- Always keep a suction-type mat in a bathtub that does not have a skid-resistant bottom.
- Always keep a nonskid mat next to the bathtub.
- Install a strong "grab bar" that offers good support for getting into and out of a tub if such a bar is not part of the bathtub installation.
- Keep soap in a soapdish; never leave it on the rim of the tub.
- Never leave a small child alone in the bathtub, even for a brief moment.
- A family with children at home or children who visit often should remove all locks from the inside of the bathroom door except for a simple hook arrangement placed high enough to be beyond the reach of small children.
- Install a night-light just outside the bathroom door.
- Used razor blades and other sharp objects should be discarded in their container, not tossed loose in a wastebasket.

The Medicine Cabinet

Drugs, both prescription and over-the-counter medications, should not be stored in the bathroom. (See The Home Medicine Chest, page 768.) The bathroom medicine cabinet should be reserved for toothpaste, shaving supplies, and other toiletries. Follow these safety rules that apply to the storage of medicines:

- Review the contents of the medicine cabinet every few months. Discard leftover prescription medicines. (Flush them down the toilet; do not put them in the garbage or wastebasket.)
- Never take a medicine in the dark.

- Keep medicines in their original container, with the labels intact.
- Make sure the medicine cabinet has a childproof lock if there are young children in the family or if they are frequent visitors.
- Never tell a child that medicine "tastes good" or is candy.
- If you take several medications, keep a chart to help remember if and when you have taken them; this helps avoid accidental overdoses.
- Used hypodermic needles (e.g., for insulin injections) should be broken and discarded in a separate container, not tossed in a wastebasket where someone else may be accidentally cut.

The Bedroom

- Never smoke in bed.
- Heating pads and electric blankets should be unplugged when not in use.
- If a medication may be needed during the night, or should be kept handy (e.g., nitroglycerin tablets), make sure that only one medicine is kept on a bedside table. Always turn on a light and verify you have the right medicine before taking it.
- A lamp that doesn't tip easily should be within easy reach of the bed.
- Eyeglasses should be kept on a bedside table.
- Fire ladders should be installed outside the window of each upstairs bedroom.
- If there are young children in the household, window guards to prevent falling from an open window should be installed. These guards should be of a type that can be removed for easy exit during a fire.
- A telephone within easy reach of the bed is a good idea, especially for people with heart disease, diabetes, or other chronic illness.
- For people with serious illness or disability, particularly if living alone, consider the use of special telephone systems with preprogrammed emergency dialing and prerecorded emergency messages.

The Living Room, Den, and Other General Rooms

- Don't overload electric outlets, and make sure that electric cords are not lying on the floor in the path of traffic.
- If electric cords have been lying under rugs or furniture for a long time, check them periodically for frayed or worn spots.
- Don't place scatter rugs on a highly polished floor unless they have a nonskid backing.

Entrance and Stairways

- A flight of stairs should have a railing, and if there is a banister, the spindles should be so close together that a child cannot wedge his head between them.

- Stairway carpeting should be firmly secured and regularly inspected for holes and worn spots.
- Stairs and landings should never be waxed.
- Safety gates should be installed at both the top and bottom of stairs in a household with young children.
- Stairs should always be kept free of any clutter.
- Light switches should be located at the top and bottom of the stairs; never go up or down stairs in the dark. A nightlight at the top and bottom of stairs is another added precaution.
- Suitable precautions should be taken to prevent visitors from mistaking the door leading to stairs for the one to the bathroom. A surprising number of serious falls occur each year from this mistake.

Basement/Utility Room/Workroom

A basement used as a laundry room and/or recreation area should have a fire-resistant ceiling. Storage areas should be free of flammable rags and newspapers. All chemicals should be stored in clearly labeled jars or metal cans that are inaccessible to children. Specific safety rules include:

- An all-purpose fire extinguisher should be conspicuously placed on a wall.
- Electric washers and dryers should be installed in a well-lighted area where water and dampness do not accumulate. Dryers should be properly vented; all electrical appliances should have proper wiring and grounding.
- Manufacturers' instructions for washers, dryers, and other appliances should be followed and necessary repairs made promptly by a licensed repair person.
- If children use laundry appliances, they should be instructed in their proper use and the use of safety switches and emergency procedures.
- Ironing should always be done on a strong, well-balanced board with a fireproof cover. The iron should be set on its heel during brief intervals between use, and should be unplugged immediately when ironing is finished.
- Never leave an iron and ironing board unattended.
- Keep all tools out of reach of children. When a child is old enough to handle them, give the proper instruction and make sure the tools are in good repair and properly sharpened. Power tools should be used with caution no matter what the age of the user.
- Wear safety goggles whenever using a welding iron, power saw and other such tools. Heavy gloves, earplugs, and proper clothing (no loose shirttails, ties, etc.) also should be used as indicated.
- Pets should be kept out of the workroom or other areas where power tools are in use.

Garden/Garage/Backyard

- A child should never be permitted to use a power mower.
- Always wear safety goggles when using a power

mower, weed cutter, trimmer, or other tools that may kick up stones, twigs or other objects.
- Never try to free an object from a mower blade or snow blower while the motor is running.
- Never leave a power mower unattended while the motor is running, even momentarily.
- Always wear protective gloves and goggles when using a power saw. Follow manufacturers' instructions and make sure the saw is in proper working order and that the blades are sharpened.
- When not in use, a garden hose should be rolled up and stored. It should never be left lying in the grass where someone may stumble over it.
- Garden tools should be put away after using. A grocery carton can be used, or they can be hung individually on a wall. Hoes, rakes, and other such tools should never be left lying on a lawn where someone may step on them.
- Pesticides should be used with extreme care and always sprayed downwind. They should not be decanted into unlabeled jars; leftovers should be discarded according to instructions, and not tossed in the garbage or flushed down the toilet.
- The cover on a well, septic tank, or cistern should be sufficently secure at all times so that it cannot be removed by children.
- Garage doors should be easy to open both from inside and outside. If electronic power lifts are used on a garage door, there should be another exit that can be used in case of power failure.
- The driveway should always be clear of bicycles, motorcycles, children's wagons, and other obstructions. Also, children should be warned not to play in the driveway.
- Don't wear loose clothes or flowing sleeves when cooking on an outdoor grill.
- Cancel a backyard barbecue if there's a high wind.
- Never attempt to pour starter or other flammable liquid onto burning or smoldering charcoal. Use an electric starter instead.
- Have a fire extinguisher nearby whenever cooking out. When using a campfire or grill in the woods or open area, dig a fire pit first and make sure that the fire is thoroughly extinguished before leaving it.

Safety in the Workplace

Next to the home, the workplace is the most common setting for accidents. Again, most can be prevented by obeying safety regulations and using common sense. If your job involves working with hazardous chemicals or materials, be particularly diligent in handling them. Also, change and shower before leaving the workplace to avoid carrying hazardous residue home. Follow these safety rules:

- If your job requires wearing protective gear, such as goggles, gloves, ear plugs, or masks, make sure that you do so. Even if your employer does not require or provide protective clothing, it's a good idea to wear it

whenever around potentially harmful substances.
- Never try to operate machinery or other equipment when you are drowsy or ill. If you are taking medication, heed any label warning about operating machinery or driving.
- Bring any potentially hazardous condition to the attention of your supervisor, union representative, or other appropriate official.
- Obey rules regarding smoking in any area where there is a danger of fire.
- A pregnant woman or one who is trying to conceive should be especially careful about exposure to chemicals, or other substances that may be harmful to her and/or her unborn child.

Farm and Country Safety

Because emergency medical assistance is not as quickly available in the country as in urban areas, people who live or work on a farm are well advised to understand the hazards they face and how to handle them. Agriculture ranks third among all major industries in the annual number of accidental deaths.

Fire prevention is of utmost importance, especially because of the built-in fire hazards and the time it may take to get help from firefighting equipment. (See the fire safety rules at the beginning of this section.) Follow these farm fire safety precautions:

- Store all flammable liquids, including sprays and fuel, in an adequately ventilated area away from direct heat and in a place that is inaccessible to children.
- Don't leave nearly empty gasoline or other fuel containers lying about.
- Don't store fuel, oil-soaked rags, and other highly flammable items in a haybarn or other building that will burn easily.
- Enforce "No Smoking" rules in all potentially dangerous areas, including barns, grain sheds, silos, and fuel-storage areas.
- Have fire extinguishers in all potentially hazardous areas, including barns and storage areas.
- Make sure that all family members and farm workers know what to do in case of a fire, e.g., the location of fire ladders and emergency exits from both home and outbuildings; the location of fire extinguishers and how to operate them.
- Use special caution during lightning and electrical storms. Make sure that all wiring is properly grounded and that all buildings have properly installed wiring and safety circuit breakers.

Hazards of farm equipment can be reduced by observing safety rules at all times. Carelessness in handling farm machinery results in more than 1,000 deaths each year and a larger number of disabling injuries.

- When operating a tractor, always use a safety belt and overturn bar.
- Never permit children to play in and around tractors, wagons, and other farm machinery.
- Do not permit a child to ride on a tractor "for fun." An older child can be taught how to operate some farm machinery, but careful adult instruction and supervision should be provided.
- Never leave a tractor or other farm machinery unattended with the motor running.
- Never attempt to make a repair or remove a stone or other object from a piece of machinery while the motor is running.
- Wear appropriate clothing, e.g., heavy boots, work pants, and safety goggles, when operating farm machinery.

Farm animals also are a potential source of danger, especially for the unwary or unsuspecting farm visitor.

- Approach any farm animal with proper caution; even a gentle cow can cause considerable injury if she is startled or is trying to protect her calf. Teach children how to approach farm animals and also not to tease or mistreat them.
- Avoid feeding animals from your hands.
- Don't try to pick up or approach a wounded or sick animal, including a pet or a wild animal, with your bare hands. An injured pet should be securely wrapped in a towel or blanket and picked up in such a manner that it cannot bite you. Avoid any wild animal that appears sick or is acting strangely; it may have rabies or some other serious disease that can be transmitted to humans.
- Make sure that pets and farm animals have up-to-date vaccinations, especially against diseases that are transmitted to humans.

Sprays and other chemicals are commonly used in farming, but regulations and recommendations regarding their use are constantly changing. Before using a leftover spray, check with your local agriculture agent to make sure that it is still permitted and that instructions for its use have not changed. The following specific precautions should be heeded:

- Never use a chemical spray out-of-doors on a windy day.
- Protect exposed skin surfaces with clothing, gloves, and goggles. Wear a mask to avoid inhalation.
- Keep chemicals in their original containers. Before entering the house after using a chemical spray, carefully wash face and hands (or shower, if possible) and change into fresh clothes.
- Follow instructions regarding length of time that should elapse between spraying and harvesting of food, and wash all food that has been exposed to chemical sprays before eating it.

Special note: Make sure that all visitors, both children and adults, adhere to safety rules regarding smoking, animal handling, the use of equipment, and other aspects of farm life.

Road and Highway Safety

Lowering the national speed limit to 55 miles per hour has resulted in a marked decline in the number of highway deaths, but even so, more than 50,000 Americans die in highway accidents each year. About one-half of these deaths are caused by driving while under the influence of alcohol or other drugs, including antihistamines that cause drowsiness or medications that impair reflexes and judgment.

Many lives could be saved or serious injury prevented by universal use of seat belts. Many states now have laws that require proper safety seats for all infants and toddlers, and a growing number are considering requiring seat belts for adults. Babies and young children always should ride in these seats, even for short distances. Holding a child on your lap is particularly dangerous; should you be thrown against the dashboard or windshield, the child will bear the force of the accident.

All cars should have regular preventive maintenance checks and be checked regularly for any sign of trouble. Brakes and lights should be tested and tires examined before starting on a trip. A spare tire and tire-changing equipment should always be carried in the trunk. A first-aid kit, flares, and a flashlight also should be carried at all times. Other car safety rules:

- Never drive when you feel sleepy, tired, or ill. Don't attempt to drive after drinking or taking any drug that may impair reflexes, cause drowsiness, or alter judgment.
- Always wear your safety belt and make sure that all passengers do the same. Babies and young children should always be securely fastened in safety seats. (See figure 5.2.)
- Know in advance what to do in a crisis. Know how to pull out of a skid on ice or a slippery road.
- Know and observe local safety regulations regarding such things as speed limits and rules of turns.
- Always be aware of what other drivers are doing. Drive defensively and remain calm when dealing with other drivers who are rude, careless, or speeding.
- Watch out for bicycle riders, motorcyclists, joggers, and animals.
- Don't be distracted by conversations, the car radio, arguments, or the scenery.
- Enforce rules regarding horseplay or poor behavior in the car. If necessary, pull off the road and stop the car and put an end to distracting behavior.
- Don't attempt to drive during a heavy downpour, snowstorm, or other bad weather that affects visibility

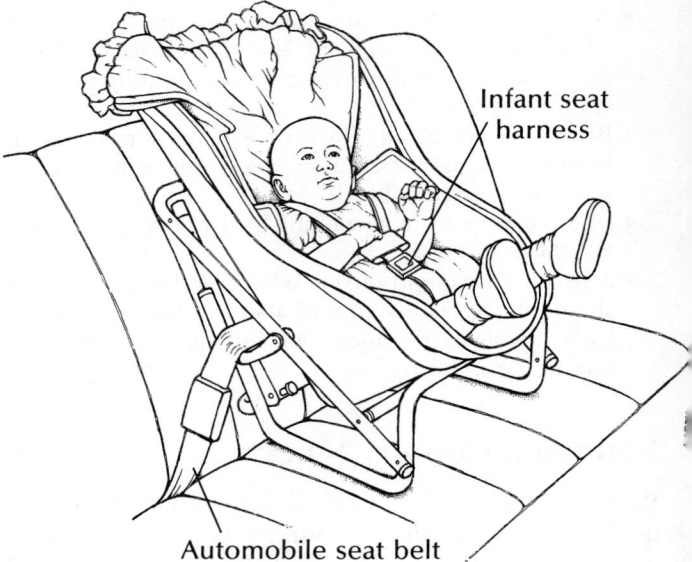

Figure 5.2. **Babies and young children should always ride in a safety seat, such as the one pictured here. The seat should be belted to the car seat, and the child should be placed in a harness in the carrier.**

and road conditions. If you must drive at such times, make sure the car is properly equipped with snow tires, chains, or other appropriate devices and that you know what to do in case of skids or other hazardous situations.
- Be sure your view is unobstructed by passengers, packages, or other objects.
- Pets should travel in carrying cases unless they are very well behaved and accustomed to riding quietly in a car. In any event, pets and passengers should not be permitted to ride with heads or other body parts hanging out of the window.
- If you come upon a car accident, proceed with caution. Turn off the motor if it is still running and try to determine if there is danger of a fire or explosion. (Do you smell gas?) If there are injuries, try to treat the victims where they are unless they are in danger of further injury or require basic life-support measures. (See Directory of First-Aid Procedures, page 105.)

Bicycle Safety

There are now more than 100 million Americans who ride bicycles or motorcycles, and each year, more than 1 million serious injuries are incurred by cyclists. One-half of these accidents involve children under the age of 14; and in 90 percent of all cycling accidents, the cyclist is at fault. Bicycles should be kept in good working order and all cyclists, children and adults alike, should know and follow the rules of the road. This means obeying the same traffic regulations and signals that apply to motor vehicles: stopping for red lights, riding with (never against) traffic, and cycling in the street or road, not on the sidewalk. Follow these safety rules:

- All motorcyclists should wear protective headgear. The same is true for bicyclists who ride on highways or crowded streets.
- Never wear loose pants or other clothing that is likely to become entangled in a bicycle chain.
- Never permit children or other passengers to ride on the handlebars. Special children's seats should be installed behind the cyclist and the child should be securely strapped into the seat.
- Bicycles that are ridden at night should be equipped with lights and special reflectors that are clearly visible to motorists.
- Never dart in and out of traffic; if there is a bicycle lane, stay in it. If not, stay to the far right-hand side of the road. When passing a car, follow the same rules and precautions that apply to motor vehicles.
- When cycling with others, ride single-file, not two or three abreast.
- Don't wear radio or tape earphones when cycling; this blocks out warning sounds from other traffic and is likely to be distracting.

Water and Boat Safety

Drowning in either boating or swimming accidents is yet another leading cause of accidental deaths in this country. Anyone who goes near the water should know how to swim. Almost everyone can learn, including very young children, older people, and those who are disabled. In addition, swimming is an excellent form of aerobic exercise. Swimming courses are widely available at local "Y's," schools, community or recreation centers, health clubs, camps, Red Cross chapters, and other organizations. But even expert swimmers should obey basic water safety rules, including the cardinal one of never swimming alone or in an unattended area. Follow these water safety rules:

- Never permit a child to play alone at the water's edge, including a shallow backyard pool.
- Always use a "buddy system," even when swimming with a group. Anyone, including an expert swimmer, can suffer a cramp or other disabling problem while in the water; this may go unnoticed by others who are not specifically looking out for him or her.
- Know your limits and don't overdo. Swimming beyond one's depth or capability is a common cause of drowning accidents.
- Don't swim after drinking alcoholic beverages.
- Never dive into a pool or other water unless you have tested the depth first.
- Don't swim in the dark, especially in the ocean.
- Don't swim in boating or fishing areas.

- Be cautious of diving into waves. Pay particular attention to the undertow, especially when the tide is turning. Don't try to swim against an undertow. Swim parallel to shore until you reach a spot where you can swim in toward shore again.
- When storm clouds gather, get out of the water and head for shelter from lightning. Don't stand under a tree, however. Lightning usually strikes at the tallest point and follows the tree trunk down to the ground and then follows the root system. Anyone near the tree or roots can easily be electrocuted.
- Young children and inexpert swimmers should wear life jackets in the water. Floats, inner tubes, and inflatable water toys are not suitable substitutes; it is easy to fall off them.
- Backyard pools should be fenced with a gate that is locked when unattended. This applies even when the pool has been drained or is iced over.

Boating safety begins with a complete understanding of the capabilities of the particular craft. All boat owners and their families should take a boat handling and safety course such as those sponsored by local units of the Coast Guard or Power Squadron or boating clubs. Never go out in a boat unless there is someone on board who knows how to handle it; this applies to all craft, from rowboats to sailboats and motorboats. In addition to the general safety rules for swimmers, boaters should also pay attention to the following basics:

- Make sure that each person on the boat is wearing a properly fitted life jacket. Children sleeping on a boat should wear one to bed. Many life jackets come with pockets. Equip each one with a flare and a mirror for signaling, as well as a whistle, which can be heard more easily across water than the voice. Attach strips of reflective tape to the back of the jacket.
- Know and follow the boating regulations that apply to your particular waterway. Watch out for other craft, especially slower moving boats that may not be able to get out of your path, even if you have the right-of-way.
- Water-skiers should always wear a life jacket and there should be two people in the motor boat: one to drive and the other to watch the skier.
- Watch for swimmers who also may be in your way.
- Don't drink while boating.
- Know the capability of your craft; if a storm is coming up, head for safer waters or port.
- Before fueling a boat, make sure that no one is smoking and that all electrical equipment and the motor are shut off. After refueling, check for any gas fumes, especially in low places, and wait a few minutes before restarting the engine to be sure the engine housing is well-vented.
- Always carry flares and other warning devices; make sure running lights and the boat radio are in proper working order. If you are an offshore boater, equip your boat with an Emergency Position Indicator Ra-

dio Beacon (EPIRB), which will automatically signal your position on a frequency picked up by ships and planes in the area, as well as by certain satellites. Take it into the water with you if the boat capsizes or sinks.

- Be prepared to do everything you can to keep the boat afloat if you begin to take on water. Even if the boat is equipped with an automatic bailing pump, carry extra bailers (gallon and half-gallon plastic bleach or milk containers with the bottoms cut out make good ones). If you spring a leak, stuff it with clothes, mattresses, rags, or whatever else is available. If necessary, go into the water with a rope around your waist to plug the hole from the outside as well.

- If your boat capsizes, do not leave it in an attempt to swim to shore. It will provide a place to rest and it will be more easily spotted by rescuers than a swimmer in open water. Try to climb onto the hull or stand on the rails to stay out of the water as much as possible.

- If the boat actually sinks, debris such as ice chests, hatch covers, mattresses, and seat cushions will begin to float free as it goes down. Gather them around you to hold onto, to rest on, and to make yourself more easily seen by rescue craft.

- Hypothermia is a serious problem in most United States coastal waters. Your respiration, pulse, and blood pressure automatically rise when you first enter cold water, especially that less than 70° Fahrenheit. Try to stay perfectly still for the first 1 to 3 minutes until this reaction begins to subside.

- Even if you are a strong swimmer, do not attempt to swim to shore. The United States Coast Guard reports that many people drown within 10 to 15 feet of a safe haven. Current, water temperature, fatigue, poor swimming ability, and panic may all work against you. Stay with the boat or the debris and try to keep as much of your body out of the water as possible.

Hiking and Camping

Getting back to nature is one of the great pleasures of modern, urban life. But all too often, the hiking or camping trip is marred by an accident that could have been prevented with proper planning and foresight. The cardinal rule for anyone planning a trek into a remote area is: Let someone know where you are and when you plan to return. Arrange regular times when you will call or contact that person; then if you fail to do so, help can be sent. If no one knows you are long overdue, chances are slim that there will be search parties out looking for you.

Another often overlooked, but basic, rule is always to carry a good map of the area. If you are planning a hiking trip into a wilderness area, contact the area forest service or other official agency and ask for a detailed map of trails, campsites, aid stations, and other important information. Follow these precautions

- Make sure that you and other members of your party are in suitable physical condition to withstand the rigors of hiking or camping out.

- Take along a first-aid kit (see the checklist of first-aid supplies, page 79) and if medication is needed, make sure you have an extra supply as well as a signed prescription.

- Wear appropriate clothes and pay particular attention to your shoes. They should be sturdy, comfortable, and appropriate for the terrain; running or jogging shoes may be lightweight and comfortable, but they are not suitable for long hikes or mountain climbing.

- Carry insect repellent and check on whether there are any animal- or insect-borne diseases (e.g., Rocky Mountain spotted fever, viral encephalitis, tularemia) endemic in the area you plan to visit. In some instances, vaccination may be appropriate.

- Never eat wild berries, plants, or mushrooms unless you are absolutely certain they are nonpoisonous. Warn children not to eat berries or plants unless they show them to you first.

- If hiking with a party, form a "buddy" system and know where your partner is at all times.

- Watch for poisonous plants such as poison ivy, and avoid contact with them. Even handling shoes or other objects that have come in contact wih poison ivy can cause a reaction.

- Use special caution in exploring caves, abandoned mines, and buildings, and avoid entering them unless you are absolutely certain they are structurally sound and not harboring a wild animal, snakes, or other hazard.

- Don't drink water from unknown sources. If you don't have your own water, boil any taken from a pond or stream for at least 3 minutes before drinking it.

- Observe and enjoy wild animals, but at a safe distance. Most animals are very wary of humans, but each year, several thousand visitors to the wild end up with serious animal bites or even worse consequences. If you are in bear country, be particularly cautious about food supplies. Never keep food in your tent or near your sleeping area and don't sleep in clothes in which you have prepared or eaten food. Food supplies should be placed in a bag and hung from a high tree branch at a safe distance from your campsite. A special warning to women campers in bear country: The U.S. Park Service has observed that a number of bear attacks have involved women who were menstruating at the time or who were wearing scented cosmetics or hair spray. Apparently bears are attracted to these scents.

- Garbage should be placed in special containers, burned, or carefully packed to carry away with you. Don't leave it strewn around your camp; it not only despoils the area, it also attracts unwelcome insects and animals.

- Before setting up camp, clear the area of leaves, branches, stones, and other hiding places for snakes, spiders, and other potentially hazardous animals or insects. Avoid cave entrances, rock piles, and other places that may be the home of nocturnal animals.

- Don't attempt to feed wild animals. If you come upon a baby animal, don't try to pick it up. Chances are it has a protective mother nearby who will not hesitate to attack if she thinks her offspring is in danger.
- Be wary of any animal—skunk, raccoon, rodent, etc.—that is behaving oddly. It may have rabies or some other disease.
- Check on whether there are poisonous snakes in the area, and if so, use special caution. Know what to do in case of a bite from a snake, spider, or other wild creature. (See the section on bites in Chapter 7, A Directory of Common First-Aid Procedures.)
- If you are hiking in an unfamiliar area, proceed with caution and make sure you are on firm ground. Mountain and rock climbing is tricky and should be undertaken only by experts or under the leadership of an experienced guide. Quicksand and alkali bogs are hazards that should be avoided; if an area looks at all suspicious, make a wide detour or test it carefully with a long pole before stepping onto it.
- Pay attention to the weather. If you are camping in an area where flash floods are a possibility, head for high ground. Avoid camping in dry river beds, even if there is no sign of rain. The flood may occur without warning and result from a heavy rainfall miles away. During an electrical storm, stay away from trees, poles and water. Avoid ditches, which may have water in them, and do not lie flat on the ground. The electrical current from lightning travels underground in search of water. Crouch down, covering as little ground as possible. If possible, get into a car with a metal roof and close the windows; the car's metal frame forms a protective "Faraday cage," but do not stand outside, close to a car.

Winter Hazards

It would be a mistake to imply that the major outdoor hazards apply to summer campers; the increasing popularity of winter outdoor activities has been accompanied by a rise in cold-weather mishaps. The same rules listed for hikers and campers apply to winter sports and outdoor activities. In addition, winter hikers, snowmobilers, cross-country skiers, and hunters, among others, should be skilled in their respective activity and know what to do in case of an emergency.

Weather reports should be heeded; modern weather forecasting has improved, but there is always the possibility of a sudden, unpredicted winter storm and there are still a surprising number of people who venture out without checking a weather report. Obviously, one should always dress appropriately and know what to do if marooned by a storm. Usually, the best advice is to stay in your car or other shelter until the worst is over or until help arrives. Other special precautions for winter sportsmen include:

- Know your terrain. If you are snowshoeing, cross-country skiing, or hiking in unknown territory, stick to established trails and don't venture out alone.
- Dress appropriately. This means wearing clothing that provides proper insulation against the cold, wind, and wetness, while allowing proper ventilation and circulation. Undergarments should be made of cotton or cotton-lined wool or polypropylene. Several layers of loose, nonconstricting wool, down, or synthetic down clothing and an outer layer of windproof/water-repellent material. Make sure head (an area of potential significant heat loss), hands, and feet are well protected. Mittens worn over gloves provide good protection for hands. Two pairs of socks—one cotton and one wool—and boots covering the ankles provide adequate protection of feet. All clothing should be nonconstricting.
- Before going out onto ice, make sure that it is thick enough to bear your weight. If in doubt, cut a hole in it and measure the thickness. If it is less than 8 inches thick, stay on land or go to a commercial ice rink.
- When sledding or snowmobiling, be particularly wary of crossing roads and railroad tracks. Avoid areas where there may be hidden obstacles, such as fallen branches, trees, fences, or other sources of danger.
- Don't go out in the cold after drinking alcohol. While you may feel a warm glow from the drink, in reality, it makes you more susceptible to the effects of cold and may alter your judgment, decision making, and behavior in a potentially dangerous situation.

SUMMING UP

MOST ACCIDENTS can be prevented with proper knowledge and attention to basic principles of safety. Many of these have been outlined in this chapter. What to do in actual medical emergencies is covered in the following chapters.

6 Basics of CPR and Life Support

A. L. Loomis Bell, Jr., M.D.

The following is a guide to the major first-aid and emergency medical procedures. They should be performed in the order outlined in Basic Principles of First Aid in Chapter 5, page 77.

BASIC LIFE SUPPORT

LIFE-SUPPORT TECHNIQUES, artificial respiration, cardiopulmonary resuscitation (CPR), and clearing obstructed airways in choking emergencies (the Heimlich maneuver) are the most important of all emergency medical procedures. Except under very unusual circumstances, brain damage is likely to occur 4 to 6 minutes after cardiopulmonary arrest; its likelihood and severity increase each minute thereafter.

AN OVERVIEW OF CPR

CARDIOPULMONARY RESUSCITATION IS more than a rescue technique for someone whose heart or breathing has stopped. Rather, it is an organized approach to assessing and dealing with a medical emergency. It requires learning the physical skills of artificial respiration (mouth-to-mouth breathing) and closed chest compressions, as well as the proper timing and a specific sequence in which to use the skills.

The sequence begins when you come across an apparently unconscious victim. You must first determine whether the victim is indeed unconscious or merely sleeping. You must then be sure that the airway—the passage between the mouth and the lungs—is not blocked by the tongue, which would prevent the victim from breathing. Then you must determine if he or she is breathing, and if there is a pulse, indicating circulation. Depending on the answers, you will start mouth-to-mouth breathing alone or chest compressions interposed with breath-

ing. You must continue until the victim revives, a trained person takes over, or you become exhausted.

In a nutshell, that is CPR. The American Heart Association, which sets the standards for CPR training, uses the mnemonic "ABC" for the major parts of this process—Airway, Breathing, and Circulation.

It is strongly recommended that those who wish to learn CPR take a formal course offered by the American Heart Association or the American Red Cross, which will allow adequate time to practice on a training manikin under close supervision of an instructor.

PERFORMING CPR

(NOTE: To help you establish a sense of timing, to make sure that you are spending adequate, but not too much, time on each step, the recommended time span for each activity is given in parentheses.)

FIRST STEPS *(4–10 seconds)*

1. Establish Unresponsiveness and Call for Help

When you come across a seemingly unconscious victim, you must first establish unresponsiveness by tapping the person firmly on the chest and shouting "Are you O.K.?" (O.K. is understood in virtually every language.) If you get no response, shake the person gently by the shoulders and shout again. (See figure 6.1.) It is important to be sure that the person really is unconscious, so that you don't do CPR unnecessarily.

At the same time, you should call out for help, even if no one is in sight. This may bring someone within earshot to your aid and this person, if not trained in CPR, may be able to phone for medical aid.

2. Position the Victim

For CPR to be effective, the victim must be flat on his or her back on a firm surface. If you find the victim lying face down, you will have to turn him over, rolling him toward you. First, take the arm that will be on the underside as he rolls and stretch it out straight over his head. Put one of your hands behind his neck to support it as you turn him. (See figure 6.2.) With your other hand, grasp his upper arm and roll him over gently.

AIRWAY *(3–5 seconds)*

1. Open the Airway

Once the person is on his back and you are sure

Figure 6.1. **Establish unresponsiveness by shaking the victim gently by the shoulders. At the same time, call out for help.**

Figure 6.2. **Support the victim's neck with one hand as you turn him over with the other.**

Figure 6.3. **In an unconscious person, the relaxed tongue blocks the airway.**

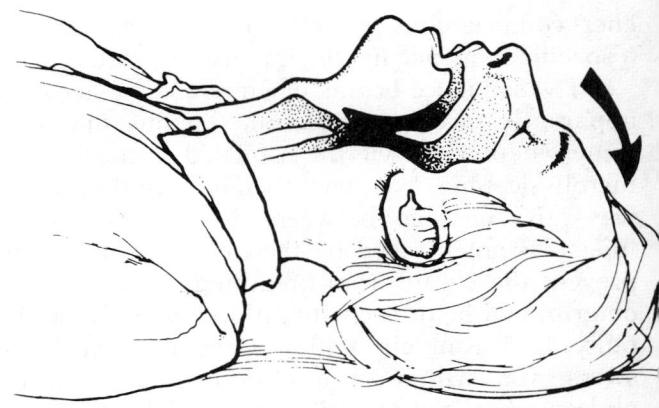

Figure 6.4. **When the neck is extended, the tongue pulls away from the back of the throat, opening the airway.**

he is unconscious, you must open the airway to be sure that he can breathe. In an unconscious person, the tongue relaxes and falls against the back of the throat, preventing air from getting from the mouth and nose to the lungs. (See figures 6.3 and 6.4.)

Kneel at right angles to the person's shoulder—on whichever side is more convenient or comfortable. Using the hand closer to the victim's head, place your palm across his forehead. Put your other hand under his neck to support it. Push down and back on his forehead with one hand while lifting up his neck with the other hand. (See figure 6.5.) You'll need to rotate his head relatively far back to stretch out the neck and open the airway, but don't extend it too far back or too forcefully. This technique should not be used in infants or in persons with suspected neck injury.

Practice tip: Lie on the floor and extend your neck back until your chin is pointing straight up and you have trouble swallowing. This is approximately the correct position for opening the airway.

2. Check for Breathing

Now, with your hands still in place, check for breathing. Looking toward his chest, bend over so that your cheek is almost touching his nose and mouth. LOOK to see if his chest is rising and falling, LISTEN for sounds of breathing, and see if you can FEEL expired air on your cheek.

Look, listen, and feel for several seconds. Sometimes, opening the airway is all that is needed and the victim will begin breathing spontaneously. If nothing happens, try opening the airway again. If you see the chest rise and fall, but do not hear or feel air, the victim is attempting to breathe, but the airway is still blocked. (See Obstructed Airway, page 93.)

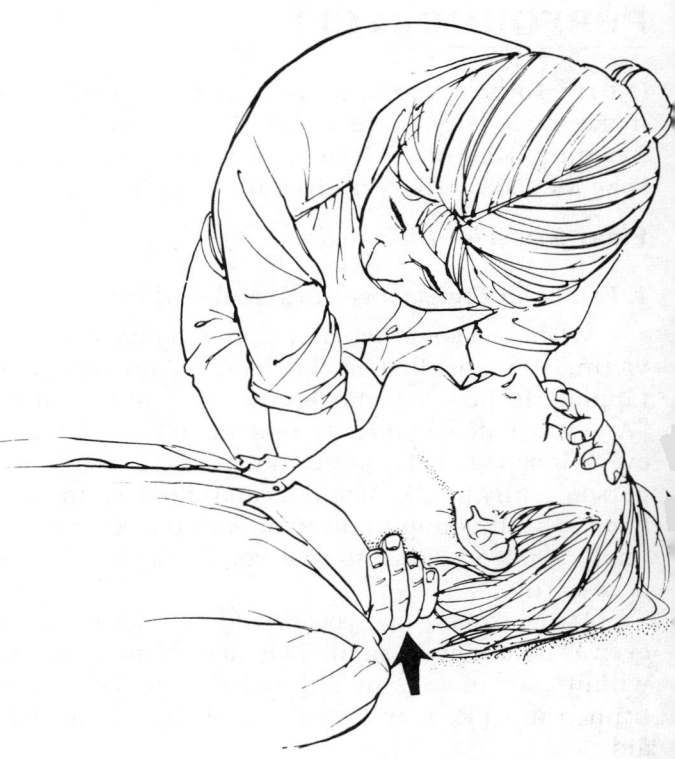

Figure 6.5. **Lift up with the hand under the neck as you push down and back with the hand on the forehead.**

GIVE 4 QUICK BREATHS *(3–5 seconds)*

If there is no evidence of breathing, the victim is not getting any oxygen, and you want initially to get as much oxygen into him as possible. Keep your hands in place on his forehead and neck to keep the airway open. Using the hand on his forehead, pinch his nostrils together tightly with your thumb and forefinger to keep the air from escaping through his nose.

Take a deep breath, open your mouth wide, and

place it completely over the victim's mouth to make a tight seal with your lips. You do not need to press down hard to get a tight seal, only to encircle completely the victim's mouth with your own. Exhale forcefully into the victim's mouth 4 times. Take your mouth away to inhale between breaths, but do it quickly so that the victim's lungs don't completely empty between your breaths.

Although you will feel some resistance from the victim's lungs, you should be able to feel air going in as you blow and to see the chest rise and fall.

Practice tip: To get a sense of what this feels like, blow against your tightly clenched fist. The resistance you feel is akin to the feeling of a blocked airway. Now make a tiny hole in your fist and blow again. You will have to blow forcefully and you will still feel some resistance, but you should feel the air going through.

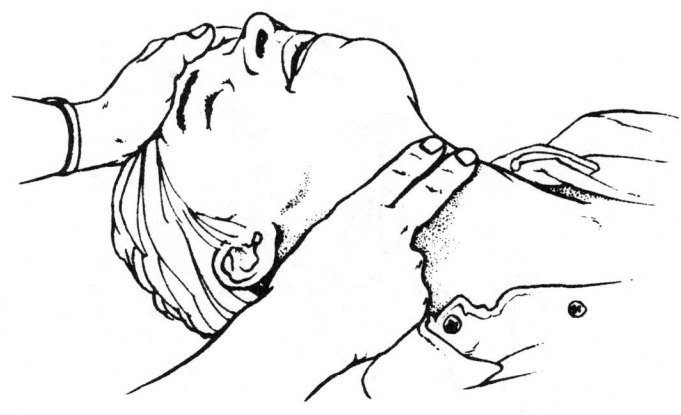

CHECK FOR PULSE *(5–10 seconds)*

Once you have given 4 quick breaths, check to see if the victim has a pulse. The easiest pulse to check is on either of the carotid arteries, which run down both sides of the neck. Keeping your other hand on the forehead, take your hand from under the victim's neck and place 2 fingers on his Adam's apple. Then slide them over into the groove between the Adam's apple and the neck muscle on the side closer to you. (See figures 6.6 and 6.7.) The carotid pulse should be felt in the space between these structures.

If you don't find a pulse immediately, move your fingers around slightly. Allow adequate time—the pulse may be slow and weak (although it may also be rapid).

Practice tip: Practice finding your own carotid pulse and then try it on a friend.

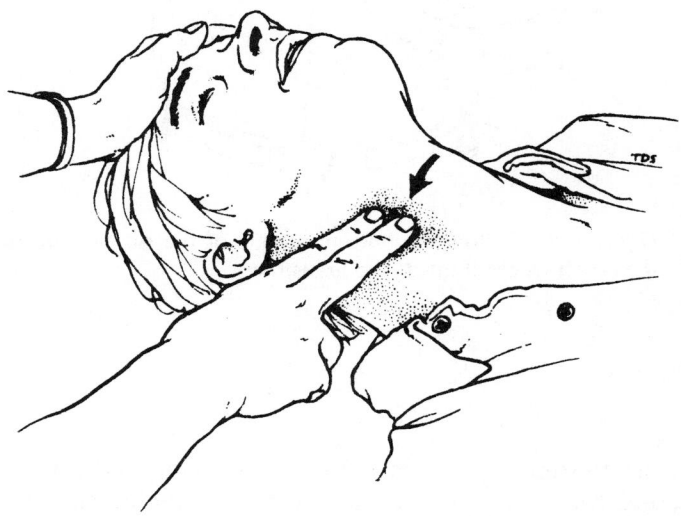

Figures 6.6 and 6.7. **Locate the carotid pulse by placing 2 fingers on the Adam's apple, then sliding them into the groove on the side of the neck toward you.**

Get Medical Help

If a second person is present, now is the time to have him or her call the Emergency Medical Service (EMS) system. At this point you can give more complete information about the victim's condition. (See introductory material about emergency medical systems.) If you are still alone, perform CPR for at least 1 minute before stopping to call EMS yourself.

Rescue Breathing

(If the victim does *not* have a pulse, skip this section and go on to Circulation.) If the victim has a pulse but is not breathing, you must now start mouth-to-mouth respiration. Just as you did before, keep your hands in position on the neck and forehead, pinch

the nostrils closed, inhale and make a seal with your mouth, and exhale air into the victim's lungs. Between breaths, turn your head to the side and look, listen, and feel for the victim's breathing.

Do this once every 5 seconds, taking your mouth away between breaths. Continue for 1 minute—12 breaths. At this point, check the pulse again and call EMS if someone has not done so. If there is a pulse, continue breathing once every 5 seconds until the victim begins to breathe on his own or medical help arrives. Check the pulse after every 12 breaths.

Circulation

If there is no pulse, you will have to create artificial

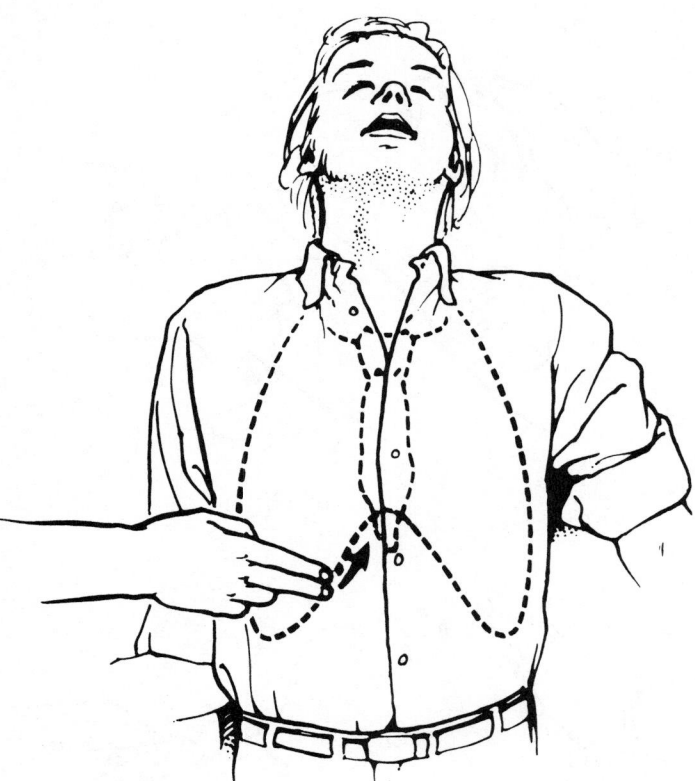

Figure 6.8. **Follow the bottom margin of the rib cage up to the notch where it meets the breastbone.**

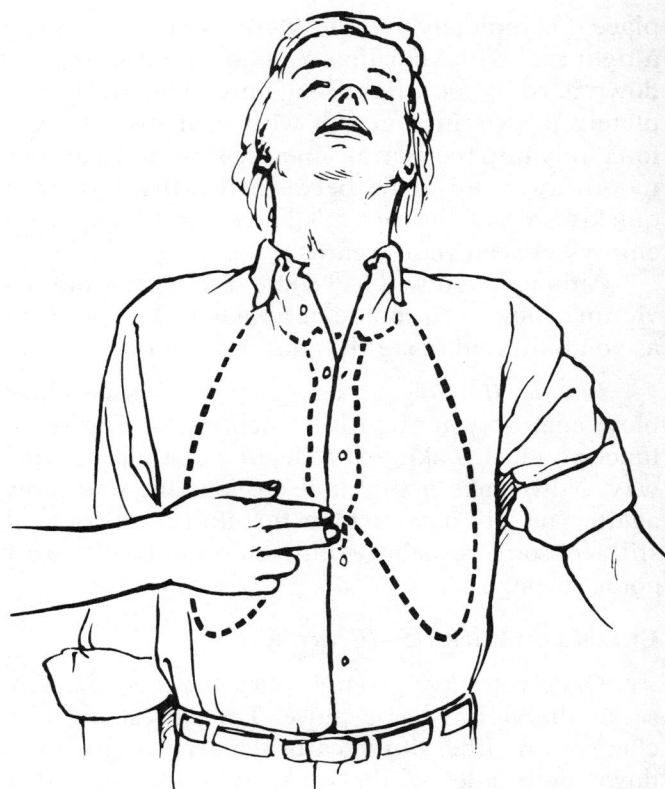

Figure 6.9. **Place the middle finger on the notch and the index finger next to it.**

circulation of the blood by compressing and releasing the chest. It may help you to imagine that by pushing down on the chest, you are squeezing the heart between the breastbone and the back bone and forcing blood out through the circulatory system. (While this may be a useful concept, the mechanism is probably more accurately described as intermittent changes in pressure in the chest. When you push down on the heart, positive pressure forces blood out through the aorta to the brain and other organs, while one-way valves prevent it from entering the veins. On release, falling pressure results in flow back into the thorax from the venous system, while one-way valves prevent it from reentering the aorta.)

Move down a little so you are kneeling next to the victim's chest, about midway between shoulder and waist. To find the correct hand position, first find the bottom margin of the rib cage, down near the abdomen. Using your hand closer to the victim's feet, follow the edge of the ribs as your fingers move up toward the center of the chest. You will feel a notch where the ribs meet the breastbone. (See figure 6.8.) Put your middle finger on this spot and then

put your index finger next to your middle finger. (See figure 6.9.)

Now place the *heel* of your other hand next to the index finger. Place your other hand on top of the first. (See figure 6.10.) You can either interlace your fingers or keep them straight, but at no time should they rest on the chest. (See figures 6.11 and 6.12.) To avoid any injury to the ribs, only the heel of your hand should touch the chest.

Shift your weight forward on your knees until your shoulders are directly over your hands and your elbows are locked. Now, bear down and come up, bear down and come up, keeping your elbows locked. In order to squeeze the heart and circulate the blood, you must depress the chest (of the average adult) 1½ to 2 inches with each compression. To get the proper speed and rhythm, count out loud as you do the compressions:

1 and 2 and 3 and 4 and 5

Practice tip: Think of your arms as pistons, moving straight up and down. The compression phase should be equal in time to the relaxation phase be-

Figure 6.10. **Place the heel of the other hand next to the index finger.**

Figures 6.11 and 6.12. **Right: Placing one hand on top of the other, either interlock the fingers or keep them straight.**

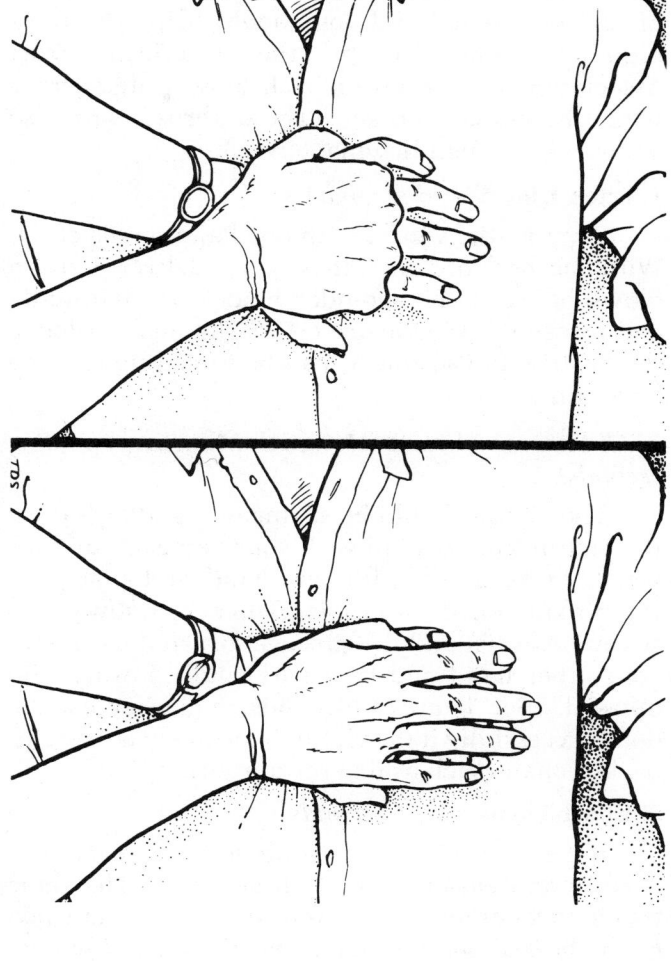

tween compressions. In other words, hold the chest compressed for the same time (about ½ second) as relaxation. Your hands should rest lightly on the chest between compressions to keep them in the proper position.

After each 15 compressions (counting to five 3 times), you must perform 2 breaths. Take your hands off the chest, place them on the neck and forehead as before, pinch the nostrils, seal the mouth, and give 2 strong breaths, watching out of the corner of your eye for the chest to rise.

Go back to the chest, find the correct hand position again, and do 15 more compressions, followed by 2 breaths. Repeat this cycle of 15 and 2 for a total of 4 times, which will be approximately 1 minute. Then check again for pulse and breathing. If neither has returned, you must continue compressions and breathing until the patient revives, qualified help comes, or you are too exhausted to continue.

OBSTRUCTED AIRWAY AND CHOKING

Conscious Victim

People who are choking may still be conscious and have circulation but are unable to breathe because something—usually food—is lodged in their throat.

Obviously, choking on food occurs with eating and often when adults have been drinking alcohol as well. Frequently, if a person is choking, he or she will clutch the throat with thumb and forefinger, a universal signal of distress. Before you do anything to assist, ask the victim if he can talk. If he can, the airway is not completely obstructed and it is best to leave him alone until he can dislodge the food or object himself by coughing, throat-clearing, or with his fingers.

If the victim cannot talk, the airway is completely obstructed and you should help. The technique recommended by the American Heart Association is a series of back blows interspersed with abdominal thrusts. (These thrusts are also known as the Heimlich maneuver.)

1. Back Blows (*4–6 seconds*)

Support the victim with one hand on his chest. With the heel of your other hand, deliver 4 sharp blows between the shoulder blades. Do it rapidly and forcefully. (See figure 6.13.) This may dislodge the obstruction so that it can be forced upward by abdominal thrusts.

2. Abdominal Thrusts (Heimlich Maneuver) (*5–6 seconds*)

The victim should be sitting or standing. Grasp the victim from behind with your hands around his waist. Make a fist with one hand and place the thumb side on the victim's abdomen, midway between the waist and the rib cage. Grasp the fist with your other hand and thrust forcefully inward and upward. (See figure 6.14.) This maneuver can be done successfully if the victim is sitting in a straight-backed chair (such as in a restaurant).

3. Chest Thrusts (*5–6 seconds*)

If the victim is especially obese or is pregnant, it is safer and easier to do a chest thrust. The same two-fist technique is used, but the victim is grasped at the breastbone instead of the abdomen. (See figure 6.15.)

Note: There have been reports of people using the abdominal or chest thrusts on themselves if no one is present to help. You can do it by leaning back against a wall, but it may be easier to lean over and thrust your body toward a chair or table edge.

Unconscious Victim

1. Back Blows (*4–6 seconds*)

If you have begun the initial steps of CPR, including attempts to open the airway, and you cannot see the chest rise and fall when you do rescue breathing, you should assume that the airway is obstructed. Back blows and abdominal or chest thrusts should be used in this case as well.

Since the unconscious victim will be lying on his back as you discover that an obstruction of the airway is preventing breathing, you will need to turn him partially over to administer the back blows. Grasping his shoulder, roll him toward you, supporting him across your thigh, and give 4 sharp blows to the back between the shoulder blades with the heel of your hand. (See figure 6.16.)

2. Abdominal Thrusts (*5–6 seconds*)

If the back blows do not dislodge the obstruction, roll the victim onto his back again. Kneeling next to or astride the victim, place the heel of one hand on the abdomen midway between the waist and the rib cage. Place the other hand on top of the first (as you would for chest compressions, but on the abdomen rather than the chest) and thrust inward and upward. Give 4 quick thrusts. (See figure 6.17.)

3. Chest Thrusts (*5–6 seconds*)

Alternatively, with an obese or pregnant victim, substitute chest thrusts. Use the same hand position

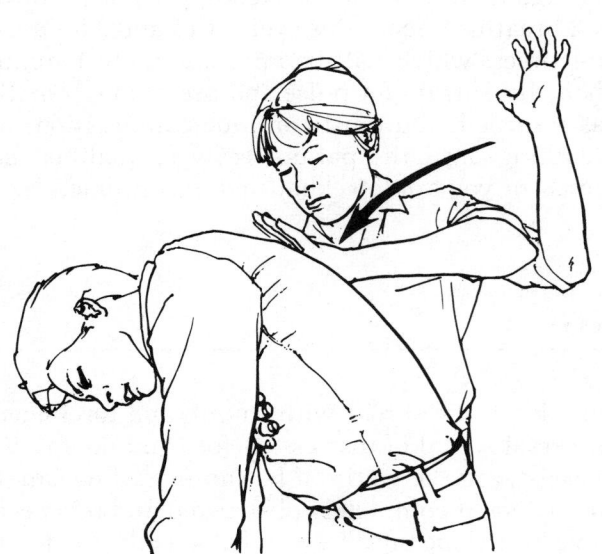

Figure 6.13. **Back blows on a conscious victim.**

Figure 6.14. **Abdominal thrusts (Heimlich maneuver) on conscious victim.**

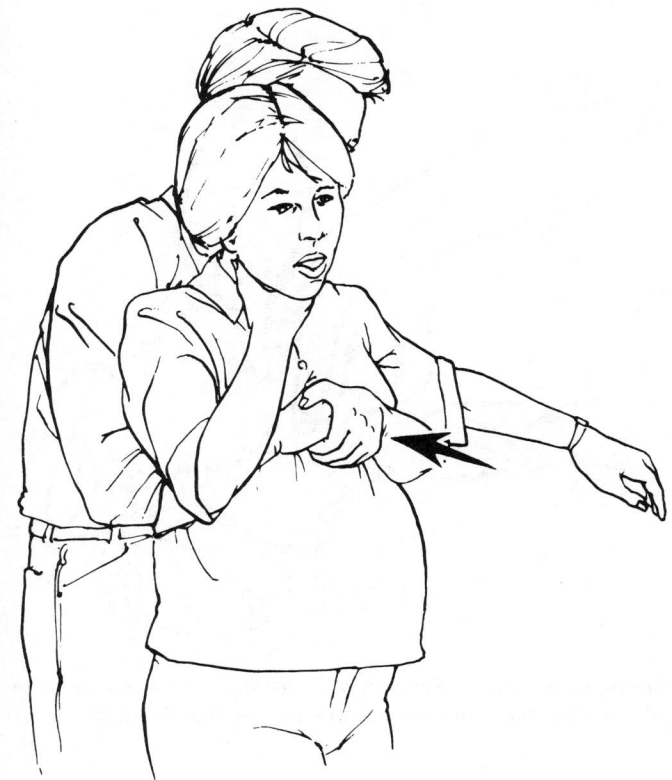

Figure 6.15. **Chest thrust for pregnant or obese conscious victims.**

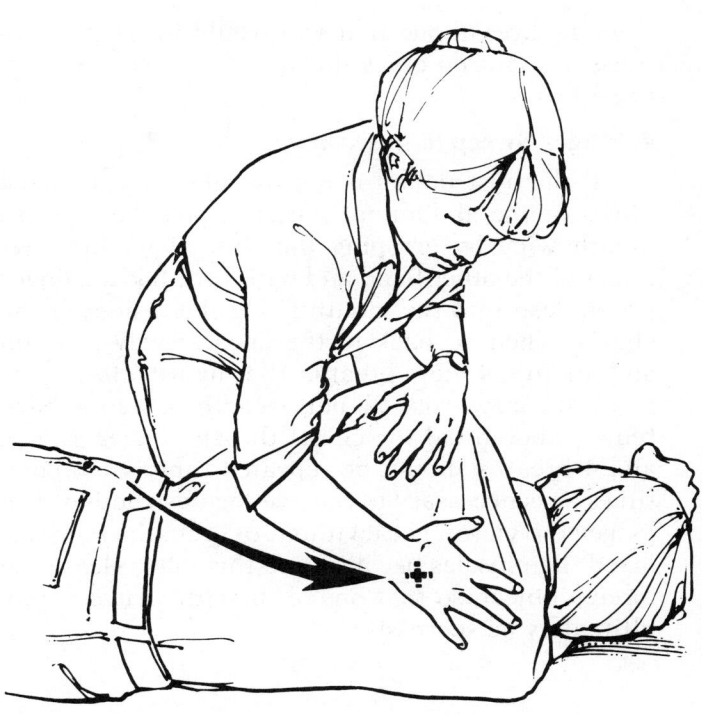

Figure 6.16. **Back blows on an unconscious victim.**

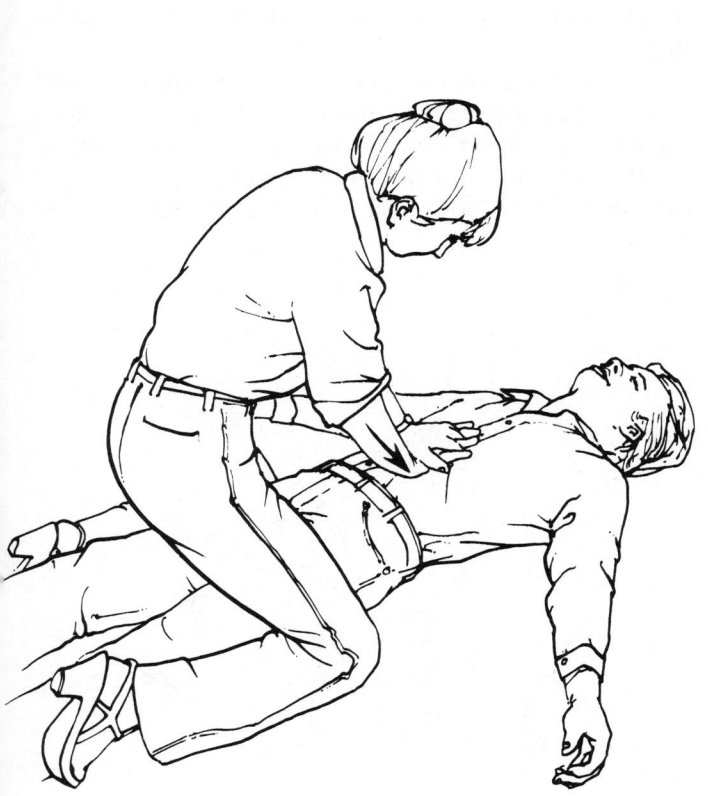

Figure 6.17. **Abdominal thrusts on an unconscious victim.**

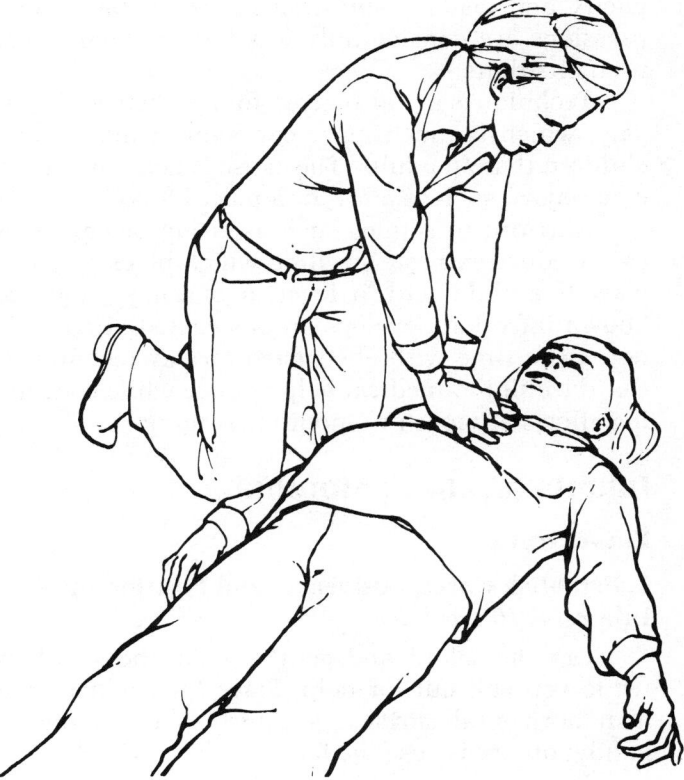

Figure 6.18. **Chest thrusts on a pregnant or obese unconscious victim.**

over the breastbone that you would for chest compressions, but do quick downward thrusts. (See figure 6.18.)

4. Finger Sweep *(6–8 seconds)*

If the obstruction is not dislodged by the back blows or the abdominal thrusts, open the victim's mouth wide by grasping the chin. Bend the forefinger of the other hand and with your hooked finger probe deep into the mouth along the insides of the cheeks. Then go back to the open airway position and attempt 4 more breaths. (See figure 6.19.)

If the airway is still not open, the 4 steps—back blows, abdominal (or chest) thrusts, finger sweep, and 4 breaths should be repeated rapidly as many times as is necessary to remove the obstruction. The longer the victim goes without oxygen, the more relaxed the muscles become, and this may release the foreign object, so that one of these maneuvers may ultimately be successful.

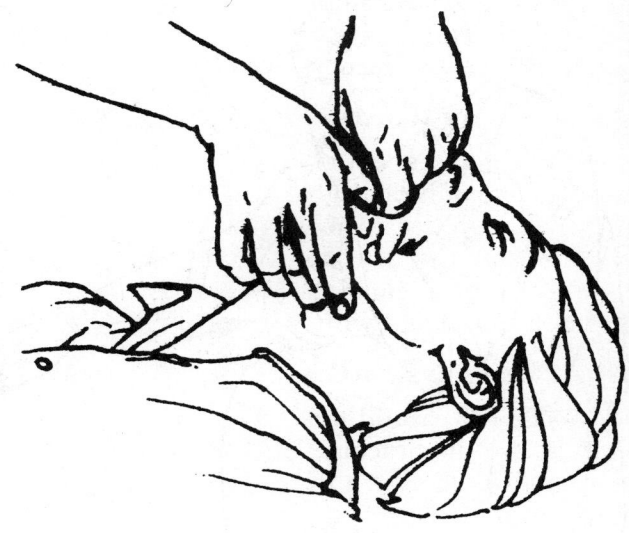

Figure 6.19. **Grasp the chin while using the hooked forefinger of the other hand to sweep the mouth for the obstruction.**

CPR ON INFANTS AND CHILDREN

CPR CAN ALSO BE USED on infants and children. Although the steps and the sequence in which they are performed remain the same, modifications have been made to compensate for the smaller lung capacity and faster respiration rate of babies. Compressions are considerably less forceful than those used on adults.

Techniques are also given for an obstructed airway, which is much more common in infants and children than in adults. The cause is generally a foreign object, such as a toy, or a piece of food.

CAUTION: Infections such as croup or epiglottis can produce extreme swelling which blocks the airway. If a child with a fever, a barking cough, or known infection develops an obstructed airway, do not waste time with obstructed airway techniques. Get the child to medical help at once while continuing efforts at mouth-to-mouth breathing.

Infants (Up to 12 Months)

FIRST STEPS

1. Establish Unresponsiveness and Position the Infant *(4–10 seconds)*

Tap the infant and gently shake the shoulder while you call out for help. Place him or her on a firm horizontal surface. A table is best if one is handy; otherwise use the floor.

2. Open the Airway and Check for Breathing *(3–5 seconds)*

With one hand on the forehead and the other under the neck, tip the head back to open the airway, but do not extend it as far as you would with an adult. (See figure 6.20.) Put your cheek over the mouth and LOOK, LISTEN, and FEEL for breathing.

Also check the lip color. If the lips are pink and you can hear or see the infant struggling to breathe, maintain an open airway, but do not start rescue breathing. If the lips are blue, not enough oxygen is reaching the blood and you must begin rescue

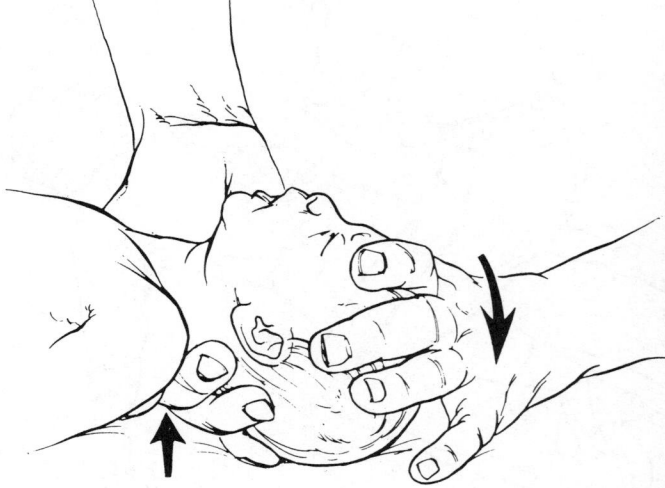

Figure 6.20. **Open the infant's airway with one hand lifting the neck while the other hand gently tips the head back.**

breathing. Like the adult victim who can talk, the infant who is crying is not completely obstructed, and may dislodge the obstruction by coughing.

Give 4 Gentle Breaths *(3–5 seconds)*

Cover and seal both the infant's *nose and mouth* with your mouth and give 4 quick, gentle puffs of breath. Too much air may distend the stomach and result in vomiting. (In contrast to those of adults, infants' faces are so small that it is easier to cover both the nose and mouth with your mouth.)

Check the Pulse and Call the EMS *(5–10 seconds)*

Since the carotid pulse is difficult to locate on infants, use the brachial pulse on the inside of the arm, midway between the elbow and the shoulder. (See figure 6.21.) If there is a pulse, continue rescue breathing, 1 breath every 5 seconds. If there is no pulse, begin chest compressions.

If someone is available to help, have him or her call the EMS. If you are alone, call after you have done 4 cycles of breathing or breathing and compressions.

Chest Compressions

Place your index and middle finger on the middle of the breastbone and depress no more than ½ to 1 inch. Count out loud as you do the compressions:

1, 2, 3, 4, 5

Since the respiration rate of infants is faster than that of adults, the compressions should be at a rate of 100 a minute, rather than adult rate of 80. Give 1 gentle breath every 5 compressions. (See figure 6.22.)

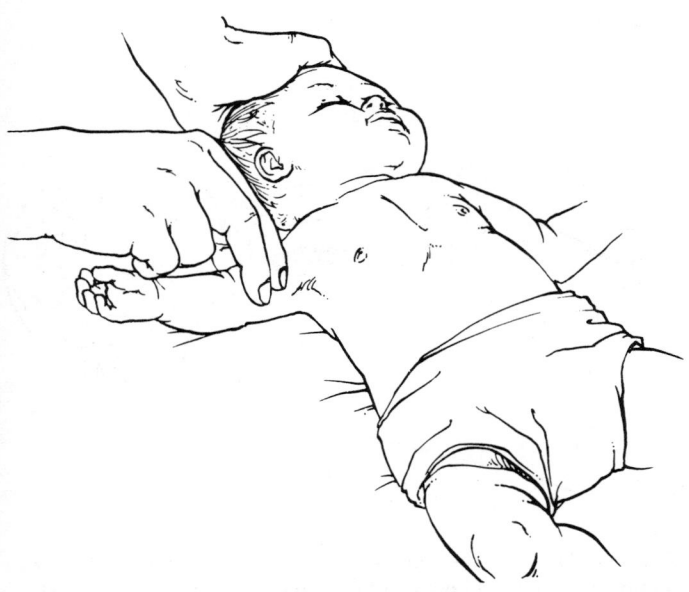

Figure 6.21. **Check the pulse on the inside of the upper arm.**

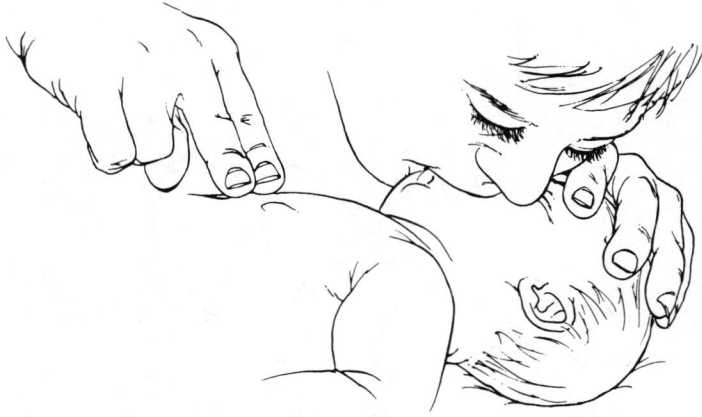

Figure 6.22. **Give one gentle breath, covering both the nose and mouth with your mouth, after every 5 compressions.**

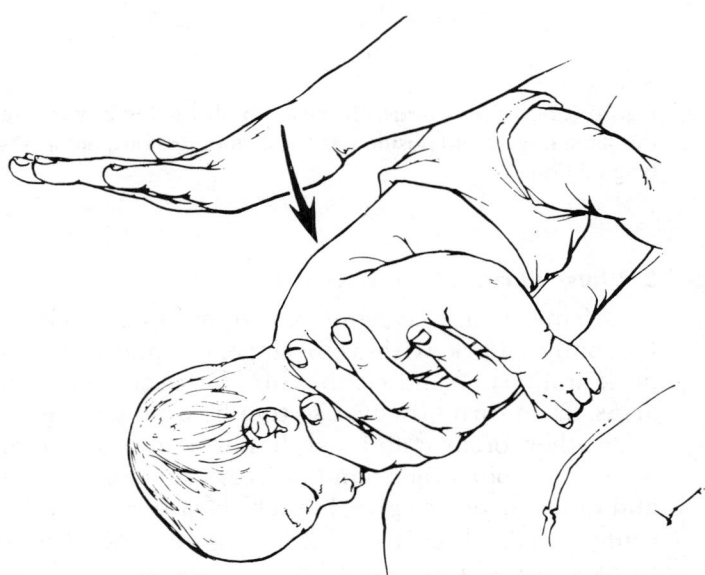

Figure 6.23. **Deliver back blows with one hand while you support the infant with the other.**

Obstructed Airway

If the infant does not have an infection (see CAUTION, page 96), and the airway is completely obstructed, a combination of back blows and chest thrusts is used, whether or not the infant is conscious. If the airway is only partially blocked and the infant is making attempts to breathe and cough, let him or her continue.

1. Back Blows *(4–6 seconds)*

Straddle the infant face down along your forearm with his head pointing toward the floor. Support the baby's head with your hand on his jaw and rest your forearm on your thigh. With the heel of your other hand, give the baby 4 rapid blows to the back between the shoulder blades. (See figure 6.23.)

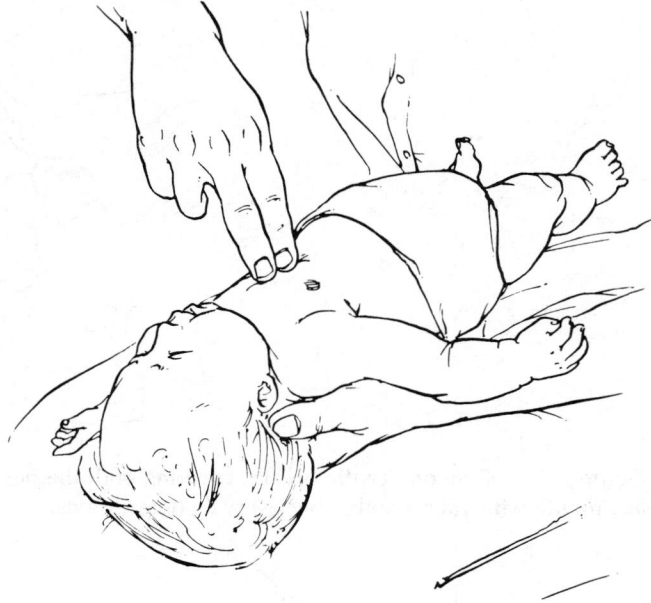

Figure 6.24. Chest thrusts to clear an obstructed airway use the same fingers and position as chest compressions, but a jabbing motion.

2. Chest Thrusts (5–6 seconds)

Using your free hand, lay your forearm along the baby's back with your fingers supporting his neck and head, sandwiching him between your two arms. Then turn him over so that he is now lying on your other forearm and rest that arm on your thigh. Now that your other hand is free, use your middle and index fingers to give 4 quick chest thrusts in the center of the breastbone. (See figure 6.24.) Chest thrusts are administered in the same location and with the same 2 fingers as chest compressions, but they are given with more of a thrusting or jabbing motion than a steady compression.

Alternate back blows and chest thrusts. The finger sweep should not be used blindly on an infant where a large adult finger can often make the situation worse. If you can see the object, however, you can try to remove it with your fingers, being very careful not to push it farther down into the throat.

Children (1–8 Years)

FIRST STEPS

1. Establish Unresponsiveness and Position the Child (4–10 seconds)

Tap the child and gently shake the shoulder while you call out for help. Place him or her on a firm horizontal surface. If the child can talk, shout "Are you O.K.?"

2. Open the Airway and Check for Breathing (3–5 seconds)

With one hand on the forehead and the other under the neck, rotate the head back and extend the neck as you would with an adult. Put your cheek over the mouth and LOOK, LISTEN, and FEEL for breathing.

GIVE 4 QUICK BREATHS (3–5 seconds)

With your hand still on the child's forehead, pinch the nostrils closed. Cover his mouth with your mouth to make a tight seal. Give 4 quick breaths.

CHECK THE PULSE AND CALL THE EMS (5–10 seconds)

Check the carotid pulse on the side of the neck, as you would with an adult. If there is a pulse, continue rescue breathing, 1 breath every 5 seconds. If there is no pulse, begin chest compressions.

If someone is available to help, have him or her call the EMS. If you are alone, call after you have done breathing or breathing and compressions for 1 minute.

CHEST COMPRESSIONS

As you would with an adult, use your hand closer to the child's feet to follow the edge of the ribs as your fingers move up toward the center of the chest. You will feel a notch where the ribs meet the breastbone. Put your middle finger on this spot and then put your index finger next to it. Place the heel of

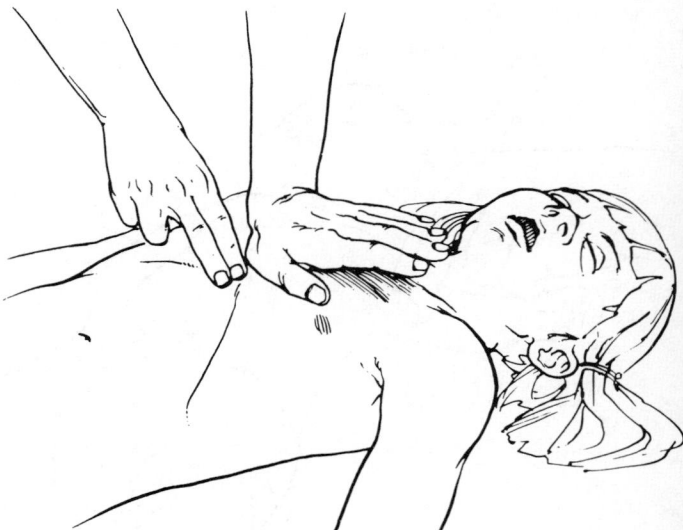

Figure 6.25. Use the same position for chest compressions on a child as you would on an adult, but only compress the chest 1 to 1½ inches.

your other hand next to the index finger. Use only one hand and be sure you use only the heel, keeping your fingers off the chest to avoid injury to the ribs. Depress the chest 1 to 1½ inches with each compression. (See figure 6.25.) To get the proper speed and rhythm, count out loud as you would for an adult:

1 and 2 and 3 and 4 and 5

Give 1 breath every 5 compressions.

OBSTRUCTED AIRWAY

1. Back Blows *(4–6 seconds)*

If the child is small, kneel on the floor and drape the child face down over your thighs, with his head pointing toward the floor. Deliver 4 quick back blows between the shoulder blades. If the child is large, you can use the same technique as with an adult, placing him on the floor on his side to deliver the back blows.

2. Chest Thrusts *(5–6 seconds)*

Roll the child carefully onto the floor so that he is on his back. Run your fingers up along the margin of the ribs until you find the notch of the breastbone. Measure up two fingers as you would to find the position for chest compressions and use the heel of one hand to deliver the chest thrusts. The position and technique are the same, but the chest thrusts require a more rapid thrusting or jabbing motion than the more steady depressing of the chest used with compressions.

OTHER LIFE-THREATENING EMERGENCIES

CARBON MONOXIDE POISONING

UNCONSCIOUSNESS from carbon monoxide poisoning is a life-threatening emergency that may require mouth-to-mouth respiration or CPR. Carbon monoxide can cause death by combining with hemoglobin, the oxygen-carrying protein of blood, and therefore depriving the tissues of oxygen. Automobiles, industrial fumes, and burning buildings are the most common sources of carbon monoxide poisoning. Signs include:

- Circumstances that indicate poisoning (e.g., a car with a running motor, or a fire, especially in a poorly vented room).
- Severe headache, disorientation, agitation, lethargy, stupor, coma.

If carbon monoxide poisoning is suspected:

- Get the victim into the open air as quickly as possible.
- Check for respiration and pulse. If both are absent, begin CPR.
- If breathing is absent but there is a pulse, begin mouth-to-mouth respiration and continue until the victim begins breathing or help arrives.
- Begin administering oxygen with an oxygen-breathing mask as soon as it becomes available.
- Get the victim to a hospital as soon as possible. Extended observation and additional emergency care will be required. There may also be other medical problems, especially neurological, cardiac, or pulmonary problems.

CARDIAC ARREST FOLLOWING ELECTROCUTION

ELECTRIC CURRENT passing through the body can cause cardiac arrest, generally from ventricular fibrillation (rapid, uncoordinated beating or quivering of the heart muscle). The longer the contact with the electrical current, the less likely are the chances of survival. The source of current may be a downed electrical wire, a defective household appliance, or lightning. A victim of suspected electrocution should be approached with caution because until the person is free of contact with the current, he or she is an electrical conductor. Therefore, NEVER touch a victim of electric shock until you are sure the power is off or contact has been broken.

- If an appliance is the source of electricity, shut off the current at the fuse box or if you can safely do so, unplug it immediately. Simply turning off the appliance is not adequate.

- If the current cannot be turned off and a live wire is touching the victim, dry your hands completely and insulate them with dry gloves or a dry cloth.

- Stand on a dry, nonconductive surface, such as a stack of newspapers, a board, or pile of clothes (NOT the earth or anything metallic or wet). If possible, pull on a pair of dry rubber boots.

- Decide if it is more practical to push the victim away from the wire or to push the wire from the victim. If your hands are well-insulated and you are standing on a dry, nonconductive surface, move the person or the wire using a nonconducting object such as a wooden pole or board. If the wire is clutched in the victim's hand, it may take considerable force to separate the two. Do not directly touch the person or the wire. (See figure 6.26.)

- Check whether the victim is breathing or has a heartbeat. If not, begin CPR immediately. Even if the victim does not revive within minutes, continue these measures until help arrives, as recovery from electric shock can be slow.

- If the victim was struck by lightning, check immediately for breathing and pulse. Since the current has passed through the body and disappeared, the rescuer does not need to worry about sustaining a shock and treatment can begin immediately.

- When breathing is reestablished, treat the victim for shock by elevating the feet and covering with a blanket.

- If the victim is conscious but has fallen from a height,

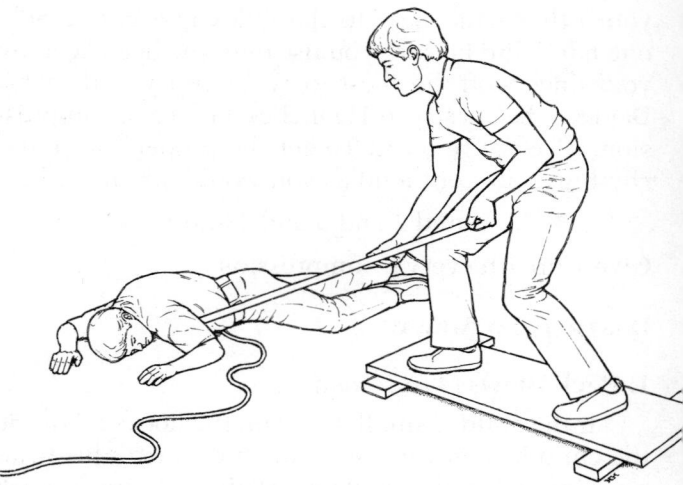

Figure 6.26. **Moving victim of electrocution. Before attempting to move victim, make sure that you are not in danger of electrocution yourself. Stand on a dry, nonconductive surface. If possible, wear dry rubber boots. Use a nonconducting object, such as a wooden pole or board, to move either the wire from the victim or the victim from the wire.**

or is a victim of high tension contact or lightning strike, check for associated injuries, such as skull, spine or extremity fractures, burns, and other injuries. Anyone who has sustained a serious electrical shock should be transported as soon as possible to a hospital emergency service.

DROWNING AND NEAR DROWNING

FIRST AID for someone who is floundering in the water or who appears to have drowned should be preceded by a realistic evaluation of the rescuer's skills, including swimming ability. Granted, there are examples of nonswimmers who have plunged into the water and succeeded in rescuing a drowning person, but there are far more examples of both the swimmer and the would-be rescuer drowning. If you cannot swim or if you doubt your ability to get the drowning victim out of the water, it is far better to summon help or try some other tactic, such as the throw, tow, or row technique recommended by the Coast Guard:

- *Throw.* From a float, shoreside dock, or boat, attach a long rope to a buoyant object such as a lifejacket, life preserver, or a large empty plastic bottle that is securely closed and throw it to the floundering swimmer and then pull him or her to shore.

- *Row.* If it is not possible to throw something to the swimmer and a rowboat or other boat is available, get to him or her as quickly as possible.

- *Tow.* Give the person an extra oar, rope, or life preserver to hold onto, and tow him or her to shore. (Don't try to haul the person into the boat; this may cause it to capsize and you'll both be in the water.)

- If none of these procedures is possible and the rescuer can safely swim to the victim's aid, make the rescue attempt. If you cannot swim, summon help.

Depending on circumstances, do the following:

- If there is a chance the near-drowning victim has a neck or back injury (e.g., from a diving, waterskiing, or boating accident), special care in maintaining neck and back alignment will be needed in getting him or her to shore. If possible, float the victim onto a board and then pull to shore. If the victim is breathing and a spinal injury is suspected, keep him or her in the water floating on the back until a board or other support can be brought to you.

- If the victim has fallen through ice into the water, do not walk on the ice to rescue him or her. Instead, have the victim, if conscious, try to rest on the edge of the ice, rather than trying to climb out, which may only result in breaking more ice. Throw a rope from shore, or use a long board or stick and try to pull the victim out and across the ice on his or her belly, to distribute the weight as evenly as possible. If the victim is unconscious, tie the rope around your waist, secure the other end, and slide out on the ice on your belly. If other rescuers are present, form a human chain, with all of you lying down, to reach the victim.

- If breathing has stopped, begin mouth-to-mouth respiration. This can be done even while the victim is still in the water by giving 4 quick breaths and then a breath every 5 seconds while you are pulling him or her to shore.

- Once the victim is out of the water, determine if there is a pulse. If not, begin CPR at once and continue until help arrives. Do not attempt to drain water from the lungs. If a back injury is suspected, do not transport except to remove from water, and then use a board if possible.

- Even if the victim is revived, observe carefully for possible complications, such as cardiac arrest, and get to a hospital as soon as possible. Water in the lungs decreases their ability to function; the body's salt and fluid balance also may be upset, leading to further complications that may not be immediately apparent. Hospital personnel should be informed whether the drowning took place in fresh or salt water as this may influence the type of aftercare.

HEMORRHAGE

AFTER ATTENDING to respiration and circulation, the next major priority is to stop any major bleeding or hemorrhaging. The bleeding may be external, from obvious cuts, punctures, or other wounds, or internal, in which case there may not be any obvious signs of hemorrhage, but it still may be a life-threatening situation.

Bleeding from Cuts, Punctures, and Other Wounds

Depending upon the nature of the wound, bleeding is classified as follows:

Arterial blood is bright red and if the artery is exposed, the blood may escape in spurts synchronized with the pulse. This type of bleeding is the least frequent but the most serious. It can usually be controlled with direct pressure.

Venous blood is dark red and flows slowly and steadily. This is the type of bleeding associated with most deeper cuts. It is controllable with direct pressure.

Capillary blood is medium red and oozes slowly. This is the type of bleeding associated with minor scrapes and cuts.

Bleeding from an ordinary cut or puncture wound usually can be controlled by applying direct pressure. Whenever tissue is cut, the body releases chemicals that interact with blood components to promote clotting (coagulation) and which also constrict or narrow the blood vessels. By applying a bandage or clean cloth to a cut or wound and holding it firmly in place, the blood flow can be slowed and the body's natural clotting mechanism will be given a chance to work.

When you are confronted with more severe bleeding or injuries, follow these steps:

1. Lay the victim down, preferably with head slightly lowered (to prevent fainting) and the legs elevated (unless a fracture is suspected or there is bleeding from the nose or mouth).

2. If possible, expose wound and elevate bleeding part to take advantage of gravity in slowing the bleeding. Put pressure directly on the wound by covering with a sterile pad, clean cloth, or other suitable material. (If nothing else is available, cover the wound directly with your hand.)

3. Don't attempt to clean wound at this point; it is more important to stop the bleeding.

4. Maintain pressure for 10 minutes. Do not remove bloodsoaked pad or cloth; instead, apply another over it. Bandage can be held in place by tying it with a strip of cloth, stocking, or by wrapping a belt around it, being careful not to cut off circulation to areas beyond the wound. (Check for pulse beyond the injury.) Transport patient to an emergency room.

If direct pressure does not control the bleeding, then continue to maintain pressure at the site of the wound and, at the same time, apply pressure at the appropriate pressure point over an artery or pulse point located above the wound. For example, if the bleeding is from a wound in the lower arm, apply pressure to brachial artery, located midway between the armpit and elbow in the groove between the biceps and triceps. Grasp the person's arm in the middle, with your fingers on the inside of the arm and your thumb on the outside, using your fingers to press the flat, inside surface. If the bleeding is in the leg or lower part of the body, the appropriate pressure point is in the crotch area to the side of the pelvic bone. (See figures 6.27A and 6.27B.) Pressing upon these pressure points will further reduce the flow of blood to the injured area and help promote clotting. However, DO NOT apply pressure to arter-

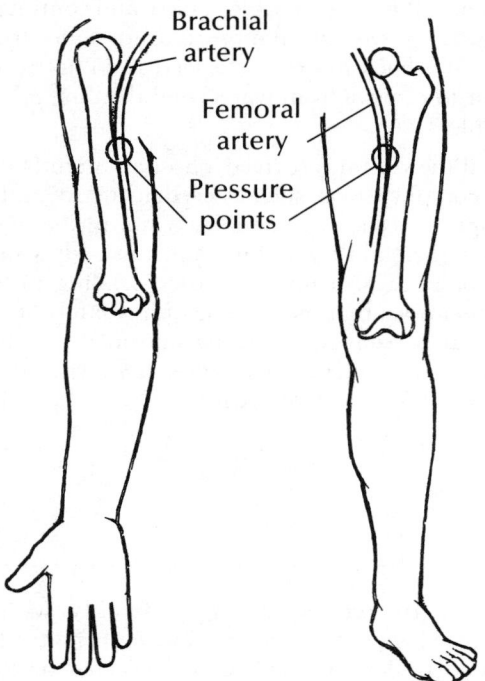

Figure 6.27. **Hemorrhaging is controlled either by applying direct pressure to the wound or by applying pressure to the major artery serving the injured area at a point above the cut blood vessel.**

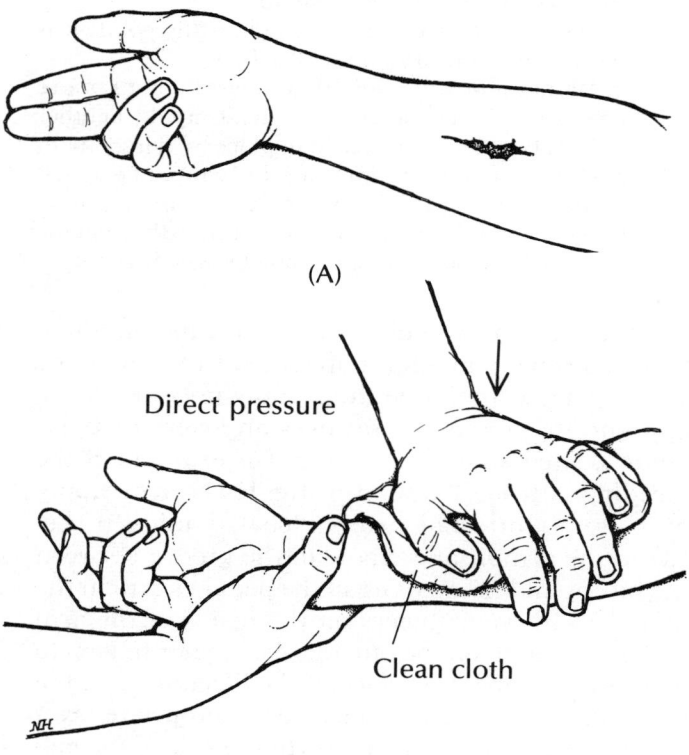

(A) **Bleeding from this type of cut usually can be stopped by applying direct pressure, as shown above. A clean cloth should be placed directly over the cut and then firm but not excessive pressure applied to it.**

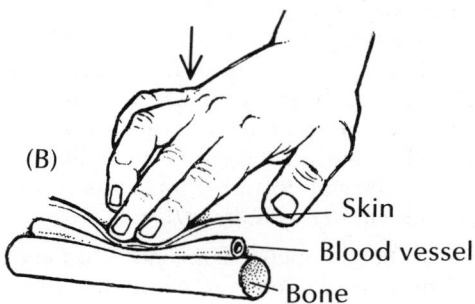

(B) **If direct pressure fails to stop the bleeding, pressure should be applied to the blood vessel at a point above the injury. The objective is to compress the blood vessel against bone to stop the blood flow enough to halt the bleeding. Pressure points for lower limbs are shown below.**

ies leading to the head or neck, as this may interfere with blood circulation to the brain. (See figure 6.28.)

Immobilize the injured part, leaving the bandages in place, and get the injured person to an emergency room or hospital. The use of a tourniquet is not advisable except with an amputation with bleeding uncontrolled by direct or proximal pressure. If a tourniquet is applied, always note the time that it is started. (See section on Amputations, Chapter 7, page 106.)

Bleeding from an Abdominal Wound

Penetration of the abdominal wall is always a serious injury, both from the bleeding and from the risk of injury to the abdominal organs. The victim should be taken to an emergency room or hospital as soon as possible after performing the following first aid:

Position the victim so that he is lying on his back. If there are no protruding internal organs, follow the steps for controlling the bleeding as outlined above. Cover wound with a sterile pad or clean cloth and apply pressure to stop bleeding. Tape or bind the bandage in place.

If internal organs are exposed, cover the wound with a moist dressing, but avoid touching it or trying to reposition it. Only gentle pressure should be applied if the wound is bleeding.

Internal Bleeding

Internal bleeding often is not readily apparent, although in some cases there may be coughing or vomiting of blood or bleeding from the rectum, urethra, or vagina, depending upon the location and nature of the injury. Other warning signs are those of hypovolemic shock, and include anxiousness, lightheadedness, or fainting; a weak, rapid pulse, shallow

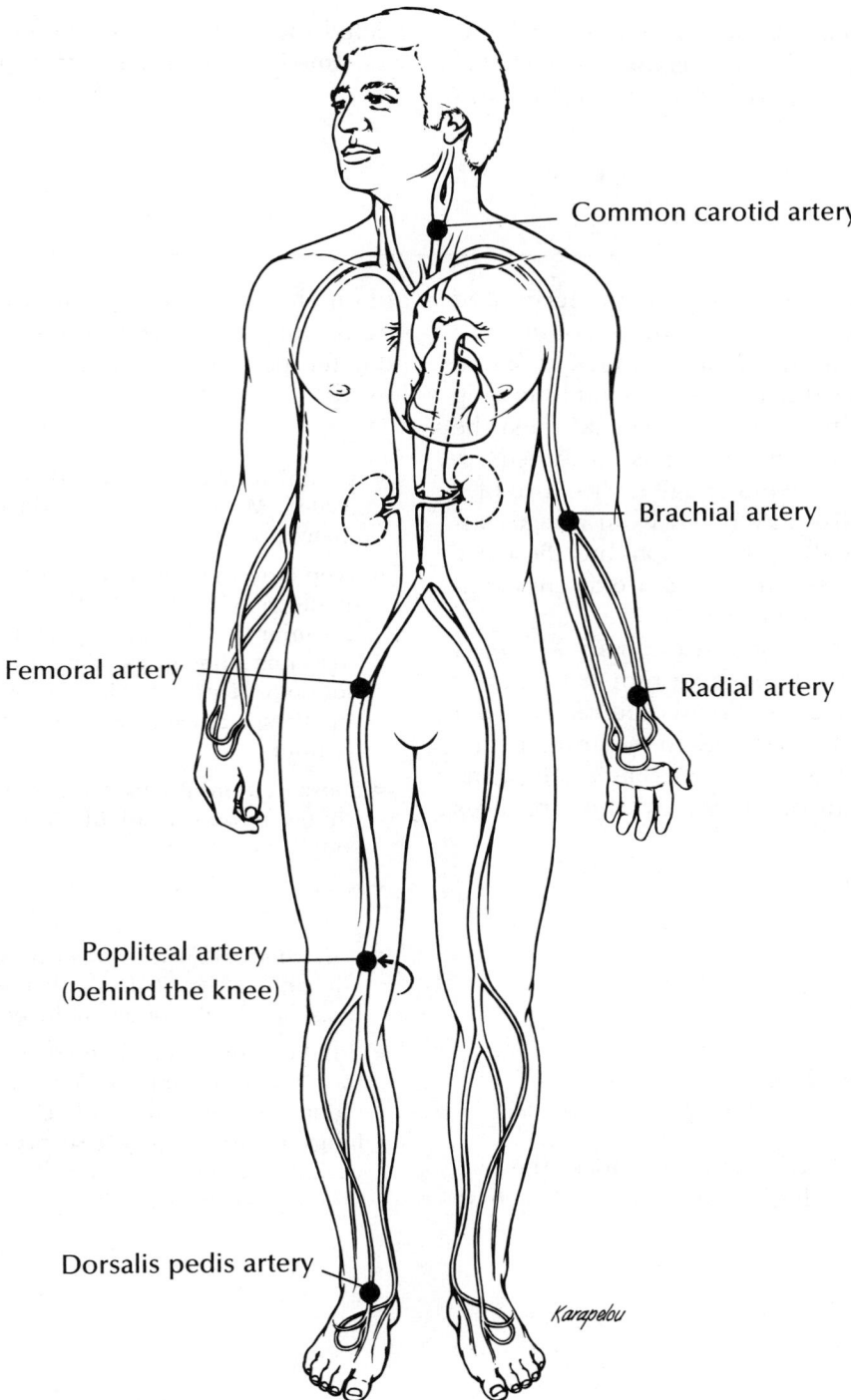

Common carotid artery

Brachial artery

Femoral artery

Radial artery

Popliteal artery
(behind the knee)

Dorsalis pedis artery

Karapelou

Figure 6.28. **The most common arterial pressure points are
illustrated here.**

breathing and shortness of breath; dilated pupils;
cold, pale, and clammy skin; and possibly abdominal swelling.

If breathing stops, mouth-to-mouth respiration
should be started; if, in addition, there is no pulse,
CPR should be administered, even though this is
usually futile if loss of blood is the cause. The victim
should lie down and be kept warm and as comfortable as possible, otherwise there are no specific
first-aid measures to stop internal bleeding. An ambulance should be called as quickly as possible. If
there is a faster way of getting the victim to a hospital emergency room, by all means do so, since
prompt medical attention is vital, even though there

are instances in which the bleeding may not be as serious as it appears. Still, there is no way of telling until the person is in expert hands; hence, any sus-pected internal bleeding should be considered a serious medical emergency until proven otherwise.

SHOCK

"TRAUMATIC HEMORRHAGIC SHOCK" is the term used to describe a slowing down, or stoppage, of life-sustaining functions caused by an insufficient blood supply to vital organs due to loss of blood following severe injury. The possibility of shock must be guarded against in anyone who has sustained serious injury, including hemorrhage or fracture of a large bone. Shock also may result from a heart attack, infection, or an allergic reaction, but these are different from traumatic shock and are discussed in the specific section devoted to each.

In the early stages of shock, the body attempts to compensate for blood loss by a redistribution of the available supply. Blood flow is redirected from the skin, muscles, and soft tissues to the brain, heart, lungs, and vital organs. In hemorrhagic shock, as well as in shock from other causes, this produces such symptoms as:

- Generalized weakness
- Cold, clammy skin that is very pale or bluish
- Sweating
- Rapid, shallow breathing
- Faint, rapid pulse
- Nausea, sometimes followed by vomiting
- Restlessness

In the early stages of traumatic shock, the victim may be alert. But don't be misled by this; first aid for shock should begin at once to improve blood circulation, safeguard oxygen supply, and maintain body temperature. These specific steps should be followed:

- Administer basic life support and control bleeding as needed. Make sure that medical help has been summoned.
- Keep movement to an absolute minimum. The victim should be lying down, with head tilted to one side (unless injury to the cervical spine is suspected). Unless breathing difficulties or pain result, elevate the feet. But do NOT raise the feet or lower the head if the victim has sustained a head, neck, back, or lower extremity injury.
- Loosen clothing and cover victim with a blanket or whatever else is available. The purpose is to conserve body heat.
- Keep the victim as calm as possible. Do not ask unnecessary questions.
- If the victim asks for water, moisten the lips but do not allow him or her to drink. Do not attempt to give sedatives, hot drinks, or alcoholic beverages.
- If the victim feels nauseated or vomits, roll him or her to the side so that the vomitus is expelled from the mouth and not inhaled back into the windpipe and lungs. If spinal injury is suspected, keep the head and neck in alignment as you roll. Get the victim to a hospital as soon as possible.

7 A Directory of Common First-Aid Procedures

Kenneth C. Fine, M.D.

THERE ARE LITERALLY hundreds of situations that, although not immediately life-threatening, require varying degrees of first aid. Others require emergency medical treatment and follow-up care. The most common, both life-threatening and not, are summarized in alphabetical order in this section. Others, such as childbirth emergencies, psychiatric crises, and similar situations involving specific disease states, are covered in the chapters dealing with those disorders.

ALLERGIC REACTIONS (ANAPHYLACTIC SHOCK)

ALLERGIC REACTIONS cover a wide spectrum from itching eyes and nasal conjestion to much more serious events. There are some people, however, who are extremely hypersensitive to particular substances and who may suffer massive systemic reactions soon after exposure to them. Signs of extreme hypersensitivity (anaphylactic reaction) include sudden widespread blotchy swelling of the skin (hives) and mucous membranes, difficulty in breathing, wheezing, increased pulse rate, a sudden fall in blood pressure with a weak and thin pulse, nausea, vomiting, and abdominal cramps. These symptoms may quickly escalate into loss of consciousness and cardiorespiratory collapse. If untreated, they may lead rapidly to death.

At the first sign of an anaphylactic reaction, the victim should be transported to the nearest emergency room, preferably, or to a doctor's office. Some people with a prior history of severe allergic reactions carry an anaphylaxis kit containing medications (adrenaline, antihistamines) and instructions on how to use them. Check for this kit and use as directed. While transporting the patient to the hospital, administer CPR if necessary. If medication is not available, the person should be rushed immediately to the nearest emergency room or doctor who can provide the proper treatment. No time should be wasted for anything else since this is a life-and-death situation.

Anaphylactic shock is seen most commonly in response to insect stings, certain medications, or foods. Anyone who has had serious allergic reaction to a sting or medication should be doubly careful to avoid all future contacts. Desensitization shots may be recommended if bee stings prompt the response. All offending medications should be avoided, as well as any drug in the same class or with a similar chemical composition. In any event, the person should wear a Medic Alert bracelet warning of the allergy.

AMPUTATIONS

THE SEVERING of any body part—a finger, hand, leg—is always a serious medical emergency. The majority of amputations involve, however, smaller distal parts, such as a finger tip or a part of an ear. Although bleeding occurs, major blood loss is usually not a problem. These cases can generally be managed easily by applying a pressure dressing, and transporting the patient and the amputated part, properly wrapped (see below), to the hospital. With larger amputations (hand, foot, arm, leg) there may be significant blood loss and shock.

The victim should be carefully evaluated for signs of respiratory distress, heartbeat, and shock at the outset, as well as the presence of other injuries. Reassure the victim and try to keep him or her as calm and quiet as possible. Observe for signs of shock and treat appropriately. Follow these first-aid measures:

- Lay victim down with head slightly lowered and the severed limb elevated.

- Control bleeding by applying pressure directly to the wound using gauze pads or a clean cloth. Once the bleeding has been controlled, place several layers of the gauze over the severed area and bandage the layers firmly in place. If bleeding is not controlled by direct pressure, apply pressure to the large feeding artery above the amputation. (For pressure points, see Chapter 6 on Basics of CPR and Life Support, page 103.)

- As soon as bleeding is controlled, check for and attend to any other serious problem, such as a head wound or cervical spine injury. When other serious injuries have been attended to, pick up the severed limb and wrap it, preferably in plastic. If plastic is not available, a clean cloth, shirt, or other material will do. If possible, pack the wrapped limb in ice.

- Rush the victim and limb to the nearest emergency room. If there is a nearby hospital or medical center with a surgery team skilled in microsurgery and reimplantation, take the victim and limb there. Advances in reimplantation techniques in recent years have greatly improved the chances of successfully rejoining the severed limb.

- Avoid applying a tourniquet except as a last resort in uncontrollable hemorrhaging. A tourniquet greatly increases the chance of tissue damage and reduces the chance of successful reimplantation. If a tourniquet is necessary, it is applied as follows:

   1. Use any flat, 2-inch-wide piece of cloth long enough to go around the arm or leg twice. Rolled bandaging is ideal, but a belt, scarf, strip torn from a shirt or other similar material will serve the purpose.

   2. Place the tourniquet just above the edge of the wound, but do not allow it to touch the wound. If the wound is very close to the joint or directly below it, place the tourniquet directly above the joint.

   3. Wrap the tourniquet tightly twice around the limb and tie a half knot.

   4. Place a short, strong stick, ruler, screwdriver, or similar rigid object on top of the half knot and tie a full knot over it. Note the time when you apply the tourniquet.

   5. Twist the stick until the bleeding has slowed enough to clot. Secure the stick in place.

   6. Do not loosen the tourniquet unless a physician tells you to do so.

   7. Transport the patient immediately to a hospital.

BITES AND STINGS

Animal Bites

Dogs are the most common source of animal bites. According to Dr. Martin Kurtz, Director of Animal Affairs at the New York City Department of Public Health, more than 1 million Americans, more than one-half of them children, are treated for dog bites each year. Children should be taught at an early age not to approach a strange dog, and dog owners should see to it that their animals are properly restrained at all times. This means using a leash and, if needed, a muzzle when walking a dog, and making sure that it is kept in a secure enclosure at other times. This not only ensures the safety of others, but also will prevent the dog from becoming lost or hit by an automobile—an all too common fate for animals that are left to roam free.

Any animal bite requires some sort of treatment, depending upon the nature of the wound.

- A small superficial bite from an animal known to be healthy, for example, a household pet, usually requires nothing more than careful washing with soap and water and application of an antiseptic, such as hydrogen peroxide, and an antibiotic cream. This is done to prevent infection, since the mouth harbors many bacteria that can be harmful if they invade the skin. If tetanus immunization is not up to date, consult your physician. If the victim has circulatory problems or diabetes, a doctor should be consulted, even if the injury is minor.

- If the bite is a puncture wound or large gash, it should be cleansed (infection is always a danger with animal bites) and, if needed, stitched shut by a doctor. The decision to close a bite depends on the type, location, and severity of the wound. A tetanus shot and antibiotics also may be needed.

- Whether or not the bite has been treated initially by a doctor, if there is any subsequent swelling, pain, increasing redness, or drainage, a doctor should be consulted.

- If the bite was unprovoked, the pet's owner should be notified. Vicious animals that are permitted to roam free should be reported to the local animal warden or health department.

- If possible, try to find the animal that inflicted the bite. Rabies is a relatively rare disease, but it is a possibility that should be eliminated. There are about 40 million dogs in the United States, and only about half of them have been properly immunized against rabies. Other, more important reservoirs of rabies are found among wild animals, such as raccoons, skunks, squirrels, foxes, rats, and bats. If the offending animal cannot be found, then immunization against rabies may be necessary. The decision to treat or not will be based on the type of animal or its behavior or both, the geographic location, and other factors. All bites should be treated promptly in an emergency room or doctor's office and should be reported to the local Board of Health.

A new rabies treatment, consisting of a single dose of rabies-immune globulin and 5 injections of human diploid cell rabies vaccine, has greatly simplified the antirabies shots. Heretofore, the shots had to be administered in the abdominal wall and required up to 25 injections.

- A number of other diseases, including tularemia (rabbit fever), and cat-scratch disease, may be transmitted by animal bites or scratches. Any flulike symptoms, fever, swollen glands, or other symptoms following an animal bite should be investigated promptly by a doctor.

- Human bites happen more frequently than is generally recognized. One of the most frequent human bites is the result of one person punching another in the mouth, only to find that the skin over his knuckles has been penetrated by his intended victim's teeth. The likelihood of a serious infection is very substantial because of the type and amounts of bacteria in the human mouth. Human bites should always be checked immediately by a doctor, who may, along with other treatment, administer antibiotics.

Bee Stings

About 1 million Americans are severely allergic to the venom of bees, hornets, yellow jackets, and fire ants. Although death from anaphylactic shock following a sting is relatively rare, it is the most common cause of death from animal, snake, or insect bites in this country. People who are hypersensitive to bee venom should be extremely careful when going outdoors in areas or at times of the year when there may be bees. Proper protection includes wearing long pants, long-sleeved shirts, shoes, and socks of subdued colors and patterns. Do not wear perfumes or colognes. Do not panic and duck when approached, but instead, walk slowly away from the insect.

Highly sensitive individuals may benefit from carrying a bee-sting treatment kit. These are commercially prepared and available by prescription. They contain adrenaline in preloaded syringes, antihistamines, a tourniquet, swabs, and other items. If a bee stings a person who has experienced widespread allergic reactions in the past and an adrenaline shot is not immediately available, he or she should be rushed to the nearest emergency room or doctor. If any signs or symptoms of generalized reaction occur, place a tourniquet 2 to 4 inches above the bite while transporting the patient or waiting for an ambulance. Desensitization shots may be recommended for hypersensitive individuals who are likely to be stung (e.g., farm dwellers, orchard owners, or other people who work outdoors in areas frequented by bees). For people who are not hypersensitive, but who wish to minimize the discomfort of bee stings, the following measures can be followed:

- Check the sting site to make sure the stinger and venom sac are not still imbedded in the skin. If so, remove by scooping under the barbed stinger with a fingernail or sharp object. Do not try to grasp and pull out, because, in honeybee stings, this may inject more venom from the venom sac.

- Apply an ice pack or flush with cold water. This will reduce swelling and ease the pain.

- Calamine lotion or a nonprescription corticosteroid cream may ease the itching and swelling. Some experts recommend applying commercially available meat tenderizers that contain enzymes. Aspirin or antihistamines may relieve moderate, localized reactions.

Jellyfish, Stingrays, and Other Sea Animals

A sting by a jellyfish, stingray, or other venomous marine creature may produce dramatic symptoms, such as severe pain, cramps, vomiting, and difficulty in breathing. With a few exceptions, however, stings from marine animals usually are not fatal. Obviously, it is not wise to swim in waters infested with jellyfish or other poisonous sea animals. If a sting does occur, the following steps should be taken:

- Try to calm and reassure the victim. If a jellyfish or Portuguese man-o'-war tentacle still adheres to the skin, carefully remove it by pulling, not rubbing it off, using a hand protected by a heavy cloth or towel. Cover the tentacle with sand before removing. Take care not to touch it with an ungloved hand, however, as it still may be capable of stinging. The barbed spine of a stingray should not be removed by a layperson.

- Watch for signs of a severe reaction. If there is widespread swelling, severe pain, difficulty in breathing, or loss of consciousness, seek immediate medical help.

- If there is no widespread reaction, thoroughly wash the injury and apply alcohol, being careful not to touch the involved area with an unprotected hand. After this, apply a thick coat of a paste of baking soda, which may be scraped off after an hour. Other local remedies that have been recommended include diluted household ammonia, lemon juice, salt water, etc. Local or generalized reactions may be quite severe and uncomfortable and all such stings of significance should be seen in an emergency room. Deaths have been reported from jellyfish or Portuguese man-o'-war bites. Stingrays are equipped with a large, barbed venomous spine that may cause significant cuts. The venom is quite toxic. Immediate care consists of washing the wound and irrigating it thoroughly with salt water, followed by immersion in hot water to deactivate the venom. Transport immediately to an emergency room.

Scorpions and Spiders

Several species of scorpions are found in the United States and Canada. Only two of these are capable of producing significant toxicity by stinging. A scorpion looks something like a small lobster and administers its venom via a stinger on its tail. The scorpions in this country are not as toxic as those found in South America and other parts of the world; a sting may cause swelling and considerable discomfort, but it is rarely fatal. In those few instances when it is, the victim is most likely to be a person who is hypersensitive to the venom or a young child. In any event, a doctor should be seen as soon as possible after a scorpion sting. Follow these first-aid measures:

- Observe carefully for signs of breathing difficulty, visual or speech problems, rapid pulse, convulsions, or signs of impending shock. If breathing and heartbeat stop, start CPR immediately.

- Apply an ice pack or cold water to the bite area to help slow spread of the venom.

- Seek medical care. An antivenin is available for serious scorpion stings, but is unnecessary in most cases.

The two most poisonous spiders in the United States are the female black widow and brown recluse. (Most other spiders in this country are harmless; if they do bite, only a local reaction is likely.) The black widow is a small, black spider with a red hourglass marking on its abdomen. The brown recluse is a small spider with a purple violin-shaped marking on its back. It usually inhabits attics or out-of-the-way places. First-aid measures include the following:

- A bite from a black widow causes little local reaction, but the spider injects a neurotoxin that produces pain, local and regional on one side; muscle spasm, and occasionally paralysis. The victim should be taken to the nearest hospital as soon as possible. Treatment usually consists of administering muscle relaxants and pain medication. An antivenin is available, but in most cases, it is not needed. If shock occurs, treat as instructed in the section on Shock, Chapter 6, page 104.

- The bite of a brown recluse spider may not become apparent for several hours or even days, at which time an enlarging, ulcerating skin lesion appears. This may be followed by fever, nausea, and a body rash. The majority of these bites do not result in serious local or systemic reactions; therefore, the initial treatment involves evaluation in an emergency room followed by conservative measures with close follow-up by a doctor. This is important since in some severe cases, the lesion may continue to erode and ulcerate, necessitating surgery.

Snakebites

More than 45,000 snakebites occur in this country each year, but only about 7,000 of them involve poisonous snakes, causing 3 to 6 deaths. Most of the fatalities are among children or members of snake-handling cults. (In fact, bee stings cause 4 times as many fatalities as snakebites.)

Every state, with the single exception of Alaska, has some variety of poisonous snake. About 60 percent of the venomous snakebites are from rattlesnakes; the rest are from copperheads, cottonmouths or water moccasins, and coral snakes. Although not all bites from poisonous snakes result in release of poison, you must assume that poison is involved and act accordingly. Emphasis is on immediate transport of the snakebite victim to a hospital for antivenin serum as quickly as possible, certainly within 4 hours (the serum is not effective if administered more than 12 hours after the bite). Follow these first-aid measures:

- Reassure the victim and keep him or her supine and as quiet as possible.
- Try to identify the snake (but don't waste time hunting for it). If the bite was inflicted by a foreign snake kept as a pet or in a zoo, its identification is particularly important because it may require a special type of antivenin.
- Do not give the victim anything to eat or drink, especially alcohol.
- Apply a venous tourniquet 2 to 4 inches above the bite. Check to make sure that a pulse is present below the tourniquet. Loosen the tourniquet for a few minutes every 15 to 30 minutes. If swelling occurs at the level of the tourniquet, remove and replace it a few inches above the swelling.
- Place the victim in a position that keeps the bitten part of the body lower than the heart.

Note: Hikers or campers who plan to spend time in a remote area with no easy access to transportation should carry a snakebite kit and be trained in its proper use. Also they should know how to differentiate between the two major types of venomous snakes. All pit vipers—rattlesnakes, copperheads, and cottonmouths—have triangular heads with a pit between the nostril and eye on both sides of the head, elliptical pupils, and two fangs. The coral snake, also called the harlequin or bead snake, is banded in red and black interspersed with white or yellow rings. It has teeth, but no fangs, and a black snout. All pit vipers have the same antivenin, while coral snakes have a different one. (The folk rhyme "Red next to yellow will kill a fellow" is helpful in remembering that coral snakes are very dangerous and in distinguishing it from the more poisonous, banded snakes of similar appearance.)

Ticks

Ticks are parasites that feed on warm-blooded vertebrates. Some ticks are harmless; others carry a variety of diseases, including Rocky Mountain spotted fever and Lyme disease, a form of arthritis, that can be transmitted to humans. Although the name Rocky Mountain implies that this disease is confined

Figure 7.1. **The two major ticks that transmit disease to humans are the wood tick and eastern dog tick. To remove a tick, apply a drop of mineral oil or alcohol, then use a pair of tweezers to remove it from the skin. Make sure that the head is completely removed. Cleanse the area with soap and water and then apply alcohol and, if needed, a Band-Aid.**

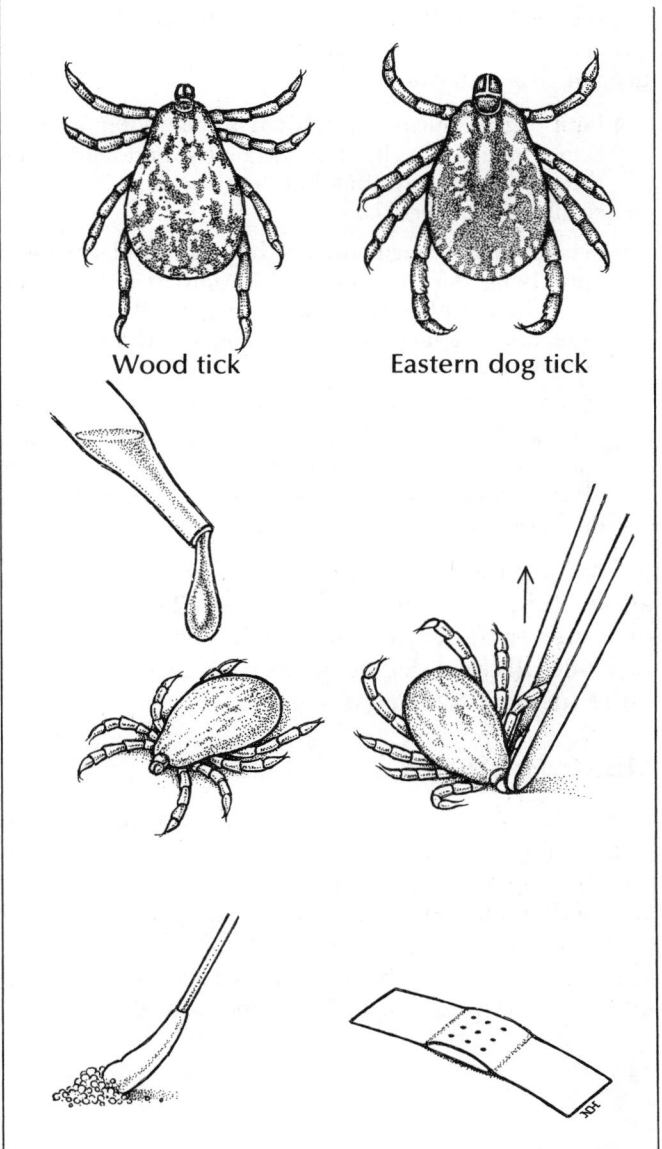

Wood tick   Eastern dog tick

to the West, in fact, it is seen in all parts of the United States, especially the East Coast. The presence of a tick on the skin or any tick bite must be dealt with promptly. Do not try to remove the tick by rubbing or pulling it out. (See figure 7.1.) This may leave the head imbedded under the skin. Instead:

- Cover the tick with a few drops of thick oil—olive or mineral oil will do fine—to suffocate and immobilize it. A few drops of kerosene or gasoline also may be used.

- Then gently remove the tick with a pair of tweezers, taking care to remove the head. Do not handle or crush the tick between your fingers. (Use the same caution in removing ticks from dogs and other pets.)

- Carefully wash the bite area as well as your hands and the tweezers with soap and water. Apply alcohol or hydrogen peroxide to the area and cover with a sterile bandage.

- Consult a doctor to see if further treatment is advised. Be particularly aware of any symptoms such as fever, rash, generalized aches and pains, headaches, or other signs of illness following a tick bite. If symptoms occur, see a doctor at once.

- In areas with heavy tick populations, prevention includes avoiding tick-infested areas, wearing proper protective clothing (long pants, boots, long-sleeved shirt), and daily body inspection for presence of ticks.

BURNS

BURNS CAN BE CAUSED by fire, heated liquids, steam, sun, chemicals, and electricity. In approaching first aid for burns, the source of the injury, extent, and degree of burns should be determined. Burns are generally classified according to their depth and degree of tissue damage.

- First-degree burns are limited to the outer layer of skin (epidermis). The skin will be red and tender and there is usually swelling but no blistering. These generally are not serious.

- Second-degree burns involve both the epidermis and underlying dermis, and in addition to redness and pain, there is blistering. These, too, usually are not serious unless a large area is involved or there is a secondary infection.

- Third-degree burns are always serious. They involve destruction of the full thickness of the skin and also may extend to the underlying tissue. The skin may be blackened or white; there usually is no pain because the nerves have been destroyed.

Widespread first-degree burns (except sunburn), all second-degree burns greater than 2 to 3 inches in diameter or those involving the hands, face, or genitals, and all third-degree burns regardless of size, require medical treatment.

Minor Burns

First aid for a minor burn (e.g., a first-degree sunburn, minor scald, or burn from a hot object) involves easing the pain, if possible by flushing the area with cool water. The burned area can be placed under a running tap, or cool, wet compresses may be applied directly to the skin. This type of burn usually heals without special treatment. Make sure the victim takes plenty of fluids. The use of aloe vera creams and aspirin or acetaminophen (e.g., Tylenol) may alleviate the symptoms more rapidly.

Major Burns

The obvious priority in cases of major burns is to remove the victim from the source of the burn by dousing flames or flushing chemicals off the skin surface. If clothing is ignited, lay the victim down and extinguish flames with water or by covering with a blanket or coat, or by having the victim roll over slowly. Running fans the flames and spreads the burns to the upper body and face. First-aid measures include the following:

- A second-degree burn that covers only a limited area (less than 2 to 3 inches in diameter) usually can be treated at home. Rinse the area with cool water and then gently wash with soap and water and rinse. Spray with an antiseptic spray and cover with a sterile dressing. DO NOT apply ointments, petroleum jelly, margarine, grease, oil, butter, or other home remedies. Avoid breaking blisters, as this increases the risk of infection.

- Larger second-degree and all third-degree burns require medical treatment. In extensive burns, check for any signs of shock and treat appropriately. Then look for other serious injuries and treat appropriately.

- Immerse the burned area in cold water or apply cold compresses briefly to bring skin temperature back to normal. Wrap the victim loosely in a clean sheet and call 911/rescue or, if not available, transport to an emergency room. Do not try to remove burned clothing or objects that adhere to the burned area, and do not apply any ointments or other medication.

- Loss of body fluids, pulmonary complications, and infection are major dangers of extensive burns. All major burns (more than 10 percent of body surface for infants and elderly; more than 20 percent of body surface for adults) should be treated in a specialized burn facility.

Chemical Burns

Follow these first-aid measures:

- Start treatment immediately by placing the burned area under cool running water and continue flushing for at least 15 minutes or longer.

- If the chemical has splashed into the eye, position the injured eye under cool running water. Make sure that the eye is open and the head is positioned so the water will not run into the other eye. (If both eyes are involved, flush them simultaneously by tipping the head back and pouring water onto both.) Continue washing for at least 15 minutes, then cover the eye with a sterile compress and transport to an emergency room.

- If the chemical container contains first-aid instructions, follow them.

- After administering first aid, cover the burn with a cool, wet dressing and transport to an emergency room.

Note: Not all chemicals cause burns. Some, such as liquid hydrocarbon (e.g., Freon) cause freezing instead. In these exposures, the victim should be treated for frostbite. (See section on Frostbite, page 120.) Other chemicals are absorbed through the skin and may produce a toxic reaction. When working with such chemicals, protective gloves and other clothing should be worn, and if the skin is exposed, the area should be washed immediately and the local Poison Control Center consulted for further guidance.

Electrical Burns

Electrical burns may be deceptively deep and should be seen in an emergency room. First-aid measures are the same as for other types of burns. Injuries associated with lightning strikes or contact with high-tension wire may be accompanied by other complications aside from the burn. These include cardiac arrest and long bone or spine fractures, and should be taken into account when dealing with this kind of victim. All electrical burns should be checked by a doctor.

Sunburn

Most sunburns are first-degree burns and, although painful, can be treated at home. If there is widespread blistering, systemic symptoms, or secondary infection, a doctor should be seen. (For information on preventing sunburn, see Chapter 31 on Skin Diseases, page 619.)

CONVULSIONS

EPILEPSY IS a common cause of convulsions; however, seizures that come on suddenly without any prior history of epilepsy may result from a head injury, poisoning, drug overdose, withdrawal from drugs or alcohol, stroke, or other causes. In a young child with a high fever, the convulsions may be due to febrile seizures or a disease such as meningitis. Most seizures last only a short time and stop on their own. Follow these first-aid procedures during the seizure:

- Protect the victim from self-injury by laying the victim down gently, preferably on a soft or padded surface. Turn the head to one side. Keep the airway open. If possible, place a rolled-up handkerchief (not a spoon or other hard object) between the upper and lower teeth to prevent the person from biting his or her tongue. However, do not try to force the mouth open to do this.

- Don't try to restrain the victim while he or she is convulsing unless there is danger of self-injury.

- If vomiting occurs, turn the head so the vomitus is expelled from the mouth and not inhaled into the windpipe and lungs.

- Keep a careful watch and begin mouth-to-mouth respiration if breathing stops more than briefly after a seizure. Make sure the airway is not obstructed. Begin CPR immediately if breathing and pulse are absent at any point.

- If poisoning is suspected, try to identify the source and contact the Poison Control Center for guidance.

- If the convulsions are related to a high fever in infants and children, lower the temperature by using cool compresses, but do not place in a bathtub.

- If the seizure continues for more than a few minutes, or if it recurs in a short time, call for an ambulance.

- Provide first aid for injuries that may have been sustained during the seizure.

After the seizure has stopped, the person will usually be confused or will fall asleep. Note the details of the attack—the presence of antecedent (prodromal) symptoms, the type of seizures (stiffening, jerking, localized, generalized), any deviation of the eyes, the loss of urine or feces—and seek medical attention to determine the cause. Anyone without a history of seizures should be brought promptly to an emergency room.

CUTS, SCRAPES, AND BRUISES

MINOR CUTS AND SCRAPES can be handled with simple first-aid measures. Most can simply be washed with cool water and bland soap and covered with a light protective adhesive bandage (such as a Band-Aid or Telfa strip). If you wish to use an antibiotic or antiseptic, avoid alcohol. Hydrogen peroxide is useful in generating oxygen at the site of the cut, but it is only a weak antiseptic. Stronger substances include iodine complexes such as Betadine and benzalkonium chloride (Zephiran).

Scrapes on the face should be washed, covered with an antiseptic or antibiotic cream, and left unbandaged. Bruises (bleeding into the tissue beneath the outer layer of skin) can be treated with a cold pack, which may reduce swelling.

DIABETIC COMA/INSULIN SHOCK

THERE ARE several types of coma in diabetic patients. One of the most common comes on relatively rapidly and is caused by an excess of injected insulin or other sugar-lowering medication and depletion of blood sugar (hypoglycemia). A second is caused by inadequate insulin, which leads to too much blood sugar (hyperglycemia) and a buildup of acid (keto-acids) in the blood, which leads to ketoacidosis. Both are serious situations, but an excess of insulin with resultant hypoglycemia is of more immediate danger to the patient and requires prompt action. If possible, try to determine whether the loss of consciousness is from too much insulin and low blood sugar or from hyperglycemia, since the treatments for the two are quite different. If you are unable to tell, treat for low blood sugar. In both instances, however, the patient should be brought immediately to an emergency room.

An insulin reaction is heralded by any of a number of rapidly developing symptoms:

- Relatively sudden onset, usually a matter of minutes
- Hunger
- Sweating
- Cold, clammy feeling
- Paleness
- Trembling, anxiety
- Rapid heart beat
- Feeling of weakness or faintness
- Irritability and change in mood or personality
- Loss of consciousness

First aid for an insulin reaction consists of administering a source of quickly absorbed sugar. If the person is still conscious, this can be taken in the form of table sugar, fruit juice, honey, a soft drink containing sugar, or any other sugar source. If the person has lost consciousness, do not try to force sugar or liquid down his or her throat. Honey or granulated sugar or a special capsule (such as D-glucose) containing concentrated sugars, which some diabetics carry, can be carefully placed under the tongue, where it will be absorbed into the body, but this may be difficult to do. In any event, the patient should be taken to a hospital emergency service as quickly as possible since a severe insulin reaction can be fatal.

Signs of hyperglycemia and ketoacidosis include:

- Increased thirst and urination, usually for one to several days. Increasing amounts of sugar are "spilled" in the urine.
- Nausea, vomiting, and abdominal pain
- Feeling of weakness or fatigue
- Dehydration (dry mouth and skin, sunken eyes)
- A fruity breath odor
- Heavy, labored breathing that is also rapid and deep
- Drowsiness or loss of consciousness

Any diabetic patient showing the above symptoms should be brought to an emergency room as soon as possible. (For more details, see Chapter 23, Diabetes and Other Endocrine Disorders, page 474.) Any acute change in alertness, consciousness, or mental status in a diabetic patient warrants immediate attention at a hospital emergency service.

DISLOCATIONS

A DISLOCATION is the disruption by displacement of the normal relationship of two bones in a joint. Dislocations most commonly occur in free-moving joints, such as the jaw, shoulder, elbow, fingers, hip, knee, and ankle. A dislocation may result from a direct blow, hyperextension, a fall, sports injury, or other accident; torn ligaments, damaged blood vessels or nerves and a fracture also may be present. Symptoms include pain, decreased function and deformity in the appearance of the joint. Follow these first-aid measures:

- Splint the joint in the position in which it was found and treat as if it were fractured.
- Improvise a sling if an arm is involved.
- Do not attempt to correct the dislocation or force the bone back into its proper position, as this may cause further injury. The person should be taken to an emergency room immediately for x-rays and treatment.

DRUG WITHDRAWAL

WITHDRAWAL SYMPTOMS may be experienced following chronic use of a wide variety of drugs that result in physical dependence. Common examples include alcohol, sedatives, amphetamines and other stimulants, and narcotics. Some people are able to stop "cold turkey" without withdrawal problems, but this is unusual. Most people need help, both emotional and often pharmacologic, in stopping an addictive substance once they are dependent upon it. This is best administered in an in-patient drug abuse treatment facility or clinic, especially since stopping may bring on withdrawal symptoms which call for special attention. These vary according to the type of drug dependency, but commonly include cold sweats, extreme restlessness, anxiety, nausea, vomiting, delusions, tremor, hallucinations, and, in extreme cases, convulsions. If these symptoms occur, the person should be taken to a hospital emergency service.

FAINTING

FAINTING (SYNCOPE) OCCURS when the blood supply to the brain is briefly inadequate and is restored within a minute or so. There are many causes of fainting, ranging from benign to serious. Some people faint at the sight of blood, after intense pain, emotional shock, or as a result of severe anxiety or fatigue. This is due to reflexes that slow the heart and dilate blood vessels resulting in a fall in blood pressure. Fainting is not uncommon during the early stages of pregnancy. Cardiovascular, neurological, and metabolic (such as hypoglycemia) problems and adverse drug reactions are still other causes of fainting. Anyone who experiences a fainting episode or "blackout" should see a doctor about the cause. Follow these first-aid measures for a fainting episode:

- Make sure the person is lying down on his or her back. Check for breathing and feel *carefully* for a pulse, since it may be slow and weak immediately after a faint. If they are absent, begin CPR. If breathing and pulse are present, raise the legs higher than the head. This promotes the flow of blood to the brain and will quickly revive the person. Loosen clothing and make comfortable.

- When the person revives, color returns to the face, and pulse is normal, suggest lying or sitting quietly for a few minutes before attempting to stand. A weak or "washed out" feeling after a faint is common.

- Determine if there are other symptoms, such as chest pain, palpitations, difficulty breathing, headache, vertigo, weakness, or loss of sensation on one side of the body or difficulty speaking, or an underlying medical condition, such as diabetes or heart disease. If so, or if this is the first episode of fainting or if more than a few minutes elapse before complete recovery, the patient should be transported to a hospital as soon as possible.

- If the faint feeling returns, have the person lie down again.

- Do not give an alcoholic drink or splash cold water on his or her face. A cold compress may be applied to the forehead.

FEVER

THE AVERAGE TEMPERATURE is 98.6°F or 37°C when measured with an oral thermometer. Slight variations in either direction are normal, especially in young children, and are not a cause for concern. An elevation of more than 1 or 2 degrees, however, is a sign of an infection or other illness. The fever may be accompanied by other symptoms or, less commonly, be the only symptom. Most fevers disappear in 1 or 2 days and require no special treatment other than taking plenty of fluids to prevent dehydration and perhaps aspirin or acetaminophen to relieve symptoms. Any high fever (greater than 103°F) or one that is accompanied by recurrent shaking or chills, or one that lasts for several days should be investigated by a doctor. Follow these steps in treating a fever:

- A doctor should be called if a very young baby (less than 1 month old) has a temperature of more than 101°F, especially if there are other symptoms.
- A child with a high fever should be lightly dressed and covered with only a light blanket, if at all.

- If a doctor approves, small amounts of aspirin or acetaminophen may be given to a child, but follow instructions as to dosage. Aspirin should not be given to children with viral illness (flu, chickenpox, etc.), as this may increase the risk of Reye's syndrome.
- If the temperature rises to 103°F, the child should be sponged with lukewarm water, allowing the water to evaporate from the skin surface, or placed in a tub of lukewarm water. Recheck the temperature frequently (every 15 minutes); continue until temperature falls below 102°F. (Do not sponge with alcohol, which has potentially harmful side effects; water is just as effective.)
- If the fever does not respond or the child has a convulsion, a doctor should be consulted.
- A fever accompanied by severe headache, nausea and vomiting, a stiff neck, change in alertness, and hypersensitivity to light may signal meningitis and should be investigated promptly by a doctor.
- Any fever not associated with the usual coldlike or flulike symptoms should be discussed with your doctor.

FOOD POISONING

FOOD POISONING may be caused by eating foods contaminated by bacteria or their toxins or, less commonly, a substance in the food itself, as in certain mushrooms, plants, or some fish. Symptoms include severe stomach cramps, nausea, vomiting, and diarrhea, usually within a few hours after eating the offending substance. In many cases, the substance is eliminated from the body by vomiting or diarrhea; if food poisoning is suspected, steps should not be taken to stop either in the early stages. In some instances, it is desirable to induce vomiting, but frequently, the symptoms do not begin until the food has left the stomach.

Most cases of food poisoning resolve themselves in a few hours or days. Follow these first-aid measures:

- Try to identify the source of the poisoning. If it is mushrooms or canned food, take the person to an emergency room without delay. The same applies if there are any nervous system symptoms, such as difficulty in speaking or swallowing, visual changes, paralysis, or difficulty in breathing.
- If vomiting or diarrhea are severe or prolonged, watch for signs of dehydration. Offer fluids, but do not give food. Antidiarrheal medication may be prescribed by a doctor if diarrhea is persistent.
- Call a doctor or go to a hospital emergency service if the symptoms persist or are severe, or are accompanied by fever, persistent localized abdominal pain, blood in the vomitus or stool, or abdominal distension.

FOREIGN BODIES

In the Eye

In trying to remove a small foreign body from the surface of the eye, take care not to rub the eye. Do not attempt to remove any foreign object that is embedded in the eyeball; instead, cover both eyes with a sterile compress. If there is difficulty closing the eye because of the size of the foreign body, protect with a small paper cup placed over the eye and taped in place and cover the uninjured eye with a

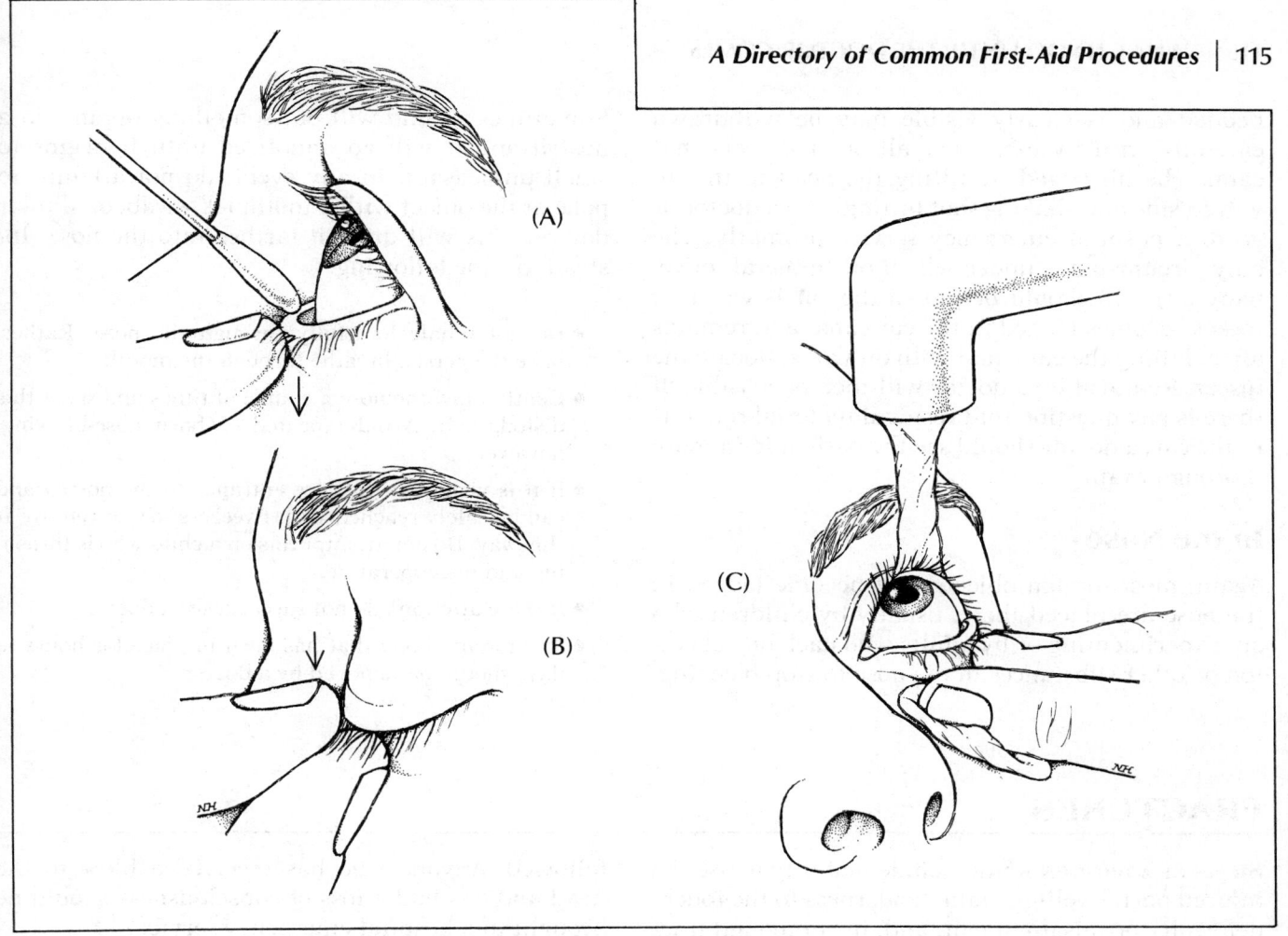

Figure 7.2. **Foreign body in the eye. If the foreign object is on the lower lid (A) gently pull lid down and have the person look upward. Use a moistened cotton swab or corner of a clean handkerchief to remove the object. If the object is not on the lower lid, gently grasp the upper lid (B) and draw it down over the lower. This will produce tears that should wash out the object. Flush out the eye by running lukewarm water directly over it (C).**

sterile compress. Get the person to an emergency room as soon as possible. Small objects on the surface of the eye can be removed as follows:

- Wash the hands carefully before attempting the removal.
- Pull the lower lid down gently so that its lining is visible; at the same time, have the person look upward.
- If the speck is on the surface of the lower lid, lift it off carefully with a slightly moistened cotton swab or the corner of a clean handkerchief or tissue.
- If the speck is not on the lower lid, gently grasp the lashes of the upper lid between the thumb and forefinger and draw the upper lid out and down over the lower one. The resulting tears may flush out a particle adhering to the upper lid.
- If the object has not drifted to the corner of the eye, lift the upper lid (as shown in figure 7.2) and have the person look downward. If the object appears on the inner surface of the upper lid, carefully remove it with a moistened cotton swab or the corner of a clean handkerchief or tissue.

- Flush the eye with lukewarm water or any ophthalmic irrigating solution. If the tearing or pain persists, or if vision does not clear, see a doctor promptly.

Note: If chemicals are accidentally splashed in the eye, tilt the head slightly toward the involved eye and position under a running tap of cool water, or pour water slowly from a glass. Rinse for at least 15 minutes, then go to a hospital emergency service.

In the Ear

The protective structure of the outer ear prevents objects from easily entering its middle and inner parts. However, children in particular often put foreign objects in the ear and there are instances in which bugs or other objects may accidentally enter it. Never attempt to remove a foreign object that has entered the ear canal by poking it with a matchstick, bobby pin, cotton swab, or similar device; this may only push it in farther or cause damage to the middle-ear structure. A soft object that is not deeply embedded and is clearly visible may be withdrawn carefully with tweezers. For all other objects that cannot be dislodged by tilting the head to the involved side and shaking (not hitting), see a doctor or go to a hospital emergency service promptly. The only circumstance under which oil (mineral, olive, baby oil, etc.) should be put in the ear is when an insect becomes lodged in the ear canal and remains alive. Filling the ear canal with oil will suffocate the insect. Removal by a doctor will then be feasible. If there is any question that residual material remains in the ear, a doctor should see the patient for a more thorough exam.

In the Nose

Again, most foreign objects that become lodged in the nose are placed there, usually by children who are experimenting or by adults who pack bits of cotton or other substances in the nose to stop bleeding.

Sometimes a child will put something organic in a nostril and it will go unnoticed until it begins to smell unpleasant. In any event, do not attempt to poke at the object with a toothpick, swab, or similar device. This will drive it farther into the nose. Instead, try the following:

- Do not inhale forcefully through the nose. Rather, have the person breathe through the mouth.
- Gently blow the nose a couple of times and see if this dislodges it. Avoid repeated or hard nose-blowing, however.
- If it is visible at the very entrance to the nostril and can be safely reached with tweezers, try to remove it this way. Do not attempt this on a child who is thrashing and uncooperative.
- If these attempts do not succeed, see a doctor.
- Any foreign body that has been in place for hours to days should be removed by a doctor.

FRACTURES

SIGNS OF A BROKEN BONE include inability to use the injured part, swelling, pain, tenderness to the touch, deformity or misalignment, and, in compound fractures, the bone protruding through the skin. A broken bone also may cause internal bleeding and injury, particularly in the case of broken ribs or pelvis.

First aid involves protecting the bone and body from further damage. No attempt should be made to "set" or straighten a broken bone; it should be splinted where it lies with a minimum of movement. If the bone has pierced the skin, bleeding should be controlled by direct pressure, a sterile dressing placed over the wound, the extremity splinted, and the victim brought to an emergency room. The victim should be observed closely for signs of shock and treated accordingly. First aid for specific types of fractures is described below.

Head Injuries

Head injuries range from bumps and scrapes to scalp lacerations, skull fracture, concussion and other brain injury, and may involve a combination of these. Minor head injuries such as bumps or abrasions, without any of the signs of possible brain injury listed below, can usually be treated by simple first-aid measures. With severe facial or head trauma, a neck injury should always be suspected and the recommendations for neck or back injury

followed. Anyone who has received a blow to the head and has had a loss of consciousness should be brought to a hospital emergency service.

If the victim is conscious and shows no sign of brain or neck injury but is bleeding from the scalp, perform the following first aid.

- Check pulse and respiration. Keep the victim lying down and do not place a pillow or other object under the head.
- Control bleeding by placing clean gauze gently over the injury; gentle direct pressure may be applied. Scalp lacerations tend to bleed profusely because of the large number of blood vessels located there, but bleeding can usually be controlled with pressure. They should be seen by a doctor.

If there are signs of brain injury—change in mental status, such as agitation, confusion, lethargy, or loss of consciousness; vomiting; amnesia about events before or after the head injury; a colorless or blood-streaked discharge from the nose or ears; speech disturbances; convulsions; paralysis; or if the eye pupils are different in size from each other—observe the above precautions. In addition:

- Administer CPR if breathing stops or if there is no heartbeat. If you are trained in CPR, use the chinlift method of mouth-to-mouth breathing if there is the possibility of neck injury.
- Observe precautions for neck or spine injury. The need to keep the neck in alignment with the rest of the spine

in cases of suspected spinal injury cannot be overemphasized.

- Watch for signs of shock. Shock generally indicates that there are other injuries, and may be the result of internal bleeding.
- Keep the victim lying as quietly as possible. Do not move unless absolutely necessary.
- Do not attempt to give any fluids.

Neck or Spine Fracture

A neck or back injury always should be suspected after any accident or fall in which abnormal forces are applied to the back (e.g., driving accident, whiplash, fall from a height and landing directly on feet or back, any accident resulting in serious head and facial trauma). Warning signs include neck or back pain, an odd position of the head or neck, feelings of numbness, weakness or paralysis in an extremity or other part of the body.

If any neck or back injury is suspected, keep the victim absolutely still. Treat where he or she lies un-

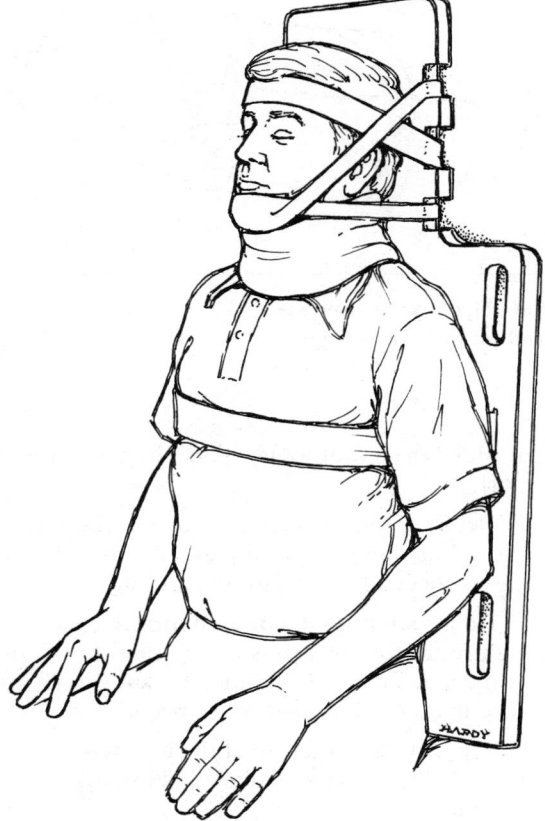

Figure 7.3. **Moving a person with a suspected back or neck injury. Before moving, stabilize the cervical spine (neck) with an improvised collar, such as a heavy towel or scarf, and slide a rigid support (door, board, table leaf) under or behind him. Secure the patient to the board with broad straps, such as wide belts or ties.**

less there is immediate danger of fire, an explosion, or other life-threatening circumstance. If movement is absolutely necessary, do so on a stretcher, board, door, or other firm object. (See figure 7.3.) To prevent the head from rotating during movement, several people should carefully lift and move the victim, making sure that the head and neck are held in a direct, straight line ("neutral position") with the spine, without any forward or backward bending or sideways turning of the head. Follow these first-aid measures:

- Check for vital signs and institute mouth-to-mouth respiration and CPR if necessary.
- Reassure the conscious victim, but do not allow him or her to move head or neck. Immobilize the individual's head and neck in the positions in which they lie. Support the back of the neck by sliding a rolled pad underneath and placing pads, pocketbooks, or other stabilizing items at the sides of the head.
- Summon emergency personnel to transport victim to hospital.

Hip or Pelvis Fracture

These fractures are particularly common in elderly people, and may result from even a minor fall. (In people with severe osteoporosis, thinning of the bones, the fracture may occur spontaneously, causing the fall, and not vice versa.) A person with a suspected fracture of the pelvis should not move, since this can cause damage to the pelvic organs. A fracture should be suspected if there is pain in the hip or groin, lower back or suprapubic area, especially with movement of the leg. Observe these precautions:

- Do not move the victim unless absolutely necessary.
- If movement is necessary, follow the same procedure as outlined for a spinal injury. Do not permit any movement of the torso and legs. With a pelvic fracture, this may be achieved by tying the legs together at the ankles and knees and transporting on a firm surface (backboard). With a hip fracture, the leg may appear to be shortened and rotated out. Do not attempt to straighten it.
- Look for signs of shock and treat appropriately.
- Call an ambulance.

Limb Fracture

A limb fracture should be suspected when there is pain, swelling, distortion, or inability to use the injured part. (See figures 7.4A and 7.4B.) Injuries to the wrist and ankle should be treated the same as the arm or leg until they are x-rayed to determine the extent and nature of the injury. The object of first

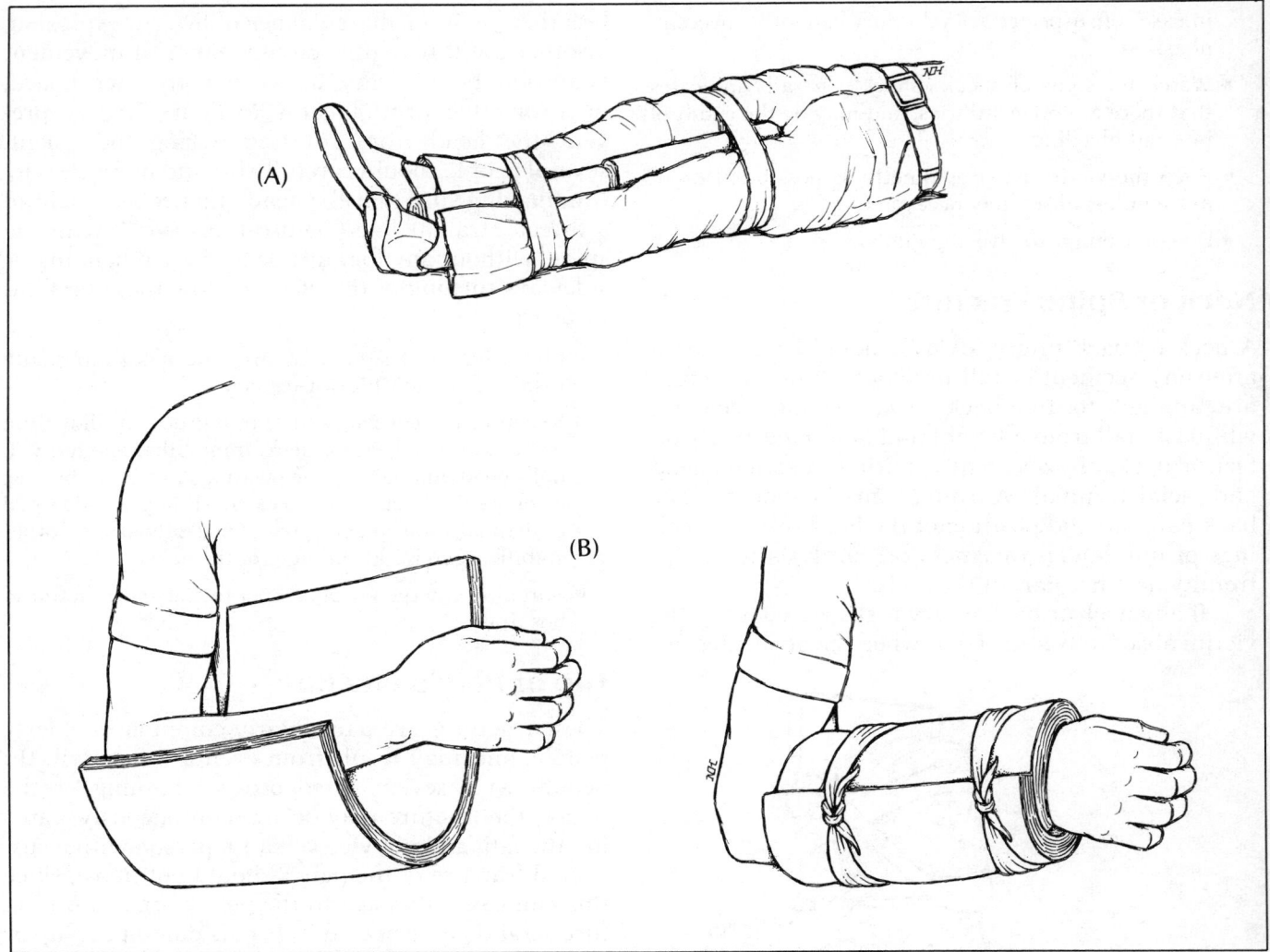

(A)

(B)

Figures 7.4A and 7.4B. **Almost any rigid object can be used for a splint. The examples shown here use rolls of thick newspapers.**

aid is to prevent further injury. Follow these steps:

- If the skin is broken at any point along the arm or leg, stop the bleeding by applying direct pressure. Take care, however, not to move the bone. Cover open fractures with a sterile dressing.

- Do not permit the victim to use or "test" the injured part.

- If the victim is lying down as the result of a fall, do not move, but keep as comfortable as possible by putting a pillow under the head and covering with a blanket.

- Immobilize the injured limb by splinting it in the position in which it is found. Almost anything that is rigid and the right length can serve as a splint: boards, broom handle, cane, branch, or tightly rolled newspapers. In the case of a leg, if a splint is not available, the uninjured leg with a roll of newspapers placed between it and the injured one can be used as a splint. To make a splint:

1. Make the splint longer than the bone it is to support.

2. Before being placed against the fractured bone, the splint should be well-padded with soft material, e.g., a sheet, cloths, items of clothing.

3. Tie the splint to the injured limb snugly but not so tightly that it constricts circulation. Leave the tops of the fingers or toes out and check regularly to make sure that circulation is not impeded.

4. Supporting a fracture of the arm with a sling will often prevent further injury and provide some relief from pain.

Miscellaneous Broken Bones

Almost any bone can be broken: jaw, cheek, nose, and other facial bones; ribs; small bones of the hands or feet, among others. These bones ordinarily do not need to be splinted. If there is bleeding, it should be controlled. Care should be taken in moving or transporting the victim to an emergency room or a doctor who can make the appropriate x-ray studies and initiate treatment.

Note: It usually takes 9 months to 1 year for a broken bone to fully heal in an adult (less time in a child). While it is not necessary to wear a cast for nearly that long, care should be taken to avoid undue stress on the bone during this time.

HEART ATTACKS

A SUSPECTED HEART ATTACK is always a serious medical emergency. The top priority is to get the person to an emergency room or hospital with a coronary care unit where lifesaving procedures can be initiated if need be. Each year, many thousands of people die needlessly from a heart attack because they delayed seeking medical help. Any severe chest pain is a cause for alarm and should be investigated immediately. While it may turn out to be indigestion or from some other cause, only a doctor can make this determination.

Warning signs of a heart attack include:

- Chest pain, which may be intense or dull and which is often described as squeezing, crushing, or a heavy feeling starting under the breastbone or on the left side of the chest and often spreading upward and to the left arm, although the right arm, shoulders, back, neck, and jaw also may be involved. Unlike the pain typical of angina, the pain of a heart attack does not subside with rest, although it may fade only to return with greater intensity.
- Shortness of breath
- Fainting
- Sweating
- Nausea and vomiting
- A feeling of impending doom

If these symptoms occur, an emergency squad should be summoned immediately. If this is not practical, transport the patient to the nearest emergency room yourself. If you suspect you are having a heart attack and no one is available, call for help; do not try to drive yourself. Follow these first-aid steps for heart attacks:

- While waiting for help to arrive, reassure the patient, but observe carefully and do not leave him or her alone.
- Have the patient sit up or lie down, whichever feels more comfortable.
- If a cardiac arrest occurs, start CPR immediately.
- Do not give anything to eat or drink unless specifically instructed to do so.

Other Types of Chest Pain

There are many causes of chest pain other than a heart attack. If the pain is accompanied by coughing and spitting up of blood, pneumonia or some other lung problem may be the cause. A collapsed lung may be signaled by a sudden, sharp pain and shortness of breath. Chest pain that is made worse by movement or a deep breath may be pleurisy or a muscular problem. Indigestion and hiatus hernia are still other common causes for chest pain. Any suspicious chest discomfort should be investigated promptly by a doctor.

NOSEBLEEDS

NOSEBLEEDS ARE COMMON, usually harmless, occurrences. Most are caused by a minor injury or by picking the nose. A nosebleed also may occur after a few days of nose-blowing during a cold or upon arrival in a high altitude area. Most will stop within a few minutes and require no further treatment. The following steps are effective in treating nosebleeds:

- Have the person sit down with the head angled slightly forward so that the blood doesn't run back into the throat. Swallowed blood may make the person nauseated or gag.

- If the blood is coming from only one nostril, press it firmly toward the midline; if in both, pinch them together. Maintain this pressure for about 5 to 10 minutes.

- If the bleeding continues when the pressure is released, insert a twist of sterile gauze or a twisted piece of clean cloth torn from a handkerchief or similar material into the nostril. Make sure that the end protrudes for easy removal. Do not use absorbent cotton or facial tissue since these are hard to remove.

- Repeat the pressure for about 10 minutes, encouraging the person to breathe through the mouth.

- If bleeding has stopped, the packing may be gently removed after 30 to 60 minutes. The nose should not be blown during that period, even gently, as this may cause the bleeding to resume.

- If the bleeding cannot be controlled within 20 or 30 minutes or if the nosebleeds recur frequently, a doctor should be seen.

- If the bleeding is a result of direct trauma to the nose, only gentle pressure should be applied and the nose should not be packed.

- If there is persistent bleeding, swelling, change in shape or alignment of the nose, or clear fluid discharge from the nose, the injury should be checked at a hospital emergency service.

OVEREXPOSURE

OVEREXPOSURE TO EXTREMES of temperature is often a matter of carelessness or a disregard of the obvious dangers of environmental climactic extremes. The very young, the old, the chronically ill, alcoholics, and drug abusers, and outdoor enthusiasts are especially vulnerable to overexposure.

Frostbite

Frostbite occurs with prolonged exposure to subfreezing temperatures. The risk increases as the temperature declines or the wind-chill factor increases. The most obvious signs of frostbite are progressive, painful loss of feeling leading to numbness, a white or blue appearance of the skin, firmness of the skin to the touch, and loss of function. Do not rub or massage the frostbitten area with anything, particularly snow, as is so often touted in home remedies. Rubbing increases the danger of tissue damage, and snow, of course, adds to the freezing. By the same token, frostbitten skin should not be exposed to intense heat from a stove, radiator, open fire, heating pad, or the like. Follow these first-aid measures:

- If aid must be administered out-of-doors, gently wrap the affected parts in a blanket, dry clothing, or several layers of newspaper.

- If treatment must be undertaken outside a hospital setting, bring the patient indoors and begin warming the frostbitten parts immediately, by immersing in warm water at a temperature of 100 to 106°F. Rewarming may take 45 minutes to 1 hour. Successful rewarming leads to progressive return of function, color, and sensation, and may result in blistering, which is normal. This process may be very painful; aspirin or acetaminophen may be given.

- If a hot beverage is available (e.g., coffee or tea), offer if the person is fully awake. Do not give alcohol.

- When the skin has been warmed, blisters may appear, but do not touch or attempt to burst them.

- Apply dry, sterile gauze for protection.

- Bring victim to an emergency room as soon as possible to evaluate the extent of damage and to determine what further treatment is appropriate.

- During transport, avoid refreezing of frostbitten part.

- Treatment of hypothermia takes precedence over treatment of frostbite.

Severe Exposure—Hypothermia

Hypothermia is the term for subnormal body temperature. Accidental hypothermia, seen most often in the very young, the old, alcoholics, and drug abusers, occurs after prolonged exposure to cold temperatures. Anyone with frostbite should be suspected of and treated for hypothermia.

In accidental hypothermia, the body temperature is increasingly lowered. The victim usually first develops severe shivering and difficulty walking and speaking, then becomes progressively confused and drowsy, and may lapse into a coma. In extreme cases, death from cardiac arrest may occur. Follow these first-aid measures:

- Check vital signs and administer CPR if indicated.

- Wrap victim in warm blankets or clothes and remove immediately to a warm shelter.

In mild hypothermia (body temperature 90° to 95°F), the person is conscious, alert, and shivering. Wrap in blankets and give a warm, nonalcoholic drink. Be aware that most household thermometers don't register below 94°F and may conceal a case of even mild hypothermia.

With more severe hypothermia (body temperature below 90°F), the patient usually stops shivering and has an altered mental status ranging from loss of alertness to unconsciousness. He or she should be transported immediately to a medical facility. If one is not available, transport to warm shelter, remove wet clothing, and wrap in warm blankets. Be careful to avoid jostling the patient when covering and transporting. Hot-water bottles and body-to-body transfer of heat may be useful as well. There is some risk of further transient decline in temperature, as well as shock, in the process of rewarming. The process may take several hours, but it can be successful, even in cases of prolonged exposure. It is a tricky, difficult procedure, however, and should only be attempted by a layperson if no medical help is available.

Sun and Heat

Overexposure to heat and humidity may lead to heat cramps, heat exhaustion, or, more seriously, heat stroke. These are three different conditions that require different treatments. All can be prevented if proper precautions are taken.

Heat Cramps. Heat cramps occur as a result of salt and water losses through sweating. Replenishing supplies of salt and water should alleviate the cramps. Stretching the cramped muscle may give immediate relief.

Heat Exhaustion (Heat Prostration). The victim will be pale, the temperature will be normal or only modestly elevated (up to 102°F), and the skin will be damp. There may be nausea, weakness, light headedness, and, in some cases, fainting, but not prolonged loss of consciousness. Painful cramps may occur after strenuous activity. Follow these first-aid measures:

- Move the victim to a cool, shady, or air-conditioned place and have him or her lie down with feet elevated.
- Loosen or remove most of the clothing.
- Administer fluids. If possible, give ½ teaspoon of salt

dissolved in a quart of cold (not iced) water or fruit juice, over a period of 30 minutes.

Heat Stroke (Sun Stroke). This is a medical emergency that occurs most often in hot, very humid weather. In classic heat stroke, which usually affects the elderly and debilitated, the victim will feel hot to the touch and the skin will be red and dry. The body's internal cooling mechanism has ceased to function; therefore, there is no sweating and body temperature is dangerously high (104°F or more). In exertional heat stroke, heat production exceeds loss and the internal temperature rises. This is the type of heat stroke seen in healthier victims, such as athletes and military recruits, and it may be accompanied by sweating.

Other symptoms of heat stroke include rapid heartbeat, confusion, agitation, lethargy, stupor, and loss of consciousness. Medical help should be summoned at once and the patient transported to an emergency room. While waiting for an ambulance:

- Move the victim indoors to an air-conditioned area or to a shady place.
- Cool the victim down by covering with sheets and soaking with cold water. A fan will help increase heat loss.
- If a thermometer is available, check the victim's temperature and stop cooling measures when it reaches 102° F.

Heat stroke can be prevented by exercising commonsense precautions during hot, humid weather. Wear light clothes, drink plenty of fluids, and avoid overexposure to the sun. Take a cool bath or shower once or twice daily; seek air-conditioned places for rest. Strenuous activity also should be avoided, especially during the hottest hours of the day. Be especially careful if you have certain types of chronic diseases (cardiovascular, neurological, or dermatological) or if you are taking certain types of medications (diuretics, phenothiazines, etc.). For more information, see Chapter 40, The Proper Use of Drugs, page 772.

POISON IVY

POISON IVY, poison sumac, and poison oak are the most common plants producing an allergic contact dermatitis—rash, itching, and blisters—in the majority of people exposed to them. In addition, some

people suffer more severe reactions, characterized by generalized swelling, headache, fever, and malaise. The best approach is to know how to recognize these plants and to avoid all contact with them. (See

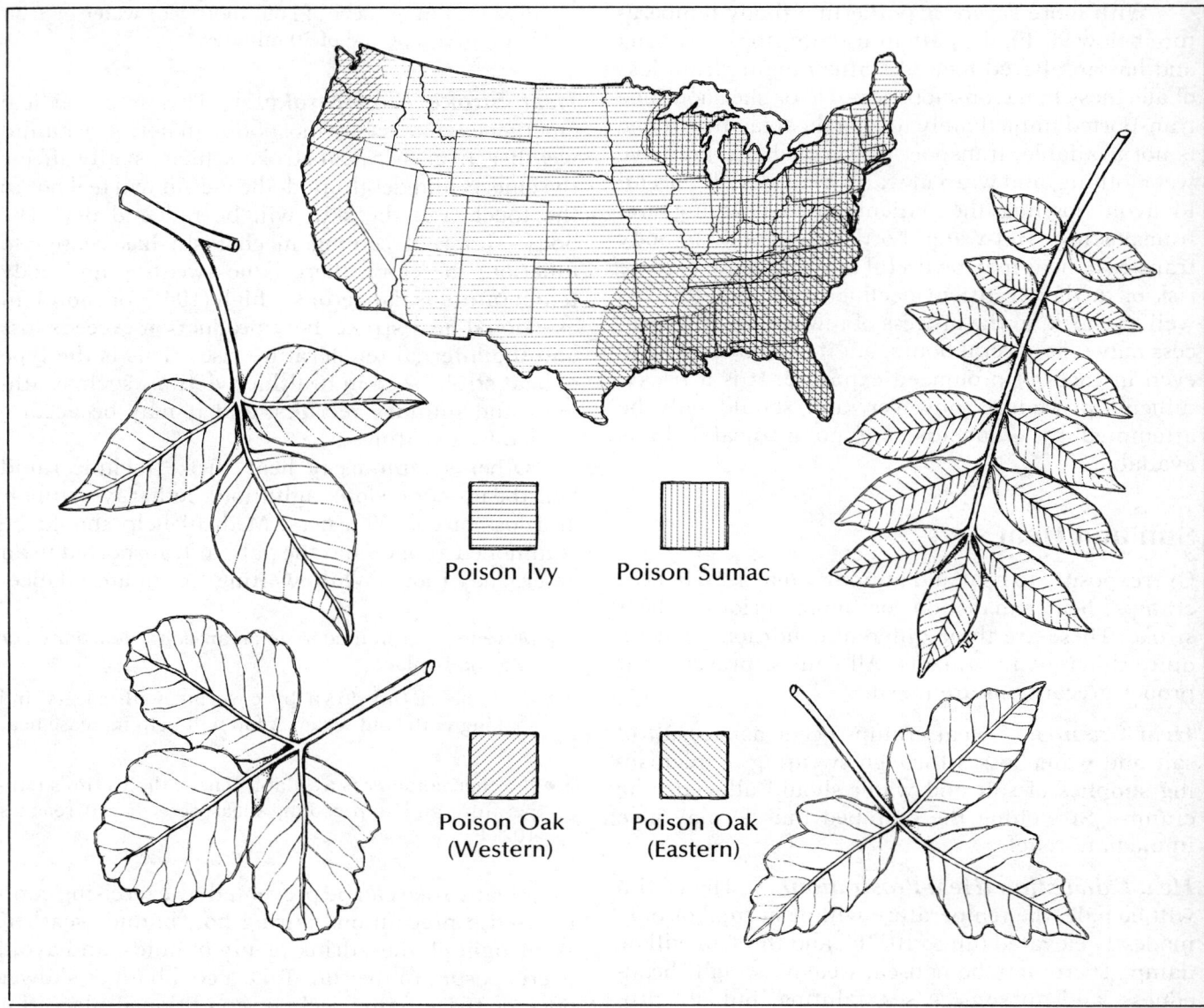

Figure 7.5. **Distribution of poison ivy, sumac, and oak in the United States.**

figure 7.5.) If exposure does occur, follow these steps:

- Remove contaminated clothing (including shoes) and wash all exposed areas thoroughly with a strong soap. Apply alcohol and then rinse with water.

- If a rash appears, apply calamine or other soothing lotion. Corticosteroid creams or lotions also will ease itching and swelling, but should be used according to instruction, should only be applied to limited areas and should not be used on young children.

- Weeping or oozing blisters should be covered with sterile gauze moistened with a mild solution of 1 tablespoon of baking soda in 1 quart of water.

- If fever or severe symptoms such as widespread rash or involvement of mouth, eyes, or genitals occur, see a doctor.

RAPE

IN RECENT YEARS, more attention has been focused on the problems of rape and sexual abuse of children. There is now greater awareness of the importance of sensitive treatment of rape victims, not only by medical personnel but also by police officials, the courts, friends, and family members. Observe these steps in caring for victims of rape and other sexual abuse:

• The victim should be assured that she is safe from further harm from her attacker.

• Injuries, such as bleeding and fractures, should be treated appropriately, but the woman should not wash or douche until seen by a doctor, as this may destroy evidence of the attack.

• The victim should be encouraged to go to a hospital emergency service as soon as possible and also to report the attack to the police. Choose a hospital that offers not only immediate medical and gynecological evaluation, but also psychological support, as well as follow-up services in all these areas. If possible, accompany her and be willing to offer further assistance and support. At the hospital, she will be checked and treated for any internal as well as external injuries. Vaginal and other specimens will be taken for evidence. Follow-up will include tests for pregnancy and venereal disease.

• If the victim is a child, prompt medical evaluation is essential. The youngster also may need extra counselling by an expert in dealing with child abuse, especially if the attack was committed by a family member or friend.

SPRAINS

A SPRAIN is an injury to the ligaments, the fibrous tissue that connects the bones at a joint. A sprain may be relatively mild or quite severe, depending upon how badly the joint was wrenched and whether the ligaments were only stretched or were torn. A serious sprain usually cannot be readily distinguished from a fracture until x-rays are taken; therefore, first aid should be similar to that of a fracture. For a less serious sprain that does not involve a torn ligament or fracture, do the following:

• Eliminate all stress on the injured part.

• Keep the sprain raised, using pillows or a sling.

• Apply an ice pack or cold, wet compresses to the injured part for several hours to keep swelling down.

• After the first 24 hours, heat may be applied. The injured part should not be used until pain and swelling subside, usually within a couple of days. If pain and swelling persist longer than this, consult a doctor.

• Apply an elastic bandage properly to provide support and immobilization without excessive compression.

• If there is pain with swelling, discoloration, or deformity, consult a doctor.

SUMMING UP

FIRST-AID PROCEDURES can be lifesaving in many different situations and, clearly, everyone over a certain age should know basic life-support techniques and other procedures. In many instances, knowing what not to do is just as important as knowing what to do. Each family member old enough to use a telephone should be instructed in how to summon help in an emergency situation, and numbers of the local Emergency Medical Service and Poison Control Center should be permanently affixed to all household telephones.

As stressed throughout this section, most accidents can be prevented. The checklists outlined in the section on Accident Prevention and Safety Precautions (Chapter 5, page 76) provide a good starting point for your family safety program. Households with young children or older people need extra precautions. The room-by-room survey of major safety features is designed to give families guidance in home safety, which extends to the yard and other areas.

This chapter is intended to outline the major first-aid procedures and preventive techniques. It is not intended to cover the hundreds of different emergency situations that may arise, but instead, to give the basic principles that should enable readers to evaluate and cope with the most common medical emergencies.

8 Poisoning

Kenneth C. Fine, M.D.

INTRODUCTION

MORE THAN 7 MILLION accidental poisonings are reported each year, with more than three-fourths involving children under the age of 5. Although most poisonings are accidental, a substantial number involve deliberate suicide or homicide attempts. Childhood poisonings have been reduced dramatically since the widespread use of childproof tops for most drug containers sold in this country, but children remain the most common victims. The aged are the second most commonly affected group; failing eyesight, the use of multiple drugs, and confusion or difficulty in remembering whether a medication was taken are among the causes of accidental poisoning in older people.

Drug overdoses among drug abusers are increasingly common incidents, affecting all classes and age groups. Mixing drugs and alcohol or the unwitting use of drugs that interact with each other are still other sources of accidental poisonings.

This section concentrates mostly on ingested poisons; inhalation and chemical spills are discussed elsewhere.

MEDICATIONS AS POISONS

ALMOST ANY MEDICATION taken in a large enough quantity can have a toxic effect. Aspirin remains one of the leading causes of accidental poisoning in young children, although this has diminished because of childproof containers. Acetaminophen (Tylenol, Anacin III, etc.) is an increasingly frequent source of acute poisoning. Other over-the-counter drugs, including sleep aids and antihistamines, can be toxic as well. With some drugs, the margin between therapeutic and toxic doses is relatively small; taking a few extra sleeping pills, for example, may be sufficient to result in coma. Altered metabolism of medications in the elderly may narrow the therapeutic margin. The need to follow label or physician instructions in taking any medication cannot be overemphasized. Leftover prescription drugs almost always should be discarded unless they are medications taken for chronic or recurring conditions. Prescriptions should not be shared, and great caution should be exercised in taking more than one drug at a time, including over-the-counter medications, birth control pills, and vitamin preparations

—things people often forget when listing their medications.

Many accidental poisonings in children involve drugs, usually those taken by their parents. As emphasized elsewhere, all medications should be stored in a safe place where children cannot get them. People often overlook the drugs left on a nightstand, in a pocketbook, refrigerator, or other unlikely places, but young children have been victims of poisoning from taking medications left in such spots.

The elderly or people with failing memories or eyesight may need extra help in keeping track of and in taking prescribed medication. Color-keyed labels, a large-print medication calendar, or a preset alarm may be helpful, but often the best solution is to have a family member, neighbor, or other reliable person supervise the medication ingestion.

There is no such thing as a "universal antidote" for poison. If an accidental ingestion occurs, call your local or regional Poison Control Center for specific information and instructions.

ACIDS AND ALKALIS

ACIDS AND ALKALIS are found in many household cleaners, such as lye, bleaches, and toilet bowl or drain and oven cleaners and such preparations as hair straighteners. Their labels are almost always marked as "poisonous if ingested," and since they clearly are unappetizing, many people don't think of them as potential dangers. But each year, young children are rushed to emergency rooms after drinking one of these products. Sometimes the poison has been decanted into another more familiar container, such as a milk bottle or soft-drink bottle, and consumed by mistake. Also, many of the original containers look very much like they might contain something good to eat or drink, at least to the eye of a young child. In any event, accidental poisoning from these household products can be prevented by making sure they are stored in a place that is inaccessible to children.

These are serious ingestions. If they occur, take the victim immediately to a hospital emergency service. Do not induce vomiting. For alkali ingestion, have the victim take milk and swallow if possible, or swish it in the mouth once and spit it out. For acid ingestion, transport immediately to a hospital emergency service.

POTENTIALLY POISONOUS SUBSTANCES COMMONLY FOUND ABOUT THE HOUSE

Ammonia	Diuretics	Laxatives	Rat poison
Acetaminophen	Drain cleaner	Lighter fluid	Room deodorizer
Aspirin	Fabric softener	Liquor	Rubbing alcohol
Bicarbonate of soda	Floor wax	Metal polish	Shampoo
Bleach	Furniture polish	Nail varnish	Shoe polish
Carpet cleaner	Hairspray	Oven cleaner	Sleeping pills/sleep aids
Cement and glue	Headache remedies	Paint	Tranquilizers
Contraceptive pills	Heart medicines	Paint thinner	Turpentine
Deodorants	Houseplants	Paraffin	Vitamins
Depilatories	Ibuprofen	Perfume	Window cleaning fluid
Detergents	Insecticides	Permanent-wave	
Diet pills	Iodine	solutions	

PESTICIDES

COMMON EXAMPLES of pesticide poisoning include accident ingestion of rodent pellets; ant, roach, and other bug poisons; garden sprays; and farm chemicals. Skin contact with these liquid or powdered products may also produce toxicity. Avoid the use of pesticides in households where there are young children and certainly never have them sitting around. If a pesticide must be used, do so when children will be away for a few days and make sure that it is a type that does not leave a harmful residue. As with all other poisonous products, pesticides should be stored in their original containers in a childproof place. If ingestion occurs, call your Poison Control Center immediately for instructions or take the child to a hospital emergency service. There are specific antidotes for this type of serious poisoning.

PETROLEUM PRODUCTS

POISONOUS PETROLEUM PRODUCTS include gasoline, kerosene, benzene, mineral seal oil, furniture polishes, paint thinners, and other solvents. In recent years, inhaling or sniffing some of these products has become popular among young people, especially drug users, because the fumes can produce a "high." This can be a deadly practice, as evidenced by the number of young people who have died from cardiorespiratory problems or suffered severe liver damage from sniffing liquid paper, glue, carbon tetrachloride, and other petroleum-based chemicals. Household petroleum products also should be stored out of the reach of children. If accidental ingestion occurs, call your local Poison Control Center for specific instructions. Serious pulmonary problems may accompany certain types of poisoning. Do not induce vomiting unless specifically instructed to do so.

POISONOUS PLANTS

THERE ARE MORE THAN 700 plant species in the United States that can cause poisoning if some part of them is swallowed. In some cases, the entire plant is poisonous. In others, there are some edible parts and some that are poisonous: in some, it may be the bulb (e.g., tulips or narcissus); in others, the berries or seeds (mistletoe berries, apple or apricot seeds); and in still others, the flower (jasmine), leaves (tomatoes or rhubarb), or roots.

Surveys have found that plants are second only to medicines as the cause of serious poisoning in children under 5. The problem is increasing, according to Poison Control Centers, because of the growing popularity of houseplants, and also the number

COMMON POISONOUS PLANTS

There are hundreds of poisonous plants in the United States. Following are some of the more common ones that are grown in gardens or used as houseplants.

Autumn crocus	Delphinium	Jimson weed (also	roots; only the stalk
Azalea	Dieffenbachia (also	called thornapple)	is edible)
Belladonna	called dumbcane)	Lantana	Monkshood
Bird-of-Paradise (seed	English ivy (berries and	Larkspur	Mountain laurel
pod)	leaves)	Lily-of-the-Valley	Poison hemlock
Buttercups	Foxglove	Manchneel	Pokeberry
Cassava	Grass peavine	Mistletoe (berries)	Purple locoweed
Castor bean	Holly (berries)	Oleander	Rapeweed
Chinaberry	Horse chestnuts	Philodendron	Skunk cabbage
Chinese evergreen	Hyacinth (bulbs)	Poinsettia	Sweet pea
Christmas pepper	Hydrangea	Potato (sprouts, roots,	Tomato plant leaves
Corncockle	Iris	and vines; only the	Water hemlock
Daffodil (bulb)	Jack-in-the-pulpit	tuber is edible)	Wisteria (seeds)
Daphne	Jasmine (flowers)	Rhododendron	Yew (needles, bark,
Deadly nightshade	Jerusalem cherry	Rhubarb (leaf and	seeds, and berries)

of families who make foraging for wild food a hobby. Wild mushrooms are particularly notorious. Although only about 100 of the 5,000 species of mushrooms found in the United States are poisonous, some of these, such as the amanitas, are particularly deadly.

Before acquiring a houseplant, make sure that no part of it is poisonous to either humans or pets. (Cats and dogs frequently like to chew on plant leaves, and although most will avoid poisonous plants, kittens and puppies may not be so wise.) Be especially wary of plants like the Jerusalem cherry that have an appetizing appearance, but highly poisonous fruits or berries.

In foraging for food, for example, during a hiking or camping trip, don't eat anything that you are unsure about. And don't let children nibble on anything that grows wild, including berries you know are safe. Many wild berries look alike and you can't expect a child to make such distinctions when you are not around. The box on page 126 lists some of the more common poisonous plants.

INDUSTRIAL POISONS

INCREASING ATTENTION AND CONCERN are being focused on the problem of industrial poisons that are finding their way into food and water supplies. In most instances, the effects are apt to be delayed, and can take the form of cancer or other diseases. But in some, the toxic effects show up relatively rapidly and may cause irreversible damage or death. Poisonings from lead, mercury, and other heavy metals are good examples. A few years ago, a number of mercury poisoning cases in Japan were traced to eating fish taken from waters contaminated by industrial waste. Lead poisoning among children remains a serious problem in the United States, not only from the practice of eating flaking paint chips that contain lead, but also from exposure to industrial wastes near factories where lead is used.

Avoiding exposure is often difficult, since individuals have little or no control over such contamination. If lead or other such poisoning is suspected, especially in a child, a toxicologist or other expert should be consulted for evaluation and treatment. In cases of suspected environmental contamination, the Environmental Protection Agency should be notified.

HANDLING POISONING EMERGENCIES

THE FIRST STEP in handling poisoning emergencies is to call the local Poison Control Center. (A directory of such centers is included at the end of this book, see Appendix A, page 838; the number is also listed in the telephone book white pages or may be obtained from Information.) This number should be affixed to all telephones and posted in a conspicuous place, such as a bulletin board next to a telephone. All family members should know when and how to call this number; it also should be called to the attention of babysitters.

In calling the Poison Control Center, be prepared to give as much information as possible. The person answering the phone will want to know your name, location, and telephone number so he or she can call back in case you are disconnected, or can summon help if needed. Give the name of the substance ingested and, if possible, the amount. If the bottle or package is available, give the trade name and ingredients, if they are listed. Note, too, any specific instructions for poisoning, including antidotes.

Describe the state of the poisoning victim. Is the person conscious? Are there any symptoms? Vomiting? Convulsions? Altered mental state? Using this information, the poison center specialist can give specific first-aid instructions. The majority of the cases called into Poison Control Centers can be handled at home if instructions are followed promptly and correctly.

First aid for a poisoning emergency follows the same priorities for any injury:

- Check first for vital signs and, if they are absent, institute mouth-to-mouth respiration or CPR.

- If the victim is having convulsions, treat as outlined on page 111.

- Follow whatever instructions were communicated by the Poison Control Center.

If you are unable to reach a Poison Control Center or a local hospital emergency department for advice (e.g., a telephone is not available), you must decide whether to attempt to dilute the poison, or induce vomiting, or do nothing but rush the person to the nearest emergency room. All households, especially those with children, should have on hand ipecac syrup, which induces vomiting. Follow these steps in the absence of specific instructions from a Poison Control Center:

- Determine the nature of the ingested substance. If there are no visible bottles or other clues, examine the mouth for signs of burns, which would indicate an acid or alkali. Smell the breath for a petroleumlike odor. DO NOT induce vomiting if either a corrosive substance (drain cleaner, lye, bleach, or other acid or alkali product) or a petroleum product is suspected. Vomiting up a corrosive material will cause further burning and tissue damage. Vomiting a petroleum product carries the danger of inhaling it into the lungs, causing chemical pneumonia. Diluting the poison by administering ½ to 2 glasses of water or milk is advised for many substances. Milk is recommended for acid and alkali ingestion if the person can swallow.

- If the ingested substance is a drug, poisonous plant, or pesticide, the best advice is usually to dilute by giving water or milk, and then to induce vomiting. This can be done by giving 1 or 2 tablespoons of ipecac syrup (see label instructions for dose) followed by water or milk. This may be repeated once in 15 to 20 minutes if the first dose does not induce vomiting. Vomiting also can be induced by inserting a spoon or, if none is available, a finger, at the back of the throat to produce a gag reflex. Collect a specimen of the vomitus for analysis. The patient should be lying on the stomach or side with the head low, not lying on the back, or if sitting, keep the head down.

- Do not induce vomiting if the person is unconscious or appears to be losing consciousness or if the nature of the ingested substance is unknown.

- Take the poisoning victim, along with the bottle or container of whatever was ingested, and any vomitus to the nearest hospital emergency department for further treatment.

A CAUTION ON HERBS AND HERB MEDICINE

HERBS ARE mankind's oldest remedies, and many are still used as the basis for modern medicine. But many herbs are also deadly; others are not particularly harmful, but neither do they possess any great healing or curative powers. A medicinal herb should be treated like any medication: Do not take it unless you check with your doctor. Be wary of herbalists and home herbal remedies and never try brewing your own. Many plants look alike, and a deadly poison can easily be mistaken for one that is harmless. For example, one bite of water hemlock, which looks very much like parsley, chervil, or coriander (all harmless), can be fatal. Following is a list compiled by the Food and Drug Administration of toxic herbs and their effects.

Common names	Botanical name of plant source	Remarks
Bittersweet. Woody nightshade. Climbing nightshade.	*Solanum dulcamara* L.	Contains the toxic glycoalkaloid solanine; also solanidine and dulcamarin.
Bloodroot. Red puccoon.	*Sanguinaris canadensis* L.	Contains the poisonous alkaloid sanguinarine and other alkaloids.
Buckeyes. Horse chestnut.	*Aesculus hippocasteranum* L.	Contains a toxic coumarin glycoside, aesculin (esculin).
Burning bush. Wahoo.	*Euonymus atropurpureus* Jacq.	The poisonous principle has not been completely identified. Laxative.
Deadly nightshade.	*Atropa belladonna* L.	Contains the toxic solanaceous alkaloids hyoscyamine, atropine, and hyoscine.
European mandrake.	*Mandragora officinarum* L.	The plant is a poisonous narcotic similar in its properties to belladonna. Contains the alkaloids hyoscyamine, scopolamine, and mandragorine.
Heliotrope.	*Heliotropium europaeum* L.	Contains alkaloids that produce liver damage.

Common names	Botanical name of plant source	Remarks
Hemlock. Poison hemlock. Spotted hemlock. California or Nebraska fern.	*Conium maculatum* L.	Contains the poisonous alkaloid coniine and four other closely related alkaloids. Produces trembling, muscular weakness, slowed heartbeat, coma, and death.
Henbane. Black henbane. Hog's bean. Poison tobacco. Devil's eye.	*Hyoscyamus niger* L.	Contains the alkaloids hyoscyamine, hyoscine (scopolamine), and atropine. A poisonous plant.
Indian tobacco. Wild tobacco. Asthma weed. Emetic weed.	*Lobelia inflata* L.	A poisonous plant that contains the alkaloid lobeline plus a number of other pyridine alkaloids. Extracts of the leaves or fruits may produce vomiting, sweating, pain, paralysis, depressed temperatures, rapid but feeble pulse, collapse, coma, and death.
Jalap root. Jalap. True jalap. Jalapa. Vera Cruz jalap. High John root. (Possibly also known as High John the Conquerer. John Conqueror. St. John the Conqueror root. Hi John Conqueror.)	*Exagonium purga* (Wenderoth) Bentham. *Ipomoea jalapa* Nutt, and Coxe. *Ipomoea purga* (Wenderoth) Hayne. *Exagonium jalapa* (Wenderoth) Baillon.	A large twining vine of Mexico, this plant has undergone many name changes. Its resin contains a powerful, drastic cathartic.
Jimson weed. Apple of Peru. Jamestown weed. Thornapple. Tolguacha.	*Datura stramonium* L.	Contains the alkaloids atropine, hyoscyamine, and scopolamine. A poisonous plant.
Lily of the valley. May lily.	*Convallaria majalis* L.	Contains the toxic cardiac glycosides convallatoxin, convallarin, and convallamarin.
May apple. American mandrake. Devil's apple. Umbrella plant. Vegetable calomel. Wild lemon. Vegetable Mercury.	*Podophyllum peltatum* L.	A poisonous plant, it contains podophyllotoxin, a complex polycyclic substance, and other constituents.
Mistletoe. American mistletoe.	*Phoradendron flavescens* (Pursh.) Nutt. *Viscum flavescens* (Pursh.)	Contains the toxic pressor amines B-phenylethylamine and tyramine.
Morning glory.	*Ipomoea purpurea* (L.) Roth	Contains a purgative resin. In addition, the seeds contain amides of lysergic acid but with a potency much less than that of LSD.
Periwinkle.	*Vinca major* L. and *Vinca minor* L.	Contains pharmacologically active, toxic alkaloids such as vinblastine and vincristine that have cytotoxic and neurological actions and can injure the liver and kidneys.
Pokeweed. Scoke. Pigeonberry.	*Phytolacca americana* L.	Contains unidentified toxic substances. Produces gastrointestinal cramps, vomiting, and diarrhea.
Scotch broom. Irish broom. Broom.	*Cytisus scoparius* (L.) Link.	Contains toxic sparteine, isosparteine, and other alkaloids; also hydroxytyramine.
Spindle-tree.	*Euonymus europaeus* L.	Violent purgative.
Sweet flag. Sweet root. Sweet cane. Sweet cinnamon.	*Acorus calamus* L.	Oil of calamus. Jammu variety is a carcinogen. FDA regulations prohibit marketing of calamus as a food or food additive.
Tonka bean. Tonco bean. Tonquin bean.	*Dipteryx odorata* (Aubl.) Willd. *Coumarouna odorata* (Aubl.) and *Dipteryx oppositifolia* (Aubl.) Willd. *Coumarouna oppositifolia* (Aubl.)	Active constituent of seed is coumarin. Causes extensive liver damage, growth retardation, and testicular atrophy in laboratory animals.

Common names	Botanical name of plant source	Remarks
Water hemlock. Cowbane. Poison parsnip. Wild carrot.	*Cicuta maculata* L.	Contains cicutoxin, an unsaturated higher alcohol. It is a violent convulsant which may produce death through respiratory failure within 15 minutes.
White snakeroot. Snakeroot. Richweed.	*Eupatorium rugosum* Houtt	Contains a toxic, unsaturated alcohol, tremetol, combined with a resin acid. Causes "trembles" in cattle; weakness, nausea, and prostration ("milk sickness") in humans who have ingested milk, butter, and possibly meat from poisoned animals.
Wolf's-bane. Leopard's bane. Mountain tobacco.	*Arnica montana* L.	Aqueous and alcoholic extracts of the plant contain choline, plus two unidentified substances that affect the heart and vascular systems. Arnica can produce violent toxic gastroenteritis, nervous disturbances, change in pulse rate, intense muscular weakness, collapse, and death.
Wormwood. Madderwort. Wermuth. Mugwort. Mingwort. Warmot.	*Artemisia absinthium* Linné	Contains oil of wormwood, an active narcotic poison. Oil of wormwood is used to flavor absinthe, an alcoholic liqueur illegal in this country because its use can damage the nervous system and cause mental deterioration.
Yohimbe. Yohimbi.	*Corynanthe yohimbi* Schum. *Pausinystalia yohimbe* (Schum.) Pierre	Contains the toxic alkaloid yohimbine (quebrachine) and other alkaloids.

Part Three

YOUR BODY AND
HOW IT WORKS

9 The Human Body and How It Works

Henry Greenberg, M.D.

INTRODUCTION

THE HUMAN BODY is often likened to a machine, but there is no machine in the world that operates so effectively and efficiently as the body. Most activities and disorders affect the entire body and, through a highly complex internal communications network, the various organ systems work in amazing harmony most of the time. These facts are often lost sight of when we describe a single organ system or disease. While the interdependent relationships become most obvious during the study of illness, they also are an integral part of the healthy organism.

Although medical scientists have been studying the human body for hundreds of years, there is still much that is not fully understood, both about how the body functions normally and about disease processes. On all levels—biochemical, intracellular, mechanical, microscopic, and macroscopic—the body functions as a whole, with each part related to all others and dependent upon an array of support systems.

While we may focus considerable attention on disease and organ dysfunction, the fact remains that for the large majority of us, the body functions very well despite all of the stress and abuse we subject ourselves to. And when illness does occur, the body's tremendous recuperative powers come into play. Many of our most common disorders—colds, headaches, digestive upsets, minor infections—are short-lived and will resolve spontaneously. The exceptions often require only commonsense attention and minimal medical treatment. The more serious life-threatening diseases—heart disease, diabetes, cancer, major infections, among others—are leading causes of death, but most people live many years before experiencing symptoms and often many years after contracting them. In the following chapters, the major organ systems and the common disorders that affect them will be described in detail. Here we will attempt to give a brief overview on how these organ systems work in harmony to sustain life, day-to-day activities, and general good health.

HOW THE ORGAN SYSTEMS WORK TOGETHER

TO GET AN IDEA of how the various body systems work together to accomplish a common activity, let's consider what happens when we eat a meal, such as breakfast. While asleep, before waking and thinking of breakfast, the major organ systems are working in concert, albeit at a low basal level. The circulatory and pulmonary systems are providing the oxygen and other nutrients required by every cell to continue functioning. The endocrine and nervous systems, with their complex, often interrelated communications networks, are regulating such vital functions as heart rate, blood pressure, temperature control, and other involuntary or autonomic processes. Metabolism, while slowed down, goes on and involves virtually every body organ. As dawn approaches, the complex circadian rhythms begin to speed up; hormone levels change and the body begins to "wake up." Sleep becomes lighter, heart and respiratory rates begin to increase, and—sometimes prompted by an alarm clock but often without any external stimuli—we waken to a new day. Since it has been 8 or more hours since the last meal, a feeling of hunger is apt to be one of the earliest sensations. The appetite center, located in the hypothalamus area of the brain, works through an intricate feedback system involving certain hormones, nerves, and sensory organs. Also, the kidneys have been performing their function of removing waste and excess fluid from the blood throughout the night; as a result, the bladder is apt to be full—a message conveyed through the nervous system. During the night, the kidneys process fluid to produce a concentrated and hence low volume of urine to facilitate uninterrupted sleep. The morning urine is darker in color than later in the day, reflecting this process.

Even before breakfast is on the table, the major sense organs—the eyes, ears, nose, and then the tongue and mouth—begin preparing the body to receive the food. The fragrance of cooking food reaches the mucous membrane lining the nose and stimulates olfactory nerve receptors, which transmit the impulse to the brain, where it is recognized as an odor. In response to odor and even just the thought of food, the brain, working through the endocrine and nervous systems, transmits messages to the glands in the mouth and stomach, which increases the flow of digestive juices in anticipation of the food. The message also may prompt a physical response: If the smell says the eggs are burning, we quickly act (requiring the coordinated effort of the nervous and muscle systems) to remove the pan from the stove. If the pan handle is too hot, the nerve endings in the skin trigger an automatic protective reaction; without even thinking, the hand is jerked from the pan before the pain sensation is perceived.

Familiar sounds associated with a meal—for example, juice being poured into a glass or cereal into a bowl—also come into play. The sound vibrations are carried through the outer ear to the eardrum, or tympanic membrane, and then into the middle ear and inner ear to the hairlike nerve cells that transmit the signals to the brain, where the sound is perceived and registered. If the sound says the coffee is boiling over, it will again prompt a coordinated conscious action.

Sight is yet another sensory response that is important in readying the body for a meal. Light from an object—a glass of juice, for example—strikes the lens of the eye and is directed to the retina. The impulse generated by the retina travels along the optic nerve to the brain, where it is perceived. If the image is one of a favorite food, the appetite center and digestive system will be further stimulated.

With the first bite of breakfast, two additional sense organs are stimulated. Food in the mouth comes in contact with the tiny taste buds on the tongue; nerve receptors in these taste organs are transmitted to the brain. All taste sensations are combinations of only 4 basic responses: sweet, sour, salty, or bitter; these plus the food odor produce the recognizable flavor.

Touch is the fifth sensory system involved in eating. The texture and temperature of food touching nerve endings in the tongue and palate further stimulate circulation of blood in the entire digestive system and also help increase the secretion of digestive enzymes.

In a marvelously coordinated, highly complex process that requires little or no conscious effort aside from chewing or swallowing, our breakfast is transformed into the fuel and other nutrients required by all individual cells. Chewing, a conscious effort involving the skeletal muscles of the jaw and mouth and the tongue, coordinated by the nervous systems, begins the actual digestive process. Food is broken down into smaller pieces and mixed with saliva and other digestive juices and mucus in the mouth. This process adds moisture, which makes swallowing easier. Saliva contains an enzyme, ptyalin, that begins to break down starches or complex carbohydrates into simple sugars that can be absorbed easily further along the digestive tract.

From the back of the mouth, food is squeezed through the pharynx, a muscular, funnel-shaped structure, into the esophagus, a foot-long tube that leads to the stomach. In 4 to 8 seconds, the bolus of chewed food passes through the esophagus and into the upper part of the stomach. The muscles in the lower esophagus, unlike those in the jaw, are involuntary and respond automatically to the stimulus of swallowing. An involuntary series of coordinated muscle waves, a process called peristalsis, moves the food through the esophagus and, in fact, the rest of the digestive tract. Rings of muscle that function as a valve between the esophagus and stomach relax to admit the food. These muscular valves then close to prevent a backflow (regurgitation) into the esophagus.

Much of the digestive process occurs in the stomach. Four or 5 times every minute, rippling waves controlled by the autonomic nervous system pass through the muscles of the stomach walls, mixing the food with gastric acids and digestive enzymes, further breaking it down. The food is reduced to a thin liquid mass and the digestive juices break down some of the nutrients into forms that can be utilized by the body. Carbohydrates continue to be broken down in the stomach; gastric juices and enzymes also begin breaking down protein and fat into forms that can be absorbed. This partially digested liquid food mass moves next through the muscular pyloric valve to the duodenum, the initial portion of the small intestine. The emptying of the stomach is a complex act, requiring an integration of feedback messages to and from the brain carried by the vagus nerve as well as by intestinal hormones released by changes in volume and acid levels.

As the food enters the upper part of the small intestine, the hormones that are stimulated by its arrival coordinate the flow of digestive enzymes from the pancreas and of bile from liver and gallbladder. The pancreatic juices and bile give the duodenum its alkaline environment, in contrast to the acidic environment of the stomach. These digestive secretions complete the breakdown of proteins and fats, processes that take longer than the digestion of carbohydrate and its conversion to glucose (blood sugar). The small intestine is about 22 feet long, and as the now liquefied and well-mixed food continues its journey, a steady flow of basic nutrients is available to the body.

The small intestine is lined with villi, fingerlike projections. These villi greatly increase the total surface area of the intestines in much the same way that fjords increase Norway's total coastline. The villi also permit each cell to come in contact with a blood capillary. These microscopic blood vessels are only one cell thick, and permit the direct exchange of biological chemicals between the intestine and the blood. (A similar physiological mechanism to increase the surface area for blood-organ interchange occurs in the lungs and kidneys. Not only does this increase physiologic capacity without increasing organ size, but it also provides a reserve capacity in case disease strikes.)

The digested nutrients pass through the villi; the sugars (from carbohydrates and some protein) and the amino acids (from digested proteins) pass directly into the bloodstream, and are carried to either the liver or muscles to be further metabolized or used as fuel. The digested fats pass from the villi to blood or the lymphatic system and enter the bloodstream through a vein.

Blood rich in digested nutrients flows from the small intestine into the liver, which, acting in concert with the endocrine and other body systems, regulates the amount of nutrients, particularly glucose, that enter the bloodstream for distribution to the individual body tissues. The liver, the largest of the internal organs, carries on a number of highly complicated chemical processes. It produces bile from old blood cells, which are being reprocessed. One of the breakdown products of hemoglobin gives bile and hence the stool its brown color. Bile is essential to the digestion of fats. The liver also manufactures a number of other substances, including cholesterol,

enzymes, vitamin A, blood coagulation factors, and complex proteins. The liver also acts as a storehouse for blood, certain vitamins and minerals, and fuel, in the form of glycogen, which is readily converted to glucose as the body needs it. It detoxifies alcohol and many other potentially harmful chemicals.

Finally, food that is not digested moves from the small intestine into the colon or large intestine. In the colon, water is extracted from the waste material and what remains moves via peristalsis through the 3 feet of the large intestine to the rectum for eventual elimination in the form of a bowel movement. Voluntary control returns at this end of the digestive tract, i.e., the direct interactions with the environment are under conscious control.

While all these various digestive processes are going on, other body systems are carrying on their respective functions in a finely tuned, coordinated manner. With each breath, the lungs take in oxygen and eliminate carbon dioxide and other gaseous wastes. The circulatory system carries oxygenated blood and other nutrients to cells throughout the body and collects their wastes. Each cell comes in direct contact with a blood capillary, which brings it oxygen and other nutrients and takes away cellular waste. The kidneys filter out the wastes and help regulate blood pressure and internal chemical fluid balance. The muscles and bones give us shape, movement, and strength and protect the internal organs. The marrow of bones is essential for the manufacture of blood components. The endocrine system produces a number of chemical messengers that coordinate many of these processes and also control such vital functions as reproduction and growth. The central nervous system provides the seat of our intelligence and emotions. It also coordinates and controls other vital functions, often in concert with the endocrine system. The immune system helps protect the body from invading microorganisms and other foreign substances. The skin also protects the body, helps regulate temperature, and carries on a number of important metabolic functions.

This is a highly oversimplified summary; in reality, most organ systems have multiple functions and some are capable of taking over for others as needed. None acts independently; the smooth functioning of one is highly dependent upon other organ systems; similarly, a breakdown of one process or system is likely to have an impact throughout the body.

The full-color atlas following page 146 illustrates the major organ systems; other illustrations appear throughout the book accompanying specific discussions. In the following chapters, each body system will be discussed in more detail. In using this book, it is important to remember that what affects one system can have ramifications in other parts of the body. Likewise, symptoms that affect one part of the body may have their origin in another, quite distant, and seemingly unrelated organ.

In looking at the human body and how it works, one of the most striking aspects is the fact that most of these highly complex processes require little or no conscious effort. The example cited here—digesting breakfast—involves the conscious act of eating. But after that, the digestive and metabolic processes involving the entire body are all automatic. Conscious actions obviously have a profound effect on health and well-being, but virtually all our vital processes can proceed smoothly without any action on our part. Few of us truly appreciate just how precise and fine-tuned the body is until something goes awry. And even then, the body often can remedy the situation on its own. This does not mean that maintaining good health requires no effort. For most people, a lifestyle that provides the basics of good nutrition, adequate rest, physical activity, and a commonsense approach to life in general will go a long way toward meeting most health needs. When something does go wrong, being able to recognize warning signs and then seeking proper medical attention will further ensure maintaining good health. The detailed discussions of the various organ systems and disorders that can affect these systems are intended to give readers a broader understanding of how the body works, with guidance on how to approach various medical problems.

10 Sexual and Reproductive Health

Raphael Jewelewicz, M.D.

THE ANATOMY OF SEXUALITY

SEXUAL ANATOMY, like skin tone, hair color, weight, and height, varies from individual to individual. While variations in size and shape may be substantial, the basic structure of the reproductive organs is the same, depending on sex.

Male Reproductive Anatomy

The external male sex organs consist of the penis and the scrotum, which contains the testes. (See figure 10.1.) The penis contains 3 cylinders of spongy tissue surrounded by a tough fibrous covering. During sexual excitement, the spongy tissues become engorged with blood, causing the penis to expand. Since the fibrous sheath covering the spongy tissues will expand only so far, the tissues press against the sheath as they fill with blood, making the penis hard. Though the penis actually extends far into the body, almost to the rectum, it contains no muscles and cannot be enlarged by exercise. However, the internal part is surrounded by muscles which can be strengthened. For most men, the head is the sensitive part of the penis, especially around the ridge that connects it to the shaft.

The major internal sex organs consist of the testes, each with an epididymis, the vas deferens, the seminal vesicles, Cowper's glands, prostate gland, and urethra. The testes produce sperm and the hormone testosterone. The sperm matures in the epididymis. The vas deferens are 2 firm tubes that extend from the epididymis to the prostate. The sperm travel through the tubes and are stored at their upper ends until they mix with the secretions of the seminal vesicles and prostate just prior to ejaculation. The exact purpose of the vesicles is unclear, but it is known that they contribute a portion of the ejaculate. The secretions of the prostate comprise most of the seminal fluid or ejaculate, giving it its whitish color. The sperm actually account for only a tiny fraction of the seminal fluid or ejaculate.

It is thought that the Cowper's glands secrete a small amount of clear, sticky fluid that is often visible prior to ejaculation. This fluid sometimes contains sperm, making withdrawal of the penis from the vagina prior to ejaculation an ineffective means of contraception.

The urethra is a tube that runs from the bladder through one of the spongy cylinders in the penis and ends in a slit at the head of the penis. Both urine and seminal fluid travel through the urethra, but not at the same time. The prostate surrounds the urethra, where it leaves the bladder, and prostate problems—such as the inflammation or enlargement that is common in men over 50—very often cause urinary difficulties.

Female Reproductive Anatomy

The female external genitalia are called the vulva, which consists of the mons veneris, a pad of fatty tissue over the pubic bone (and covered with pubic hair in women and in girls who have started to menstruate); and the labia majora, two folds of fatty tissue that touch to protect the urinary and reproductive openings that lie between them. (See figure 10.2.) The internal organs begin just inside the labia majora. The labia minora or inner lips come to-

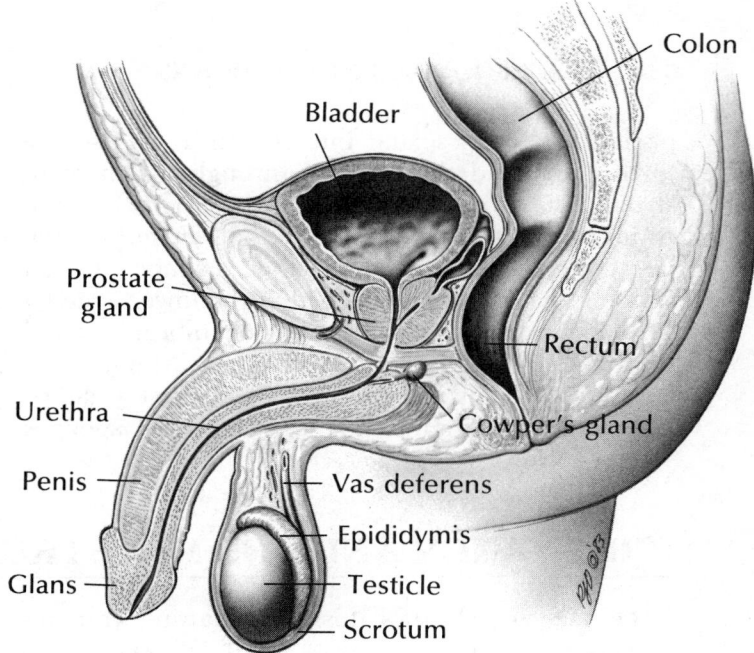

Figure 10.1. **Male sexual organs.**

gether at the intersection of the mons veneris. The fused portion or prepuce covers the clitoris. The clitoris is made of erectile tissue similar to that of the penis; it fills with blood and swells during sexual arousal. The visible part of the clitoris is the size of a pencil eraser. The rest of it, hidden under the skin, is connected to veins throughout the pelvis that also become congested with blood during sexual arousal. The clitoris is directly or indirectly involved in all female orgasms.

Within the labia minora are the urethral meatus, through which a woman urinates, and the opening to the reproductive tract or vagina. Two small Bartholin's glands, which keep the opening of the vagina moist, are also located here.

The vagina is a 5-inch-long tube into which the

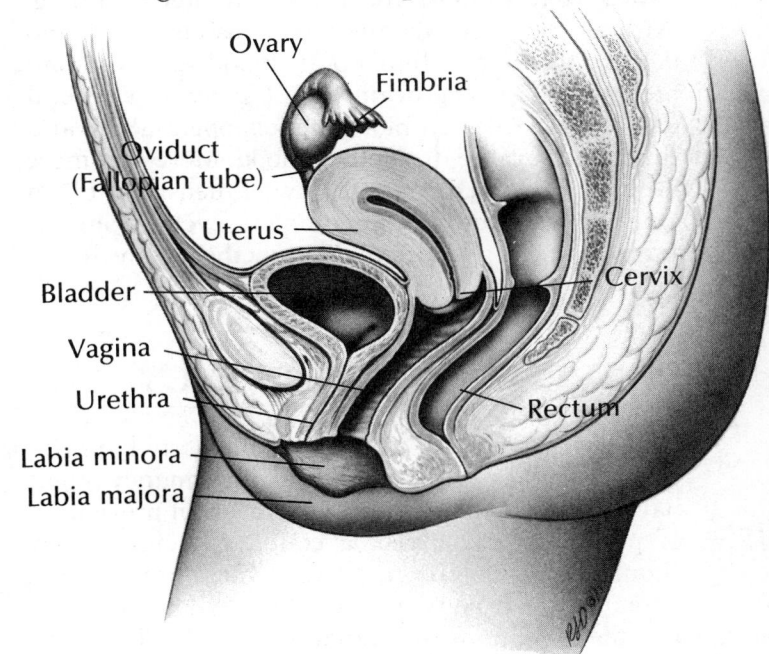

Figure 10.2. **Female pelvic organs.**

penis fits during sexual intercourse. It is also the birth canal and the channel through which menstrual fluid flows from the uterus. In its normal state, its walls gently touch each other, but during intercourse and childbirth they expand. In all women, the opening is fringed at the lower edge by a semicircular strip of mucous membrane called the hymen, which is ruptured during the first intercourse. Because the vagina is relatively short, tampons, diaphragms, and contraceptive sponges

cannot get "lost" in it.

The cervix is the closed end of the vagina, actually the neck of the womb or uterus. Its ordinarily tiny opening allows sperm to pass into the uterus and menstrual fluid to pass out. The uterus is about the size and shape of an inverted pear. It is a hollow organ with a unique inner surface—endometrial tissue—that thickens and is shed each month during the menstrual period. A fertilized ovum or embryo implants itself to develop there.

PREGNANCY AND THE MENSTRUAL CYCLE

EVERY 28 TO 32 DAYS, inside a mature woman's body, an ovum or egg (one of about 250,000 in each ovary) begins a several-day-long journey down one of the 4-inch-long Fallopian tubes, moved along to the uterus by thousands of slowly moving cilia (hairlike projections). The ova normally alternate ovaries and Fallopian tubes each month. The release of the egg from the ovary is called ovulation. If fertilization is to occur, it usually does so in the Fallopian tubes. Five days before ovulation, the uterus begins to prepare itself for a possible pregnancy; blood vessels in the area swell, providing a rich supply of blood to nourish the soft, spongy tissue of the uterine lining, which will cushion the egg when it arrives; and the uterine glands secrete nutrients to nourish the egg.

For the first 3 days after it enters the uterus, the minuscule egg—a single cell barely visible to the naked eye—floats freely. If it has been fertilized, it will implant itself in the uterine lining and begin to develop. If not, the ovaries stop producing the hormones that support the thickened uterine lining. Without these signals, the blood vessels shrink and deprive the uterine lining of its blood supply. Small pieces of the lining begin to fall away over several days. The weakened blood vessels open, a few at a time, discharging droplets of blood. More and more drops are released, and the flow of menstrual blood empties the uterus. The complete cycle, from the time the egg is released to the time the uterine lining

is entirely shed, takes about 18 days. Over the next 10 days or so, the uterus begins to ready itself for another egg and a new opportunity for pregnancy.

Menstrual flow ordinarily amounts to 4 to 6 tablespoons of vaginal and cervical secretions, tissues, and blood. The reproductive cycle in a mature woman usually occurs regularly, and cycles ranging from 20 to 36 days are considered within the normal range. Physical and mental stress as well as medication can upset the reproductive cycle and delay menstruation.

If egg and sperm meet and join together, fertilization takes place. The fertilized egg, called an embryo at first and then a fetus, implants itself in the uterine wall and continues to grow and develop during pregnancy, nourished by the rich blood supply to the uterus.

All ova carry 23 genetic information sets called chromosomes. These, when combined with the 23 chromosomes of sperm, create potential for a new individual with a normal complement of 46 chromosomes. The chromosomes that the ova carry are all known as type X; those carried by the male chromosomes may be X or Y. If the embryo is XX, it will be female, if XY, it will be male. Thus, the father's contribution to the embryo determines its sex. Specialists in the study of the fetus are able to determine at about 3 months what sex it will be.

PREVENTING PREGNANCY

NO COUPLE SHOULD ENGAGE in sexual activity unless they first consider the effect that a pregnancy might have and plan accordingly. This means if prevention of pregnancy is part of a couple's decision, they should agree on the method of birth control and agree to use it consistently. Those whose lifestyles include more than one sexual partner should be pre-

pared to use contraceptive methods themselves and not assume that their partners will attend to it. Due to the widespread choice of contraceptives, the ability of sexually active people to prevent unwanted pregnancy has increased significantly over the last 25 years. The methods vary in ease of use, safety, and effectiveness. The individual or couple choosing contraception should consider all of these factors.

Despite the relative ease of obtaining contraceptives—they are available through prescriptions or over-the-counter in drugstores, Planned Parenthood clinics or by mail order, and most states no longer limit the sale of contraceptives to persons over a certain age—there are still large numbers of unwanted pregnancies. This indicates that although people can obtain information about pregnancy prevention, they either cannot use it or they do not want to. To be sure, the available information can be overwhelming and confusing. What follows is information about the various methods of preventing pregnancy—what they are, how they work, and how convenient they are.

There has been much written about the safety of some methods of contraception. Recommendations based on long-term studies of the newer methods are just beginning to appear, along with guidelines for certain age groups or people in certain health categories. Ironically, the methods that have the greatest number of questions about safety are the most convenient. These include the pill and the intrauterine device (IUD). Less convenient and with less health risk potential are the barrier methods: the diaphragm, the cervical sponge, the cervical cap, and the condom.

The fact remains that contraception is very much an individual decision, to be made on the basis of the individual's pattern of sexual activity, age, health, desired family size, and religious convictions.

Birth Control Pills

Birth control pills (oral contraceptives) are made by combining (synthetic) hormones similar to the ones made in the ovaries. There are two types of pills currently manufactured in the United States: a combination pill with both synthetic progesterone (progestin) and synthetic estrogen; and mini-pills which contain only progestin.

The pill essentially works by interfering with a woman's normal fluctuations in hormone levels which in turn prevents the egg from maturing and being released. It also acts on the climate of the cervix, uterine lining, and Fallopian tubes, making them all inhospitable for egg, sperm, or embryo.

Combination pills are packaged in several ways; the most common is the 21-day pack. One pill is taken each day for 21 days, none during the next 7 days of the average 28-day cycle during which menstruation occurs. There are also 28-day packs with 21 active pills followed by 7 inactive ones (placebos). The mini-pills must be taken every day. With the exception of sterilization, combination pills are the most effective method of birth control, provided that they are properly used. Mini-pills are slightly less effective but are still highly reliable.

Serious possible side effects are more likely to occur in women over age 30 to 35. These include an increased risk of heart attack, stroke, and formation of blood clots in the veins (thrombosis). These side effects are more likely to occur among women who smoke; thus, the pill is not recommended for women who smoke. Women with a history of blood clots, high blood pressure, severe diabetes, or breast or uterine cancer also should not take the pill. Though there is no evidence indicating that recent use of the pill will affect the health of a fetus should pregnancy occur, many physicians recommend that women who want to get pregnant stop taking the pill at the end of a cycle and wait a few months, using some other contraceptive method, before attempting to conceive. The pill should not be taken if there is any chance that a woman is already pregnant.

The pill is available only by prescription; a woman should have a checkup first to be sure the risk of side effects is minimal. She should contact her doctor promptly if, while on the pill, she develops signs of a serious side effect. Possible symptoms include chest pain, shortness of breath, unusual coughing, pain in the legs, severe headaches, breast lumps, dizziness or faintness, muscle weakness or numbness, speech disturbances, vision changes or loss of vision, severe depression, or yellowing of the skin.

Certain drugs, including ampicillin, sulfa drugs, antihistamines, some antidepressants, sedatives, medication for epilepsy, tuberculosis, and arthritis can decrease the effectiveness of the pill. When taking these drugs, a woman should switch to another birth control method or use a backup method.

The pill can also interact with insulin, anticoagulants, certain tranquilizers, Demerol (a pain controller), and tuberculin skin tests. They can alter laboratory test results, so the patient should tell her doctor if she is on the pill, even if the test is for a totally unrelated problem.

Women on the pill may have relief from heavy bleeding and painful menstrual cramps, although some bleeding between menstrual periods, or "breakthrough bleeding," can occur, especially when this birth control method is first begun. Periods are regular, light, and predictable and a woman can manipulate them to accommodate vacations or even events where having one would be inconvenient. Iron-deficiency anemia is less common among pill users than among other women because of the decreased amount of menstrual blood. Since the pill suppresses ovulation, users have a lower incidence of ovarian cysts. Ovulation pain does not affect these people and many find that acne improves.

Disadvantages beyond those already mentioned include some 50 side effects and complications. In some cases, the relationship has not been clearly defined. However, the pill has been associated with breast tenderness and swelling; skin changes, including increased oiliness, sun sensitivity, and pigment (color) changes; increased vaginal discharge; increased yeast infections; weight gain; fluid retention; headaches; nausea and vomiting; bronchitis and viral infections; urinary tract infections; fibroid tumors; circulatory disorders; gallbladder disease; liver problems; high blood pressure; birth defects; ectopic pregnancy; infertility; breast milk quantity and quality changes; depression; thyroid gland changes; eye problems; changes in the chemical and metabolic processes in the blood; vitamin and mineral deficiencies, and sugar metabolism changes. Despite the long list of possible complications, most women are able to tolerate the pill, explaining why it is the second most common form of contraception in the United States, exceeded only by sterilization.

Women with the following conditions should not take the pill:

- Blood clotting disorders
- Heart attack, stroke, angina, or coronary disease
- Impaired liver function
- Vascular disease
- Known or suspected cancer of the breast, uterus, cervix, ovaries, vagina, or elsewhere in the female reproductive tract
- Pregnancy or suspected pregnancy

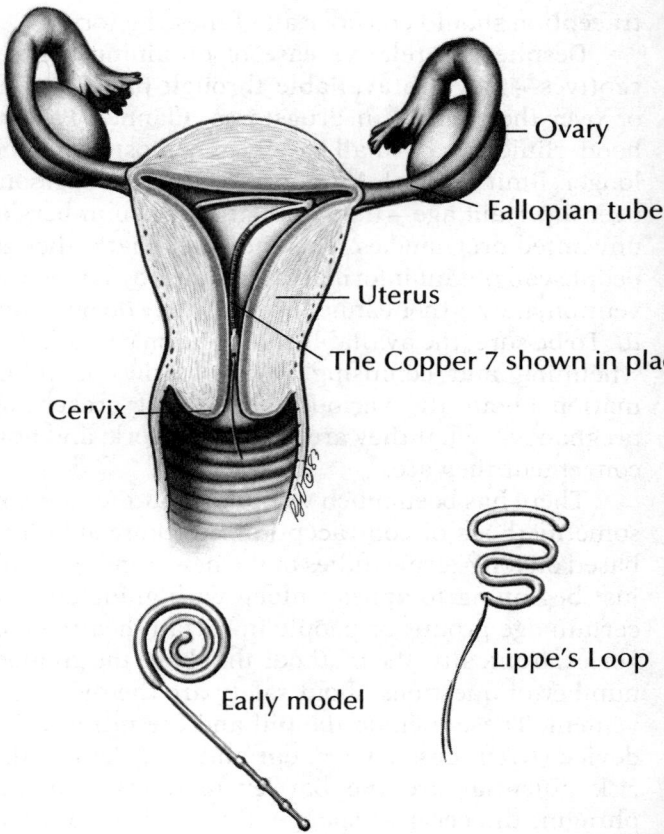

Figure 10.3. **Several types of IUDs are available; the type used depends upon a woman's anatomy and physician preference.**

The Intrauterine Device

The IUD, loop, or coil has been used as a birth control device for centuries. It is said that Arabs traveling on long caravan journeys put pebbles into the wombs of their camels to prevent them from becoming pregnant and thus unable to carry heavy loads.

In more modern times, it has been used as a birth-control device by millions of women worldwide, but with growing controversy regarding potential adverse effects. As of this writing, only one IUD is marketed in the United States; others have been voluntarily removed from general use by their manufacturers because of a large number of liability suits brought by women who claim they have suffered adverse effects from using an IUD. As a result, many women have had their IUDs removed; others, who want to continue using this method of birth control but whose physicians will no longer prescribe an IUD, are going to Canada to have them inserted.

Where they are available, IUDs come in various forms. (See figure 10.3.) The only one that is being marketed in the United States as of this writing is a flexible plastic device with the hormone progesterone embedded in the plastic. An IUD insertion usually requires two visits to a gynecologist or family planning clinic, one to provide a thorough medical history, including a physical exam, blood test for anemia, Pap smear, wet smear, and gonorrhea culture. The second visit is for the insertion.

Insertion can be somewhat painful for women who have not had children. Sometimes, a doctor or family planning specialist will inject a painkiller into the cervix just before insertion. Pain may persist for 24 to 48 hours afterward and there may be a slight blood flow after insertion. The first period following insertion may be particularly heavy.

Removal of an IUD must be done by a trained specialist during an office visit. Occasionally the device, which can be left in place for several years, shifts and must be surgically removed. An IUD is a very reliable means of birth control with only 1 to 6 pregnancies occurring per 100 women who use it. No one is quite sure how IUDs work. One theory is that the device irritates the uterus so much it triggers the body's defense mechanisms, which absorb the sperm or the fertilized egg. Another is that the fertilized egg may not be able to attach itself to the irritated uterine lining. Still another is that the IUD works by dislodging the fertilized egg. Another theory is that the IUD speeds movement of the egg through the Fallopian tube, and the egg enters the uterus too immature to implant itself successfully in the lining.

Though an effective contraceptive measure, the IUD has been beset with problems and controversies surrounding its use. Recent studies have found that the IUD markedly increases the risk of infertility, surrounding its use. Recent studies have found that the IUD markedly increases the risk of infertility. The following is a partial list of the common problems linked to IUD use:

1. *Safety*—Infections are not uncommon. The Dalkon Shield, one common IUD, was taken off the market in this country and many women had them removed when it was discovered that the strings that lead out of the cervix help promote infection. Similar problems were found with the Majzlin Spring and the Birnber Bow.

2. *Pelvic Inflammatory Disease* (PID)—A higher percentage of women who use an IUD tend to get PID than those who do not. The theoretical reason is that the device chronically irritates the uterus, which may impair its ability to defend itself against infection. Another theory is that the IUD strings help promote infection. PID is a serious disease, often requiring hospitalization. It can spread beyond the uterus to the Fallopian tubes and ovaries where a massive infection may be very dangerous. Generally, doctors recommend that women with recurring pelvic infections, especially those with multiple sexual partners, should not use an IUD.

3. *Expulsion and Perforation*—Some women cannot tolerate an IUD, and it is expelled within the first 3 months of use. The woman is usually aware that the device has been expelled. About 20 percent of the time, however, women do not realize it. For this reason, many doctors recommend using another method of birth control during the first 3 months that the device is in place.

The IUD may also perforate the uterus and sometimes will even work its way into the abdomen. When a wearer checks for and cannot find the strings that indicate that the IUD is in place, she should seek medical attention. A specialist can locate the device with special instruments, or, if necessary, with ultrasound. If a perforation has occurred or if the IUD has entered the pelvic cavity, most doctors will want to remove it immediately to prevent infection or injury to other pelvic organs.

4. *Ectopic Pregnancy*—If a woman wearing an IUD becomes pregnant, it is more likely to occur in a Fallopian tube. This is called ectopic pregnancy and can result in severe internal bleeding and possibly shock, due to tearing of the wall of the Fallopian tube as the embryo grows there instead of in the uterus. Such pregnancies usually require surgery to remove the fetus and placenta and repair any damage. The chances of future pregnancies are generally greatly reduced. Some doctors feel that women who have never had children are at greatest risk of complications and advise against using an IUD.

If an IUD wearer becomes pregnant and the embryo develops in the uterus, there is a 50 percent chance that she will miscarry. If the IUD is removed, the chance of miscarriage drops to 25 percent. Pregnancy with an IUD in place also increases the chance of infection, premature delivery, and stillbirth.

Because PID and ectopic pregnancies are related to the IUD, many doctors are reluctant to prescribe it for the woman who has never had children but who plans to. There are also conflicting viewpoints on the effect of the IUD on fertility in general. One feeling is that there is no effect; another is that women who use IUDs are slower to recover fertility after one is removed; a third is that the longer a women wears an IUD, the less chance she has of becoming pregnant after its removal. The indications are that a woman who wears an IUD but who plans to have a family might want to consider another birth control method.

The Diaphragm

The diaphragm is a rounded rubber cup stretched over a flexible metal ring. The user spreads sperm-killing jelly or cream in the cup, bends the diaphragm in half, and slips it into her vagina, pushing it until it reaches the cervix. When the diaphragm is released, it spreads out to cover the cervix, with the spermicidal cream or jelly inside. A diaphragm acts in two ways to prevent pregnancy—it provides a physical barrier for the passage of sperm into the cervix, and the spermicidal cream or jelly kills sperm on contact. Diaphragms, which must be fitted by a physician or other health-care practitioner, come in several sizes and types. (Creams and jellies are available without a prescription in drugstores.) Ideally, a woman should have a choice among several types of diaphragms. There are coil spring, flat spring, arcing and bowbent types. Some health practitioners favor one over another, and sometimes a woman's physical condition—medical problems or poor vaginal muscle tone—may require one type or another. When properly in place, the diaphragm lies at an angle in the vagina with the back part of the rim fitting closely behind the neck of the womb (cervix) and the soft rubber part covering the neck of the womb completely. The front part of the diaphragm lies behind the pubic bone.

The diaphragm may be inserted up to 3 hours before intercourse. (Many couples make its insertion part of their love play.) It must be left in place 6 hours after intercourse so that the spermicide will kill any sperm before it is removed.

A well-fitted diaphragm cannot be felt once the woman is accustomed to its presence. Its size should be the smallest that will properly cover the cervix. One too large may cause irritation; one too small will not protect properly.

The health professional who fits a woman with a diaphragm should give her instructions and make sure that she is beginning to develop some comfort with its use before she leaves the office. The first few times it is inserted at home can be trying. But skill develops quickly. If the woman continues to have difficulty inserting it, she can ask her doctor for an inserter, a plastic device on which the diaphragm is stretched and then placed into the vagina.

The diaphragm is removed by inserting a finger under the metal rim to break the suction that holds it in place and slipping it out. The inserter can also be used to do this.

Spermicides

The diaphragm should be used with spermicidal cream or jelly; type and brand chosen is up to the user. Most brands contain similar, equally effective, ingredients. Creams tend to provide more lubrication than jellies. Most spermicides have a slight fragrance and a chemical flavor. Some have recently come on the market with fruit flavors and fragrances; others are now available without any flavor or fragrance.

Some spermicides are manufactured to be used alone. They are inserted with a small plunger deep in the vagina so that the material is in front of the cervix. Although these products are stronger than those manufactured for use with a diaphragm (and may, in fact, be especially good protection with a diaphragm), there is some risk that they will not disperse well enough to cover the cervix properly. If use of the diaphragm is objectionable, it is better to use another contraceptive method than to rely on the contraceptive cream or jelly alone.

Contraceptive Foam and Tablets

Contraceptive Foam. This is used by itself to act as a barrier to sperm during sexual intercourse. It usually comes in a purse size aerosol can with an inserter. The can must be shaken thoroughly and the foam inserted near the cervix shortly before intercourse. Some manufacturers claim this can be done from 1 to 3 hours beforehand, but the effectiveness of the foam depends on its bubbles' ability to trap and kill sperm. And the user has no way of knowing how long the bubbles will last.

Contraceptive Tablets. A few manufacturers market tablets or suppositories, available in drugstores, which are inserted in the vagina shortly before intercourse. Vaginal secretions activate the tablet and the foam is released. There is always the danger that the tablet will not dissolve completely and that contraceptive protection will thus be incomplete. This method is less preferred than others where the barrier to sperm attempting to enter the cervix is more certain. Purchasers should make sure they are buying contraceptive tablets, not feminine hygiene suppositories, which are often displayed nearby.

Condoms

The condom is the only contraceptive device that can be used by the male partner. It is a sheath made of thin rubber or lamb's gut that fits over the penis. Rolled onto the erect penis just before intercourse, the condom is a barrier that prevents the ejaculate from entering the vagina. Some condoms have a reservoir tip to catch the semen. The rubber at the open end of the condom is thicker, helping it to stay on the man's penis. Condoms come in one size and fit most men. They are available in a range of varieties: regular latex, thinner latex, or sheep gut; they can be dry or lubricated with a wet or dry lubricant; some are colorless, opaque or transparent, or brightly colored; with ribbed, textured, and raised surfaces. Condoms are less expensive than some other barrier contraceptive methods; and they are a highly effective means of birth control if a couple is motivated to use them every time they have intercourse. They also protect both partners against sexually transmitted diseases. In recent years, condoms have been displayed more openly in pharmacies and other stores, and women now make up a good number of purchasers.

Cervical Caps

The cervical cap is not approved for manufacture and sale in the United States by the Food and Drug Administration as of this writing. However, cervical caps have been imported from England for experimental use here for several years. They are thimble-like devices, sometimes with a one-way valve to release cervical secretions, which fits over the cervix that swells slightly, holding the cap in an airtight seal. It is used with spermicidal cream or jelly, and should not be worn for more than 72 hours at a time. In this country, researchers are experimenting with variations individually molded to precisely fit the cervix of each user. These models, which must be inserted by a doctor or nurse, are designed to be worn for 6 months at a time.

Contraceptive Sponges

A recent entry in the mechanical contraception field is the contraceptive sponge. This rounded device, made of polyurethane, is impregnated with spermicide. Inserted into the vagina and pushed up to the cervix, it is held in place by the vaginal muscles. The manufacturer says it can be used for repeated intercourse over 24 hours. Some doctors, however, advise against leaving the sponge in place this long. It is removed by grasping a ribbon loop attached to it and pulling gently to break the suction. Like the diaphragm and cervical cap, insertion and removal of the sponge may take getting used to.

Withdrawal (Coitus Interruptus)

A contraceptive method practiced by many couples, withdrawal of the penis just before ejaculation is a highly unreliable birth control technique. Not only is the timing of withdrawal difficult to judge, but even during foreplay, sperm may be present in the fluids secreted by the male before ejaculation. If these enter the vagina, conception can take place.

Natural Family Planning or Rhythm Method

Natural family planning takes advantage of the fact that a woman is able to become pregnant only when ovulation occurs during the menstrual cycle. If the rhythm method is used, she must determine when that time is, and either avoid intercourse or use a separate type of contraception during these days. For the rest of the cycle, she is unlikely to become pregnant, at least in theory. A woman undertaking to determine her safe and unsafe days keeps records of the pattern of her cycle by following one of the methods described below. The unsafe days begin 1 week before ovulation (which is usually 14 days before the onset of menstruation) and last for at least 3 days afterward.

There are 3 ways to calculate the time of ovulation: (1) The calendar method: The woman keeps an accurate record of the lengths of her cycles for at least 12 months. Then she subtracts 18 from the number of days in the shortest cycle (14 from ovulation to the onset of menstruation, plus 4 for the average sperm life span) and 11 from the longest (14 from ovulation to the onset of menstruation, less 1 for egg life span and 2 for safety). The results are the first and last unsafe days in the woman's cycle, counting the first day of the period as day 1. (2) The temperature method: In most women, body temperature is slightly elevated just after ovulation and does not fall again until the next period starts. The woman must take her body temperature each day upon awakening, before engaging in any activity, and develop a chart. Safe days begin 2 days after the monthly temperature increase, which indicates ovulation. (3) Mucus inspection method: A woman's cervical mucus changes consistency in the course of her menstrual cycle, going from sparse, just after menstruation, to thick, to thin during ovulation. By studying her mucus over several cycles, a woman will discover when these changes occur and be able to determine the pattern of her cycle.

A combination of methods is probably advisable, studied under the guidance of a physician or family planning specialist. As cycles, sperm life spans, and egg life spans vary from individual to individual and month to month, it is best to consider that there will be about 11 unsafe days per cycle for each woman. Several groups offer information on Natural Family Planning. The largest is Natural Family Planning Federation of America, Inc., Suite A, 1221 Massachusetts Avenue N.W., Washington D.C. 20005.

Sterilization of Men (Vasectomy)

About 10 million men have been sterilized in this country since the late 1960s with a simple, in-office or outpatient procedure called vasectomy. In this procedure, which takes 20 minutes and is done under local anesthesia, the doctor makes a small incision in the scrotum and cuts the vas deferens, the tubes that carry sperm. (See figure 10.4.) Soreness lasts only a few days. Sterility is not achieved until all the sperm that may be stored in the testicles have been eliminated—a process that may take several weeks. Therefore, an alternative means of contraception should be used until tests show that semen is sperm free.

Vasectomy has no effect on a man's general health or his virility. It should not be undertaken, however, if there is a possibility that the man will want to father more children. Some reversals are possible, depending on the condition of the cut tubes.

Sterilization of Women

Female sterilization is a surgical procedure that may be performed under general or local anesthetic. It is the ligation or tying of the Fallopian tubes so they cannot carry an egg into the uterus to be fertilized. Alternative methods include cutting away a portion of the tube, and coagulation (burning) to close the tubes. (See figure 10.5.)

In recent years, a technique called laparoscopic tubal ligation has become popular. It is an abdominal procedure done under local anesthesia with a visualizing instrument, called the laparoscope, and a

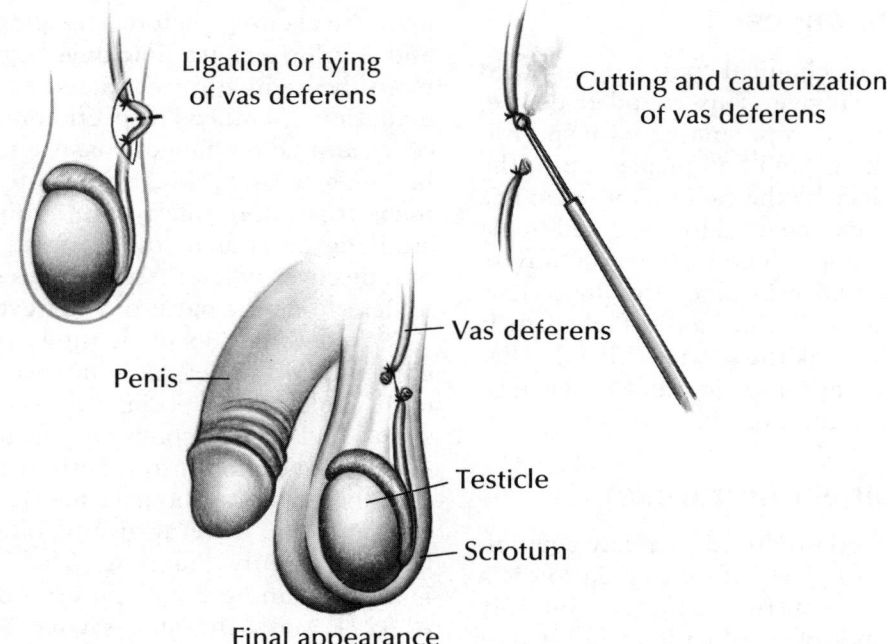

Figure 10.4. **The 2 methods of vasectomy are shown here; the drawing in the middle illustrates the final appearance of the vas deferens following the cutting of the tube and cauterization.**

cauterizing instrument introduced through tiny incisions in the abdomen. The abdominal cavity is filled with gas to isolate the reproductive organs, and the Fallopian tubes are burned in one or more places.

In minilaparotomy—another abdominal procedure—an instrument is inserted through the cervix to elevate the uterus. An incision in the abdomen directly above it enables the doctor to reach and tie, cut, or burn the Fallopian tubes. Most women experience pain and discomfort for 24 to 48 hours.

Sterilization is the most effective means of birth control and is now the most popular form of birth control in the United States. Even so, it should be considered only by couples whose families are complete. Although some operations have been successfully performed to restore fertility, reversal cannot be guaranteed.

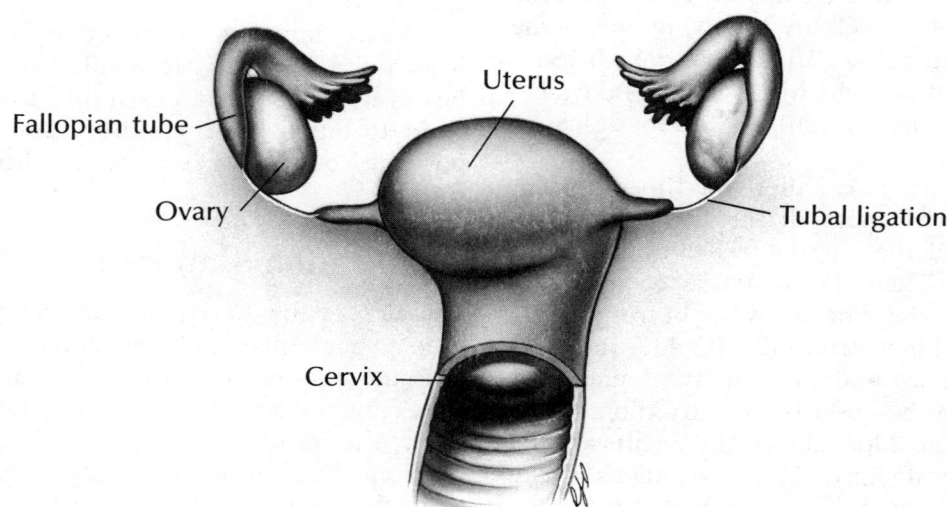

Figure 10.5. **In female sterilization, the Fallopian tube may be either tied (ligated) or cut and cauterized, to prevent passage of the ovum into the uterus.**

ABORTION

ABORTION DOES NOT HAVE a particularly savory history, although it has been practiced in many countries and societies for centuries, often with dire results for the woman. Before 1974, botched illegal abortions claimed the lives of thousands of women in this country each year. This has been changed by the 1974 Supreme Court ruling that legalized abortion. Initially, the court ruled that for the first 3 months of pregnancy, a woman's decision to have an abortion would be between her and her doctor. Eventually, it permitted abortions from the third to the sixth months in order to protect the health of the woman.

But legalization does not make a woman's or a couple's decision to have a therapeutic abortion any easier. It is still a painful choice for many, bringing emotional, moral, and religious beliefs and conflicts to the surface. A woman or a couple may want to consult a physician or the skilled, unbiased counselors in a family planning center to aid them in making a decision.

Legal abortion is a relatively safe procedure; the risk of death is substantially less than that involved in carrying a pregnancy to term. The most important consideration is the duration of the pregnancy; the later the abortion is performed, the greater the risk to the woman.

A woman who suspects she is pregnant should have a pregnancy test as soon as possible. Some of the newer tests can detect a pregnancy within a few days of a missed period. A woman who uses an at-home test first should have it backed up by a test given by a health-care professional. If an abortion is to be performed, the earlier in the pregnancy the better.

Types of Abortions

Vacuum Abortion. This is performed at 4 to 12 weeks of pregnancy and requires a local or general anesthesia. The cervix is dilated, a vacuum tube is inserted, and the uterine contents are suctioned out.

Menstrual Extraction. This is a procedure similar to a vacuum abortion that is done very early in pregnancy immediately after tests determine that a woman is pregnant. A syringe is used to extract the uterine contents. Dilation of the cervix is not necessary, and anesthesia is not usually used.

Intraamniotic Injection of Hypertonic Saline. This is performed at 14 to 20 weeks of pregnancy. It is a procedure whereby a hollow needle is inserted into the amniotic sac, which is filled with the fluid that surrounds the fetus. A drug that causes fetal death is then injected. Fetal death is followed by uterine contractions that cause expulsion of the fetal tissues. This can be accomplished with vaginal suppositories of prostaglandins, which cause uterine contractions and expulsion of the fetus and placenta.

POSTCOITAL CONTRACEPTION

VARIOUS HOME METHODS will not prevent pregnancy following unprotected intercourse. Douching, for example, may have the effect of pushing live sperm further up the vagina into the cervix. There are some new medical treatments available, however, for women who have been raped, have forgotten to use contraception, have used it improperly, or used a method that failed (broken condom or expelled IUD, for example).

The Morning-After Pill

A synthetic estrogen called DES has been approved by the Food and Drug Administration for use in emergency cases. Administered in large doses, it works by making the uterine lining an inhospitable place for the egg to implant itself. It can produce unpleasant side effects such as nausea and vomiting, headaches, menstrual irregularities, and breast tenderness. DES has been implicated in certain reproductive abnormalities by daughters of women who took DES to prevent a threatened miscarriage—a practice that was stopped in the early 1970s. Recent research also has found an increased incidence of breast cancer among women who took DES.

Postcoital IUD

The postcoital insertion of the copper IUD apparently prevents implantation of the fertilized egg in the uterine wall. Most experts feel that the sooner the IUD is inserted for this purpose, the better, but some have been inserted many days afterward (about the time it takes for egg implantation in the uterine wall).

GENETICS OF REPRODUCTION

PERHAPS THE MOST troubling question involving pregnancy and childbirth is: Will the baby be normal? Increasingly, medical science is finding that the answer to this question lies in genetic heritage. Genes are the chemical information each person inherits from his or her parents, from the moment sperm and egg combine. They determine what people look like, how they grow, whether the individual will have certain diseases or be resistant to others. Twenty-three bits of genetic information or chromosomes in the ovum combine with 23 chromosomes in the sperm to form a 46-chromosome embryo that has the potential to be a completely new individual. By the time this happens, many questions about inherited characteristics have already been answered, although the answers may not become clear for many years.

Science is slowly unraveling just how much information the genes contain and where the gene for certain characteristics is located on the chromosomes. There may be remarkable findings in the next few days that will enable medical science to control heredity—including diseases and personal characteristics—far beyond present-day imagining.

As cells divide and form organs, bones, teeth, nerves, muscles, skin, and features, there are many opportunities for nature to slip. The fortunate fact is that 11 out of 12 babies are born normal. But in 1 out of 12 births, there is an inheritance that nobody wants: a genetically linked disease.

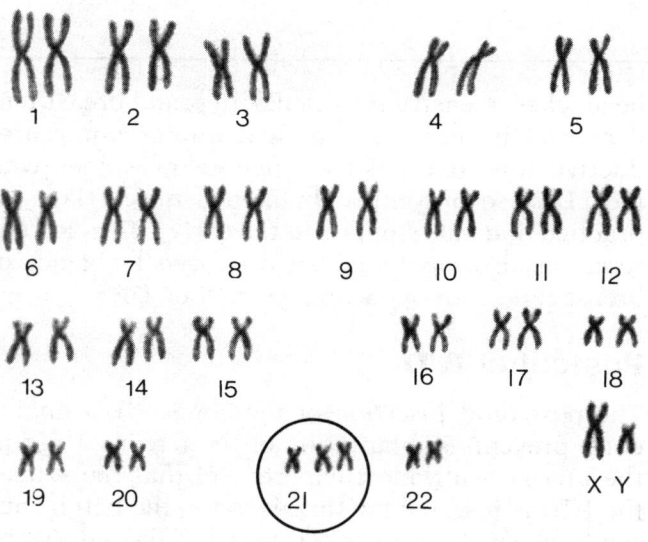

Figure 10.6. **The chromosomal pattern of Down's syndrome or Trisomy 21. Note the abnormal 3 chromosomes for pair No. 21.**

Genetic diseases number in the thousands and afflict between 12 and 15 million people. Most people are familiar with Down's syndrome (see figure 10.6) or remember the deformed babies born after mothers took Thalidomide. But many genetic diseases are not those usually associated with chromosomal changes. These diseases—which yearly handicap or take the lives of adults—are just beginning to be recognized as having genetic origins. They include some types of early heart disease, diabetes, high blood pressure, allergies, and peptic ulcers. Some are correctible by diet, medication, or surgery in the early months and years of life or in adulthood. Others, however, can cripple, maim, and kill in infancy or early childhood, disable the individual, or shorten his or her life.

The actual process of transmission of genetic disorders is fairly well known. Genetic defects are transferred to the new individual within the genes of his or her parents in one of the following ways.

Dominant Inheritance

One parent has a single faulty gene that dominates its normal counterpart in the other parent's genetic makeup. If this is the case, there is a 50 percent risk that each of their children will manifest the defect. There is an equal likelihood that each child will not receive the abnormal gene.

Dominant inheritance diseases tend to show considerable variability: different children will have different degrees of symptoms, from none to very severe. Currently, there are almost 2,000 confirmed or suspected dominant disorders, among them achondroplasia, a form of dwarfism; chronic simple glaucoma, a major cause of blindness if untreated; Huntington's disease, a progressive degenerative disease of the nervous system; familial hypercholesterolemia, a type of high blood cholesterol that appears early in life and often leads to a heart attack during young adulthood; and polydactyly, or extra fingers and toes.

Recessive Inheritance

Both parents of a child with one of these diseases appear to be normal. But by chance, both carry the same harmful gene, although neither may be aware of it. Unfortunately, the child who inherits the defective genes from both parents may have a significant birth defect. When both parents are carriers of a harmful recessive trait, each of their children will run a 25 percent chance of not inheriting the gene from either parent; a 50 percent chance of receiving

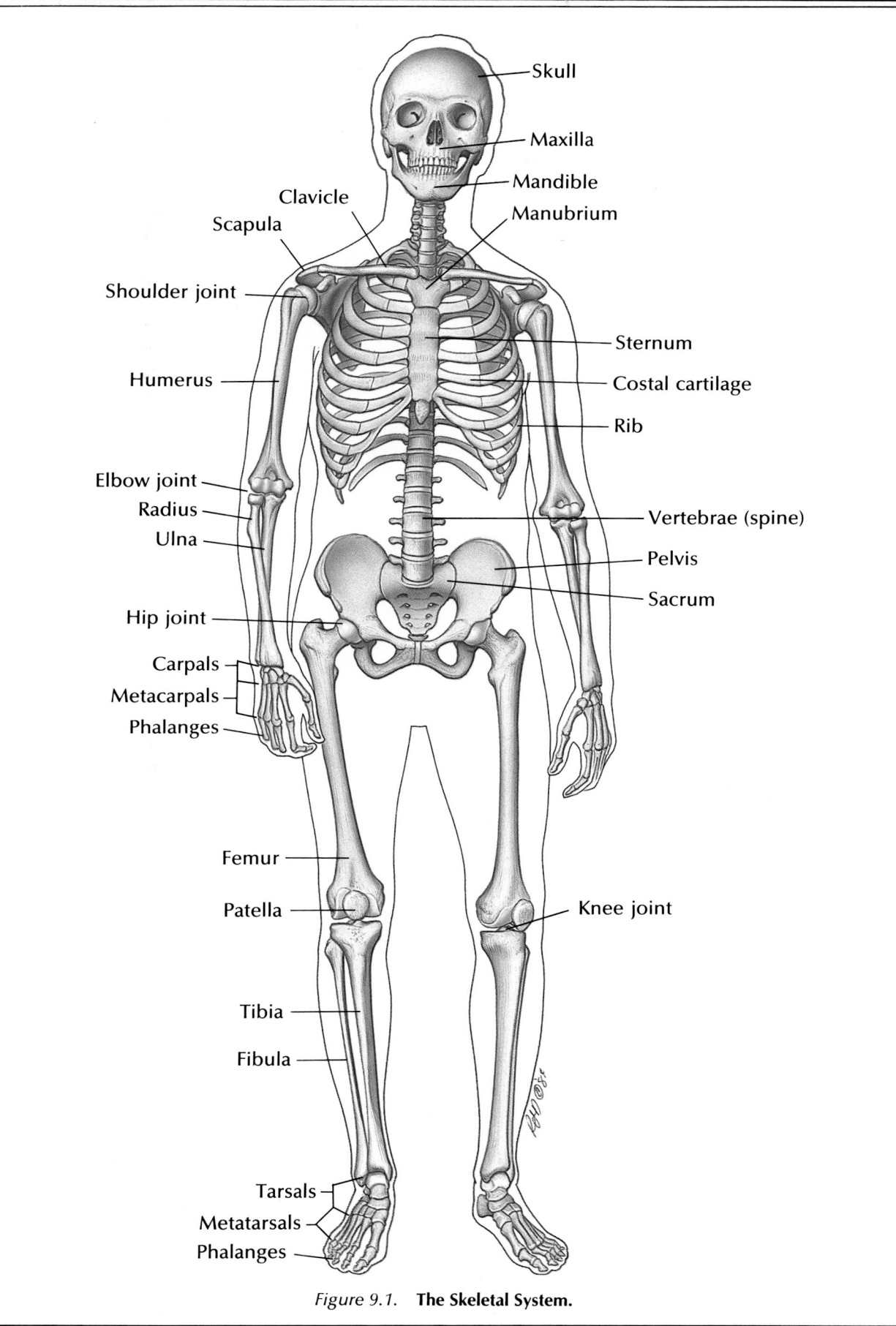

Figure 9.1. **The Skeletal System.**

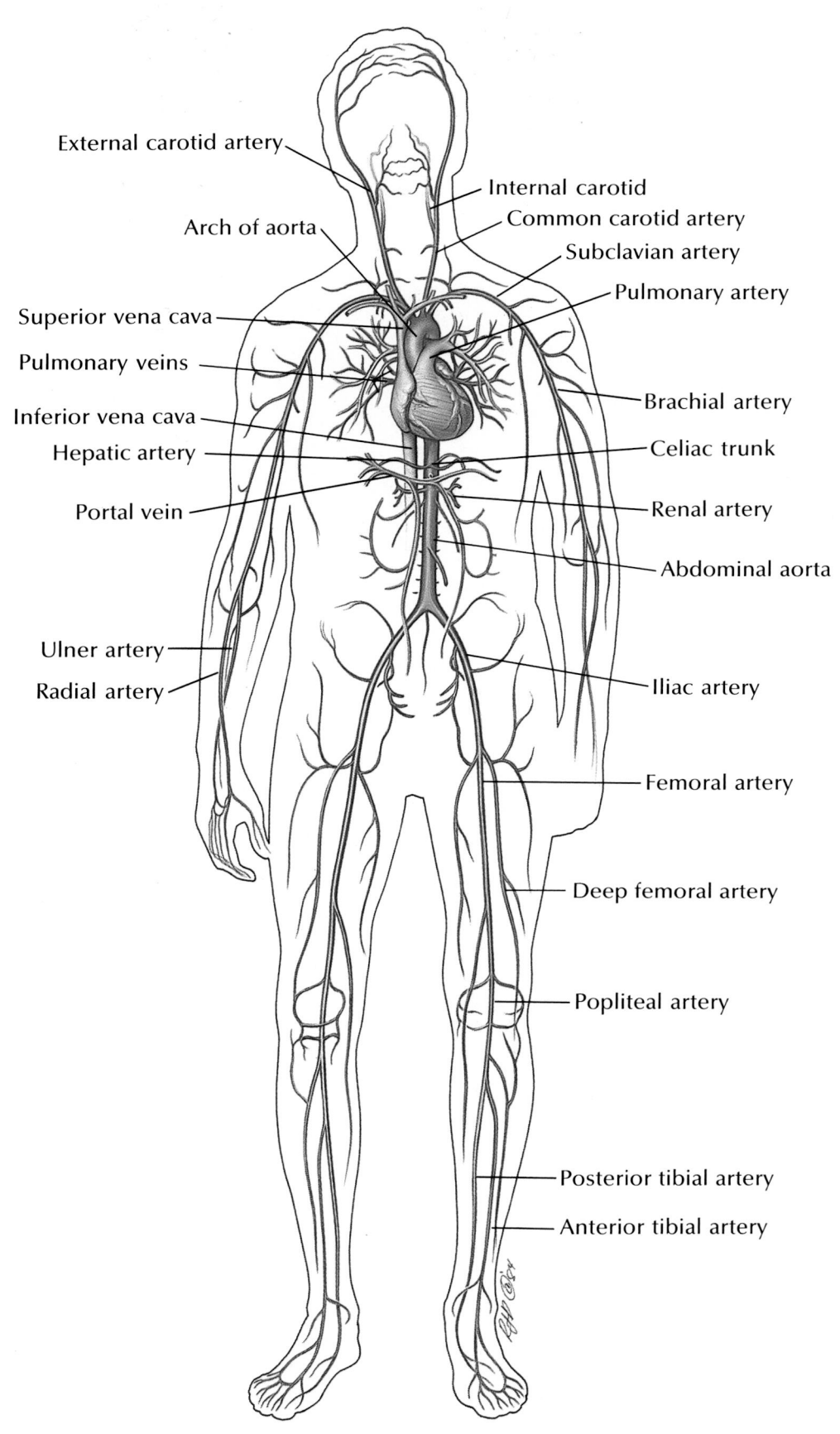

External carotid artery

Internal carotid

Common carotid artery

Subclavian artery

Pulmonary artery

Arch of aorta

Superior vena cava

Pulmonary veins

Brachial artery

Inferior vena cava

Celiac trunk

Hepatic artery

Portal vein

Renal artery

Abdominal aorta

Ulner artery

Radial artery

Iliac artery

Femoral artery

Deep femoral artery

Popliteal artery

Posterior tibial artery

Anterior tibial artery

Figure 9.2. **The Circulatory System.**

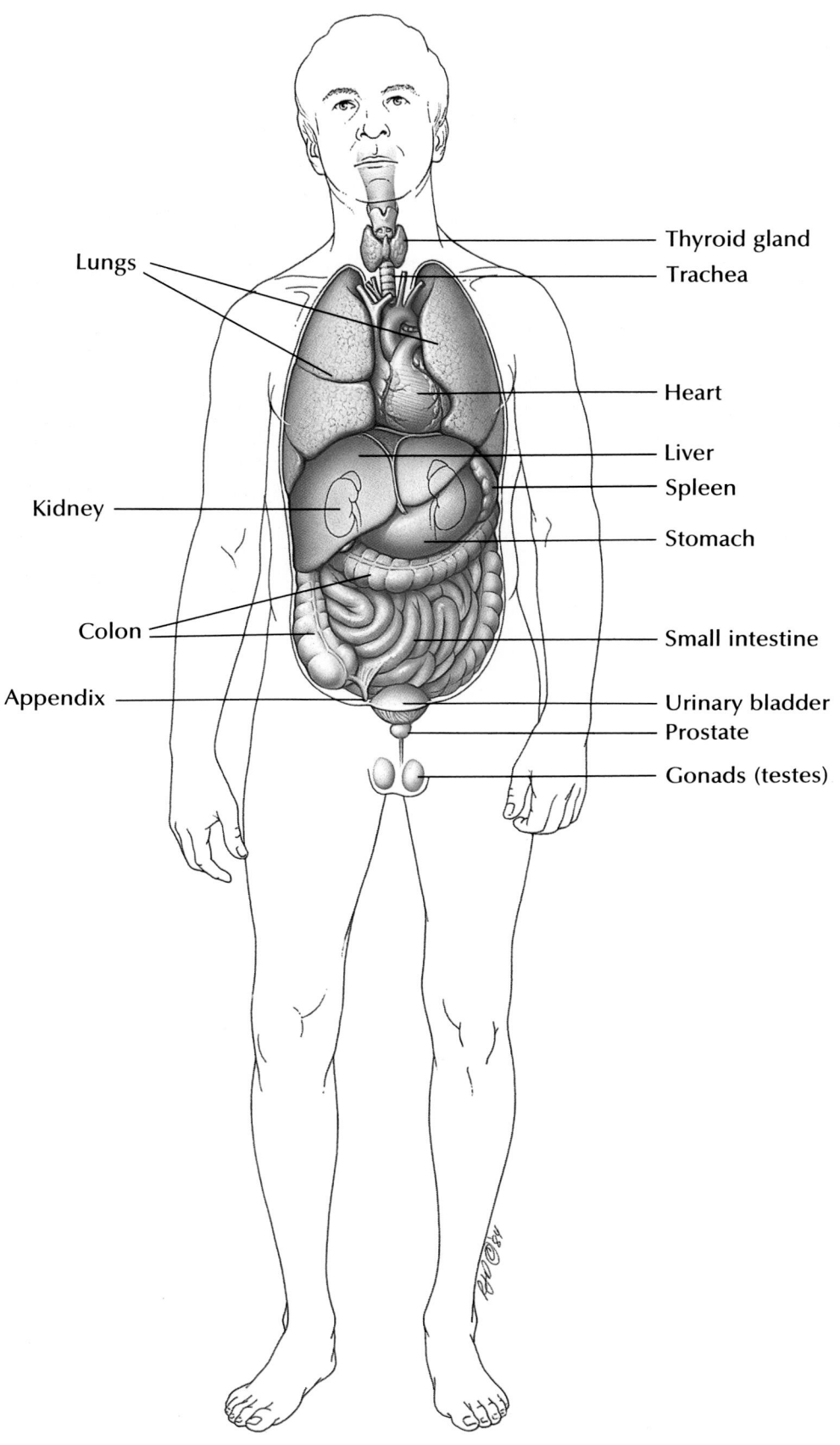

Lungs

Thyroid gland

Trachea

Heart

Liver

Spleen

Kidney

Stomach

Colon

Small intestine

Appendix

Urinary bladder

Prostate

Gonads (testes)

Figure 9.3.   **The Internal Organs.**

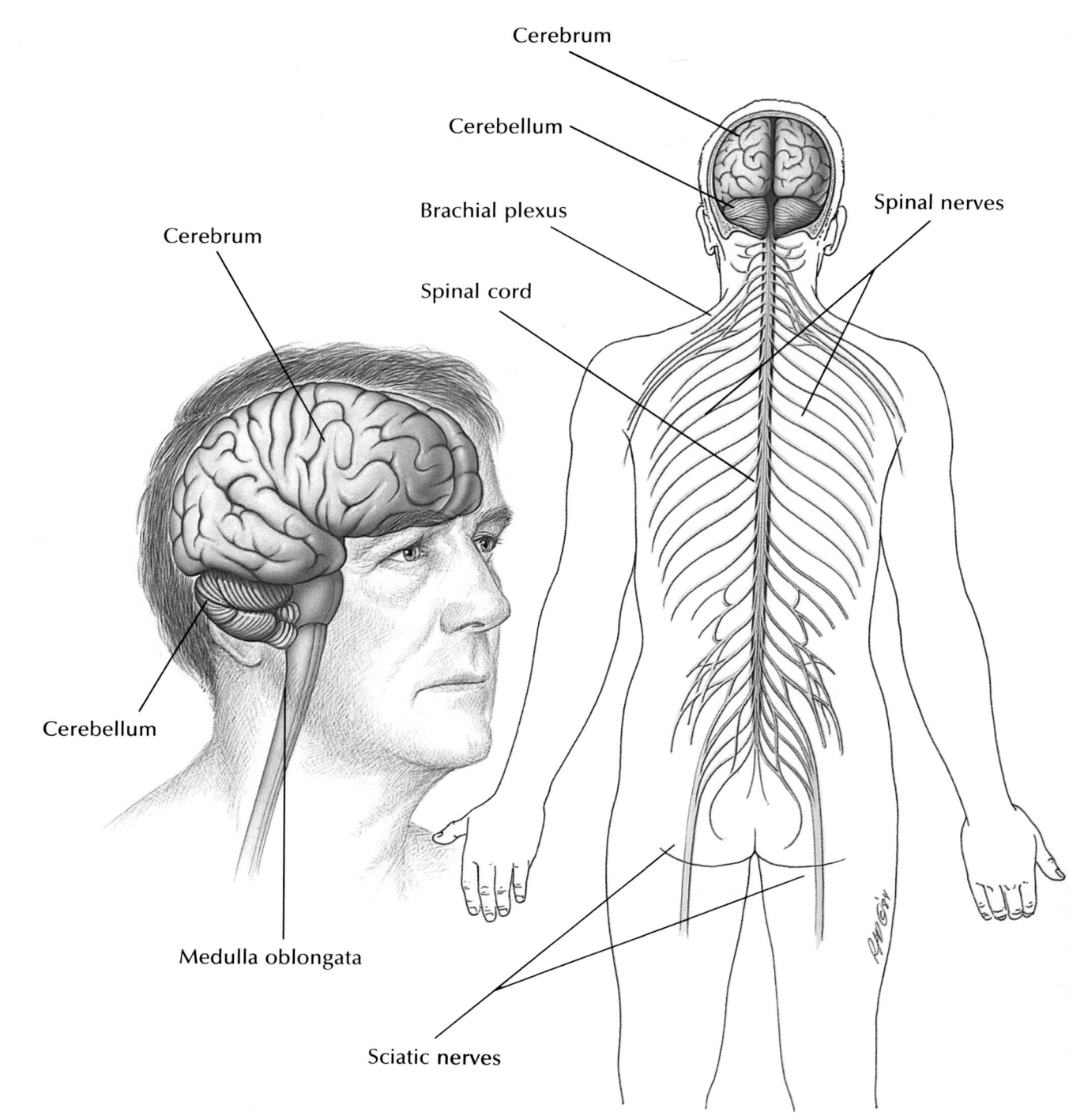

Figure 9.4. **The Nervous System.**

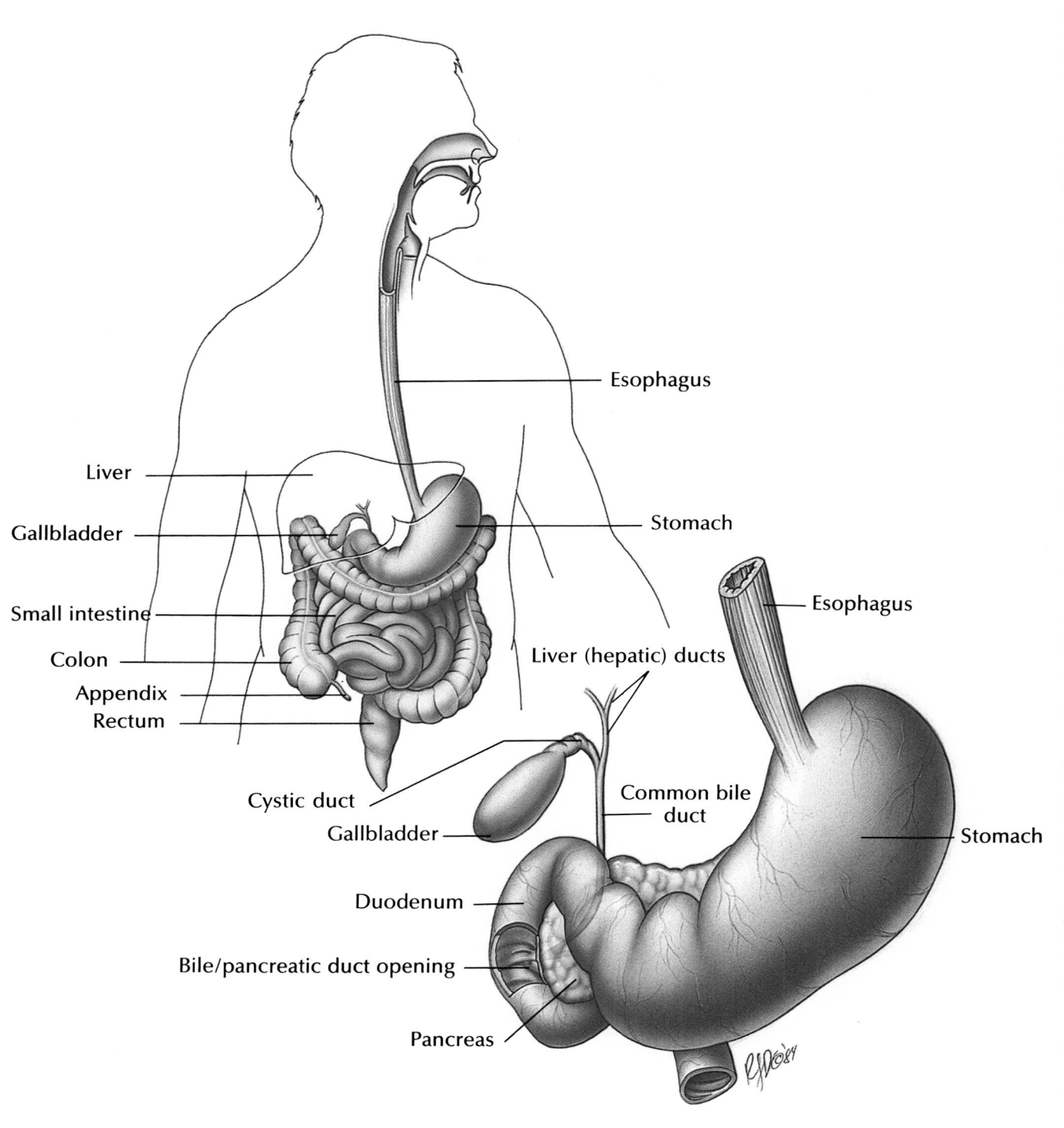

Esophagus

Liver

Gallbladder

Stomach

Small intestine

Colon

Liver (hepatic) ducts

Appendix

Rectum

Esophagus

Cystic duct

Common bile
duct

Gallbladder

Stomach

Duodenum

Bile/pancreatic duct opening

Pancreas

Figure 9.5. **The Gastrointestinal System.**

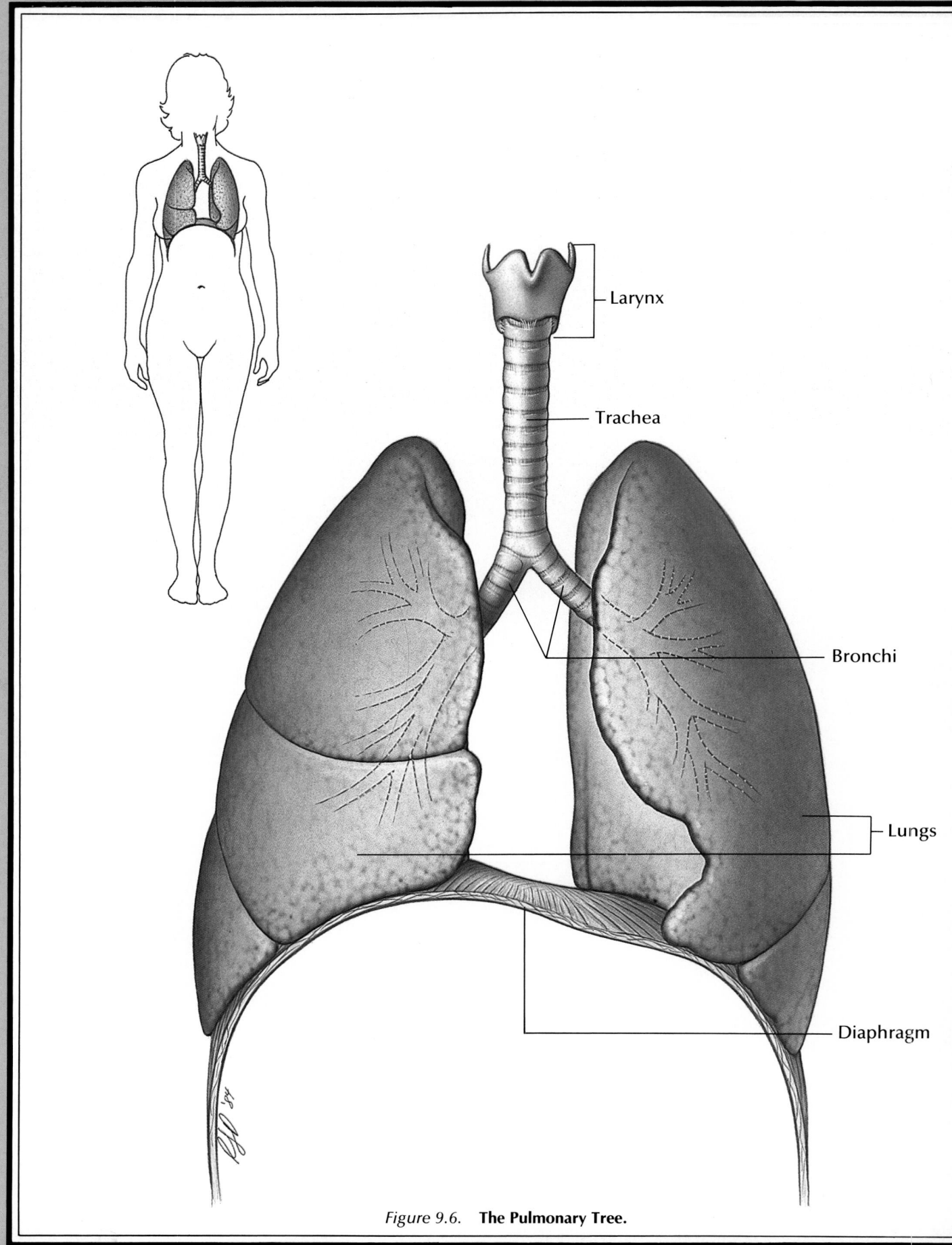

Figure 9.6. **The Pulmonary Tree.**

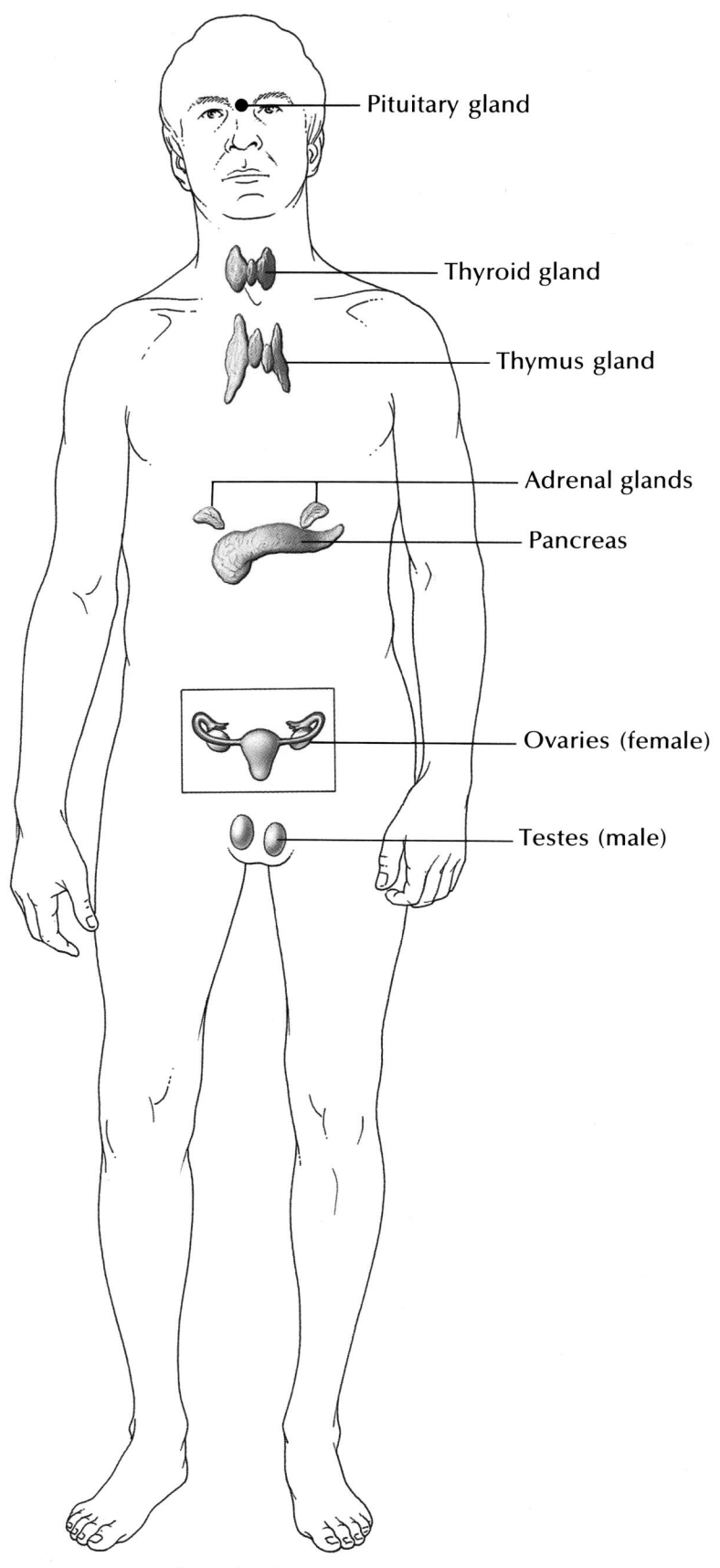

Pituitary gland

Thyroid gland

Thymus gland

Adrenal glands

Pancreas

Ovaries (female)

Testes (male)

Figure 9.7. **The Endocrine System.**

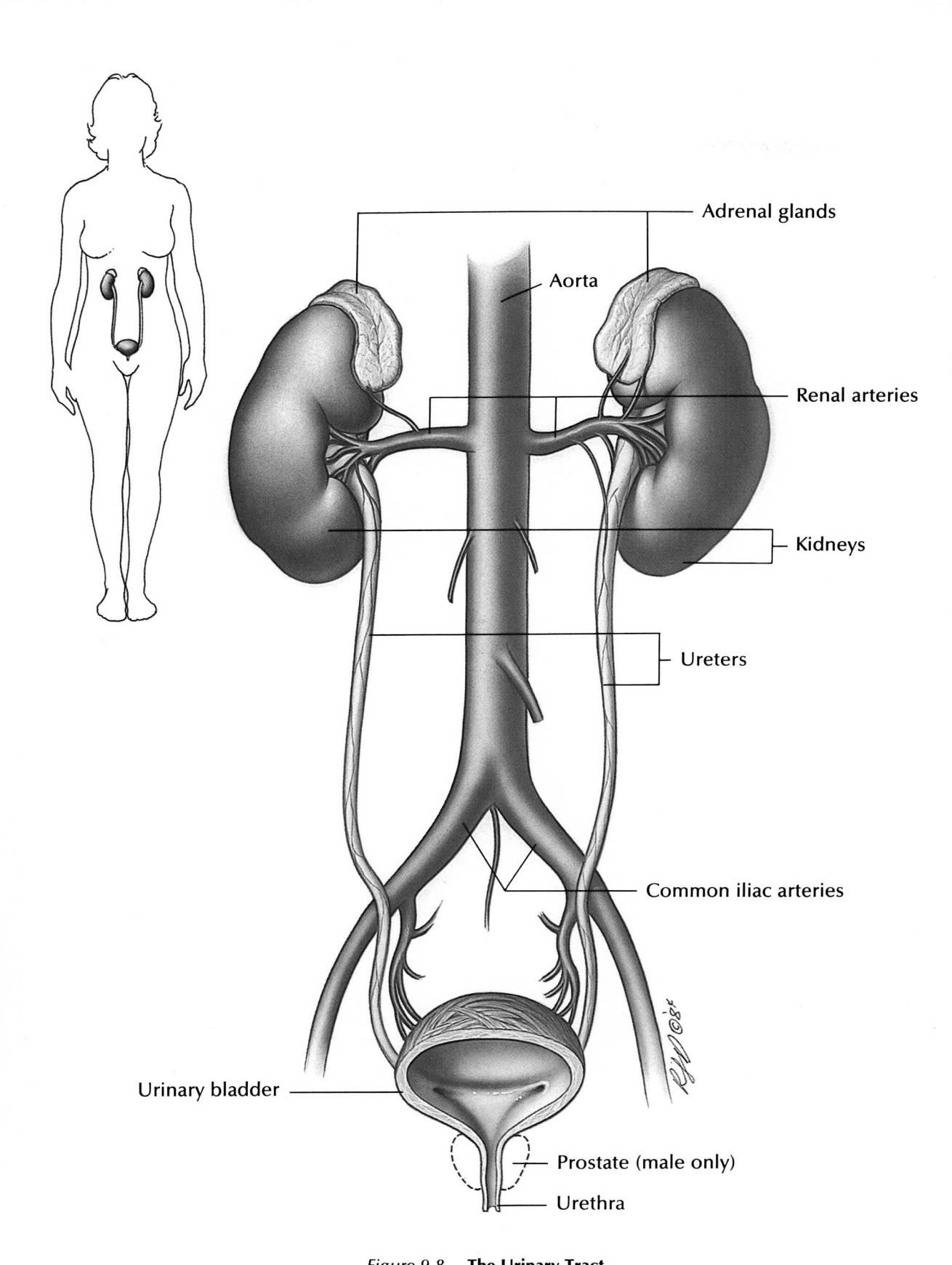

Adrenal glands

Aorta

Renal arteries

Kidneys

Ureters

Common iliac arteries

Urinary bladder

Prostate (male only)

Urethra

Figure 9.8. **The Urinary Tract.**

only a single defective gene, in which case they will become a carrier, like the parents; or a 25 percent chance of receiving the gene from both parents and getting the disease. Should a carrier-child eventually marry another carrier, he or she runs the same risk as his or her parents of transmitting the disease to the next generation.

Recessive inherited diseases tend to be severe and often cause death early in life. Among some 1,300 confirmed or suspected recessive disorders are: cystic fibrosis, which affects the function of mucous and sweat glands (new treatments have been developed which are able to prolong the life of a child with cystic fibrosis, but most do not live beyond young adulthood); galactosomia, or inability to metabolize milk sugar, which can be treated by diet; phenylketonuria, a liver enzyme deficiency that can cause mental retardation if not recognized in time, but which can be treated by diet; and diseases that strike members of particular ethnic groups. These include sickle cell disease, a blood disorder that affects primarily blacks; thalassemia, a blood disorder that affects persons of Mediterranean heritage; Tay-Sachs disease, a fatal brain disease that primarily affects infants of Eastern European (Ashkenazic) Jews; and Gaucher's disease, a chronic disorder that affects the spleen, liver, bones, and blood, primarily in offspring of Eastern European Jewish couples. Some experimental work in blood transfusions and marrow transfusions prolongs the lives of children with these blood diseases, but no completely successful treatment has yet been found.

X-Linked Inheritance

Normal women have 2 X chromosomes. Normal men have one X and one Y chromosome. A woman who is normal may be a carrier of a faulty gene on one of her X chromosomes. In such a case, her sons each have a 50/50 risk of inheriting that gene and manifesting the disorder of the faulty X chromosome. Each daughter has a 50/50 chance of becoming a carrier of the disease and, like her mother, being unaffected by the disease, but capable of transmitting it to her male offspring. Scientists have found that fathers do not contribute faulty genes to their children in this way. There are some 240 confirmed or suspected disorders transmitted by a gene or genes in the X chromosome. They include: agammaglobulinemia, or lack of immunity to infection; color blindness, or inability to distinguish certain colors; and hemophilia, a defect in blood-clotting mechanisms.

Multifactorial Inheritance

A large group of genetic disorders result from the interaction of many genes with other genes or with environmental factors. The pattern of transmission is less well defined, but it is known that the probability of recurrence in other children in the family is low. With one affected child in the family, chances of another having the same defect are 5 percent or less. Some defects thought to be multifactorial include: cleft palate and/or lip and congenital dislocation of the hip, both correctable by surgery; spina bifida (open spine), sometimes with hydrocephalus—water on the brain; pyloric stenosis, narrowed or obstructed opening from the stomach into the small intestine, often correctable by surgery; diabetes mellitus; and congenital heart defects, which may often be corrected by surgery.

The probability of genetic disease in a particular child can be determined to a certain extent by medical genetics, a relatively new and developing field. Both the National Genetics Foundation and the National Foundation/March of Dimes offer methods for a couple to trace their health history through this new knowledge.

The National Genetics Foundation offers, for a small fee (about $10), a three-generational family health history to be completed by the couple. When it is returned to the foundation (555 West 57th Street, New York, New York 10019), counselors evaluate it and their report may offer information that will be useful in preventing or controlling genetic diseases in the couple's children. The National Foundation/March of Dimes, which has local chapters in communities around the country, has a free Family Medical Record form available to be filled out and then shared with one's own family physicians or other counselors. Its chapters or its national office (1275 Mamaroneck Avenue, White Plains, New York 10605) also have a brochure called "A Family Health Tree" that helps gather and record the family medical genealogy.

There are also medical genetics counseling services at about 60 university-based centers around the country. Individuals may be referred by their physicians or may decide to go themselves.

The process includes giving a complete family and personal medical history to the counselor, and evaluation of the mother's and father's health by the physician specializing in genetics, who may order certain tests to uncover the presence of genetic abnormalities. A genetic workup is intended to determine the probable existence of a genetic problem occurring or reoccurring and to offer prospective parents choices for prevention and treatment.

Genetic counseling can help answer questions like:

- Whether the parent, a child, or another relative has an inheritable genetic disease.

- Whether the prospective parents are statistically likely to carry a genetic disorder in their genes even though they may not show it. (But they could pass it on to a certain percentage of their offspring.)

- What the chances are of children in a particular family having a genetic problem.

- Where treatment and care for this disorder can be obtained.

The genetic counselor's work is to marshal the facts and present possibilities and probabilities of genetic disease in a couple's offspring. It is then up to the parents-to-be to make their own decisions about whether to have children or whether to adopt.

Diagnosis of some genetic disorders during the early part of pregnancy is possible with amniocentesis, a low-risk method performed during the fourth month of pregnancy on an outpatient basis in a hospital that has the specialized laboratory facilities and qualified personnel. Ultrasound equipment, using high-frequency sound waves, completely without pain, locates the position, size, and structure of the fetus and the placenta in the womb. (Ultrasound is used by itself to make early diagnosis of multiple births and certain congenital defects.) The ultrasound information makes possible the guided insertion into the abdomen of a syringe, which enters the amniotic sac (containing the fetus) and withdraws some cells discarded by the fetus. The test takes a short time, and discomfort is minimal. Usually a local anesthetic is used on the mother's abdomen. During the next few weeks, the sample of fluid is analyzed biochemically and/or the fetal cells are cultured and their chromosomes examined. Amnio-

centesis can rule out only certain specific problems, for example Down's syndrome. In every pregnancy, there is perhaps a slight risk that the baby will be born with some abnormality. At this time, there are many genetic diseases for which there are no prenatal tests.

Within the next few years, it is expected that first trimester pregnancy diagnosis will be available. In one method, chorionic villus biopsy, cells gently suctioned off the fingerlike attachments of the amniotic sac to the uterus can be examined as early as 6 to 8 weeks into the pregnancy. Its advantages over amniocentesis are that it can be performed earlier in the pregnancy, and will require only that an ultrasound guided tube be inserted through the woman's cervix, instead of requiring the insertion of a needle through the abdomen. A few medical centers are also using, on an experimental basis, fetoscopy, or insertion of a viewing instrument directly into the womb to observe the fetus and take blood samples.

In fact, genetic science is proceeding in two directions to control genetic diseases: research and treatment. There is research going on now to unscramble the mysteries of the structure and position of all the genes on the 46 chromosomes. The major aims of this work are to discover how these genes are "switched on and off" to promote normal development, and to discover just what goes wrong to cause genetic diseases. Eventually, there may be vaccines for protecting against these diseases, early warning for many diseases that occur in adulthood, an understanding of the basis of inherited disease, and therapies that will help more children and adults lead better, healthier lives.

INFERTILITY

INFERTILITY IS an increasingly common problem among American couples, and as a growing number of couples decide they are ready for parenthood, they are seeking help. There are several reasons for their infertility.

1. More people than ever are starting families. Therefore, more infertility is turning up in the population. While birth rates began to rise in the United States beginning in 1947, the largest number of births actually occurred between 1956 and 1961. Now, in the mid-1980s, the average age of these people is 25, the height of the fertile years. The number of couples trying to have a baby means more who are finding that they cannot do so.

2. There are more infertile women among the current generation than among previous populations in their reproductive prime. Some theories as to why

this is include: the recent rise in sexually transmitted diseases that result in pelvic inflammatory disease and infertility; women entering the work force and being exposed to potential occupational hazards that affect their reproductive ability; and the possible increased exposure of American couples to environmental toxins that decrease fertility.

3. Women are delaying childbearing into the later reproductive years; a woman's fertility begins to decrease in her thirties.

4. The use of oral contraceptives and the IUD may account for some infertility. Between 1970 and 1975, approximately 20 million women used oral contraception. When they discontinued taking the pill, whether because of a desire to become pregnant, or because of adverse publicity, it took longer for them to become pregnant. And, the IUD may reduce fertil-

ity, either by chronic uterine irritation or by promoting infection or tubal pregnancy.

5. Since many couples delayed childbearing until their later reproductive years, they condense the time during which they would like to conceive into a much shorter period. Faced with diminished reproductive years, many couples decide to seek help to start their families if pregnancy does not occur soon after they decide to have a child. In addition, some people who have been sterilized are now attempting to have the operations reversed. These add to the flow of people seeking fertility counseling and services.

6. Finally, more couples are aware that help is available for infertility problems, thus, more are seeking it.

What Is Infertility?

About one-half of all fertile couples trying to conceive will do so within 1 month, and about three-quarters within the first 6 months. An additional 5 to 10 percent will become pregnant within the following year.

Infertility is defined as the inability to get pregnant after 1 year or more of regular sexual activity without the use of contraception, or the inability to carry a pregnancy to a live birth. (See Infertility in Women, page 152.) Some specialists use 2 years as the cutoff point. If a pregnancy has never occurred, the condition is called primary infertility. If a couple cannot seem to start another pregnancy after the birth of a child, it is called secondary infertility. The causes of primary and secondary infertility may be different. Sterility is defined as the absolute inability to conceive children.

Infertility is fairly common. About 10 to 18 percent of the population, or 1 out of every 6 couples, is infertile at any given time. A woman is at the height of her fertility in her mid-twenties. Her ability to conceive declines until she reaches 30 and drops more rapidly after that. A man's fertility decreases slowly until about the age of 40, and then decreases more rapidly.

Women in their thirties will probably want to seek help more quickly than younger women, for their chances of getting pregnant are declining with the passage of time. Those who are not menstruating regularly may want to seek treatment as well, since irregular cycles may mean they are not ovulating. Such women are not likely to conceive without treatment. A woman who has a history of pelvic disease, or a man who had mumps as an adult might also want to forgo the waiting period.

Seeking Help

Diagnosing the many possible causes of infertility is a time-consuming task. A couple (or individual) should look for a doctor who specializes in infertility and who may work with a health-care team that can help educate and support a couple through the procedures involved.

Infertility was not recognized as a medical subspecialty for certification by the American Board of Obstetrics and Gynecology until about 10 years ago. Since then, the number of health-care professionals interested in infertility services has increased. Even so, there are probably not more than 200 of them in the United States. Most are associated with medical schools. The American Fertility Society, 1608 13th Avenue S., Suite 101, Birmingham, Alabama 35205, has a list of fertility specialists and centers available to the public.

A specialist may not be necessary for the preliminary steps in determining that a fertility problem exists, so the family doctor, the woman's gynecologist, or the man's urologist may be a suitable place to start.

If a couple (or individual) does seek fertility services, they should know that they are committing themselves to a process of several months, during which their intimate lives may very well become subject to scrutiny, along with their bodies and feelings. It is a trying time for most people. Determining whether pregnancy is probable, and what must be done to make it possible, requires far more cooperation on the part of the patients than in almost any other medical specialty. However, many of the causes of infertility can be diagnosed and treated, so if a couple is eager to have a baby—or to find out for sure that they cannot—the effort (which is expensive, and may not be covered by medical insurance) is well worth it.

The First Step

An interview with both partners is the first step. A family history is taken to detect possible genetic disorders. A health history of each partner is also taken, with particular attention to medical conditions that might affect fertility: mumps, measles, whooping cough, diphtheria, rubella, thyroid disease, tuberculosis, epilepsy, and the presence of infections. The doctor will ask about use of certain medications that may be spermicidal, as well as the use and abuse of alcohol, tea, coffee, or "recreational" drugs—all of which affect sperm count.

A sexual history of each partner follows. Questions for the woman may include when she began menstruating (menarche) and what her periods are like; whether she has pain between periods (indicative of ovulation); whether she has previously been pregnant, has miscarried, or has had therapeutic

Sample Chart

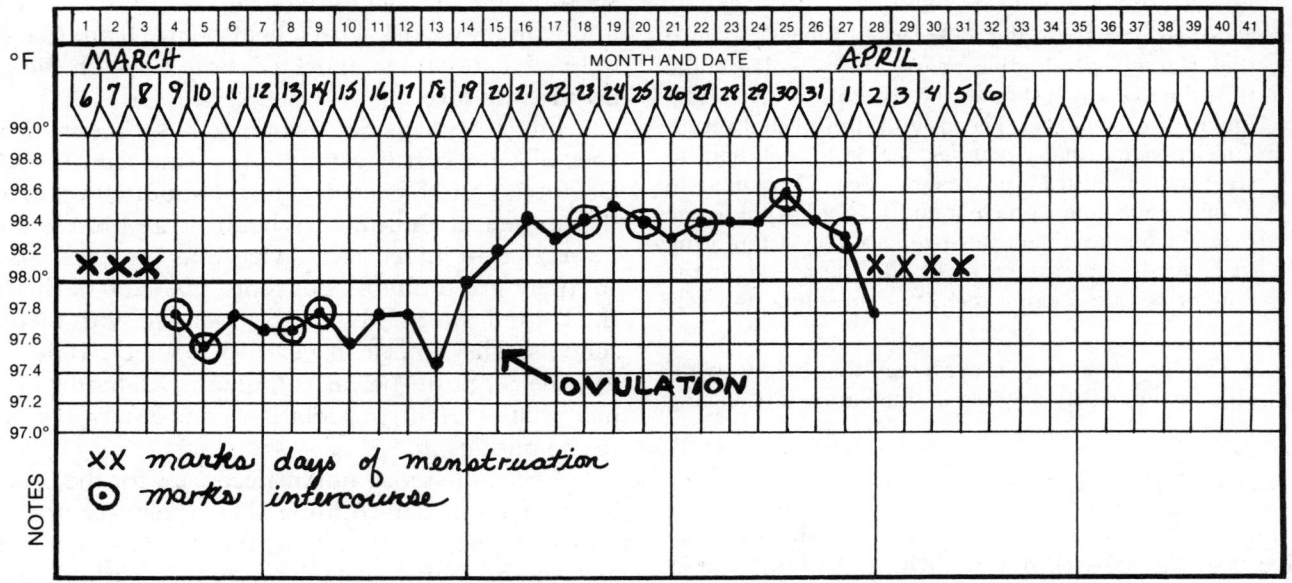

Figure 10.7.   **Sample temperature chart.** © Serono Laboratories, Inc., 280 Pond Street, Randolph, Massachusetts 02368.

abortions. She is also likely to be asked about the use of lubricants (some, such as Vaseline, retard the movement of sperm) or contraceptives, whether she has had pain during intercourse, and whether she has had pelvic infections. (Pelvic inflammatory disease may cause blockages that interfere with the passage of ova through the Fallopian tubes.) She will be taught how to measure and record her basal body temperature upon awakening each morning. The chart developed will help determine if she is ovulating. (See figure 10.7.)

Questions for the man may include whether there were problems in the normal descent of his testicles; whether he had surgery (orchiopexy) to help them descend; whether he has been circumcised and at what age.

Both partners will likely be asked about their sexual behavior: how often they have sex, orgasmic patterns, preferred positions, masturbation, or other sexual techniques. A small number of infertility cases are solved on the spot when it is learned that the couple is not engaging in vaginal intercourse.

The Physical Examinations

Both partners undergo extensive physical examinations. The doctor will be looking for normal development of sexual organs and secondary sex characteristics (pubic hair growth and breast development). A careful examination of the woman's abdomen may reveal scars from operations she has not mentioned. A bi-manual examination will confirm the presence of a normal healthy uterus and ovaries, or any problems of shape and size which may exist. The man's genitals will be examined for abnormal development or displacement of organs. Blood, glands, and urine will be tested for the presence of sexually transmitted diseases. As the workup progresses, more sophisticated tests will be done.

The process of infertility workup is a trying one for both the man and the woman. Often, they wonder if the problem is not a psychological one, and this is a reasonable question that can only be answered by going through the workup.

The goal of achieving pregnancy comes to dominate the couple's lives, and sometimes leads to depression. Intercourse comes to be less an expression of interest and affection than a job to be done in preparation for tests or when it is most likely to result in pregnancy.

A woman sometimes becomes less interested in sex and enjoys it less. She develops a new point of view toward her partner. She sees him as either supportive or unsympathetic, cooperative or difficult. Their relationship may be permanently altered by the revelations of this ongoing crisis.

A man sometimes questions his own "manliness" because fertility and virility are closely intertwined in our society. Sex-on-schedule becomes a problem for the male partner who just may not feel like it at the necessary time. Sometimes he develops performance problems or feels anger and resentment toward his partner. Both people may feel at various times that they are failures. The fertility specialist and the health-care team may or may not be sensitive to these problems. A doctor may seem rushed and unavailable to answer questions, which may have more to do with these perfectly legitimate feelings than with the tests that he or she is comfortable discussing.

Some fertility practices now include a nurse practitioner whose job it is to provide facts and support at a more leisurely, individualized pace than may be possible for a doctor.

Tests for Men

It makes sense for the man to be tested first. If he is the cause of the couple's infertility, the reason will be his sperm. Infertility in a woman may be due to a variety of causes. It used to be thought that if a couple could not conceive, it was because the woman was "barren." Now it is known that the man may also be infertile. Being infertile has nothing to do with male sexual prowess (virility), but with the presence of healthy sperm in the semen that are capable of traveling to meet the ovum. This is determined by semen analysis. The man provides the semen by masturbating into a sterile container or into a special condom during intercourse, and bringing the specimen to the doctor's office or hospital within 2 hours of collection.

Absence of sperm or low sperm count can be due to any infection associated with high fever that occurs after puberty. Mumps has long been associated with infertility in a man. Sexually transmitted diseases, like syphilis and gonorrhea, can affect the sperm and, if untreated, may make a man sterile. In actuality, men with low sperm counts may not have trouble fathering a child, while men with high sperm counts may. But the quality of sperm, as seen under the microscope in the laboratory, is the most important factor. The sperm must be moving rapidly and easily, and it must have few abnormalities. If a man tests at fewer than 60 million sperm per milliliter of ejaculate (a condition called oligospermia), he may have difficulty becoming a father. Occasionally, sperm count will reveal the complete absence (azoospermia) of live sperm in the specimen.

Sperm Delivery.

Sexually transmitted diseases may result in blockage of the seminal vesicle or other portions of the male reproductive tract through which sperm pass. Injury or accident can also cause blockage. In addition, about 500,000 vasectomies are performed in the United States each year, and these men are voluntarily sterile. Block-

ages can be cleared; vasectomies may sometimes be reversed.

In addition, a small percentage of men have a condition called retrograde ejaculation, in which the sperm enter the bladder instead of continuing out through the urethra. This condition can sometimes be treated.

Impotence (inability to maintain an erection), premature ejaculation, and the inability to ejaculate can all make it impossible for a man to impregnate a woman. These conditions may have an organic cause, or a psychological component. Sex therapy has been effective in treating the latter.

Sperm Antibodies.

Occasionally, a man has had an injury or infection that allows the sperm to enter the surrounding tissue where they are killed by his own antibodies. If the man's injury or infection can be treated, his own antibodies should cease attacking his sperm.

Some women are allergic to sperm and they develop antibodies to fight it. An allergy to sperm in a woman can sometimes be dealt with by having her partner use a condom for intercourse for some time and then, when her antibodies have lessened, by having sex without a condom at the time of ovulation.

Other Reasons for Male Infertility.

There are numerous causes of male infertility, some of which are illustrated in figure 10.8. If the man's testicles did not descend into the scrotal sac before puberty, sperm production will be affected. The testicles function at a slightly lower temperature than the rest of the body's organs and need to be in the scrotal sac to produce sperm. Hormone therapy or surgery can make the testicles descend, but it is best done in childhood. Sometimes there are abnormalities in the testicles themselves that affect sperm production. These usually cannot be surgically corrected.

Another condition that can cause higher temperatures and lower sperm count in the testicles is a varicocele, a twisted vein in the testicle that affects blood flow. This condition can be corrected surgically. There may be other temporary conditions that the man himself may control—extensive use of hot tubs and saunas, long, hot showers, and athletic supporters. They all may slow growth of sperm. This situation will reverse itself in a short time when the environment changes.

Other conditions that may affect function of the testicles and reduce or eliminate sperm in a man's semen include:

- Injury to the reproductive organs from a serious accident, which could result in a reduction or cutoff of blood supply to the area and death of the surrounding

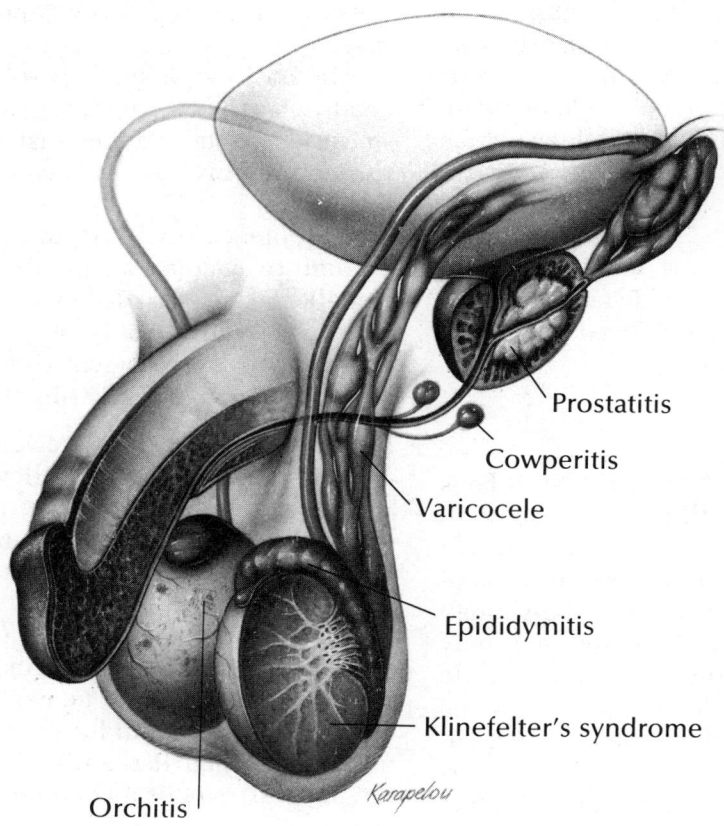

Prostatitis

Cowperitis

Varicocele

Epididymitis

Klinefelter's syndrome

Orchitis

Figure 10.8. **Common causes of male infertility.**

tissues (occasionally this may occur with a hernia operation).

- Radiation, which may make a man temporarily infertile.
- Chronic illness, including alcoholism or drug abuse. Heavy, long-term use of marijuana has been implicated in cases of lowered sperm counts.
- Stress, which may reduce fertility.
- Hormonal imbalances, which can also cause infertility. If they are treated, fertility may return.
- Pollutants such as toxic pesticides, herbicides, and industrial chemicals.

Sperm Mobility. Many of the factors that cause a reduced sperm count may also affect the ability of sperm to move successfully along the female reproductive tract to fertilize an ovum and start a pregnancy. Infections of the prostate gland (which produces the milky fluid that constitutes most of the ejaculate), or surgical removal of the gland will affect sperm mobility. Chronic illness will also affect the ability of the sperm to move vigorously, as will hormonal problems.

Infertility in Women

If the male reproductive system appears in order, study of the woman begins. The first question to determine is what happens to the man's sperm in the woman's body; this is answered by the Huhner Test. This test first involves the collection of cervical mucus, done painlessly with a small spadelike instrument in the doctor's office, within 2 hours after the woman has had intercourse. The examination of the mucus under a microscope seeks to establish whether there are a sufficient number of live sperm present and whether she has produced sufficient mucus to ease the passage of sperm through her genital tract and into her Fallopian tube where fertilization might take place.

Problems in Female Conception. A woman may be unable to conceive because of abnormalities of her uterus, Fallopian tubes, or ovaries (see figure 10.9). She may be unable to produce an ovum, or her reproductive organs may be damaged by disease. Occasionally, the woman's uterus or ovaries may

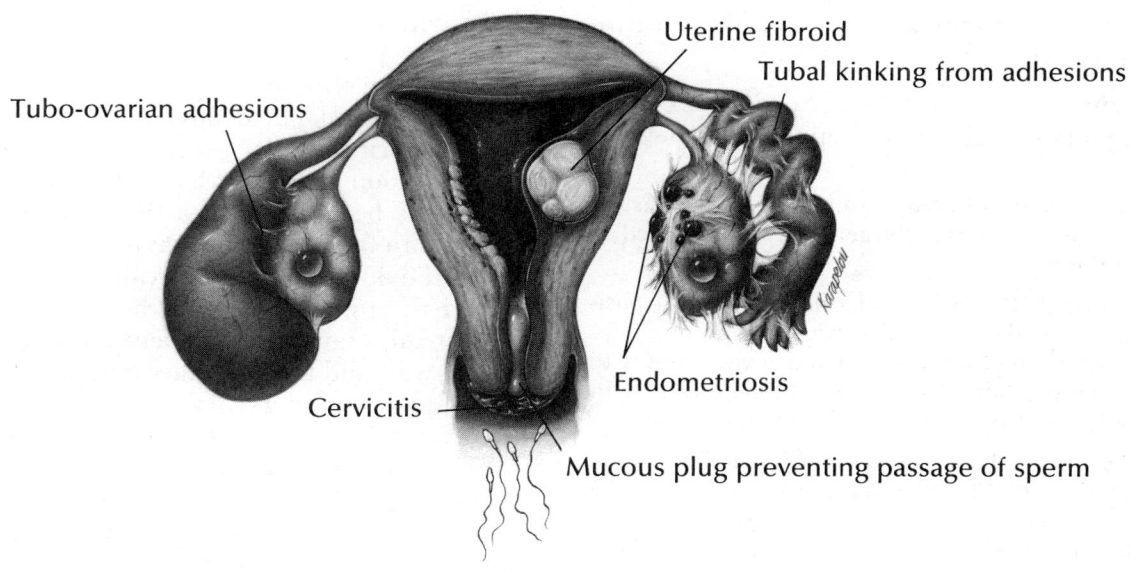

Tubo-ovarian adhesions

Uterine fibroid

Tubal kinking from adhesions

Cervicitis

Endometriosis

Mucous plug preventing passage of sperm

Figure 10.9. **Common causes of female infertility.**

not have developed normally; in such a case, she may not menstruate or menstruate only occasionally.

Sometimes a woman with normal menstrual periods still is not producing an ovum with each menstrual cycle. This can be determined by a basal body temperature chart, which the woman develops at home by taking her own temperature before getting up in the morning. When a woman ovulates, her temperature rises slightly, and remains slightly higher in the second half of the menstrual cycle than in the first half. Her chart at the conclusion of a menstrual cycle will show this rise or lack of it.

Female infertility is often the result of hormonal imbalance. Hormones produced by the hypothalamus stimulates the pituitary gland which, in turn, stimulates an ovum's maturation and its release from the ovary into the Fallopian tube where pregnancy may occur. Estrogen and progesterone prepare the lining of the uterus for implantation of the fertilized ovum. When fertilization does not occur, the woman's body stops producing these hormones, and menstruation occurs. Initially, tests are done to determine if these hormones are being produced. If progesterone cannot be found in a blood test, there is a good chance that ovulation is not occurring. It is not necessary that a woman ovulate 12 times a year in order to become pregnant, and women who do so less frequently can still conceive. But the chances of a pregnancy occurring are increased with regular ovulation.

Another hormone sought in a blood test is prolactin. Produced when a woman breast-feeds, it prevents a nursing mother from becoming pregnant.

However, sometimes this hormone is produced in women who are not nursing, and it prevents both menstruation and ovulation. This condition can be caused by a tumor of the pituitary gland, a condition that, if successfully treated, will result in restoration of the woman's menstrual periods, and the probability that she will again ovulate. Sometimes the condition is not caused by a tumor and can be treated with a drug to restore the woman's fertility.

Another reason for female infertility is that a woman's body may not be giving itself enough time in the menstrual cycle for implantation to take place. In other words, there may be too few days each month when she is ready to accept the fertilized egg, allowing normal development. This can be determined by measuring progesterone levels in a woman's blood at regular intervals through the second half of a cycle. The condition can be treated with hormones, a treatment that sometimes results in overstimulation of the ovaries that may produce multiple births.

General Conditions Affecting Female Fertility. Women who have lost a great deal of weight frequently have a cessation of menstrual periods. In the severe dieting disorder, anorexia nervosa, periods are altogether lacking. The condition is treated by encouraging the affected woman to eat enough so that her periods will begin again. Chronic illness or substance abuse (alcohol, drugs) tends to decrease the activity of the ovaries. In many disorders of the endocrine system such as severe diabetes, thyroid abnormalities, or adrenal gland insufficiency, there may be cessation of menstruation or ovulation. Exposure to x-rays or radioactive materials is a rare cause of infertility.

The Uterus.   Several uterine conditions may make pregnancy difficult or impossible. They include:

- *Fibroids*—These are benign tumors that can distort the shape of the uterus. Surgery may be required to remove them.

- *Tipped uterus*—Normal wombs lie in a typical position, their closed end facing forward and pointing upward. A tipped uterus faces back and down. Surgery to correct the position has had only limited success in improving fertility and is not recommended.

- *Endometriosis*—This condition usually affects women between 30 and 40 and reduces their fertility. The same tissue that lines the uterus and that is expelled each month during menstruation may grow elsewhere in the pelvic cavity. If this happens in the Fallopian tubes or on the ovaries, fertility may be affected. The misplaced tissue is as responsive to hormonal signals as the tissue in the uterus; it grows and deteriorates in the same way and often causes scarring and adhesions. It is not fully understood how endometriosis interferes with fertility. Research indicates that the errant tissue may have some influence on the ovum after it is released from the ovary. Treatment of endometriosis includes treatment with hormones or sometimes surgery.

The Fallopian Tubes.   In the normal woman, an egg travels down the Fallopian tube—an alternate tube each month—from the ovary to the uterus. Little hairlike projections called cilia float the egg along to meet the sperm at a point near the womb. The journey is aided by a slight squeezing of the walls and the egg is nourished by delicate cells that line the tube.

Damage to the Fallopian tubes makes it difficult or impossible for an ovum to be conducted to the uterus every month, and may result in a woman's inability to conceive. Sometimes, if the tubes' lining is damaged, a conception can occur too high and pregnancy will begin there instead of in the uterus. An ectopic pregnancy, as this is called, requires surgical removal to prevent rupture of the tube and other serious complications. Some doctors try to leave the tube intact but often it is damaged beyond repair. Should a woman have only one functioning Fallopian tube, her chances of becoming pregnant are reduced by half.

To determine whether the Fallopian tubes are functioning properly, fertility specialists can call upon a variety of tests.

One test is a laparoscopy, a minor surgical procedure performed under general anesthesia through a small incision just beneath the umbilicus. After the bladder has been emptied, a thin hollow needle is inserted into the abdominal cavity and a gas, either carbon dioxide or nitrous oxide, is then gently pumped through it and into the abdomen, which will distend, leaving space between the front abdominal wall and the intestines and pelvic organs.

A laparoscope—a small, telescopelike instrument with its own lighting system—is then inserted into the abdominal cavity, and the doctor is able to inspect the pelvic organs. The passage of a colored fluid pumped into the uterine cavity and into the Fallopian tubes will permit the doctor to see whether the tubes are open or closed and whether there is blockage. A decision to perform surgery to restore fertility can be made at that time. At the end of the procedure, the laparoscope is removed, the gas drawn out, and the incision closed with a stitch or two. The procedure takes less than one-half hour.

Another test is insufflation of the Fallopian tubes. When carbon dioxide, a gas readily absorbed into the body, is blown gently through the uterus, it will escape through the Fallopian tubes. This test enables the physician to determine whether the tubes are open. The tubes are muscular, so there is bound to be some resistance, but the properly open tubes will accept the gas at a steady rate. Sometimes the physician will listen with a stethoscope on the abdomen to determine the rate at which the gas is escaping.

Yet another test is called a hysterosalpinogram. A water-soluble fluid, opaque to x-rays, is injected in the uterus while an x-ray film is made. As the uterus fills with the fluid, it enters the tubes and goes toward the ovaries. Abnormalities and blockages can be revealed this way. The procedure is often performed under general anesthesia. Sometimes a woman is able to become pregnant after the procedure has been performed, her infertility having been caused by a minor blockage which the liquid has removed. Adhesions and other conditions revealed by this test can often be corrected surgically or with antibiotics.

WHEN THE COUPLE REMAINS INFERTILE

OUT OF A GROUP of couples who believe they are infertile, a large proportion will conceive while undergoing tests. Another group will be helped by removal of blockages, treatment of endometriosis, or induction of ovulation with fertility drugs. For some couples, however, the tests reveal an absolute inability to have children.

Adoption has been the traditional solution for the infertile couple, and, although there are fewer infants available than there once were (due to the increased use of contraceptives, changing ideas about unwed motherhood, and the legalization of abortion), a couple might first look into this means of having the opportunity to raise a child. Public and private agencies throughout the country can be called on for information about beginning the procedure.

Another alternative is artificial insemination. The male partner's semen is collected and placed in the cervix or uterus of the female partner around the time of ovulation. Reported pregnancy rates, however, are low.

Artificial insemination by donor sperm should take place only if both partners want it. Donors are usually chosen for physical similarities to the couple. Physical history to rule out disease is required of donors, as is a good semen count. Medical students, interns, and residents are often donors. Insemination procedures are usually done more than once, sometimes with a different donor each time. Often, the partner's sperm may be mixed in with the donor sample. This method of artificial insemination usually has better results.

IN VITRO FERTILIZATION

THIS NEW CONCEPT has held public attention since the birth of the first "test-tube" baby several years ago. It is still highly experimental and used only when there is no other alternative. It requires, of course, that the woman be capable of producing ova and ovulating. The woman receives hormones to stimulate ovarian activity just after her menstrual period. This is intended to produce as many ova as possible. Just before ovulation, the woman enters the hospital, where the ova are obtained by laparoscopy. After a short incubation, a sperm sample is added, either from her partner or from a donor. Should fertilization occur, the developing embryos are incubated—this is where the test-tube labeling of the procedure came from—until they reach the 2- to 8-cell state. They are then transferred to the uterus. The woman may receive more hormones to decrease the possibility of miscarriage. Hormone levels continue to be measured until it is certain that the pregnancy is in progress. *In vitro* fertilization is costly, running $6,000 or more per attempt.

SEXUAL BEHAVIOR
Alexander Levay, M.D., and Lawrence Sharpe, M.D.

INTRODUCTION

THE IMPORTANCE OF healthy sexual functioning to total well being and the emotional pain and suffering of people with sexual problems are at long last being recognized. The past decade has brought revolutionary changes in attitudes, knowledge, and treatment of sexual problems.

The vast majority of sexual problems originate in one or more of the following areas: physical, psychological, interpersonal, informational, circumstantial, and psychiatric. There is almost always some overlap between these categories, but it is helpful to view the problem along these lines to understand the difficulties involved and arrive at an appropriate treatment plan.

THE PHYSICAL ASPECTS OF SEXUALITY

THE SEXUAL RESPONSE cycle consists of four sequential stages. Assuming a healthy sexual drive and the presence of sexual desire, adequate stimulation leads to an initial arousal stage involving an erection in the man and genital engorgement and vaginal lubrication in the female. This continues into the plateau stage, in which sexual arousal and continued pleasurable tension are heightened, followed by the third stage—orgasm in the woman and ejaculation in the man. The final stage is one of resolution, in which the genitalia return to their previously nonstimulated state. The first three stages are accompanied by other physical changes, such as muscle tension and rises in blood pressure, pulse, and respiratory rates. These also return to normal during the fourth stage.

In both sexes, sexual arousal is not subject to voluntary control. Instead, it is controlled by the autonomic nervous system, which also mediates a number of other involuntary responses, such as rage, fear, and anxiety. Therefore, if these responses occur before or during the sexual response cycle, it can be blocked or aborted.

External factors can also interfere with the autonomic nervous system, resulting in sexual impairment. Nerve damage, such as that which may occur during radical prostatic surgery, may lead to impaired sexual functioning. Some medications that directly affect the autonomic nervous system, such as the beta-blocking drugs used to treat high blood pressure and heart disease, can also hinder sexual functioning. Certain metabolic and vascular diseases, such as diabetes mellitus, can also affect the autonomic nervous system and cause sexual dysfunction.

The role of hormones in sexual functioning is not fully known. Adequate testosterone (the male sex hormone that is produced by the testes and which is also secreted, in smaller amounts, by the adrenal glands in women), however, appears essential for adequate sexual desire in both sexes. Men who are unable to achieve an erection should have their blood levels of testosterone measured. If testosterone levels are normal, however, extra hormone supplements will not improve sexual function. In fact, they may have an opposite effect by leading to a reduction in the naturally produced hormone. There is some evidence that the peaking of estrogen associated with ovulation may increase sexual response in women, but this interaction requires further documentation.

THE PSYCHOLOGICAL ASPECTS OF SEXUALITY

THE GREATEST INHIBITIONS to healthy sexual function are feelings of guilt and anxiety and a negative feeling toward sexuality. Women, for example, often fear that it is not "proper" to be sexual or to respond overtly to a partner's stimulation. The healthy and sexually comfortable woman is able to accept full responsibility for her own sexuality, is knowledgeable about sex and about her body's sexual responsiveness, and is able to satisfy her needs in a sexual relationship. Such a woman understands that her arousal and satisfaction will also be arousing and satisfying to her partner and will add to their joint sense of pleasure and closeness.

Both sexual partners should focus on their own personal pleasure and be able to communicate this pleasure as well as recognize and respond to the needs and pleasures of the chosen partner. Sex is a moment-to-moment pleasurable act involving many forms of activity, including oral and other touching stimulation as well as intercourse. Sexual pleasure is greatly enhanced by a high level of intimacy and love, so that each partner is able to communicate about innermost sexual desires, fantasies, and preferences, and is able to please the other without compromising his or her own pleasure. If sexual activity is used to satisfy aims other than mutual support and pleasure—for example, to dominate or control a partner or to fulfill a sense of duty—the sexual relationship is invariably placed in jeopardy.

Unfortunately, a negative attitude against masturbation persists in our society. Most men masturbate as a normal part of sexual development and when they lack a sexual partner. Women do so less frequently, although this seems to be changing with the increased acceptance of female sexuality. A negative attitude toward masturbation among women is often associated with negative feelings about one's body image and sexuality. Such women not only find it impossible to contemplate masturbation, but also frequently find it difficult to be touched in the genital area or to touch their partners' genitals.

Once anxiety, guilt, or other negative feelings interfere with sexual functioning, both partners begin to think of sex in terms of performance. This stage of sexual dysfunction may be characterized by:

1. *Performance anxiety*, in which the individual is highly anxious about moment-to-moment performance activity.
2. *Goal orientation*, in which one of both partners direct their concerns to a specific goal, usually orgasm.
3. *Spectatoring*, in which either or both partners keep checking their own or their partner's current state of excitement and response.

THE INTERPERSONAL ASPECTS OF SEXUALITY

OPEN, ANXIETY-FREE communication is the basis of the best interpersonal relationships, yet many couples have difficulty in communicating about sexual matters. Frequently, partners know little about one another's sexual fantasies, preferences, dislikes, fears, and vulnerabilities. In many relationships, certain aspects of a partner's preferences are never revealed and are either totally repressed or allowed expression only outside the relationship.

In contrast, sexual dysfunction may be an initial symptom of an unidentified interpersonal problem. For example, one partner may have an unconscious need to totally dominate the other, a situation that may manifest itself in sexual problems.

Sexual dysfunction almost invariably leads to interpersonal problems, which then further aggravate the sexual difficulties. This can create uncertainty as to whether the sexual difficulties are the cause or the result of the couple's problems. If sexual problems are the cause, solving them usually restores harmony. When the sexual problems are secondary to an underlying interpersonal problem, however, solving the sexual problem often, ironically, aggravates the interpersonal one. In such situations, counselling may be required.

THE INFORMATIONAL ASPECT OF SEXUALITY

PEOPLE STILL DO not know many facts about sex. Myths, negative attitudes, and misconceptions persist. Even when accurate information is available, many people resist using it in their own personal sex lives, possibly because of uncertainty or guilt.

THE CIRCUMSTANTIAL ASPECTS OF SEXUALITY

MANY SEXUAL PROBLEMS seem to be associated with extraneous circumstances and problems of daily living. Work, children, hobbies, sleep patterns, and numerous obligations all may intrude upon the time available for sex. For some couples, such conflicts may be a sign of underlying interpersonal problems, but where the problems are truly circumstantial, simple measures may solve them. For example, many couples have difficulties in finding time together for sexual activity. The pressure of work and work-related activities often take priority. They fall into the habit of having sex before falling asleep at night—a time when they are most tired and least open to lovemaking. Or one partner may like to retire early and get up at the crack of dawn, while the other has an opposite late-to-bed, late-to-rise pattern. Recognizing and dealing with these difficulties can often solve the problem.

Variations in sexual activity during the life cycle clearly occurs in both sexes. The sudden explosion of sexual awareness in adolescence is severely modified by social factors, availability of partners, and attitudes toward sexuality. Possible changes in sexual responsiveness during the menstrual cycle and at the menopause require further study. The myth that sexual ability and activity ceases with advancing age has been disproved and, although sexual activity changes with advanced age, there seems to be no reason why it should not continue throughout life.

At times of severe emotional stress, such as following the death of a loved one, or the breakup of a relationship, sexual desires and abilities are likely to change. In some people, there is an increased need for sexual expression. For others, loss of libido is a common component of mourning.

THE PSYCHIATRIC ASPECTS OF SEXUALITY

CHANGES IN SEXUAL activity often indicate a more serious psychiatric disorder. Loss of interest in sex is a common symptom of depression. The sudden ap-pearance of excessive sexual desire, increased sexual activity, and promiscuity may indicate a manic disorder. Bizarrely diverse sexual behavior may be part of a schizophrenic disorder. Exhibitionism in the elderly may signal dementia. Other inappropriate sexual behaviors, such as the compulsive seeking of new sexual partners, may be precipitated by a variety of severe life-stress situations.

HOMOSEXUALITY

HOMOSEXUAL BEHAVIOR IS a complex phenomenon. In some people, it may be related to as yet undefined intrauterine hormonal influences. In these people, there appears to be a lifelong pattern of homosexual interests. For others, homosexual behavior appears to be related to psychological influences in the patient's early development, such as fear of heterosexual relationships.

Homosexuality is not an illness, nor is it necessarily associated with "femininity" in the male or "masculinity" in the female. Homosexuals of both sexes share the same sexual concerns and problems of interpersonal relationships as heterosexuals. Homosexual relationship patterns can vary from extreme promiscuity to stable long-term relationships.

Some people may seek medical or psychiatric help if they experience distress specifically from their homosexual concerns. These include adolescents with homosexual impulses who have not acted upon them or people who have been functioning homosexually but wish to function heterosexually. Others may be functioning heterosexually but have homosexual impulses, and still others may mistakenly develop fears of homosexuality because of sexual problems, such as loss of sexual desire or impotence in a heterosexual setting.

Many of these people need only simple reassurance. Others, however, should undergo therapy. In general, psychotherapy concentrates on dealing with the problems entailed in being homosexual in a predominantly heterosexual society. Other patients may want to shift to a heterosexual orientation. About 1 out of 3 male homosexuals can be helped to shift his sexual orientation provided he still has heterosexual dreams or fantasies, he has had one or more successful heterosexual encounters, and he had his first homosexual experience after the age of 16.

PARAPHILIAC BEHAVIOR

THIS TERM COVERS a wide range of sexual behavior, including nonconsenting partners (such as children or animals), inflicting pain or severe humiliation, exhibitionism, or using fetish objects.

In modest forms of fetishism, such asking that the partner wear a garter belt, the person often only requires reassurance about the meaning and consequences of the fetishism. But if the paraphiliac behavior interferes with healthy sexual functioning or with other aspects of daily life for either partner, or inflicts harm on others, therapy should be sought.

PRINCIPLES OF TREATMENT

THE PREFERRED TREATMENT for all sexual problems involves both sexual partners, with each assuming a degree of responsibility for the sexual activity. After a couple seeks professional help and the problem has been defined, partners should understand the treatment goals and the steps involved in achieving them. Some of the more obvious myths are easily dispelled by reassurance and the sharing of information. Other problems may require specific therapies, some of which are outlined in the following sections.

Before seeing a sex therapist or counsellor, his or her qualifications should be checked. Because few states require licensing, unqualified and untrained individuals often set themselves up as therapists. In general, it is best to seek a suitably qualified, trained, and experienced therapist via a family physician or the treating specialist. Other reliable sources of referral include county medical societies and teaching hospitals, some of which have departments of sexual medicine.

SENSATE FOCUS EXERCISES

Sensate Focus I. Each partner is required to be totally receptive for 15 to 20 minutes while the other partner explores, stimulates, and caresses all parts of the body except the genital areas and breasts. All types of manual and oral stimulation may be used. The touching should include all types from light touch to stroking or rubbing, and can include using other parts of the body besides the hands, such as the lips or hair. Partners should take turns in initiating sensate focus exercises.

Sensate Focus II. The exercises are continued but now include the genital areas. Feedback from the partner is encouraged so that those aspects of stimulation found most pleasurable are inte-

grated into the stimulating exercises. Orgasm and penetration is still prohibited, but in some instances, oral-genital contact is encouraged.

Sensate Focus III. The exercises are continued and penetration and continued activity to orgasm is encouraged, depending on the specific sexual dysfunction.

The sensate focus exercises in the sequence outlined here are valuable for any couple that wishes to resume sex after a period of inactivity. They also help enhance sexual activity when it has become routine and unimaginative. Couples are not advised to proceed to the next exercise stage until the previous one has been mastered.

THE SEXUAL DYSFUNCTIONS

Sexual Dysfunctions in Men

Among men, sexual dysfunction is often associated with anxiety resulting from the misconception that all sexual activity must lead to intercourse, ejaculation, and orgasm by the partner. If this expectation is not met, the sexual act is considered a failure. Since the sexual response cycle is not under voluntary control, people with this self-imposed expectation are particularly vulnerable to anxieties and a self-fulfilling prophecy of failure.

Premature Ejaculation. This is probably the most common sexual dysfunction and the most easily treated. It occurs in men who, once aroused, cannot regulate their level of sexual stimulation or time the ejaculation. Characteristically, these individuals ejaculate immediately prior to or immediately after penetration. This often leads to performance anxiety as well as frustration on the part of the partner, who is denied sufficient arousal time, especially if sexual activity ends with male ejaculation. Persistence of premature ejaculation frequently results in sex becoming a dreaded and frustrating experience by both partners. Impotence may occur and either or both partners may experience a lack of sexual desire.

Treatment of premature ejaculation depends upon the factors involved; for example, whether there is a loss of desire or impotence. Under these circumstances, sex almost invariably becomes goal directed and is no longer pleasurable for either partner. Thus, the couple is usually advised to stop aiming for intercourse, but all other forms of love-

making are encouraged in whatever manner the couple finds comfortable. The goal of sexual activity becomes moment-to-moment pleasure, rather than genital performance. Ejaculatory control is just a matter of learning, which can be easily mastered when secondary anxiety is removed. The aim of treatment is to consistently reduce anxiety so that the new techniques can be practiced.

By practicing the sensate focus exercises (see accompanying box), each partner receives stimulation by the other, but the genital area is initially excluded. In most instances, the man is surprised to find he has been able to maintain the erection for up to 15 minutes of stimulation without ejaculation.

When the genital area is included (Sensate Focus II), the man should concentrate on the immediate preejaculatory period, when he feels that ejaculation is imminent. Within seconds, this leads to the emission phase, in which the semen enters the urethra and there is an accompanying feeling that ejaculation will occur even if all stimulation ceases. Once these phases are identified, the man can assume some control because stopping thrusting activity and/or stimulation during the first part of the preejaculatory phase will lower the level of excitation and prevent ejaculation from occurring. After 15 to 30 seconds, stimulation can be resumed until the preejaculatory sensations occur again.

Once the man knows that he can identify the preejaculatory phase, the stop-and-go technique should be done randomly three or four times before it occurs. This prevents undue concentration on the preejaculatory phenomena and allows full involvement in the pleasure of lovemaking. If the preejaculatory sensations do occur, the man simply asks his partner to momentarily stop the stimulation.

As the man gains a sense of control over the point of ejaculation, he can then decide when he wishes to ejaculate. Sensate Focus III exercises are based on essentially similar principles, and by the time they are part of the couple's regular sexual activity, the problem of premature ejaculation should be cured. This process usually takes about 6 to 8 weeks of twice-weekly exercises.

Occasional instances of premature ejaculation may occur during the early stages of the exercises, but this should not be considered a failure. With reassurance and continued practice, the problem usually disappears.

Retarded Ejaculation. This disorder also entails an inability to time the ejaculation, but here the erection is maintained for an excessive length of time. When ejaculation finally occurs, satisfaction is experienced but the timing is perceived as unsatisfactory for both partners. In some cases, ejaculation does not occur at all. The striving and inability to time the point of ejaculation, and the woman's feeling that she is inadequate to help her partner, can lead to distress, not only in the sexual activity, but also in the relationship.

Treatment involves attempting to reduce anxiety and goal orientation and the teaching of techniques of control over the timing of ejaculation. The same sensate focus exercises are suggested for retarded ejaculation as in other sexual disorders. After the couple has achieved a pleasurable state of lovemaking with low anxiety, the man should demonstrate whatever methods he uses to experience ejaculation by masturbation for his partner. When these techniques have been mastered, the couple can move on to phase III of the sensate focus exercises. The man should withhold penetration until he senses that ejaculation is inevitable. To facilitate this, the woman should adopt the astride position, but once the exercises have been completed, the partners may switch positions so that the man can better control the moment of ejaculation.

Erectile Dysfunction. This disorder, commonly referred to as impotence, is characterized by an inability to achieve and maintain an erection. In some men, the problem is caused by a disease, such as diabetes, or the result of prostate or other surgery. More often, however, the problem is psychological rather than physiological. Anxiety may interfere with the arousal process at any time during lovemaking. Some men are unable to respond in a normally sex-

ually stimulating environment, while others may experience anxiety later on in the arousal stage. For some men, the problem occurs in all situations with any partner, while others experience it only in certain specific situations, such as when attempting an extramarital affair. In some cases, the man has never had an erection with a sexual partner, but is able to have one when masturbating.

Men with erectile problems usually engage in spectatoring and are constantly checking the size of their erection. They are particularly sensitive to their partner's comments, activity, and attitude toward the penis. The problem may result in a loss of sexual desire and prompt a couple to avoid sex.

Once a physiological cause for the problem has been ruled out, treatment should be directed to alleviating anxiety. In fact, the level of anxiety is often so severe that it takes longer to establish a nonthreatening, pleasurable milieu than in other male sexual dysfunctions.

Although there may be feelings of disappointment and anxiety, neither sex partner should harbor feelings of inadequacy or guilt. Continued intimate contact and maintenance of emotional warmth is encouraged without the "need" for intercourse.

Again, sensate focus exercises are recommended. For some patients, simply reducing anxiety and removing the "need" for intercourse is enough to restore erectile function. Once an erection occurs, the couple should stop the stimulation until it disappears and then renew the activity to regain the erection. This shows the couple that erections can come and go, and that the pleasurable aspect of lovemaking is paramount. This also shows that the erection is not under conscious control but is the most obvious outcome of adequate stimulation in a relaxed, nonanxious man. The partner's role is to help provide and maintain the nonanxious environment. She should also learn to accept the other pleasurable aspects of lovemaking and not to demand intercourse and an erect penis from her partner.

If a man finds pleasurable, moment-to-moment sensations invariably lead to spectatoring, he should try to concentrate on other aspects of his partner, such as her attractiveness, her enjoyment, or even the freckles on her forehead. When even this does not work, the pleasuring of the man should stop for the time being and he should concentrate on giving his partner sexual pleasure by nonpenile means. In this way, the partner is not left disappointed and the man does not experience a total sense of "failure." The sensate focus exercises are continued until the anxiety is reduced and the normal sexual response cycle can be established.

For those men whose problem is organic, two types of penile prostheses are available—one is a semirigid silastic rod that allows a semirigid penis, able to engage in intercourse, and the other one is a hydraulic implant that allows the man to achieve an erect penis when he wishes.

Sexual Dysfunctions in Women

The most significant difference between male and female sexual dysfunction is that women can perform sexually and pretend to have an orgasm, whereas it is impossible for a man to simulate an erection. With increased awareness among women of the sexuality, however, the level of performance anxiety is now raised in both sexes. A woman has a greater capacity for physiological responsiveness in sexual activity than a man, enabling her to achieve an orgasm early in the arousal stage and to have more than one orgasm during the same sexual activity—factors that theoretically should protect against sexual problems. Certain attitudes regarding female sexuality, however, have contributed to a variety of sexual dysfunctions.

Anorgasmia. The failure to achieve orgasm is the most common female sexual dysfunction. With the changes in cultural attitudes toward female sexuality and the wider dissemination of sex information, most women now expect to be fully responsive and orgasmic. They are therefore concerned if they are not, and are likely to seek professional help.

There are three different types of anorgasmia:

1. *Primary,* in which the woman has never had an orgasm in any sexual situation, including masturbation. Paradoxically, this type is the most responsive to treatment.
2. *Secondary,* in which a woman who has been orgasmic in the past becomes anorgasmic. This is more difficult to treat with sexual therapy alone because psychological and interpersonal factors not directly connected to the sexual experience usually play a role.
3. *A situational condition* in which the anorgasmia occurs under specific conditions, such as when the children are still awake, or when with specific individuals. Frequently, these anxiety-provoking concomitants are easily identified and treated.

In some instances, the male partner becomes anxious because he looks upon his partner's inability to climax as a sign of his own sexual inadequacy. Thus, the striving anxious woman and the striving anxious man create a situation in which achieving a specific goal becomes the principal reason for sexual activity, with frustration the inevitable result.

The woman with primary anorgasmia is generally uninformed about her own sexuality and is often apprehensive about expressing her own sexual needs. Approaches to treatment include education about female sexuality, assertiveness in expressing one's own sexual needs and the use of masturbatory exercises to help the woman become comfortable with her sexuality. Lonnie Barbach's *For Yourself* is a useful book for women to learn more about their sexuality. Women are encouraged to examine their own genitalia by hand and with the use of a mirror, and to identify the position of her clitoris and her other anatomical features. It is also useful for a woman to identify and learn to use the pubococcygeal muscles—the muscles that control the genitourinary area. A woman can identify these muscles by inserting two fingers into the vagina and tightening the muscles around them. (Stopping urination in midstream is another method of identifying the muscles. Repeated tightening and relaxation of these muscles is recommended both to enhance sexual pleasure and also to overcome incontinence that often occurs following childbirth.)

Women are also encouraged to explore their physiological responses to sexual stimulation by masturbating at times when they are free from interruption and other concerns. The increased knowledge of sexual responsiveness plus the repeated masturbation help most women to become orgasmic by self-pleasuring.

During this period, sexual activity with the partner should be continued and sensate focus exercises by the couple instituted. This allows the woman to practice the knowledge she is gaining through self-exploration and self-stimulation in a couple situation and also avoids resentment on the part of the man, who may feel he is to blame for his partner's lack of responsiveness. The man should also learn about female anatomy and his partner's needs and responses and put this to use. The importance of clitoral stimulation during intercourse should be recognized and practiced. Women who are easily orgasmic during masturbation but not in intercourse should show her partner her preferences for sexual stimulation.

Arousal Stage Problems. These are often related to the degree of lubrication. Physical changes in the degree of lubrication can occur with illness, certain drugs, aging, and other factors. Most can be treated successfully by the use of creams, oils, and artificial lubricants. Inadequate lubrication in a healthy, premenopausal woman, however, reflects either psychological problems associated with sexual response or inadequate arousal techniques used by the partner. Sensate focus exercises and masturbation also are useful in resolving arousal problems.

Dyspareunia. This is persistent or recurrent genital pain during intercourse. It is rare in men and is usually associated with a penile disorder. Women who experience painful intercourse should be carefully examined for a physical cause that may include vaginitis, urinary tract infection, localized vaginal scarring (as occurs after episiotomy), broad ligament injuries, prolapse, endometriosis, and ovarian tumors. During breast feeding and after menopause, hormonal changes may result in a thinning of vaginal tissues, leading to painful intercourse. If there is no organic cause for the dyspareunia, it is usually associated with inadequate lubrication or other forms of sexual dysfunction, especially vaginismus—the involuntary contraction of the vaginal muscles. Often there is a general aversion toward all sexual activity, but particularly sexual intercourse.

Treatment involves ruling out an organic cause of the dyspareunia and making sure there is adequate stimulation and lubrication before intercourse. If the problem persists, the same approach as for vaginismus (see below) may be recommended.

Vaginismus. This is the sudden contraction of the muscles of the lower outer third of the vagina, which can occur at any point in the sexual response cycle. In some women, it occurs before sexual response begins and is precipitated by the knowledge that her partner is about to begin sexual activity. Usually, vaginal penetration cannot occur, and when penetration is forced, pain frequently results, leading to further muscle contractions.

The underlying cause of vaginismus, as with the other dysfunctions, is anxiety. The causes of the anxiety range from fears associated with earlier painful intercourse, rape or rape-like situations, or penetration associated with injury, violation, or impregnation.

Vaginismus, when not due to organic factors, can usually be treated by the use of dilators, or in milder cases, the woman's and the partner's own fingers. Both partners should understand that the vaginal contraction is an automatic response outside the woman's control.

The man should be directly involved in the treatment, although the final responsibility rests with the woman. Each day, she inserts one of a set of graduated dilators into her vagina and maintains it in position for at least 15 minutes. After she uses the dilators she is also encouraged to insert her own fingers and to allow her partner to insert his fingers into the vagina. This helps to remove painful associations and to resensitize the vagina to pleasurable stimuli. Sensate focus exercises should also be practiced until intercourse can be practiced without discomfort or difficulty. The establishment of full sexual activity and enjoyment is usually rapid, once the initial aversion to penetration has been overcome.

Lack of Sexual Desire

A significant number of people experience a lack of sexual desire, even though they have normal sexual function. A variety of factors can lead to loss of libido, including physical illness, hormonal abnormalities, depression, and interpersonal problems. Treatment involves identifying the underlying problem and resolving it.

11 Pregnancy and Birth

Phyllis Leppert, M.D.

PLANNING PREGNANCY

PREGNANCY IS a unique period of change and growth, terminating in the delivery of a new human being into the world. If all goes well—and in the great majority of cases it does—this period is among the most fulfilling of a woman's life.

There is never a "perfect" time to have a baby; instead, the best time to have a baby is when you and your partner want one. Pregnancy and parenthood inevitably require considerable adjustment in a woman's—and a couple's—lifestyle. Physiologically, however, the optimal years for childbearing are those between 18 and 35. Medical science has shown that women who become pregnant in their early teens or after the age of 35 have an increased risk of problems during pregnancy. A very young mother has a far greater than average risk of bearing a low-birth-weight (and consequently frail) infant. After age 35—and particularly after age 40—there is a greater risk of complications during pregnancy and of having a child with a congenital anomaly, such as Down's syndrome.

Pregnancy is a demanding experience, both physically and emotionally, and it takes time, effort, and money to raise a child. A couple should therefore be very sure that both partners are ready before planning a pregnancy and that the child is not being born "to save the marriage," for example, or to satisfy demands for a grandchild.

Preferably, a woman should begin to prepare herself before conception for the demanding work of pregnancy and labor. If she is not at her ideal weight, she should make every effort to become so. If she feels that she is flabby and out of condition, she should exercise and tone her muscles. She will need the physical strength during the months ahead. Since the vulnerable first trimester of intrauterine life may begin before she is aware of it, she should give up smoking and reduce her intake of alcohol. Most important, she should check with her doctor about the safety of any drugs, both prescription and over-the-counter, that she may be taking. About 20 percent of birth defects are caused by environmental factors (drugs, viruses, and vitamin excesses and deficiencies) and approximately 60 percent result from the interaction of an environmental factor with a genetic predisposition. A woman who is planning a pregnancy, or who is already pregnant, should be aware of these hazards and take steps to guard against them in every way she can.

Pregnancy is necessarily a time of waiting, but it need not and should not be a time of simply passive waiting. It is a time to learn as much as possible about what is happening in the body, what will happen in labor, what to expect in caring for the newborn infant, and how to prepare.

THE BEGINNING: FERTILIZATION AND IMPLANTATION

FERTILIZATION OCCURS when a male sperm (spermatozoon) enters the Fallopian tube and penetrates the layer of cells surrounding the egg, or ovum (see figure 11.1). The ovum contains chromosomes from the mother which unite with the chromosomes from the father contained in the sperm. Together, these chromosomes make up the nucleus of the new cell. Each parent supplies one-half the full complement of chromosomes, which determine all the physical characteristics, such as hair color, eye color, and sex, that the baby will exhibit. The female sex is determined by two X chromosomes, while the male carries an X and a Y chromosome. Thus, if the mother contributes one of her chromosomes, it must be an

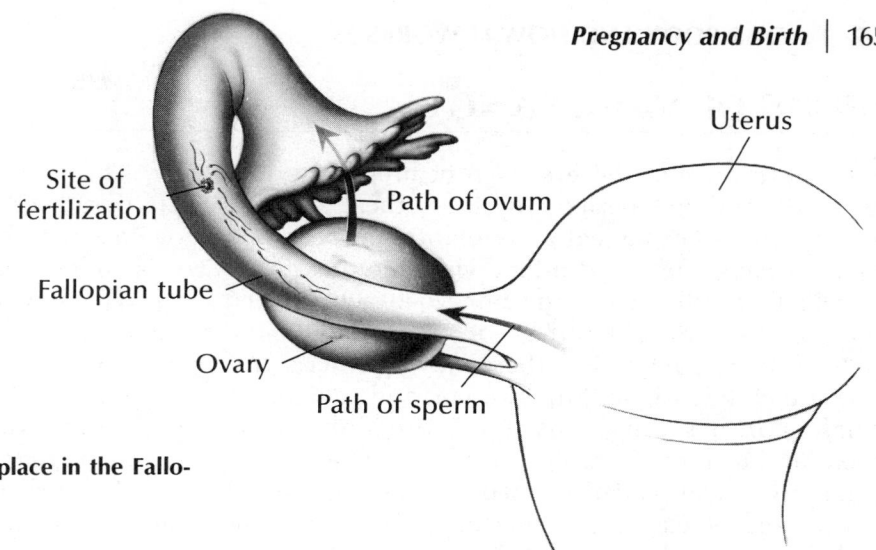

Figure 11.1. **Fertilization ordinarily takes place in the Fallopian tube, as illustrated here.**

X. The father can contribute either an X or a Y, and therefore it is the father who determines the sex of the resulting embryo.

As soon as the egg has been fertilized, the outer layer of cells alters, preventing any other sperm from entering. Within 1½ days, the fertilized egg divides into 2 complete cells. Over the next 3 days, they move gradually down the Fallopian tube toward the uterus (see figure 11.2), at the same time dividing into a mulberrylike cluster of many smaller cells. By the end of the first week, the fertilized egg has implanted itself in the uterus and rapid growth and change begin.

Although the distinction is essentially arbitrary, it is customary to refer to the fertilized egg as an embryo for the first 8 weeks; after that and until birth, it is called a fetus. During the embryonic period, all the major organ systems are formed; during the fetal stage, differentiation of tissues takes place.

Figure 11.2. **View of female reproductive organs showing actual size before pregnancy is established.**

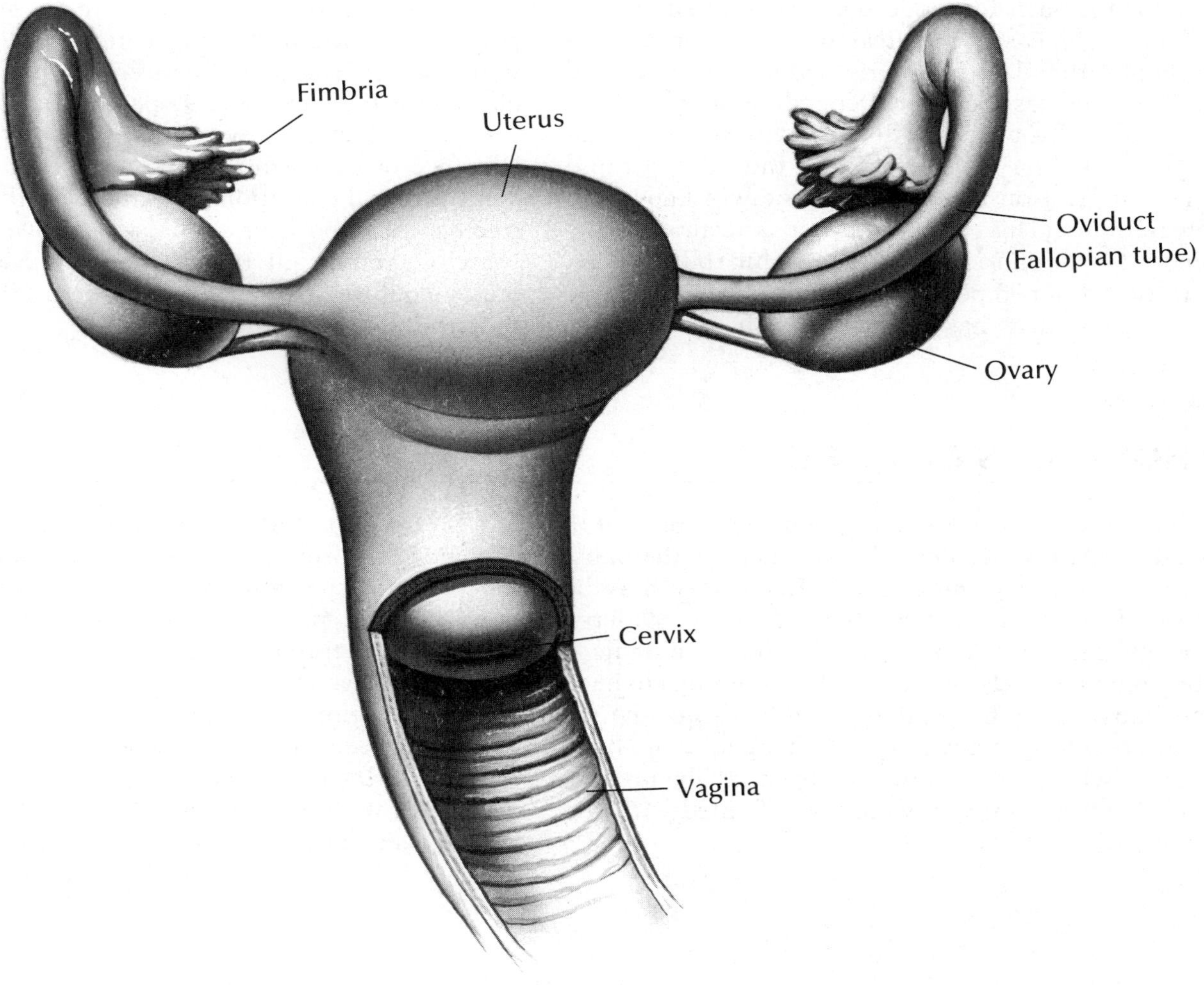

SIGNS OF PREGNANCY

FOR MOST WOMEN, the first sign of pregnancy is a missed menstrual period. In some, there may be some slight spotting, called implantation bleeding, about 7 days after conception, when the tiny group of cells that will become the embryo attaches to the uterine wall. Shortly after—or even before—the date of the missed period, there may be other signs. These include fatigue; full, swollen, and sometimes tingling breasts; sensations of pressure in the pelvic area; and a frequent desire to urinate. Often these signs are accompanied by nausea, and in a small percentage of cases, by vomiting. This is the so-called morning sickness, which can, in fact, occur at any time of the day. If a woman has been taking her basal body temperature in order to determine the date of ovulation, she will have another sign to go by. The temperature normally rises by $\frac{1}{5}$ degree Centigrade ($\frac{2}{5}$ –$\frac{3}{5}$ degree Fahrenheit) at the time of ovulation. If the rise is sustained for 20 days or more, it is almost certain evidence of pregnancy.

These symptoms of pregnancy are the result of the hormonal changes that take place in a woman's body at the time of conception and in the days and weeks that follow. Not all women will experience all of them. However, a woman is likely to have a strong suspicion that she is pregnant even before her doctor or other health professional confirms that she is. In fact, one study of a very early biochemical test for pregnancy found that the positive tests correlated very well with the woman's own feeling that she was pregnant.

DETERMINATION

WHEN THE EGG HAS BEEN fertilized and has become implanted in the uterus, the tissue surrounding it (the chorion) produces a hormone that enters the mother's bloodstream and is excreted in her urine. The presence of this hormone, chorionic gonadotrophin, is the basis for modern pregnancy testing. The hormone can easily be detected in blood or urine as early as 6 to 9 days after a missed menstrual period and in some cases earlier. Depending on which test is performed, a woman will know within a few hours or days whether she is pregnant. Indeed, if a rapid screening test on urine is done, she will know in a few minutes. (This rapid test is not as accurate as the blood test for chorionic gonadotrophin, but even so, it is more than 95 percent accurate.)

A great deal has been written in the popular press concerning home pregnancy tests. Sold in kit form, these tests are based on the hemagglutination inhibition technique. If a woman is pregnant, an indicator particle (the red blood cells of a sheep, coated with human gonadotrophin) will react with the urine to produce a positive test result: a dark ring at the bottom of the test tube that is provided with the kit. The manufacturers of the testing kits claim that they are 96 to 99 percent accurate. However, such factors as vibration, sunlight, heat, the presence of detergents and some medications, and some medical conditions can influence the test, producing a false-positive and false-negative result. It is therefore important that a woman have her pregnancy confirmed by a doctor or in a clinic, where more reliable tests are used.

PROVIDERS OF CARE

ONCE THE PREGNANCY has been confirmed, if a woman has not decided who will deliver the baby, she should do so immediately. Her choice may be affected not only by what type of care provider—obstetrician, family physician, or nurse-midwife—she prefers, but also by where she would like to have the baby—at a hospital or childbirth center. (In large cities with many hospitals, her choice of physician may be affected by which hospital she prefers, since a given doctor may only be affiliated with one or two.)

In the United States, most women receive their prenatal care from physicians—either obstetricians (doctors who specialize in the care and treatment of women during pregnancy and childbirth), or family practitioners trained to do uncomplicated obstetrics—and have their babies in a hospital. About 2 percent of women are cared for by certified nurse-midwives, registered nurses who have received extra training in the care of normal pregnant women and who work with obstetrician "backup" in case complications should arise. A few women receive their care from lay midwives. Some of these women are very competent, but the requirements for licensure vary from state to state. A woman planning to use the services of a lay midwife should check her qualifications carefully, as well as the qualifications of the doctor providing backup support. (A few lay midwives have no such support; it would be foolhardy to use their services.)

The out-of-hospital childbirth center movement began in the mid-1970s as a reaction against hospital procedures that were perceived as stressing technology at the expense of human needs. In the 1980s, however, largely in response to changing patient wishes, the concept of family-centered childbirth has become an integral part of care in most hospitals. Many have childbirth rooms (labor-delivery-recovery rooms), in which the father may stay with the mother throughout labor and delivery, and which make the transfer to a delivery room during the second stage of labor unnecessary. As to technology, most women do not object to modern fetal monitoring techniques once they understand the reason for their use. Delivery in hospitals provides the assurance that, if a problem occurs—and studies show that 10 to 15 percent of women in labor develop some serious problem—it can be treated speedily. Childbirth centers, on the other hand, are equipped to handle only normal births, even though there have been a few cases in which emergency cesarean sections have been performed at childbirth centers. If a complication develops during labor, the woman will have to be sent from the center to a hospital,

and precious time may be lost in transit.

If a woman is considering a childbirth center for her prenatal care and for labor and delivery, she should inquire as to the qualifications of the staff and the reputation and nearness of the backup hospital. While some centers provide excellent care, standards vary widely, and there are no uniform regulations. The center should provide patients with written guidelines detailing the circumstances under which transfer to other facilities will be made. If a woman has any doubts about the standard of care, she should check with the local health department.

Home births enjoyed something of a vogue a few years ago but are now less common, perhaps because of the growing flexibility of hospital practices. Home delivery is safe only for "normal" births; the problem is that a birth can be safely said to be "normal" only after the event. In addition, it is more difficult to ensure an adequately germ-free environment to protect both the mother and baby against the danger of infection.

It is important for a woman to have confidence in those who care for her during childbirth. Therefore, if she chooses a midwife, she should meet with the backup physician several times during pregnancy.

(Note: For convenience' sake, we will use the term "doctor" to refer to the health-care provider—physician or midwife—caring for the pregnant woman in the prenatal period and during labor and delivery.)

PRENATAL EXAMINATIONS

THE VALUE OF ROUTINE prenatal examinations in ensuring the health of both mother and fetus has been established beyond doubt. Every study that has considered the impact of regular, consistent prenatal care, begun in the first trimester (the first 3 months), shows unequivocally that such care prevents many complications and assures that, if they do arise, they will be treated before they become serious. Where there is early prenatal care and continued care throughout pregnancy, the risk of stillbirth and infant mortality is reduced by 75 percent.

The First Prenatal Examination

This is usually carried out in the second month of pregnancy, by which time the pregnancy will have

been confirmed. It includes a discussion of the woman's medical history (past illnesses and operations, past pregnancies, miscarriages, and abortions), her family history of disease (heart and kidney disease, diabetes, sickle cell anemia), and the child's father's history of disease, the family history of twins, and the history of the present pregnancy itself. A physical examination is done to assess the woman's health and to check for any general disease. A pelvic examination is performed to check the size of the uterus and to detect any abnormalities or misplacement.

The first prenatal examination includes a Pap smear to detect any possible cancerous or precancerous condition of the cervix, and a vaginal culture to check for gonorrhea, trichomonas (a common parasite), and, sometimes, yeast infections. Blood is drawn for tests. These routinely include a complete blood count, a rubella (German measles) test, blood type and Rhesus (Rh) factor tests, and a test for syphilis (if this is demanded by law, as it is in most states). Depending on the medical history and the findings of the physical examination, other tests may be necessary. If the woman has had genital herpes, she should let the doctor know. Although a past history of herpes does not ordinarily threaten the developing fetus, a flare-up at the time of delivery can expose the baby to the virus as it passes through the birth canal. Herpes infection in the newborn can create grave problems, resulting in mental retardation, blindness, neurological problems, and even death. If a mother develops an active herpes infection near the end of pregnancy, delivery should be by cesarean section to protect the baby from exposure to the virus.

Most doctors encourage the father to attend all or any part of the initial examination. It is a good opportunity to discuss any problems that may have arisen and to anticipate future concerns, particularly plans for the birth itself.

DUE DATE

ON THE BASIS OF physical examination and the history, the doctor will, in most cases, be able to tell when the baby is due. This calculation of the due date, or estimated date of confinement, is based on the date of the last menstrual period and the size of the uterus.

A normal pregnancy is usually calculated to last for 40 weeks (280 days) from the first day of the last menstrual period, or 38 weeks (266 days) from the day of conception. The due date is, of course, only an approximation. A baby may be born anywhere from 3 weeks before the due date to 2 weeks after it, and the pregnancy will still be a completely normal one and the baby considered "full term." In fact, only 1 baby in 20 arrives precisely on the day due.

The calculation of the due date may be made harder by the fact that, after contraceptive pills are discontinued, the monthly cycle is often irregular.

Moreover, some women habitually have irregular monthly cycles.

Ultrasound, a technique that uses high-frequency sound waves to visualize internal organs, can be used to determine the expected duration of the pregnancy. However, a due date calculated by ultrasound can be off by 10 to 14 days. Even this innovation in modern obstetrics technology cannot tell exactly when a baby is to be expected.

Pregnancy is arbitrarily divided into 3 periods or trimesters. The first trimester ends at 12 weeks, the second lasts from weeks 13 to 27, and the third from weeks 28 to 40. Most doctors speak of "numbers of weeks completed" (reckoned from the date of the last menstrual period) rather than of "trimesters" when referring to the progress of a pregnancy.

PRENATAL FOLLOW-UP EXAMINATIONS

MOST WOMEN, following the initial examination, should see the doctor once a month until they are in the seventh month of pregnancy. In the eighth month, 2 or 3 visits are usually scheduled; in the final month, weekly visits are the rule. Of course, if some special situation suggests it, the visits may be more frequent.

At the follow-up visits, the doctor will monitor weight and blood pressure and measure the growth of the uterus. A urine sample will be checked for the presence of protein and glucose. By the twelfth week of pregnancy (and occasionally by the tenth), the fetal heartbeat can be heard through an ultrasonic fetal stethoscope. This, too, will be checked at each visit. The internal pelvic examination done at the first visit is usually not repeated until the last month of pregnancy, unless special circumstances dictate it. For example, a woman who has had a previous premature baby will be checked for the early cervical changes that precede a preterm birth, so that steps can be taken to avert premature labor.

GENETIC COUNSELING AND PRENATAL TESTING

BECAUSE MANY COUPLES are now delaying pregnancy until relatively late in life, and because the likelihood of congenital defects increases with the mother's (and possibly the father's) age, the prenatal diagnosis of congenital defects has become an increasingly important part of modern obstetrical care. The number of conditions that can be diagnosed prenatally has increased greatly. Since it is not feasible to do all possible tests in any one case, it is important to obtain accurate family medical histories from both father and mother to determine which specific tests should be done.

Diagnostic tests are usually recommended for women who will be 35 years or older when they give birth. Testing is also recommended when the family history of either parent indicates a risk of a congenital defect, or when a previous baby has been born with a chromosomal abnormality (Down's syndrome, for example) or a defect such as spina bifida, in which the spinal neural tube fails to close.

The majority of prenatal diagnostic tests are conducted on the amniotic fluid that surrounds the fetus in the uterus and is obtained by a technique called amniocentesis. Although there are rarely complications, there is some slight risk of damage to the fetus, so that the test is not routinely done if a woman is younger than 35 or if there is no reason to suspect a possible defect.

The main purpose of prenatal testing is to detect birth defects early enough so that the pregnancy can be terminated before the legal limit for abortion (24 weeks' gestation) if the parents so choose. (If a defect is found, and the parents decide to proceed with the pregnancy, the knowledge provided by the diagnosis will help them prepare for the special considerations of caring for the child.) However, 95 percent of these tests reveal no abnormality in the fetus, so prenatal testing also has the result of reassuring couples at high risk for a particular abnormality that their child will not have it. Prenatal diagnostic testing does not guarantee that a child will be born normal; it can rule out the presence of particular problems, but a tested fetus runs the same risk of birth defects (4 percent) that all babies do.

Amniocentesis

During amniocentesis (usually carried out under local anesthesia), the doctor inserts a long, thin needle through the abdomen into the uterus and extracts a small amount of amniotic fluid (less than an ounce). A sonogram (see Ultrasound, following) is used to guide the needle, and afterward the small needle hole in the amniotic sac readily seals itself.

The amniotic fluid, which contains cells shed from the fetus's skin and gastrointestinal tract, is tested chemically and then the cells are grown in tissue cultures in the laboratory and analyzed for abnormalities—a process that usually takes about 4 weeks.

The amniotic fluid may show an elevated level of alpha-fetoprotein (a protein produced by the fetus's liver). This suggests one of a number of abnormalities: failure of the brain or the spine to close properly; failure of the abdomen to close; obstruction in the urinary or gastrointestinal tract. The cultured cells are examined to detect possible defects in the chromosomes, such as the extra chromosome that is present in Down's syndrome. The cells can also be subjected to a variety of tests to identify some 70 metabolic problems. Diagnosis of the presence or absence of a fetal defect is correct in 99.4 percent of cases.

Doctors are currently developing a technique to enable them to detect genetic abnormalities in the first trimester. This will make it more important than ever to discuss genetic counseling and follow-up with the doctor at the first prenatal visit.

Ultrasound (Sonography)

Ultrasound is one of the most widely used diagnostic tools in pregnancy, and one of the safest. It has been used in more than 1 million pregnancies with no evidence of harm to either mother or baby. The technique uses painless, high-frequency sound waves (much like the sonar used by ships) to produce a picture of the fetus in the uterus. It is useful in the detection of major malformations and it can give important information about the age of the fetus and can show the presence of twins. The procedure provides a picture, called a sonogram, similar to that given by an x-ray, but with no risk of radiation damage to the fetus. Some highly sophisticated types of ultrasound equipment are capable of providing a succession of images of the fetus that can reveal many structural defects, including heart anomalies.

Fetoscopy

This prenatal diagnostic technique is largely a research tool. The fetoscope is a long, narrow fiberoptic tube that can be inserted into the uterus through an incision in the woman's abdomen, allowing the doctor to actually see the fetus. It can be used to draw blood samples from the fetus to aid in the diagnosis of hereditary blood disorders including thalassemia (Cooley's anemia), sickle cell anemia, and hemophilia.

THERAPEUTIC ABORTION

AN ABORTION IS TERMED therapeutic when it is done to safeguard a woman's physical or emotional health. Otherwise the procedure is known as legal termination of pregnancy.

Pregnancy may be terminated by dilation of the cervix and removal of the fetus by suction up to 16 weeks from the last menstrual period. The earlier in pregnancy this is done, the safer. The procedure may be performed under general or local anesthesia, whichever is preferred, and may be done in a hospital, an abortion clinic, or a well-equipped medical office. The tissue specimens should be sent to a pathologist to be certain that the pregnancy was not an abnormal one.

Between 16 and 24 weeks' gestation, the fetus may be aborted by the injection of saline (a highly concentrated salt solution) into the uterus. Alternatively, a gel that contains prostaglandins may be inserted as a suppository into the vagina. This causes the uterus to contract, as in labor, and after 12 to 24 hours the fetus is expelled. Late pregnancy terminations are carried out in hospitals to ensure the safety of the procedure, since complications of hemorrhage and infection may occur.

SPECIAL TESTS DURING PREGNANCY

Blood Glucose Screening

If a pregnant woman is over 25, has a family history of diabetes, gains weight very rapidly, or shows glucose in the urine, she should be tested for a type of diabetes that occurs during pregnancy. Known as gestational diabetes, this disorder occurs because of changes in glucose metabolism during pregnancy, which are largely due to the action of a hormone produced in the placenta called human placental lactogen. (See Hormonal Changes, page 179.)

Gestational diabetes can usually be taken care of by a special diet, though in some cases insulin injections are necessary. This complication of pregnancy causes the fetus to grow larger than normal, contributing to difficulties at birth. Further, if gestational diabetes is not controlled in pregnancy, the newborn may have difficulties with glucose metabolism.

Rhesus-Factor Titers

Most people have in their blood a compounding factor called the Rhesus (Rh) factor. These people are considered to be Rh-positive, while those who lack this factor are Rh-negative. There can be a problem of Rhesus incompatibility if a mother is Rh-negative and the baby is Rh-positive, having inherited positive genes from the father. (If both the mother and the baby are Rh-negative, there is no problem. This sometimes happens even if the father is Rh-positive, but carries a recessive gene for a negative Rh factor.)

As the fetus grows in the uterus, some of the red blood cells that it produces pass through the placenta into the mother's bloodstream, and her system produces antibodies to the Rh factor. Recrossing the placenta, these antibodies destroy the fetus's red blood cells. The baby may be born with erythroblastosis, a blood condition in which the red cells are abnormal. It can lead to anemia, or jaundice, or both. In severe cases, the baby may be stillborn.

Most Rh-negative women are able to have at least one healthy baby. However, with subsequent pregnancies, the level of antibodies—and thus the risk to the fetus—rises. Even so, the chances of an Rh-negative woman having an affected baby are only about 1 in 20, and then only in a third or later pregnancy.

Rh-negative women are given a series of blood tests (Rh titers) during pregnancy, the frequency depending on whether antibodies are present, and in what numbers. If a test shows that the antibodies are increasing in number, labor may be induced to prevent the fetus's blood from being totally destroyed. After an affected baby is born, its blood can be "exchanged" for Rh-negative blood. This transfusion technique has saved the lives of thousands of infants.

It is also possible to prevent the occurrence of Rh disease with an injection of Rhesus gammaglobulin given to a woman at risk within 72 hours after the delivery of an Rh-positive baby. The gammaglobulin destroys the fetal blood cells in the mother's bloodstream and prevents the production of antibodies that would affect subsequent pregnancies. All Rh-negative mothers should have a gammaglobulin injection after every pregnancy, whether it goes full term or is terminated by miscarriage or abortion.

HIGH-RISK PREGNANCIES

WOMEN WITH SERIOUS medical conditions such as high blood pressure, diabetes, heart or lung disease, or thyroid or neurological problems, are at risk for a variety of complications during pregnancy. Pregnancy may have an adverse effect on the disease, and by the same token, the disease may affect the pregnancy and its outcome. Before becoming pregnant, these women should consult with their doctors about having a baby. In some cases, they may be advised against it, period. However, with the modern maternal and fetal medical care, many of the complications of high-risk pregnancies can be successfully handled.

CARE DURING PREGNANCY

A PREGNANT WOMAN, in addition to seeing her doctor regularly, can do a great deal herself to ensure her health during pregnancy and labor, and to give her baby the best chance of being born strong and healthy.

Weight Gain

A generation ago, pregnant women were cautioned not to gain much more than the probable weight of the baby. More recent studies have shown that a minimum weight gain during pregnancy of 24 pounds is better for the mother and for the growth and development of the baby. Women who gain less are likely to have low-birth-weight babies who are more vulnerable to infection than babies of normal size. A woman who is underweight when she becomes pregnant should gain more than the minimum—up to 30 pounds. A woman who is overweight should not choose this time to go on a weight-loss diet, even though she is more likely than mothers of appropriate weight to have a difficult labor. Cutting back on nutrients during pregnancy shortchanges both mother and fetus. Moreover, if body fat is lost, toxins that have accumulated over time, such as pesticides, will be released into the bloodstream, and these may have an adverse effect on the fetus.

During pregnancy, a number of changes take place in a woman's body. These adaptations prepare the mother for lactation and create the best possible environment for the growth of the fetus. In the early months, the uterus expands, anticipating future fetal growth. The volume of circulating blood doubles, facilitating the flow of oxygen and nutrients across the placenta to the fetus. Breast tissue develops and storage fat is laid down in preparation for lactation. Then, as the pregnancy progresses, the placenta grows and the amniotic fluid accumulates, surrounding and protecting the growing fetus.

These changes add weight. (See table.) By the

APPROXIMATE WEIGHT GAIN DURING PREGNANCY	
Fetus	7.5 (pounds)
Placenta	1.5
Amniotic fluid	2.0
Uterus	2.5
Breasts	1.0
Extra blood	3.5
Body fluids	2.0
	20.0

time of birth, if the baby is an average 7½ pounds, there will be a weight gain of 20 pounds simply from being pregnant. An additional 4- to 5-pound gain provides a nutritional reserve for both mother and fetus.

If because of poor advice, bad eating habits, or lack of food, a pregnant woman does not get an adequate diet, the growth of her baby may be jeopardized. One might expect the mother's store of nutrients to be tapped to supply the fetus, but this is not the case. Rather, if a woman's nutrition is inadequate, her body may not adapt well to pregnancy. For example, there may not be an adequate increase in blood. As a result, the placenta will not grow as it should and will be unable to transport nutrients properly. So, even though the necessary nutrients are available in the mother's reserves, they may not reach the fetus in normal quantities and the baby may be born underweight.

It appears that the body protects the mother's reserves at the expense of fetal growth because these reserves are essential for breast-feeding. Even if the baby grows in the uterus more slowly than normal, and is born smaller, it has a better chance of survival if there is enough breast milk later on.

During the first 3 months of pregnancy, a woman should gain 2 to 3 pounds. From the beginning of the fourth month, and until term (the end of the 9 months), a steady gain of about ¾ of a pound per week is desirable, although a "spurt" of 2 pounds is not unusual. When the gain is steady, there is no worry about exceeding the optimal weight, and thus no temptation to reduce food intake in the final months when most of the weight gained represents fetal growth.

A sudden, large weight gain in the second half of pregnancy (together with raised blood pressure and a leakage of protein into the urine) is a warning signal of preeclampsia, a not uncommon complication of pregnancy that should be checked with the doctor. (See Preeclampsia, page 184.) Loss of weight or a failure to gain in the final months is also a sign that complications may have arisen. However, a small weight loss often occurs when labor is imminent. This is probably due to a decrease in fluid retention caused by a drop of production in the placenta of the hormone progesterone, which normally promotes retention.

Diet

To gain 24 pounds during her pregnancy, a pregnant woman will have to eat somewhat more than she has been accustomed to. If there is no change in her activity level, she will need an extra 300 to 500 calories, bringing the total caloric intake to 2,300 to 2,500. If she is exercising less, she will need proportionally fewer calories.

In addition to extra calories, a pregnant woman's diet must provide certain specific nutrients that are essential to proper fetal growth and development. Unfortunately, the nutrients in greatest demand during pregnancy are often those in shortest supply. Table 11.1 lists the nutrients that are essential, the foods from which they are derived, and the minimum number of daily servings that are necessary. Additional servings may be needed to meet the increased caloric intake. In general, the closer a food is to its natural state, the more nutritious it is.

Nutrition

Protein is essential for building fetal tissues. A pregnant woman should increase her protein intake to 76 grams daily. For the protein to be used in fetal tissues, sufficient calories must also be consumed to meet the daily energy requirement of both mother and baby. In order to get sufficient *calcium*, necessary for the baby's bone and tooth development, pregnant women should drink 4 cups of milk or the equivalent daily. Young women in their teens and

Table 11.1 **ESSENTIAL NUTRIENTS DURING PREGNANCY**

Nutrients	Food groups	Minimum number of servings daily during pregnancy
Protein and iron	Meats, including organ meats, fish, poultry, eggs, nuts, legumes in combination with grains	4
Calcium and protein	Milk (all forms), yogurt, cheese, cottage cheese, ice cream	4
Vitamins A and C	Citrus and other fruits, green leafy vegetables, red and orange vegetables, potatoes and other tubers	5
B vitamins	Whole-grain and enriched grain products, fortified cereals	4
Fluids	Water, unsweetened fruit juices, vegetable juices, beverages	6

early twenties, who are still developing bone themselves, will need 5 cups of milk daily to meet their own and their baby's needs.

Iron is necessary for the manufacture of hemoglobin, the molecule within red blood cells that carries oxygen. Not only does the woman's extra blood volume require extra iron, but the fetus must build up a rich reserve of iron against the first few months of life. Unfortunately, iron is present in only marginal amounts in the average diet and menstruation further depletes a woman's iron reserves. Many women are iron-deficient even before pregnancy. Iron supplements (30–60 milligrams daily) are frequently prescribed.

Folic acid and *pyridoxine*, two of the B vitamins, are particularly important in pregnancy. Folic acid is necessary for protein synthesis in the early months; both vitamins are needed for proper development of the fetal nervous system. Folic acid is the scarcest vitamin in the human diet, however, and reserves may be especially low in women who have been taking contraceptive pills. Supplements are recommended, either through fortified foods or directly in tablet form.

The need for other B vitamins, and for vitamins C, A, and D, also increases in pregnancy, but these are normally present in sufficient quantities in a well-balanced, extra-calorie diet.

Liquids are needed in increased quantities during pregnancy. The requirement—over and above milk—is at least 6 glasses a day. Latest studies show that there is no harm in drinking moderate amounts of caffeine-containing products (coffee, tea, cocoa, cola) during pregnancy, but it is wise to limit consumption to 3 or 4 cups per day.

Vegetarian women must pay special attention to nutritional requirements during pregnancy. Those following a strict vegetarian diet with no animal products, such as eggs, cheese, and milk, will need vitamin and mineral supplements. Sufficient calories and protein can be obtained from a meatless diet if care is taken to balance foods properly. Complete proteins can be derived from dairy products, and from legumes and grains when these are combined at the same meal to provide a proper balance of amino acids. A woman who consumes no dairy products should eat generous amounts of green leafy vegetables, nuts, and seeds. She should also take supplements containing iron, calcium, vitamin D, and the B vitamins (including, most important, vitamin B_{12}, which is only found in animal products).

Medications

Virtually all drugs can cross the placenta and thereby reach the fetus. Many drugs are known to be potentially harmful, and some of them produce serious birth defects. Moreover, 85 percent of the drugs currently on the market have never been tested for safe use during pregnancy. Therefore, a pregnant woman should take no medication—not even an over-the-counter laxative or cold remedy—that has not been prescribed or approved by her doctor. Medications prescribed by a woman's dentist, or by a doctor other than the one attending the pregnancy, should not be taken without approval. The only exceptions to this rule are:

1. Acetaminophen (such as Tylenol). This may be taken as directed for the relief of cold or flu symptoms, headaches, and muscle strain, or a fever. If these symptoms persist for more than a day, however, a pregnant woman should call her doctor. A high fever (over 101°F) should be treated by a doctor and should be brought down as quickly as possible. Self-medication with aspirin should be avoided, be-

cause aspirin interferes with the blood-clotting mechanism and its use can result in bleeding in both mother and fetus. Moreover, aspirin inhibits prostaglandin, a hormonelike substance important in the development of the fetal circulation.

2. Gelusil or Mylanta may be taken for the relief of heartburn if other measures are not effective. (See Heartburn, page 176.)

3. Preparation H may be used for relief from hemorrhoids. The use of these medications should be discussed with the doctor during the regular prenatal visits.

Alcohol, Tobacco, etc.

Heavy alcohol consumption during pregnancy retards fetal growth and may result in severe birth defects, including mental retardation. It is *not* known, however, exactly how the extent of fetal damage relates to the quantity of alcohol consumed. To be on the safe side, women are advised not to drink during pregnancy, particularly during the first trimester.

Cigarette smoking during pregnancy interferes with the supply of blood, and consequently of nutrients, to the fetus. Women who smoke have an increased risk of stillbirth and premature or low-birth-weight babies. Some studies have shown that children of mothers who smoke cigarettes during pregnancy score lower on tests measuring neurological and intellectual function than those of nonsmokers and are more likely to be hyperactive. There is also a higher incidence of sudden death (crib death) among babies born to women who smoke.

Addictive drugs such as heroin, cocaine, and methadone cross the placental barrier. The infant of an addicted mother will be born addicted and may suffer seizures during the period of withdrawal after birth. Marijuana may cause chromosomal changes in the fetus, with possible growth retardation.

Exercise

Keeping fit and promoting good muscle tone is an important part of health care during pregnancy. Exercise prepares the body for labor, promotes good bowel function, aids in sleep—and makes a woman feel better.

As long as the pregnancy is progressing normally, a woman should be encouraged to get regular exercise. If she enjoyed tennis or jogging, for example, before she became pregnant, there is no reason why she should not continue these activities. Late in pregnancy, however, exercise that is weight-related and puts strain on abdominal muscles, knees, and ankles may be increasingly uncomfortable. Some form of exercise that is not weight-related (swimming, or bicycling, for example) may be preferable. Very hot saunas (temperature higher than 180°F) should be avoided because the heat causes blood vessels to dilate and excessive body fluids to be lost in perspiration. Sports that might result in a heavy fall should be avoided unless a woman is very proficient. A woman should be aware that, as pregnancy progresses, her body's center of gravity shifts forward, and this affects her balance.

In many schools, church halls, and Ys, special exercise classes are held for pregnant women. These offer the advantages of a carefully planned exercise program, a trained instructor, and the company of other women. Exercises at these classes generally concentrate on the following areas:

- Strengthening the abdominal muscles, to make it easier to support the weight of the fetus, to prepare for labor, and to aid in regaining a flat abdomen after delivery;
- Strengthening the muscles of the back to help avoid low back pain, which is a common problem in pregnancy when back muscles are strained by the added weight (see page 176);
- Strengthening the muscles of the pelvic floor in preparation for labor and to prevent bowel and bladder problems after delivery;
- Maintaining good posture, which also helps relieve or prevent back pain.

Many instructors also include breathing exercises and specific relaxation techniques.

Personal Hygiene

Bathing and showering as usual can continue throughout pregnancy. If late in pregnancy, however, the bag of waters (the membranes containing the amniotic fluid) has broken, or there appears to be a leak of amniotic fluid, a woman should not take a bath. (If she suspects that the membranes have ruptured, she should call her doctor. See page 186.)

A woman should not douche during pregnancy. Not only do many commercial douching preparations contain iodine, which is potentially harmful to the fetus, but douching may cause an infection present in the vagina to be carried to the uterus. A bothersome vaginal discharge should be reported to the doctor. (See page 176.)

Intercourse

Unless a woman has been counseled otherwise, sexual intercourse can continue normally in pregnancy, although it is usually not advised in the last month. If there is vaginal bleeding or a suspected leak from the bag of waters, intercourse should be discontinued until the woman has been checked by her doctor.

It is very common to experience some brief abdominal cramping after intercourse. If this continues or worsens over a 1-hour period, a woman should contact her doctor, since it is possible that the cervix may be dilating. Semen contains prostaglandins, which can initiate uterine contractions.

Especially in the last months, it is important to avoid excessive pressure on the abdomen. Couples should adopt positions that are comfortable as well as satisfying.

Partners may find that their appetite for sexual relations changes in response to the emotional and physical events of pregnancy. Some may desire sexual intimacy more frequently than before, others less often. If there is a conflict, open and honest communication, and understanding of the other's needs, will help work out the problem.

EMOTIONAL CHANGES

PREGNANCY IS A TIME of heightened emotional response. Sudden changes of mood, which may startle both the woman and those around her by their strength and volatility, are completely normal in pregnancy. It is also completely normal to have negative feelings about pregnancy itself. A woman should anticipate that at times she may feel impatience and apprehension, even resentment and repugnance, about many aspects of pregnancy and the coming birth. These feelings are best frankly acknowledged; they are temporary and will not affect a woman's ability to be a loving mother.

Very vivid dreams, some of which may be bizarre or frightening, commonly occur in pregnancy. Dreaming is one way in which the mind deals with concerns that may not be consciously acknowledged; such concerns are present in most pregnancies and disturbing dreams are entirely normal.

TRAVEL

A HEALTHY PREGNANT WOMAN can travel as usual. In the last month, however, she should not travel to any great distance from the hospital or other place where the baby is to be born. Many airlines will not accept a woman who is more than 32 weeks pregnant as a passenger without a doctor's certificate. When traveling by car, a pregnant woman should adjust her seat belt so that the lower strap lies across the pelvic bones rather than across the abdomen. It also helps to stop every 2 hours or so, stretching and moving about to relieve pressure from the enlarged uterus on pelvic organs and large blood vessels to the legs.

X-RAYS

EXPOSURE TO X-RAYS should be kept to a minimum. Prenatal exposure to the amount of radiation used in a diagnostic x-ray does not cause birth defects. However, higher amounts can do so and there may be evidence of a risk of childhood leukemia associated with even low doses.

To protect against exposure to the fetus in an as-yet-undiagnosed pregnancy, a woman of childbearing age should have nonemergency abdominal and pelvic area x-rays only during the menstrual period and the few days afterward, and such examinations should be postponed if she knows she is pregnant. The abdominal area should be protected with a lead apron during *all* nonabdominal x-rays. All nondental x-rays should be taken by a qualified radiologist who is aware of the woman's condition.

The need for x-rays in the later stages of pregnancy—to confirm a diagnosis of multiple pregnancy, for example—has largely been superseded by ultrasound. X-rays are still used, however, when the fetus is in a breech (feet-first) position, to determine whether the mother's pelvis is wide enough to permit a vaginal delivery. The benefits to mother and fetus in such cases can outweigh any potential danger from exposure to radiation.

DENTAL CARE

GOOD ORAL HYGIENE, with brushing and flossing as usual, should continue in pregnancy. If tooth loss is associated with pregnancy (as in the adage, "a tooth is lost for every child") it is because women tend to neglect their teeth at this time, not because calcium is drawn from the mother's teeth for fetal bone development.

Frequently, gums tend to swell and bleed. This condition, pregnancy gingivitis, is due to elevated hormone levels; in most cases the gums return to their previous state after delivery.

Dental x-rays should be kept to a minimum and the abdomen should be covered with a lead apron. Local anesthesia may be used, but general anesthesia should be avoided if at all possible because there is a risk of oxygen deprivation for the fetus. A pregnant woman may feel faint in the dental chair, due to the weight of the fetus pressing on the inferior vena cava, the main blood vessel returning from the lower limbs. If this is the case, a small pillow or rolled-up towel can be placed under the right hip, tipping the weight of the uterus to the left so that the blood flow is not blocked.

COMMON DISCOMFORTS AND SYMPTOMS

Fatigue

The most widely experienced symptom in the first 3 to 4 months of pregnancy is an overwhelming feeling of tiredness. Women may sleep many more hours than usual and still lack energy. This fatigue is quite normal and becomes less of a problem during the second trimester of pregnancy.

Toward the end of pregnancy, many women have difficulty sleeping at night, and this may again cause fatigue. When the abdomen is large, the fetus active, and the bladder needs to be emptied frequently, sleeping for long stretches becomes difficult.

Measures such as a warm drink at bedtime and exercise during the day are helpful. If sleeplessness becomes a real problem, and a woman's general health is suffering, the doctor should be consulted. There are sedatives, tested and found safe during pregnancy, that may be prescribed if other measures fail.

Morning Sickness

About 50 percent of all pregnant women feel some nausea during the first 3 months of pregnancy. Of these, about a third experience one or more episodes of vomiting. This is commonly known as morning sickness, although it may occur at any time of the day, or may last throughout the day. The cause is still unknown. Morning sickness usually clears up, often suddenly, after the third month.

Small amounts of food eaten every hour or two, including a high-protein snack at bedtime (to provide for nourishment in the early morning hours) may be very helpful. Highly flavored foods and those with strong odors are best avoided, as are greasy or fatty foods. Most doctors prefer to avoid medication for the treatment of simple nausea and vomiting in early pregnancy. However, severe or prolonged cases which interfere with good nutrition and normal living require medical help.

Heartburn

Many women experience a burning sensation in the center of the lower chest or upper abdomen, or taste an acidic substance in the throat in the later months of pregnancy. This sensation, called heartburn, is caused by reflux (flowing back) of stomach contents into the esophagus. It occurs more frequently in later pregnancy when there is a higher level of the hormone progesterone, which causes muscle tissue to relax. Thus the muscle that closes off the esophagus from the stomach becomes relatively lax, allowing the stomach contents to back up into the esophagus.

Taking a swallow of milk or sucking on a peppermint may be enough to wash the material back down, relieve the burning feeling, and get rid of the acid taste. Foods that appear to cause heartburn should be avoided. If nighttime heartburn is a problem, elevating the head of the bed slightly or using an extra pillow may be beneficial—gravity will help keep the stomach contents in the stomach. If warranted, Gelusil or Mylanta may be used to relieve the discomfort.

Constipation

The hormone progesterone also acts on the smooth muscle of the bowel during pregnancy, causing it to be somewhat more sluggish in its action than usual. Moreover, the uterus, increasing in size, presses on the bowels and displaces them upward and backward, contributing to the tendency toward constipation. The best remedy for this condition is prevention: a diet high in foods that promote good elimination. Fresh fruit and vegetables, plenty of fluids, whole-grain breads and cereals, and foods high in bulk and fiber should be included in the diet. Exercise is very effective in keeping the bowels moving regularly. If the problem persists even with proper diet and exercise, the pregnant woman should discuss it with her doctor, who may prescribe a mild laxative.

Backaches

A high backache may be caused by strain on the muscle carrying the newly acquired weight of increased breast tissue. A good support bra and attention to proper posture will often relieve this. A low backache, very common in pregnancy, occurs when a woman tries to compensate for the additional weight of the uterus by throwing her shoulders back, thus placing strain on the back muscles. Attention to posture and regular exercise to strengthen the muscles of the back and abdomen are helpful in cases of low backache. The back should also be supported when driving or sitting for any length of time. An extra-firm mattress or a bed board may be necessary if the pain becomes severe.

Vaginal Discharge

An increased vaginal discharge which is pale and mucuslike is normal in pregnancy and helps to lubricate the vagina during delivery.

There are two common causes of an abnormal discharge that may produce discomfort or irritation. The fungus infection *candida* produces a thin, white discharge; infection with trichomonas parasites produces a frothy, yellowish one, often with an unpleasant odor. Both these conditions should be reported to the doctor. They can usually be cleared up easily with vaginal suppositories.

Gonorrhea and syphilis can cause vaginal discharge, among other symptoms. These sexually transmitted diseases must be treated promptly, for the health of both mother and fetus. If a woman has active herpes at the time of delivery, her baby is usually delivered by cesarean section, to avoid infection in the passage down the birth canal.

Vaginal Bleeding

Some spotting or staining is common at the time of the first two missed menstrual periods. In some women, spotting continues throughout pregnancy. It is usually not cause for alarm. Bright red vaginal bleeding, however, is a serious symptom and should be reported promptly to the doctor. Bleeding in the early months may indicate a threatened miscarriage (see page 181) or an ectopic pregnancy (see page 182). In the later months, bleeding may be a sign that the placenta has partially separated from the uterus, jeopardizing the fetus's survival (see page 185). Immediate hospitalization is imperative in such a case.

Occasionally, there is bleeding from the cervix, as a result of erosion or the presence of a polyp. Sexual intercourse may aggravate these conditions.

Round Ligament Pains

The uterus is held in place by round ligaments. As pregnancy progresses and the uterus enlarges, these ligaments become stretched and may at times cramp. The pain is typically sharp and stabbing and is felt on one side of the abdomen and toward the groin area. Occasionally, the pain may be felt on both sides of the abdomen simultaneously. Massage of the area, the application of heat, or a simple change of position (particularly the adoption of the "fetal position" with knees pulled up to the chest) will be effective in relieving the spasm. These round ligament pains are quite common in pregnancy and, although uncomfortable, are not cause for alarm.

Leg Cramps

Leg cramps are often bothersome during pregnancy, especially at night. Stretching the leg out as far as possible and "pointing the heel" may relieve the muscle cramp, as may standing with all the weight on the affected leg. If these cramps occur frequently, supplemental calcium tablets may be prescribed.

Sometimes in late pregnancy, the enlarged uterus presses on nerves extending from the pelvis to the legs, causing pain. Pulling the knee to the chest may help relieve this.

Varicose Veins

Varicose veins often appear for the first time in preg-nancy, usually in the legs but sometimes also around the vulva. Varicose veins in the legs can be prevented to some extent by avoiding socks or stockings with tight bands that tend to constrict the veins.

A woman who already has varicose veins when she becomes pregnant should begin to wear good support stockings immediately and should continue to do so throughout her pregnancy. Unless preventive measures are taken, the extra weight, carried on legs whose veins are relaxed by the hormone progesterone, will inevitably cause a worsening of the varicose veins. In addition to wearing support stockings, a woman should put her feet up whenever possible and avoid standing or sitting for long periods of time.

If a varicose vein becomes tender, red, and swollen, a clot may have formed. Medical attention should be sought immediately.

Hemorrhoids

Hemorrhoids are a fairly common complaint during pregnancy and in the days immediately following delivery. They are, in fact, varicose veins of the rectum or anus, and cause discomfort and sometimes bleeding. Occasionally they can be very painful. Hemorrhoids are aggravated by constipation and the passing of hard stools. Preventing constipation is therefore the most important measure. The pain can be relieved by the use of a topical ointment (such as Preparation H).

Sciatic Pain

Sciatic pain, a sharp, needlelike sensation going from the buttocks down the side of the leg, occurs when the fetus's position puts pressure on the sciatic nerve. A change of position, the application of heat, or the knee-to-chest position may temporarily relieve this.

Edema

Edema is a swelling of the tissues, caused by retention of fluid. All pregnant women normally have some edema. Usually the feet and legs swell the most, since both gravity and the weight of the uterus contribute to sluggish circulation of blood and body fluids in the lower limbs. Obviously, standing or sitting for any length of time will make the condition worse. Elevating the legs will help decrease the swelling, as will lying on the left side. This position shifts the weight of the uterus off the inferior vena cava.

As long as the blood pressure remains normal and there is no protein in the urine, edema is no threat. If, however, either of these two conditions changes, there is a danger of preeclampsia (toxemia of pregnancy), a potentially serious complication of pregnancy (see page 184). Thus, if a woman in the later part of pregnancy experiences edema of the face and hands, together with headaches, blurred vision, and/or high abdominal pain (signaling rising blood pressure and the excretion of protein), she should see a doctor immediately.

Tingling Sensations

Tingling or a sensation of pressure in the vagina is a common problem toward the end of pregnancy. It occurs because the position of the fetus puts pressure on the nerves in this area. While uncomfortable, it is no cause for alarm.

Tingling or numbness of the arms, hands, or fingers also occurs in the later months of pregnancy. The nerves that supply these upper extremities traverse the bronchial plexus, which is pressed upon by the enlarging breasts. Shrugging the shoulders or swinging the arms in a circular fashion can help relieve the sensation.

INFECTIOUS DISEASES

PREGNANCY UNFORTUNATELY does not confer immunity to the common infectious diseases. Among the most serious is the mild childhood complaint, German measles (rubella), which, if contracted during the first 16 weeks of pregnancy, may severely affect the fetus. The risk of fetal blindness, deafness, and a number of congenital defects of the heart and brain is so great that most doctors recommend that the pregnancy be terminated in such cases. Standard tests early in pregnancy include one for past infection with rubella. If a woman is found not to be immune, she should avoid any possible source of contagion and should be immunized after delivery. (It is not considered safe to give rubella vaccine during pregnancy.)

Another infection that may occur in pregnancy is influenza. Since a high temperature may be fatal to the fetus or cause premature labor, a fever of more than 101°F that persists for more than 24 hours should be reported to the doctor.

PREPARATION FOR CHILDBIRTH

THE CONCEPT OF ACTIVE PREPARATION for childbirth is a relatively recent one. A decade ago, few hospitals or clinics offered such classes. Today, courses are available at most such institutions and there are, in addition, a number of similar courses being offered by highly qualified private instructors.

There are two main, general approaches to prepared childbirth—one originated in Great Britain by Dr. Grantly Dick-Read, and the other a psychoprophylactic method developed in Russia by Lamaze and adapted in the United States by Elizabeth Bing. They differ to some extent in emphasis and technique, although both include mental and physical components of training. Many preparation-for-childbirth classes combine elements—or variations—of both methods.

The philosophy behind the Dick-Read method is that ignorance of what occurs in childbirth produces fear; this leads in turn to tension and, inevitably, to an increase in the experience of pain. Teachers concentrate on overcoming fear by providing accurate information about the process of childbirth, and by teaching deep relaxation and different breathing techniques appropriate to the different stages of labor. In addition, the classes include information on breast-feeding and exercises to promote suppleness.

Psychoprophylaxis (Lamaze) is a highly structured training that places great stress on breathing techniques, on the premise that intense concentration on breathing patterns reduces the experience of pain. Relaxation is taught in such a way that it becomes a conditioned response. At the start of classes, women are helped to eliminate their fear and doubt about childbirth. They are then taught to respond to labor contractions as helpful stimuli rather than "pains." Classes provide information on the anatomy and physiology of pregnancy and labor and teach exercises to strengthen the abdominal and pelvic floor muscles.

The baby's father is included in most preparation-for-childbirth classes, so that the entire preparation for birth can be shared. The father's support during labor is of even greater benefit if he, too, knows what to expect and is prepared for each stage of the process.

Classes usually start in the seventh month of pregnancy, meeting weekly for 1½ to 2 hours. Teachers of all methods agree that at least 6 sessions should be devoted to the labor itself.

For most women who have had training, the pain of labor is experienced as a side effect. With the aid of breathing and relaxation techniques, and with emotional support from their partners and attendants, many are able to cope with the pain without medication. Others require pain relief and should feel no sense of self-reproach at this.

Preparation-for-childbirth classes anticipate, and contribute to, a normal, easy labor. However, a woman should be aware that not all labors are easy and normal. It may prove necessary to deliver the baby by cesarean section, or by forceps or suction. This does not mean that a woman has "failed" during labor to apply what she learned in her classes.

HORMONAL CHANGES IN THE EARLY MONTHS

AFTER FERTILIZATION, ovulation stops and the ovary develops a glandular area known as the corpus luteum. This in turn produces the hormone progesterone, which helps in the formation of the placenta and is active during the first 4 weeks after conception. After that time, the production of progesterone is largely taken over by the placenta. During pregnancy, the function of progesterone is to promote relaxation of the smooth muscle of the uterus and to prepare the milk-producing glands in the breast for nursing.

After the eighth week of pregnancy, the corpus luteum begins to produce a hormone known as relaxin, which may help prepare the cervix for labor, although its exact role is uncertain.

In addition to progesterone, the growing placenta secretes the hormones chorionic gonadotrophin, estrogen, and human placental lactogen. During pregnancy, estrogen enlarges the ducts of the breasts, and promotes the growth of the blood vessels of the endometrium, the lining of the uterus. Increased estrogen secretion is probably responsible for the slight enlargement of the pituitary gland that occurs during pregnancy.

Another hormone secreted by the placenta, human placental lactogen, ensures that the fetus is constantly supplied with the proper amount of nutrients, and provides alternate fuel sources (that is, other than glucose) for the mother.

During pregnancy, the thyroid gland enlarges slightly and secretes increased levels of its hormone, thyroxine, which increases the basal metabolic rate —a determination of the body's energy needs in the resting state—by 25 percent. This provides for the energy needed for fetal growth and for the chemical changes taking place in a woman's body.

Pregnancy results in an increase in the levels of the parathyroid hormones (which ensure proper calcium balance in the body) and in the amount of cortisol produced by the adrenal glands. Like thyroxine, cortisol is bound to a protein, allowing an adequate amount of it to circulate in the bloodstream.

The secretion of another adrenal hormone, aldosterone, also increases in pregnancy and counters the sodium loss produced by the increased progesterone level, thus maintaining a healthy level in the bloodstream of this important mineral. (For additional information on hormones, see Chapter 23, page 474.)

THE FIRST TRIMESTER—WEEKS 0–12

DURING THE FIRST 3 MONTHS of pregnancy, the body undergoes a number of changes that help provide the proper environment for the growth and development of the fetus. The uterus enlarges to about 3 times its usual size, in preparation for the future growth of the fetus. Breasts also enlarge noticeably; they will become considerably heavier by the end of the pregnancy. The volume of circulating blood doubles.

By the end of the twelfth week, the fetus has developed from a minute oval disk into a recognizably human form. It already possesses most of its organs and tissues. The heart has begun to beat and can be heard through a Doppler stethoscope. (See figures 11.3 and 11.4.)

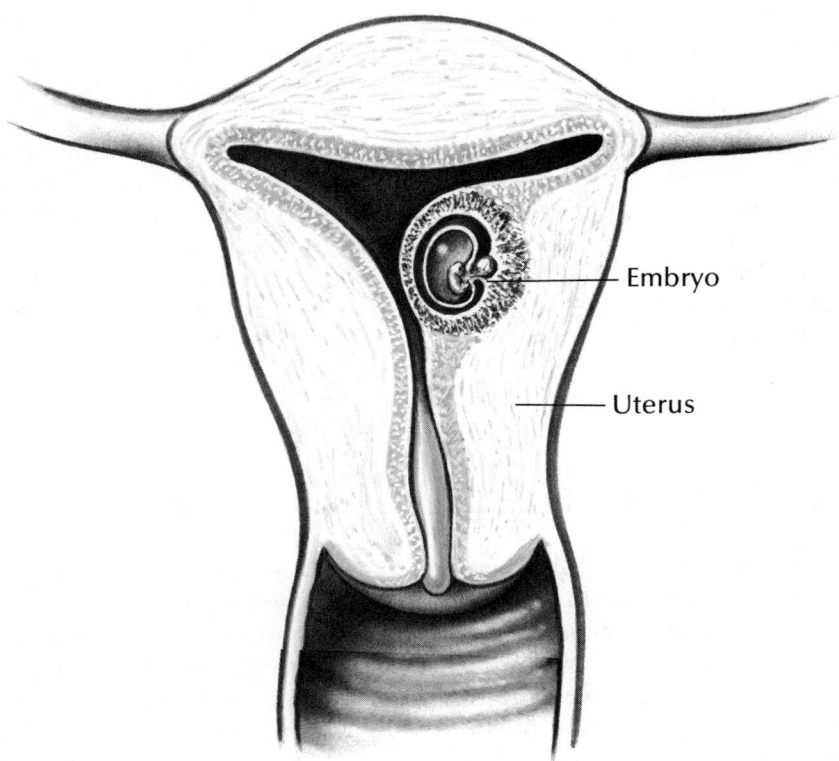

Figure 11.3.   **Implanted embryo at 6 weeks (actual size).**

Figure 11.4.   **The embryo at 10 weeks (actual size). Note enlarged size of uterus and the development of distinct body parts.**

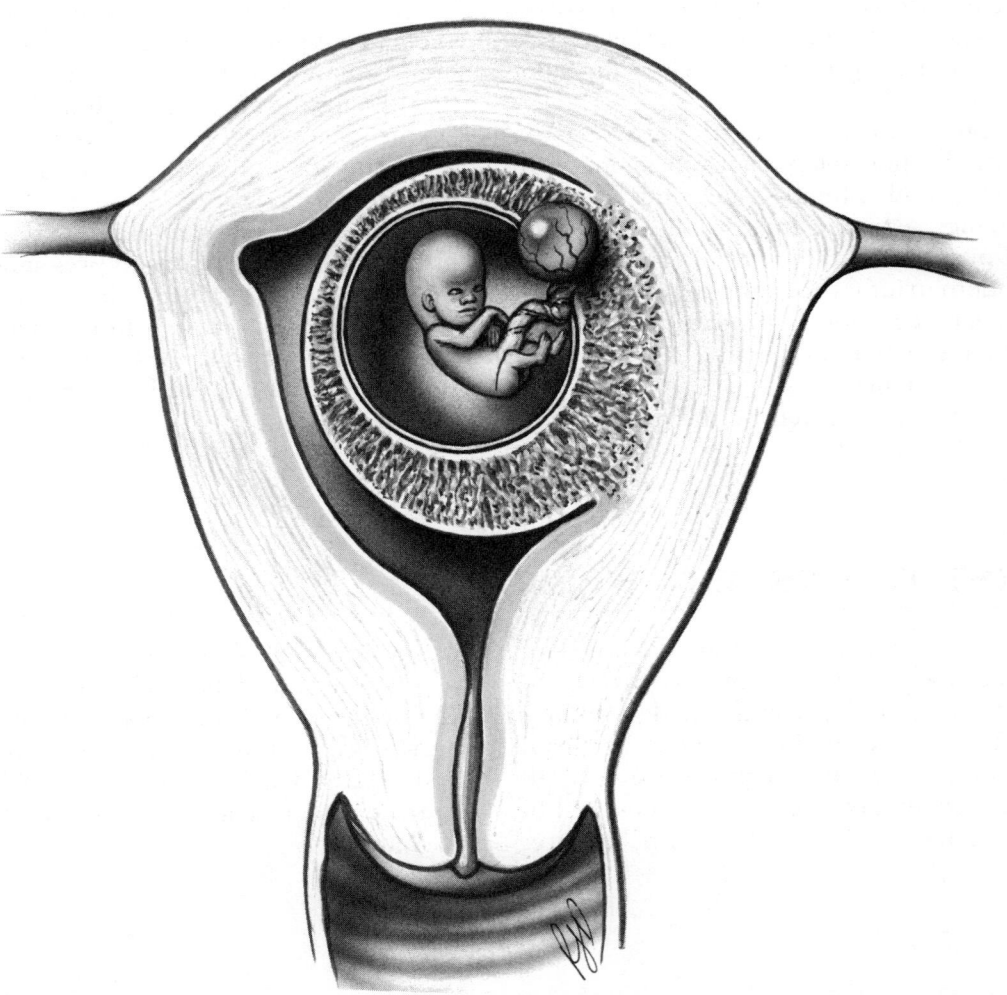

THE COURSE OF PREGNANCY BY TRIMESTER

Development of the Embryo

Day 9. The inner layers of the cell (endoderm and ectoderm) become differentiated. The amniotic cavity appears.

Days 13–15. The yolk sac develops and the amniotic cavity expands.

Day 20. The fetus is suspended on a body stalk through which it receives nutrients.

Day 28. The body stalk develops into the umbilical cord, joining the placenta and embryo. Oxygen, carbon dioxide, and nutrients are exchanged through the placenta. The amniotic sac expands further and its outer layer merges with the inner layer of the trophoblast. Gallbladder, liver, and stomach begin to form; areas of the brain start to develop.

Day 32. Head parts—nose, mouth, eyes, ears, brain—are developing. Divisions of the heart are recognizable and the first heartbeats occur. Thyroid, larynx, and trachea start to develop.

Days 35–37. Arm and leg buds lengthen. Regional divisions of the brain are recognizable. Lung buds and the kidneys begin to form. The skin and the eyes develop; the nostrils are recognizable.

Days 40–42. The stomach is recognizable. Cells are being laid down to form the skeleton. The heart parts fuse to form the 4 chambers.

Days 46–49. The beginnings of fingers, toes, and eyelids are evident. The nervous system is forming and muscle fiber begins to develop. Adrenal gland and thyroid cells become more mature. The tail disappears.

Fetal Growth and Development

Week 8. Centers of bone growth are established and ossification begins. Nose and upper jaw grow rapidly and the two sides of the lips and palate fuse. Tooth buds appear.

Week 12. The eyelids meet and fuse. The inner ear is almost completely formed; the lens of the eye develops rapidly. External genitals are evident as swellings. Hair follicles and the dermis become distinct.

Week 16. The bulge of the forebrain is distinguishable from the cerebellum and brain stem. The epidermis becomes thicker.

Week 20. The ovaries and testes are structurally established. The tubules of the kidneys branch out.

Week 24. Eyebrows and eyelashes are evident; the fetus is covered with downy hair. The bronchial tube continues to branch. The palms of the hands and the soles of the feet develop skin ridges.

Weeks 28–32. The eyelids separate. The testes begin to descend to the scrotum. Fat is deposited under the skin. At 28 weeks, all the vital organs have been formed; further development is mainly that of greater size.

PROBLEMS IN THE FIRST TRIMESTER

Miscarriage

About 20 percent of all pregnancies end in a miscarriage, known medically as spontaneous abortion. Three-quarters of these occur in the first trimester, generally between the sixth and the tenth weeks.

The usual signs of a threatened miscarriage early in pregnancy are vaginal bleeding, often accompanied by cramping. With bed rest, the process may stop and the pregnancy may continue normally. It may, however, continue and become what is called an "inevitable abortion," meaning that the fetus has died and miscarriage cannot be prevented by any medical means. Bleeding becomes heavy; there are strong uterine contractions and progressive dilation of the cervix. The fetus, amniotic sac, and placenta may be expelled entirely (this is a

IMPORTANT WARNING SIGNS

Medical help should be sought immediately if any of the following emergencies occur during pregnancy:

Bright red vaginal bleeding

Severe abdominal pain

Fever over 101°F

Continuous headache or blurred vision, with swelling of the face and hands, in the latter half of pregnancy.

"complete abortion") or only partially (an "incomplete abortion"). An incomplete abortion must be completed by a doctor, to prevent serious infection. Usually, a dilation and curettage (D&C) is performed, cleaning the uterus so that it will heal. Occasionally a fetus dies but is retained in the uterus. This is a "missed abortion." The death of the fetus can be determined by ultrasound techniques. If a missed abortion occurs early in pregnancy, a D&C is usually done. Later, labor may be induced.

Among the causes of miscarriage are fetal abnormality, a structural defect of the uterus, or maternal hormonal imbalance. (A fall seldom results in miscarriage because the fetus is well protected within the uterus.)

In the great majority of miscarriages, the fetus is found to be abnormal. Genetic defects, maternal syphilis, drugs, and stress so severe that it affects the hormone balance are among the causes of abnormalities that result in miscarriage. Excessive caffeine and alcohol use, heavy smoking, and poor maternal nutrition also play a role. The high rate of abnormality among miscarried fetuses is, in its way, a reassurance that a pregnancy that reaches the sixth month will most likely result in a healthy baby.

Grief and anger are common—and completely normal—reactions to a miscarriage. The feelings of grief are often complicated by guilt, which may cause tension between the woman and the baby's father. They may, for example, needlessly reproach themselves and each other for having exercised too strenuously, had intercourse too frequently, or neglected some aspect of care. They need to realize that such factors are not responsible for a miscarriage.

Many women fear that the miscarriage signals an inability to carry a fetus to term, but in most cases a subsequent pregnancy will be normal. Some women, however, have "habitual abortion," a series of consecutive miscarriages. Since this may be due to a hormone imbalance or other treatable condition, a woman who has had 3 or more spontaneous abortions should be given tests to determine the cause.

Intercourse can usually be resumed within 2 to 4 weeks after a miscarriage, or when the cervix has closed. After 1 or 2 normal menstrual cycles have been completed, another pregnancy can be planned.

Hydatidiform Mole

In about 1 in 1,500 pregnancies, the embryo dies or fails to develop; instead, the chorion—the tissue surrounding the egg—develops into grapelike sacs or vesicles. This condition, which is called a molar pregnancy or Hydatidiform mole, is more common in Oriental than in Occidental women, and in women over 45, and is due to a chromosomal defect in the fertilized egg.

The woman with a molar pregnancy may have uterine bleeding and high blood pressure; the uterus will be larger than is usual for the age of the fetus. Ultrasound is used to confirm the condition and, if there is no spontaneous abortion, the pregnancy will be terminated by suction curettage. It is highly unlikely that a subsequent pregnancy will be molar, but a woman should wait a year before attempting to conceive again.

About 10 percent of women who have had a molar pregnancy later develop choriocarcinoma, a relatively rare form of cancer that can be treated successfully with chemotherapy.

Ectopic Pregnancy

Sometimes the fetus grows in a Fallopian tube, or in an ovary, or in the wall of the uterus. (See figure

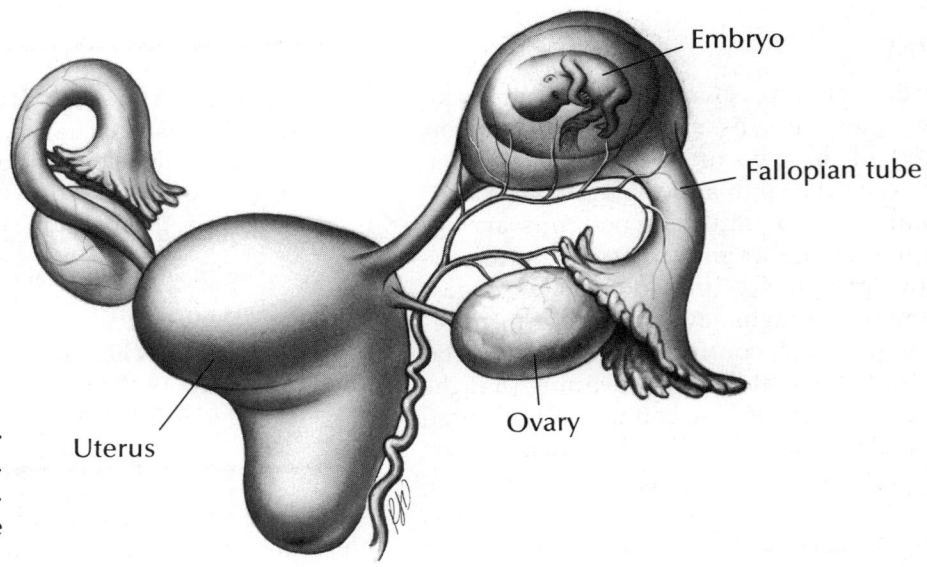

Figure 11.5. **Ectopic or tubal pregnancy, with developing embryo in the Fallopian tube instead of the uterus.**

11.5.) Doctors are not certain what causes ectopic pregnancy, as this condition is called, but it occurs more frequently when the tubes have been damaged by pelvic infections. Women who have used intrauterine contraceptive devices are also more susceptible.

An ectopic pregnancy is suspected when a woman has vaginal spotting together with lower abdominal pain, especially on one side. Blood tests for human chorionic gonadotrophin, ultrasound examinations, and a pelvic examination confirm the diagnosis. Treatment of an ectopic pregnancy is surgical. If there has been rupture of the tube or ovary, removal may be necessary. If there has been no rupture, it may be possible to remove only the misplaced embryo, thus preserving the affected tubes.

Some studies indicate that there is a slightly increased risk of subsequent ectopic pregnancy. Others, however, suggest that the risk is as high as 50 percent.

THE SECOND TRIMESTER—WEEKS 13–27

MOST WOMEN FEEL extraordinarily healthy during the second trimester. (See figures 11.6 and 11.7.) The discomforts experienced earlier have for the most part disappeared. The pregnancy is very noticeable to others and the mother usually becomes conscious of the fetus's movement at about the 20th week. As the fetus grows, movement becomes more energetic and may even wake the mother at night.

During the second trimester, the fetus grows from 3 to 14 inches in length, and by 27 weeks weighs a little more than 2 pounds.

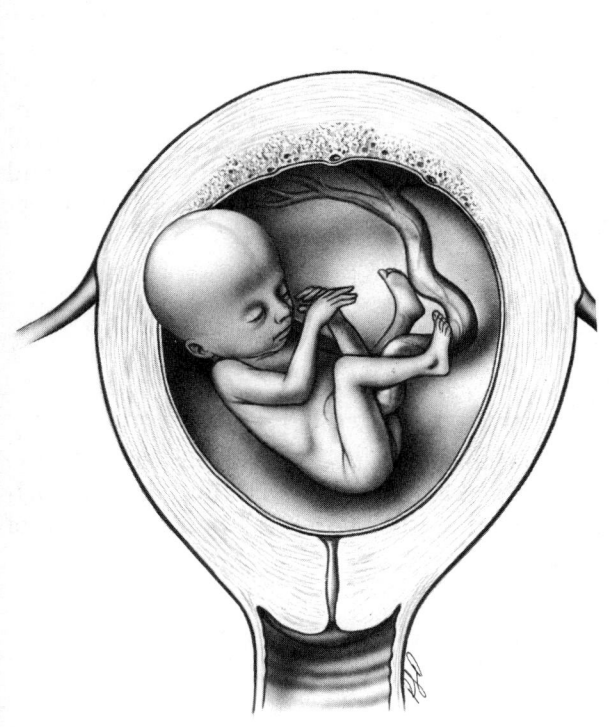

Figure 11.6. **The fetus at 14 weeks.**

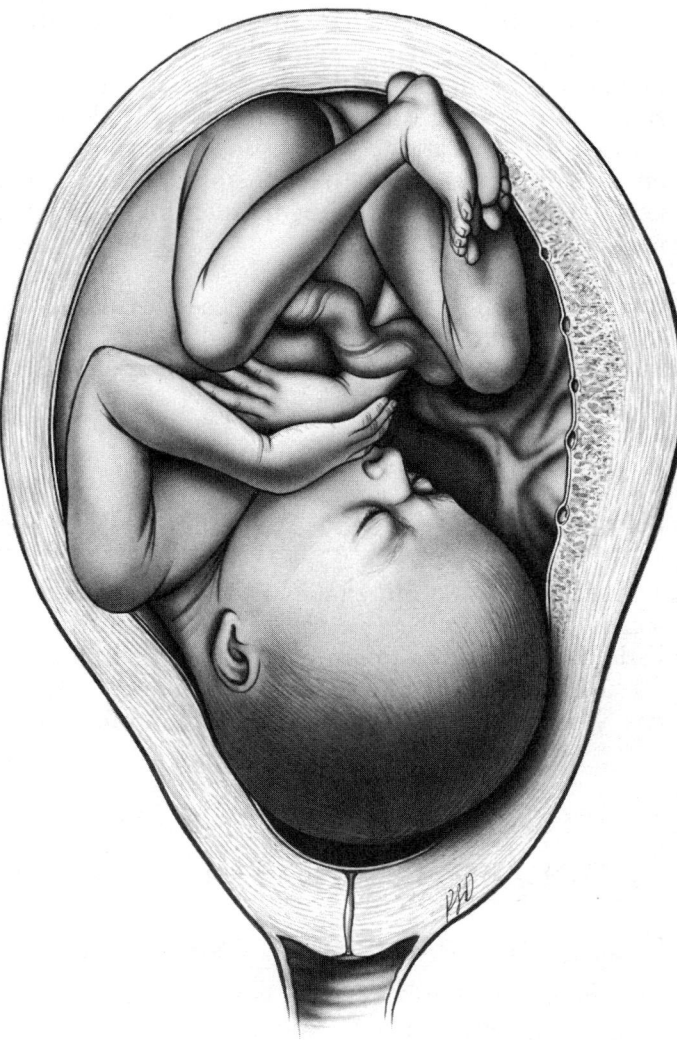

Figure 11.7. **The fetus at 24 weeks.**

PROBLEMS IN THE SECOND TRIMESTER

Premature Labor

In about 5 percent of all pregnancies, labor begins before term, sometimes well before the expected date of confinement. The outcome for the infant depends greatly on how premature the labor is, on what kind of neonatal care is available, and on the infant's weight and functional development. Of babies born at 25 weeks' gestation (slightly less than 2 pounds), about 50 percent survive—given appropriate treatment in a modern neonatal unit. (At a birth weight of 3 pounds or more, an infant has a better than 90 percent chance of survival.) Long-term follow-up studies of such premature infants show that those who live are normal in intelligence and, after some catch-up growth in the first year, in development also.

Poor general health, heavy cigarette smoking, and inadequate nutrition increase the likelihood of premature labor. Specific causes include syphilis, preeclampsia (see page 184), thyroid disturbances, diabetes, and abnormalities of the placenta. Occasionally, premature labor is triggered by physical trauma, such as a bad fall. Even more rarely, an emotional shock may be responsible. However, in nearly half the cases, there is no identifiable explanation.

Premature contractions are a serious complication of pregnancy. If allowed to proceed to full labor, they can result in miscarriage, fetal death, or prematurity, depending upon the stage of pregnancy. If

at all possible, steps should be taken to halt the contractions. This may involve giving a drug that will stop the contractions. Bed rest, sometimes for the remainder of pregnancy, is also mandatory in most instances.

Older women appear to be particularly susceptible to developing premature contractions. In any event, contractions are always a signal to call your doctor immediately.

The first sign of premature labor is usually the beginning of regular uterine contractions. Sometimes there is vaginal bleeding, increased vaginal discharge, or vaginal pressure. Premature rupture of the membranes (the amniotic sac) occurs in 20 to 30 percent of all premature deliveries and, occurring early, may be the first abnormal sign.

Examination by the doctor is imperative. It will probably be recommended that a woman in premature labor enter a medical center equipped for the care of premature infants, if such a facility is available. The doctor may decide to proceed with delivery or, if appropriate (only about 25 percent of the time), may administer a drug to suppress labor.

It is almost impossible to stop premature labor that is associated with vaginal bleeding or rupture of the membranes. However, if premature rupture of the membranes occurs in the second trimester and *no labor ensues*, it is sometimes possible for the pregnancy to continue to term.

THE THIRD TRIMESTER—WEEKS 28–40

THE FINAL STAGE of pregnancy is, not unexpectedly, somewhat uncomfortable. The fetus grows from a little over 2 pounds to an average of 7 pounds and the uterus continues to enlarge (see figure 11.8). A few weeks before the onset of labor the abdomen

commonly changes shape as the fetus "drops"; the fetus's head descends to—or even through—the pelvic inlet and there is some reduction of volume of amniotic fluid.

PROBLEMS IN THE THIRD TRIMESTER

Preeclampsia and Eclampsia

The cause or causes of preeclampsia (toxemia of pregnancy) are not fully understood. The early symptoms, which occur in about 5 percent of all pregnancies, are elevated blood pressure, blurred vision, edema of the face and hands, and protein in the

urine. Treatment with bed rest, fluids, and a well-balanced, high-protein diet can usually control the problem. If preeclampsia becomes severe, however, it can lead to seizures in the mother and it will be necessary to induce labor or deliver the baby by cesarean section.

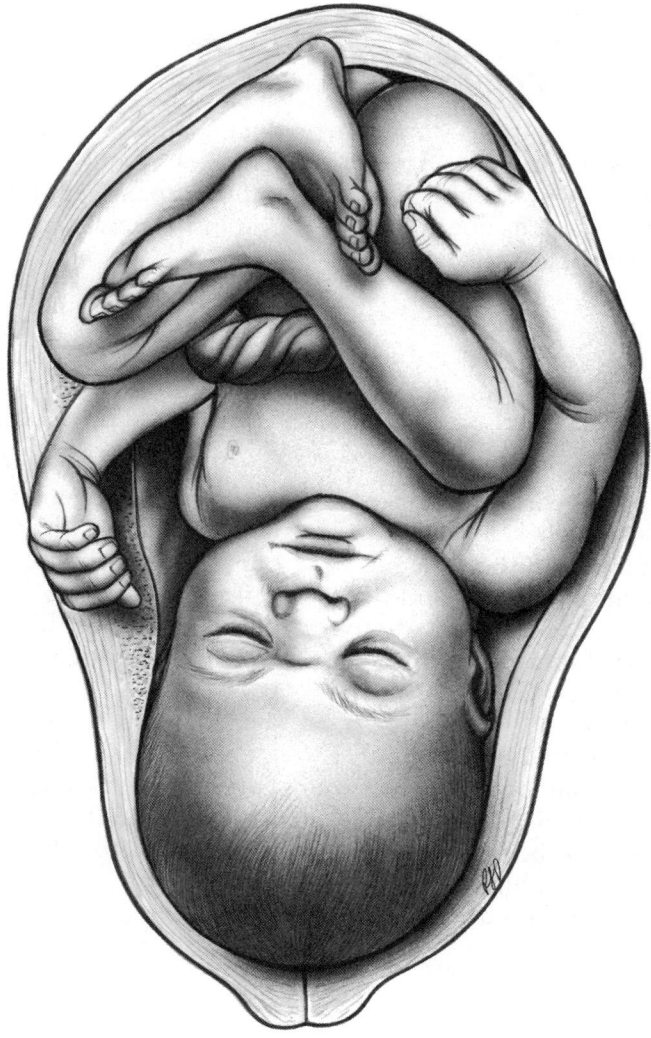

Figure 11.8. **Full-term fetus in position for normal birth.**

Preeclampsia is more common in young women having their first baby, in women with preexisting high blood pressure and kidney disease, and in those carrying twins. Only the end of the pregnancy completely cures the condition.

Placenta Previa

In this condition, the placenta lies in an abnormally low position in the uterus, and may completely block the cervix. Bleeding in the second and third trimesters, usually without pain, is the sign of placenta previa; the condition is best diagnosed by ultrasound. In order to continue the pregnancy as long as possible, a woman with this condition will be confined to bed and asked to refrain from sexual intercourse. If the placenta is found to be completely overlying the cervix, the only way to deliver the baby safely is by cesarean section.

Placenta Abruptia

Occasionally, the placenta suddenly tears away from the wall of the uterus. The tear may be very small, or may involve the entire placenta, producing bleeding, great pain, and shock. This condition is life-threatening for both mother and fetus and should be treated as an obstetrical emergency. Placenta abruptia may occur in women with high blood pressure or dietary deficiency with severe anemia. Sometimes it is the result of an extremely short umbilical cord, or it may occur following extreme trauma, such as an automobile accident.

False Labor

Many women, especially those who have already borne a child, experience episodes of false labor in the final weeks of pregnancy. These contractions of the uterine muscles often occur very close together and may continue for several hours. The contractions of false labor do not cause the cervix to dilate, as do the contractions of the first stage of labor itself. If there is a question about whether the labor is "true" or "false," it can often be settled by changing position, walking about, or taking a glass of warm milk. False labor will then usually stop as abruptly as it started.

Premature Rupture of the Membranes

Occasionally at 38 to 40 weeks' gestation—that is to say, at term—the membranes rupture, releasing the amniotic fluid. Labor almost always begins within 12 hours of this occurrence. A woman should inform her doctor of what has happened; doctors will await the natural onset of labor in these circumstances, inducing labor only if 24 hours pass without the occurrence of strong, rhythmic contractions. Labor is induced to prevent infection, both of the membranes and in the newborn.

LABOR AND DELIVERY

AT 36 WEEKS' GESTATION, the cervix starts to soften and at the same time, or a little earlier, the uterine muscles become more strongly cohesive.

Just before the onset of labor, the body begins to produce prostaglandins in large amounts and these are responsible for the first contractions. Once active labor has begun, oxytocin (produced by the pituitary gland) acts on the uterine muscles to strengthen and speed up their contracting force.

Normal labor may last up to 24 hours with a first baby. Subsequent labors may be shorter—3 to 12 hours. A woman should inform her doctor or midwife when the first signs of labor begin and should prepare to go to the hospital or childbirth center when rhythmical uterine contractions are occurring every 5 minutes.

When she arrives at the hospital, the woman will have a vaginal exam to determine the degree to which the cervix has dilated and the position of the baby's presenting part (usually the head, but sometimes, in breech birth, the buttocks or feet) in the pelvic inlet. Few hospitals today routinely give enemas to laboring patients, or shave their pubic hair. If a woman has not eaten for some hours and is dehydrated, an intravenous drip of glucose and water may be started. Since hospitals have different procedures, and doctors have different preferences, a woman should discuss these preliminary routines with her doctor ahead of time.

THE THREE STAGES OF LABOR

The First Stage

The first stage of labor is said to start with the first rhythmic contraction of the uterine muscles. It ends when the force of these muscles has overcome the resistance of the long-closed but very soft cervix and the cervix is fully open (dilated). The first stage is the longest, lasting from 12 to 14 hours, on the average, for first babies, 8 to 10 hours for subsequent ones. (See figure 11.9.)

At the onset of labor, a woman will often notice that a plug of mucus, and a slightly red-tinged, watery discharge, is expelled from the cervix. This is the so-called "show."

The contractions usually begin mildly, lasting 10 to 20 seconds, and coming at 20- to 30-minute intervals. As labor progresses and the cervix gradually dilates, the contractions come closer together and last longer. Toward the end of the first stage, they may last 40 to 50 seconds and occur at 1- or 2-minute intervals. Many women find this the most difficult part of labor. If the membranes have not ruptured earlier, the doctor may break the bag of waters toward the end of the first stage.

The Second Stage

The second stage of labor lasts from the time that the cervix is fully dilated until the baby is born. This second stage usually takes about 2 hours with a first baby; with subsequent births, it may last only 5 to 30 minutes. (See figure 11.10.)

Unlike the first stage, when the woman has been largely passive, in the second stage the pressure of the baby's head on the pelvis brings about an urge to push or bear down with the contractions. With the expulsive force of the uterine contractions supplemented by the woman's pushing efforts, the baby passes through the pelvis and is born.

An episiotomy, preceded by a local anesthetic, is frequently performed to shorten the second stage of labor and prevent tears in the skin. There are two types of episiotomy: "midline" (an incision from the vagina toward the rectum) and "medio-lateral" (across the vagina). The medio-lateral episiotomy is more painful, but there is usually no threat of splitting to the rectum. In the United States, the midline episiotomy is the procedure most frequently done.

Many hospitals now have combination labor-

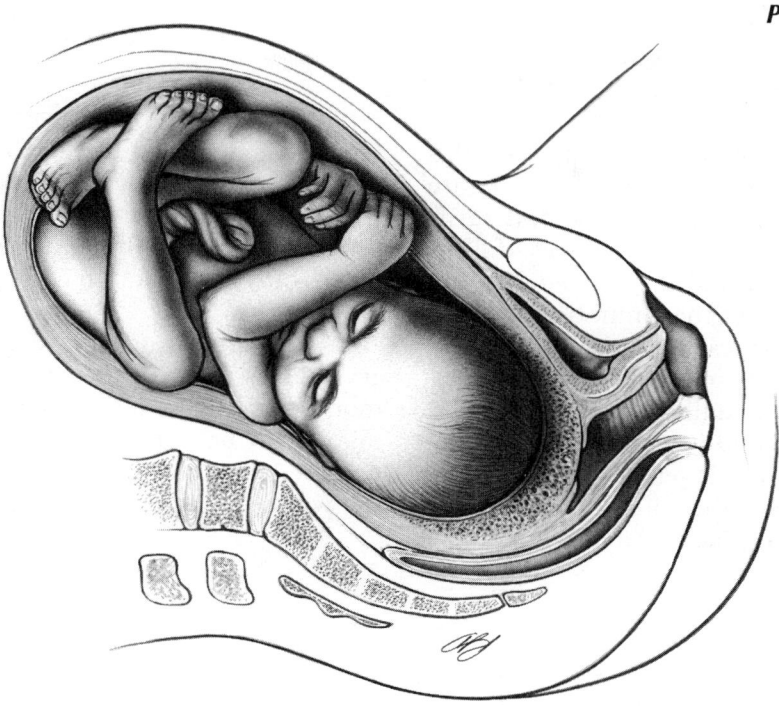

Figure 11.9. **First stage of labor.**

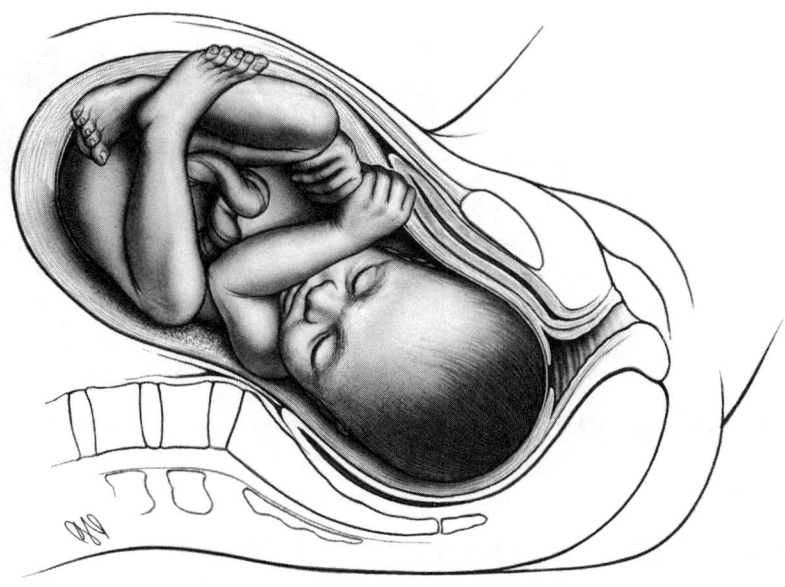

Figure 11.10. **Second stage of labor with baby moving through fully dilated cervix.**

delivery-recovery rooms, making it unnecessary for a woman to be moved during the second stage of labor. If a problem is anticipated during the delivery itself, a woman will be taken to a delivery room, where surgical and emergency equipment are available, about 10 minutes before delivery.

The Third Stage

The third stage of labor is that between the birth of the baby and the delivery of the placenta (afterbirth). Normally, this stage takes only 5 to 10 minutes. If the placenta is not delivered within half an hour, however, the doctor may have to remove it surgically.

After the third stage, the episiotomy—if this incision has been made—is sutured. Usually, an injection of pitocin (oxytocin) is given to the new mother to stimulate uterine contraction and thus stop the bleeding.

THE NORMAL SEQUENCE OF BIRTH

IN THE NORMAL SEQUENCE of birth, the baby's head is born slowly, usually facing downward (see figure 11.11). When the whole head has emerged, it turns spontaneously sideways. The shoulders follow quickly and then the body and the legs emerge, together with the remainder of the amniotic fluid. The umbilical cord that attaches the baby to the placenta is clamped and cut, usually before the placenta itself is delivered. Usually a baby will take a breath and begin to cry loudly as soon as it is completely born, but sometimes a gentle rubbing of the back is necessary to start the infant breathing. It may also be necessary to place a small catheter in the baby's nose and mouth to suction out mucus so that the baby may begin to breathe.

The newborn's eyes are usually treated with silver nitrate or penicillin ointment to prevent possible gonorrheal infection. (In most states, this is required by law.)

The baby's condition will be checked and, if everything is normal, the infant will be given to the mother, or will be placed in a bassinet. A premature infant will be placed immediately under a radiant heater; after examination by a pediatrician, he or she will be transferred to an incubator.

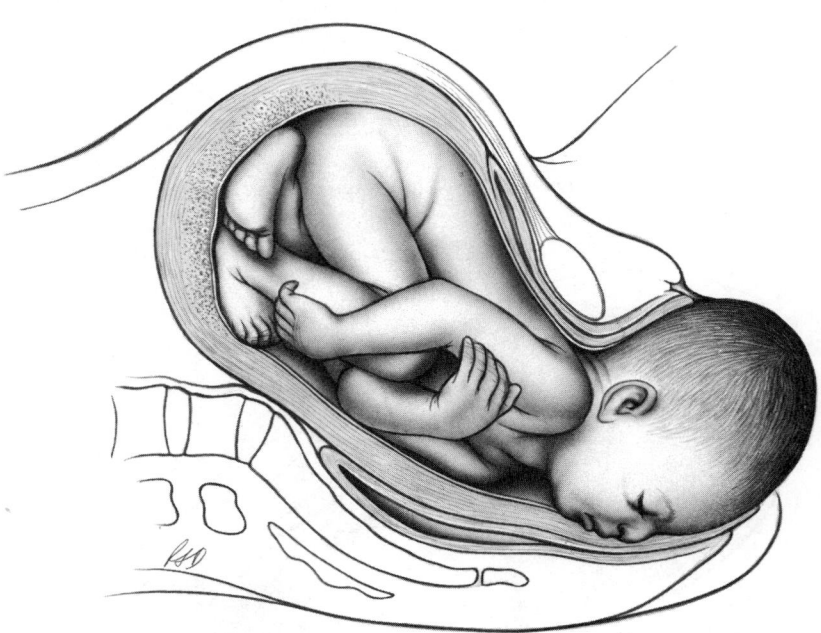

Figure 11.11. **First stage of birth, with baby facing downward for journey through birth canal.**

RELIEF OF PAIN DURING LABOR AND BIRTH

ANY DRUG GIVEN to the mother for the relief of pain during labor will pass across the placenta and may adversely affect the newborn. For this reason, pain-relieving drugs and anesthetics are used conservatively in modern obstetrical practice.

In early labor and in the second, active phase, medications such as meperidine (Demerol) may be given by injection to lessen the pain of the contractions. With the pain somewhat relieved, a woman may be able to use relaxation breathing techniques more effectively.

The form of anesthesia generally used to control the pain of labor today is the epidural or peridural block, a local anesthetic given by injection in the middle of the back. The anesthetic blocks feeling completely from the waist down, relieving the woman of pain—but also of the sensation of her contractions. However, with coaching from those attending her, she will be able to bear down in time with the contractions during the second stage of labor.

Occasionally a nerve-blocking procedure is done in the area around the cervix—a pericervical block. This anesthesia must be given with great care; the fetal heart rate may drop below normal if the fetus absorbs some of the medication from the mother.

SPECIAL CONSIDERATIONS AND COMPLICATIONS OF BIRTH

Fetal Monitoring

In many, if not most, hospitals, an external fetal monitor will be put in place early in labor, to remain until the baby is born. The device is held in place by two straps around the woman's abdomen. (See figure 11.12.) A Doppler ultrasound device records the fetal heart rate continuously and another device, a tocodynameter, records the uterine contraction pattern; the measurements are recorded on a moving strip of paper similar to the familiar ECG record. If electronic fetal monitoring is not done, an attendant will monitor the fetal heart at frequent intervals with a fetoscope.

Continuous monitoring of the fetal heart rate permits early detection of possible complications, so that they can be treated before they become serious. Monitoring is safe, not uncomfortable—a woman can change position and even walk about while the monitor is in place—and is essential in high-risk pregnancies.

If the fetal heart rate suddenly dips, or there are other signs of fetal distress, internal monitoring devices will be used. A small electrode will be attached to the fetus's scalp and a catheter will be inserted into the uterus through the vagina. These devices enable the doctor to determine more accurately the pattern of the fetal heart rate and the force of the uterine contractions.

Induction of Labor

If there are medical problems such as high blood pressure, or obstetrical problems such as premature rupture of the membranes followed by a long latent period, or the baby is more than reasonably overdue, labor may be induced. This is done by placing the hormone oxytocin—normally produced by the pituitary gland during the first stage of labor—into an intravenous solution that is slowly infused into the bloodstream through a large vein in order to initiate contractions. If it is necessary to induce labor when the cervix is hard and thus not easily dilatable, prostaglandin, a hormonelike substance, may be inserted into the vagina in gel form to soften the cervix prior to the start of the oxytocin infusion.

Once labor has started and the cervix has begun to dilate, an induced labor progresses in the normal fashion. Induction of labor, done properly and for good medical or obstetrical reasons, is an entirely safe procedure.

Augmentation of Labor

Labor should progress in a certain specific time frame. When it slows down or stalls, it is important to augment it—that is, to speed up the dilation of the cervix—by infusing oxytocin. Dysfunctional labor, if allowed to continue without treatment, jeopardizes the baby.

Figure 11.12. **Fetus during labor with fetal monitors in place.**

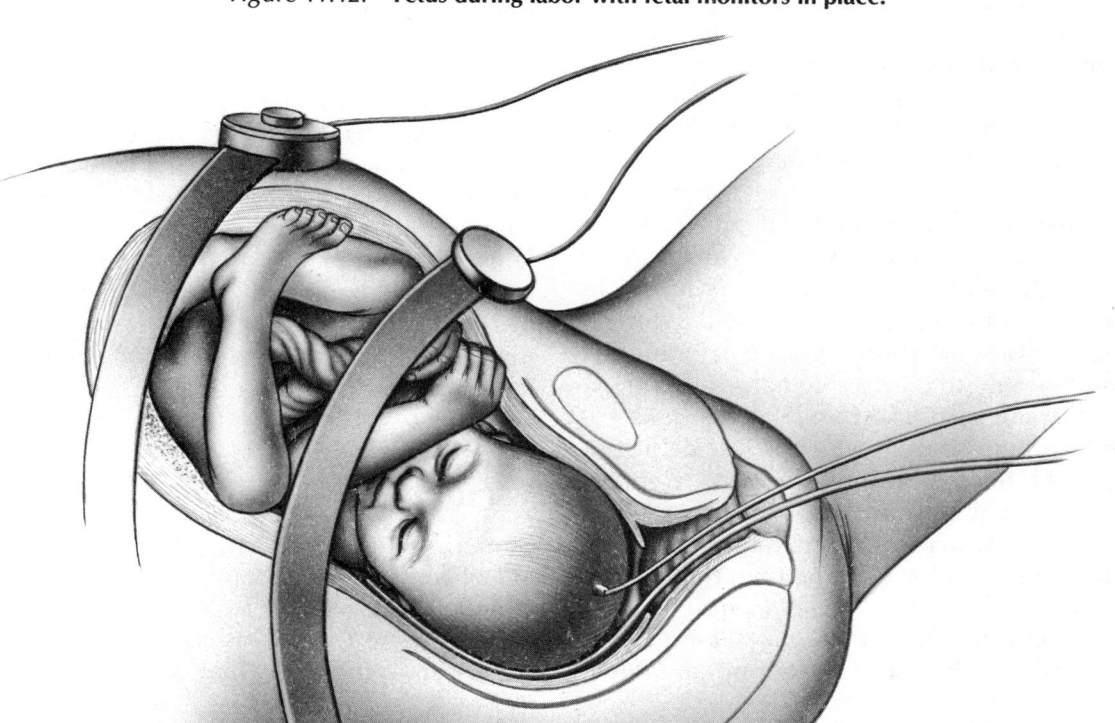

Cesarean Birth

The great majority of cesarean births are unexpected, performed because the baby is in distress and must be delivered quickly. Signs of fetal distress that will be noted on the electronic monitor include a slow or very rapid heart rate, a deceleration of the heart rate, and a heartbeat that does not fluctuate normally. The presence of meconium (a fetal bowel movement in the uterus) and hypoxia (lack of oxygen in the fetal bloodstream) are other signs of distress. An emergency cesarean section may also be prompted by a delivery complication such as placenta previa.

A woman who has looked forward to a vaginal delivery may find this unexpected outcome extremely disappointing; the father may feel helpless and useless. To help ease the couple's emotional trauma it is very important that the doctor provide a full explanation of why it was necessary to do the emergency cesarean section.

Not all cesarean sections are emergencies, of course. In some cases it is known from the beginning that the procedure will be necessary, as with a serious illness such as diabetes that would make labor hazardous to the mother and baby. In others, the necessity for the procedure becomes apparent late in pregnancy. For example, the operation will be done when it is found that a baby is too large to pass safely through the mother's pelvic bones. It will also be done when a baby is very small, especially when such a baby is breech, because the small head is easily injured during vaginal delivery.

The major risk to a baby born by cesarean section is premature delivery and the susceptibility to hyaline membrane disease, a life-threatening disease of premature lungs. This may occur when, for example, the operation is scheduled in advance and the due date is incorrectly estimated. To guard against premature delivery, the doctor will draw some amniotic fluid and measure the amounts of two fatty substances, sphingomyelin and lecithin, contained in it. This measurement gives an accurate assessment of the maturity of the baby's lungs. In some centers, fetal maturity is determined by ultrasound. Delaying the operation until the beginning of labor is another way to ensure the baby's maturity.

Many cesarean sections are now done under regional (epidural) anesthesia, which is less debilitating than general. Some hospitals allow the woman's partner to remain with her during the procedure. The operation is performed by making an incision through the abdominal wall, opening the uterus, and removing the baby and the placenta. The incision on the skin may be a crosswise Pfannenstiel incision (a "bikini" incision) or an up-and-down midline incision. The former is far less destructive of abdominal muscle tissue and the scar has the further, cosmetic advantage that it can be hidden by even a brief bathing suit. The incision on the uterus is usually on the lower part, and vertical; this reduces the risk of rupture should the woman attempt to deliver vaginally in a subsequent pregnancy.

Any abdominal surgery may produce a temporary paralysis of the gastrointestinal tract. For this reason, a woman who has had a cesarean section will be fed intravenously for 1 or 2 days after the operation.

A woman who has had an uncomplicated cesarean delivery will be discharged from the hospital within 4 to 8 days. It will, however, take 4 to 6 weeks before she recovers her normal well-being and energy.

Increasing numbers of babies are being delivered by cesarean section. It has taken the place of traumatic forceps deliveries, which, in the past, too often resulted in the birth of damaged or stillborn infants, and which are no longer being done. Surgery is much safer now than previously; however, some doctors may be too ready to perform it. A realistic rate for cesarean section ranges from 12 to 30 percent of all deliveries, with large teaching hospitals and specialists in maternal-fetal medicine at the high end of the scale because they care for more women with problem pregnancies.

Subsequent Births. While it may be possible to deliver a second or even a third infant vaginally, it may also be the case that the problem that made the previous cesarean section necessary persists, making a vaginal delivery unsafe. The possibility of vaginal birth must be discussed with the doctor. Important considerations are the woman's medical history, her state of health, and her understanding that, if the "trial of labor" is unsuccessful, she will have to undergo another cesarean delivery. (In a "trial of labor," labor is allowed to progress, as for a vaginal delivery; surgery is performed only if problems arise.) The labor should take place in a hospital with a blood bank and operating room immediately available should another section be necessary. About half the women who elect to deliver vaginally after a previous cesarean section are successful.

Forceps Delivery and Vacuum Extraction

Sometimes it is necessary to deliver a baby with the aid of forceps or a vacuum extractor. The forceps, which are curved in a handlike shape, are placed on either side of the baby's head as it is beginning to come through the vaginal opening. Gently pulling on the forceps, the doctor is then able to lift the baby out. In a vacuum extraction a small plastic suction cup is placed on the baby's head. A vacuum is then created, which enables the doctor to lift the baby out of the birth canal by drawing on the cup.

Breech Birth

A breech birth is one in which the baby presents with the feet or buttocks first, rather than the head. (See figure 11.13.) If such a baby is small (under 5½ pounds) or large (over 8 pounds), or if the head, as seen by x-ray, is not well tucked into the chest but is extended upright, a vaginal delivery is not safe.

A breech presentation is the one occasion in modern obstetrics in which x-ray is employed to determine the configuration of the woman's pelvic bones. It is important to be sure that the pelvic bones are sufficiently wide apart to allow the baby's head to be born quickly and easily after the body has emerged.

Dysfunctional or slowed labor occurs more frequently with a breech birth than with the normal head-down presentation; a cesarean delivery may be necessary. In many hospitals, women delivering first babies as breeches routinely have cesarean sections, as they are considered safer.

Multiple Births

Twins are formed either from 1 egg (identical twins) or from 2 fertilized eggs (fraternal twins). Identical twins, less common than fraternal twins, have the exact same genetic makeup and are consequently always of the same sex, though they may differ in size. Examination of the placenta and membranes at the time of birth can help determine if twins of the same sex are fraternal or identical.

Twins occur in about 1 of 80 pregnancies. The likelihood of bearing twins is higher for black women, and for women who were themselves twins or had twins in their immediate families. Twins are also more commonly born to older women and to women with 4 or more previous pregnancies.

Pregnancy is uncomfortable for a woman carrying twins, and delivery may be difficult. Premature birth is more likely and the perinatal mortality rate is higher. The second-born twin is usually at higher risk. In some instances, twins are more safely delivered by cesarean section. For example, if one baby is breech and the other is vertex, cesarean delivery will prevent their heads from becoming locked together, as would be the case in a vaginal delivery. An ultrasound examination early in labor can help the doctor decide whether the position of twins warrants a

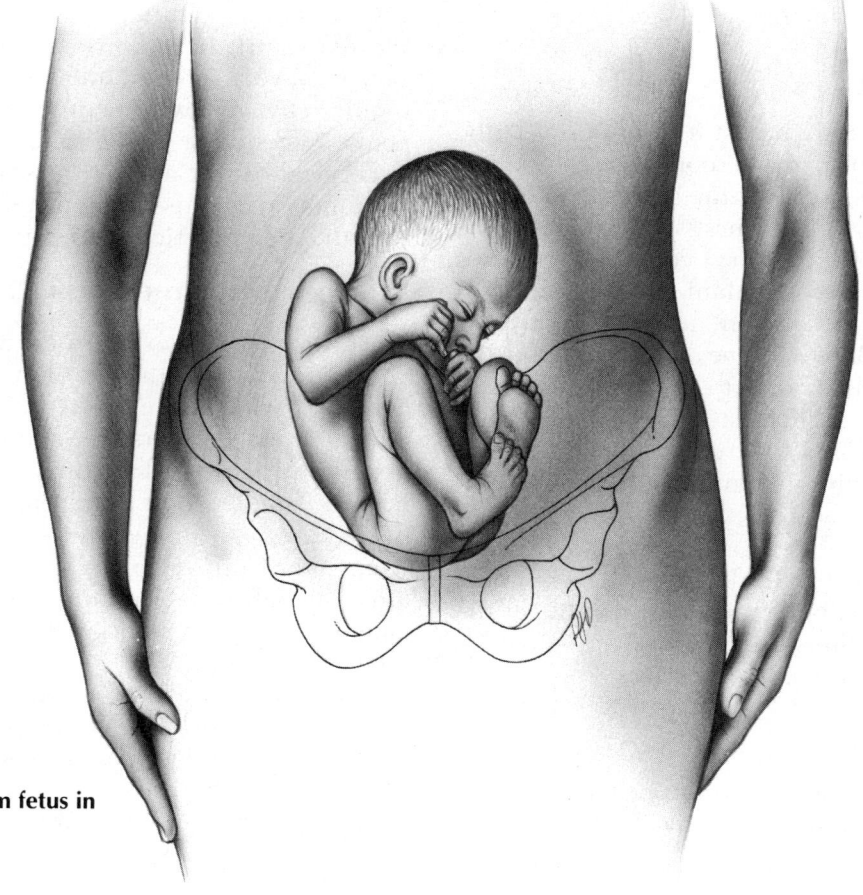

Figure 11.13. **Full-term fetus in the breech position.**

cesarean delivery, or whether a vaginal birth is preferable.

Triplets and Other Multiple Births. These are rare events although, with the use of fertility drugs, more common than in the past. Depending on the circumstances, triplets may be delivered vaginally or by cesarean section. The criteria are always those of the safety of mother and infants.

Emergency Delivery

On rare occasions, a baby is born in a car or taxi on the way to the hospital or childbirth center. In such cases, the person accompanying the laboring woman should be as calm and reassuring as possible. No attempt should be made to stop or slow the birth. The mother's perineum should not be touched—doing so could easily lead to infection—and the umbilical cord should not be cut. If the placenta delivers before the hospital is reached, the baby and the placenta should be wrapped up together, with the cord intact. The baby should be encouraged to nurse immediately; the sucking action prompts the release of oxytocin, causing the uterus to contract and preventing further bleeding.

Almost all babies born unexpectedly in this manner will cry quickly. If there is mucus in the nose or mouth, which may prevent the baby from breathing, the baby should be turned on its side and the back gently rubbed.

THE POSTPARTUM PERIOD

TODAY, MOST WOMEN who give birth in the hospital remain for 3 to 4 days after giving birth. This allows time for the uterus to begin to heal and return to its nonpregnant state, and for the episiotomy, if done, to heal. Few childbirth centers have overnight facilities; women who choose to give birth at a center must be prepared to return home with the newborn on the day of delivery. Some hospitals have 24-hour discharge for normal birth.

Breast-Feeding

Most doctors encourage breast-feeding, even if the mother must return to work soon after the baby's birth. Breast milk is ideal for the baby's nutritional needs; it and colostrum (the first secretion from the mother's breasts after delivery) contain antibodies that will help the newborn infant resist infection in the early months. The decision, however, is the new mother's to make. Babies thrive on formula, too.

Initially, tenseness, anxiety, or fatigue may interfere with successful breast-feeding. Once well-established (usually in 4 to 6 weeks after the birth), however, breast-feeding is neither difficult nor uncomfortable. For many women, it is a very rewarding experience.

Probably the greatest difficulty for new mothers in starting breast-feeding is that they do not get the help and support that they need from others—nurses, doctors, other women, partners.

Circumcision

Circumcision is a minor surgical procedure in which the foreskin of the penis is removed. It is usually done before the baby leaves the hospital, but not until he is more than 2 days old. Couples of the Jewish faith may wish to have their sons circumcised according to tradition, in a ceremony performed on the eighth day of life. While the procedure is probably painful for the baby (no anesthesia can be used), it does not take long and healing is quick.

Circumcision became an almost routine procedure in this country during the years following World War II. It is, however, not medically necessary to have a son circumcised, nor is circumcision required by any law. The procedure does not prevent penile infection or penile cancer. Moreover, the rate of cervical cancer among the sexual partners of uncircumcised men is no higher than usual, provided that the men practice good hygiene.

Postpartum Emotions

Most women feel exhilarated after the birth of a child and relieved that the long months of waiting are over. Some, however, experience a sense of anticlimax when they first see the new baby. This is a normal response and a woman should not reproach herself if the rush of maternal feelings she has expected does not immediately occur. In many cases, women feel a little "blue," usually on the third day after the baby is born. This transitory depression is usually simply an emotional rebound to the excitement of the birth.

Serious depression persisting after a birth, or beginning several weeks postpartum, is not common. It may be due to endocrine imbalance resulting from thyroid disease, or to other metabolic and endocrine conditions that are not yet understood.

A woman who feels severely depressed in the postpartum period should seek medical help promptly.

Postpartum Checkup

It is important to return to the doctor's office for an examination 4 to 6 weeks after birth. The postpartum checkup includes a pelvic examination to assess the size of the uterus—it should have recovered its prepregnancy size—and proper healing of the perineum.

Postpartum exercises to strengthen the abdomen and the muscles of the pelvic floor should be discussed at this time, if they have not already been started. Toning the muscles not only helps a woman to regain her figure but also aids in preventing such problems as prolapse of the uterus later in life. The question of contraception and the planning of future pregnancies should also be discussed at this time. Nursing a baby should not be relied upon as a method of contraception since, although a woman may not have her period during the months that she is nursing, it is quite possible that she may ovulate. Sexual intercourse may be resumed as soon as the placental site is healed—usually in 3 weeks. Some couples prefer to wait until all postpartum bleeding and spotting has ceased.

12 Infancy and the Early Years

Stephen Atwood, M.D.

INTRODUCTION

"THE CHILD IS the father of the man," wrote the English poet William Wordsworth. Today, everyone knows what he meant, but there were times in history when few people considered what it meant to be a child. Each society places its own stamp on the character of childhood, which intimately affects how a child develops and what kind of person he or she becomes.

In medieval times, childhood almost did not exist—as you can tell by looking at medieval paintings. The Christ child is almost always shown as a miniature adult, perched securely on his mother's lap and often dressed in adult clothing. Those children who survived to the age of about 7 were put to work and treated as adults—a situation that persisted until concern about child labor arose during the Industrial Revolution.

We now know that childhood is a period very different from later years, a time of striking growth and change in both body and mind. It is a continuum of developments that begin long before birth and proceed until a child is ready to assume independent responsibility for him- or herself.

The stage of dependence in human beings is far longer than in any other animal—just as the potential for intelligence appears to be greater. During infancy and childhood, people learn about themselves, about their culture, and how to respond to the expectations of others.

In today's society there is tremendous interest in the study of child development, in part because it provides an adult with fascinating insights into his or her own makeup. The process of interacting with a developing child also provides opportunities for new growth and development in an adult. This is what parents discover, and something nonparents rarely share.

Mothers have traditionally and physiologically been most closely bound to this developmental process. The responsibilities of breast-feeding, as well as daily child care, impose demands few anticipated before their first child. As a result, many parents describe new inner growth and knowledge of themselves to a degree hardly matched at any other time of their lives.

It is an opportunity, however, that far too many fathers have missed in the past. Today there is a new emphasis on the vital role that a father plays in a child's development, and increasing attention to the problems of fatherhood. Fathers are likely to feel shut out of the mother-child relationship, particularly if the mother is breast-feeding. If the mother spends more time with the infant, it is natural that the infant will pay far more attention to the mother during the first year or two. In fact, there is evidence that at birth infants prefer women; they pay more attention to higher voices than to lower ones.

In the past, American society has encouraged this alienation by taking the attitude that fathers are incompetent or even dangerous to their infants, and by such practices as shutting them out of the delivery room and shielding the babies in the nursery from fathers by a wall of glass. Unfortunately, these practices continue even today in some places. It is now recognized, however, that in feeding and diapering an infant and playing with older children, a man plays a vital role in his child's development and also learns important things about himself. Because cuddling and nutrition equal love to an infant, fathers should have as much opportunity as possible to share in providing them. At the same time, any primary caregiver needs relief from the unrelenting demands of child care, and the other parent should be prepared to help.

Child development may be a continuum, but as any parent knows, no two children are alike. Each child has individual strengths and weaknesses and learns different skills at an individual pace. Certainly there are recognizable patterns in child development, but the range of normal is very wide. Therefore, it is unfortunate that parents tend to compare their children with others, and are discouraged when their child does not seem to be keeping up in one area or another.

In the early years, the child development "experts" in the playground or nursery tend to pay particular attention to developments in the area of motor skills, so that a child who is concentrating on the perceptual and language skills that are more difficult to recognize may be regarded as "slow." Good parents try very hard to disregard the attempts of strangers and friends to criticize their child's development; only a parent can see all the strengths of a developing infant.

Be sensitive to the fact that the developmental stages mentioned below are only guides to the average, not necessarily the norm. A child may spurt well ahead in some areas and lag in others. These spurts and lags are normal, unless a lag persists for a very long time. The normal baby learns at his own pace. Just as an adult learns something best if he is truly interested, attempts to force an infant to learn something before he exhibits independent interest in it may result in a shaky foundation in that particular skill.

The section on the first year is divided month by month. Because a child is like no other, it is wise to read the entire section rather than concentrating on the particular age of an infant. For the reasons mentioned above, some of the developmental stages your infant is going through now may not appear in the section about the month he or she has reached to date.

THE FIRST YEAR OF LIFE

An Overview of What to Expect

A baby's first year is exciting. Even discovering how to smile at daddy's face represents an important and intricate set of accomplishments. Furthermore, such accomplishments draw immediate and satisfying responses from the parents, rewarding both parents and infant for their efforts. While the thought of caring for an "uncommunicative" infant may be frightening at first, sensitive parents quickly learn that their infant can communicate, that cries have different meanings and that a baby has an ability to react and adapt to the needs of the entire family.

Most of the developments of the first year are miraculously programmed into an infant's nervous system, and the infant proceeds on his own. The process is remarkable and mysterious to any adult, but it will not happen without their loving and active interaction. Many studies of children who have spent their first years in uncaring situations, such as institutions, have established this. Even an infant who is kept well-nourished, clean, and healthy will develop into a passive, uninterested, and unintelligent child unless regularly babbled to, cuddled, given toys to grasp and contemplate, and communicated to with eye-to-eye contact.

The two big landmarks of the first year are *sitting*, which is often achieved at around 6 months, and *walking*, which often begins around the first birthday. The ability to transfer items from one hand to the other is also an important milestone. While no two children are alike in development, the process does follow several general patterns:

1. Development proceeds from generalized activity of the whole body to specific individual responses. A month-old baby moves his entire body wildly when he sees something he wants; an older infant simply smiles and reaches.

2. Large-muscle control proceeds from head to toe. First the infant learns to control his head, then he crawls on his belly, dragging his legs by pulling with his arms, and finally he controls his legs and feet in walking. Fine muscle control begins with flexion and proceeds to extension. A newborn infant is all curled up; by his first year he should be sitting and standing tall and reaching and picking up objects with accuracy.

3. Movements proceed from symmetry to asymmetry. A normal newborn uses both arms and both legs equally; by the first year a child has learned to control each side of the body separately and uses the two hands differently.

Many infants and toddlers undergo development tests for one reason or another. A child's pediatrician will also be observing his or her spontaneous motions and reflexes. A specific reason for seeking testing is an obvious delay in some aspect of development such as sitting, walking, or speech.

The results of such tests should be viewed with great caution, particularly if they seem to reveal mental abnormality. While it is important to avoid lengthy uncertainty on such a matter, it is wise to be very certain about the result, because often dire predictions are proved wrong. Furthermore, once a child is viewed as "retarded" it is all too easy for a parent unwittingly to turn that into a self-fulfilling prophecy.

There are many reasons why the tests may be wrong. Most of the norms have been established using Caucasian babies and may not apply to other ethnic groups. Nearly all of the norms are based on infants who were not premature, physically handicapped, twins or triplets, or small at birth—and may not be useful for these groups. Finally, in many cases it has never been established that the things these tests measure are actually predictive of mental development. A child is pure potential, and beyond evidence of very gross abnormality no one can say for certain what kind of potential a particular child represents.

The First Month

Birth. This is not the beginning, of course, but just a milestone in a developmental process that began 9 months before. Many things that happen to a mother during pregnancy may have an impact on her child. (See Chapter 11 on Pregnancy and Birth, page 163.) For several hours after birth, the medication present in the mother's blood during delivery will affect an infant. The baby also may be jaundiced for the first few days because of a by-product of the breakdown of extra red cells he or she needed in the uterus but no longer needs after delivery. The newborn baby's liver, which is responsible for removing these by-products from circulation, may still be too immature to perform this function properly.

Although it may be a difficult process, what happens during birth rarely harms a baby. A baby's head is soft and is normally molded and misshaped during its passage through the birth canal. Newborn infants may also have a soft swelling (called a caput succedaneum) at the top of the head, which is not a sign of brain damage. The head will form into a pleasing shape over several weeks. An abnormally small or large head can be a warning sign of brain damage, but this, too, can often be a false alarm. A small head may be inherited. Napoleon, because of the odd shape and size of his head, was thought to be the person in his family least likely to succeed.

Dry skin is normal for a baby in the first few days after birth. Many newborn babies look like little monkeys, their skin covered with soft, furry hair. This is called lanugo, and gradually disappears. Immature babies make rapid, jerky but not rhythmic movements that are sometimes worrisome to parents. These are normal and common.

Nearly half of babies are born with the umbilical cord around their necks, but this ordinarily does not cause problems. Many infants gasp or even choke and turn blue just after delivery, which also usually has no lasting effect. Studies have shown that many babies who were severely deprived of oxygen at birth are normal at 1, 5, and 10 years of age.

All newborn babies are given Apgar scores, named after the anesthesiologist and pediatrician who devised them. The purpose of the test is twofold: (1) to determine what measures must be taken to support the baby in the first minutes of life; and (2) to give some idea of what problems the child may encounter in the future. The tests measure heartbeat, breathing, reflexes, muscle tone, and whether the skin is a healthy color. The Apgar score has not proven as meaningful in predicting future development as was originally thought. The best signs of a baby's future development are wide-open alert eyes and a responsive face when the baby is awake.

Perception.

It is not true, as even doctors used to think, that babies are deaf and blind at birth. A newborn will focus on a parent's face and follow it with his or her eyes. Even on the delivery table, newborns will focus on their mother, and would rather look toward a picture of a normal face than one in which the features have been garbled. Loud noises will cause a startle or a shudder, and a newborn will respond to the sound of a soft, high voice. By 4 weeks of age, a baby may show by his behavior that he recognizes his mother and father.

Reflexes.

A newborn baby also has a remarkable variety of reflexes to test. If you touch the cheek or skin around the mouth, a newborn will open its mouth and turn toward your finger, "rooting" for a nipple to suck. If you touch a newborn's foot or hand, it attempts to make a grasp—which may be surprisingly strong.

One of the most famous reflexes is the Moro reflex. When an infant's head falls back or he startles, he will throw out his arms and legs, extend his neck, and cry briefly. Then he will bring his arms together rapidly, as if to clasp the branch of a tree or his mother. It is easy to believe that this reflex evolved because it helped protect an infant from falling. The other fascinating motion is the walking reflex: If you hold a small baby's legs down and allow one foot to touch a bed, he will lift that foot and set the other down, and so on, in a walking movement. This reflex will disappear completely later in infancy and is not related to learning to walk.

Nutrition and Feeding.

The decision to breast-feed or bottle-feed is important, and should ideally be made jointly by both parents. The success of their choice will depend on mutual support.

Except in unusual circumstances, it is exceedingly advisable to breast-feed. If it is impossible to sustain breast-feeding for long, whatever breast milk the mother can provide is better than none at all. Breast milk is easier to digest than any other source of food, and contains all the nutrients necessary for normal growth for as long as 6 months. It also contains immune factors from the mother's body, which are not found in formula and which can help protect an infant from infection while he is nursing and create favorable conditions inside the infant's digestive tract. Furthermore, breast milk seems to protect an infant against allergies. Breast-feeding also provides an automatic and wonderful atmosphere for communication between mother and child.

On the other hand, there are many circumstances such as adoption and maternal illness which make breast-feeding impractical or impossible. Mothers who cannot breast-feed should not feel inadequate or guilty. Millions of infants have been raised on formula to become completely healthy and well-adjusted adults. The standard infant formulas (Enfamil, Similac, SMA, and the like) are all equally good nutritionally. These prepackaged formulas are more expensive than powdered or concentrated formulas, but the latter run the risk of being nutritionally inadequate if they are not mixed carefully. If there is any reason for concern that tap water is contaminated, it should be sterilized before mixing with the concentrated or powdered formula. Cow's milk is indigestible to the immature digestive system of most young infants, and may provoke allergies to milk.

Babies should be fed in the first 6 to 12 hours of life, when the sugar in the first breast fluid, called colostrum (or a bottle of sugar-water) can revive them from the stress of delivery. It takes 3 to 5 days for normal milk to replace colostrum. Formula feeding can begin on day 1 or day 2 of life.

During the first few weeks, nutritional needs are

erratic, but infants will signal their hunger by crying. Eventually, infants put themselves on a schedule, but "demand feeding" is the best policy until that happens. As a rough average, most babies want to eat every 2 to 3 hours at this age, and take about 10 minutes to empty 80 percent of the milk in one breast. They may continue sucking a dry breast much as a bottle-fed baby would suck a pacifier.

Transient weight loss during the first week is normal, while the colostrum is maturing into breast milk and while the baby is losing excess fluid accumulated *in utero*. After 1½ weeks, regular weight gain should begin. Bottle-fed babies tend to begin gaining right away, and their mothers should be careful not to feed them more than they actually want, in order to avoid excessive weight gain. The compulsion to urge a baby to finish the bottle is best ignored. Formula can be kept refrigerated safely for at least 24 hours.

It is not necessary to give an infant vitamin supplements, whether he is breast-feeding or drinking formula. Breast milk contains an ample supply of vitamins if the woman who provides it is eating a well-balanced diet with plenty of fruit juice, fresh fruit, and vegetables. The vitamin content of prepared formulas is carefully controlled to be adequate for an infant's needs. Feeding supplemental vitamins may even be dangerous, because there have been isolated reports of toxic reactions to vitamins A and D in infants who took excessive amounts of them.

It is also unnecessary to give a baby water, except perhaps if he is extra thirsty on a very hot day. Both formula and breast milk contain as much water as he needs, and extra water may diminish his appetite for nourishing liquids. Once breast-feeding is well established, it is safe for a breast-feeding mother to give a supplemental bottle of formula, if she wishes, for her own convenience or reassurance that the infant will take from a bottle during times that she is unable to breast-feed. This supplement of formula is not necessary, however. The same goals may be accomplished by giving the infant expressed breast milk in a bottle. Bottle-feeding of either breast milk or formula gives the father the opportunity to have the important experience of feeding the infant.

Breast-fed and bottle-fed infants are burped or bubbled because air coming in with their food may create a false feeling of fullness and may contribute to crampy abdominal pains. Bottle-fed babies should be fed with the bottle in a tilted position with the nipple down, so the baby always gets milk and not air from the nipple. To prevent spitting up after feedings, tilt the baby at a 30-degree angle for a few minutes before burping; the milk then tends to settle and the air can come up.

Health Matters. Newborn babies may appear to sleep nearly all the time, but recent studies show that from the beginning they sleep as little as 12 hours a day. Their eyes may be closed most of the time, but they are often aware of what is going on around them.

Some infants are born with "stork bites," areas where a collection of tiny capillaries show through their transparent skin at the nape of the neck or in the scalp. These will disappear in the first 2 years, as the infant's skin thickens. So will a visible vein across the bridge of the nose, which turns blue when the infant strains or is flushed.

All babies have soft spots on their heads which may not close until 18 months. This soft spot, called the anterior fontanelle, is the place where the skull has not yet joined. The brain must grow more rapidly than the bones of the skull can grow, so they fuse later in infancy. The open fontanelle gives the skull more flexibility during delivery or when the baby hits his or her head.

The soft spot will pulse with the heartbeat. When an infant is active or has a fever, it will pulse more rapidly. The fontanelle may be touched and will not be harmed by gentle poking or washing. A fontanelle that bulges outward or one that is very sunken, however, is abnormal and reason for the infant to see a doctor.

In a hospital nursery, infants' hands used to be covered with mittens to prevent scratches from their own fingernails, which are not trimmed to avoid causing infections. There is no need to cover the baby's hands at home, but the nails should be trimmed with blunt-nosed scissors, while the baby is asleep.

Also in the hospital, the stump of the umbilical cord is painted with a disinfectant dye to kill bacteria. Unless there is a foul odor or inflammation around the stump, there is no cause for worry while it remains in place. In most cases the stump falls off painlessly after about 1 week.

Pediatricians today do not recommend circumcision for any but religious reasons. However, if the infant has been circumcised, healing can be speeded by a gentle application of petroleum jelly to the penis when the diapers are changed.

The nature of a baby's stools are a matter of concern to most parents. Many factors about an infant's elimination seem very unusual to an adult. Diarrhea or constipation may occur in the first month but only rarely. Breast-fed babies are believed to be particularly free of problems related to their stools.

Many babies strain with each bowel movement, but they seem to outgrow this. This is because they cannot specifically control the muscles of defecation—when it comes to a bowel movement, it's all muscles or nothing. Many newborns, particularly breast-fed newborns, have green or yellow loose bowel movements. A bottle-fed baby's movements will begin to appear more ordinary within a few days, but a breast-fed baby may have loose, greenish-yellow stools until he or she is weaned. Four to six stools a day is not an unusual number at this age; some babies have one after each feeding.

The two real health problems of concern at this time are infections and gastrointestinal allergy. When stools are excessively frequent, watery (not just loose), foul-smelling, and green, call the doctor. Blood and mucus in stools are further signs of trouble, particularly if the blood is reddish black.

Sometime near the end of the second week is a good time for an infant to have his or her first office visit to the pediatrician. At this time the doctor will check the infant's weight, height, and head circumference, and record them on a growth chart appropriate for the baby's age. (Examples are on pages 209 and 210.) The curved lines indicate the range within which the measurements for 90 percent of all children will fall at a given age. What matters most is not where on the chart a child's measurements fall at a certain age—smallness and largeness are not usually matters of health—but the *rate* at which the baby grows over a period of months. A child's growth rate should follow the shape of the gentle upward curve seen on the growth chart.

The pediatrician at this visit will be primarily concerned with an infant's growth and with problems that the parents may want to ask about. As mentioned above, whether an infant is growing normally is about the only predictive statement a pediatrician can make at this time. The pediatrician cannot predict future intelligence or achievements, and at almost any stage of development a doctor cannot be sure that an infant who does not appear to be up to average in certain accomplishments is not simply a slow starter. The features of best predictive value for an infant's future are alertness and responsiveness, qualities that a doctor has no good way to measure, but which a parent is often able to judge.

SPECIAL HEALTH PROBLEMS

Intensive Care. Having an infant delivered straight into the intensive-care unit is an anguishing experience. Knowing that the baby has serious problems and also being unable to feed and handle the baby are understandably difficult situations for all parents. For the baby, an intensive-care nursery is a stressful environment in itself, with constant noise, light, and the cries of other infants (which often provoke stress and crying in a baby). It is especially important at this time that parents spend as much time with the baby as possible, touching and holding and trying to provide the infant with meaningful stimulation.

Preemies and "Small-for-Dates." In the past, doctors used to lump infants born early and infants born too small into the same category. Today it is recognized that these are two different problems, with different characteristics. A premature infant may be normal for gestational age, but clearly not at the same developmental stage as an infant who has had 9 full months in the womb. On the other hand a "small-for-date" infant is one that is born at the right time, but is unusually small—perhaps indicating a medical problem in the mother or malnutrition of some kind.

Premature infants are at especially great risk of respiratory distress syndrome, immaturity of the structure and function of some organs, and brain hemorrhage. Small-for-date infants, too, are at risk of some anomalies, which may have caused or contributed to their small size.

Premature infants sleep more than infants born at term; in fact, they appear to sleep nearly all the time. Their cries are feebler and higher-pitched, their movements are more jerky, and they often do not indicate when they are hungry. The reflexes of a premature infant are different than those of a term baby; the reflexes of a small-for-date infant may also be abnormal, and different again from those of a preemie.

Handicapped Infants. A handicap obvious at birth allows the parents to begin immediately to adjust the child's environment to provide maximum opportunity for development. This environment for development is bound to be different from that of fully normal children, and there are special problems to watch for.

Handicapped children are often overprotected at home, treated like invalids who must have everything done for them. This is understandable, but in the long run it works to the child's detriment. A physical or sensory handicap is made worse when a baby lacks normal opportunities to practice and learn. The parents of a handicapped child are very wise to seek any way possible to provide the child with intellectual stimulation, and to be sensitive to the things the baby can learn and wants to learn. However, parents should also be sensitive to the risk of overstimulation, and try not to set individual goals too high.

Handicapped children may also be socially deprived, by being isolated from other children and lacking their stimulation. They may be further deprived if they are separated from their parents to go to special schools, and they invariably have to learn to deal with insensitive and prejudiced statements from others. The parents of a handicapped child do well to seek out play groups and other situations in which their infant can be exposed to playmates in a positive way. A continuing and important question may be whether to have the child go to a special school or join a regular classroom.

Blind children are particularly at risk of "pseudoretardation," of being raised with the self-fulfilling expectation that they lack potential. Unwittingly, parents may delay in giving them solid foods, which may cause difficulty in learning to chew and eat. Toilet training may also be delayed, and without thinking about it, parents may miss the opportunity to teach a blind child to dress him- or herself when ready to learn. A blind child may be stopped from putting things in his mouth—a developmental experience. (See The Seventh Month, page 205.) Parents of blind children should be encouraged to read to them, since this is an essential part of intellectual growth. The first month is not at all too early to begin planning how to rear a blind child in the most positive, stimulating way.

The same may be said of deaf children, who are often treated as retarded and who may, in fact, develop slowly since they are deprived of a sense that is so important for learning. Early recognition of deafness with suitable substitutions of other sensory stimuli will do the most for future normal development.

It is particularly important to choose a handicapped child's pediatrician carefully. The pediatrician should seem comfortable with the handicap and be willing to provide the time and effort needed to give such a child continuity of care. Family counseling is often important to help resolve feelings of guilt and ambivalence in families with handicapped children. Sending the handicapped child to a temporary school or camp may be a necessary and welcome break for everyone concerned.

Sudden Infant Death Syndrome (SIDS). In the United States, some estimates indicate that as many as 2 of every 1,000 infants under 1 year of age die suddenly after being put to bed in what seemed to be a perfectly healthy condition. Fortunately, in recent years, doctors, the police, and the public have become sensitive to the fact that SIDS is indeed an unexplained cause of death, and that parents, above all, need support, not blame for what has happened. There is suggestive evidence that infants who die of SIDS were not as normal as they appeared beforehand, and hope that high-risk infants can be identified and saved.

SIDS tends to strike in the second or third month of life and is rare after the sixth month. The risk of SIDS is not uniform: Oriental infants are at very low risk, Caucasian and Hispanic-origin babies have about half the average rate, and black and American Indian babies are at particularly high risk. Factors that increase the risk of SIDS include low birth weight or premature birth, poor socioeconomic conditions, a mother who smoked or took narcotics during pregnancy, and a family history of SIDS or a "near-miss" (when an infant was rescued from a cessation of breathing). Some victims of SIDS were slow to grow after birth.

There is no known cause of the fatal disorder, and it is not even agreed whether SIDS is one disease or many. Most normal infants have brief pauses in breathing as they sleep, but the vast majority do not die of SIDS; therefore, theories that SIDS is directly due to such pauses are controversial. Studies of infants who died of SIDS show some slight abnormalities in the arteries leading to their lungs, and studies of infants who later died of SIDS have revealed a variety of abnormalities of breathing reflexes and heart function. There is no clear picture as yet.

The breathing patterns of many infants suspected of being at risk of SIDS can be tracked during the night using home monitors, but the value of these monitors has yet to be established. For the moment, the most important aspects of dealing with SIDS come after the tragedy has happened—making sure that the grief-stricken parents find comfort and understanding support.

The Second Month

This is a leveling-off time, when the family has begun to adjust to life with a new baby. The parents get organized and the baby may begin to fall into recognizable behavior patterns. (See table 12.1, page 213.)

A baby's "good periods" may alternate with fussy periods during this time, and the infant may find ways of quieting himself from crying: sucking fingers, turning, or looking for and finding a mobile. It is normal and very common for a baby this age to begin sucking his fingers. This kind of behavior is an early and important sign of self-sufficiency.

Finger-sucking is not a sign of inadequate mothering or inadequate nutrition. Nearly every infant needs some extra sucking, and thumbs and fingers are natural sources. A pacifier is an adequate substitute, and some dentists believe, better for future tooth development.

Many infants have a spell of fussiness every day in the late afternoon or early evening. The child psychologist Anna Freud referred to this period as "ego disintegration," a time when an infant is fatigued from a long day of trying to come to terms with his environment and himself, and loses control of emotional equilibrium. An infant of this age has no idea how to relax, and thus gets fussy.

Unfortunately, this crotchety period often corresponds with the time when the baby's mother and/or father arrives home from work outside the home, perhaps suffering some ego disintegration of their own. Parents should understand that this fussiness never indicates their infant is rejecting them; instead, it is part of a normal 24-hour cycle. They should be encouraged to play with their infants despite the fussiness. It can turn into a gratifying encounter, because the cranky period often evolves into a time of playful alertness.

By the end of the second month, the majority of babies smile at something that pleases them, and make noises other than crying. What an infant can see at this age is a matter of disagreement. Some studies suggest that such a baby cannot see objects 6 or 8 feet away, but many pediatricians and parents think they can, if they are interested.

Most infants begin to show a strong preference for a particular sleeping position at this age or earlier. However, a decided preference for using one side of the body—sucking on one breast, sleeping and lying on one side, turning the head in only one direction, sucking on only one hand—may be cause for concern at this stage. While some normal infants may already show strong normal "sidedness," asymmetry may also be a sign of a neurological problem.

There is little need to worry about an infant's sleeping position. Unless there are pillows or too many covers in the bed, an infant will not bury him- or herself in bedclothes if he or she lies on the stomach. (Using heavy pajamas or a baby sleeping bag in the winter prevents the need for extra covers.)

A normal infant of this age will not breathe through the mouth unless desperate for air. However, infants may develop stuffy noses just like anyone else, due to dry air, dust, or the fuzz from blankets. A humidifier in the baby's room may help and it may also help to elevate the head of the bed a few inches so the baby can swallow nasal secretions. In the case of serious accumulations of mucus in the nose, some pediatricians recommend that a few drops of a solution of ¼ teaspoon of salt in 8 ounces of water sterilized by boiling for 3 minutes be used as nosedrops to wash out the nose. This treatment is not universally accepted, however. Some practitioners believe it only increases the irritation of the nose, leading to further mucus production.

Infants are constantly scratching themselves on the face, but these scratches heal quickly without any scars.

Sometimes between the fourth and tenth weeks many infants develop an acnelike rash on the face and neck, consisting of pimples with white centers. The rash comes and goes, sometimes becoming worse when a baby is hot or has been crying. It is thought to be associated with hormone changes as the mother's hormones disappear from the infant's system. Parents need not do anything about this rash, which will disappear spontaneously within a few weeks.

It may be very tempting for the parent of a formula-fed infant to prop the bottle in the baby's mouth and leave him or her alone. This practice should be avoided. The baby could conceivably choke while the parent is out of sight and earshot. In addition, it can seriously interfere with a child's chance for normal development. For bottle-fed, as well as breast-fed, babies, feeding is an important time for loving communication with the parent and for important eye-to-eye contact. Being left alone with the bottle is a cold, unstimulating way to gain nourishment, and may lead to behavioral problems later on if food becomes an infant's only source of gratification.

A parent should also get into the habit of keeping one hand on the baby whenever the infant is on a changing table or some other place where he or she could fall. It is difficult to know when a child will begin to turn him- or herself over.

Fortunately, because their skulls can give to absorb the impact of a fall, infants can survive the most frightening falls unharmed. However, if an infant is unresponsive after a fall, vomits often, or if the pupils of his eyes do not respond to a direct light, he may have a concussion or some other trauma to the brain, and should see a doctor immediately.

Vaccinations. The second month is the time for an infant's first vaccinations. At this time he will be inoculated with the first dose of the DTP and OPV vaccines. The first, DTP, protects him against diphtheria, tetanus, and pertussis (or whooping cough). The second protects against polio.

The goal of vaccination is to mimic the natural infection by stimulating the immune system to react and learn to recognize the infectious agent, in a way which causes no harm to the patient. Immunization usually provides total protection against a disease, in many cases for a lifetime. For some diseases, such as tetanus, protection from a vaccine is only partial and an individual requires revaccination some years later.

No vaccine can be completely safe, in part because no child's immune system is totally predictable. Vaccines often cause transient and trivial side effects such as fever and rash or tenderness at the site of injection. An allergic reaction at the site of injection is rare, but can happen. Serious adverse reactions are exceedingly rare.

In any case, the risk to the child of the vaccine is overwhelmingly outweighed by the dangers, including death, from contracting one of the diseases the vaccine would have prevented. Unfortunately, in places where doctors and parents have become lax about vaccination practices, some "forgotten" diseases such as polio and whooping cough have begun to maim and kill children as they did at the turn of the century. In most areas of the United States, children cannot enter school by law without having completed their vaccinations.

Vaccinations should not be administered when a baby is ill or feverish. However, a minor cold or allergy is not reason to suspend a vaccination schedule. In general, immunological abnormalities and any treatments designed to reduce the immune system should contraindicate the use of vaccines containing live viruses (such as those against measles, mumps, rubella, and polio).

The Third Month

This is often a magical turning point in a baby's development. Something happens in an infant's nervous system that seems to take the place of the need to cry; the baby has an increased ability to interact with the world in other ways. The importance of this level of achievement is underscored by the fact that this is the age at which children raised in institutions, without getting sufficient stimulation, begin to show signs of deprivation.

A 3-month-old baby begins to reach out to the world with both arms, and instead of crying, to coo and gurgle. The whole body may become involved in the pleasure of seeing a smiling face; the baby may coo, kick, and reach out all at once. A baby of this age may whimper when hungry, rather than crying, and may even be able to wait a few minutes. This ability to wait in anticipation of an expected reward is an important step, representing a level of understanding and trust not present in a younger infant.

By the third month, an average infant may spend long periods lying on his back, playing with fingers or a mobile hung over the crib. The baby can grab one hand with the other and play with his hands as if they were toys. The baby begins to understand that hands are extensions of himself.

An average infant this age may be able to hold his head up for long periods, and should certainly be able to hold it up for some period without bobbing. He may also begin to be able to help maintain his own shape while sitting up. A 3-month-old infant can usually follow an object with his eyes in a full 180° arc.

Feeding time may also become playtime. By now, it is his most receptive time, and an infant may remove his mouth from the nipple at this stage to watch what is going on around him. Many parents begin to wonder in the third month when to introduce solid foods.

For a baby, solid foods are defined as anything that is fed with a spoon: cereals, fruits, vegetables—all those puréed baby foods that can be bought in bottles or prepared in a blender. Because the baby gets them by spoon, not in a bottle, eating them requires a certain level of neurological coordination. Very few infants have reached this stage by 3 months. By far the majority are still at the sucking stage and simply don't know how to work their tongues in order to swallow food from a spoon. Thus, most solid food winds up being spit out. Putting any solid food in a bottle is dangerous, because it may cause the infant to choke. It may clog the nipple, and if the nipple is enlarged to accommodate the solid food the child may gulp in too much at once. Furthermore, mixing solid foods with milk represents an increase in calories, and can easily set the stage for later obesity. At this age, a happy, healthy child can continue to receive all the nourishment he or she needs from milk or formula.

Unfortunately, the introduction of solid food is often regarded as a sort of landmark in development, and a mother may begin to feel inadequate when she learns that someone else's baby of the same age is already on solid foods. Reacting to this kind of competition is for the benefit of the parents, not the infant, and should be recognized as such. Indeed, it may even work to the detriment of the infant. The American Academy of Pediatrics recommends delaying the introduction of solid foods until sometime between the fourth and sixth month.

By the third month, an infant will be alert most of the day with several daytime naps. Nighttime sleep usually lasts for 10 or 11 hours, although the infant may still require a nighttime feeding. Sleep cycles in infants are consistent with their character in general: An active, noisy baby may be an active and noisy sleeper. Infant sleep also seems to run in cycles, periods of deep sleep alternating with periods of semialertness, during which an infant may cry out, suck a finger, rock or bang his head, move about, and settle down again. It is not necessary to respond to all of these noises. Most often the infant is not truly awake and falls asleep again without assistance.

During the third month, some fathers may seem to lose interest in the intimate details of their child's progress and tire of having a wife totally wrapped up in an infant. This is less likely to happen if the father has been involved in the baby's development up to this point. At any rate, this is a good time to locate a good baby-sitter and have an evening away from home.

The Fourth Month

If an infant was born with hair, it probably has begun to fall out by the fourth month, and will continue to come out for several more months. The hair at birth has little relation to the infant's permanent hair and is not an indication of his or her lifelong hair color. Because the permanent hair may be growing in at the same time, this hair loss may not be noticeable.

A 4-month-old infant is beginning to be aware of both sides of the body, and this may be the end of symmetry in motion. The baby can turn his or her head to look in any direction and is making a few recognizable noises, primarily vowel sounds such as "ooh" and "ah." As many as 4 hours a day may be spent sucking (in addition to eating), which may indicate early teething but may also be just a normal part of a growing curiosity about things.

In some infants, this is the time for teething, which begins with the lower front incisors. The erupting teeth cause swelling and irritation of the gum, which can be relieved temporarily by rubbing the gum with a clean finger or ice. Sucking actually adds to the infant's distress because it causes blood to rush to the area, and the swelling increases. The baby may begin to rub the gums (which helps reduce the pain) and may begin to chew.

Is the distress really teething? If rubbing the gums causes a sudden yowl, the answer is probably yes. Continuing to rub will cause the infant to settle down. Giving a little liquid baby acetaminophen or aspirin also helps relieve the pain temporarily. Be aware, though, that the teeth that begin erupting at 4 months may not actually appear for weeks.

By now, the baby may be ready for solid foods: Refer to the discussion about solid foods under The Sixth Month, page 204. If the baby was vaccinated as scheduled during the second month, now is the time for the second dose of DTP and OPV.

The Fifth Month

By the end of the fifth month, most infants can smile spontaneously. They reach for objects and can get a firm grasp when you hand them a rattle. Most infants can perceive and look at an object the size of a raisin, and they laugh and squeal. By this time, particularly active infants will have begun to outgrow their molded chairs, and can easily flop or clamber out of them.

This is the age when infants begin waking up very early in the morning, at 5 or 6 A.M. Keeping them up later at night only makes the parent and not the baby more tired in the morning. And it will not help to force an extra night feeding, which they probably have outgrown by now. The only thing that may prevent a baby from turning into a human rooster is to install a dark shade in the baby's room.

This is also the age of discovery, of exploring things by manipulating them and by mouthing them. Watching something is no longer enough: a 5-month infant wants to feel its shape with both hands and mouth. A child who may seem ready to eat solid foods may still be more interested in mouthing new textures than in consuming the food. (See The Sixth Month, page 204.) The attention span for play increases to more than 1 hour.

By five months, a baby discovers and manipulates his or her genitals. This may be difficult for a parent or grandparent to watch impassively, but it is wise to resist the urge to prevent such behavior, which is a natural part of an infant's exploration. Trying to prohibit it may only heighten the baby's excitement about this newly discovered area.

Sores and ulcerations on the genitals are not due to this manipulation but to diaper rash and should be treated vigorously. The solution is to avoid plastic-coated diapers or rubber pants and not to use strong detergents or bleaches when washing the diapers and to change diapers often (including the middle of the night). Some (but by no means all) pediatricians recommend using cornstarch or baby powder to absorb ammonia and an anti-ammonia rinse before drying the diapers. Applying a protective ointment to the sores may also be recommended. Exposing the area to the open air also helps; if possible, let the baby play diaperless on a sheet placed over a waterproof pad. If the problem persists, consult the doctor.

Infants of this age also begin to be capable of discovering and mouthing objects and substances that are potentially harmful. Any parent who has not baby-proofed the house should do so now. (See the sections on Poisoning and Safety in Chapter 8, page 124.)

Every house with children in it should also contain ipecac syrup, which is used to induce vomiting after poisonings, and a list of poisons and their antidotes. Use the ipecac only after consulting a doctor or the nearest poison control center. The telephone number of the poison control center should be prominently posted. Ipecac should be given by the table-spoon—2 times, 15 to 20 minutes apart—with water or milk administered after each dose.

The Sixth Month

By this time, the average child has begun to babble extensively. Although adults may not recognize much of what is said, the 6-month infant can understand a few words, and probably makes two recognizable sounds—mama and dada—although neither have any meaning to the child yet.

At this age, a baby's individual progress should become obvious. A very active child may have begun to crawl, drawing his belly and legs along on the ground by pulling with his hands. An active baby may sit for minutes at a time and will enjoy stepping with one leg after another while being held upright. An average child can roll over alone, and will be able to sit upright without having his or her head loll one way or another.

Other babies may have discovered the fascinating game of dropping things usually before they discover the game of picking them up. The activity usually generates a response from parents, and provides an early experience in "cause and effect" for the baby, who enjoys this new "control" over his or her environment. The activity also represents progress in developing the fine muscles of the hands, which here parallels the development of the large muscles needed for locomotion.

Even the average child will be able to move backward and forward, making most babies too active to be fed or diapered easily at this stage. Don't expect an infant of 6 months to stay put.

By this age, a child's eye color is predictable. Blue eyes will have remained blue; eyes destined to be brown will be turning a muddy color.

By the sixth month, nearly all babies are ready for solid foods. A sign of readiness is the baby's ability to turn his head or push your hand away when he does not want any more to eat.

Some of the reasons for waiting until now to introduce solids have been stated earlier; one of the most important is that by the age of 6 months the digestive system is mature enough to be able to handle most of them. Nonetheless, milk will remain the mainstay of an infant's diet for many months to come.

It is a good idea to introduce foods gradually, a week at a time, starting with a one-grain cereal such as dry rice (a 6-month baby is not ready for wheat). Dilute it approximately 1 part cereal to 6 parts water—using cow's milk adds calories and may cause an allergic reaction. Progress slowly in this fashion to strained vegetables and fruits. (Try the vegetables first, because infants are more likely to like the sweet fruits and starting them on fruits too soon might contribute to a sweet tooth.) By introducing foods at least a week apart, you have time to watch for an allergic reaction.

Allergic reactions to food may appear to be indigestion, but they may also include a runny nose, wheezing, mood changes, and various skin reactions. Using an elimination diet, a parent can withdraw the food suspected of causing the allergy, wait for the symptoms to clear, and then reintroduce it. If the symptoms appear suddenly, the allergy is confirmed. (However, children are often able to tolerate an allergenic food after a wait of several months.)

Orange juice is especially likely to cause problems; some babies vomit the juice and continue to do so every time it is offered. A day or two later the stools may become frequent and loose, and the child may be fussy and full of gas. Some parents delay the introduction of fruit juices until a baby is able to drink them from a cup, around the ninth or tenth month. Many infants younger than 6 months are allergic to eggs, and egg whites and meat should be held until even later because their proteins are the most difficult to digest.

Strained baby foods may be prepared at home, but care should be taken to make certain the infant gets enough iron. If there is any question about the iron content of the baby's diet, use baby-food dry cereals. Also, avoid adding salt to the baby's portion.

An infant may balk initially at the idea of solid foods because the taste and texture are unfamiliar. Because a baby is so interested in manipulating things at this age, it helps to give him a spoon and a cup or a biscuit to play with while feeding him by spoon. In any case, the child may be more interested in playing with his food than in eating it. The feeding should be fun, not a battle; if the child objects violently to the food, stop trying and wait a few days.

At first, breast milk or formula will continue to be the mainstay of the infant's diet. A breast-feeding mother should let the baby empty one breast, in order to maintain her milk supply, then offer the baby some solid food, and continue with the other breast if he is still hungry.

When should a breast-fed baby be weaned? The answer is very individual and, for some people, very controversial. Certainly breast milk is the most beneficial form of nutrition for an infant, and in some societies babies breast-feed until the age of 2 or 3. There is good reason to wean sometime in the second half of the first year, however. Infants adapt more easily to the idea of using a cup sometime before their first birthday than they do afterward.

The American Academy of Pediatrics advises

that infants weaned from the breast should continue to be given formula until they are 1 year old. One way to begin weaning is to add a supplementary bottle of formula. Used to replace one meal, this bottle a day will start to slow down the flow of milk. However, many mothers prefer to wean their infants directly to a cup, which should happen sometime around the ninth month.

The introduction of solid foods may bring on an infant's first bout of constipation. Bright blood in the stool may accompany this, indicating a crack around the anus that is slightly bleeding. The first step in treating this is to soften the stool by feeding the infant prune juice, prunes, or some unrefined sugar like molasses. Next, the anus should be coated with petroleum jelly 2 or 3 times a day and, if it fails to heal, the infant should be taken to a doctor.

During this period an infant's invisible secondary or permanent teeth are undergoing enamel formation. Babies at this stage should be given some fluoridated water, or fluoride drops, along with their usual diet. Fluoride is incorporated into the outer layers of enamel and makes the baby's teeth more resistant to cavities.

An infant ready to eat solid foods is also ready to swallow objects he is playing with. Infants can also choke on biscuits or cookies if they eat them while lying on their backs; they should not be fed anything while lying down, nor should they ever be left unattended while eating.

To extract a swallowed object, first whack the infant on the back, holding him or her face down over your knees. You may try to extract it with your fingers, but this runs the risk of pushing it farther down. As a last resort, try the Heimlich maneuver. (See page 97.)

The sixth month is time for an infant's third course of DTP and OPV vaccines.

The Seventh Month

By the seventh month, many infants have begun to move around and can no longer safely be left alone. Crawling ability improves, while some babies prefer to bump across the floor on their buttocks. Many have also begun to pull themselves to a standing position, an experience they may find very exciting but slightly frightening at first, since they will not yet know how to get themselves down.

The scope of the arms and hands is also greatly increased. The baby uses each hand independently, perhaps without a preference for one or the other. Most love to bang toys or other objects together, and to compare differences in their size and shape. The baby also may be very interested in poking at things. All unused electric outlets in the home should by now have plastic covers.

A baby at this age may also have discovered the delightful game of dropping something and calling to a parent to pick it up. Retrieving an object over and over may provide great glee to the child, but doing it is much less entertaining to the parents. There is no way to recommend how often a parent should yield to this obviously manipulative behavior.

Because of a baby's increasing manual dexterity, feeding time often becomes a game. The baby may want to eat with his hands—or to smear food all over, to splutter it all over the bib or let it ooze slowly down his chin. Is this experimenting with textures or simply teasing Mama? Who can say? However, what may seem like disinterest in food should probably be viewed as an important stage in the development of independence.

Most babies seem more interested in eating with their fingers, and it is wise to go along with this desire. There is not as much need to worry about "good" nutrition at this stage as many parents might think. The absolute minimum requirements for a healthy diet at this stage are (1) 1 pint of milk or its equivalent as cheese, ice cream, or a calcium substitute; (2) 1 ounce of fresh fruit juice or 1 piece of fruit; and (3) 2 ounces of iron-containing protein, such as an egg or meat. Rather than turning mealtimes into battles and food into a symbol of something else, it is good for a child to start learning to fulfill his own needs.

This may be a good time to begin the gradual transition to feeding liquids in a cup. A good way to start is to offer a baby some expressed breast milk or formula in a cup, and gradually to increase the amount the infant takes from the cup as the amount from a breast or bottle is decreased. By the tenth or eleventh month, the baby can be taking most liquids from a cup.

Teething is usually active during this period. (See page 212.) The first tooth, in the lower jaw, is usually the worst. Besides rubbing at the gums and mouth, infants like to put their fingers in their ears. If they persist in tugging at the ear and seem cranky or irritable, they may have an ear infection and should be seen by a doctor.

The Eighth Month

How far the average baby has come! By now, most babies can feed themselves crackers and play peek-a-boo. An attempt to take away a toy may be met with resistance, and if something is placed out of sight or reach, the baby will try to find it. The baby finds it very easy to pass a toy from one hand to the other and is probably imitating some of the sounds adults make while playing with him or her. Long since, the baby has learned how to sit without support and to bear some weight while being held upright.

It is a time of wonderful achievements for an infant—and also may be a time of frustration and worry for the parents. Most babies are into everything they can reach, and if mobile they can easily get hurt or trapped. It is time to reevaluate the entire house in terms of baby safety. (It is not a bad idea to get down on the floor and crawl around a little to see what dangers are on the baby's level. This "primal" activity can be entertaining and educational for others to watch as well.) Other young children in the family, sensing the infant's propensity to mouth anything, may start to offer things like worms, pills, and other unsuitable items. (See page 212.)

As mentioned above, some babies simply get "trapped" in a standing position: They pull themselves up and don't know how to sit back down without falling. At this age many infants do not know that they can bend, and may fall over straight backwards to get a sound bang on the back of the head. Parents are well advised to be sure there is soft carpeting under any piece of furniture the infant may pull him- or herself up by or be placed upon. It may also be wise to teach the infant how to sit down from a standing position, by gently bending him at the waist over and over until he or she catches on. Buffers in the crib are also a wise investment.

The danger is not always unintentional. Infants may have learned how to test their parents by their interest in danger zones, and this is a time for parents to begin learning how to set limits. It is important to the parent to decide which battles are worth fighting, since a persistently strict attitude may be unnecessarily harsh for the baby.

At this point, an infant may begin to use food aggressively, refusing to be trapped in the high chair, throwing food around, and demanding food from other plates. This is no time to try to push food into a child, because he or she may begin to use it as a way to test parents as well. If a baby is routinely disrupting family meals, it may be better for all concerned to feed him separately.

Babies of this age may be very stubborn, particularly when they are tired. Few children want to stop playing when bedtime comes, but no baby should be allowed to become exhausted. On the other hand, a very active baby may want to get up in the middle of the night. There is no way to solve this problem. Some parents go along with the baby, others refuse to go into the room after he or she has been put to bed.

By this age, many babies have adopted a toy or blanket that they carry everywhere with them. This habit is perfectly normal and a healthy sign that the child is finding a way to become more emotionally independent as physical independence increases. If the child keeps tripping on a beloved blanket, it will be just as loved if it is cut in half. (And one piece can be washed while the other is hugged.) If for some reason it is desirable that affection be transferred to another object (for instance, if a special doll or toy has parts that could be swallowed), pin or sew it to a replacement until the new one begins to take on the same adored dog-eared, smelly quality.

The Ninth Month

By this point, many infants can sit up by themselves and can reach a standing position with some effort. With this new ability may come an understanding and perhaps a fear of heights. However, children are usually excited about the idea of standing, and may insist on standing up while eating or being dressed.

A very active baby may already be crawling and may have learned to crawl up stairs. Coming down is far more frightening than going up, and the baby may get stuck a few steps up. Installing stair carpets is certainly a good idea; putting a gate at the top and bottom of the stairs is essential.

With the ability to sit and lean forward with hands free, a 9-month-old baby has complete freedom to explore all of his or her body and delights in the process.

Sometime between the ninth and twelfth month, babies who are still breast-feeding may begin to lose interest in it, and this is an appropriate time to take them up on the lapse of interest. In some instances weaning may actually be psychologically more difficult for the mother, who recognizes the growing independence of her infant. Babies already on solid foods may now be ready to tolerate meats and fruit juices.

Sometime around this age, almost every infant begins to cry when separated from parents, and may cling desperately or wail piteously at the prospect of separation. Strangers are frightening and not to be trusted, particularly if they stare. Before an "ordeal" such as a visit to relatives, it may help to warn the hosts beforehand and talk to the child and hold him or her close during the visit.

The Tenth Month

By their tenth month, almost all children can pull themselves to a standing position and stand up while holding onto something. Many can walk sideways holding on to a piece of furniture such as a sofa, and pull themselves up to a sitting position from lying down without help. Some children can stand alone, at least for a moment.

It might seem that babies would first crawl, then creep, next stand, and finally walk. But babies tend to learn to stand and then to creep—as if they feel the need for more experience at ground level before they actually walk erect.

Some babies at this age begin to test out their independence from their parents, creeping away but checking back often to see if the parent is still there, or calling out for reassurance that the parent is still in the next room. Careful babies will test out adventures such as standing alone or crawling up stairs, only going as far as the point where they can easily get back down.

Babies only recently weaned may show a very sudden spurt in motor development during the tenth month. They may also begin to rock their bodies, particularly when they go to bed. This is apparently akin to the need to suck the thumb. Trying to stop this rocking behavior goes against the child's needs; if the rocking and banging of the crib is disturbing the rest of the family, oil the crib, install rubber castors and put a thick carpet under it. A spell in the rocking chair with a parent, and a bedtime story, may also help.

Ten-month-old babies can often begin to help with their dressing, lifting their legs and arms, and many of them can identify body parts by name. However, children of this age are still too young to dress themselves.

Many relatives or "old school" baby-sitters may begin to make a younger mother feel she is inadequate if she is not toilet training her child near the end of his first year. In some cultures, children are routinely forced to learn toilet training in their first year. The questions surrounding toilet training are always difficult but it does seem best for the child if the practice is not forced on him or her.

There may be some sphincter control in a 10-month-old baby, but it is still a reflex. Few babies are mature enough to need or understand toilet training in the tenth month. They may passively submit at this age, but the consequence is likely to be rebellious "accidents" and the retention of feces in the second year.

The Eleventh Month

Most babies of 11 months are well on their way toward the first independent step, although most will not attain it in this month. Many babies of this age will have fashioned their own walker from a lightweight chair or their own stroller. The average baby will be able to drop and pick up toys with one hand while supported by the other. Some child-rearing experts do not recommend the use of walkers since they are associated with many accidents and may be detrimental to the child's neuromuscular development. It may be best to use them only judiciously, and not in excess. Many babies wait until this age to start "cruising," walking side to side while pulling themselves along a bed or sofa with their hands.

The child's feet may look quite peculiar at this stage. Most infants begin to stand on what appear to be rolled-over feet. As they begin to balance with their legs wide apart, their feet splay out and they look like walking ducks. Don't worry: As a toddler learns to walk he or she gains balance, no longer needs a wide base, and has stronger feet and arches. A toddler learning to walk needs to be able to grip with his or her toes; shoes with very soft soles or bare feet are much better than hard soles.

By the eleventh month, many children know quite a few words and can identify things by name, although they may still be speaking gibberish. A child this age has a mature grasp, thumb and forefinger, and has little trouble holding onto small objects like a raisin. They also have no trouble putting small objects in their mouths. It's best to keep such objects out of reach since they are a perfect size to block the windpipe if the child chokes on them. They may be able to put on their own socks and untie shoes.

About this age, many babies begin to be aware of the difference between good and naughty, and to test out the word "no." This is a pattern that will become very familiar in the early part of the second year. Around the first birthday, a baby may begin to say "no" over and over, accompanied by appropriate head shaking. Infants get so taken up with this that they may spend all day refusing to be changed, refusing to eat, refusing a bath, and so on. (For more about this negativism, see the section on The Second Year, page 214.)

The Twelfth Month

As they near their first birthdays, many children are now well into the experiment of trying to walk, although they would rather crawl to get around. When a baby falls over while trying to walk, the resulting tears are more likely from disappointment rather than pain; reassurance and a new start is what's needed most.

Most babies don't need hard walking shoes. And parents shouldn't buy a 1-year-old baby shoes "large enough to grow into." If the baby is pigeon-toed or seems to stumble too much, have the doctor check his gait. An infant may seem to lose a fraction of an inch as he or she starts to stand, because the vertebrae settle with the new posture.

Weight gain may stabilize for a time because the baby is paying more attention to movement than to eating, and exercising more than formerly. At the same time, the baby may not yet be digesting solid food completely. All this is normal, and signs of undigested food in the stool are not normally a cause for concern.

Do not be discouraged if the baby is not speaking yet. One in 4 normal, healthy children will not speak 3 adult words (other than "mama" and "dada") until 4 or 5 months from now. The only reason for concern is if a child is not turning around at the sound of a voice and is not imitating sounds—signs of a possible hearing problem.

The negativism of the second year begins in earnest now for many children, and is a perplexing behavior. A particularly active child may begin to have tantrums at night and scream inconsolably when faced with even the simplest decision, such as whether or not to eat a piece of fruit. Most first-time parents are utterly at a loss at some of this behavior, and few parents can really help at these times. The tantrums reflect a child's turmoil in learning to sort out yes from no, mine from yours, and good from bad. It is usually best to let the tantrum run its course, and be ready to reassure an exhausted and confused toddler afterward.

Idiosyncracies may often be common at this time; an infant may absolutely refuse a food eaten with relish 6 weeks earlier. A diet may consist of a good breakfast, a not-so-good lunch, and no dinner at all. Probably the best policy at this time is to let the baby satisfy himself; no child will starve for a harmful period if good food and love are available. As mentioned in more detail in the section on the seventh month, a child can be well-nourished on a surprisingly small diet.

PROBLEMS DURING THE FIRST YEAR

Crying

In the first months, crying is virtually the only way an infant has to communicate. Crying often signals hunger, but not always. The infant may be too hot or too cold, wet, frightened, or simply irritable. A baby may cry particularly often during the first few days home from the hospital, adjusting to new routines.

Young babies often cry for long periods at a time when nothing appears to be wrong. Some pediatricians point out that a baby has no other way to relax or let off steam from the enervating process of learning about the world. Imagine what it is like, not understanding anything he sees or hears, dependent on someone else for every comfort. Of course life is fatiguing, and crying may simply reflect that. Infants who don't fuss don't appear to sleep as well as those who do.

In the United States, serious nutritional problems are rarely the reason for a child's crying, and severely malnourished children are listless and dull. The most serious causes of crying are ear infections, sudden obstruction of the bowel due to gastrointestinal abnormalities, or infections, particularly if accompanied by fever. In most cases, however, there are other signs of the illness. The baby looks sick and often shows a sudden disinterest in food. The onset of crying in such situations is often sudden.

The "Spoiled" Child

Some children seem to cry just to bring a parent to them, and in some cases this is true. A "spoiled" child is not a bad child, nor are the parents bad parents. The baby has simply learned precociously how to manipulate the environment in order to satisfy desires, and crying is a major weapon. Parents are driven to respond to this crying out of feelings of guilt, love for the child expressed as overprotectiveness, or fear of harm to the infant. As the child's demands become ever more difficult to meet, the parents' guilt and anger increase.

Some pediatricians feel a baby cannot be spoiled by being picked up whenever he or she cries; some say this is true only if it is done before the baby is 3 months old. Others say the age makes no difference; a parent who always responds to a cry with attention or feeding will not change after 3 months of this behavior. No doctor would advocate leaving a child to cry without attention, but once a parent is satisfied that nothing obvious is wrong, it sometimes may be a good idea simply to let the child cry for a while. A pacifier may help; many babies who do not need food are calmed by suckling.

Colic

Some infants younger than 4 months cry for as long as 12 to 14 hours a day. This distressing problem is known as colic, and it is a condition without a known cause. Pediatricians even disagree about whether or not colic is a disease. Some think it is caused by immaturity of the digestive system, food allergies, or chronic abdominal gas; others think it is hypersensitivity to a noisy, turbulent environment; still others think it is a combination of these factors. Certainly colic is more common in active, sensitive infants, and can be exacerbated by the very tension it causes in the parents.

Some babies with colic let out sudden shrieking cries; others just cry normally, but for hours on end. The infant may seem in great pain, draw up his legs and pass gas.

Colic is not dangerous unless it is caused by a serious condition. These diseases are ruled out by examination of the baby, measurement of temperature, and occasionally examination of the stool for blood or x-ray studies of the abdomen. One serious cause of colic is intussusception, a sliding of one part of the bowel over another, in the same way a radio antenna can collapse into itself. The blood vessels supplying that part of the bowel may become kinked and blocked, which can lead to tissue damage and bowel obstruction and, ultimately, blood in the stool. The only treatments for most cases of colic are temporary measures to comfort the infant. Sometimes drugs are prescribed to prevent intestinal spasms, but they don't always work and it is not desirable to give a baby drugs for obscure causes. It sometimes helps to place the baby on his or her stomach or to swaddle him or her tightly in a blanket. Holding the baby upright or close to the chest in an infant carrier also helps in some cases. Taking the baby for a car ride also may help. Some parents have tried putting the baby on top of a spinning washing machine; the constant vibrations seem to be soothing. A most interesting theory has come from recent research in Sweden, which studied colic in breast-fed babies. They found that if the mother stopped eating milk products, the baby's colic would disappear, in most cases, within 8 days. A return to milk caused a resumption of colic within 8 hours. Pediatricians who have also tried this therapy report success in close to 70 percent of cases.

Some pediatricians jokingly refer to colic as a condition caused by the baby and affecting parents. Perhaps one of the more serious problems with colic is that it interferes with the development of a good relationship between parents and baby. It is important to get a break now and then from the stress of a constantly crying baby, either by having each parent take turns or by engaging a reliable sitter for a few hours several times a week. Also, it's heartening to know that the problem always resolves itself within a matter of months.

Failure to Thrive

Is my baby growing properly? This question troubles nearly all new parents. In the large majority, the answer is yes. Obviously, some children are smaller than others; what matters is the rate at which they grow. As long as a child's growth tends to follow a steady upward curve (see growth charts 12.1–12.4), the child is growing well regardless of

Chart 12.1. Girls: Birth to 36 Months Physical Growth NCHS Percentiles[a] (Weight).

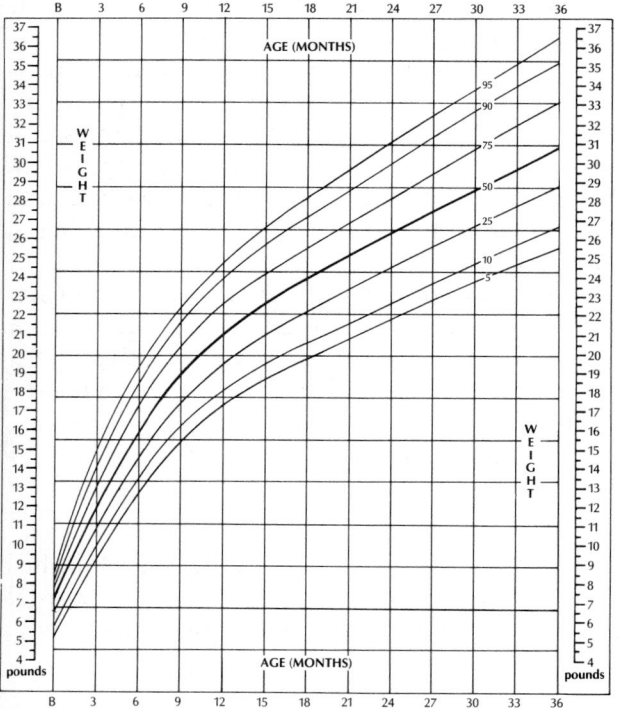

[a]Adapted from: Hamill PVV, Drizd TA, Johnson CL, Reed RB, Roche AF, Moore WM: Physical growth: National Center for Health Statistics percentiles. AM J CLIN NUTR 32:607-629, 1979. Data from the Fels Research Institute, Wright State University School of Medicine, Yellow Springs, Ohio. © 1982 ROSS LABORATORIES

Chart 12.2. Girls: Birth to 36 Months Physical Growth NCHS Percentiles[a] (Length).

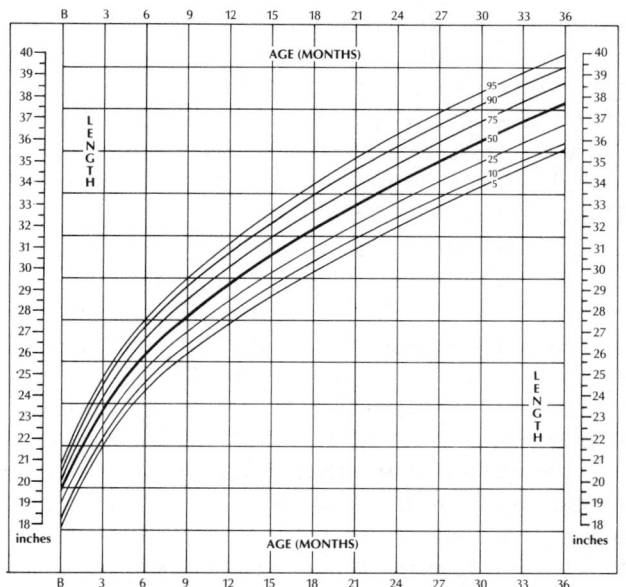

[a]Adapted from: Hamill PVV, Drizd TA, Johnson CL, Reed RB, Roche AF, Moore WM: Physical growth: National Center for Health Statistics percentiles. AM J CLIN NUTR 32:607-629, 1979. Data from the Fels Research Institute, Wright State University School of Medicine, Yellow Springs, Ohio. © 1982 ROSS LABORATORIES

Chart 12.3. Boys: Birth to 36 Months Physical Growth NCHS Percentiles[a] (Length).

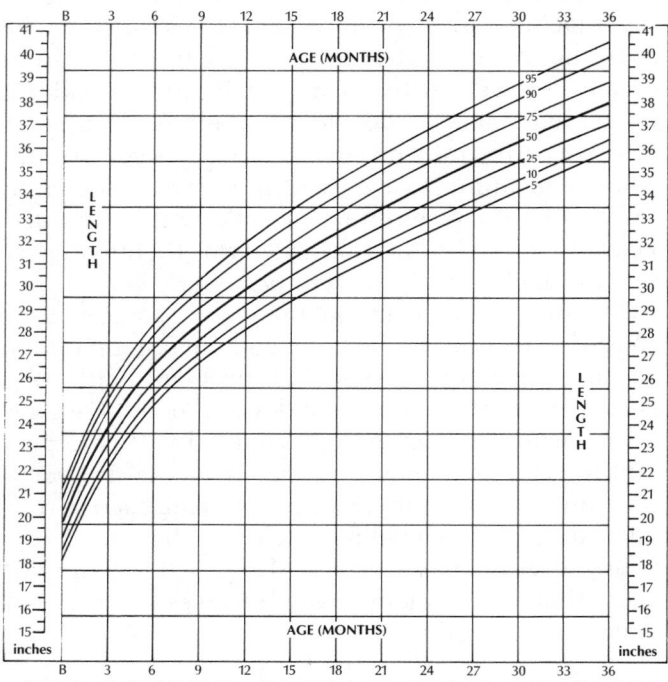

[a]Adapted from: Hamill PVV, Drizd TA, Johnson CL, Reed RB, Roche AF, Moore WM: Physical growth: National Center for Health Statistics percentiles. AM J CLIN NUTR 32:607-629, 1979. Data from the Fels Research Institute, Wright State University School of Medicine, Yellow Springs, Ohio. © 1982 ROSS LABORATORIES

Chart 12.4. Boys: Birth to 36 Months Physical Growth NCHS Percentiles[a] (Weight).

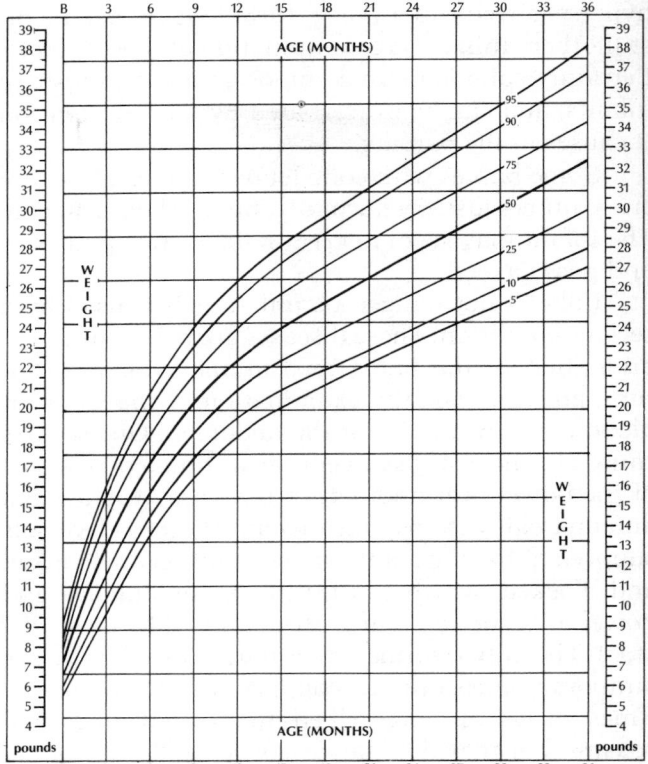

[a]Adapted from: Hamill PVV, Drizd TA, Johnson CL, Reed RB, Roche AF, Moore WM: Physical growth: National Center for Health Statistics percentiles. AM J CLIN NUTR 32:607-629, 1979. Data from the Fels Research Institute, Wright State University School of Medicine, Yellow Springs, Ohio. © 1982 ROSS LABORATORIES

size. A persistent failure to follow the curve, however, reflects failure to thrive. Therefore, determining true failure to thrive is difficult and usually requires measurements over a period of months.

The major cause of failure to thrive is inadequate nutrition, usually because of some feeding problem. The difficulty may be due to the mother's nervousness during feeding or to chronic overfeeding, which ironically causes the baby to spit up too much of what is eaten. Malabsorption, in which the baby does not properly digest food, is another nutritional cause of failure to thrive. (See discussion on Diarrhea following.)

The problem may also be due to disorders of the heart, kidneys, thyroid, lungs, adrenal glands, nervous system, and intestines. Testing for these conditions may require hospitalization, so before resorting to this, a pediatrician will ask parents to keep a careful diary of how much the infant is eating and when, in order to rule out nutritional causes.

Failure to thrive that is caused by nutritional problems is cured relatively easily by finding ways to provide more calories and to reverse the downward trend in growth. Once the underlying cause is detected and corrected, most babies quickly catch up.

Vomiting

All babies spit up, and vomiting may be difficult to distinguish from ordinary spitting up. The baby who grows normally despite frequent spitting up is probably not a cause of alarm. But true vomiting is a danger sign, particularly if it involves projectile vomiting. The food will be forcefully vomited up, shooting across the room. This projectile vomiting is an indication of an obstruction at the stomach outlet, which prevents food from passing into the small intestine. Instead, it is forcefully vomited up. Fortunately, this can be easily corrected with surgery to open the pyloric sphincter between the stomach and small intestine.

Other causes of vomiting include viral stomach infections, food allergies, and accidental ingestion of drugs or other toxic substances, among others. Diseases of the liver and kidney also may cause persistent vomiting.

Diarrhea

It is often very difficult to tell whether an infant has diarrhea or simply has frequent loose but normal stools. What is most important is the consistency:

Diarrhea is a bowel movement that is too watery. A frequent number of stools per day is not often abnormal. Many healthy babies have a reflex that gives them a bowel movement soon after every meal.

Too much water in the stool will show up as a water ring on the diaper. Other signs of poor intestinal absorption, which is the cause of diarrhea, are stools that have an abnormal amount of fat—making them very foul-smelling and grayish. This problem is known as steatorrhea. Children with malabsorption of this type often also have unusually large appetites, because calories are passing right through them.

Most acute infections that cause diarrhea are brief and don't cause failure to thrive. The more serious problem is dehydration. While a child can always recover from the calorie loss that occurs during sustained diarrhea, dehydration may damage the intestinal lining and interfere with future ability to absorb food.

The treatment for viral diarrhea is to stop all milk products except breast milk and to give clear fluids for 24 hours, to make sure the baby stays well-hydrated. Clear fluids are continued as regular formula, diluted half and half with water, or other binding foods such as bananas, rice cereal, or toast are introduced. The best clear fluid to use is one developed to prevent dehydration in children in the Third World countries, where infant diarrhea is the most common cause of infant death. There is no reason to take true diarrhea with dehydration less seriously in North America, and these fluids are readily available from pharmacies and supermarkets, sold under the names Enfalyte (sold as a powder to be mixed with water) and Pediatlyte RS (which is a premixed formula). There is no place for medicines —either antibiotics or antidiarrheals—in the treatment of the child with acute viral gastroenteritis.

Diarrhea that persists for days and days may be due to lactose intolerance, the inability to digest lactose, which is the prominent sugar in milk. Lactose intolerance is less common in breast-fed babies than in those on formula. The treatment is clear fluid followed by soy formula, which is free of lactose and thus easier to digest if the child lacks the enzymes needed to digest lactose.

Another cause of malabsorption is cystic fibrosis, an inherited disease most common among Caucasian families of central European descent. In about one-half of cases, it shows up during infancy. Cystic fibrosis is a disease of the mucus-secreting and other exocrine glands in the body, which causes obstruction of the lungs and prevents the pancreas from secreting the enzymes responsible for digestion of fats. Because a child with cystic fibrosis has diffi-culty breathing, and also is unable to digest fats, the result is often steatorrhea and failure to thrive.

Fever

A fever is almost always a sign of infection. Many infants run frighteningly high temperatures—104 to 105°F (40 to 40.5°C)—whenever they have any fever at all. In recent years, some medical specialists have begun to believe that in an otherwise healthy child, a sudden fever may simply be a healthy reaction during which the body fights off a mild infection. A mild temperature, in and of itself, usually is no reason for panic or measures to bring it down. A doctor should always be consulted, however, especially if the temperature occurs in a newborn under two months of age. But other symptoms of illness in an older child usually must show up before a fever is considered serious. Is breathing difficult? Is the baby pulling on his or her ears? Does he or she cry when urinating? Is there severe diarrhea or a stiff neck? If not, many doctors prefer to let the baby's natural defenses fight off an infection, and reserve antibiotics or other treatments for more serious illness. In short, in most babies, a fever need not be treated for its own sake.

Unless there is evidence of complications or the child looks and acts seriously ill, most parents can treat the feverish child themselves. Before giving a baby or young child acetaminophen or aspirin, however, check with a doctor. If the fever is high (over 103 or 104° F; 39.4 or 40° C) it can be lowered by giving an antipyretic. Sponging the baby with lukewarm water is a questionable practice. (Don't use rubbing alcohol; the fumes may be hazardous and the alcohol can be absorbed through the skin.)

It is particularly important to keep the baby from becoming dehydrated, so plenty of fluids should be given. The danger of dehydration increases if there is vomiting or diarrhea. If there is nausea and vomiting, carbonated soft drinks like ginger ale seem to stay down best. Some babies don't want to drink when they have a fever or feel sick, and they may almost have to be force-fed by spoon.

The serious danger of a high fever is convulsion. The above measures should prevent it. Only a few children have seizures with high fevers; but if seizures do occur, a doctor should be seen. (Convulsions are discussed on page 223.)

Siblings

Older sisters and brothers are a wonderful asset to a child's development. They provide him with a measure of stimulation and companionship that parents can never offer an only child. They are examples for a baby to copy, from his first tentative steps to his last days in school. Depending on the age of the siblings, they may also be an immeasurable help to a busy mother in caring for an infant.

Siblings can also, however, be a problem and even a hazard to a younger infant. Their reaction to a new baby depends on their age and birth order. If a sibling is still a preschooler, the introduction of a baby into the home is a cause for a considerable amount of jealousy, hostility, and competition—all of which is completely normal. Parents should try to channel these emotions into harmless or even beneficial outlets.

Preschoolers often want to touch or poke the new baby. Unless they jab extremely hard at his eyes, ears, mouth, or urogenital region, there is little chance of harm. This behavior arises from normal curiosity about the infant and uncertainty about how to interact with the baby. As soon as the sibling begins to show interest in a baby brother or sister, rather than steering him away from the baby, it is a very wise idea to examine the baby together, showing the sibling how to stroke and cuddle the baby gently. If the sibling can be included in everything the parents do with the infant at some stage early on, the child will feel brought in rather than left out.

Breast-feeding is a particularly troubled time at first for a preschool sibling, who may be very jealous of the attention the baby is getting. The sibling may even attempt to feed at the other breast. Whatever a mother's reaction to this, it should not be horror or a scolding. Cuddling one child while feeding another may be a very comforting response. Of course, parents should try to provide a period of single-minded attention to the older sibling, as often as they can.

When an infant is at the precarious stage of learning to stand and walk, older siblings often seem to take pleasure in distracting the baby or even causing a fall. This may be a sign of intentional competition, and care should be taken to discourage such behavior; children need a more or less harmless way to express their competitiveness, and the baby will not suffer from having to try again.

On the other hand, other children are much more fascinated than adults are in the repetitive and "childish" games an infant needs in order to practice babbling speech and manual manipulation. They can endure repetitive games much longer than a parent can. As long as siblings understand how to avoid harming an infant, and as long as they do not justifiably feel neglected by their parents, their play with the baby should be encouraged.

Cerebral Palsy

Severe cerebral palsy may be detected in the newborn, but milder forms of this neurological disease may not be noticeable until years later. Telltale signs in newborns include abnormal stiffness, particularly on one side, or kicking with only one leg. Later signs may include walking or creeping with one leg trailing behind, or standing always on tiptoe.

The risk of cerebral palsy is increased by extreme prematurity and episodes of prolonged cessation of breathing or convulsions shortly after birth. Cerebral palsy evolves into a condition in which a child is unable to control some of the muscles, but it has a wide range of severity. There also may be mental impairment, but this varies greatly from child to child. In rare cases the symptoms of cerebral palsy disappear gradually.

Teeth

Many infants do not develop teeth until near the end of their first year or later. However, the problems that cause unsightly or unhealthy teeth often have their origins in the earliest months or even before birth. Letting a baby fall asleep with a bottle promotes tooth decay, which is caused by the interaction between bacteria in the mouth and sugar, either in the milk or juice. The prolonged exposure to the sugar promotes the formation of plaque, which causes decay.

Even though the first teeth are only "baby teeth" destined to fall out at age 6 or 7, their condition sets the stage for the permanent teeth. If they fall out prematurely due to decay, the permanent teeth may be displaced and, besides being unattractive, may not function well. Also, decayed teeth at any age are frequently painful and may interfere with normal nutrition.

At an early age, a pacifier or nothing at all is better than a bottle for quieting or putting the baby to sleep. If the infant is in the habit of a bottle at bedtime, try filling it with water. At the very least, remove the bottle after the baby has fallen asleep. (For a discussion of teething, see The Seventh Month, page 205.)

THE PRESCHOOL YEARS

BY THEIR FIRST BIRTHDAYS, most children are well on the road to their first true independence—the ability to walk. The years before they enter school are a time of increasing emphasis on self-mastery, and a

Table 12.1 PATTERNS OF DEVELOPMENT[a]

At 3 months	Lifts head and chest, with arms extended, from prone position; reaches for (and usually misses) objects; waves at toys; beginning to have some head control when pulled to sitting position; smiles, listens to voices, coos, and says aah and ngah; listens to music.
At 6 months	Rolls over, lifts head, sits briefly; may support most of weight when pulled to standing position; bounces actively; reaches for and grasps objects, transfers them from hand to hand; makes polysyllabic vowel sounds, babbles; responds to change in environment, recognizes parents, prefers mother.
At 9 months	Sits alone with back straight; pulls self to standing position; beginning to crawl; picks up objects with thumb and forefinger; can uncover hidden toy and tries to retrieve dropped objects; says mama and dada; responds to name, plays pat-a-cake, peek-a-boo; waves.
At 12 months	Walks when held by hand or hanging onto objects; picks up small objects; says a few words; plays simple ball games.
At 15 months	Walks alone, crawls upstairs; stacks 2 blocks; makes lines with crayon; can put small objects in box, names familiar objects; follows simple commands.
At 18 months	Runs stiffly; sits on small chair; walks up stairs holding hand or bannister; stacks 3 blocks, imitates scribbling; empties objects from containers; names parts of body; identifies pictures; feeds self; asks for help; kisses parents; may complain when needs changing.
At 24 months	Runs well, walks up and down stairs one step at a time; opens doors, climbs; stacks 6 blocks, makes circular scribbling, folds paper; puts 3 words together; handles spoon; listens to stories; helps undress self.
At 30 months	Jumps; stacks 8 blocks; makes vertical and horizontal strokes, tries to draw circles; knows full name and uses pronoun "I" to refer to self; helps put things away; engages in pretend play.
At 36 months	Rides tricycle; balances on one foot; goes up and down stairs alternating feet; uses blocks to build bridges; copies a circle; counts 3 objects; repeats 3 words of short sentence; plays simple games with other children; helps in dressing; washes hands.

[a] Adapted from *Nelson Textbook of Pediatrics*, Richard E. Behrman and Victor C. Vaughn III, editors, W. B. Saunders Co., 1983. Reprinted by permission of the publisher.

time to begin slowly to understand concepts of social interaction and the difference between private and public behavior.

Even more than during the first year, a toddler should be understood in terms of the particular developmental stage. Actual calendar age may be more or less irrelevant, and the age categories used below should be considered only as rough guides. Of more importance are the subject categories, which represent specific problems or stages of progress toward maturity.

The Second Year

By the first birthday, a healthy baby will weigh approximately 3 times the birth weight. During the second year, the baby will exercise more and, for a variety of reasons, eat less. The diet also will be transformed to include more solid food. A slowing of growth is normal and healthy, as the growth charts on pages 209–210 demonstrate. The average child will gain only 5 or 6 pounds in his second year.

Sometime between their first and second birthdays, the substantial majority of infants master the following skills: They imitate housework and learn how to do simple tasks such as putting away their toys. They learn to drink from a cup and eat with a spoon. They learn to wash their hands. They scribble spontaneously with a crayon, and they can build a tower 4 blocks high that will stand without toppling.

Perhaps more exciting is the progress of a toddler during the second year in the important areas of speech and mobility. At some point he or she speaks 3 "adult" words, and begins to combine words in pairs. The toddler can point to a body part, and name familiar objects. By the second birthday, most toddlers can stand, walk forward and backward and up and down stairs, and can kick a ball as well as throwing it overhand with some rudimentary aim. Judging by the average skills of a 1-year-old baby, this second year is clearly a portentous one.

The fifteenth month is time for the child's MMR (measles, mumps, rubella) vaccine; the eighteenth month is time for the fourth DTP vaccination and polio vaccine.

Speech. Sometime during the second year, toddlers begin to voice some of their wants in intelligible speech. The development of language proceeds in a fairly standard pattern: Single words in the first 6 months of the second year, phrases, adjectives, and adverbs in the second half. Suddenly in the 6 months after the second birthday, many toddlers will erupt into a stream of sentences and ideas that they seem to have been formulating for some time.

If a toddler does not start to speak any words during the second year, a hearing problem may be the reason. (See The Twelfth Month, page 207.) There are other explanations for delayed speech. A very active child, to whom learning motor skills is most important, may learn to talk in a rush after the second birthday. In large families, the hubbub and activity may cause a toddler to withdraw; gentle encouragement to experiment with sounds is often all that is needed. Alternatively, a child with many siblings may not feel pressed to speak because he and his companions communicate effectively in other ways. A bilingual family sometimes confuses a small toddler, and often delays the development of speech.

A special problem, ironically, is the family so intent on having their baby speak that they inhibit him. Each utterance may be followed so swiftly with an exaggerated response, or a demand for progress, that the child becomes intimidated. Particularly if a child has started to speak, and then stops, a family should reconsider whether they are exerting too much pressure.

Perception. The average 1-year-old is beginning to understand concepts of reality that are quite sophisticated. At this age a youngster can follow the arc of a ball after it has dropped out of the line of sight and understand where it has gone. The same is true of objects that have been purposely hidden from view; at some point at the end of the first year or fairly early in the second year, a child will know enough to go to where something has been hidden, move the obstruction aside, and retrieve it.

Walking. A toddler's progress in learning to walk can be judged by 3 factors: width of gait, balance, and the ability to walk and do something else at the same time. The width of gait narrows gradually as walking improves. Balance becomes more steady; it takes a lot of practice to avoid falling after losing one's balance. But walking really becomes a confirmed skill when an infant can stop concentrat-

ing on it in order to turn and listen, or bend over to pick something up and examine it.

An improving ability to walk brings about a dramatic change in a toddler's posture. At first, a child's feet turn out almost at right angles; soon they begin to draw in toward the parallel. A learning walker balances by thrusting his belly out front and his bottom out back. As the back muscles strengthen, this posture should gradually become more erect—but not until about age 4 or 5. One of the things to ask a child's doctor at this stage is for an assessment of the child's gait and whether it will need to be corrected. Standing with slightly bowed legs is also normal for the early months of walking.

Falls. No child learns to walk without plenty of spills. Perhaps it is fortunate that at the start of the process, most children appear to be fearless. Also, fortunately, the skull does not close until 18 months of age in most children, and can absorb much of the impact of a fall without harm to the brain. Nonetheless, a parent must take a fall very seriously if it causes unconsciousness or a dazed attitude. A doctor should be consulted without delay.

Preventive measures are always preferable. A toddler can be taught not to fall straight backward like a board by gently but repeatedly bending him from a standing into a sitting position. Children also learn by imitation; showing a toddler how to back down a set of stairs, one step at a time, may help prevent a fall.

Negativism. This is the hallmark of the second year. By saying "no" over and over, and intentionally provoking it from parents, a child tests limits and begins to resolve priorities. Between the ages of 1 and 2, a toddler will often repeatedly do something he knows will provoke a parent's anger, and seem to be almost begging for punishment. Why? It is the essence of the child's growing independence; the starting point of the journey that ends years later with separation from his parents. The most important and most difficult job for the parent is to be consistent in the use of "no." Inconsistency will only confuse the child and lead to more testing and negative behavior.

Negativism is particularly evident at mealtime. An infant may refuse certain types of food or solid food altogether, and may regress to the bottle or try to breast-feed. These are all signs of confusion about growing independence, and are best met with a sense of humor.

Tantrums. Some children dissolve into tears and inconsolable screams when they realize their parents are about to leave them temporarily. Another child may kick and scream at having to choose whether or not to watch "Sesame Street." These tantrums are inexplicable to an adult; the child obviously cares intensely about something, but it may seem a trivial issue. Many people (primarily nonparents) think such tantrums reflect a serious disturbance in a child and parental neglect. Nothing could be further from the truth. They are another sign of a child's mounting confusion about independence.

Children having real tantrums at this age can seldom be calmed down or distracted by a parent's coddling. However, they may cool off by themselves quite suddenly, and return to playing placidly with the nearest toy. The best parental approach seems to be to stay nearby or hold the child while the tantrum runs its course, and be available for consolation and cuddling afterward. It is important not to reinforce this behavior by yielding to a child's demands after a tantrum.

Fears. Sometime during the second year all children become clinging and afraid of strangers, relatives, and particularly doctors. A sensitive doctor will examine a nearly 2-year-old while the child sits on a parent's lap or stands in front of the doctor. A parent should always be nearby. People who stare a toddler in the eye at this stage or ask direct questions are particularly fearsome. This is a wholly normal stage, but relatives should be warned about it before a visit.

Many children also develop a fear of the bathtub sometime during their second year. This is serious only if the parents react as if it were serious. To help overcome this fear, a parent should resume temporary use of the bathing table or sink used previously, or take a bath with the child.

Child Abuse. The second year is the beginning of the first stage at which child abuse most commonly occurs. (The second stage is during adolescence.) Both times are periods when children are testing their own independence, and child abuse may represent an adult's own turmoil at this separation.

Any parent undoubtedly has been frustrated to the point where he or she can understand why some people succumb to child abuse. But most parents do not abuse their children and understanding the frustration does not excuse or condone the practice. Most people who actually give in to this urge have been abused themselves as children. (This is discussed in more detail in The Third Year, page 217.)

Nutrition. During the second year, mealtime becomes playtime for most youngsters. A baby will have a great time waving an empty cup, banging a spoon, and all the while picking, pushing, squishing, throwing, or examining the food that was meant to be eaten. More food will actually get into the mouth if it is presented a few bits at a time rather than as a small "mountain" in a bowl. At around 15 months, most babies begin to master eating with a spoon. Avoid helping too much as the baby struggles with the spoon. This is a learning process like any other, and the best way to learn is to practice. It's a good idea, though, to spread some paper or other protective cover under the child's chair.

Eating development provides an excellent demonstration of the way a baby is preprogrammed for each successive stage. In order to master feeding himself, a baby must be able to sit erect and hold his head up firmly. This was learned several months ago. Eating also requires sophisticated use of the hands, which has progressed from a clumsy pawlike grasp of a block to a delicate thumb-and-forefinger hold on a raisin or pea.

Hard (teething) biscuits are particularly appropriate at this stage. They provide something for the baby to hold, to rub against sore gums, and they gradually soften in the mouth so they don't need to be chewed. As teeth develop, a baby progresses from mouthing food to chewing it. By the time a baby can really chew, the digestive system has been thoroughly prepared to handle regular table food.

Thus, during the second year, a baby's diet progresses from mainly breast milk, formula, and cow's milk to the same (well-balanced) diet the rest of the family consumes. What is a well-balanced diet for a child nearing the age of 2? Perhaps the best way to ensure a nutritious diet for the entire family is to be certain adequate amounts of foods from the basic four groups are eaten each day. (See the Nutrition section in the Fundamentals of Health, Chapter 16, page 293.)

By the time a child is eating table food, some parents switch from whole milk to low-fat milk. Although it is still a controversial point, some doctors believe that even at this early age, consumption of a high-fat diet begins the atherosclerotic process (hardening of the arteries). As long as a child eats sufficient meat, eggs, and vegetables to provide essential fatty acids, neither the high-cholesterol fat nor the extra calories in whole milk are needed for normal growth. However, changing to skim milk before these other foods are part of the child's diet can be dangerous and interfere with the child's normal growth.

How much should a child eat at this age? Trust his or her instincts. Young children eat to satisfy their hunger, which is how the body signals its need for nourishment. As long as a child is offered a selection of foods comprising a well-balanced diet, he or she will consume the proper amounts. Remember, eating habits become well entrenched early and may last for life. Many adult eating problems are formed early in life, often as a result of being urged to eat despite a lack of hunger, or because food is used as a reward for good behavior.

During this period of increasing independence, the matter of how much and what to eat can easily become the cause of battle between child and parents. The more you can avoid such confrontations, the better. Respect likes and dislikes by giving a child nutritional alternatives.

Obesity. To many parents (but more often grandparents), the perception of a healthy baby is one who is chubby, with rolls of body fat. But as the baby begins to walk and exercise more, the body fat should begin to give way to muscle and lean tissue. A grandparent may worry that the baby is getting too skinny, but in the United States, overweight is a more serious and common health problem than being underweight.

Although the precise causes of obesity are unknown, it is exceedingly rare that it's a glandular or organic problem. Metabolism may play a role, but faulty eating habits or chronic overeating without adequate exercise are what add the extra pounds.

What should be done about an obese 1- or 2-year-old? Certainly, a crash diet is not the answer. The best approach is to provide a balanced diet that offers a reduced caloric intake but is still consistent with nutritional needs and normal growth. Let the child's growth in height catch up with his weight. Achieving this may well require modifying the entire family's eating habits, including preferences for snack foods. It's very hard to mollify a hungry toddler with a carrot when a parent is munching on a cookie!

Another strategy is to increase the child's level of exercise, although most toddlers are active on their own. Exercise alone will not cause a significant weight loss in a person who is chronically overeating (unless he's a marathoner) but, accompanied by diet changes, it will speed weight loss and help control the appetite.

Thumb- and Finger-Sucking. Many parents worry that children who continue to suck their thumbs or fingers in their second year may be developing a bad habit. However, this behavior is completely normal and probably essential at this age; in fact, it is one of the few self-reliant ways that a 1-year-old has of handling tension. Some children may also need a "comforter," some well-worn beloved object to hold while sucking. Studies have found an increase in the amount of finger-sucking in the second year, which begins to subside by 2½ years. Most of the children studied showed none of

the problems parents fear, such as distorted mouths and a persistent habit of thumb-sucking into the school years.

Toilet Training. While it is possible to rush a 1-year-old to the toilet in time to catch a bowel movement, most experts agree it's not a good idea, probably even less so than it was in even younger children. At least a 10-month-old baby is compliant; toddlers in their second year are independent and often resistant, and the toilet, like the high chair, is apt to become a battleground. A child may hold back movements, wet his pants after getting off the potty, or hide in a corner while having a bowel movement —all signals of too much parental control. At a later stage, a child will naturally want to learn toilet habits and training will be easier and less fraught with implications.

Sleep Problems. A 1-year-old eventually tests all limits, including bedtime. A toddler who has tantrums every evening probably is being allowed to stay up too late. Parents should avoid keeping the child up so long that he or she is exhausted and irritable and asks to go to bed. If this is happening, the parents should begin to be gently firm about an earlier bedtime.

A 1-year-old is also old enough to sleep through most nights without crying. Any crying bouts—particularly if they are regular and repeated—should not be met with a response that is too quick, too predictable, or overly sympathetic. Unless a child is seriously ill, this is probably another attempt to test parents' limits, and represents a certain vacillation about independence.

In many cultures, children are allowed to crawl in and out of their parents' bed freely until the age of 4 or 5. In our society, the practice is less common. Parents need to establish their own response to this activity and work to modify the child's behavior to satisfy his or her needs, as well as the parents'. The knotty question of when and how to go about removing the child from the bed before he or she begins to mature psychosexually should always be considered.

The Third Year

During their third year, most children fully master eating with a spoon, undressing and dressing (perhaps with some supervision), and washing their hands. A child of this age typically plays games such as tag with other children, can build a tower of 8 blocks—twice as tall as last year—and can draw a line that is almost straight vertical.

Motor skills become quite sophisticated: Most

children at the age of 3 can jump in place, do a broad jump, pedal a tricycle, and stand on one foot for a second or two.

As to behavior, this is the period when the positives of independence begin to outweigh the negatives—even from the child's point of view. Many children by the age of 3 separate from their mothers without any fuss. It is also a time for imitation, and parents can capitalize on this behavior to teach their toddler many important things.

Speech. At some point 9 in 10 of all normal 2-year-olds begin to combine different words, follow directions, and identify a body part when it is named. Most of them can also name familiar objects in a picture. Many mothers notice that at this age their children begin to understand and use plurals.

Several reasons for a delay in speech were mentioned in the previous section on The Second Year. Other problems to be sensitive to during this year are stuttering, hesitation in speech, and regression to baby talk. It has already been mentioned that parents may cause speech delays by putting too much pressure on a child to learn language. So can older siblings, who often are only learning to speak properly themselves. They may mimic and tease a toddler's attempts to speak, or pressure him too hard to imitate them. If parents become aware of this, they may want to limit their own active reinforcement of their infant's babble, to let up on some of the pressure. The arrival of a new baby in the family can also cause some regression in the speech of a 2-year-old, as he tries to reclaim some of the attention lost to the new sibling.

Perception. This is a time of sorting for many children. They learn to group toys by their size and color. They may also, with positive interaction from a parent, begin to learn pronouns and the concepts behind them: his, mine, ours, theirs, sharing, possession.

Breath-Holding. One of those heart-stopping gambits a toddler may try out at the age of 2 is to stop breathing until the eyes roll up and skin turns grayish-blue. Like the tantrums of the previous year, this behavior is another sign of the turmoil going on inside a child. Usually it occurs after a tumble or a reprimand.

Unfortunately, the breathing reflexes at this age are not mature enough to force respiration immediately as they would in an adult who attempts breath-holding. However, the brief period without oxygen does not damage the brain and the spell has no permanent effect. Breath-holding does not cause epilepsy, as some people mistakenly believe.

The children who bring on such spells are usu-ally manipulative and overprotected; if encouraged in such behavior with too much sympathy and concern, or compliance to demands, the children will soon learn how to control their parents. This is the time, if ever, to learn to set limits on a toddler's behavior.

Foreign Objects and Pica. Two-year-olds enjoy exploring their own orifices; yet again, parents must be on guard against their own instinctive negative reactions about manipulation of the genitals, which is still a very normal behavior. Manipulating them often includes trying to insert objects into the urethra and rectum, as well as into the nose and ears, not to mention the mouth. Free at last to roam, a 2-year-old can try to put almost anything appropriately small almost anywhere an adult can imagine.

One-sided drainage from the nose and a foul-smelling discharge are warnings that a foreign object may be lodged inside. (Use discretion in trying to remove such an object yourself; the problem probably requires the help of a doctor.) It's also amazing what children this age try to swallow; most swallowed foreign objects are probably coughed up without notice. But choking accidents do occur and parents should know how to respond. (See Basics of CPR and Life Support, Chapter 6, page 96.) If something small enough still to permit the flow of air becomes lodged in a child's larynx, it may be several days before any symptoms appear. The child may then develop hoarseness, a cough, and problems in swallowing and in breathing.

Another potentially serious problem is pica, the propensity of some children to eat nonfood items such as dirt, paint chips, turpentine, and medications. This behavior reaches a peak during the third year. It does not affect all toddlers, but can lead to brain damage from lead paint and a wide range of poisonings. Do everything you can to keep such dangerous objects away from toddlers; some 600,000 poisonous ingestions occur in the United States annually, and poisoning and accidents are the leading cause of death in children. (See Poisoning, Chapter 8, page 124.)

Child Abuse. Child abuse is more widespread than most people realize, and often involves people other than parents. Be particularly aware that baby-sitters can be child abusers. It is also vital to consider child abuse if a child avoids a particular person habitually, or if he or she shows injuries of a kind that cannot easily be explained. Doctors are often reluctant to point out the possibility of sexual abuse of a child, but if pain in the genital area is not explained by a foreign object it must be considered.

Children at this age are the most common victims of child abuse of all kinds.

Every parent has understandable feelings of irritation and wishes for independence from a child, but if these wishes are translated into physical aggression, the parent as well as the child is in dire need of help. Most communities have counseling centers and hot lines to help with child abuse problems; it is a wise idea to know the number, just in case. Many families affected by child abuse seem to adjust well afterward if they have cooperated with counseling.

Nutrition.   Most children by the third year are eating more or less their parents' diets. For information on a balanced diet, see page 293.

Toothbrushing.   As mentioned above, children are great imitators, a factor that can be used to teach proper toothbrushing, perhaps with the help of the dentist. Like other habits, this one, instilled properly now, should last a lifetime. Cleaning of the teeth, on the other hand, should start when the first tooth is present, even if the child is only 7 months old.

Toilet Training.   Most 2-year-olds at some point exhibit an active interest in using the toilet, and it is appropriate to wait for them to express this interest before trying to teach them how to use it. This is the time at which toilet training should be quickest and easiest. But it is wise not to place too much emphasis on the task or make it a focus for attention or rebellion. A child can too easily turn this into a tease. Treated sensitively, a child will come to see toilet training as a very exciting aspect of independence and will be eager to attain it.

There is no one method of toilet training; a straightforward, low-key approach usually works best. When the child seems ready, start by setting him or her fully clothed on the potty seat at a regular time. Next, take the child to the potty when he or she needs changing. Place the stool in the potty, which helps the child see what is supposed to go into the bowl. If there are older children to imitate, a child will soon get the idea. Parents, unfortunately, frequently feel uncomfortable allowing the child in the bathroom while they use the toilet. By doing so, they deprive the child of an important example as well as some aspects of gender identity. Do not, however, push the child into pants too quickly, or attempt night training before the child asks to be helped. Using adult-style pants too soon is risking that the child may be overly upset with occasional accidents. And if the child has to adjust to a new situation, such as the birth of a sibling or a change of dwelling, expect a regression in toilet skills. The appropriate reaction is to point out that this is all right and that the parents understand why it has happened.

Constipation.   For some children, bowel training seems to represent a kind of threat: They have an unspoken fear about letting part of themselves go down the drain. This translates into retention of bowel movements, so that when the movement finally comes it may be hard and very painful. When bowel movements hurt, the sphincter closes reflexively, and the problem becomes a vicious cycle.

The most important thing for a parent is to assure the child that the problem will go away, that he need not worry about any "failure to perform," and that he may wear diapers again until bowel movements become natural and comfortable. At the same time the parent should use a stool softener which will substantiate the promise that bowel movements won't hurt anymore. Occasionally the problem becomes so severe that a suppository or an enema is needed, but this is rare and too harsh a solution for a common problem. They should be avoided whenever possible.

In some cases, retention of feces and occasionally bowel incontinence are part of a severe psychological problem on the part of the child, who uses this behavior to get back at parents for some cause of resentment. If a child has formerly expressed interest in toilet training and seems distressed by his own constipation, this is unlikely to be the problem.

Diarrhea.   Intermittent loose stools are a very common problem in 2-year-olds, which seem to be brought on by any change in the child's equilibrium: teething, illness, traveling, new foods. Unless the child is failing to gain weight normally, the problem probably reflects the normal immaturity of a 2-year-old's intestinal tract and an inability to deal fully with solid foods. If such bowel movements are no more frequent than 4 or 5 a day, and unless they contain blood or are accompanied by other symptoms, they probably do not merit serious concern. If they persist or lead to even mild dehydration, a doctor should be consulted.

Hyperactivity.   What is the difference between an "active" child and a hyperactive one in need of medical treatment? This question nags teachers, parents, and doctors. Unfortunately, children are sometimes labeled as hyperactive and treated with drugs when the problem does not merit such an approach. Before a child is assumed to be hyperactive, a careful medical evaluation should be done to rule out other problems.

At one time hyperactivity was called "minimal brain damage" until a number of pediatric specialists pointed out that no connection between hyperactivity and brain damage had ever been detected. The condition is very difficult to define because so many normal children are constantly on the move.

However, the hyperactive or "hyperkinetic" child literally never stops. Nothing can hold his attention; he seems to be driven from one activity to the next without completing anything.

The accepted treatments for established hyperactivity include drugs such as methylphenidate or dexamethasone, but they should be used only in extreme cases. Often, the problem is more psychological than physical; parents may have become so "battle-scarred" by dealing with a very active child that they frustrate him by their inattention. In other cases, what a teacher takes for hyperactivity may be a learning disability or language problem. (For more information on psychological problems of childhood, see Chapter 36 on Mental and Emotional Health, page 723.)

The Fourth and Fifth Years

Before about the third birthday, a preschool toddler has been concentrating on learning inner controls; afterward, the focus changes. The period approaching the start of regular school is one of introspection and attempts to understand the meaning of a child's own achievements. Three- and 4-year-olds are constantly questioning their parents about themselves and the world around them. Their questions become ever more difficult to answer. Why is the sun? When is next week? Where does the wind go? and Why? Why? Why?

By the time they start kindergarten, virtually all children can dress themselves without supervision. They understand colors and what to do to relieve hunger, coldness, and fatigue. Most 4-year-olds can tell you what a common word means and what household objects are made of. Average 4-year-olds can balance on 1 foot for 10 seconds, hop on 1 foot, and catch a ball bounced to them.

Most children have developed handedness by the time they start regular school. Fortunately most parents and teachers no longer make it a battle of wills to force a naturally left-handed child to write with the right hand. Left-handedness is not a sign of backwardness, as some people still assume. The composers Johann Sebastian Bach and Maurice Ravel, and the author of *Alice in Wonderland*, Lewis Carroll, are among the many famous figures of history who were left-handed.

Speech. A 3-year-old child begins to abandon baby talk entirely, although there may still be trouble with certain combinations of sounds. The child by now understands fully the difference between "mine" and "yours."

Don't be surprised if a 3-year-old begins to use rude words. He or she has learned them from older playmates who know they are considered unacceptable. Practicing them at home may be a way of taunting parents, who have two choices: to be firm about the use of "dirty" words around the house or avoid turning them into attractive taboos by paying them too much attention.

Imagination. The fourth and fifth years are magical times when a child is able to explore various imaginary possibilities and to some extent live in a pretend world no adults can enter. A particularly common part of this fantasy world is an imaginary friend. This enchantment is an important time in a child's development.

Imaginary friends are a good way for a child to try out various personalities without being committed to them. Fantasy companions may be very good or horrendously bad. Sometimes these fantasy friends are blamed for the child's own acts. This is normal, not pathological. For one thing, a child can find out easily what parents will allow by letting a ghostly friend get away with them. It makes sense for a parent to say what he would do if sometime he found the child himself being naughty like that.

Many 3-year-olds also try out lying and stealing to see what happens. Of course, such behavior should not go uncorrected, but it is a mistake to interpret it as an indication of a future problem.

Sex. No parent should be surprised by stumbling on a group of preschoolers examining each other's genitals or giggling in a nervous, conspiratorial way about some bathroom or primitive sexual joke. Three-year-olds are merely exploring the nature of their physical differences from each other, and are far too immature to understand or act on any of them. As with reactions to masturbation, it may be difficult for an adult to avoid showing shock at such a moment. But children at this age already have some built-in guilt and prohibition about this early sexual exploration, and any effort to scold or prohibit them will increase their guilt and lead to attitudes of shame whose permanent consequences can hardly be imagined. Ideally, a self-assured parent can, in a constructive way, ensure that, while the children are exploring each other, the things they deduce are accurate and positive.

Siblings. Many 3- and 4-year-olds suddenly become siblings. It is important to ensure that they receive adequate support and attention while one parent is caring for a newborn infant.

When a toddler causes a younger infant to cry in the course of play, the parent's response is often to comfort the infant and shout at the toddler. But it may be the toddler who needs comfort more at this time; a scolding will be seen as a rejection, and will exacerbate feelings of jealousy toward the infant. (For more information on sibling rivalry, see page 211.)

Meals. By the time a child has fully mastered the use of a spoon and cup, it is appropriate to move him from the high chair to a chair with the family at the dining table. This usually happens sometime at age 3 or 4, and the transition is likely to cause some disruption in family mealtimes.

More now than ever, when a child's eating practices are obvious to both parents and other siblings, eating behavior and standards should be enforced. A child should understand that he or she must eat what is served, choose from among acceptable alternatives, or not eat at all.

The further question of table manners now enters the picture. Food should not become a literal weapon any more than it should be a figurative one. The traditional and time-honored response to serious misbehavior at the table is to send a child to his room until he is ready to finish quietly—which usually happens well before dessert is served. Dessert, however, should not be withheld as punish-ment; temporary banishment from society sends a clearer message.

Night Toilet Training. By the time a child enters kindergarten, daytime toilet training should be complete. The need for a healthy child to wear diapers to kindergarten would, of course, be a cause for ridicule and a sign of serious problems in the child.

Before the fifth birthday, most children will probably be night-trained, but at their request. The need to stay dry all night must come from deep within, or night training cannot work, because it is a matter of unconscious control. This may not occur until sometime after the third birthday. But night training is also a matter of physical maturation. Some children with small bladders or incomplete neuromuscular control may continue to wet the bed for several more years. Many normal children wet the bed occasionally even after training. (For more information about bed-wetting, see Chapter 36 on Mental and Emotional Health, page 725.)

THE SCHOOL YEARS

ENTRY INTO SCHOOL is an obvious milestone on the road to total independence. While many 5- or 6-year-olds are frightened on the first day of school, the average child is pleasantly excited, particularly if the parents have been giving school the appropriate buildup. In fact, on the first day of school separation anxiety may be more difficult for the parent than for the child.

Sometime before school begins, at 4½ or 5 years, a child should have his fifth DTP/OPV vaccine. Most states require children to be vaccinated before starting school. This is the last dose of DTP, and it's a good idea to get it out of the way. Other than a tetanus and diphtheria vaccination in the mid-teens, this is the last vaccination a child needs under ordinary circumstances.

From now on, probably the best indication of a child's social and intellectual progress will come from teachers. This kind of judgment is what schools are for, of course, and teachers are experts at comparing and judging children's potential.

Nutrition

For better or worse, a child's eating habits are fairly well established by school age. However, significant new peer pressures will enter into the youngster's culinary desires. Before long, the child will want to eat what peers do, which may not be what parents have offered previously. In this situation, parents must judge how much of a stigma a child will suffer by not conforming and weigh this against their nutritional standards. Remember, however, school-children are likely to trade or scrounge to get what they want to eat. Older children with mobility and an allowance can buy what they like, which usually ends up being fast-food burgers, fries, and other fare that are fortunately nutritionally acceptable, as long as they don't represent the child's entire diet. The best fall-back position is to provide the best possible diet for meals that are still consumed at home—breakfast and dinner.

Summing Up

By the time a child starts school, most of the important early developmental milestones have been passed. The next few years are marked by continued physical growth, but at a slower rate than during infancy and early childhood. Personality traits become more established and, as the child progresses in school, intellectual development broadens. The next few years are generally smooth ones; the next trying period for both parent and child occurs during puberty and adolescence, which are covered in the next chapter. Following is a directory of common childhood diseases. Others may be found in chapters dealing specifically with groups of diseases

(e.g., childhood diabetes is discussed in Chapter 23 on Diabetes and Other Endocrine Disorders; leuke-mia and other childhood cancers are covered in Chapter 20 on Cancer.)

DISEASES OF CHILDHOOD

Introduction

American children are, on the whole, far healthier than ever before and among the healthiest in the world. One hundred years ago, 2 children out of 10 could be expected to die before their first birthday from diseases such as dysentery, diphtheria, measles, and whooping cough. Today these diseases are becoming rare in the United States, thanks to our higher standard of living and effective immunization, but are still more widely known in Third World countries.

Infant mortality has dropped from about 75 per 1,000 live births 50 years ago to only 11 per 1,000 (although it remains a more serious problem among lower-income families). In fact, if a child survives the first day, the odds are very high of surviving the first year and the rest of a normal life span. Today the vast majority of infant deaths are not due to diseases but to accidents.

Therefore, a child's illness today is rarely cause for serious concern. However, some problems remain common enough to merit special attention and it is wise to be aware of possible complications.

Acute Appendicitis

Appendicitis is the most common cause for abdominal surgery in a child, and one of the few indications for emergency surgery in children over the age of 2. About 4 of every 1,000 children under the age of 14 have to undergo an appendectomy to remove the appendix. Appendicitis is more common in boys than in girls, and is rare under the age of 2, although when it occurs in that age group it is usually more serious.

The appendix is a narrow, dead-end tube that leads from the cecum, where the large intestine begins, in the right lower abdomen. Appendicitis is most often caused by an obstruction, although the causes for the obstruction vary. In the young child, the progression of the disease is often so fast that the first sign may be the intense generalized abdominal pain caused by perforation of the wall of the appendix, without the crampy, spasmodic pains and sometimes constipation that may precede it in older children and adults. Because a ruptured appendix causes release of fecal material from the digestive system into the abdominal cavity, it may prove fatal unless surgery is performed immediately or antibiotics are administered intravenously.

Typically, appendicitis causes pain in the lower right abdomen or occasionally in the right pelvis. It is exacerbated by movements. Children with acute appendicitis may hold their hands over their navels when asked where it hurts; infants tend to lie quietly with the hips flexed.

Surgery is the only treatment for acute appendicitis, and only under the most dire circumstances should it be delayed more than a few hours. However, a doctor must take time beforehand to ensure that appendicitis is indeed the problem and avoid unnecessary surgery. Postoperative recovery is rapid and the child usually can resume activities within 3 to 4 days. Whether or not the appendix has perforated, the prognosis after surgery is excellent. (For more information, see the section on Appendicitis in Chapter 25 on Disorders of the Large Intestine, page 531.)

Asthma

While there is no universal definition for asthma, and apparently a wide range of causes, most doctors agree that it is some form of hyperreactivity of the breathing passages. Asthma affects 5 to 10 percent of children, but the outlook for outgrowing the condition is very good. About half of asthma sufferers recover completely by adulthood.

About 85 percent of asthmatic children have their first symptoms by the age of 5. The course and severity of the disease are difficult to predict, although most children have only occasional mild episodes of wheezing and coughing that are handled with relative ease. Injections of epinephrine or theophylline are effective, but aerosol inhalants containing drugs such as isoproterenol, which prevent an attack, are increasingly popular.

There seem to be three elements that contribute to obstruction of the breathing passages in asthma: spasm of smooth muscle cells, swelling and inflammation of the mucous membranes, and the secretion of mucus and other substances into the breathing passages. Most children also show signs of an allergic component, and emotional factors often seem to be involved in bringing on wheezing attacks.

Asthma is worse during respiratory infection and contact with air pollutants, household dust, animal dander, molds, and numerous other substances. (For more information, see the section on Asthma in Chapter 22 on Respiratory Diseases, page 461.)

Chickenpox

Chickenpox is caused by the varicella zoster virus, a member of the herpes virus family. The disease is highly contagious and commonly affects children between the ages of 5 and 9. Other children in the family are very likely to catch it when one child falls ill, which usually happens between January and May. Patients are infectious beginning about 24 hours before they show the characteristic rash.

The incubation period is 11 to 21 days, and the symptoms begin with a slight fever and malaise, usually before the typical rash appears. The rash begins as small, red bumps that progress to a cloudy, fluid-filled blister on top of a reddish patch which eventually breaks and forms a scab. The lymph glands may also swell. The severity of the disease ranges from a rash and not much else to many hundreds of bumps and a fever as high as 105° F (40.5° C). The symptoms are usually worst in the first 3 or 4 days, while the rash is erupting.

The vast majority of children recover fully in 1 to 2 weeks. Serious complications such as pneumonia and encephalitis are rare and are seen mostly in adolescents and adults who contract the disease. The usual treatments are aimed at minimizing scratching by keeping the child's fingernails short and perhaps having a young child wear mittens. In order to prevent a bacterial infection in addition to the rash, regular antiseptic baths and frequent changes of clothing are advisable. A child with chickenpox should be isolated until all of the lesions are scabbed over.

As a viral infection, chickenpox is not subject to any active treatment; antibiotics have no effect. The only thing to do while waiting out the course of the illness is to comfort the child and control the fever. However, a precaution is necessary: There has been an association between the use of aspirin in children and the incidence of Reye's syndrome, which can be fatal. To be safe, use acetaminophen to control fever due to chickenpox. (See Reye's Syndrome, page 227.) A new vaccine against chickenpox is undergoing tests in humans, but is not expected to be approved for general use until 1986 or later.

Colds

Most colds are caused by viruses, although a concomitant bacterial infection may sometimes cause complications. Everybody suffers an occasional cold; why a cold comes on at a particular time is unknown. In the northern hemisphere, there are 3 peak seasons: September, when school starts; late January; and toward the end of April. Most children have 2 or 3 colds a year, although some may have more, particularly during their second and third years. Colds may be virtually endemic in nursery schools.

Colds are most severe in children younger than 4 years, who usually have a fever a few hours before other signs appear. Persistent sinusitis as a result of colds, however, is more common in older children. The first symptoms, besides fever, are irritability, restlessness, and sneezing. During the first 3 days the ears are also congested in many cases. Older children characteristically notice dryness of the nose, followed by sneezing, chills, muscle aches, a runny nose, and often a cough. Colds usually last between 4 and 10 days.

It is virtually impossible to prevent colds, other than with a good diet and sensible habits, such as washing hands and not sharing glasses or other eating utensils. Ideally, young infants should not be exposed to people with colds.

There is no cure, other than time, for the common cold. Antibiotics do not affect its course and there is no good evidence that bed rest hastens recovery, although it may ease symptoms. Aspirin or acetaminophen relieves pain and fever. Nasal decongestants such as ephedrine, epinephrine, and phenylephrine, used as nosedrops, are popular and often effective in relieving symptoms. The addition of antihistamines to cold medications is only occasionally helpful.

It is wise to give nosedrops about 15 minutes before feeding and at bedtime, administering 1 or 2 drops to each nostril while the child is lying on his or her back. Another 1 or 2 drops may be added 5 or 10 minutes later, to allow the medication to reach deep into the nose. Bottles of nosedrops should be used by only one person for one illness, since they quickly become contaminated. Older children may use nasal sprays, but caution is advisable; they quickly become overused and may ironically lead to a chronic nasal stuffiness. No medication put directly into the nose should be used for more than 2 or 3 days.

Devices exist to draw fluids from an infant's nose by suction. Parents should be careful not to overuse them since they may cause irritation of the nasal mucosa. However, they may be useful in clearing the nose so an infant can nurse. The best drainage usually comes by laying the infant tilted up slightly on his or her back. Anticough medications are unwise with colds, because the cough is necessary to clear the throat and lungs. A humidifier may be useful to ease breathing; if croup occurs, taking the child into a steamy bathroom will usually relieve the coughing. (See the section on Croup in Chapter 21 on Infectious Diseases, page 432.)

Most children with colds lose their appetites; this is temporary and can be treated lightly. They should, however, be given plenty of fluids of their choice. A child who has just recovered from a cold may be unusually susceptible to other infections, and it is wise to restrict contact with other children for a day or two after the symptoms have disappeared. (See the section on Colds in Chapter 21 on Infectious Diseases, page 430.)

Convulsions

Convulsions range in severity, from benign febrile ones to those caused by infections of the central nervous system. Convulsions may begin with a few jerky movements; breathing may become slow and irregular and a child may give out a few feeble cries. The neck becomes rigid, pupils dilate, and there may be drooling. There may be a change in skin color and slight movements of the fingers, toes, and eyelids. (For first-aid measures, see page 111; for more information on seizure disorders, see the section on Epilepsy in Chapter 29 on Nerve and Muscle Disorders, page 594.)

Convulsions with Fever. About 3 percent of children suffer convulsions during an episode of fever, usually at age 1 or 2. During this period, most seizures that occur at the onset of fever are benign, although a more serious problem should always be ruled out by a doctor. These benign "febrile" convulsions can be prevented by controlling the fever, although frequently the seizure will be the first sign that the child has a fever. Phenobarbital will prevent the recurrence of these seizures, but it must be taken daily for 2 years or more. Most pediatricians do not recommend its use, particularly if the child has had less than 3 seizures, since the complications of the drug may be greater than those of the seizures. Benign febrile convulsions are short, generalized, leave no residual effect, occur in children between the ages of 6 months and 6 years, and do not go on to epilepsy or delayed mental development. However, children who have had more than one such convulsion during one febrile illness should be observed carefully during an infection and steps should be taken to control any fever.

Ear Infections

Children are unusually vulnerable to two kinds of ear infections, those of the outer ear, or otitis externa, and those of the middle ear, or otitis media.

Otitis externa. This infection, also called "swimmer's ear," often begins with itching and proceeds to extreme pain in the ear canal. Swelling of the ear canal and a foul discharge are other signs of external ear infection. A child with otitis externa should see a doctor promptly, since medications will cure the infection and ease the pain rapidly.

The most common treatment is with antibiotic drugs. Some children, particularly if they swim often, are bothered by outer ear infections frequently, and may benefit from a preventive ear wash with dilute alcohol or acetic acid immediately after every swim. (For more information, see the section on Ear Infections in Chapter 21 on Infectious Diseases, page 432.)

Otitis media. About one-third of all children under the age of 6 develop otitis media at some time. It often results from obstruction of the eustachian tube which provides drainage from the middle ear into the back of the throat and to the nose; this kind of obstruction is common among infants and younger children for reasons that are unclear but may have to do with poor cartilage development, or some other functional abnormality that gradually improves with age. Contamination of the middle ear may also occur during vigorous nose blowing, sneezing, or swallowing while the nose is obstructed.

The most common signs of middle ear infection are pain in the ear, fever, and temporary loss of hearing. Through an otoscope, a doctor can see if the eardrum is swollen. Treatment is usually started with a broad-spectrum antibiotic, such as amoxicillin, since most infecting organisms are sensitive to this drug. Pain medications are usually comforting. Complete healing may take 6 weeks or longer. (For more information, see the section on Ear Infections in Chapter 21 on Infectious Diseases, page 432.)

Epiglottitis

Epiglottitis is a relatively rare but potentially fatal infection of the epiglottis, the lidlike structure in the throat that prevents food from entering the windpipe. It sometimes becomes infected as a complication of a respiratory infection. Symptoms include rapid development of a sore throat, fever, difficulty breathing, and a muffled quality to the child's voice. The sore throat is so severe that children with epiglottitis will not eat and will drool rather than swallow their saliva. When epiglottitis occurs, the child should be rushed immediately to the hospital for emergency treatment, which will include intravenous antibiotics and insertion of a breathing tube to keep the airway open or, alternatively, making an opening in the trachea to permit breathing. (For a further discussion, see the section on Epiglottitis in Chapter 21 on Infectious Diseases, page 434.)

Head Lice

Head lice (pediculosis capitis) are a common infestation among schoolchildren. Although many people mistakenly associate head lice with unhygienic conditions, in reality they are seen in all social classes. They are spread by direct contact and by sharing combs, hats, and other such items.

Head lice cause severe itching and this is the first and major symptom. Most infestations are confined to the scalp hair, although sometimes the lice also may be in the eyebrows and lashes. The lice are large enough to be seen, as are the nits (eggs), which appear as tiny white sacs firmly glued to a hairshaft.

The lice are easily eradicated with a shampoo which should be applied as directed. A second application may be needed in about 10 days to destroy any remaining lice. The nits should be combed out with a metal or fine-toothed comb. Bed clothing, caps, combs, brushes, and other such items should be washed in hot, soapy water. Children should be kept home from school at least until the first treatment is completed. (Other skin parasites are discussed in Chapter 31 on Skin Diseases, page 633.)

Influenza (Flu)

Influenza, or flu, is often taken lightly because it is so common. However, flu is a potentially serious disease with many complications, and a child with it should be observed carefully.

The highest incidence of flu occurs in children 5 to 14 years old; about half of them eventually catch any new variety. Infection is transmitted from one person to another by airborne flu viruses. The usual incubation period is about 3 days after a child's nasal passages come into contact with the virus. The most common signs are abrupt onset of fever (102 to 106° F; 38.8 to 41.1° C), chills, headaches, muscle pain, and malaise. Some flu sufferers also have diarrhea. The fever may last anywhere from 2 to 5 days. Sometime after the second day, respiratory symptoms become predominant and fever and muscle aches subside. A dry hacking cough usually sets in around the fourth day, and may persist for 1 or 2 weeks. Febrile convulsions may be associated with the high fever in small children. (See Convulsions, above.)

Influenza vaccines exist for many strains. These are safe and effective, but routine immunization is not recommended for anyone but the elderly and children with serious chronic respiratory disorders. Treatment should include bed rest and restricted activity in all but the very mildest cases. Fluid intake should be increased, particularly during the fever. Acetaminophen is useful for fever control and relief of discomfort.

In most cases, an attack of the flu is benign, but complications to watch for include febrile convulsions, chest pain, and prolonged high fever, which may be a sign of pneumonia.

Kawasaki's Disease

Kawasaki's disease, also called mucocutaneous lymph node syndrome (MLNS), was first identified about 20 years ago in Japan, and since then a few hundred cases have been reported in the United States. It is a rare disease, affecting mostly young children under the age of 5. The illness begins with a low-grade fever (102° F; 38.8° C), irritability, lethargy, and sometimes colicky abdominal cramps. Lymph nodes in the neck are swollen throughout the course of the disease. Within a few days, a rash appears, mostly on the trunk, followed a few days later by a reddening of the lips, tongue, and other mucous membranes. There is swelling of the hands and feet and scaling of the skin on the palms and soles. The disease may last from 2 to 12 weeks.

The major complication of Kawasaki's disease involves the arteries, particularly those of the heart. The coronary arteries may become inflamed in 5 to 20 percent of cases, leading to various heart problems. Other possible complications include joint inflammation and pain, and liver involvement. The causes are unknown and there is no specific treatment other than relieving the symptoms with high doses of aspirin, and keeping a careful watch for cardiac and other complications.

Measles

Measles is a serious childhood disease that is endemic throughout the world. It is caused by a virus and, fortunately, can now be prevented by routine immunization during infancy. Since introduction of the measles vaccine, the disease is now rarely seen but is more common among adolescents who were not immunized during their early childhood.

Early symptoms of measles are a low-grade fever, a slight cough, coldlike symptoms, and conjunctivitis (pinkeye). Within 2 or 3 days a rash will appear on the face, usually concurrent with an abrupt rise in temperature to about 105° F (40.5° C). For a while the child may appear desperately ill, but within a day or two, the symptoms usually subside.

Treatment for measles includes bed rest, adequate fluid intake and, if laryngitis and cough are excessive, humidification of environmental air. The chief complications of measles are pneumonia and encephalitis.

Mental Retardation

Mental retardation is a rather imprecise term used to describe a child with a deficit in intellectual capacity that limits learning and the development of skills needed for self-care. About 3 percent of the total population can be classified as mentally retarded, but only about half are actually diagnosed as such. The others have enough intellectual ability to function reasonably well and to achieve varying degrees of independence as adults.

There are many causes of mental retardation, including congenital or chromosomal abnormalities, infections, birth injuries, toxic substances, accidents, metabolic or hormonal disorders, and nutritional deficiencies. In up to 80 percent of all cases, the causes for retardation are unknown. Some forms of retardation, such as Down's syndrome, may be accompanied by other abnormalities or congenital defects. Some retarded children have a normal appearance, while others may have characteristic facial or physical abnormalities. Also, there are many degrees of retardation, ranging from profound to borderline. (See box.)

Except in Down's syndrome and cases of severe and obvious abnormalities, mental retardation is often difficult to diagnose in infancy and early childhood. All children develop at different rates, and doctors are understandably reluctant to label a child as retarded when, in fact, the baby is simply developing at a slow rate. Therefore, a diagnosis of retardation may be delayed until the second or third year, depending upon the type and degree.

While most forms of mental retardation cannot be cured, all retarded children should be helped to reach their full potential. All but the very severely retarded can learn at least some skills, such as speech, how to dress and care for their basic physical needs, and even some reading skills. From very early infancy on, the mentally retarded child should have multisensory stimulation: mobiles and other visual objects, toys, music and other auditory stimulants, things to touch and explore. Love and attention are particularly vital; a retarded child may not demand attention, but the more that is given, the greater the likelihood of advancement. In recent years, a number of special classes and support groups for parents of the mentally handicapped have been formed in all parts of the country to teach parents some of the special skills needed by a retarded child.

Often there is a tendency not to "push" a mentally handicapped child, but if any degree of in-

---

LEVELS OF MENTAL RETARDATION

Although there is no clear agreement as to the precise levels of mental retardation, the following classifications, as outlined in Nelson's classic *Textbook of Pediatrics*, are generally accepted by most experts.

Level (IQ)	Characteristics and Potential
Mild (52–67)	Ninety percent of retarded children fall into this range. Most need special classes, but many can learn elementary reading and arithmetic. With training, may be able to function independently as adults.
Moderate (36–51)	Can usually attain self-care skills and most can attend classes for the trainable. May be semi-independent as adults in supervised living or sheltered workshop settings.
Severe (20–35)	Can learn simple conversational skills and minimal self-care skills (eating, dressing, toilet training). Supervision required, even as adults; may be institutionalized.
Profound (below 20)	Total supervision required. Some may achieve toilet training, but only very minimal self-care skills are possible. Language development may be minimal.

[a] Adapted from *Nelson Textbook of Pediatrics*, Richard E. Behrman and Victor C. Vaughn III, editors, W. B. Saunders Co., 1983. Reprinted by permission of the publisher.

---

dependence is to be achieved, this is necessary. Crawling, walking, and the development of other motor skills are often difficult or delayed, but very important. Toilet training is possible for all but the most profoundly retarded. Speech also may be difficult to learn, but with persistence and patience, most retarded children can learn to communicate effectively.

Behavior is another area that should not be neglected. If a retarded person is to achieve any independence, he or she must learn to conform to the rules and demands of society. Teaching things like manners and restraint of impulsive or aggressive behavior may be time-consuming and frustrating, but such social skills are necessary if the person is to cope outside a family or sheltered environment.

Mononucleosis

This viral disease commonly affects adolescents and young adults. Since it can be transmitted via direct contact with saliva, it's commonly referred to as "the kissing disease," although a younger child may catch it by putting a hand that is carrying the virus into the mouth.

The incubation period is vague and may be longer than a month. The first signs of infectious mononucleosis are malaise, fatigue, headache, nausea, and abdominal pain, which may last for 1 or 2 weeks. Sore throat and fever up to about 102° F (38.8° C) set in later. The lymph glands swell, and some patients have a rash.

Because of its insidious onset, mononucleosis may first be recognized by its complications: hepatitis and pneumonia.

No specific treatment is available or necessary for most cases of mononucleosis, although rest is advisable. As long as there are no complications, children uniformly recover without incident, although fatigue may persist for months after recovery. (See also the section on Mononucleosis in Chapter 13 on Adolescence and Sexual Maturity, page 247.)

Mumps

A painful enlargement of the salivary glands is the chief sign of mumps, a contagious viral disease. It is spread by direct contact, through infectious saliva, and also through the air. Epidemics occur at all times of the year, although slightly more often in the winter and spring. However, now there is a safe mumps vaccine that can be given after the age of 15 months, so there is little need for anyone to suffer from the disease.

One mumps infection seems sufficient to protect a person for life, and infants gain a temporary immunity from their mothers' immunity through the placenta, a protection that lasts 6 to 8 months.

Mumps is far more severe if it is contracted in adulthood and can occasionally cause infertility in men. The disease usually begins with fever, muscle pain in the neck, headache, and malaise. There is pain and swelling in the parotid (salivary) glands in front of and below the ear. Swelling of these glands

proceeds rapidly, and is usually visible, reaching a maximum in 1 to 3 days and then subsiding within 1 week. The swelling may be accompanied by a moderate fever no higher than 103 or 104°F (39.4 or 40° C). In men and adolescent boys, the infection may spread to the testes, causing painful swelling and, in some cases, infertility.

Psychoses

Childhood psychoses are relatively rare. They generally are divided into two categories: early onset, which appears during infancy or the preschool years; and late onset, which appears during or just before adolescence.

Autism. This disorder often is not diagnosed until it becomes evident that the child's speech development is seriously delayed. In reviewing development to that point, it often is noted that the baby was not particularly cuddly or outgoing. The autistic child is usually withdrawn, and prefers solitary play, often with a favorite toy or object in a ritualist or repetitive manner, to human contact. Head banging, rocking, teeth grinding, or blank staring are common, although children who demonstrate these activities may not be autistic. Many autistic children develop ritualistic behavior and any disruption of a compulsive routine may result in explosive rage. Self-mutilation, even to the point where it is life-threatening, is fairly common. There is often diminished response to pain and other stimuli. Speech is usually absent or limited to nonsense rhyming or nonsense babbling.

The cause of autism is unknown, although it is now believed to be a neurophysiologic disorder. While it is difficult to measure the intelligence of autistic children, some appear to have low IQs, while others who have some language skills appear to fall in the normal range. Contrary to popular belief of only a few decades ago, it is not caused by parental neglect or actions. In some cases, a child appears to be developing normally, and then will inexplicably regress, often after the birth of a sibling or some other event.

The outlook for autistic children is guarded. Some, particularly those who at one time appeared to be developing normally and then regressed, may eventually become marginally self-sufficient and independent. But most require lifelong shelter and care.

Psychoses in Older Children. Psychoses appearing in older children and adolescents tend to resemble adult mental illness and usually require the same approaches to treatment. Drug therapy, psychotherapy, family counseling, and behavior modification are among the approaches to treatment. In general, the outlook is better for this age group than for the autistic child. (Other psychological problems seen in childhood and adolescence are discussed in Chapter 36 on Mental and Emotional Health, page 723.)

Reye's Syndrome

Reye's syndrome is a relatively rare but serious disease that appears to be related to a variety of viral infections, particularly chickenpox and influenza. Its cause is unknown, although some studies have found an increased risk after the use of aspirin during a viral illness.

It is most common in children over the age of 6. Although the death rate from the disease is dropping, due largely to improved treatments and a greater awareness of the early symptoms which has led to earlier treatment, about 30 percent of children who contract it still die.

The disease is characterized by brain swelling (edema) and fatty infiltrates in the liver. It seems to involve dysfunction of certain energy-producing cells known as mitochondria. Typically, a child with Reye's syndrome has been healthy until developing episodes of particularly persistent nausea and vomiting after an ordinary viral infection. Hours to days later, the child may become hyperactive or combative, followed by sleepiness, altered consciousness, stupor, convulsion, and coma. Death may follow rapidly; survivors usually recover completely, but neurological damage has been noted in some.

All patients suspected of having Reye's syndrome should be taken to a hospital emergency room without delay. Intensive care, which may include mechanical ventilation and drugs to relieve brain swelling, may be required to halt progressive deterioration.

Rubella

Rubella (German measles) is an infection worth particular attention because of its danger to an unborn infant. It is not a particularly dangerous disease to a child who catches it after birth, but a fetus who contracts rubella in the womb may develop severe congenital defects, including blindness, deafness, and heart defects. The rubella immunization given to most children as part of their routine vaccinations is important primarily in reducing the risk that these children will transmit the disease to others, particularly pregnant women, or that young women will be unprotected from the disease when they reach their childbearing years. Women who have not been im-

munized against rubella should do so before becoming pregnant. The vaccine should not be given, however, if there is any chance that the woman is already or about to become pregnant since it may transmit the disease to the fetus.

Scarlet Fever

Scarlet fever is no longer feared as a potentially lethal disease, as was the case before the discovery of antibiotics. It also is not as common as in the past, probably because the widespread use of antibiotics against the causative streptococcus organism prevents widespread outbreaks of the disease.

Scarlet fever is so named because of the characteristic pink-red rash, which occurs most on the chest and abdomen but may cover the entire body, and a strawberry tongue, with bright red showing through the whitish coating. The red skin, which blanches when pressed, also feels rough, like sandpaper. The incubation is 2 to 5 days and the symptoms usually appear rapidly: a high fever (103 to 104° F; 39.4 to 40° C), vomiting, headache, sore throat, and chills, followed in 12 to 48 hours by the rash. After a week or so, the rash will fade and the skin will flake or peel, a process that may continue for several weeks.

Treatment of scarlet fever is similar to that of any streptococcal infection. Penicillin is the drug of choice; erythromycin may be given to children who cannot take penicillin. Therapy should continue for a full 10 days, even if the symptoms subside. Other susceptible family members should be examined and treated, if appropriate. Isolation is no longer considered necessary. Bed rest may be wise during the acute period, but is not necessary if the child is not very sick. Liquids should be given, especially during the feverish stage; other symptoms such as sore throat and headache may be treated with aspirin or acetaminophen.

Sore Throat

Sore throat (acute pharyngitis) is a common complication of upper respiratory tract infections, and may occur whether or not a child has tonsils. Pharyngitis occurs at all ages, but is most common between 4 and 7. It is most commonly caused by viruses, although the bacterium *Streptococcus* may also be a cause, leading to "strep throat."

Viral sore throat usually comes on fairly gradually, along with fever, malaise, and lack of appetite. Most commonly the sore throat reaches a peak 2 or 3 days after the other symptoms, often accompanied by hoarseness, cough, and a runny nose. The illness may last less than 24 hours and rarely persists more than 5 days.

Streptococcal pharyngitis, seen most commonly after the age of 2, often begins with headache, abdominal pain, and vomiting. There may be a fever as high as 104°F (40° C). The throat usually becomes sore hours after the first symptoms; the degree of pain ranges from slight to severe enough to impair swallowing. Fever may continue as long as 4 days and the child may feel ill for as long as 2 weeks. The doctor may notice that the tonsils are also involved. (See Tonsillitis, following.)

There is no drug treatment for a viral sore throat, and most doctors will delay antibiotic treatment until obtaining results of the throat culture, which can prove that a sore throat is caused by *Streptococcus* bacteria. If the throat is infected by *Streptococcus*, penicillin or erythromycin treatment usually relieves the discomfort within a day. However, since strep throat can lead to serious complications, most notably rheumatic fever, it is extremely important to continue the antibiotic therapy for a full 10 days to ensure that the microorganism has been completely destroyed.

Most children with sore throats prefer to stay in bed. Warm compresses on the neck and saline solution gargles, as well as the inhalation of steam, may also help. Since swallowing may be painful, the child should not be forced to eat. However, liquids should be offered and things like chicken soup or cold drinks may be soothing. (For more information, see the section on Acute Sore Throat in Chapter 21 on Infectious Diseases, page 431.)

Tonsillitis

Infection of the tonsils can be either acute, as noted above, or chronic. The latter is particularly important because the tonsils are important to the development of the immune system. They serve naturally as defenses against infection, and only when these defenses are breached can a tonsil infection begin. Because of this relatively recent understanding, tonsillectomy operations for children are not as common as they were during the past, although there are still children who may benefit from their removal.

Chronic tonsillitis may cause recurrent or persistent sore throat and obstruction to swallowing or breathing, as well as a sense of dryness and irritation in the throat. The child may have bad breath. However, the signs of chronic tonsillitis are far from obvious, and most doctors are very cautious in making the diagnosis.

Tonsillectomy is usually indicated only in children who have had tonsillar or peritonsillar abscesses, or who have tonsils so large that they obstruct breathing or lead to cardiac failure. Only very rarely should a child younger than 2 have a tonsillectomy. Frequent sore throats is not a valid reason for tonsillectomy; removal of the tonsils has not been proven to solve the problem. Formerly many children were thought to have abnormal and dangerous enlargement of the tonsils; however, the normal tonsils are relatively larger in children than in adults, and this is not a valid reason to remove them.

Whooping Cough

Whooping cough (Pertussis), which is caused by the *Bordetella pertussis* bacterium, is now a rare disease, thanks to widespread DTP immunization during infancy. Still, several thousand cases are reported in the United States each year. It most commonly attacks very young children, with a very high mortality rate. The most common whooping cough patient in this country, however, is an adolescent or young adult who was not properly immunized in the first year or who has some immunological problem. The disease, however, is rarely serious once the child has passed his first birthday.

Pertussis is from the Latin for "intensive cough" and this is the most striking characteristic of the disease. At first, there may only be a runny nose, mild cough, and low-grade fever. But as the disease progresses, the nasal discharge becomes thicker and more profuse, leading to severe upper respiratory congestion in a young baby. This stage usually lasts 1 to 2 weeks before progressing to the next (paroxysmal) stage. Typically, the child will cough forcefully 5 to 10 times during a single expiration. This is followed by a sudden intake of air and a whooping sound as it is inhaled against the narrowed glottis. During these coughing spells, the face may turn red or blue, the eyes bulge, the tongue protrude, and there may be drooling. Vomiting may accompany the coughing. Understandably, these attacks leave the child exhausted. This stage may last 2 to 4 weeks or even longer; weight loss is common. The coughing attacks gradually become less frequent and disappear, but a cough may persist for several months after recovery.

Pneumonia is one of the most serious potential complications of whooping cough, causing more than 90 percent of the deaths from the disease in children under the age of 3.

Administration of erythromycin during the early stage of the disease may prevent it progressing to the paroxysmal or coughing stage. But once the cough begins, antibiotics do not seem to shorten its duration. Hospitalization for suction to remove the secretions from the upper nose and upper respiratory tract may be necessary in very young children,

RECOMMENDED SCHEDULE FOR ACTIVE IMMUNIZATION OF NORMAL INFANTS AND CHILDREN

Recommended age	Vaccine[a]	Comments
2 months	DTP, OPV	Can be initiated earlier in areas of high endemicity
4 months	DTP, OPV	2-month interval desired for OPV to avoid interference
6 months	DTP (OPV)	OPV optional for areas where polio might be imported (e.g., some areas of southwestern United States)
12 months	Tuberculin test	May be given simultaneously with MMR at 15 months (see text)
15 months	Measles, mumps, rubella (MMR)	MMR preferred
18 months	DTP, OPV	Consider as part of primary series—DTP essential
4–6 years[b]	DTP, OPV	
14–16 years	Adult tetanus and diphtheria	Repeat every 10 years for lifetime

[a] DTP—diphtheria and tetanus toxoids with pertussis vaccine. OPV—oral, attenuated poliovirus vaccine contains poliovirus types 1, 2, and 3. *Tuberculin test*—mantoux (intradermal PPD) preferred. Frequency of tests depends on local epidemiology. The Committee recommends annual or biennial testing unless local circumstances dictate less frequent or no testing (see tuberculosis for complete discussion. MMR—live measles, mumps, and rubella viruses in a combined vaccine (see text for discussion of single vaccines versus combination). Td—adult tetanus toxoid (full dose) and diphtheria toxoid (reduced dose) combination.

[b] Up to the seventh birthday.

Reproduced by permission of the American Academy of Pediatrics.

The Recommended Schedule for Active Immunization of Normal Infants and Children, from the "Report of the Committee on Infectious Diseases," 19th Edition, 1982. Reprinted by permission of the American Academy of Pediatrics.

and oxygen also may be required. Fluids should be given to prevent dehydration, and even though the disease is exhausting and a child may not feel like eating, maintaining nutrition is important, especially in an infant.

Worms

Infestation with various intestinal worms is common in children throughout the world. In this country, the most common worm infection is enterobiasis, or pinworms, an essentially harmless infection that often causes more social than medical problems. Pinworm infections are particularly common in nursery schools and kindergarten; an entire classroom may be affected in a short period.

Pinworms are transmitted from person to person by ingesting the eggs, which may be carried on fingernails, clothing, bedding, or even in dust and the air. Typically, the female worm crawls out through the anus at night to deposit her eggs there. This causes severe itching; the child usually scratches the area and some of the eggs become embedded under the fingernails. These are ingested, allowing the parasites' life cycle to continue. Some also may be transmitted to others by hand-to-mouth contact with contaminated food or other objects. Since the eggs are very small, they also may be inhaled in dust.

The major symptoms of pinworms are itching in the anal area, restlessness, and difficulty sleeping. An infection can be diagnosed by placing adhesive tape over the anal area, removing it, and then examining it under a microscope for eggs. Worms also may be observed in the stool or in the perianal area.

Complications include secondary bacterial infections of the area that is constantly scratched and vaginal involvement in young girls. Treatment is with a single dose of pyrantel pamoate, followed by a second dose in 2 weeks. Petroleum jelly may be applied to the anal area to relieve the itching. Other family members also should be treated, especially if they have symptoms. Careful washing of bedding and clothing is advised, but there is no evidence that cleanliness plays a major role in either getting or eradicating pinworm infections.

Other worm infections that are relatively common in this country include the following.

Roundworms (Ascariasis). Roundworm infections are most common in tropical areas, but even so, some estimates indicate as many as 4 million cases of ascariasis, mostly among children, occur in this country each year. Roundworm eggs are passed in the feces and harbored in the soil, where they may remain for months or even years. They are transmitted to humans by hand-to-mouth contact; perhaps by eating without washing hands that have been in contact with the contaminated soil, or by eating raw food containing the eggs.

Most people do not suffer any serious consequences of roundworm infections, although in unusual instances, the parasite may cause lung problems, intestinal obstruction, or nutritional deficiency. Roundworm infections are diagnosed by examining the stool for eggs. Treatment is with drugs to kill the adult worms in the intestinal tract.

Hookworms. Hookworms are very common worldwide, but are rarely seen in this country, limited to the subtropical areas of the Southeast. The hookworm eggs are passed in the feces and develop into larvae in the soil. Humans are infected by drinking contaminated water or by coming in direct contact with contaminated soil (usually by walking barefoot) and having the larvae penetrate the skin. Most hookworm infections are asymptomatic; when symptoms occur, they may include itching where the larvae enter the skin, abdominal pain, loss of appetite, a feeling of fullness, and diarrhea. Anemia also may occur in severe infections and represents one of the most serious complications of hookworm infections. Diagnosis is made by examining the stool for eggs; treatment involves giving iron for any anemia and drugs to eradicate the worms. (Other parasitic infections are discussed in Chapter 21 on Infectious Diseases, page 449.)

13 Adolescence and Sexual Maturity

Karen Hein, M.D.

INTRODUCTION

ADOLESCENTS, no matter how they may seem to parents or even health professionals, are neither big children nor small adults. In fact, little that is applicable in childhood or in adulthood, in psychological or physiological terms, is relevant at this stage of development.

But 3 factors do characterize adolescents as a group. The first is a marked change in the rate of physical growth and development. At no other period beyond the first year of life is physical change so noticeable. A second factor is the marked rate of mental development, which is characterized by alterations in the mode of thinking and consequently in the ways in which the individual interacts with the surrounding world. Common to both these factors is the notion of change, and it is important to remember that change is the one constant in adolescence. The consideration of what is normal or abnormal—physically or psychologically—must always be made in the context of the individual adolescent's stage of growth and development.

A third factor that distinguishes adolescents as a group is their role in society. Because they are neither dependent children nor fully accountable adults, their role is ambiguous in the extreme. The ambiguity is reflected in current legal debates: Should an adolescent murderer, for example, be treated differently from an adult who commits a similar crime (and, if so, in what ways should the treatment be different)? Should contraceptives be prescribed for minors without parental knowledge and consent? Should status offenses—acts that are not against the law when committed by adults but for which youngsters can be punished, often severely—be kept on the books?

For health-care professionals, adolescents are further distinguished by the fact that, until very recently, they have been apart from the mainstream of medicine. There has been no obvious place where they could receive medical care. Although this situation is changing, and the special health needs and conditions of adolescents are being recognized and treated in new ways, it is still unfortunately true that many people do not see a doctor during the whole span of their adolescent years.

PSYCHOLOGICAL CHANGES

DURING ADOLESCENCE, a large number of psychological and developmental changes take place. In these few short years, an adolescent comes to terms with bodily changes, copes with sexual development and its accompanying emotions, establishes and confirms a sense of identity, incorporates formal learning into the patterns of living, and achieves independence and emancipation from the family. The corresponding tasks required of a parent of an adolescent are to help the youngster complete his or her emancipation, and to provide support and understanding while at the same time setting standards and limiting dangerous or harmful behavior. Parents must provide a favorable and appropriate environment for healthy development, be firm but not punitive, and accept and respect the adolescent's struggles toward independence. It is not surprising that this is often a stressful period for the entire household, since changes in the adolescent require that other family members change as well.

The Family

Within the family, the adolescent's primary psychological task is to move from the position of total dependence occupied as a child to one that is largely independent—physically, emotionally, and economically.

In early adolescence (the years from 9 to 12 approximately), the youngster still spends most of the time not taken up by school with the family, looking to the parents not only for food and shelter but also for many forms of recreation. Generally, at this stage of development, girls are more interested in emulating their mothers, and boys their fathers, in contrast to later stages when rivalry develops between the same-sex parent and child.

It is characteristic in early adolescence for a youngster to try out new behaviors, new styles of clothing, and so on within the family. While parents may be alarmed at what seems excessive forwardness or ostentation, they must realize that the youngster is looking for some kind of parental approval of the new behavior before trying it in the world outside the family. A girl of 10, for example, may "practice" flirting with her father; it may be years before she is ready to flirt with a boy of her own age.

Middle adolescence (ages 13 to 16) is typically the period when the struggle for independence is most overt. Middle adolescents demand (and deserve) a space at home—a room or part of a room that is private to do with as they wish. Issues that commonly arise in middle adolescence center on questions of autonomy: how late to stay up, where to go out and with whom, when to return, and who is in control of spending money. Limit-testing is also characteristic of the period: The adolescent tries out a new skill (for example, budgeting money for recreation), exceeds the limit, and then, having learned from the consequences, sets a boundary. Each limit has to be experienced before it is adopted.

Often in middle adolescence the youngster will choose an adult outside the family (a teacher or a counselor, for example) as a role model, or select such a person as a surrogate parent. Parents and the family situation are frequently the subjects of detailed, critical analysis during middle adolescence. An idealized parent or family is constructed in the teenager's mind, and then compared with the actual parent or family. Many family values and rules are challenged for the first time. Political and religious beliefs, economic choices, parenting style, and household organization all become subjects of review by the middle adolescent. The parent may feel such a critique unjustified, but teenagers need to question the "givens" before they can move on to the next phase of more independent living.

Late adolescence is characterized by an ability to look at the family in a new way. Late adolescents (ages 17 to 20) come to grips with their role in the family and the economic and physical focus begins to shift from the parents' house to their own living quarters. Even if they are still living under their parents' roof and are still dependent on them financially, by the late teens most adolescents have reached their emotional and financial emancipation.

Peer Group

The composition of the peer group, its typical activities, and its importance in the youngster's life all change markedly from early to middle to late adolescence.

Psychologically, younger adolescents need friends to play with, to learn from, and to compete with. An early adolescent's peer group is usually of the same sex, a hierarchy of friends with one or two intimates. Peer activities tend to revolve around sports and undertakings that involve adults as leaders—scouting and athletic teams, for example.

In middle adolescence, there is a distinct change. The peer group includes both sexes and the group's activities characteristically involve risk-taking behavior. This behavior—experimenting with drugs, riding motorcycles without helmets, swimming in areas that are off limits, and the like—is viewed as dangerous by adults, and with good reason. The teenager, however, may either be genuinely unaware of the possible results of such risky activities, or may simple choose to ignore them. There is little that parents can do except to restate their concerns, set reasonable limits, and wait out this stage

of development, realizing that risk-taking is an essential part of adolescent growth, and normal when limited in duration. If such potentially self-destructive behavior continues into the late teenage years, however, there is cause for concern.

The peer group of late adolescence is typically composed of concentric circles. At the center are one or more intimates, either friends or sexual partners. Next comes a circle of close friends and beyond that again a circle of acquaintances. The pattern approximates that of a typical adult social life. Adolescents are now testing newly found ideals—trust, sharing, commitment to a relationship—with real people, rather than focusing on such ideals in the abstract.

Societal Role

From age 9 to 16, the adolescent's chief role is that of a student. This role defines the adolescent as part of a group larger than the family or peer group. Membership in a group is an actual developmental milestone in adolescence; society expects everyone to belong somewhere outside of the family. The "loner" is often isolated because of some serious emotional problem. Acute or chronic depression or a major personality disorder may underlie failure to join a group.

If not in school, an adolescent will likely be a member of some other group—a religious organization, the armed forces, or a political group, for example. Even social protest, while an expression of an individual's values and ideals, may unite a youngster with others in a group.

After age 16, many will abandon the student role, either by graduating or by dropping out, but they will still be a member of a group. For many, the group will now be the labor force. Those who continue their education will retain the student role, with its privileges and its frustrations, for several years.

Interests

The interests of the younger adolescent tend to conform to those of the peer group as a whole. At this stage, there is typically a preoccupation with "heros," whether in sports, music, entertainment, or the community. By the middle years, however, a youngster's interests become more individual, reflecting personal tastes rather than those of friends. There is often a great depth of interest in the activity that an adolescent engages in alone, whether it is some form of artistic expression, sports, or a self-imposed "self-improvement" plan.

By late adolescence, most youngsters have some realization of what they do well, and of how they will be able to use their interests and abilities in the world of work. There occurs a merging of interests with a career goal. Drastic changes in career plans between the late teens and the early twenties often represent a shift from an idealized version of self, talents, and interests to a more realistic assessment of what a given job or profession entails, how well suited the adolescent is to that pursuit, and what the financial and emotional trade-offs will be. Sometimes the earlier plan was based on what parents or others thought was suitable, rather than on the youngster's own preferences.

INTELLECTUAL CHANGES

DURING ADOLESCENCE, marked changes occur in the area of cognition, that is, the developing of knowledge that includes both awareness and judgment. Gradually, a comprehensive, abstract cognitive structure develops, radically changing the way adolescents think about the world—and, therefore, the way they make decisions about behavior.

Until about age 12, most situations are viewed concretely; youngsters are concerned with objects and with the here-and-now. Many young adolescents are no more able than a 5-year-old to think in terms of abstractions or to understand the implications or future consequences of an action. This ability often doesn't develop until middle adolescence. But by the age of 15, about half of all adolescents have reached a level of development that allows them to think "futuristically." This ability is not uniform, however, even in those who exhibit it, and there remain areas where thinking is at a more primitive level. For parents, this unevenness of cognitive development is often perplexing. They must realize that adolescents may sometimes think and act like children because certain areas of their cognitive development are still at a childlike stage.

MORAL DEVELOPMENT

MORAL REASONING also evolves dramatically during adolescence, although different levels of ability may appear under different circumstances.

Laurence Kohlberg of Harvard University has developed a widely quoted description of the stages of moral development in children, adolescents, and adults. For the sake of simplicity, 3 stages can be distinguished that apply to adolescents. The first is the "egocentric" stage, in which a person's chief concern is himself, and the "morality" of an action is judged by whether it will benefit or hurt him. This type of reasoning is characteristic of children.

The second stage may be called "legal-centric," where moral thinking centers on rules or the legality or illegality of action. There is a realization that laws apply to all and should be obeyed whether or not there is a likelihood of being punished. By middle adolescence, this is the predominant type of moral reasoning.

In the third stage, moral behavior is characterized by an adherence to principles, which may at times go beyond the requirements of the law. Tests have shown that older teenagers are able to look at dilemmas in their lives, and those of friends and family, in terms of abstractions—reciprocity, justice, the equality of individuals, and so on. Yet, interestingly, decision making about sexual matters frequently remains at a lower level. This may be because many parents and teachers try to help teenagers reach the highest level of reasoning of which they are capable—in all matters except sexual decision making. Here adults often resort to "scare tactics," using moral reasoning that approximates Kohlberg's lowest level, where the consequences of an action to self are paramount. Consequently, teenagers have less practice in the higher levels of moral reasoning about sex than they do in many other situations.

PHYSICAL DEVELOPMENT

Height and Weight

During adolescence, height increases by 25 percent and weight almost doubles, a growth rate second only to that of a newborn infant. A boy who, at the age of 11, weighs an average 78 pounds and mea-

Chart 13.1. Girls: 2 to 18 Years Physical Growth NCHS Percentiles[a] (Stature).

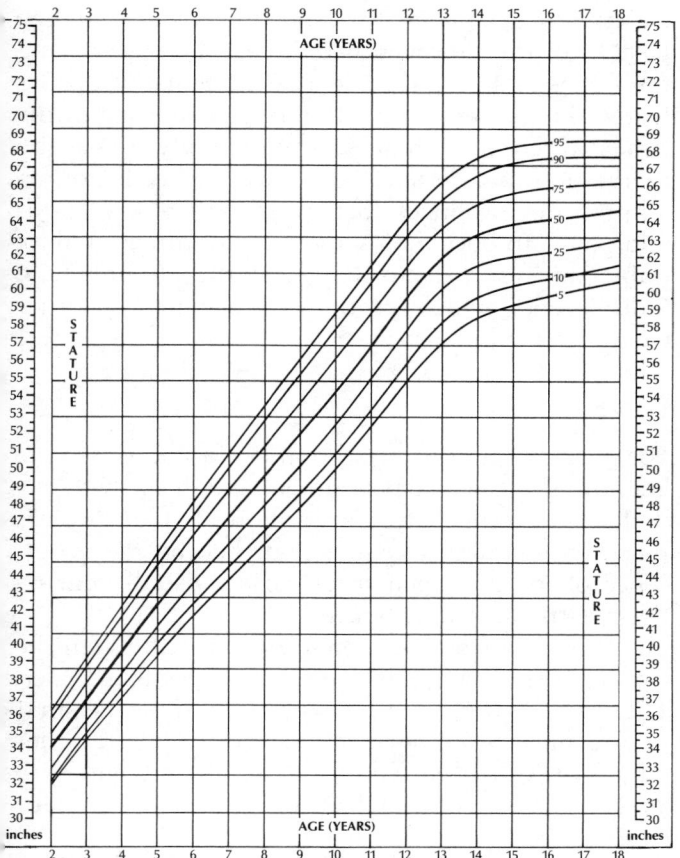

[a]Adapted from: Hamill PVV, Drizd TA, Johnson CL, Reed RB, Roche AF, Moore WM: Physical growth: National Center for Health Statistics percentiles. AM J CLIN NUTR 32:607-629, 1979. Data from the Fels Research Institute, Wright State University School of Medicine, Yellow Springs, Ohio. © 1982 ROSS LABORATORIES

Chart 13.3. Boys: 2 to 18 Years Physical Growth NCHS Percentiles[a] (Stature).

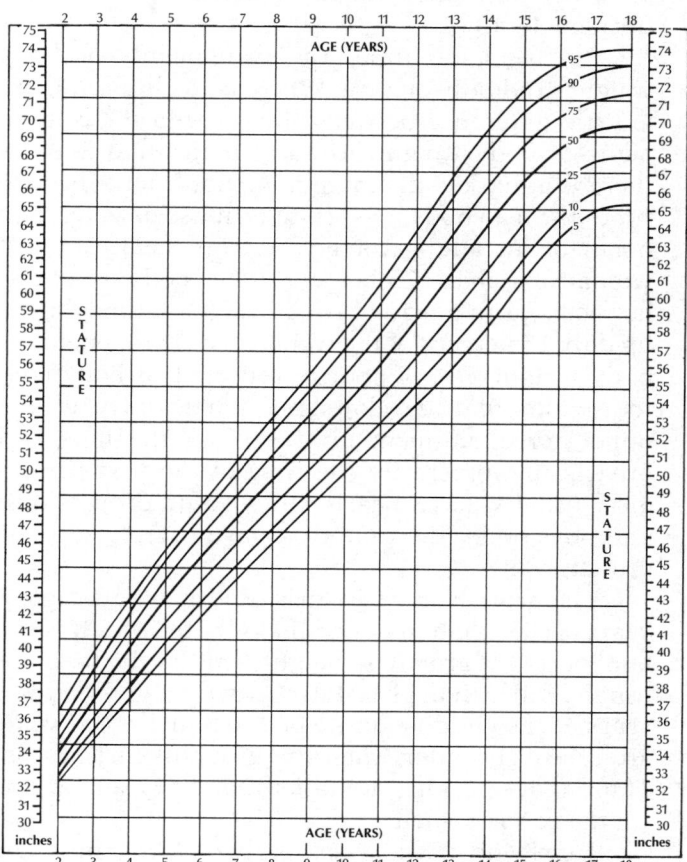

[a]Adapted from: Hamill PVV, Drizd TA, Johnson CL, Reed RB, Roche AF, Moore WM: Physical growth: National Center for Health Statistics percentiles. AM J CLIN NUTR 32:607-629, 1979. Data from the National Center for Health Statistics (NCHS) Hyattsville, Maryland. © 1982 ROSS LABORATORIES

Chart 13.2. Girls: 2 to 18 Years Physical Growth NCHS Percentiles[a] (Weight).

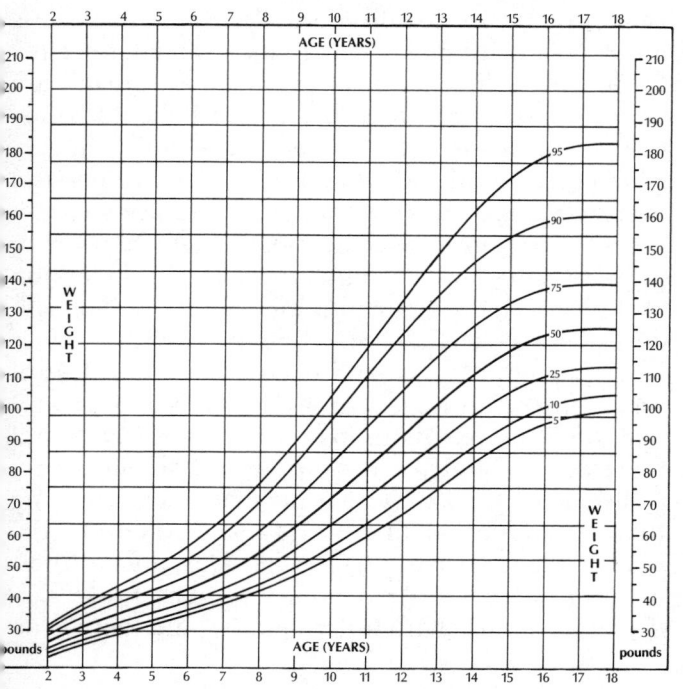

[a]Adapted from: Hamill PVV, Drizd TA, Johnson CL, Reed RB, Roche AF, Moore WM: Physical growth: National Center for Health Statistics percentiles. AM J CLIN NUTR 32:607-629, 1979. Data from the Fels Research Institute, Wright State University School of Medicine, Yellow Springs, Ohio. © 1982 ROSS LABORATORIES

Chart 13.4. Boys: 2 to 18 Years Physical Growth NCHS Percentiles[a] (Weight).

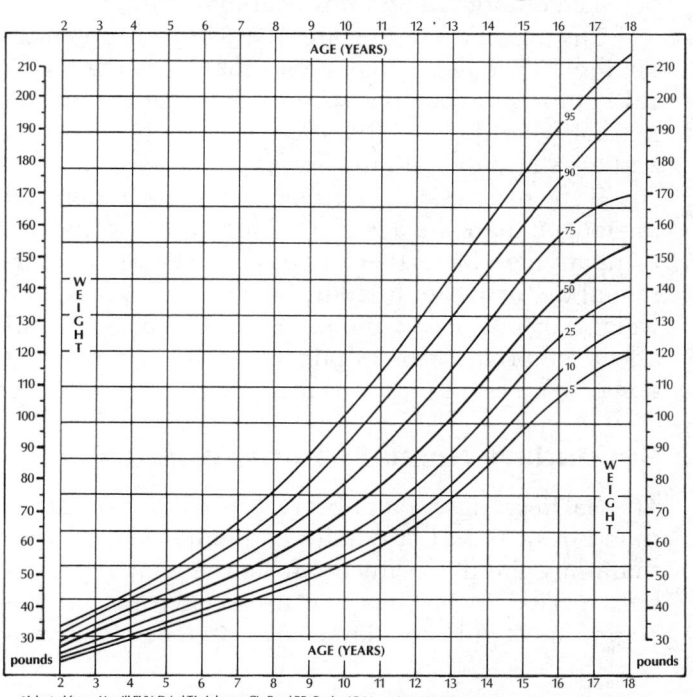

[a]Adapted from: Hamill PVV, Drizd TA, Johnson CL, Reed RB, Roche AF, Moore WM: Physical growth: National Center for Health Statistics percentiles. AM J CLIN NUTR 32:607-629, 1979. Data from the National Center for Health Statistics (NCHS) Hyattsville, Maryland. © 1982 ROSS LABORATORIES

sures 56 inches will, within 7 years, weigh 150 pounds and measure almost 70 inches. The same dramatic changes hold for girls. (See charts 13.1 through 13.4.)

At the same time, the components of body weight gradually change. Whereas in children there is little difference between the sexes in the components of body weight, in adult males and females there is a marked distinction. An adult male has 1½ times the lean body mass (that is, muscle, water, and bone) of an adult woman. A trim, healthy adult woman may have 25 percent of her body weight as fat, whereas in a man of equal weight, fat may make up only 15 percent of the weight. The components of body weight are, of course, reflected in body contour—muscular development, particularly of the upper torso, in men; fat tissue on the hips and breasts in women. By the time of the first period, girls usually have nearly fully adult proportions, and boys do by the time they have completed their growth spurt.

The growth spurt in girls occurs, on average, 2 years earlier than in boys, and for both sexes it is the final period of growth in height. This is why boys are usually taller than girls. Boys, growing for an extra 2 years at the childhood rate of 2 to 3 inches per year, are relatively taller when the growth spurt begins. Thus, at age 12, girls are taller than boys, and at age 15, the reverse is true.

A girl who matures very early may be taller than her peers from 8 to 12, but ultimately shorter than average, since the take-off point for her growth spurt was lower. Socially, she may feel isolated from her friends her own age, but may be accepted by adolescents 4 or 5 years older, increasing the discrepancies between emotional and physical maturation.

The problems of the late-maturing boy are more apparent. The delay may be normal from the medical standpoint, but the social consequences of late maturity can profoundly affect a boy's body image and his standing with his peers.

If the progression of puberty stops, or is delayed for longer than the age ranges indicated on the accompanying chart, there may be a genetic or hormonal disturbance. In addition, chronic illness, low weight, or prolonged and excessive exercise may all affect the progression of puberty, causing a slowing down or arrest of maturation.

Secondary Sexual Characteristics

The earliest signs of puberty are chemical rather than physical. In both males and females, the hypothalamus gland is primed during the fetal and newborn period to be sensitive to sex steroids. At the beginning of puberty, the sensing device in the hypo-thalamus causes chemical signals (gonadotrophins) to be released in the pituitary gland. In females, the ovaries then begin to produce more estrogens and this, in turn, affects the deposition of fat and the growth of the uterus, the lining of the vagina, and the breasts. In males the rise in gonadotrophins leads to a greater production of testosterone in the testes which, in turn, affects many body tissues (an increase in muscle mass and red blood cells, for example) and produces further growth of the testes and penis. In both males and females, the growth of pubic hair results from changes in the adrenal gland (adrenarche) which precede or accompany other early signs of puberty.

Girls

For girls, the first external marks of puberty are the beginning of breast development and the growth of a little pubic hair. These are followed, 1 or 2 years later, by a spurt in height, and then by the occurrence of the first menstrual period, usually during the twelfth year. (See figure 13.1.)

It is important to remember that, although the timing varies, the sequence itself proceeds in order. Thus, a girl would not be expected to have her first period until after her growth spurt. On the other hand, if several years have passed since the growth spurt and menstruation has not begun, it is cause for concern.

It is not uncommon for the breasts to develop unevenly, with a noticeable difference in size lasting for many months. Girls should be reassured that, in most women, the breasts eventually will be symmetrical. In some rare instances, one breast will fail to develop, or the two will remain markedly asymmetrical, giving rise to considerable self-consciousness and a poor self-image. Sensitivity to an adolescent's feelings of self-consciousness and body image are very important at this time. The girl should be assured that this is not a sign of disease and that surgical correction is possible if the difference persists even when growth is complete. There are two approaches to surgical correction—augmentation to make the small breast match the larger, or reduction of the larger one. Augmentation is preferred for several reasons: It is a simple operation with a lower risk of complications, and it does not entail loss of sensitivity or future lactation. In contrast, breast reduction often results in loss of both sensitivity and function, especially if the nipple and areola are repositioned. Reduction also involves more scarring than augmentation. Many girls also worry about the size of their breasts. Size in no way affects their function (small-breasted women produce milk as efficiently as those with fuller figures), and there is no

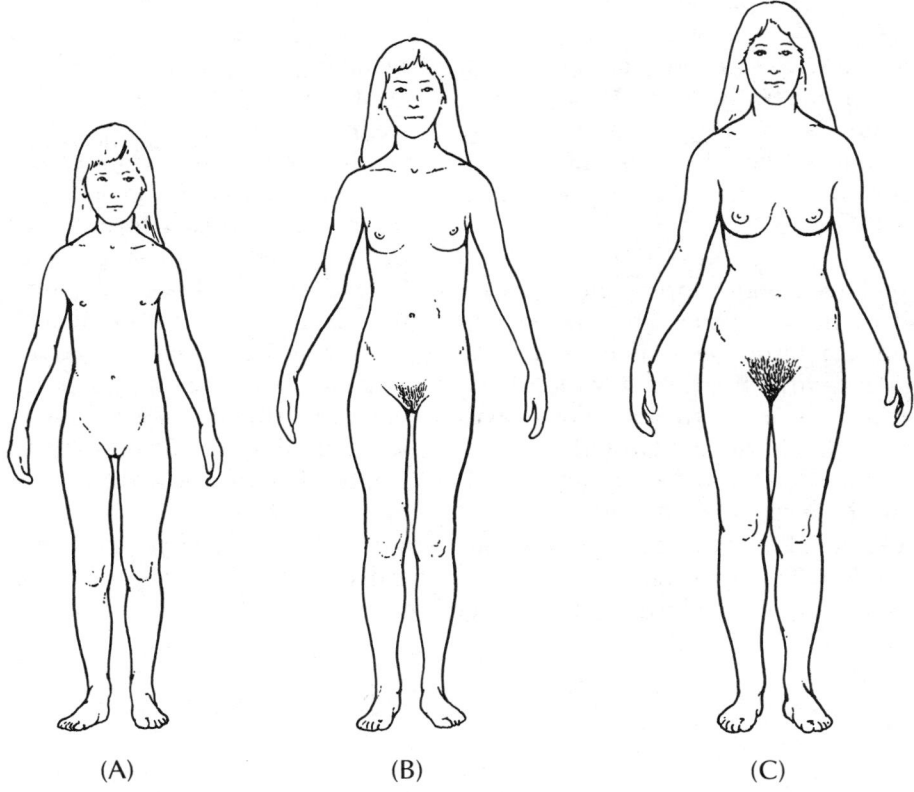

(A)   (B)   (C)

Figure 13.1. **Changes during puberty in girls. (A) shows a typical girl before the onset of puberty; in (B) the breasts are beginning to develop and there is the beginning of pubic hair. There is also increased height and body fat. (C) shows a fully developed female figure at about age 17 or 18.**

correlation between breast size and pleasure in sexual relations. Rarely, a girl with extremely large breasts may have a surgical reduction, if activities such as running are curtailed by the amount of tissue, or if she is very self-conscious about the size. But she should understand that this is a serious operation with long-term consequences and should not be undertaken for minor cosmetic appearance. And, of course, young women who are very self-conscious about small breasts also can undergo augmentation surgery. This, however, should be discouraged in the young, since small breasts often grow markedly with any weight gain later in life. For example, many women who were size A in their teens and twenties find they are size B or C in their thirties, especially after childbirth.

The other major event of puberty, the beginning of menstruation, is preceded by an increase in vaginal discharge, either white or yellow, which may come and go over several months. The blood of the first and subsequent periods may be red or brownish in color. The darker color is merely an indication that the blood has remained in the uterus for a time

and thus been exposed to oxygen before flowing through the vagina with other menstrual products.

Menstrual irregularities are very common in the first 6 months to 1 year (or even 2 years in some cases) after menarche, the beginning of menstruation. There may be several periods within a short span of time, or no periods for many months. Such irregularities are usually due to absence of ovulation and therefore the absence of progesterone, a hormone produced in the ovary after ovulation occurs. Painful menstruation is not usual in the early months.

Whether to use tampons or pads should be the adolescent's choice, although many girls find tampons awkward to insert at first. A girl should be reassured that since the hymen does not normally cover the entire vaginal opening, tampons can be used at any age. She should also be aware of the necessity of intermittent use of tampons and the need to change them regularly, not only for hygienic reasons but because of the remote possibility of toxic shock syndrome.

Boys

Enlargement of the testicles is the first sign of puberty in boys, and it generally begins at age 11½. After that, pubic hair begins to grow and then the penis gets longer and thicker. In boys, the growth spurt occurs, on average, at age 14—2 years later than in girls. (See figure 13.2.)

Rapidly growing teenage boys (and girls, to a lesser extent) often have a leggy appearance because the long bones of their extremities grow faster and earlier than do the vertebrae. Their shoe, pants, and shirt sizes change dramatically; for a few months at the height of their growth spurt, their rate of growth is double what it was in childhood. Growth changes in the larynx make voice changes a common hallmark of boys in midpuberty. They will also begin to grow body hair and facial hair in a distribution pattern that tends to follow family lines.

Although boys are capable of having an erection in infancy, the capacity for ejaculation comes with the changes of puberty. The first ejaculation may occur at any time from age 8 to 21, although it usually occurs between ages 11 and 15. Ejaculation may occur during masturbation, spontaneously in association with sexual fantasies, or at night as a "wet dream." In contrast to menarche, the first ejaculatory experience is often greeted as a major positive life event. A few boys are confused, however, thinking that they have urinated accidentally.

Two-thirds of normal boys develop some breast tissue at about the time of the growth spurt. Gynecomastia, as this tissue is called, may be on one side or both, painless or uncomfortable. The breast tissue usually disappears within 6 months, but it may be noticeable for up to 2 years. While acutely embarrassing to most boys, gynecomastia does not generally indicate any kind of underlying hormonal problem.

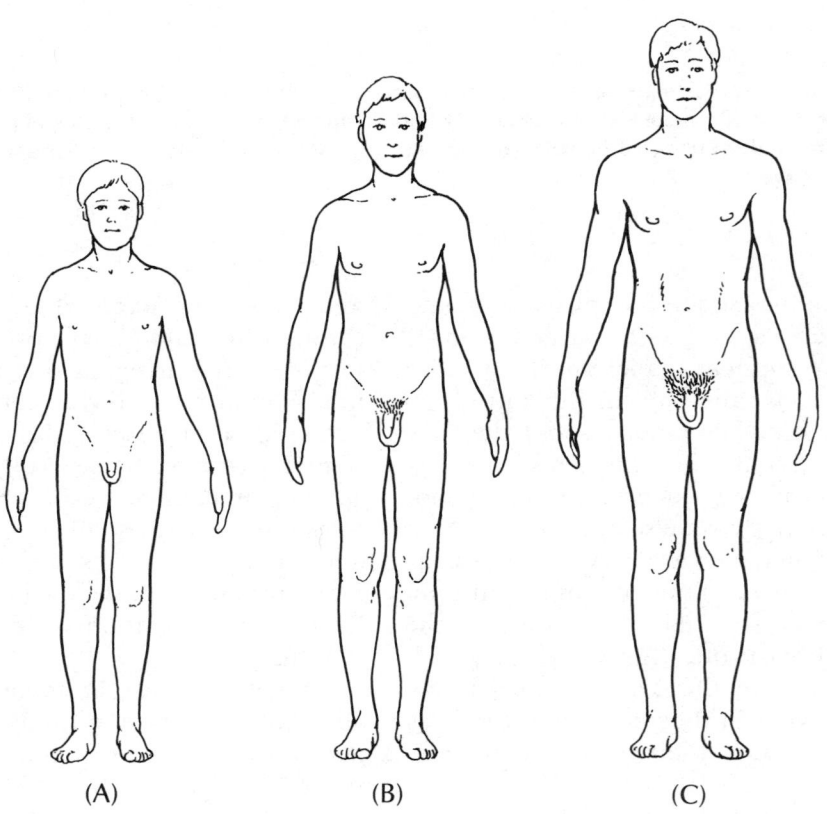

(A)   (B)   (C)

Figure 13.2. **Changes during puberty in boys. (A) shows a boy at about age 9 before the onset of puberty. In (B) secondary sex characteristics are beginning to develop; e.g., the beginning of pubic hair and enlargement of the penis and testes. There is also increased height and muscle development. (C) shows a fully developed male at about age 18.**

ADOLESCENT SEXUALITY

The Role of Parents

Parents, for all their good intentions, often find that their sons' and daughters' emerging sexual maturity—and the expression of this maturity in sexual activity—is a difficult topic to deal with in a straightforward way. As a result, many teenagers lack essential factual information. They may say that they have all the facts, having gotten them from friends and from school sex education programs. In general, however, they do not know as much as they need to about such things as bodily changes, the mechanism of intercourse, contraceptives, or the transmission of venereal disease.

Adolescents generally express respect for their parents' views on many topics, but not on sexuality. Here parents are seen as handing out judgments while withholding information. (Where facts are not freely provided, a lack of respect for attitudes is readily understandable.) In addition to facts, many teenagers look to their parents for a dialogue about the feelings that lead up to and accompany sexual behavior. It may not be appropriate for adolescents to discuss the details of their sexual experiences with their parents, any more than it would be for parents to share details of their own sexual practices. But discussion of emotions is another matter.

As much for factual information as for anything else, adolescents often turn to pornographic magazines and movies for their explicit depiction of sexual organs and sexual acts. There are, however, a number of good publications that parents can provide for their adolescent children if they themselves are uncomfortable with explicit discussions of sex. (See Suggested Reading, page 256.) Ideally, of course, discussions of bodily functions, including information about reproductive organs and the changes that can be expected at puberty, should begin at the preschool age.

Sexual Activity

Of the approximately 40 million young Americans between the ages of 10 and 20, some 12 million have had sexual intercourse. This single figure is misleading, however. It does not take into account differences among age groups (of 15-year-old girls, 14 percent have had intercourse; by the age of 19, the figure is 50 percent). Nor is it an indication of how many are having regular sexual relations, since it includes all those who have had intercourse only once or a few times as well as those who are sexually active. (See chart 13.5.)

Most teenage girls report that their experience of first intercourse is basically a negative one. They find it frightening, uncomfortable, or even painful. Teenage boys, on the other hand, generally maintain that the experience was positive and enjoyable, both for themselves and for their partners. Thus, there still seems to be a "double standard" concerning sexual experience.

Patterns of Relationships

Robert Sorensen, in a book on adolescent sexuality,

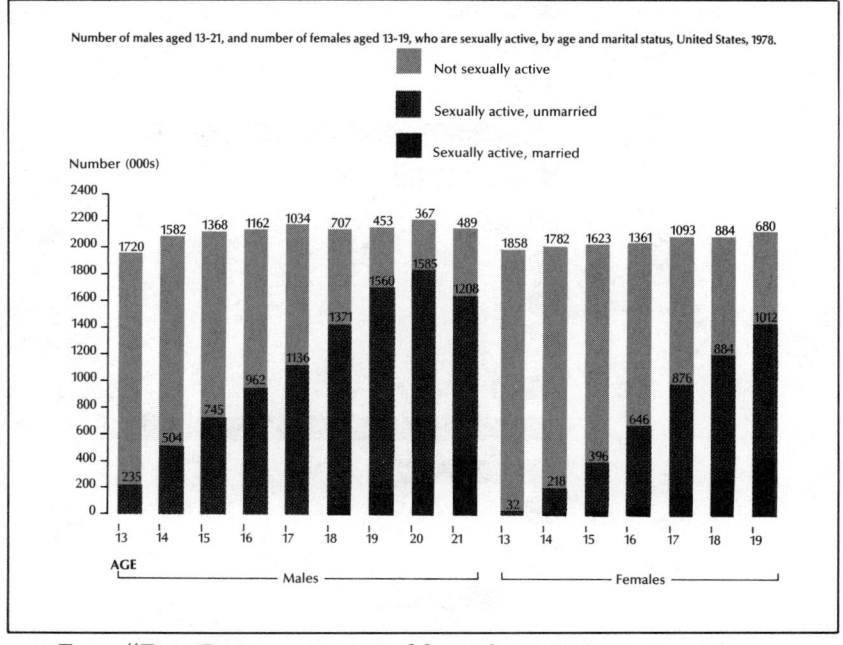

Chart 13.5.

From "Teen Pregnancy—A Problem That Won't Go Away," The Alan Guttmacher Institute, New York, 1983.

describes the intimate sexual relationships of most American teenagers as "serial monogamy"—a series of emotional commitments for an undefined period of time that is tacitly understood not to be "forever." During that time, there are no other sexual partners. Adolescents involved in such relationships generally have no more than 2 or 3 sexual partners during the course of the teenage years.

This pattern contrasts sharply with that adopted by a much smaller group of adolescents, whom Sorensen calls the "sexual adventurers." Sexual adventurers comprise about 15 percent of the adolescent population. During the mid- and late-adolescent period they have many sexual partners—an average of 16—and may have 2 or more partners at a given time. As a group, these teenagers seem to find adolescence particularly tumultuous. Their truancy rate is high, they have an increased risk and rate of venereal disease, their drug use is higher than average, and their attitudes toward parents, school, and adult society in general tend to be more negative. For these adolescents, unlike the majority, the pattern of sexual behavior is part of an overall picture of "being in trouble."

Pregnancy and Parenthood

More than 10 percent of adolescent girls between the ages of 15 and 19 have had a pregnancy, and an esti-mated one-third of all 19-year-olds have been pregnant at least once. Slightly more than 50 percent of all young women have had sexual intercourse by the age of 19, so these figures indicate that 4 in 10 adolescent girls who are sexually experienced will become pregnant before they leave their teens. (See chart 13.6.)

Of the approximately 1.2 million teenage pregnancies that occur annually, three-quarters are not intended. About 25 percent of these pregnancies are terminated by induced abortion (prior to 1973, when abortion was legalized, only half that number were aborted), and another 10 percent end in miscarriage. However, two-thirds (approximately 560,000) result in live births. Since only some 10 percent of the infants are given up for adoption, the vast majority of teenage girls who bear a child take on the role of mother. While some marry, teenagers account for almost half of all out-of-wedlock births.

Factors that influence a pregnant teenager's decisions about her future and her baby's include her own views about abortion and her desire (or lack of it) to have a child; her perception of her relatives' reactions; her partner's reaction; and perceived support from friends and neighbors, or the lack of such support. Depending on her own cognitive development, she may be more concerned with immediate issues (the discomfort of abortion, or the desire to please her partner or her parents) than with long-

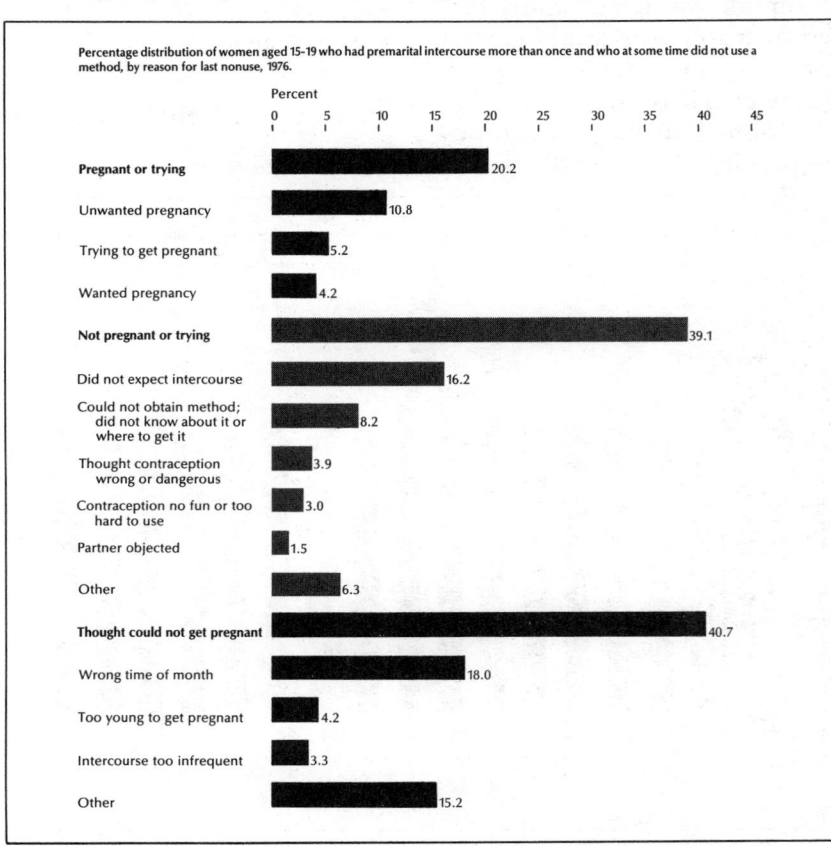

Chart 13.6.

From "Teen Pregnancy—A Problem That Won't Go Away," The Alan Guttmacher Institute, New York, 1983.

term considerations (the difficulties of raising a child). Preoccupation with the present rather than with the future is characteristic of early- and mid-adolescent development.

Federally funded teen-parent clinics have been established, and most offer nutritional advice, counseling, social services, and school support, as well as continuing medical care. There are fewer complications in these pregnancies than there were a decade ago and the rate of perinatal illness has dropped sharply. Nevertheless, young women still have a higher than average risk of bearing low-birth-weight babies, and the younger the woman, the higher the risk.

The social "risks" of teenage parenthood remain great. Marriages hastily entered into to legitimize a child often break up quickly; young mothers frequently drop out of school. Without adequate education or training, they find it hard to compete in the job market and many become dependent on welfare for support. About half the money paid out by the Aid to Families with Dependent Children program goes to families in which the woman gave birth while still in her teens. The children of these young mothers are also affected. Their cognitive development tends to suffer and often they, in their turn, become teenage parents.

Contraception

Of the approximately 4.5 million sexually active teenage girls, 2.5 million have had contraceptives prescribed for them. Overall the use of contraceptives, including over-the-counter methods, has risen 35 percent among adolescents during the last decade. About 1.5 million teenagers use family clinics as their source of contraception (there are now some 5,000 such clinics around the country); another 1.2 million consult private doctors. (See charts 13.7 and 13.8.)

It is not the case that adolescents are having intercourse at an earlier age and in greater numbers *because* contraception is readily available. In actuality, a large percentage of adolescents do not obtain contraception for almost a year after they become sexually active (this is reflected in the fact that about half of all premarital first pregnancies occur during the first 6 months of sexual activity). Further, a re-

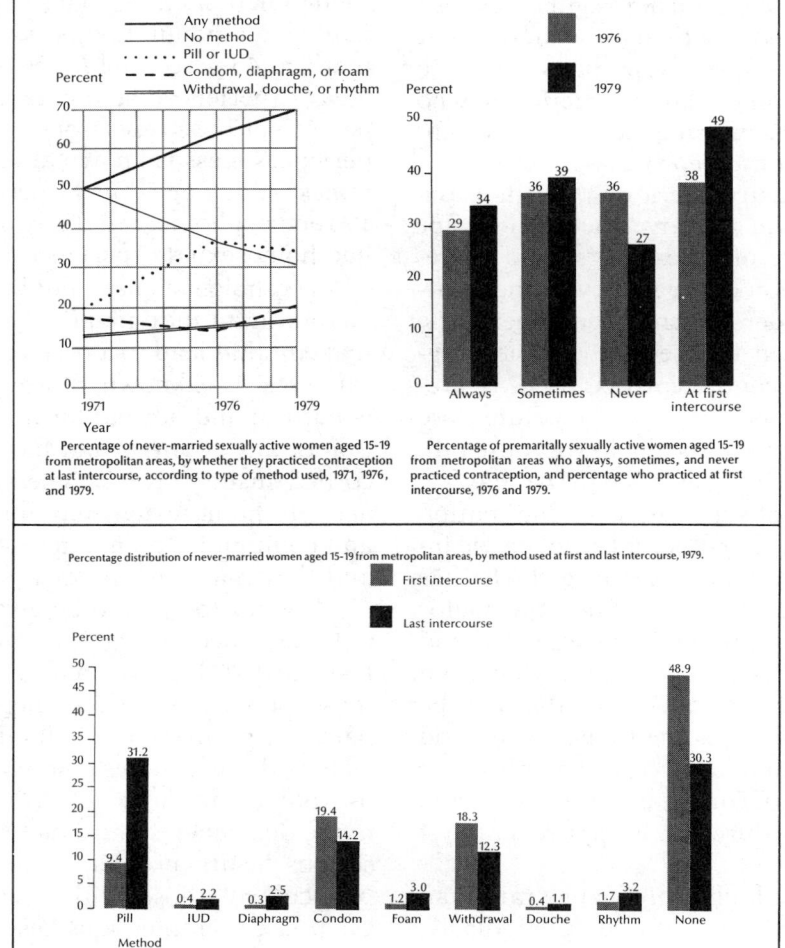

Chart 13.7.

Percentage of never-married sexually active women aged 15-19 from metropolitan areas, by whether they practiced contraception at last intercourse, according to type of method used, 1971, 1976, and 1979.

Percentage of premaritally sexually active women aged 15-19 from metropolitan areas who always, sometimes, and never practiced contraception, and percentage who practiced at first intercourse, 1976 and 1979.

Chart 13.8.

Percentage distribution of never-married women aged 15-19 from metropolitan areas, by method used at first and last intercourse, 1979.

From "Teen Pregnancy—A Problem That Won't Go Away," The Alan Guttmacher Institute, New York, 1983.

cent study shows that 10 percent of adolescent patients visiting a family planning clinic for the first time did so because they feared they were pregnant.

Special Considerations. For a teenage girl, the choice of a contraception method must depend on her motivation and the frequency with which she has intercourse. Her partner should be involved in counseling as well as in the decision making.

Oral contraceptives are a safe, appropriate choice for many teenage girls, especially those who have intercourse frequently. The newer contraceptive pills contain doses of hormones that are much lower than those used when oral contraceptives were first introduced, and the risk of death as a result of childbirth or abortion is much greater than the risk of life-threatening disease from using these contraceptives. The only real risk now appears to be for women over 35 who are also cigarette smokers, or who have specific contraindications for their use, such as a history of cancer or heart disease. For the vast majority of women under the age of 20, provided that they have established regular ovulation, there appear to be no long-term effects on fertility when oral contraceptives are taken.

Oral contraceptives, requiring regular, conscientious use, are not a good method for an adolescent who has intercourse infrequently, perhaps only once or twice a year, or for one who is forgetful or who doesn't follow directions in using medication in general. In the past, oral contraceptives were often prescribed to relieve menstrual cramps and tension. There are now new and effective medications for these purposes; the use of "the pill" should be restricted to the prevention of pregnancy or the treatment of specific disorders, such as endometriosis. The 1-year standardized failure rate (or the pregnancy rate) with oral contraceptives, used as prescribed, is less than 1 percent for the medium dose pill and about 2 to 3 percent for the lowest dose pill.

Users of intrauterine devices (IUDs) have a slightly increased risk of salpingitis—inflammation of the Fallopian tubes—and other forms of pelvic inflammatory disease. For an adolescent girl who has her whole reproductive life ahead of her, this factor deserves serious consideration. Moreover, IUDs tend to cause very heavy periods and more than the usual cramping. On the other hand, devices that can be fitted for uterine size (such as the Lippes loop), and the new copper-containing devices, are highly effective—and the question of compliance does not arise. With IUDs, the 1-year failure rate is approximately 4 to 6 percent.

Diaphragms have a higher pregnancy rate than IUDs because they are often not used regularly. Pregnancy rates vary from 5 to 15 percent. Usually the diaphragm is selected by an adolescent girl because of fears or prejudices about other contraceptive methods. When properly fitted and used conscientiously, it has many advantages and no known adverse medical consequences. It is important that a diaphragm be refitted if the user gains or loses more than 10 pounds.

Condoms and contraceptive vaginal foams—easily available, nonprescription contraceptives—can each be used separately, but they provide more protection if they are used together. The 1-year failure rate for condoms used alone is 9.6 percent, and for foams, 17.9 percent. New contraceptive vaginal suppositories and sponges contain the same chemical ingredients as those found in foams, but in a form that may make their use more convenient.

In comparison to these methods of contraception, about 70 percent of women become pregnant in a year using no method of contraception.

Homosexuality

Transient homosexual fantasies and behavior are not uncommon in heterosexual adolescents. Although homosexuals make up only 10 percent of the adult male population, studies have shown that as many as 45 percent of American males aged 16 to 19 have experienced a homosexual advance, and 17 percent of boys report one or more homosexual experiences. Less is known about homosexuality in females, at any age, but 11 percent of girls aged 16 to 19 report a homosexual advance and 6 percent have had homosexual experiences.

Psychologists have not been able to identify any factors in an individual's psychological or physical makeup that lead to a preference for a partner of the same sex. It is known, however, that homosexuality is natural and normal for a minority of the population of any country, and has been since earliest recorded history. Nevertheless, adolescents who are actively homosexual may find that family, friends, and community do not accept the preference easily, and they may wish to seek professional counseling.

The doctor should be aware of a teenager's sexual preferences in order to watch for certain sexually transmitted diseases that are more common in homosexuals. These include hepatitis B and intestinal parasites such as Giardia lamblia and Chlamydia, as well as those diseases commonly found in the heterosexual community. More recently, acquired immune deficiency syndrome (AIDS) has emerged as a serious health problem among male homosexuals, particularly those with many sex partners. (See Chapter 21 on Infectious Diseases, page 446.)

Sexual Fantasies

Fantasies may occur at any time of day or night and are entirely normal. In fact, they seem to be important in adolescent development, because they provide an opportunity for "trying out" sexual thoughts and desires which may be inappropriate to express overtly.

Masturbation

This normal, natural, and healthy activity begins in childhood, continuing throughout life. The vast majority of Americans of both sexes and all ages masturbate, giving themselves pleasure and releasing sexual tensions. Many adolescents, however, feel guilty about the practice, especially since warnings and myths about masturbation seem to persist. Despite age-old myths, there is no evidence that masturbation is associated with hair falling out, pimples erupting, the onset of madness, or any other ill effect. Masturbation should not be discouraged but rather should be restricted to an appropriate time and place, when personal pleasures can be enjoyed alone or in the company of an intimate.

SEXUAL MOLESTATION

Rape

In those incidents of rape that are reported to the police—and a great many, for one reason or another, are not—anywhere from one-quarter to one-half of the victims are adolescent girls. A teenage victim of rape is far more likely to be blamed for the incident than is an older woman, not only by the police, but also, unfortunately, by medical personnel and by family members. The old myths about rape—that the woman "asked for it" by dressing in a seductive fashion, or by walking in a dangerous neighborhood late at night—still have credence for many when the victim is an adolescent. It should be stressed that dressing in extreme fashions, and testing limits by keeping late hours and venturing into new neighborhoods, are part of normal adolescent behavior, and should not be construed as sexual invitations.

The immediate medical needs of a teenage rape victim are, of course, the same as those of a woman of any age. Estrogens (usually diethylstilbestrol or DES) may be given within 72 hours to bring on the period and ensure that pregnancy does not occur. Antibiotics—specifically, oral doses or injections of penicillin—should be given to prevent venereal infection. A pelvic examination is usually necessary to be sure that any internal injury is detected and treated. Equally important is counseling by a professional familiar with "rape-trauma syndrome."

The response to rape, rape-trauma syndrome, appears to differ between adolescents and older women. An adolescent's response in the days immediately following the rape is often one of phobia: fear of being alone, of the dark, of dying of an unknown disease, of going out of the house to school or to attend extracurricular activities. Some of the fears may seem to be related to the life-threatening experience of the rape itself, but others may appear quite irrational. This period of extreme and generalized fearfulness may last for days, weeks, or months. It is often followed by a stage of denial which usually lasts for about 6 months but may continue for many years. The adolescent at this stage may deny that the incident ever happened; she does not want to talk about it, or her response to it. This stage may be followed in turn by one in which a number of psychosomatic complaints appear—headaches, abdominal pains, and insomnia, for example. Renewed contact with a doctor or a psychiatrist can then be helpful, since the youngster may now be ready to discuss the incident.

Incest

Webster defines incest as "sexual intercourse between two persons too closely related to marry legally," that is, between family members. From a child's or an adolescent's point of view, however, the definition should be broadened to include those who are *perceived* as being family members, even if they are not in fact related by blood or marriage. Incest cuts across socioeconomic and racial lines and is much more common than was previously thought.

For an adolescent victim of incest (or, as is frequently the case, of repeated acts of incest) there is often, in addition to the abuse itself, a further distress: The perpetrator of the act is someone who in all other areas is a source of love and support. The most common pairings are father-daughter, stepfather-daughter, uncle (or other adult male)-niece. More rarely, the act involves an older brother and a sister. Male victims, however, also exist and should not be forgotten, since they may be less willing to seek help.

In the past, incest was surrounded by silence. The alternatives for the victims were to run away from home, to wait until they had homes of their own to move to or, more rarely, to retaliate with violence. Today, there is a slowly growing willingness to discuss the problem and to try to organize care and help for victims.

ROUTINE MEDICAL CARE

SOME 22 PERCENT OF TEENAGERS aged 12 to 15, and 15 percent of 16- to 17-year-olds, have no source of regular medical care. This lack is particularly striking, and unfortunate, among pregnant teenagers: Only 53 percent of pregnant women aged 15 to 19 receive first-trimester medical care (as against 81 percent of women aged 25 to 34). The availability of medical care for adolescents varies regionally and racially. Rural adolescents and members of minorities receive significantly less care than urban and suburban white teenagers.

Many teenagers continue to see their pediatrician throughout adolescence. The American Academy of Pediatrics has recently redefined pediatrics as the care of children from birth through age 21. In recognition of the special needs of adolescents, pediatricians are now receiving extensive training in such areas as adolescent sexuality and school problems, and may be particularly well qualified to continue providing medical care during adolescence.

Some adolescents change doctors, receiving their medical care from a general practitioner, internist, or gynecologist, or from a specialist in adolescent medicine. (The new subspecialty of adolescent medicine is attracting a growing number of doctors.) Other possible sources of health care are teen clinics and health services within schools, which are often more accessible to teenagers than the traditional doctor's office. In choosing a doctor it is important to look for one who is comfortable in dealing with adolescents, willing to accommodate an adolescent's schedule, aware of the need for privacy and for the assurance of confidentiality, and willing and able to deal with both body and mind.

Confidentiality is an all-important issue in an adolescent's medical care. An agreement should be made between the doctor and the adolescent patient concerning matters of confidentiality and the disclosure of information contained in medical records. In general, adolescents will agree that information about a life-threatening condition should be transmitted to their parents, and that parents, if paying the bills, should know about the timing, but not the content, of appointments. (At some point in adolescence, youngsters should assume responsibility for making and keeping their own medical appointments.) Parents, for their part, should expect that areas of sensitivity, such as problems connected with sexual activity or drug use, will remain confidential between doctor and patient. In making such an agreement, the degree of privacy and confidentiality should be the adolescent's choice, not the parents' or the doctor's.

It is desirable that adolescents have a physical checkup twice a year during the years of rapid growth, and once a year during the years that precede and follow. An annual examination is important not only to check growth and development and investigate specific complaints, but also to detect the common asymptomatic conditions of adolescence.

The First Pelvic Examination

The timing of an adolescent girl's first pelvic examination depends less on her age than on gynecological considerations. She should have an initial visit by at least age 18, but sooner if she has irregular periods, severe cramps or abdominal pain, vaginal discharge, or unusual bleeding; if she has a need for contraception; or if her mother took the drug DES during pregnancy (see page 247). A teenager's desire to know that she is "normal" is an entirely appropriate reason for a pelvic examination. (It would not be appropriate, however, for a parent to ask that a pelvic exam be done to ascertain virginity, even if virginity could be established with certainty by such an exam, which it cannot.)

An adolescent may be somewhat apprehensive about her first internal examination, but if she knows what to expect and has a physician who will explain step by step what is happening, the experience will be less threatening. Although a mother might want to accompany her daughter, it may be better if she were not present during the actual exam unless her daughter specifically prefers her presence. Information that is important for the doctor to have, such as her history of sexual activity, is best obtained before the pelvic examination during discussion with the doctor without a parent present.

The first visit should begin with a complete family and medical history, including menstrual and

CHECKLIST FOR ROUTINE MEDICAL SCREENING DURING ADOLESCENCE

Past medical history
Family history of illness
Composition of family *(siblings, stepparents, etc.)*
Medical/social history *(sexual activity, use of drugs, personal interests, sports, hobbies)*
Special diets, food omissions, patterns of eating
Activity level, including sleep patterns
Physical examination:
    Height and weight
    Blood pressure
    Review of systems *(heart, lungs, gastrointestinal system, genitourinary system, neurological function, etc.)*
    Nutritional status
    Teeth and gums
    Skeletal examination *(for scoliosis, sports-related injuries)*
    Vision *(acuity, color-blindness)*
    Hearing
    For females: menstrual history, breast examination, pelvic examination, Pap smear
    For males: testicular examination

Immunizations: measles and rubella *(if not given in childhood)*; diphtheria-tetanus booster at age 15 *(or 10 years after last booster)*

Laboratory tests that should be done during adolescence include:

    Blood test for anemia *(twice a year during the growth spurt, otherwise once a year)*
    Urinalysis or urine culture *(once or twice during the teen years if there are no urinary tract symptoms; more frequently if symptoms occur)*
    Liver function tests *(for those using drugs; frequency of tests depends on the drugs used, the amounts, and the route)*
    Skin tests for tuberculosis *(annually for inner-city dwellers and those with known exposure, especially if female)*
    Blood test for sickle cell anemia *(once)*
    Tests for venereal disease *(frequency depends on the sexual history: the number of partners and the number of sexual encounters; it should be remembered that venereal diseases are often asymptomatic)*

---

sexual history, and a record of height, weight, and blood pressure. The physical portion of the exam should include an examination of the thyroid, breasts, abdomen, and lymph nodes (in the neck, armpits, and groin), for the presence of any swelling, tenderness, or unusual lumps or masses. Breast self-examination should also be taught. The doctor should also be able to feel if the liver, bladder, or bowels are enlarged or distended.

Next the doctor will examine the vagina and the cervix (the neck of the uterus) by inserting an index finger, then the index and third finger together, covered by a disposable rubber glove. To judge the position, size, and texture of the vagina and uterus, the examiner will place his or her other hand on the lower abdomen so that internal organs are felt be-tween the two hands. A vaginal speculum, a simple instrument that spreads and separates the walls of the vagina, will allow the doctor to use a light to see into the vagina and cervix, to assure that the color, shape, and amount of discharge are normal. The doctor may also insert a gloved finger into the rectum to detect any abnormalities. Samples will be taken for routine laboratory tests, which may include urine to check for presence of sugar or protein, a Pap smear to check for cervical cancer, and blood to check for anemia and other common disorders. If the Pap smear is normal, it should be repeated the following year and then at intervals of a few years until adulthood. At that time it should be part of the annual gynecological exam.

CONDITIONS AND COMPLAINTS OF PARTICULAR RELEVANCE

Sleep and Sleepiness

Patterns of sleep among adolescents are different from those in both children and adults. First, in adolescence there is 40 percent less deep sleep (during which there is no evidence of dreaming) than in earlier years. The reduction of this deep or nonrapideye-movement sleep may be associated with hormonal activity, specifically with the release of many of the growth-related hormones during sleep. The mechanism is not yet clear, but there may well turn out to be a biological basis for the old notion that sleep is needed for growth.

Second, daytime sleepiness increases in adolescence and is perfectly normal. Comparison with records made at the turn of the century shows that today's teenagers sleep less at night than did their Victorian counterparts. Adolescents may be deprived of some of the hours of sleep they need by the demands of homework and social and other activities. This deprivation is evidenced in daytime sleepiness and the well-known teenage habit of rising late on weekends, which is too often taken as a sign of laziness.

Acne

Almost all teenagers suffer acne to some extent, but only rarely is it permanently scarring. It probably causes more psychological than physical problems and is particularly vexing coming at a time when concerns about appearance are very real. Parents can help by assuring their teenagers that acne usually doesn't last more than a few years and many cases clear up in months.

Popular notions to the contrary, poor personal hygiene is rarely a major contributing factor in the cause of acne; food (even the popular villains nuts and chocolate) is seldom a consideration. Rather, in both sexes acne is caused by an increase during adolescence of the male sex hormone androgen, which results in an increase in sebum, a fatty substance secreted by the sebaceous glands of the skin. Androgen also stimulates the growth of the cells in the top layer of skin, which may block the sebum from flowing freely and causes it to form plugs. If a plug extends to the skin surface and is exposed to air, it turns black, resulting in a blackhead. If it is below the surface, it will appear as a whitehead.

Mild acne may be treated by cleaning the affected areas daily with water and mild soap or a medicated wash. Over-the-counter medications containing drying agents, such as alcohol, and peeling agents, such as benzoyl peroxide (5 to 10 percent), can usually be used safely, once or twice a day. However, if peeling or redness becomes severe, the use of drugs should be discontinued and a doctor consulted. Exposure to small amounts of sunlight may help dry the skin, too, but excessive burning and tanning are associated with increased risk of skin wrinkling and cancer later in life.

There are several approaches to the treatment of moderate to more severe acne. The first is to decrease the growth of bacteria on the skin by using antibiotics such as tetracycline by mouth or erythromycin directly on the skin. Another is to apply retinoic acid (a derivative of vitamin A) to cause some mild scaling and peeling of superficial skin and to keep the irritating bacteria and sebum from accumulating. Retinoic acid and related products should only be used under the direction of a physician familiar with its use and side effects.

Dysmenorrhea (Painful Menstruation)

Medical understanding and treatment of dysmenorrhea has changed greatly during the last few years. Once thought of as a psychosomatic problem, dysmenorrhea is actually the result of high levels of prostaglandins, which occur in cycles and cause the muscles of the uterus to contract. (The force of a contraction during menstrual cramping can be as intense as that of a labor pain, though usually much briefer.) Several prescription medications now available are extremely effective in preventing menstrual cramps. They contain prostaglandin-inhibitors, which block the formation and action of these substances. Medication can be started on the first day of the period, and can be used for a day or two when the cramps are at their worst; it has minimal side effects when used for a brief time. Oral contraceptives, once widely prescribed for the relief of dysmenorrhea, need no longer be used—unless contraception is also desired.

The leading cause of school absenteeism among teenage girls is dysmenorrhea, which is experienced by more than half of them. The problem tends to be at its worst in adolescence, improving over the years, and especially after a pregnancy.

Iron-Deficiency Anemia

As the body grows, the number of red blood cells must increase enormously so that the new tissues are supplied with necessary oxygen. Hemoglobin levels change dramatically during adolescence, especially among males. Whereas the average hematocrit (the percentage of red blood cells in the total blood count) in a child is 35 to 37 percent, in an adult male it should be 45 to 50 percent.

Increased quantities of iron are needed to keep up with the demand for increased numbers of red blood cells. An inadequate supply of iron in the diet may manifest itself as iron-deficiency anemia, the most common nutritional disease of adolescence. Normal menstruation accounts for a monthly blood loss of only 2 to 3 tablespoons; only in cases of severe menstrual bleeding does iron lost in this way contribute to anemia. In girls as in boys, accelerated growth is the chief responsible factor.

Tuberculosis

Tuberculosis (TB) is no longer a major public health hazard, as it was through the end of World War II. In adolescence, however, as in infancy and old age, there is an increased risk of activation of the disease. Girls are more likely to be affected than boys. It is no longer thought necessary for most adolescents to be screened annually for TB, but screening is advised for teenagers living in inner cities or institutions, or when a family member has had a positive skin test. If the BCG immunization against tuberculosis was administered during childhood, there is no reason for annual TB screening.

Diethylstilbestrol Exposure

Diethylstilbestrol (DES), a drug used to control spotting and bleeding, was given to pregnant women from the 1940s through 1971, when a link was noted between the drug and a rare cancer in daughters of women who had taken it. There may be some young girls coming into their teens in the 1980s who were exposed. A substantial number, but not all DES daughters, have been found to have vaginal adenosis, a congenital condition in which a type of tissue that normally lines the uterine cavity is found in the vagina. Those with adenosis are also at a somewhat increased risk of developing a rare form of vaginal cancer, called clear cell adenocarcinoma, and possibly cervical cancer. About 400 cases have been recorded among DES daughters. They may also have certain structural abnormalities, such as an extra piece of tissue over the cervix or a small uterine capacity, which affects their ability to carry a pregnancy.

Daughters whose mothers may have taken DES should be examined early on by a gynecologist, preferably one experienced in DES screening, for possible congenital defects, and should be carefully monitored for the development of any malignancy. Fourteen is the recommended age for this exam, or earlier if menstruation has started or if there is vaginal bleeding or other unusual symptoms. In boys, maternal exposure to DES may result in small or undescended testes, and in benign abnormalities of the genital tract, and they, too, should be examined.

Mononucleosis

This syndrome—which includes a sore throat, swollen lymph nodes, and sometimes an enlarged spleen or liver, together with prolonged fatigue and lethargy—is particularly apparent among teenagers although an asymptomatic infection is common in children. It is commonly caused by the Epstein-Barr virus, which, like other viruses, can be transmitted in many different ways and not just by kissing, as is often thought. Mononucleosis cannot be treated with anything more specific than rest. If the liver is affected, then some specific instructions, such as no alcohol, may be given. The sore throat associated with mononucleosis may be a separate infection, caused by streptococcal bacteria, and should be treated specifically.

Chronic Inflammatory Bowel Disease

Many adolescents experience intermittent abdominal pain, diarrhea, or cramps, which seldom have serious implications, but an adolescent who has bloody stools, prolonged diarrhea or abdominal pain, or growth failure, should be evaluated for regional enteritis (Crohn's disease) or ulcerative colitis, which often begin in adolescence. Similar symptoms may be caused by intestinal parasites or various bacterial infections.

Asthma

Asthma (reactive airway disease) is a long-term condition that commonly starts in childhood. Asthma attacks—periods of breathlessness and sometimes audible wheezing that may go away after a few minutes or be long and exhausting—are triggered by a variety of conditions (such as exercise or cold air) that result in contractions and swelling of the bronchioles in the lungs.

Although most attacks seem to happen for no apparent reason, some are caused by viral infections or allergic reactions to such things as pollen, mold spores, animal dander or house-dust mites, or foods like eggs and shellfish; by psychological problems of tension or anxiety; or by physical causes, such as changes in temperature, the presence of smoke or fumes, overexertion, or (as doctors frequently forget) by sexual activity.

Asthma is one of the conditions where it is important for adolescents to assume responsibility for their own medication. They can do a lot to control their condition by being aware of what triggers it (keeping a diary if necessary), avoiding situations that lead to attacks, and using prescribed medications (inhalants or pills) that can control or eliminate the reaction of the airways.

Seizures

There are two times in the life cycle when seizures are likely to begin: infancy and adolescence. Sometimes those that begin in childhood are caused by a form of epilepsy called petit mal, and they can increase during adolescence. The seizures may only last 5 to 15 seconds and are characterized by a momentary lapse, when the youngster may become quiet and stare vacantly. Afterward, he or she may be unaware that anything has happened. The presence of petit mal can be confirmed by an electroencephalogram (EEG). This type of seizure usually ends by the late teens.

Grand mal is the more commonly recognized form of epilepsy, which may begin as late as adolescence or early adulthood. It is characterized by seizures during which the body jerks and the victim may fall and lose consciousness. Grand mal epilepsy can generally be controlled by drugs, such as phenobarbital and dilantin, but dosage is a delicate balance that is affected by growth, so that a teenager with grand mal epilepsy should see a doctor regularly. (See Epilepsy, page 594.) In most states, teenagers with epilepsy can apply for a driver's license if their seizures have been controlled for 2 years prior to application.

Migraine Headache

Although they can begin in childhood or middle age, migraine headaches often occur for the first time in adolescence. The problem is more common in girls than in boys, and there is frequently a strong family history of the complaint. Migraines, like other types of headaches, are increased in frequency by stress. They can be triggered by foods such as chocolate, red wine, or certain cheeses. Attacks, which are characterized by intense pain caused by dilation of blood vessels in the head, can last several hours or even days, followed by periods of freedom. They may be accompanied by nausea, vomiting, and extreme sensitivity to light.

A mild analgesic or a drug that constricts the blood vessels may be prescribed for persistent attacks, but aspirin, rest in a dark, quiet room, and reduction of stress with relaxation techniques are often enough to control the headache.

Scoliosis

Scoliosis, a sideways curvature of the spine, may appear in adolescence for no apparent reason. It affects nearly 10 times as many girls as boys, and there may or may not be a family history of it. In a small number of cases, scoliosis may be caused by birth defects, such disorders as cerebral palsy and polio, or certain structural bone problems such as a difference in the length of the legs.

Curvature of the spine seldom causes problems initially but can be permanently disabling if it progresses and is not treated. All adolescents should be screened for scoliosis every year during the growth years. If progressive or severe, the condition may be treated with the use of a low-profile brace which does not show under most clothing, or a Milwaukee brace which is more visible and cumbersome, or surgery. Exercises and careful observation are also extremely important in the treatment of scoliosis.

Hepatitis

Adolescents are at increased risk for infectious hepatitis (hepatitis A), an acute viral infection that particularly affects the liver and is spread by means of food, water, and kitchen utensils and other objects contaminated by feces. Hepatitis symptoms can range from mild to severe, and include fever, headaches, nausea, vomiting, muscle aches, and general weakness. This flulike stage is often followed by jaundice, caused by an accumulation in the blood of bile that cannot be processed properly by the weakened and sometimes enlarged liver. Little can be done for hepatitis A except bed rest and avoidance of substances like fat, drugs (including many prescribed medications), and alcohol, which tax the weakened liver.

Adolescents as well as adult drug users are at high risk for serum hepatitis (hepatitis B). Dirty needles, however, are not the only means by which hepatitis B is transmitted; the virus may be present in saliva, in semen, and in other secretions. Carriers of serum hepatitis may not have any symptoms, and thus have no idea of the danger they pose to others. Hepatitis B vaccine is now available for people who are at particularly high risk of exposure to this virus. In some countries, such as China, the new vaccine is being offered routinely to children born to mothers who show evidence of previous infection.

Urinary Tract Infections

Cystitis, an infection that results in an inflammation of the membrane lining the bladder, is a common problem among teenage girls. The symptoms include frequent urination, which may cause pain or a burning sensation, and urgency, especially at night. The urine may be cloudy, bloody, or foul-smelling. Frequent sexual intercourse, during which the urethra and walls of the bladder can be inadvertently bruised, may play a part in the problem but recurrent cystitis is also seen in the absence of intercourse. Cystitis is usually treated by antibiotics and by drinking large quantities of liquids, which helps to flush out the bladder, and is important in prevention as well. It is important to have a urine culture done so that the specific bacterium responsible for the infection can be identified and an appropriate antibiotic prescribed.

In teenage boys, infections are usually of the

lower urinary tract and are frequently caused by venereally transmitted organisms, such as Chlamydia.

Venereal Diseases

Teenage girls appear to be at a special risk for developing complications of venereal disease. The absence of some hormones such as progesterone during puberty may affect the transmission of organisms like gonococci and Chlamydia and thus local infection may more likely spread from the initial entry site to the uterus and Fallopian tubes.

In adolescents, as in older women, venereal disease may be asymptomatic for days, weeks, or months, during which time it may be transmitted to sexual partners. A sexually active teenage girl should have regular tests and examinations for the common venereal diseases.

Nonspecific urethritis is not a new venereal disease, but one that is being recognized increasingly in males of all ages. A number of organisms may cause the problem, among them Chlamydia, which is readily treatable with oral tetracycline. Any burning on urination or drip from the penis should receive medical attention.

When any venereal disease is diagnosed, it is important that all sexual partners be identified and treated. To teenagers in particular, identifying partners may be considered "snitching," but they must realize that the only hope of preventing complications in themselves and their partners and bringing these epidemic diseases under control is to treat all known cases.

Thyroid Problems

Both hyper- and hypothyroidism are common in adolescence. Changes in weight and menstrual irregularities are the most usual symptoms, with hyperthyroidism generally leading to weight loss and amenorrhea (absence of menstruation), and hypothyroidism to weight gain and menorrhagia (profuse menstrual flow).

Normal teenagers sometimes experience a transient enlargement of the thyroid gland. This, and any other swelling in the neck, should be brought to a doctor's attention.

Changes in Visual Acuity

As the body undergoes the growth spurt, the eye and its components also change in shape. These changes affect visual acuity, necessitating corrective lenses or a change in the prescription lenses worn during childhood. The development or worsening of myopia (nearsightedness) is a common problem.

Hearing Loss

High-frequency hearing loss (the inability to hear in the range of 4,000 herz) is a recently documented problem among adolescents. The loss may be permanent and may be due to chronic exposure to loudly amplified music. If compounded by exposure to environmental noise—subway trains, jackhammers, and heavy machinery, for example), these minimal losses can contribute to moderate or profound hearing loss in adulthood.

Chronic Handicapping Conditions

Many of the chronic handicapping conditions of childhood persist into adolescence. Moreover, many of the diseases that begin in adolescence become chronic in adulthood.

If treating a chronic handicapping condition means frequent doctor appointments, appliances, medication, or hospitalization, the treatment may be viewed as worse than the condition or disease. A teenager who feels isolated from peers by medical treatment is likely to choose to suffer long-term consequences rather than to agree to the short-term disruption.

It is important to remember that all teenagers, whether they are handicapped or not, must negotiate the same psychological tasks. The needs of an impaired adolescent for independence from family, and for peer group association, are the same as those of a nonimpaired contemporary. Too often, parents and doctors forget that these teenagers need the same social outlets and experiences as other adolescents.

Sports Injuries

Each year, during the short high school football season, there are an estimated 1 million injuries. Such a rate of disability and impairment—some of it temporary but some, unfortunately, permanent—would never be tolerated in an adult workplace. Football is not alone; other competitive sports that carry a high risk of severe injury include wrestling (especially if radical weight-change programs are adhered to) and soccer, or any contact sport where youngsters of vastly different weights, stages of development, and strengths play together.

There are many things that parents can do to minimize the risk of injury. A pretraining physical examination should be given to all teenage athletes, of both sexes, regardless of the sport in which they participate. This examination is necessary to detect any specific orthopedic problems or growth considerations that might make a specific sport inadvisable. Dysfunction or absence of one of a paired organ (for example, eye, kidney, testicles) should be grounds for limiting contact sports that might injure the remaining organ. Second, proper protective clothing should be provided, and every effort made to see that it is used. Third, youngsters of varying levels of development should not be permitted to engage in contact sports together. Finally, parents should examine their own attitudes to determine whether parental pressures to perform and excel are behind a youngster's participation in competitive sports.

NUTRITION AND ASSOCIATED PROBLEMS

TEENAGERS REQUIRE enormous numbers of calories for growth, as well as for daily activity. (See tables 13.1 and 13.2.) They also require an increased intake of iron, calcium, and phosphorus, considerably more per kilogram of body weight than in childhood or the adult years. Adolescence, then, is a time when good nutrition is of great importance. It is also a time when skipped meals, indiscriminate consumption of "junk food" (not necessarily synonymous with "fast food"), and food faddism are common. Misunderstandings about "natural foods" and food supplements often result in wasted time and money, as parents and teenagers battle over what can or cannot be considered healthy or reasonable in the diet.

Calories in the teenage diet should break down approximately like this: 58 percent from carbohydrates, 12 percent from protein, and 30 percent from fat (of the fats, only 10 percent should be saturated fats). The form of the carbohydrates—whether simple or complex—is not important calorically or nutritionally, although those carbohydrates that contribute to dental cavities should be avoided. The caloric intake should be spread over the day, rather than concentrated in one meal, to avoid problems of lightheadedness and weakness after exertion.

Excessive salt should be avoided, as this may contribute to high blood pressure in susceptible individuals. Vitamins, minerals, trace elements, and

Table 13.1 CALORIC EQUIVALENTS OF ACTIVITIES

Activity	Approximate energy spent
Sleeping, sitting, watching TV	Less than 1 cal/min
Strolling 1–2 mph	2–4 cal/min or 120–140 cal/hr
Bowling, walking 3 mph, cycling 6 mph	4–5 cal/min or 240–300 cal/hr
Cycling 8 mph, table tennis, badminton, volleyball, tennis (doubles), many calisthenics, and ballet exercises	5–6 cal/min or 300–360 cal/hr
Walking 4–5 mph, cycling 10–12 mph, ice or roller skating, tennis (singles), waterskiing, light basketball	6–8 cal/min or 360–400 cal/hr
Jogging 5 mph, downhill skiing, vigorous basketball, paddleball	8–10 cal/min or 400–600 cal/hr
Cross-country skiing, cycling 13 mph, squash, handball, running 6 mph	10–11 cal/min or 600–660 cal/hr

Table 13.2 CALORIE ALLOWANCES BASED ON THE 1980 RECOMMENDED DIETARY ALLOWANCES FOR ADOLESCENTS [a]

Sex	Age (years)	Median body weight (kg)	Median energy allowance (kcal/day)	Range of kcal/day	Estimated kcal/kg body weight
Male	11–14	45	2,700	2,000–3,700	60
	15–18	66	2,800	2,100–3,900	42
Female	11–14	46	2,200	1,500–3,000	48
	15–18	55	2,100	1,200–3,000	38

[a] Food and Nutrition Board, National Academy of Sciences, National Research Council. *Recommended Dietary Allowances*, 9th edition, 1980. Reprinted by permission of Elsevier Science Publishing Co., Inc., from Assessment and Conservative Management of the Overfat Adolescent, by Carruth, B. and Iszler, J. in *Journal of Adolescent Health Care*, Vol. 1 pp. 289–299. Copyright 1981 by The Society for Adolescent Medicine.

fiber are normally present in adequate quantities in an average well-balanced diet (the possible exceptions are iron and calcium) and under normal circumstances there should be no need for an adolescent to take vitamins or mineral supplements.

Parents are often concerned about adolescents' patronage of fast food restaurants. If they are consumed as part of a balanced diet (58 percent carbohydrates, 12 percent proteins, 30 percent fat), there is nothing intrinsically wrong with fast food items, except that certain combinations, if eaten exclusively, provide inadequate amounts of vitamin A or vitamin C. The allowance for these vitamins will generally be met through foods consumed at other meals in the course of the day.

Weight

The normal range of weight for height in adolescence is a very wide one and only extremely high or low weight calls for medical attention.

In early puberty there is a redistribution of fat in both boys and girls. Fat accumulates on the buttocks and around the abdomen. This is the first in a series of bodily changes that culminate in the growth spurt and is an essential step in proper growth. Although the young adolescent commonly views this new plumpness as a sign of becoming overweight, any attempt at dieting at this stage should be discouraged.

Obesity

Obesity in adolescence, as at any age, is seldom the result of an endocrinological imbalance. Rather, it stems from a pattern, usually established in childhood, of eating too much, or exercising too little, or both.

The treatment of obesity in adolescence is complicated by the fact that calories are required for growth—in the obese adolescent as in a youngster of normal weight. The guidance of a doctor or nutritionist is advisable for any weight-reduction plan during the growth years.

The obese teenager should follow a plan that combines exercise with diet and is geared to maintaining body tone at the same time that weight is *gradually* reduced. The balance of protein, carbohydrate, and fat that is required for growth should be maintained. Rather than cutting down drastically on any one food category, the goal should simply be to eat less of everything, while maintaining an active lifestyle. Exercise programs are an excellent way to modify weight. They should include both stretching and strengthening movements, as well as sustained exercise performed at a level high enough to burn off excess calories. (See table 13.1 for caloric equivalents of activities.)

Self-help groups can be useful, in conjunction with a medically approved regimen for weight loss. If possible, an adolescent should join a group of others of the same age since the concerns of overweight teenagers—social acceptance and patterns of eating, for example—differ from those of adults and are best discussed with peers.

Anorexia Nervosa

Anorexia nervosa and other forms of eating disorders are a growing problem, in reality as well as in awareness. Although anorexia affects primarily females, it is now known to affect some adolescent boys.

Among the symptoms of anorexia nervosa are extreme weight loss (approximately 25 percent of the preillness or ideal weight may be lost), a high level of physical activity (ballet dancing and running are among the activities favored), and the development of ritualistic eating and behavior patterns. The ritualism most commonly centers on food—the way it is prepared, arranged, and eaten; its type; and its amount. Body image distortion is common: In the face of a 25 percent weight loss, a youngster will continue to maintain that she is fat and when asked to sketch her diameter with her hands, will greatly overestimate. Menstrual irregularities may follow the weight loss and commonly outlast it, continuing into the twenties and even thirties. Among the serious complications of this condition are electrolyte imbalance (particularly a low level of potassium), cardiac arrhythmias and, when there is frequent self-induced vomiting, severe tooth erosion. If allowed to persist, anorexia nervosa can lead to death; with proper attention and intervention the mortality rate has been lowered to 5 percent.

If weight loss is profound and long-lasting, the body's compensatory mechanisms begin to wear down. Temporary muscle weakness can become permanent, even extending to the heart muscle. The gastrointestinal tract may show signs of chronic irritability and sensitivity, especially if purgatives were used for long periods of time. Bloating, mucus in the stool, flatulence, and cramps can last for years after prolonged low weight, even in the absence of obvious nutritional deficits.

When weight loss or low weight become life-threatening, or seem likely to leave the individual permanently impaired, hospitalization is necessary and supervised feeding, or tube or intravenous feeding, may be required.

Some doctors believe that a disturbance in the

hypothalamus gland triggers some of the weight loss and the menstrual irregularities, and may in fact be responsible for many of the behavioral problems. However, most feel that anorexia is the result of a combination of circumstances: a vulnerable youngster (one who has unreasonably high expectations of herself), a particular type of family (upwardly mobile, often of the middle or upper class, with high expectations and standards), and adolescence itself. The usual onset of anorexia is around the time of puberty; in rare cases, it may begin at any time up to the early twenties.

Individual psychotherapy in conjunction with family therapy is successful in treating many cases of anorexia nervosa. Self-help groups for anorexics can also be very helpful, when combined with knowledgeable medical assistance. With increased medical knowledge of anorexia, more and more patients are being treated as outpatients and are able to resume functional lives.

Bulimia

Bulimia—"an oxlike appetite"—is a problem that is increasingly being recognized by health professionals. The syndrome involves eating enormous amounts of food (binge eating) and purging or inducing vomiting shortly thereafter. Typically, the bulimic is an adolescent or college-aged woman.

Bulimics are usually in the normal weight range, but maintain that they use purging for fear of becoming obese or to relieve bloated feelings. The binging–purging may occur as rarely as once a month, or as often as several times a day. In the latter case, the victim's daily life can be dominated by the necessity to find a place to binge and purge in privacy. Electrolyte imbalance is a common complication; if there is repeated vomiting, exposure to stomach acids may completely erode the teeth, leaving nothing but small stubs. Occasionally, the parotid glands or the whole face appear swollen. Commonly, the symptoms of bulimia will be found in conjunction with those of anorexia.

The true frequency of this condition is unknown, since considerable shame surrounds it and victims are reluctant to bring the problem to medical attention, or to let their families or roommates know of it. However, some surveys of college students suggest that up to 20 percent of college-aged women suffer from bulimia to some extent. Psychotherapeutic techniques similar to those found effective for anorexia nervosa are currently being used to treat this condition.

DRUGS AND SUBSTANCE ABUSE

TEENAGERS HAVE conflicting reputations about drugs. On the one hand, they are accused of taking drugs that have not been prescribed for them, and on the other, of not taking drugs that have been prescribed.

Noncompliance

Although teenagers are commonly charged with noncompliance (failure to take prescribed medication as prescribed or at all), their compliance rate is about the same as that of adults. Few people of any age who are asked to take medication for any length of time actually do so; most discontinue or take the medicine irregularly after 3 months.

With adolescents, part of the noncompliance problem stems from the difficulty of arriving at the proper dosage of medication. Whereas drug dosages have been calculated accurately both for small children and for adult men and women, the same is not the case for adolescents. In calculating drug dosages for teenagers it is necessary to look not only at weight (the basis for dosage in children) but also at sex and the degree of physical development. For example, a drug that is fat-soluble may have a longer and more pronounced action in a 14-year-old girl with adult female fat distribution than it will in a less-developed girl or a boy of the same weight. Until the correct dosage is arrived at, a teenager may suffer a worsening of the condition due to undermedication, or the signs of toxicity from too high a level of a drug.

For many teenagers—those with chronic diseases such as asthma, for example—compliance with drug therapy is essential. There are several ways in which adolescents can be encouraged to take medication regularly and as directed. First, the adolescent should understand what the medication is for, the dosage, the possible side effects, and the consequences of not taking the medication as prescribed. This information should be given directly to the patient, as well as to the parent. Second, teenagers should be responsible for taking their own medication, or at the very least, this issue should be discussed between parent and child. In rare circumstances it can be dangerous to have control of medication become part of the teenage dependence/ independence struggle that commonly takes place at this time. Teenagers may find it helpful to keep track of signs, symptoms, and use of medication in a journal if they are at a stage when dose is changing or the disease or problem for which they are taking the medicine is poorly controlled.

Substance Abuse

Experimentation with drugs, as with sex, seems to be a normal part of adolescence in the United States today. Sixty percent of teenagers have tried marijuana at least once, 71 percent have had at least one drink, and nearly all (93 percent) have smoked cigarettes on at least one occasion. A distinction must be made, however, between the daily, prolonged, or heavy use of drugs on one hand, and occasional use on the other.

The age at which both occasional and heavy use of drugs begins is dropping. Marijuana, alcohol, and tobacco are the substances most used, but the list is a long one, including many types of opiates, stimulants, and depressants. Currently, cocaine is becoming a more favored drug.

A number of factors are known to be statistically related to drug use. In one large survey of teenagers enrolled in school, those high school students who had above-average drug habits also had trouble in adapting to the school environment. Their academic performance is poor and they have a high rate of truancy and dropping out. Those who spend many evenings out for recreation, have heavy time commitments to a job, or who have relatively high incomes are also likely—statistically—to be higher-than-average drug users.

Excessive drug dependence may indicate a growing depression or some other serious emotional disturbance. If dependence is accompanied by social withdrawal or isolation, falling grades, or a change in activity level that persists for more than a few weeks, parents should seek the advice of a school counselor, physician, or other professional skilled in handling adolescent problems.

The behavior engaged in while intoxicated or "high" on alcohol and other drugs may be even more dangerous than the immediate effects of drug use on the body. Drunk driving is the leading cause of death among young people in this country, despite the growing number of states that have increased the legal drinking age.

Recently, both health professionals and the general public have been made aware that some drugs, especially cocaine that is "free-based" or smoked, can be almost immediately lethal. This fact was forcefully impressed upon the public with the highly publicized cocaine-related deaths of two young professional athletes in the summer of 1986.

Of course, the best protection against drug abuse is to not use these substances. This is the basis of the Just Say No campaign. Enlisting youngsters to promote anti-drug efforts directed at their peers appears to be a more successful strategy than having adults attempt to enforce drug bans. Still, there are practical steps that parents can take to minimize dangers of alcohol or drug experimentation. For example, on occasions when it seems likely that young people may be using alcohol, parents can take action to make sure that no one who consumes alcohol will drive afterward. This may entail designating an abstainer as the driver or hiring a car service. They also can provide nonalcoholic beverages for parties and can make sure that young people know about local laws regarding substance use and possession. Parents also can do all that is possible to assure that there are adequate recreational facilities in the community where young people can gather and socialize. In addition, parents should be aware how greatly their own patterns of drug use influence their youngsters' views on the subject.

A new "epidemic" that seems likely to occur in the 1980s is the use of prescribed and nonprescribed medication by teenage athletes in an attempt to improve performance. Interviews with players in the National Football League during the mid-1970s revealed that more than half used amphetamines before and during a game. Further, there have been increasing reports of the use of androgens, such as testosterone, by both male and female athletes. As with other types of drugs, use by young adults is likely to be followed by increasing use by adolescents. There is little evidence that these drugs dramatically improve performance, but their side effects are sometimes very dangerous, and include changes in blood pressure, blood volume, body hair, salt balance, and (although rare) benign and malignant liver tumors.

LEADING CAUSES OF DEATH IN ADOLESCENCE

THE TEENAGE YEARS are among the healthiest of the life span. Yet unfortunately, while the mortality rate for all other groups in the population shows a steady decline, that for adolescents is on the increase. The leading causes of death in adolescence are not illnesses, but rather environmental and behavioral factors. Each year, approximately 18,000 teenagers die as the result of accidents (most of them automobile accidents), about 5,600 from homicide, and about 5,000 from suicide. The rate for suicide has more than tripled during the last decade in the United States, as in other Western industrialized countries. It is probably in fact higher than this "official" figure, since many suicides are not reported as such.

Depression and Suicide

Until recently, doctors did not believe that depression afflicted children and adolescents. This view has changed; it is now clear that, although some of the manifestations of depression differ in children and adolescents, no age is immune.

It is important for both parents and adolescents to differentiate between depression that is a transient mood change (a feeling of sadness and despair that is a normal response to a difficult life situation) and true depression. The majority of teenagers experience depression as a mood-swing, lasting several hours to several days. During these times, a parent can try to "take the pulse" of a teenager by checking on the depth of despair, the duration and effects of the youngster's mood, and any mounting concerns. Gentle reassurance about the family's support, interest, and concern are appreciated, and necessary, during such times.

The signs of true depression may include complaints of insomnia, headache, stomachache, weakness, and dizziness; acting-out behavior; feelings of sinfulness, worthlessness, hopelessness; inability to concentrate; isolation from family and friends; school failure or school avoidance; and sudden or heavy use of drugs or alcohol. The adolescent's level of development and maturity will affect how the condition is expressed. For example, in order to experience hopelessness fully, it is necessary to have a conceptualization of the future. But it is frequently not until midadolescence that the changeover from concrete to abstract thought processes occurs, which permits a time sense that includes past, present, and future. Thus, young teenagers will not express true hopelessness about the future until they are able to think about the abstraction of a time beyond the moment.

Suicide is the most feared potential outcome of severe depression. Suicidal thoughts and behavior may be associated with other psychiatric disturbances, with poor impulse control, or with attempts to manipulate what appears to be an intolerable situation or environment, but depression is one of the major triggers. There may be some triggering event —the real or perceived loss of a significant person, failure at school or in athletics, an unwanted pregnancy, or the fear of punishment—that, in retrospect, is seen to be the "cause" of the suicide; equally, there may be no such event. For each youngster who commits suicide, there are an estimated 50 to 200 who attempt it. Those who survive may be affected psychologically and physically, and are likely to make additional attempts or to succeed at suicide in the future. It is believed that females outnumber males in suicide attempts, but that males more commonly complete the act, perhaps because they use more violent methods—guns or knives or hanging, rather than pill ingestion.

Warning signs that an adolescent is at risk of suicide include, in addition to the physical and emotional symptoms of depression, preoccupation with death, suicidal thoughts and threats, and making plans suggestive of imminent death—giving away possessions, for example. *All* threats should be taken seriously, since there is no way of determining the actual risk involved. Parents should not be afraid to convey to a teenager their impression that he or she is unhappy or distraught. Often this is helpful to a youngster—and certainly it never "causes" a suicide. Parents should not, however, attempt to deal with a severely depressed adolescent's problems themselves, but should make every attempt to see that the youngster gets professional evaluation. This may take the form of individual psychotherapy or family therapy, very rarely including drug therapy with antidepressant medication.

SCHOOL PROBLEMS

IN ADOLESCENCE, "school problems" fall into two general categories: school avoidance or truancy and learning difficulties, or similar problems occurring within the school setting itself.

A teenager who is consistently truant is, statistically, likely to have a history of "being in trouble" in general. In some cases, an educational plan with emphasis on behavioral management can be worked out among the family, the school, and medical personnel. In others, family or individual psychotherapy proves effective, depending on the nature of the underlying problem. Bear in mind, however, that while completing school has traditionally been viewed as a stepping stone to the workplace, the situation has now changed. In times when job opportunities are limited—for the educated and the uneducated alike—and when teachers themselves are leaving the profession for work in industry, it is not surprising that many adolescents are disillusioned about the value of schooling.

Within school, undetected hearing loss or loss of visual acuity may contribute to academic underachievement. In addition, some specific problems—attention disorders and hyperactivity, for example—may persist from childhood into adolescence. Such problems sometimes can be helped with medication, but this requires a thorough evaluation by a team skilled in diagnosing and treating such disorders.

Out-of-Control Behavior

Whether or not an adolescent's behavior is out of control depends on who is making the definition—the parents, the school authorities, or the youngster himself. Is such behavior actually a problem for the youngster, or is it a problem for others? Behavior that clearly puts a young person or someone else at risk of serious injury, however, obviously requires immediate intervention.

Much behavior that is seemingly out of control is an exaggerated expression of the universal adolescent striving for autonomy—the desire of youngsters to think and act according to their own standards and beliefs. Frequently, adolescents view autonomy as being "all or nothing." A specific instance of conflict with parents or authorities will be blown up out of all proportion and the whole question of ultimate independence seems to be at stake. In such a situation, extreme ("out-of-control") behavior is more than likely to occur.

How much expressed anger is acceptable to a given family, school, or community may be a factor in defining behavior as out-of-control. Like small children, adolescents are very direct in their expressions of hostility, but such directness may be considered inexcusable in their age group. Similar judgments may be passed on expressions of frustration and depression, and on the risk-taking behaviors that are typical of adolescence.

Problem or negative behavior may also be a reaction to undue pressure from parents to achieve scholastically, athletically, or socially. Feelings of inadequacy or inability to achieve what is expected may be expressed as rebellious rejection of parental standards and expectations. Parents should recognize that there may be a considerable mismatch between their expectations of an adolescent and the youngster's actual interests and talents.

Adolescents do not, in general, enjoy being "out of control." They know when they have exceeded limits and usually learn from the experience. For their part, parents should use discrimination in limit-setting, choosing a few areas of vital importance rather than applying equally stringent rules to situations of varying degrees of seriousness. When adolescents understand which areas are of real importance to parents, *and vice versa*, the setting of limits can be the subject of a true negotiation.

ADOLESCENT MEDICAL CARE AND THE LAW

THERE ARE TWO GENERAL legal guidelines for providing health care to a minor (in most states, a person under the age of 18) without parental consent. First, if the situation is considered a medical emergency and the time spent in obtaining parental consent would cause dangerous physical deterioration, or cause the teenager to flee from needed care, it is legal to provide services. Second, medical care can be provided without parental consent to those adolescents who are considered to be legally emancipated—that is to say, those who are living away from home, or who are supporting themselves or serving in the armed services, or who are married or have borne a child. In addition, in all 50 states teenagers of any age can legally be tested and treated for venereal disease without their parents' knowledge or involvement.

Recent federal guidelines mandating parental notification (but not consent) for prescribed contraceptives have been overturned by the courts. Unresolved are questions about abortion—a teenager's right to have a first-trimester abortion without her parents' knowledge and consent, and parents' right to insist that their daughter have an abortion against her wishes. Most federal rulings support the teenager's right to treatment without parental consent or notification, but many state and local jurisdictions are enacting more restrictive guidelines, substituting a court-appointed parent "substitute" if a parent is not involved.

A concept currently emerging in the medical care of minors is that of the "mature minor." Essentially this means that the doctor or other health-care professional should be the one to determine whether a minor is sufficiently mature to be treated without the parents being informed. The judgment of maturity, under this legal concept, would be made according to such factors as the adolescent's understanding of the nature and consequences of the treatment, whether or not the teenager initiated the medical appointment, and qualities of responsibility and initiative in general. Unfortunately, the majority of doctors and most hospitals still tend to be more restrictive in providing health care to adolescents than the law in fact requires.

SUGGESTED READING

For Pre- and Early Adolescents

Boys and Sex and *Girls and Sex* (revised), by Wardell B. Pomeroy. Delacorte Press, NY, 1981.

Facts About Sex for Today's Youth (revised), by Sol Gordon. Ed-U Press, Fayetteville, NY, 1981.

Facts About VD for Today's Youth (revised), by Sol Gordon. Ed-U Press, Fayetteville, NY, 1979.

Love and Sex and Growing Up, by Corrine B. Johnson and Eric W. Johnson. Bantam Books, Inc., New York, NY, 1974.

Love and Sex in Plain Language (revised), by Eric W. Johnson. Bantam Books, Inc., New York, NY, 1974.

Teensex? It's Okay to Say No Way. Planned Parenthood Federation of America, Inc., New York, NY, 1981.

Threshold: A Doctor Gives Straightforward Answers to Teenagers' Most Often Asked Questions About Sex, by Thomas Mintz and Lorelie Mintz. Walker and Company, New York, NY, 1978.

What Teens Want to Know but Don't Know How to Ask. Planned Parenthood Federation of America, Inc., New York, NY, 1981.

"What's Happening to Me?" by Peter Mayle. Lyle Stuart, Inc., Secaucus, NJ, 1975.

For Older Adolescents

Commonsense Sex: A Basis for Discussion and Reappraisal, by Ronald M. Mazur. Beacon Press, Inc., New York, NY, 1973.

Conception, Birth and Contraception: A Visual Presentation (second edition), by Robert J. Demarest and John J. Sciarra. McGraw-Hill Book Company, New York, NY, 1976.

The Facts of Love: Living, Loving and Growing Up, by Alex Comfort and Jane Comfort. Crown Publishers, Inc., New York, NY, 1979.

Growing Up with Sex: A Guide for the Early Teens, by Richard Hettlinger. Seabury Press, Inc., New York, NY, 1980.

Learning About Sex: The Contemporary Guide for Young Adults, by Gary Kelly. Barron's Educational Series, Inc., Woodbury, NY, 1977.

For Parents

The Flight of the Stork, by Anne C. Bernstein. Delacorte Press, New York, NY, 1978.

How to Talk to Your Teenagers About Something That's Not Easy to Talk About. Planned Parenthood Federation of America, Inc., New York, NY, 1982.

How to Tell Your Child About Sex (#149); *Sex Education: The Parents' Role* (#549); *Talking to Preteenagers About Sex* (#476). Public Affairs Committee, Inc., New York, NY.

Sex Education at Home: A Guide for Parents. Parenthood Center of Syracuse, Inc., Syracuse, NY, 1974.

Your Child and Sex: A Guide for Parents, by Wardell B. Pomeroy. Delacorte Press, New York, NY, 1976.

General

Abortion to Zoophilia: A Sourcebook of Sexual Facts, by Anne Mandetta and Patricia Gustaveson. Carolina Population Center, Chapel Hill, NC, 1975.

The Family Book About Sexuality, by Mary S. Calderone and Eric W. Johnson. Harper & Row Publishers, Inc., New York, NY, 1981.

Sex Facts. Planned Parenthood Center of Syracuse, Inc., Syracuse, NY, 1977.

Sex Talk, by Myron Brenton. Stein & Day, Briarcliff Manor, NY, 1977.

Straight Talk About Love and Sex for Teenagers, by Jane Burgess-Kohn. Beacon Press, Inc., Boston, MA, 1979.

14 The Middle Years and Aging

Joseph G. Sweeting, M.D.

INTRODUCTION

THE WESTERN MIND, particularly the American mind, is fond of order. Ambiguity and uncertainty are not well tolerated. Perhaps this is why Americans dislike the subject of aging—since except for the certainty that aging begins at conception and ends at death, there are few absolutes.

When does middle age begin? Who is old? It all depends. Popular wisdom calls 40 the beginning of the middle years and the government has decreed that 65 is the age of retirement or the beginning of old age. But what of today's "young couple" who are enrolling their first child in kindergarten as they turn 40? Who would think to call them "middle aged"? And who (except for the very young) would describe vigorous, creative men or women at the peak of productivity as "old," although their calendar years might number 70 or 75?

From the medical point of view, 55 might be a better, though still arbitrary, number for the beginning of the middle years. This is close to the point when people begin to notice physical changes about which they seek medical advice. The age-specific problems that bring many people to geriatric specialists begin to manifest themselves by age 75.

Part of the difficulty of definition may lie in changing lifestyles and new perceptions of what is appropriate to certain age groups. Perhaps our language and its emotional content have not caught up with our way of life.

In the not-too-distant-past, most people married and had children in their late teens and early twenties, watched the third generation appear in their forties, and often died before reaching what we think of today as old age. In 1900, only 4 percent of the population was over 65. Then along came improvements in sanitation and diet, discovery of antibiotics, and other medical advances that lengthened life-expectancy and gave us a much larger, healthier group of older people (about 12 percent of the population in 1980).

At the same time, the postwar baby boom created an unprecedented number of youth in the 1960s, and suddenly there was a new age distribution in the population. Between 1960 and 1970 there was a 48 percent increase in the number of people aged 15 to 24. Since 1970, the percentage of population for all ages over 17 has increased, while the percentage for those under 17 has decreased. This portends a steady rise in the median age (16.7 in 1830; 28 in 1970; 30 in 1980) and in the percentage of population over 40 (36.3 percent in 1970; 38.2 percent in 1980).

The relatively neutral words associated with maturity and advanced age took on a negative emotional overlay in the late 1960s and the 1970s, in part because the media explosion that paralleled the youth boom deluged the public with advertising directed at the largest market—the young. Anyone who could not be described as young or youthful and attractive was by inference old or getting old and unattractive, and "middle-aged" and "old" were used pejoratively. Now that these same people, still a major target of advertisers, are getting older, this unfortunate image may change.

No matter how the perception of age may be changed in the popular mind, chief among the problems of defining the middle years and old age is that aging is a highly individual process. It doesn't happen to any two people in exactly the same way at exactly the same rate from any point of view—biological, psychological, sociological, or spiritual.

Even the experts—physicians, psychologists, physical therapists—have trouble guessing ages and often miss by 10 to 15 years. They look for clues such as skin quality, facial expression, gestures, locomotion, body contours, and voice, but these clues are affected by many factors other than age. General health, heredity, occupation, environment, mood, fatigue, weight, and a host of other things can add or subtract years from appearance. Even within the individual, different body systems may age at vastly different rates so that one system may show fewer signs of age than another.

Subjectively, many people claim that they feel the same inside no matter what their age. Of course, prolonged ill-health, grinding poverty, enforced retirement, and similar misfortunes may precipitate feelings of being old, but for those who enjoy reasonably good health and who remain active and productive, the inner sense of youth remains constant.

Constant, too, is the interest in and search for a way to lengthen life. In one respect this has been accomplished. More people are living longer; life-expectancy continues to rise. But life span, the maximum number of years people might expect to live under the best of circumstances, has remained about the same throughout recorded history. People just don't live much past 100, no matter what. Even in those remote societies where longevity is noteworthy and widespread, 110 seems to be about the limit.

Why should this be so? If it is possible to have greater numbers of people living productively into their eighties and nineties, why is it not possible to extend life indefinitely? If accident and disease are avoided, why must the body nevertheless deteriorate? Is growing old part of a natural cycle, or is it the ultimate disease, capable of being understood and subject to cure? Right now, no one can say for sure, but there are several theories of aging, each of which may provide a piece to the puzzle of why we grow old.

THEORIES OF AGING

EVERY SPECIES has a definite life span. A mouse lives about 3½ years; a horse, about 30; and a chimpanzee about 60. The maximum human life span appears to be about 110 years, though the verified record is 113 years. Why species have a set number of years continues to baffle gerontologists, but as they have sought the reason, they have unveiled much about the process of aging.

For instance, one of the prevalent theories of aging is that our cells are increasingly damaged, the older we get, by what are called free radicals, a by-product of oxygen metabolism. Though oxygen is essential to life for the great majority of species, its breakdown as it passes through cells results in substances that attack and destroy membranes. The more this happens, the less efficiently cells function. One result is the accumulation of a substance called lipofuscin in tissues, particularly in the brain—one theoretical cause of senility. Liver spots, brown splotches often found on the skin of elderly people, are the most obvious example of the accumulation of lipofuscin.

Though the cells of all animals are damaged by free radicals, some species have a greater amount of substances, dubbed free radical scavengers by gerontologists, to combat the bad effects of free radicals than do other species. One of these substances is called superoxide dismutase. Humans, it turns out, manufacture about twice as much superoxide dismutase as do chimpanzees, our closest relatives. Generally, the longer-lived species manufacture free radical scavengers in greater amounts than do shorter-lived species. Other free radical scavengers are thought to be vitamin E, vitamin C, and selenium, though this has not been proven. Indeed, that free radicals have an influence on longevity and life span is just one theory of aging among many.

Generally, aging theories fall into two camps. One postulates that aging is under the influences of the cells. The other theorizes that there is an aging clock somewhere in our brains, probably in the hypothalamus. How the clock works remains a mystery, but it is thought to be closely tied to hormonal secretion.

The cellular theory of aging came into being in the 1950s with the work of Leonard Hayflick, a well-known gerontologist at the University of Florida. Hayflick discovered that certain cells seem to have limited life spans. Experimenting with cells from a human fetus, he noticed that a population will double approximately 50 times before dying out. Before this point was reached, though, cell division became very erratic and many mutations showed up. What was most tantalizing about the research was that the limit of 50 doublings appeared to be programmed into the cells. One of the experiments involved freezing a cell population after it had doubled 20 times and then thawing it out. After thawing, the cells divided about 30 more times, for a total of 50, before dying.

One of the reasons that the cells stopped dividing was that their hereditary material ceased being able to make perfect copies of itself. One of the keys to successful growth and reproduction is that DNA be able to duplicate itself. If it cannot do this, mutations appear. One of the results of these mutations is the development of cancerous cells. An offshoot of the cellular theory of aging is that the older a cell population grows, the more mistakes its DNA makes and the less able it is to repair the damage. Just as the longer living species have more free radical scavengers than do shorter living ones, longer living species appear to have a greater ability to repair errors in their cells' DNA than do shorter living ones.

The hypothalamus, a pea-sized structure in the middle of the brain, controls to a large extent the secretion of a number of hormones and neurotransmitters, the brain's chemical messengers. It is the hypothalamus that releases the hormones that result in such dramatic events as puberty, ovulation, menstruation, and menopause. Gerontologists have noted that the sudden death of Pacific salmon shortly after spawning is precipitated by a huge release of hormones. The same thing happens with the octopus.

Hormonal release in humans, though to a much less dramatic extent, may be responsible for the gradual deterioration and slowdown that marks the aging process, according to the theory of aging that holds that our bodies are programmed to age. The hormonal release results in an imbalance that affects our immune system, metabolism, and reproductive ability, among other things. At the same time, neurotransmitters decrease with age, leading to such conditions as Parkinson's disease or perhaps to senility.

Overriding all the theories of aging, of course, is the hereditary factor, the information that is built into our genes that says that we as humans have the capacity to live 110 years, whereas a mouse has the capacity to live only 3½ years. Gerontologists cannot hope to, nor do they strive to, increase those limits. But they do hope to learn enough about the aging process to enable us to live out our genetically endowed life span to the fullest possible.

NORMAL EFFECTS OF AGING

GIVEN WHAT IS KNOWN at present, if accidents and disease could be completely avoided and stress kept to a minimum, the average well-nourished person would show superficial signs of aging in the forties, would begin to notice slightly reduced organ function in the mid-seventies, and would die sometime between 90 and 100. Indeed, about 15 percent of the population who live to age 75 have a life pattern very similar to this.

The adage "you are as young as you feel" or the class-reunion compliment "you haven't changed a bit" are perhaps reasonable descriptions from a psychological point of view. They point to the importance of attitude in maintaining vitality. However, there are specific biological changes that take place in a more or less predictable fashion which are related to aging and happen independently of disease or other negative influences. Look at the physical differences in the average man or woman at 3 stages of life.

There are functional changes that cannot be seen and the effects of which may hardly be noticed by the individual. The decline in organ function may be hastened by disease or retarded by observing a healthful lifestyle, but it occurs, nonetheless. This decline does not seriously affect the ability to lead a normal life, rather it decreases the ability to handle the stress of insults to the body whether caused by accident or disease.

In most cases, organ function tends to decrease gradually after maturity. However, the more complex processes that require the integrated activity of several systems show a much higher rate of decline than do functions accomplished by a single organ system. This means that in part, aging is a breakdown or diminution in effectiveness of the many regulatory mechanisms, for it is these mechanisms that trigger the necessary activity to counteract stress.

For example, the speed of nerve conduction changes by only about 15 percent between ages 30 and 90, whereas maximum breathing capacity, which involves coordination between the muscular and nervous systems, decreases by about 60 percent between the ages of 30 and 80. Likewise, while muscle strength may decline very little with age, coordination of muscle groups shows significant change. (Additional information about each of the following changes can be found in the corresponding chapters.)

Vision

Frequently the first change in function to be noticed is the onset of farsightedness (presbyopia). Along with this decrease in acuity comes a need for more light in order to see well, a longer time of adjustment when moving from light to dark, and a decrease in visual fields. These changes occur because with age the eye becomes less elastic and, therefore, less able to change its focusing characteristics. Sooner or later all people experience these changes to some degree.

For a considerable number of people, advanced age will also bring cataracts and chronic glaucoma. Both of these conditions can and do occur as congenital conditions or, in rare cases, from other causes in early life. However, they are far more common in middle and late years—glaucoma after age 35 and cataracts after age 40.

Loss of vision is one of people's greatest fears, yet few are well informed about eye diseases and even fewer have regular examinations. It is important to seek medical attention as soon as possible in the presence of any change in vision, however minor it may seem. With eyesight, haste may be the only way to prevent waste.

Glaucoma. Glaucoma is the result of abnormally high pressure (not related to high blood pressure) within the eye caused by a buildup of fluid when normal drainage is blocked. This pressure inside the eyeball squeezes the blood vessels that nourish the retina and optic nerve, causing some of the nerve cells to die. As more and more cells are damaged, the field of vision narrows, producing "tunnel vision," and finally blindness.

It is estimated that 1 in 50 Americans over 35 and 3 in 100 over 65 have glaucoma. It may run in the family (if so, regular checkups from age 30 are recommended), it may be a concomitant of diabetes, or it may result from increased susceptibility caused by the use of certain drugs prescribed for high blood pressure or cortisone preparations applied to the eye. Most often, however, the cause is unknown.

Since glaucoma can be well advanced before significant symptoms appear, it is important to have an examination at least every 2 years. An optometrist can measure pressure with a tonometer, and if any abnormality is discovered, the patient will be referred to an ophthalmologist, a physician specializing in diseases of the eye and the only one qualified to monitor and treat the condition. The symptoms and treatment for both acute and chronic glaucoma are discussed in detail in Chapter 33 on Eye Disorders, page 651.)

Cataracts. Senile cataracts, seen in virtually all people who live to very old age, are caused by degeneration. A clouding of the lens, they may result from exposure to x-rays, microwaves, and infrared radiation, as well as from aging. Cataracts begin as a small white spot on the lens, caused by a chemical alteration in the protein of the lens which changes it from transparent to opaque. As the cataract grows, vision gradually begins to cloud. More and more light will be required for reading, episodes of blurred vision and double vision may occur, and night driving becomes difficult.

Surgery is the only treatment for cataracts. Once a dreaded procedure, this surgery is now quite simple and is frequently done on an outpatient basis.

Hearing

Changes in hearing are usually noticed later than changes in vision. There is a progressive decrease with age in the ability to hear well (presbycusis). At first it is only the high pitches that are missed, but later other sounds become difficult to differentiate. Presbycusis is thought to occur because of progressive loss of tiny hairlike structures on the inner ear's nerve cells.

Hearing loss can result from the natural process of aging, as well as from injury and disease. The most common hearing problem noted by older people is difficulty following a conversation in a noisy environment. There seems to be a loss of the ability to "focus" the hearing. Many types of hearing loss can be either cured or ameliorated by surgery or the use of hearing aids.

There are many kinds of hearing loss, but all of these can be classified as one of two types: conduction deafness and nerve or perceptive deafness (also called sensorineural deafness). Sometimes impairment is mixed, with involvement of both conductive and nervous apparatus. Some hearing problems can be improved by surgery, some by the use of a hearing aid, and some not at all. Correct diagnosis is critical to success.

Conduction deafness is caused by a disruption in the transfer of sound waves from the external ear through the middle ear to the nerve in the middle ear. The most easily corrected form of conductive hearing loss is that caused by a lump of ear wax. Once this obstruction is flushed out by the doctor, hearing usually returns to normal. But the most common source of conductive deafness is in the middle ear where tiny bones transmit and augment vibrations from the eardrum to the middle ear. An infection in the middle ear may damage these structures, or an overgrowth of bone around the stirrup-shaped ossicle (otosclerosis) may keep that tiny structure from vibrating, so that no message is sent to the inner ear. This condition can be corrected by surgery, and in general, conduction deafness is amenable to treatment.

Nerve deafness may be partial or complete. While there may be ways to compensate for partial damage, nerve damage is not reparable. It may result from simple wear and tear, from infection of the mother during pregnancy (German measles), from high fevers and some childhood infections, from certain drugs such as gentamicin, from blows to the head, and from middle ear infection—to name only a few possible sources. However, the single most pervasive cause of perceptive hearing loss is noise. The ears are designed to recover well from temporary or brief exposure to loud noise, but prolonged exposure to intense noise damages the nerves in the inner ear and the loss sustained is not recoverable.

Hearing aids can help in some cases in both conductive and nerve deafness, but each condition will require a different type of aid. Over-the-counter shopping for a hearing aid can be useless and very expensive. A hearing specialist, not a salesman, should prescribe the appropriate device.

The Cardiovascular System

The heart is capable of sustaining normal activity of healthy persons throughout life. However, because of age-associated thickening of the lining of the heart and of the heart valves, and thickening and loss of elasticity of the blood vessels (arteriosclerosis), the heart becomes less efficient, while at the same time it must work against greater resistance. This limits the ability of the heart to vary its output, so that acute or prolonged stress such as surgery, infection, or blood loss, which could be easily tolerated by the young, can precipitate heart failure in an older person.

The level of blood pressure throughout life is one of the important factors that determine how rapidly the blood vessels become thickened. If there has been no history of hypertension in the early or middle years, the mild elevation of blood pressure that occurs in old age is not a matter for grave concern.

It is important to realize that blood pressure readings can be quite labile (readily open to change). Many people become unduly alarmed because they are told of an elevated blood pressure reading on the first visit to a new doctor or in a storefront clinic. These pressures often drop to near normal levels within a short time; what is important is a sustained level of hypertension. Pressures recorded at home in a relaxed atmosphere may be more accurate than those taken in a doctor's office.

If sustained hypertension is present, it is almost always possible to control it with some combination of diet and medication. Patients, however, tend eventually to discontinue their treatment regimens because they have no overt symptoms. Since high blood pressure can begin as early as childhood, close cooperation over the years between doctor and patient is important in order to prevent long-term complications such as heart disease and stroke.

Strokes occur when the blood supply to the brain is drastically reduced or cut off—from arteriosclerosis, a blood clot (embolism), or a burst vessel (aneurysm). While a stroke can occur at any age, they are far more common in those over 50, particularly in those with chronic, untreated hypertension and those with severe atherosclerosis. Strokes precipitated by an embolism or an aneurysm may have nothing to do with age (but at least 50 percent will be associated with hypertension). Those that result from hardening of the arteries are attributable in part to age-related changes.

Although the deleterious effects of arteriosclerosis may be ameliorated or slowed by proper diet and exercise and a good genetic background, there is no "cure" for the condition.

The Lungs

Like the heart, the lungs will support normal life activity into old age, but numerous changes in the lungs and the lung cavity make them less efficient and less able to respond to the added demands of infection, heavy physical exertion, and surgery, etc. Consequently, the old are at much greater risk of pulmonary complication or respiratory failure in these situations.

The changes that occur are primarily due to a stiffening of the lungs and a decreased ability to clear the air passages of mucus. Changes in the rib and spine, such as demineralization, curvature of the spine, and a weakening of the chest muscles all can contribute to the decreased pulmonary reserves seen in older people.

The Kidneys

The kidney can effectively control fluid volume, remove toxic substances, and maintain acid-base balance throughout life, but with age it is less able to handle volume overload or depletion, large amounts of toxic substances or an extreme acid or base imbalance. This happens because the number and size of filtering units (the nephrons) decrease with age and the blood supply may be decreased. The kidneys lose about one-third of their efficiency by age 70, but usually retain the ability to keep the level of certain waste products, such as urea, at a normal level in the blood. When presented with the increased demands associated with infections and injuries, however, the aging kidney may quickly fall behind in its blood-filtering ability, and levels of urea and other potentially toxic materials will begin to accumulate in the blood.

The Digestive System

The food we eat is normally broken down into an absorbable form by the action of the stomach and upper intestinal tract. The pancreas and liver contribute vital enzymes and other digestive materials to permit the small intestine to absorb the nutrients. Virtually all absorption of food materials is complete by the time the intestinal contents reach the cecum, which is where the small and large bowel (colon) come together. The colon is mainly concerned with absorbing fluids and salts back into the body so that the stools become formed.

These digestive processes normally change very little as people age. When they have been measured, the levels of digestive enzymes along the intestinal tract are not much different at 65 than at 25. What does tend to happen frequently is a decrease in the motility of the intestine as one ages. This contributes to the greater frequency of constipation seen in older people.

While constipation alone can certainly be an annoyance, it rarely leads to any serious health consequences. The regular use of laxatives and enemas is a poor way to deal with this problem. An increase in the amount of bulk in the diet (found in whole-grain products, fruits, and vegetables) is a prerequisite in overcoming constipation. So-called "bulk expanders," such as ground psyllium seed, are readily available and provide a much better supplement in the treatment of constipation than do ordinary laxatives.

Certain illnesses of the intestinal tract are more common in older people. Ulcers, gallbladder problems, and cancers can occur at any age, but are more frequent in the older person. The symptoms of digestive disease can be quite varied and even well-qualified physicians with access to modern diagnostic facilities may have trouble sorting them out. The major symptoms include abdominal pain, change in bowel habits, signs of internal bleeding, jaundice, and weight loss. Any of these requires medical evaluation.

The Endocrine System

The internal glandular system of the body is incredibly complex and is concerned with the regulation of a wide variety of functions, such as level of blood sugar, blood pressure, reactions to stress, and production of urine. It is likely that all major bodily functions are in some way affected by hormones from the endocrine glands.

Although a number of rare illnesses have been attributed to an imbalance of hormones, the most common, by far, is diabetes. In younger people, this is usually due to a deficiency of insulin from the pancreas and is called juvenile diabetes. In older people, it may be due to a resistance to the action of insulin, rather than to a lack of it, a condition known as adult-onset diabetes. Obesity clearly aggravates this type of diabetes and weight reduction alone will often return the blood sugar levels to normal.

The most obvious change in hormone production seen in people as they age relates to decreases in the sex hormones. (For more information, see Sexual Changes, page 264.)

Muscles and Locomotion

Strength remains almost undiminished in an active person well into the sixties, and any diminution is usually the result of decreased use (poor conditioning) rather than to actual muscle-cell loss. Endurance, however, is partly controlled by the capacity of the heart and lungs, and as circulation and breathing capacity decreases, the ability to sustain effort without stopping to rest is impaired. Flexibility and coordination do tend to decrease with age, even in the physically fit. A healthy, physically active man of 65 may well be able to pick up as heavy a load as he could at 35, but he will not have the ability to coordinate rapid movements, as would be demanded in many sports. Likewise, many healthy women can continue to swim effectively in their sixties, but the more rapid, coordinated movements required in rope jumping generally would not be possible.

Bones

The major changes associated with bones in normal aging is a loss of calcium. This demineralization is a more serious problem in women after menopause. Older women may lose twice as much calcium as men and, therefore, are more prone to fractures, par-

ticularly fractures of the hip. Sometimes, the demineralization of the spinal column leads to small compression fractures that cause the spine to squeeze into itself. The end result is a loss in height of as much as 1 inch or more in both men and women.

The Brain and Nervous System

There is remarkably little change in the physical appearance of the brain associated with aging. A decrease of 5 percent or less in brain size may be noted by age 60. This cell loss has very little to do with change in normal mental function. What may be noticed is the increased reaction time that comes with age. It takes a little longer for impulses to flash from eye to brain to spinal cord—the fast tennis serve may become harder to hit, for example.

Increased caution is wise with ascending years. One of the consequences of the slower travel time of impulses is a tendency to dizziness or loss of balance upon sudden movement. This happens commonly in older people when they arise from bed too quickly, and it can be the cause of bumps and falls.

Finally, memory may change—which is not to say disappear. (Changes in memory are discussed on page 265.)

COMMON COMPLAINTS OF AGING

MANY OF THE THINGS that people worry about as they begin to age have nothing to do with illness or disease. These complaints have to do with changes in appearance, stamina, sexual function, emotions, memory, and intelligence. Understanding the changes, knowing what one must adjust to and what one can alter, is important to psychological well-being, if nothing else.

Perhaps the most important factor in dealing with change of any kind is attitude. Self-acceptance is both antidote and cure for much of the discomfort that accompanies aging.

There are two stock characters in drama which are meant to evoke pity—the very young trying to appear grown up and the aging or old trying to simulate youth. Both of these characterizations violate our sense of the appropriate. Since people continue to feel "young" inside, the changes in physical appearance, emotional tenor, endurance, etc., sometimes violate the personal sense of the appropriate. If one feels the same, why shouldn't one look the same?

The shock of realization that one is no longer

young is universal, coming to most Americans sometime between 40 and 50. It seems to hit hardest those who find their jobs to be dull and meaningless or those who have put a low value on their work. For those who enjoy their work, who feel useful and productive, the apprehension of the fact of aging is less jarring.

Since aging changes will occur in a highly individual fashion, deciding what is appropriate in light of the changes is a most individual task. Those whose work requires a youthful appearance may want or need to "interfere" with the sagging and drooping through cosmetic surgery, while those for whom appearance has no relationship to work may be quite content with things as they are. Faced with the possibility of a shortened life, a once sedentary and overweight individual may launch upon a rigorous physical fitness and weight-loss program, while a similarly disposed person whose life is not threatened may be happy with a continued inactive life and a few extra pounds.

The decreases in strength, stamina, and mobility that are frequently the subject of complaint, especially by sedentary types, do occur in those over 75, but before that time much depends upon the individual. It is altogether possible for a well-conditioned marathon runner of 70 to have far more stamina than a sedentary smoker of 30. The housewife who has continued to do most of her housework without benefit of laborsaving devices may be much stronger than a young woman in her twenties with all the household gadgets.

All of which is to say that there is great individual variation, and changes up until old age are relative to the individual. The marathoner's best time at 70 will be less than his best time at 30, but will be better than the time of a nonrunner of 30. The 60-year-old housewife may not be able to do as much at 60 as she could at 30, but she may be able to do far more than her sedentary 25-year-old counterpart. The aging changes in bones, vision, and cardiopulmonary capacity do occur, but in the healthy and physically fit, taste and motivation are usually well adapted to capacity. If a person in midlife begins to feel weak and creaky, it is an alterable condition.

Changes in Appearance

The changes in the body outlined previously will come, but for those who don't want excessive change—a "spare tire," flabby arms, a stooped back, or a halting gait—there are simple, if not easy answers. Exercise and good nutrition will keep weight normal, muscles taut, and body flexible. (For more information, see Chapter 16 on Fundamentals of Health, page 292.)

Changes in the skin are another matter. The benefits of exercise and good nutrition will accrue to the skin in some measure because of improved circulation, provided all the exercise is not taken unprotected in the sun. The skin, however, requires a special kind of attention if it is not to become leathery, overly wrinkled, and excessively blemished.

With aging, the skin gradually becomes drier and thinner. This dry, thin skin wrinkles deeply and shows veins and pigmentation changes readily. To prevent undue or premature dryness, treatment should begin early—long before the need is apparent. (For more information on prevention and care of dry skin, see Chapter 31 on Skin Disorders, page 622.)

Even with the best of care, however, the skin will wrinkle eventually, the entire contour of the face will sag a bit, and more and more blemishes will appear. For those who would like to improve upon these ravages of time, there are a number of things that can be done.

The flat brown spots that frequently begin to appear in the middle years on exposed areas of the skin—"liver spots" or "age spots"—can be camou-flaged with a cover cream or stick. (They will fade somewhat if bleaching creams are faithfully applied, but those who use such creams are often subject to blotching when exposed to the sun.) The warty-looking brown or black growths that may be more annoying can be removed by chemical peeling, burning, use of electric needles, or excision. If the excision is necessarily deep, there may be tiny white scars. For wrinkles and sagging, however, the only useful treatments are surgical. (See box on Cosmetic Surgery, page 266.)

Sexual Changes

Both men and women experience sexual changes and some change in sexual function beginning in the middle years. For those who remain healthy and sexually active, most changes are gradual and, if correctly understood, bring only slight changes in function.

Menopause is, of course, a significant change in women. It generally occurs sometime between ages 45 and 55 and is the end result of a gradual diminution of estrogen until there is no longer enough output to stimulate growth of the lining of the uterus. Perhaps as many as one-third of women experience menopause as a sudden event—one month they menstruate and the next month they don't. Most women, however, have several months or years of changes in flow and irregular periods before the menses cease altogether.

Since menopause occurs at a time when many other dramatic changes in lifestyle may be occurring, including such major markers as loss of parents, and since women vary greatly in their emotional response to these changes, a variety of symptoms may be attributed to menopause which are actually the result of other factors, such as stress.

There are two symptoms directly attributable to menopause—hot flashes and genital atrophy. A few women will have neither in any recognizable sense.

Hot flashes may be mildly annoying for some and a real but transitory problem for others. The "flash" is a sudden sensation of heat in the face, neck, and upper chest, often accompanied by sweating and followed by a slight chill. For those troubled with frequent, severe flashes or persistent sweats, relief is generally readily achieved by taking supplementary estrogen.

Genital atrophy, which comes along much later than the hot flashes, is a slow process that may not be noticed at all, especially in those who remain sexually active without long periods of abstinence. In all women, however, there is some shrinking of tissues and some decline in the secretion of lubricating fluids.

Men do not have a radical change in hormonal output, as do women. There are very gradual changes in hormone production, but the "male menopause" about which so much has been written is more properly called "midlife-crisis." This is probably not related to sexual changes, but to other physical and emotional upheavals that may affect sexual performance. Between 40 and 50, men are apt to find a gradual reduction in the desire for sexual activity and some loss in sexual responsiveness. While both of these will occur in all men over time, they may in the early years be attributable to boredom, mental or physical fatigue, preoccupation with business interests, excessive eating or drinking, or panic resulting from a transient occurrence of impotence.

After age 50, there are changes in sexual response which require minor adjustments in sexual habits. Penile erection will take longer to achieve and may require direct partner involvement. There may also be a decrease in expulsive pressure at ejaculation and in volume of fluid expelled. In later years there may also be a reduced demand (perhaps only once in 3 or 4 coital experiences) for ejaculation.

None of these changes alters the ability to enjoy a satisfying sex life. It is important that they be understood by both partners, however, so that they not be interpreted by the woman as waning interest or by the man as performance failure.

In later life, both men and women may experience some difficulty in resuming sexual activity after prolonged abstinence. In the woman over 55, a period of more than 1 year of sexual continence encourages the Widow's syndrome, a reduction in the elasticity of the vaginal walls with a corresponding reduction in the facility for vaginal expansion. The production of vaginal lubrication may be slowed and severely reduced, and finally, the vaginal barrel constricts and the labia are thinned. These symptoms can be reduced within a period of 6 weeks to 3 months, given a knowledgeable and understanding partner, and if necessary, some modest medical assistance in the form of estrogen replacement and advice on the use of lubricants.

In men there is likewise a Widower's syndrome. A man in his late fifties, after more than 1 year of continence, may find that he cannot achieve or sustain an effective erection, even if he has not experienced sexual dysfunction before. This unexpected failure often leads to a period of partial or complete impotence. A cooperative and sexually knowledgeable partner can reverse the syndrome by providing repeated episodes of unhurried and nondemanding sexual interplay. (For a discussion of prostate problems in older men, see Chapter 38 on Disorders Common to Men, page 763.)

Changes in Memory and Intelligence

Memory loss, intellectual decline, and confusion are not normal parts of aging. Researchers can now demonstrate that while there is some decline in memory and certain intellectual function, the changes are inconsequential for those who remain physically and emotionally healthy. Indeed, crystallized intelligence, the ability to use an accumulated body of information to make judgments and solve problems, actually rises throughout life in healthy, active people.

Key factors in maintaining or improving mental capacities in later life are social involvement and flexibility. Those people who remain active participants in family and society and who demonstrate in midlife a capacity to enjoy new experiences and to tolerate ambiguity generally are most successful.

Just as with physical activity, some aspects of mental activity may require adaptation. However, it is possible that much of the seeming decline in memory may be merely an increased sensitivity to and fear of the problem. If a young person is forgetful it is attributed to distractions, carelessness, or a "scatter-brained" personality, whereas a similar forgetfulness in an older person is assumed to herald senility.

With age, more time may be required to assimilate new information or to solve a complicated problem. There may be some small deficits in short-term memory which require a few "tricks" to compensate. Noted behavioral scientist B.F. Skinner, at 79, wrote a book with Margaret E. Vaughn called *Enjoy Old Age*, which lists a number of ways to improve memory and generally circumvent many of the small inconveniences caused by process changes.

Alterations in mental function can be produced by a variety of circumstances that are common to aging. Medications, infections, anemias, abnormal blood chemistry, elevated or lowered blood sugar, cardiopulmonary insufficiencies, malnutrition, sight or hearing deficits, and other problems can bring about sudden confused states.

In such cases an improvement in the underlying cause will bring a reversal of the decline in mental function. For example, tranquilizing drugs frequently administered after surgery and for depression can cause confusion, even delirium, in the elderly. Infections such as endocarditis and tuberculosis, and numerous cardiovascular problems, including heart attack, congestive heart failure, and vascular occlusion can do the same. Bleeding, dehydration, kidney failure, brain disorders, pain, even the trauma of hospitalization, can cause demented behavior which is completely reversible.

A recent study indicated that specific training

COSMETIC SURGERY

Francis C. Symonds, M.D.
Associate Professor of Clinical Surgery

Cosmetic surgery is now a $1.5 million business in this country. Once for the rich and the celebrated, it is now fairly common for others as well, although most of the cost must be borne by the patient, since many of these procedures are not covered by insurance. Some 15 to 20 percent of cosmetic surgery patients are men.

Any surgical procedure carries with it at least some risk, and the more complicated the procedure, the greater the risk. The risks attendant to cosmetic surgery are statistically small, but they should be taken into account before undergoing any sort of treatment.

The choice of an experienced and qualified surgeon is critical. The surgery can be performed either by a surgeon who specializes in plastic and reconstructive surgery or by a specialist in another field, such as dermatology or otolaryngology (ear, nose, and throat), who is also qualified (and board certified) to perform those surgical procedures related to his or her specialty. (For more information on finding a qualified surgeon, see Chapter 2 on The American Health-Care System, page 18.)

Not every person is a good candidate for every procedure. Factors such as general health, weight, allergies, skin type, and color may make surgery inadvisable. Additionally, the prospective patient's attitude and expectations will weigh heavily in a doctor's evaluation. For those who have psychological problems—feelings of failure or rejection, low self-esteem, and the like—cosmetic surgery is often seen as the answer to the basic problem, which it is not. When the physician senses that the patient will be dissatisfied with the result, he or she is apt to recommend against the procedure.

For the person who wants improvement but doesn't expect miracles, however, these procedures can make significant changes in appearance. In some cases the improvement may be temporary (5–10 years) and may need to be repeated. In the case of eye surgery and such reconstructive procedures as a nasoplasty or chin augmentation, there may be no need for additional work in the future.

The cost is considerable, ranging from $1,000 to $8,000, depending on the procedure, in which facility and by whom it is done, and on geographical location. In many cases the surgery is not covered by insurance, and payment is generally required beforehand. Some procedures are routinely done on an outpatient basis, some are optional, and some require a short hospital stay. Most require several days of seclusion while the initial healing takes place.

Dermabrasion. For removal of fine wrinkles around the mouth, eyes, and brow, dermabrasion is often chosen. It is basically like sanding a surface to make it smooth. A skin planing tool that looks much like a dentist's drill is used to sand off the wrinkled areas which have been injected with local anesthesia. This will leave raw surfaces of pink skin which will require about 2 weeks to return to normal. The procedure itself takes only about ½ hour.

Skin Peeling. Chemical peeling of surface skin is called chemosurgery. A form of carbolic acid is applied, which burns off a layer of skin (none too comfortably) and a scab forms. When the scab comes off after about 10 days, there is a new, unblemished layer. The color initially may be rather dark or red, but will return to normal after some weeks or months.

The one universal proscription that accompanies this procedure is no sun exposure for 6 months. Skin peeling is sometimes done with a facelift to add the finishing touch. Those with fair skin are the best candidates. Black, brown, and Oriental skin may develop irregular pigmentation.

Eyelid Surgery. Eyelid surgery, or blepharoplasty, is needed when excessive skin on the upper lid and bags below the eye give a look of perpetual tiredness or dissipation. This problem can be hereditary or may result from aging.

Incisions are made in the fold of the lid and just below the lower lash line, excess tissue is removed, and the incision is stitched. The procedure takes only a little more than 1 hour to complete and is frequently done on an outpatient basis, provided there is someone to help the patient through the very important follow-up care for the first 24 hours. Looks have usually returned to normal after 2 weeks, and many people return to work wearing dark glasses after 1 week's time. (See figure 14.1A–14.1C, page 268.)

Complications: Most of the possible complications of eyelid surgery are temporary. There is always the danger of hematomas (swellings filled with blood) in facial surgery, but they usually cause no permanent damage. Some people have excessive tearing, but this usually subsides quickly, certainly by the time healing is complete. Double vision caused by muscle disturbances or swelling of the conjunctiva may be a problem for the first few hours after surgery.

Complications are rare, but may require prolonged medication or additional corrective surgery. The inability to close one's eyes completely may occur in the first few days after surgery. Sometimes this persists for a few weeks or months. When this happens, the doctor will prescribe drops to relieve the irritation that occurs when the eyelid cannot perform its function of distributing the tears over the eyeball.

Occasionally, small cysts will form along the incision, but these can be easily removed. The most unpleasant complication and the most difficult to correct is ectropion, a turning out of the eyelid caused by removing too much skin from the lower lid. This is corrected by reconstruction with skin grafts.

Facelift. Increasingly there are new facelift procedures that can be performed on an outpatient basis, but for a few patients who are subject to special risks, surgeons still prefer a hospital stay of 2 or more days. The procedure is sometimes done under general anesthesia, but more often under local with preoperative sedatives. It requires from 1½ to 4 hours, making it more risky than the shorter, simpler procedures.

Incisions are made under the hairline and around the ears, fatty tissue is removed, and the loose facial and neck skin is tightened. (See figure 14.2A–14.2C, page 269.) In addition to the regular facelift, there may also be eyelid surgery, or chin augmentation, or a chemical peel for a "finishing touch."

The face is heavily bandaged for 2 days and more lightly for the next few days. The patient will be on a liquid diet for a few days and will probably not feel like socializing for a few weeks until the scars have begun to heal and the puffiness disappears. About 21 days of relative seclusion is common, though a few who do very well can get by with 2 weeks.

Complications: Although rare, complications can occur. Infections (very rare), scarring, facial nerve injury, skin sloughs (loss of facial tissue), hair loss around incisions, and hematomas are possible problems, each of which is usually amenable to treatment. Keloid scars are difficult to treat, but hypertrophic scars not only improve with time, but can often be lessened by injection of small amounts of steroid compounds.

Nose and Chin. Rhinoplasty (a nose job) is the most frequently performed cosmetic procedure and is often performed under local anesthesia with intravenous sedation. Healing is usually uncomplicated and prompt, and most patients can return to light normal activity within 1 or 2 weeks.

Nose surgery is generally accompanied by only minor problems. A diminished sense of smell (and, therefore, taste) is not unusual, but seldom persists more than a few weeks. Congestion and skin irritations from the bandages are other nuisance factors. The most serious complication is bleeding, which can occur anytime up to 12 or 14 days after surgery. Though the hemorrhage is controlled with medicated packing, occasionally it will be severe enough to require hospitalization and more aggressive methods of control.

Chin augmentation is often done along with rhinoplasty. Through an incision inside the mouth or under the chin either a soft or a firm prosthesis is implanted. Although it is unlikely, the chief risk in chin augmentation is extrusion of the implant. Should this happen, the implant can be replaced.

Breast Augmentation, Reduction, and Reconstruction and Body Contouring. These procedures are considered more risky than a facelift. Each of them results in scarring that may be visible, though most patients consider the scars better than the original condition. Other complications may also occur: disturbances of circulation, skin abscesses, wound separation, hardening of tissues surrounding implants, fluid accumulation under the skin flaps, and thrombophlebitis. Blood transfusion is occasionally necessary and recovery can be a long and painful process.

A new technique in body contouring called suction lipectomy is still controversial. Since skin elasticity is important for attractive shrinkage over the reduced areas, those over 30 are generally not good candidates for this procedure.

Hair Transplant. Hair transplant is the only safe method of surgically restoring hair to the balding pate. The procedure consists of punching out a small plug of flesh from a part of the scalp that is well-supplied with hair, and placing this sterilized plug in a hole (prepared by the same punch) on a bald part of the scalp. Sometimes a few sutures are required to secure the plug. The head is bandaged, the patient goes home, and the crusts that form around the implanted plugs fall off within 2 weeks.

Usually the transplanted hairs fall out, but after about 100 days or so, new hair begins to grow in the transplanted follicles. Good coverage may require several sessions, and the amount of cover will depend upon the degree of baldness and the richness of the hair supply from which the transplants are taken. The average patient requires between 250 and 300 plugs implanted at a rate of 10 to 60 per procedure over a period of 2 to 3 months.

Hair transplant is painless for most, mildly uncomfortable for a few. When done properly by a qualified physician, there are rarely either rejections or complications. In the hands of nonmedical "hair specialists," the complications can be legion.

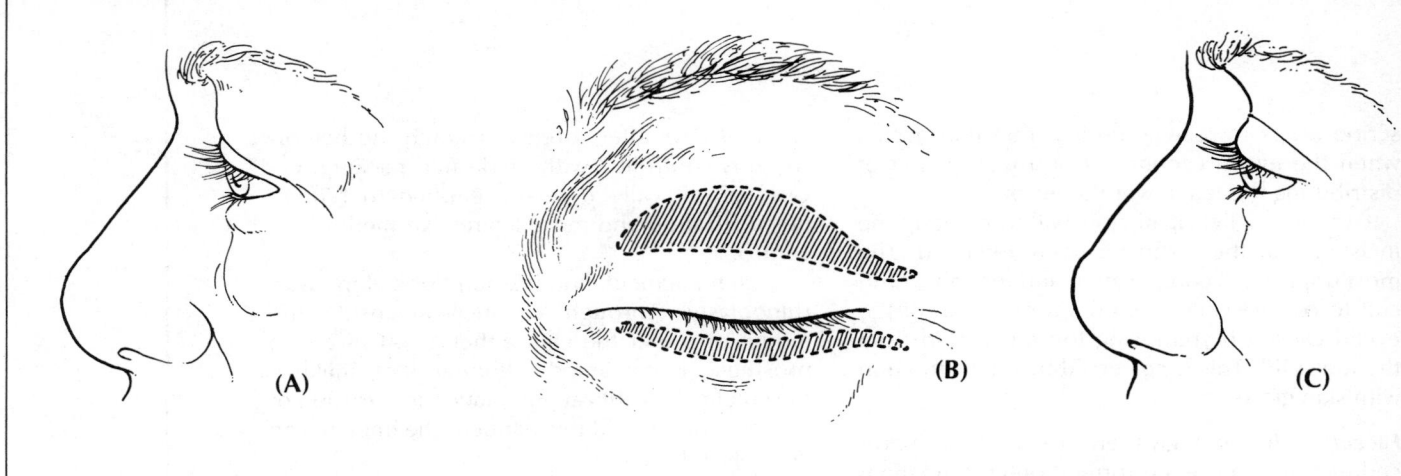

Figure 14.1. **(A) Before surgery. Note the drooping upper eyelid and baggy appearance under the eye. (B) The operation. Incisions are made in both the upper and lower eyelids, and fatty deposits along with excess skin are removed. (C) After the operation. Both the upper and lower eyelids have a firmer, more youthful appearance, and the bags under the eyes have been removed.**

can indeed improve intellectual performance that appears to be declining for no particular reason. In only a small number of people are signs of mental decline not subject to improvement, and most of these are true losses, resulting from stroke or Alzheimer's disease. The old caveat "use it or lose it" is equally as applicable to the mind as to muscle.

Mood

Mild depression at one time or another is common to all ages, but it sometimes becomes an unrecognized but constant fact in later years. Major life changes seem to come fast and furious from midlife on, and it would be miraculous to escape any depression at all. It is important to recognize the common symptoms of depression, and to admit and report them, for they can be managed successfully through a variety of means.

What does it mean to be depressed? It is not the normal short-lived "feeling blue" over a major disappointment, nor is it the normal grief all people experience at the loss of a mate, though it can grow out of either experience.

Depression is recognized by physical and emotional symptoms that usually appear as a group, but may be seen as only one or two symptoms, particularly when it is long-term. All of the following symptoms are typical of depression; any of them can exacerbate an existing medical problem or can actually precipitate a heretofore unknown condition:

- Sleep disturbance—waking in the middle of the night or very early in the morning, or being unable to fall asleep
- Loss of appetite and a corresponding loss of weight, or conversely, constant nibbling and weight gain
- Inertia—the feeling that nothing is worth the effort
- Withdrawal from social contact
- Crying at inappropriate times
- A feeling that nothing in the body is working very well

Sometimes the only thing needed to counteract depression is counseling and some changes in daily routine or environment. At other times there may be a need for medication, usually a mood-elevating drug. There is a type of depression related to senile dementia which is quite another thing, a part of the disease state rather than an affective disorder.

Eyesight and Hearing

It is a rare person indeed who lives to a great age with no noticeable diminution of sight and hearing. For some reason, the necessary adjustment of wearing glasses or using other visual aids is far more acceptable to most than that of wearing a hearing aid, even though miniaturization and technological advances have made hearing aids almost invisible.

In these two areas great strides have been made in surgical procedures to correct many of the problems that appear with age. And where correction or repair is not sufficient, a host of devices are available

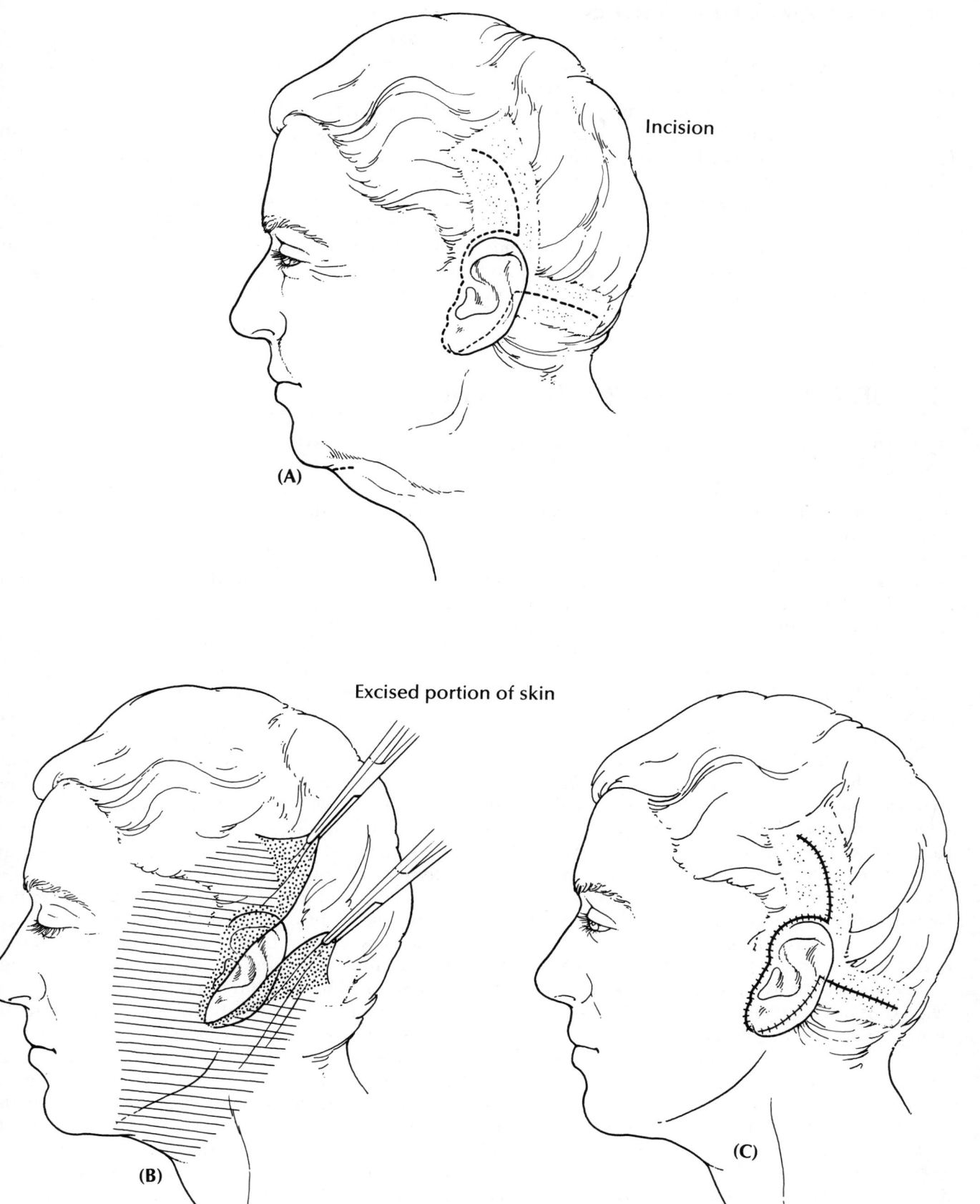

Incision

(A)

Excised portion of skin

(B)

(C)

Figure 14.2. **(A) Typical incision for facelift to tighten sagging skin on the face and neck. (B) The skin is pulled up and back. The excess is cut away, and the edges are stitched together. (C) The scars are hidden by the hair line. Note the firmer throat and jaw line and more youthful contour.**

to make living with sight or hearing impairment quite tolerable. There is no excuse for allowing either poor sight or poor hearing to impinge seriously on normal living and continued social contact. (Chapters 33 and 34 on The Eyes and Diseases of the Ear, Nose, and Throat explain what happens to these organs and how improvements are made medically.)

The National Association for the Visually Handicapped and the Deafness Research Association, both in New York, and the American Speech and Hearing Association in Washington, D.C., can provide information on how to live successfully with sight and hearing deficits.

Besides glasses and hearing aids, there are amplifiers for telephones, overlays for telephone dials with large, easy-to-read numbers, speed-dialing systems that require pushing only one button, special cassette libraries for those who cannot see well enough to read, and many other free or inexpensive devices that ameliorate the problems of failing eyesight or hearing.

MAJOR ILLNESSES AFFECTING THE AGING

WITH THE EXCEPTION of early childhood illnesses, middle-aged and elderly people get most of the same diseases everybody else does. There are some diseases, such as osteoporosis, adult-onset diabetes (diabetes mellitus), and Alzheimer's disease, which rarely appear before the early part of middle life. There are others, such as heart disease, cancer, and arthritis, which appear with greater frequency in the aging. All in all, though, the major difference in the young and the old with regard to disease is the way in which the disease presents itself and the decreasing ability with age to withstand insults to the body.

In the case of cancer, heart disease, diabetes, and arthritis (which are covered in detail in their respective chapters), the aging may have less to fear than the young. It is perhaps easier for someone in later life to alter lifestyle to accommodate heart disease and arthritis than for the younger person. And cancers, for the most part, progress much more slowly in the old than in the young. For example, lymphosarcoma (cancer of the lymph system) is frequently fatal in young adults, seldom in those who first contract the disease after 65. So being old and sick isn't all bad news, though being sick is not to be desired at any age, and the older the body the less reserve to counteract disease.

The good news is that the vast majority of illnesses common to later life can be managed effectively and need not drastically affect the quality of life until very near life's end. It's more a matter of exchanging the stresses of "getting ahead" for the stresses of "getting on." The awful specter of spending declining years in a nursing home with reduced mental capacity is a fate that befalls only 5 percent of the elderly. At least 15 percent of those over 75 lead fully active and healthy lives to the very end, and 82 percent of American elderly are classified as being in moderately good health.

Osteoporosis

Osteoporosis is the loss of calcium from the bones, which causes them to become porous, so that if they are subjected to pressure from weight-bearing or the pulling of muscles, they may collapse. This results in the shortened and stooped stature often seen in the aged, especially in older women.

Everyone loses some bone through demineralization, shrinking in height just a bit. And all old bones are more brittle than young bones. Osteoporosis, however, is noticeable in far more women than men and in some women much more than in others.

Most likely to be afflicted are small-boned women of northern European background and those whose mothers or maternal aunts or grandmothers had the problem. Large, heavy women, blacks, and dark-skinned women of southern European origin are somewhat protected, as are those who do heavy physical work throughout life.

The symptoms of osteoporosis are chronic back pain caused by compression fracture of the vertebrae, persistent muscle spasms, and bone fractures due to minor falls, the most common and the most serious of which is a hip fracture.

The disease probably begins long before the symptoms are present. Even with clinical symptoms it is difficult to diagnose. There is no readily available way at this time to objectively measure calcium loss; blood and laboratory tests shed no light on this condition. While calcium levels in the blood can be easily measured, they tell little about the amount of calcium in the bones. For x-rays to show degeneration, calcium loss must be extensive—too late to do much in the way of prevention.

Because it occurs after menopause in women, the lack of hormones and sex steroids may be related. On the other hand, poor nutrition, especially inadequate calcium intake over the years, or a predisposition to malabsorption of calcium are more likely the culprits.

Since doctors do not know how to replace calcium in bones once it is gone, nor do they know why it disappears from some more than others, it seems wise for all people, and especially for women at higher risk, to take special care to include adequate calcium in a well-rounded diet. (See box on nutrition, page 272.) Regular exercise throughout life is also recommended, based on the theory that the protection apparently afforded women to do heavy physical work is conferred by the exercise they get.

Alzheimer's Disease

Perhaps the single greatest fear of aging is the fear of dementia, either through cerebral accident (stroke), Alzheimer's disease, or some other type of neurological problem. (Stroke, the greatest of the enemies, is discussed in Chapter 19 on Cardiovascular Disease, page 385.)

Alzheimer's disease, first described by a German neurologist in 1907, has only recently become widely recognized as perhaps the chief cause of what has traditionally been called senile dementia. It affects about 5 percent of the population over 65 in its severe form and another 10 percent in mild or moderate forms, but it is not limited to the elderly. It has been seen as early as the mid-forties, when it is called "presenile dementia."

No one knows yet what sets it off or what can be done to allay the mental and physical decline. Some of its victims suffer memory loss, learning and concentration disabilities, incontinence, inability to communicate, disorientation in time and space, decreased physical coordination, mood swings, personality changes, and deteriorating overall health with eventual total incapacitation and death. Those with mild or moderate disease can still attend to many of their personal needs. They may be able to jog or play tennis, but they will not be able to conduct business or supervise a household, and they will require constant attention to be sure that memory lapses and the like do not put them at hazard.

Alzheimer's disease is usually diagnosed by exclusion, since no laboratory procedure or biochemical marker can confirm it. Other disorders that cause dementia must first be eliminated, including the reversible ones discussed earlier. Less common causes of dementia that the physician will consider are loss of brain tissue from a series of small strokes, and normal pressure hydrocephalus, in which there is some loss of brain tissue associated with some increased fluid accumulation inside the brain.

In a recent analysis of 78 elderly patients with dementia, 68 percent had Alzheimer's disease; 8 percent suffered from depression; 5 percent had multiinfarct dementia; 5 percent had vitamin B_{12} deficiency; 4 percent had normal pressure hydrocephalus; and the remaining 8 percent had 6 other, very rare conditions.

In recent years there has been a marked increase in interest in Alzheimer's disease and a considerable increase in research funding. Doubtless researchers will uncover more about possible causes which may, in turn, lead to finding a cure.

LIFESTYLE CHANGES

Planning for Retirement

Just as a healthy body in later years depends upon care and attention to the body in youth and middle age, a successful retirement depends upon years of preparation. It has been said that one should plan for retirement, but not on retiring. As life expectancy increases, this becomes more important because most people can expect at least 14 or 16 years to fill up in some way—more if early retirement or longevity enter the picture.

For those who "retire" at 50 or 55 as do many government workers, there is usually a plan to enter a second career, often something that can continue indefinitely as long as good health allows. Some people actually leave work early, taking decreased benefits, in order to make such a major change while still relatively young.

Those who retire at 65, especially those who have not particularly enjoyed their work, often dream of a respite—of having nothing special to do, of having free time for whatever they like. Or for those to whom work has been everything, the idea of retirement is a nightmare, not a dream. For them, to lose their jobs is to lose their identity.

For everyone, retirement represents a major change, one that is largely unimaginable to both worker and extended family; for this reason it is critical to give serious thought to the matter years before it is at hand.

There are a host of things that will help in planning for retirement years:

- People who know they still want to work should start laying the groundwork several years ahead by being involved in that activity part time, as a volunteer, as a consultant, or as a hobbyist.
- They should examine their skills and see where they can be used, not only for personal profit, but for community service.
- They should expand their social network. Those who have failed to take time for family, friends, and community should begin immediately to remedy the situation.
- They might start helping others, as a way of learning things that will be valuable later on.
- They must evaluate their financial position and be prepared to change their style of living by choice rather than necessity.
- They can try out proposed changes in living situations (for a month on vacation, for example) before committing to a change, thinking about the emotional debits and credits, as well as the financial implications of planned changes.

People are meant to be active, useful, loved, amused, and purposeful. To the extent that a foundation is laid to ensure these possibilities, retirement will be an interesting and productive period rather than a time of hopelessness and despair.

Attitude, Attitude, Attitude

As in all of life, attitude will be a major factor in how one views the middle years and aging. The human body and mind are very plastic and are capable of infinite variation.

What, then, can most usefully be done to bolster or improve attitude and thus life? Those who are approaching middle age can:

1. Remain involved with family, friends, and community. Those who have never been joiners will probably not suddenly become activists, but even "loners" can find one-to-one or small group activities of interest and of service.

NUTRITION

There is wide acceptance of the idea that good nutrition is important at all stages of life. What is less commonly realized is that the precise definition of good nutrition for particular periods of life is not completely clear. For the aging person it appears important to eat a wide variety of foods that contain all of the known dietary requirements. A diet that contains daily servings of protein, fruits, vegetables, and grains should accomplish this. (For more information, see Chapter 16 on Fundamentals of Health, page 293.)

Diets that focus on one constituent, such as the high-protein diets, are at best ineffective and may be detrimental. The intestinal tract seems to require more rather than less bulk as people age, so that low-residue diets (those that have little fiber from fruits, vegetables, whole grains, etc.) are apt to promote constipation. There has been a swing away from the excessive focus on trying to keep slim as one ages, and it seems clear that a modest weight gain is both common and appropriate.

The best established "special requirement" of the aging person is the need for extra calcium, especially for women who are at high risk of developing osteoporosis. (See page 270.) Calcium is found in milk, dark green vegetables, and meats, so that these foods provide excellent nutrition for the older person.

Some people lose their ability to digest milk as they grow older, and develop gas or diarrhea when they drink it. For them, as well as for anyone else who has trouble taking in adequate amounts of calcium-

rich foods, there are a number of simple tablets, often made from the shells of shellfish, that are an excellent and inexpensive form of calcium supplement. Physical activity seems to help in getting calcium from the blood into the bones and should be a partner to calcium intake.

Many people have been convinced of the need for extra vitamins in the diet. It seems natural to think that as one ages, extra vitamins should be taken. In reality, there is meager evidence that a healthy, active older person requires vitamin supplements. It is almost certainly inadvisable to single out certain vitamins, such as vitamin E or vitamin C, and take large amounts of these in the hope of preventing some particular illness. Mineral supplements, with the possible exception of calcium, fall into the same categories as vitamins: They are unnecessary with a balanced diet.

The renewed interest in nutrition in recent years has been highly beneficial. On occasion, however, it has been exploited in a way that leads to unnecessary or unwise treatment. There is no firm evidence that nutritional deficiencies can be reliably diagnosed by analyzing hair, fingernails, or the like. Such procedures usually lead to unbalanced prescriptions for one or more "deficient" vitamins or minerals. If there is a specific deficiency, such as a lack of iron in the blood, it will usually be detected by a standard blood test.

As people grow older, good nutrition is obviously important, but its pursuit should not become the major theme in their thoughts or activities.

2. Choose their environment carefully and thoughtfully. Some people have never been particularly fond of children and might therefore welcome an age-restricted retirement community. But for those to whom contact with multiple generations is vital to well-being, a retirement villa might be a great mistake.

3. Start in the middle years to expand interests and horizons. The greater the number of interests, the larger the circle of potential friends and acquaintances, the greater the opportunity for new learning, the less the chance of becoming bored. Recent studies show that variety of interests may be even more important than family history of longevity as a predictor of life expectancy.

4. Maintain a daily routine, even after retirement, including regular and adequate nutrition. Recent studies show that a few extra pounds (within limits, of course) may be beneficial in later years.

5. Plan for the retirement years, but not to retire. One can experiment over a period of several years with what might be done after leaving a primary job to fill up the time interestingly and usefully, to augment the income (which is usually less than before), to fulfill dreams.

6. Focus on the positive aspects of life. If something unpleasant comes along that they don't like, they can find out how to change it, and if it can't be changed, they can find out how best to adjust to it.

With only moderate changes in wording or emphasis, the foregoing advice might as well be given to high school or college graduates about to launch out on their own as to those approaching retirement. It's much the same except that the mature person comes to the changes of later life with a great store of wisdom, a fairly well-developed sense of self, and it is hoped, a sense of accomplishment. That's a much richer lode to mine than the young person has.

Robert Browning may have been right after all in his invitation to "grow old along with me—the best is yet to be, the last of life, for which the first was made."

Part Four

MAINTAINING
PERSONAL HEALTH

15 Determining Your Health Quotient

John L. Roglieri, M.D.

INTRODUCTION

ALL OF US are familiar with the concept of using a quotient to measure intelligence. The abbreviation IQ has become so much a part of our vocabulary that it might be forgotten that these letters stand for intelligence quotient. Intelligence quotient is your intellectual age as measured by tests, divided by your chronological age as determined by the calendar. The result is usually multiplied by 100.

A health quotient, on the other hand, could be defined as your "health age" divided by your calendar age. Obviously, these two quotients are quite similar. The major difference between them is that there is nothing you can do to change your intelligence quotient. The health quotient, however, is only created in order to show you how you can improve your chances of living a longer and healthier life by changing your lifestyle.

The concept of "health risk" goes back to the ancient Greeks and to Hippocrates. The ancients used many tools, including the oracle at Delphi, in order to determine their chances for good health and longevity. Not much progress was made in this field over the next 1,800 years. In the nineteenth century, finally, the risk of early death from certain diseases was associated with a specific occupation. For example, it was noted that the workers who made their living cleaning out chimneys frequently died early from cancer of the scrotum. Later it was determined that certain carbon products related to incomplete combustion were the causative agents for this disease, and that it could be prevented if the chimney sweeps washed the soot off each day after work.

It is only relatively recently that significant progress in risk appraisal has been made. Several social and technological advances have made the process more effective and worthwhile. These include newer mathematical and biostatistical methods, the increasing power and decreasing cost of computers to support statistical analysis, greater allocation of public money for epidemiologic research, and much greater understanding of the disease processes themselves.

Using these new techniques, two California researchers showed in 1972 that health status and longevity could be significantly affected by simple, everyday living habits. Their results showed that health could be improved by sleeping 7 to 8 hours a night, having no more than 7 alcoholic drinks each week, not smoking, and maintaining normal body weight by moderate dietary habits, eating regular meals and not taking snacks, and having breakfast every day. It appeared that the more of these favorable health habits people pursued, the healthier they were and the longer they lived. This study was rather straightforward and the results yielded a simple guideline that could be followed by everyone, regardless of age, sex, or race.

Some 12 years earlier, a more formal program had begun, which is still under development. This approach, called health hazard appraisal, formalizes the concept of recognition, risk assessment, and risk reduction. It is intended to give more specific advice to individuals based on their age, race, and sex.

HEALTH HAZARD APPRAISAL AND ITS APPLICATIONS

EVERYONE IS SUBJECT to the risk of death, and naturally the risk increases with age. Health hazard appraisal offers a quantitative approach to assessing the risk for each individual. In general, however, applicable data bases have not been developed for the very young or the very old. The target population for health hazard appraisal has been Americans between the ages of 10 and 73 years. In round numbers, the population at risk in the United States is approximately 200 million older children and adults.

The risks that are considered in health hazard appraisal make up an extensive list. Included are family history, the individual's past medical history, current levels of blood pressure, cholesterol and weight; exercise habits; smoking habits; economic and social status; religion; miles traveled per year; use of alcohol, drugs, and prescription medication; seat belt use; ownership of weapons; and other related lifestyle factors. (See sample on page 281.)

The objective of health risk appraisal is to advise individuals of their most likely causes of death over the next 10 years. For example, teenagers are at much greater risk for death in automobile accidents or drownings, while middle-aged men are at greater risk due to heart attack and arteriosclerosis.

The first step, then, is to identify the most likely causes of death for each patient. Then the risk factors that are related to each of these causes are calculated for the individual, based on responses to a standardized lifestyle questionnaire. The last step is counseling to help individuals go about reducing their most serious personal risk factors through improved health habits.

In its most common form, health hazard appraisal is used to derive an appraisal age that, because it relates directly to a person's actual age, is generally easier to understand than a health quotient. Appraisal age is derived by adding to or subtracting from a person's chronological age a number of years equal to the risk of death he or she incurs as compared to others of the same chronological age, sex, and race.

To understand the concept, it is helpful to use a few specific examples, but first, a few words on how the "average American"—the standard against which everyone is measured—is derived. To begin with, basic health statistics covering all Americans are gathered by various researchers and government agencies. The data they derive represent the "average" American, who may not be the "typical" American at all. For example, the typical American may no longer smoke cigarettes. But the average American smokes because, statistically, the 6 billion cigarettes smoked in the United States each year are apportioned across the board. Likewise, the average American has some hereditary medical burden (such as a family history of heart disease); sometimes drives without seat belts; sometimes drinks excessively; has some high blood pressure, high blood sugar, and elevated cholesterol; and so on. For this reason, it is statistically impossible for the average American to live an optimally healthy life.

Obviously, some Americans are at greater than average risk because of heredity, occupation, weight, diet, smoking, and other lifestyle excesses. And those who are especially fortunate *and* attentive to their health can enjoy less than average risk. We can use appraisal age to demonstrate all three cases: average, worse than average, and better than average.

For example, a 35-year-old American who is average in terms of eating, drinking, sleeping, exercising, and other health habits, may have an appraisal age of 37 years. This means that the life expectancy for this person would be the same as that of a 37-year-old of the same sex and race whose health habits are exemplary.

On the other hand, if this same individual were to smoke excessively, go overboard with alcohol, drive a high-powered sports car several hundred miles weekly without seat belts, gain weight, and develop high blood pressure, he or she could be living with an appraisal age of 42 years. Finally, if this 35-year-old maintained ideal body weight; took regular aerobic exercise; enjoyed alcohol, salt, fat, and red meats with discretion; avoided cigarettes; drove a safe family sedan only on weekends and always with seat belts; and otherwise exemplified American prudence and sobriety, he could lower his risk to that of the average 32-year-old.

After a person's appraisal age has been determined, an "achievable age" is developed as an educational and motivational tool. The achievable age represents a lower risk that could be obtained by adopting various lifestyle changes prescribed by the physician. In determining this target age, the physician will take into consideration the individual's inherited risk factors and other problems over which he or she may have no control. Going back to the earlier example, the physician may determine an "achievable age" of 36 years. On the other hand, people who have inherited a remarkably favorable family history and coupled it with exemplary lifestyle habits may have achievable ages even younger than their calendar ages.

In practice, appraisal and achievable ages are determined using very specific criteria and data—not merely "some smoking" or "moderate exercise." For example, a 41-year-old American white male might have the following characteristics: His blood pressure is 180/94, cholesterol is 220, he has no family history of diabetes, he walks 1 mile per day, he smokes 1 pack of cigarettes per day, and he is 15 percent overweight. In an average week he drinks 18 ounces of alcohol. He drives 15,000 miles per year using seat belts 80 percent of the time. He has never been arrested and does not own a gun. He has no family history of gastrointestinal cancer, but he has had some rectal bleeding.

For this patient and for all 41-year-old white American males, the most likely causes of death in the next 10 years are (in order of probability): heart attack, lung cancer, cirrhosis, motor vehicle accident, suicide, stroke, homicide, cancer of the colon or rectum, pneumonia, and alcoholism.

Of 100,000 41-year-old white American males, 4,552 will die in the next 10 years from all of the above causes. However, for every 100,000 white American males 41 years of age who have the same characteristics as the man in the example, 8,144 will die. This greater risk is, again, because of unfavorable habits like smoking, excessive drinking, and driving without seat belts. This larger risk of death (8,144 out of 100,000) is equal to that of white males in the 47-year-old age group who have exemplary health habits but who, by virtue of increased age, have increased odds of death. Accordingly, the man in the example has an appraisal age of 47 years.

A health appraisal will also point out the relative risk of each cause of death. The 41-year-old in the example has a risk of heart attack that is 2.7 times higher than normal. His other risks of death are higher than normal by the number of times in parentheses: lung cancer (1.9), cirrhosis (2.0), motor vehicle accident (2.2), stroke (2.8), rectal cancer (3.0), and pneumonia (3.3).

By eliminating the lifestyle habits that lead to this survival disadvantage, this patient can aim for an achievable age of 41 years. This would represent a 44 percent reduction in his overall risk of death within the next 10 years.

A demonstration of the difference between appraisal age and achievable age can be a strong motivating factor. The term "health hazard intervention" has been used to describe a patient's actions in improving health characteristics and reducing risk. The general approach to patient care based on health hazard appraisal and health hazard intervention has given rise to a whole new medical philosophy known as prospective medicine.

PROSPECTIVE MEDICINE

PROSPECTIVE MEDICINE is based on a view of health and disease which includes 6 separate stages. In stage 1, a person is not at any risk. In stage 2, a risk develops because of a change in age or a change in personal environment. At this point, the individual has come close to an agent of disease but has not yet become involved (and may not become involved) with that agent. In stage 3, the person is clearly at greater risk because now the agent of disease is present. If this agent is allowed to continue without intervention, disease or injury may be inevitable. In stage 4, the individual develops signs that are not apparent to him or her but can be perceived by a physician who is attentive to the indications of early disease. In stage 5, the person develops symptoms and is aware that something is abnormal. The final stage 6 is disability or death.

Conventional medicine generally aims at providing crisis intervention in stages 5 and 6, after symptoms have appeared. Many physicians use periodic screening in the absence of symptoms, and this could provide more intervention in stage 4, where there are signs but no symptoms. Health hazard appraisal and prospective medicine aim for intervention in stages 2 and 3, by calling to a patient's attention the possibility of an unhealthy personal environment long before signs and symptoms are present.

For example, before puberty, a healthy American boy (with no congenital heart defects) has essentially no risk of heart disease. He is in stage 1. After puberty and especially in the late teen years, he may move into stage 2, by developing unfavorable habits like smoking and overeating or eating a high-fat diet of hot dogs, hamburgers, french fries, and other foods favored in that age group. In his twenties, he might develop high blood pressure and a sedentary lifestyle and lead into stage 3. In stage 4, he might develop an abnormal electrocardiogram as the first sign of clinical heart disease without any symptoms. Stage 5 might bring the onset of chest pain, an indication he has reached an advanced stage of disease without being aware of it. Finally, an overt heart attack or even death may follow very closely and represent stage 6.

It is not at all uncommon for patients to first seek medical advice when they develop chest pain. Individuals involved in prospective medicine, on the other hand, are advised several decades earlier to modify or eliminate unhealthy habits.

HOW HEALTH HAZARD APPRAISAL DATA ARE OBTAINED

INFORMATION NEEDED for health hazard appraisal is developed from the bottom up. The first step is to determine the major causes of death in the next 10 years by age (in increments of 5 years), sex, and race. From this information comes the average probability of death from each major cause for each 5-year age, sex, and race group. The third step is to associate the particular risk factors (and their intensity) with each of these causes of death. Finally, there must be demonstrated effective methods for addressing and modifying the identified risks.

Information on the major causes of death comes from U.S. government mortality statistics. The average probability of death is calculated for each age group from census and death records for the total population. These tables have been developed and updated by Geller and Steele under the aegis of the Methodist Hospital in Indianapolis. More recently the Department of Health and Human Service's Centers for Disease Control has assumed the task of maintaining and updating this information.

The determination of relevant risk factors is made by expert panels on each of the major diseases identified. The risk intensity comes from such long-term studies as the Framingham Heart Study, critical prognostic reviews of professional experience, available data presented by experts in the various diseases, conferences held at university medical centers, and underwriting manuals from life insurance companies.

Through this approach, health hazard appraisal brings the benefits of large population studies and results to bear in individual cases in clinical situations. By reducing their discussion to hard-and-fast mathematical terms, the patient and physician are freed from open-ended moralistic and judgmental discussion, interaction, and negotiation. Using a fixed time period (10 years) brings to the method a sense of immediacy. The discussion is not about what might happen to a teenager in middle age, in the sixties, or after retirement. No matter what the patient's age, the method focuses on the next decade. Achievable age brings squarely into focus an individual target for each patient, and the steps required to reach that target can be very clearly specified by the physician.

VARIATIONS OF HEALTH HAZARD APPRAISAL

HEALTH HAZARD APPRAISAL has become widely available in many forms. In its simplest application, the individual completes a standardized history questionnaire, such as the sample included in this chapter. The appraiser then enters the appropriate data and the calculations are performed, increasingly using computer technology. Depending on the method of application and applicable overhead, the cost of health appraisal can range from $5 to $10. (A list of names and addresses of firms that offer appraisals directly to the public is also included at the end of this chapter.)

PROBLEMS WITH HEALTH HAZARD APPRAISAL

THERE ARE SOME theoretical and minor practical problems with health hazard appraisal. The first of these results from labeling a patient "at risk." Many patients may be overwhelmed by a pessimistic projection of their future and may simply give up. One patient told me, for example, that the 1964 Surgeon General's report on smoking made him so nervous about his own prospects that he went from smoking 2 packs of cigarettes a day to 3! In a more formal analysis, employees at a Canadian steel mill who were found through widespread screening to be hypertensive, showed increased absenteeism in the year following their unsought diagnosis, as compared to the year before.

In other people, the projection of probable disease and the chances of death may create excessive anxiety which, if unmitigated by appropriate behavioral changes, can result in stress-related illness.

One other problem in health hazard appraisal is the inability to guarantee results in any individual.

It is always difficult to extrapolate from group statistics to the odds for a single person. For example, while the incidence of lung cancer in nonsmokers is extremely low, we continue to see patients who develop this disease without ever having taken a single puff. Moreover, neither health hazard appraisal nor any other technique will identify these people prior to the onset of disease. Accordingly, participants in appraisal must be aware that they are improving their odds, but not buying a guarantee.

Finally, health hazard appraisal clearly identifies a major role in health maintenance for the individual. Many persons will insist that their own health is the responsibility of the physician. Still others delegate their health problems to a parent, child or, most commonly, a spouse. Such people will obviously incur conflict with a health promotion strategy imposed on them by a physician or, more important, by an employer.

HOW TO USE A HEALTH HAZARD APPRAISAL

PERHAPS THE GREATEST BENEFIT to be derived from a health hazard appraisal is that it pinpoints those areas or habits that represent the greatest risk. It also enables a systematic approach to lifestyle change. Throughout this book, diseases are discussed in terms of risk. In Chapter 19 on Heart and Blood Vessel Disease, for example, the factors that increase the risk of a heart attack are outlined in detail. The hazards of smoking, alcohol, and other substance abuse are discussed at length in Chapter 18, page 340. Stress is yet another important factor that should be taken into consideration in evaluating an overall health quotient. (See Chapter 17 on The Effects of Stress on Health, page 327.)

There is also the question of whether it is worth-

while to make the effort to change a habit. How do we evaluate the merits of changing a habit, say, of quitting smoking? Do these benefits outweigh the pleasure gained from smoking? Obviously, these are highly personal considerations that can be likened to any investment. Changing a habit (quitting smoking, eating less, starting exercise, etc.) involves an individual investment and an opportunity. The payback may be immediate or long-term. If the cost of change, in the eyes of the concerned individual, is greater than the cost of not changing, then why bother?

Tables 15.1–15.12 are designed to help you evaluate the benefits to be derived from changing a health habit that represents a risk factor.

SAMPLE HEALTH HAZARD APPRAISAL QUESTIONNAIRE

THE FOLLOWING is a sample of the questionnaire used by the Prospective Medicine Center of Indianapolis, Indiana. Dr. Jack H. Hall, president of the Prospective Medicine Center and author of the book *Prospective Medicine*, was instrumental in developing the first health hazard appraisal at Methodist Hospital in the early 1960s.

A recognized pioneer in the field, Dr. Hall has since developed the health hazard appraisal into an

adaptable health tool, using computers to analyze the results. His center provides computerized health hazard appraisal services to physicians, medical centers, and business health programs throughout the United States.

The computerized analysis informs the respondent of his or her appraisal age (as compared to actual age) and also outlines areas of particular risk and makes specific recommendations for change.

SAMPLE QUESTIONNAIRE

Name _____

Address _____

_____

Birthdate _____

Weight _____ lbs.

Systolic *(upper reading)* blood pressure *(if known)*

_____

Diastolic *(lower reading)* blood pressure *(if known)*

_____

Cholesterol level *(if known)* _____

Your mileage per year as both a passenger and as a driver in an automobile or any other motor vehicle (national average is 10,000 miles per year)

_____

Is your natural mother alive? _____

1. No   2. Yes   3. Do Not Know

Is she now over 70, or was she at the time of death? _____

1. No   2. Yes   3. Do Not Know

If she is dead, did she die of Heart Disease? _____

1. No   2. Yes   3. Do Not Know

Is your natural father alive? _____

1. No   2. Yes   3. Do Not Know

Is he now over 70, or was he at the time of death? _____

1. No   2. Yes   3. Do Not Know

If he is dead, did he die of Heart Disease? _____

1. No   2. Yes   3. Do Not Know

Has any member of your immediate family (parents, brothers, sisters, or children) ever committed or attempted Suicide? _____

1. No   2. Yes   3. Do Not Know

Has any member of your immediate family (parents, brothers, sisters, or children) had or have Diabetes? _____

1. No   2. Yes   3. Do Not Know

Have you ever been told that you have Diabetes? _____

1. No   2. Yes with treatment   3. Yes without treatment

Approximately how much of time do you wear your seat belt? _____

1. None   2. 20%   3. 40%
4. 60%   5. 80%   6. 100%

Approximately how many alcoholic drinks do you have per week? (one drink equals 1 12 oz. beer, 4 oz. of wine, or 1 oz. of hard liquor) _____

1. Nondrinker   2. Have Stopped Drinking
3. 1–2 Drinks Per Week   4. 3–6 Drinks Per Week   5. 7–24 Drinks Per Week
6. 25–40 Drinks Per Week   7. 41 or More Drinks Per Week

Do you or have you ever taken any of the drugs or medications listed here before driving in your car? If your answer is YES, please indicate the type of drug or drugs you have taken or are presently taking. _____

1. Do Not Take Any   2. Mood Elevators
3. Amphetamines, Diet Pills   4. Tranquilizers, Sedatives, Sleeping Pills, Nerve Pills
5. Narcotic Pain Pills   6. Antihistamines   7. Marijuana, LSD

Have you ever been arrested for a violent act or threat of a violent act? _____

1. No   2. Yes

Do you carry a weapon? (Includes carrying a weapon while at work) _____

1. No   2. Yes

How much exercise do you have each day? _____

1. Walking less than 5 blocks or climbing up less than 5 flights of stairs. (Sedentary—No Sports)
2. Walking 5–15 blocks or climbing up 5–15 flights of stairs. (Little—Light Sports)
3. Walking 15–20 blocks or climbing up 15–20 flights of stairs. (Acceptable—Active Sports)
4. Walking more than 20 blocks or climbing up more than 20 flights of stairs. (Substantial—Strenuous Sports)

Do you smoke? _____

1. No   2. Yes

Did you previously smoke? _____

1. No   2. Yes

If either of the above answers were YES, please list the amount that you now smoke per day or previously smoked per day _____

1. 40+ Cigarettes   2. 20–39 Cigarettes
3. 10–19 Cigarettes   4. 1–9 Cigarettes
5. Heavy Pipe   6. Light Pipe
7. Heavy Cigar   8. Light Cigar

Prospective Medicine Center, Indianapolis, IN.

If you have stopped smoking, please list the number of years that you have stopped _____

    1. 1 year   2. 2 years   3. 3 years
    4. 4 years   5. 5 years   6. 6 years
    7. 7 years   8. 8 years   9. 9 years
    0. More than 9 years

What would you consider your economic and social status to be? _____

    1. Low   2. Average   3. High

Are you often depressed? _____

    1. No   2. Yes

Do you frequently have crying spells? _____

    1. No   2. Yes

Do you frequently think of ending your life? _____

    1. No   2. Yes

Do you have an annual proctosigmoidoscopy (examination of your bowel with a lighted instrument) or screening of stool specimen for blood 3 times a year? _____

    1. No   2. Yes

Have you had any bleeding from your rectum? _____

    1. No, have not had any bleeding   2. Yes, have had some bleeding   3. Yes, have had some bleeding, but my doctor knows about it.

Have you ever had polyps or growths in your rectum? (not piles or hemorrhoids) _____

    1. No   2. Yes   3. Do Not Know

Do you have or have you had an Ulcerative Colitis? (bloody diarrhea with pus and mucus and sores inside the rectum) _____

    1. No   2. Yes, 10 or more years   3. Yes, under 10 years

Have you had Bacterial Pneumonia? _____

    1. No   2. Yes

Have you had or do you have Emphysema? _____

    1. No   2. Yes

Have you ever had Rheumatic Fever? (Inflammation of the heart and/or joints) _____

    1. No   2. Yes, with treatment   3. Yes, without treatment

Have you ever been told that you have a Heart Murmur? _____

    1. No   2. Yes, with treatment   3. Yes, without treatment

Please list any other significant problems which you feel may affect your life expectancy.

_____

_____

Prospective Medicine Center, Indianapolis, IN.

_____
_____
_____

In the past 12 months, have you experienced any of the following:

Insert appropriate number in each space at right:
(1) No   (2) Yes

Death of Spouse _____
Change in health of a family member _____
Death of a close family member _____
Death of a close friend _____
Trouble with your in-laws _____
Change in number of arguments with your spouse _____
Sexual difficulties _____
Marital separation _____
Marital reconciliation _____
Divorce _____
Marriage _____
Revision of personal habits _____
Change in sleeping habits _____
Change in eating habits _____
Minor violation of law _____
An outstanding personal achievement _____
Personal injury or illness _____
Change in responsibilities at work _____
Change in work hours or conditions _____
Trouble with boss _____
Fired from job _____
Change to a different line of work _____
Business readjustment _____
Change in your financial status _____
Change in residence _____
Change in living conditions _____
Change in number of family get-togethers _____
Begin or end school _____
Change in schools _____
Foreclosure of a mortgage or loan _____
Retirement _____
Spouse begins or stops work _____
Mortgage over $30,000 _____
Mortgage or loan less than $30,000 _____
Pregnancy _____
Son or daughter leaves home _____
Gain of a new family member _____
Change in social activities _____
Change in church activities _____
Change in recreation _____
Vacation _____
Christmas _____
Jail term _____

The following questions are for females only

Has your mother or any sisters or aunts ever had breast cancer? ____

1. None had   2. One had   3. Two or more had

Has your doctor ever told you that you had a lump or cyst in your breast that was NOT cancer? ____

1. No   2. Yes

Does your doctor examine your breasts at least once a year? ____

1. No   2. Yes

Do you examine your breasts at least once a month? ____

1. No   2. Yes

What is your current menstrual status? ____

*1. Still menstruating   2. Natural menopause
3. Surgical menopause at under 35 years
4. Surgical menopause at over 35 years*

How many times have you been pregnant? ____

1. None   2. 1–2 times   3. 3 or more times

If you have been pregnant, what was the age of your first pregnancy? ____

1. Under 20   2. 20–24   3. 25 or over

At what age did you begin to have regular sexual intercourse? ____

*1. Never   2. Before 20   3. Between 20–25
4. After 25*

Prospective Medicine Center, Indianapolis, IN.

Are you Jewish? ____

1. No   2. Yes

Has your cervix been removed? ____

1. No   2. Yes

Has your uterus been removed? ____

1. No   2. Yes

Have your ovaries been removed? ____

1. No   2. Yes, one   3. Yes, both

Have you had any ABNORMAL vaginal bleeding in the past year? ____

*1. No
2. Yes, between menstrual periods.
3. Yes, during or after sexual intercourse.
4. Yes, periods have stopped, but having bleeding every once in a while.
5. Yes, taking estrogens, bleed when off.
6. Yes, taking estrogens, bleed whether on them or off.*

Please indicate the results of any Pap smears, cancer smears, that you have by inserting the most appropriate answer ____

*1. I have not had a Pap smear in the past 5 years.
2. I have had 1 normal Pap smear in the past year.
3. I have had 1 normal Pap smear in the past 5 years.
4. I have had 3 normal Pap smears in the past 5 years.
5. I have had 5 normal Pap smears in the past 5 years.
6. I have had a Pap smear in the past year, but it was abnormal.
7. I have had a Pap smear in the past year, but I do not know the results.*

CALCULATING THE RISKS

HEALTH RISK APPRAISALS are usually evaluated in conjunction with statistical tables that show the risk of dying for certain population and age groups. The following tables show these risks, as well as a breakdown of what is involved in changing habits that are detrimental to health.

Table 15.1 **WHITE MALES**[a]

Top Ten Causes of Deaths per 100,000 that Can Be Expected over Next Decade for Each Age Group

Cause	(Age)	15	20	25	30	35	40	45	50	55	60	65	70
Aircraft accidents		—	23	28	29	—	—	—	—	—	—	—	—
Alcoholism		—	—	—	—	—	54	—	—	—	—	—	—
Arterial disease		—	—	—	—	—	—	—	—	—	435	771	1,292
Bronchitis/emphysema		—	—	—	—	—	—	—	132	275	509	829	1,164
Car accident		709	599	395	305	269	256	242	236	237	—	—	—
Cirrhosis		—	—	35	81	161	274	398	497	578	603	532	—
Colorectal cancer		—	—	—	—	41	78	161	298	509	782	1,108	1,461
Coronary disease		—	—	62	214	601	1,355	2,567	4,248	6,694	9,859	13,910	19,429

[a]Author's assessment.
Adapted from *Odds on Your Life* by John L. Roglieri, M.D., Seaview Books, New York, 1980. © John L. Roglieri, M.D.

Table 15.1 **WHITE MALES (continued)**

Top Ten Causes of Deaths per 100,000 that Can Be Expected over Next Decade for Each Age Group

Cause	(Age) 15	20	25	30	35	40	45	50	55	60	65	70
Diabetes	—	—	—	—	—	—	90	149	235	359	532	714
Drownings	70	52	37	—	—	—	—	—	—	—	—	—
Electrocution	18	21	—	—	—	—	—	—	—	—	—	—
Falls	24	24	—	—	—	—	—	—	—	—	—	—
Fire	—	22	—	—	—	—	—	—	—	—	—	—
Firearms accidents	28	—	—	—	—	—	—	—	—	—	—	—
Homicide	116	147	143	144	136	112	95	—	—	—	—	—
Leukemia	21	—	—	—	—	—	—	—	—	—	—	—
Lung cancer	—	—	—	39	120	317	675	1,160	1,851	2,606	3,212	3,530
Machine (noncar) accidents	34	40	36	39	43	—	—	—	—	—	—	—
Pneumonia	—	—	—	—	37	61	94	149	251	404	687	1,280
Poisonings	41	53	48	38	—	—	—	—	—	—	—	—
Prostate cancer	—	—	—	—	—	—	—	—	—	421	799	1,389
Stomach cancer	—	—	—	—	—	—	—	—	—	—	—	456
Stroke	—	—	25	41	78	142	238	413	754	1,355	2,485	4,484
Suicide	230	296	263	247	244	250	265	274	287	—	—	—
Other causes	382	495	571	171	1,193	1,524	2,378	617	5,635	7,894	7,326	13,858
Total deaths	1,673	1,772	1,643	1,901	2,752	4,423	7,203	11,203	17,306	25,227	35,403	49,057

Table 15.2 **BLACK MALES** [a]

Top Ten Causes of Deaths per 100,000 that Can Be Expected over Next Decade for Each Age Group

Cause	(Age) 15	20	25	30	35	40	45	50	55	60	65	70
Alcoholism	—	—	71	153	205	226	284	290	—	—	—	—
Arterial disease	—	—	—	—	—	—	—	—	—	—	564	928
Car accidents	393	496	447	370	351	348	340	352	—	—	—	—
Cirrhosis	—	64	179	335	524	708	812	814	768	600	—	—
Colorectal cancer	—	—	—	—	—	—	—	323	508	690	995	1,327
Coronary disease	—	48	133	376	902	1,728	2,980	4,670	7,008	8,977	12,175	16,741
Diabetes	—	—	—	—	90	130	200	—	447	609	790	999
Drownings	145	122	110	89	—	—	—	—	—	—	—	—
Epilepsy	19	—	—	—	—	—	—	—	—	—	—	—
Esophageal cancer	—	—	—	—	—	137	255	409	505	486	—	—
Fire	26	38	—	—	—	—	—	—	—	—	—	—
Firearms accidents	31	—	—	—	—	—	—	—	—	—	—	—
Homicide	733	1,168	1,200	1,054	986	824	657	570	476	—	—	—
Hypertensive disease	—	—	—	—	—	—	—	—	—	—	3,278	811
Lung cancer	—	—	—	—	235	595	1,187	1,916	2,604	2,948	—	—
Machine (noncar) accidents	23	—	—	—	—	—	—	—	—	—	—	—
Pneumonia	26	42	79	135	185	250	343	443	571	693	1,006	1,538
Poisonings	36	83	90	74	—	—	—	—	—	—	—	—
Prostatic cancer	—	—	—	—	—	—	—	—	507	919	1,768	2,857
Stomach cancer	—	—	—	—	—	—	—	—	—	448	598	807
Stroke	—	37	88	176	313	492	772	1,200	1,885	2,705	4,181	6,263
Suicide	137	237	232	172	132	—	—	—	—	—	—	—
Other causes	531	909	1,282	1,839	2,629	3,613	4,950	6,939	9,501	11,127	13,644	17,149
Total deaths	2,100	3,244	3,911	4,773	6,552	9,051	12,780	17,923	24,780	30,202	39,614	52,798

[a] Author's assessment.

Adapted from *Odds on Your Life* by John L. Roglieri, M.D., Seaview Books, New York, 1980. © John L. Roglieri, M.D.

Table 15.3 **WHITE FEMALES** [a]

Top Ten Causes of Deaths per 100,000 that Can Be Expected over Next Decade for Each Age Group

Cause (Age)	15	20	25	30	35	40	45	50	55	60	65	70
Arterial disease	—	—	—	—	—	—	—	—	—	—	299	672
Breast cancer	—	8	36	85	170	320	504	673	804	887	952	1,027
Car accidents	229	162	111	95	95	93	94	97	—	—	—	—
Cervical cancer	—	—	13	24	37	48	—	—	—	—	—	—
Cirrhosis	—	—	13	32	76	132	190	240	260	261	253	—
Colorectal cancer	—	—	—	—	39	80	144	255	416	604	843	1,182
Congenital circulatory defects	9	—	—	—	—	—	—	—	—	—	—	—
Coronary disease	—	—	15	39	112	263	548	1,081	2,118	3,770	6,610	11,815
Diabetes	—	—	—	—	—	—	63	110	208	342	544	828
Drownings	8	—	—	—	—	—	—	—	—	—	—	—
Fire	10	8	—	—	—	—	—	—	—	—	—	—
Hodgkin's disease	—	8	—	—	—	—	—	—	—	—	—	—
Homicide	14	44	39	39	39	—	—	—	—	—	—	—
Hypertensive heart disease	—	—	—	—	—	—	—	—	—	—	—	315
Leukemia	14	13	16	19	—	—	—	—	—	—	—	—
Lung cancer	—	—	—	22	70	161	289	439	608	709	714	698
Ovarian cancer	—	—	—	—	—	76	142	209	278	321	342	364
Pneumonia	9	10	—	—	—	—	—	—	118	183	326	677
Poisonings	14	14	14	—	—	—	—	—	—	—	—	—
Rheumatic heart disease	—	—	—	—	—	—	—	—	131	184	—	—
Stroke	10	15	25	46	81	136	212	329	568	993	1,898	3,933
Suicide	56	82	93	99	111	128	133	125	—	—	—	—
Other causes	180	245	325	458	685	1,038	1,555	2,297	3,432	4,747	6,531	9,099
Total deaths	579	609	699	958	1,515	2,475	3,874	5,855	8,941	13,001	19,312	30,610

[a] Author's assessment.
Adapted from *Odds on Your Life* by John L. Roglieri, M.D., Seaview Books, New York, 1980. © John L. Roglieri, M.D.

Table 15.4 **BLACK FEMALES** [a]

Top Ten Causes of Deaths per 100,000 that Can Be Expected over Next Decade for Each Age Group

Cause (Age)	15	20	25	30	35	40	45	50	55	60	65	70
Arterial disease	—	—	—	—	—	—	—	—	—	—	443	843
Breast cancer	—	—	52	121	189	320	530	692	745	722	824	962
Car accidents	102	93	83	76	76	—	—	—	—	—	—	—
Cervical cancer	—	—	28	64	101	142	180	222	256	—	—	—
Cirrhosis	—	36	91	172	258	343	395	374	347	269	—	—
Colorectal cancer	—	—	—	—	—	—	159	304	466	601	900	1,239
Coronary disease	—	18	48	162	382	777	1,462	2,501	4,063	5,548	9,146	14,568
Diabetes	—	—	—	39	73	122	341	469	731	920	1,272	1,739
Drownings	12	—	—	—	—	—	—	—	—	—	—	—
Fire	19	23	—	—	—	—	—	—	—	—	—	—
Homicide	189	243	229	192	166	139	—	—	—	—	—	—
Hypertensive heart disease	—	—	—	—	92	137	192	277	410	613	887	
Leukemia	19	17	—	—	—	—	—	—	—	—	—	—
Lung cancer	—	—	—	—	76	200	341	471	556	570	585	595
Nephritis/nephrosis	—	—	—	—	—	—	—	—	233	269	—	475
Pneumonia	17	26	38	53	74	107	134	171	—	284	478	842

[a] Author's assessment.
Adapted from *Odds on Your Life* by John L. Roglieri, M.D., Seaview Books, New York, 1980. © John L. Roglieri, M.D.

Table 15.4 **BLACK FEMALES (continued)**

Top Ten Causes of Deaths per 100,000 that Can Be Expected over Next Decade for Each Age Group

Cause (Age)	15	20	25	30	35	40	45	50	55	60	65	70
Poisonings	25	34	30	—	—	—	—	—	—	—	—	—
Stroke	22	37	64	134	239	398	632	939	1,495	2,162	3,949	6,648
Suicide	39	58	56	44	—	—	—	—	—	—	—	—
Uterine cancer	—	—	—	—	—	—	—	—	—	—	352	—
Other causes	359	572	822	1,033	1,586	2,261	3,098	4,210	5,675	6,725	9,332	13,181
Total deaths	818	1,157	1,485	2,090	3,245	4,901	7,307	10,545	14,844	18,490	27,894	41,979

Table 15.5a **INVESTMENT VALUATION MODEL FOR LIFESTYLE DECISIONS**[a]

Lifestyle habit	Investment	Opportunity cost (loss)	Payback	Present value	Benefits
Smoking	"Withdrawal"	Relaxation; sedation; stimulation; "fun," "taste," etc.; avoiding cravings	13 years	Individual	Money saved; improved hygiene; social acceptability; freedom from fear; freedom from smokers' symptoms (cough, pneumonia, hoarseness)
Heavy drinking	Withdrawal	Sedation; tranquilization; easy sociability	Immediate, unless liver disease advances	Individual	Sobriety; productivity; domestic tranquility; improved appearance; respect and self-respect; freedom from symptoms, illnesses, and hazards of alcoholism
Overeating	Dietary restraint	Stress relief; convenience; enjoyment	Indeterminate	Individual	Respect and self-respect; more energy; better looks; freedom from fear of disease; fewer aches and pains; reading, sleeping
Careless driving	Public transportation; seat belts; slow down	Convenience; "comfort"; enjoyment	Immediate	Individual	Security; freedom from DWI citations
Sedentary life	Exercise; getting into shape	Time Rest	Immediate	Individual	Respect, self-respect; improved appearance; more energy; weight control
Stress mismanagement	Active management	Passivity (drugs, psychiatrist)	Immediate	Individual	Money saved; freedom from side effects; improved sleep

[a]Author's assessment.
Adapted from *Odds on Your Life* by John L. Roglieri, M.D., Seaview Books, New York, 1980. © John L. Roglieri, M.D.

Table 15.5b **LIKELY EXTENSION OF LIFE DUE TO LIFESTYLE CHANGE**

Lifestyle habit	Likely life extension (years)[a]	Lifestyle habit	Likely life extension (years)[a]
Quit smoking	2–9	Drive carefully	2–6
Quit heavy drinking	3–11	Manage stress	1–5
Achieve ideal body weight	1–3	Multiple changes[b]	1–11
Exercise	1–2		

[a]Author's assessment.
[b]Changes are usually linked, e.g., quitting smoking or drinking may lead to better stress management; increasing exercise may lead to weight loss and stress management, etc. Most experts agree that any combination of changes is likely to extend life beyond a decade.
Adapted from *Odds on Your Life* by John L. Roglieri, M.D., Seaview Books, New York, 1980. © John L. Roglieri, M.D.

Table 15.6   **LIFESTYLE INVESTMENT FORMULA EVALUATOR** [a]

Habit: Smoking   **Change: Quit**

	COSTS			BENEFITS	
Investment	Lost opportunity		Payoffs		Joy along the way
Cost to you of withdrawal	Cost to you of lost pleasures	Immediate	Later		
0 (easy) down to −10 (most difficult)	−1 point each Energy, stimulation ____ Handling, manipulating ____ Extra pleasure ____ Relaxation ____ Calming ____ Social ease ____ Appetite suppression ____ Other ____ ____	+1 point each No cough ____ No shortness of breath ____ No bronchitis ____ No pneumonia ____ No hoarseness ____ No cancer fear ____ No heart-attack fear ____ No guilt ____	*Extra years of life (from table)* Number of years ____ times personal value (½ to 2) equals ____		+1 point each Mastery of own life __ Social acceptance __ Example for kids __ Domestic tranquility (spouse) ____ (kids) ____ Convenience ____ Money saved ____ Aesthetics (breath, teeth, fingers, etc.) ____ Improved sense of smell, taste ____ Other ____
MAXIMUM: −10	MAXIMUM: −5	MAXIMUM: +5	MAXIMUM: +5		MAXIMUM: +5

YOUR VALUES:

PERSONAL TOTAL:

RESULT: any minus total = unmotivated; 0 to +1 = indifferent; +2 to +5 = motivated; more than +5 = highly motivated

[a] Author's assessment.
Adapted from *Odds on Your Life* by John L. Roglieri, M.D., Seaview Books, New York, 1980. © John L. Roglieri, M.D.

Table 15.7   **BENEFITS OF QUITTING SMOKING IN TERMS OF LIFE EXPECTANCY** [a]

If you are age	And you smoke, your 20-year death risk is (per 100,000)	If you quit, your 20-year death risk will fall to	If you survive, you will have increased your life by (years)
Male			
35	9,420	4,370	4
45	24,146	13,942	6
55	51,176	33,858	9
65	90,875	73,052	13
Female			
35	5,629	4,729	2
35	11,898	9,998	4
55	28,802	25,141	9
65	67,719	67,026	9

[a] Author's assessment.
Adapted from *Odds on Your Life* by John L. Roglieri, M.D., Seaview Books, New York, 1980. © John L. Roglieri, M.D.

Table 15.8 **LIFESTYLE INVESTMENT FORMULA EVALUATOR**[a]

Habit: Heavy drinking   Change: Quit

COSTS			BENEFITS	
Investment	Lost opportunity	Payoffs		Joy along the way
Cost to you of withdrawal	Cost to you of lost pleasures	Immediate	Later	
0 (easy) down to −10 (most difficult)	−1 point each Social ease _____ Business ease _____ Relaxation _____ Taste _____ Calming _____ "Courage" _____ Other _____ _____	+1 point each No hangover _____ No blackouts _____ No stomach trouble _____ No heartburn _____ No jaundice _____ No DT's _____ No shakes _____ Other _____	Extra years of life (from table) Number of years _____ times personal value (½ to 2) equals _____	+1 point each Social acceptance _____ Sober driving _____ Better job performance Domestic tranquility _____ Improved appearance _____ Self-respect _____ Other _____
MAXIMUM: −10	MAXIMUM: −5	MAXIMUM: +5	MAXIMUM: +5	MAXIMUM: +5

YOUR VALUES:

PERSONAL TOTAL:

RESULT: any minus total = unmotivated; 0 to +1 = indifferent; +2 to +5 = motivated; more than +5 = highly motivated

[a]Author's assessment.
Adapted from *Odds on Your Life* by John L. Roglieri, M.D., Seaview Books, New York, 1980. © John L. Roglieri, M.D.

Table 15.9 **LIFESTYLE INVESTMENT FORMULA EVALUATOR**[a]

Habit: Sedentary lifestyle   Change: Regular aerobic exercise

COSTS			BENEFITS	
Investment	Lost opportunity	Payoffs		Joy along the way
Cost to you of withdrawal	Cost to you of lost pleasures	Immediate	Later	
0 (easy) down to −10 (most difficult)	−1 point each Time _____ Rest _____ Relaxation _____ Comfort _____ Other _____	+1 point each More energy _____ Less appetite _____ Fewer aches and pains _____ Lower blood pressure _____ Fewer anxiety symptoms _____ Other _____	Extra years of life (from table) Number of years _____ times personal value (½ to 2) equals _____	+1 point each Improved appearance _____ Sense of well- being _____ Self-respect _____ Better sleep _____ Less fear of heart attack _____ Easier weight control _____ Quit smoking _____ Other _____
MAXIMUM: −10	MAXIMUM: −5	MAXIMUM: +5	MAXIMUM: +5	MAXIMUM: +5

YOUR VALUES:

PERSONAL TOTAL:

RESULT: any minus total = unmotivated; 0 to +1 = indifferent; +2 to +5 = motivated; more than +5 = highly motivated

[a]Author's assessment.
Adapted from *Odds on Your Life* by John L. Roglieri, M.D., Seaview Books, New York, 1980. © John L. Roglieri, M.D.

Table 15.10 **LIFESTYLE INVESTMENT FORMULA EVALUATOR**[a]

Habit: Stress mismanagement   Change: Improved coping

COSTS				BENEFITS	
Investment	**Lost opportunity**	**Payoffs**			**Joy along the way**
Cost to you of withdrawal	Cost to you of lost pleasures	Immediate	Later		
0 (easy) down to −10 (most difficult)	−1 point each Passivity _____ Crutch (drug) _____ (cigarette) _____ (psychiatrist) _____ Emotional release (outburst) _____ Other _____	+1 point each Calming _____ Lower blood pressure _____ Less need for tobacco _____ Decreased drug dependence _____ Fewer symptoms of stress _____	*Extra years of life (from table)* Number of years _____ times personal value (½ to 2) equals _____		+1 point each Money saved _____ Freedom from side effects _____ Better sleep _____ Mastery of self _____ Improved performance _____ Other _____
MAXIMUM: −10	MAXIMUM: −5	MAXIMUM: +5	MAXIMUM: +5		MAXIMUM: +5

YOUR VALUES:

PERSONAL TOTAL:

RESULT: any minus total = unmotivated; 0 to +1 = indifferent; +2 to +5 = motivated; more than +5 = highly motivated

[a] Author's assessment.
Adapted from *Odds on Your Life* by John L. Roglieri, M.D., Seaview Books, New York, 1980. © John L. Roglieri, M.D.

Table 15.11 **LIFESTYLE INVESTMENT FORMULA EVALUATOR**[a]

Habit: Overeating (to obesity)   Change: Moderate (to ideal bodyweight)

COSTS				BENEFITS	
Investment	**Lost opportunity**	**Payoffs**			**Joy along the way**
Cost to you of withdrawal	Cost to you of lost pleasures	Immediate	Later		
0 (easy) down to −10 (most difficult)	−1 point each Taste _____ Act of eating _____ Relaxation _____ Satiation _____ Convenience _____ Other _____	+1 point each "Energy" _____ No shortness of breath _____ Less "arthritis" _____ Less back pain _____ Lower blood pressure _____ Less risk of diabetes _____ Less risk of heart disease _____	*Extra years of life (from table)* Number of years _____ times personal value (½ to 2) equals _____		+1 point each Respect _____ Self-respect _____ Better looks _____ Less fear of disease _____ No guilt _____ Other _____
MAXIMUM: −10	MAXIMUM: +5	MAXIMUM: +5	MAXIMUM: +5		MAXIMUM: +5

YOUR VALUES:

PERSONAL TOTAL:

RESULT: any minus total = unmotivated; 0 to +1 = indifferent; +2 to +5 = motivated; more than +5 = highly motivated

[a] Author's assessment.
Adapted from *Odds on Your Life* by John L. Roglieri, M.D., Seaview Books, New York, 1980. © John L. Roglieri, M.D.

Table 15.12 **LIFESTYLE INVESTMENT FORMULA EVALUATOR**[a]

Habit: Careless driving		Change: Wearing seat belts; driving more carefully		
COSTS			**BENEFITS**	
Investment	Lost opportunity		Payoffs	Joy along the way
Cost to you of withdrawal	Cost to you of lost pleasures	Immediate	Later	
0 (easy) down to −3 (most difficult) for each:	*−1 point each* Comfort _____ Convenience _____	*+1 point each* Less risk of death _____	*Extra years of life (from table)* Number of years _____	*+1 point each* Security _____ Example for kids _____
Wear seat belts ___	Other _____	Less risk of	times personal value	Fewer minor
Drive sober _____	Convenience _____	death _____	(½ to 2) equals _____	accidents _____
Use public	Other _____	No DWI risk or		No threat to
transportation _	Convenience _____	fear _____		others _____
Drive less _____	Time _____	Less risk of		Save money _____
Slow down _____	Other _____	death _____		Read, sleep _____
	Convenience _____	Save money _____		Exercise
	Convenience _____	Reduce risk _____		Save fuel _____
	Time _____	Reduce risk _____		
MAXIMUM: −10	MAXIMUM: −5	MAXIMUM: +5	MAXIMUM: +5	MAXIMUM: +5

YOUR VALUES:

PERSONAL TOTAL:

RESULT: any minus total = unmotivated; 0 to +1 = indifferent; +2 to +5 = motivated; more than +5 = highly motivated

[a]Author's assessment.
Adapted from *Odds on Your Life* by John L. Roglieri, M.D., Seaview Books, New York, 1980. © John L. Roglieri, M.D.

A GUIDE TO HEALTH HAZARD APPRAISALS[a]

In recent years, a number of health hazard appraisal systems have been developed. Following are some of the appraisal services and a brief description of what each offers.

1. *Prospective Medicine Center, 3901 North Meridian St., Indianapolis, IN 46208.* The Health Hazard Appraisal offered by this center is modeled on the one developed by Methodist Hospital in Indianapolis, widely regarded as the prototype of all subsequent appraisals. (A sample questionnaire appears on page 281.) The individual completes the questionnaire, which is then evaluated by computer. The Automated Personal Risk Analysis lists the major health hazards faced by the individual and offers specific recommendations for reducing and eliminating each one.

2. *U.S. Public Health Service Hospital, 3100 Wyman Park Dr., Baltimore, MD 21211.* This questionnaire is similar to the one developed by Methodist Hospital in Indianapolis, but has several additions, such as questions on depression and medication. The analysis is almost exclusively quantitative.

3. *Interhealth Life Extension Institute, 1185 Avenue of the Americas, New York, NY 10036.* Content and format are similar to Methodist Hospital questionnaire, but includes more questions on the individual's state of health. Analysis indicates risk of death in next 10 years.

4. *Institute for Lifestyle Improvement, University of Wisconsin, Stevens Point Foundation, 2100 Main St., Stevens Point, WI 54481.* This appraisal includes more questions on women's health, and ranks the respondent's risk in graph form.

5. *St. Louis County Health Department, 504 East Second St., Duluth, MN 55805.* Questionnaire is similar to Methodist Hospital's, and analysis is quantitative data presented in graphic format.

6. *Medical Datamation, 5433 Strong Ridge Rd., Belle-*

[a]Adapted from "A Shopper's Guide to Appraisal Instruments," by William L. Beery, Edward H. Wagner, Victor J. Schoenbach, and Robin M. Graham, and published in *Promoting Health*, Vol. 2, No. 4, copyright 1981, a publication of the American Hospital Association and "Selected Health Risk Appraisals," published in *Healthpointer*, a publication of the National Health Information Clearinghouse and the U.S. Department of Health and Human Services.

vue, OH 44811. Several questionnaires are offered, covering different ages and groups. Analysis gives probable life expectancy, recommends changes in behavior, and also analyzes "indicators of comfort and satisfaction."

7. *Center for Health Promotion, U.S. Centers for Disease Control, 1600 Clifton Road, Atlanta, GA 30333.* Questionnaire ranks likely causes of death and gives effects of behavior change in terms of longevity.

8. *Well Aware About Health, P.O. Box 43338, Tucson, AZ 85733.* Questions are designed to provide health education; analysis ranks most likely cause of death and also provides educational material about individual health hazards.

9. *General Health, Inc., 1046 Potomac St., NW, Washington, DC 20007.* Questionnaire format is similar to Well Aware About Health, but with more emphasis on mental health and occupational hazards.

10. *HEART Evaluation and Risk Tabulation, U.S. Air Force School of Aerospace Medicine, Brooks Air Force Base, San Antonio, TX 72235.* Concentrates on cardiovascular risk; analysis is quantitative, with explanations of ways to reduce risk.

11. *Wisconsin Center for Health Risk Research, University of Wisconsin Center for Health Sciences, 600 Highland Ave., Room J5/224, Madison, WI 53792.* Questionnaire evaluates health profile and compares respondent's risks with those of the average population. Specific recommendations on risk reduction also are offered.

12. *University of California at San Francisco, Room 1699 HSW, San Francisco, CA 94143.* A health risk assessment by the department of Epidemiology and International Health.

13. *Portland Adventist Center, 10123 Southeast Market St., Portland, OR 97216.* "Life Chec" computerized health appraisal.

14. *Pacific Research Systems, P.O. Box 64218, Los Angeles, CA 90064.* Nutrition, health, and activity profile.

15. *Institute for Personal Health, 2100 M St., NW, Suite 316, Washington DC 20007.* Personal health appraisal program.

16. *Control Data, Life Extension Institute, P.O. Box O, Minneapolis, MN 55440.* Personal medical history and health risk profile.

17. *International Health Awareness Center, 148 East Michigan, Kalamazoo, MI 49007.*

Self-scored health appraisals are offered by the following organizations:

1. *St. Louis Medical Center, Department of Health Promotion, 1325 South Grand Blvd., St. Louis, MO 63104.* "General Well-Being Questionnaire."

2. *Blue Cross/Blue Shield of Michigan, Department 1909, 600 East Lafayette, Detroit, MI 48226.* "Go to Health."

3. *Preventive Medicine Institute, Strang Clinic, 55 East 34th St., New York, NY 10016.* "Health Action Plan."

4. *University of Rhode Island Health Services, Health Education Department, Roosevelt 4th Floor, Kingston, RI 02880.* "Health Graph."

5. *Public Affairs Pamphlets, 381 Park Ave. South, New York, NY 10016.* "Health Hazard Appraisal: Clues for a Healthier Lifestyle."

6. *National Health Information Clearinghouse, P.O. Box 1133, Washington DC 20013.* "Healthstyle."

7. *Center for Consumer Health Education, 1900 Association Drive, Reston, VA 22091.* "Life Score for Your Health."

8. *Northwestern Mutual Life, Advertising and Corporate Information, 720 East Wisconsin Ave., Milwaukee, WI 53202.* "The Longevity Game."

9. *Shealy Pain and Health Rehabilitation Institute, 1919 South Fremont, Springfield, MO 65804.* "Personal Stress Assessment Test."

10. *Health Education Center, 200 Ross St., Pittsburgh, PA 15219.* "Your Health Profile."

11. *Kansas Department of Health and Environment, Building 321, Forbes Field, Topeka, KS 66620.* "Your Lifestyle Profile."

16 The Fundamentals of Health

Robert Lewy, M.D.

PART I: A HEALTHY LIFESTYLE

GOOD HEALTH is a goal toward which we all strive, since the quality of life is determined, in great measure, by physical well-being. But to decide which course to follow toward improving or maintaining personal health is no easy task. It is virtually impossible to read a newspaper, watch television, listen to the radio, or browse in a bookstore without being bombarded by information from experts and so-called experts on the art of staying healthy.

Are vitamins the elixir of the Fountain of Youth? Will a spa, gym, or fitness center provide the optimal exercises to keep us in shape, or is jogging or running more sensible? Should we worry about our weight, our cholesterol intake, the food we eat, the air we breathe? If we give up that cocktail before dinner, eat "natural" foods, get regular medical checkups, and follow the advice in a best-selling exercise manual, do we have any real assurance of living a longer, healthier life?

Unfortunately, the answers to these questions are all too often provided by entrepreneurs, by advertisers touting their products, or by well-meaning, but ill-informed advisors.

The truth is that longevity can be markedly increased and the quality of life improved by following such simple health habits as avoiding smoking, drinking only in moderation, eating a well-balanced diet, controlling weight, reducing stress, and exercising regularly. By understanding the basic principles of healthy living and by applying these principles with sense and moderation, people can vastly improve the quality, and may well increase the length, of their lives.

DIET AND NUTRITION

HEART DISEASE AND CANCER are responsible for the vast majority of chronic illnesses and premature deaths in America today. While enormous strides have been made in the treatment and cure of these diseases, medical science is now moving in a different direction—toward their prevention.

Diet as a means of prevention has received a lot of attention, both in the medical community and in the popular press. While the American Heart Association and other groups have been advocating for many years a diet lower in cholesterol and fat and higher in complex carbohydrates to combat heart disease, evidence has been mounting that virtually the same diet could also reduce the risk of cancer.

Many of our natural foods have been altered, refined, and treated with chemicals. Our diet, once rich in fiber and nutrients, has changed to include excessive amounts of processed food high in fat, salt, and sugar. The refining process reduces the food's fiber content and depletes it of essential vitamins and minerals. A diet of low-fiber, high-sugar, high-fat processed food predisposes the individual to obesity and to breast and colon cancer, as well as to cardiovascular disease, hypertension, and kidney stones. An excess of sodium may exacerbate hypertension.

It is far healthier to replace some of the animal protein in the diet with the vegetable protein in legumes, grains, nuts, and seeds; to eat whole-grain products rather than refined foods; to emphasize fresh rather than processed foods in the diet, and to increase potassium intake while cutting down on sodium consumption by eating fresh fruits and vegetables.

In order to change our diet, we need to know something about the essential nutrients, both caloric and noncaloric, that should be a part of any diet plan.

Essential Nutrients

Protein. Every body cell contains protein, which maintains body tissues and supports growth, and is made up of chains of building blocks called amino acids. There are 22 different amino acids, and the body is able to manufacture all but 9 of them. These 9 are called essential amino acids, which must be supplied by food.

Most animal protein contains all the essential amino acids. To derive sufficient protein from vegetable sources, combinations of plants must be eaten. (See page 303.) Ten to 15 percent of the daily caloric intake should come from protein, since protein is essential to almost all bodily functions.

In muscle tissue, protein permits contraction; in the hair, skin, and nails, it forms a protective outer layer; it provides elasticity to blood vessel walls and serves as a framework for the minerals in bones and teeth. Without protein, there can be no growth or replacement of tissues. It also regulates the balance of body fluids and helps in the production of antibodies.

Carbohydrates. Carbohydrates are the body's main source of energy. They are readily digested and changed into blood sugar (glucose), which provides fuel for the muscles, brain, and other body tissues. Without carbohydrates, the body relies on fat and protein as sources of energy, putting a burden on the kidneys. The American diet is too low in complex carbohydrates, such as those found in bread, cereals, and whole grains. Instead, most carbohydrate intake is from highly refined and sweetened foods which provide the body with little more than sugar. Actually, the body has no need for sugar (except perhaps the psychological need of some to satisfy their "sweet tooth"), if sufficient complex carbohydrates are eaten to provide fuel.

Nutritionists recommend that carbohydrates, especially those with complex starches, natural sugars, and fiber found in fruits, vegetables, grains, cereals, beans, legumes, peas, nuts, and seeds, should make up about 55 to 58 percent of the individual's daily caloric intake.

Fats. A certain amount of fat is necessary to support and protect internal organs, to provide insulation against extreme heat and cold and, in women, to help control hormone balance. This is body fat, and the body can manufacture it, if necessary, from protein and carbohydrates. In fact, that's exactly what it does if an individual consumes more calories than needed for daily activities.

Dietary fats (those you eat) are also necessary. They transport the fat-soluble vitamins (A, D, E, and K) to the tissues. One kind of dietary fat—polyunsaturated—is especially necessary because it provides linoleic acid, which the body needs to manufacture fats properly. To get this essential fatty acid, the human body requires only 1 tablespoon of a polyunsaturated fat a day, yet most adults consume from 6 to 8 times that amount. Polyunsaturated fats are corn, cottonseed, safflower, sesame, soybean, and sunflower seed oils.

Besides polyunsaturated, there are 2 other types of dietary fats—saturated and monounsaturated, determined by their chemical makeup. The differences between them are important for their effects on the amount of cholesterol found in the bloodstream. (For more about cholesterol, see page 300.)

Saturated fat tends to raise cholesterol in the blood and is found primarily in dairy and animal products. The marbling in a prime steak, as well as the border of fat around the edge, is saturated fat, as is butter, and margarine that is made primarily of hydrogenated (hardened) oil. Saturated fats are generally solid at room temperature, with 2 notable exceptions—coconut oil and palm oil—which are both vegetable fats. They are often used in commercial baked products and nondairy creamers.

Monounsaturated fat, like polyunsaturated fat, also lowers serum cholesterol, but not as much. The 2 major monounsaturated fats are peanut oil and olive oil. This type is also found in peanuts and olives themselves, and in peanut butter, as well as in avocados and cashews.

Other Nutrients

Fiber. Fiber is the chemical substance that makes up the cell walls of plants, giving them structure and stability, but other, nonstructured substances found in plant starches are considered fiber as well. Generally, dietary fiber can be defined as anything that cannot be broken down by enzymes in the digestive tract. Fruits, vegetables, whole-grain cereals and breads, nuts, and seeds are all good sources of fiber.

Different types of fibers act in different ways, but most of them are important to the diet because they absorb many times their weight in water and pass through the digestive tract undigested, resulting in softer and bulkier stools and lessening the chance of constipation. Because fiber swells in this way, it gives the feeling of being full, thus helping to control food intake and weight.

Fiber has been shown to be of some help in controlling blood sugar levels in diabetics and is associated with reducing the amount of cholesterol and triglycerides in the blood, although it is not known whether this will reduce the risk of heart disease. Some researchers have noted that in countries where the diet is normally high in fiber, there are relatively few cases of cancer of the colon and rectum, diverticulosis, and other intestinal diseases, but a definitive link has yet to be established.

While it is generally agreed that fiber is beneficial in the diet, the benefit depends on the source of the fiber. The natural sources of fiber mentioned earlier—fruits and vegetables, nuts, seeds, and whole-grain products—also provide vitamins, minerals, and other essential nutrients, and emphasizing them in the diet means deemphasizing proteins and fats. Packaged fiber supplements, on the other hand, add nothing but bulk. In either case, adding too much fiber to the diet too quickly can have some undesirable side effects, among them excess flatulence and bloating. Large doses of fiber can result in sigmoid volvulus (enlarging and twisting of the sigmoid colon) and can aggravate existing cases of ulcerative colitis or ileitis. (For additional information on adding fiber to the diet, see Chapter 25 on Disorders of the Large Intestine, page 524.)

Vitamins. Vitamins are organic substances required in the diet in only minute amounts to assist in the body's processing of nutrients and participate in the formation of blood cells, hormones, chemicals, and genetic materials. They fall into two categories: fat soluble and water soluble. Fat-soluble vitamins—A, D, E, and K—are absorbed by the body with the aid of fat and then stored in body fat. Therefore, it is not necessary to consume them daily, as long as adequate amounts are stored in the body. For the same reason, it is possible to consume too much of these vitamins (by megadosing on supplements), in which case they can build up to toxic levels. Rarely are deficiencies of fat-soluble vitamins found with a balanced diet, except in those with certain disorders that interfere with the digestion of fats.

Water-soluble vitamins—C and all the B vitamins—are a different story. Because they are used up quickly or excreted in urine and perspiration, they are not stored and should be consumed daily. They break down quickly and can be partially lost through premature harvesting, long and improper storage, processing, overcooking, and cooking in water. Ideally, fruits and vegetables should be ripened on the vine and eaten raw and unpeeled immediately after harvest to get the greatest amount of vitamins from them. (There are a few exceptions, such as carrots, which actually provide more vitamin A if they are cooked.) But these ideal conditions

VITAMIN FACTS [a]

Vitamins	U.S. RDA for adults and children over four	Some significant sources	Some major physiological functions	Some deficiency symptoms	Some overconsumption symptoms
		FAT-SOLUBLE VITAMINS			
VITAMIN A (*retinol, provitamin carotenoids*)	5,000 IU	*Retinol:* liver, butter, whole milk, cheese, egg yolk. *Provitamin A:* carrots, leafy green vegetables, sweet potatoes, pumpkin, winter squash, apricots, cantaloupe, fortified margarine.	Assists formation and maintenance of skin and mucous membranes, thus increasing resistance to infections. Functions in visual processes and forms visual purple. Promotes bone and tooth development.	**Mild:** night-blindness, diarrhea, intestinal infections, impaired growth. **Severe:** xerophthalmia.	**Mild:** nausea, irritability, blurred vision. **Severe:** growth retardation, enlargement of liver and spleen, loss of hair, rheumatic pain, increased pressure in skull, dermal changes.
VITAMIN D (*calciferol*)	400 IU	Vitamin D fortified dairy products; fortified margarine; fish oils; egg yolk. Synthesized by sunlight action on skin.	Promotes ossification of bones and teeth, increases intestinal absorption of calcium.	Rickets in children; osteomalacia in adults, rare.	**Mild:** nausea, weight loss, irritability. **Severe:** mental and physical growth retardation, kidney damage, mobilization of calcium from bony tissue and deposition in soft tissues.
VITAMIN E (*tocopherol*)	30 IU	Vegetable oil, margarine, shortening; green and leafy vegetables; wheat germ, whole grain products; egg yolk; butter, liver.	Functions as antioxidant protecting vitamins A and C and fatty acids from destruction; and prevents cell-membrane damage.	Almost impossible to produce without starvation; possible anemia in low-birth-weight infants.	Nontoxic under normal conditions.
		WATER-SOLUBLE VITAMINS			
VITAMIN C (*ascorbic acid*)	60 mg	Broccoli, sweet and hot peppers, collards, brussels sprouts, strawberries, orange, kale, grapefruit, papaya, potato, mango, tangerine, spinach, tomato.	Forms cementing substances, such as collagen, that hold body cells together, thus strengthening blood vessels, hastening healing of wounds and bones, and increasing resistance to infection. Aids in use of iron.	**Mild:** bruise easily, bleeding gums. **Severe:** scurvy.	When megadose is discontinued, deficiency symptoms may briefly appear until the body adapts. Newborns whose mothers took megadoses will show deficiency symptoms after birth until the body adapts.
THIAMIN (*vitamin B₁*)	1.5 mg	Pork, liver, meat; whole grains, fortified grain products; legumes; nuts.	Functions as part of a coenzyme to promote carbohydrate metabolism, production of ribose, a constituent of DNA and RNA. Promotes normal appetite and normal functioning of nervous system.	Impaired growth, wasting of tissues, mental confusion, low morale, edema. **Severe:** beriberi.	None reported.

[a] Used with permission from the National Dairy Council, Rosemont, IL.

VITAMIN FACTS (continued)

Vitamins	U.S. RDA for adults and children over four	Some significant sources	Some major physiological functions	Some deficiency symptoms	Some overconsumption symptoms
RIBO-FLAVIN (vitamin B_2)	1.7 mg.	Liver; milk, yogurt, cottage cheese; meat; fortified grain products.	Functions as part of a coenzyme assisting cells to use oxygen for the release of energy from food. Promotes good vision and healthy skin.	Lesions of cornea, cracks at corners of mouth.	None reported.
NIACIN (nicotinamide, nicotinic acid)	20 mg	Liver, meat, poultry, fish; peanuts; fortified grain products. Synthesized from tryptophan (on the average 1 mg of niacin from 60 mg of dietary tryptophan).	Functions as part of a coenzyme in fat synthesis, tissue respiration, and utilization of carbohydrate for energy. Promotes healthy skin, nerves, and digestive tract. Aids digestion and fosters normal appetite.	Skin and gastrointestinal lesions, anorexia, weakness, irritability, vertigo. **Severe:** pellagra.	None reported for nicotinamide. Flushing, headache, cramps, nausea for nicotinic acid.
FOLACIN (folic acid)	0.4 mg	Liver; legumes; green leafy vegetables.	Functions as part of coenzymes in amino acid and nucleoprotein metabolism. Promotes red blood cell formation.	Red tongue, diarrhea, anemia.	May obscure the existence of pernicious anemia.
VITAMIN B_6 (pyridoxine, pyridoxal, pyridoxamine)	2.0 mg	Meat, poultry, fish, shellfish; green and leafy vegetables; whole grains, legumes.	Functions as part of a coenzyme involved in protein metabolism, assists in conversion of tryptophan to niacin, fatty acid metabolism, and red blood cell formation.	Irritability, muscle twitching, dermatitis near eyes, kidney stones, hypochromic anemia.	None reported.
VITAMIN B_{12}	6.0 mcg	Meat, poultry, fish, shellfish; eggs; milk and milk products.	Functions in coenzymes involved in nucleic acid synthesis and biological methylation. Assists in development of normal red blood cells and maintenance of nerve tissue.	**Severe:** pernicious anemia, neurological disorders.	None reported.
BIOTIN	0.3 mg	Kidney, liver; milk; egg yolk; most fresh vegetables.	Functions as part of a coenzyme involved in fat synthesis, amino acid metabolism, and glycogen formation.	Fatigue, depression, nausea, dermatitis, muscular pains.	None reported.
PANTOTHENIC ACID	10 mg	Liver, kidney, meats; milk; egg yolk; whole grains; legumes.	Functions as part of a coenzyme involved in energy metabolism.	Rare because found in most foods. Fatigue, sleep disturbances, nausea.	None reported.

are rarely met except by those fortunate enough to have their own gardens. Nevertheless, attempts should be made to preserve as much as possible by buying only in quantities that can be used immediately and by cooking (preferably steaming) as little as possible. In many cases, frozen fruits and vegetables, especially those meant to be cooked in a sealed plastic bag, may be a better bet than those improperly shipped and stored.

Supplements and Megadoses.
When an entire day's requirement of vitamins amounts to less than

⅛ teaspoon, it is obvious how easy it is to overdose. Megadoses of vitamins—many times more than the Daily Recommended Dietary Allowance (RDA) amount established by the Food and Nutrition Board of the National Academy of Sciences—are at best a waste of money; at worst, extremely dangerous. There is not one shred of evidence to substantiate the claim that vitamin C can cure or prevent the common cold, or that vitamin E can cure impotence, prevent heart disease, or slow the aging process.

If the diet is well-balanced, the healthy adult has no need for additional intake of vitamins and minerals. Varying the diet, rather than taking supplements, is the preferred way to correct a vitamin deficiency in otherwise healthy adults. Exceptions are pregnant women, who should take an iron/folic acid supplement; patients suffering from illness, trauma, or anemia; and those on chronic drug therapy (including the contraceptive pill), who require additional vitamin E, B₆, and folic acid. Folic acid deficiency, especially among pregnant women, is the most common vitamin deficiency in the United States, but easily correctable with supplements. Its natural sources include liver, dark-green leafy vegetables, dried beans, peas, and wheat germ.

Minerals. Minerals are inorganic substances needed in small or even minute amounts to aid in such important functions as formation of bones and teeth, red blood cells, cell membranes, and genetic material, as well as assisting with many metabolic processes in the body. They are divided into major, or macro, minerals, needed in larger amounts, and trace, or micro, minerals, needed in very small amounts. The macrominerals are calcium, phosphorus, magnesium, potassium, sulfur, and chloride. The trace minerals are iron, copper, iodine, zinc, fluoride, chromium, cobalt, manganese, molybdenum, selenium, nickel, tin, vanadium, and silicon.

All of the minerals necessary to keep the body functioning are found in foods and, with the possible exceptions of iron and zinc, a well-balanced diet should provide all that is necessary. Supplements are rarely necessary; megadoses can produce serious health risks. Furthermore, increasing mineral intake with supplements may distort the ratio among various minerals, which can actually result in mineral deficiency. For example, an excess of phosphorus decreases the body's ability to absorb calcium. If too much phosphorus is taken, there may be a calcium deficiency, even if calcium is taken in appropriate amounts.

Minerals are, for the most part, not destroyed by cooking, food processing, or by exposure to air, and dietary mineral deficiencies are rare, with 2 major exceptions: iron and calcium. Iron is the most commonly deficient mineral in the United States. This condition is present in children, especially during infancy and adolescence, and is prevalent among the poor. Children who are iron deficient have a reduced attention span and therefore are likely to perform poorly in school. According to a government survey,

MINERAL FACTS

Nutrient	RDA for adults and children over four [a]	Some significant sources	Some major physiological functions	Some deficiency symptoms	Some overconsumption symptoms
	MACROMINERALS				
CALCIUM	1,000 to 1,500 mg [b]	Milk and milk products, green leafy vegetables, citrus fruits, dried peas and beans, sardines and shellfish.	Helps build strong bones and teeth. Helps blood clot. Helps muscles and nerves function normally. Needed to activate certain enzymes which help change food into energy.	Rickets in children; osteoporosis in adults.	Drowsiness, calcium deposits.

[a] The RDA ranges, established by the Food and Nutrition Board of the National Academy of Sciences National Research Council, are for healthy people. The lower figures represent the RDA for children, the higher figures are the maximum for adults and should not be exceeded since the toxic levels may not be much higher.

[b] The RDA for calcium is under study. This is the amount now recommended by the Food and Drug Administration and is higher than the former RDA.

MINERAL FACTS (continued)

Nutrient	RDA for adults and children over four [a]	Some significant sources	Some major physiological functions	Some deficiency symptoms	Some overconsumption symptoms
PHOSPHORUS	1,000 mg	Meat, poultry, fish, eggs, dried peas and beans, milk and milk products, egg yolk, and whole-grain bread and cereal.	With calcium, helps build strong bones and teeth. Needed by certain enzymes which help change food into energy.	Weakness, bone pain, decreased appetite (rare).	Upset of the calcium-phosphorus ratio, hindering uptake of calcium.
SODIUM	450 to 3,300 mg	Processed foods, ham, meat, fish, poultry, eggs, milk.	Helps maintain water balance inside and outside cells.	Water retention (edema); loss of sodium through extreme perspiration can cause muscle cramps, headache, weakness.	High blood pressure, kidney disease, cirrhosis of the liver, congestive heart disease.
CHLORIDE	700 to 5,100 mg	Table salt, same as sodium.	Part of hydrochloric acid found in gastric juice and important to normal digestion.	Upset balance of acids and bases in body fluids (very rare).	Upset acid-base balance.
POTASSIUM	775 to 5,625 mg	Bananas, dried fruits, peanut butter, potatoes, orange juice.	With sodium, helps regulate body-fluid balance, transmission of nerve impulses.	Muscular weakness, irritability, irregular heartbeat (rare but may result from prolonged diarrhea or use of diuretics).	High levels of potassium can cause severe cardiac irregularities and can lead to cardiac arrest.
MAGNESIUM	200 to 300 mg	Leafy green vegetables, nuts, soy.	Activator for enzymes that transfer and release energy in the body.	Muscular tremors, twitching and weakness. Deficiency is sometimes seen in people with severe disease, prolonged diarrhea, or alcoholism.	Upset of the calcium-magnesium ratio, leading to impaired nervous-system function. Especially dangerous for people with impaired kidney function.
SULFUR		Wheat germ, dried beans, beef, clams.	In every cell as component of several amino acids.	Unknown.	Unknown.
TRACE MINERALS					
IRON	10 to 18 mg	Liver, meat products, egg yolk, shellfish, green leafy vegetables, peas, beans, dried prunes, raisins, apricots, whole-grain and enriched bread and cereal.	Combines with protein to make hemoglobin, the red substance in the blood that carries oxygen from lungs to cells, and myoglobin which stores oxygen in muscles.	Iron-deficiency anemia: pallor of skin, weakness and fatigue, headache, shortness of breath.	Toxic buildup in liver, pancreas, and heart (very rare).
IODINE	90 to 150 mcg	Iodized salt, seafoods.	Necessary for normal function of the thyroid gland.	Thyroid enlargement (goiter). Newborns: cretinism.	Could cause poisoning or sensitivity reactions.
ZINC	10 to 15 mg	Meats, fish, egg yolks, and milk.	Element of the enzymes that through the red blood cells move carbon dioxide from the tissues to the lungs.	Loss of taste and delayed wound healing. Children: growth retardation and delayed sexual maturation.	Gastrointestinal symptoms, such as nausea, vomiting, bleeding, and abdominal pain. Pregnant women: premature labor and stillbirth.

MINERAL FACTS (continued)

Nutrient	RDA for adults and children over four [a]	Some significant sources	Some major physiological functions	Some deficiency symptoms	Some overconsumption symptoms
COPPER	2 mg	Organ meats, shellfish, nuts, fruit, dried legumes, raisins, mushrooms.	Occurs as part of important proteins, including enzymes involved in brain and red blood cell function. Also needed for making red blood cells.	Rarely seen in adult humans. Infants: hypochronic anemia with abnormal development of bone, nervous tissue, lungs, and pigmentation of hair.	Gastrointestinal symptoms such as vomiting and diarrhea can occur as a result of eating foods cooked in unlined copper pots.
FLOURINE	1 to 4 mg	Flouridated water and foods cooked in flouridated water, fish, meat, tea.	Contributes to solid tooth and bone formation, especially in children. May help prevent osteoporosis in older people.	Tooth decay.	Mottling of enamel of teeth.
CHROMIUM	.03 to .20 mg	Dried brewer's yeast, whole-grain cereal, liver.	With insulin, it is required for utilization of glucose.	Diabeteslike symptoms.	Unknown.
SELENIUM	.03 to .20 mg	Seafood, egg yolk, chicken, milk, whole-grain cereals.	Interacts with vitamin E; prevents breakdown of body chemicals.	Unknown in humans.	Unknown.
MANGANESE	1.5 to 5 mg	Bran, coffee, tea, nuts, peas, beans.	Needed for normal tendon and bone structure; part of some enzymes.	Unknown in humans.	Unknown.
MOLYBDENUM	.06 to .50 mg	Legumes, cereals, dark green vegetables, kidney, liver.	Forms part of the enzyme xantine oxidase.	Unknown in humans.	Loss of copper; joint pain similar to gout.

as many as 20 percent of adolescent boys may be iron deficient, and estimates are even higher among women during childbearing years. Women lose iron through menstruation and have an increased need for it during pregnancy and breast-feeding, when supplements are advisable.

The most abundant mineral in the body, calcium is necessary for bones and teeth; a deficiency can result in rickets (in children) or osteoporosis (in older people, especially postmenopausal women).

Elements to Deemphasize

Fats. A diet high in fats has for a long time been implicated as a contributing cause in cardiovascular disease. In 1984, the American Cancer Society issued a report stating that excessive fat intake increases the chance of developing cancers of the breast, colon, and prostate.

Fats currently constitute about 40 percent of the

American diet, while most experts agree that they should be limited to no more than 30 percent. They should be divided equally among the 3 types: 10 percent (or less) from saturated fat, 10 percent from polyunsaturated, and 10 percent from monounsaturated. Reduction in fats, especially saturated fats, can be accomplished by:

● Reducing the amount of meat consumed, using leaner cuts, and trimming all fat from meats and skin from poultry

● Steaming, broiling, poaching, or stir-frying rather than deep frying or sautéeing foods

● Limiting the amount of butter used, or replacing it with liquid corn oil or margarine

● Using part-skimmed cheeses instead of high-fat ones

● Using low-fat yogurt and ice milk in place of whole milk yogurt and ice cream

● Dressing salads with lemon juice or "lite" dressings or limiting the amount of dressing used

Cholesterol. Cholesterol is a waxy-type alcohol found naturally in all animal tissues (but not in plants) and essential to many of the body's chemical processes. It is manufactured by the body and stored in the liver and it also comes from the food we eat. While a certain amount of it is essential, too much in the blood (called serum cholesterol) encourages development of atherosclerosis, a thickening and loss of elasticity of the artery walls. This condition is characterized by deposits of fatty plaque which project above the surface of the inner layer of the arteries, thus decreasing their diameter and interfering with normal blood flow and nourishment of tissues.

Because cholesterol is a fatty substance and thus not soluble in water, it cannot travel in the bloodstream by itself. Rather, it is transported by fatty proteins called lipoproteins. In recent years, scientists have noted 3 different types of lipoproteins—high-density (HDL), low-density (LDL), and very-low density lipoproteins (VLDL). HDLs are sometimes referred to as "good cholesterol," since they help remove cholesterol from the artery walls and deposit it in the liver where it can be more safely

Table 16.1 **CHOLESTEROL AND FAT CONTENT OF SELECTED FOODS**

FOOD ITEM—100 Gram Serving	Total fat (gm)	Saturated fat (gm)	Monounsaturated fat (gm)	Polyunsaturated fat (gm)	CHOL (mg)
[1]Beef, approx. 6% fat, cooked	6.10	2.70	2.72	0.48	91.0
[1]Lamb, approx. 7% fat, cooked	7.00	2.95	2.69	0.42	100.0
[1]Veal, approx. 6% fat, cooked	6.70	2.04	1.90	0.67	99.0
[3]Chicken, light meat without skin	4.51	1.27	1.54	0.98	85.0
[3]Chicken, dark meat without skin	9.73	2.66	3.56	2.26	93.0
[3]Turkey, light meat without skin	3.22	1.03	0.56	0.86	69.0
[3]Turkey, dark meat without skin	7.22	2.42	1.64	2.16	85.0
[1]Pork, fresh, 30% fat, cooked	30.60	11.68	15.24	3.54	89.0
[1]Frankfurter, all beef, cooked	30.00	12.70	14.80	1.20	51.0
[1]Herring, canned, smoked, pickled	13.60	2.56	8.06	2.16	97.0
[1]Fish, 6% fat	4.00	1.08	1.07	1.55	66.0
[1]Fish, 12% fat	13.40	2.28	3.17	4.56	84.0
[1]Salmon, pink, canned	5.90	0.98	1.75	2.66	35.0
[1]Sardines, canned, drained	11.10	3.00	3.57	3.22	140.0
[1]Tuna, canned, oil packed, drained	8.20	1.63	1.66	4.45	65.0
[1]Tuna, canned, water packed	0.80	0.19	0.13	0.20	63.0
[1]Clams, cooked	2.50	0.48	0.45	0.53	63.0
[1]Crab meat, cooked, canned	2.50	0.37	0.54	1.02	101.0
[1]Lobster, cooked	1.50	0.14	0.15	0.46	85.0
[1]Oysters, cooked	2.20	0.75	0.42	0.84	45.0
[1]Scallops, cooked	1.40	0.23	0.14	0.53	53.0
[1]*Shrimp	1.10	0.13	0.12	0.44	150.0
[2]*Eggs, whole	11.15	3.35	4.46	1.45	548.0
[2]*Egg, yolk	32.93	9.89	13.16	4.28	1602.0
[2]Egg, white	—	—	—	—	—
[2]Egg substitute, frozen	11.11	1.93	2.43	6.24	2.0
[2]Creamer-poly perx	10.00	1.50	4.60	3.90	0.0
[2]Cream, Half and Half	11.50	7.16	3.32	0.43	37.0
[2]Cream, light, coffee or table	19.31	12.02	5.58	0.72	66.0
[2] Buttermilk, cultured	0.88	0.55	0.25	0.03	4.0
[2]Milk, skim	0.18	0.117	0.047	0.007	2.0
[2]Milk, 1% fat, protein fortified	1.17	0.73	0.34	0.04	4.0
[2]Milk, whole, producers	3.66	2.28	1.06	0.14	14.0
[2]Cheese					
*American, processed	31.25	19.69	8.95	0.99	94.0
*Cheddar	33.14	21.09	9.39	0.94	105.0
Cottage, creamed	4.51	2.85	1.28	0.14	15.0
Cottage, dry curd	0.42	0.273	0.110	0.015	7.0

stored or excreted. LDLs and VLDLs have the opposite effect, by keeping cholesterol in circulation.

While the average person has only about 30 percent HDL, a number of factors can affect this percentage. Losing excess weight generally raises the amount of HDL, as does strenuous exercise. Age and sex also have an effect, since before menopause, women have higher HDL levels than men of the same age, but this evens out later.

The most important factor that affects the HDL/LDL ratio is diet. A diet high in saturated fats causes the liver to produce more VLDLs and LDLs,

while one high in polyunsaturated fats increases the amount of cholesterol transported by HDLs and decreases that carried by LDLs and VLDLs.

The average American consumes 450 milligrams of cholesterol a day, rather than the 300 that is recommended. Foods that are high in cholesterol include egg yolks (the yolk of a large egg contains 250 to 275 milligrams; the white contains none), whole milk, whole-milk cheeses, whole-milk yogurt, cream, sour cream, ice cream, butter, and organ meats, especially liver. (See table 16.1.)

Table 16.1 CHOLESTEROL AND FAT CONTENT OF SELECTED FOODS (continued)

FOOD ITEM—100 Gram Serving	Total fat (gm)	Saturated fat (gm)	Monounsaturated fat (gm)	Polyunsaturated fat (gm)	CHOL (mg)
* Cream	34.87	21.97	9.84	1.26	110.0
Parmesan, grated	30.02	19.07	8.73	0.66	79.0
* Ricotta, made with part skim milk	7.91	4.93	2.31	0.26	31.0
* Swiss	27.45	17.78	7.27	0.97	92.0
[2]Yogurt					
Plain, low fat	5.25	1.00	0.43	0.04	6.0
Plain, skim milk	0.18	0.116	0.049	0.005	2.0
[2]Sherbet, orange	1.98	1.23	0.57	0.07	7.0
[2] * Ice cream, vanilla, regular	10.77	6.70	3.11	0.40	45.0
[2] * Ice milk, vanilla, hardened	4.30	2.68	1.24	0.16	14.0
[4]Oil					
Corn	100.00	12.70	24.20	58.70	0.0
Cottonseed	100.00	25.90	17.80	51.90	0.0
Safflower, linoleic	100.00	9.10	12.10	74.50	0.0
Sesame	100.00	14.20	39.70	41.70	0.0
Soybean	100.00	14.40	23.30	57.90	0.0
Olive	100.00	13.50	73.70	8.40	0.0
Peanut	100.00	16.90	46.20	32.00	0.0
* Coconut	100.00	86.50	5.80	1.80	0.0
* Palm	100.00	49.30	37.00	9.30	0.0
[4] * Lard	100.00	39.20	45.10	11.20	95.0
[4] * Margarine, hard, stick, corn	80.50	13.20	45.80	18.00	0.0
[4]Margarine, soft, tub, corn	80.40	14.10	31.60	31.20	0.0
[4]Mayonnaise, safflower and soybean	79.40	8.60	13.00	55.00	—
[4]Peanut Butter	50.60	9.66	23.28	15.18	0.0
[4]Almonds	54.20	4.31	36.84	10.12	0.0
[4]Cashews	45.70	9.20	26.44	7.42	0.0
Peanuts	48.70	9.30	22.40	14.61	0.0
Walnuts	64.00	6.94	9.90	41.81	0.0
Olives, black	13.80	1.96	10.01	1.24	0.0
[2] * Butter	81.11	50.49	23.43	3.01	219.0
MCT oil	100.00	100.00	—	—	—

[1]Goodhard/Shils. *Modern Nutrition in Health and Disease*, 1980.
[2]Agriculture Handbook No. 8–1, 1976.
[3]Agriculture Handbook No. 8–5, 1979.
[4]Agriculture Handbook No. 8–4, 1979.
* Does not appear on *Cholesterol Restricted Diet*.

Proteins. Most Americans consume twice the amount of protein they need, and much of it in forms that are also high in fat and sodium. The recommended amount of protein is 12 percent of daily caloric content. This translates into no more than two 3-ounce servings of meat, fish, or poultry a day, or the equivalent in vegetable proteins. (See Complementary Proteins, below.)

Simple Carbohydrates. Sugar, like starch, is a carbohydrate. It is consumed in vast quantities by the average American—as much as 128 pounds per person annually—much of it in processed foods. Since sugar contains nothing but calories, the person who relies on sucrose (refined sugar) as the main source of carbohydrates is deprived of the fiber, vitamins, and minerals found in complex carbohydrates such as breads, rice, pasta, fruits, and vegetables. Sugar is a major cause of tooth decay. It also raises blood sugar in diabetics or individuals genetically predisposed to the disease.

Sodium. Sodium, which appears in foods in many forms, including the most common, sodium chloride, or table salt, has often been implicated as contributing to high blood pressure. Although the link has not been firmly established, there is increasing evidence that sodium is a contributing factor in a complex set of conditions that lead to hypertension. People who have been diagnosed as hypertensive need to restrict carefully their intake of sodium, according to guidelines prescribed by their doctors. For those with normal blood pressure, reducing the amount of salt added in cooking and at the table (replacing it with herbs, spices, and lemon juice, for example) and avoiding salty snack foods and canned foods that are high in sodium should be sufficient.

Salt-Cured, Smoked, and Nitrite-Cured Foods. There is some evidence that conventionally smoked foods such as hams, some varieties of sausage, and fish absorb some of the tars that arise from incomplete combustion. These tars contain carcinogens that are similar to the carcinogenic tars in tobacco smoke, and should be consumed only in moderate amounts. Many smoked meats on the market have nitrate levels that are substantially reduced from what they were a decade ago, and the meat processing industry is experimenting with liquid smoke, which may be less hazardous. Therefore, this warning may apply only to traditionally prepared meats and fish.

Although the evidence is still somewhat limited and inferential, the American Cancer Society suggests that salt-cured and pickled foods may increase the risk of stomach and esophageal cancer and should be used in moderation.

Other Food Additives. Ironically, a number of food additives with ominous sounding, polysyllabic chemical names like carboxymethylcellulose, sorbitan monostearate, and alpha-tocopherol are perfectly safe, while common household items like sugar, salt, and caffeine are even more prevalent as food additives and may have serious effects. The effects of salt and sugar have already been mentioned. The easiest way to avoid them is to follow the dietary guidelines in this chapter, which stress fresh or frozen fruits and vegetables, while avoiding processed meats, snack foods, and the "empty carbohydrates" in such foods as commercially prepared desserts and other sweets.

Caffeine as a natural substance and as an additive is beginning to receive a lot of attention. It is naturally present in or added to everything from aspirin to chocolate, where it is often consumed unsuspectingly. Cola drinks are a major source of caffeine consumption, especially among children, where they can pack a lot more punch than they do for adults with their greater body weight. Fortunately, many of the major brands are now available in caffeine-free forms.

Among the ill effects attributed to excessive caffeine consumption are anxiety attacks, indigestion, diarrhea, rapid heartbeat, and fibrocystic breast disease. Perhaps the most serious are birth defects. Studies in animals have shown that caffeine consumed in large amounts during pregnancy may result in abnormalities of the fetus. Structural abnormalities were reported when pure caffeine was fed to the mother, while behavioral abnormalities lasting until weaning were noted when large amounts of coffee were administered. Other preliminary studies have shown a high risk of miscarriage and still and premature births among heavy coffee drinkers. In light of this, the Food and Drug Administration has advised women to avoid coffee and caffeine during pregnancy.

Foods to Emphasize

Complementary Proteins. Foods high in carbohydrates have already been mentioned as good sources of vitamins, minerals, and fiber, while being low in fat and devoid of cholesterol. They can also make good low-cost substitutes for animal protein. To provide all the essential amino acids necessary for the body to manufacture protein from these carbohydrates, they must be used in specific combinations. The box on this page shows how.

Foods Rich in Vitamins A and C.
Vitamin A is thought, based on laboratory tests on animals and on population studies of people whose diets are rich in this vitamin, to lower the risk of cancers of the larynx, esophagus, and lung. Foods rich in vitamin A and carotene, a form of the vitamin, include carrots, tomatoes, spinach, apricots, peaches, and cantaloupes.

Studies of people whose diets are rich in vitamin C, or ascorbic acid, show that they are less likely to get cancer of the stomach and esophagus. While it is uncertain whether the protection comes from the vitamin itself or from other constituents of the foods which contain vitamin C, the American Cancer Society recommends including at least one source of this vitamin in the daily diet. Good sources are broccoli, cabbage, tomatoes, berries, cantaloupe, mango, papaya, strawberries, and all citrus fruits.

Cruciferous Vegetables.
Some epidemiological studies suggest that vegetables of the mustard family (which have 4 leaves surrounding their flowers, suggesting a cross) may reduce the risk of cancer, particularly of the gastrointestinal and respiratory tracts. They may also be very effective in protecting against chemically induced cancers, as shown in tests on laboratory animals. Cruciferous vegetables include broccoli, Brussels sprouts, kohlrabi, and cauliflower.

Calcium.
Calcium is an essential mineral needed to form bones; it is also required in minute amounts by all body cells. Growing children and pregnant or nursing women require large amounts of calcium; so do older women who are prone to develop a thinning of the bones. Calcium protects against osteoporosis, a condition in which the bones become weak and porous and thus have an increased tendency to fracture. Older women, particularly those who are fair-skinned, small in stature, and not active, and some older men are prone to develop this condition. In general, men, who have denser bones than women, and premenopausal women (who are thought to be protected by estrogen) don't develop this condition as often. The National Institutes of Health recommends that postmenopausal women take 1,000 to 1,500 milligrams of calcium per day. The best sources are milk and milk products and canned fish that contain edible bones, such as sardines. (CAUTION: Sardines, especially those packed in oil, are high in cholesterol, fat, and sodium, and should be used sparingly by those on physician-prescribed low-sodium diets or at high risk for heart disease.)

COMPLEMENTARY PROTEINS

Combine	With
Legumes	Grains or nuts and seeds
Grains	Legumes
Nuts and seeds	Legumes

Dairy products such as milk, yogurt, eggs, or cheese can be used alone as a source of protein or used to complement any of the 3 elements above.

Legumes include:
Peas: black-eyed, chick, cow, field, lentils
Beans: aduki, black, cranberry, fava, kidney, limas, marrow, mung, navy, pea, pinto, and soy (*Beans can be used as sprouts; soy can be used as tofu*)

Grains include:
Barley, corn, oats, rice, rye, wheat (*Grains can be used as sprouts or baked into breads; wheat includes bulgur and wheat germ; corn includes grits*)

Nuts and seeds include:
Nuts: almonds, beechnuts, Brazil nuts, cashews, filberts, pecans, pine nuts, walnuts
Seeds: pumpkin, sunflower

(For additional information, see Chapter 14 on The Middle Years and Aging, page 257.)

The Balanced Diet—Putting It All Together

The percentages and guidelines given for proteins, carbohydrates, fats, and other dietary elements need to be translated into daily servings in order to be useful. The following chart suggests the minimum number of daily servings and portion sizes for the average adult. The number of servings does not differ for children, but the serving sizes may be smaller. Additional servings of low-fat, low-cholesterol foods may be needed to meet energy requirements of some children and adults, according to their weight and level of activity.

GUIDELINES FOR A BALANCED DIET

Food	Servings	Serving size	Examples
Fish, poultry, meat, complementary proteins, eggs (limit to 3 per week), peanut butter	2	3 oz. cooked for meats, etc.; 1 C. for complementary protein; 4 T. peanut butter	Chicken, turkey, fish, lean beef, veal, pork, lamb
Vegetables and fruits (whole and juice); use at least one source each of high vitamin A and vitamin C	4 or more	4 oz. for juice; medium-sized fruit or vegetable or ½ C.	High in vitamin C: broccoli, cabbage, tomatoes, berries, cantaloupe, mango, papaya, citrus
			High in vitamin A: apricots, broccoli, cantaloupe, carrots, chard, chickory, corn, escarole, kale, mango, papaya, peas, rutabagas, spinach, string beans, sweet potatoes, watercress, winter squash
Breads and cereals	4 or more	1 slice bread; ½ C. cooked cereal, 1 C. dry	Whole wheat, French bread, English muffins, Italian bread, oatmeal, pumpernickel, rye, biscuits, muffins, matzoh, melba toast, pasta
Dairy products	2 or more	8 oz. milk or yogurt; 1 oz. hard cheese; ⅓ C. cottage cheese	Skimmed milk, buttermilk, low-fat yogurt and cheese, cottage, farmer's, baker's hoop, part skimmed mozzarella and ricotta cheeses
Polyunsaturated oils	2 or more	1 T.	Corn, cottonseed, safflower, sesame, soybean, sunflower

Weight Loss

Excess weight affects many of the body's systems and may be at the root of a number of diseases. Obesity is associated with high blood pressure, elevated levels of blood fats, and certain types of diabetes, all increasing the risk of heart disease. People who are obese, especially those 40 percent overweight, have an increased risk of cancer of the uterus, gallbladder, kidney, stomach, colon, and breast.

Most overweight people would like to lose weight, but food habits, which are formed in childhood, are strong patterns of behavior and difficult to break. Those who do attempt to break ingrained habits often think in terms of a "magic diet," which they try for a brief period of time, perhaps losing some weight, only to quickly return to old eating habits.

If diets don't work, why are they so popular? Because it is easier to follow a diet—for a while—than to change eating habits. And most diets do work, for a while. The dieter loses 10 pounds, feels good about the weight loss, but is bored with the menu plans, if the diet is a rigid one; or feels "deprived" of old favorites, like desserts. Soon the 10 pounds come creeping back.

Modifying eating habits may be a lot harder than, for example, giving up smoking or cutting back on drinking. People *have* to eat; they don't have to smoke or drink. But, like smoking and drinking overeating is learned behavior. At one time or another in just about every household, food is used by parents to bribe, to reward, to celebrate, and to manipulate. It takes on far more significance than simple nutrition. So as adults, some people overeat because they're angry, sad, nervous, procrastinating, bored, tired, lonely, or because the food is there and they shouldn't waste it—for virtually any reason but because they're hungry. Does this mean that dieters can't enjoy food? Quite the contrary. It means they can enjoy it for the best reason—because they're hungry—and they can enjoy it even more because they eat it consciously.

The second important reason diets don't work is that most dieters don't exercise. Most know by now that exercise burns up calories and helps shed weight faster. But many people choose to go on a more stringent diet rather than to take the trouble to exercise. With this method, the weight comes off reasonably quickly at first, but then begins to slow down. In a few months, it's back. They've reached the set point. The body, probably in response to a time when food was not as abundant, was designed to conserve energy. It expended energy, or burned calories, at a certain level (metabolism). When food was less available, the body compensated by burning calories at a lower rate. That's set point: the body's attempt to keep weight steady by compensation.

Exercise, on the other hand, changes the set point. It can increase the level at which calories are burned and keep it at that level for several hours after exercise. In other words, people who take a brisk 30-minute walk after dinner will not only burn up the calories that walking normally burns up, but when they stop, their bodies will continue to burn calories at a higher level, even while they come back and settle down in front of the TV. Even better, if they walk *before* dinner, they will decrease their appetite. People who exercise moderately have smaller appetites than either people who don't exercise at all or those who exercise vigorously.

Finally, the advantage of exercise is that it has the potential to alter body composition favorably by increasing the ratio of muscle to fat, primarily by decreasing stores of body fat. Without exercise, a person will lose both fat and muscle. With exercise, he or she will lose more fat in relation to muscle. Not only does this make the body thinner and more shapely, but since it takes more calories to maintain muscle than it does to maintain fat, if two people are exactly the same weight, but one has more muscle than the other, the person with more muscle can eat more without gaining weight.

Acceptable Weight. Many dieters have placed great emphasis on tables that attempt to determine "ideal" weight by sex and height, using the weight on the table as their goal. Actually, the answer is not so simple. The ratio of muscle to fat is as important

as total weight, but difficult to measure.

A skin fold test—a gentle pinch in a place where body fat typically accumulates, such as the upper arm, or the abdomen just above the navel—gives a general indication of excess body fat. If the skin fold in one of those places is more than 1 inch thick, the individual is overweight.

Weight-Loss Methods. If weight loss is necessary, a sensible approach and a moderate loss of 1 or 2 pounds per week is recommended. Fad diets that emphasize one category of food and promise rapid weight loss can cause chemical imbalance in the body and result in irreversible medical conditions. One such diet, popular a few years ago, that consisted almost entirely of protein, resulted in a number of cases of severe kidney damage and in depletion of electrolytes, a potentially fatal condition.

For the individual who is severely obese and must lose a large amount of weight rapidly, it is imperative to have a complete medical evaluation and to diet under careful supervision of a physician. For those who are moderately overweight, a slow and steady approach, using a balanced combination of essential nutrients, is the only safe method of weight loss. Diet pills and appetite suppressants, which may appear to be effective at the outset, serve no purpose unless used as an adjunct to sensible eating habits. For some, hypnosis may be helpful in boosting resolve, but it is not magic.

Whether the individual follows a diet prescribed by a physician, a nutritionist, or a weight-reduction group is a matter of personal choice. Some dieters may find it easier to diet with a group, which often helps to boost motivation by providing peer support

HEIGHT AND WEIGHT STANDARDS

Following are 1983 Metropolitan Life tables showing desirable weight by height and size of frame, for those 25 to 59 years old, in shoes with one-inch heels and wearing five pounds of clothing for men, three pounds of clothing for women.

MEN				WOMEN			
Height	Small	Medium	Large	Height	Small	Medium	Large
5' 2"	128-134	131-141	138-150	4'10"	102-111	109-121	118-131
5' 3"	130-136	133-143	140-153	4'11"	103-113	111-123	120-134
5' 4"	132-138	135-145	142-156	5' 0"	104-115	113-126	122-137
5' 5"	134-140	137-148	144-160	5' 1"	106-118	115-129	125-140
5' 6"	136-142	139-151	146-164	5' 2"	108-121	118-132	128-143
5' 7"	138-145	142-154	149-168	5' 3"	111-124	121-135	131-147
5' 8"	140-148	145-157	152-172	5' 4"	114-127	124-138	134-151
5' 9"	142-151	148-160	155-176	5' 5"	117-130	127-141	137-155
5'10"	144-154	151-163	158-180	5' 6"	120-133	130-144	140-159
5'11"	146-157	154-166	161-184	5' 7"	123-136	133-147	143-163
6' 0"	149-160	157-170	164-188	5' 8"	126-139	136-150	146-167
6' 1"	152-164	160-174	168-192	5' 9"	129-142	139-153	149-170
6' 2"	155-168	164-178	172-197	5'10"	132-145	142-158	152-173
6' 3"	158-172	167-182	176-202	5'11"	135-148	145-159	155-176
6' 4"	162-176	171-187	181-207	6' 0"	138-151	148-162	158-179

and requiring accountability. Weight Watchers and TOPS (Take Off Pounds Sensibly) offer sensible, well-balanced diet plans, plus plenty of tips and moral support from group leaders and members. Overeaters Anonymous, not a diet plan per se, is for those who feel they are compulsive overeaters. It is modeled on Alcoholics Anonymous, where members admit that they have not been in control of their lives and vow to change, one day at a time, sharing their stories with others in the group.

There are no foods that are inherently fattening. The basic principle of weight gain is simple: People gain weight because they consume more calories—through any combination of foods—than they expend. They can change this ratio by consuming less or expending more, or both. A change in food intake equivalent to 3,500 calories will result in a weight loss of 1 pound. Thus, by consuming 500 fewer calories a day, dieters can lose 1 pound per week. They can do the same by burning up 500 calories per day through exercise.

How many calories a person needs to consume to lose weight at the rate of 1 to 2 pounds per week, then, depends on body weight to begin with and on amount of physical activity. A reducing diet is just a guideline. The basic balanced diet that appears on this page is, without additional foods, a reducing diet. It will provide about 1,200 calories, the average amount needed by most women to lose 1 to 2 pounds per week. Taller women and most men can lose the same amount on a 1,500- to 1,800-calorie diet. To make up the additional calories, they may add another 2 or 3 servings of bread, cereal, or a starchy vegetable and another tablespoon of margarine, oil, or mayonnaise, or 1½ tablespoons of salad dressing or peanut butter.

Consuming the day's allotted calories in 3 average or even 6 smaller meals is preferable to eating the same amount in only 1 meal. A single meal per day provides more calories at one time than the body can use, and leads to fat storage.

Once acceptable weight has been reached, caloric intake can be adjusted to maintain it. One way to figure maintenance level intake is by this formula:

Acceptable weight (pounds)	×	10 for light activity 15 for moderate activity 20 for heavy activity
Age		
25–34		Subtract 0
35–44		Subtract 100
45–54		Subtract 200
55–64		Subtract 300
65+		Subtract 400

What about alternatives to dieting? Procedures that wire the jaw or result in a partial or total bypass of the stomach or small intestine or both are for the morbidly obese—those in danger of dying from complications of being grossly overweight. Total GI bypass has resulted in some cases in failure to absorb amino acids properly, leading to liver failure, hepatic coma, and death. Any surgery carries with it the risk that fluids will collect in the lungs, making the patient subject to pneumonia and other respiratory disorders and that blood will pool in the extremities, raising the risk of clots.

Table 16.2 **A TYPICAL DAY'S MENU** [a]

1,200 calories	1,600 calories
Breakfast	
1 serving fruit or fruit juice	1 serving fruit or juice
1 serving bread or cereal	2 servings bread or cereal
1 serving cheese, egg, fish, or milk	1 serving cheese, egg, fish, or milk
Coffee or tea, if desired	Coffee or tea, if desired
Lunch	
1 serving fish, poultry, meat, cheese, egg, or peanut butter	1 serving fish, poultry, meat, cheese, egg, or peanut butter
2 servings bread	2 servings bread
2 servings nonstarchy vegetable	2 servings nonstarchy vegetable
1 serving fruit	1 serving fruit
Dinner	
1 serving meat, fish, poultry	1 serving meat, fish, poultry
1 vegetable high in vitamin A	1 vegetable high in vitamin A
1 starchy vegetable or serving bread	1 starchy vegetable or serving bread
Other vegetables as desired	Other vegetables as desired
1 serving fruit	2 servings fruit
1 serving milk	1 serving milk
Additional foods	
1 tablespoon oil used at any time	2 tablespoons oil used at any time
1 additional glass of milk (unless already chosen as protein source)	1 additional glass of milk (unless already chosen as protein source)

[a]Developed by Bureau of Nutrition, New York City Department of Health.

EXERCISE AND FITNESS

ALTHOUGH MANY MORE AMERICANS are now walking, running, playing tennis, and engaging in other active sports, most still do not get sufficient exercise. They drive to work and to stores, use elevators instead of stairs, become spectators rather than participants at sports, and do little heavy labor on their jobs. Inactivity is common among all age groups, despite the findings of several studies that there is a link between the sedentary lifestyle and an increased risk of heart attack. Only about 40 percent of all Americans, children as well as adults, exercise with any frequency, and those who do often do not exercise vigorously enough.

Not only can the lack of exercise be a risk factor for heart disease, but the presence of exercise can have a very positive effect on the other risk factors. It tends to lower blood pressure, helps control weight, increases levels of high-density lipoproteins (the "good" cholesterol) in the blood, and may help control diabetes. Some people who exercise find that it helps them control stress, and many smokers give up the habit after they start exercising.

In addition to benefiting the cardiovascular system, regular exercise may enhance a person's sense of well-being, improve muscle tone and flexibility, and provide more energy. There is a decidedly lower death rate among the elderly who exercise.

Aerobic Exercise

Muscles work by converting fuel to energy. In some activities, the muscles are able to provide this energy through a chemical process that does not involve oxygen, and thus they are called anaerobic. Aerobic exercise, on the other hand, requires oxygen and is dependent on the cardiovascular system to supply it to the muscles while they work. Like all muscles, the heart becomes more efficient and better conditioned the more it is used, and this is why aerobic exercise promotes cardiovascular fitness.

Not all sports and other forms of exercise promote cardiovascular fitness. Some promote strength, endurance, flexibility, or physical skill—a combination of coordination, agility, and speed. Good aerobic exercises include brisk walking, running or jogging, bicycling, swimming, skating, and jumping rope. Anaerobic exercises include bowling, golf, weight lifting, doubles tennis, and volleyball. Although the latter two may seem strenuous, the level of activity is not sustained long enough to be aerobic.

Designing a Fitness Program

Ideally, a cardiovascular fitness program should be flexible, graduated, individually tailored and, if necessary, supervised. The 3 key factors in designing a program are intensity, duration, and frequency. Cardiovascular conditioning occurs when the program involves sustained effort for a *duration* of at least 30 minutes per day, at a *frequency* of at least 3 days per week, beginning at an *intensity* of approximately 70 percent and increasing to 85 percent of the maximum heart rate.

Maximum heart rate, or the maximum an individual's pulse rate can attain, is calculated by subtracting his or her age from 220. (See table 16.3.) So, for example, a 40-year-old has a maximum heart rate of 180. Exercise should be carried out at a rate that will raise the pulse to between 70 and 85 percent of this number, or 126 to 153 beats per minute.

Exercise below 70 percent of the maximum heart rate gives the heart and lungs little conditioning; anything above 85 percent is dangerous. The area in between is known as the "target zone"—the goal for which an individual should strive. For those who have not exercised regularly, it may take several months to raise the rate above 70 percent, and it is wise not to do this any way but gradually.

Individuals can determine whether they are within their target zones by taking their pulse immediately after exercise. The easiest way to do this is to place 2 or 3 fingers lightly over the carotid artery, located on the left and right sides of the Adam's apple, count the pulse for 10 seconds, and multiply by 6. If the pulse is below the target zone, the rate of exercise should be increased; if above, it should be reduced. Pulse rate should be checked once a week during the first 3 months of exercising and periodically thereafter.

Exercisers should be aware that some medications and medical conditions may affect the maximum heart rate and the target zone. For example, some medicines given to lower blood pressure also lower the maximum heart rate and thus the target zone. Diabetes may also have an effect on these guidelines. Anyone taking medications should consult a physician to determine whether this rate should be adjusted.

The optimal frequency for those beginning an exercise program is 2 to 4 times a week. In fact, 3 times a week is really all that is necessary at any stage. Although the "training effect" on the body increases somewhat if the exercise is done more often,

Table 16.3 **DETERMINING TARGET ZONE**

Age	Target zone—70–85% (beats per minute)	Average maximum heart rate (100%)
20	140–170	200
25	137–166	195
30	133–162	190
35	130–157	185
40	126–153	180
45	123–149	175
50	119–145	170
55	116–140	165
60	112–136	160
65	109–132	155
70	105–128	150

CALORIE EXPENDITURES FOR SELECTED PHYSICAL ACTIVITIES

Activity	Calories per hour
Walking—2 mph	200
Walking—4 mph	350
Jogging	600
Running	800–1,000
Cycling—5 mph	250
Cycling—10 mph	450
Dancing	200–400
Tennis	400–500
Swimming—breast/backstroke	300–650
Swimming—crawl	700–900
Skiing	600–700
Skating (fast)	300–700

frequency also increases the chance of joint and muscle damage, particularly with exercises like running. Those who walk or swim, where there is less chance of injury, or those who are exercising for weight control, may want to exercise more frequently.

Duration is a variable that can be manipulated for beginners who are out of shape and may have trouble sustaining exercise at target zone intensity for 30 minutes. They could begin below the target zone for 30 minutes and gradually work their way up. This is probably the least demanding but, aside from burning some calories, it will not have much of an effect. On the other hand, exercising at proper intensity, even if only for 5 or 10 minutes, can provide some training effect. So the beginner will do better to start at his or her target zone of intensity and gradually build up duration. Interval training, alternating exercise of high intensity and low intensity or rest periods, is another way to start.

In order to maintain the training effect, as the individual continues to exercise and the heart becomes better conditioned, either the intensity or the duration must be increased. A bicycle rider, for example, would either have to pedal longer, pedal faster, or begin cycling up hills or in a lower gear to increase the resistance. (See below for examples of how to begin and upgrade a training program.)

EXERCISE PRECAUTIONS

- Do a few warm-up exercises first to stretch the muscles, tendons, and ligaments, flex joints, and increase the blood flow.

- Start slowly and increase speed, distance, and duration gradually.

- Avoid exercise on days when the wind chill factor is below −20° F, when the temperature is above 90° F, or when the humidity is above 80 percent.

- Stop exercising if you feel dizzy, breathless, or nauseated, or if you feel pain in a joint or muscle.

- Seek medical help at once if you have pain in the center of your chest that lasts more than 2 minutes and that may be accompanied by pain in the arm, shoulders, neck, or jaw.

- Wait at least 2 hours after a heavy meal before exercising, and at least 4 hours after consuming alcohol. Alcohol followed by exercise can cause irregularities of the heartbeat and dehydration.

- Drink water before, during, and after exercising, especially on a hot or humid day.

SAMPLE EXERCISE PROGRAMS

The table on page 309 shows sample exercise programs for 3 individuals: a healthy 25-year-old man, a healthy 45-year-old woman, and a 65-year-old man who has had a heart attack. They are meant only as examples, not prescriptions.

The 25-Year-Old Man. Although running is an aerobic exercise that many people find enjoyable, it is frequently too strenuous for the unconditioned. Those who have not been exercising regularly should begin with a 3-minute walk, alternating with a 3-minute jog. Each week the jog interval should be increased 1 minute and the walk interval decreased 1 minute until the individual is able to jog continuously for 30 minutes. From this point, 5-minute increments can be added every other week until the jog lasts 46 to 50 minutes. At this point, speed can be increased by alternating 5 minutes at a fast pace with 5 minutes at a moderate pace.

On a "perceived exertion" scale of 1 to 10, representing levels of not-at-all fatigued to extremely fatigued, the individual should reach 7 or 8 for this exercise.

The limitation of running is its absence of upper-extremity conditioning. To balance this, the individual might consider rowing as an alternate exercise. To start, the rowing machine should be set at the lowest resistance point and the setting should be increased with each 3-minute set, until a perceived exertion level of 7 or 8 is reached. After 2 or 3 weeks, the exerciser should try to begin each set at the second lowest resistance level, using that as the base level if it is comfortable. If it is not, the initial setting should remain at the lowest level for a few weeks.

The 45-Year-Old Woman.

Aerobic dance—simple dance—and calisthenic movements performed at a fast pace are excellent aerobic activities involving most muscle groups. Important considerations are a good initial stretch program and an equally good postexercise stretch. Often these are built into class or tape routines. Individuals should start with a beginning class and if they experience pain in a particular part of the body, they should not do specific routines that increase pain in that area until the pain abates. Swimming is an excellent alternate exercise. Both the crawl and the backstroke are good

and should be alternated with rest periods. As training progresses, 1 or 2 laps can be added.

The 65-Year-Old Man.

Walking is an excellent aerobic exercise that can be beneficial to anyone at any level of conditioning as long as an appropriate level of exertion is reached.

The exercise program of anyone who has had a myocardial infarction (heart attack) should be based on a symptom-limited exercise stress test (meaning the test is stopped as soon as chest pain is felt). During exercise, regular pulse checks (a 10-second pulse multiplied by 6) should be used to maintain and to avoid exceeding the target heart rate set by a physician on the basis of the stress test.

Any recurrent chest pain, weakness, dizziness, or excessive fatigue should be immediately followed up with a physician visit and possibly a repeat exercise stress test. If available, a supervised program at a YM/YWCA, YM/YWHA, or community center is preferable to individual exercise, at least for the first year following a heart attack.

Like jogging or running, walking does not usually provide upper body conditioning, but arm calisthenics are a good alternative. For a post-heart attack patient, they should first be performed with EKG monitoring and the appropriate frequency and numbers of repetitions of each activity determined by the physician. Arm activities can include shoulder flex—extend; elbow flex—extend; arm swing, front to back; and arm "bicycle" motion.

Table 16.4 **SAMPLE EXERCISE PROGRAMS**

Participant	Primary exercise	Starting level	Warm up	Cool down	Secondary exercise	Secondary starting level	Frequency (days/week) Prim.	Sec.
25-year-old healthy male	Running	Jog/walk 3 min/3 min for total of 24 min	Stretching exercises for 3 min, then walk for 2 min, increasing pace from slow to brisk	Slow down from brisk to slow walk in 2 min, then stretching exercises for 3 min	Rowing machine	15-min total, alternating 3 min rowing with 2 min rest	2	2
45-year-old woman	Aerobic dance	30-min "beginners" class or tape	Stretching exercises for 5 min	Stretching exercises for 5 min	Swimming laps (25 yards each)	3 laps at moderate exertion level, alternating with 30 sec rest, for total of 12 laps	2–3	1–2
65-year-old male, post-heart attack	Walking	Walk for 15 min, rest for 5, walk for 15	Stretching exercises for 2 min	Stretching exercises for 2 min	Arm calisthenics[a]	Each of 4 exercises to fatigue, rest for 2 min, repeat set of 4	3	2

[a]See accompanying text.

Stress Testing

Anyone who is over 35 or has a known medical problem should check with a physician before beginning an exercise program. If the individual is over 35 and has been sedentary, is obese, is a smoker, has a high cholesterol level or a family history of heart disease, the doctor may recommend a stress, or exercise tolerance, test. A stress test may also be recommended for anyone under 35 who has high blood pressure, diabetes, or a history of chest pain or other symptoms of heart disease.

A stress test measures the performance of the cardiovascular system during exercise. It is used as a diagnostic tool for those suspected of certain types of heart disease and to assess the individual's level of cardiovascular fitness in order to design an individualized fitness program.

During the stress test, which can be performed in the physician's office, a hospital, or a stress testing facility, the individual will be required to pedal an exercise bicycle or to walk on a treadmill while the pulse rate, blood pressure, and perhaps the oxygen consumption are being monitored, and while an electrocardiogram is being taken. The test will begin slowly and will eventually take the individual up to his or her maximum heart rate.

Since there is some risk involved in this procedure, it is important that it be performed by a trained health professional in a facility that is equipped for any emergency that might arise. If the person being tested is at high risk of heart disease or has had any symptoms that might indicate heart disease, it is preferable to have a physician perform the test. In either case, the results should be interpreted by a physician, preferably a cardiologist.

Deciding How and Where to Exercise

Thousands of new gyms and physical fitness centers have opened in the last decade, providing a number of options for pursuing an exercise regime. For the gregarious, the camaraderie of a gymnasium or center may serve an important purpose. Other advantages will be a place to change and shower, the availability of exercise equipment, guided instruction, and a schedule (not to mention an investment) which may encourage self-discipline.

Exercising independently, on the other hand, will probably save money, will eliminate the necessity of traveling to and from the facility, and will probably make scheduling easier.

In evaluating an exercise training center:

- Look for aerobic exercise facilities (treadmills, exercise bicycles with resistance controls, a pool at least 60 feet long, a running track)
- Note the types of instruction available (swimming, running, aerobic dancing, as opposed to yoga, weight lifting, and calisthenics)
- Consider the quality and background of instructors (ideally, they should have a degree in physical education or exercise physiology)
- Note the physical facilities, particularly whether the dressing rooms, showers, and lockers are clean and adequate
- Visit at least twice at the hour when you would be most likely to use the facilities, to see how crowded they are.

YM/YWCAs and YM/YWHAs and municipal facilities, although usually inexpensive, are often quite adequate. A posh setting does not always mean that the center is oriented toward cardiovascular fitness.

Exercise in Rehabilitation

Postcoronary patients who exercise regularly recover more completely and more rapidly from an initial heart attack. Carefully prescribed aerobic exercises are extremely useful for patients with angina pectoris (chest pain). With exercise, asthmatics and individuals with chronic lung disease can improve their respiratory capacity, diabetics can lower their blood sugar levels and insulin requirements, and obese adults who become diabetic often are freed of the disease when they achieve normal weight via exercise and diet.

SMOKING

CIGARETTE SMOKING is the single most preventable cause of illness and death in the United States today. Cigarette smoke itself contains more than 4,000 compounds, including tar, carbon monoxide, nicotine, and cancer-causing benzopyrene, benzopyrelene, arsenous oxide, and radioactive polonium. The major immediate effects of smoking can range from tachycardia (abnormally fast heartbeat) to arrhythmia (variation of the heart's normal rhythm) to increased blood pressure and bronchial constriction. But by far, the greatest risks the smoker faces are the risks of coronary heart disease and cancer.

Smokers have a 70 percent greater chance of developing coronary heart disease than do nonsmokers—the risk increasing in direct proportion to the number of cigarettes smoked per day. Even people who smoke 1 pack per day have twice the risk of heart attack and 5 times the risk of stroke as nonsmokers.

Studies have shown that the carbon monoxide ingested by smoking, in addition to reducing the blood's oxygen level, causes changes in body tissues that may leave smokers prone to heart disease. The smoker with a blood level of carbon monoxide above 5 percent faces a 20-fold risk of coronary heart disease over the individual with a level below 3 percent. Smokers who switch to cigarettes with low tar and nicotine will only somewhat lower the level of carbon monoxide in their blood. The heart disease risk of smokers who quit, on the other hand, will begin to decline immediately. Within 10 to 15 years, the ex-smoker's chance of early death from heart attack is no greater than that of someone who never smoked.

Clearly, one of the most important preventive health measures an individual can take is to avoid or give up smoking. There are a number of methods, ranging from cold turkey to hypnosis. Groups like the American Cancer Society run low-cost stop smoking clinics for those who feel they would do better with face-to-face counseling and peer support, and supply literature on quitting for those who want to go it alone. Research has not been able to show that any one method is more successful than any other method, but some methods do seem to work better for some people than for others. Chapter 18 on Smoking, Alcohol, and Substance Abuse, page 340, has tips on quitting.

ALCOHOL

ALCOHOL is the most commonly used recreational drug in the United States. Taken in moderation, it can be compatible with a healthy lifestyle. But alcohol abuse is the cause of problems that reach far beyond drinkers themselves. The Department of Health and Human Services has defined alcoholism as "the nation's number one health problem"—a problem that is a major cause of disrupted family life, automobile and industrial accidents, poor job performance, and increasing crime rates.

Cirrhosis of the liver, overwhelmingly a result of alcohol abuse, is the seventh leading cause of death in the United States. In addition, alcohol has been implicated as a contributor in 50 percent of fatal automobile accidents, 53 percent of fire deaths, 45 percent of drownings, 22 percent of home accidents, and 36 percent of pedestrian accidents. Violent crimes attributed to alcohol abuse include 64 percent of murders, 41 percent of assaults, 34 percent of rapes, 30 percent of suicides, and 60 percent of child abuse.

The financial toll of alcohol abuse is heavy, too. American industry loses over $25 billion per year due to the accidents, absenteeism, and medical expenses of alcoholic workers.

The pregnant woman who drinks heavily risks giving birth to a child with fetal alcohol syndrome (FAS)—a pattern of physical and mental defects which may include malformed facial characteristics, growth deficiency, heart defects, poor neurological coordination, and mental retardation. FAS has become a problem of large proportion, since there are an estimated 1 million alcoholic women of childbearing age in the United States. A 1984 study, funded by the National Institute of Child Health and Human Development, looked at data from more than 31,600 pregnancies and found that consumption of at least 1 to 2 drinks daily was associated with a substantially increased risk of producing a growth-retarded infant. Even though an occasional drink may not cause a problem, alcohol has no positive effects on pregnancy to recommend it, and thus pregnant women, or those who wish to get pregnant, are advised not to drink at all.

Finally, the American Cancer Society reports that heavy drinkers, especially those who also smoke cigarettes, are at an unusually high risk for oral cancer and cancers of the larynx and esophagus.

Is it safe to drink at all? For some people, light to moderate drinking does not seem to have any serious effect. The problem is in knowing how much and for whom. Some people, for example, can develop cirrhosis of the liver with only 1 drink per day, while 10 drinks per day will not lead to cirrhosis in others (although this amount may have other serious consequences). At what point does social drinking become alcoholism? The test on page 312, from the National Council on Alcoholism, may be helpful in identifying some signs. Those who score 4 or more should seek help promptly.

For those who still want to enjoy an occasional drink, there is much that can be done to promote a healthy, positive attitude toward alcohol. The following suggestions for moderate use of alcohol are

Table 16.5 **WHAT ARE THE SIGNS OF ALCOHOLISM?**[a]

YES	NO	
☐	☐	1. Do you occasionally drink heavily after a disappointment, a quarrel, or when the boss gives you a hard time?
☐	☐	2. When you have trouble or feel under pressure, do you always drink more heavily than usual?
☐	☐	3. Have you noticed that you are able to handle more liquor than you did when you were first drinking?
☐	☐	4. Did you ever wake up on the "morning after" and discover that you could not remember part of the evening before, even though your friends tell you that you did not "pass out"?
☐	☐	5. When drinking with other people, do you try to have a few extra drinks when others will not know it?
☐	☐	6. Are there certain occasions when you feel uncomfortable if alcohol is not available?
☐	☐	7. Have you recently noticed that when you begin drinking you are in more of a hurry to get the first drink than you used to be?
☐	☐	8. Do you sometimes feel a little guilty about your drinking?
☐	☐	9. Are you secretly irritated when your family or friends discuss your drinking?
☐	☐	10. Have you recently noticed an increase in the frequency of your memory "blackouts"?
☐	☐	11. Do you often find that you wish to continue drinking after your friends say they have had enough?
☐	☐	12. Do you usually have a reason for the occasions when you drink heavily?
☐	☐	13. When you are sober, do you often regret things you have done or said while drinking?
☐	☐	14. Have you tried switching brands or following different plans for controlling your drinking?
☐	☐	15. Have you often failed to keep the promises you have made to yourself about controlling or cutting down on your drinking?
☐	☐	16. Have you ever tried to control your drinking by making a change in jobs or moving to a new location?
☐	☐	17. Do you try to avoid family or close friends while you are drinking?
☐	☐	18. Are you having an increasing number of financial and work problems?
☐	☐	19. Do more people seem to be treating you unfairly without good reason?
☐	☐	20. Do you eat very little or irregularly when you are drinking?
☐	☐	21. Do you sometimes have the "shakes" in the morning and find that it helps to have a little drink?
☐	☐	22. Have you recently noticed that you cannot drink as much as you once did?
☐	☐	23. Do you sometimes stay drunk for several days at a time?
☐	☐	24. Do you sometimes feel very depressed and wonder whether life is worth living?
☐	☐	25. Sometimes after periods of drinking, do you see or hear things that aren't there?
☐	☐	26. Do you get terribly frightened after you have been drinking heavily?

If you answered "yes" to any of the questions, you have some of the symptoms that may indicate alcoholism.

"Yes" answers to several of the questions indicate the following stages of alcoholism:
Questions 1–8—early stage
Questions 9–21—middle stage
Questions 22–26—the beginning of final stage.

[a] Used with permission from the National Council on Alcoholism, Inc.

especially important for parents of teenagers and young adults:

• Put a negative value on drunkenness. Getting "bombed" or "plastered" is socially acceptable behavior at many gatherings; in fact, it's the goal of some events. And getting drunk is tolerated in certain people (e.g., a famous writer or that member of the family who always gets drunk). It's necessary to make clear that drunkenness is not acceptable, and certainly not attractive or chic. Being able to "hold one's liquor" isn't a sign of prowess for either men or women; if anything, it reveals a dangerously high tolerance which comes from overuse.

• Put alcohol in its proper place. The healthy use of alcohol lies in its power as a social lubricant; it is an adjunct to living, not an end in itself. Alcohol should be enjoyed in moderation at social events and as an accompaniment to meals. Parties and family gatherings should be planned around enjoyable activities, good food, and good conversation rather than the drinks to be served. Good hosts and hostesses do not try to push alcohol on their guests; they always take "no" for an answer.

- Serve a variety of beverages at social functions. Whether at home or at the worksite, nonalcoholic alternatives should be available for abstainers and safe drinkers alike. Drinkers can enjoy an alcoholic drink for sociability and for its mellowing effect, then switch to something nonalcoholic for the rest of the evening.

- Set comfortable drinking patterns. Some experts suggest avoiding a habitual pattern of drinking every day. By varying the drink, the time, even the place, the drinker avoids making alcohol a necessary habit, one intimately associated with a certain time of day or a certain way of drinking. For example, if drinkers find themselves trapped by the after-work ritual of cocktails, they can substitute some other activity for it on occasion. Instead of having a martini, they can try a hot bath or a cool shower, playing music, talking to a friend on the phone, or moving meal time up 1 hour earlier.

- Recognize that it's all right to say "no." No one has to explain his or her drinking behavior at any time. The growing American concern with fitness and with a natural, healthy life has made abstinence an acceptable alternative. And safe drinkers can test their own drinking habits by abstaining occasionally, asking themselves: Do I feel perfectly comfortable doing without alcohol?

- Prohibit driving while drinking. Partygoers should make return transportation arrangements beforehand. One spouse or one member of the group can abstain at the party in order to drive home. And friends can tell friends, ahead of time, "If I ever have too much to drink, don't let me drive." Permitting a friend to take the wheel when drunk, out of fear of making a scene, is permitting possible suicide or murder. A drunk driver isn't necessarily an alcoholic; he *is* a menace to himself and others.

- Present a healthy role model to children. Total abstainers can produce alcoholic offspring; however, alcohol abuse is often related to family drinking patterns. The children of alcohol abusers are at high risk of becoming alcoholic themselves. Because family patterns of drinking—both good and bad—affect children's behavior, parents must be conscious of the role models they present. Parents can be educated and aware of the problems of alcohol and drug abuse and communicate that awareness, without moral overtones, to their children. They can discourage drunkenness in themselves and their friends. They can refuse to drive when they've been drinking. They can present moderation and abstinence as part of a healthy and appealing lifestyle.

- Avoid drinking alone. On tests designed to diagnose alcohol abuse, one question often is: "Do you drink alone?" The reason for this is not because the presence of other people will magically protect the drinker against alcoholism, but because alcohol abusers often isolate themselves with their drinking. They are having a "love affair" with the bottle, and prefer its company to the companionship of their friends. Also, solitary drinkers are more apt to gulp drinks, sneak extra ones, or generally overindulge. Drinking alone abandons the social benefits of alcohol.

- Don't drink to avoid problems. Family troubles, crises in love relationships, and problems at work can all seem like reasons to escape into drinking. But no problems are ever solved by a bout with the bottle. "Escapist drinking" is symptomatic of alcoholism; people who find themselves using alcohol in this way should talk to a good friend, member of the clergy, family member, or doctor they trust.

(For more information, see Chapter 18 on Smoking, Alcohol, and Substance Abuse, page 346.)

DRUG ABUSE

ALTHOUGH THE ILL EFFECTS of drugs have not been entirely defined, there is sufficient evidence to determine that their use is not compatible with a healthy lifestyle. Nevertheless, there is an increasing tendency toward "recreational" drug use, when drugs become part of a social setting, as alcohol often is.

Although not everyone who tries drugs goes on to use them regularly, the progression of drug use usually follows the same pattern, from experimentation, in which the individual has one or perhaps a few experiences with a particular drug (out of curiosity or because of peer pressure); to occasional use, which is usually unplanned and generally occurs in

social situations where the drug is readily available; to regular use, where drug-taking is routine. Finally, in drug dependency, the individual's psychological and physical well-being is so closely linked to the chosen chemical that it becomes a necessity. At this stage of addiction, physical withdrawal signs occur if the drug is abruptly discontinued.

The most popular drugs are the psychotropics such as marijuana, hashish, and cocaine, which have in common the ability to distort sensory experience and produce pleasurable mood swings. According to the National Institute on Drug Abuse, changes in the way marijuana is grown have greatly increased concentrations of THC, its major psychoactive ingredient. Strengths of THC, which were in the range of 0.1 percent to 0.2 percent in the mid-1960s, are now reported in concentrations as high as 13.49 percent. Even the more commonly available marijuana (about 5 percent THC), is 25 to 50 times more potent now than it was 20 years ago.

Drug experimentation and use typically begins in adolescence, where alcohol and marijuana are the most common drugs, and where cocaine, on the rise in the 20 to 40 age group, seems also to be becoming more popular. Pediatrician Donald Ian Macdonald of the University of Florida, writing in the *American Journal of Diseases of Children*, has described 4 stages among adolescents as they begin to experiment with drugs: learning the mood swing, seeking the mood swing, preoccupation with the mood swing, and doing drugs to feel okay.

In the first stage, teenagers, giving in to peer pressure, begin to experiment and find they like the pleasurable high they get. Unfortunately, the few who experiment and decide against further use are outnumbered by those who enjoy the feeling of being high and decide to continue use, Dr. Macdonald points out. Nevertheless, many of them remain in the first stage. Since there are few behavioral changes, other than the efforts to cover up, it may be difficult for parents to detect drug use at this stage. One clue, according to Dr. Macdonald, is tobacco use. Those adolescents who admit that their friends smoke, even if they deny their own use, are identifying with a high-risk peer group who have already caved in to peer pressure to smoke.

It is those who reach the second stage, when they begin to use drugs to deal with stress and negative feelings rather than to increase positive feelings, who may have a predisposition to dependence. In this stage, deterioration in school performance, lack of motivation, irritability, and dramatic mood swings are common. The adolescent's group of friends may change, as he or she is drawn to others who share the habit. Unfortunately, parents often respond to this stage in inappropriate ways, denying the problem, blaming the child's friends or environment, and refusing to acknowledge that the child may be the source of his or her own problems. In that way, they are enabling the teenager to continue use.

Stage 3, preoccupation with the mood swing, represents a major problem, when the adolescent is in trouble in a number of areas and may be supporting—through theft, dealing, unwitting or disbelieving parents, or even an afterschool job—a habit of $50 to $60 a week. Finally, drugs lose the ability to produce euphoria for the user and are taken just to ward off guilt and depression. At this point, relationships with the family—even the family itself—may have broken down completely.

Contributing to adolescent drug abuse is a fact that is not always considered: Youngsters at this age do not have a fully developed value system, nor the capacity for moral judgment that is a strong deterrent against succumbing to peer pressure to experiment. Thus, parents who allow their children to experiment on the grounds that it is something all teenagers do are unwittingly failing to help their children develop the wherewithal to exercise judgment. Without realizing it, they become addicted—often multiply addicted to combinations of drugs, frequently adding alcohol to their drug addiction. (For more information, see Chapter 13 on Adolescence and Chapter 18 on Smoking, Alcohol, and Substance Abuse.)

THE HEALTHY WORKPLACE

WORK—a job, a career, a profession—whatever we choose to call it, is a major part of the lives of most adults. It is not only where we spend 8 or more hours per day, 5 days per week or more, it is often the major source of our identity. In some cities, it is the center of social life. For some people, it even takes the place of a social life.

The work environment—both social and physical—can have a profound effect on our lives. The effect can be positive, if we derive satisfaction from the work, if we learn how to control stress, to keep frustration to a minimum, and if we work in a safe environment.

Stress

Stress on the job can result from the nature of the job itself (such as flight control and stock trading, where workers must constantly make crucial decisions rapidly); from imposed irregularities (such as rotating work shifts); or from having to do boring and repetitive tasks with little chance for decision making (such as assembly line work). It may also be created by management practices or be the result of the personalities of workers themselves.

Various methods for controlling stress, both on and off the job, are discussed in Chapter 17 on The

Effects of Stress on Health, page 327. Stress and muscle tension can build up even in nonstressful jobs just from sitting or working in one position for long periods of time. The exercises on page 319 are designed to relieve muscle tension and strain.

Occupational Safety

Many American workers are exposed daily to some kind of occupational health hazard—to carcinogenic agents, pulmonary irritants, or to the job-related pressures of noise, crowding, and stress. Every year, 100,000 Americans die from occupational illness—a figure probably underestimated, since the link between job and disease is often unrecognized or unreported. Nevertheless, this is more than twice the number that die in motor vehicle accidents. There are approximately 125,000 new cases of occupational diseases annually, while 5.3 million workers are stricken by disabling injuries.

Occupational exposure to toxic chemicals, and to the physical hazards of excessive radiation, noise, and vibration can produce chronic lung disease, cancer, degenerative diseases to vital organs, birth defects, and genetic changes. Some hazards can cause stillbirth, miscarriage, impaired fertility, or sterility.

These health effects are often linked to particular jobs. For example, workers involved in manufacturing the pesticide dibromochloropropane have an infertility rate 2 to 3 times that of the general population.

It is difficult to estimate how much cancer is caused by exposure in the workplace—perhaps as much as 20 percent of all cancers can be traced to occupational exposure. Of the more than 63,000 chemicals manufactured or used in American industry, approximately 160 could meet criteria for proven carcinogens. Among them are arsenic, asbestos, chromium, coal products, dusts, iron oxide, mustard gas, nickel, petroleum, and ionizing radiation. Another 2,000 could be listed as potential carcinogens. Of the 1 million people who have worked in industries where there is heavy asbestos exposure, 30 percent will die from cancer.

The Occupational Safety and Health Act passed in 1970 established the Occupational Safety and Health Administration (OSHA) in the Department of Labor, with responsibility for mandating and enforcing health and safety standards for the workplace. Scientific support for OSHA is provided by the Department of Health and Human Services' National Institute for Occupational Safety and Health (NIOSH). Although this is a start, NIOSH is dreadfully understaffed to handle the magnitude of its job.

The 90 million workers subject to OSHA services are distributed in 5 million workplaces of which over 60 percent (3.1 million) employ less than 20 people. Most of the remaining 1.9 million employers have less than 100 workers.

It becomes obvious, then, that protection against occupational hazards cannot be left to OSHA, but requires the cooperation of employers, employees, unions, the medical community, and state and local governments, to:

- Set and enforce standards
- Educate employees and employers to recognize hazards
- Properly train employees who work with dangerous substances and to monitor their exposure
- Provide protective clothing and equipment
- Design and maintain industrial equipment with safety in mind
- Identify those workers who are at risk and to recognize early signs of disease
- Isolate dangerous processes within the worksite, to limit exposure
- Substitute less hazardous materials whenever possible
- Use specialized ventilation systems to eliminate hazardous fumes and dusts in the work environment

Much of the technology to reduce occupational risk is already at hand; it is a matter of employing it. For some hazards, such as asbestos, the likelihood of disease is very high among exposed workers, so that a concentrated effort in a few industries can produce a large benefit.

Some 20 states have now passed "right to know" laws, mandating that employees be allowed access to information about the chemicals with which they work. The table on pages 316–318 identifies major industrial chemicals and their risks. If others can't be depended upon to protect the worker, workers themselves must be aware of the risks to which they are exposed. Right-to-know laws encourage workers to assume responsibility for their own health and safety and to inform their doctors about the potential hazards of their workplace.

The Office Environment

With the advent of "office automation," visions of a computer screen on every desk have produced a number of unfounded fears about the dangers of computer viewing screens (called VDTs or CRTs) as a source of radiation. Actually, studies have shown that they give off no more than the minuscule

Table 16.6 **THE WORK ENVIRONMENT**[a]

Agent, pollutant, or source	Disease, effect, illness, or injury	Types of workers affected
Acrylonitrile	Lung cancer, colon cancer	Manufacturers of apparel, carpeting, blankets, draperies, synthetic furs, and hair wigs
4-aminobiphenyl	Bladder cancer	Chemical workers
Anesthetic gases	Miscarriages, birth defects, decreased alertness, increased reaction time, reticuloendothelial cancer, lymphoid cancer	Physician-anesthetists, nurse-anesthetists, other operating room personnel
Arsenic	Poorly differentiated epidermoid bronchogenic carcinoma, skin cancer, scrotal cancer, cancer of the lymphatic system, hemangiosarcoma of the liver	Workers in the metallurgical industries, sheep-dip workers, pesticide production, copper smelters workers, children living near copper smelters, people living where arsenical insecticide was sprayed, vineyard workers, insecticide makers and sprayers, tanners, miners (gold miners)
Asbestos	Asbestosis (pneumoconiosis), cancer of lung, GI tract, larynx, mesothelioma	Asbestos factory workers, textile workers, relatives of asbestos workers, people who live near asbestos factories, rubber-tire manufacturing industry workers, miners, insulation workers, shipyard workers
Auramine	Bladder cancer	Dyestuffs manufacturers, rubber workers, textile dyers, paint manufacturers
Benzene	Aplastic or hypoplastic anemia, leukemia	Rubber-tire manufacturing industry workers, painters, shoe manufacturing workers, rubber cement workers, glue and varnish workers, distillers, shoemakers, plastics workers, chemical workers
Benzidine	Bladder cancer, pancreatic cancer	Dyeworkers, chemical workers
Beryllium	Berylliosis (pneumoconiosis)	Beryllium workers, electronics workers, missile parts producers
Bis-chloromethyl ether *(BCME)*	Bronchogenic cancer	Workers in plants producing anion-exchange resins (chemical workers)
Cadmium	Lung cancer, prostatic cancer	Cadmium production workers, metallurgical workers, electroplating industry workers, chemical workers, jewelry workers, nuclear workers, and pigment workers
Carbon disulfide	EKG changes, hypertension, neurological abnormalities, decreased sperm counts, menstrual disorders, increased spontaneous abortions	Rayon manufacturers, textile workers, paint industry workers
Carbon monoxide	Neurological and behavioral disturbances	Miners, workers in the iron and steel industry and in gas plants and tunnel workers
Carbon tetrachloride	Liver and kidney damage	Plastic workers, dry cleaners

[a] Used with permission from the Institute of Medicine of the United States National Academy of Sciences, Washington, D.C.

Table 16.6 **THE WORK ENVIRONMENT (continued)**

Agent, pollutant, or source	Disease, effect, illness, or injury	Types of workers affected
Chloromethyl methyl ether *(CMME)*	Lung cancer	Chemical workers, workers in plants producing ion exchange resin
Chloroprene	Central nervous system depression, lung, liver, kidney injuries, lung and skin cancer, miscarriages	Workers in rubber-producing plants
Chromium	Bronchogenic cancer	Chromate-producing industry workers, acetylene and aniline workers, bleachers, glass, pottery, pigment, and linoleum workers
Coal dust	Pneumoconiosis	Miners, gashouse workers, stokers and producers
Coal tar pitch volatiles	Lung cancer, scrotal cancer	Steel industry workers, aluminum pot-room workers, foundry workers
Coke oven emissions	Lung cancer, kidney cancer	Steel industry workers, coke plant workers, children born of female steel industry workers
Cold temperatures	Chilblains, erythrocyanosis, immersion foot, frostbite, general hypothermia	Farmworkers, sailors, fishermen, telephone linemen
Cotton dust	Byssinosis ("brown lung disease")	Textile workers
Decaborane	Neurological and behavioral disturbances	
Dibromo-3-chloropropane	Sterility, impotence	Pesticide production workers/applicators
Hair spray	Chronic lung disease	Hairdressers
Heat	Decreased alertness, decreased psycho-motor coordination	Steelworkers, railroad workers, foundrymen
Hematite	Lung cancer	Miners
Inadequate lighting	Eye strain, fatigue, headache, eye pain, lachrymation, congestion around the cornea, "miner's nystagmus"	Miners, office workers
Kepone	Weakness, tremors, numbness, tingling, blurred vision, temporary memory loss, loss of balance	Kepone (insecticide) plant workers, agricultural workers
Lead	Miscarriage, birth defects; defects in hearing, eye-hand coordination; anemia, acute encephalopathy, "lead colic" (abdominal pain), decreased male fertility, decreased muscular strength and endurance, end stage renal disease, wrist drop, hostility, depression, anxiety	Lead production workers, lead battery plant workers, smelter workers, firing range attendants, welders, solderers
Leptophos	Weakness, tremors, numbness, tingling, blurred vision, temporary memory loss, loss of balance	Insecticide production workers, agricultural workers
Manganese	Neurological and behavioral disturbances	Steel workers, ceramic makers, electric arc welders, battery makers, drug makers, food additive makers, foundry workers, glass makers, match, paint, and varnish makers, ink makers, water treaters

Table 16.6 **THE WORK ENVIRONMENT (continued)**

Agent, pollutant, or source	Disease, effect, illness, or injury	Types of workers affected
Mercury	Nephrosis, pneumonitis, bronchitis, chest pain, shortness of breath, coughing, neurological and behavioral disturbances	Dental assistants, dental hygienists, chemical workers
Methyl butyl ketone	Peripheral neuropathy	Solvent workers, varnish and stain makers, wax makers, adhesive makers, dope (glue) workers, explosive makers, garage mechanics, celluloid makers, dyemakers, oil and lacquer processors, shoemakers
2-naphthylamine	Bladder cancer, pancreatic cancer	Dyeworkers, rubber-tire manufacturing industry workers, chemical workers, manufacturers of coal gas, nickel refiners, copper smelters, electrolysis workers
Noise	Headaches, hearing losses	Factory workers, construction workers, textile workers
Polybrominated Biphenyls (*decabromobiphenyl*) Polybrominated Biphenyl Oxides (*decabromobiphenyl oxide*)	Hypothyroidism	Chemical plant workers where PBB and PBBO are manufactured
Radiation	Cancer of paranasal and mastoid sinuses, cancer of the skin, pancreas, brain, stomach, breast, salivary glands, thyroid, GI organs, bronchus, lymphoid tissue; leukemia, multiple myeloma	Uranium miners, radiologists, radiographers, luminous dial painters
Silica	Silicosis (pneumoconiosis)	Workers in mines and quarries, steelworkers; workers in iron foundries, glass and ceramics industries
Thorium dioxide	Angiosarcoma of the liver	Chemical workers, steel workers, ceramic makers, incandescent lamp makers, nuclear reactor workers, gas mantle makers, metal refiners, vacuum tube makers
Tin	Neurological and behavioral disturbances	Aluminum and steel workers, welders, solderers
Toluene diisocyanate (*TDI*)	Pulmonary sensitization	Adhesive workers, isocyanate resin workers, organic chemical synthesizers, insulation workers, paint sprayers, lacquer workers, polyurethane makers, rubber workers, textile processors, wire coating workers
Trichloroethylene	Neurological and behavioral disturbances	Operating room personnel
Ultraviolet radiation	Conjunctivitis, keratitis, skin cancer	Farmers, sailors, arc welders
Vinyl chloride	Angiosarcoma of the liver, chromosome aberrations, cancer of the lung, brain, lymphatic and hematopoietic systems, gall bladder, and liver; lymphoma, miscarriages, birth defects	Plastics factory workers, vinyl chloride, polymerization plant workers, pregnant women living in communities near PVC plants

amount produced by fluorescent lights—and less than color TVs.

VDTs have also been accused of harming the eyes. Again, government and industry studies have shown that there is no truth in this. However, under some circumstances, they may cause eyestrain, which is simply muscle soreness that affects the muscles of the eyes. There are no serious or long-term effects, but precautions can be taken to keep the strain at a minimum. Since glare is a major source of strain, screens should not be placed where light from windows or fluorescent fixtures can bounce off them. Screens that don't come equipped with one can be fitted with an antiglare filter.

The lighting in many offices is actually too bright for the computer screen, washing the image out and causing the operator to squint, adding to eyestrain. According to the American Optometric Association (AOA), the ambient lighting level should be between 30 and 50 foot-candles, and the brightness control on the VDT screen should be set at 4 times the level of room light.

Having to change focus to look from the copy to the screen and back can also induce eyestrain. Computer and word processing operators should use a copy stand to hold notes and reference materials vertically at the same height and distance from the eyes as the screen. The optimal distance away from the screen is 14 to 24 inches. Finally, NIOSH recommends that operators take a 15-minute break every 2 hours to work on other tasks.

Fatigue, muscle, and back strain, and possibly circulation problems, can result from long hours at the VDT terminal. Most of these stem from trying to put today's computers into yesterday's offices. For example, the best height for keyboards is no more than 26 to 28 inches off the floor. Conventional office desks are 30 to 32 inches. The AOA recommends that VDTs be placed so that the top of the screen is 10° below eye level and the middle of the screen is 20° below. (How high that is, of course, depends upon how far away from the screen the operator sits.)

Proper chairs—ones that allow correct vertical alignment of the vertebrae and provide lower lumbar support—are important in preventing fatigue and back strain. Seat height should be between 16 and 22 inches and the angle between the seat and the backrest should be between 80 and 110°. In order not to restrict circulation to the legs, the ideal chair seat should pitch downward at a slight angle of about 3° and should have a "waterfall edge," dropping off sharply to keep pressure off the underside of the thighs.

EXERCISES TO DO AT A DESK[a]

Exercise	Cause for tightness, tension, or strain	Description of exercise
1. Eye movements	Constant focusing on small print	Keeping head stationary. 1. Let eyes look up and look down. Repeat 4 x's. 2. Look to right and to left, 4 x's. 3. Have eyes make a clockwise circle (as if you are tracing the numerals on a clock). Reverse to make a counterclockwise circle. Between 1, 2, and 3 close eyes and relax.
2. Neck stretch	Holding receiver of telephone with head and shoulder	Tilt head to right as if listening to shoulder with right ear. Hold onto head and stretch gently. Reverse and do on left.

[a]Adapted from *The Executive Body: A Complete Guide to Fitness and Stress Management for the Working Woman*, by Nancy Burstein, Simon and Schuster, 1984 © Nancy Burstein, used with permission.

EXERCISES TO DO AT A DESK (continued)

Exercise	Cause for tightness, tension, or strain	Description of exercise
3. Head rolls	Long periods of typing or writing	Make a circle with the head by tilting head to right side, drop forward, tilt to left side, and drop to the back. Reverse circle starting on left.
4. Shoulder lifts	Long periods of typing or writing	1. Lift right shoulder, lift left shoulder, drop right shoulder, drop left shoulder. 2. Lift and drop both shoulders together.
5. Rolling down the spine	Sitting for extended periods of time	1. Drop head and roll down the back articulating each vetebra until you reach the tail bone. 2. Reverse and roll up.
6. Hip lifts and rotations	Lack of movement during the day causes inflexibility	1. Lift right leg up 4 inches, replace foot on floor. Repeat 6 x's and do on left side. 2. Lift right leg and make circle outwards 8 x's. Reverse and make circle inwards. Repeat exercise with left leg.
7. Ankle flexes and circles	Wearing high-heeled shoes or constricting footwear	1. Lift right foot and point toes to floor. 2. Point toes to ceiling (flex). Repeat 8 x's and do on left foot. 3. Lift right foot and circle ankle outwards 8 x's. Reverse and make circle inwards. Repeat exercise with left foot.

PART II: PREVENTIVE HEALTH SERVICES

AS A NATION, Americans are healthier today than ever before in history. We have a greater knowledge of the causes of health problems, and new methods for the treatment of illness and injury are continually being developed.

We take almost for granted the seemingly miraculous cures available—ranging from vital organ transplant to the reattachment of severed limbs. But unfortunately, the glamour and drama of the "pound of cure" has almost totally eclipsed the un-glamorous "ounce of prevention." Although we may never see headlines proclaiming them, the gains in life expectancy which have occurred in the twentieth century were achieved more by prevention and health promotion measures than by treatment and curative medicine. The eradication of smallpox was accomplished not by finding a cure, but by deploying a vaccine against the disease. Medicine is now coming to realize that victory over today's major killers—heart disease, cancer, stroke, and others—

must be achieved more by prevention than by cure.

From the viewpoint of cost-effectiveness, prevention of disease is the best investment a nation or a person can make. Yet less than 5 percent of the annual federal budget is expended in disease prevention.

On an individual basis, most people wait until illness strikes before seeing a physician, and little realize that the means of protecting or promoting their health lies within their own hands. Medicine's capacity for the prevention of disease is steadily increasing. Planned, organized, and scheduled preventive visits to the doctor should be a top priority for all health-conscious people.

ADULT HEALTH SCREENING

JUST AS EVERY CHILD should receive health supervision on a regularly scheduled basis, so should the adult plan for preventive health care. But the concept of the "complete annual physical" for apparently healthy adults is now outmoded, both in frequency and in content. In these days of spiraling medical costs, it is not just a luxury, it is an inefficient use of scarce medical resources.

What has caused this change in philosophy in the health community is the realization that early diagnosis of some diseases (that is, before symptoms are apparent) has not been shown to alter the natural history of these diseases in a way that benefits the individual. Two exceptions that come quickly to mind are most (though not all) forms of cancer, and heart disease, especially hypertension and coronary artery disease. But there are other major diseases, such as diabetes, where early detection will probably not have an effect on outcome: It will not prevent the disease from developing, make it any less severe, make it more amenable to cure, alter longevity, or improve quality of life. The same can generally be said for lung cancer, brain tumors, and possibly glaucoma.

That is not to say that the complete physical is never warranted. For adults, it is appropriate at age 18, then again at 21, in order to establish a baseline against which to measure changes throughout future years. From ages 30 to 60, every 5 years is sufficient, followed by every 2 years from ages 60 to 74. From age 75 onward, when many major diseases begin to take their toll, it is appropriate annually.

Midway between the annual visit to the doctor and the habit of seeing the doctor only when ill, lies the happy medium—the periodic screening for individual risk factors. Screening is intended to identify unrecognized disease, to keep track of the progress of recognized disease, and to make changes in treatment as necessary. The frequency of the screening varies with the patient's age and sex, based on the likelihood of a particular disease being present at a particular time. Family history, environmental exposure, and past medical history can, of course, influence the content and frequency of risk factor screening.

Whether or not screening is recommended at all for a particular symptom or disease should be based on whether there is an effective method of treating the disease and whether the results outweigh any adverse effects of intervention; whether detection of the disease during the asymptomatic period can substantially affect the seriousness of the disease or the patient's life span; whether the prevalence and seriousness of the disease or condition justify the cost of screening; whether the screening process is relatively easy to administer; and whether resources for follow-up are generally available.

When there is a family history of a particular disease, screening for that disease may be recommended with more frequency or at an earlier age. For example, cardiovascular disease and some forms of cancer appear to run in families. In those families with a history of heart disease, even children may evidence hypertension (high blood pressure) and elevated levels of cholesterol. With early detection and with diet modification, serious future problems may be prevented.

When 2 or more close relatives (parents, children, or siblings) have had cancer or have had a familial disease which predisposes patients to cancer, early testing will generally be recommended. Heavy smokers and persons exposed to environmental hazards (carcinogenic chemicals such as coal tar and asbestos) should have regular checkups.

There are more than 3,000 traits and diseases commonly known to be controlled by heredity and, for many of them, preventive measures and early detection can vastly decrease the severity of illness.

The chart on page 322 lists common diagnostic tests and when they should be performed on patients who are free of symptoms, are not at high risk, and have no family history of the diseases that these tests are designed to detect.

COMMON DIAGNOSTIC TESTS AND WHEN THEY SHOULD BE PERFORMED

Name of test	Age at first test	Comments	18	19	20	21	22	23	24	25	26	27	28	29	30	31
Blood tests (anemia, diabetes, thyroid); hyperthyroid	18	Repeat tests not indicated unless symptoms; hyperthyroid for post-menopausal women														
Blood pressure	3–4	Annually	•	•	•	•	•	•	•	•	•	•	•	•	•	•
Breast exam	20	Should be supplemented by self-exam each month			•			•			•			•		
Chest x-ray		Not recommended except for those with symptoms or at high risk, such as heavy smokers														
Cholesterol	5						•				•					•
Color perception (color blindness)	5	Not necessary to repeat														
Dental	3–4	Every 6–12 months; x-rays every 2–3 years	•	•	•	•	•	•	•	•	•	•	•	•	•	•
Electrocardiogram	20–40	Should be done once as a baseline before age 40. Not necessary to repeat until age 50 unless symptoms. After 50, every 3 years.				•										
Eye (visual accuity)	5	Annually until age 18	•		•		•		•		•			•		
Hearing	5	Once during adolescence. No need for further tests unless there are symptoms.														
Mammography	35–40															
Occult Blood Stool test	40–50															
Pap test	16–17	Another, 1 year later. If both are negative, then at least every 3 years.				•			•			•			•	
Pelvic exam	16–17					•			•			•			•	
Physical exam including history	18	For schedules before age 18, see Chapters 12 and 13				•									•	
Prostate	40															
Rectal (digital)	30															
Sigmoidoscopy (also called proctosigmoidoscopy)	50	Again at 51; if both are negative, then every 3–5 years														
Testicular exam	15	This should be supplemented by self-examination each month.					•			•			•			•

36	37	38	39	40	41	42	43	44	45	46	47	48	49	50	51	52	53	54	55	56	57	58	59	60	61	62	63	64	65	66	67	68	69	70	71	72	73	74	75
									•		•		•		•		•		•		•		•		•		•		•		•		•		•		•		•
•	•	•	•	•	•	•	•	•	•	•	•	•	•	•	•	•	•	•	•	•	•	•	•	•	•	•	•	•	•	•	•	•	•	•	•	•	•	•	•
		•			•	•	•	•	•	•	•	•	•	•	•	•	•	•	•	•	•	•	•	•															
•					•					•					•					•					•					•					•				
•	•	•	•	•	•	•	•	•	•	•	•	•	•	•	•	•	•	•	•	•	•	•	•	•	•	•	•	•	•	•	•	•	•	•	•	•	•	•	•
														•			•			•			•			•			•			•			•			•	
•		•		•		•		•		•		•		•		•		•		•		•		•		•		•		•		•		•		•		•	
			•		•		•		•		•		•	•	•	•	•	•	•	•	•	•	•																
													•	•	•	•	•	•	•	•	•	•	•	•	•	•	•	•	•	•	•	•	•	•	•	•	•	•	•
•			•		•		•		•		•		•		•		•		•		•		•																
•		•	•	•	•	•	•	•	•	•	•	•	•	•	•	•	•	•	•	•	•	•	•	•	•	•	•	•	•	•	•	•	•	•	•	•	•	•	•
		•		•		•			•				•			•			•		•	•	•	•	•	•	•	•	•	•	•	•	•	•	•	•	•	•	•
		•	•	•	•	•	•	•	•	•	•	•	•	•	•	•	•	•	•	•	•	•	•	•	•	•	•	•	•	•	•	•	•	•	•	•	•	•	•
		•	•	•	•	•	•	•	•	•	•	•	•	•	•	•	•	•	•	•	•	•	•	•	•	•	•	•	•	•	•	•	•	•	•	•	•	•	•
															•	•			•			•			•			•			•			•				
•	•			•	•	•	•	•	•	•	•	•	•	•	•	•	•	•	•	•	•	•	•	•	•	•	•	•	•	•	•	•	•	•	•	•	•	•	•

Screening for Cardiovascular Disease

More Americans die from cardiovascular disease than from any other cause. It is responsible for nearly 50 percent of all deaths, many of which could be prevented by early screening followed by intervention. Men with elevated serum cholesterol levels and elevated blood pressure who are cigarette smokers are at the greatest risk. Diabetes is another major risk factor. Contributing factors to heart disease are physical inactivity, obesity, stress, and family history of heart disease. Before menopause (scientists are not sure why) women have a much smaller risk of coronary heart disease than men. After menopause, their risk begins to rise, but never equals men's.

Screening for heart disease should include blood pressure monitoring for all patients, including children. Adults with normal blood pressure should have theirs checked at least every 2 years, while those at risk should be monitored more frequently. HDL and LDL cholesterol levels in the blood (see Diet and Nutrition section for additional information) should be measured every 4 or 5 years for the well patient, and annually for the patient at risk. A smoking history should be obtained on the initial visit and repeated periodically, and weight should be monitored. Finally, the physician should be aware of stresses that affect the patient.

Screening for Cerebrovascular Disease (Stroke)

Although well over one-quarter of a million people survive strokes each year, about one-third remain disabled for life with paralysis, speech disorders, and loss of memory. The risk factors for stroke are similar to those for coronary heart disease—high blood pressure, a diet high in saturated fats and cholesterol, diabetes, and smoking. Chief among them is high blood pressure (hypertension), which is responsible for more strokes than any other single cause. Since blacks have more than a 40 percent greater chance of having high blood pressure than whites, they are also much more prone to stroke.

Cancer Screening

Cancer is the second most common cause of death in this country. Almost half of the cancer fatalities come from cancer of the lung, the large intestine, or the breast.

Factors that affect the content and frequency of cancer screening are use of alcohol, smoking habits, diet, exposure to radiation (including sunlight), occupational exposure to chemicals, water and air pollution, and hereditary tendency.

Familial forms of cancer include all the major ones—lung, skin, breast, colon, and uterine. This does not mean that every individual who has had a family member with cancer is at a higher risk of developing that disease. "Familial" in this case refers to two or more documented cases of close relatives developing the same form of cancer. There are also familial diseases that predispose patients to cancer, for which early testing should be done.

Virtually every patient with familial polyposis of the colon (multiple polyps in the colon) will develop colon cancer by age 50, and thus should have the stool tested for blood at age 10 rather than at age 40, the recommended age for those at average risk. Women exposed to the drug DES because their mothers took it during pregnancy are at a higher than normal risk for developing a form of vaginal cancer, and should have a gynecological exam earlier than most teenagers.

Because of the hazards of radiation, routine chest x-ray is not recommended for the patient who is free of symptoms. However, those at risk of lung cancer and those with symptoms may require a combination of chest x-rays and regular sputum analysis.

Breast cancer occurs in 1 out of every 11 women. Modern methods of detection permit early identification before it has spread to the lymph nodes. Women in the high-risk category are those with family history of breast cancer, women over 50, single women, and those with previous breast cancer. All women over 20 should perform breast self-examination on a monthly basis. Between ages 20 and 40, a breast physical examination is recommended every 3 years, and over age 40, annually. Low-dose mammography is recommended for all women over 50, and the American Cancer Society also recommends a baseline mammogram for all women between the ages of 35 and 40.

Cancer of the cervix, if detected early, is curable. The Pap test detects abnormalities in cervical cells. In low-risk women, after 2 negative tests a year apart, the Pap smear will be repeated on a less frequent schedule. In higher-risk women (those with family history of cancer, sexually active teenagers, women who began having sexual intercourse at an early age, the Pap smear may be performed on a more frequent schedule.

Cancer of the colon and rectum (colorectal cancer) is the second most common malignancy in America. Early detection of colon cancer by means of digital rectal examination and sigmoidoscopy can reduce mortality. For those over 40, annual digital rectal examination is recommended. Over age 45, a fecal occult blood test to detect polyps or other causes of rectal bleeding is recommended. Over age

50, proctosigmoidoscopy examination (a "procto") is recommended every 3 to 5 years if the patient is free of symptoms. (For additional information, see Chapter 20 on Cancer, page 395.)

IMMUNIZATION OF ADULTS

EVEN PARENTS who dutifully follow a prescribed immunization schedule for their children often forget about themselves. While most vaccinations do not have to be repeated beyond childhood, some are advisable periodically or when necessary for known exposure, for international travel (see table 16.7), and for those at high risk of certain diseases.

Tetanus and Diphtheria.   While there is little incidence of tetanus (lockjaw) in this country, those cases which do occur (about half of which are fatal) involve a laceration or wound in or around the home or yard. Over two-thirds of these cases occur in people over 50, which would indicate that large numbers of people over 40 are not adequately immunized. Tetanus boosters for adults are recommended every 10 years.

Poliomyelitis (Infantile Paralysis).   Although polio has been practically eradicated in this country, outbreaks can occur among unimmunized people, and the traveler to underdeveloped areas may be at further risk. Routine immunization against polio is not recommended for adults over 18, with the exception of travelers to countries where polio exists, members of special population groups with disease caused by wild polio virus, and laboratory and health-care workers who may be exposed to polio virus. Three doses of inactive polio virus (trivalent type) should be given at intervals of 1 to 2 months, with a fourth dose 6 to 12 months later. Pregnant women and patients with immunodeficiency diseases should not take oral polio vaccine.

Influenza (Flu) Vaccine.   Adults at high risk of Influenza A and B should be vaccinated annually. This includes those with chronic heart and respiratory conditions, cancer, kidney disease, diabetes, anemia, or conditions that alter immunity. Influenza vaccine is also advised for those over 65, and for healthy younger adults who work in close contact with persons at high risk. *Individuals who are sensitive to eggs should not be given influenza vaccine.*

Pneumococcal Vaccine.   Patients with certain chronic conditions are at risk of developing pneumococcal infections, principally pneumonia. Those susceptible include patients with sickle cell anemia, certain malignancies, cirrhosis of the liver, kidney failure, disorders of the spleen; alcoholics; diabetics; persons with congestive heart failure or chronic pulmonary disease; and those who have had their spleens removed, have had organ transplants, or have immunosuppressive diseases. Immunization consists of a single dose of vaccine. Booster doses should not be given, nor should the vaccine be given during pregnancy.

Rubella Vaccine.   Rubella (German measles) can cause birth defects if it occurs during the first trimester (first 3 months) of pregnancy. For that reason, women of childbearing age who have never been vaccinated against rubella and who are anti-

Table 16.7   **SELECTED IMMUNIZATION FOR INTERNATIONAL TRAVEL**

Immunizing agent	Indications	Schedule
Cholera vaccine	Travel to countries with legal requirement	Two shots at 1-week intervals, 2 months before leaving
Plague vaccine	Travel to plague endemic areas	
Polio vaccine	Unimmunized or partially immunized persons traveling to developing countries	Complete course of oral polio vaccine
Rabies vaccine	Extensive travel in developing countries	
Smallpox vaccine	Not indicated	
Typhoid vaccine	Extensive travel to rural areas of developing countries	
Yellow fever vaccine	Travel to Africa or South America	
Immune serum globulin	Extensive travel to rural areas of developing countries, as protection against hepatitis A	

body negative by testing, should receive a single dose of vaccine. Pregnancy must be avoided for 3 months following injection, and the vaccine should never be taken by a pregnant woman.

Hepatitis B Vaccine. Health-care workers, physicians, dentists, and others who come in contact with contaminated needles are at risk of getting hepatitis B, a virus infection that affects the liver. Others at risk are users of illegal drugs, sexually active male homosexuals, and hemophiliacs who get frequent blood transfusions. The vaccine is administered in 3 separate doses and provides protective immunity to over 90 percent of vaccinated individuals.

SUMMING UP

HOW WE LIVE OUR LIVES has a profound effect on our health. By living prudently, we have the capacity to improve the quality of our lives immeasurably, to reduce the risk of disease, to counteract the effects of some disorders, and to better our chances of living a longer life that is mobile, productive, and relatively pain-free in old age.

By avoiding smoking, drinking only in moderation, exercising regularly, learning to handle stress, maintaining ideal body weight, and following a prudent diet, we can substantially reduce our risk of premature cardiovascular disease and cancer—together responsible for more than 70 percent of the deaths in this country. By making efforts to control our work environment, we can reduce our risk of occupational diseases. And finally, we can better our chances of surviving those diseases we can't prevent by having periodic screening for diseases likely to occur in our sex and age group.

17 The Effects of Stress on Health

Stanley S. Heller, M.D., and Kenneth A. Frank, Ph.D.

STRESS HAS ALWAYS BEEN a part of life: Prehistoric humans faced a constant struggle with their environment to find food, shelter, and a safe haven from a multitude of enemies. In the Middle Ages, plague and famine decimated entire populations. Until this century, infections such as tuberculosis, diphtheria, and smallpox were major killers. Today, people living in industrialized societies have conquered most of these scourges of the past, but this does not mean that stress is also a thing of history. Instead, we face a new set of stresses, many of them of our own creation, which are believed to contribute significantly to our most serious health problems. As Alvin Toffler points out in *Future Shock*, if anything characterizes our culture, it is change—pervasive, accelerating change. And this change all too often is translated into stress.

A growing number of researchers are convinced that stress contributes to diseases, both physical and psychological ones. It is not known what proportion of diseases are the direct consequence of stress, but the list in which it is thought to be a factor is long and varied: heart disease, ulcers and other digestive disorders, diabetes, psychological problems, asthma, high blood pressure, migraine, arthritis and other diseases with an autoimmune component, dermatitis, recurring attacks of genital herpes, and perhaps even certain cancers.

WHAT IS STRESS?

EVERYONE HAS an intuitive concept of what stress means, but a precise definition is difficult because one person's stress may well be another's pleasure. The late Dr. Hans Selye of Montreal, a pioneer in stress research, defined stress as a state of being, brought about by any of a large number of possible stressors. Others define it as the need to adapt or change because of something that happens. Some adaptations are not stressful; for example, if it gets cold, you adapt by putting on a coat or sweater—hardly a stressful situation. But if you are cold and don't have a coat or sweater or adequate shelter, you may indeed experience stress. In other words, stress can be regarded as the state of being in which a person is forced to adapt in a way that is difficult or unpleasant.

Not all stress is necessarily bad or detrimental. Indeed, all of us need a certain amount of stress to add variety and spice to life, to prod us to achieve goals. A marathon runner, a symphony conductor, a fisherman pulling in a huge salmon are all visibly under stress at the peak of their respective performances. But while they may be panting and sweating, with pulses racing and all senses in "high gear," they also may be experiencing an exhilarating high. Dr. Selye referred to such positive stresses as "eustress." Many psychologists make a similar distinction, noting that there is a great difference between stress and distress, and that it is the latter that is likely to be detrimental to health and well-being.

How a person reacts to both stress and distress also is a key to its effect. How much control the individual has over the situation appears to be an important key. A Swedish study, for example, found lower levels of stress-related hormones among commuters who boarded the train early enough to control their environment by choosing their seats, taking time to stow their briefcases and coats, and not worrying about having to stand. In contrast, those who boarded the train after it was already crowded and had to either scramble for a seat or stand had higher levels of stress-related hormones, even though they had shorter commutes.

Predictability is another factor. Animals warned by a beep tone that an electrical shock is about to come have 6 times fewer ulcers than those that are shocked without warning. Intensity is still another consideration: An air traffic controller and traffic cop may work at the same rate, but the stakes are higher for the air controller; so is the incidence of stress-related disease.

Individual perception of what constitutes stress varies from person to person. Some people thrive on deadlines and cannot seem to get started until one becomes pressing. Others fall to pieces if they are required to work within any kind of time frame. Noise and the hustle of on-going activity may be sweet music to some and unbearable distractions to others. These are just a few of the variables that make stress difficult to define and measure; still, it must be considered an important factor in assessing overall health and well-being.

THE PHYSIOLOGY OF STRESS

STRESS IS ASSOCIATED with the "fight-or-flight response," which occurs automatically in reaction to perceived danger. This perception prompts the pituitary, the body's master gland, to release adrenocorticotrophic hormone (ACTH), which in turn stimulates the adrenal gland to pour out corticosteroid hormones and epinephrine. These almost instantaneous responses cause the pulse to quicken, muscles to tense, blood pressure to rise, the senses to sharpen, all in preparation to either flee or fight. This may be appropriate, and even lifesaving, in situations involving real danger. But all too often, we react with a full "fight-or-flight" response in situations that do not warrant it. Most people don't punch the boss or race out of the office screaming, even though their bodies may be primed to do so. Instead, they may develop psychiatric symptoms, a tension headache, or abdominal pains.

During the late 1950s, Dr. Selye subjected experimental animals to a variety of stressors, such as starvation, extreme heat and cold, or surgery. In each case, he noticed the same syndrome: A reaction of alarm, followed by an adaptation phase and, if the stress continued, eventual exhaustion and death. "No living organism," he wrote, "can exist continuously in a state of alarm." Since then, researchers have learned considerably more about the physiologic changes brought about by stress and the long-term effects. For example, rises in the levels of stress-related hormones, such as cortisol, epinephrine, and testosterone, vary from person to person and also according to the degrees of stress. In some people, the hormonal responses are fleeting; in others the altered levels may persist for weeks or even months. There is growing evidence that these hormonal changes may lead to disease. In experimental animals, for example, cortisol has been shown to raise the level of cholesterol and other lipids in the blood and to increase the development of atherosclerosis and other signs of damage to the blood vessels. Similarly, patients who take corticosteroid drugs for arthritis, asthma, and other conditions have an increase in atherosclerosis.

Studies in animals have shown that cortisol and epinephrine can depress the immune system, making them more susceptible to disease. In one particularly intriguing study, researchers at the University of Rochester found that animals that learn to associate the taste of saccharin with a drug that suppresses their immune system will eventually show immune suppression when they taste saccharin without the drug: Clearly, the mind can in some way affect the immune system. Of course, common folklore has long held that people are more likely to fall ill when they are upset or otherwise subjected to stress. The examples are legion: Catching a bad cold before an important date or event; suffering a heart attack or developing a serious illness in the aftermath of the death of a loved one; contracting diabetes or other disease on the heels of a viral infection or some other stress are but a few of the more common ones.

The consequences of stress are by no means limited to physical illness. People under significant stress are at high risk of alcohol or drug abuse, overeating or smoking, immersion in cults, or other potentially self-destructive behavior, including suicide. Depression and other manifestations of mental illness also are closely related to stress. (See Chapter 36 on Mental and Emotional Health, page 709.)

THE SOCIAL READJUSTMENT RATING SCALE[a]

Life event	Mean value
1. Death of a spouse	100
2. Divorce	73
3. Marital separation	65
4. Jail term	63
5. Death of close family member	63
6. Personal injury or illness	53
7. Marriage	50
8. Fired at work	47
9. Marital reconciliation	45
10. Retirement	45
11. Change in health of family member	44
12. Pregnancy	40
13. Sex difficulties	39
14. Gain of new family member	39
15. Business readjustment	39
16. Change in financial state	38
17. Death of close friend	37
18. Change to different line of work	36
19. Change in number of arguments with spouse	35
20. Mortgage or loan for a major purpose (home, etc.)	31
21. Foreclosure of mortgage or loan	30
22. Change in responsibilities at work	29
23. Son or daughter leaving home	29
24. Trouble with in-laws	29
25. Outstanding personal achievement	28
26. Spouse begins or stops work	26
27. Begin or end school	26
28. Change in living conditions	25
29. Revision of personal habits	24
30. Trouble with boss	23
31. Change in work hours or conditions	20
32. Change in residence	20
33. Change in schools	20
34. Change in recreation	19
35. Change in church activities	19
36. Change in social activities	18

Life event	Mean value
37. Mortgage or loan for a lesser purpose (car, TV, etc.)	17
38. Change in sleeping habits	17
39. Change in number of family get-togethers	16
40. Change in eating habits	15
41. Vacation	13
42. Christmas	12
43. Minor violations of the law	11

Preventive Measures

The following suggestions are for using the Social Readjustment Rating Scale for the maintenance of your health and prevention of illness:

1. Become familiar with the life events and the amount of change they require.
2. Put the scale where you and the family can see it easily several times a day.
3. With practice you can recognize when a life event happens.
4. Think about the meaning of the event for you and try to identify some of the feelings you experience.
5. Think about the different ways you might best adjust to the event.
6. Take your time in arriving at decisions.
7. If possible, anticipate life changes and plan for them well in advance.
8. Pace yourself. It can be done even if you are in a hurry.
9. Look at the accomplishment of a task as a part of daily living and avoid looking at such an achievement as a "stopping point" or a "time for letting down."

---

[a]Adapted from T. H. Holmes and R. H. Rahe. "The Social Readjustment Scale," *Journal of Psychosomatic Research*, Vol. II, 1967, 213–18. © 1967, Pergamon Press, Inc. Reprinted with permission.

MEASURING STRESS

GIVEN THE FACT that there are so many variables involved in stress and an individual's response to it, it is somewhat difficult to measure stress and predict its effect in a given individual. Even so, a number of self-rating tests have been devised that alert individuals to the possibility of stress-related health problems. One of the most useful of these is the Social Readjustment Rating Scale, developed by Drs. Thomas Holmes and Richard Rahe of the University of Washington. In their work with thousands of patients, these researchers and their colleagues determined that most people consider the death of a spouse, even a former one to whom they are no longer married, as life's most stressful event. In further research, Drs. Holmes and Rahe rated 42 other common life events, and then set about to follow their patients for several years to determine what effects on health these life events would have over time. Their studies suggested that an accumulation of 200 or more stress points in a single year greatly increased the likelihood of a major illness. A score of 300 or more carried an 80 percent likelihood of a major illness or accident within 2 years; scores between 150 and 300 translated into a 50-50 risk.

In reviewing the list of life events, 3 important patterns emerge. First, there is a pattern of losses. Many of these are losses because of death, alienation of affection, or geographical moves. There are also abstract losses, such as the loss of job status; and finally, there are the losses, perhaps most devastating, of self-esteem. The second pattern is of threats—threats to status, to the likelihood of achieving goals, to health, and to security. The third pattern involves change, both for better and for worse. Even some things that happen automatically with the passage of time or recur year after year—for example, Christmas and school closing—are stressful.

The usefulness of this stress rating scale can be found in its title, namely, the word *readjustment*. While many of the life events listed are inevitable, others can be avoided, planned, or postponed. In other words, some of the major stresses do not happen automatically or randomly; they take place when we make them happen. Insofar as is possible, it is wise to put some months or even years between these "heavy happenings." For example, a person getting divorced or remarried this year might postpone an anticipated job change until next year, or at least, make such a decision with the realization that it may increase the risk of illness. Someone who has just married, moved to a new home, and started a new job might well consider postponing pregnancy for at least a year or so.

PERSONALITY AND STRESS

IN RECENT YEARS, a good deal has been written about the possible role of personality type in disease. Much of this stems from the research and writings of two San Francisco heart specialists, Drs. Meyer Friedman and Ray Rosenman. By interviewing heart-attack patients, Drs. Friedman and Rosenman began to see a behavior pattern, which they called "hurry sickness." Later they described this as a "chronic, incessant struggle to achieve more and more in less and less time." The Type A person always tries to do more than one thing at a time and is impatient with slowness in others. He or she is likely to behave competitively in situations that do not call for competition. Type As have their own pattern of speech: They talk fast, interrupt others, and finish sentences for those who speak more slowly. They may be quick-tempered, compulsive, suspicious, and hostile.

In contrast, Type B behavior is more relaxed, less competitive, and not so driven by time and the need to succeed. Drs. Friedman and Rosenman found that people with this personality type did not seem to be as susceptible to heart attacks as Type As. Over the last 25 years, the question of personality and heart disease has been the subject of continuing research and controversy. Some studies seem to indicate that it is a major factor, while others do not. Recent studies at Duke University and elsewhere have attempted to identify those components of Type A behavior that may be the most detrimental. Two long-term Duke studies pinpointed hostility as a key factor: people who tended to be suspicious and hostile had a higher incidence of heart attacks, as well as a higher death rate from other causes.

Why should Type As be more disease-prone than the calmer Type Bs? This important question has not been fully answered, but a growing body of evidence seems to point to many of the same physiologic changes that are produced by stress. In Type A individuals, the levels of stress-related hormones are higher than normal; conceivably, this could produce the same detrimental effects on blood pressure, blood vessels, blood lipids, and other body systems as stress.

Type A Women

Until recently, men have been the focus of most studies relating personality and disease. But, according to Drs. Friedman and Rosenman, there are Type A women, but they are different from Type A men. Women, for example, are more likely to turn their stress inward on themselves rather than release it in sudden outbursts of anger, which is typical of Type A men. In fact, Type A women often come across as excessively polite, when, in fact, they are only hiding feelings of anger or hostility. Type A men tend to be very driven and focused on a single goal; in contrast, women have difficulty setting priorities, assigning equal rank to career, family, marriage, and home, resulting in incredible pressure and feelings of guilt and overload. Studies have found that even women who have achieved executive rank or high professional status are likely to devote 40 or more hours a week to managing a household and caring for a family. It is little wonder that working women are experiencing an increase in stress-related illness.

Type A Children

Studies have found that children as young as 3 years exhibit the behavior patterns typical of Type A personality. Whether this is an inherited characteristic or one molded by environment is open to debate; there is mounting evidence to support both theories, indicating it may well be a combination of factors. Dr. Karen Matthews, a psychologist at the University of Pittsburgh, did one study in which a group of toddlers were instructed to stack blocks on top of each other in the presence of their mothers or other women. The women, regardless of their own behavior patterns, tended to encourage the Type A children to do more, while they expressed praise and satisfaction for the performance of the Type B children. Dr. Matthews theorizes that Type A children are more emotionally responsive than others, and therefore elicit the very behavior that urges them on. Dr. Friedman, for his part, believes that Type A behavior can grow out of a child's feelings that parental love depends on what he or she does—getting high grades, winning at sports, excelling in any assigned task—rather than for what the child is.

In contrast, there are a number of studies linking the behavior pattern with consistently higher levels of stress-related hormones, and hormonal responses to stressful situations seem to be excessive in Type A people. Given the fact that the Type A profile can be detected in children barely old enough to talk, it is a distinct possibility that it is not fundamentally a behavioral problem, but instead, the product of an inborn, physiological syndrome, interacting with life's conditioning experiences.

Modifying Type A Behavior

Regardless of the roots of Type A behavior, one important question is whether or not attempts should be made to modify it. Again, there is no clear agreement among the experts. Some people feel that there is not enough evidence to indict Type A behavior as a cause of disease; therefore, attempts to change may be just another stress without beneficial results. Also, ours is a success-oriented, competitive society, and the Type A person is rewarded by achieving many of the goals that we hold in such high esteem: money, status, and power, among others. Add to this the fact that many, if not most, Type A people enjoy their hectic, fast-paced lives and have no desire to change. What's more, studies have found that many either deny or overlook the more undesirable facets of their behavior. Most prefer to think of themselves as competent and competitive rather than compulsive and hostile; as conscientious and productive rather than time-slaves and workaholics; as verbal and self-assured rather than loud-mouthed and overbearing. In any event, in Western society Type A drive is more likely to succeed. One recent study from Canada showed that about 60 percent of the top corporate executives have Type A behavior. (In contrast, in Japan, where corporate philosophy is more cooperative than competitive, the Type A pattern is far less prevalent than in North America.)

Some experts assert that it is futile, and perhaps contrary to the best interests of the person involved, to try to force a Type A to become a Type B. The people who seek professional help because of stress related to this behavior pattern are often the families or close associates of Type A people rather than the individuals themselves; many Type As don't want to change their way of life, they simply want to avoid the detrimental effects. One of the more successful treatment strategies is to identify those specific Type A characteristics that seem to be the most damaging and then to try to modify them, rather than undergoing a complete revision in behavior. Thus, someone who harbors excessive hostility may enter group therapy aimed specifically at overcoming this facet of behavior. A person who consistently hyper-responds may benefit from relaxation

STRESS SELF-ANALYSIS TESTS

THE FOLLOWING is a 4-part test; the first 3 parts are designed to measure your vulnerability to certain types of stress and to increase awareness of the effects of stress. The fourth part is designed to test how well you cope with stressful situations.

PART ONE

Read and choose the most appropriate answer to each of the 10 questions as it actually pertains to you.

1. When I can't do something "my way," I usually do it the easiest way.

    (a) Almost always true _____
    (b) Usually true _____
    (c) Usually false _____
    (d) Almost always false _____

2. I get "upset" when someone in front of me drives slowly.

    (a) Almost always true _____
    (b) Usually true _____
    (c) Usually false _____
    (d) Almost always false _____

3. It bothers me when my plans depend upon others.

    (a) Almost always true _____
    (b) Usually true _____
    (c) Usually false _____
    (d) Almost always false _____

4. Whenever possible, I tend to avoid large crowds.

    (a) Almost always true _____
    (b) Usually true _____
    (c) Usually false _____
    (d) Almost always false _____

5. I am uncomfortable having to stand in long lines.

    (a) Almost always true _____
    (b) Usually true _____
    (c) Usually false _____
    (d) Almost always false _____

6. Arguments upset me.

    (a) Almost always true _____
    (b) Usually true _____
    (c) Usually false _____
    (d) Almost always false _____

7. When my plans don't "flow smoothly," I become anxious.

    (a) Almost always true _____
    (b) Usually true _____
    (c) Usually false _____
    (d) Almost always false _____

8. I require a lot of room (space) to live and work in.

   (a) *Almost always true* _____
   (b) *Usually true* _____
   (c) *Usually false* _____
   (d) *Almost always false* _____

9. When I am busy at some task, I hate to be disturbed.

   (a) *Almost always true* _____
   (b) *Usually true* _____
   (c) *Usually false* _____
   (d) *Almost always false* _____

10. I believe that "All good things are worth waiting for."

   (a) *Almost always true* _____
   (b) *Usually true* _____
   (c) *Usually false* _____
   (d) *Almost always false* _____

To score:
1 and 10: a=1 point, b=2 points, c=3 points, d=4 points;
2 to 9: a=4 points, b=3 points, c=2 points, d=1 point

This test measures your vulnerability to stress from being frustrated. Scores in excess of 25 seem to suggest some vulnerability to this source of stress.

PART TWO

Circle the letter of the response option that best answers the following questions.

How often do you:
1. Find yourself with insufficient time to complete your work?

   (a) *Almost always* _____
   (b) *Very often* _____
   (c) *Seldom* _____
   (d) *Never* _____

2. Find yourself becoming confused and unable to think clearly because too many things are happening at once?

   (a) *Almost always* _____
   (b) *Very often* _____
   (c) *Seldom* _____
   (d) *Never* _____

3. Wish you had help to get everything done?

   (a) *Almost always* _____
   (b) *Very often* _____
   (c) *Seldom* _____
   (d) *Never* _____

4. Feel your boss (parent, professor, etc.) expects too much from you?

   (a) *Almost always* _____
   (b) *Very often* _____
   (c) *Seldom* _____
   (d) *Never* _____

5. Feel your family/friends expect too much from you?

   (a) *Almost always* _____
   (b) *Very often* _____
   (c) *Seldom* _____
   (d) *Never* _____

6. Find your work infringing upon your leisure hours?

   (a) *Almost always* _____
   (b) *Very often* _____
   (c) *Seldom* _____
   (d) *Never* _____

7. Find yourself doing extra work to set an example for those around you?

   (a) *Almost always* _____
   (b) *Very often* _____
   (c) *Seldom* _____
   (d) *Never* _____

8. Find yourself doing extra work to impress your superiors?

   (a) *Almost always* _____
   (b) *Very often* _____
   (c) *Seldom* _____
   (d) *Never* _____

9. Have to skip a meal so that you can get work completed?

   (a) *Almost always* _____
   (b) *Very often* _____
   (c) *Seldom* _____
   (d) *Never* _____

10. Feel that you have too much responsibility?

   (a) *Almost always* _____
   (b) *Very often* _____
   (c) *Seldom* _____
   (d) *Never* _____

To score:
a=4 points, b=3 points, c=2 points, d=1 point.

This test measures your vulnerability to overload. Scores in excess of 25 seem to indicate vulnerability to having too much to do.

PART THREE

Answer all questions as is generally true for you.

1. I hate to wait in lines.

   (a) *Almost always true* _____
   (b) *Usually true* _____
   (c) *Seldom true* _____
   (d) *Never true* _____

2. I often find myself racing against the clock to save time.

   (a) *Almost always true* _____
   (b) *Usually true* _____
   (c) *Seldom true* _____
   (d) *Never true* _____

3. I become upset if I think something is taking too long.

    (a) *Almost always true* _____
    (b) *Usually true* _____
    (c) *Seldom true* _____
    (d) *Never true* _____

4. When under pressure, I tend to lose my temper.

    (a) *Almost always true* _____
    (b) *Usually true* _____
    (c) *Seldom true* _____
    (d) *Never true* _____

5. My friends tell me that I tend to get irritated easily.

    (a) *Almost always true* _____
    (b) *Usually true* _____
    (c) *Seldom true* _____
    (d) *Never true* _____

6. I seldom like to do anything unless I can make it competitive.

    (a) *Almost always true* _____
    (b) *Usually true* _____
    (c) *Seldom true* _____
    (d) *Never true* _____

7. When something needs to be done, I am the first to begin even though the details may still need to be worked out.

    (a) *Almost always true* _____
    (b) *Usually true* _____
    (c) *Seldom true* _____
    (d) *Never true* _____

8. When I make a mistake, it is usually because I've rushed into something without giving it enough thought and planning.

    (a) *Almost always true* _____
    (b) *Usually true* _____
    (c) *Seldom true* _____
    (d) *Never true* _____

9. Whenever possible, I will try to do two things at once, like eating while working or planning while driving or bathing.

    (a) *Almost always true* _____
    (b) *Usually true* _____
    (c) *Seldom true* _____
    (d) *Never true* _____

10. When I go on a vacation, I usually take some work along just in case I get a chance to do it.

    (a) *Almost always true* _____
    (b) *Usually true* _____
    (c) *Seldom true* _____
    (d) *Never true* _____

To score:
a = 4 points, b = 3 points, c = 2 points, d = 1 point.

This test measures the presence of compulsive, time urgent, and excessively aggressive behavioral traits. Scores in excess of 25 suggest the presence of one or more of these traits.

PART FOUR

How well do you cope with stress? This scale was created largely on the basis of results compiled by doctors and researchers who have sought to identify how individuals effectively cope with stress. It is an educational tool, not a clinical test. Its purpose is to inform you of ways in which you can effectively and healthfully cope with stress.

Follow the instructions given for each of the 14 items listed below. When you have completed, total your points and place the score on the bottom line.

_____ 1. Give yourself 10 points if you feel you have a supportive family around you.

_____ 2. Give yourself 10 points if you actively pursue a hobby.

_____ 3. Give yourself 10 points if you belong to some social or activity group that meets at least once a month (other than your family).

_____ 4. Give yourself 15 points if you are within 5 pounds of your ideal bodyweight, considering your height and bone structure.

_____ 5. Give yourself 15 points if you practice some form of deep relaxation at least 3 times a week (meditation, imagery, Yoga, etc.).

_____ 6. Give yourself 5 points for each time you exercise 30 minutes or longer during the course of an average week.

_____ 7. Give yourself 5 points for each nutritionally balanced and wholesome meal you consume during the course of an average day.

_____ 8. Give yourself 5 points if you do something you really enjoy which is "just for you" during the course of an average week.

_____ 9. Give yourself 10 points if you have some place in your home that you can go in order to relax and/or be by yourself.

_____ 10. Give yourself 10 points if you practice time management techniques in your daily life.

_____ 11. Subtract 10 points for each pack of cigarettes you smoke during the course of an average day.

_____ 12. Subtract 5 points for each evening during the course of an average week that you take any form of medication or chemical substance (including alcohol) to help you sleep.

_____ 13. Subtract 10 points for each day during the course of an average week that you consume any form of medication or chemical substance (including alcohol) to reduce your anxiety or just calm you down.

_____ 14. Subtract 5 points for each evening during the

course of an average week that you bring work home—work that was meant to be done at your place of employment.

_____ 15. Now calculate your total score. A perfect score would be 115 points. If you scored in the 50–60 range, you probably have adequate coping strategies for most common sources of stress. However, you should keep in mind that the higher your score, the greater your ability to cope with stress in an effective and healthful manner.

WORK AND STRESS

PARTICULAR KINDS OF WORK seem to cause special stress, and the effects on health are manifested in an all-too-common pattern: fatigue, insomnia, eating disorders, nervousness, feelings of unhappiness, abuse of alcohol or drugs. Stress is often related to the nature of the job or imposed irregularities. Rotating shift work, in which hours are erratic or inconsistent with the normal sleep cycle, produces both physical and mental stress by constantly upsetting circadian rhythms that control specific hormonal and other responses. Jobs that involve little variation but require constant close attention, for example, assembly-line work or jobs requiring repetitive tasks with dangerous equipment, seem to be particularly stressful. In one study in a sawmill, people who ran the equipment had much higher levels of stress-related hormones than workers who did not come in contact with machinery, even though their jobs also may have been boring and repetitive.

As might be expected, the personality and management techniques of the supervisor are important factors in determining the level of job-related stress. One study of personnel management techniques among bosses showed that the only factor that correlated with high blood cholesterol levels in employees was a boss who was more concerned with petty details than with overall effectiveness and productivity.

Some of the most extensive work on jobs and stress has been a coordinated group of studies in the United States and Sweden, directed by Dr. Robert A. Karasek of Columbia University. Dr. Karasek's study began with the U.S. Labor Department's official list of occupations. The Karasek research team specifically asked people in each category to rate the amount of psychological demand in their job—how hard and fast they had to work, how hectic they found the job, whether they felt they had more than they could do at any one time. The researchers also asked people about the "decision control" they felt in their work: whether they had any say about working conditions, whether the job had variety and required skill, whether they were learning new things on the job.

Then the Karasek team sought out the rates of cardiovascular illness in the different professions. In a half dozen studies comparing job categories with heart disease in the United States and Sweden, their results have been consistent: occupations with high psychological demand and low control are associated with high rates of heart disease.

While their research is too limited to imply that particular occupations cause a high risk of heart disease, Dr. Karasek and his co-workers do feel that they have found a way to define a high-stress job, and have shown a link between such stress and heart disease.

People who may be in high-stress jobs (depending on their particular circumstances) are assembly-line workers, freight-handlers, punch-press operators, and garment stitchers. Why? Because people in such occupations have high psychological demand but low control over their work. The same is probably true of many cashiers, telephone operators, and nurse's aides, because they must take on a responsibility and demand without being allowed to interact in a meaningful way with clients or customers. In many cases, Dr. Karasek adds, the homemaker with small children and an unhelpful spouse may also be in a very high-stress situation: too much to do, too little time, work that is seen as unstimulating, and no way to escape.

At the very worst end of the spectrum—so stressful it tends to "fall off the charts" in Dr. Karasek's study—is assembly-line work. Time demands are inexorable, control is almost nonexistent, and the work is routine and dull. Heart disease rates among assembly-line workers are particularly high.

Low-stress jobs would tend to be those with low demand: forestry, natural science, auto repair. Surprisingly, Dr. Karasek's scheme would categorize doctors, lawyers, and top executives as having relatively low-stress occupations, because they may have high demand but they also, in general, have a high level of control over their work. Also surprisingly, because it defies popular wisdom, people at the top of these professions have relatively low rates of cardiovascular disease.

POST-TRAUMATIC STRESS DISORDER

PEOPLE WHO HAVE BEEN THROUGH extraordinarily stressful events—war combat, witness to a murder, survival of a natural catastrophe, among others—often develop a specific syndrome referred to as "post-traumatic stress disorder." Very often, the symptoms do not appear for months or even years after the event. Some of the most important research in this field has involved survivors of Nazi concentration camps; more recently, the syndrome has been identified in a large number of Vietnam War veterans.

People with post-traumatic stress disorder are irritable, easily depressed, and have difficulty relating to others. During the day they are easily startled and may have flashbacks to the traumatic event; nights are often disrupted by recurring nightmares.

In one study of survivors of a maritime explosion with a heavy death toll, the focus was on survivors who had shown no anxiety reactions and who seemed initially to recover without incident. Four years later, however, about 70 percent exhibited the typical reactions.

Stress researchers have found 4 distinct phases in the disorder. First, the survivor recognizes that he or she has been through a living nightmare and cries out in anguish. This is followed by a period of denial and numbness, which gives way to a period of oscillation between numbness and repetitive flashbacks to the traumatic event. Eventually, the survivor must either come to terms with the experience or enter a kind of psychological retreat in which he or she refuses to accept the implications of the experience. Individual psychotherapy can be very helpful in sorting out the meaning of the experience; group therapy with others who have had similar experiences is also helpful.

TECHNIQUES TO OVERCOME STRESS

STRESS MANAGEMENT and the development of effective coping techniques are the keys to overcoming stress. While it may be possible to eliminate some stressors, it is highly unlikely in our fast-paced, ever-changing society that their number can be significantly lowered.

How people manage their own stress, like the nature of stress itself, is a very individual matter. In general, people benefit most from the technique for which they are best suited psychologically, or which "fits" them best. Some might wish to talk at length to another individual who can help them understand the roots of their problem. Although psychoanalytic psychotherapy is usually costly in terms of time and money, many experts believe that the changes effected by this approach are the deepest and most lasting. A person under stress is often suffering because of a vulnerability resulting from his early life experience. For example, the loss of a spouse might be unduly distressing because it reactivates old feelings and memories about the painful loss of a parent in early childhood. The loss of the spouse, while deeply disturbing, may be felt as overwhelming, as if the person were once again the relatively helpless, dependent young child who was earlier abandoned. Through the process of a guided self-exploration, other stresses may be similarly understood in terms of their subtle connections to the childhood past. Insight into the origins of such stress reactions may lead to reductions in stress, and may facilitate the development of more realistic and adaptive coping behaviors.

Others may wish to seek the support of group therapy. Groups are extremely valuable in providing needed social support and a feeling that one is not alone in his or her distress. Groups may also provide the opportunity for catharsis, offer members useful information, and promote the acquisition of new, more adaptive socializing and interpersonal skills. Groups are particularly helpful to adolescents, the bereaved, and people who have experienced excessive trauma.

Many of us can borrow from the coping techniques that have helped others survive almost unimaginable horror, such as imprisonment in a Nazi death camp. Studies of survivors have identified two major coping techniques: (1) Those who cope best refuse to accept the notion that they are doomed; and (2) endurance is a group activity—those who cope best do so by seeking and gaining the support of others. These coping strategies are echoed repeatedly in studies of people who survive against great odds, such as patients with normally fatal cancer. Survivors refuse to see themselves as victims and they refuse to accept the logic of the situation forced on them.

There are also a number of teachable coping techniques designed specifically to reduce stress. These include the following:

Relaxation Training

Relaxation, by definition, is the opposite of stress. Relaxation therapy may be as simple as sitting for 10 minutes in a reclining chair with eyes closed and the phone off the hook and repeating the word "one" silently while exhaling. Or it may be a period of almost ritualistic deep muscle relaxation or transcendental meditation. Practiced regularly in a quiet, uninterrupted setting, relaxation therapy can produce benefits that extend long beyond the relaxation period. For the religious, prayer often serves a similar stress-relieving function.

Another short-term approach is called Stress Management Training. In general, it utilizes a number of behavioral techniques to reduce stress. First one is taught to practice deep muscle relaxation. Subsequently, one is helped to imagine anxiety-arousing situations in order to learn to identify muscular tension cues in the body. Next one learns to terminate or to cope with the anxiety thus aroused, with a relaxation response. With practice one can learn to identify muscular tension cues in daily life and to condition relaxation as a coping response. This technique has also been used to diminish the stress component of the Type A behavior pattern, e.g., time urgency. In related behavioral techniques, one can imagine anxiety-arousing situations, and practice Type B, rather than Type A, behaviors, while practicing relaxation. Many mental health practitioners, some working in hospital settings, are skilled in helping people to learn these skills in order that they may then practice them on their own for self-help.

Another approach which has been used for reducing stress, including the stress component of the Type A behavior pattern, is called Cognitive Restructuring. Ideally, one is helped to identify muscular tension cues as in the stress management program outlined above. However, in this approach people are taught to recognize such stress responses as a reaction to some prior event. One can then be helped to identify the meaning, or interpretation placed on the event, which results in stress. A guided critical evaluation of such beliefs, or interpretations, then follows, leading to the replacement of unreasonable with reasonable beliefs, or self-statements as they are called. For example, a Type A person might interpret the boss's comment, "Complete this as soon as you can," to mean "Complete this immediately." This places him under time pressure and

stress. A more reasonable self-statement would be substituted, like "Do this when you get the chance." This more relaxed interpretation is consistent with the boss's requirement, but offers a more relaxed and less stressful interpretation. Cognitive Restructuring, when taught by a skilled professional, may also be utilized as a self-help technique once mastered. Behavioral, cognitive, and interpretive techniques are used alone and in combination by mental health professionals in order to help people master stress.

Exercise

Regular vigorous aerobic exercise has been found to reduce the level of stress-related hormones and to promote a renewed sense of well-being. For example, physicians at West Point Military Academy have noted that there are fewer psychiatric disorders among young people who were accustomed to regular exercise before entering the academy. Dr. Selye found that rats trained to a high degree of physical fitness had a substantially increased level of resistance to laboratory stresses. In addition to relieving stress, regular aerobic exercise has numerous other health benefits, such as cardiovascular conditioning, a more efficient uptake of insulin (an important consideration for people with diabetes), and weight control.

Biofeedback Training

This increasingly popular method of stress reduction can be an excellent coping technique. Biofeedback training involves learning to control normally involuntary body functions, such as slowing the heart rate, lowering blood pressure, halting the vascular or muscle spasms that trigger certain pain syndromes. The training is accomplished by placing sensors on the skin that measure muscle activity (muscle contractions are a sign of tension) or skin temperature (an indication of arterial blood flow) and then watching a bleep or squiggle on a monitor or listening to a tone. By watching the monitor, the subject learns the physiological signs that indicate arousal or anxiety. As the training progresses, the subject learns to control the physical responses to stress: chest pains, migraine headaches, irritable bowel syndrome, or asthma are among the stress-related disorders that can be effectively treated by biofeedback training in some individuals. A word of caution, however: As with many unconventional therapies, patients must be cautious in determining whether the practitioner is, indeed, legitimate. Biofeedback training is now offered in special clinics affiliated with major medical centers or institutions; these are likely to be directed by qualified health professionals. Be wary of practitioners who urge patients to buy expensive equipment or sign a long-term contract for a number of treatments. If there are doubts, the credentials can be checked by writing the Biofeedback Society of America, 4301 Owen Street, Wheatridge, Colorado 80033.

Social Support

The importance of social support in times of stress cannot be overemphasized. Numerous studies have found that the people who are most likely to recover from a serious injury or illness are those who have close personal relationships. Concentration camp inmates were constantly giving gifts to each other; nothing of particular value, but something unexpected to demonstrate caring. Dozens of stories are told of people on the verge of starvation who recovered and regained a will to live, thanks to an un-

expected gesture of comfort and humanity. "Some minimal fabric of care, of giving and receiving, is essential to life," writes one student of the survivors. "Survival is a collective act." Effective support need not involve advice or saying "the right thing," but rather being able to convey feelings of understanding.

A number of recent studies have found that people who are socially isolated, for example, Asian immigrants who have been uprooted from family and friends, are more likely to have heart attacks than are their counterparts who have been able to maintain their traditional social structure. While we may tend to idealize the "strong, silent type" who seems to be totally self-reliant, there is growing evidence that people with weak personal attachments and a tendency to "go it alone" are much more vulnerable to stress and its consequences. Some people find release and comfort in pets; a number of recent studies have found that pet owners have a reduction in stress-related illnesses.

COPING STRATEGIES

SPECIFIC COPING STRATEGIES that have emerged from stress-management studies include:

1. The "good coper" almost immediately seeks human attachment, perhaps of a transient nature, to guide his or her priorities and to clarify options. The cancer patient may develop a deep attachment to a nurse; the grieving spouse accepts the comfort of a neighbor or maiden aunt. Many people facing stress suddenly renew an old friendship that has been neglected for years.

2. Copers tend to regulate the time and amount of stressful information reaching them, so that their transition from denial to acceptance (and fighting) can be gradual.

3. People facing several stressful problems at the same time deal with them one at a time. If there is one basic problem that looms unmanageably large, they break it into manageable units, and aim toward intermediate goals that are attainable. The accident victim or heart attack patient does not immediately focus on running a marathon, but on taking that first step.

4. Successful copers seek information relevant to

their problem from a variety of sources. In planning for the future, they create alternate strategies: Plan A and Plan B. In time, they commit themselves to a single plan and pursue it vigorously, but not without researching the alternatives.

5. Good copers concentrate on their expectations for the future, usually hopeful ones. A coper does not bemoan a job lost, but looks toward the challenge of the next one.

Hans Selye, the pioneer of stress research, offered sound advice from his own personal experience in facing serious illness. "Death is inevitable," he wrote, "but it is quite possible not to worry about it all the time. Having faced death before, I am fully determined to go on working as long as health permits, and I constantly make plans that could not possibly be accomplished in 10 or 20 years." The thought that his plans would survive him was not a source of stress or depression; instead he drew comfort from the knowledge that the research he had carried out with such enthusiasm and conviction would be continued by others long after his death.

SUMMING UP

THERE IS INCREASING EVIDENCE that stress and how we cope with it is an important factor in health. A large number of diseases are now believed to be directly related to stress, and survival and recovery against sometimes overwhelming odds is often tied to specific coping techniques. While it may not be feasible or even desirable to change personality traits radically, recognizing and altering those components that are the most harmful may be beneficial. Learning how to reduce excessive stress to manageable proportions is a major step toward survival in today's stress-filled world.

18 Smoking, Alcohol, and Substance Abuse

Eric Josephson, Ph.D.

INTRODUCTION

THE ABUSE OF DRUGS—including tobacco and alcohol—is now widely recognized as one of the greatest of all public health problems. This chapter deals with the effects of drugs most likely to be abused and with ways of preventing and treating such abuse (see also Chapter 40 on Proper Use of Drugs, page 772). The health and social problems presented by drug abuse are infinitely complex for society and, above all, for the individuals and families involved. While there are no easy solutions, the effort to prevent and treat those problems is by no means hopeless.

Any drug is subject to abuse, an ambiguous term which refers to the harm that repeated use of the drug can do to one's health and personal relations at home or at work. Some drugs lend themselves to abuse more than others. There are many occasional and moderate drinkers who are unharmed by alcohol, but there are relatively few occasional and moderate smokers or heroin users; most people who use these drugs become addicted to them.

To be addicted to a drug, whether physically or psychologically, or both, means that to be denied the drug is highly unpleasant, even painful, sensations that addicts try to avoid unless they are determined to kick their habits. Unfortunately, both terms—abuse and addiction—have become heavily loaded and people labeled as drug abusers or addicts are often the targets of stern moral judgments, disapproval, and punishment—responses that create their own problems and complicate attempts at rehabilitation and prevention.

Whatever the definition and by any calculation, the number of casualties resulting from drug abuse, and the social costs of those casualties, are enormous; the personal costs are immeasurable. Thus, although the number of cigarette smokers in the United States has declined sharply during the past 20 years, more than 50 million Americans continue to smoke and 300,000 of them die prematurely every year. The cost of this habit in terms of medical care and time lost from work has been estimated at upward of $50 billion per year. Two-thirds of all adults drink alcoholic beverages and it is estimated by the National Institute on Alcohol Abuse and Alcoholism that among them 10 percent are problem drinkers or alcoholics. The cost of alcohol-related diseases and accidents, which claim about 200,000 lives every year, has been estimated at between $40 billion and $100 billion annually—a range that reflects the difficulty of making such estimates. Smoking and drinking are expensive in every sense of the term.

Fewer people use drugs such as heroin, cocaine, and marijuana than use cigarettes or alcohol—perhaps chiefly, although not entirely, because they are illicit. But these drugs also take their toll, particularly among the young. Public concern about "the drug problem" has tended to focus on the illicit drugs precisely because young people are most likely to use them and also because of drug-related crime. The cost of illicit drug abuse to our society has been estimated at more than $100 billion a year. Included in this figure are the costs of extensive efforts, so far only partially successful, to control and punish trafficking in these drugs, to prevent people from using them, and to treat those who have become addicted to them.

To some experts, there is ambiguity and inconsistency in our society's response to a drug such as heroin, used by relatively few people, yet the target of endless "wars," while drugs such as tobacco and alcohol, used by far more people with far greater loss of life, are legally and readily available. To be sure, prohibitions against alcohol and tobacco were tried in the past and are considered to have been failures (although the alcohol prohibition, for example, may have helped reduce cirrhosis death rates). It seems unlikely that such prohibitions will be tried again, at least in the foreseeable future. It is also unlikely that prohibitions now in effect against drugs such as heroin, cocaine, and marijuana will be repealed, although such a policy has its advocates. On the other hand, there is growing recognition that it is not just the illicit drugs that present health and other social problems.

If we include alcohol, tobacco, and prescription and over-the-counter mood-altering drugs, as well as the illicit drugs now popular, most people in our society can be described as drug-takers; few are entirely drug-free. People take drugs for pleasure, to relieve pain, to cope, to sleep, to wake, to find themselves, to lose themselves, even to destroy themselves.

Many closely related factors help determine just what drugs people take and how. Among those factors are:

- Age (for example, young men are more likely to drink, smoke, and use illicit drugs)

- Sex (women, especially older women, are more likely to use tranquilizers)

- Heredity (even if they are adopted by nondrinkers, the sons of alcoholics are 4 times as likely to become alcoholics themselves as the sons of nonalcoholics raised in adoptive families)

- Religion (Orthodox Jews, for example, almost never become alcoholics)

- Culture (the French consume 5 times as much alcohol per capita and have 8 times the cirrhosis death rate of the Norwegians)

- The influence of peers (which may start young people off on drugs, but which may also help people of any age stop)

These are just some of the factors, not all of them fully understood, which influence drug-taking and abuse.

SMOKING

THROUGH EXTENSIVE epidemiological and clinical studies, researchers have shown that smoking is a health hazard of the first order. Yet, although the proportion of cigarette smokers has declined considerably during the past 20 years, there are still more than 50 million smokers in the United States today. Among men, the proportion of smokers fell from 52 percent in 1965 to 38 percent by 1980; among women there has been less of a drop, from 34 to 29 percent in the same period. As for those in their teens, when smoking for so many begins, a nationwide survey of high school seniors showed that there has also been a greater decrease in the proportion of smokers among boys than among girls; indeed, girls now are more likely than boys to smoke cigarettes.

Most smokers say they would like to stop, and with good reason: The Surgeon General of the United States has stated that "cigarette smoking is clearly identified as the chief preventable cause of death in our society." Smokers can expect shorter life spans than nonsmokers: for example, the life of a 25-year-old who smokes 2 packs per day will be 8.3 years shorter than that of a nonsmoker.

Smokers are 3 times more likely to die of cancer

than nonsmokers. Smoking is the number one cause of lung cancer; more than 85 percent of fatalities in this category are due to cigarette smoking. It is a major cause of cancers of the oral cavity; smokers are 6 times more likely to contract cancer of the mouth, larynx, throat, and esophagus than nonsmokers. (This risk is increased if the smoker is also a heavy drinker.) It is also the chief cause of pulmonary diseases and is one of the leading causes of heart disease. It is a contributory factor in cancers of the bladder, kidney, and pancreas. It complicates conditions of peptic ulcer, hypertension, and sleep disorders.

Tobacco has some adverse effects on health in whatever form it is ingested. Low tar/nicotine cigarettes offer the promise of reduced risks, but they are not risk-free. First of all, tests to determine tar/nicotine levels are done using smoking machines, not people. Real smokers may inhale more deeply, more often, or may cover the ventilation holes in the filter or paper (which are designed to dilute the smoke). Also, some smokers who switch to low tar/nicotine brands will actually smoke more cigarettes to achieve their previous levels of nicotine in the body. And the smoke from low tar cigarettes can still inflame and clog airways in the lungs, leading to bronchitis and emphysema. Cancer specialists warn that there is no such thing as a "safe" cigarette.

Pipe and cigar smokers reduce their risk of lung cancer because they don't usually inhale; their risk is only slightly higher than that of nonsmokers and much lower than that of cigarette smokers. But those who switch from cigarettes to pipes or cigars may continue inhaling; inhalers have the same or higher chance of lung cancer than cigarette smokers. And pipe and cigar smokers are at equal risk of contracting cancers of the mouth, lip, larynx, and esophagus as cigarette smokers. Users of snuff also increase their risk of cancer of the oral cavities.

Smokers say they smoke for many reasons—to be sociable or sophisticated, for example, or for the ritualistic pleasure of lighting and handling cigarettes. But the real reason most people smoke is that they are addicted to a powerful drug found in tobacco—nicotine. This addiction is manifested in increasing tolerance to the drug (moving from initial aversion to increasing dosages, leveling off at 1 to 4 packs per day); dependency which reveals itself as a craving when the smoker has to do without cigarettes for a period of time; and distinct withdrawal symptoms.

As smoke is inhaled, the nicotine in it passes through the membrane of the lung tissue and rapidly enters the bloodstream. The heart pumps about 15 percent of this nicotine directly to the brain, which absorbs all of it, a process taking about 7 seconds. When the nicotine hits the brain, the brain signals the release of substances called catecholamines, which include adrenaline. The effect is to raise the heart rate and blood pressure; this change in the body's metabolism is the "lift" that smokers crave. For every puff, the smoker gets a "shot" or "fix" of nicotine. Throughout the day, smokers unconsciously maintain an appropriate level of nicotine in their brain by varying the amount of cigarettes they smoke and the way they smoke them (e.g., stubbed out quickly or smoked to the butt). In this way, they try to keep the "lift" effect without inducing the unpleasant side effects of smoking, like nausea and dizziness.

Addicted smokers must keep a continuous amount of nicotine circulating in the blood and going to the brain. If that amount falls below a certain level or if smokers stop smoking, they experience withdrawal symptoms. The physical symptoms of withdrawal include headache, nausea, constipation or diarrhea, falling heart rate and blood pressure, fatigue, drowsiness, and insomnia. Among the psychological symptoms are an inability to concentrate, irritability, anxiety, depression, and craving for smoking.

Smokers who want to quit should remember the addictive nature of the drug nicotine and be prepared to accept withdrawal symptoms as a natural consequence of stopping. Withdrawal, they should remember, is a temporary condition that, though unpleasant, is not harmful. Every tobacco user, no matter how addicted, *can* stop smoking.

In addition to nicotine, cigarette smoke contains 2 other significant elements: gases and tars. There are many different gases, including hydrogen cyanide, nitrogen oxide, and ammonia, but the most dangerous one is carbon monoxide (CO). Carbon monoxide has a stronger affinity, by 200 times, for red blood cells than does oxygen. Since red blood cells are meant to carry oxygen throughout the body, this means that CO is replacing oxygen and depleting the body's supply of it. While nicotine stimulates the heart to beat faster, CO prevents the distribution of life-giving oxygen needed for this extra work. It is no wonder that smokers become breathless when they must make an extra spurt of activity, such as running for the bus. In addition to breathlessness, the effects of CO include impaired vision, hearing, and judgment.

Nicotine's stimulant effect releases free fatty acids in the bloodstream while CO promotes their deposit inside the arteries. These fatty deposits, or plaque, cause atherosclerosis, a form of hardening of the arteries, which is a leading cause of heart attack, stroke, and other circulatory diseases.

The smoker's heart is also affected by nicotine's tendency to strain the heart while CO reduces its oxygen supply. Cigarette smoking has been identified as one of three major, controllable risk factors contributing to heart attack; the other two are high blood pressure and high cholesterol levels in the blood. Smokers who also have one or two of the other risk factors are in greater danger of heart attack, and the risk increases with the number of cigarettes smoked. In general, heart and blood vessel diseases are the leading cause of death for smokers. Nicotine constricts blood vessels and is a major risk factor of peripheral vascular disease, in which blood vessels leading to arms and legs narrow and eventually become blocked. In severe cases, loss of limbs results.

Cigarette smoke contains tars, solid chemical particles which, when inhaled, condense as sticky resins in the lungs. At the same time, cigarette smoke produces more mucus in the lungs and anesthetizes the tiny hairs, or cilia, which line the airways and sweep the mucus and foreign matter toward the throat. When a smoker sleeps, the cilia begin to recover and to move the accumulated mucus and impurities out of the lungs. This is why the smoker awakes with a hacking "smoker's cough." Cigarette smoke also impairs the functions of the pulmonary enzyme system and the lymphocytes whose jobs it is to keep the lungs clean.

Eventually the cilia in the lungs of heavy smokers are destroyed. The accumulated mucus becomes a breeding ground for infections, which the lungs can no longer adequately ward off. As a result, smokers are more susceptible to colds, respiratory infections, and chronic bronchitis. They are 2½ times more likely than nonsmokers to get acute respiratory illness. In addition, smoking is the leading cause of emphysema, an irreversible condition which reduces the lungs' elasticity and destroys the air sacs, reducing the amount of lung surface available for the exchange of oxygen. Average adults spend 5 percent of their energy for breathing; emphysema victims use up to 80 percent of their energy just to get enough oxygen just to stay alive.

There are about 4,000 chemicals present in tar, of which a number are known to produce cancer. Some are complete carcinogens and will cause cancers independently. Others are cocarcinogens, acting with other chemicals present in smoke to produce cancer. Still others affect cancers already present, causing them to grow faster.

Cancers begin when tars produce abnormal cells in the mouth, larynx, esophagus, and lungs, and these irregular cells develop into lesions. When the cancer is fully developed, it may spread to other parts of the body. Unfortunately, lung cancer can become far advanced before it produces noticeable symptoms, and the cure rate is very low—about 10 percent. But the Surgeon General's Report (1979) states that "lung cancer is largely a preventable disease." The prevention consists of not smoking.

Smoking affects pregnant women and their unborn children in several ways. First, babies of smoking women have lower birth weights than those of nonsmokers—an average of 6 ounces less. This is due to the twin action of nicotine's constriction of blood vessels and CO's depletion of oxygen. Long-term effects of lower birth weight include shorter stature at age 7 and impaired reading ability. Second, smoking mothers have a greater risk of spontaneous abortion and stillbirth. Smokers of 1 or more packs per day will increase the chance of infant mortality by 50 percent.

Smokers themselves are not the only ones affected by tobacco smoke. Although the evidence so far is not as conclusive as it is for smokers, nonsmokers exposed to tobacco smoke—as in the case of nonsmokers married to smokers—may also be at risk. Several studies suggest a positive relationship between so-called "passive" or involuntary smoking and the incidence of lung cancer.

Health Benefits of Quitting

Many of the adverse effects of smoking are reversed when the smoker quits, according to statistics provided by the American Cancer Society. After 10 to 15 years of not smoking, the ex-smoker's risk of a shortened life expectancy, and of cancer of the lungs, larynx, and mouth approach that of people who have never smoked. Over a period of 7 years, the risk of bladder cancer decreases to that of a nonsmoker. Stopping smoking reduces the immediate risk of cancer of the esophagus and the pancreas. The risk of coronary heart disease drops after 1 year; after 10 years, it's the same as for nonsmokers. The effects of not smoking on bronchitis and emphysema are an immediate improvement in breathing and a slowing of the deterioration of lung function.

Smoking Habits and Quitting

In its 1983 statement of health goals for the United States, the Department of Health and Human Services (DHHS) says that it would like to see the proportion of adults who smoke reduced to below 25 percent by 1990 (in 1979 it was 33 percent); DHHS would also like to see the proportion of youngsters

12 to 18 years of age who smoke reduced to below 6 percent (in 1979 it was 12 percent).

It will not be easy to achieve these goals because it is not easy to stop smoking. Many people who have tried to do so relapse within a short time. And many who finally succeed in kicking the cigarette habit do so only after a number of unsuccessful attempts.

Most smokers begin smoking in their teenage years, mimicking their friends' smoking behavior as a sign of independence and maturity. In fact, peer pressure may be necessary for those first cigarettes, since the sensations are mostly unpleasant in the beginning. Smoking is definitely learned behavior; once learned, it is used in different ways for different situations. For some people, the first step in quitting is an awareness and identification of their smoking habits and a conscious effort to replace old habits with new ones.

Some people smoke for its stimulant effect; it gives them a lift or appears to get them going. In fact, while smoking's initial effect is as a stimulant, its long-term effect is as a depressant. Instead of a cigarette, these smokers can take a brisk walk, do a few stretches at their desks, or just open a window and breathe fresh air. Ten minutes in the morning of a gentle exercise like yoga will provide the wake-up benefits of smoking, in a healthier way.

Smoking is sometimes used for the pleasure of handling the paraphernalia of cigarettes. Smokers may make a ritual of tapping the cigarette, lighting up with matches or a lighter, or gesturing with a cigarette. Even stubbing out the cigarette can have a meaning—for example, that a piece of work or a conversation is ended. Lighting up again indicates a willingness to continue to listen, to prolong a conversation, or to tackle another job. For the cigarette, smokers can substitute other objects to keep their hands busy, for example, "worry beads," a pen or a pencil, or a pair of eyeglasses.

Some people smoke to ease times of stress, when they're anxious, angry, or upset. For them, the cigarette is a tranquilizer. It is also a literal smokescreen, behind which they can hide their feelings. Smokers who use smoking as this kind of coping mechanism will have to face the fact that cigarettes do not resolve the conditions that produce stress; they are merely a kind of diversionary tactic. Finding some definite substitute—eating or drinking a healthy snack, for example—has eased many through difficult moments. Others decided that instead of picking up a cigarette, they would pick up the telephone and talk to a friend about what's bothering them.

Smoking is often used in order to relax, as a re-ward for getting a job done, and to enhance the pleasures of eating, driving a car, or conversation. Closely related to this enhancement factor is the smoker's desire to maintain a level of nicotine in the brain. Smokers know that there is no real replacement for the specific rewards of smoking. Therefore, they must remind themselves that the pleasures of not smoking—improved health, energy, and self-confidence, for example—will one day far outweigh the satisfactions of an addiction.

Some smokers reach for a cigarette merely out of habit; they may light up or finish a smoke without being aware of it or taking much pleasure in it. People whose smoking is on "automatic" may not find it hard to quit once they make an effort to be conscious of each cigarette they smoke. Habit smokers may find it helpful to cut down gradually, becoming more and more aware of when and how cigarettes are smoked. Smokers can ask themselves, "Can I do without this cigarette?" The answer is often yes.

For those who have been completely addicted to cigarettes, smoking is a continual act of craving. These are the chain-smokers whose craving begins as soon as one cigarette is stubbed out. They may wake in the morning and, despite a hacking cough, reach for a cigarette before they're out of bed. For these smokers, quitting is undoubtedly hard and must generally be done "cold turkey," since cutting down is almost impossible. Many of these smokers throw away the pack after a firm talk with their doctor or after reading a report on the health consequences of smoking. They must quit smoking as a conscious act of will, replacing the addiction to smoking with a turning toward health and self-control.

Those who want to quit smoking can take heart in the fact that more than 30 million people have done so successfully since the Surgeon General's report on smoking in 1964. Although smoking cessation programs of one kind or another are helpful for some, most people who stop do so on their own.

The box on page 345 has some helpful tips for going it alone. In addition, a number of organizations offer helpful literature: a "Helping Smokers Quit Kit" is available from the Office of Cancer Communications, National Cancer Institute; local chapters of the American Cancer Society, the American Heart Association, and the American Lung Association have various materials; and a report on "Smoking or Health: It's Your Choice" can be obtained from the American Council on Science and Health. (See Directory of Resources, Chapter 41, pages 799–800, for addresses.)

HOW TO QUIT

Of the almost 2 million Americans who quit smoking every year, about 95 percent do it on their own. No one method of quitting works for everyone: some stop "cold turkey," others cut-down gradually. Many smokers are helped by joining low-cost smoking cessation clinics, such as the ones offered by the American Cancer Society, the American Lung Association, the Seventh Day Adventist Church, local hospitals, and others, or a commercial one such as SmokEnders. (Other programs are listed in the Yellow Pages under "Smokers' Information & Treatment Centers.")

Stop-smoking clinics generally provide education about smoking, group support, and a firm target date for quitting. Other methods for cessation include individual and group counseling, hypnosis, behavior modification, and the use of nicotine chewing gum or other drugs to medicate withdrawal.

Smokers have found a wide variety of ways to help themselves put down cigarettes and get through the early, difficult period without relapsing. Here are a few of the methods some ex-smokers have found effective:

1. *List your reasons for quitting.* Concentrate on reasons that are personally very important to you, such as: "I have bad breath," or "My kids will see me smoking and start smoking themselves." After quitting, if craving and withdrawal is making you uncomfortable, you can use your list to remind you about the unacceptable and unappetizing aspects of smoking.

2. *Emphasize immediate benefits.* If the long-term health benefits of quitting aren't sufficient motivation because they are too abstract or removed, concentrate on the immediate rewards of not smoking, such as cleaner breath, improved stamina, awakening without a hacking cough, fresher clothes and hair, and the absence of littered ashtrays.

3. *Study your smoking habit.* Keep a smoking diary to determine when and under what circumstances you smoke (e.g., on arising, with coffee, with friends) and to note your mood (jittery, relaxed, depressed, tired, hungry). If you plan to quit by cutting down gradually, keep track of each cigarette you smoke on a piece of paper wrapped around your cigarette pack and secured with a rubber band. The act of unwrapping and recording will help you become more conscious of your smoking.

4. *Plan your quitting.* Set a date several weeks in advance and plan ahead. Some people are helped by tapering off, which may lower nicotine dependency, before the actual target date. Talk to friends who have quit and learn what to expect. Ask your doctor for advice.

5. *Enlist the help of friends and family.* Don't be afraid to ask others not to smoke in your presence. When someone offers you a cigarette, politely but firmly decline.

6. *Get rid of all cigarettes and other smoking accessories.* Give away, or throw away, your favorite ashtrays and lighters, both at home and at work.

7. *Examine your diet.* Since smoking depresses the appetite by dulling the sense of taste and smell, one of the immediate advantages of not smoking is being able to truly taste and smell food again. But because of this, and because ex-smokers may satisfy their oral craving with food, many people gain weight when they quit.

Try to avoid high-calorie foods and to keep a supply of low-calorie snacks on hand while reading or watching television, but don't be overly concerned in the beginning. The early period of quitting is not a good time for a stringent diet, since it creates an atmosphere of self-denial which may only lead to a relapse. In any event, weight gain is *not* an inevitable result of quitting. You can return to your normal weight once you get used to your new, and healthier, lifestyle.

8. *Increase your exercise.* Exercise will help minimize the weight gain and provide an immediate sense of physical well-being, calming jittery nerves, and relieving tension. In fact, some people have quit smoking after they started to jog or swim and discovered their breathlessness or lack of stamina.

9. *Avoid situations in which you normally smoke.* Identify times when you are most likely to smoke, and plan other rituals, such as taking a walk after dinner instead of having a second cup of coffee and a cigarette.

10. *Reward yourself.* The financial rewards for quitting are an immediate incentive, and some people begin putting away their former cigarette money to save for a trip, stereo records, or new clothes. Others use the money to buy a special treat every day or so, like a new paperback, fresh flowers, or a taxi ride home from work. Smokers who quit deserve to pamper themselves. And they have the immediate satisfaction of knowing that by doing something good for themselves every day they don't smoke, they are overcoming a serious addiction.

ALCOHOL USE AND ABUSE

IN THE UNITED STATES TODAY, approximately two-thirds of all adults drink alcoholic beverages, most in moderation and with little, if any, damage to their health. The rest abstain. Among those who do drink, perhaps as many as 10 percent drink to such an extent and with such frequency that they experience serious health and behavioral problems. Some of these drinkers are alcoholics, but just how many is difficult to estimate because of differences of opinion even among experts about how to define and measure problem drinking and alcoholism, let alone how to deal with it.

Although there is increasing public concern about drinking problems and alcoholism, reflected in the movement to raise the drinking age and pass tougher laws against drunken driving (or better enforce those that exist), there is no evidence that such problems are becoming more prevalent. To be sure, per capita consumption of alcoholic beverages in the United States has increased since World War II, but that level of consumption and the health problems resulting from it are still well below what is reported in a number of other countries, such as Germany, France, and Italy.

Nevertheless, about 10 percent of all deaths in the United States may be directly alcohol-related, and alcohol may play a role in many more. Cirrhosis of the liver, largely attributable to heavy alcohol consumption, ranks among the 10 leading causes of death. Alcohol abuse leads to increased risk of injury and death to drinkers, their family members, and others, especially by fire and motor vehicle and other accidents. Alcohol abuse is associated with brain damage, cancer, heart attacks, and high blood pressure. Alcohol abuse is also associated with work problems, spouse and child abuse, rape, assault, murder, and suicide.

Not all of the items in this grim list can be attributed to alcohol alone, but it plays a significant part. Nor can they all be attributed to alcoholism. In considering the problems associated with drinking, it is important to distinguish between those problems related to chronic heavy drinking and those related to occasional heavy consumption of the drug; not all drunken drivers are alcoholics.

How Alcohol Works in the Body

Alcohol is found in so many familiar beverages that it is easy to overlook the fact that it is a drug. It is, in fact, a tranquilizer, one of a family of sedative-hypnotic drugs. As a nonprescription drug, it is sold over the counter to anyone over each state's legal age limit.

The temperate and occasional use of the drug alcohol appears to have no negative effects on a healthy person. In moderate doses, alcohol has some beneficial effects; it relaxes, stimulates the appetite, and provides a mild sense of euphoria. In large doses, however, alcohol becomes a toxic drug. Its toxicity can be felt in the short-term, in a hangover, or in the long-term, in alcoholism or alcohol-related diseases such as cirrhosis.

Alcohol's toxicity may be due to the fact that it acts as a foreign substance in the body's metabolism. Unlike carbohydrates, fats, and proteins, which can be manufactured by the body, alcohol is basically an introduced substance. It can be called a food, because it is a concentrated source of calories, but it is poor nourishment, containing no significant amounts of needed nutrients, vitamins, or minerals.

Unlike most foods, which are prepared for digestion by the stomach so that their nutrients can be absorbed by the large intestine, 95 percent of alcohol is absorbed directly through the stomach wall or the walls of the duodenum and the small intestine. From there, alcohol passes quickly into the bloodstream; absorption from an empty stomach will be complete in about 20 minutes.

The absorption rate can be affected slightly. "Watery" drinks such as beer are absorbed more slowly. Food, especially fatty foods, delays absorption. Carbonated beverages speed up the emptying of the stomach into the small intestine where the alcohol is absorbed more quickly. Other factors that affect absorption, with unpredictable results, are the drinker's physical and emotional state (such as fatigue or stress) and individual body chemistry.

Alcohol moves from the bloodstream into every part of the body that contains water, including major organs like the brain, lungs, kidneys, and heart, and distributes itself equally both inside and outside of cells. Only about 5 percent of the alcohol is eliminated from the body through breath, urine, or sweat; the rest is oxidized, or broken down, by the liver.

When alcohol passes through the liver, it is broken down by enzymes, the final products of which are carbon dioxide and water. The liver processes alcohol at about one-third of an ounce of pure ethanol per hour—less than 1 ounce of whiskey—while the unprocessed alcohol continues to circulate. This means that the alcohol from 2 cocktails, each about 1½ ounces, taken 1 hour before dinner, will still be in the body 3 to 4 hours later, though in diminishing amounts.

It is because the liver processes alcohol at this fixed rate that sobering up strategies such as drinking black coffee or taking cold showers do not work. Caffeine can't speed up the elimination of alcohol from the body; it has often been noted that feeding coffee to an intoxicated person simply produces a wide-awake drunk. This is, in fact, a dangerous tactic, since it may delude both the drinker and friends into thinking he or she has sobered up sufficiently to drive a car.

Within a few minutes of ingestion, alcohol reaches the brain where its initial activity is to stimulate and agitate; this may account for the euphoria or "glow" effect produced by the first drink. But the initial phase of stimulation gives way to one in which alcohol acts as a depressant. It is this depressant effect which makes alcohol a sedative, which calms and tranquilizes; an anesthetic, which numbs; and finally a hypnotic, which induces sleep.

Alcohol first depresses those functions in the brain which have to do with inhibition and judgment. As inhibitions are released the drinker may feel friendlier, more gregarious, more expansive. A host's suggestion to "have a drink and loosen up" has a biological basis, though the "loosening up" is, of course, temporary and chemical. Sexual inhibitions may also be released, which gives alcohol the reputation as an aphrodisiac; in fact, alcohol impairs sexual function, performance, and eventually desire. With increased consumption, some drinkers suffer Jekyll-and-Hyde personality changes; they may become aggressive or cruel. Radical mood changes are also typical during intoxication—from euphoria to self-pity, for example.

Alcohol next affects motor ability, muscle function, reaction time, eyesight, depth perception, and night vision. Since these are the abilities needed to operate a vehicle, and since *even moderate amounts of alcohol produce some impairment*, the rule is that drivers should not drink and drinkers should not drive.

If a drinker continues to imbibe, the alcohol will continue to depress the functions of the lungs and the heart, slowing breathing and circulation. Death can occur when alcohol paralyzes the breathing functions completely. However, this state is seldom reached because the body rejects the alcohol by vomiting it, or because the drinker reaches the comatose stage before he can imbibe a fatal dose.

The natural penalty for overindulgence is the hangover, which is a combination of headache, stomach upset, and dehydration. The headache is a result of alcohol's ability to dilate blood vessels; the stretched vessels and nerves are now painfully returning to their former state. Stomach upset occurs because the gastric juices have been altered by the presence of so much alcohol. Dehydration is the result of alcohol's influence as a diuretic; the stimulated kidneys process and pass more water than is being ingested.

During a hangover, the body is actually in a state of withdrawal from alcohol. Some people are tempted to medicate this withdrawal with more alcohol or with a similar depressant drug like Valium. However, this simply keeps alcohol circulating in the blood and delays its elimination from the body. The use of amphetamines or "uppers" merely masks hangover symptoms. The best cure for a hangover is simple: aspirin, liquids, sleep, and time. Bland foods, especially in liquid form, may also help. The best prevention for a hangover is even simpler: moderation or abstinence.

Physical Effects of Alcohol Abuse

Since alcohol permeates so easily into every cell and organ of the body, it is not surprising that the physical effects of chronic alcohol abuse are wide-ranging and complicated. When large doses of alcohol bathe the body's fluids, the result is metabolic damage in every cell. Alcohol damages the liver, the central nervous system, the gastrointestinal system, and the heart. Alcoholics who continue to drink decrease their life expectancy by 10 to 15 years.

Other effects of alcohol abuse include impaired vision, impaired sexual function, sluggish circulation, malnutrition, water retention (resulting in weight gain and bloat), pancreatitis, skin disorders such as middle-aged acne and permanent dilation of blood vessels near the skin resulting in "brandy nose," weakening of both bones and muscles, and a decreased resistance to infection.

The Liver. Because the liver is the organ that breaks down alcohol in the body, it is a chief site of alcoholic disorders. Alcohol's effect on the liver is direct and toxic, interfering with cell function. At first, a condition develops called "fatty liver," in which the cells become infiltrated with abnormal fatty tissue, resulting in an enlarged liver. The next stage is alcoholic hepatitis (distinguished from serum or infectious hepatitis), in which liver cells swell, become inflamed, and die, causing blockage. Fatty liver and hepatitis are reversible stages, although the mortality rate for the latter is between 10 and 30 percent. The final stage—cirrhosis—is, however, irreversible and often fatal. In cirrhosis, fibrous scar tissue forms in place of healthy cells, obstructing the flow of blood through the liver. As a result, the various functions of the liver deteriorate. (Cirrhosis is found in 10 percent of the alcoholic population.)

A diseased liver cannot convert stored glycogen into glucose, thus lowering blood sugar and producing hypoglycemia. It has impaired abilities as a detoxifier of the bloodstream, so that it cannot adequately eliminate toxic substances (including drugs and alcohol) and dead red blood cells. It cannot manufacture bile (for digestion of fat), prothrombin (for blood clotting and the prevention of bruises), globulin (for warding off infection), and albumin (for maintaining healthy cells). Alcohol in the liver alters the production of digestive enzymes, preventing the absorption of fats and proteins and decreasing the absorption of the vitamins A, D, E, and K. The decreased production of enzymes also results in diarrhea.

The Brain and Central Nervous System.
Alcohol interferes with the supply of oxygen to the brain. This oxygen deprivation may be one of the causes of blackout, or temporary amnesia during drunkenness. Alcohol abuse destroys brain cells, producing deterioration and atrophy of the brain (though recent studies show that brain cells may actually regenerate in alcoholics who remain abstinent). It alters the brain's production of RNA, one of the genetic "messengers," and of such substances as endorphins and serotonin, natural opiates that may one day provide a key to the addictive process.

A neurological disorder called Wernicke–Korsakoff's syndrome is the result of vitamin B deficiencies produced by alcoholism and of the direct action of alcohol on the brain. Symptoms include amnesia, loss of short-term memory, disorientation, hallucinations, emotional disturbances, as well as double vision and loss of muscle control. Other effects on the central nervous system include mental disorders, such as increased aggression, antisocial behavior, depression, and anxiety.

The Digestive System.
As large amounts of alcohol enter the body, they bathe the mouth, esophagus, and stomach and produce inflammation. There is strong evidence of a direct link between cancer of these organs and alcohol consumption, especially among heavy smokers. Alcohol increases the stomach's digestive enzymes, which in turn irritates the stomach wall by altering its mucous lining. This can produce heartburn, nausea, gastritis, and in some cases, ulcers. The stomach of a chronic drinker loses its ability to move food and expel it into the duodenum, thus leaving some food always in the stomach, causing sluggish digestion and vomiting. In addition, as it moves through the digestive tract, alcohol continues to have an inflammatory effect on the small and large intestines.

The Heart.
Studies that show that moderate daily drinking is good for the heart should be viewed with caution, since the risks may outweigh the benefits. Even a one-time binge may produce irregular heartbeats, and alcohol abusers show increased risk of high blood pressure, heart attacks, heart arrhythmias, and heart disease. Alcohol is also the cause of a small percentage of the cases of cardiomyopathy, a disease of the heart muscle. There is a good recovery rate, even in the late stages, if the patient stops drinking.

Withdrawal Symptoms.
These are acute and life-threatening effects occurring from 3 to 6 days after alcohol leaves the body of a chronic alcoholic, usually one who has been ingesting a fifth of liquor a day. Withdrawal phenomena include sleep disorders like insomnia, visual and auditory hallucinations, disorientation, alcoholic convulsions, epileptic seizures of the *grand mal* type, and delirium tremens accompanied by acute anxiety and fear, agitation, fast pulse, fever, and extreme perspiration.

Fetal Alcohol Syndrome

One effect of alcohol that every woman drinker should be aware of is fetal alcohol syndrome (FAS), a cluster of irreversible birth abnormalities which is the direct result of heavy drinking during pregnancy.

Alcohol, like most other drugs, passes easily through the mother's placenta and into the bloodstream of the fetus. Once there, the alcohol acts just as it does in the mother's body; it depresses the fetus's central nervous system and must be metabolized by the liver. However, since the infant's liver isn't developed fully, it isn't an efficient metabolizer. As a result, the alcohol stays in the infant's body, even after it has been eliminated from the mother's. An intoxicated mother produces intoxication in her unborn infant; newborns may suffer from alcoholic withdrawal.

Children born with fetal alcohol syndrome typically are smaller in size, have smaller heads, and have deformities of limbs, joints, fingers, and face, and heart defects. They may also have cleft palate and poor coordination. For some, FAS does not show up until adolescence, when they may exhibit hyperactivity and learning and perceptual difficulties. These latter impairments are symptoms of minimal brain dysfunction (MBD), which affects between 5 and 10 percent of school age children, according to a study by the National Institute of Alcohol Abuse and Alcoholism.

Fetal alcohol syndrome is caused by excessive drinking during pregnancy, especially in the first 3 months when the fetus's central nervous system is developing most fully. "Excessive" in this case means 6 or more drinks per day, but can also include occasional binge drinking, which has proved just as harmful as heavy daily consumption. There is evidence, however, that even moderate amounts of alcohol may prove harmful to the unborn infant.

Since scientific investigation has not yet determined what the safe level of alcohol consumption is—or if there is a safe level—most doctors advise their pregnant patients: Don't drink at all during pregnancy. The first weeks of gestation are crucial in the development of fetal alcohol syndrome, so women who are likely to conceive are also urged to abstain from alcohol.

Profile of Alcoholism

The reasons why one person develops alcoholism and another doesn't have been the subject of much study. Researchers have examined as possible causes home environment, biological susceptibility, learned behavior, youthful social practices, and the existence of an "alcoholic personality." However, this research has produced no certain predictors of alcoholic drinking. What is clear is that alcoholism is an equal-opportunity disease, afflicting both men and women, black and white, Hispanic and Oriental, rich and poor, young and old. The alcoholic may be a housewife, a businessman, a skid row inhabitant, a high school student, or a college teacher. And being successful and happy, at home or in business, is no guarantee against alcoholism.

Like cancer, alcohol is not one disease, but many; there may be as many alcoholisms as there are alcoholics. And there may be as many definitions of the disease as there are researchers, clinicians, and field workers.

As a disease, alcoholism can be seen independently of moral issues. For many years, alcoholics were viewed as morally defective persons; they were objects of scorn or pity, but not of needed help. Their problem was seen as an absence of willpower, not the presence of a compulsion. Accepting alcoholism as a disease clears the way for understanding, treatment, and recovery. At the same time, sober alcoholics can and must take responsibility for their own recovery. And since alcoholism, like diabetes, is treatable but not curable, that recovery will be a lifelong one.

Some alcoholics begin drinking to the point of intoxication from their first drink, behaving in ways destructive to their health and relationships. For most others, the disease is progressive, beginning with acceptable social drinking. In the early stages of the progression, the alcoholic comes quickly to depend on the mood-altering qualities of alcohol. There is a drink for every mood; a drink to perk up or calm down, to celebrate or to mourn, to be solitary or to be social. The alcoholic soon doesn't need a special occasion to drink; alcohol must be ingested every day, or at prescribed periodic times, such as weekends.

At this stage, alcoholics may start a party early by gulping a few quick ones in the kitchen. They may order doubles when they're out. They feel uncomfortable on occasions when alcohol isn't served. Consumption at this point may be limited and controlled; perhaps 2 strong drinks before dinner, moving up to heavier social drinking of 3 to 5 per day.

In the middle stages, there is an increasing compulsion to get to the first drink of the day. The hour at which the drinker has that first drink may move up to lunch, or earlier on weekends. The drinker prefers alcohol-related activities and friends who drink as he or she does. An increasing tolerance for alcohol is balanced by increasing lack of control, which leads to drunkenness and blackouts. A blackout is a term designating a kind of amnesia, in which the drinker continues to function (e.g., make dinner, drive an automobile), but will remember none of it later on. It is not uncommon for the drinker to go in and out of a series of blackouts during one drinking episode.

One drink sets up a craving for more in the alcoholic. This craving is independent of the drinker's judgment of what is good for him or her, or what is socially appropriate. That is why members of Alcoholics Anonymous say: "It's the first drink that gets you drunk." This loss of control may not inevitably result in drunkenness each time; that is a function of the unpredictability of the drinker's behavior. But sooner or later that "first drink" will lead to an episode of drinking too much. And as the disease progresses, the certainty of getting drunk increases.

Drinkers begin to be secretly ashamed and worried about their lack of control. They may try to control their drinking or stop completely, attempts that often fail. They may switch brands or kinds of alcohol, for example, from hard liquor to beer. They may make a "geographic cure," moving to a new city or a new job in an attempt to cut down. They are hoping that some external formula will successfully alter their drinking behavior.

Sooner or later, the alcoholic will exhibit signs of denial, which is one of the chief psychological symptoms of the disease. Denial is the mechanism that allows the drinker to keep drinking: it says that he or she is not an alcoholic. In the midst of growing problems, all directly linked to alcohol, drinkers will blame everything except booze for their plight. Rationalizations for drinking come into full bloom. The drinker will offer reasons for drinking or for getting drunk: an unhappy love affair, financial difficulties, problems at work. What the drinker cannot see, because of denial, is that heavy drinking, far from being the effect of these problems, is the cause.

Drinkers will explain that they got drunk because they were tired, anxious, or depressed. What they do not know is that alcohol, in the amounts they are now consuming, produces fatigue, anxiety, and depression. The more anxious they feel, the more they drink, thus ensuring a continuation of the anxiety. They also become irritable or angry, and go into rages against those closest to them. This reflects their growing self-loathing and lack of self-esteem.

At this stage, physical symptoms may include stomach upset, minor tremors in the hands, and increased tolerance for alcohol. The alcoholic may decide to medicate the morning hangover and shaking hands with more alcohol or tranquilizers.

In the final stages, alcoholics are obsessed with alcohol to the exclusion of everything else. They will drink despite the pleading of family and the advice of doctors. They may begin round-the-clock drinking, despite an inability to keep down those first few drinks in the morning. By now, tenuous relationships with family and work may be severed. But lost jobs, lost family, and severe health problems are not a deterrent to continued drinking.

Now the alcoholic suffers from a host of nameless fears, sometimes including fear of crowds or public places. Constant remorse and guilt can only be alleviated, the alcoholic believes, by more drinking. Debts, legal problems, and homelessness may be added to the anxiety. Physically, alcoholics in the late stages are addicted. Deprived of alcohol, they show clear withdrawal symptoms—shakes, delirium tremens, even convulsions. They may have a collection of illnesses, ranging from cirrhosis to mental disturbances. Unless alcoholics receive help at this stage, usually hospitalization or residence in a therapeutic community, their futures hold only insanity or death.

It is important to stress, however, that it is not necessary for a person to reach this last stage in the progression of alcoholism before deciding to get help. Many men and women have realized that they had problems with alcohol before they lost their jobs or families, began drinking in the morning, suffered DTs, or had to be hospitalized. For them, the labels "early stage" or "late stage," "problem drinker" or "alcoholic" were less important than the fact that their growing powerlessness over alcohol was causing them pain.

Diagnosis of Alcoholism

In some cases, the "diagnosis" of alcoholism is made by the courts, as when a judge hands down a drunk driving sentence accompanied by a requirement to attend Alcoholics Anonymous, or enter a rehabilitation program. The emergency rooms of hospitals make such diagnoses when a man or woman shows up, suffering from alcohol poisoning or withdrawal. Some doctors, however, may miss the diagnosis of alcoholism, in part because patients will rarely admit to excessive consumption; one-half of the alcoholics seen by doctors won't be accurately diagnosed.

Families may diagnose alcoholism directly, when they are forced to hospitalize the alcoholic, or indirectly, when one partner leaves the other because of drinking. However, families may also suffer from symptoms of alcoholism denial, which allow them to avoid diagnosis completely. In the beginning, denial takes the form of excuses given to bosses, colleagues, or friends about the alcoholic's behavior. Spouses may lie or cover up for lateness, missed appointments, or irresponsibility. In this way, families learn to be "enablers," enabling the alcoholic to continue drinking.

In the later stages, the pattern of denial and enabling becomes so entrenched that family members lose their own perspective. The alcoholic may make many promises that he or she will quit drinking. When these promises are broken, the spouse makes more demands, in effect trying to control the alcoholic's drinking for him or her. These attempts, of course, often fail. The spouse's attitude becomes one of suspicion, anger, and despair. The alcoholic feels like a failure and continues to drink. The environment of the home is now a deeply unhappy one; this is why alcoholism is called "the family disease."

At this point, the most helpful thing that a spouse, family members, and friends can do for the alcoholic is to stop enabling him or her. For alcoholics to admit that they have a problem, they must see that they are powerless over alcohol and that their lives have become unmanageable because of it. However, it is difficult for them to reach this point if the people around them protect them from the consequences of their actions. Every crisis in their lives—a missed work day, a crucial blackout, a child's forgotten birthday—is a chance for alcoholics to see what alcohol is doing to their lives. If family members let them experience these doses of reality, they may be able to come to their own moment of truth concerning alcohol.

Husbands, wives, family members, and friends can help the alcoholic stop drinking if they do several things. First, they must abandon any wishful thinking that the alcoholic will one day be able to drink safely, recognizing that alcoholism is nearly always progressive. Second, they must accept the alcoholic for what he or she is—a sick person who cannot control drinking. Third, they must stop enabling the alcoholic to continue drinking by rescuing him or her from mistakes. Finally, they must seek information about alcoholism, knowing that it is a treatable disease, with a good recovery rate once the alcoholic stops drinking.

Treatment of Alcoholism

The treatment of alcoholism takes many forms because there are many kinds of alcoholics, all of whom have special needs. Sources for treatment include hospitals, alcoholism units within hospitals, private clinics designed solely for the care of alcoholics, residential alcoholic rehabilitation facilities, and private practitioners such as alcoholism counselors, psychologists, and psychiatric social workers.

For a small minority of alcoholics, a brief stay (3–10 days) at a detoxification center may be necessary. Candidates for detoxification are those who suffer withdrawal symptoms because of their addiction to alcohol. At the center, the alcoholic's body can clear itself of the toxic effects of alcohol. The patient is cared for with rest, good diet, abstinence from alcohol, and careful medical attention, which may include medication to reduce anxiety and to manage withdrawal symptoms. A detoxification unit may be a hospital unit, a section of a nonmedical alcoholism treatment community, or a separate facility.

If longer-term care is needed, the alcoholic can recover at a rehabilitation center or in the inpatient treatment unit of a hospital. Such centers provide an alcohol-free environment, continued medical care, group, individual, and family therapy, classes about alcoholism, and regular Alcoholics Anonymous meetings. Outpatient care is also available to those patients who can return to home and work while continuing to receive therapy. The purpose of these centers is not to "dry out" the alcoholic, but to provide a therapeutic setting in which a bridge back to life can be built.

Many alcoholics do not require the services of a detoxification center or a rehabilitation program. For them, a first step toward recovery is a thorough physical examination by a doctor to diagnose possible alcohol-related conditions. The doctor can ease the alcoholic's mind by giving him or her a clean bill of health or by setting up a schedule of continuing care to manage chronic health problems.

The early recovery period is one that must be accepted with patience by the alcoholic and family and friends. For most alcoholics, the compulsion to drink will be gone, but occasional thoughts of drinking may continue for awhile, especially at the cocktail hour or at times of stress. These drink desires need not be alarming if the alcoholic realizes they are a natural reminder of years of drinking, and will diminish and disappear after a time.

Mood swings are also typical in early recovery. One moment the alcoholic may feel relieved, elated, "on a pink cloud," and the next moment discouraged or tearful. Like drink desires, these mood changes disappear after a few months and give way to a more balanced emotional condition. What the alcoholic needs most in the early stages is plenty of rest, good nutrition, and patience with his or her recovery rate. Alcoholics who choose to join a fellowship such as Alcoholics Anonymous, will also have the support of recovered alcoholics who can share their common experiences about the recovery process.

To help the alcoholic stay sober, a drug called Antabuse (disulfiram) is sometimes administered; it is taken daily, by mouth. Antabuse intervenes in the liver's metabolism of alcohol, preventing the breakdown of acetaldehyde. Even a small sip of alcohol produces an accumulation of acetaldehyde and the result is nausea and vomiting, severe headache, breathing difficulties, blurred vision, lowered blood pressure, and an impending feeling of death.

Antabuse works only with the patient's full consent and the clear understanding of what its effects will be if he or she drinks. The drug neither alters the alcoholic's mood nor removes the urge to drink. It is not an instant solution to the problems of alcoholism, nor a complete therapy. But it is a deterrent and can be a useful part of treatment if it makes the patient feel "protected" from alcohol while learning to live a sober life. Antabuse is administered only until the patient feels ready to live without it; it is not a long-term solution.

Sometimes mood-altering drugs, such as tranquilizers, are administered during recovery to quell anxiety. However, careful physicians will be aware of the dangers of substituting another drug addiction for an alcohol one, and of the problems of reinforcing the dependency on chemicals in alcoholics.

Some emotional conditions, for example, a manic depressive psychosis, require pharmacological solutions. But as a general rule, sobriety should be drug-free.

Living Sober

Quitting drinking is, of course, the crucial first step in recovering from alcoholism. But it is not the only one. Learning to live without chemicals requires adjustments in attitudes, values, and lifestyles. For example, if serious psychological disturbances have developed because of drinking, then psychiatric counseling designed for alcohol abusers may be in order. Other alcoholics may require occupational rehabilitation or vocational guidance to allow them to reenter the work force.

Abstinence is the absence of alcohol or drugs; sobriety is a way of life. In this sense, recovery begins where formal treatment leaves off and is a lifelong process. In developing this new way of life, many factors may play a part. Recovered alcoholics are urged to stay away from the people, places, and things that are associated with their drinking days. After they have been sober for a while, alcoholics can make new friends and new activities by returning to school, going back to work, taking up a new or an old hobby, doing volunteer work, or renewing a lost association with their church or religious group.

Substituting positive addictions for alcohol is also helpful. Walking, jogging, sports, or a regular schedule of exercise promotes well-being and self-esteem and provides a healthy outlet for energy. There is some evidence, in fact, that exercise releases chemicals in the brain that produce a natural "high." For the alcoholic, exercise—even if it is just a walk after supper—can be a natural tranquilizer.

Prevention of Alcohol Abuse

In view of the heavy costs of treatment, it makes sense to begin to focus on the prevention of alcohol abuse and alcoholism. An enlightened public policy about drinking, addressing such topics as the legal drinking age, liquor labeling, laws governing drunk driving, and public education, is necessary. But individuals should be aware of their own drinking patterns and be responsible for their alcohol use.

The National Institute on Alcohol Abuse and Alcoholism defines moderate drinking as averaging not more than 2 drinks per day, and estimates that 15 million adults (15 percent of America's drinkers) have more than that amount. Fifteen percent of the men and 3 percent of women have more than 4 drinks per day; this group risks developing a serious drinking problem. And anyone, even safe drinkers, can become a statistic if one night's overindulgence leads to drunk driving, a family argument, an accident, or an incapacitating hangover the next day.

Efforts toward moderation don't have to be prohibitionist or puritanical. Americans need to view moderation or abstinence as life-enhancing choices rather than negative self-denial.

In its statement of goals for 1990, the U.S. Department of Health and Human Services has said that by that time it would like to see the per capita consumption of alcohol no higher than current levels, no increase in the proportion of adolescent drinkers, a reduction in the cirrhosis death rate and in the number of deaths from alcohol-related accidents, a reduction in the number of infants born with fetal alcohol syndrome, and increased public, and especially adolescent, awareness of the risks associated with heavy alcohol use.

In view of alcohol's generally accepted place in our society, its likely continued—if somewhat more restricted—availability, and the difficulties of providing treatment for alcoholics, it will not be easy to achieve these goals. Thus, it is too early to assess the effects of the current campaigns to raise the drinking age and punish drunken driving. As for treatment, the majority of problem drinkers and alcoholics are not presently getting formal treatment services, apart from what Alcoholics Anonymous has to offer. Such treatment as is available to them seems to be most effective for socially stable, middle-class alcoholics and least effective for those without families or home to support them, i.e., skid row drunks.

The need to provide more—and more effective—services is self-evident. Meanwhile, the major burden of coping with this complex drug problem will continue to fall where it has always fallen, on the individuals and families most directly affected. If they want help, they can get it in one form or another, and any help will be better than none.

There are a variety of sources of information about alcoholism. The first contact may be with a doctor, clergyman, social worker, or psychologist. The Yellow Pages lists resources under the heading "Alcoholism." The local chapter of the National Council on Alcoholism gives information and referrals. Alcoholics Anonymous and Al-Anon Family Groups are listed in both the white pages and the Yellow Pages of the telephone directory. For printed materials, contact the National Clearinghouse of the National Institute on Alcohol Abuse and Alcoholism. (For more information, see Directory of Resources, Chapter 41, page 798.)

PSYCHOTHERAPEUTIC DRUGS

THE USE OF MOOD-ALTERING DRUGS is, like alcohol use, an ancient human custom. For example, Indians of South America have for centuries anesthetized themselves against the rigors of high-altitude life by chewing the leaves of the coca bush, from which cocaine is derived. In our century, major pharmacological advances have made available drugs for many purposes—to calm or excite, to decrease or increase appetite, and to alter the way in which we see, hear, touch, or taste. Some of the drugs have legitimate medical uses. (See Chapter 40 on Proper Use of Drugs, page 772.) But for some people, their mood-altering qualities create dependency or addiction.

This phenomenon has in turn led to the notion that there is widespread abuse of medically prescribed psychotherapeutic drugs, particularly antianxiety drugs such as Valium or Librium, sedatives, and antidepressant drugs such as Elavil and Tofranil—to name some of the better known ones. This notion has been fed by sensational reports in the mass media. Such reports are exaggerated. Data available on prescribing by physicians and drug-taking by their patients (likely to be older women) indicate that the practices of physicians as well as the attitudes and drug-using behavior of the general public tend to be moderate or conservative. This does not mean that there are not some physicians who overprescribe and some patients who abuse the psychotherapeutic drugs that are prescribed, but such cases are less common than is generally believed. As said before, any drug—licit or illicit, prescribed or nonprescribed—is subject to abuse.

Information about drug abuse is available from the National Clearinghouse for Drug Abuse. (See Directory of Resources, Chapter 41, page 801.)

Sedative-Hypnotic Drugs

Sedative-hypnotic drugs depress the functions of the central nervous system. They fall into two major classes: the barbiturates (e.g., Seconal, Nembutal, Tuinal) and the benzodiazepines (e.g., Valium, Librium). These latter are called the "minor tranquilizers" to distinguish them from the "major tranquilizers" like Thorazine, which are used in the treatment of some psychoses. Sedative-hypnotics can be used both as tranquilizers and sleeping pills, according to the dosage. They are prescribed to quell anxiety, produce calm, and promote sleep; in addition, they are used as anticonvulsants and muscle relaxants.

Barbiturates are classed as short-acting or long-acting, depending on how long it takes for the liver and kidneys to metabolize the drug, and therefore how long it continues to circulate in the bloodstream. Abusers tend to prefer the shorter-acting barbiturates such as Seconal and Nembutal, which are also the most addictive and have the most deleterious health consequences.

Barbiturate abusers may also abuse amphetamines, trying to negotiate a balance between the sedative effects of barbiturates and the stimulant effects of amphetamines. Barbiturate hangovers are commonly medicated with "speed" or "uppers" to create a sense of wakefulness and alertness. This kind of cross-addiction makes strenuous and injurious demands on the body.

Barbiturates and tranquilizers have been called "solid alcohol" because they exert a similar depressant effect on the central nervous system. In small doses, the sedative-hypnotics produce relaxation and mild euphoria; in larger doses, the effects are slurred speech, slowed reflexes, unsteady gait, mental confusion, drowsiness and, eventually, unconsciousness. An overdose results in a severe depression of breathing and heart functions, and may lead to kidney failure, coma, and death.

Because alcohol and barbiturates are so similar, their combined effect can be fatal; they should, therefore, never be taken at the same time. Even a small dose of barbiturates can be dangerous if alcohol is also ingested. Lethal overdoses can occur if users become confused and accidentally take more than they intended, or deliberately take more when the desired effect (e.g., sleep) is not attained.

The effects of overuse are wide ranging and include nausea, hangover symptoms, confusion, low blood pressure, and depressed breathing functions. Barbiturate addicts, like alcoholics, become obsessed with the use of the substance and will neglect their family, work, and health in its favor. They can become anxious, insomniac, paranoid, and suicidally depressed.

Sedative-hypnotics can create psychological dependency in susceptible users and physical dependency with regular use. First, abusers come to depend on the drug to medicate the normal stresses of life, to enjoy the mild "high" and to sleep. Then the drugs produce tolerance in the body, so that larger doses are required to produce similar effects. Finally, if the drug is discontinued, the user suffers withdrawal symptoms.

Withdrawal from barbiturates and some benzodiazepines (notably Valium) can be severe and life-threatening, resembling alcoholic withdrawal, with delirium tremens, rapid pulse, weakness, convulsions, anxiety, restlessness, hallucinations, and temporary psychoses. Death can result from seizures and from exhaustion during the psychotic stage. Withdrawal should only be attempted with a doctor's assistance, and preferably in a hospital, where it can be safely managed by slowly decreasing the amount of the drug in the system.

Amphetamines

Amphetamines were first sold in the marketplace in 1932 as the inhalant Benzedrine, a nasal decongestant. They were issued to U.S. troops in World War II, where their stimulant effect was used to increase endurance and to combat fatigue, and after the war, they were medically prescribed as antidepressants and diet drugs. Today, their medical uses are mostly limited to treating narcolepsy (a sleep disorder) and hyperactivity in children, in whom the drug has the paradoxical effect of sedation.

Amphetamines produce an intense alertness and a false confidence in the user's sense of perseverance, energy, and abilities, especially mental abilities. Amphetamine users become talkative, excited and restless, and feel capable of working tirelessly or having special insights. In fact, neither performance nor thinking tasks are substantially improved by amphetamines. But their euphoric effects and ability to counteract fatigue make them popular with truck drivers, students, performers, and athletes, among others.

There are three classes of amphetamines—amphetamine, dextroamphetamine, and methamphetamine. This latter class, called "speed," is the most potent. Amphetamines are usually taken orally, in pills called "bennies," "pep pills," "diet pills," or "uppers." It is also possible to inject amphetamines, a method that produces a faster and stronger effect. Chronic amphetamine abusers—called "speed freaks"—often choose this method.

Amphetamines create the sensation of energy by activating adrenaline, which stimulates the central nervous system. The side effects of these drugs include decreased appetite, decreased saliva and nasal mucus, enlarged nasal and bronchial passages, increased heart rate and blood pressure, and faster breathing. In larger doses, effects include irregular heartbeat, restlessness, dizziness, anxiety, and aggressive or violent behavior.

While many people have used amphetamines in low doses with no apparent ill effects, others have become quickly hooked on the drug's effects. Although amphetamines are not physically addicting, they can produce tolerance and psychological dependence. Users may feel that they can only function normally when they are "speeding." They may require larger doses and may spend days staying on an amphetamine bender. When a bender is finished, users "crash," experiencing enormous fatigue, depression, anxiety, and hunger. They may attempt to sleep and, failing that, medicate their lack of sleep with barbiturates. This stimulant-sedative cycle causes dual addiction in some users.

Chronic amphetamine abusers suffer excitability, extreme restlessness, exhaustion from lack of sleep, and loss of appetite which results in malnutrition and vitamin deficiencies. Psychological effects include anxiety, depression, thoughts of suicide, paranoia, and persecution mania. Abusers tend to be antisocial and exhibit aggressive or violent behavior. Abstinence from amphetamines produces a slow (6 months to 1 year) diminishment of these symptoms, but recovery is complete.

ILLICIT DRUGS

ALTHOUGH THEY ARE NOT intrinsically more dangerous than alcohol, tobacco, or the psychotherapeutic drugs and are used by fewer people, the illicit drugs such as marijuana, cocaine, and heroin have aroused most public concern. This concern has prompted the federal and state governments to undertake large-scale efforts to block the trafficking in these drugs and to punish the traffickers, to discourage young people from using them, and to support a variety of treatment services for those who become addicted to the drugs.

The drugs themselves are not as new as they may seem; opiates (of which heroin is one type), cocaine, and cannabis (or marijuana) have been used in one form or another in many parts of the world for centuries. What is unprecedented is the explosion of youthful experimentation with and use of such drugs which has taken place just during the past decade or so; in this regard, the United States leads the world.

At present it is estimated that more than 20 million people—most of them in their teens and twenties—are current users of marijuana. A nationwide survey undertaken in the late 1970s showed that 1 in 10 high school seniors used marijuana daily, although this proportion has since declined. According to recent surveys, more than 4 million people are users of cocaine—well over half of them in the 18 to 25 age group. As for heroin, the most notorious of all drugs, it is difficult to get valid estimates of the numbers of people involved, but there may be as many as half a million people addicted to it.

Many factors have contributed to the spread of youthful drug-taking—among them the increasing availability of the drugs (despite efforts to enforce their prohibition) and perhaps most important, the influence of peers (a complicated process that involves the seeking out by young people of friends who use drugs as well as the models of drug-taking which those friends provide).

For occasional users of drugs such as marijuana, as in the case of occasional drinkers, there is relatively little danger. For chronic, heavy users of any of the illicit drugs, there are serious health hazards, e.g., increased danger of accidents and even premature death. Thus, during the last decade, hospital emergency rooms have reported sharp increases in cocaine-related visits; the number of individuals entering drug abuse treatment for cocaine dependence has increased fivefold; and deaths related to cocaine use have increased threefold.

Even though the use of one drug does not necessarily or automatically lead to use of another, there is also the risk that heavy consumption of any one of these drugs will expose users to an environment associated with the use of other illicit drugs. Heroin addicts are particularly at risk for engaging in criminal behavior (which may precede as well as accompany experiences with the drug), overdoses, and premature deaths. Perhaps most troubling is the problem of multiple drug use, particularly common among heavy users of any of the illicit drugs.

Cocaine

Like the amphetamines, whose effects it closely resembles, cocaine is a stimulant of the central nervous system. It is derived from the leaves of the coca bush which grows in Bolivia and Peru where it has been used for centuries by some to combat the effects of hunger, hard work, and thin air. In the mid-nineteenth century its effects were praised by Freud, among others, and it was, until 1906, a chief ingredient in Coca-Cola. Used occasionally for anesthetic purposes, in recent years it has mostly been taken as a "recreational" drug. Because of its high cost, it is a status drug, one often associated with celebrities. However, increasing information about the ill effects of its chronic use has tarnished its image of glamour.

The usual method of ingesting cocaine is by sniffing or "snorting" it into the nose, where it is absorbed by the mucous membranes. It can also be swallowed or injected. The effects of cocaine are immediate and short-lived. It raises the breathing rate, heart rate, blood pressure and body temperature, and dilates the pupils. Like caffeine, cocaine produces wakefulness and reduces hunger. Psychological effects include a feeling of well-being and a grandiose sense of one's own abilities and powers, mixed with anxiety and restlessness. As the drug wears off, these temporary sensations of mastery are replaced by a correspondingly low feeling of depression.

Cocaine may not be physically addicting in the way that heroin is, but it can produce psychological dependence, since users seek to medicate the unpleasant aftereffects of depression with more cocaine. Chronic users suffer stomach disorders, loss of appetite which results in malnutrition and weight loss, and ulcerated linings of the nose as a result of sniffing the drug. Long-term use may produce psychological conditions such as paranoia, sleeplessness, restlessness and anxiety, hallucinations, and a condition known as formication, in which insects or snakes are perceived to be crawling under the skin.

Marijuana

Marijuana is a psychoactive (mind-altering) drug, derived from the plant *Cannabis sativa*, or hemp, which is grown wild and cultivated in many areas of the world. Marijuana can be put in foods and eaten, but generally it is smoked in cigarettes, or "joints," which are made up of the dried leaves, flowers, and small stems of the plant. The active ingredient in marijuana is delta-9-tetrahydrocannabinol (THC); a cigarette may contain up to 4 percent THC, a substantial rise from the 0.4 percent content of cigarettes in the early 1970s. Hashish, or hash, is the resinous part of *Cannabis*, pressed into cakes and smoked.

The psychological effects of marijuana are a mild sense of well-being, a disconnected sense of time, a dreamy consciousness and self-absorption, and a reduced ability to think and communicate clearly. Many users also report feelings of acute anxiety, panic, paranoia, and hallucinationlike sense distortions. Physical effects include faster heartbeat (increased by as much as 50 percent), bloodshot eyes, dry mouth and throat, decreased motor abilities and reaction time, altered depth perception, and impaired short-term memory.

There is little evidence that marijuana is physically addicting. However, dependence may result with regular long-term use. That this dependence may be harmful is clearly seen in teenage users, in whom heavy use results in impaired learning abilities (both verbal and mathematical), reduced attention span, and lowered problem-solving skills and reading comprehension. In addition, heavy use (between 1 and 3 times per day) may interfere with acquiring necessary social skills at a crucial time of development. Teenagers may turn to the isolation and escapism of the drug rather than developing healthy coping mechanisms.

Teenagers are introduced to marijuana use by their friends. The social pressures to use the drug are subtle, reinforced by the ritual of rolling and smoking a "joint" and by the fact that marijuana is illegal, enhancing its value as a rite of passage into an adult world. Marijuana use is most often preceded by alcohol use and smoking, although the relationship cannot be said to be causal. Heavy marijuana users are more likely than moderate ones to go on to use other drugs, such as barbiturates, amphetamines, LSD, or cocaine.

Studies have shown that one possible long-term health effect of marijuana use is cancer. Any smoke, tobacco or marijuana, has an inflammatory effect on the lungs, irritating air passages and impairing pulmonary function. In addition, marijuana smoke contains several of the carcinogenic tars of tobacco smoke, and marijuana smokers hold the smoke in the lungs deeply and for a longer length of time than most cigarette smokers, exposing more lung tissue. Chronic marijuana use results in metaplasis, a precancerous condition of the lung cells. While research continues in this important area, marijuana users should consider the substance as both a powerful drug and a possible carcinogen.

Women who are pregnant should not use marijuana, because, like many other drugs, marijuana enters the baby's bloodstream through the mother's placenta. The infant, like the mother, receives the effects of the drug. Breast-feeding mothers should also abstain from marijuana since evidence indicates that the drug is carried in breast milk. Other studies show that effects on fetuses may include a larger-than-normal number of spontaneous abortions and stillbirths, as well as infants with lighter birth weights.

Opiates

Opiates are derived from the opium poppy, grown mostly in Asia, and include opium, morphine, and heroin. Opiates were both legal and widely available in the nineteenth century and were thought by doctors and the general population to have beneficial effects on a variety of disorders, including diabetes, diarrhea, and "women's troubles." They were often used during the Civil War as a painkiller, producing addiction among many soldiers.

Opiates can be ingested, inhaled, or injected (a method called "mainlining"). They act as painkillers and tranquilizers and produce euphoria in experienced users; pleasurable sensations are not usually reported by those using opiates for the first time. It may be that the chief pleasure addicts find comes from relief at holding off withdrawal symptoms, which are acute and painful.

The discomfort of heroin withdrawal—shakes, sweating, tremors, hot and cold flashes, anxiety, and craving—have often been dramatically portrayed in literature and the media. But as unpleasant as these symptoms are, they are usually not life-threatening and are less severe than withdrawal from chronic alcoholism or barbiturate abuse.

Unlike alcohol, which produces alcoholism only in susceptible individuals in a period of time ranging from 5 to 10 years, opiates rapidly produce addiction in almost any regular user. Effects of chronic use are increasing tolerance for the drug, psychological and physical addiction manifested in an intense craving, and a host of physical ailments including liver dysfunctions, pneumonia, lung abscesses, and brain disorders. Injecting the drug, especially with contaminated needles, can result in skin abscesses and ulcers, phlebitis, extensive scarring, and bacterial endocarditis. An overdose of opiates depresses the central nervous system to the extent that breathing and heart rate can slow or stop, causing death.

Heroin addicts are often treated with methadone, a synthetic opiate. Methadone eases withdrawal and, when administered as part of outpatient care at clinics and hospitals, is believed to help the addict stay off the street and begin recovery. But a methadone maintenance program actually substitutes one addiction for another, and sooner or later the addict has to withdraw from methadone. Non-drug treatment programs, such as therapeutic communities, work well as long as the addict remains in residence. But the rare statistics on graduates of these programs show that the relapse rate is extremely high. A craving for heroin can be triggered in times of stress, anxiety, or depression, even if the addict has been abstinent for years. Research continues on the possible social, psychological, and biological causes of heroin addiction, and on appropriate treatment and recovery programs.

Psychedelic Drugs

Psychedelic is a term meaning "mind-manifesting" or "mind-expanding." The psychedelic drugs include lysergic acid (LSD or simply "acid"), peyote and mescaline, which are derived from a cactus plant, and psilocybin, which comes from certain mushrooms. The main effects of psychedelics are psychological rather than physical, and vary according to the user's mood, expectations, and the environment in which the drug is used. These effects are highly unpredictable and include distortion of sense perceptions, difficulty in speaking or communicating, a suspended sense of time, a feeling of motor paralysis alternating with hyperactivity, a depressed appetite, and loss of sexual desire. A "bad trip" causes the user to feel out-of-control and paranoid, to experience panic, or to see other people as grotesque distortions.

Psychedelics do not produce physical or psychological addiction. However, in some individuals the drugs may trigger a psychosis that lasts beyond the drug's effects and may require therapy or institutionalization. It isn't known whether the drugs produce this state or uncover a previous tendency.

LSD users are also susceptible to "flashbacks" of the drug experience up to a year afterward, during which time such things as visual or sensory distortions can occur again. The long-term effects of heavy use include impaired mental function and impaired ability to reason abstractly.

Inhalants

Inhalants are volatile substances which, while never intended to be used as drugs, are abused because of their mind-altering effects. The chief abusers of inhalants are children from 7 to 17, who sniff these household products because they are easily available at home or at the supermarket.

The inhalants include solvents like gasoline, cleaning fluids, liquid shoe polish, lacquer, nail polish remover, and airplane glue; aerosols like spray paint, insecticides, and hair spray; and anesthetics like nitrous oxide (laughing gas). Also abused are the volatile nitrates such as amyl nitrate, which heart patients use to treat chest pains because it dilates blood vessels and speeds up the heart rate. Amyl nitrate is contained in covered vials (called "poppers" or "snappers") which are popped open and inhaled. Butyl nitrate is the over-the-counter version of amyl nitrate.

Inhalants temporarily stimulate before they depress the central nervous system. Their immediate effects include a dreamy euphoria which may last a few minutes to a few hours, mental confusion, hallucinations, dizziness, nausea, lack of coordination, fatigue, loss of appetite, and blackouts.

Death, which can occur from first-time use, may result from instant heart failure, from sniffing the substance in high concentrations, resulting in displacement of oxygen in the lungs, and suffocation from the depression of respiratory functions. Long-term effects include weight loss, fatigue, muscle fatigue and, in certain cases, damage to the nervous system, liver, kidneys, blood, and bone marrow.

Teenagers and Drugs

Statistics from the National Institute on Drug Abuse show that while marijuana use by young people may be declining, almost two-thirds of American teenagers will experiment with an illicit drug before they finish high school, and more than one-third will have used an illicit drug other than marijuana. In the 1981 nationwide survey of senior high school students, 7 percent were daily users of marijuana, 6 percent drank alcohol daily, and 20 percent smoked cigarettes daily.

In the United States, teenagers' involvement with drugs follows a clear-cut sequence. Beer and wine are the first substances tried by young people. Tobacco and hard liquor are used next. The use of marijuana rarely takes place without the prior use of liquor or tobacco. The use of illicit drugs such as psychedelics or heroin is usually preceded by marijuana. This sequence does not mean, however, that teenagers will inevitably progress to using drugs further along in the sequence. Researchers today no longer accept the "stepping stone" theory of addiction, in which use of marijuana was assumed to inevitably lead to the use of hard drugs, especially heroin.

Marijuana users are most actively involved with the drug in their early twenties, but use begins to decline by age 23. For many drug users, the process of growing up—getting married, beginning to work, or becoming a parent—is a natural brake on the use of illicit drugs. Other users will replace marijuana and other illicit drugs with alcohol or will abuse prescription drugs.

Certain influences identify groups at greater risk of drug use. Cigarette smoking is almost exclusively determined by peer pressure, although parents who smoke slightly increase the chance of their children smoking. Teenagers who use hard liquor often learn drinking patterns from their parents. Marijuana use is usually initiated through friends and peers. Use of illicit drugs other than marijuana is usually associated with poor relationships with parents, by exposure to parents and peers who misuse drugs, and by depression or psychological distress.

Parents cannot prevent their children from using or experimenting with drugs, but they can do several things to reduce the chances for abuse. Parents need to provide accurate information about drugs and alcohol long before the child reaches adolescence. (A small percentage of children, for example, will begin using alcohol by the age of 10 or 11). This information should be presented with the same care that discussions about religion or sexuality are given. Lectures or scare tactics are rarely successful.

The parents' own use of alcohol and drugs will provide a model for values and behavior. Keeping lines of communication open is crucial, because drug-using adolescents will be forced by a lack of communication to further isolate themselves with their drugs.

Finally, parents must give their children a sense of themselves as valuable individuals, capable of making the right choices. Responsibility, self-esteem, and good judgment are better tools for coping with adolescence and its bewildering options than overprotective parents.

If parents suspect their children are using or abusing drugs, they can look for these changes in behavior which *may* signal drug involvement, according to the Department of Health and Human Services:

- Abrupt change in mood, or attitude
- Sudden decline in attendance or performance at work or school
- Sudden resistance to discipline at home or school (such as ignoring curfews)
- Unusual flare-ups of temper
- Increased borrowing of money from parents or friends
- Stealing from home, school, or employer
- Heightened secrecy about actions or possessions
- Associating with a new group of friends, especially with those who use drugs

Parents should remember, however, that adolescence is a turbulent time and these changes may not necessarily be drug-related. Positive proof of drug use may only come from self-revelation by the teenager, by the presence of drug paraphernalia in the teenager's room, or by obvious drug intoxication.

When discussing drug use with children, support, understanding, and firmness are in order; ac-

cusations, sarcasm, and blame will only make the child feel more isolated and defensive. It is important for parents to create an atmosphere of calm discussion, emphasizing mutual caring and reiterating family values on drug and alcohol use. If the drug situation cannot be handled by the family alone, then parents can turn to school counselors, the family doctor, adolescent drug treatment centers, social workers, and drug abuse information centers.

A major question regarding the recent increase in illicit drug use in the United States is whether it will somehow end, like epidemics of disease in the past (some of which declined without the benefit of medicine). Is it a passing fad? Will today's young generation give up their illicit drugs of choice as they become older? On such questions there is no agreement among experts. Some have taken reports of a decline in daily marijuana use by high school seniors as evidence that at least the marijuana epidemic has peaked—encouraged by warnings about the drug. But to other experts, drugs such as marijuana have become a permanent part of the drug landscape, whether they become licit or remain illicit. Meanwhile, the campaign to warn young people of the dangers of marijuana use continues. It is reflected in the rise of parents' groups organized to combat youthful drug use, paralleling the movement against drunken driving. Whether this campaign will be successful remains to be seen.

As for the "harder" drugs such as cocaine and heroin, it is difficult to assess the effectiveness of efforts to prevent trafficking in them, to discourage their use, and to treat those who become addicted. So far, relatively little progress has been made. For heroin addicts in particular, federal and state governments have helped provide a variety of treatment services, ranging from methadone maintenance programs to drug-free therapeutic communities. Do they work in terms of freeing addicts from the drug? For some addicts—perhaps those with most to gain by kicking the drug—these programs do indeed work; for others—perhaps those with the least to gain outside the world of illicit drugs—they do not.

SUMMING UP

IN VIEW OF human curiosity and inventiveness regarding mind-altering substances of one kind or another, drug problems are not likely to go away. What can be done about those problems? One way to prevent drug abuse is to try to make the drug unavailable, but this is more easily said than done, as our earlier experiment with prohibition of alcohol dem-

onstrated. Another alternative is to restrict the drug's availability; this is illustrated by the recent movement to raise the drinking age, and by the tendency of most physicians to be conservative in prescribing antianxiety drugs to their patients.

Still another way to deal with drug abuse is somehow to dissuade people (especially young people) from starting to use drugs nonmedically or, for those who have started, to persuade them to stop. This, too, is more easily said than done. Yet, since the Surgeon General's first report in 1964 warning about the health hazards of smoking, more than 30 million Americans have stopped smoking cigarettes; most of them are doing it on their own. The recent leveling of youthful interest in marijuana may also be due in part to warnings about the dangers of using that drug.

The prevention and treatment of other forms of drug abuse have so far been less successful; many of those dependent on alcohol or heroin or on combinations of drugs are more likely than not to come from or end up in broken family and work situations. Their treatment may require the reconstruction of lives as well as some degree of drug freedom—no easy task. That treatment takes various forms, ranging from the temporary prescription of substitute or antagonistic drugs to participation in voluntary support groups of former abusers or addicts. It is difficult to assess the relative effectiveness of different methods of treatment; some work well with certain individuals and not with others. But the combination of individual determination to end the addiction, support from family or friends, and a helping hand from health professionals and from others who have experienced similar problems can prove effective. Any treatment is better than none.

Part Five

DISEASE, TREATMENT, AND PREVENTION

19 Heart and Blood Vessel Disease

J. Thomas Bigger, Jr., M.D.

INTRODUCTION

CARDIOVASCULAR DISEASE remains our leading health problem despite numerous advances and a decade of declining death rates. It is still the leading cause of death in the United States, claiming more than 1 million lives a year. In addition, at least 42 million Americans have some form of heart or blood vessel disease. Millions of these people have no symptoms; in fact, many do not know that they have a potentially serious illness until they suffer a heart attack, stroke, or sudden death.

The two most common forms of cardiovascular disease are hypertension (high blood pressure), a condition that affects an estimated 37 million Americans, and coronary artery disease, the progressive narrowing of the blood vessels that nourish the heart muscle, which may result in chest pain (angina pectoris) and numerous other outcomes, including heart attacks and sudden death. Very often, the two conditions coexist. Coronary artery disease is the major cause of heart attacks (myocardial infarction), which afflict about 1.5 million Americans each year. High blood pressure increases the risk of a heart attack and is also the leading cause of stroke (cerebrovascular hemorrhage occlusion), a potentially life-threatening or disabling event suffered by a half million people each year, with a mortality of more than 170,000.

Other major forms of cardiovascular disease include congenital heart defects, rheumatic heart disease and other infections, disorders of the heart valves, and heart muscle disease. Abnormalities, such as congestive heart failure or disturbances in heart rhythm (cardiac arrhythmias), which result from heart disease, also may become life-threatening. Advances in diagnosing and treating cardiovascular disorders in their earliest stages have greatly improved their prognosis in the last few years. For example, rheumatic fever was once a major cause of heart disease, particularly among the young. But the widespread use of antibiotics to treat streptococcal throat infections—the leading cause of rheumatic heart disease—has greatly diminished its incidence and severity. Implantable artificial devices, such as pacemakers and prosthetic heart valves, now make it possible for people to lead nearly normal lives who only a few years ago would have been seriously disabled or doomed to an early death. Major advances in heart surgery make possible the repair of most congenital heart defects; other procedures, such as coronary artery bypass operations, can provide often dramatic relief from disabling angina or may prevent heart attacks and death. In this chapter, the major forms of heart disease and their treatments, risk factors, and possible means of prevention will be discussed.

HOW THE HEART WORKS

THE HEART is one of nature's most efficient and durable pumps. Throughout life, it beats an average of 60 to 80 times per minute, supplying oxygen and other essential nutrients to every cell in the body and removing waste for elimination through the lungs or kidneys. The heart is a muscular, hollow organ weighing 11 to 16 ounces in the average adult. It is about the size of 2 clenched fists and is divided into 4 chambers, the left and right atrium and the left and right ventricle. (See figures 19.1A and 19.1B.) Blood that has circulated through the body flows into the right atrium from the venous system. This blood, which is depleted of oxygen and loaded with carbon dioxide, flows into the right ventricle, which pumps it through the pulmonary artery into the lungs. In the lungs, the carbon dioxide is removed and a fresh supply of oxygen is added; the oxygenated blood then travels through the pulmonary vein into the left atrium and on to the left ventricle. This chamber is the heart's major pump, responsible for pumping the oxygenated blood into the aorta and eventually, all parts of the body through a vast network of arteries, arterioles, and capillaries before it returns via the venules and veins—a total of about 60,000 miles

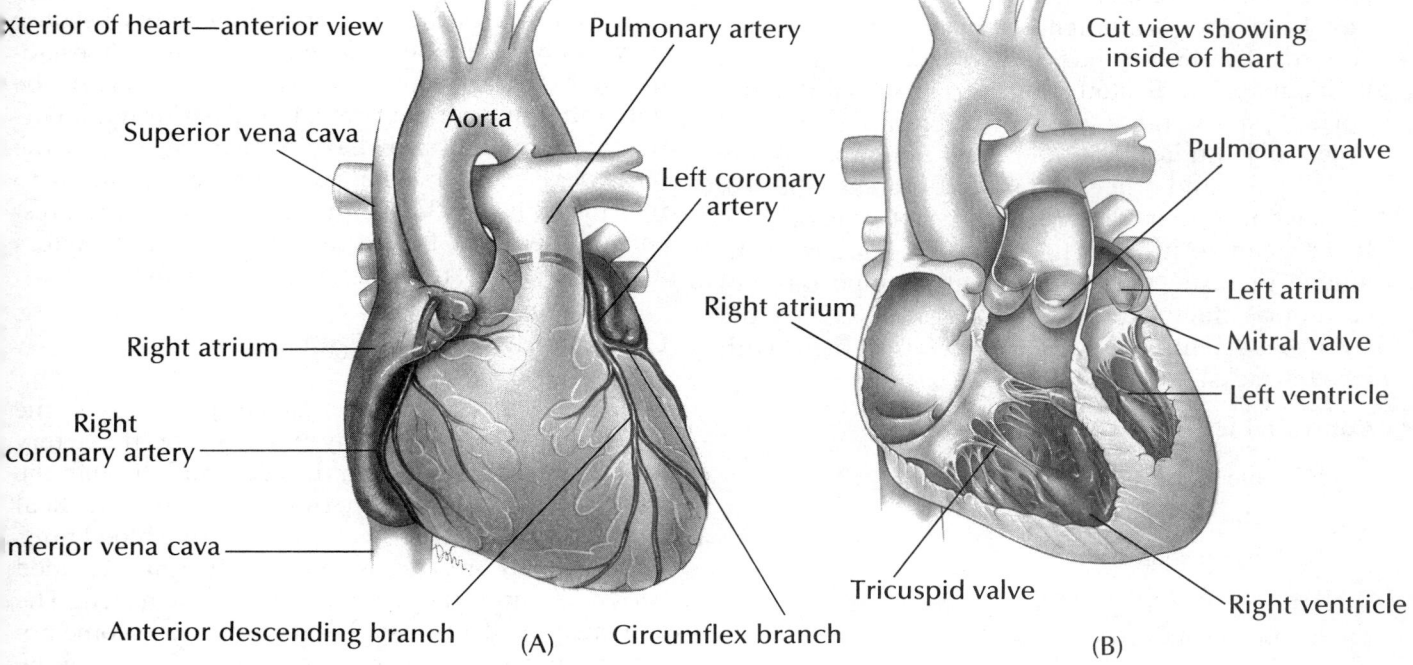

Figures 19.1A and 19.1B. **The normal heart.**

of blood vessels. In a normal, healthy adult, each ventricle pumps about 3 ounces of blood per beat, which adds up to about 2,100 gallons per day. A system of valves keeps the blood moving in the right direction through the heart.

Normal cardiac rhythm is maintained by the heart's electrical system, centered primarily in the group of specialized pacemaker cells in the sinus node. The impulse that arises in the sinus node is transmitted to specialized atrial conducting fibers to activate the cells in the A–V node, the "gateway" to the ventricles. As the cardiac impulse enters the A–V node, it slows dramatically; but when it emerges from the node into an area called the His bundle, the conduction speeds up dramatically and excites the network of conducting fibers on the inner surface of the ventricular chambers, thereby stimulating the muscle of the heart's pumping chambers (ventricles) to contract.

A system of valves keeps the blood moving in the right direction through the heart. The coronary arteries, so named because they encircle the heart like a crown, supply the heart muscle (myocardium) with oxygen and other nutrients.

When the freshly oxygenated blood leaves the heart, it passes through the aortic valve into the aorta, the great artery that arches over the heart and forms the main trunk of the arterial system. The aorta carries blood through the chest and abdomen, and other arteries branch from it to carry blood to all parts of the body. The arteries branch into smaller vessels called arterioles, which conduct blood from the arteries to the capillaries, the smallest blood vessels that transmit oxygen and nutrients to the individual body cells and collect waste products to transmit to the venous system for the return journey to the heart and lungs.

WHO GETS HEART DISEASE?

UNTIL THE MIDDLE of this century, most people regarded heart disease as an inevitable part of aging, or the result of events that people had no control over, such as rheumatic fever or congenital defects. This opinion has changed as a result of a number of large-scale population (epidemiologic) studies in which lifestyle and patterns of disease are investigated. One of the most notable and quoted of these has been the Framingham Heart Study, which started in 1948 and has followed more than 5,000 residents of the Boston suburb from which this important study takes its name. Framingham and other such studies have identified a number of lifestyle habits and other factors that increase the risk of cardiovascular disease. These risk factors are listed below. Although there is some disagreement among the experts as to the relative importance of certain risk factors, the ones with asterisks have the strongest scientific evidence associating them with heart attacks.

Controllable Risk Factors

High blood pressure *

Cigarette smoking *

High blood cholesterol *

Type A personality

Environmental stress

Obesity

Diabetes

Sedentary lifestyle

Uncontrollable Risk Factors

Age *

Sex *

Heredity *

As indicated, some of these risk factors, such as sex or age, are beyond our control. In contrast, the controllable risk factors are so designated because they can be altered by changing diet and other habits, or by controlling a disease state. It should be noted that one cannot predict whether or not a particular individual will have a heart attack on the basis of risk factors; there are always exceptions to the rule. But the chances are increased by the presence of these risk factors, and the more risk factors in an individual, the greater the likelihood.

Controllable Risk Factors

High Blood Pressure. Blood pressure is the amount of force exerted by the blood on the artery walls as it is pumped from the heart and through the circulatory system. Hypertension is the medical term used to describe an elevated resting blood pressure. If blood pressure is too high over an extended period of time, the arteries will be damaged. The detrimental effects usually take years to become apparent, and by that time, the consequences may be irreversible. Many studies have identified hypertension as a leading risk factor in heart attacks; it is also the major cause of stroke.

HOW TO TAKE YOUR OWN BLOOD PRESSURE

Home monitoring of blood pressure is useful for both patient and physician. By keeping track of daily or weekly changes in blood pressure, you can help your doctor determine whether you should take medication to lower it or if the drugs you are already taking are working. Often, blood pressure readings taken in a doctor's office or clinic will be higher than those taken at home. Once a patient has learned to monitor his or her own blood pressure, it may not be necessary to make repeated trips to a doctor's office or clinic simply for a blood pressure measurement. Most people can quickly learn to take their own blood pressures, especially if one of the several automated sphygmomanometers is used. These devices have an inbuilt sensing device that removes the need to use a stethoscope.

For convenience, blood pressure is measured in millimeters of mercury, which correspond to the height that blood traveling through an artery would spurt if it weighed as much as mercury. Traditionally, blood pressure is expressed in two numbers, such as 120/80. The higher number is the blood pressure during systole, the contraction of the heart that pumps blood into the arterial system. The lower number is during diastole, when the heart is relaxed between beats.

Following is a step-by-step procedure for taking your blood pressure using a nonautomated sphygmomanometer and stethoscope. A similar procedure is followed if you use an automated device except you do not use a stethoscope and the blood pressure will appear on a digital readout.

1. Pick a quiet spot. You have to use your ears to "hear" the blood pressure. Anything that diminishes your hearing will alter the true reading.

2. It is customary to take the pressure seated and most information on treatment is taken from seated measurements. Blood pressure will vary in the lying, sitting, and standing positions.

3. Sit next to a table so that when you rest your forearm flat on the table, your upper arm (where the cuff will be placed) is at about the same level as your heart. Having your arm above your heart will lower the reading (and vice versa), but the changes are relatively minor.

4. Use your fingertips to locate the brachial artery in the crook of your elbow by feeling for the pulse, a little to the inside of the center of the elbows' crease. Get to know this spot, since it is the best place for the stethoscope. If you can't feel it, just set the stethoscope in the general area just above the elbow crease, to the inside of center.

5. Slip on the deflated cuff, placing the stethoscope over the artery. Use the ring and velcro wrap to make the cuff snug.

6. Place the stethoscope in your ears. Most people need to have the tips tilted slightly forward, but you may have to experiment to find the position that gives the loudest sound. You can test this before putting on the cuff by gently tapping the stethoscope with your finger and finding the best position for the ear pieces.

7. Once the cuff and stethoscope are set, get the manometer (pressure gauge) in a good viewing position and you are ready to inflate the cuff.

8. You will want to inflate the cuff roughly 30 points (millimeters of mercury) above your expected systolic pressure in order to get the most accurate readings. This value has been determined by trial and error. Since most people know about where their pressure is, it is easy for them to decide how high to inflate.

9. Once the cuff pressure is greater than your systolic pressure, you should not hear any sound in the stethoscope. In effect, you have made a tourniquet for your arm and cut off all of the blood supply. This is why it feels uncomfortable.

10. Now, keeping your eyes on the gauge, gradually release the pressure in the cuff using the release on the bulb. It takes practice to learn how to release slowly so that the pressure falls 2 to 3 points with each heartbeat.

11. As the pressure in the cuff falls, it will continue to act as a tourniquet as long as its pressure is greater than the pressure in the artery. As soon as the arterial pressure drops below the cuff pressure, a pulse beat gets through, and you hear the sound of that pulse in your stethoscope. Read the gauge level at the time you hear the first sound. The first recorded sound is the systolic pressure. If you also concentrate on feeling, you can learn to sense this first beat. It gives a good check on your sound readings.

12. Continue to let air out. The thumping sound, corresponding to the amount of the pulse wave that gets through the tourniquet, will first get louder as more blood gets by. Then, as the cuff pressure approaches diastolic pressure, the sounds gets faint. Listen carefully until the sounds disappear. The gauge reading at the time of the last sound is the diastolic pressure. Note at this time, you no longer feel a pulse in your arm inside the cuff. This is because the tourniquet effect of the cuff disappears when its pressure is the same as or less than the diastolic pressure.

13. Optional check. Wait a minute and repeat the measurement. This time, readjust your initial cuff pressure to exactly 30 points above your previous systolic pressure. Slow the pressure fall to as close to 2 points per beat as you can.

14. Record date, time, systolic and diastolic pressures.

15. You can increase the value of the data by also measuring your weight and your pulse. This helps you and your doctor to interpret any changes in pressure. So will notes on any unusual related events such as menstrual periods, taking of other medicines, a recent argument, or physical exertion.

—Jay Meltzer, M.D.

A blood pressure measurement is expressed in two numbers, for example, 120/80, an ideal reading. The higher number is the systolic pressure, or the amount of force, as measured in millimeters of mercury, that is exerted against the artery walls during the heart beat (contraction). The lower number is the diastolic pressure, which is the force existing while the heart is resting between beats. While there is no clear agreement as to what constitutes high blood pressure, most experts now agree that consistent readings of 140/85–90 or higher are too high, and that the person should either take steps to lower the blood pressure, or at the least, should be carefully followed in case it becomes higher.

About 37 million Americans have high blood pressure; most of these do not have any symptoms and would be unaware that they have a potentially life-threatening disease if it were not detected during a routine checkup or examination for other disorders. There has been marked improvement in the detection and treatment of high blood pressure in recent years, thanks to widespread public education programs. Even so, substantial numbers of hypertensive Americans are either untreated or are not having their blood pressures adequately controlled.

In 90 percent of all cases, there is no detectable cause for the high blood pressure. Contrary to popular belief, hypertension is not a result of life stress, even though blood pressure does go up during periods of stress. Heredity appears to be a factor; the disease tends to run in families, and children of hypertensives often develop high blood pressure at an early age. Obesity is also a major risk factor for developing hypertension, and losing weight may bring blood pressure into the normal range. High salt intake plays an important role in the development of hypertension. Consuming too much salt (sodium) causes high blood pressure in people who are predisposed to the disease. Conversely, sharply restricting sodium can lower blood pressure in hypertensives.

Sustained high blood pressure has several adverse effects on the cardiovascular system. It causes the heart to work harder and, over a period of time, can lead to an enlarged heart and impairment of pumping function (heart failure). The sustained high pressure against the artery walls promotes arteriosclerosis, or hardening of the arteries. These damaged blood vessels often cannot deliver enough oxygen to vital organs, particularly the brain and the heart itself. Damage to blood vessels in the kidneys are a particularly important and common result of prolonged hypertension, and kidney failure is a common complication of untreated high blood pressure.

Cigarette Smoking. Although most people are well aware of the association between cigarette smoking and lung cancer and other pulmonary diseases, many still do not realize that smoking is also a major risk factor in heart attacks. In fact, the latest Surgeon General's report on Smoking and Health estimates that 225,000 of the American deaths from cardiovascular disease each year are directly related to smoking—many more than the total number of cancer and pulmonary disease deaths attributed to smoking.

Smoking harms the heart in several ways. Nicotine, one of the major addictive substances in tobacco, increases the heart rate and blood pressure, causing the heart to work harder. When nicotine, a powerful stimulant, is inhaled, it goes to work almost immediately by signaling the adrenal glands to pump out epinephrine (adrenaline), which causes the heart to beat faster and blood pressure to rise. It also narrows or constricts the capillaries and arterioles, which raises blood pressure and also reduces circulation to the fingers, toes, and other surface areas. At the same time, the amount of oxygen available to the heart is reduced—a factor that is potentially serious in someone whose heart muscle is already receiving inadequate blood flow because of coronary artery disease.

Carbon monoxide, an odorless gas that makes up 1 to 5 percent of cigarette smoke, has a great affinity for hemoglobin, the molecule in the red blood cell that carries oxygen. When carbon monoxide is inhaled into the lungs, as it is when smoking, it competes with oxygen in binding to hemoglobin. Because it has a greater affinity for hemoglobin than oxygen, it replaces some of the oxygen that would normally circulate with the blood. When carbon monoxide binds to hemoglobin it forms a molecule called carboxyhemoglobin; in its presence, oxygen binds even tighter to hemoglobin, further reducing the availability of oxygen to the body cells. Carbon monoxide also may cause degenerative damage to the heart muscle itself, a finding that has been verified in laboratory animals but not humans. Studies also suggest that carbon monoxide may alter blood vessel walls, making them more susceptible to the buildup of cholesterol and other fatty deposits.

Although more studies are needed to verify all of these adverse effects, there is clear evidence that the combination of increased levels of adrenal hormones, accelerated heartbeat, and higher blood pressure increases the possibility of anginal attacks and disturbances in heart rhythm. Some researchers believe that this explains the increased incidence in sudden death among smokers. In addition, smokers who have any of the other cardiovascular risk factors have a greatly increased incidence of heart attacks.

The question of passive smoking, i.e., inhaling the smoke of others without actually smoking yourself, is one of continuing controversy among both the public and researchers. Tobacco contains a glycoprotein, a substance to which about 1 out of 3 people are sensitive. Research with laboratory animals has found that when this glycoprotein is inhaled, it increases the clotting activity (platelet clumping) of the blood. This in turn is thought to injure the blood vessel walls and promote the development of atherosclerosis. Since nonsmokers who are exposed to cigarette smoke involuntarily inhale this glycoprotein, it is conceivable that they also suffer from its harmful effects. (The same substance is found in many vegetables, but since it is altered by the digestive process, it does not produce the same effect as when inhaled.) This effect has not been proved in humans, but some researchers feel the evidence is strong enough to warrant stricter regulation of smoking in public places.

Smokers often ask whether low-tar, low nicotine cigarettes reduce the cardiovascular risk. The answer appears to be "no." In fact, some of the filter cigarettes increase the amount of carbon monoxide that is inhaled, making them even worse for the heart than unfiltered brands.

Stopping Smoking. The best thing that a smoker can do to improve his or her cardiovascular health is to quit. More than 30 million Americans have stopped smoking since the first Surgeon General's report in 1964. Unfortunately, they have been replaced by new smokers—increasingly, women and young people; today, an estimated 50 million Americans continue to smoke. Nicotine is a powerful addictive substance; no one disputes that quitting is difficult. But many people find that stopping is easier than they had anticipated. About 95 percent who succeed in breaking the habit do so on their own. Quitting "cold turkey"—all at once—is the most effective way of stopping, but for many, other methods or aids are helpful. (See section on How to Quit, Chapter 18, page 345.)

High Blood Cholesterol. Framingham and a number of other studies have consistently found that high levels of cholesterol, a fatty substance that is consumed in the diet and also manufactured by the body, is a major factor in developing atherosclerosis—the narrowing of arteries through a buildup of fatty plaques. Cholesterol is an essential substance, needed for the function of all cells, reproduction, and other vital roles. Since the body can manufac-

ture all of the cholesterol it needs, it is not necessary to consume large amounts of it. The typical American diet, however, tends to be very high in cholesterol, which is found in eggs, red meat, whole milk, cheese, and other foods high in saturated fats. (In general, saturated fats are those that are solid at room temperature, as opposed to polyunsaturated fats, such as vegetable oils, that are liquid or soft.) People who consume large amounts of cholesterol and saturated fats tend to have higher levels of blood cholesterol, and also a higher incidence of atherosclerotic disease of their coronary and other arteries.

The total amount of blood cholesterol is not the only important factor in assessing the risk of coronary heart disease; the type of molecule on which it is transported is also a factor. Since cholesterol is a fatty substance (lipid) that is not soluble in blood, which is mostly water (and fats and water do not mix), it must be attached to a water-soluble substance before it can travel through the blood. This substance is a protein, which, when combined with the lipid, forms a molecule called a lipoprotein.

There are different types of lipoproteins, which are often classified by their size or density as determined by high-speed centrifugation. The heaviest is the high-density lipoprotein (HDL), which has the highest portion of protein. The low-density lipoprotein (LDL) is lighter than HDL, and carries a larger amount of cholesterol. The very-low density lipoprotein (VLDL) carries the largest amount of triglycerides, a lipid that is important in fat metabolism and the manufacture of cholesterol.

Recent studies indicate that HDL carries lipids away from the body cells, and is therefore important in preventing the accumulation of cholesterol and other fats along the artery walls. Thus a high level of HDL in relationship to LDL is now considered desirable. LDL, however, seems to transport cholesterol to the cells, and a high LDL level is thought to be a major factor in developing atherosclerosis. The higher the ratio of HDL to LDL cholesterol, the better. Factors that influence this ratio include heredity, sex, exercise, diet, and cigarette smoking. Some families, for example, enjoy a high level of HDL cholesterol, while others with an inherited disorder called familial hypercholesterolemia have extremely high levels of LDL—and unfortunately, often die of heart disease at an early age unless they are identified and treated while still in their teens or young adulthood. Women seem to have a higher HDL to LDL ratio than men—a factor some experts think may help explain the lower incidence of heart attacks in premenopausal women. People who engage in very vigorous exercise, such as long-distance runners or swimmers, also have high HDL levels, as do vegetarians. Smokers tend to have low HDL and high LDL cholesterol.

In the United States, the average total cholesterol is about 220 milligrams per deciliter of blood (mg/dl), a figure that is much higher than what is found in less-developed countries where there is a low incidence of coronary artery disease. There is no "normal" or "safe" level of blood cholesterol; studies have found, however, that as blood cholesterol increases above 100 mg/dl, the risk of coronary disease rises sharply as a nonlinear function of cholesterol concentration. For example, people with a cholesterol measurement of 300 mg/dl or more tend to have a very high incidence of heart attacks. Doctors now generally recommend that people who have a total blood cholesterol of 200 mg/dl or more attempt to lower it.

Lowering High Cholesterol.
For most people, the best way to lower total cholesterol (and improve their HDL:LDL ratio) is to reduce their intake of saturated fats and to increase exercise. In the average American diet, 40 percent of the total calories consumed are in the form of saturated fats. The American Heart Association recommends that this be lowered to 30 percent, with the majority coming from polyunsaturated fats. The AHA further recommends that cholesterol consumption be limited to 300 mg/day, considerably less than the average of 500 mg that is now consumed. Foods that are particularly high in cholesterol and saturated fat include egg yolks, organ meats (liver, sweetbreads, etc.), red meats, butter, cheese, and whole milk.

Although vegetable fats do not contain cholesterol and most are unsaturated, there are exceptions that should be avoided by people who are trying to lower their cholesterol. These include palm and coconut oils, and unsaturated fats that have been hardened (hydrogenated) to make solid margarines or vegetable shortenings. (There is a third type of fat, monounsaturated, that lowers blood cholesterol levels, but not as much as polyunsaturated fats.)

Increasing exercise tends to raise the levels of HDL cholesterol, although there is no evidence that exercise alone lowers total cholesterol. Since losing weight often reduces total cholesterol, this may explain why some people who undertake exercise programs may show a marked lowering of cholesterol. For those people who still have very high cholesterol levels despite dietary and other lifestyle changes, lipid-lowering drugs may be recommended. This is particularly true of people with familial hypercholesterolemia.

Type A Personality.
Personality and the ability to cope with stress have long been suspected as important health factors. Some epidemiologic studies conducted over the last 30 years have found that Type A personalities—people who overreact to even minor stresses, who tend to be driven by a heightened sense of time urgency and ambition, and who are often aggressive, hostile, or compulsive—have a higher-than-normal incidence of heart attacks, when compared to the calmer, more easy-going Type B personality. Other large-scale studies do not confirm this finding.

Whether Type A behavior may promote heart disease is unknown. Also a rationale for a link between personality type and heart disease is not well defined. Recent studies at Duke University Medical Center have found that Type A persons tend to overrespond to any challenge, no matter how large or small. This overresponse is characterized by increases in heart rate and blood pressure, and the release of adrenal hormones. It is theorized that the frequent surges of epinephrine and other adrenal hormones, which increase stress in the cardiovascular system, may cause minute injuries to the artery walls, making them more susceptible to atherosclerosis.

Modifying Type A behavior is often difficult, especially in our success-oriented society which rewards drive and ambition. Most Type As actually enjoy their fast-paced lives and are reluctant to change. The key is to identify those aspects of Type A behavior that seem to be the most destructive and to modify them while retaining the more beneficial ones. Learning to relax for varying periods of time and curbing the tendency to overrespond are two important starting points. Regular physical exercise has helped many Type As modify their behavior. Behavior modification, relaxation techniques, and biofeedback training are among the approaches that are being used to alter the more destructive elements of Type A behavior. (For a further discussion, see Chapter 17 on Effects of Stress on Health, page 327.)

Stress.
Environmental stress and our ability to cope with it is closely related to personality type. Stress in this instance is defined as an imbalance between excessive psychological or physical demands and the ability to cope with them. A certain amount of stress is a normal part of living, and without it, life would be rather dull. But there are some people who overrespond to almost any type of stress. Deciding what to buy at the supermarket, solving a simple problem, and making a major life decision all are approached with the same feelings of intensity and

anxiety. Such people have a low capability to cope with their environment.

Of course, there are some types of stress that place almost overwhelming demands on anyone's ability to cope. Examples include the death of a spouse or child, the loss of a job, major illness, or a culmination of stressful events. In any event, stress produces both physical and psychological responses. The heart beats faster, blood pressure rises, muscles tense, the hands become cold and clammy, and we may break into a cold sweat. These physiological responses to stress are characteristic of the "fight or flight" response triggered by the autonomic nervous system—a response that can be lifesaving in times of danger. The psychological effects are characterized by feelings of tension, apprehension, or nervousness. People who respond appropriately to stress are those who perform well in almost any situation; signs of poor coping include constant feelings of irritation or pessimism. Fatigue, loss of appetite (or overeating), inability to concentrate or perform at usual levels, and vague unexplained symptoms such as headaches or gastrointestinal upsets are other common signs of inability to cope with stress.

The adverse effects of stress on the cardiovascular system are similar to those seen in Type A behavior. Excessive amounts of adrenal hormones are released, heart rate and blood pressure rise, and cardiovascular symptoms, such as palpitations or chest pain, may occur. If these occur only occasionally, they probably do not produce illness or lasting harm. Theoretically, constant inability to cope with stress can lead to serious illness and may set in motion some of the processes that lead to heart disease, but this theory has not been proved.

Obesity. Obesity, defined as being 20 percent or more above ideal weight (see Chapter 16 on The Fundamentals of Health, page 305), has been shown to lead to premature death from a number of causes, including heart disease. A recent report from the Framingham Heart Study asserted that obesity should be considered a major cardiovascular risk factor in its own right, rather than one that contributes to other risk factors such as diabetes or hypertension, as has been the tendency in the past. Obesity increases the work load on the heart; other ways in which it may directly promote heart disease are unknown.

Diabetes. Diabetes mellitus, defined as an inability to metabolize carbohydrates (and, to a lesser extent, proteins and fat), may be caused either by an insufficiency of insulin or by the body's inability to use effectively the insulin it produces. As a result,

the level of sugar (glucose) in the blood rises, some of which may be excreted in the urine. Poorly controlled diabetes is characterized by extreme swings in blood sugar, going from very high to very low.

Diabetic patients have a much higher incidence of cardiovascular disease than nondiabetics. People with poorly controlled diabetes tend to have a wide range of related complications, including high blood lipids, coronary disease, and other circulatory disorders affecting both the large arteries (e.g., arteriosclerosis) and the microcirculation, leading to hemorrhages of the tiny blood vessels in the eye and diminished circulation to the extremities, especially the feet. Most diabetes experts believe the risk of these complications can be minimized by maintaining normal levels of blood sugar. This requires careful attention to diet and exercise and, in patients who require insulin or other antidiabetic drugs, careful self-monitoring to ensure the proper dosages. Not smoking is also doubly important for diabetic patients. (See Chapter 23 on Diabetes and Other Endocrine Disorders, page 474.)

Sedentary Lifestyle. Although it has not been proved that a sedentary lifestyle causes heart disease, or that exercise can prevent it, there is a statistical link between physical activity and cardiovascular health. There is also a widespread popular belief that exercise and physical fitness result in better health. Studies conducted among people whose jobs involve physical activity (dock workers, postmen, London bus conductors, among others) and among those who engage in regular exercise for recreational or health reasons have found that exercisers do have a lower-than-average incidence of heart attacks. A lack of physical activity can contribute to obesity and an increase in body fat in relationship to lean muscle tissue. It also leads to a lowered capacity in the oxygen-transport system, and may affect ability to cope with stress. People who exercise regularly not only have improved cardiovascular function, they also have an enhanced sense of well-being. Even though it is not known whether exercise can help prevent a heart attack, other health benefits make the effort worthwhile.

Uncontrollable Risk Factors

Age. Although heart disease is not caused by aging, per se, it is more common among older people. This is primarily because coronary disease is a progressive disorder; it has been demonstrated that atherosclerosis often begins at an early age and may take 20 or 30 years to progress to the point where the coronary arteries are blocked enough to cause a heart attack or other symptoms. But heart disease is not an inevitable part of aging—many people live to be 90 or more and still have healthy, vigorous hearts, and there are societies in which heart attacks are rare, even among the very aged.

Sex. Men, particularly in middle age, have a higher incidence of heart attacks than women in the same age range. After menopause, however, the incidence rises among women, and after the age of 60, it is about the same as that for men of the same age.

It is not known why younger women enjoy a lower incidence of heart attacks than men. The possible protective role of estrogen and other female sex hormones has been studied extensively, but without conclusive proof that they are responsible for the lower heart attack rate. Women who have their ovaries removed at an early age or who have a premature menopause do not seem to develop heart disease at an earlier age than women who go through menopause in their late forties or early fifties. But a small number of women who take oral contraceptives containing estrogen have an increased incidence of heart attacks and strokes, especially if they also smoke. Also, men who have been given female hormones do not have a reduction in heart attacks, as might be assumed if they had a protective role.

Other factors may explain the lower incidence in women. They tend to have higher levels of HDL cholesterol, which is considered protective against coronary disease. Until recently, women did not smoke in as great a number or as heavily as men. Now, however, the traditional roles are changing and it is interesting to note that as many facets of women's lives are undergoing change, their incidence of heart attacks at an earlier age is increasing.

Heredity. Family history is another cardiovascular risk factor over which we have no control. It has long been recognized that heart disease seems to run in some families. If parents, uncles, siblings, or other close family members have suffered heart attacks before the age of 50 or so, the chances of others following suit is significantly increased. Some risk factors, such as high blood pressure or the very high cholesterol that is characteristic of familial hypercholesterolemia, are hereditary. Although family history cannot be changed, steps can be taken to minimize the chances of a heart attack by identifying and then changing these risk factors at an early age.

TYPES OF CARDIOVASCULAR DISEASE

THERE ARE many different diseases of the heart and blood vessels, some very serious and others relatively benign. Fortunately, most people even with serious heart disease can lead relatively normal lives, thanks to modern treatment and rehabilitation efforts. Treatments vary widely according to the type of disease; they may include drugs, surgery, lifestyle modification, exercise, and diet. But no matter what the form of treatment, it is important that the patient be an informed partner in his or her own health care. The past tendency to leave therapeutic decisions entirely up to the doctor is changing; increasingly, the trend is to include the patient and often family members in treatment planning.

Coronary Heart Disease

This disorder, also known as coronary artery disease or coronary atherosclerosis, involves the progressive narrowing of the arteries that nourish the heart muscle. The narrowing is due to a buildup of fatty plaque (atheromas) along the artery walls. These deposits are composed mostly of cholesterol, other lipids, and fibrous tissue, such as collagen. Coronary disease appears to be a lifelong process in some people, beginning at an early age and progressing slowly until the vessels become so occluded that the heart muscle no longer gets adequate nourishment. The cause is unknown, although it is seen most frequently in people who live in developed industrialized nations. A diet high in cholesterol and saturated fats, and other disease states, particularly high blood pressure and diabetes, seem to promote the process. Smoking and the other cardiovascular risk factors discussed earlier also may contribute to the disease.

A coronary artery must be narrowed to less than 30 percent of its original size before there is a serious reduction in blood flow to the heart muscle, served by the vessel. (See figure 19.2.) Generally, about 5 percent of the total cardiac output of blood goes through the coronary arteries; thus there is adequate coronary blood flow to meet normal demands at rest even if the vessels are 70 to 90 percent occluded. If the coronary arteries are seriously blocked, however, blood flow may not be adequate for any increased demand such as that of exercise or an emotional upset. If the heart muscle cannot get enough oxygen—a state known as myocardial ische-

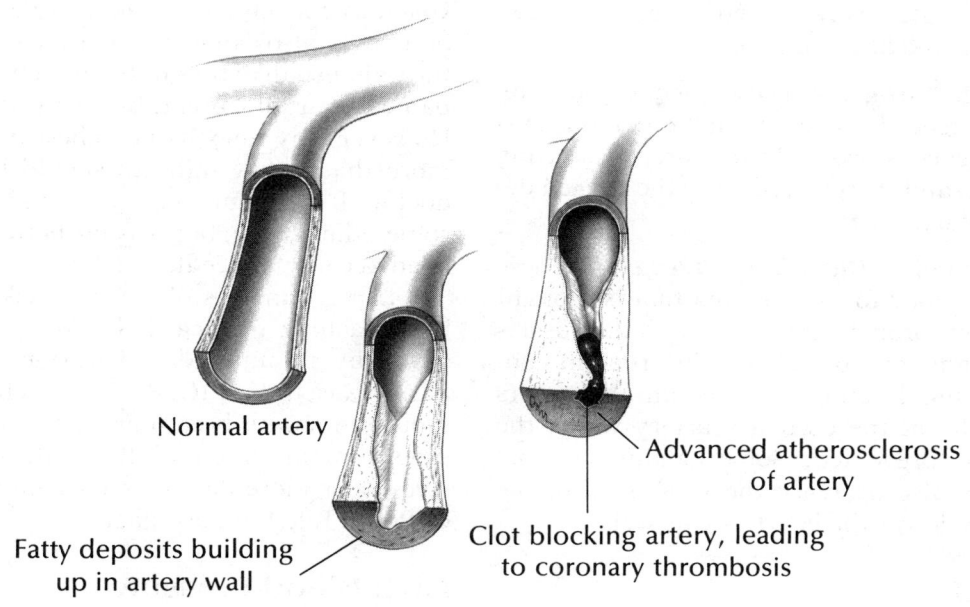

Normal artery

Fatty deposits building
up in artery wall

Advanced atherosclerosis
of artery

Clot blocking artery, leading
to coronary thrombosis

Figure 19.2. **Progression of coronary disease.**

mia—symptoms such as chest pain (angina) or shortness of breath may result.

A heart attack is a common manifestation of coronary artery disease. This can occur when an artery becomes completely blocked, either by a clot (coronary thrombus) or by atherosclerotic plaque. The medical term for a heart attack, myocardial infarction, literally means heart muscle death. Very often, a heart attack occurs without warning; indeed many people who suffer heart attacks are unaware that they have diseased coronary arteries until they are stricken. In some instances, there may have been symptoms, such as chest pain, but they may have been misinterpreted as something else, such as indigestion. (There also are some people who have "silent" heart attacks with symptoms so mild that they are unaware of the fact.) Until a few years ago, about half of all heart attack patients died, most before they even reached the hospital. These figures have changed dramatically in the last decade; more than two-thirds now survive, thanks in large part to improved medical care both before reaching the hospital and in special coronary care units.

Angina

Angina pectoris, the medical term for pain behind the sternum (breastbone), is a common manifestation of coronary artery disease. The pain is caused by reduced blood flow to a segment of heart muscle. It usually lasts for only a few minutes, and an attack is usually quickly relieved by rest or drugs, such as

nitroglycerin. Also, it is possible to have myocardial ischemia without experiencing angina.

Typically, angina is a pressing or squeezing pain that starts in the center of the chest and may spread to the shoulders or arms (most often on the left side, although either or both sides may be involved), the neck, jaw, or back. It is usually triggered by extra demand on the heart: exercise, an emotional upset, exposure to cold, digesting a heavy meal are common examples. There are, however, some people in whom an attack may occur while sleeping or at rest. This type of angina may be caused by a spasm in a coronary artery, which most commonly occurs at the site of atherosclerotic plaque in a diseased vessel.

Most people with angina learn to adjust their lives to minimize attacks. There are cases, however, when the attacks come frequently and without provocation—a condition known as unstable angina. This is often a prelude to a heart attack, and requires special treatment, primarily with drugs.

In most instances, drugs are recommended for the treatment of angina before surgery is considered. The major classes of drugs used to treat angina include the following.

Nitrates. These come in several forms: as nitroglycerin tablets to be slipped under the tongue during or in anticipation of an attack; as ointment to be absorbed through the skin; as long-acting medicated skin discs; or as long-acting tablets. The latter 3 forms are used mostly to prevent rather than relieve attacks. The nitrates work by reducing the oxygen requirements of the heart muscle.

Beta-Blocking Drugs. These agents act by blocking the effect of the sympathetic nervous system on the heart, slowing heart rate, decreasing blood pressure, and thereby reducing the oxygen demand of the heart.

Calcium-Channel Blocking Drugs. These drugs are prescribed to treat angina that is thought to be caused by coronary artery spasm. All muscles need varying amounts of calcium in order to contract. By reducing the amount of calcium that enters the muscle cells in the coronary artery walls, the spasms can be prevented. Some calcium-channel blocking drugs also decrease the work load of the heart and some lower the heart rate as well.

Heart Attack

The pain of a heart attack differs from that typically associated with angina. The pain usually does not recede with rest, and will last 30 or more minutes. The pain may vary from mild to excruciating. Sweating, nausea, vomiting, dizziness, or fainting also may occur. Many heart attack patients describe a feeling of impending doom experienced with the onset of the pain and other symptoms. In 10 percent or more of all cases, however, there may be no pain or other obvious symptoms and the person may not even know he or she had a heart attack until it is detected during an electrocardiogram at some later time.

Anyone who suspects a heart attack should seek immediate emergency treatment. The best course is to summon the local emergency medical squad. If one is not available, the patient should be taken as quickly as possible to the nearest emergency room or hospital that has a coronary care unit. The patient obviously should be driven, and not try to drive himself. If the patient arrives at the hospital early (less than 4 hours after onset) it is often possible (80 percent of the time) to dissolve the clot in the coronary artery that is responsible for the heart attack. This will decrease heart damage considerably and will also reduce mortality and disability.

Each year, thousands of heart attack victims make the mistake of delaying getting medical help, sometimes with fatal results. They may think the pain will pass or that it is from indigestion or some other cause. It is not easy to distinguish the pain of indigestion or heartburn from a heart attack, although there may be a telltale burning sensation that extends into the back of the throat. Pain caused by muscular or skeletal disorders is usually pro-

voked by movement or taking a deep breath. Stress or anxiety also can lead to chest pain; in these cases, the pain usually stays in the midchest and is accompanied by rapid breathing, palpitations, and fear. However, any unexplained chest pain that lasts for more than a few minutes should be checked by a doctor. It may turn out to be indigestion or from some other cause, but it is far better to be safe than dead because of needless delay.

Large numbers of heart attack victims die before reaching medical help. Many of these can be saved by prompt administration of cardiopulmonary resuscitation (CPR). This technique combines mouth-to-mouth breathing and external heart massage to maintain circulation until medical help arrives. (For more details, see Chapter 6 on Basics of CPR and Life Support, page 88.)

High Blood Pressure

About 37 million Americans have hypertension, or high blood pressure. In most cases, the cause is unknown, but in 10 percent of patients, the disease can be traced to specific causes, most commonly kidney abnormalities, adrenal gland tumors, or a congenital narrowing of the aorta. These cases can be treated by correcting the underlying cause. In the remaining 90 percent, the hypertension cannot be cured, but it can be controlled by salt restriction, drugs, and lifestyle changes.

In the large majority of hypertensives, the disease is classified as mild to moderate, with diastolic pressures (the lower of the two numbers in a blood pressure reading) between 85 and 104 millimeters of mercury (mm Hg). Doctors still do not agree on when to initiate drug treatment for mild hypertension, although most now agree that persistent diastolic readings above 85 millimeters of mercury should, at the least, be carefully monitored and treated by lifestyle modification. This will include weight loss, if appropriate, exercise, and reduction in salt intake. In many people with mild hypertension, this approach will be sufficient to lower the blood pressure to within the normal range. If not, drugs may be needed. In the last 20 years, a large number of antihypertensive drugs have been developed, and these have truly revolutionized the treatment of the disease. Classes of antihypertensive drugs include the following.

Diuretics. Commonly called "water pills," these drugs lower blood pressure by reducing the body's sodium and water volume. The most commonly used diuretics in treating hypertension are the thiazides; if these fail to lower the blood pressure adequately, a different diuretic or other drugs to take with a thiazide may be prescribed.

Beta-Blocking Drugs. These drugs, which block the sympathetic nervous system hormones to reduce the constriction of blood vessels, may be prescribed alone or with other drugs, usually a thiazide diuretic.

Vasodilators. These drugs relax the muscles in the blood vessel walls, causing them to dilate, or widen. Vasodilators are usually prescribed along with a diuretic or beta-blocking drug.

Centrally Acting Drugs. These agents decrease the heart rate and lower the amount of blood pumped with each beat by decreasing sympathetic nervous system activity, which controls involuntary muscle action. They are usually taken with a thiazide.

Angiotensin Converting Enzyme (ACE) Inhibitors. These drugs block the formation of angiotensin, a naturally occurring substance that constricts blood vessels. They also decrease the body's ability to retain salt and water.

Drugs prescribed for hypertension should be taken exactly as instructed, and usually for a lifetime. Although they will lower blood pressure, they do not cure the disease; once stopped, the blood pressure will go back up, sometimes higher than before. Side effects or adverse reactions are common with these drugs, but usually can be minimized by adjusting the dosage or substituting other drugs. Any side effects, which may include dizziness when standing (orthostatic hypotension), fatigue, depression, impotence, among others, should be reported to the treating physician. In any event, the patient should not stop taking the drugs or alter the dosage without first contacting his or her doctor. This is particularly important with the beta-blocking agents because abrupt cessation can provoke a heart attack.

Most people with high blood pressure do not experience any symptoms unless the disease has progressed to a serious stage. Headaches, visual changes, difficulty in breathing, and other signs of congestive heart failure, ministrokes (transient ischemic attacks), strokes, and kidney failure all are possible outcomes of untreated or poorly controlled hypertension. People who are under treatment for hypertension should have their blood pressure checked at periodic intervals (blood pressure machines are now available for home use), and see their doctors regularly.

Congestive Heart Failure

Congestive failure, which is characterized by an inability of the heart to pump enough blood, may be caused by prolonged high blood pressure, damage from a heart attack, or a primary disease of the heart muscle (cardiomyopathy, or heart-valve disease). Early symptoms include difficulty in breathing, especially at night or when lying down, and easy fatigue. When the heart cannot pump enough blood, the body retains salt and water, and blood volume increases, resulting in a backup into the lungs and other tissues (thus the term congestive failure). Later in the course of heart failure, swelling of the feet and ankles may occur.

Early diagnosis and treatment are important to prevent further deterioration of the heart muscle. Treatment depends upon the cause of the problem, and may include lowering of high blood pressure, surgery to replace diseased heart valves, salt restriction, weight loss, and a program of exercise and rest. Drugs most commonly used to treat congestive failure are digitalis (cardiac glycosides), diuretics, and vasodilators.

Cardiac Arrhythmias

Arrhythmias, or irregular heartbeats, are disturbances in the normal beating pattern of the heart. From time to time, everyone experiences a skipped heartbeat, palpitations, or other irregularities, most of which are not serious. The heart speed usually is dictated by the demands placed upon it; when a person is excited or undergoing physical exercise, the heart will beat faster to deliver more blood. In contrast, when we are resting or asleep, the heart slows down. This regulation is primarily accomplished in the sympathetic nervous system.

Normally, the heart beats at a steady 60 to 80 beats per minute, although it may speed up to 200 or more beats during periods of intense exercise. A number of factors can disturb the heart's normal rhythm, causing it to beat too fast (tachycardia) or too slow (bradycardia). These include cigarette smoking, anxiety, excessive caffeine, and the use of certain drugs. Some cardiac abnormalities, such as congenital defects, coronary disease, or heart valve disorders, can result in arrhythmias, as can thyroid disease and some lung disorders.

Most cardiac arrhythmias are temporary and benign; some, however, may be life-threatening and require treatment. A very common chronic arrhythmia is atrial fibrillation, in which the atria beat 400 to 600 times per minute. The ventricles usually beat irregularly at a rate of 170 to 200 times per minute in response to this rhythm. Atrial fibrillation is seen in many types of heart disease; once established, it usually lasts a lifetime.

One of the most serious arrhythmias is ventricular tachycardia, in which there are 3 or more consecutive impulses that arise from the ventricles at a heart rate of 100 beats or more per minute. This type of arrhythmia is dangerous because it may degenerate further into a totally disorganized electrical activity known as ventricular fibrillation, during which the heart's action is so disorganized that it quivers and does not contract, thus failing to pump blood. If the fibrillation is not stopped and normal rhythm restored within 2 or 3 minutes, death will result. (See section on Sudden Cardiac Death for a more detailed discussion.)

Chronic cardiac arrhythmias may be treated with drugs or devices that either slow or speed up the heart rate. These include the following.

Quinidine and Procainamide. These drugs, which are similar and may be used interchangeably, slow the heart rate by converting abnormal rhythms back to the normal sinus rhythm. They achieve this result by slowing the rate of conduction of electrical impulses and decreasing the excitability of heart muscle.

Digitalis. Drugs derived from digitalis glycosides may be prescribed to decrease the ventricular rate in atrial fibrillation. This slowing of heart rate is achieved by slowing conduction and increasing refractoriness in the A–V node, the structure that governs impulse traffic from the atria to the ventricles.

Beta-Blocking Drugs. These drugs, commonly used to treat angina and high blood pressure, slow the sinus node firing rate and slow A–V conduction. These drugs may be prescribed to treat a variety of supraventricular tachycardias, arrythemias arising from areas above the ventricle, particularly the atrium or the A–V node.

Lidocaine. This drug may be used to treat the ventricular arrhythmias that sometimes follow a heart attack or occur during surgery. It can only be given intravenously and is effective and safe when administered by this route.

Calcium-Channel Blocking Drugs. These agents are used to treat coronary spasm and angina. Two of them, verapamil and diltiazam, also may be used to treat a variety of supraventricular tachycardias.

Atropine. This drug increases heart rate by blocking some of the vagus nerve impulses to the heart. It is sometimes used to treat the bradycardia that may result from a heart attack or other conditions.

Pacemakers. Implantable electronic cardiac pacemakers also are used to regulate the heartbeat. These devices, which are implanted under the skin with tiny electrodes leading to the heart, are generally used to control bradycardia. One type of pacemaker, the synchronous model, takes over when the heart rate falls below a certain level. New pacemakers pace both the atria and ventricles and provide a reasonable simulation of normal heart rhythm. Modern pacemakers have long-lived batteries and can function for 7 or 8 years before they need changing.

Sudden Cardiac Death

Every minute, another American succumbs to sudden cardiac death, an age-old phenomenon that is often referred to as the major challenge confronting modern medicine. It remains the leading cause of death in industrial countries, striking all ages and social and economic groups.

Sudden cardiac death is 3 to 4 times more common in men than women; it is the leading cause of death in men 20 to 64 years of age. In about 25 percent, there are no previous symptoms of heart disease. Because most victims of sudden death die outside a hospital, doctors have tended to consider it a complex problem over which they had no control. But in recent years, it has become increasingly clear that most cases of sudden cardiac death are not the inevitable outcome of coronary artery disease, but instead, the result of ventricular fibrillation, which is reversible if treated in time. This realization has led to renewed efforts to identify people who may be at risk of ventricular fibrillation, and to take appropriate preventive action.

One of the major problems lies in identifying the types of arrhythmias or other circumstances that are most likely to culminate in ventricular fibrillation. In recent years, a number of studies have shed new light on possible risk factors for fatal arrhythmias. For example, certain patterns of ventricular premature complexes (VPC) are a warning sign of increased risk of ventricular fibrillation. But VPC alone do not appear to increase the risk of sudden death significantly in most patients; the situation changes, however, when they are accompanied by certain other factors. For example, if these complexes appear in recent heart attack patients or in people with serious coronary artery disease, the risk of sudden death increases. Patients who have been resuscitated from an episode of sudden cardiac death have a high risk of a repeat episode. Patients who have VPC during exercise testing or an attack of angina also are at higher risk of sudden death, as are those who have sustained ventricular tachycardia.

Episodes of fainting and VPC complexes in patients with mitral valve disease are still other risk factors. Recent studies have demonstrated that appropriate drug therapy can prevent further episodes of dangerous VPC and recurrent sudden death in patients who have been successfully resuscitated.

To date, most of the emphasis in identifying factors that may trigger sudden cardiac death have centered on the heart. A number of researchers propose, however, that there are other triggering mechanisms that should be considered. These include various neurological and psychological factors. The release of adrenal and other hormones can alter heart rhythm; the same is true of certain nervous system responses and interactions. Some researchers have suggested that the lowered incidence in sudden cardiac death among heart attack patients who take beta-blocking drugs may be explained by the action of these drugs to block the sympathetic nervous system. Studies of laboratory animals indicate that psychological stress also can provoke cardiac arrhythmias. Further studies are needed to define more specifically the mechanisms and factors outside the heart that may provoke sudden death. But even though many questions remain to be answered, a growing number of physicians feel that many cases of sudden death can be prevented or delayed.

Heart Valve Disease. A series of valves direct the flow of blood through the heart's chambers. Blood returning to the heart flows into the right atrium and then flows through the tricuspid valve into the right ventricle, and out the pulmonary valve into the pulmonary artery and into the lungs. Blood returning from the lungs to the left atrium passes through the mitral valve into the left ventricle, and is then pumped through the aortic valve into the great arteries. (See figures 19.3A–19.3E.) All of these valves are composed of thin leaflets that, when closed, prevent a backflow of blood, and when open, permit the blood to move forward to its next destination. When a valve fails to close properly, as is the case in a common disorder called mitral valve prolapse, there is a regurgitation or backflow of blood. A valve that fails to open properly—a condition called valvular stenosis—impairs the forward flow of blood to the body. In either case, the heart has to work harder to pump enough blood to the body, eventually leading to heart muscle damage. Congestive heart failure, syncope (fainting), and arrhythmias are common signs of valve disease.

A number of conditions can lead to heart valve disease. Congenital defects and infections, such as rheumatic fever, are among the most common. In many cases, people can have a diseased heart valve for many years without suffering any symptoms or

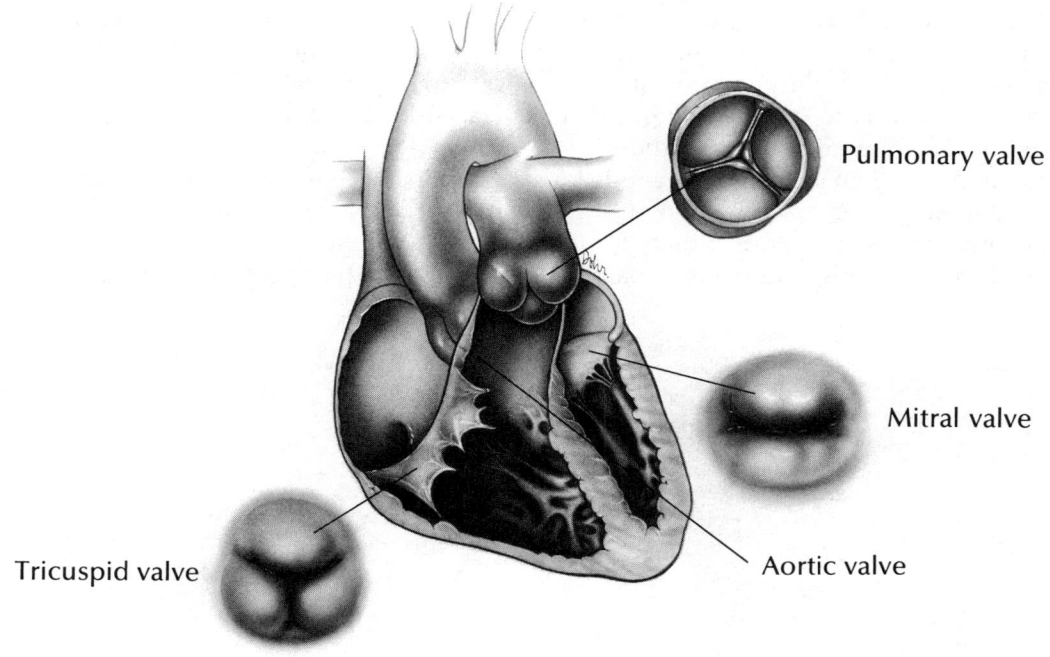

Pulmonary valve

Mitral valve

Tricuspid valve

Aortic valve

Figure 19.3A. **Normal heart valves.**

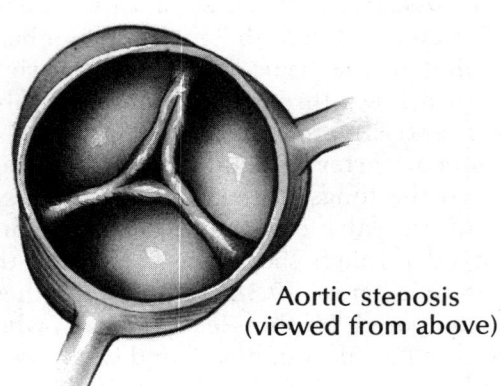

Aortic stenosis
(viewed from above)

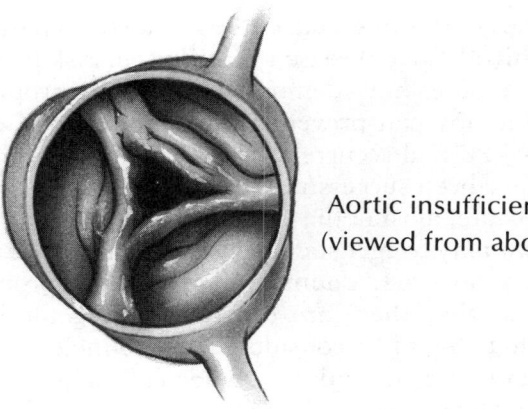

Aortic insufficiency
(viewed from above)

Figure 19.3B. **Disorders of the aortic valve.**

even being aware of the problem. Diseased valves can be detected by murmurs or other unusual sounds heard through a stethoscope. Ultrasound examination of the heart, also called echocardiography, in which sound waves are used to map internal structures, is also helpful. The most precise diagnosis is made by cardiac catheterization and angiocardiography.

Rheumatic heart disease, although greatly diminished since the advent of antibiotics to treat streptococcal infections, still affects nearly 2 million Americans and causes about 8,000 deaths per year. Rheumatic fever is seen most often in children 5 to 15 years of age and usually follows a streptococcal throat infection. This is why it is so important to diagnose these infections accurately and then to use appropriate antibiotic treatment. If this is done, most cases of rheumatic fever will be prevented.

Depending upon the type of valvular problem, patients often can go for many years without any special treatment. A common example is a condition called mitral valve prolapse. Up to 7 percent of the population has mitral valve prolapse, which, for unknown reasons, is most common in women, particu-

larly those with scoliosis and certain other skeletal abnormalities. In most people, it is not medically serious although it may cause worrisome symptoms such as palpitations and chest pain. These can usually be controlled by prescribing a beta-blocking drug.

In other forms of valvular disease, digitalis or other drugs to slow the heartbeat and increase its output may be prescribed. A diuretic may be added to prevent retention of salt and water; a salt-restricted diet may be recommended for the same reason. Anticoagulant drugs may be prescribed to prevent blood clots and antiarrhythmic drugs may be used to maintain a normal heart rate and rhythm.

Since diseased heart valves are highly susceptible to a serious infection called bacterial endocarditis, it is important to take antibiotics before any dental or surgical procedure that may release bacteria into the bloodstream. Depending upon the severity of the disease, a doctor also may recommend avoiding strenuous activities and taking frequent rest periods during the day to minimize the work load on the heart.

When the heart valves are seriously damaged

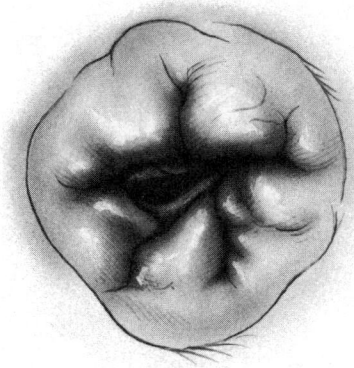

Stenosis of mitral valve
with insufficiency

Figure 19.3C. **Mitral valve disorders.**

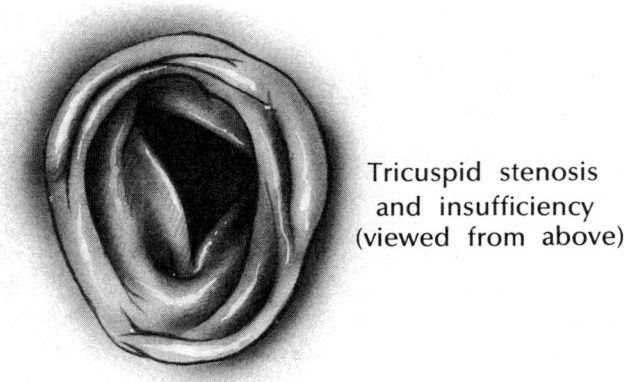

Tricuspid stenosis and insufficiency (viewed from above)

Figure 19.3D. **Disorders of the tricuspid valve.**

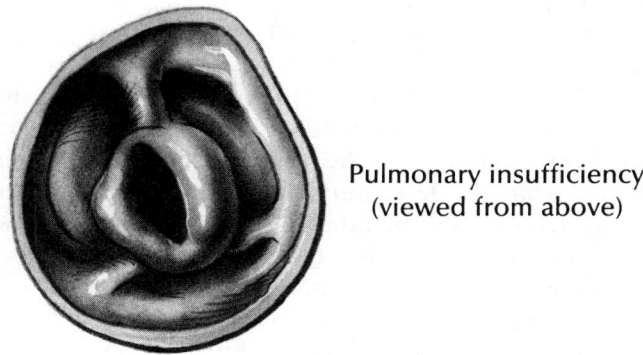

Pulmonary insufficiency (viewed from above)

Figure 19.3E. **Disorders of the pulmonary valve.**

and impairing blood flow to the rest of the body or causing heart muscle damage, surgery to replace the defective valve may be recommended. Over the last few years, a number of durable and highly efficient artificial valves have been developed from animal parts and/or plastic and metal.

Congenital Heart Defects

The development of the fetal heart is a very complex process in which a large number of defects may occur. The human heart begins to develop from a single tube in about the third week of pregnancy and starts beating at about the fourth week (even though a fetal heartbeat usually is not detected until the tenth to twelfth weeks). The tube twists and divides in such a fashion as to form the 4 chambers, valves, and other parts. Since the developing fetus gets its oxygen from the mother's blood, the fetal circulation bypasses the lungs via a short vessel linking the aorta and pulmonary artery called the patent ductus arteriosus. In the normal course of events, this ductus closes shortly after birth and the infant heart, lungs, and circulatory system begin functioning on their own.

Since the development of the heart is a complex process that can be adversely affected by many circumstances, it is understandable that defects occur with some frequency. Disturbances in the mother's oxygen supply, infections, drugs, cigarette smoking, and nutritional deficiencies are among the many factors that can harm the fetal heart, especially if they occur during the first 3 months when the heart is undergoing its basic formation. About 1 baby in 100 is born with some sort of congenital defect. Genetics or heredity also may play a role in causing heart defects. In about 97 percent of these babies, the specific cause of the abnormality cannot be identified; in a small minority, the defect can be traced to specific

causes, such as the mother's having rubella (German measles) during the first trimester of pregnancy, or chromosomal abnormalities, such as Down's syndrome.

Most congenital heart defects involve either an obstruction to blood flow or an abnormal routing of blood through the heart chambers. A small number of babies are born with disturbances of the heart's normal rhythm; for example, there is a condition called congenital heart block in which the electrical impulses responsible for normal contractions of heart muscle are blocked in the A–V node, where the impulses pass from the atria to the ventricles.

Some congenital heart abnormalities may be so mild that they are barely noticeable. Others may correct themselves in time. Still others are serious enough to be life-threatening or to interfere with normal growth and development. Specific congenital heart defects include the following.

Cyanotic Heart Disease. Some malformations result in an abnormal shunting of blood from the right to the left side of the heart, or a right-to-left shunt. As a result, some of the unoxygenated (venous) blood will flow into the aorta instead of the pulmonary artery, hence into the general circulation, without first passing through the lungs. Infants with this condition are commonly referred to as "blue babies" because the unoxygenated blood gives a bluish tinge to the lips, skin, and nails.

Specific right-to-left shunts include tetralogy of Fallot, a malformation that has 4 distinct components: an opening between the right and left ventricles (ventricular septal defect), a narrowing of the pulmonary artery or valve (pulmonary stenosis), an enlargement of the right ventricle, and an aorta that receives blood from both ventricles. Normally, the aorta—the great blood vessel that arches from the top of the heart and forms the main trunk of the arterial system—receives oxgenated blood from the right ventricle. Another right-to-left shunt occurs when the aorta and pulmonary artery are transposed (e.g., arising from the wrong sides of the heart). Thus, the aorta receives venous blood returning from the body and the pulmonary artery receives blood from the left ventricle. Transposition of the great arteries will be fatal in a relatively short time unless there is a mixing of oxygenated and venous blood. For example, the channels that are present in the fetal heart that permit blood to circulate without flowing to the lungs may remain open instead of closing, as normally happens shortly after birth. (See figures 19.4A–19.4D.)

Still another congenital abnormality resulting in cyanosis is a failure of one or both chambers on the left side of the heart to develop. This defect does not hinder the fetus, but after birth, when the heart and lungs must function on their own, abnormal left heart chambers may mean that the heart is unable to receive blood from the lungs and send it to the rest of the body. The outlook for babies born with these types of abnormalities is usually poor.

Many of the congenital deformities that cause "blue babies" can now be corrected surgically at an early age, greatly improving their chances of normal development.

Left-to-Right Shunts. In a left-to-right shunt, some oxygenated blood will flow back into the right side of the heart through defects in the walls separating the atria and ventricles and/or the great arteries. The 3 most common defects causing left-to-right shunting are patent ductus arteriosus, in which the duct between the aorta and pulmonary artery in the fetal heart fails to close shortly after birth; and atrial septal defect and ventricular septal defects, which are abnormalities in the walls separating the left and right heart chambers. Left-to-right shunts do not cause the blue baby syndrome, but as the lungs and vascular system become more developed, symptoms of heart failure may appear.

Valvular Stenosis. Congenital narrowing (stenosis) of one or more of the heart valves results in an obstruction of blood flow. Most commonly, the problem is caused by a fusing of the valve leaflets, which

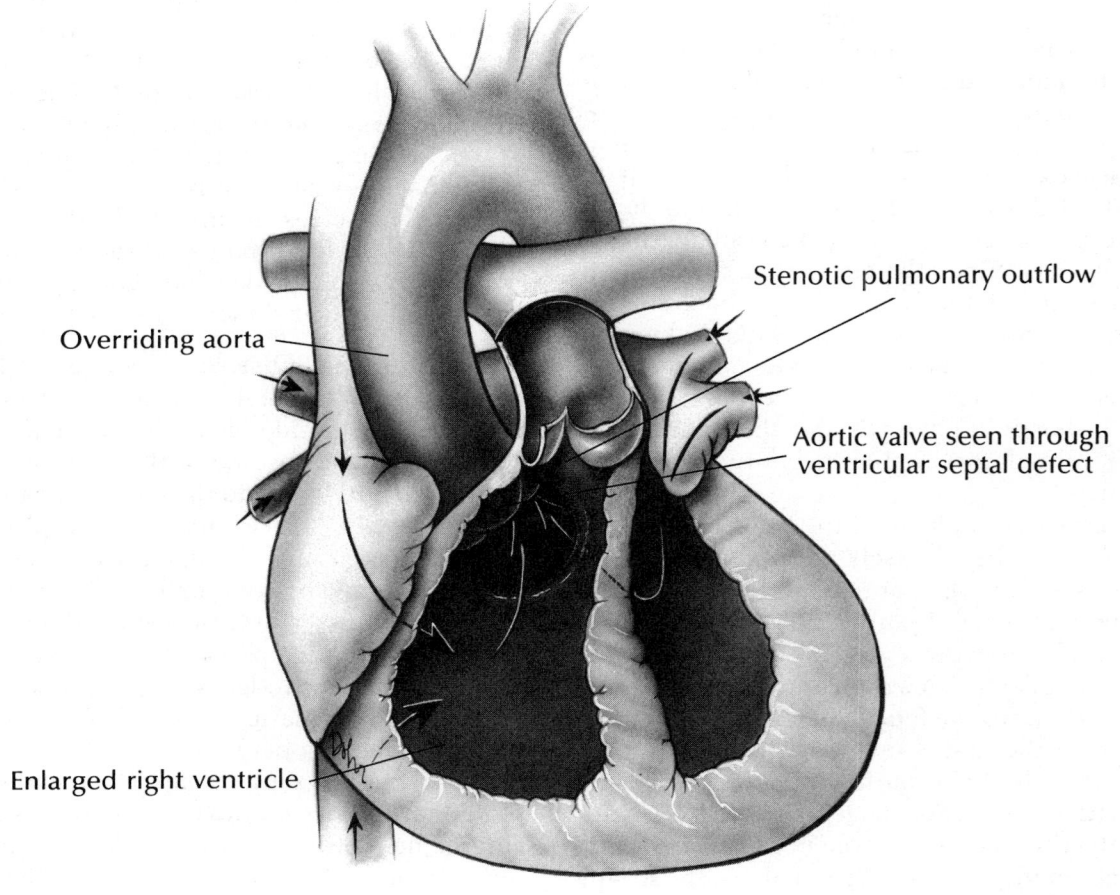

Figure 19.4A. **Tetralogy of Fallot. This malformation has 4 components: ventricular septal defect, pulmonary stenosis, an overriding aorta, and enlargement of the right ventricle.**

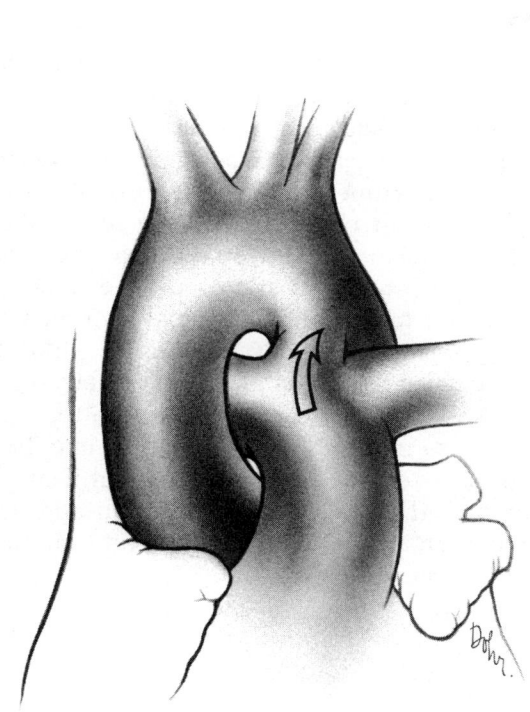

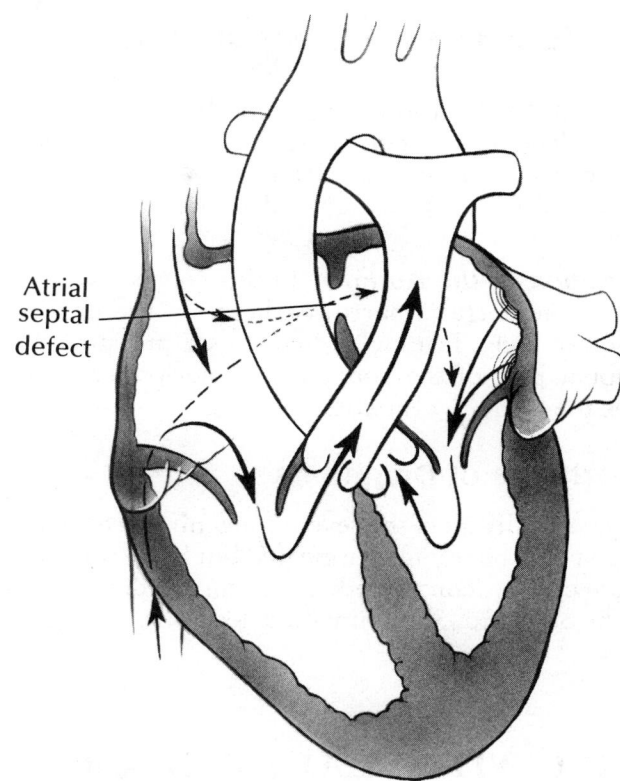

Figure 19.4B. **Patent ductus arteriosis. Duct between the aorta and the pulmonary artery in fetal heart fails to close after birth.**

Figure 19.4C. **Atrial septal defect. An opening in the wall separating the left and right atria results in increased blood volume on right side of heart, leading to enlargement of the right chambers and pulmonary artery.**

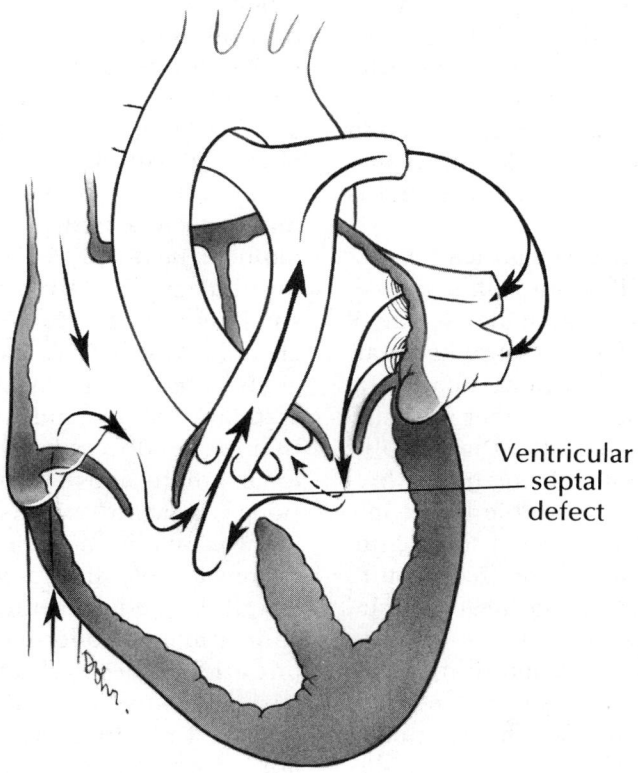

Figure 19.4D. **Ventricular septal defect. Opening between the right and left ventricles results in movement of some blood from the left to the right ventricle and then out the pulmonary artery.**

prevents them from opening properly. In order to supply blood to the body, the heart muscle must pump harder than normal, leading to a thickened, overworked heart. This can lead to eventual heart failure.

Coarctation of the Aorta. In this congenital deformity, the aorta is narrowed between the upper and lower body, leading to high blood pressure in the upper part of the body. This abnormality also causes the heart to overwork.

Importance of Diagnosis

Today, virtually all of the severe congenital heart defects can now be treated surgically, but before an operation can be considered, an accurate diagnosis must be obtained. Sometimes a defect is not readily apparent and is only recognized when the baby fails to grow or develop normally or shows symptoms of heart failure. Unusual fatigue, difficulty in breathing, and blueness are signs of possible heart defects. Often a heart murmur can be heard through a stethoscope, but not all children with congenital heart defects have murmurs. Also, many heart murmurs are not significant. Diagnostic procedures include a careful history-taking and physical examination. Depending on individual circumstances, a number of diagnostic tests, such as chest x-rays, electrocardiogram, and echocardiography (a test that uses sound waves to map internal structures) may be required. If these tests are not conclusive, or if surgery is contemplated, cardiac catheterization and angiography is performed. (See Chapter 4 on Diagnostic Tests and Procedures, page 55.)

LIVING WITH HEART DISEASE

VERY OFTEN, people who have a heart attack or are diagnosed as having heart disease are both stunned and frightened. Although 1 out of every 5 Americans at some point develops heart disease, most people harbor the notion that "it won't happen to me." When it does, there often is a tendency either to deny that anything is wrong or to move to the opposite extreme and become a cardiac cripple. Mental attitude is one of the most important factors in making a suitable recovery from a heart attack and adjusting to the fact that one has a chronic disease that is likely to last for life.

Most people with heart disease can lead a productive, relatively normal life, but some adjustments may be required. This is particularly true of heart attack patients. Even after a severe heart attack, most survivors can return to work, depending on the nature of the job, or engage in other pursuits. There are, of course, exceptions. Jobs that involve the safety of others, for example, airline pilots, firemen, or policemen, may not be suitable for people who have had a heart attack because of the significant probability of a recurrence. Jobs that require strenuous labor also may be inappropriate or special rehabilitation training may be needed.

In general, cardiovascular rehabilitation involves at least 4 stages: treatment of and recovery from the acute disease (for example, a heart attack); psychological adjustment to the nature of the disorder; lifestyle adjustments (stopping smoking, exercise conditioning, dietary changes, behavior modification); and long-term maintenance and medical follow-up. The course of treatment is dictated by the nature of the disease. Psychological adjustment is not as clear-cut: Some people accept the situation with determination and optimism; others become very depressed or adopt a defeatist attitude. Still others deny that anything is wrong. Professional counselling or group therapy with other heart patients may be appropriate and should be extended to spouses and other family members if needed.

Cardiovascular rehabilitation is an often-neglected aspect of treating heart disease. Once the initial crisis is passed and recovery is underway, many doctors and patients avoid discussing what happens next. All too often, a patient will leave the hospital with instructions to "lose weight, stop smoking, and try to get more exercise," without a clear idea of how to go about accomplishing these goals. What's more, heart attack patients are understandably afraid and many harbor misconceptions that are holdovers from past practices. At one time, for example, most heart attack patients were cautioned to avoid exercise, advice that doctors now know is invalid for the majority of patients. In recognition of these shortcomings, a growing number of hospitals, medical centers, physician groups, and organizations are offering formal cardiovascular rehabilitation programs, many of which begin while the patient is still hospitalized and continue after discharge. Unfortunately, most insurance policies do not cover outpatient rehabilitation, so there may be economic stricture on participating on a long-term basis. However, there are alternatives. For example, many YMCAs now offer physician-supervised cardiovascular rehabilitation programs at a modest cost. Local chapters of the American Heart Association usually can provide information about such programs and also can check on whether they are properly structured and supervised.

Lifestyle adjustments are perhaps one of the most important factors in living with heart disease. All too often, heart attack patients assume that they can no longer engage in pleasurable activities of the past, including athletics and sex. For the large majority of patients this is not true. The extremes, such as running a marathon, may no longer be feasible, but then, most people who have never had a heart attack cannot do these things, either. The important thing is to examine carefully what is important to making as full a recovery as possible, and then following through in instituting the necessary changes. Stopping smoking is high on the list of necessary lifestyle adjustments for those who smoke and have heart disease. Losing excess weight, altering eating habits to lower cholesterol, and increasing physical activity are examples of other positive lifestyle adjustments that are important in living with heart disease. Some of these require only common sense and determination; others, such as exercise conditioning and dietary changes, may require professional guidance. In fact, no one with heart disease should undertake an exercise program without medical clearance and a diagnostic exercise test. (See page 57.) By the same token, a person should not be afraid to exercise within reason because he or she has had a heart attack. Heart attack patients who engage in exercise conditioning, either in a supervised setting or individually following a doctor's prescribed regimen, find they not only feel better, but are able to resume previous activities faster and with more confidence. (See Model Exercise Conditioning Program, page 383.)

Backsliding to one's former ways is a constant danger, especially as time goes by. Since a previous heart attack is very often a precursor to recurrences, it is important to do everything possible with an eye to prevention. There is no guarantee that adopting a healthier lifestyle will, indeed, prevent future heart attacks or other cardiovascular problems, but it would be foolish not to make the effort.

CORONARY ARTERY BYPASS SURGERY

AN ESTIMATED 170,000 AMERICANS undergo coronary artery bypass surgery each year. This operation, once considered an ultimate achievement in cardiovascular medicine, is now almost routine in many medical centers. Indeed, there is a good deal of controversy over whether it is now being used unnecessarily to treat coronary disease that could be controlled just as effectively by more conservative, less costly medical therapies.

There remains some disagreement among doctors as to the indications for coronary bypass surgery. Studies have conclusively demonstrated that the operation prolongs life in patients who have a severely blocked left main coronary artery. It is also indicated in most cases in which 3 major arteries are diseased. There is less agreement about when it is appropriate for other patients. In general, it is recommended for people with disabling angina that cannot be controlled by conventional therapy who are also good candidates for surgery.

The operation itself is relatively simple. A segment of healthy blood vessel, usually a vein from one of the legs, is interposed between the aorta and the blocked coronary arteries. (See figure 19.5.) During the operation, which takes about 2 hours, circulation is maintained by a heart–lung machine. Coronary bypass patients usually spend 2 or 3 days in an intensive care recovery unit following the operation, and another week in the hospital. Costs of the operation range from $15,000 to $25,000, depending on individual considerations and the part of the country.

Most people who undergo the operation report feeling vastly better afterward. Very often, the patient may have suffered from disabling angina or other cardiac limitations before the operation. With an increased blood supply to the heart muscle, these problems should be eliminated or minimized. (It should be noted that not all people with severe coronary disease are suitable candidates for surgery, and also, that the operation is not always successful in achieving its intended goals.) As with any surgical procedure, the operation involves some risk; nationwide, about 1 to 3 percent of bypass patients do not survive the operation or recovery. The risk is highest for people who have heart failure or are debilitated by age or other medical conditions. Women do particularly poorly.

The skill and experience of the surgical and recovery teams also are important considerations. Patients considering coronary bypass surgery always should determine whether the surgeon performs this particular operation regularly (at least 2 or 3 times per week) and whether there is a skilled recovery team and a special recovery unit.

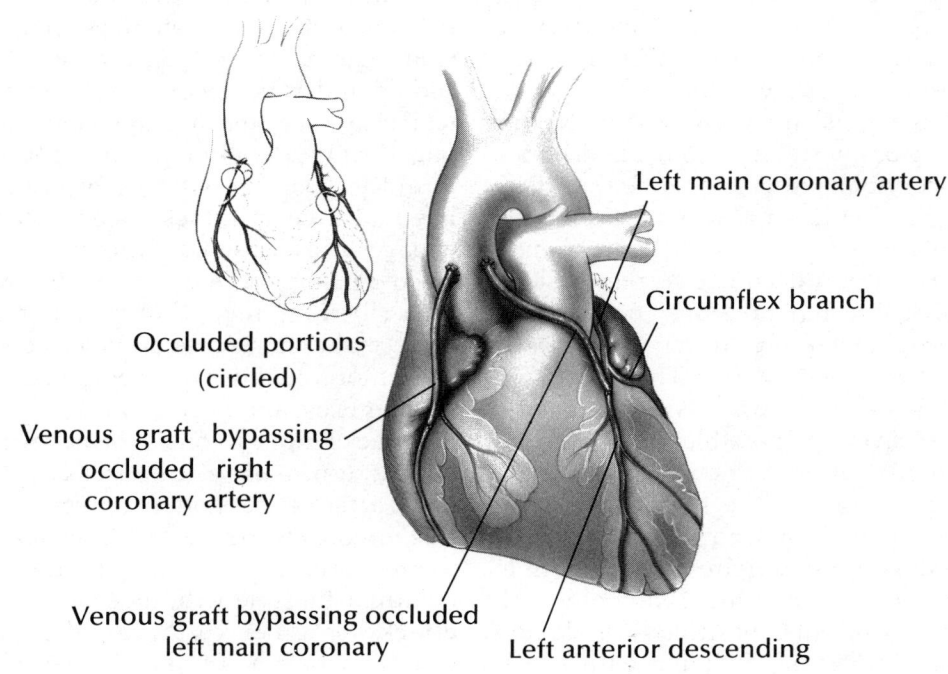

Left main coronary artery

Occluded portions
(circled)

Circumflex branch

Venous graft bypassing
occluded right
coronary artery

Venous graft bypassing occluded
left main coronary

Left anterior descending

Figure 19.5. **Coronary bypass surgery. This drawing shows 2 graits, one of the left main coronary artery and the other of the right coronary artery.**

Although bypass surgery greatly improves the way most patients feel, it is not a cure for heart disease. Unless other preventive steps are taken, the processes that caused the artery disease will continue. In fact, the grafts seem to become diseased even faster than the natural coronary arteries. Therefore, it is particularly important for bypass patients to follow a prudent lifestyle following the operation.

ANGIOPLASTY

ANOTHER PROMISING NEW TREATMENT for atherosclerotic arterial diseases that is being used increasingly in this country is transluminal angioplasty. It is being used to treat severely blocked coronary arteries as well as arteries diseased with atherosclerotic plaques in other parts of the body.

The technique involves threading a catheter with an inflatable balloon-like tip through the artery until it reaches the area of blockage. The balloon is then inflated, flattening the fatty plaque and widening the arterial opening. (See figure 19.6.) The procedure has several obvious advantages: It is done under a local anesthesia and, although invasive, it does not involve surgery or the use of a heart–lung machine. It is not as costly as coronary bypass surgery, nor does it involve more than 1 or 2 days of hospitalization under ordinary circumstances.

Unfortunately, it is not appropriate for all types of coronary artery disease, nor does it work in all patients who undergo the procedure. Some studies have put the success rate at about 60 percent; patients who undergo an unsuccessful angioplasty still may require coronary bypass surgery. However, as more physicians gain experience in the procedure and it is performed at more centers, the results are expected to improve. It also should be noted that it is not a cure for the disease. In a significant number of patients, the occlusions reform, and a repeat angioplasty may be required after 2 or 3 years.

Angioplasty is also being used to treat blockages in the arteries of the legs and the carotid artery, the major vessel carrying blood to the brain.

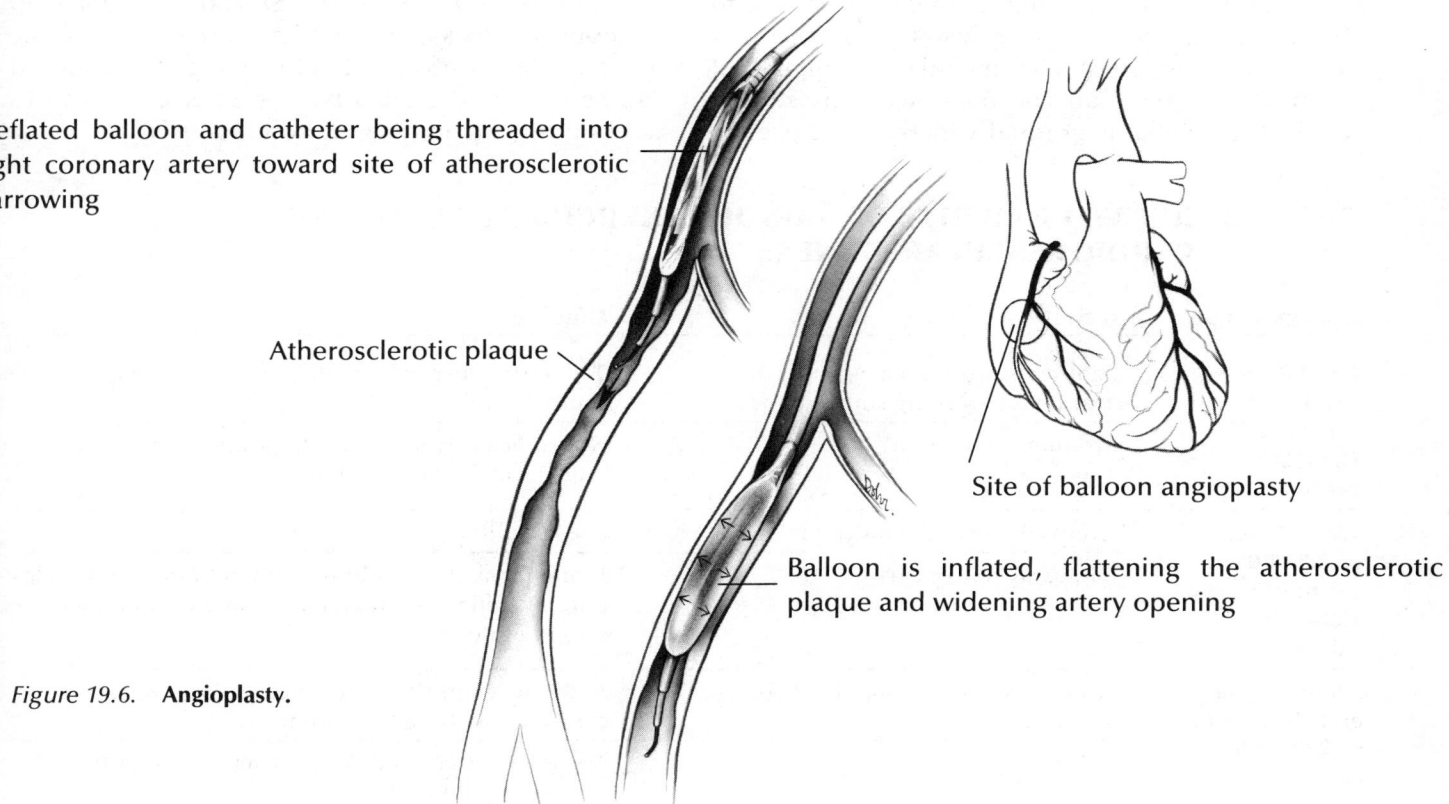

eflated balloon and catheter being threaded into
ght coronary artery toward site of atherosclerotic
arrowing

Atherosclerotic plaque

Site of balloon angioplasty

Balloon is inflated, flattening the atherosclerotic
plaque and widening artery opening

Figure 19.6. **Angioplasty.**

EXERCISE CONDITIONING

THE ROLE OF EXERCISE in the possible prevention and treatment of heart disease is a subject of increasing interest to both the general public and medical researchers. Studies have found a statistical link between a sedentary lifestyle and increased incidence of heart attacks, but to date, not much is known about the processes involved. Most people agree that physical fitness, defined as having enough stamina to exercise at or near one's biological potential, is important in the way we feel, both physically and emotionally. People who are physically fit tend to have more energy and a heightened sense of well-being. Formerly sedentary people who take up exercise conditioning are often amazed at the difference it makes, both in the way they feel and also in such areas as increased productivity, improved ability to relax, and disposition.

In recent years, exercise conditioning has become a part of many cardiovascular rehabilitation programs. Exercise programs for heart patients should be directed by a physician experienced in this area and individualized to meet specific patient needs. (Other people undertaking exercise conditioning should follow the precautions outlined in Chapter 16 on Fundamentals of Health, page 308.)

The following tables outline a model exercise conditioning program for both heart patients and healthy people. There should be at least 3 and preferably 5 exercise sessions per week. Note: Do not undertake this or any exercise program without appropriate medical clearance.

Table 19.1 **MODEL EXERCISE CONDITIONING PROGRAM**

Weeks	Distance (miles)	Time goal (min/mile; healthy)	Distance (miles)	Time goal (min/mile; heart patients)
1–2	1–2	15	1	20
3–4	2–2.5	12–15	1	17–30
5–6	2.5–3	12	1	15
7–8	3–3.5	12	1.5	15
9–10	3.5–4	12	1.5	14

In each succeeding 2-week period, increase distance and/or decrease time until conditioning goal has been reached. To maintain fitness, exercise 20 to 30 minutes in heart target range 4 or 5 times per week. Each session should include 10 minutes of warm-up and 10 minutes of cool-down exercises.

Start by walking; gradually increase the pace as indicated below. If there are no orthopedic problems and if your doctor approves, jogging can be added gradually after 9 or 10 weeks. Start by walking a lap or couple of blocks, jog for a few yards, then resume walking. If no problems develop, the distance jogged can be increased gradually over a period of 8 to 10 weeks until you are jogging continuously.

Table 19.2 **RELATIVE MERITS OF VARIOUS EXERCISES IN INDUCING CARDIOVASCULAR FITNESS**

Energy range	Activity	Comment
1.5–2.0 Mets[a] or 2.0–2.5 cal/min or 120–150 cal/hr	Light housework such as polishing furniture or washing small clothes	Too low in energy level and too intermittent to promote endurance
	Strolling 1.0 mile/hr	Not sufficiently strenuous to promote endurance unless capacity is very low
2.0–3.0 Mets or 2.5–4.0 cal/min or 150–240 cal/hr	Level walking at 2.0 miles/hr	See "strolling"
	Golf, using power cart	Promotes skill and minimal strength in arm muscles but not sufficiently taxing to promote endurance; also too intermittent
3.0–4.0 Mets or 4–5 cal/min or 240–300 cal/hr	Cleaning windows, mopping floors, or vacuuming	Adequate conditioning exercise if carried out continuously for 20–30 minutes
	Bowling	Too intermittent and not sufficiently taxing to promote endurance
	Walking at 3.0 miles/hr	Adequate dynamic exercise if low capacity
	Cycling at 6 miles/hr	As above
	Golf—pulling cart	Useful for conditioning if reach target rate; may include isometrics depending on cart weight
4.0–5.0 Mets or 5–6 cal/min or 300–360 cal/hr	Scrubbing floors	Adequate endurance exercise if carried out in at least 2 minute stints
	Walking 3.5 miles/hr	Usually good dynamic aerobic exercise
	Cycling 8 miles/hr	As above
	Table tennis, badminton, and volleyball	Vigorous continuous play can have endurance benefits but intermittent, easy play only promotes skill
	Golf—carrying clubs	Promotes endurance if reach and maintain target heart rate, otherwise merely aids strength and skill
	Tennis—doubles	Not very beneficial unless there is continuous play maintaining target rate—which is unlikely; will aid skill
	Many calisthenics and ballet exercises	Will promote endurance if continuous, rhythmic, and repetitive; those requiring isometric effort such as push-ups and sit-ups are probably not beneficial for cardiovascular fitness

[a]**Met** = multiple of the resting energy requirement; e.g., 2 Mets require twice the resting energy cost, 3 Mets triple, etc.

Note: Energy range will vary depending on skill of exerciser, pattern of rest pauses, environmental temperature, etc. Caloric values depend on body size (more for larger person).

From Lenore R. Zohman, M.D., *Beyond Diet: Exercise Your Way to Fitness and Heart Health*, CPC International, Englewood Cliffs, N.J.

Table 19.2   **RELATIVE MERITS OF VARIOUS EXERCISES IN INDUCING CARDIOVASCULAR FITNESS (continued)**

Energy range	Activity	Comment
5.0–6.0 Met or 6–7 cal/min or 360–420 cal/hr	Walking 4 miles/hr	Dynamic, aerobic, and of benefit
	Cycling 10 miles/hr	As above
	Ice or roller skating	As above if done continuously
6.0–7.0 Mets or 7–8 cal/min or 420–480 cal/hr	Walking 5 miles/hr	Dynamic, aerobic, and beneficial
	Cycling 11 miles/hr	Same
	Singles tennis	Can provide benefit if played 30 minutes or more by skilled player with an attempt to keep moving
	Water skiing	Total isometrics; very risky for cardiacs, pre-cardiacs (high risk), or deconditioned normals
7.0–8.0 Mets or 8–10 cal/min or 480–600 cal/hr	Jogging 5 miles/hr	Dynamic, aerobic, endurance-building exercise
	Cycling 12 miles/hr	As above
	Downhill skiing	Usually ski runs are too short to significantly promote endurance; lift may be isometric; benefits skill predominantly; combined stress of altitude, cold, and exercise may be too great for some cardiacs
	Paddleball	Not sufficiently continuous but promotes skill; competition and hot playing areas may be dangerous to cardiacs
8.0–9.0 Mets or 10–11 cal/min or 600–660 cal/hr	Running 5.5 miles/hr	Excellent conditioner
	Cycling 13 miles/hr	As above
	Squash or handball (practice session or warmup)	Usually too intermittent to provide endurance building effect; promotes skill
Above 10 Mets or 11 cal/min or 660 cal/hr	Running 6 miles/hr = 10 Mets 7 miles/hr = 11.5 8 miles/hr = 13.5	Excellent conditioner
	Competitive handball or squash	Competitive environment in a hot room is dangerous to anyone not in excellent physical condition; same as singles tennis

STROKE

ALTHOUGH STROKES affect the brain and fall under the province of a neurologist, they are listed among the cardiovascular disorders because most are caused by a vascular problem. Many of the risk factors for a heart attack also apply to stroke.

In recent years, there has been a marked decline in stroke as high blood pressure control has improved; even so, it remains a major cause of death and disability. Strokes are usually caused by a marked reduction in blood flow to the brain, leading to brain-tissue death (cerebral infarction). Progressive narrowing of the arteries, or arteriosclerosis, and high blood pressure are major causes of strokes; the immediate precipitating factor is frequently the complete closure of a blood vessel by a clot or piece of fatty plaque (cerebral thrombosis or embolism). Less common are strokes caused by cerebral hemorrhage, usually resulting from high blood pressure or a rupture in a weakened blood vessel in the brain.

Strokes are most common in older people between the ages of 60 and 80. In addition to high blood pressure and arteriosclerosis, the risk of stroke is increased by diabetes, obesity, high blood lipids, and smoking. A stroke may come on suddenly or during sleep. But in a large number of cases, there are warning signs that call for prompt action. These signs, known as ministrokes or transient ischemic attacks (TIAs), are temporary spells of impaired brain function due to brief but marked reduction in blood flow to the brain. TIA symptoms include temporary weakness or paralysis on one side, difficulty in speaking, loss of vision in one or both eyes, double or blurred vision, weakness or paralysis on one side of the face, dizziness, and hearing loss, among others. The particular symptom or symptoms depends upon the part of the brain that is being temporarily deprived of oxygen. Very often, the problem stems from serious narrowing of the carotid artery in the neck, the major vessel supplying blood to the brain. These symptoms may be so fleeting that they are ignored or quickly forgotten; however, if properly diagnosed and treated, a full-blown stroke may be prevented or its damage minimized. Preventive measures include lowering blood pressure if it is higher than normal, prescribing low doses of aspirin or other drugs to prevent the formation of clots, and surgery. Increasingly, operations to bypass seriously blocked arteries or to reposition blood vessels to supply the brain with adequate oxygen are being performed to prevent impending strokes.

As in heart attacks, there is a wide range of damage that can be caused by a stroke. When they are mild or affect certain parts of the brain, full recovery can be expected; more frequently, there are lasting effects ranging from minor speech impairment or sensory loss to total paralysis. And, of course, about 170,000 per year are fatal. The type and extent of damage depends upon the site of the cerebral infarction. If the stroke occurs in the left half of the brain, the dominant hemisphere, results may include speech impairment (aphasia) and paralysis of the right side of the body. Cerebral infarction in the right hemisphere may cause loss of spatial perception, making tasks like eating or dressing difficult, as well as possible left-side paralysis. A stroke in the brain stem can have varied effects, including sensory loss, uncoordination, and paralysis or weakness on one or both sides. Brain scans are now used to pinpoint the exact area of infarction and also may help identify other causes of the symptoms, such as a brain tumor or injury.

Cerebral Hemorrhage

Cerebral hemorrhage is not as common as cerebral thrombosis or obstruction, but it is more likely to be fatal. The bleeding usually occurs when a blood vessel ruptures, often as a result of high blood pressure. Depending upon the site of the hemorrhage, the bleeding may destroy brain tissue directly or form masses of extravascular blood, compressing parts of the brain, which in turn may reduce the supply of oxygen to the distorted areas. (See figure 19.7.) This type of stroke usually comes on suddenly with a se-

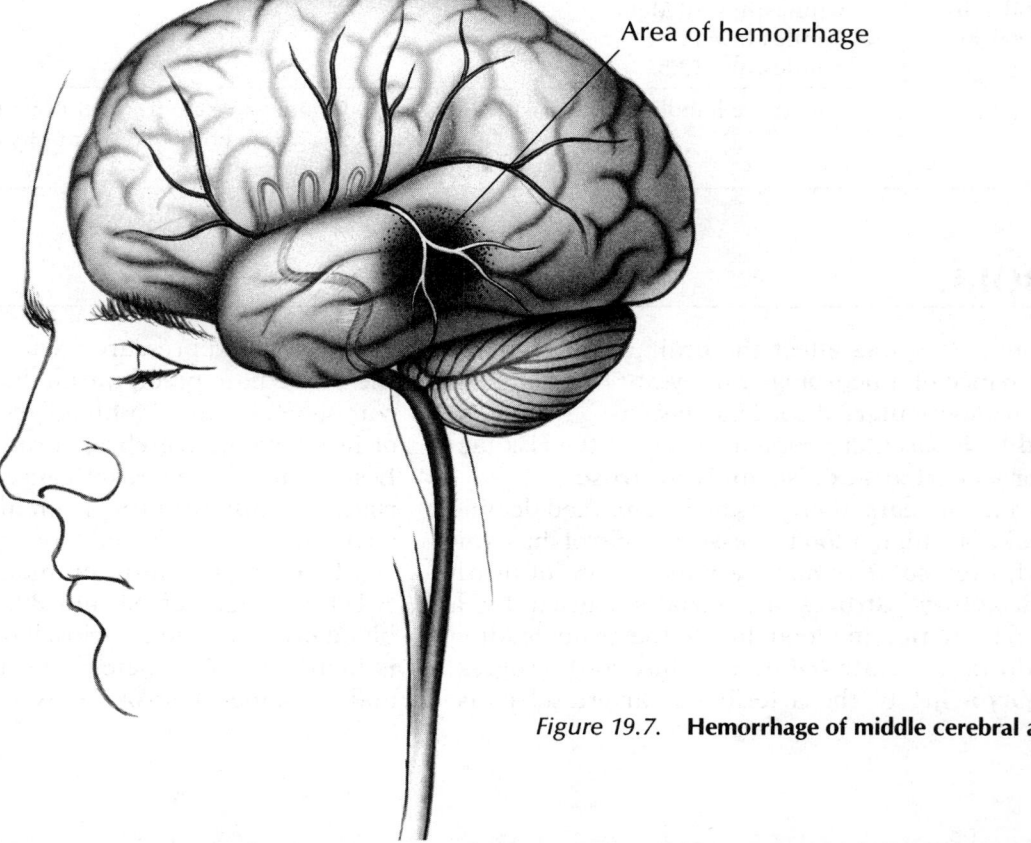

Area of hemorrhage

Figure 19.7. **Hemorrhage of middle cerebral artery.**

vere headache, change in neurological function, and loss of consciousness. If the bleeding is directly into the brain (intracerebral hemorrhage), the outlook is generally poor. This type of stroke has a high mortality rate and survivors are likely to be permanently disabled.

If bleeding occurs in the subarachnoid space—between 2 of the 3 membranes covering the brain—the outlook is significantly better. This type of stroke is usually caused by a rupture of an aneurysm, a thin-walled bleb that forms in a congenitally weak segment of cerebral blood vessel. This type of aneurysm is often found near the base of the brain, and bleeding is confined to the space surrounding the brain. Because the skull is rigid, the space-occupying clot will compress the underlying brain

tissue. There may be neurological symptoms and sensory loss in addition to severe headache. Since these aneurysms generally are too small to show up on brain scans, arteriography usually is required to locate them. The mortality rate from this type of stroke is about 50 percent, with most dying before they can reach a hospital. Among the survivors, treatment aimed at preventing future hemorrhages is important. People who have one cerebral aneurysm are likely to have more; finding them and eliminating the risk of their rupturing is the best course of prevention. This may be done surgically or, if surgical removal is not indicated, the danger may be lessened by blocking off the parent blood vessel. If high blood pressure is present, lowering it to normal is crucial.

OTHER TYPES OF CARDIOVASCULAR DISEASE

HEART ATTACKS AND STROKE are the most common of the life-threatening cardiovascular diseases, but there are a number of other conditions that should be considered in any review of this system. Some of these involve diseases arising in other organ systems that affect the cardiovascular system. Examples include diabetes and other endocrine diseases, various blood disorders, chronic pulmonary diseases, kidney failure, certain rheumatoid diseases, syphilis, and some types of cancer. These are discussed in greater detail in the chapters dealing with the primary disorders. Covered in this section are cardiovascular disorders that may not occur as frequently as heart attacks, hypertension, or stroke, but are still relatively common or serious enough that people should at least be aware of the warning signs.

Infective Endocarditis

Endocarditis is one of several inflammatory conditions affecting the heart. As its name implies, endocarditis is an inflammation of the heart's inner lining, the endocardium. In bacterial endocarditis, colonies of microorganisms form wartlike growths on the endocardium, usually the portion that lines the heart valves. These colonies, which also contain blood cells and other material such as fibrin (a protein instrumental in blood clotting), can eventually destroy the heart valves; the bacteria also may travel through the bloodstream to other parts of the body. (See figure 19.8.) In some cases, emboli may form, resulting in pulmonary embolism, heart attack, or stroke, depending upon where they finally lodge.

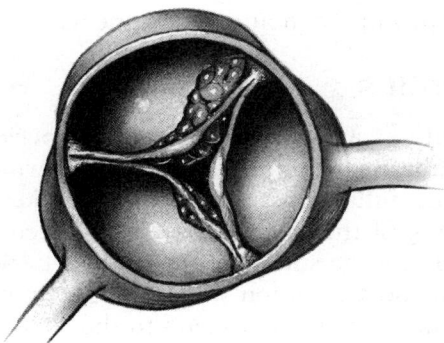

Figure 19.8. **Bacterial endocarditis.**

Endocarditis most often occurs in patients who already have a damaged heart valve or congenital abnormalities of the heart. Artificial heart valves are also likely to become infected. In recent years, there also has been an increase in subacute endocarditis among drug addicts who use contaminated needles and other items.

The most common causative bacterial agents are streptococcus or staphylococcus. But many other bacteria and certain fungi and rickettsiae (parasitic microorganisms that are neither viruses nor bacteria) also may cause endocarditis.

If endocarditis is recognized and treated in its early stages, the recovery rate is good. Frequently, however, the disease smoulders undetected until it has an opportunity to cause serious damage to one or more heart valves. Possible warning signs include weakness, fatigue, a slight fever, and aching joints. There is often a heart murmur indicating an abnormal valve or other heart defect. In some cases, the disease comes on suddenly, with fever, chills, and rapid destruction of the involved heart valve. Blood tests and cultures should be performed to identify the invading microorganism so that aggressive treatment with the most effective antibiotics can begin. If a heart valve has been seriously damaged, surgery to replace it with an artificial valve may be needed.

There has been an increase in endocarditis in recent years, especially the types caused by staphylococcus, fungi, and rickettsiae. Since the disease is most common in people who already have damaged heart valves, congenital heart defects, or artificial heart valves, it is particularly important that they follow the American Heart Association's guidelines for preventive antibiotic treatment, especially before and after any procedure that may permit bacteria to enter the bloodstream. This includes surgery and routine dental work, such as oral surgery or the cleaning of teeth and gums. Anyone who has had rheumatic fever, valvular disease, or has a congenital heart defect or an artificial heart valve should be attuned to the warning signs of endocarditis and see a doctor promptly should they appear.

Pericarditis

Pericarditis is an inflammation of the pericardium, the membrane forming the outer covering of the heart. The inflammation causes a thickening and roughening of the membrane and an accumulation of fluid in the sac surrounding the heart. (See figure 19.9.) The most common symptom is pain under the breastbone, which may extend to the left side of the

chest and to the left shoulder. The pain often becomes worse with a deep breath and is relieved when sitting or leaning forward. When the doctor listens to the heart and chest with a stethoscope, a grating sound can be heard, caused by a rubbing of the roughed pericardium surfaces with each heartbeat.

Most pericarditis in this country is caused by a viral infection. The disease also may be caused by bacteria, fungi, or parasites. There is also a noninfectious pericarditis; causes include disease of the underlying heart muscle, injury, and other diseases, such as rheumatoid arthritis, lupus erythematosus, or kidney failure.

Early detections and treatment are important to prevent potentially serious complications. For example, untreated bacterial or chronic pericarditis may cause the pericardium to lose its elasticity, causing a constriction of the heart. If the heart is unable to function normally because of pericardial constriction, surgery to remove part of the pericardium may be required. Another potentially serious complication of pericarditis, especially that caused by a bacterial infection, injury, or tumor, is cardiac tamponade, which is caused by an accumulation of fluid in the pericardial sac, resulting in excessive pressure on the heart. If untreated, blood pressure will drop along with cardiac output. This is an emergency situation that is treated by puncturing the pericardial sac to remove the fluid.

Myocarditis

Myocarditis is an inflammation of the heart muscle,

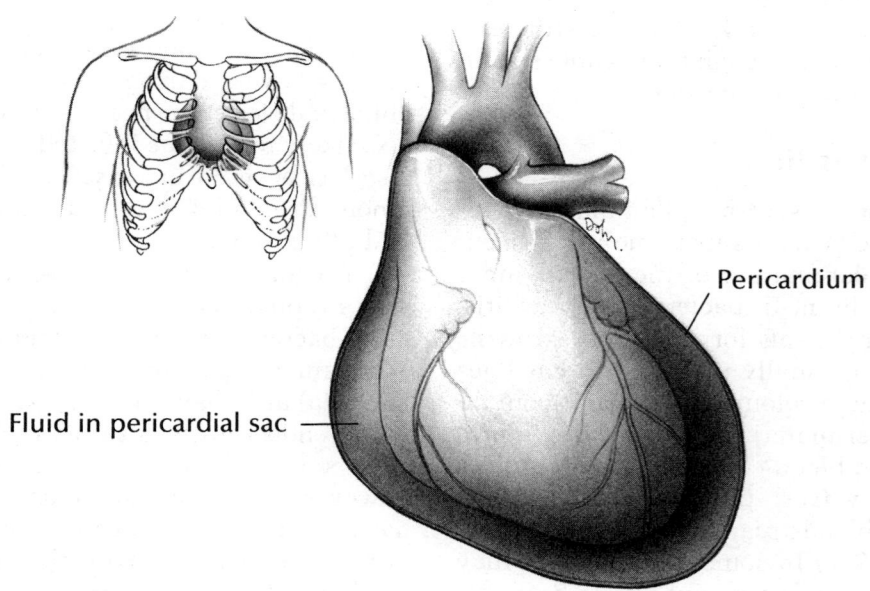

Fluid in pericardial sac —

Pericardium

Figure 19.9. **Pericarditis.**

usually as a result of other generalized infection or inflammatory disease. Most cases, especially those in young people, are caused by viruses. Other causes include bacteria, rickettsiae, parasites, an adverse drug reaction, arsenic or other toxic substances, or other diseases.

The most common symptoms are disturbances in heart rhythm. If there is generalized weakening of the heart muscle, there also may be symptoms of heart failure. Myocarditis should be suspected if these symptoms appear during a widespread viral infection, especially if there is no previous history of heart disease.

Most cases of myocarditis are self-limiting and the heart symptoms will clear up as the overriding infection subsides. In some cases, drugs may be prescribed to treat specific cardiac symptoms, such as arrhythmias or heart failure. Rest to reduce the heart's work load is important, as is avoiding alcohol and other substances that may be toxic or irritating to the heart.

Heart Muscle Disease

There are 2 major categories of cardiomyopathy, or heart muscle disease: primary cardiomyopathy, defined as changes in the structure or function of the heart muscle that cannot be attributed to a specific cause, and secondary, which is associated with disorders of the heart or other organs.

Congestive cardiomyopathy is the more common primary form of heart muscle disease. For unknown reasons, the heart becomes enlarged and weakened and is unable to pump effectively. Symptoms of heart failure develop. Blood flows more slowly through the heart, causing clots to form.

Some of these may adhere to the endocardium (mural thrombi); these may lead to pulmonary embolism, stroke, heart attack, or other circulatory blockages. The drugs used to treat congestive failure may work initially, but with decreasing effectiveness. Selected cases of cardiomyopathy with end stage heart failure can be treated effectively with heart transplantation.

Hypertrophic cardiomyopathy, in contrast to the congestive type, involves an enlargement or overgrowth of the heart muscle, usually that of the left ventricle, but sometimes the right chamber is also involved. In one form of hypertrophic disease, the septum—the wall between the 2 ventricles—becomes enlarged and obstructs the flow of blood from the left ventricle into the aorta. The mitral valve also may be distorted by the thickened septum, leading to mitral insufficiency. The major symptoms are shortness of breath, dizziness or fainting, chest pain, and cardiac arrhythmias. The condition usually can be diagnosed by characteristic physical findings, electrocardiogram, echocardiogram, and, if doubt still exists, cardiac catheterization and angiography. Beta-blocking drugs or calcium-channel blockers usually can control the symptoms and reduce the obstruction. If drug treatment is inadequate, surgery may be indicated.

Patients with cardiomyopathy should avoid cigarette smoking or drugs that may have a toxic effect on the heart. Maintaining normal weight and blood pressure are important because this reduces the heart's work load. The causes of primary cardiomyopathy are unknown, although there appears to be an inherited susceptibility to the hypertrophic subaortic stenosis.

PERIPHERAL BLOOD VESSEL DISEASES

THERE ARE 2 MAJOR categories of blood vessel diseases: peripheral arterial diseases, which are disorders of the vessels carrying blood from the heart to all parts of the body, and peripheral venous diseases, which are disorders of the vessels carrying deoxygenated blood back to the heart.

Arterial disease may result from obstruction, which impedes the flow of blood; from disorders of the arterial muscles, causing them to either constrict or dilate; or from aneurysms, weakened vessel segments that fill with blood and balloon outward. As discussed earlier, the formation of atherosclerotic, or fatty, deposits along the inner arterial walls is the most common arterial disease. When the coro-

nary arteries become seriously obstructed by these deposits, a heart attack or symptoms of coronary disease are an all too common result; when arteries supplying blood to the brain are blocked, a stroke may ensue. Similarly, arteries supplying other parts of the body also may become partially or fully obstructed, leading to a condition referred to as chronic occlusive arterial disease.

Arteriosclerosis Obliterans

When the lower limbs are affected by occlusive arterial disease, the disorder is referred to as arteriosclerosis obliterans. (See figure 19.10.) The typical

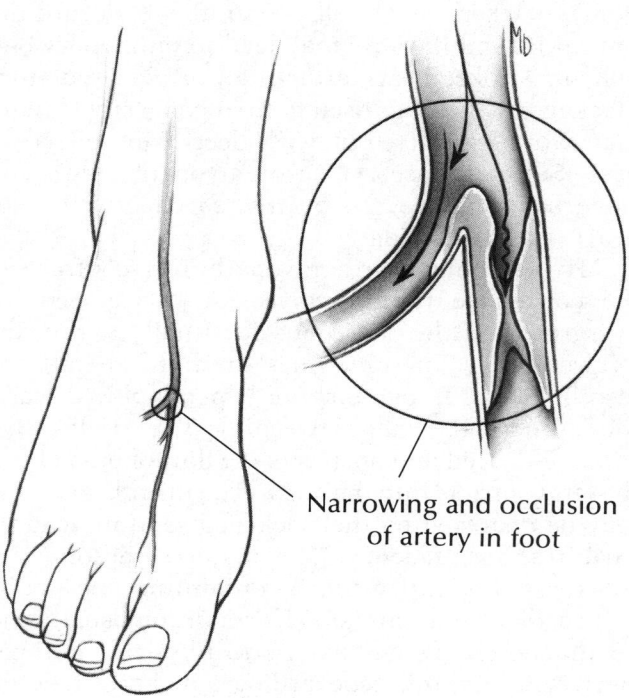

Narrowing and occlusion
of artery in foot

Figure 19.10. **Arteriosclerosis obliterans.**

patient is a man over the age of 50 who smokes, has high blood cholesterol, and who may also have diabetes or high blood sugar. There are, of course, exceptions; people with a family history of early arteriosclerosis, diabetics, hypertensives, or people with very high blood lipids may develop arteriosclerosis obliterans at an earlier age.

In the early stages of arteriosclerosis obliterans, the major arteries carrying blood to the legs and feet become progressively narrowed by fatty deposits. Smaller collateral blood vessels that branch off the major arteries increasingly take over supplying blood to the limb. But these collateral vessels are often inadequate to meet extra demands, such as walking for more than a short distance. Thus, one of the early symptoms of arteriosclerosis obliterans is cramplike pains, aching, or muscle fatigue in the calves that occur during exercise. These symptoms are referred to as intermittent claudication. The site of the pain is determined by which arteries are occluded. Blockage of the lower abdominal aorta or iliac arteries may cause pain in the hips, thighs, and calves. If the femoral artery is involved, the symptoms are likely to be in the calf; blockages in the popliteal, anterior, or posterior tibial arteries will produce symptoms in the lower leg and foot. As the disease progresses, discomfort may occur even when resting.

Eventually, the skin that is chronically deprived of sufficient oxygen and nutrients will begin to break down, resulting in superficial ulcers. These ischemic ulcers are usually small in the beginning and are generally located on the foot, toes, or heel. In severe cases, gangrene may develop, resulting in amputation of the affected part.

Arteriosclerosis obliterans can be diagnosed by feeling the pulses and studying the pattern of circulation to the lower limbs. The sites of occlusion can be located precisely by injecting an opaque contrast substance into the vessel to make it visible on x-ray films. (See Chapter 4 on Diagnostic Tests and Procedures, page 55.)

Treatment depends upon the severity of the disease. If the patient smokes, stopping completely is an essential first step since smoking not only hinders the delivery of oxygen, it also impairs development of collateral circulation. Vasodilating drugs that widen the blood vessels may be prescribed, but very often, these are of little benefit in peripheral vascular disease.

Exercise is an integral part of the overall treatment program. Patients often are instructed to walk or use an exercise bicycle for ½ hour 2 or 3 times per day, resting if pain or discomfort occurs. Studies have found that following a graduated walking program can improve collateral circulation and improve symptoms in some patients.

If the arterial disease is related to other conditions, such as diabetes or high blood pressure, treatment will obviously include controlling these other underlying conditions. (See Chapter 23 on Diabetes and Other Endocrine Disorders, page 481, for a more detailed discussion of the circulatory disorders accompanying this disease.)

Foot care is particularly important for patients with circulatory problems. Wearing comfortable, properly fitted shoes and socks and protecting the feet from injury or infection are crucial. This means inspecting the feet carefully at least once a day and getting prompt medical attention for any problems such as corns, calluses, injuries, or signs of infection. These are trivial, self-healing problems in people with a healthy circulation, but for patients with impaired blood flow to the lower limbs, they can become major infections that threaten the loss of a foot.

If medical measures are not sufficient, surgery may be advised. There are 2 major types of operations: revascularization, in which the blocked arteries are bypassed with either healthy blood vessels taken from elsewhere in the body (usually a vein in the leg) or synthetic material; or endartectomy, which involves opening portions of the diseased artery and removing the atherosclerotic deposits. A newer technique called angioplasty involves inserting a catheter with a balloon tip into the diseased artery and inflating the balloon at the sites of occlusion to flatten the fatty deposits and widen the artery opening.

Buerger's Disease

Buerger's disease, or thromboangiitis obliterans, occurs most often in men who smoke. The disease is characterized by an inflammatory response in the arteries, veins, and nerves, which leads to a thickening of the blood vessel walls caused by infiltration of white cells. The first symptoms are usually a bluish cast to a toe or finger and a feeling of coldness in the affected limb. Since the nerves are also inflamed, there may be severe pain and constriction of the small blood vessels controlled by them. Overactive sympathetic nerves also may cause the feet to sweat excessively, even though they feel cold. As the blood vessels become blocked, intermittent claudication and other symptoms similar to those of chronic obstructive arterial disease often appear. Ischemic ulcers and gangrene are common complications of progressive Buerger's disease.

The cause of Buerger's disease is unknown, but since it occurs mostly in young men who smoke, it is thought to be a reaction to something in cigarettes. The most important treatment is to stop smoking; if this is done early in the disease before serious blood vessel or nerve damage has occurred, the symptoms usually improve markedly. If pain and circulatory problems persist, an operation to sever the sympathetic nerves that cause the small blood vessels to constrict may be performed.

Raynaud's Phenomenon

Raynaud's phenomenon is characterized by spasms of the arteries in the fingers and toes, causing a lack of blood flow to the affected parts. The spasms are usually triggered by cold or, less frequently, emotional factors. The problem is confined to the fingers and toes and, in most cases, can be relieved by rubbing or warming them. In some cases, the circulation may be impaired enough to cause sores or ulcers to form; in a small minority, these may progress to gangrene and amputation.

There are 2 types of Raynaud's phenomenon: primary, in which there is no evidence of other underlying disease; and secondary, in which the condition is complicated by other disorders, such as lupus erythematosus, rheumatoid arthritis, or scleroderma (hardening of the skin). Sometimes Raynaud's may accompany Buerger's disease. It also may be job-related; for example, it sometimes occurs in people who work with vibrating machinery, pianists or typists, or people whose circulation is impaired by excessive exposure to a cold, damp environment.

Primary Raynaud's may be uncomfortable or annoying, but rarely leads to serious problems such as chronic ulcers or gangrene. Avoiding cold is often all that is needed to keep it in check. Treatment of Raynaud's related to other diseases or environmental conditions is managed by controlling the underlying cause.

ANEURYSMS

AN ANEURYSM is a weakened segment of a blood vessel—usually an artery—that fills with blood, causing it to balloon outward. Aneurysms may be caused by a congenital weakness in the vessel wall, high blood pressure, arteriosclerosis, injuries, infection, and other diseases.

Symptoms will depend upon the location of the aneurysm. Common sites include the abdominal aortic artery, the intracranial arteries supplying blood to the brain, and the aorta supplying blood to the chest area. Many aneurysms are asymptomatic and are discovered by feeling or on x-ray films during a routine examination. When symptoms occur, they include a pulsating sensation; there may be pain if it is pressing on internal organs. If the aneurysm is in the chest area, for example, there may be pain in the upper back, difficulty in swallowing, coughing or hoarseness.

A ruptured aneurysm usually produces sudden, severe pain and, depending upon the location and amount of bleeding, shock, loss of consciousness, and death. Emergency surgery is necessary to stop the bleeding. In some cases, the aneurysm may leak blood, causing pain without the rapid deterioration characteristic of a rupture. Also, clots often form in the aneurysm, creating a danger of embolisms in distant organs.

In some cases, the aneurysm may dissect into the wall of an artery, blocking some of its branches. Dissecting aneurysms usually occur in the aortic arch, near its origin as it leaves the heart, or start in the descending thoracic portion of the aorta after it gives off the branches to the head and arms. Symptoms vary according to the part of the body that is being deprived of blood; they are usually sudden and severe and require emergency treatment. Medical treatment is often quite successful and consists of instantly lowering the blood pressure and keeping it at low values.

PERIPHERAL VENOUS DISORDERS

THE VENOUS SYSTEM, which returns the oxygen-depleted blood to the heart via a network of increasingly larger blood vessels, often must work against gravity, especially in returning blood from the lower part of the body. Coordinated muscular contractions and, in medium-sized veins, a system of one-way valves help keep the blood flowing in the right direction. But these vessels are not aided by the pumping action of the heart or the elastic tension that enables the arteries to function. Thus, many of the disorders arising in the venous system are related to a breakdown in their ability to maintain blood flow.

Varicose Veins

Varicose veins are a very common, usually benign, condition that affects one or more of the large veins in the legs. For reasons that are poorly understood, the veins become distended, either because of an inherent weakness in the walls or a malfunction of some of the one-way valves, permitting a backflow and pooling of blood. (See figure 19.11.) Obesity, pregnancy, constriction of the veins with garters or tight clothing, and an inherited tendency are among the contributing causes of varicose veins. Contrary to popular belief, sedentary jobs or jobs that involve standing do not, in themselves, seem to cause varicose veins although they may aggravate a preexisting varicosity.

Most varicose veins do not require medical treatment. In some cases, however, the circulation may be hindered enough to cause swelling of the foot and ankle, discomfort, or a feeling of heaviness. Itching and scaling may develop in the skin in the affected area; if untreated, this may eventually develop into a skin ulcer.

For most people with varicose veins, wearing specially fitted elastic stockings is all that is needed. The stockings should be carefully fitted to the individual, providing the most pressure in the lower-

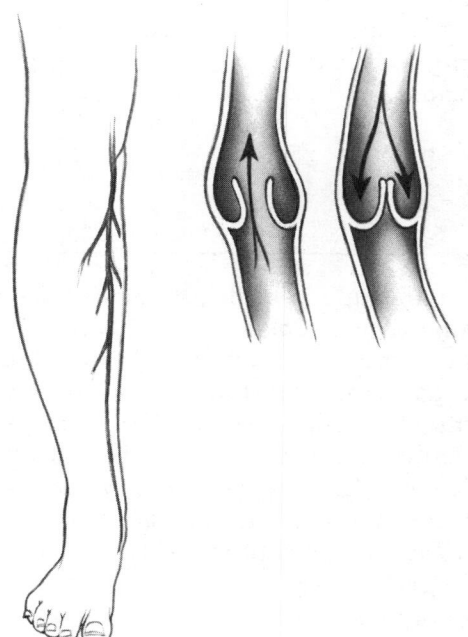

Normal vein with functioning valves
to prevent backflow of blood

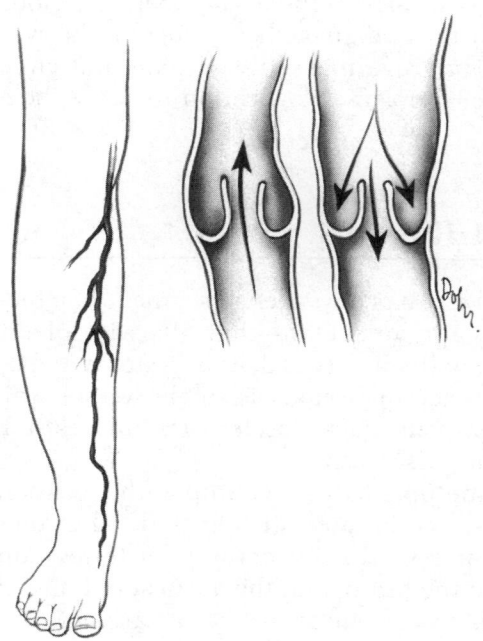

Varicosed vein with faulty valve

Figure 19.11. **Varicose veins.**

most part of the leg. The stockings should be put on when first arising in the morning, preferably before getting out of bed. Exercise, such as walking or cycling, also helps promote better circulation from the lower part of the body. Resting with the legs elevated will help promote circulation; in contrast, sitting with the legs crossed can aggravate the condition.

There are some cases in which removal may be desired. Even when there are no symptoms, some people may be bothered by the cosmetic appearance of the bulging, discolored veins and want them removed. Pain and development of chronic ulcers also may be an indication for removal. In these cases, the varicosities may be removed surgically or, alternatively, injected with a sclerosing agent and wrapped firmly for a few days until the inflammation subsides.

Phlebitis

Phlebitis is a general term used to describe inflammation of a vein. Very often, the inflammation is accompanied by formation of a clot (thrombus), which occludes blood flow through the vein. This condition is known as thrombophlebitis or venous thrombosis. (See figure 19.12.) There are two general types of thrombophlebitis: a superficial condition that is painful but not life-threatening; and deep thrombophlebitis, a potentially serious condition involving an interior blood vessel. About 300,000 Americans are hospitalized each year because of deep thrombophlebitis, the major danger being that a portion of the clot will break away and travel through the venous system to the lungs, forming a pulmonary embolism. If one of the large pulmonary vessels is blocked, death may result.

Superficial phlebitis is most likely to develop in people with varicose veins, patients who are bedridden, or in pregnant women. There may be obvious swelling and a red streak along the involved vein; there also may be heaviness and pain in the leg. The discomfort is usually eased when the leg is elevated and worsened when it is lowered. Deep thrombophlebitis is more likely to cause pain, tenderness, and swelling of the entire limb. Unfortunately, deep thrombophlebitis may occur without producing

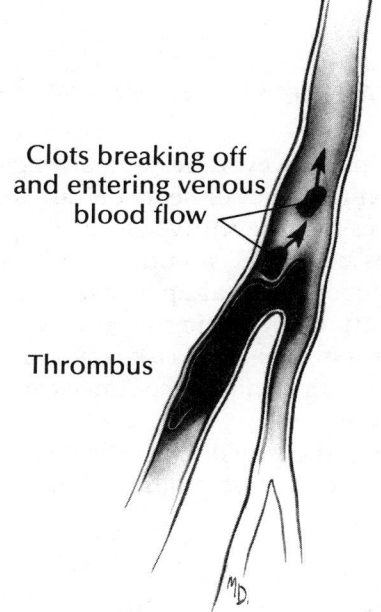

Figure 19.12. **Thrombophlebitis. Inflamed vein occluded by a clot (thrombus) with parts of the thrombus breaking off and entering the venous blood flow. This can lead to a life-threatening pulmonary embolism if the clots lodge in the lungs.**

symptoms until pulmonary embolism signals its presence.

Superficial thrombophlebitis is generally treated with periods of rest with the leg elevated, nonsteroidal anti-inflammatory drugs and, if needed, antibiotics. Warm compresses may ease the inflammation and elastic stockings or bandages may be recommended to reduce the swelling.

Deep thrombophlebitis is usually treated with anticoagulant drugs to reduce the formation of clots and to permit the clots that already have formed to dissolve. Bed rest with the leg elevated may be necessary. Anticoagulant drugs may be prescribed for up to several months to prevent recurrence. If these drugs are used for long-term treatment, patients are cautioned not to take any other medication, especially things like aspirin, that may interact with them. Patients on anticoagulants should have periodic blood tests and also should be alert for any signs of abnormal bleeding, such as bloody or tarry stools, blood in the urine, or excessive bleeding of the gums or small cuts.

People susceptible to phlebitis (or any other circulatory or cardiovascular problem) should not smoke since this promotes clot formation. Moderate physical activity is recommended to maintain muscle tone and promote circulation.

OUTLOOK FOR THE FUTURE

NEW TREATMENTS are constantly being developed that hold great promise for heart patients. Artificial hearts, heart and heart–lung transplants, and new operative procedures, including the use of laser surgery to unclog occluded arteries, are but a few of the advances that are either here or under development.

The real hope, however, lies in learning more about the underlying causes of heart disease and then taking the necessary preventive steps.

As stressed earlier, a number of lifestyle factors have been identified that appear to increase the risk of a heart attack. Adopting a prudent lifestyle that avoids or minimizes these risk factors has long been advocated by physicians, the American Heart Association, and others.

Changing the way one lives is not easy; even so, there have been major modifications in diet, exer-cise, and smoking among men in recent years. There has also been a marked improvement in detection and treatment of hypertension. There is little doubt that these positive changes have contributed to the substantial decline in premature cardiovascular mortality that has occurred over the last decade. Science may eventually give us more cures for the many forms of heart disease; in the meantime, there is considerably more that each one of us can do to help minimize the risk of a heart attack or other cardiovascular disease.

SUMMING UP

CARDIOVASCULAR DISEASE remains our leading cause of death and sickness in this country. A number of risk factors have been identified that appear to increase the likelihood of heart attacks, strokes, and other cardiovascular diseases; there is increasing evidence that reducing as many of these risk factors as possible also lowers the risk of disease and premature death. Many of these are related to lifestyle; for example, not smoking, maintaining ideal weight, engaging in regular physical exercise, consuming a diet low in saturated fats, cholesterol, and total calories, and controlling stress. Others involve controlling other diseases, such as diabetes or high blood pressure, which contribute to additional cardiovascular disorders. Some, such as age or sex, are beyond our control but serve as warning signs to pay attention to minimizing the controllable risk factors. Prompt diagnosis and treatment is a vital element in combating cardiovascular disease; the earlier the treatment, the greater the chances of preventing a life-threatening event such as a heart attack or stroke. And early treatment of heart attacks and strokes often can minimize their damage.

In this chapter, we have summarized the major types of cardiovascular disorders. For additional information on cardiovascular complications related to other diseases, such as diabetes, refer to those specific chapters.

20 Cancer

Robert N. Taub, M.D.

INTRODUCTION

ALTHOUGH WE TEND to speak of cancer as a single disease, it is actually more than 100 different diseases, all characterized by the uncontrolled growth and spread of abnormal cells. There is probably no other disease that is more feared than cancer or surrounded by misconceptions and mystique. A large segment of the general public is unaware of the fact that the outlook for people with cancer has been steadily improving in recent decades, and today, there are more than 5 million Americans who have had cancer. Nearly 3 million of these have survived more than 5 years and are considered cured. Contrast this to the outlook at the beginning of this century, when most people who developed cancer died within a few years. By the 1930s, only 1 out of 5

cancer patients lived 5 or more years after being treated. The 5-year survival had improved to 1 out of 4 during the 1940s, and in the 1960s, it was 1 out of 3. Today, 38 percent, or 3 out of 8 cancer patients survive 5 or more years, and when adjustments are made to account for deaths from other causes, the actual cancer survival rate is now 46 percent. In addition, the American Cancer Society estimates that about 145,000 of those who die of cancer each year could have been saved by earlier diagnosis and treatment.

In all, about 910,000 new cases of cancer are diagnosed yearly in the United States and the annual death toll from the disease is about 462,000 people. (These statistics do not include the 400,000 cases of skin cancer, which has a very low death rate, that occur each year.) Ironically, despite the very real gains in treating cancer and improved survival rates, the total number of cancer deaths has been increasing. In 1930, for example, there were 143 cancer deaths per 100,000 people; today, the figure is nearly 180 per 100,000. This is ironic because the major reason for this is the marked increase in lung cancer—now the leading cancer killer in men, and rising alarmingly among women. Also, since the incidence of cancer increases with age, the growing number of Americans over the age of 65 is reflected in the rising total of cancer deaths.

Many myths persist about cancer. While no one can yet say that cancer has been conquered, or that it is not a serious, life-threatening disease, public attitudes about it often exaggerate its worst aspects. Many people, for example, still believe that cancer is a hopeless disease, despite the fact that nearly half of today's cancer patients can expect to be alive and free of any sign of the disease in 5 years—a statistic that is much more optimistic than the outlook for heart attack patients. Feelings of hopelessness and intense fear often cause many people to delay seeking a diagnosis until the disease has reached an advanced, less treatable stage. Many people also have an unrealistic notion of what is involved in cancer treatment; there is a popular myth that the cure can be worse than the disease, so why bother. Again, this misconception does not take into account the many advances in all forms of cancer therapy—surgical, radiologic, chemotherapeutic, and combinations of all three—that have taken place in recent years. While cancer therapy is often rigorous and can be debilitating and uncomfortable, many people are successfully treated with a minimum disruption of their normal lives. Others may be quite ill during the intensive treatment stage—something that is true for many diseases—and then recover to resume their careers and other pursuits. Pain is another common area of misconception; most people assume that cancer inevitably involves intense pain. While some types of cancer do produce pain, others involve little or no pain and, in any instance, many types of cancer pain can be controlled or minimized. Indeed, there are many diseases such as arthritis and certain neurological disorders that can be more painful than most forms of cancer, yet are not as feared or as firmly associated with pain in the public mind.

Overcoming these common fears and misconceptions regarding cancer is important both for the individual cancer patients and society as a whole. It is important to realize that persistent cancer should be viewed as any other chronic disease—an unfortunate occurrence in anyone's life, but one that for vast numbers of people can be effectively dealt with, often for many years. The more an individual knows about the disease, the more he or she will be able to make informed decisions regarding such factors as where to go for treatment, what to avoid, how to judge whether a particular approach is the most suitable, and what to expect at each step along the way.

CELL BIOLOGY OF CANCER

BEFORE DISCUSSING the specifics of cancer diagnosis and treatment, an understanding of the basics of cell biology related to cancer is important.

Each of the specialized tissues of the body is composed of cells that are the ultimate units that carry out functions, such as metabolism of nutrients, locomotion, transport of oxygen, excretion of waste materials, reproduction, and intelligence. For each tissue, replacement of worn out or injured cells, or increasing the number of certain types of cells in response to environmental stimuli, may be essential. For example, the body is able to increase its production of red blood cells (which carry oxygen) sevenfold or greater in response to bleeding. Another example: Certain white blood cells (granulocytes) are produced much more rapidly when infection is present. Also, removal of portions of the liver or of endocrine organs is often followed by regeneration of the needed cells.

Regulation of this process is complex and may be different for each type of tissue. In general, cells are of 3 types: those that are capable of renewing themselves without limit ("stem cells"); those that are "committed" to dividing a defined number of times, but are limited in their ability for self-renewal; and cells that continue to function, but have become so specialized that they are no longer capable of cell division ("end cells"). Stem cells are most active in those tissues where cells are continually going through cycles of "shedding" and replacement. Examples include the skin, the blood, and the endothelial cells that line the intestinal tract. These are controlled by an internal feedback system that determines the balance between old and dying cells, and the progeny of the stem cells. This control system, and the ability of these cells to obey signals and stop growing, is what distinguishes the behavior of normal tissues from the uncontrolled growth of cancer cells. The cells that are "committed" are those that may grow until the body or organ reaches a specific (usually adult) size or stage and then stop dividing. If the need arises, cells in such tissues are able to resume growing by mobilizing new stem cells, as might be the case if part of the organ is damaged or removed. Liver, kidneys, and certain hormone-producing glands, such as the thyroid, are examples of organs that contain tissues that can generate new cells in response to their injury or removal. Static or "end" cells lose their ability to divide and grow after reaching a certain stage of development. Muscle and nerve cells are examples of tissues composed mainly of static cells. If damaged or diseased, their regenerative capacities are so limited that replacement does not occur.

Cancer cells, unlike other body cells, lack controls to stop the growth process, and therefore continue to grow without restraint. Also, cancer cells may not be "shed" or lost in the body at the same rate as normal cells. They then compete with normal, healthy tissue for nutrients, and also encroach on the space or territory of other cells in the body. Contrary to popular belief, cancer cells do not grow faster than normal cells, but they can persist longer and may divide more times during their long life, causing the tumor to increase in size and displace surrounding normal tissue.

Many cancers are very slow-growing and may be present for many years before causing symptoms. Cancer of the prostate is an example. It is rarely seen in men in their forties, but by age 85 or 90, most men have some form of prostatic cancer, although it is usually localized and not a serious medical problem. Cancers in children tend to grow faster than those in adults; at that stage of life, all body tissues are growing rapidly and the cancer may grow at a similar rate.

CAUSES OF CANCER

THE CAUSES OF CANCER remain unknown. While the final common pathway is loss of control of cell growth, the reason for this loss of control can only be speculated upon. Viral infections, ionizing radiation, chemical substances in the air and diet, and vitamin deficiencies have all been implicated. In the laboratory, some cancers develop in two or more stages, requiring exposure to a chemical "initiator" to start the process, then to a "promoter" to move cancer growth forward. It is generally thought that the defect in cancer cells resides in DNA (deoxyribonucleic acid), the material that controls the genetics and heredity pertaining to each cell. Recently, there have been dramatic advances in our understanding of how DNA may contribute to the cause of cancer. Genes composed of DNA that are responsible for specific hereditary traits in normal cells have been shown to be altered or rearranged in characteristic ways in cancer cells. Links are actively being sought between these genes, termed "oncogenes," and specific cancers.

CANCER DIAGNOSIS

THE IMPORTANCE of timely diagnosis, preferably while the cancer is still in a localized stage, cannot be overemphasized. A cure is always easier to achieve if the cancer has not spread to adjacent tissue or distant organs. Fortunately, modern cancer diagnosis makes it easier to detect early cancer and, in many cases, to determine its type, making more accurate and definitive treatment possible. For example, some types of breast cancer are influenced by estrogenic hormones; this can be determined by a test at the time of diagnosis. Knowing this, the treating physician can tailor the treatment to this particular type of disease and thereby increase the chances of a cure.

Specific cancer symptoms depend upon the type and location of the disease. The classic 7 warning signals listed below are the most common signs of possible cancer; however, these signs should not be construed as a definite indication of cancer, nor does their absence rule out the possibility.

COMMON WARNING SIGNS OF CANCER

- Change in bowel or bladder habits
- A sore that does not heal
- Unusual bleeding or discharge
- Thickening or lump in breast or elsewhere
- Indigestion or difficulty in swallowing
- Obvious change in wart or mole
- Nagging cough or hoarseness

Other possible signs include a persistent, low-grade fever, unusual tiredness, unusual and persistent headaches accompanied by visual or behavior changes and other symptoms, nagging pain in the bones or elsewhere that has no apparent cause, excessive bruising, pallor or other signs of a blood disorder. Loss of appetite and weight loss also may be warning signs of cancer. All of these symptoms are associated with many diseases, however; the diagnosis of cancer is often a process of elimination, and a biopsy—the microscopic examination of tumor or other abnormal cells—is needed before a final diagnosis can be made.

The diagnosis of cancer, or any disease, begins with a complete medical checkup. This starts with a medical history, during which the doctor will ask a number of questions, not only about the current symptoms or illness, but also about past illnesses, family history, and other background information that may prove useful. Since some types of cancers have a strong genetic predisposition, questions about family history may be important. Some types of cancers are linked to environmental factors, such as chemicals, asbestos and other workplace substances. Certain habits, most notably smoking, increase the likelihood of cancer; in fact, the American Cancer Society estimates that smoking accounts for about 30 percent of all cancers, including more than 75 percent of all lung cancer. It is also a major factor in cancers of the mouth, pharynx, larynx, esophagus, pancreas, and bladder.

The history-taking will be followed by a physical examination, with particular attention to the area of suspected cancer. In many instances, special diagnostic tests will be required. (See Chapter 4, Diagnostic Tests and Procedures, page 47, for details of specific tests.) The most common of these are x-ray studies, which may include examinations of particular organs (e.g., mammography of the breasts); CT scans of the head, chest, or body; visual examination of internal organs using fiberoptics or other endoscopes (e.g., colonoscopy of the large intestine); cell (cytology) examinations (e.g., Pap smears of the cervix or bronchial tissues); laboratory analysis of blood, urine, and other body fluids; ultrasonic examination; and determination of the distribution of injected radioactive tracers. Although these tests provide important clues and are useful in eliminating other disorders, a diagnosis of cancer usually must be confirmed by a biopsy. Depending upon the cancer site, this may be done in a doctor's office (skin and certain superficial cancers), outpatient clinic, or hospital.

Modern cancer diagnosis involves a second, very important step called staging. No longer is it considered enough to simply diagnose the presence of cancer; it is also important to determine the extent or stage of the disease. In general, most cancer staging is based on size of the tumor, involvement of nearby lymph glands, and any evidence of metastases or spread to other parts of the body. After the stage of disease is determined, the physician can then best determine the type and extent of treatment. For example, breast cancer that is limited to a small, localized lump without any lymph gland involvement or evidence of metastases can be treated much more conservatively than a cancer that has spread to the lymph glands and perhaps other parts of the body. Similarly, a localized (*in situ*) cancer of the cervix may be treated with laser surgery, freezing, cauterization or simple surgical excision; these treatments may then be followed by a short course of radiation therapy to further ensure that the cancer has been totally eliminated. In contrast, a cancer that involves a larger portion of the cervix and uterus will require a hysterectomy and perhaps additional radiation treatments and cancer chemotherapy.

TYPES OF CANCER TREATMENT

CANCER THERAPY falls into 3 major categories: surgery, radiation, and chemotherapy. Surgery to remove the primary tumor and surrounding tissue remains the major cancer treatment. It is estimated that 220,000 cases of cancer are curable each year with surgery alone. About 90,000 cases per year are curable with radiation therapy alone, and most cases of leukemia, multiple myeloma, and certain other cancers are treated by chemotherapy alone. Increasingly, however, combinations of treatments are being used to produce both a higher cure rate and to minimize the adverse effects of a single therapy. For example, radiation therapy may be administered before surgery to reduce the size of a tumor and to lessen the extent of the operation. Anticancer drugs may be combined with surgery and/or radiation to treat distant spread and to increase the possibility of a cure.

All therapy involves a risk of side effects; in the case of cancer, so much has been said about the adverse effects of treatment that many people fear it almost as much as the disease. While cancer therapy is far from pleasant, many people are surprised to find that it is not as bad as they have been led to believe. New surgical techniques, improved methods of administering radiation, and combinations of anticancer drugs all have reduced the side effects. In addition, treatments for some side effects, such as new drugs to control or minimize nausea and vomiting during cancer chemotherapy, also have been developed. Reconstructive plastic surgery is being used increasingly to minimize the effects and disfigurement of cancer surgery. Breast reconstruction and new approaches to treating bone cancer are two examples of techniques that have been developed to improve the quality of cancer survival without compromising the treatment.

In treating cancer, some harm to normal tissue is inevitable. Most of the side effects associated with both radiation therapy and chemotherapy stem from harm to normal tissue while attempting to destroy the cancer. Loss of hair, for example, is a temporary but often distressing side effect of both radiation therapy and anticancer drugs, both of which damage the hair follicle cells. Recent studies have found that this side effect may be prevented in some cases by applying cold packs to the scalp while the anticancer drugs are being administered. More accurate beaming of the radiation doses also has reduced hair loss and damage to normal tissues. Nausea and vomiting can now be countered by a variety of newer, more effective drugs, including corticosteroids and tranquilizers. Tetrahydrocannabinol, known as THC, the active ingredient in marijuana, has also been used in some cases. Anemia and fatigue, also common side effects of radiation and chemotherapy because of the adverse effects of these treatments on the blood-producing cells in bone marrow, can be reduced by more precise dosing schedules and the use of combined therapies and supplementary blood transfusions when needed.

In addition to the 3 major forms of cancer therapy, a number of still experimental treatments are being studied. For example, a number of researchers are seeking ways to stimulate or manipulate the immune system to fight the cancer. One experimental approach involves giving an agent such as interleukin-2, a hormone that stimulates immune cells (lymphocytes). Interferon, another naturally occurring body chemical, is also being studied for treating certain cancers. Genetic engineering to produce substances called monoclonal antibodies, which are specific antibodies that have been developed by a genetic fusing of several different types of immune cells, also appears promising against certain cancers. It should be emphasized, however, that these treatments are still in the experimental stage; when used, they are generally administered in conjunction with traditional cancer therapies, and very often are reserved for those patients for whom other treatments have not been successful.

As an increasing number of cancer patients survive for longer periods, a number of long-term effects are becoming more apparent. These include infertility, an increased risk of developing other cancers and other adverse effects. Research is constantly attempting to find improved treatments with fewer side effects. It should be emphasized, however, that in weighing the risk of certain death from nontreatment against the potential benefit of a long-term disease-free survival that may or may not produce long-term adverse effects, there is little doubt that for most people the treatment is worthwhile.

WHERE TO GO FOR CANCER THERAPY

ONCE CANCER has been diagnosed, the patient and his or her family face many important and often difficult decisions. People who have been diagnosed as having cancer are understandably afraid. Very often, they feel isolated and confused as to where to turn for help. It is helpful to realize at the outset that there are numerous sources of aid of all kinds, ranging from medical and psychological to financial and rehabilitative. In fact, there are so many avenues of assistance now open to the cancer patient that simply sorting them out and making the right decisions can be a bewildering task. From the beginning, the cancer patient should realize that this is not a time to try to shoulder the burden alone—fears and feelings should be shared with close family members or someone in whom he or she can confide. While all important decisions ultimately rest with the patient, knowing that there are others to whom one can turn for advice and comfort is a major factor in embarking on a course of cancer treatment.

One of the most important early decisions that must be made involves where to go for treatment. The answer depends upon many factors: the nature of the disease, geographic location, economics, and the wishes of the patient. The first inclination is often to get another opinion or to seek out the best authority in this type of cancer. Getting a second opinion is a valid approach if it is sought with the proper motivation, namely, to confirm the diagnosis and stage of disease and to better inform the patient so that he or she may participate in treatment decisions. But there is also a tendency to seek out a doctor who will echo what the patient wants to hear, and there are people who will go to half a dozen physicians in search of an opinion that matches their own. This can be a dangerous course, especially if it leads to an unproved or unorthodox therapy that is of little or no value. Unfortunately, cancer quackery is a multibillion-dollar business and continues to thrive because it caters to desperate people who are acting with less than the best information.

Most cancers are initially detected by regular family physicians. This person may or may not be experienced in cancer treatment, and cancer is one disease that always should be treated by an experienced physician with up-to-date knowledge and appropriate resources. Many cancers can be effectively treated by a family physician working in a community setting. But most cases will also require the expertise of other specialists: A diagnostician, cancer surgeon or specialist, radiation therapist, chemotherapist or hematologist, rehabilitation therapists, psychologists, and financial counselors are but a few of the many specialists that the cancer patient may encounter. With so many people involved in treatment and rehabilitation, it is vital to have a primary physician who can function as an overall advisor or treatment team leader. This role usually falls to the primary-care physician, who may be an internist, family physician, pediatrician, gynecologist, or some other medical specialist who ordinarily fills the role of family doctor. There may be some instances, however, in which this is not an appropriate role for the physician. The patient may want someone who is more experienced in cancer care, or the physician may not feel comfortable in the role. In such instances, another physician to oversee and coordinate the treatment process should be sought.

Finding the right doctor for this role may in-volve interviewing two or three different physicians and carefully checking their qualifications before making a decision. This may seem a time-consuming process, especially at a time when one feels a great urgency to move ahead. But the time and effort should be expended at the outset, before irreversible decisions have been made, because it is much easier to change at the beginning than it is halfway through treatment. Finding the right doctor often appears more difficult than it really is. Very often, a family physician will refer cancer patients to the appropriate doctor(s). A physician's educational and professional training can easily be checked in one of two medical directories: the *Directory of Medical Specialists* and the *American Medical Association Directory*, which are found in most libraries. The state or local county medical society, the state chapter of either the American College of Physicians or the American Academy of Family Physicians also can give background information about doctors or suggest names of specialists. Local chapters of the American Cancer Society or the National Cancer Institute are still other sources of names and information. (See Directory of Resources, page 799.)

Once a primary physician has been selected to coordinate the treatment process, the actual course of treatment can be planned and started. Increasingly, cancer—even complicated or unusual forms of the disease—can be treated locally. The National Cancer Institute coordinates a network of community hospitals throughout the United States where the newest cancer treatments can be administered by local physicians who have computer access to the institute's vast resources. The important consideration is whether or not the treatment physician is experienced in the particular type of cancer involved, and also, whether he or she will tap into the available resources. Cancer treatment is changing at a rapid rate, and many doctors simply may not be aware of the latest advances. Patients should not hesitate to question their doctors about their experience and knowledge—many of the cancer therapies available today did not exist even a decade ago; unless a doctor has made special efforts to keep abreast of new therapies, he may not even know that his approach is out of date.

When to Go to a Specialized Cancer Center

Although most cancers can be treated locally, there are instances in which a patient may want to seek a referral to a specialized cancer center. Some centers have built a particular expertise in treating certain forms of cancer. A large medical center or teaching hospital may be better equipped to handle an unusual or complicated case. There may be some instances in which a patient will go to one institution for the diagnosis and staging, to another for the treatment, and to still another for follow-up and rehabilitation. An important factor is the experience of the physicians involved. It is not necessary to seek out the most famous doctor who specializes in this particular cancer, or the one who treated some noted personality. But it is important to make sure your doctor has had experience in treating other patients with similar problems. Once such a physician

has been found, then the question of where to go usually resolves itself.

The National Cancer Institute has designated 21 Comprehensive Cancer Centers throughout the United States that carry out investigative cancer treatment and research, and a number of other institutions that are Clinical Cancer Centers or Cancer Research Centers. These centers offer a full range of cancer therapies, including those that are still under investigation. An experimental treatment is not indicated, however, if there is an established therapy that has been proved to be safe and effective.

COMPREHENSIVE CANCER CENTERS

The following is a list of institutions that have been designated Comprehensive Cancer Centers by the National Cancer Institute (NCI). This means that they have met NCI criteria for programs in prevention, diagnosis, and treatment of cancer, and are qualified to participate in nationwide clinical studies. The centers also have advanced cancer treatment facilities.

Alabama

Comprehensive Cancer Center,
University of Alabama in Birmingham,
University Station, Birmingham, AL 35294
(205) 934-6612

California

UCLA Jonsson Comprehensive Cancer
Center, UCLA Center for Health
Sciences, 10833 Leconte Avenue,
Los Angeles, CA 90024
(213) 825-5412 (professional),
(213) 824-6017 (public)

University of Southern California,
Comprehensive Cancer Center, 2025
Zonal Avenue, Los Angeles, CA 90033
(213) 244-7626

Connecticut

Yale University Comprehensive Cancer
Center, 333 Cedar Street, New
Haven, CT 06510 (203) 436-3779

District of Columbia

Cancer Research Center, Howard
University Hospital, 2400 Sixth Street
NW, Washington, DC 20059
(202) 636-5700

Vincent T. Lombardi Cancer Research
Center, Georgetown University
Medical Center, 3800 Reservoir Road
NW, Washington, DC 20007
(202) 625-7066

Florida

Comprehensive Cancer Center for the
State of Florida, University of Miami
School of Medicine, Jackson
Memorial Medical Center, 1475 NW
12 Avenue, Miami, FL 33136
(305) 547-7707 ext 203

Illinois

Cancer Center, Health Sciences
Building, 303 East Chicago Avenue,
Chicago, IL 60611
(312) 266-5250

Illinois Cancer Council, 36 South
Wabash Avenue, Suite 700, Chicago
IL 60603
(312) CANCER-1 (Illinois
only), (312) 346-9813 (out-of-state)

Rush-Presbyterian-St. Luke's Medical
Center, 1753 West Congress
Parkway, Chicago, IL 60612
(312) 942-6642

Cancer Research Center, University of
Chicago, 905 East 59th Street,
Chicago, IL 60637
(312) 947-6386

University of Illinois, PO Box 6998,
Chicago, IL 60608
(312) 996-8843, (312) 996-6666

Maryland

The Johns Hopkins Oncology Center,
600 North Wolfe Street, Baltimore,
MD 21205
(301) 955-3636

Massachusetts

Sidney Farber Cancer Institute, 44
Binney Street, Boston, MA 02115
(617) 732-3150, (617) 732-3000

Michigan

Comprehensive Cancer Center of
Metropolitan Detroit, 110 East Warren
Avenue, Detroit, MI 48201
(313) 833-0710 ext 378

Minnesota

Mayo Comprehensive Cancer Center,
200 First Street SW, Rochester, MN
55901
(507) 284-8285

New York

Roswell Park Memorial Institute, 666
Elm Street, Buffalo, NY 14263
(716) 845-4400

Columbia University Comprehensive Cancer Center,
College of Physicians and Surgeons,
701 West 168th Street, New York, NY 10032
(212) 305-6904

Memorial Sloan-Kettering Cancer
Center, 1275 York Avenue, New York, NY 10021
(212) 794-7984

North Carolina

Comprehensive Cancer Center, Duke
University Medical Center, Durham, NC 27710
(919) 684-2282

Ohio

The Ohio State University
Comprehensive Cancer Center, Suite
302, 410 West 12th Avenue,
Columbus, OH 43210
(614) 422-5022

Pennsylvania

Fox Chase/University of Pennsylvania,
Comprehensive Cancer Center, 7701
Burholme Avenue, Philadelphia, PA 19111
(215) 728-2717

Texas

The University of Texas Health System
Cancer Center, M.D. Anderson
Hospital and Tumor Institute, 6723
Bertner Avenue, Houston, TX 77030
(713) 792-3030

Washington

Fred Hutchinson Cancer Research
Center, 1124 Columbia Street,
Seattle, WA 98104
(206) 292-6301

Wisconsin

The University of Wisconsin Clinical
Cancer Center, 600 Highland Avenue,
Madison, WI 53706
(608) 263-8600

Avoiding Cancer Quackery

It seems almost unthinkable that unscrupulous individuals would set out to profit by offering desperate cancer patients treatments that are of little or no value. The sad reality is that cancer quackery is a multibillion-dollar-a-year business and many thousands of unsuspecting cancer patients or their families are misled into turning to useless unproved treatments. Many purveyors of cancer quackery come across as caring, sincere people who are eager to help, especially where the established medical community is failing. Even well-educated, otherwise sophisticated people fall victim to quackery or unproved treatments, many of which may be given at the expense of lifesaving therapy. The laetrile clinics in Mexico, unproved treatments with megavitamins, gadgets that have been rejected by federal or other regulatory agencies or the medical establishment

are but a few examples of the kinds of cancer quackery that continue to thrive. In checking out an unorthodox approach, there are certain warnings that should raise suspicion as to the worthiness of the treatments. Questions that should be resolved include:

- Is there a verifiable track record? Has the treatment been reported in the medical literature or reputable publications? Bona fide experimental treatments are carefully monitored and controlled by various governmental agencies or peer review committees made up of physicians or scientists who are experts in the area under study. Experimental treatments offered outside this framework should be approached with extreme caution or avoided entirely. Ask if the treatment has been described in medical or other publications. Be wary of self-published booklets. Also, if the only reports seem to be limited to sensational popular publications or publicist statements, the legitimacy should be questioned.

- Is the doctor or treatment center situated outside the jurisdiction of regulatory agencies? Clinics located just over the border in Mexico or other places that are beyond the reach of United States authorities always should be viewed with suspicion.

- Can you check the practitioner's background? Are his or her degrees legitimate? Many cancer quacks look and act very professional, and some have medical degrees. Check to see if the doctor is, indeed, a licensed physician—the *American Medical Association Directory*, the *Directory of Medical Specialists*, or the county medical society can provide such information. A large number use the title "doctor" but have degrees in areas that are unrelated to medicine: Doctor of Metaphysics (Ms.D), Doctor of Naturopathy (N.D.). Others claim membership in obscure organizations or purport to be "nutritionists," an area in which there are now large numbers of fringe practitioners.

- Does the treatment sound logical? While many laypeople may lack the medical knowledge to understand fully or judge an approach to treatment, the physician should be able to explain it in such a way that the patient and family can understand it and can follow its logic. Be aware, however, that many quacks are very convincing and can make even the most illogical treatment sound bona fide. A "secret" approach that the practitioner does not want to share with the medical community all too often smacks of quackery.

- Does the practitioner claim that his or her treatment is being boycotted by the medical establishment or that he or she is being persecuted by organized medicine? This is a common ploy among medical quacks, who feed upon their victims' doubts of established medicine. It is important to recognize that there are still many gaps in our medical knowledge, especially concerning cancer. And there are instances in which little can be done to overcome the disease. While it may be comforting to turn to someone who offers a treatment that has been shunned by the medical establishment (very often, the claim is that medical professionals fear a loss of income, prestige, or power) in the hopes that it will work where conventional therapies have failed, the chances of success are nil.

These are but a few of the questions that should be resolved before resorting to unproved therapy. While affiliation is not always the most reliable criterion—many excellent physicians are not part of a teaching institution or medical center and not all physicians who are, are necessarily the best qualified in certain areas—it also is an indication of reliability. If there are any doubts at all regarding the legitimacy of a practitioner or treatment, consult your family physician or local medical society; they at least can check on the background and qualifications.

CANCER EMERGENCIES

HERETOFORE, WE HAVE concentrated on treatment approaches to cancer in situations that are not immediately life-threatening; while promptness may be an important element, it is not the most vital consideration. There are, however, cancer-related emergencies that require immediate treatment. In some instances, these emergency situations may be the first obvious sign of the underlying cancer. Examples include internal bleeding; intestinal obstruction, such as might occur in colon cancer; compression of the spinal cord; metabolic imbalances, such as dangerously high levels of calcium; or encroachment on other vital organs, such as a condition called superior vena cava syndrome, a complication of lung cancer in which the major vein carrying blood to the heart is compressed, resulting in a buildup of body fluid in the upper part of the body. In such emergency situations, resolving the immediate problem takes precedence over treatment of the cancer itself.

DIFFERENT TYPES OF CANCER

AS NOTED EARLIER, there are more than 100 different types of cancer, and most are distinctly different diseases. Not all can be discussed in detail here; instead, the most common types will be briefly reviewed.

Lung Cancer

This is the most common form of cancer seen in the United States, accounting for 144,000 new cases and 125,000 deaths, according to 1985 statistics compiled by the American Cancer Society. At the turn of the century, it was a very rare cancer, but as the popularity of smoking increased among men, so did the incidence of lung cancer. Today, it is the leading cancer killer of both men and women. As of 1985, the lung cancer death rate overtook the mortality for breast cancer in women. Again, the rise is attributed almost entirely to cigarette smoking. Exposure to asbestos and certain other work-place substances also increases the risk, but again, the disease is more common among smokers who are exposed to these substances.

The symptoms of lung cancer include a persistent cough, blood-streaked sputum, chest pain, and recurring pneumonia or bronchitis. Unfortunately, by the time lung cancer is diagnosed it is usually well advanced. The overall cure rate is low, only about 9 percent survive 5 or more years. Since lung cancer grows more slowly in women, they usually live somewhat longer than men, but the overall mortality is about the same.

Early diagnosis of lung cancer is difficult. By the time a lung tumor is visible on x-rays, it often is already well advanced. Even so, yearly chest x-rays are advised for smokers. Periodic Pap smears of the sputum are also advised for smokers. Stopping smoking obviously is the best preventive for lung cancer; those who cannot stop are advised to switch to low-tar, low-nicotine brands. While these cigarettes are not without risk, the lung cancer mortality among people who smoke them is somewhat lower than for those who smoke regular brands. The total number of cigarettes smoked also is important; studies have found that the more a person smokes, the greater the chance of developing cancer.

There are 4 main types of lung cancer, each with its own cellular abnormalities: squamous cell; adenocarcinoma; undifferentiated small cell (oat cell); or undifferentiated large-cell cancer. The large majority are either squamous cell cancer or adenocarcinoma. Of the 4 types of lung cancer only squamous cell has an identified precancerous stage, during which abnormal cells that are not yet cancerous are detected in the sputum. These cancers tend to develop mostly in the central part of the lung; they do not spread to other parts of the body as rapidly as other types of lung cancer and they also are the most treatable by surgery and radiation.

Adenocarcinoma is a type of lung cancer in which the tumor cells form glandular structures (adeno means "gland"). It frequently starts in the smaller bronchi, and it often spreads into the pleural spaces between the lung and chest wall. Surgical removal of the tumor is the major treatment, which may be followed by radiation therapy or chemotherapy. If the cancer has invaded the chest wall, this may require removal of ribs and part of the supporting structures, followed by extensive repair and reconstruction using a meshlike substance or muscle and skin grafts. In selected cases, this extensive surgery is successful in eliminating the disease.

Small, or oat cell lung cancers are so named because of the small, round, or oval shape of the abnormal cells, which resemble oat grains under the microscope. This is the most aggressive of all lung cancers; the spread to distant organs often has taken place by the time it is diagnosed. Surgery usually is not of value in treating oat cell cancer and, until recently, the outlook for most patients with this form of the disease was poor. In recent years, however, regimens using several different anticancer drugs have been developed that have extended the survival of many patients with oat cell lung cancer far beyond the previous 2 months; the median survival is now 2 years, and a number of patients can now expect to reach the 5-year survival point.

Large-cell lung cancer is the rarest form of the disease; in fact, there is some dispute over whether it is a distinct type of cancer or a variation of squamous cell and/or adenocarcinoma. In general, large-cell cancers are similar to adenocarcinoma and the treatment is similar.

Most lung cancer patients also have some degree of heart or pulmonary dysfunction related either to smoking or age, or both. Very often, these coexisting conditions limit the type of cancer therapy that can be undertaken. Or there may be instances in which surgical procedures may be performed in the same operation (for example, lung surgery and a coronary artery bypass). In any event, evaluation of the lung cancer should be combined with a careful examination of the cardiovascular system as a whole as well as pulmonary function and tests for other underlying lung disorders, such as emphysema or chronic obstructive pulmonary disease.

Most lung cancer patients who undergo surgery can expect to be discharged from the hospital in about 7 to 10 days, although full recovery may take several weeks or longer, depending upon the extent of the surgery and general physical condition. Many patients are able to resume normal or near-normal physical activities following lung surgery, but this depends upon how much lung tissue was removed, the condition of the other lung, and their overall physical health. If the cancer recurs after surgery, the outlook has generally been regarded as poor. However, even in this situation newer regimens of combination chemotherapy can reduce the size of the tumor, alleviate pain and other symptoms, and possibly prolong survival of the patient.

Breast Cancer

Breast cancer remains the most common form of the disease among women, accounting for 115,000 new cases each year and about 37,000 deaths. About 1 out of every 11 women will develop breast cancer at some point in their lives. It is most common in women over the age of 50, although about one-third of all cases occur in women 39 to 49 years old, and it may also occur in younger women. The risk seems to be higher among women whose mothers, sisters, and other close relatives have had the disease; women who have never had children; and women who had their first baby after the age of 30. The risk is somewhat higher in women with a history of cystic breast disease. Also, having had cancer in one breast increases the risk of getting it in the second.

The causes of breast cancer are unknown. Recent epidemiological studies suggest that diet may be a factor; women in population groups that consume a diet rich in animal fats appear to have a high incidence of breast cancer. The mechanisms whereby diet may cause breast cancer are unknown, however. There also are some women whose cancers are related to hormone levels; a history of cancer, particularly breast cancer, is often a contraindication for estrogen replacement therapy or the use of oral contraceptives. Contrary to popular myths, breast cancer is not caused by blows, bruises, childbirth, nursing, or sexual relations.

Warning signs include any persistent breast changes, such as a lump that does not go away, a thickening of tissue, dimpling or pulling of the skin, any change in breast shape or contour, nipple discharge, a retraction or scaliness of the nipple, pain, or tenderness.

Early detection and treatment are extremely important in curing breast cancer. About 90 percent of localized breast cancer is now cured, compared with 50 to 70 percent 5-year survival for more advanced disease. All women should practice monthly breast self-examination. (See figures 20.1–20.4.B.) For menstruating women, this should be done in the first half of the menstrual cycle when the breasts are easiest to examine. Postmenopausal women should pick a certain time of the month that is easy to remember and be diligent about the self-examination. In addition, all women over the age of 20 should have their breasts examined at least once every 2 or 3 years by a physician, and annually after the age of 40.

Mammography, special low-dose x-rays of the breast, is now considered one of the most important screening and diagnostic tools for breast cancer. It is recommended for most women who have suspicious breast lumps; it is not only useful in determining the likelihood of cancer in a lump (even though a biopsy is needed for certain diagnosis), it also can detect other suspicious growths that may be too small to feel (palpate). For cancer screening, the American Cancer Society now urges that all women have a baseline mammogram between the ages of 35 and 40, and then on an annual basis, if possible, after 40. Previously, the American Cancer Society had recommended annual mammograms only for women over the age of 50 or for certain high-risk categories. This recommendation was changed after analyzing breast cancer data indicating that large numbers of women in their forties also could benefit from mammography screening.

At one time, there had been concern that the radiation involved in mammography might, in itself, increase the risk of breast cancer. Extensive studies involving thousands of women have not found any increased incidence of breast cancer, leading the American Cancer Society, National Cancer Institute, and other experts to conclude that the potential benefits in early detection outweighed any possible risks. Also, the newer low-dose mammography machines use very little radiation—only a fraction of what would be absorbed in an ordinary chest x-ray, for example.

A number of other tests are being studied to see if they may be useful in detecting early breast cancer. Ultrasound, which uses high-frequency sound waves to map internal structures, is being used experimentally. Thermography, which involves measuring minute variations in heat generated by various body tissues, also has been studied as a breast-cancer screening device. The idea is that cancer generates more heat than normal tissue; therefore, the detection of "hot spots" within the breast would raise a suspicion of cancer. So far, thermography has not proved accurate enough to be very useful in screening for breast cancer. Newer techniques, such as graphic stress telethermometry, which also involves studying heat patterns in breast tissue, may prove more useful, but so far are used only on a limited, experimental basis. Still other avenues of research include blood analysis for certain chemical markers that may indicate breast cancer. While these appear highly promising, more study is needed before they can be recommended for general use.

Definitive diagnosis of breast cancer requires a biopsy. In some cases, this can be performed in a doctor's office in a procedure called a needle biopsy. A local anesthetic is injected into the breast and a hollow needle is inserted into the lump in an attempt to draw off, or aspirate, fluid from it. If fluid can be withdrawn and the lump disappears or col-

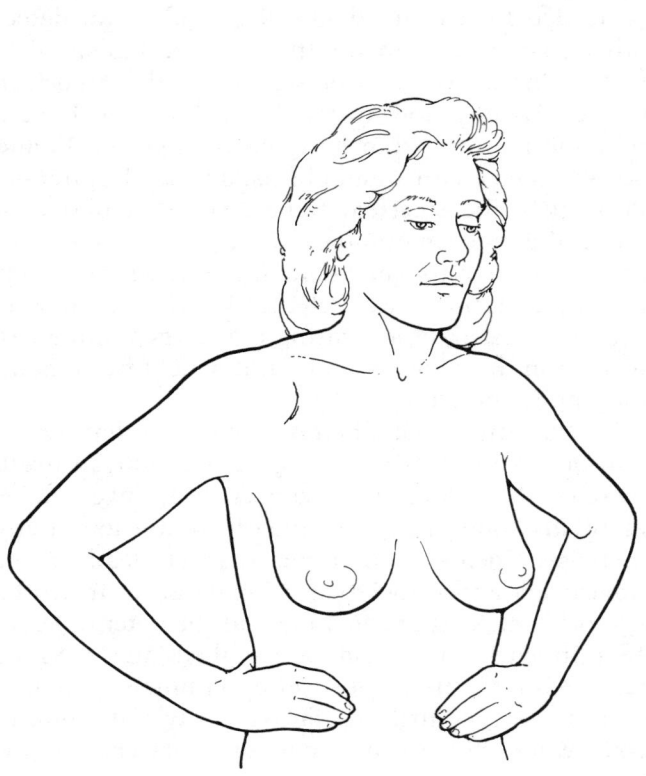

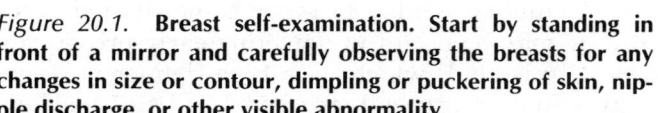

Figure 20.1. **Breast self-examination. Start by standing in front of a mirror and carefully observing the breasts for any changes in size or contour, dimpling or puckering of skin, nipple discharge, or other visible abnormality.**

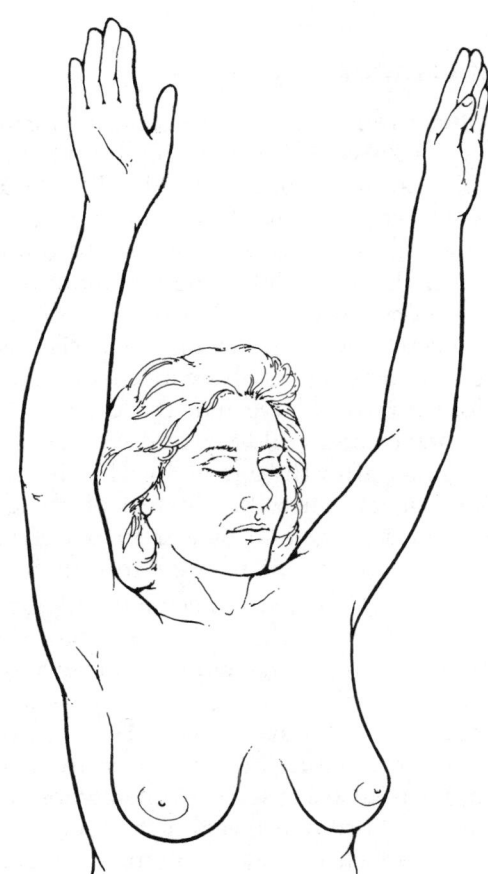

Figure 20.2. **Raise your hands above your head and, again, carefully observe the breasts in a mirror for any changes.**

lapses, it is probably a benign cyst. The fluid is sent to a laboratory for analysis; if it does not contain abnormal cells, no further tests will be required. If the lump does not collapse, or if the laboratory report is positive, or if fluid cannot be obtained, a more extensive biopsy may be required. This usually involves removing the lump and small amounts of surrounding tissues for laboratory analysis. (An estrogen-receptor test to determine whether the tumor is stimulated by estrogen should be done at the same time.) This procedure is done in the hospital, and either a local or general anesthetic will be used. At one time, it was standard to remove the suspicious tissue, send it for an immediate laboratory analysis and if it was cancerous, to do a mastectomy at the same time. Although this practice is still followed by some doctors, it is no longer the most common approach. Since the large majority—upwards of 80 percent—of breast biopsies are negative and also since a number of other considerations may enter into the treatment, a two-step procedure is now favored by many doctors and women. A biopsy is done

in the first procedure; if it is positive, the woman and her physician have an opportunity to discuss the various treatment options to arrive at what seems best for the individual patient. This does mean having two operations with the risks involved, but many women prefer to take this relatively small risk in order to have an informed voice in the treatment decision.

There are several different types of breast cancer, distinguished mostly by their rate of growth and tendency to spread throughout the body. Breast cancer usually spreads through the lymph system. The lymph glands that are affected first are those near the armpit, under the sternum (breastbone), or along the upper spine. In evaluating and staging breast cancer, these lymph nodes also should be examined. Enlarged nodes under the arm, for example, may or may not be cancerous; only a biopsy can determine this.

Treatment of breast cancer remains a subject of continuing medical debate and controversy. Recent large-scale studies have found that in some cases of

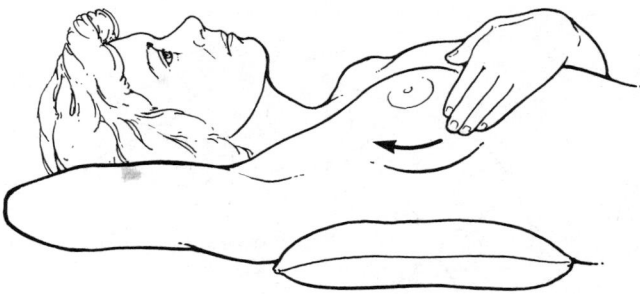

Figure 20.4A. **Lying down with one arm tucked behind your head, again carefully examine the breast for any lumps, thickening, or other changes. Repeat on both sides.**

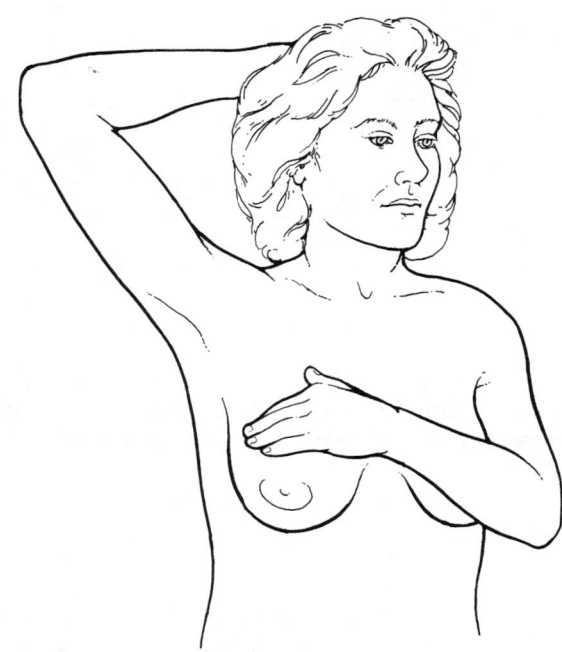

Figure 20.3. **With your arm behind your head, carefully examine the breast for any lumps, thickening, or other changes. Repeat on the other side.**

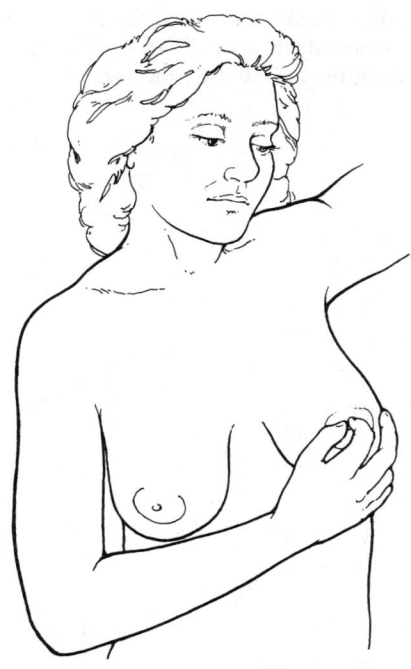

Figure 20.4B. **Finally, squeeze the nipple gently for any discharge.**

small, localized cancers, removal of the lump and surrounding tissue followed by radiation and/or cancer chemotherapy produces a cure rate comparable to the long-time standard treatment by radical or modified radical mastectomy, which involves removal of the breast, varying degrees of underlying tissue, and the lymph glands from the armpit. (See figures 20.5 and 20.6.) Some doctors still feel, however, that the best chance of survival rests with mastectomy. Before undergoing treatment, a woman should understand the extent of her disease and discuss with her doctor the most appropriate treatments. She also should make certain that an estrogen-receptor test is done at the time of the biopsy to determine whether hormone manipulation will increase her chances of survival. Some breast cancers are promoted by the presence of estrogen; in these cases, surgical or chemical removal of the sources of this female sex hormone may be important in preventing a recurrence or spread.

Many breast cancers that are too large or widespread for surgical cure, or that have recurred after surgery, can often be controlled for long periods, sometimes many years, by hormonal therapy and chemotherapy. Often, too, chemotherapy may be given for several months after mastectomy, especially if the lymph glands in the armpit were found to be involved. Such treatment, called "adjuvent" chemotherapy, can decrease the risk of recurrence, especially in premenopausal patients.

Women who undergo a mastectomy now have the prospects of breast reconstruction, which mini-

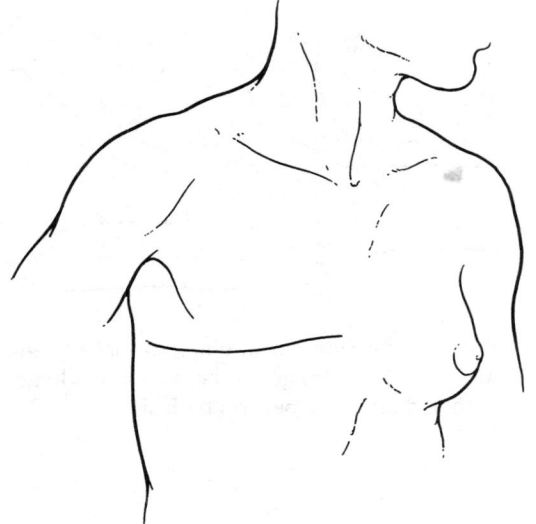

Figure 20.5. **Appearance of the chest wall following a simple or modified radical mastectomy. In a simple mastectomy, only the breast is removed. In a modified radical, the breast and lymph nodes from the armpit are removed.**

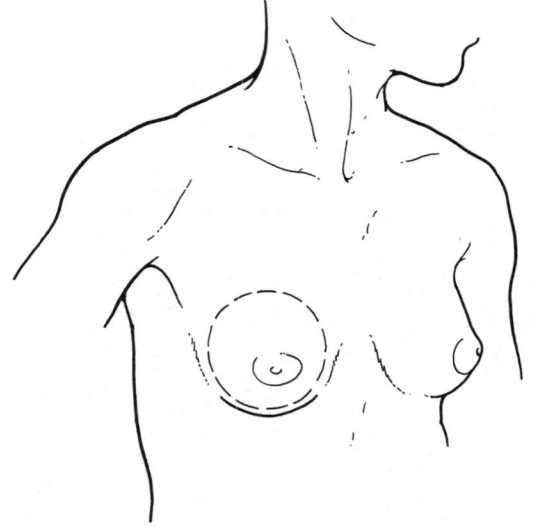

Figure 20.6. **Breast reconstruction following a subcutaneous mastectomy in which the skin and nipple are left intact.**

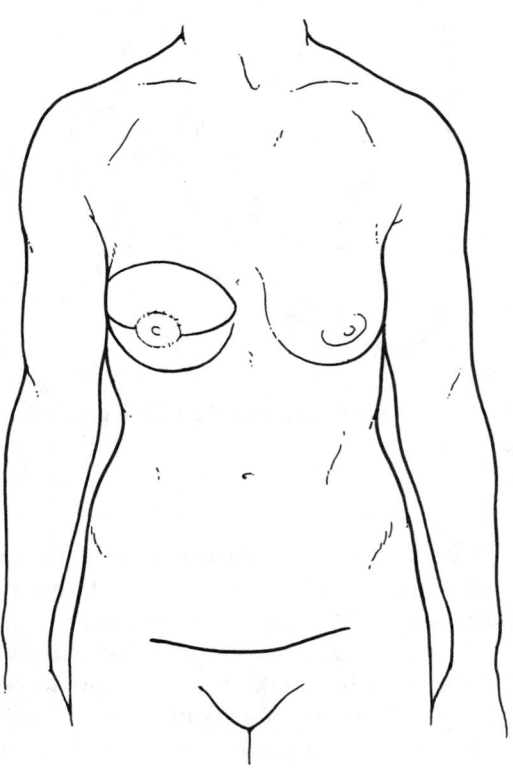

Figure 20.7. **Breast reconstruction following a modified radical mastectomy, using an implant and reconstructed nipple.**

mizes the disfigurement associated with this operation. Timing of the reconstruction depends upon the extent of the cancer and preference of the woman and surgeon. It usually follows the mastectomy and any additional therapy, such as radiation treatments; in some cases it can be done at the time of initial surgery. (See figure 20.7.) But even if reconstruction is not done at the time of the mastectomy, it can be planned then, a step that often makes the later operation easier because of placement of the scar and other steps. Reconstruction usually involves implanting a soft silicon prosthesis, either under the skin or increasingly, under the pectoral (chest) muscle. Alternatively, a breast may be constructed from fatty tissue that is removed from the abdomen or other part of the body and transplanted in the breast area. Improved plastic surgery techniques and wider acceptance of breast reconstruction by cancer surgeons have made this an increasingly important part of treatment and rehabilitation of mastectomy patients.

Volunteer organizations such as Reach to Recovery, which is supported by the American Cancer Society, are also useful in helping women adjust to breast cancer and its treatment. Many YWCA branches and other such groups also sponsor rehabilitation groups and services for women with breast cancer. Reach to Recovery volunteers are available to call on a woman while she is still in the hospital, but the visit must be requested by the patient's physician. (Some women have the mistaken

Figures 20.8 and 20.9. **Simple everyday tasks, such as brushing or combing your hair, can serve as useful postmastectomy exercises. At first, a stack of books or a few pillows may be used to give the arm needed support. Reaching above your head also helps regain use of the arm and prevents swelling. This exercise should be performed standing facing a wall and slowly reaching along the wall until the arms are above the head.**

notion that the volunteer visits are automatic; if such a visit is desired and the doctor has not made the request, the patient can ask that he or she do so.) The volunteer brings a kit containing a breast prosthesis that can be worn home from the hospital, information about exercises to help recover arm function and prevent swelling, and, perhaps most important, the assurance that although breast cancer is a devastating experience, it does not mean the end to femininity, personal relationships, sexual attractiveness, and other aspects that are personally important. (See figures 20.8 and 20.9.) Recognizing that breast cancer can also be difficult for the patient's spouse or other loved ones, there also are volunteer organizations and counseling services for them. (See Directory of Resources, page 799.)

Colon and Rectal Cancers

Cancers of the large bowel, which includes the colon and rectum, are the second most common types, with 126,000 new cases per year and 58,000 deaths.

These cancers are highly curable when detected and treated in an early stage; unfortunately, many people delay seeking medical attention, even when there are symptoms. Warning signs of colon/rectal cancer include a change in bowel habits (e.g., any change in the frequency, shape, or size of stools); blood in the stool, rectal bleeding, lower abdominal pain, a feeling of discomfort, or urge to defecate when there is no need. Difficulty in passing stools or intestinal blockage are signs of an obstructed bowel that may be caused by a tumor.

Colon cancer occurs most commonly in people with a family history of the disease, a personal or family history of polyps in the colon or rectum, and ulcerative colitis and other colon disorders. Recent studies have linked an increase in colon cancer to a diet high in fat and low in fiber. In addition to having any suspicious signs of colon cancer checked promptly by a doctor, the American Cancer Society recommends 3 periodic screening tests to detect bowel cancer in its early stages. A digital rectal examination by a physician is recommended annually after the age of 40. Since many bowel cancers occur in the lower rectum and can be felt by a doctor during this examination, this easy, inexpensive test could save many lives.

Second, the American Cancer Society recommends that a stool guaiac test, an examination of small stool samples smeared on specially treated paper to detect occult (hidden or microscopic) blood in the feces, be performed annually after age 50. This is a test that patients can do at home and then send the stool sample to a laboratory for analysis. Since most bowel cancers give off small amounts of blood in the stool, this test can detect such bleeding at an early stage. (It should be noted that a positive guaiac test is not a definite sign of cancer; many other conditions, including hemorrhoids, result in blood in the stools. However, such bleeding warrants medical investigation.) Finally, the American Cancer Society recommends that proctosigmoidoscopy—the examination of the lower 25 to 35 centimeters of the rectum and colon using a flexible, lighted tube—be performed every 3 to 5 years after the age of 50, providing that examinations in 2 successive years are negative.

A small cancer may be present in the colon for a long period, even years, without producing symptoms. But as the cancer enlarges, characteristic growth patterns will produce different symptoms. A cancer growing on the right side of the colon near the small intestine, for example, tends to grow into the interior of the intestine (the lumen). These cancers may grow large enough to produce right-sided pain. They may also produce slow but frequent internal bleeding, and may cause iron deficiency anemia; in fact, unexplained anemia in an older person is often caused by right-sided colon cancer.

The lumen on the left side of the colon is narrower and cancer developing in this area has a tendency to encircle the intestinal wall. Partial intestinal blockage, marked by increasing constipation, abdominal bloating, or distention, are signs associated with this cancer. Cancers on the left side of the colon also may cause bleeding, but anemia is less common than with growths on the right side.

Rectal cancers are often associated with diarrhea, which may be streaked with blood. The patient also may experience a sense of fullness or urgency, resulting in repeated attempts at a bowel movement. These sensations are caused by the cancerous growth, which is perceived as an incomplete bowel movement. If any of these tests are positive, further examinations of the entire colon may be needed. These may include a barium enema, in which a chalky, opaque substance that can be visualized on x-ray film is infused into the colon, or colonoscopy,

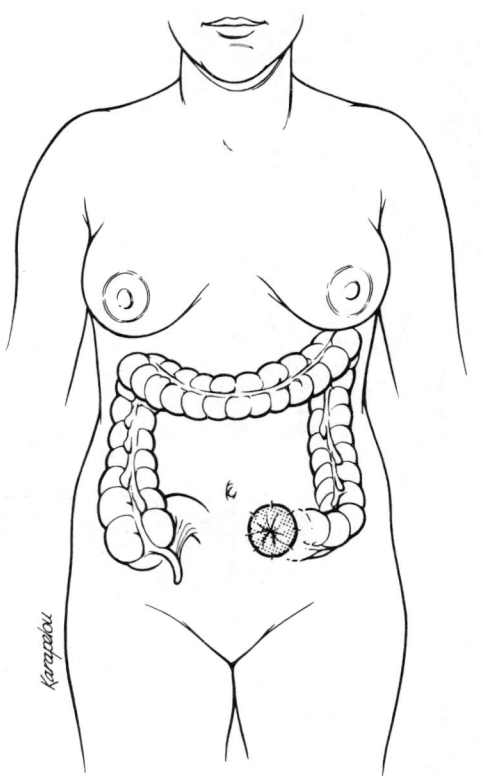

Figure 20.10. **Front view of a stoma opening in the abdominal wall for emptying of colon.**

in which a long, flexible tube is inserted into the colon and the mucous membranes then observed. (See Chapter 4 on Diagnostic Tests and Procedures, page 59.) Small samples of tissue can be removed for biopsy study during a colonoscopy. If the cancer is detected and treated in an early stage, 80 percent of all patients can expect to survive 5 or more years. This falls to less than 30 percent if the cancer has spread beyond the bowel to other parts of the body.

The most common treatment for bowel cancer involves surgical removal of the diseased area. In some cases, this may mean creation of a colostomy —an artificial opening in the abdomen for elimination of body wastes. The colostomy may be temporary to give the colon a chance to heal, or permanent if the lower part of the rectum has to be removed. (See figure 20.10.) Although many people automatically associate colon cancer with a colostomy, only about 10 to 15 percent of all patients actually require a permanent colostomy. And most of these patients find they can lead normal lives once they learn how to manage their colostomies. Embarrassment and fear have kept many people from seeking prompt medical attention for bowel symptoms in the past; fortunately, this is changing as more people have talked openly about their personal experiences with this type of cancer, and also as the general public has become more aware of the importance of early treatment.

Advanced or recurrent bowel cancer is usually not surgically treatable; radiation therapy or chemotherapy then can be used. The results have so far been disappointing, but several promising regimens of combined chemotherapy and radiation are currently being evaluated.

Gastric and Other Gastrointestinal Tract Cancers

In addition to the colon, cancer can affect any of the other gastrointestinal organs. In this country, these other gastrointestinal cancers are not as common as colon cancer, but in some parts of the world they are among the leading cancer killers. For example, gastric or stomach cancer is relatively rare in this country, but in Japan, it is one of the more common malignancies. Similarly, liver cancer is one of the rarer cancers among Americans, but worldwide, it is one of the most common forms of the disease, especially in areas where hepatitis is endemic.

Sites most commonly affected by cancer in the upper gastrointestinal tract are the pancreas, stomach, liver, and esophagus, in that order. According to American Cancer Society estimates for 1984, there were about 25,000 new cases of pancreatic cancer; 24,900 of stomach (gastric) cancer; 13,300 of liver and biliary cancer; and 9,100 of esophageal cancer. Cancer of the small intestine is quite rare, with only about 2,000 cases per year.

Cancer of the Pancreas. The pancreas is a dual-purpose gland that produces digestive juices and enzymes in its larger, exocrine portion, and the hormones insulin and glucagon in its endocrine portion, the "islets of Langerhans," small dots of tissue which are scattered throughout the larger gland. Symptoms of pancreatic cancer include severe upper abdominal pain, often radiating to the back; weight loss; jaundice and severe itching; or gastrointestinal bleeding, depending upon the location of the tumor. Various digestive symptoms, such as nausea and vomiting, loss of appetite, and loose stools, also occur.

The less common endocrine pancreatic cancers may cause a variety of symptoms related to hormonal imbalance: overproduction of insulin resulting in low blood sugar (hypoglycemia), diabetes, and Cushing's syndrome. Very often, tumors in the endocrine pancreas are benign and their removal will reverse the symptoms.

Pancreatic cancer usually occurs during middle-age and is slightly more common in men than women. There has been a marked increase in this type of cancer in the last few decades, but reasons for this are unknown.

The general outlook for pancreatic cancer is poor. By the time most pancreatic cancers are diagnosed, they already have metastasized to the liver or lungs. Treatment consists of radiation therapy, chemotherapy and, if indicated, palliative surgery to relieve symptoms such as duct obstruction. If the cancer is confined to the pancreas, the gland may be surgically removed, followed by chemotherapy and/or radiation therapy. The diabetes resulting from removal of the pancreas is treated with insulin injections; pancreatin is administered to replace the natural pancreatic enzymes needed for digestion.

Stomach Cancer. Worldwide, stomach cancer is quite common, but in the United States its incidence has declined markedly in the last 40 years. Epidemiological studies have implicated diet and other environment factors. For example, stomach cancer can be induced in laboratory animals by feeding them large amounts of nitrates and nitrites, compounds that occur in certain foods and which also are used to make bacon and other cured meats. It is very common in Japan, Chile, and parts of eastern Europe; Japanese coming to this country continue to have a high incidence of stomach cancer, but it is less common among their children and in succeeding generations. The disease occurs twice as often in men as women, and is rarely seen in persons under the age of 40. A family history of stomach cancer also increases the risk, as does gastritis. A stomach ulcer does not seem to be a predisposing factor, although there is a somewhat higher incidence of gastric cancer among patients who had part of the stomach removed some years earlier because of peptic ulcers.

Stomach cancers cause few or minimal symptoms in their early stage. Later symptoms are often similar to those of an ulcer or may include vague feelings of fullness, loss of appetite, indigestion, weight loss, nausea, and anemia. Diagnosis can be made by inserting a gastroscope to view the inside of the stomach and also to remove tissue samples by biopsy. If the cancer is detected while it is still localized, surgical removal can result in cure. Very often, however, the cancer has spread to other organs by the time of diagnosis, which decreases the outlook. In such instances, cancer chemotherapy and/or radiation therapy will be used to reduce the tumor size and extend survival.

Liver Cancer. Cancer originating in the liver is relatively rare in this country, accounting for only

1 or 2 percent of all cancers. (Far more common is involvement of the liver from cancers that have metastasized from other areas of the body.) In contrast, in some parts of the world, most notably in parts of Africa and Asia, it accounts for 20 to 30 percent of all malignancies and, in some areas is the leading cancer killer. In this country, it occurs most often after the age of 40 or 50, and is more common in men than women.

Causes of liver cancer are unknown, but it occurs most often in population groups with a high incidence of viral hepatitis and certain other chronic liver diseases, including cirrhosis. The consumption of mycotoxins, the metabolites of certain fungi (for example, aflatoxins) that frequently contaminate food, particularly in tropical areas, is another possible cause. There is also some speculation that male sex hormones may play a causative role, but this has not been proved.

Liver cancer is often undiagnosed until autopsy because its symptoms are assumed to be a progression of cirrhosis or other preexisting disease. Pain and a swelling in the upper abdomen are among the most common symptoms. Jaundice may occur if the tumor is blocking a bile duct; anemia and abnormal blood chemistry are other signs of possible liver cancer. Liver scans using radioactive tracers can locate tumor sites; a biopsy is required, however, to confirm a diagnosis of liver cancer.

Until recently, liver cancer was almost always fatal within a few months. In recent years, the outlook has improved somewhat for patients with small, localized tumors that can be surgically removed, followed by chemotherapy.

Cancer of the Esophagus. Esophageal cancer is yet another gastrointestinal cancer that is relatively rare in this country, but common in other parts of the world, most notably parts of Asia where it is one of the most common malignancies among men. Even in this country, it occurs most frequently in men.

Difficulty in swallowing (dysphagia) is the most common—and often only—symptom of esophageal cancer. Any swallowing problem, including one that occurs only intermittently, should be checked promptly by a doctor. Other possible symptoms include pain under the breastbone or in the back and neck. If the esophagus is seriously blocked, there may be a spitting up of blood-flecked food. Diagnosis is made by visual examination of the esophagus using a fiberoptic instrument and removal of tissue for biopsy. In a large number of cases involving cancer of the lower portion of the esophagus, the disease actually originates in the stomach.

Early diagnosis and treatment is important because rapid spread to the liver and lungs is common. About half of all esophageal cancers originate in the middle portion of the esophagus, with the remainder about evenly divided between the upper and lower third of the organ. The outlook is best for the lower cancer; poorest for those in the upper portion. Cancers that are localized in the lower third of the organ may be surgically removed; this operation is more difficult or impossible if the cancer involves the upper portion. Radiation and, more recently, chemotherapy are used both following surgery and also to treat inoperable cancers.

Cancer of the Small Intestine. Cancer in the small intestine is quite rare; only about 2,000 cases occur each year. The risk appears to be increased by chronic small intestine disorders such as celiac sprue or regional enteritis. Symptoms include fever, intestinal bleeding, loss of weight and appetite, and abdominal pain. Treatment is surgical removal of the affected area; radiation therapy and chemotherapy also may be administered.

Cancer of the Uterus and Other Female Reproductive Organs

Cancer of the reproductive organs was once one of the most common causes of cancer death among women, but the incidence has declined in recent decades, thanks largely to public education and widespread use of Pap smears to detect early precancerous changes. Now there are an estimated 55,000 new cases each year, and about 10,000 deaths. The most common cancer sites are the cervix, or the mouth of the uterus, and the endometrium, the lining or body of the organ. Endometrial cancer is seen mostly in older women between the ages of 50 and 64. The risk seems to be increased by a history of infertility, failure to ovulate, late menopause, obesity, and prolonged estrogen therapy after menopause. Cervical cancer usually occurs at an earlier age, but is now most common in the lower social and economic groups. The risk also is increased by a history of viral genital infections, such as genital warts and perhaps herpes; becoming sexually active at an early age; and having multiple sex partners.

Ovarian cancer is rarer than uterine cancer; there are about 18,000 new cases diagnosed each year. It also has a higher mortality rate, resulting in more than 11,000 deaths per year. Cancers of the vagina and other female genital organs are very rare. In the last decade, there have been reports of a slight increase in precancerous changes in the vaginal tissue among young women whose mothers took DES, an artificial estrogen that was given until the late

1960s to prevent a miscarriage. These young women should have regular gynecological checkups, but early reports of increases in vaginal cancer have been exaggerated.

Regular Pap smears—the microscopic examination of cells shed from the surface of the cervix—have been instrumental in the dramatic decline in cervical and uterine cancer deaths. By detecting cervical cancer in its early localized or even precancerous stages, treatment with laser, freezing, burning (cauterization), or local excision is usually sufficient to cure the disease. Women who are at risk of developing either cervical or uterine cancer should undergo yearly gynecological examinations. The American Cancer Society recently relaxed this recommendation for women with a history of normal Pap smears and no risk factors, saying they are probably safe having a gynecological examination and Pap smear every 2 or 3 years until age 50 and annually thereafter. The American College of Obstetricians and Gynecologists recommends, however, that women over the age of 20 or 25 who are sexually active undergo an annual pelvic examination, noting that cancer is only one of many conditions that doctors look for.

In discussing uterine cancer, the question of hormone therapy inevitably arises. Studies have found that long-term estrogen replacement following menopause appears to increase the likelihood of endometrial cancer. This prompted a marked decline in the use of postmenopausal hormones in the 1970s. In recent years, the trend has reversed somewhat, largely because of an increase in osteoporosis (thinning of the bones) among older women. There is now a greater tendency to give women who are likely to benefit from estrogen therapy small doses of the hormone with periodic interruption of the estrogen with a second female hormone, progesterone, which causes the shedding of the endometrium similar to what occurs during menstruation. This prevents a buildup of the endometrial tissue, which, in theory, should also prevent endometrial cancer. In addition, women on long-term estrogen therapy are advised to have annual endometrial biopsies and periodic pelvic examinations. In younger women, hormone manipulation does not seem to increase the risk of uterine cancer. Women who use oral contraceptives seem to have a lower incidence of cancer than women who use other forms of birth control.

A precancerous condition (carcinoma *in situ*) affecting the cervix is relatively common among young women, especially those in their thirties who have borne children. It has no specific symptoms and is usually detected by an abnormal Pap smear or sometimes visually during a pelvic examination.

Treatment depends upon the age of the woman, extent of the diseased tissue, and the probability that it may develop into invasive cancer or spread to other parts of the body. If there is no indication of spread, the diseased tissue may be removed by surgery, laser surgery, electrical cautery, or cryosurgery. These treatments are frequently followed by radiation therapy to ensure that any abnormal cells that may have spread to nearby tissues are destroyed. A hysterectomy may be recommended for a postmenopausal woman or a woman who has completed her family.

Treatment of established cervical cancer depends upon the extent of the disease. If it is localized, with no evidence of spread, removal of the cancer and surrounding tissue followed by radiation therapy and perhaps chemotherapy may be sufficient. A hysterectomy may be indicated if a large portion of the cervix is involved or if the disease has spread to the uterus.

Uterine cancer is usually treated surgically with removal of the uterus and, depending upon age and other circumstances, the ovaries and Fallopian tubes also may be removed. If the woman has not yet reached menopause, the ovaries may be left intact. In postmenopausal women, the tendency is to remove them, thus ending the risk of later ovarian cancer. In some cases, radiation may be used instead of or in addition to surgery. If the cancer has spread, chemotherapy may be given. If diagnosed early, the 5-year survival is 81 percent for cervical and 88 percent for endometrial cancer. If treatment is delayed until the cancer has spread to adjacent tissue, however, the 5-year survival drops to 57 percent for cervical cancer and 75 percent of endometrial cancer.

Ovarian cancer is much more difficult to detect in its early stages, largely because there are no obvious early symptoms and no simple screening test. Masses on the ovaries can be felt during a pelvic examination, but these usually are not cancer. Vague abdominal pain is the most common symptom of ovarian cancer, but this often does not occur until the disease is advanced. Treatment is usually with surgery followed by radiation and/or chemotherapy.

Leukemia

Leukemia, or blood cancer, is the most common malignant disease associated with childhood, but in reality, it is much more common among adults. There are about 24,000 new cases of leukemia per year, about 21,500 in adults, and 4,000 to 5,000 in children. The death toll is about 16,000 yearly.

The causes of leukemia are unknown, although there appears to be an increased risk from exposure to radiation, chemicals, and drugs. In addition, viruses akin to some viral diseases seen in mammals have been implicated in the causation of leukemia. Recently, there has been much experimental work that implicates chromosomal changes and unusual genes termed "oncogenes" as responsible for some of the manifestations of leukemia, and for the cell abnormalities underlying the disease.

Children with Down's syndrome (mongolism) and other genetic diseases also may have an increased incidence of leukemia. Also, siblings of patients with acute leukemia have an approximately fivefold increased risk of developing the disease.

Leukemia is characterized by the production of abnormal, immature white cells (leukocytes). As the disease progresses, these abnormal leukocytes eventually interfere with the production and function of the healthy white blood cells (granulocytes) that are important in fighting bacterial, viral, and other infections. Other cells of the blood, including the red blood cells, which transport oxygen, and blood platelets, which are needed for clotting, are also markedly affected.

There are several types of leukemia. In children, the most common type is acute lymphocytic leukemia; in adults, acute granulocytic and chronic lymphatic leukemia are the most common.

Early detection is often difficult because the symptoms are vague and similar to those of other less serious diseases. Acute leukemia often comes on suddenly, especially in children. At first parents may think the child has only a cold, but the symptoms will progress rapidly and include swollen lymph nodes, spleen, and liver, which become enlarged as white blood cells accumulate in these organs. Weight loss, pallor, fatigue, easy bruising, nosebleeds, and other bleeding and repeated infections are symptoms associated with leukemia. As the disease progresses, the fatigue and bleeding problems become more pronounced. Pain, especially in the joints, swollen and bleeding gums, and various skin disorders also occur. In chronic granulocytic leukemia, there may be gradual progressive enlargement of the spleen, often to 10 times normal size or greater. The chronic leukemias may progress slowly for years without apparent symptoms. However, many of these cases eventually transform into a disease resembling acute leukemia, which ends in death in a few months.

The diagnosis of leukemia may be suspected from observing abnormal cells in blood smears under the microscope. However, the blood smear may only show mild abnormalities. The definitive diagnosis can only be made by examining the cells of the bone marrow, which is obtained by aspiration or biopsy. This procedure is usually done in an outpatient setting, and involves insertion of a needle into the marrow cavity within a bone, such as the hip or sternum (breastbone) to remove a sample of cells. With adequate local anesthesia given by injection of novocaine or similar agents, the procedure can be performed with only a small amount of discomfort. (See Chapter 4 on Diagnostic Tests and Procedures, page 54.)

The bone marrow is always abnormal in acute leukemia, and usually contains many cells that are clearly abnormal, or that have failed to differentiate from the more primitive "blast" form into the mature, functioning peripheral blood granulocyte or lymphocyte. On occasion, because immature leukemic blood cells may resemble their normal counterparts, special stains or immunologic tests must be done to confirm the diagnosis.

Treatment of Leukemia. Some of the chronic leukemias can be managed conservatively for many years without the necessity for treatment. Not so with acute leukemia; treatment should be instituted as soon as the diagnosis is made.

At one time, acute leukemia was always thought to be fatal, usually within months. Today, an increasing number of patients are being cured of the disease through chemotherapy. During chemotherapeutic treatment, sufficient amounts of these drugs are given to destroy nearly all cells, both normal and leukemic, which are contained in the patient's bone marrow. Theoretically, leukemic cells are known to divide more slowly than their normal counterparts. Thus, if the entire marrow is ablated, healthy regenerating cells are more likely to repopulate the marrow. It is generally true, however, that unless a complete remission is obtained which lasts 4 or more years, relapse is inevitable. Repeated relapses are associated with progressively poorer responses to therapy and progressively shorter duration of remissions.

The management of leukemia has been greatly improved by the advent of many anticancer drugs known to be effective against the disease. Among these drugs are vincristine, methotrexate, 6-mercaptopurine, cytosine arabinoside, daunorubicin, and L-asparaginase.

Often during the period of treatment, patients must remain in the hospital for 6 weeks or longer because the reduction in their peripheral leukocyte count makes them highly susceptible to infection, and reduction in platelets predisposes them to bleeding. During this time, patients often are maintained with frequent transfusions of red blood cells, or component therapy with transfusions of platelets or granulocytes.

More recently, an experimental procedure known as bone marrow transplantation has been introduced. Patients with refractory disease are treated with high doses of radiation or chemotherapy to remove all cells from the bone marrow; subsequently, bone marrow·cells, removed from a compatible donor, are injected and reseed the marrow with healthy cells. It is still an experimental procedure and is fraught with hazard. Not only is the grafted bone marrow frequently rejected by its new host, but often, the marrow contains immunocompetent cells that can mount a "graft versus host" reaction against the recipient, sometimes with a fatal outcome. However, in selected patients, this experimental therapy has reversed an otherwise hopeless situation.

The outlook for childhood lymphocytic leukemia has been greatly improved; some centers now achieve more than 95 percent complete remission rate, with a 50 to 75 percent long-term survival. The nationwide average ranges from 27 to 35 percent cure. The outlook is not as good for lymphocytic leukemia in adults or for acute granulocytic leukemia. However, even in these diseases, the statistics are improving as new and better drugs are being developed. (See also the Leukemia section in Chapter 26 on Blood Disorders, page 542.)

Urinary Tract Cancers

Urinary tract cancers usually originate in the bladder, accounting for 40,000 cases per year with 10,800 deaths. In addition, there are 19,700 cases of kidney cancer each year, with about 8,900 deaths. Men are affected more often than women, and these cancers are also more common in whites than blacks. The causes are unknown, but the risks seem to be increased by tobacco use, certain industrial chemicals and dyes, saccharin, and cyclamates, chronic urinary tract infections, and hormones.

The most common early warning sign is blood in the urine (hematuria); other symptoms include urinary urgency, painful urination, abdominal or back pain, loss of weight and appetite, persistent fever, and anemia. The diagnosis of bladder cancer usually can be made through direct examination of the bladder using a cystoscope, and biopsy of suspicious tissues. Tests for kidney tumors include an intravenous pyelogram and abdominal CT scanning (see Chapter 4 on Diagnostic Tests and Procedures, page 72). Since kidney and bladder cancer often spread to other organs, additional tests such as chest x-rays and bone scans also may be performed.

Bladder cancer is usually treated surgically. If the cancer is in an early, superficial stage, transurethral electrosection is the favored method. A long, telescopic instrument is passed through the urethra into the bladder, and electrical current is used to cut away the tumor. The procedure can be repeated as often as needed to control regrowth of the tumors. Regular follow-up is advised for life since the recurrence frequency of superficial bladder cancer exceeds 60 percent. Frequently, with recurrent superficial bladder cancers, instillation of chemotherapeutic or immunotherapeutic agents into the bladder will reduce the tendency to recur.

Kidney cancer is best treated by removal of the diseased organ. Since most kidney cancers affect only one organ, the patient can function well with the remaining one. Even if cancer affects both kidneys, the tumors may be removed with the salvage of sufficient functioning kidney tissue. Thus far, there is no good therapy developed for the patient with metastatic kidney cancer. Immunotherapy trials with interferon or tumor vaccines are promising, although still experimental. Chemotherapy and hormone manipulation are rarely successful.

Cancers of the Prostate and Male Reproductive Organs.

Prostatic cancer is the second most common cancer in men, with about 86,000 new cases per year, resulting in 25,500 deaths. Cancers of the testes and other male reproductive organs are relatively rare, with only 5,000 new cases per year and 500 deaths. Prostatic cancer is seen mostly in older men, with an average age of 73 at the time of diagnosis. In contrast, most testicular cancer occurs in young men.

The cause of prostatic cancer is unknown, but predisposing factors include heredity and male sex hormones, and perhaps viral, sexual, and dietary factors. For example, a high-fat diet seems to increase the risk.

Early prostate cancer usually develops without any symptoms. Therefore, a rectal examination, in which a doctor inserts an index finger into the rectum to check the prostate for any unusual swelling or nodules, should be performed yearly after the age of 40. About half of the prostatic nodules detected in a digital examination turn out to be cancerous. Diagnosis is confirmed by a biopsy, performed by inserting a hollow needle into the prostate and withdrawing a tissue sample for microscopic examination.

Difficulty in urination is a common system of more advanced prostatic cancer. The prostate gland, about the size of a walnut, encircles the uppermost part of the urethra, the tube that carries urine from the bladder for elimination. Any prostate enlargement will encroach on the urethra and obstruct the flow of urine. Occasionally, blood in the urine may result, but more often the patient may experience a painful or burning sensation when urinating or a weak or interrupted urinary flow. The presence of these symptoms does not necessarily mean cancer, however. The prostate gland becomes enlarged by benign growth in most older men, and can cause symptoms similar to those of cancer.

Prostate cancer, when not detected early in its course, characteristically spreads to the bony skeleton; the onset of arthritislike pain in the back or legs results. Treatment depends upon the stage of the disease and whether there is evidence of spread to other organs. Patients with localized disease have a good chance of living out their normal life expectancy, with surgical removal of the prostate gland or by irradiation of the tumor. The surgical approach, known as a radical prostatectomy, was previously associated with a high risk for impotence because the pelvic nerves would be severed. Recent surgical advances have been developed, however, that allow radical prostate removal without resultant impairment of sexual function. An alternative treatment involves the insertion of radioactive iodine seeds into the prostate—a procedure that results in impotence 5 percent of the time. External radiotherapy may also be utilized, but fails to control the disease in about one-third of patients and results in impotence in 40 percent of men.

Advanced prostate cancer requires systemic treatment. Since the cancer depends upon male hormone (testosterone) stimulation in 80 percent of cases, hormone therapy is the best palliation. Removal of the testes accomplishes this task. Alternatively, administration of female hormone pills (estrogen) may be employed. Side effects of both of these treatments include impotence and loss of libido. Estrogen pills result in breast swelling, fluid retention, and an increased incidence of cardiovascular disease. A third form of hormone management that spares cardiovascular side effects and avoids castration has now been developed. LHRH analogues can be administered daily to stop testosterone production by the testes without the dangerous side effects of estrogen pills. In recent years, anticancer drugs also have been used to treat advanced prostatic cancer, with good success in slowing the tumor growth rate and relieving symptoms.

Testicular cancer occurs most often between the ages of 15 and 34, and is one of the most common cancers seen in young men. Most testicular cancers arise in the sperm-producing cells. The cause is unknown, but the cancers occur more frequently in young men with a history of undescended or late-descended testes. Early signs include a swelling or lump in the testicle, and sometimes pain or discomfort. All young men should learn testicular self-

examination (see figure 20.11) and practice it each month or so. Any suspicious swelling or hard lump should be checked by a doctor.

Treatment of testicular cancer depends upon the stage of the disease. In all cases, the diseased testicle is removed surgically; if the cancer has spread to other organs, as is often the case, additional surgery, radiation, or chemotherapy may be indicated. When treated in its early, localized stage, nearly 100 percent of all patients can expect to be cured. Even when the disease has spread, effective surgery, radiation, or chemotherapy can result in survival rates of 85 percent. Testicular cancer is, indeed, one of the "success stories" in the development of adjunctive cancer treatment principles.

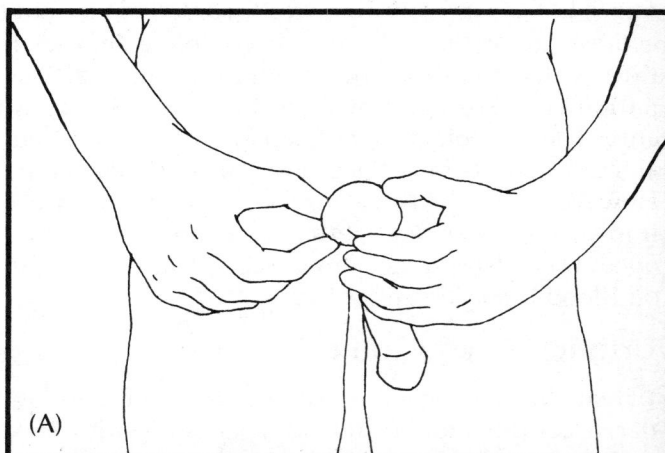

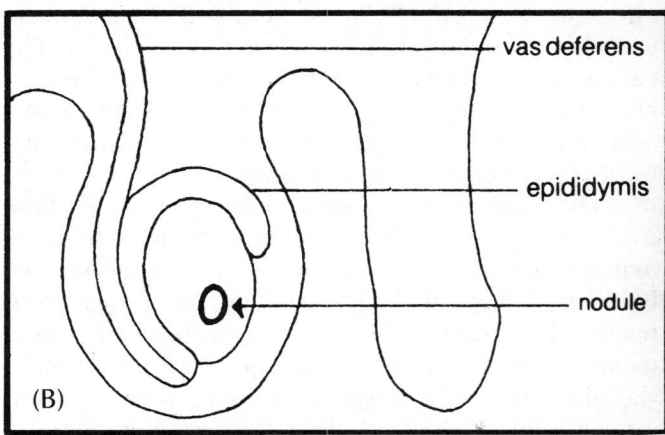

Figures 20.11A and 20.11B. **Testicular self-examination. Support the testicles with your left hand and feel each with your right. You will be able to feel the tubular structure (epididymis) which covers the top, back, and bottom of each testicle. This structure is smooth to the touch. You will be able to gently separate it from the testicle with your finger and examine the testicle itself. If a hard mass is found in either testicle, a doctor should be seen promptly.**

Management of metastatic testicular cancer depends upon the cell type found. Seminoma is sensitive to radiation and small doses of radiation to the abdomen and chest suffice. Cell types other than seminoma (non-seminomatous germ cell cancers) respond to additional surgery with or without chemotherapy. Surgery is employed to remove the involved lymph nodes situated in the back of the abdomen. Residual cancer, if present, responds remarkably well to multiple-drug chemotherapy programs delivered over a 4- to 6-month interval.

Cancer of the penis is very rare in this country, but is relatively common in many parts of the world. Personal hygiene and the widespread practice of male circumcision in the United States are cited as 2 possible explanations for the low incidence of penile cancer. Early symptoms are usually the appearance of painless nodules, warty growth, or ulcer on the penis. Pain and bleeding are later symptoms. Small superficial tumors can be treated by circumcision or radiation therapy; more extensive cancers may require more extensive surgery, including removal of all or part of the penis.

Cancer of the Bone and Connective Tissue

Cancers arising in the bones and connective tissues (sarcomas) are relatively uncommon, with about 2,000 new bone cancers and 1,750 deaths, and 5,000 connective tissue cancers with 1,650 deaths each year. Most of these cancers occur in young people under the age of 20.

Pain and swelling in the bones and joints are the most common symptoms of bone cancer. Osteosarcoma, which originates in the cells that form bone tissue, is seen most commonly in the legs, especially in or near the knees. Eventually, this type of cancer softens the bones, resulting in spontaneous fractures. Ewing's sarcoma, which develops in the bone marrow, usually affects the shafts of long bones. In addition to generalized pain, patients with Ewing's sarcoma may also have fever, weight loss, and feelings of generalized malaise and fatigue. Diagnostic tests include bone scans, x-ray studies, and bone biopsy. Very often, bone cancer has spread to distant organs, especially the lungs, by the time it is diagnosed. Cancer chemotherapy has dramatically improved the ability to treat the spread of bone cancer. The survival rate for treated patients with localized osteosarcoma is over 70 percent. A usual treatment strategy is to remove the cancerous bone surgically and then administer anticancer drugs to treat the cancer that may spread to the lungs and other organs. In some cases, the affected limbs can be salvaged by removing only the tumor and inserting a metal prosthesis to strengthen the bone. This is followed by cancer chemotherapy.

Ewing's sarcoma, which is not as common as osteosarcoma, is usually treated by radiation therapy followed by anticancer drugs. In some cases, surgical removal of the diseased limbs may be performed. A newer approach to treatment involves the use of chemotherapy alone as the initial treatment, followed in 2 or 3 months by radiation and/or surgery.

Soft-tissue sarcoma, which involves the connective tissue of the joints and other skeletal parts, is usually treated by a combination of surgery, radiation, and chemotherapy.

Lymphomas, Hodgkin's Disease, and Multiple Myeloma

About 40,000 of these cancers are diagnosed each year, with non-Hodgkin's lymphomas being the most common. Lymphomas and Hodgkin's disease, which are cancers of the lymph nodes, can strike at any age, but are most common in children and young adults. In contrast, multiple myeloma, a cancer of the bone marrow that affects the blood plasma cells, occurs most often after the age of 50.

Hodgkin's disease often begins as a swelling of a lymph node in the neck area or just under the collarbone. It tends to spread downward, involving the lymph tissue in the chest, and then the spleen and lymph nodes in the abdomen and pelvis. If the spleen is involved, the liver may also be affected. In adults, the disease often spreads to the lungs, bones, and bone marrow. Diagnostic tests include x-ray studies using a CT scanner of the chest and abdominal lymph nodes, the bones, and liver. Ultrasound has also been used. X-ray studies of lymph vessels and nodes injected with special dyes to make them visible on x-rays (lymphangiogram) are occasionally performed. A bone marrow biopsy, as well as biopsy of the lymph tissue, usually is needed to determine the exact diagnosis as well as the extent and stage of the disease. Other types of lymphoma are differentiated by location and type of cancer cells. Burkitt's lymphoma, for example, is characterized by large abdominal masses that result in kidney damage, and by central nervous system involvement. Treatment usually involves radiation therapy to the involved lymph nodes, and depending upon the extent of the disease, chemotherapy. Dramatic improvements have been made in recent years in treating both Hodgkin's disease and other forms of lymphomas. If the disease is diagnosed in an early stage, most patients with these cancers now survive for 5 or more years.

Multiple myeloma, the most common of a group of cancers affecting the plasma cells, differs from many other cancers in that the altered cells continue to function, manufacturing abnormal antibodies and releasing them into the bloodstream. The bones and bone marrow are among the first tissues to be attacked and eroded by the proliferating cells. Thus, bone pain and thinning similar to that of osteoporosis is one of the first symptoms of multiple myeloma. The bone destruction often results in a rise in calcium in the blood and urine, leading to metabolic problems, kidney damage, and other symptoms. As the plasma cells continue to proliferate, the number of white and red blood cells will be reduced, resulting in anemia. Smaller amounts of normal antibodies and gamma-globulin are produced, leading to increased vulnerability to infection, one of the most dangerous problems faced by myeloma patients. While there is still no cure for multiple myeloma, an increasing number of patients are able to live reasonably normal, productive lives while being maintained on various drug regimens. Several anticancer drugs help in suppressing the disease, and antibiotics are given to help prevent infection. Other drugs may be needed to control calcium levels and treat bleeding problems. The average survival is now 4 years, and many patients are living longer. In the past, most myeloma patients died within a few months. (These cancers are also discussed in Chapter 26 on Blood Disorders, page 545.)

Cancers of the Mouth, Pharynx, and Larynx

Cancers of the oral cavity and larynx account for about 6 percent of all cancers; each year, there are about 27,000 new cases of oral cancer, with about 9,000 deaths, and 11,000 cases of larynx cancer, with 3,700 deaths. These cancers are seen most often in men over the age of 45. Most have used tobacco in some form—chewing tobacco or snuff seems to be as dangerous as smoking in causing oral cancers. Heavy alcohol use also increases the risk, especially of cancer of the pharynx.

Cancers of the mouth and pharynx, which encompasses the area behind the nasal cavity, the soft palate, and the back wall of the throat, are easy to see and diagnose. Dentists are often the first to notice the telltale signs of mouth cancer. These include the formation of whitish patches (leukoplakia) or reddened, velvety patches (erythroplakia) on the mucosal lining of the mouth and throat. If untreated, these patches may produce ulcerations, small and painless at first, but painful as they grow larger and begin to invade underlying tissue. These ulcerations may at first be mistaken for canker sores,

which may be very painful but are harmless. Any sore or ulceration that does not heal in 2 weeks should be seen by a doctor.

Treatment of mouth cancer usually involves a combination of therapies that has greatly improved the survival rate in recent years. Depending upon the size and location of the tumor, treatment may begin with surgical removal of the tumor and surrounding tissue, followed by radiation therapy. The radiation may be administered externally or through radioactive needles implanted into the tumor and surrounding tissue. Lymph nodes in the neck are often removed because of the high probability of spread to these areas. Radiation also may be administered to the neck. If the tumor is very large, radiation may be given first to shrink it, followed by surgical removal. Cancer chemotherapy has also been shown to improve survival in many patients, and is now used increasingly in addition to surgery and radiation.

At one time, mouth and neck surgery was quite disfiguring. Now a variety of plastic surgery techniques is changing this, making rehabilitation much easier.

Cancer of the pharynx, in its early stages, may be mistaken for chronic infection of the upper respiratory tract. The eustachian tube, which connects the nasopharynx and the middle ear, may be pressed by the tumor, leading to a feeling of a blocked ear. A mild sore throat, difficulty in swallowing, and slight bleeding from the throat are other common symptoms. Again, if these symptoms persist for more than 2 weeks, they should be checked by a doctor. In some cases, there may be no warning symptoms; instead, a hard lump will develop on one of the neck lymph nodes. This is very often a sign that pharynx cancer has spread to the lymph nodes, and prompt medical attention is required. Diagnosis is by biopsy; if positive, this will be followed by a number of x-ray studies to determine the stage of cancer development.

Radiation is the most common treatment for pharynx cancer. More advanced cancers may require surgical removal in addition to radiation. Chemotherapy also may be administered before radiation or surgery in advanced cancers.

Hoarseness is the major symptom of cancer of the larynx (voice box). A number of other less serious conditions, including infection, allergy, and injuries, can produce hoarseness. But any persistent hoarseness lasting more than a few weeks should be evaluated by a doctor, particularly if the person smokes or uses tobacco. Cancers arising on the vocal cords are not painful until late in the disease, or unless adjacent tissues are involved. By that time, there also may be a chronic cough and difficulty in breathing.

Diagnosis is confirmed by direct examination

through a laryngoscope and biopsy. If the cancer is confined to the vocal cords, the large majority of cases (more than 85 percent) can be treated successfully with radiation therapy. Some early cancers are also treated by limited surgery using laser beams. These treatments remove the cancer yet preserve the ability to speak normally. In more advanced cancer, or disease that persists despite radiation therapy, removal of the larynx (laryngectomy) is usually necessary. While this operation usually cures the cancer, it does result in the loss of normal speaking. Other means of speaking can be taught by speech therapists. These include using a variety of electronic or vibrating aids to produce speech, or learning to trap air in the throat or esophagus and using the tongue, lips, and cheeks to produce sounds.

Thyroid Cancer

Thyroid cancer is the most common of the malignancies affecting the endocrine glands (with the exception of the ovaries). About 10,000 new cases are diagnosed each year. The outlook is generally good; about 1,100 deaths each year are caused by this type of cancer and most people with thyroid cancer can expect to be cured or to have the disease adequately controlled.

The most common sign of thyroid cancer is a painless lump in the neck. The lump differs from the more common goiters and benign nodules in several respects: It is usually solitary and will have a hard consistency. Scanning tests using radioactive iodine will not show an increased uptake of the substance. Recent and rapid enlargement and childhood x-ray treatments to the area also increase the suspicion of thyroid cancer.

Thyroid cancer occurs more commonly in women than men and is seen most often in young adults. Most thyroid cancers grow relatively slowly and although spread to distant organs occurs, this is not usual, at least in the early stage of the disease.

Treatment depends upon the type and location of the cancer. The most common type is papillary carcinoma, in which the cells form short cordlike structures interspersed with abnormal cancerous thyroid gland tissue (follicles). This tumor often remains localized for years, then may spread to lymph nodes in the neck, and then to the lungs. If the tumor is small and confined to a single thyroid lobe, treatment usually involves removal of the affected lobe. Since this type of cancer is highly dependent on thyroid-stimulating hormone (TSH) and often develops in an underfunctioning lobe, treatment also may involve giving thyroid hormone to suppress its growth. Larger papillary tumors require more extensive surgery, often removal of the entire thyroid gland and destruction of any remaining tissue with radioactive iodine. This is followed by lifetime replacement of thyroid hormone.

Medullary (solid) thyroid cancer, in which the cells do not form recognizable thyroidlike structures, tends to run in families and often is associated with various hormonal disorders. Treatment involves removal of the entire thyroid; if the parathyroid glands are also diseased, they too will be removed. In some cases the adrenal glands—small, hormone-producing glands located atop each kidney—also will develop tumors called pheochromocytomas. If this is the case, they should be removed before the thyroid surgery to prevent a hypertensive crisis during the operation. Since there is an inherited tendency to develop medullary thyroid cancer, other family members should be screened periodically.

Follicular thyroid cancer is more common in older people, especially women who have had earlier radiation therapy of the neck. The cells of this tissue form follicles resembling those on the normal thyroid. Nevertheless, this type of thyroid cancer spreads to other organs more frequently than other types. Treatment is similar to that of papillary cancer; any metastases may be treated with radioactive iodine or chemotherapy.

Brain Cancer

Brain cancer can occur at any age, but is most common among young and middle-aged adults. There are about 13,000 cases of brain cancer diagnosed each year and about 10,400 deaths. The most common type of brain cancer is a glioma, a tumor that arises in the supportive tissue of the brain. Other frequently involved sites are the pituitary, an endocrine gland that lies at the base of the brain; the meninges, the membranes surrounding and covering the brain and spinal cord; and the cranial nerves.

The most common signs of brain tumor are related to increased intracranial pressure, either from the tumor mass or from a buildup of fluid. Symptoms include headache, nausea, visual changes, convulsions, and mental symptoms, such as lethargy, personality changes, psychotic episodes, and impaired mental function. The tumor usually can be detected with CT scans or other brain studies. Other tests may be performed to determine if there are cancers elsewhere in the body, since the brain is a frequent target of metastasis.

In recent years, there have been considerable advances in the treatment of brain cancer. In those tumors that are localized and do not extend into a vital part of the brain, surgical removal of the cancer (or as much of it as possible) followed by radiation therapy and/or chemotherapy is resulting in prolonged, relatively symptom-free survival for a growing number of patients. Localized tumors that do not infiltrate the brain may be cured by surgical removal. In inoperable cancers, radiation therapy to reduce the size of the tumor and chemotherapy may halt the progress of the disease for variable lengths of time. Drugs to reduce brain swelling and edema also may be given to relieve symptoms.

Cancers confined to the spinal cord are much less common than brain tumors, and they usually involve the meninges. The most common early symptoms are pain from compression of the nerve roots; sensory loss, muscular weakness and wasting, and paralysis are symptoms of more advanced disease. X-rays may show bone damage and distortion of the spine. Tumors on the surface of the spinal cord may be removed surgically, depending upon their location and degree of damage. Inoperable cancers are treated with radiation therapy.

Eye Cancer in Children

Retinoblastoma is a congenital cancer of the retina that usually becomes apparent before the age of 2 or 3. The disease is rare, and 80 percent of all cases can be cured if diagnosed and treated early. In about one-third of the cases, both eyes are affected. A large percentage of cases are hereditary; the disease also occurs more frequently in children with certain chromosomal abnormalities.

Early symptoms include crossed eyes (strabismus) or a yellowish or white spot in the pupil. The tumors often can be seen by careful examination of the eye; a CT scan also may detect small, calcified tumors in other parts of the eye. Treatment depends upon the extent of the cancer. If only one eye is involved, it may be removed along with as much of the optic nerve as possible. The other eye will then be examined periodically. If both eyes are involved, the one that has the more extensive disease often will be removed and the other treated with laser surgery, freezing (cryotherapy), radiation, and chemotherapy in an effort to eliminate the cancer and yet preserve as much eyesight as possible. Following treatment, the child should undergo periodic examination to determine if the cancer has recurred, either in the

other eye or distant parts of the body. Since retinoblastoma often has a hereditary pattern, siblings also should be examined periodically.

Skin Cancer

Skin cancer is the most common of all human malignancies, with more than 400,000 new cases diagnosed each year. But since almost all non-melanoma skin cancers can be easily cured, they usually are not included in cancer statistics. Most skin cancers are caused by overexposure to the sun, and are seen most often in whites with fair skin and blue eyes. Skin cancer is most common in the south and southwest, where the sun is strong and people spend more time outdoors with little protective clothing. Skin cancer usually can be treated easily with topical anticancer drugs or surgical removal.

The most dangerous type of skin cancer is malignant melanoma, which affects about 22,000 people a year and results in 7,400 deaths. This type of cancer starts in the melanocytes, the cells that produce pigment. It occurs most often in fair-skinned whites who spend a good deal of time in the sun. There also seems to be a hereditary predisposition to developing melanoma; some families may have several members with numerous moles in the skin, each of which carries a risk of malignant melanoma.

Malignant melanomas can start in any skin area that contains pigment-producing cells, but body moles are common sites. Any mole that bleeds, changes in size or color, or forms nearby spots of pigment should be checked. Also, any new mole that appears after the age of 30, or that is tender or itches should be seen promptly by a doctor, preferably a dermatologist.

Some superficial melanomas spread mainly along the skin surface. In contrast, a more aggressive type, termed nodular melanoma, is raised and lumpy, and tends to invade the underlying tissue earlier in the course of the disease than the superficial types. Melanomas are treated by complete surgical removal of the cancer and surrounding tissues. The overall 5-year survival is now 68 percent, a marked improvement over 20 years ago, thanks largely to early detection and greater awareness of the disease.

LIVING WITH CANCER

A DIAGNOSIS OF CANCER almost always produces intense fear and feelings of hopelessness—a response that is normal for any life-threatening illness. Fortunately, public attitudes toward cancer are changing,

making it easier for the cancer patient to share his or her fears and concerns with others. Until recently, however, even the word cancer was avoided as if the disease were a punishment or source of shame.

Attitude and emotional strength are important elements in successfully fighting cancer. Numerous studies have found that the patients who respond best to treatment are those who can cope with the stress of cancer and assume responsibility for seeking treatment and following up. A good psychological outlook seems to contribute to a better medical prognosis, although it is not fully understood why this should be. Doctors stress the importance of making sure that even during intense treatment, each day also provides some source of pleasure and diversion. Family and friends are vital in helping provide this, but much also depends upon the patient. The ability to at least temporarily lose oneself in music, books, hobbies, or some other source of pleasure and interest is as important as following treatment protocols.

A willingness to share worries and fears of the future may also be an important element in living with cancer. Many people are reluctant to discuss the disease and its prognosis for fear of worrying others or being a burden. In reality, the silence can be a burden for both the patient and loved ones. It has only been in recent years that death and dying have been discussed openly; heretofore, even doctors avoided the subject with the mistaken notion that a facade of good cheer and silence would somehow spare the patient and make death easier. We now recognize that this is not true, that many people need to discuss their feelings about death and to be surrounded by caring loved ones when that time comes.

CANCER REHABILITATION

AS EMPHASIZED EARLIER in this chapter, up to half of all cancer patients can now expect to be alive and free of the disease 5 or more years after treatment. But many cancer patients never feel they are truly "free" of the disease. There may be the constant physical reminders and lingering fears of recurrence. Treatment often alters a body function, requiring learning new ways of speaking, walking, eliminating body wastes, and so on. Rehabilitation is an essential part of modern cancer therapy and, in most cases, should be planned as part of the overall treatment.

The first large-scale cancer rehabilitation program was started in 1952 with the founding of the International Association of Laryngectomees. This organization is dedicated to helping people who have had their larynx removed learn new ways of speaking. Another well-known rehabilitation program, Reach to Recovery, was also founded in the 1950s to help women cope with a mastectomy to treat breast cancer. Today, following the lead of these two organizations, there are now programs for ostomy patients, amputees, and the terminally ill. (See Directory of Resources, page 804.) These groups are largely made up of volunteers who have experienced the disease. They operate on the premise that someone who has already been through the diagnosis and treatment is best equipped to help new

patients cope. In addition to volunteer efforts, legislation has been passed to promote cancer rehabilitation and to prevent job discrimination against former cancer patients. The goal of all cancer rehabilitation programs is to return patients to a point where they can function to the best of their abilities. Some cancer patients are unable to return to their former jobs, but many can. Very often, however, there is a reluctance to hire former cancer patients and other employers are reluctant to take back an employee who has undergone cancer treatment. Hostility of fellow workers, diminished fringe benefits, including health insurance, and exclusion from promotions are among the problems reported by recovered cancer patients returning to work. Employers often assume that cancer patients will continue to require time off, even though studies have found that recovered cancer patients often have better work records than those who have not had the disease.

Older people are not the only ones who encounter problems in returning to normal life; youngsters who have undergone cancer treatment also find it difficult to return to school or normal activities. Counselling both the patient and teachers (or employers and co-workers in the case of adults) can help overcome many of the misconceptions and rehabilitation problems.

PAIN

MOST PEOPLE automatically associate cancer with pain, even though there are some types of cancer that cause little or no discomfort. Others may involve a moderate amount of pain, but less intense than the pain experienced in some forms of arthritis, certain nerve disorders, and other less-feared diseases. This moderate cancer pain usually can be controlled by aspirin, acetaminophen, or other non-narcotic painkillers. About a third of patients undergoing active treatment experience severe pain; the problem is more pronounced in people with advanced, untreatable cancers. About 60 to 80 percent of these patients have severe pain, at least part of the time.

Drugs remain the major avenue of pain relief for patients suffering from chronic cancer pain. A large number of nonnarcotic medications produce substantial relief; many patients, however, require stronger medications. During the past decade, newer guidelines have been emerging regarding the use of narcotic medications. Because these drugs are addictive, in the past, some physicians had opposed their use for anything other than short-term indications, such as immediately following surgery. It is now recognized by many oncologists that these drugs, properly used, can ease the pain of cancer for months or years while maintaining the patient in a lucid, functional state. Often, medications given at strictly prescribed intervals, combined with antidepressant drugs and mild sedatives, have been very effective in producing a high degree of pain control with only modest impairment of functioning.

For advanced end-stage cancer pain, physicians now feel strongly that morphine, methadone, and similar opiate derivatives should not be withheld.

There are some alternative methods of pain control that also may be considered for cancer patients. These include:

- *Electrostimulation.* This involves implanting electrodes at certain places in the body and then using an external transmitter to stimulate the electrodes and prevent pain messages from being delivered to the brain. Alternatively, the stimulation may be applied to peripheral nerves. There are major disadvantages to these approaches: Although the techniques are initially effective in most patients, this tends to wear off in time. The treatment also tends to be costly and require close supervision by trained personnel.

- *Neurosurgery.* There are a number of operations in which pain can be relieved by selective destruction of sensory nerves. So far, these operations are experimental and not widely available.

- *Behavior modification.* These include relaxation training, biofeedback, hypnosis, and cognitive control. In recent years, behavior modification as a means of pain control, especially in the milder cases, has attracted attention in many centers.

THE HOSPICE MOVEMENT

No DISCUSSION OF CANCER is complete without recognizing that death remains an outcome in more than half of all cases. Increasingly, death has become a topic of open discussion, not only among health professionals but also among patients and their families. The resurgence of the concept of "death with dignity" and all its attendant ethical and moral considerations reflects our changing attitudes toward death and dying.

Although all of us must eventually die, modern medical technology has made it possible to prolong life far beyond what was formerly possible. The employment of this technology, which can be enormously expensive, has led many to question when and how it should be used. Should heroic methods be used to prolong the life of patients for whom death is inevitable and who are no longer capable of enjoying being alive? Many of us would respond "no" (especially if the prospects of death are still remote), while others strongly feel that life is so precious that it should be maintained at any cost, regardless of the condition or ultimate outcome. These are difficult questions for which there are no easy answers.

The hospice movement attempts to resolve the conflict for families facing death of a loved one. A hospice is defined as a place for patients who can no longer be treated. The goal is to provide comfort and an atmosphere that makes death easier. The hospice may be situated in a special section of a hospital, a separate facility, or even in the patient's home, with medical personnel and help available as needed. The number of hospices in this country is growing and recent changes in Medicare laws may increase the movement by providing some funding for hospice and at-home care. (For a more complete discussion, see page 22.)

CANCER PREVENTION

MOST CANCERS in this country are believed to be related to lifestyle or factors in the environment, and large numbers undoubtedly could be prevented by judicious changes in personal habits or environmental conditions. In addition, ongoing research is constantly revealing new facts about the possible causes of cancer; once we understand the biological processes involved, the potential for preventing cancer will increase even more. Until that time, however, the best means of reducing the cancer toll is to avoid unnecessary exposure to known cancer-causing agents. Clearly, this involves free choice, a factor that makes prevention of any kind difficult.

According to the latest Surgeon General's Report, 1 out of every 4 cancer deaths in the United States today can be directly linked to tobacco use. Simply stopping smoking could conceivably save more than 100,000 lives per year that are now lost to cancer. These facts have been well-known since the first Surgeon General's Report in 1964, yet 50 million Americans persist in smoking. Indeed, when the number of cardiovascular deaths attributed to smoking—about 225,000 a year—are added to the cancer toll, it is clear that tobacco use is by far the leading cause of preventable death in this country. Thus, the most effective step anyone can take in preventing premature death is to stop smoking, or better still, never start smoking. (See How to Stop Smoking, Chapter 18, page 345.)

The role of diet in cancer has come under increasing study in recent years. It appears that the high-fat diet consumed by the majority of Americans may possibly contribute to the development of colon and breast cancers, and possibly cancers of the prostate and uterus as well. A number of epidemiological studies have found increased incidences of these cancers among people who have a high-fat diet, and a correspondingly low incidence among vegetarians and others who consume a low-fat diet. The mechanisms are unknown, but it is theorized that the consumption of fat stimulates an increased production of bile acids, some of which have been found to promote cancer. In addition, fats increase the production of certain hormones; people who are overweight tend to have a higher incidence of hormone-related cancers, particularly cancers of the prostate and uterus. This also may be a factor in the type of breast cancer that is estrogen-sensitive. Animal fat also acts as a storage place for many fat-soluble chemicals, some of which may be cancer-causing. PCBs and dioxin are two examples that have been in the news of late. These chemicals may be consumed in a high-fat diet; they also are stored in body fat. Some researchers believe that prolonged exposure to them increases the risk of cancer.

There has been considerable controversy in recent years over the possible role of food additives in causing cancer. Some food dyes, for example, have been banned from food because they have been shown to cause cancer in animals. The same is true of some artificial sweeteners, such as cyclamates. Cured meats, which contain nitrites and nitrates, are suspected of increasing the risk of cancer, and many authorities urge that their consumption be minimized.

On the other hand, certain dietary components also may protect against cancer. Dietary fiber or roughage is one often-cited example. Populations that consume high-fiber diets tend to have a low incidence of intestinal cancer, perhaps because the fiber helps speed the passage of waste through the colon. A high-fiber diet also promotes the excretion of fats and bile acids.

The possible protective role of certain vitamins is also under study. Both human and animal studies suggest that there may be an increased susceptibility to several chemically induced cancers when the diet is deficient in vitamin A. Since vitamin A is fat soluble and toxic levels can build up in the body if too much is consumed, doctors recommend that it be consumed in foods rather than as vitamin supplements. Liver, green and yellow vegetables, and carrots are high in vitamin A; including an assortment of these foods in the diet should provide adequate intake.

Animal studies also have found that vitamin C may inhibit the formation of certain cancer-causing chemicals in the body, thus lowering the risk of cancers of the stomach and esophagus. Again, adequate dietary amounts appear to be sufficient to provide the protective effect.

Research has found that people living in areas where the soil and water have low levels of selenium—a trace mineral—have an increased cancer rate; however, there is not enough evidence at this point to recommend selenium supplements. Iron deficiency has long been associated with an increased risk of esophageal cancer, but a normal diet provides enough of this mineral for most people.

The link between certain occupational hazards and cancer has long been documented and is the subject of continuing medical controversy. One of the earliest examples dates to the eighteenth century when it was found that cancer of the scrotum in English chimney sweeps could be prevented if they washed off the soot after work. As our society has become increasingly industrialized, with tens of thousands of chemicals and other pollutants released into the environment, the concern over environmentally caused cancer has grown. A large number of substances, ranging from asbestos to chemicals such as vinyl chloride, industrial dyes, and acids all are known carcinogens. Protecting workers and the rest of the population from these substances, and at the same time enabling industry to function, has become one of the leading social and economic problems of the day. Passage of the Occupational Safety and Health Act and creation of the Occupational Safety and Health Administration (OSHA) and the National Institute for Occupational Safety (NIOSH) in 1970 have formalized the government's role in protecting workers from occupational hazards. The Environmental Protection Agency has a similar charge in attempting to minimize harmful pollutants in the environment. While these governmental efforts are constantly under criticism from both sides as being either too stringent or too weak, they do represent a framework in which to begin reducing environmental and occupational hazards.

Radiation hazards, both from medical and other sources, represent still another area of environmental concern. Exposure to ionizing radiation, such as that used in medical x-rays, may pose a danger of cellular damage. Whenever radiation is used, the potential benefits must be weighed against the possible risks. Medical diagnosis, and even the treatment of cancer, have progressed greatly because of the use of radiation. But overuse and misuse can well outweigh the potential benefits. This is why routine chest x-rays are no longer recommended as part of an annual physical unless there are clear indications that they may prove beneficial. Radiation therapy is no longer used for relatively benign conditions such as acne or tonsillitis because of the increased risk of cancer. In addition, the dosage of radiation administered by modern x-ray machines has been reduced markedly.

Exposure to the sun is still another environmental cancer hazard. Ultraviolet light can cause cellular damage, and is the most common cause of skin cancer. A commonsense approach to sun exposure can prevent most cases of this relatively harmless but potentially disfiguring cancer. People with fair skin should be particularly careful to limit their sun exposure. And while most skin cancers are not life-threatening, it should be noted that one form, malignant melanoma, is. This type of cancer has risen dramatically in recent decades, very likely because of the increase in sun exposure.

The role of certain viruses and other disease-causing agents in cancer is yet another area of ongoing research. The link between some sexually transmitted viral diseases, most notably genital herpes and venereal warts, and an increase in cervical cancer has been noted. More recently, the association between certain homosexual practices and the development of autoimmune deficiency syndrome (AIDS), which leads to sarcomas, lymphomas, and other types of cancer, has caused great public concern. There seems little doubt that changing sexual mores may increase the risk of some cancers, but the precise mechanisms involved are still unknown.

A number of other cancer-causing agents could be cited. In fact, the list is so long that many people complain that it seems as if everything they like can cause cancer or some other disease. Obviously, it would be folly to go through life worrying about the cancer-causing potential of virtually everything we eat, drink, or touch. At the same time, following a prudent lifestyle that avoids known carcinogens that are not essential to life and happiness would seem a wise course to follow.

SUMMING UP

EVEN THOUGH CANCER remains one of our most feared diseases, and the second leading cause of death among Americans, great strides have been made against it in recent decades. With today's knowledge and treatment, nearly half of all Americans who are diagnosed as having cancer can potentially be cured of the disease. There have been dramatic breakthroughs in recent years in our understanding of how cancer cells develop. The best prospects for a cure lie in early diagnosis and treatment—factors that require a greater public awareness of warning signs and knowledge of where to go for the most effective treatment. In addition, 25 percent of all cancers could be prevented by eliminating all tobacco use. Thousands of other cases could potentially be prevented by dietary measures or reducing environmental carcinogens. While it seems unlikely that we will ever fully eliminate cancer as a threat to human health and life, it increasingly is a disease that we can control.

21 Infectious Diseases

Harold C. Neu, M.D.

INTRODUCTION

WE LIVE IN a virtual sea of microorganisms. There are teeming numbers of bacteria, viruses, and fungal spores in the air, on the skin, on hair follicles, and around the base of the teeth. The intestines alone harbor billions of useful bacteria. Much of humankind's relationship to the microbes is one of mutual tolerance, and in many cases, one of beneficial symbiosis.

Causes of Infection

Yet serious infections do occasionally strike. What happens to upset the usual harmonious balance between man and the microbes? Two events must occur. First, there must be an invasion of the body—via the skin or the mucous membranes—by a *virulent* microbe, one capable of producing disease. (Only a minority of the microbes are virulent.) Second, there must be a weakening or compromising of the immune-defense system, which normally attacks and destroys invading germs.

Every one of the body surfaces—the skin, the conjunctiva or outer surface of the eye, the mucous membranes of the upper and lower respiratory tract, and the lining of the genital tract—harbors a characteristic group of bacterial flora that differs from the flora in or on other parts of the body. The pathogenic (disease-producing) organism must first survive on one of these sites in competition with the normal flora already there. Then, for infection to occur, the organism must penetrate deeper into the tissues to produce damage. We have recently learned that bacterial pathogens produce disease partially because of their ability to attach to our mucosal cells through specific surface-to-surface interactions. For example, some bacteria cause disease by multiplying on the epithelial cells (which constitute the surface covering of the skin, organs, and other internal tissue); there they produce toxins, or poisonous substances that diffuse throughout the victim and cause characteristic illness. For example, *Corynebacterium diphtheriae* can infect the lining of the throat, generating a toxin that infiltrates the body, sometimes damaging the heart.

Some toxins produce disease locally. *Vibrio cholerae*, for example, yields a toxin that does not damage the lining of the intestine but instead causes a change in the enzymes that disrupts the intestines' ability to retain water. The result is the severe diarrhea characteristic of cholera. Other bacteria penetrate our mucosal barriers, multiply, and kill the local cells. An example is the Shigella bacterium that causes dysentery, another severe diarrheal disease. Yet other bacteria, such as streptococcal pharyngitis (commonly referred to as strep throat), can penetrate into subepithelial cells, or they may actually spread throughout the body, as is the case with the typhoid bacillus.

Some of the virulent microorganisms even have the ability to establish themselves as part of our normal bacterial flora. *Streptococcus pneumoniae*, for example, colonizes in the throat during the winter, often producing no noticeable symptoms. But if it gets down into the lung, it can generate disease. Another organism, *Branhamella catarrhalis*, lives harmlessly all the time in the throats of many people but can cause disease in the ears of children or in the sinuses of some adults.

Another sinister talent of some virulent microbes is that they can be ingested intact by the very cells that are supposed to protect us—the white blood cells and the macrophages—and survive within these. The tuberculosis bacterium has this capacity. Other microorganisms produce substances called endotoxins that are actually part of their own cell wall; they can cause severe damage to humans when killed by the immune defense system or when they die within us. Endotoxins are associated with the life-threatening shock that occurs when bacteria get into the bloodstream from some infection in another part of the body.

As for viruses, they can cause as many diseases as bacteria, ranging from severe encephalitis (inflammation of the brain) to hepatitis and venereal disease. Structurally less complex than bacteria, viruses' effects are expressed mainly by their attachment to surface structures and their influence on the genetic system. Unlike bacteria, viruses are parasitic and grow only within cells. What they do—and why they are so harmful to man—is invade a cell, multiply within it and thereby kill it, and then move on to other cells.

The virus's damaging parasitic ability is often determined by its coating or surface. This explains why simple substances like hypochloric acid, or household bleach, can kill a virus—it damages the all-important surface properties of the organism. But antibiotics are ineffective against viruses.

Viruses can grow only in certain types of cells. Influenza virus, for example, restricts itself to respiratory epithelium; it won't grow in the cells of other tissue. The polio virus has an affinity for the nervous system. Herpes simplex Type 1 virus prefers to grow in and around the mouth; herpes simplex Type 2 in and on the genital organs.

Reactions to a viral invasion range widely. The cells may accept the virus and live symbiotically with it. At the other extreme, the virus will take over the cell and kill it. There can be a change in the genetic structure of the cell hyperplasia—followed by the death of the cell or by a malignant change of the cell, generating the growth of a tumor. And the length of time between a virus invasion and the appearance of a disease can range from hours to years; in the latter case, the microbes are known as "slow viruses." They mainly cause devastating diseases of the central nervous system.

The third major group of infection-causing organisms are the fungi (plural form of fungus, Latin for mushroom)—yeasts, molds, and mushrooms. Though lacking chlorophyll, fungi structurally resemble plants: They have cells complete with nuclei, mitochondria, and more than one chromosome (bacteria lack these traits). Extremely diverse, they live on soil, on plants, and in water. On occasion, they live on people, where they generate many diseases, both on the skin and within the body.

The Body's Defenses Against Infection

The skin itself is an effective physical barrier to germ invasion. Its specific antimicrobial properties are not known, but its mild acidity along with the normal bacteria living there creates a hostile environment for opportunistic microbes. Within the body, membranes are bathed in secretions—cervical mucus, prostatic fluid, and tears—that are toxic to many organisms. The respiratory tract has formidable defenses: an aerodynamic filtering system in the tracheal–broncheal tree; small hairs (cilia) in the nose that continually sweep out invaders; a layer of mucus that traps invaders; coughing to expel organ-

isms. Ninety percent of inhaled microbes are expelled within 1 hour.

The gastrointestinal tract also is hostile to invading microbes. There is acid in the stomach that destroys many. Enzymes secreted by the pancreas and intestines are lethal to others. Cells on the surface of the intestine slough off continuously, facilitating the purge of unwanted visitors. And the intestines move in such a way, via peristaltic action, as to help rid themselves of microorganisms.

The urinary tract is protected by local antibodies and a very frequent and effective flushing mechanism, urination. The kidney has a chemical environment particularly hostile to bacteria. And men have the prostate gland, whose secretions also act to destroy microbes. In women, the vagina has no particular cleansing ability but estrogen stimulates increased deposits of glycogen there. Beneficial bacteria thrive on the glycogen, producing lactic acid, an inhibitor to harmful bacteria.

If all the physical and biochemical barriers fail to expel or neutralize an invasion by dangerous microbes, there is a second line of defense—the immune-defense system. This is a complicated group of organs, nodes, vessels, specialized cells, and blood proteins that stand ready to mount a rapid reaction to disease-producing organisms and the toxins they generate. Basically, the system consists of several types of white blood cells and a blood protein called complement.

The white blood cells are manufactured by the billions in the bone marrow. Those called leukocytes can sense, trap, engulf, and destroy unwanted agents, a process known as phagocytosis. (See figure 21.1.) Cells known as lymphocytes make antibodies, or instruct other white blood cells called macrophages to kill bacteria, or have other specialized functions.

Antibodies are proteins that circulate in the blood and in fluids between tissues. They bind to invading organisms, neutralizing their pathologic effects and enhancing their destruction by phagocytic white blood cells. A vital talent of lymphocytes is their ability to remember each and every specific invader. After the pathogens have been destroyed, a few lymphocytes will imprint their identity and pass this information along to other "memory" lymphocytes indefinitely. Then when the same microbe tries to invade again, the memory lymphocytes quickly spring into action before a serious infection sets in. This is called acquired immunity and is the basis of vaccination. (See figure 21.2.)

Antibodies activate another part of the complex immune defense—the so-called complement system. Complement consists of distinct proteins that, like

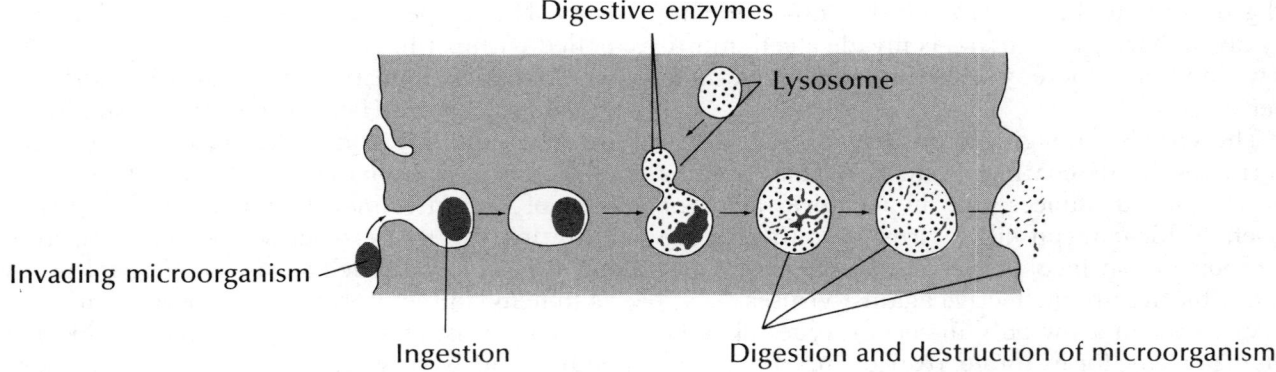

Figure 21.1. **During phagocytosis, the macrophage travels to the site of infection and first adheres to the invading agent and then proceeds to surround and ingest it. It then releases enzymes that kill the bacteria.**

antibodies, circulate in the bloodstream and in the fluid between tissues. Normally present in low amounts, they multiply rapidly when activated and help the white blood cells ingest invading organisms. In certain circumstances, complement attacks bacteria and other cells by actually making a hole in the cell wall which allows the contents to spill out and the cell to be killed.

Cellular and Humoral Immunity. The body's defense system employs 2 specialized types of lymphocytes, T cells and B cells. These cells are the ma-

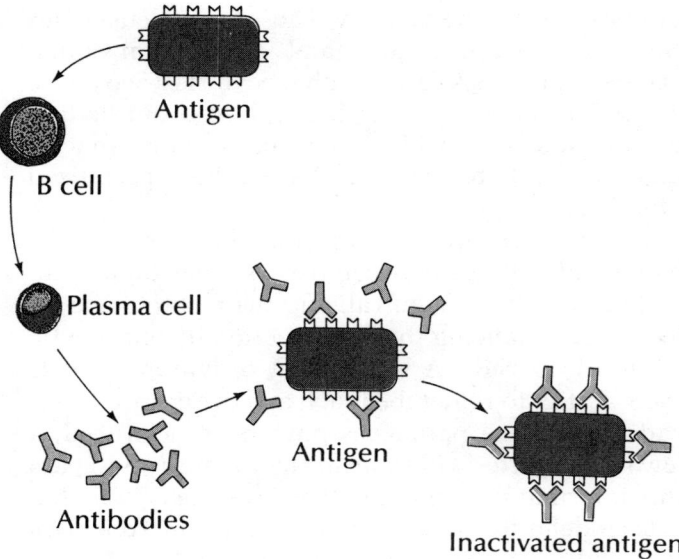

Figure 21.2. **Antigen–antibody response. The antigen stimulates a B cell, which has been programmed to recognize it, to transform itself into a plasma cell, which in turn produces antibodies. These antibodies attach to the antigen, making it harmless.**

jor components of the lymphoid tissue, which is located in the lymph nodes, spleen, gastrointestinal tract, and bone marrow—all sites that are ideally suited to timely intervention against invading organisms.

T cells are responsible for cell-mediated or cellular immunity. They work by attaching themselves to the invading agent and destroying it. (See figure 21.3.) B cells are responsible for humoral immunity, the process by which they produce antibodies that attack the foreign agent. Cellular immunity is most effective against things like parasites, cancer cells, transplants of foreign tissue, and fungi, while humoral immunity comes into play during bacterial or viral infections.

There are thousands of different T cells, each one programmed to respond to a particular antigen. Following phagocytosis, these cells go into action, a process known as T-cell sensitization. A sensitized T cell begins to grow and divide, producing a clone population. Within the clone population there are subsets of T cells: suppressor, helper, killer, and memory T cells, so named because of their individual functions in fighting the foreign invasion.

There also are thousands of different B cells, and like T cells, each is programmed to respond to a specific antigen. They differ from T cells in their method of response. Once activated, the B cells are transformed into cells that produce specific antibodies. These antibodies travel through the blood and lymph to the specific site where the foreign invasion has taken place, where they go into action to destroy it. (See figure 21.4.)

When a microbe successfully evades all the body's defense mechanisms, the result is infection. There is usually local inflammation and generalized

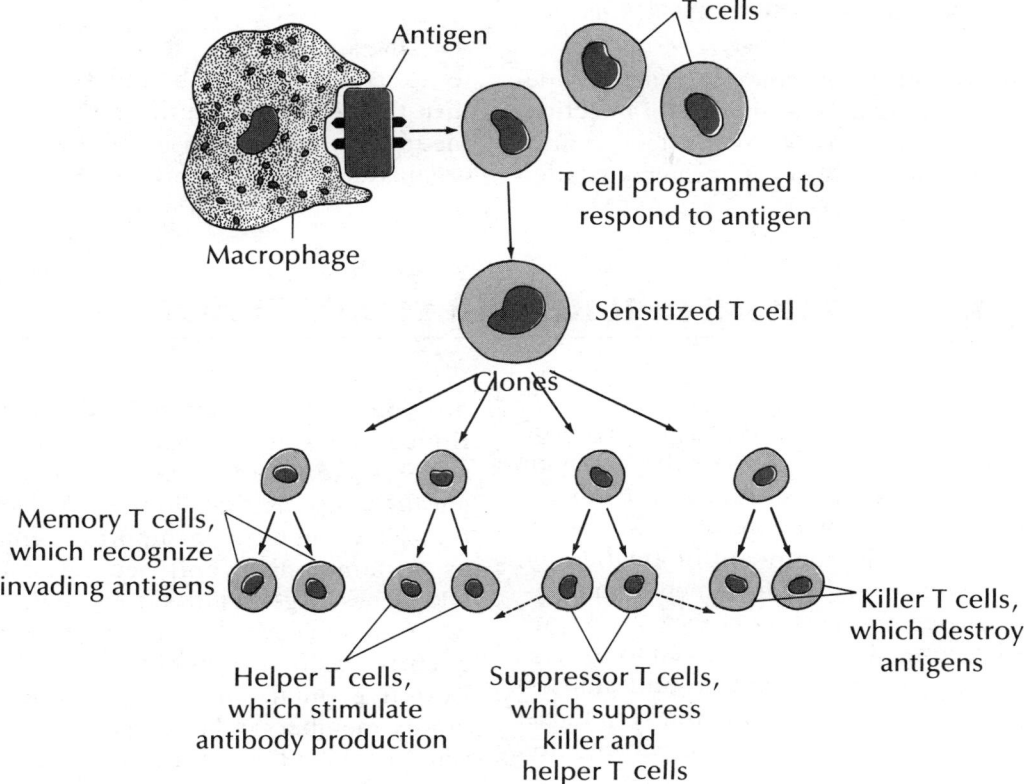

Figure 21.3. **After an antigen is released by a macrophage, the T cell programmed to respond to it becomes sensitized. It enlarges and divides, forming 4 types of T cells, each with a specific function in cellular immunity.**

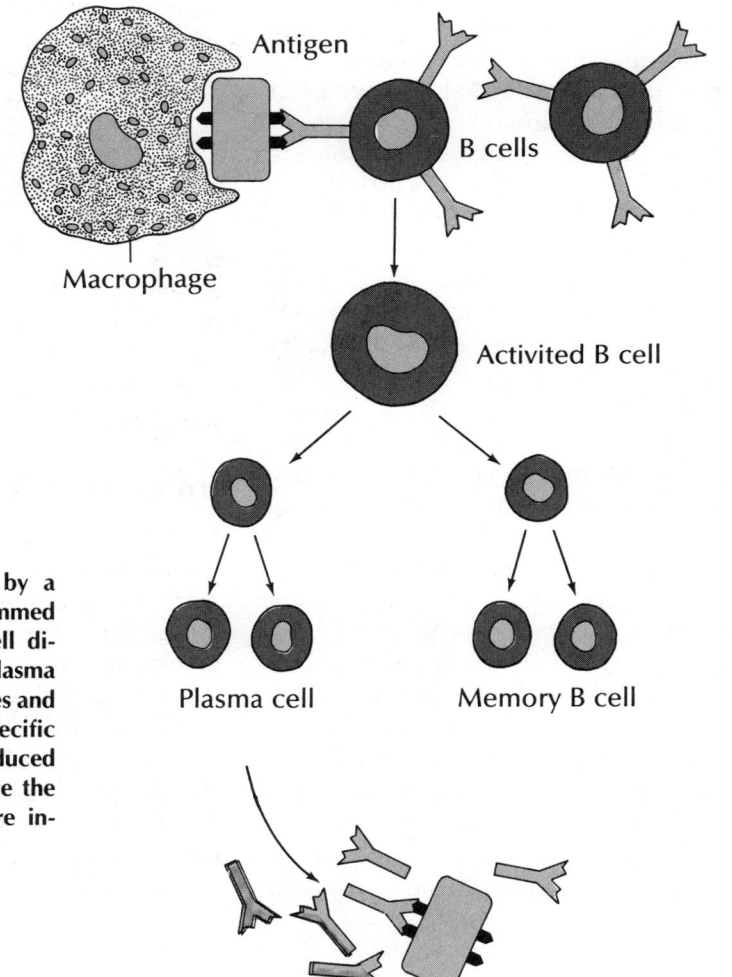

Figure 21.4. **An antigen released by a macrophage activates a B cell programmed to recognize it. The activated B cell divides, producing B cells that form plasma cells, which in turn produce antibodies and memory cells, which seek out the specific invading antigen. The antibodies produced by the plasma cells go on to produce the antigen–antibody complexes that are instrumental in humoral immunity.**

fever, plus a host of other possible reactions depending on the particular type and site of infection. Fortunately, except for most viruses, effective antimicrobial drugs can usually do what the body failed to do itself—destroy the invasive organism and return the person to health. In the following sections, the major infectious diseases that affect the various organ systems will be reviewed.

INFECTIONS OF THE UPPER RESPIRATORY TRACT

Colds

Although the common cold is mild and goes away on its own, it is the leading cause of visits to physicians and of school and job absenteeism. A few colds are complicated by bacterial infections of the sinuses or middle ear, necessitating prompt antibiotic therapy, but most colds require no drug treatment at all.

Colds are caused by the rhinovirus, corona, and scores of other viruses. The viruses attach to the epithelial cells lining the nasal passage and sinuses, provoking the discharge of large amounts of mucus. The same virus can reinfect the same person time and again.

The cold season in the United States begins in late August or early September, continues through the winter, and fades away in April and May. Scientists don't know why colds tend to be seasonal but they speculate that the congregation of children in schools may be an important reason. Cold weather also may make the lining of the nasal passage drier and more vulnerable to viral invasion.

Young children are the most susceptible to colds, and therefore the spread of colds usually occurs in schools and in households with children. Cold viruses are probably spread mainly by the hands; children rub their itchy, running noses, picking up the virus, and then later touch another person's hand. After exposure to the virus, it usually takes 2 to 3 days for a cold to develop. Symptoms are nasal discharge, some obstruction of nasal breathing, swelling of the sinuses, sneezing, and a sore, scratchy throat that prompts occasional coughs. Fever is usually slight but can climb to 102° F among infants and young children.

Colds usually last about 1 week, but in about 25 percent of cases, they persist for 2 weeks. Smoking can prolong the ordeal. A physician can do nothing for the uncomplicated cold. It does no good to do a culture to identify the infecting virus because there are no drugs to prescribe for colds, regardless of the causative organism. Both antibiotics and antihistamines are useless except to relieve symptoms, such as fever. Some cold remedies sold over the counter in pharmacies and supermarkets—especially those containing phenylephrine or epinephrine—will help promote nasal secretions and relieve obstruction. But decongestants should not be used for more than a few days. A sore throat is best relieved by warm gargle solutions, hot liquids, or even cough drops that have some cough-suppressing activity. Aspirin or acetaminophen and bed rest can help relieve headaches or generalized muscle pain.

To avoid spreading a cold, the victim should frequently wash his or her hands with soap and water. Despite popular opinion, it's doubtful that exposed family members or co-workers can gain any protection by taking large doses of vitamin C; most careful studies fail to show any benefit from this tactic. Even doses as high as 3 grams per day failed to prevent colds among volunteers exposed to rhinovirus. The best way to sidestep a cold is to avoid finger-to-nose or finger-to-eye contact, especially after being around someone with a cold.

No vaccine against the common cold may ever exist, mainly because there are so many viruses—more than 100—that cause the condition. In any event, a cold is a self-limiting illness that lasts only a few days in a normally healthy person. It may be more serious in the very young, the elderly, or people with a chronic disease, such as diabetes, heart disease, or chronic obstructive pulmonary disease, or whose immune systems have been weakened by chemotherapy or disease. These patients should contact a doctor when they have a cold since treatment may be required to prevent complications.

Influenza (Flu)

Like a cold, influenza is an acute viral infection of the upper respiratory tract, but it causes greater illness and discomfort. It starts abruptly, usually with a high fever (up to 103° F), a dry cough, and often a headache. Muscle and back pain set in, and the victim may feel sick enough to want to stay in bed. The cough eventually produces mucus and the nose may become congested, the throat sore, and eyes sensitive to light. There can even be nausea and vomiting. The fever lasts for 2 to 3 days and the other symptoms persist for a week to 10 days, leaving the victim feeling tired for a few days longer.

Whereas scores of viruses provoke colds, flu is caused by only two main viruses—influenza A and influenza B—but these two are continuously forming new strains, which are often named for their assumed place of origin (thus the Russian and Hong Kong flus). New types of influenza A cause epidemics every 2 to 4 years, whereas influenza B occurs sporadically or in localized outbreaks. Type B is associated with the development of Reye's syndrome in children (a rare but dangerous disease affecting the brain and the liver).

The flu viruses spread to other persons easily, either by direct contact—handling articles that the infected person has contaminated with nasal secretions or sneezes and coughs—or by breathing the airborne microbes. Symptoms appear after an incubation period of 1 to 2 days. The viruses infect the nose, throat, trachea, and can enter the small airways in the lung. Like the cold viruses, the flu viruses are most easily spread in places where people congregate indoors, such as schools and nursing homes, and are thus most likely to cause illness in the winter and spring. Reinfection by the same strain of virus is rare since the body builds up immunity after an attack.

Influenza strikes people of all ages at unpredictable intervals. Its greatest danger is that it reduces resistance to bacterial infection, especially among the elderly and those with chronic lung disease. The result can be bacterial bronchitis or serious-to-fatal bacterial pneumonia.

Unless the patient is one of those vulnerable to bacterial complications, a visit to the doctor is usually unnecessary, especially since there's no drug that can eliminate the virus. The patient should get plenty of bed rest, use vaporizers to ease congestion, take aspirin or aspirin substitutes to relieve muscle pain and headache, and avoid cigarettes and alcohol. Smoking worsens coughing while alcohol kills off white blood cells and predisposes the patient to bacterial pneumonia. Lots of nonalcoholic fluids, however, are recommended: they help loosen the secretions in the respiratory tract and decrease the chances of complications like bronchitis, ear infection, and sinusitis. They also are important to counter the dehydration that may accompany a fever.

Children with influenza (or other viral illnesses) probably should not receive aspirin: There is a statistical association between aspirin and the subsequent development of Reye's syndrome.

For people susceptible to developing serious complications of the flu, an annual vaccination is highly recommended. The vaccine, which is periodically reformulated to match the newest strains of the influenza viruses, has gradually improved in effectiveness and the number and seriousness of side effects have also been reduced. The U.S. Centers for Disease Control recommends the vaccine for any person over the age of 65 and for all residents of nursing homes. In addition, people with chronic respiratory disease, cardiopulmonary disease, or any disease involving the blood, kidneys, or body chemistry (metabolism), as well as medical and nursing home personnel, should also be vaccinated. The time to get vaccinated is in the late fall or early winter—October to December. The vaccine is not recommended for children or for people who are allergic to eggs.

There is also a prophylactic antiviral prescription drug for the flu—amantadine—but it's effective only against the influenza A virus. It should be taken about 2 weeks before the flu season by anyone with chronic lung disease or anyone who is taking medication that lessens natural immunity. It is also recommended for all the elderly. If a flu epidemic strikes before a person has been vaccinated, he or she should start taking amantadine and be inoculated as soon as possible. The amantadine should be taken for 2 weeks following vaccination to provide protection until antibodies develop.

Acute Sore Throat (Pharyngitis)

The pharynx—that part of the throat between the nasal passages and the larynx, or voice box—can be invaded by bacteria, viruses, or a combination of both. The result is a sore throat that can make breathing, swallowing, and speaking painful and difficult.

It is important to differentiate viral and bacterial infections, since the latter can cause serious complications. Illness stemming from streptococcal bacterium, for example, can lead to rheumatic fever, causing damage to the heart, or it can lead to acute nephritis, damaging the kidney. Therefore, the physician may do a culture to determine the cause of pharyngitis if an infection persists for more than a few days.

A large proportion of people who have a cold or the flu develop the symptoms of pharyngitis. And like colds and the flu, most throat infections occur during the colder months—the respiratory disease season. They are most prevalent among school-age children.

A common cause of pharyngitis among young adults is infectious mononucleosis, which causes fever, enlargement of the nasal passages, headache, generalized body ache, and, occasionally, enlargement of the spleen. Gonorrhea bacteria can also cause pharyngitis among those who engage in oral sex.

If pharyngitis is caused by a virus, there's no prescription drug for it, but if it stems from bacteria, an antibiotic can quickly overcome it.

The main drug for a sore throat caused by a streptococcal bacterium ("strep throat") is oral penicillin. Some physicians prefer injecting a long-acting penicillin—benzathine—since one shot lasts 2 weeks and the patient is freed of having to take penicillin pills several times a day. Patients allergic to penicillin will receive erythromycin instead. If a patient gets a prescription for an oral antibiotic, it is vital that he or she takes the full 10-day course of the drug, even though the symptoms may clear earlier than that. Failure to take the full 10-day course of drugs, especially in the case of streptococcus infection, can result in secondary rheumatic fever.

Acute Laryngitis

A very common condition, laryngitis is an infection and inflammation of the larynx, or voice box. It is usually caused by a virus. The main symptom is hoarseness, which may escalate into voice loss for a few days. There's nothing to do for it but rest the voice and avoid irritants like tobacco smoke and alcohol.

Croup

Acute laryngotracheobronchitis, or croup, is usually caused by a virus but can be bacterial (the causative agent usually being one of the pneumonia microbes). It primarily affects children 3 months to 3 years of age, reaching its peak among 2-year-olds. The infec-tion—which causes inflammation and swelling of the nasal passages, larynx, and trachea (the windpipe)—results in hoarseness, cough, and a classic labored, shrill breathing sound. Attacks usually occur at night, awakening and alarming the child, who will sit forward and make a sound similar to crowing or barking.

The symptoms of croup fluctuate rapidly and unpredictably. One hour the child may sound terrible, another he may be breathing almost normally; morning may bring relief only to be followed by a worsening at night. But fortunately the symptoms usually clear up in 3 or 4 days, although they can sometimes persist for a week. A panicky child should be comforted and relieved of anxiety as much as possible. The best home treatment is to use a steam kettle, vaporizer, or steam from a shower to relieve congestion, although this therapy has no scientifically proven benefit. If the child's breathing appears dangerously impaired, and especially if his lips start turning blue, he should be rushed to the hospital.

If croup stems from a virus, it is generally not dangerous, but if the causative agent is a bacterium called *Haemophilus*, or if the condition is actually a masked case of epiglottitis, the consequences can be dire. *Haemophilus* is a bacterium that can cause a variety of acute diseases, including meningitis, or inflammation of the lining of the brain and spinal cord; inflammation of the epiglottis—the structure in the throat that prevents food from entering the windpipe—can impair breathing and swallowing. Fortunately, both conditions are readily treatable with antibiotics.

EAR INFECTIONS

Swimmer's Ear

This is a superficial bacterial infection of the external ear canal, frequently the result of excess moisture (thus its name) or of an infection of the inner ear. Unless there is extensive inflammation, the only treatment necessary will be antibacterial ear drops. Often, diluted household vinegar will suffice. In cases of severe swelling, the physician may place a cotton wick with a 50 percent aluminum solution (Burrow's solution) in the ear for 1 or 2 days before starting topical treatment. Antibiotic drops should be discontinued as soon as there is improvement because they can cause dermatitis.

Malignant External Otitis

This is not a malignancy, but instead, it is a bacterial infection of the external canal that has spread into surrounding tissue and causes a persistent draining. There is severe pain and tenderness, but rarely fever or an increase in white blood cell count (a sign of infection). This infection can cause damage to the facial nerve on the side next to the affected ear, resulting in paralysis on that side of the face. In rare instances, it can also cause osteomyelitis (bone inflammation) and even brain abscess and death.

The condition, most prevalent among the elderly who pick at the ear canal, can now be successfully treated with antibiotics and local surgical removal of wasted tissue. Since some physicians are unfamiliar with this illness, any person with persistent ear pain should see an ear specialist (otolaryngologist) or infectious disease expert.

Otitis Media

At some point between the ages of 6 months and 3 years, most children will develop an infection of the middle ear, or otitis media. Like colds and flu, it is seasonal, striking most often in winter. It can be caused by an allergy or a functional, anatomic abnormality, but usually results from infection. Children who have their initial attack during their first year are much more likely to have recurrent bouts throughout childhood.

The most common cause of otitis media is infection by 1 of 3 kinds of bacteria—*Haemophilus, Streptococcus pneumoniae*, and *Branhamella catarrhalis*. Local symptoms include earache, hearing impairment, disturbance of balance, and vertigo, while generalized signs are fever, irritability, and vomiting. Otitis should be suspected in any small child with unexplained fever, particularly if a tug on the ear brings a painful response.

Examination of the color, contour, and structural changes of the middle ear enables a physician to diagnose otitis media. The most common treatment is an oral antibiotic or sulfa drug, but if the condition is serious or persistent, the doctor may suction out the fluids using a small needle (aspiration). If a child continues to have ear pain or fever 48 hours after starting drugs, the inner-ear fluid should be cultured to make sure the proper medication is being used. Decongestants do little good and, in fact, may prolong an attack.

Because half of all children with otitis will have persistent fluid within the middle ear even after an acute infection has cleared, all children should have return visits to the physician. Even though this fluid does not harbor bacteria, it can impair hearing at a crucial, language-learning stage of development. If fluid is found during the follow-up visit, the doctor will probably prescribe another course of drug therapy or may recommend that an otolaryngologist implant small drainage tubes.

To prevent recurrent infections, the dry winter air in the home should be moisturized with a humidifier. Infants should not be fed while lying down. In some cases, prophylactic antibiotics may be prescribed. (Also see discussions in Chapter 12 on Infancy and the Early Years, page 223, Chapter 22 on Respiratory Diseases and Lung Health, page 461, and Chapter 34 on Diseases of the Ear, Nose, and Throat, page 674.)

SINUSITIS

SINUSITIS IS USUALLY a complication of a cold or other viral infection of the nose and throat, although some cases of acute infection of the sinuses' mucous membranes may follow dental treatment. In a few instances, sinusitis is associated with hay fever or anatomical obstructions that block drainage of fluids.

Even though it usually comes on the heels of a viral infection, sinusitis most often is bacterial. This happens because the viruses change the characteristics of the cells lining the sinuses, allowing normally harmless bacteria that enter through the nose and mouth to settle and multiply. Long episodes of infection can lead to irreversible changes in the mucosal lining of the sinuses and result in chronic sinusitis.

The symptoms of sinusitis are facial pain, headache, yellowish discharge from the nose, obstruction of smell, and a nasal speaking tone. If the frontal sinuses over the eyes are involved, there can be swelling of the eyelids and excessive tearing. In almost all older children and in about half of adults, there will also be fever.

Sinusitis is difficult to distinguish from a cold. The doctor should carefully examine the throat, nose, ears, sinuses, and teeth. In a dark room, the doctor will shine a light in the mouth to see if it shows up in the maxillary sinuses behind the cheekbones and in the frontal sinuses. Lack of "transillumination" probably indicates infection. X-rays will reveal trapped air and fluid and thickened mucosal walls of the sinuses. Culturing nasal secretions is of little value. In severe cases, a fluid sample will be taken from the sinuses via a needle passed through an anesthetized facial area; this will relieve pressure and provide material for a culture so that the infectious agent can be identified.

If the infection is bacterial, an antibiotic or a drug combination that includes a sulfa drug will be prescribed. In severe cases, the patient may be hospitalized for intravenous administration of more powerful antibiotics. All drugs must be taken for at least 10 days. If the pain is severe, codeine may be prescribed. Using decongestant nose drops and inhaling steam may be helpful in many cases.

Unfortunately, once sinusitis becomes chronic, there often is permanent mucosal damage. This may require surgery to promote drainage and remove excess mucosal tissues.

There are no proven ways to prevent acute sinusitis. Common sense dictates prompt use of decongestants when symptoms develop or during bouts of the common cold, flu, and other upper respiratory infections. Allergies should be well controlled. Good dental hygiene and prompt treatment of tooth problems will reduce the chance of sinusitis developing as a complication of dental disease.

EPIGLOTTITIS

THE TINY EPIGLOTTIS is a lidlike protuberance in the throat. Fortunately, it rarely becomes infected, but when it does, it is life-threatening because breathing becomes completely obstructed.

The typical patient is a child under the age of 5 who has a sore throat and unexplained fever for several hours; suddenly he experiences severe difficulty in breathing. The condition is often confused with croup; one way to distinguish between the two disorders is that croup involves a barking cough and difficulty in speaking, whereas epiglottitis does not. The latter also occurs in slightly older children.

When infected, the epiglottis appears markedly swollen and cherry red. X-rays will confirm an enlargement, but time is critical so there should be no delay in starting treatment if epiglottitis is even suspected. The causative agent is almost always the bacteria *Haemophilus influenzae*.

Treatment may involve emergency placement of a tube into the windpipe to facilitate breathing. Intravenous antibiotics will be started immediately. Dramatic improvement usually occurs within a couple of days.

INFECTIONS OF THE MOUTH

Gingivitis and Periodontitis

Both gingivitis and peridontitis involve a buildup of destructive plaque on the gums and between the gums and teeth. One of the culprits is bacteria, but antibiotics are reserved for severe cases of ulceration and tissue death. Good dental hygiene, a balanced diet, and the cessation of smoking are the best preventive tactics. (See Chapter 35 on Maintaining Oral Health, page 689, for more details.)

Stomatitis

Stomatitis, commonly referred to as canker sores, involves an inflammation of the mouth's membrane lining (the oral mucosa) with attendant chancre-like sores that are painful and recurrent. Easily confused with herpes simplex infections, stomatitis, like herpes, often occurs during periods of stress. Since the cause of stomatitis remains unknown—scientists are not even sure an infectious organism is at work—there is no proven treatment.

Hairy Tongue

The tongue becomes discolored—from yellow to black—due to a suspected infection (the specific cause has yet to be identified). The condition often follows the use of antibiotics or certain mouthwashes. There is no known treatment, but hairy tongue goes away on its own.

Molar Abscesses

Infection from these sores can spread into the body, producing serious and even life-threatening conditions. For that reason they should be promptly treated with antibiotics and surgery to drain out the pus.

Cold Sores (Herpes Simplex)

The "cold sores" or fever blisters caused by the herpes simplex virus most often turn up among children aged 1 to 5 and among young adults. Besides oral pain, an attack will cause sudden fever, chills, and irritability. There are often accompanying sore throat and sensitive gums. The blisters themselves appear on the lips, tongue, and the floor and roof of the mouth; they eventually come together to form irregularly shaped ulcers.

In initial or primary infections, fever and pain may persist up to 1 week and the sores will take as long as 2 weeks to heal. The first attack may initially be mistaken for strep throat or mononucleosis. There is now a topical drug called acyclovir that speeds the healing of the sores; it is also in pill form. Even though an outbreak will completely clear, the

herpes virus stays dormant in the body and can precipitate new attacks at almost any time. There is no way to eradicate the virus and prevent recurrence, which often follows emotional stress or fever caused by another infection.

BRONCHIAL INFECTIONS

Acute Bronchitis

This is an inflammatory disease of the trachea (the windpipe) and its large branch-off tubes in the lungs (the bronchi), the tracheal-bronchial tree. Associated with acute upper respiratory tract infections, the disorder occurs mostly in the winter. The usual cause is a virus, and the major symptom a cough. It starts out dry but changes to produce a thick mucous discharge, or sputum. During deep breathing, there may be pain below the breastbone (sternum).

Since there is no drug for the infecting viruses, treatment centers on controlling the cough, with codeine preparations and plenty of fluids to prevent dehydration. Adding moisture to the air helps clear the bronchi as well as the nasal passages. Of course, if the cause is a bacterium, antibiotics will be prescribed.

Chronic Bronchitis

Chronic bronchitis is usually caused by smoking or

repeated bouts of acute bronchitis. It develops slowly and insidiously over many years. Typically, it affects middle-aged and older men. It is characterized by a chronic cough that produces gradually increasing amounts of sputum or phlegm. The condition usually worsens in the winter and is often exacerbated by acute invasions of bacteria—pneumococcus and *Haemophilus* being the most common. These infections should be cleared promptly with antibiotics, which should be taken for at least 10 days.

If the victim of chronic bronchitis is a cigarette smoker, breaking the habit should be the first step in any treatment plan. Cough suppressants should not be used since coughing removes secretions. In fact, the physician may suggest regular postural drainage—lying with the head lower than the chest—to expedite clearance of the sputum. Bronchodilators may also be used. (Also see discussion in Chapter 22 on Respiratory Diseases and Lung Health, page 454.)

LUNG INFECTIONS

Pneumonia

This is lung inflammation caused by a wide variety of bacteria, viruses, fungi, and other types of organisms. It occurs when these germs somehow evade the impressive range of defenses against them in the upper respiratory tract (see Introduction) or enter through the mouth, evading the epiglottis. The latter can happen when we lose consciousness, have a seizure or stroke, or undergo general anesthesia. All of these events can weaken or paralyze the reaction of the epiglottis, permitting microbes to enter the windpipe and find their way down into the lung during respiration. Smoking is another culprit since it damages the small hairs (cilia) that line the respiratory tract and sweep out invading germs. Malnutrition or conditions like kidney failure or sickle cell

disease also impair the lung's ability to get rid of microorganisms. Viral infections of the upper respiratory tract can predispose a person to pneumonia because the viruses—like cigarette smoke—paralyze the protective cilia.

To diagnose pneumonia, the physician will first listen to the chest, checking for fine, crackling noises, and then tap it, being alert for characteristic dull thuds. A certain diagnosis cannot be made, however, without chest x-rays, which will show patches in the lung where air sacs are filled with fluid and debris instead of air (see figure 21.5). To determine the particular infective agent, lab tests can be done on blood and sputum samples, but the results are not 100 percent accurate.

Most viral pneumonias are mild. Symptoms in-

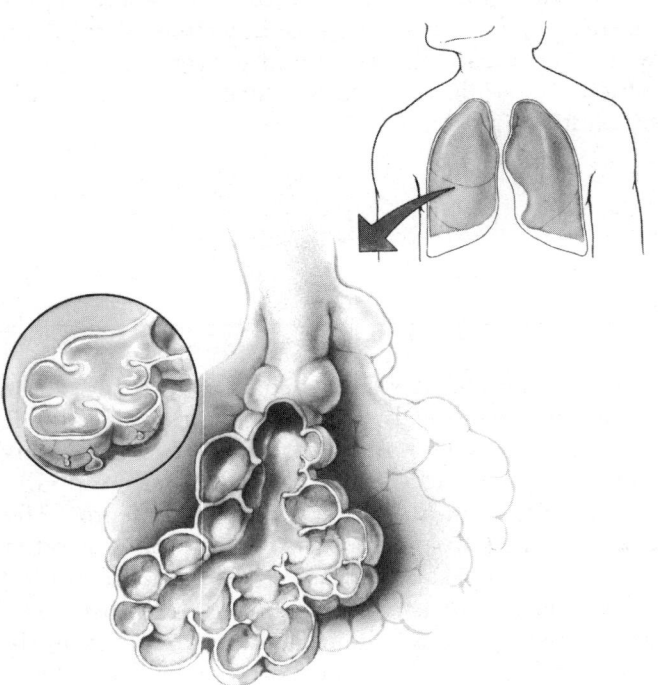

Figure 21.5. **Lungs affected by pneumonia. The enlargement shows a close-up of inflamed lung tissue, with an accumulation of mucus and fluid.**

clude fever, headache, malaise, chills, and cough. Bacterial pneumonia, which is more dangerous, usually causes attacks of shaking chills, high temperature (up to 105° F), rapid breathing, and coughing, at first dry but then producing rust-colored sputum. Headache, nausea, and vomiting may also occur.

Among children 12 and under, the most frequent cause of pneumonia is the bacteria pneumococcus. Among adolescents and young adults, the most frequent infective agent is a bacterialike microbe called *Mycoplasma pneumoniae;* symptoms at first are like those of a chest cold, with a dry cough and then a sputum-producing cough. Fortunately, antibiotics are effective against it. But even after the infection has cleared, coughing can persist for several days or weeks.

Bacterial pneumonia can also be a complication of influenza A. Often the symptoms of the flu have disappeared, then suddenly the patient is worse with fever, cough, and shortness of breath. The recuperating victim this time has a full-fledged case of bacterial pneumonia and all its distressing symptoms. These secondary infections are most often caused by the pneumococcus, *Haemophilus,* or worst of all the *Staphylococcus.* This microbe can be deadly so doctors usually prescribe antibiotics that can destroy all three of the possible microorganisms.

A recently discovered form of pneumonia is Legionnaire's disease, caused by the *Legionella pneumophila* bacterium. This disease can occur in epidemics—as the first known one did, which occurred in 1976, among American Legionnaires meeting in Philadelphia—or in sporadic cases. After an incubation period of 2 to 10 days, the victim develops fever, general muscular pain, chills, abdominal pain and diarrhea, nonproductive cough, sore throat, and sometimes headache and confusion. The disease progresses rapidly and hospitalization is necessary. The treatment is administration of the antibiotic erythromycin.

Pneumonia caused by bacteria that usually live in the mouth but are somehow aspirated into the lung (during unconsciousness, for example) is slow to develop and hard to diagnose. At first there is loss of appetite, fever, and some weight; then the patient will usually start producing foul-smelling sputum. The disease is extremely serious and requires hospitalization so that intravenous antibiotics can be given for 2 or 3 weeks. After the patient goes home, oral antibiotics should be continued for up to several months.

Pneumonia caused by pneumococcus—by far the most prevalent type of bacterial pneumonia—can now be prevented with a vaccine. It is recommended for anyone with chronic lung disease and for everyone over the age of 60. People who have had their spleen removed or damaged, and sickle-cell disease patients, should also be vaccinated. (Also see Chapter 22 on Respiratory Diseases and Lung Health, page 466.)

Tuberculosis

Tuberculosis, which is spread by small salivary droplets containing the tubercle bacillus, usually affects only the lungs but can sometimes attack other parts of the body. The symptoms are quite general—loss of appetite and consequent weight loss, low-grade fever, fatigue, chills, night sweats, and coughing. Many victims don't realize they are infected and discover it accidentally when they have a chest x-ray done for another purpose. Babies and adults with impaired immunity are the most susceptible.

There are two good diagnostic skin tests—the Tine and PPD (purified protein derivative)—which will produce swelling and hardness at the injecting site within a couple of days if the bacillus is present. The tests are not 100 percent accurate; they miss about 10 percent of cases, and people on steroids will not have a positive reaction even if they have tuberculosis.

Two highly effective drugs—isoniazid and rifampin—are used to treat tuberculosis, but they must be taken for 9 months. A reduction in coughing and infectivity, however, results just 2 weeks after the drugs are started.

Tuberculosis is now rare in the United States, but it remains a serious and highly infectious dis-ease, and anyone living with a patient should be examined for infection as soon as possible. The disease is seen most commonly among people with compromised immune systems, alcoholics or others who are poorly nourished, or people living in crowded, unsanitary conditions.

CARDIOVASCULAR INFECTIONS

Infective Endocarditis

The surface of the heart valves and the heart's chambers are lined with a thin membrane called endocardium. If it becomes infected with bacteria, the valves can grow distorted, leading to heart failure and death. Fortunately, such infections are uncommon, but with more people undergoing open-heart surgery, the incidence of endocarditis is rising. The use of intravenous drugs, preexisting heart valve disease, and old age are other risk factors (in later years, the valves stiffen and become more susceptible to infection).

Infective endocarditis usually develops slowly and there may be weeks of general ill health—fever, fatigue, weight loss, and muscle aches—before an accurate diagnosis is made. Most victims also have heart murmur. Diagnosis is made by a blood culture: The most common causative agents are *Streptococcus* or *Staphylococcus*. Effective treatment requires the use of high dosages of a powerful antibiotic or a combination of 2 drugs, usually for 4 to 6 weeks.

The only way to prevent endocarditis is to give antibiotics prophylactically 30 to 60 minutes before a highly susceptible person—anyone with heart valve disease or a prosthetic valve—undergoes any procedure that might enable bacteria to enter the bloodstream. These include a tooth extraction, oral surgery, D&C, IUD insertion, cesarean delivery or abortion, gum treatments, and many surgical procedures. Penicillin or erythromycin should probably be taken 6 hours after the procedure. (See Chapter 19 on Heart and Blood Vessel Disease, page 387.)

Myocarditis and Pericarditis

The outside of the heart is lined with a tough, thin membrane called the pericardium. This external sac is vulnerable to infection and inflammation by bacteria, fungi, and viruses—as is the heart wall (myocardium) itself—but viruses are the most frequent culprits, especially the Coxsackie B. Attacks usually occur in the summer, or they can be complications of other diseases.

The main symptom of both disorders is pain in the center of the chest, which may radiate to the neck, shoulders, and upper arms. Since most pericarditis is due to viruses, the only therapy is bed rest.

Myocarditis, an inflammation of the heart muscle, is fortunately rare since it may lead to irregular pulse and circulatory disturbances. Most myocarditis is viral and there's little to do but get complete bed rest under a doctor's observation. Unfortunately, permanent damage to heart muscle often results. (See Chapter 19 on Heart and Blood Vessel Disease, page 388.)

INFECTIONS OF THE NERVOUS SYSTEM

Meningitis

Difficult to prevent or diagnose, meningitis is an infection and inflammation of the membranes covering the brain and spinal cord, the meninges. It is an extremely serious disease which can end in permanent disability or death unless swiftly diagnosed and treated. Children are the main victims but it can strike at any age.

In most cases, meningitis is caused by bacteria—principally by one of three: *Neisseria meningitidis* (or meningococcus), *Streptococcus pneumoniae* (or pneumococcus), or *Haemophilus influenzae*. These get to the meninges via the bloodstream from a distant infection in the lung, intestine, heart, etc., or by direct invasion from an infection already in the nervous system. In premature infants and babies, the invading bacteria are usually strains of group B *Streptococcus* and *Escherichia coli*, which grow normally in the vagina of the mother. Among children 3 months to 5 years of age, the most common agents are *Haemophilus* and *Streptococcus*.

The symptoms of meningitis are high fever, stiff neck, nausea, and confusion. Confirmation can be made only by examining the cerebrospinal fluid for the telltale microbe, which means there must be a spinal tap or lumbar puncture. Fortunately, doctors have a large number of effective drugs for meningitis, including the relatively new cephalosporin antibiotics, which enable them to treat successfully nearly all cases caught early enough. If the bacterium is meningococcus *(Neisseria meningitidis)*, people in close contact with the patient should receive prophylatic antibiotics, preferably rifampin, for 2 days. And if the bacterium is *Haemophilus*, which predominantly infects children, prophylactic rifampin should be given to youngsters 5 and under who live with or have had close physical contact with the patient.

Viral meningitis tends to be less threatening than the bacterial type. Most common in the summer, it is caused by several viruses that cause summer diarrhea and one transmitted by hamsters and other rodents. In most cases, patients recover on their own without aftereffects. Even so, a spinal tap should be done to ensure that the person does not have a bacterial disease requiring antibiotics. On rare occasions, fungi will cause meningitis; the most common is cryptococcus, a fungus spread in pigeon droppings. (See page 447 in this chapter.)

Encephalitis

When viruses infect and inflame the brain cells, the result is the very serious disease, encephalitis. It's fortunate that encephalitis is rare in the United States because—with one exception—there is no treatment. That exception is encephalitis caused by the herpes simplex Type 1 virus, which produces cold sores. Symptoms include fever, headache, drowsiness, and confusion; for some reason, there are usually no cold sores present. A certain diagnosis can only be made by taking a sample of brain tissue. Two good drugs exist for the condition; both must be given by intravenous drip in the hospital. (The genital herpes virus—herpes simplex Type 2—is not implicated in encephalitis but in about 10 percent of cases it does lead to viral meningitis.)

INFECTIONS OF THE SKIN AND SOFT TISSUES

Impetigo

Impetigo is a skin infection caused by *Streptococcus* or *Staphylococcus* bacteria. It can occur anywhere on the body, but usually confines itself to the area around the nose and mouth of children. At first, the skin reddens and becomes itchy; then small blisters and pustules form, resembling chickenpox. When they break, they leave a tan crust. The crust should be removed by gentle washing, followed by application of an antibiotic ointment. If infection persists or spreads, an oral antibiotic may be prescribed.

Impetigo is highly contagious, and infected persons should wash their hands often and try not to scratch the sores. Also in the interest of prevention, skin abrasions, cuts, and insect bites should be kept clean with antiseptics since these predispose one to impetigo.

Toxic Shock Syndrome

Toxic shock syndrome, which is caused by toxins from *Staphylococcus* bacteria, is actually a type of blood poisoning, but the causative bacteria are believed to enter the body through a break in the skin. It was first associated with use of superabsorbent tampons in young women, but since then, there have been cases of it in children, older women, and men. More recently, a few cases have been associated with vaginal barrier contraceptives (diaphragms or contraceptive sponges) and there also have been some reports of sexual partners both contracting the disease, although it is not considered a sexually transmitted disorder.

It causes a general reddening of the skin, especially on the palms of the hands, fever, and often diarrhea, vomiting, and confusion. A drop in blood pressure and diminished circulation to the hands and feet also may occur. Diagnosis is made by culturing the blood and vaginal secretions. Treatment is with an antibiotic, preferably a semisynthetic penicillin.

The best preventive tactic is to avoid superabsorbent tampons; this is especially true of women who have already had toxic shock because the disease tends to recur. Tampon users should change them frequently and perhaps intersperse tampon use with napkins. It should be noted, however, that toxic shock is a rare disease; women should be aware of the warning signs, but most will never develop the disease.

Erysipelas

Erysipelas is a superficial skin disorder that mainly affects children and the elderly. It is usually a complication of streptococcal respiratory infection. Sores caused by the *Streptococcus* bacteria usually break out on the bridge of the nose and on the cheeks; they are painful and bright red and there is accompanying fever. Penicillin, or its substitute, erythromycin, will usually cure it.

Cellulitis

Cellulitis is a serious skin infection, which occurs when the bacteria infect deeper levels of the skin. Streptococcal or staphylococcal microbes enter the skin through a cut, puncture, ulcer, or sore, producing enzymes that break down the skin cells. The affected area becomes hot, red, and swollen, and there is accompanying fever, chills, and a general ill-feeling. In contrast to erysipelas sores, those caused by cellulitis do not produce elevated edges, sharply demarcating them from surrounding tissues. Because it tends to spread via the lymph nodes to other parts of the body, cellulitis is a potentially serious disorder requiring prompt therapy—either with penicillin or erythromycin.

Gas Gangrene

Gangrene means death of an area of tissue; gas gangrene refers to such a condition due to infection with the bacterium *Clostridium*. The microbe usually enters the body through a wound or cut. When infection sets in 1 to 2 days later, the local pain can be intense and the fever high; there is also marked swelling and discoloration of the skin, with a watery discharge. Surprisingly, there is usually little offensive odor, unlike other types of gangrene.

Potentially a very serious infection, gas gan-

grene must be treated promptly. Extensive surgery is required to remove all involved skin, subcutaneous tissues, and muscle. Antibiotics are also given, and in some cases, high-pressure oxygen therapy (hyperbaric oxygen) is beneficial.

Lymphadenitis

Lymphadenitis involves infection and inflammation of one or more of the lymph nodes. It usually occurs as a result of a nearby infection. The nodes may swell to several times their normal size and become quite painful. Most common among children, lymphadenitis usually is caused by *Staphylococcus* and affects the nodes in the neck, groin, and armpit. Antibiotics can successfully cure nearly all cases. It should be noted that there are many causes for swollen lymph nodes, including tuberculosis, cancer, cat-scratch fever, venereal disease, and other illnesses. Any persistently swollen lymph gland requires a careful diagnostic study.

Bites

Animal and human bites that penetrate the skin introduce bacteria that can set up serious infections and should therefore receive immediate attention. A bite that tears open tissues should be washed with soap and water and kept under running water for a few minutes to wash out the animal's or person's saliva. A bite victim should be taken promptly to a physician's office or hospital emergency room, where the damaged tissue will be removed and antibiotic therapy initiated.

If the bite is from a wild animal or a stray dog or cat, rabies infection is a possibility; immunization should be started immediately if the animal is found to be infected or appeared sick at the time of attack. If the animal cannot be examined, a physician should decide if immunization is wise. (Bites are also discussed in the Directory of Common First-Aid Procedures, Chapter 7, page 107.)

GASTROINTESTINAL INFECTIONS

ACUTE INFECTIONS of the intestines and colon can be caused by bacteria, viruses, fungi, or parasites. The main symptom in all cases is diarrhea. Although rare among adults in industrialized nations, gastrointestinal infections are a leading cause of death among small children in all countries, including the United States. Infections sometimes break out in epidemics in the United States following floods and

other disasters that contaminate drinking water.

Eating raw meat or fish and unwashed raw fruits and vegetables increases the chances of getting an intestinal infection. So does the excessive consumption of antacids, which upset the acid-alkali balance in the stomach and intestines. Drugs to halt the diarrhea or those that reduce intestinal motility and cause constipation increase the length of time the walls of the intestines are exposed to bacteria-laden fecal matter, also increasing the risk of infection. (Note: Hepatitis, a serious inflammation of the liver, is discussed in Chapter 24 on Disorders of the Digestive System, page 519.)

Traveler's Diarrhea (Tourista)

Traveler's diarrhea, which has a long list of humorous nicknames, is any acute intestinal infection encountered by travelers who may not have resistance to local microorganisms. About 20 to 50 percent of all Americans who travel to Mexico and other developing countries contract traveler's diarrhea. Despite humorous appellations like Montezuma's revenge or G.I. trots, the condition is no laughing matter, forcing a third of its victims to take to bed and another 40 percent to suspend scheduled activities. Typically, the illness sets in 4 to 6 days after arrival, with an abrupt attack of abdominal cramps and watery diarrhea (3 to 15 stools per day). In 3 to 5 days or so the diarrhea lessens and the patient can gradually resume normal activity. Some beleaguered travelers suffer repeated episodes on the same journey.

The leading cause of traveler's diarrhea is variants of the *Escherichia coli* bacterium which comes in a variety of forms and is part of our normal intestinal flora. Foreign variants the body has not been exposed to before produce toxins that interfere with the intestine's ability to absorb water. Other causative bacteria include *Vibrio parahemolyticus* (found in shellfish, lobsters, shrimp, and crab), *Shigella*, and *Salmonella*. The latter two usually cause fever as well as diarrhea, and *Salmonella* and *Vibrio* can cause vomiting.

The best preventive measure against traveler's diarrhea is to avoid the local drinking water (ice cubes included). Wine, beer, and carbonated sodas are safe. Can you brush your teeth with the hotel tap water? Yes, since most toothpastes contain antibacterial substances—but don't swallow any of the water while gargling. All raw foods should also be avoided, but fruits and vegetables are safe if peeled just before consumption.

Another preventive step is to take tetracycline or doxycycline prophylactically before the trip; studies show this affords protection in 70 percent of cases. (Be aware, though, that tetracycline causes some people to have allergic-type photosensitive reactions to the sun.) There is an alternative drug, a combination trimethoprim and sulfa agent called Bactrim or Septra, that doesn't cause photosensitivity but can produce a skin rash. A less expensive prophylactic—Pepto-Bismol—can be purchased over the counter at pharmacies and supermarkets; it can also help relieve symptoms once they develop.

Taking Bactrim can make an attack end sooner. Over-the-counter agents like Kaopectate are of little help and can actually be worse than nothing, especially if the diarrhea is bloody.

Campylobacter Infection

This bacterium, which seems to be infecting more people all the time, is found in every country and is usually passed on to humans from puppies and kittens. It can also contaminate water, milk, and some foods. One to 7 days after exposure, the bacterium colonizes the intestines, sometimes causing diarrhea so severe that doctors may mistake it for ulcerative colitis. Generally, though, the illness is milder, marked by fever, abdominal pain, nausea, vomiting, malaise, and, of course, diarrhea (often bloody). Recovery occurs within a week, often without treatment. The drug erythromycin is used, however, when campylobacter disease occurs in epidemics at nursery schools and other institutions: It cuts down on the number of infectious organisms shed in the feces and thus helps contain the epidemic. Campylobacter can be cultured from the feces of an ill person, and occasionally from the bloodstream.

Bacillus Cereus Infection (Food Poisoning)

Normally, the *Bacillus cereus* bacterium does not cause disease, but occasionally produces acute attacks of diarrhea and vomiting. It contaminates certain foods, particularly fried rice and pasta sauces, and an infection is often called food poisoning. The disease can cause either vomiting or both vomiting and diarrhea. Fortunately, the illness is not common, contagious, or dangerous, and no drug treatment is required.

Rotavirus Infection

Rotavirus causes about one-half of all diarrheal illness among infants; it attacks people of other ages, too. It usually strikes between the ages of 6 and 24 months, causing low-grade fever, vomiting, and watery diarrhea. Fluids must be given in adequate amounts to replace those lost through the bowels: In severe attacks, this can require intravenous administration of solutions in the hospital. The best preventive measure is breast-feeding since the mother's milk contains antibodies protective against the rotavirus in most cases. There is no therapeutic medication, but vaccines are being developed.

Norwalk Virus Infection

This organism causes sporadic outbreaks as well as epidemics of diarrheal illness among both adults and school-age children, usually in the winter and spring. The infection is spread by contaminated water (including swimming pools) and foodstuffs, especially oysters and other shellfish. Symptoms, which set in after an incubation period of 12 to 48 hours, vary widely, ranging from loss of appetite, nausea, and vomiting to fever, severe abdominal cramps, severe diarrhea, and headache. Normally, the attack fades quickly and complete recovery occurs without treatment. Among the debilitated elderly and infants, however, the course of the disease can be more threatening. Pepto-Bismol lessens the severity and duration of the symptoms.

Typhoid Fever

Contracted mainly by visitors to developing countries, typhoid fever is a highly transmissible and dangerous disease caused by the *Salmonella typhosa* bacterium. It is acquired from food or water contaminated with human waste containing the microbes; dairy products and undercooked meats are the most common sources. Sickness usually develops after an incubation period of 1 or 2 weeks but can be delayed for up to 60 days after exposure. Symptoms appear gradually, starting with dull headache, lethargy, and sometimes either constipation or diarrhea. Fever increases for a couple of days and reaches a very high plateau of about 105° F; frequently, it will remain there for some 3 weeks.

Diagnosis of typhoid can be made by a culture of the blood and stool and by blood tests. Three drugs are effective against it, but it will take nearly a week for fever to recede after therapy begins. When the illness clears, the patient should still be periodically tested for typhoid for up to 6 months to make certain he is not still harboring the microbes and is an unwitting "silent" carrier of the disease. This is especially true of patients with gallstones—a favored nesting site for *Salmonella typhosa*.

Antibiotics

Occasionally, antibiotics will cause mild diarrhea. In a few cases, the condition becomes serious; this occurs when the antibiotics suppress the normal intestinal bacteria so much that a type of Clostridium bacteria overgrow the intestines, producing a toxin that damages the colon. Diarrhea is watery and profuse and there may be abdominal pain and high fever. If antibiotics are being taken, they should be stopped. Vancomycin, Flagyl, or bacitracin are used for treatment when this occurs.

INFECTIONS OF THE JOINTS AND BONES

Infectious Arthritis

Although uncommon, bacteria can invade a joint and cause arthritis. Among children, such an occurrence is usually a complication of a preexisting infection or wound; among adults, preexisting osteoarthritis or rheumatoid arthritis are common predisposing factors. Sometimes the infection is confined to a single joint, causing swelling, tenderness, and pain when the joint is moved.

Mumps, chickenpox, rheumatic fever, and other disorders also can cause swelling and pain in the joints, but these symptoms clear when the disease is cured, and are not the same as infectious arthritis. A diagnosis of infectious arthritis is confirmed by culturing fluid from an affected joint. One of many bacteria may be the cause, including the gonococcus, which has a unique tendency to cause red sores on the hands and feet, especially among young women, in addition to causing severe pain in the wrists and ankles. In men, the gonococcus will often attack a single joint, usually the knee.

Left untreated, infectious arthritis can permanently damage affected joints. Antibiotics should be given in large doses, preferably intravenously in a hospital setting, and the fluid surrounding the joints should be drained regularly. (Arthritis due to gonococcus, however, can be treated with oral ampicillin.) Surgery is generally not necessary or particularly helpful. (See Chapter 28 on Arthritis, page 581, for more details.)

Osteomyelitis

Osteomyelitis is a bacterial infection of the bone and bone marrow. It is most prevalent among people with poor health and nutrition. It strikes children more often than adults, causing severe pain and tenderness, particularly when the joint near the infected area is flexed. There is also fever, drowsiness, and dehydration.

Osteomyelitis is usually a secondary infection following an infection elsewhere in the body; the primary infection is usually caused by a wound, surgery, an open fracture of a bone, or the presence of a foreign body, such as a bullet or surgical plate. To confirm a diagnosis, blood tests, x-rays, and CT bone scans may be done. In some forms of the disease, such as infection of the vertebrae, a biopsy may be necessary. Treatment consists of long-term (4 to 6 weeks) administration of antibiotics and, sometimes, surgery as well. Recurrences are common, and the disease can even become chronic. Fortunately, osteomyelitis is rare in the Western world.

URINARY TRACT INFECTIONS

Infections of the Urethra and Bladder

After respiratory tract illness, urinary tract infections (UTIs) are the leading cause of physician visits in the United States. Women are far more frequent victims than men (except among the elderly), and it has been estimated that as many as 10 percent of women will suffer an infection of the urethra, bladder, ureters, or kidneys every year.

The infectious agents, usually bacteria, commonly gain access to the urinary tract by migrating up the urethra, which carries urine from the bladder to outside the body. Women are more susceptible to infection because their urethras are only about 1.5 inches long, compared with 8 or 9 inches in men, so that the microbes' migratory journey is much easier. Women's urethral openings are also near anal and vaginal sources of infectious agents, and women lack the protection of prostate fluid.

Urination, an effective flushing mechanism, is nature's principal weapon against UTIs. Bacteria are able to invade when the urethra or bladder becomes swollen or irritated, or when an obstruction—such as a swollen prostate gland in men and pregnancy in women—prevents complete emptying of the bladder. Activities that can lead to UTIs include sexual intercourse, use of bubble baths, diaphragms, douches, or other irritants; in many instances, however, there is no identifiable activity associated with the infection.

Nearly 85 percent of urinary infections are caused by *Escherichia coli*, a bacterium normally present in the intestines. (Other bacteria and chlamydia also cause UTIs in sexually active young women.) *E. coli* can be easily transferred from the anus to the urethra of women. Lower abdominal pain and a burning sensation during urination are the principal symptoms among children; adults will also experience painful and frequent urination, and the urine will often be bloody and foul-smelling. If the kidneys are infected, there can also be fever and pain in the flanks. Men may also have low-back pain, and women can experience malaise. Occasionally, there are no symptoms, especially if the infection is in the kidneys.

Diagnosing a UTI depends on analysis and culture of the urine. Proper collection is crucial yet often not done. A "clean catch" specimen requires collecting urine only at midstream, and ideally, the urine should have been in the bladder for several hours.

If the patient has had the symptoms of UTI for 2 days or less, the treatment is often a single injection or large oral dose of an antibiotic, amoxicillin (a special penicillin) or the combination drugs Bactrim or Septra. If the woman has had the illness for more than 2 days, or if she has hemorrhagic cystitis (severe infection of the bladder), or if a culture taken 2 days after the single dose reveals the continued presence of infecting microbes, then a conventional 4- to 7-day course of antibiotics is recommended. With all therapy, the patient should also drink plenty of water.

As for prevention, there are measures that seem to help some women avoid repeated infections. Drink plenty of fluids so that urination will be frequent, and be sure to completely empty the bladder during each voiding. Keep the genital and anal areas clean with frequent washing with mild soap and water, and after a bowel movement, wipe from front to back to avoid introducing bacteria from the anus into the vagina. Empty the bladder before and immediately after intercourse, and avoid feminine hygiene sprays, bubble bath, and douches. If these fail, and if the infections are related to sexual intercourse, prophylactic antibiotics may be prescribed. (See also Chapter 37 on Disorders Common to Women, page 754.)

Kidney Infection

This is the most serious urinary tract infection and

often requires hospitalization. Infectious organisms almost always reach the kidneys by migrating up the urinary tract, although they are occasionally borne via the bloodstream from another infection site in the body. Fever rises rapidly upon infection, often reaching 104° F and producing chills and trembling, which may be accompanied by nausea and vomiting. Some patients feel as if they have to urinate constantly even though the bladder is empty. The urine is cloudy and may be tinged with blood. Pain, usually sudden and intense, is felt in the back just above the waist and gradually spreads down into the groin.

Initial treatment consists of intramuscular or intravenous antibiotics for several days. If the patient shows marked improvement, he or she can go home and continue oral antibiotic therapy for 2 weeks. Two days after the last dosage, a urine culture should be done to make sure no residual bacteria are present (up to 30 percent of patients relapse after apparent recovery). If the examination reveals persistent infection, antibiotics should then be taken for 4 to 6 more weeks.

Prostate Gland Infection

Because the prostate gland encircles the urethra in men, an infection of the gland interferes with discharge of urine and semen. Bacteria reach the gland by migrating up the urethra, and when infection occurs, the symptoms are fever, pain in the lower back and groin, and frequently painful urination. The prostate gland becomes very tender and sensitive, a fact that becomes obvious when the physician examines the gland by reaching a gloved finger through the anus.

A diagnosis of prostate infection is made by examining specimens of urine and prostate secretions. The latter are gathered by massaging the prostate after the bladder is empty and catching the few drops that trickle down the urethra. Treatment with antibiotics is usually rapidly effective. Chronic prostatitis requires antibiotic therapy for up to 3 months.

SEXUALLY TRANSMITTED DISEASES

Gonorrhea

With 2.5 million cases per year, gonorrhea is the most serious communicable disease in the United States. Caused by the *Neisseria gonorrhoeae* bacterium, the illness is confined largely to those between the ages of 20 and 30. Many people carry the bacterium without any signs of illness; in one study, 2 percent of all women studied at random were asymptomatic carriers.

Though sexual intercourse is the predominant means of transmission, gonorrhea bacteria may spread in other ways. It has recently been shown that the bacteria can survive for up to 4 hours on dry, inorganic surfaces. If a pregnant woman is infected, the disease may be passed to her baby during delivery. In these cases, the disease often attacks the infant's eyes and may cause blindness; this is why prophylactic eye drops are used on newborns.

Gonorrhea manifests itself 2 to 6 days after the bacteria invade the urethra. Among men, the main symptoms are burning upon urination and discharge from the penis of a purulent, yellowish liquid that looks like pus. Women may have a cloudy discharge from the vagina, some discomfort in the lower abdomen, or abnormal bleeding from the vagina. There can also be pain during urination. Frequently, there will be no noticeable symptoms at all, and unless the infection is somehow discovered, the person becomes a silent carrier of the disease.

Among people who engage in oral or anal sex, the mouth, throat, and rectum can also become infected. Often infection at these sites causes only very mild symptoms or none at all. If the throat is infected, symptoms may include a sore throat and tonsillitis; a constant urge to move the bowels, with an associated purulent discharge, are signs of anal gonorrhea.

The major complication of gonorrhea in women is pelvic inflammatory disease (PID)—a major cause of infertility. PID occurs when the bacteria work their way up from the cervix to infect the Fallopian tubes through which the egg must pass before it reaches the uterus. When Fallopian infection occurs—and it does in nearly 15 percent of women with gonorrhea—it happens fairly soon after the bacteria have invaded or during menstruation. If untreated, gonorrhea can also spread through the bloodstream and infect other parts of the body.

A certain diagnosis of gonorrhea requires a culture. With men, however, a doctor can usually make an accurate assessment on the basis of symptoms and a microscopic exam of the puslike discharge.

Such short-cut diagnosis with women is risky because there are so many bacteria normally inhabiting the vagina that resemble gonorrhea under the microscope.

The mainstay of treatment has always been and remains penicillin injection but the dosages have become much higher because the microbes have built up resistance. A second drug, probenicid, is now given orally to slow the excretion of the penicillin. In cases of allergy to the penicillin drugs, tetracycline may be used.

Strains of the *Neisseria gonorrhoeae*, totally resistant to penicillin, have recently been imported into the United States from Africa and the Philippines. These strains show up with varying incidence mainly in West Coast cities, and must be treated with alternative antibiotics.

Because of the growing problem of resistance, a repeat culture should be taken within 1 week after penicillin treatment to be sure the microbes are gone. This is especially true if the germs were in the anus, a location that makes them difficult to treat. The disappearance of symptoms is no guarantee of cure.

Another precaution that some experts advocate is a simultaneous course of tetracycline or erythromycin therapy over and above the penicillin–probenicid combination. These drugs would eradicate an infection by *Chlamydia trachomatis* microbes, which often simultaneously invade the genital tract along with *Neisseria gonorrhoeae*.

Chlamydial Infections

This increasingly common venereal infectious agent can invade almost any part of the genital tract of either sex as well as the anus. It is thus the cause of many cases of nonspecific urethritis, cervicitis, epididymitis, and other infections. When it infects the Fallopian tubes, it can cause sterility. It can also be transmitted to the newborn, causing eye infection or pneumonia. It is the most common cause of pelvic inflammatory disease (PID) in young women. Any sexually active young woman who has abdominal pain, vaginal discharge, and fever should make certain that her gynecologist checks for chlamydia. Both sex partners must be treated for chlamydia, just as they must for gonorrhea.

The most common diseases involving chlamydia are:

- *Nonspecific urethritis (NSU)*. Sometimes referred to as nongonococcal or postgonococcal urethritis, this is an illness that resembles gonorrhea but in which the cultures fail to show *Neisseria gonorrhoeae*. Certain diagnosis can only be made by culturing the discharge—a task that used to be impractical but that thanks to recent technological advances in diagnostic equipment is becoming more routine. The treatment is oral tetracycline for 1 to 2 weeks.

- *Rectal infections*. Chlamydia can cause rectal infections among people who engage in anal intercourse. It can cause rectal bleeding and severe soreness and swelling of lymph nodes in the pelvic area; there is also malaise, fever, and a general feeling of ill health. Untreated, it can cause serious complications in the genital area. Therapy consists of tetracycline.

Syphilis

Syphilis, the most serious venereal disease but far less common than gonorrhea, is caused by the bacterium *Treponema pallidum*, which lives only in humans. Today it is perhaps most prevalent among homosexual men. The bacteria easily penetrate the mucous membranes of the mouth, vagina, and the penis's urethra. The incubation period lasts 2 to 3 weeks but can be as long as 8 weeks. The first telltale sign of infection is the appearance on the genitals of a hard, painless, red, protruding sore or ulcer called a chancre (pronounced "shanker"). Occasionally the chancre will show up in the rectum or on the tongue, lips, or breast. In women, if the sore develops in the vagina or cervix it may go unnoticed. Another symptom at this early or primary stage of syphilis is some swelling of the lymph nodes nearest the chancre. A diagnosis can be made only by microscopic examination of a scraping from the chancre.

Secondary syphilis develops 2 to 6 weeks after the chancre heals and is characterized by flulike symptoms: fever, headache, loss of appetite, general malaise. There can also be enlarged lymph nodes, joint pain, and a skin rash of small, red, scaling bumps that do not itch. A diagnosis at this stage can be by a simple blood test.

The third and final stage of the disease is called latent or late syphilis. During this phase the disease flares up without warning, attacking almost any organ and mimicking many chronic conditions. It frequently affects the brain, causing paralysis, senility, insanity, loss of sensation in the legs, and rarely, blindness. Nerves to a joint can be destroyed. The large blood vessel leading from the heart (the aorta) can be damaged, as can the heart valves. Rarely in the United States does syphilis progress to the third stage.

Syphilis can also be passed along by a mother to her newborn. The usual signs of infection are skin sores or lesions, a runny nose, severe tenderness over the bones, and deafness. If umbilical cord blood is examined at the time of birth, antibiotic therapy can quickly eliminate infection, preventing any serious aftereffects.

Among adults, injections of penicillin will readily cure syphilis. If the nerves are infected, the physician may hospitalize the patient so that megadoses of the drug can be administered intravenously. Syphilis is highly contagious during its first and second stages, and any person who suspects or knows he or she has an infection should immediately notify all sexual partners.

Genital Herpes

Genital herpes is caused by the herpes simplex Type 2 virus, a close cousin of the Type 1 virus that causes cold sores. New cases of genital herpes develop among hundreds of thousands of Americans every year. It strikes all social and economic classes and is spreading in epidemic proportions.

The widely publicized epidemic has inspired exaggerated fears about the disease, leading many of its victims to fall into despair and adopt isolated lifestyles. True, there is no cure for the infection and once a person contracts genital herpes he or she will always harbor the virus. But herpes usually only spreads to sexual partners during active manifestation of the disease, and though most people suffer recurrences, each successive episode is briefer and milder. Among many people, recurrences stop altogether.

Spread by any form of sexual contact, the virus invades the body through tiny breaks in mucosal linings. About 6 days later the first symptoms will surface. Mild tingling and burning may precede the actual appearance of skin sores. Within a matter of hours, water blisters develop, often extensively. In women, the blisters or vesicles usually involve the external genitalia (the labia, skin around the rectum, and foreskin of the clitoris) as well as the vagina and cervix, which protrudes into the vaginal canal of the end of the uterus. There is often watery discharge and pain during urination.

Among men, the blisters break out on the penis and sometimes the testicles, and there will be a discharge of painful urination. Occasionally, the penis will swell painfully, narrowing the urinary opening.

Both men and women may experience low-grade fever, headache, generalized muscle ache, and tender, swollen lymph nodes in the groin. In a couple of days, the vesicles become pustular (pus-producing) and coalesce into large, painful ulcerlike sores. These crust over, dry, and heal without treatment or scarring. The entire episode, from the appearance of the blisters to the disappearance of all symptoms, lasts about 3 weeks. But the herpes can still be contagious for up to 2 weeks after symptoms fade. (The virus is most infectious in the blistering stage but can also be transferred during the tingling period just before the sores appear.)

The symptoms go away, but the virus does not. It travels along the nerves to the deep nerve centers (ganglia) at the base of the spinal cord near the buttocks. Here it goes into a silent period of inactivity or latency; when activated, it travels back down the nerves causing a new outbreak in the same area involved in the initial attack and sometimes on the buttocks, thighs, and abdomen as well. Anywhere from 50 to 75 percent will suffer a recurrent infection within 3 months of the initial episode. As time passes, attacks will come further apart and be less severe.

What causes reactivation of the latent viruses is not known for sure, but chronically ill or stressed people seem to have the most attacks. Other precipitating factors are thought to be menstruation, pregnancy, emotional distress, local trauma to the genitals, and even sexual intercourse itself.

The most serious complications of genital herpes affect women. Viral genital infections increase the risk of later cervical cancer. There is also a chance of passing along herpes to a baby born during an active infection. Consequently, any woman who has had the disease should have periodic Pap smears to detect cervical cancer at its earliest stages, and pregnant women should be watched closely for signs of an active infection near the time of delivery. If there is danger of passing the infection to the baby, a cesarean section is advised. A systemic herpes infection in a newborn can cause serious problems, including blindness, neurological problems, mental retardation, and even death.

Diagnosis of genital herpes can be confirmed by a microscopic examination of a scraping from a sore and by culturing such a specimen in a laboratory. Although there is no drug that cures an infection, acyclovir lotion applied to the affected area will relieve the pain and make the person less contagious by reducing the period during which viruses are shed. The same antiviral drug taken in pill form will also have the same ameliorative effects. Oral acyclovir can prevent recurrent attacks while it is being taken. But once the drug is stopped, the herpes may flare up again. In some cases acyclovir lotion used prophylactically when a patient senses a recurrence coming on will weaken the attack. The lotion is applied to the area where the blisters occurred in earlier outbreaks.

Symptoms may also be relieved somewhat by the use of local anesthetics and drying agents. The genital area should be bathed twice daily with mild soap and water and then gently pat-dried. Soaking in salt water is not recommended because it can sometimes worsen the condition. Lidocaine ointment, a local anesthetic, can help some people during the most painful part of an attack.

As for preventing herpes, sexual activity should be forsaken from the very first inkling or sensation that an attack is imminent to up to 1 week after all symptoms have disappeared (2 weeks in the case of the initial infection). The use of the condom is wise but not a guarantee of preventing spread.

Because genital herpes is so widespread, considerable stigma and emotional trauma have been associated with the disease. While no one relishes the thought of having an incurable, recurring disease, much of the hysteria over herpes is unwarranted. Except in unusual circumstances, the disease is more uncomfortable than serious.

Vaginitis

Infections of the vagina without involvement of the urinary tract can afflict all women, but are most common among the sexually active. Though a variety of microbes cause the disease, the symptoms are generally similar, including a discharge, itching and burning, pain during intercourse, and vaginal odor.

Infections caused by the protozoan *Trichomonas vaginalis* produce a profuse, malodorous, yellow, purulent, and often frothy discharge. Sores can develop on the cervix. Treatment is a large single dose of Flagyl. The sexual partner has to be treated, too.

Fungal vaginitis is caused by *Candida albicans* and produces a white discharge that resembles cottage cheese. There is no distinct odor. The predominant symptom is itching of the vulva. The disease can be successfully treated with one of several drugs or ointments.

Another common infective agent is the bacterium *Gardnerella vaginalis* (also known as *Haemophilus vaginalis* or *Corynebacterium vaginale);* it is associated with what is often called nonspecific vaginitis. It produces a white or grayish foul-smelling discharge that coats the vaginal walls. There may also be burning and itching. Sulfa drugs or antibiotics usually will eradicate this infection fairly quickly.

Acquired Immune Deficiency Syndrome (AIDS)

Acquired immune deficiency syndrome is a relatively new and lethal sexually transmitted disease that mainly afflicts promiscuous young male homosexuals in large cities. Researchers in both France and the United States have identified a virus, HTLV-III, that causes AIDS. As its name indicates, the disease's primary characteristic is a breakdown and failure of the immune system; it is not the suspected virus itself that kills the patient but the gross weakening of the immune system that the virus causes. This in turn opens the body to "opportunistic" infections and disorders that are normally warded off. The most common of these devastating opportunistic diseases are Kaposi's sarcoma, a rare form of skin cancer, and pneumonia caused by the virulent protozoa, *Pneumocystis carinii*. Others include meningitis, herpes simplex infections, and several other serious, uncommon bacterial, viral, and even fungal conditions.

AIDS usually begins with the development of fever of unknown origin, weight loss, fatigue, shortness of breath, diarrhea, and neurological disorders. Sometimes the lymph nodes will be swollen. The breathing problem can progress slowly or rapidly; a careful lung examination should be made to determine the cause, which is nearly always an infection. Lung infections should be treated immediately with antibiotics.

Although the bacterial infections and some of the other opportunistic diseases that plague AIDS patients can sometimes be successfully treated, more than half of all victims become progressively weaker, emaciated, prone to recurrent infections, and eventually die. For this reason, preventive measures become all important. Restraint in promiscuous sex is important. Although at this writing the most common victims have been male homosexuals, a number of experts fear that it may be spreading to the heterosexual population as well. Cases involving female prostitutes have been reported; the fear is they may transmit AIDS to heterosexual men who in turn will pass it on. Since the disease also can be transmitted via blood transfusions, homosexuals are discouraged from donating blood except for research purposes. A recently developed blood test can detect antibodies to the AIDS virus; however, this is not a diagnostic procedure.

AIDS, which can be transmitted by blood as well as saliva, semen, and other body fluids, also strikes heroin addicts who use contaminated syringes. Cases also have occurred in hemophiliacs. Another group that appears slightly at risk for contracting the disease is people from Haiti, although some investigators do not believe Haitians are more susceptible than anyone else. There also have been outbreaks in parts of Africa.

AIDS is under intensive study in Europe and the United States, and both a treatment and a vaccine may be developed for the disease within a few years. Indeed, the AIDS story is unfolding so fast that almost anything we write today may well be outdated before it can be published.

INFECTIONS CAUSED BY FUNGI

Histoplasmosis

This disease is caused by the inhalation of a fungus, *Histoplasma capsulatum*, which is most prevalent in the Mississippi, Ohio, and Missouri valleys and flourishes in soil enriched by bird, chicken, and bat droppings. (See figure 21.6.) In 80 percent of cases, it is a benign, self-limiting disease marked by headache, chills, fever, and sometimes lumps on the leg. There is also a cough and some chest pain, and unless a culture is done, the physician is more likely to suspect a virus. A few people develop a more severe lung disease, but antifungal medication can cure it.

Coccidioidomycosis

This is an acute respiratory disease endemic to the southwestern United States. It is caused by inhaling the fungus *Coccidioides immitis*, which is most prevalent in California's San Joaquin valley (the disease is often called San Joaquin or Valley Fever), but it can occur as far north as San Francisco.

About 2 weeks after inhaling the fungal spores, the patient develops fever, a nonproductive cough, and starts to lose weight. There may be pain when taking deep breaths (pleurisy), and lumps on the legs may show up. Diagnosis is established by finding the fungi in sputum, pleural fluid, or other specimens.

Most patients recover without treatment and with only a little scarring of the lungs. In a few people, though, the disease becomes progressive and can lead to a dangerous form of chronic meningitis. This requires therapy with a very potent antibiotic, amphotericin B, which must sometimes be administered via a special chamber implanted in the head.

Cryptococcosis

The fungus that causes this disease—*Cryptococcus neoformans*—is found throughout the world. It often occurs in pigeon droppings. In most people, it causes a simple form of pneumonia that clears up by itself, but in a few victims, chronic meningitis can result. This is manifested by chronic headaches, afternoon fever, personality changes, and other nonspecific symptoms. Meningitis usually develops among those who have an underlying disease such as Hodgkin's disease, leukemia, or AIDS. Diagnosis is made by examining the spinal fluid, and treatment is with the antifungal amphotericin B.

Candida (Monilia)

This disease is usually caused by *Candida albicans*, a fungus that we all carry at one time or another. In

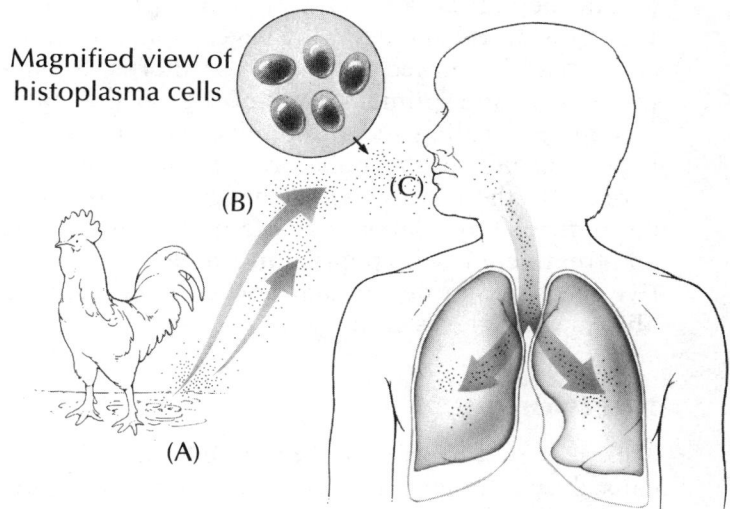

Life cycle of histoplasmosis.

Figure 21.6. **Life cycle of histoplasmosis. (A) The histoplasma fungus grows in soil enriched by droppings from infected chickens, birds, bats, or other animals. (B) The spores are released into the air. (C) When the spores are inhaled, they migrate to the lungs, resulting in symptoms typical of histoplasmosis.**

some circumstances, though, the organisms proliferate, producing symptomatic infection of the mouth, intestines, vagina, or skin. When the mouth or vagina are infected, the disease is commonly called thrush.

Vaginitis caused by *Candida* often afflicts women on birth control pills or antibiotics. There is itching and a white, cheesy discharge. Among narcotic addicts, *Candida* infections can lead to heart valve inflammation.

Diagnosis of *Candida* infections is confirmed by cultures and blood tests. Treatment can be with amphotericin B or flucytosine.

Aspergillosis

Caused by the ubiquitous *Aspergillus* fungus, this lung disease usually strikes people whose immune system has been weakened. It occurs most often among people with cancer (Hodgkin's and leukemia particularly) or people who have had a kidney transplant. It also may produce symptoms in people who are sensitive to the fungus, which is particularly common in decaying vegetation. Infection produces fever and cough. Treatment is with amphotericin B. In some cases, surgery may be needed to remove the fungus ball.

Sporotrichosis

Sporotrichosis occurs most often among gardeners and farmers. It is caused by a fungus—*Sporothrix*—that lives in soil and decaying vegetation. Infectious spores can be picked up from rose thorns, Sphagmum moss, and splinters from rotting wood. A painless but nonhealing and gradually expanding sore or ulcer appears at the puncture site, and infection spreads to the nearest lymph nodes. Diagnosis can be confirmed by a laboratory exam of a pus sample, and treatment is with potassium iodide. As a preventive measure, gardeners and horticulturists should always wear gloves on the job.

Ringworm

This is not a worm infestation but an infection caused by a fungus, usually a species of *Trichophyton*. Doctors call the infections Tinea. On the scalp, the fungi cause round, bald, scaly patches. The skin flakes and itches. A highly infectious disease that mainly afflicts children, ringworm of the scalp can become epidemic within a school or community. Diagnosis can be made by using an ultraviolet light or by examining a hair under the microscope.

Body ringworm appears as a round or oval sore that is red, scaly, and itchy. The patch gradually grows bigger until it is about an inch across. The central area heals, leaving a red ring on the skin. There are oral and topical drug treatments for ringworm of both the body and scalp.

Athlete's Foot

Another form of ringworm, athlete's foot is a fungal infection caused by *Trichophyton mentagrophytes*. It causes a dry scaling and fissuring of the skin between the toes and on the arch; it can also produce scaling and thickening of the soles. Secondary bacteria infections are not uncommon. People who spend many hours in sweaty socks and shoes are particularly susceptible (thus its name). Sterilization of footwear and antifungal foot baths are of little benefit. Also, avoid ointments, because the best strategy is to keep the feet dry (especially the skin between the toes). Air the feet often; use dry, absorbent socks, and wash the feet daily. If possible, wear sandals or open-toe shoes. If the infection persists, a doctor should be consulted for antifungal medication.

RICKETTSIAL INFECTIONS

RICKETTSIAE ARE MICROORGANISMS that are bigger than viruses but smaller than bacteria. They live within the cells of their hosts, which include ticks and other insects that pass them along to humans. Rickettsiae cause a variety of relatively uncommon illnesses characterized by fever, headache, malaise, and rash.

Rocky Mountain Spotted Fever

Rocky Mountain spotted fever is much more common in the Carolinas and in the islands off Massachusetts than in the western mountain region from which it derives its name. It is caused by rickettsiae transmitted by ticks and therefore shows up mainly in the summer between May and Labor Day, when adult ticks are active and people are most apt to be camping or hiking in the woods.

After an incubation period of about 1 week, a victim will experience abrupt and severe headache, chills, prostration, and muscular pains. Fever reaches 104° F within a few days and remains high, though morning remissions can occur. On about the fourth day of fever, a rash appears on the ankles, wrists, palms, and soles, and moves on to the trunk.

A physician can make a diagnosis by a blood test, but the test is often negative early in the course of illness so it is best to be treated with tetracycline if Rocky Mountain spotted fever is suspected. Chloramphenicol is another effective drug to use in children under 8, a group for whom tetracycline is not recommended. Delay in starting antimicrobial therapy is dangerous since this can be a rapidly progressing and ultimately fatal disease.

Typhus

Caused by *Rickettsia prowazekii* and transmitted by lice, typhus still exists in parts of Yugoslavia, the Soviet Union, and other places where people are crowded together in conditions of poor hygiene. About 2 weeks after infection, the victim suffers a severe headache and high fever; after 3 to 4 more days, a pinkish rash spreads over the body (except for the face). Early treatment with tetracycline or chloramphenicol is highly effective.

PARASITIC INFECTIONS

SEVERAL TINY and not-so-tiny members of the animal kingdom can cause serious illness in man. These include tapeworms, roundworms, flukes, and single-cell organisms called protozoa. Once a parasite establishes itself within the body, it is almost impossible to eliminate it without treatment. Relatively rare in the United States, parasitic infections strike Americans mainly while traveling abroad.

Malaria

Malaria is caused by the protozoa *Plasmodium* and transmitted by the bite of an infected anopheles mosquito. The disease is rare in the industrialized world but fairly common in many tropical countries. Once inside man, some malaria forms multiply in the liver and then reenter the bloodstream, causing the red blood cells to rupture. At the time the cells rupture, the characteristic chills, high fever (up to 106° F), and sweating develop. There is usually accompanying headache, weariness, and nausea. These symptoms appear anywhere from 10 to 40 days after the bite occurs. (See figure 21.7.)

A diagnosis of malaria is confirmed by a blood test and seeing the plasmodium in the blood. But the best time to observe the parasite in a blood sample is

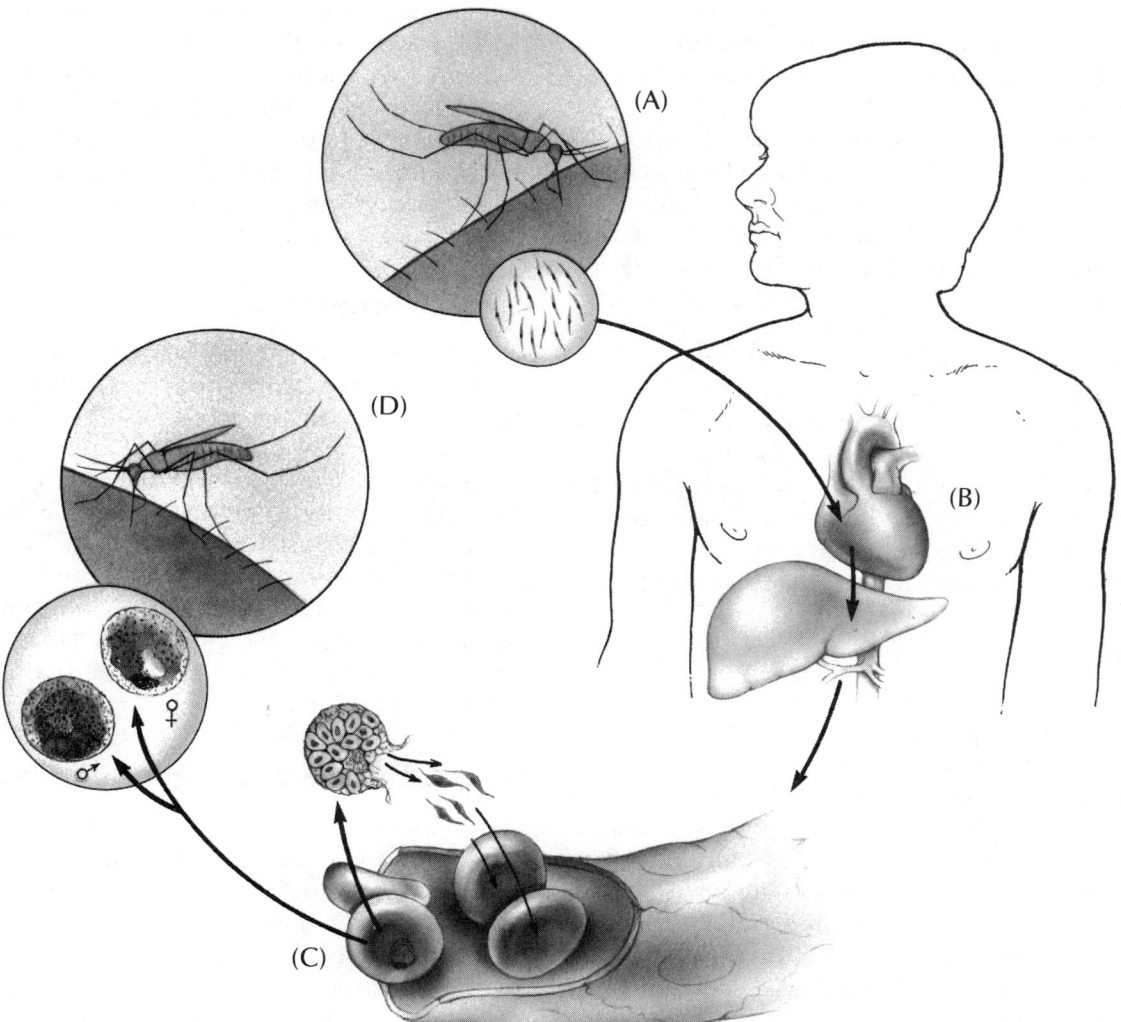

Figure 21.7. **Life cycle of malaria.**
(A) The mosquito starts the infective stage by injecting the malaria sporozoites with its saliva while sucking blood from its victim. (B) The sporozoites travel through the bloodstream to the liver where they mature and infect red blood cells. (C) The infected red blood cells pass the disease on via asexual reproduction to other red blood cells, or alternatively, divide into male and female cells (sexual reproduction). (D) Another mosquito starts the cycle anew by acquiring the sexual reproductive stage when withdrawing blood. The male and female cells complete their reproductive stage in the mosquito, and the resulting sporozoites are then transmitted when the mosquito bites again.

before the fever goes up. Treatment is with one of several effective drugs now available.

For people planning to travel to malarial areas, the drug chloroquin can be taken prophylactically; in areas such as Colombia and Southeast Asia and Kenya, where chloroquin-resistant protozoa have evolved, the drug Fansidar should be used instead. The drugs have to be started before departure and continued for 6 weeks after returning. Travelers should also use insect repellents.

Amebiasis

This is a disease of the intestinal tract caused by the tiny protozoa, *Entamoeba histolytica*. Spread person to person or indirectly via contaminated food or water, the organism dwells in the colon and rectum, where it produces ulcers and inflammation. It primarily afflicts homosexual men and visitors to countries with poor sanitation.

Most patients have a gradual onset of symptoms with increasing numbers of stools, reaching as many as 15 per day. Stools are semi-solid to liquid and often carry blood. There may be fever, local bowel tenderness, and cramping abdominal pain. If microbes invade the liver, there will be tenderness over this organ.

Diagnosis is confirmed by examining a fresh stool specimen. It is important that a specimen be taken before antibiotics, antacids, antidiarrheal agents, enemas, and intestinal radiocontrast agents (used in colon x-rays) are given since they all can interfere with recovery of the parasite. A successful diagnosis may require examination of several stool specimens. Fortunately, there is an excellent drug for amebiasis—metronidazole (Flagyl).

Giardiasis

Giardiasis is an infection of the small intestine caused by the protozoa *Giardia lamblia*. The disease is spread by fecal-oral routes, either directly between sexual partners, or indirectly via contaminated food or water. It occurs most often among male homosexuals and travelers to the Soviet Union and other countries with polluted water or among campers who drink from streams in which beavers live. The symptoms are abdominal discomfort with passage of lots of gas and stools that are foul in odor and float to the top of the toilet-bowl water. A diagnosis is made by looking at a fresh stool specimen to see if the parasite is present.

Some people who have recurrent, unexplained abdominal discomfort may have the *Giardia* parasite lodged in their duodenum, just below the stomach. The doctor can confirm a diagnosis by examining duodenal contents, obtained either by aspirations through a gastric tube or by having the patient swallow a nylon string to which the parasites attach themselves. The infection can be cured with Flagyl.

Pinworms

Pinworms account for the most common parasitic disorder among children in the United States. Pinworms colonize in the lower intestinal tract, and at night, the female worm crawls out to deposit eggs within skin folds. This leads to the characteristic sign of this infection—intense anal itching. Diagnosis can be made by placing a piece of cellophane tape in the area around the anus to pick up eggs, which can be seen under a microscope. Infections will go away on their own, but reinfection is common. A single dose of pyrantel pamoate will eradicate pinworms in about 90 percent of cases; a follow-up dosage should be taken 2 weeks later. Everyone in the family must be treated for an infestation to be wiped out. All sheets should be washed frequently to kill any eggs or worms that may be on them.

Hookworms

Nearly 25 percent of the world's population is infected with hookworms but the parasites are now relatively rare in the United States. They are contracted primarily by walking barefoot in soil contaminated with hookworm larvae; they penetrate the skin and migrate to the intestine, where they attach by their mouths and suck blood. The most common symptom is abdominal pain, but they can cause a silent anemia that is severe and can stunt the growth of children. Diagnosis is by laboratory detection of the hookworms' eggs in the stool. Several effective drugs are available.

Threadworm (Strongyloidiasis)

Threadworm, or Strongyloides, is endemic in the tropics and is generally found in the same climatic and sanitary conditions favorable to the spread of hookworm. It can also occur in unsanitary, crowded institutions anywhere. Like the hookworm, it dwells in the intestine and can cause epigastric pain and tenderness, vomiting, and diarrhea. Diagnosis is made by detecting the larvae in the stool, and treatment is with oral thiabendazole.

This disease can persist for decades. Some American soldiers who served in Burma during World War II didn't have the infection diagnosed for 30 years. Their only symptom was intermittent, unexplained abdominal pain.

SUMMING UP

THE DEVELOPMENT of vaccines, antibiotics, and other drugs effective against a wide range of disease-causing microbes has greatly diminished the incidence of most infectious diseases. Unfortunately, many microorganisms have developed resistance to some antibiotics, and other new infectious diseases, such as AIDS, have appeared. Thus, diligence is required on the part of both patients and physicians in preventing and treating infectious diseases.

22 Respiratory Diseases and Lung Health

Robert B. Mellins, M.D.

INTRODUCTION

THE HUMAN RESPIRATORY SYSTEM begins functioning within moments of birth, and from that time on, it provides clean, filtered air, warmed to body temperature, to the circulatory system. It will also remove used air, eliminate impurities, and enable the individual to speak and perform a variety of other tasks.

The respiratory system is composed of millions of parts. With luck and some care, the lungs will serve a lifetime, breathing in and out 15 times per minute for an average of 78 years or more. With each breath, air is inhaled through the nostrils or mouth to the throat (pharynx), past the tonsils and adenoids, which are air filters against infectious agents.

The air passes through the voicebox (larynx) and the windpipe (trachea) before entering a branching system of bronchial tubes in each lung. During this time it is warmed or cooled to body temperature.

In all of the breathing passages, air is filtered and impurities are trapped by mucus, a sticky fluid that comes from tiny gland cells in the passage linings. Mucus also moistens dry air so that the lungs cannot be dried by the air reaching them. Mucus moves, to keep it fresh and filtered of the impurities it traps. This is done by microscopic, hairlike projections that grow out of the passageway walls, called cilia.

There are millions of cilia in every square inch of mucous membrane along every part of the respiratory tract. The cilia move in a coordinated pattern that carries the mucus from the bottom of the lungs toward the throat. Impurities are moved up and out of the lungs into the nasal passage, where they can be sneezed out, or to the throat, where they are coughed out or swallowed.

Of course, these impurities, cast into the air from sneezes and coughs, may be taken into others' vulnerable respiratory systems and produce illness. Damaged cilia cannot carry out this function and certain substances—including cigarette smoke and various gases in the air—slow down the cilia, opening the way for disease.

The bronchial tree brings the purified air into the lungs. There is a bronchus for each lung, and each bronchus further divides into 2 secondary bronchi. Each of these divides, through 20 divisions. Air then enters more than 1 million small passageways called bronchioles. These lead to even smaller ducts to the alveoli. There are about 300 million alveoli, small sacs with walls the thickness of bubbles.

Oxygen flows from the alveoli to the blood vessels in the lungs, directly through the alveolar walls. From the bloodstream, oxygen enters those cells of the body that need it. Through chemical reactions, the oxygen generates heat and other forms of energy to maintain the body. A by-product of this process is carbon dioxide, which returns from the cells to the bloodstream and then to the alveoli, back through the bronchial tree, through the throat and nasal passages, and out.

The main responsibility of patients toward their lungs is to provide the best possible conditions for their operation: avoiding pollutants, including tobacco smoke, and keeping the body fit through good nutrition, and appropriate exercise for age and ability, in order to maintain resistance to airborne disease.

As the body's only major internal organ exposed to the outside, the lungs—particularly those of children, the elderly, and those with medical conditions—are vulnerable to mistreatment. In addition to its gas exchanging function, it is now recognized that the lung serves important nonrespiratory functions. Some of these functions are focused on fighting infection; others are concerned with processing a wide variety of chemicals carried to the lung by the blood. These are generally referred to as the metabolic activities of the lung. These activities are important in health, e.g., in forming angiotensin II— one of the most powerful natural substances that maintain blood pressure—and in disease, e.g., by inactivating excessive amounts of substances, such as serotonin, involved in blood clotting.

DIFFICULTY IN BREATHING

FEELING OF BREATHLESSNESS or shortness of breath (dyspnea) is an unpleasant sensation that may be a symptom of a number of diseases, ranging from asthma and bronchitis and other respiratory disorders to heart disease and defects in the lungs or chest wall. In general, there are 2 types of dyspnea: obstructive, which is caused by obstruction of the air passages, and restrictive, which may be due to defects in the lung or chest that prevent the lungs from fully expanding. In restrictive disorders, there usually is no difficulty in breathing when the person is at rest, but even moderate physical activity may produce labored breathing and a feeling of breathlessness.

Shortness of breath is an early symptom of heart disease. The heart muscle does not receive adequate oxygenated blood or the heart itself is unable to pump enough blood to meet the needs of the brain and other vital organs. Although the body responds by overbreathing (hyperventilation) when there is insufficient delivery of oxygen to the tissues, this can lead to increasing the acidity of the body's internal chemistry, which in turn stimulates more breathing. Anemia, in which the blood lacks sufficient hemoglobin to transport oxygen, also produces dyspnea. An upset in body chemistry, such as the acidic state that occurs in diabetic acidosis, leads to labored breathing. Anxiety also can lead to hyperventilation and a change in body chemistry. Treatment of shortness of breath depends upon the cause. In diabetic acidosis, for example, restoring the normal acid/alkaline balance of the body's chemistry will stop the dyspnea. In any event, feelings of breathlessness or difficulty in breathing are a warning sign to seek medical attention.

CHRONIC PULMONARY DISEASES

EVERYONE KNOWS SOMEONE who has chronic lung disease: breathlessness on exertion; "smoker's cough"; lingering coughs and respiratory problems after a cold; frequent colds; pulmonary diseases—chronic bronchitis and emphysema (chronic obstructive pulmonary disease [COPD]). Their respiratory systems have undergone significant changes and those with COPD have limitations on their lungs' ability to function.

Ordinarily, the respiratory tract takes in air when the lungs—which are very flexible—inhale, and the chest expands. The particles inhaled, from polluted air, cigarette smoke, or someone else's sneeze or cough, are trapped in the bronchial passages by mucus, which also keeps the passages lubricated.

The cleaned air flows into the innermost portion of the lungs, the alveoli, through the bronchial passages. The alveoli are thin enough to pass oxygen to the blood vessels and to retrieve waste gases from the circulatory system. Then the waste gases are expelled as the chest contracts and the lungs return to their original size. This process, which relies on the flexibility and permeability of the lungs, takes place about 15 times per minute. (See figure 22.1.)

Chronic bronchitis and emphysema are conditions in which this process is impaired, sometimes to a great degree. (See figure 22.2.)

Chronic Bronchitis

Many people suffer a brief attack of acute bronchitis, or inflammation of the airways with fever, coughing, and spitting when they have colds. Chronic bronchitis is the term used when this spitting and coughing continues for months and returns each year, lasting longer each time.

In chronic bronchitis, the airways have become narrowed and partly clogged with mucus that is not moving along as it normally does, propelled by small, hairlike projections in the airways called cilia. Air has trouble entering and leaving lungs that have chronic bronchitis.

Cigarette smoke has been associated with irritating the airways, causing them to narrow, and paralyzing the cilia. Those who quit smoking find that chronic bronchitis is lessened after a while. From

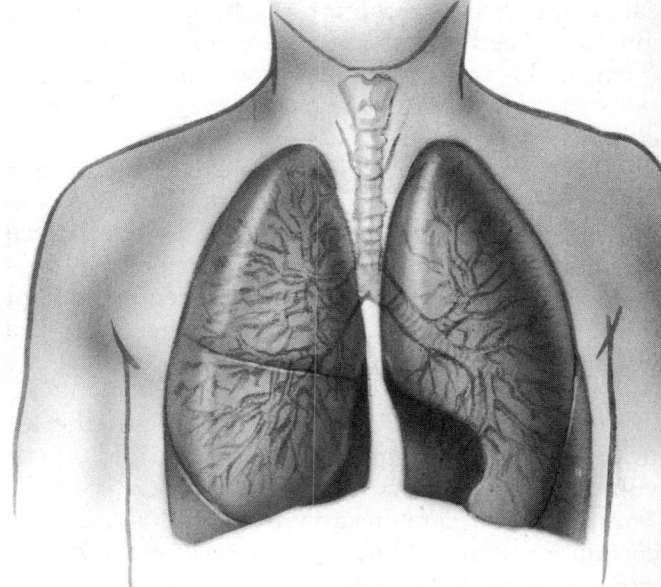

Figure 22.1.   Normal lungs.

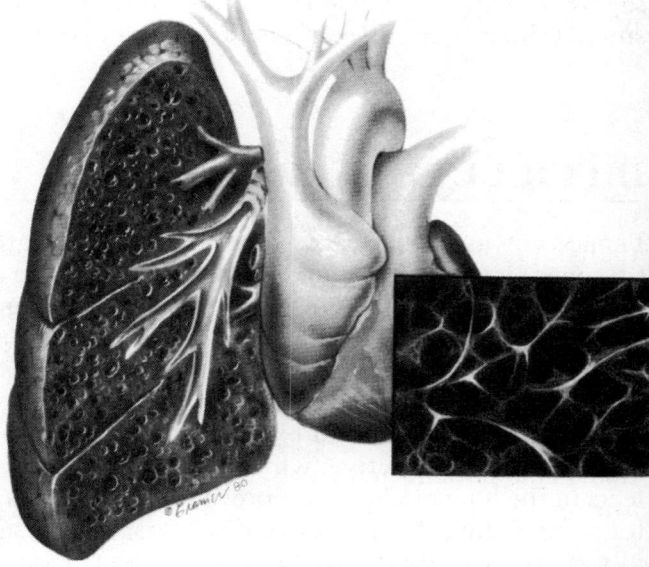

Figure 22.2.   A cross-section of lung tissue and enlargement showing the characteristic breakdown of alveolar sacs that occurs in chronic obstructive lung diseases.

chronic bronchitis, there is a possibility of a progression to a life-threatening lung disease, emphysema.

Emphysema

Emphysema is characterized by loss of the normal elasticity of the lung that helps to hold the airways open. With progressive inelasticity of the lungs, the small airways collapse on expiration, making it impossible to fully exhale stale air. The people in this country who have emphysema follow a pattern: They are primarily men, between 50 and 70, who have been heavy smokers for years. In the past, women did not develop emphysema as often as men, but this pattern is changing as women continue to become heavy smokers. Half of the people in this country who have emphysema are over 65; nearly all the rest are over 45. Frequently, those with emphysema live in areas where pollution is a constant problem.

Our current understanding is that there is a delicate balance between natural substances that fight disease but can also destroy lung tissue (proteases) and other substances that prevent this destructive process, e.g., alpha-l-antitrypsin. Some people are born with a deficiency in their ability to produce alpha-l-antitrypsin, which makes it more likely they'll get emphysema, and at an earlier age. But a major cause of both chronic bronchitis and emphysema is smoking.

Emphysema may masquerade for years as something else. A person with emphysema has probably had several very bad colds each winter for a few years, each accompanied by a heavy cough, and perhaps by chronic bronchitis. The cough often persists and becomes chronic.

Emphysema develops slowly. Slight morning and evening difficulty in breathing may be followed sometime later with the beginnings of interference in activities. A short walk may be enough to bring on breathlessness; walking up stairs is difficult. Eventually, as the lungs become less and less able to carry out inhaling, exhaling, and gas exchange, there may come a point when every breath requires a major effort and the patient is disabled and unable to carry out normal activities.

Shortness of breath is the symptom that most commonly prompts a person to seek medical attention. The patient may mistake the problem for asthma or heart disease. In fact, emphysema may lead to serious cardiovascular problems. Because the disease interferes with the passage of blood through the lungs and into the circulation, the heart must work harder. It may enlarge and eventually lead to heart failure.

Although emphysema cannot be cured, there are a number of treatments that enable patients to live more comfortably with the disease. For example, patients can learn to:

- Control their breathing to make it easier on their lungs.
- Do exercises that strengthen the diaphragm and abdominal muscles to help in the breathing process, or take medications that strengthen the force of the respiratory muscles, much as digitalis improves the force of the heart muscle.
- Clear the lungs of excess mucus by lying in special positions that help drainage.
- Build strength with a walking and exercise program.
- Use appropriate combinations of medicines, breathing aids, and living patterns to make life more comfortable.

Bronchiectasis

Bronchiectasis is now a relatively rare disorder in which the bronchi are chronically dilated or expanded as a result of chronic inflammation. This leads to an accumulation of mucus in the breathing tubes, increasing the danger of infection and inflammation of lung tissue. The disease may be caused by a congenital abnormality, but more commonly, it is a result of other diseases or circumstances. At one time, tuberculosis was a common cause; today, more likely causes include pneumonia, cystic fibrosis, chronic bronchitis, sinusitis, emphysema, measles, silicosis, lung abscess, or lung cancer. Aspiration of foreign objects into the lungs, for example, the inhaling of vomitus into the lungs during surgery, also may cause bronchiectasis.

The affected areas may be localized, confined to one portion of the lung, or they may be scattered throughout both lobes. Only in rare instances will the entire lung be involved. As the disease progresses, the bronchi become thick-walled sacs, with cystlike spaces. The normal structures of the bronchial walls may eventually be destroyed, leading to a spread of the infection and hemorrhage.

The most common symptom of bronchiectasis is a chronic cough, which may produce large amounts of thick, foul-smelling sputum. (In some cases, however, there is very little coughing and minimal production of sputum.) The foul smell is caused by death of the affected lung tissue.

Complications of bronchiectasis include recurring pneumonia, abnormal lung function, and frequent lung infections. The onset is often insidious; the disease may follow a bout of severe flu, whooping cough, or pneumonia. At first, the cough occurs sporadically, usually in the morning, the late afternoon or after going to bed. A change in posture may provoke a spell of coughing. Initially, the cough may be dry, but as the disease progresses, it is likely to produce increasing amounts of sputum. Shortness of breath during exercise may occur. Other signs include a clubbing, or thickening of the fingertips.

Diagnosis is made though bronchography, or special x-ray studies of the lungs, such as CT scans. The sputum should be studied to identify the presence and type of any infecting microorganisms.

Treatment usually involves controlling the infection with antibiotics. In some instances, the diseased area may be removed surgically if it is confined to one area of the lung. Patients should be alert to signs of recurring episodes so that antibiotic therapy can be resumed promptly. In some cases of chronic bronchiectasis, long-term antibiotics may be given as a preventive measure.

HEART AND LUNG DISEASE

Cor Pulmonale

Some of the most frequent abnormal lung conditions are associated with heart disease because these two organs are close, both in position within the body and in function. Cor pulmonale (CP)—failure of the right side of the heart due to lung dysfunction—is one of these conditions.

The heart nestles between the two soft lungs, beating freely, yet protected against pressure or injury. Normal pressure maintained in the chest cavity by the lungs helps move blood through the heart. Reserves of blood in the lungs, and their ability to move that blood through the circulatory system and to assist the heart's functions during violent exertion, tie the heart and lungs together as an integrated system.

Normally, the right side of the heart is weaker than the left, since the pressure required to push blood through the lungs is much less than that required to pump blood to the rest of the body. Normal lungs help this side of the heart function. But when the patient has emphysema, silicosis, or another severe lung disease which inhibits the lungs' function, it becomes much more difficult to pump blood through the lungs, and increasing pressure or force is required by the right side of the heart. Even though the heart muscle becomes overdeveloped to compensate, eventually it fails. Outward signs include swelling (edema) of the lower extremities and of the liver.

Lung Embolism and Infarction

The cardiopulmonary system circulates blood through the body in a continuing, uninterrupted manner. But sometimes matter foreign to the bloodstream—an embolus—plugs an artery. Infarction is the process of tissue damage caused by the blood supply being cut off to a region of the body by an embolus or a thrombosis (local clotting).

The lung is the organ most subject to embolism because all of the blood from every part of the body must come to it on each circuit. It is less vulnerable to infarction, unless already damaged by pulmonary or cardiac disease. Thrombosis does occur in the lung arteries. (See figure 22.3.)

The most common place emboli form that reach the lung is the wall of the heart. The next most common source of lung emboli is the lower extremities. Emboli can form there after an operation, a prolonged stay in bed, or following an injury because the prolonged inactivity increases the chances of clots forming in the deep veins of the leg. Tiny pieces of these clots may break away, travel through the venous system, and lodge in the lungs. This is one reason why surgery patients are encouraged to be up and about as soon as possible, or to keep their legs elevated to prevent blood pooling and clotting. If a large embolus enters the lungs, or smaller emboli enters lungs already congested by lung disease, and there is considerable infarction, the patient may quickly fall unconscious and die. If the patient survives a first embolism, his or her body has fought it by concentrating white blood cells at the site. Normal function may be restored in a few weeks. But physicians consider patients who survive an initial embolism as being vulnerable to more, because the source of the clots may set free more of them to lodge in the lungs.

Lung embolism is more frequent in women than in men, and in both sexes over age 45. The majority of lung embolisms are accompanied by heart disease or occur postoperatively. (It is in order to prevent this that patients are gotten out of bed earlier than in the past.) Others may follow trauma, infections, pregnancies, one-side paralysis (usually from stroke), cancer, and varicose veins.

Infarction may be treated medically with anticoagulants, relief of chest pain, and cough control. Oxygen is often administered. Under exceptional

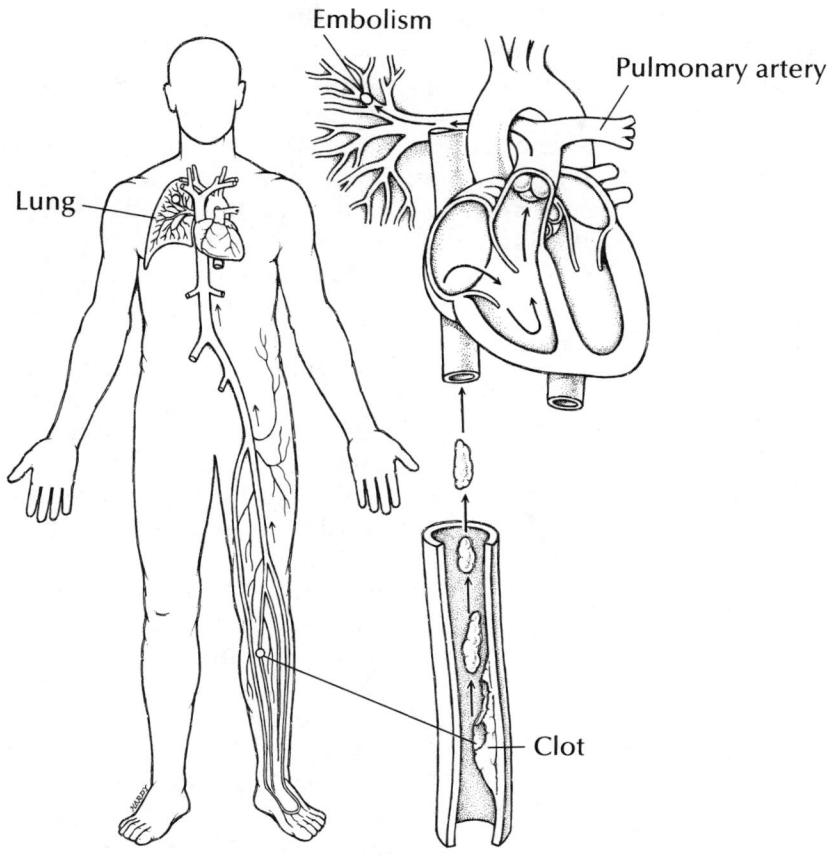

Figure 22.3. **Development of a thrombosis (clot) in the leg, with a piece of the clot breaking off and traveling through the heart and the pulmonary artery to lodge in the lungs, which causes a pulmonary embolism.**

conditions where a surgical team can be mobilized immediately, the clot or clots might be removed from the pulmonary artery. Open heart surgery and surgery to remove thrombi from the lining of the heart or from major arteries are also performed.

Circulation of blood in the extremities is re-duced when the body remains in one position for a long time, and this predisposes people to peripheral embolism. For this reason, it is important to stand and move about or do exercises periodically to break up a period of confinement, such as a long airplane ride.

CHRONIC LUNG DISEASE AND SMOKING

CLEARLY, CHRONIC OBSTRUCTIVE PULMONARY DISEASE (COPD) wreaks havoc with lives. And there is a definite link established between the development of COPD and smoking.

- As there is between COPD and lung cancer as well as cancer of the oral cavity, esophagus, larynx, urinary bladder, kidney, and pancreas.

- As there is in low-birthweight babies, candidates for respiratory infections, when the mother smokes during and after pregnancy.

- As there is in the startling fact that lung cancer has surpassed breast cancer as the leading cause of cancer in women in this decade.

More than 20 years ago, when the U.S. Surgeon General issued the first report linking smoking and illness, it became clear to the medical community that smoking, sickness, and premature death were related. But 53 million people—one-third of all adult Americans—still smoke. Every year, 340,000 of these people die prematurely from diseases caused by cigarette smoking. Cigarette smoking accounts for an estimated $13 billion in direct health-care expenses every year: medical, surgical, nursing, hospital, and home-care costs. In addition, the American economy loses $25 billion every year through lost productivity from workers who fall ill from smoking-related diseases. Clearly, quitting smoking is the best thing anyone who smokes can do to promote lung health. (See How to Quit Smoking, Chapter 18, page 345.)

Marijuana Use: Its Health Effects

Marijuana smoke contains many of the same respiratory irritants found in tobacco smoke. In addition, it contains other substances not found in tobacco smoke, such as delta-9-tetrahydrocannabinol (THC) and other compounds, some of which are irritating to the lung.

There are more than 30,000 studies that document the irritant and disease-producing effects of tobacco smoke on the lungs and other parts of the body. Habitual marijuana smoking may be harmful in the same way.

In a recent survey, the National Institute on Drug Abuse said there were 23 million current users of marijuana in the United States and 55 million who had used it at some time in the past. In the age bracket 12 to 17, there were 4 million current users versus 2.8 million tobacco users. Between 18 and 25, there were 11 million marijuana users versus 13 million for tobacco; age 26 and over, there were 8 million users and about 34 million who used tobacco.

The way Americans smoke marijuana is of particular concern for lung health. Smoke concentrators, called "bongs," "carburators," "power hitters," and "buzz bombs" have been developed to concentrate the smoke and deliver it under pressure to the lungs, thereby delivering a higher dose of THC and other constituents, and potentially more lung irritation. In the United States, where illicit marijuana is relatively expensive, the preferred smoking technique for marijuana cigarettes is deep puffs and holding smoke in the lungs for 10 to 60 seconds, presumably to increase the delivery of THC.

Studies conducted over the last 20 years have suggested that these practices inflame the airways, create carcinogenic changes in respiratory cells, and make the lungs and respiratory system more vulnerable to infection and disease because of fungus and bacteria contamination of the marijuana. The presence of known carcinogens in marijuana smoke suggests that inhalation of the smoke from marijuana into the lungs has the potential for causing lung cancer.

In the United States, a higher percentage of marijuana smokers than nonmarijuana smokers also smoke tobacco, and sometimes tobacco is mixed with marijuana for smoking. Research suggests that those who smoke marijuana and tobacco are at greater risk for respiratory tract irritation than those who do not. (For more details, see Chapter 18 on Smoking, Alcohol, and Substance Abuse, page 355.)

LUNG DISEASES IN INFANTS AND CHILDREN

THE LUNGS are the organs that cause the most problems in newborns, infants, and young children. Episodes of illness related to the lungs result in more children's hospitalizations, time lost from school, and family disruption than any other category of disease.

Babies have one-tenth of the air sacs they will have as adults. Injuries to the lungs or disease suffered early in life can therefore have serious effects. Young children also may have many, often severe, lung infections like pneumonia, bronchiolitis, or croup. They develop chronic conditions like asthma. Serious diseases like cystic fibrosis and sickle cell anemia make themselves known in childhood.

Children are also explorers. They have accidents in which they swallow or inhale (aspirate) various objects; choking may result or, if an object is re-

tained in the respiratory system, the child can become gravely ill.

Respiratory Distress Syndrome

Respiratory distress syndrome (RDS), also known as hyaline membrane disease, used to take the lives of as many as 25,000 to 30,000 infants each year. Because the medical community now better understands how the disease develops, and because of better treatments, the death rate has been reduced. Instead of the 65 or 75 percent mortality rate in RDS babies of the past, many medical centers are now reporting that 75 percent or more of the infants with RDS live.

RDS occurs in premature infants primarily, with more boys affected than girls. It also may occur in the full-term infants of diabetic mothers or those who deliver by cesarian section. Some newborn infants, probably because of immaturity, lack a vital substance—surfactant, a type of lubricant, which prevents the alveoli from collapsing every time the infant exhales.

The infant shows signs of respiratory distress within the first hours after birth—perhaps even in the delivery room. Tests show abnormalities in the lungs and in the blood serum because there is insufficient oxygen.

Treatment includes administering carefully measured concentrations of oxygen, intravenous fluids, and sometimes mechanical breathing apparatus to keep the lungs from collapsing. After a few days, over two-thirds of RDS babies improve greatly. Their breathing becomes less strained, they become more active, and the amount of oxygen in the blood becomes normal. About 25 percent simply do not respond to treatment; it remains for researchers to find out why.

Medical research has made great strides in helping RDS babies survive. Both the development of artificial surfactant and perfection of the means of providing oxygen to the tiny lungs have consumed the time and talents of a large number of researchers and reduced the mortality rate of RDS by more than half.

Bronchopulmonary Dysplasia

Bronchopulmonary dysplasia (BPD) is a disease that develops primarily in infants who have been treated for RDS. However, a small percentage of cases occurs in infants who have no history of RDS. It is the small lungs' reaction to the lifesaving intensive treatment with oxygen and mechanical ventilators. BPD is diagnosed by x-raying the baby's chest while he or she recovers from RDS. Once BPD has been diagnosed, there is no special or speedy cure. The baby's lungs will repair themselves over time, but the infant will require continuing hospitalization. Parents of BPD babies are advised to be patient, loving, and careful with their babies after discharge, since the lungs are somewhat more vulnerable than those of other babies for some time.

Other lung conditions may occur as a result of the birth process. The delivery room procedure of suctioning the infant when he first makes his appearance helps avoid respiratory problems related to aspiration of substances present in the birth canal.

Pneumothorax

Air leaks from the lungs into other parts of the chest cavity can occur in newborns, and it is a potentially serious problem. Small air leaks occur in 1 to 2 percent of all births. Babies are normally born with collapsed lungs, and considerable pressure is generated as the newborn's body works to inflate them with the first few breaths. There is no problem whatsoever for about 98 percent of newborns. But in some babies, the lungs do not open completely at once, and the pressure may cause small ruptures in the alveoli (smallest, most plentiful breathing sacs). The leaked air may be removed from the chest cavity by the attending physician, and the continuous removal of leaked air is necessary until the ruptures heal. One technique of treating RDS, called continuous distending pressure, is useful in that it keeps the lungs from collapsing, but it may occasionally precipitate air leaks because of pressure on the lungs. Newer techniques, which ventilate the lungs at lower pressures, are now being developed.

Congenital Lobar Emphysema

A newborn's bronchial tubes may be improperly developed, or there may be a substance partially blocking one of them. In the affected lobe of the lung, air is able to enter, but not to leave. The lobe becomes distended and there are air leaks. The baby, who is usually between 1 week and 1 month old, experiences shortness of breath and wheezes. He may begin to show signs of cyanosis (bluish lips and fingernail beds). In a limited number of cases, surgery on the lung is necessary.

Perinatal Asphyxia

It has been known for over 300 years that infants being born can survive with insufficient oxygen for longer periods than adults. The air-deprived newborn is capable of temporarily using energy sources that do not require oxygen, thought to be carbohydrate-rich glycogen, stored in the heart. It is also true that between the time the placenta (birth sac) separates from the uterus—and the mother's oxygen supply—and the time the infant's lungs start respiration on their own, there is a lapse. (Researchers believe this change may stimulate the infant's first breath.)

Sometimes, however, labor is especially long and difficult, or the fetus may be positioned abnormally in the birth canal so his backside or leg is born first. Sometimes the second born of twins may have decreased oxygen supply for an especially long time. Sometimes the mother may have a condition, such as high blood pressure, which may affect the fetal blood supply. Smoking by the mother is also associated with this condition. The result is that the newborn is not able to start up his own lungs without help.

It takes coordinated effort on the part of the health-care team to see that such babies are born fairly rapidly and that their lungs are activated. Fetal monitoring gives the team information about the existence of fetal asphyxia. Emergency resuscitation procedures are carried out. Mothers-to-be at high risk for this condition should ideally give birth in a large medical facility where this kind of skilled help is available.

Choanal Atresia

Infants can breathe only through the nose for the first few months. When an infant is born with a bony obstruction in the nasal passage, respiration can be difficult and the obstruction must be removed.

Stridor

Stridor is a medium-pitched, almost musical sound originating primarily in the larynx or trachea and produced by some babies when they inhale. Although it is troubling to parents, it is usually not serious and does not require treatment. It is often associated with croup, in which case it is self-limiting. It can also be congenital and, in this case, it usually improves and disappears with age.

Drug Withdrawal

The newborn of a mother who is a drug addict may be born with an imbalanced metabolism that affects breathing and that may continue for several weeks until the drugs have completely disappeared from the infant's body.

Pulmonary Immaturity (Wilson-Mikity Syndrome)

Infants of low birth weight (less than 3 pounds, 5 ounces) may have underdeveloped respiratory systems. It takes time and patience for the infant's respiratory system to improve in its ability to sustain life, and there is considerable risk in this condition. Usually, the baby's respiratory system is appropriate for his age by the time he is 6 months to 2 years old. Some infants are born with such underdeveloped lungs (pulmonary hypoplasia) that they are not able to survive.

Structural Malformations

Defects in the face, mouth, chest wall, diaphragm, heart, and major blood vessels may lead to respiratory problems in an infant. Great care in feeding and positioning and possible correction by surgery are indicated.

Sudden Infant Death Syndrome

Every year, some 10,000 seemingly healthy infants are put to bed and are later found dead, about 3 infants out of 1,000 live births. Sudden infant death syndrome (SIDS) is the largest single cause of infant mortality beyond the newborn period.

SIDS infants are usually 2 to 4 months old. The syndrome is rarely seen after the age of 6 months. Boys die more often than girls, and there are fewer cases in the summer than in the other months. A significant number of SIDS infants have low birth weights. However, maternal smoking is now recognized as a greater risk factor for SIDS than low birth weight. Low socioeconomic status is a predisposing factor, although SIDS occurs in all groups. Genetic factors have not been demonstrated but there is a tendency for SIDS to occur more than once in families. Sometimes a sleeping child is found not breathing (in an apneic condition) and may be resuscitated. The relationship between these near-SIDS cases and actual SIDS cases is uncertain.

There are many suggested causes of SIDS and many other possibilities under investigation; however, there is not conclusive proof. At present, a disturbance of normal sleep patterns and a combination of biochemical and neurological abnormalities or immaturity of cardiorespiratory control are the focal points of much research.

Families who want to know more about SIDS or who want to share their experiences with other families who have lost a child to SIDS may want to contact the National Foundation for Sudden Infant Death Syndrome or its local chapters.

Bronchiolitis

An infant's small airways (bronchioles), which carry air into the lungs, are much narrower than later in childhood or in adult life. When the infant's airways are partially or completely obstructed by an inflammation due to a virus, the infant can have great difficulty taking in fresh air and may incompletely expel used air from the lungs. An acute infection may develop, characterized by wheezing, efforts to clear the small lungs by exhaling heavily, and rapid breathing. This is bronchiolitis.

Most cases of bronchiolitis are reported in January and February, and there is usually someone else in the household who has a respiratory infection at the same time as, or shortly before, the infant gets sick.

When bronchiolitis is severe, the infant is usually hospitalized and observed carefully. Oxygen may be administered and intensive care is provided if complications develop. Within 2 or 3 days, bronchiolitis has usually run its course. It is frightening, but rarely fatal.

Cystic Fibrosis

Cystic fibrosis is a severe, genetically determined disease which involves both the lungs and gastrointestinal tract, as well as other organs. It occurs in about 1 in 2,000 live births among white children, and at a far lower rate in black and Asian children. Boys and girls get cystic fibrosis equally.

Cystic fibrosis is transmitted to a child when both parents carry the recessive gene but do not have the disease. When such a couple has children, there is a 25 percent chance that one of their children will develop cystic fibrosis. There is a 50 percent chance that the child will carry the gene but will not have the disease, and a 25 percent chance that the child will be totally unaffected.

The glands that secrete sweat and mucus are affected in this disease. The mucus is very thick and sticky and blocks airways and bile ducts. In addition, the sweat is very salty, and the child may suffer from salt depletion and heat prostration when he or she sweats during hot weather. Children with cystic fibrosis have repeated bacterial infections. Fever, cough, difficulty in breathing, fast respiration, flaring of the nostrils, poor appetite, and reduced activity are typical features of acute cystic fibrosis. Lung collapse, excessive mucus in the bronchi, or abscesses are possible. Sometimes, because of the air that is chronically trapped in the chest, the child gets a barrel-chested appearance.

Cystic fibrosis is diagnosed with a sweat test, which measures the amount of salt in the sweat. If the test is positive, there should be a second test. Then, since the child's siblings stand a chance of also having cystic fibrosis, they should be tested, too. Sometimes additional tests are used as well.

At present, 50 percent of those diagnosed as having cystic fibrosis as infants or young children live only until their late teens and twenties. However, an increasing number of children and young adults with cystic fibrosis are only mildly affected and are living into adult life. Research is continuing in this country, Canada, Australia, and Europe.

Cystic fibrosis is treated at home with antibiotics, special exercises for draining of sputum, breathing and physical exercise, and aerosols, as well as with diet therapy. Surgery is sometimes performed to correct physical complications.

Croup

Colds can be the forerunners of other unpleasant but short-lived conditions in youngsters' respiratory systems. When an infant or young child develops a cold with a cough, runny nose, and a low-grade fever, then wakes up several nights later with difficult, noisy breathing, and a harsh cough, he or she has developed the viral infection called croup. Other symptoms may include rapid breathing, pulled in breastbone, vomiting, and a sore throat. Steam from a hot shower in a closed bathroom can quickly relieve the symptoms, as can cold night air. Mild viral croup unaccompanied by fever can usually be treated at home if the child's pediatrician agrees. Using moist heat—humidification—at home is usually sufficient to relieve mild viral croup in a few days.

Children who have croup with fever or who show signs of severe breathing difficulties, restlessness, or signs of insufficient oxygen, like cyanosis (blue lips or nails), are usually admitted to the hospital. There, moist air is given either in special "croup rooms" or with a face mask or croup tent. Oxygen is often given, and some hospitals also give inhaled or injected medication similar to that used to open airways and relieve acute asthma episodes. In one form of severe croup, which has a bacterial rather than a viral cause, the child's airway may swell and start to close. This condition is called epiglottitis. An artificial airway may then have to be inserted through the nose past the pharynx to the larynx to enable the child to breathe, or an airway created surgically. The child will be placed in intensive care for observation and given antibiotics.

Croup is a frightening illness for the parents and the child. The child needs gentle handling and reassurance, and the parents should feel free to ask the pediatrician questions to assure their own understanding of what has happened, so they can comfort the child. Croup is rarely fatal. (Also see Chapter 21 on Infectious Diseases, page 432.)

RESPIRATORY PROBLEMS THAT AFFECT ALL AGES

Asthma

More than 10 million Americans—4 million of them children under 16—have or have had asthma during their lives. In most, the disease fades after some time. Asthma tends to occur in each generation of a family, and may occur in more than one member of the family.

In children, asthma may be diagnosed at age 3 or younger. In infants, it is usually the aftermath of flu, a cold, or virus infection. Bronchiolitis (a viral inflammation of the small airways which occurs in young children during the cold months) is sometimes followed by asthma, and the symptoms of asthma resemble those of the viral infection. After observing the child and noting more than 2 episodes, most doctors assume the child has asthma. (See figures 22.4A and 22.4B.)

Asthma is rarely fatal, but it can be disruptive. For although it can be controlled through medication and other means, it cannot be cured. Many children with asthma—about half—"outgrow" the disease as they enter their middle teens. Many of those diagnosed young show improvement once they reach the age of 6 or so, when the airway normally begins to widen. Boys more frequently suffer from asthma than do girls. In some children, asthma is replaced by allergy-related diseases, such as hay fever, as the asthma recedes.

Asthma episodes are responsible for 8 million school days lost each year; 24 million days of restricted activity for both children and adults; and 12 million bed rest days.

What Is Asthma? Ordinarily, the lungs work by taking in air and distributing oxygen to the circulation. Air circulates through a network of bronchial tubes. Cilia—small fine, hairlike projections within the bronchial tubes—carry out mucus and irritants such as smoke particles and dust, to be coughed up and out. At the end of the bronchial tubes, elastic air sacs called alveoli expand to take air in, contract to let it out. Surrounding the alveoli are the capillaries, or small blood vessels, which receive oxygen from the alveoli, and give up carbon dioxide to be exhaled.

The common denominator of asthma in allergic and nonallergic individuals is a hyperactive response of the breathing tubes. During an asthma episode, several things go wrong. The bronchial tubes narrow both through muscle spasms and swelling of the bronchial tissues. Mucus clogs the smaller tubes. Stale air is thus trapped.

Asthma episodes can be mild or severe. They can last for a few minutes or for days. They can happen anywhere, at any time—but they do happen most often at night.

When the episode is over, breathing returns to normal; the chest may be a little sore. Medical science is very familiar with the manifestations of asthma, and research is under way to learn more about these mechanisms so that asthma can be cured. Meanwhile, there are certain areas of knowledge about the disease that help control it.

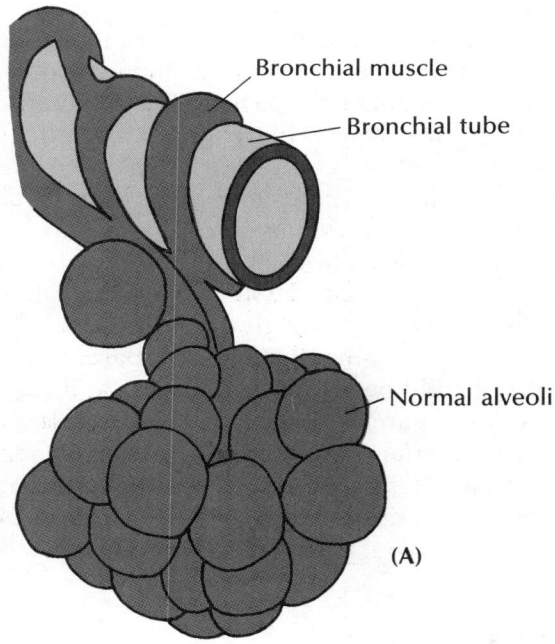

Bronchial muscle

Bronchial tube

Normal alveoli

(A)

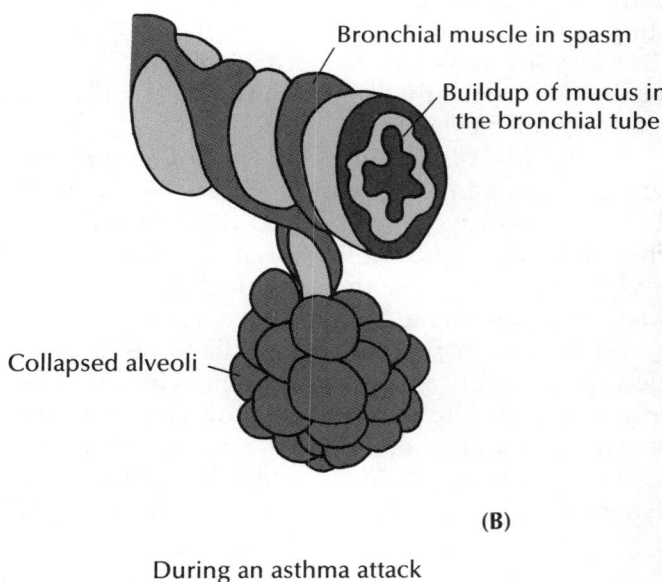

Bronchial muscle in spasm

Buildup of mucus in the bronchial tube

Collapsed alveoli

(B)

During an asthma attack

Figures 22.4A and 22.4B. **The normal bronchial tube and alveoli and the same structures during an asthma attack are shown. The spasm prevents the vital exchange of air in the tiny alveoli, leading to the gasping feeling of not being able to breathe properly.**

- Asthma patients have often had viral infections prior to the first onset of asthma. Flu, colds and viruses, bronchitis, tonsillitis, and sore throat are often forerunners.

- The asthma patient is often sensitive to various stimuli or trigger factors around the house, school, or workplace: tobacco smoke, air pollution, paint and paint thinners, hair sprays, perfume, cleaning fluids, liquid chlorine bleach, spray starch, dust, room deodorizers, spray furniture polish. He or she may be sensitive to changes in weather: sudden blasts of cold air, humid climates, changes in seasons, walking the dog on a cold night. Patients may be allergic to foods, such as nuts, peanut butter, chocolates, eggs, orange juice, fish, and milk. They also may be sensitive to plants or plant products like pollens, grasses, hay, ragweed, mold spores. Animals may trigger an episode: rabbits, cats, dogs, birds and feather products like down comforters, chickens, hamsters, gerbils. Physical exertion may induce an episode: running too fast, running up stairs. Emotions may intensify asthma: excitement, sadness, worry, laughing too hard, crying, coughing, getting very angry, breathing too hard (hyperventilation).

How to Control Asthma. Once the causative factors have been identified, there are a number of ways to treat an asthma episode: preventive medication—oral or inhaled—to dilate the bronchi and relieve breathing; airway clearing exercises; mild exercise to accustom the body to activity before more vigorous activities are undertaken; psychotherapy to help patients deal with social and emotional problems caused by asthma; immunotherapy to desensitize allergic patients. It takes some experimenting to determine what will work best for a particular patient. (See the box below for examples of typical medications.)

While some over-the-counter medications (primarily antihistamines) may be helpful in controlling asthma episodes, others are not, and many may cause sleepiness or other side effects. Therefore, the patient's physician is the best one to give advice and medication.

Sometimes, a child's asthma episode is so severe that the parents want to take him to the hospital. They should call their physician first, and follow his or her directions. Children with asthma do sometimes have to be hospitalized. But there is much that can be done at home.

The American Lung Association suggests these steps when a child appears to be starting an asthma episode:

- Reassure the child by the tone of voice, and by acting calm and self-confident.

- Give medication prescribed by the physician for the start of an episode.

- Give liquids to prevent dehydration (the amount necessary varies from patient to patient). Then,

- Let the child do his favorite breathing and relaxation exercises.

- Try to determine what triggered the episode and remove it—or the child—from the area.

ASTHMA MEDICATIONS

Epinephrine or adrenaline—This substance, which is also made by the body's own adrenal glands, helps open airways quickly. As a medication, it is given by injection or inhalation for severe asthma or an acute attack of asthma. Since it has side effects that must be overseen by a physician, it is usually used for emergencies only.

Inhaled bronchodilators—These agents are used in aerosol form or in hand-held metered dose inhalers. They resemble adrenaline and include isoproterenol, metaproterenol, isoetharine, and albuterol. Using 1 or 2 "puffs" of these bronchodilator agents may relieve spasm and wheezing of the acute episode and are particularly helpful for exercise-triggered wheezing.

Theophylline bronchodilators—These liquid, tablet, or capsule medicines help relax and open the airway, are available in rapid-acting and sustained-release forms. Most individuals with chronic, regular asthma use sustained-release preparations.

Adrenergic bronchodilators—Some inhaled agents are also available in pill or liquid form and are useful for those who cannot use inhaled medication or tolerate theophylline. These include metaproterenol, albuterol, and terbutaline.

Cromolyn sodium—This inert white powder, delivered by a special inhaler called a spinhaler, is very useful for milder asthma and allergy-induced asthma. It is not a bronchodilator and must be taken regularly where it functions as a prophylactic or asthma-preventing agent. In addition to its effect in allergic asthma, cromolyn or Intal seems to stabilize the overreactive airways characteristic of asthma.

Cortisone—This is a very effective anti-inflammatory agent which may be used by aerosol spray as beclomethasone (Vanceril, Beclovent) or triamcinolone, and in tablet or liquid form as prednesone (Medrol or Decadron). Intravenous cortisone is also used in severe problems. The side effects, which can include weight gain and hypertension, must be carefully monitored.

- Carry out postural drainage or other techniques, if suggested by the child's physician, to help get mucus out of the lungs.
- Decide whether the physician now needs to be called, or whether the episode is under control.

The Asthmatic Child in School and the Community. Parents should let the child's teacher know that he or she has asthma, what triggers it, and what needs to be done for the child in case of an episode. A child's friends should also be told. They can be very supportive, and their knowledge helps the child feel better accepted.

Children, with their physicians' approval, can participate in many sports and activities; typically those which are not carried out in dusty or pollen-laden areas, and which enable the child to rest briefly. For example, baseball, cheerleading, and bicycling are all activities in which they can often participate. Swimming is considered especially good exercise for asthmatic children. Before engaging in strenuous physical activity, they should do warm-up exercises to get their bodies ready for activity. Children with asthma should not be excused from chores or school responsibilities. Those who wheeze a great deal during vigorous exercise or sports may be able to prevent this by taking medication before the activity.

For more information about learning self-help techniques for living with asthma, contact the local American Lung Association chapter.

Common Cold

The cold is the most common of all upper respiratory diseases. It would not be unusual for a person to have 50 or more in a lifetime.

Over 100 different viruses have been identified as causing colds. They are present in the nose and throat during a cold and are carried in droplets expelled by infected persons when they talk, sneeze, or cough. Cold viruses are also sometimes spread by contact. Colds have different names, depending on where in the upper respiratory tract the infection strikes: nose colds are known as rhinitis; those affecting the throat are called pharyngitis; in the voicebox, they are known as laryngitis.

It appears that most colds are caught indoors, and during the colder months, probably because more people come into contact with each other's viruses. Fatigue and poor nutrition are predisposing conditions. Chilling has been identified as a potential factor as well. Children get colds more often than do adults.

By the time the patient's cold symptoms appear—1 to 3 days after the virus has invaded the body—he or she has likely already infected others.

About 48 hours after, the scratchy throat appears; other symptoms may occur, including running or obstructed nose, reduced taste and smell, a moderate headache, and feelings of achiness and lethargy. Children may have fever, but this is less common in adults.

Colds are unpleasant but not dangerous. For the most part, cold symptoms build, peak, and slowly disappear. Science has no cure for the common cold, and few ways of making the sufferer more comfortable. Some patients ask about antibiotics to treat a cold, but these are effective only against bacterial infections—which may follow a cold—but not against colds, which are viral infections.

The allergic reactions that accompany some colds may be relieved with antihistamines. Even though they are sold over the counter, antihistamine products may contain ingredients that can have a long-term adverse effect for certain patients. Those with other medical conditions should consult their physician. The physician, too, should be consulted if there is no relief in the cold symptoms after several days. Bacterial infections, bronchitis (inflammation of the lining of the bronchial tubes which connect the windpipe with the lungs), or pneumonia can sometimes follow a cold because of the body's lowered resistance.

Bed rest is useful mostly because it keeps the cold sufferer away from other people who might become infected. It is recommended for people with lowered resistance who might develop complications: young children, the elderly, those with chronic diseases, and those who repeatedly get colds. But although bed rest may constitute a pleasant compensation for *having* a cold, it is not strictly necessary. Fluids are recommended, as is aspirin should there be fever.

Some physicians recommend supplemental vitamin C to prevent or cure colds, but this idea has not been conclusively proved by scientific studies. A balanced diet may be just as effective as large doses of vitamin C.

Feeding a cold, starving a cold, building the body by sleeping in cold places or taking cold baths, sweating out a cold, or taking laxatives are likewise not scientifically proved as having an effect on the progress of a cold. Patients should do whatever common sense indicates will make the cold feel better, and anticipate its end in several days. (Also see Chapter 21 on Infectious Diseases, page 430.)

Influenza

For most of us, influenza is a lower respiratory infection to be endured for a few days. But there have

Columbia University
School of Public Health &
Institute of Human Nutrition

Health & Nutrition NEWSLETTER

$2.00

Introductory Issue

INTRODUCTORY ISSUE

Clearing Up the Confusion Over Cholesterol

By now, virtually every health-conscious American is well aware that too much cholesterol circulating in the blood is unhealthy. Yet considerable confusion surrounds the cholesterol issue. Here are answers to the most commonly asked questions regarding cholesterol.

Q. *Just what is cholesterol and what is its purpose?*

A. Cholesterol is a fatlike, waxy substance that is a building block of all cell membranes. Your body also needs cholesterol to manufacture sex hormones, bile, myelin (the fatty sheath surrounding nerves) and vitamin D. Without it, we would not survive.

Q. *If cholesterol is so important, shouldn't it be included in our diet?*

A. No. The body is capable of manufacturing all of the cholesterol it needs, even if it is totally lacking in the diet.

Q. *There seems to be a lot of confusion over sources of cholesterol. What foods are high in cholesterol?*

A. Cholesterol is found only in animal products. Egg yolks, fatty meats, whole milk, butter, and liver, brains and other organ meats are particularly high in cholesterol. No vegetable product, including oils, contains cholesterol. Thus, advertising messages that products such as peanut butter or margarine contain no cholesterol are somewhat superfluous; unless animal fats have been added, vegetable products obviously contain no cholesterol.

Q. *If the body needs cholesterol, why is high cholesterol a problem?*

A. In all aspects of nutrition, too much can be just as harmful as too little. In the case of cholesterol, the body needs about 1000 mg. a day to carry on its essential functions. The body, under normal circumstances, manufactures 500 to 1000 mg. of cholesterol a day, depending upon the body's requirements, and the amount consumed in the diet. If the diet provides an excessive amount of cholesterol, the amount circulating in the blood rises. For most people, this is the root of the problem. A high level of circulating cholesterol leads to atherosclerosis, or hardening of the arteries. The process starts with the development of fatty streaks in the lining of the arteries. As time passes, more of the excess cholesterol is deposited along these fatty streaks. This calcifies, or hardens, forming accumulations of fatty plaque called atheromas. Sometimes ulcerations develop in these atheromas and blood clots form that can block the vessel entirely. If this happens in a coronary artery—the blood vessels that nourish the heart—a heart attack results. Or a piece of the clot or atheroma may break off, travel through the blood stream and block an artery in the brain, causing a stroke. Progressively narrowed coronary arteries also cause attacks of angina; a diminished

continued on next page

Cholesterol/Fat Content of Foods

Food	Chol. (mg)	Sat.	Fats (gm) Mono.	Poly.
1 oz. lean beef	26	0.9	0.8	0.1
1 oz. fatty beef	27	2.2	2.0	0.2
1 oz. veal	28	0.9	0.8	0.1
1 oz. chicken (dark meat)	26	0.8	1.0	0.6
1 oz. chicken/turkey (white meat)	22	0.3	0.3	0.2
1 oz. pork	28	0.9	0.8	0.1
1 oz. beef liver	83	0.1	0	0
1 oz. lean fish	28	0	0.1	0.1
1 oz. fatty fish	25	0.9	1.1	1.1
1 oz. water-packed tuna	11	0	0	0
1 oz. lean lamb	17	0.1	0.2	0.2
1 egg	274	1.7	2.2	0.7
1 t. margarine (1.6/1.9 poly/sat)	0	1.4	3.3	2.4
1 t. corn oil	0	0.6	1.1	2.6
1 t. safflower oil	0	0.4	0.6	3.3
1 t. veg. oil	0	0.7	1.0	2.6
2 t. avocado	0	0.8	2.1	1.3
1 t. butter	12	1.9	1.4	0.2
2 oz. 5% fat cheese	20	1.6	1.0	0.1
2 oz. cheddar	56	12.0	6.0	0.5
1 cup whole milk	34	4.8	2.4	0.1
1 c. 2% milk	22	2.4	2.0	0.1
1 c. skim milk	4	0.3	0.1	0
1 c. 1% yogurt	14	2.3	1.0	0.1
1 c. ice cream	56	16.8	9.6	0.3

Kinds of Fat

Mostly Polyunsaturated
Corn oil
Cottonseed oil
Fish
Margarine (especially corn oil or soft)
Safflower oil
Soybean oil
Sunflower oil

Mostly Monounsaturated
Avocado
Cashews
Olives and olive oil
Peanuts and peanut oil
Peanut butter
Poultry
Vegetable shortening

Mostly Saturated
Butter
Cheese
Chocolate
Coconut and coconut oil
Egg yolk
Lard
Meat
Palm oil

continued

supply of blood to the brain can lead to permanent brain damage; clogged arteries in the legs lead to difficulty in walking or, in advanced cases, amputation.

Dietary Factors

Q. *How much cholesterol should be consumed in the diet?*

A. The American Heart Association recommends that the total dietary intake be limited to 300 mg. a day. Even this may be too much for people with very high cholesterol levels in their blood or for those with a hereditary disease called familial hypercholesterolemia, in which the body manufactures far too much cholesterol. The typical American diet, high in red meats, whole milk, eggs, butter and other animal products, provides much more than the recommended 300 mg. a day. Since cholesterol is part of the cell membranes, it cannot be removed in the way that fat can be trimmed off meats. The accompanying table lists the cholesterol content of typical foods.

Q. *Are there other factors that raise cholesterol?*

A. Yes: the consumption of fats also plays an important role. Fats are made up of chemical compounds called fatty acids. These fatty acids may be saturated, monounsaturated or polyunsaturated—terms that refer to the number of hydrogen atoms in the fatty compound. Saturated fats contain the most hydrogen atoms; monounsaturated fats can hold two more hydrogen atoms; and polyunsaturated can carry four more. All fats contain a combination of these three fatty acids, but in differing ratios. Butter, fats on red meat and other hard fats contain more saturated fatty acids than corn, safflower or other vegetable oils, for example. Avocado, olive or peanut oils are high in monounsaturated oils. (See accompanying list.)

Studies have found that a diet high in saturated fats raises cholesterol, while one high in polyunsaturated and monounsaturated fats lowers it. A healthy diet should contain about equal amounts of all three fats. The body requires only about a tablespoon of fat a day; the typical American diet, however, provides six to eight tablespoons. Also, food processing can transform polyunsaturated and monounsaturated fats into saturated ones. For example, hard margarine is made by adding hydrogen to the liquid corn or other vegetable oil—soft margarines will have more unsaturated fats than firm ones. You should check food labels for the ratio of unsaturated to saturated fats (it should be 3 or 4 to 2) and for terms such as hydrogenated oils, which means that the original oils have been saturated.

HEALTH & NUTRITION© is published monthly by G.S. Sharpe Communications, Inc., 606 West 116th Street, New York, N.Y. 10027. Copyright© held by the Columbia University School of Public Health, 600 West 168th Street, New York, N.Y. 10032. All rights reserved. Photocopying and other reproduction prohibited without written permission. Postmaster should send address changes to G.S. Sharpe Communications at address noted above.

Editor: Robert J. Weiss, M.D., Dean Emeritus and Delamar Professor of Public Health, Columbia University School of Public Health

Co-Editor: Myron Winick, M.D., Director, Columbia University Institute of Human Nutrition

Editorial Director: Genell J. Subak-Sharpe, M.S.   Managing Editor: Rebecca Smith

Assistant Editor: Jane Margaretten-Ohring   Art Director: Marjorie Katz

Type: Steintype

To subscribe, send a check or money order ($18 for one year, $34 for two years) made out to HEALTH & NUTRITION to: Columbia University School of Public Health
Subscription Dept; Box 5000-MJ
Ridgefield, NJ 07657

All subscription correspondence should be sent to this address.

Good vs. Bad Cholesterol

Q. *"We hear a lot about "good" vs. "bad" cholesterol. What does this mean?*

A. Cholesterol is a fat-like substance, which means it is not soluble in water. Blood is made up mostly of water, and since fats and water do not mix, in order for cholesterol to travel through the body via the blood, it must be attached to a molecule that is water-soluble. So cholesterol is attached to a protein, forming a compound called a lipoprotein. These lipoproteins come in different sizes and densities, or weights. The smallest, but most dense is the high density lipoprotein, or HDL. The largest but lightest is the very low density lipoprotein, or VLDL. In between is the low density lipoprotein, or LDL. HDLs carry cholesterol away from body tissue and back to the liver.

LDLs carry cholesterol from the liver and to the tissues; it also tends to collect along the artery linings, leading to atherosclerosis. (VLDLs carry mostly triglycerides, another fat-like compound and their role in artherosclerosis is unknown.) The ratio of total cholesterol to HDL is what's important. A person can have a relatively low level of total cholesterol, but still develop atherosclerosis if the level of HDL cholesterol is low. In general, anyone whose ratio of total cholesterol to HDL cholesterol is more than 4.5 to 1 should be treated to improve the balance.

Q. *How can I find out what my cholesterol ratio is?*

A. Most laboratories now measure the different types of cholesterol and calculate the ratio. When you have your blood cholesterol checked, make sure that your doctor instructs the laboratory to measure the LDL and HDL cholesterol ratio.

Q. *What factors influence the level of HDL cholesterol?*

A. Diet, of course, is an important factor. Vegetarians seem to have a very favorable LDL/HDL ratio. Premenopausal women have higher HDL levels than men or older women. People who exercise regularly—runners, swimmers or others who get at least 20 minutes of vigorous exercise three or four times a week, have higher HDL levels than sedentary people. Certain types of fiber, especially pectin which is found in apples, root vegetables and the pith of oranges, lowers LDLs and raises HDLs.

Oat bran is another good source of cholesterol-lowering fiber. Caution is urged, however; to avoid intestinal problems, do not abruptly add large amounts of these soluable fibers to the diet.

Q. *What is considered a healthy cholesterol level?*

A. There is still some debate about this, but a recent National Institutes of Health consensus panel recommended that anyone with total cholesterol levels above 200-300 mg/dl should attempt to lower it, either by life-style changes, such as diet and exercise, or with cholesterol-lowering drugs, or a combination of the two. Obviously, the higher the cholesterol, the more aggressive the treatment. Until recently, a cholesterol level of 200-300 mg/dl was considered normal, even though this is much higher than normal levels in many parts of the world where heart disease is rare. In recent years, the American Heart Association and others have recommended that everyone strive for a total cholesterol of less than 200 mg/dl, and the lower the better.

Cutting Cholesterol — Shopping and Cooking Tips

1. Select lean (choice grades) of meat. Trim away all fat. Avoid regular ground beef; instead, use trimmed ground round, such as that made for steak tartar.

2. Bake, broil or roast meats, using a rack. Add tomato, lemon juice, broth, wine or water to prevent drying.

3. When making meat sauce or stews, brown meat separately and drain before adding to other ingredients. Cook stews, gravy, etc., ahead of time, chill, remove hardened fat, and reheat.

4. Reduce portion size of meats by serving small amounts with stir-fried vegetables or in stews or pasta dishes.

5. Limit egg yolks to one or two a week. In cooking, use egg white plus a teaspoon of polyunsaturated oil instead of whole egg.

6. Always read nutrition labels on processed foods. Avoid those containing shortening, palm or coconut oils, or hydrogenated oils.

7. Instead of sour cream, use low-fat plain yogurt, buttermilk or low-fat cottage cheese in dips or for baking. A teaspoon of cornstarch will prevent curdling.

8. Use skim milk or 1% fat milk instead of whole milk. For baking, a tablespoon of oil can be added to a cup of skim milk for added texture and moistness. Non-fat dry milk can be added to skim milk for extra thickness in sauces, cream soups, etc.

9. Use a pan spray instead of fat to grease pans and for sautéing foods.

10. In cooking, fats and oils usually can be reduced by a third to a half without changing taste or texture.

11. Instead of cream cheese, use low-fat cottage cheese blended with low-fat yogurt or skim milk.

12. For more cooking tips, menus or recipes, consult *Jane Brody's Good Food Book* (Norton); *The American Heart Association Cookbook* (David McKay); *Don't Eat Your Heart Out Cookbook* (Joseph Piscatella, Workman Publishing Co.) or *Lean Cuisine* (Barbara Gibbons, Harper & Row).

PART TWO

Answer all questions as is generally true for you by circling the letter of the response.

1. I hate to wait in lines.
   - (a) Almost always true
   - (b) Usually true
   - (c) Seldom true
   - (d) Never true

2. I often find myself racing against the clock to save time.
   - (a) Almost always true
   - (b) Very often true
   - (c) Seldom true
   - (d) Never true

3. I become upset if I think something is taking too long.
   - (a) Almost always true
   - (b) Very often true
   - (c) Seldom true
   - (d) Never true

4. When under pressure, I tend to lose my temper.
   - (a) Almost always true
   - (b) Very often true
   - (c) Seldom true
   - (d) Never true

5. My friends tell me that I tend to get irritated easily.
   - (a) Almost always true
   - (b) Very often true
   - (c) Seldom true
   - (d) Never true

6. I seldom like to do anything unless I can make it competitive.
   - (a) Almost always true
   - (b) Very often true
   - (c) Seldom true
   - (d) Never true

7. When something needs to be done, I am the first to begin even though the details may still need to be worked out.
   - (a) Almost always true
   - (b) Very often true
   - (c) Seldom true
   - (d) Never true

8. When I make a mistake, it is usually because I've rushed into something without giving it enough thought and planning.
   - (a) Almost always true
   - (b) Very often true
   - (c) Seldom true
   - (d) Never true

9. Whenever possible, I will try to do two things at once, like eating while working or planning while driving or bathing.
   - (a) Almost always true
   - (b) Very often true
   - (c) Seldom true
   - (d) Never true

10. When I go on a vacation, I usually take some work along just in case I get a chance to do it.
   - (a) Almost always true
   - (b) Very often true
   - (c) Seldom true
   - (d) Never true

TO SCORE: a = 4 points, b = 3 points, c = 2 points, d = 1 point

This test measures the presence of compulsive, time urgent and excessively aggressive behavioral traits. Scores in excess of 25 suggest the presence of one or more of these traits.

Parts One and Two of this test are adapted from *Controlling Stress and Tension*, by Daniel A. Girdano and George S. Everly, Jr., Prentice-Hall Inc., 1979 and are reprinted with permission from the publisher.

How Well Do You Cope With Stress?

Stress has always been an unavoidable part of life, but unlike the stresses faced by our ancestors, today's problems are often of our own making.

The following self-analysis tests are designed to measure your vulnerability to stress and also to increase your awareness of its effects. Part Three is designed to measure how well you cope. If you find you are in the vulnerable zones on these tests, you should take preventive steps to both reduce your stress level and improve your coping techniques.

PART ONE

Read and choose the most appropriate answer for each of the 10 questions as it actually pertains to you.

1. When I can't do something "my way," I usually adjust to it the easiest way.
   - (a) Almost always true _____
   - (b) Usually true _____
   - (c) Usually false _____
   - (d) Almost always false _____

2. I get "upset" when someone in front of me drives slowly.
   - (a) Almost always true _____
   - (b) Usually true _____
   - (c) Usually false _____
   - (d) Almost always false _____

3. It bothers me when my plans depend upon others.
   - (a) Almost always true _____
   - (b) Usually true _____
   - (c) Usually false _____
   - (d) Almost always false _____

4. Whenever possible, I tend to avoid large crowds.
   - (a) Almost always true _____
   - (b) Usually true _____
   - (c) Usually false _____
   - (d) Almost always false _____

5. I am uncomfortable having to stand in long lines.
   - (a) Almost always true _____
   - (b) Usually true _____
   - (c) Usually false _____
   - (d) Almost always false _____

6. Arguments upset me.
   - (a) Almost always true _____
   - (b) Usually true _____
   - (c) Usually false _____
   - (d) Almost always false _____

7. When my plans don't "flow smoothly," I become anxious.
   - (a) Almost always true _____
   - (b) Usually true _____
   - (c) Usually false _____
   - (d) Almost always false _____

8. I require a lot of room (space) to live and work in.
   - (a) Almost always true _____
   - (b) Usually true _____
   - (c) Usually false _____
   - (d) Almost always false _____

9. When I am busy at some task, I hate to be disturbed.
   - (a) Almost always true _____
   - (b) Usually true _____
   - (c) Usually false _____
   - (d) Almost always false _____

10. I believe that "All good things are worth waiting for."
   - (a) Almost always true _____
   - (b) Usually true _____
   - (c) Usually false _____
   - (d) Almost always false _____

TO SCORE:

1 and 10: a = 1 point, b = 2 points, c = 3 points, d = 4 points

2 to 9: a = 4 points, b = 3 points, c = 2 points, d = 1 point

This test measures your vulnerability to stress from being frustrated. Scores in excess of 25 seem to suggest some vulnerability to this source of stress.

PART THREE

How well do you cope with stress? This scale was created largely on the basis of results compiled by doctors and researchers who have sought to identify how individuals effectively cope with stress. It is an educational tool, not a clinical test. Its purpose is to inform you of ways in which you can effectively and healthfully cope with stress.

Follow the instructions given for each of the 14 items listed below. When you have completed it, total your points and place the score on the bottom line.

_____ 1. Give yourself 10 points if you feel you have a supportive family around you.

_____ 2. Give yourself 10 points if you feel you actively pursue a hobby.

_____ 3. Give yourself 10 points if you belong to some social or activity group that meets at least once a month (other than your family).

_____ 4. Give yourself 15 points if you feel you are within five pounds of your ideal bodyweight, considering your height and bone structure.

_____ 5. Give yourself 15 points if you practice some form of deep relaxation at least three times a week (meditation, imagery, Yoga, etc.).

_____ 6. Give yourself 5 points for each time you exercise 30 minutes or longer during the course of an average week.

_____ 7. Give yourself 5 points for each nutritionally balanced and whole-some meal you consume during the course of an average day.

_____ 8. Give yourself 5 points if you do something you really enjoy "just for you" during the course of an average week.

_____ 9. Give yourself 10 points if you have some place in your home that you can go in order to relax and/or be by yourself.

_____ 10. Give yourself 10 points if you practice time management techniques in your daily life.

_____ 11. Subtract 10 points for each pack of cigarettes you smoke during the course of an average day.

_____ 12. Subtract 5 points for each evening during the course of an average week that you take any form of medication or chemical substance (including alcohol) to help you sleep.

_____ 13. Subtract 10 points for each day during the course of an average week that you consume any form of medication or chemical substance (including alcohol) to reduce your anxiety or just calm you down.

_____ 14. Subtract 5 points for each evening during the course of an average week that you bring work home; work that was meant to be done at your place of employment.

_____ Now calculate your total score. A perfect score would be 115 points.

If you scored in the 50-60 range, you probably have adequate coping strategies for most common sources of stress. However, you should keep in mind that the higher your score, the greater your ability to cope with stress in an effectve and healthful manner.

Part Three was created by George S. Everly, M.D. and is adapted with permission from *Stress*, a pamphlet by the Public Health Service.

Tips on Cutting Your Drug Costs

Americans spend about $15 billion a year on prescription drugs, and even more on nonprescription products, such as aspirin, antacids, laxatives and other medications. Yet, according to the National Council on Patient Information and Education, 50 percent of all prescriptions filled are taken incorrectly. As a result, the drugs either do not have the desired effect or the improper use leads to adverse reactions.

Questions You Should Always Ask

1. What is the name of the drug and what is it supposed to do?
2. How and when do I take it—and for how long? Should I use all the medication or stop when I start to feel better?
3. Should the drug be taken before or after meals? Does three times a day mean every eight hours, or with each meal?
4. What foods, drinks and other medicines or activities should

continued on next page

For More Information On Your Drugs

There are many books, pamphlets and organizations that provide information about drugs. These include:

Medication Information Leaflet for Seniors
These leaflets are written in cooperation with the Food and Drug Administration, and provide information about specific drugs. For information, contact:
A.A.R.P. Pharmacy Service
National Headquarters
1 Prince Street
Alexandria, Va. 22314
(703) 684-0244

Using Your Medicines Wisely: A Guide for the Elderly
A free booklet, available by sending a postcard with publication number DHHS Pub. No. (ADM) 82-705, to:
National Clearinghouse for Drug Abuse Information
Room 10-A43
5600 Fishers Lane
Rockville, Md. 20857
(301) 443-6500

General Information on the Use of Medicines
An educational booklet published by the United States Pharmacopeial Convention. For a free copy, write:
Alice E. Kimball
USP Convention, Inc.
12601 Twinbrook Parkway
Rockville, Md. 20852
(301) 881-0666

The Medicines Your Doctor Prescribes, A Guide for Consumers
Published by the Pharmaceutical Manufacturers Association, with up to 25 free copies available by writing:
Publications Department
Pharmaceutical Manufacturers' Association
1100 15th Street, N.W., Suite 900
Washington, D.C. 20005
(202) 835-3400

Ten Guides to Proper Medicine Use
Published by the Council on Family Health and available free (for the first copy; 50 cents for subsequent copies) by writing:
Council on Family Health
420 Lexington Avenue
New York, N.Y. 10017
(212) 210-8836

Questions & Answers

Bell's Palsy

Q. Can you tell me what causes Bell's Palsy? I recently had an episode, which went away in a few days, but it was very alarming. I would like to know how to prevent a future attack.

A. Bell's Palsy is a type of muscle paralysis affecting one side of the face. The exact cause is unknown, but some experts think that a virus may be implicated. The facial nerve swells and since a portion of it is encased in a bony sheath, it has no room to expand. This leads to the facial paralysis, which in 90 percent of patients, is temporary and will resolve itself without any treatment. In some patients, however, the pressure on the nerve may be so severe that it is destroyed. In such instances, treatment—either with steroid drugs or surgery to expand the bony canal through which the nerve travels—may be needed to prevent permanent paralysis.

Tetanus Booster Shots

Q. How often should you have a tetanus booster? I am 52 years old, and I haven't had a tetanus shot since I was in the army more than 30 years ago.

A. Although tetanus, or lockjaw, is rare in this country, there are scattered cases reported each year. Most of these involve people over the age of 50 and occur as a result of a cut or wound suffered in and around the home or yard. About half prove to be fatal. The Centers for Disease Control in Atlanta recommends that all adults have tetanus booster shots every 10 years. If you haven't had one for 30 years, you should see your doctor or local Department of Health, which can advise you where to get a shot.

In addition, anyone who suffers a puncture wound or cut from a possibly contaminated source should have a tetanus booster shot if more than two or three years have elapsed since the last immunization. Exceptions, of course, are people who are allergic to horse serum, who should not have the tetanus vaccine derived from this source under any circumstance since it may provoke an anaphylactic reaction.

Do you have a question for HEALTH & NUTRITION? If so, send it to: Health & Nutrition Editors, G.S. Sharpe Communications, 606 West 116th Street, New York, N.Y. 10027.

Cutting Drug Costs *(cont)*

I avoid while taking this drug?
5. Are there any side effects, and what do I do if they occur?
6. Is there any written information available about the drug?

Information You Should Provide

In addition to asking the right questions (and of course, following instructions), you should always tell your doctor and pharmacist the following:
1. All the other medications, including birth control pills, nonprescription drugs, vitamin pills, and so forth, that you are taking. Don't forget that alcohol is a drug, too, and many medications interact with alcohol.
2. Any adverse reactions you have had to drugs in the past.
3. Any allergies you may have.

Other Cost-Saving Steps

Do comparison shopping. Drug prices vary tremendously from store to store. By making a few phone calls and asking the cost of filling your prescription, you may be able to save a third of the price, or more.

Check on dosages and quantities. Often, drugs come in several dosages, and large-dosage pills may be scored so they are easy to break into halves. If the large-dose pills cost only slightly more than those of lower dosage, you can save money by buying them and dividing them into your dosage.

Check your memberships. Several organizations, most notably the American Association of Retired Persons, offer drug discounts to members. A.A.R.P. membership costs $5 a year and is available to anyone aged 50 or older. Drug discounts also are available through many labor unions, the Arthritis Foundation and the American Diabetes Association.

Avoid unnecessary nonprescription drugs. Americans spend millions of dollars each year on unnecessary vitamins, cold pills, laxatives and other remedies. The same questions you ask about prescription drugs apply to over-the-counter products. Always read the labels and follow instructions for use. Also, many nonprescription products are available in generic form. For example, 50 generic acetaminophen pills may cost $1.99, compared to $4.49 or more for Tylenol and other brand-name acetaminophen. The same is true of aspirin, calcium pills and many other such products.

Save your drug receipts. Most people have no idea how much they spend on drugs, and they may be overlooking a potential tax deduction. Also, some insurance policies reimburse drug costs after meeting a certain deductible amount.

Expect to pay more for special services. Home delivery or 24-hour prescription service, while convenient, adds to your cost.

Check into ordering by mail. Any medication that you take regularly usually can be ordered in quantity and at a lower cost by mail.

Ask your doctor about generic equivalents. Brand name drugs almost always cost more, but in many instances, there are virtually identical generic, or unbranded, equivalents.

Introductory Issue

A Buyer's Guide to Athletic Shoes

Today's emphasis on physical fitness has led to a proliferation of specialized athletic shoes—for running, walking, aerobic dancing, basketball and tennis. Many people make the mistake of buying one pair of shoes and then wearing them for various activities, or digging out an old pair of tennis shoes and wearing them for jogging. This can lead to a variety of problems, ranging from shin splints to foot pain.

Physicians, athletes and footwear experts advise wearing shoes designed to fit specific activities. It is a good idea to go to a store that specializes in athletic shoes; it is more likely to have trained salespersons who can help you select the shoe best suited for your particular activity.

Whatever sport you choose, buy only well-established brand names made by manufacturers with the research and experience needed to produce good quality footwear. In shopping for athletic shoes, you get what you pay for. A good shoe will cost at least $40, and many are in the $50 to $60 range.

Matching the Shoe to the Sport

Pick your favorite sport, or sports—if your time and budget allow—and use the following guidelines to select a shoe.

Walking. A walking shoe should be lightweight with a smooth inside surface to prevent blisters and soreness, padding to cushion the Achilles tendon and a plastic, reinforced cup at the rear, known as a counter, to support the ankles and heel. For best traction, the sole should be rippled or pebbled. A walking shoe, like all athletic shoes, should bend easily at the ball when compressed between two hands.

Running. A running shoe should be cushioned from heel to toe, have a flexible sole and a good heel counter for support.

Aerobic dancing. An aerobics shoe should be well-cushioned, especially under the ball and front half of the foot. The upper part should provide good support and have an extra layer of leather or synthetic material for reinforcement at the ball of the foot and toes. Pick a shoe with a good heel counter to prevent wiggling of the foot during exercise.

Tennis. A tennis shoe should have a reinforced upper and be made of the synthetic material Gore-Tex or leather and nylon mesh for adequate ventilation in warm weather. Outer soles vary with the type of court played on; for hard courts select a rubber or polyurethane surface with treads for traction, for clay courts, choose a smoother sole.

Basketball. A basketball shoe should have rugged, reinforced leather at the front, ankle and heel sections, and full-sole cushioning. For good support, pick a shoe with high tops, ankle padding and extra arch support.

Special Considerations

People with foot problems, such as corns and calluses, deformities or diabetes may require special inserts, padding or custom fitting. Check with your podiatrist and shoe retailer to see what adjustments are required for comfortable exercise.

Top-Rated Athletic Shoes*

The following shoes were recommended by athletes and sport-shoe dealers both for suitability and value. Take time to make sure any shoe fits well before purchasing.

Shoe	Cost
Walking	
Rockport Pro Walker	$75
Nike EMW	$54
Running	
Brooks Chariot	$62
Nike Venue	$60
Saucony Shadow	$60
New Balance 470	$53
Aerobics	
Nike Air Controller	$50
Reebok Charisma	$46
Saucony Limelight	$45
Avia 440	$42
Tennis	
Prince Leather 647	$60
Reebok ACT 600	$60
New Balance CT 650	$58
Kappa K-120	$43
Basketball	
Adidas Forum	$100
Nike Air Jordan	$65
Converse Weapon	$60
New Balance 480	$55

What To Do About A Bad Back

At one time or another, four out of every five Americans suffers from back pain. In fact, back pain is second only to headache in the list of chronic pain problems.

In the large majority of people, the pain originates in the lower back, or lumbar region. Studies have found that only 15 percent of cases involving lower back pain are caused by ruptured disks, arthritis, tumors, injuries or other defects. In the large majority of cases, however, the problem lies in a weakness of the muscle and other structures supporting the back. This means that most episodes of lower back pain can be prevented by strengthening these supporting structures.

Most episodes of back pain are caused by either a muscle spasm, pinched nerve or combination of the two. The spinal column is made up of 24 separate vertebrae and nine that are fused to form the lowermost portion. The vertebrae are held in place by ligaments; nerve roots pass through the openings at each side of the individual vertebra. A sudden wrench of the back or failure of the supporting structures can result in a "pinched" nerve. The sciatic nerve, which passes from the lumbar area down to the legs and toes, is commonly affected, with symptoms such as twinges, burning or numbness in the buttocks, legs and toes.

A muscle spasm is another common cause of back pain. The spasm, which may result from either physical or psychological stress, is a protective reflex. But as the spasms intensify, circulation to the area is reduced, resulting in an inflammatory process and further pain. Underexercised muscles also are particularly vulnerable to spasms.

Treatment of Back Pain

Most episodes of back pain will subside with rest, hot baths, aspirin or other anti-inflammatory drug, or medication to relax the muscle spasm. (If a structural defect, such as a ruptured disk, is involved, other treatments, including surgery, may be recommended.)

Exercises to strengthen the supporting back muscles also are vital in overcoming a "bad back." The five exercises illustrated here are basic to most bad-back regimens. They take about 10 to 15 minutes each day; they can be done first thing in the morning while lying on either a firm mattress or the floor. Each exercise should be performed slowly; avoid fast or jerking movements, and if an exercise provokes pain, do not attempt to continue it. If pain persists, you should see your doctor. Also, although these exercises are safe for most people, if you have a particular back problem, you should check with your doctor first.

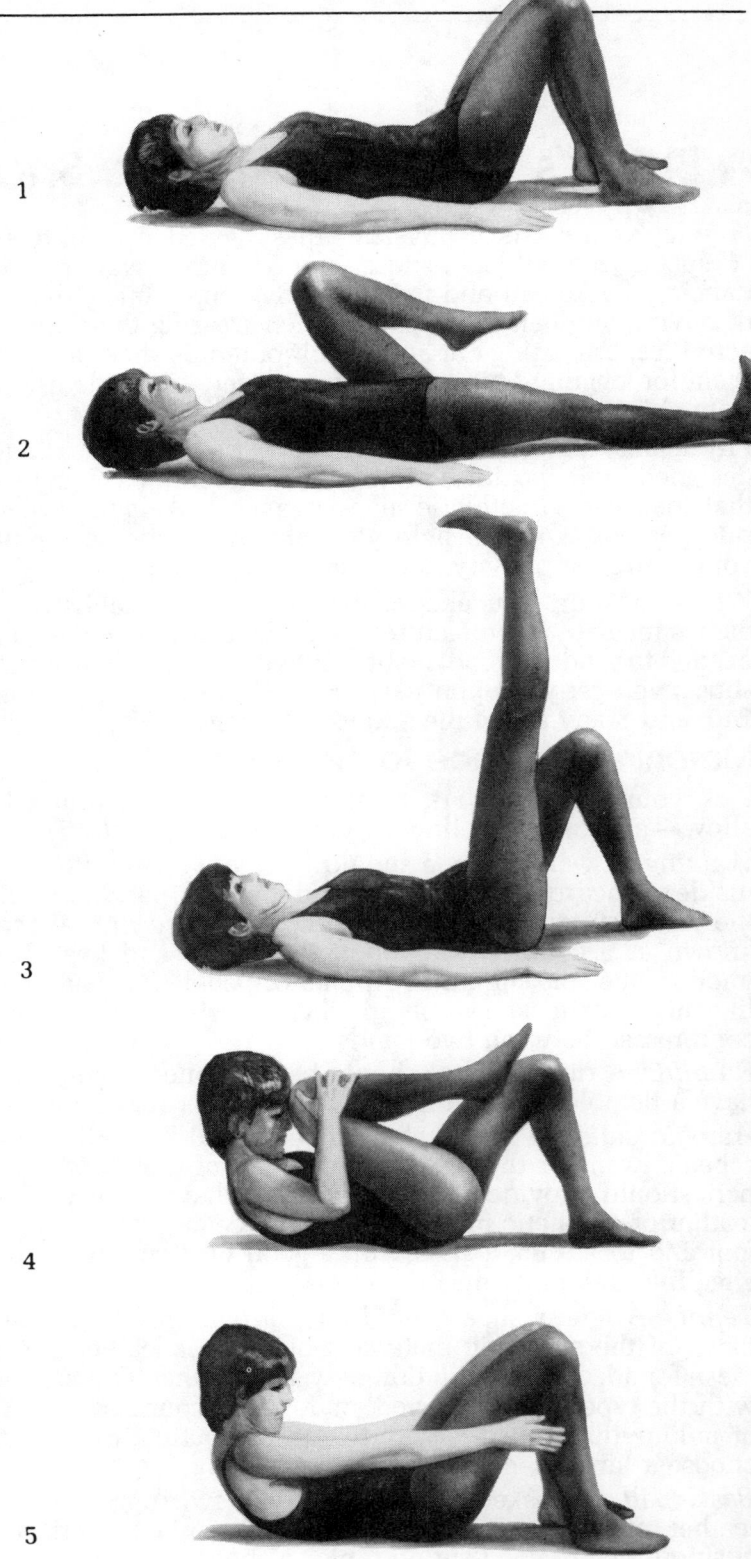

1

2

3

4

5

1. **Pelvic tilt.** Pull in your stomach so that the small of your back is flat on the floor. Tighten your buttocks and raise your hips. Hold for a count of 10. Relax. Repeat up to 20 times.

2. **Lower back stretch.** Bring one knee as close to the chest as possible. Return it slowly to the starting position. Relax. Repeat up to 10 times for each leg.

3. **Leg raises.** Bring one knee to the chest. Extend the leg, then bend the knee and return to the starting position. Relax. Alternating legs, repeat up to 10 times.

4. **Knee-to-forehead.** Grasping one knee with both hands, bring it to the chest. At the same time, raise the shoulders off the floor and touch your forehead to the knee. Return slowly to the starting position. Repeat, alternating legs, up to 10 times.

5. **Bent-leg sit-ups.** With the arms extended, raise the upper part of your body about 30 degrees off the floor. Relax and repeat up to 20 times.

been more than 200,000 deaths associated with flu epidemics in the United States (from 1968 to 1982), many of them among those over 65, or those with medical conditions for whom a lower respiratory infection could be dangerous. Included in this second group are heavy smokers and adults and children with severe asthma, heart disease, tuberculosis, cystic fibrosis, neuromuscular and orthopedic disorders that impair breathing functions, and infants who have been treated for respiratory distress syndrome (RDS). Also, those with chronic renal disease, diabetes or other diseases of the metabolism, severe chronic anemia like sickle cell anemia, and conditions that interfere with the body's immune systems. Included in this group are those with some malignancies or those receiving immunosuppressive therapy.

These people should be vaccinated annually. In addition, some communities elect to vaccinate annually health-care workers and others who perform vital services, or who may come into contact with many sick people. One dose will be recommended for most adults in these groups. Children under 12 who have not been vaccinated since 1978 when the viral strain changed should receive 2 doses.

Pregnant women who have these high-risk conditions may also be vaccinated, but the woman's physician may advise her to wait until the second or third trimester of her pregnancy, when the developing fetus is known to be less vulnerable to outside influence. There is no evidence to suggest that current flu vaccines carry any maternal or fetal risk.

Influenza outbreaks are caused by a virus that may change its structure from time to time. A person who has been vaccinated against one strain of virus, or who has developed antibodies to it after a previous illness, may still get the flu when the virus changes.

Every year, the U.S. Public Health Service studies initial cases of flu and develops a vaccine for the latest strain. Thus, it is important for patients at risk to be revaccinated every year.

Temporary adverse reactions to flu vaccine include side effects such as fever, fatigue, and muscle pain which starts 6 to 22 hours after vaccination and continues for a day or two. These symptoms occur primarily in children under 12 who have not been previously vaccinated. Immediate allergic responses such as skin eruptions are probably due to residual egg protein from the medium in which the vaccine is grown. Those allergic to eggs should not receive the vaccine.

Occasionally, more serious reactions to flu vaccine are reported. The information comes from the U.S. Public Health Service, which records and re-

ports statistics and trends to the health-care community and the interested public. Sometimes, patients in high-risk groups who should be vaccinated wonder if they aren't risking more severe illness by doing so. During the average flu season, most physicians counsel such patients that the odds that they'll get influenza if they are not immunized are much higher than are the odds they'll have a negative reaction to the vaccine.

Can Flu Be Prevented? During flu epidemic years, communities sometimes reduce the number of large meetings, under the impression that this will control its spread. It can only delay the spread of influenza and is not a necessary practice.

Some patients are candidates for an antiviral drug, amantadine hydrochloride, which can prevent Influenza A, the most common type, in someone who has not been vaccinated but who especially needs protection during a flu outbreak. However, this is not a substitute for vaccination if the patient is in a high-risk category. It protects only against strain A, not the other common strain, B, and must be taken every day during the epidemic—usually for 6 to 8 weeks. It may be useful in high-risk groups to provide protection between the time of vaccination and when active immunity develops: 10 to 14 days. But its administration must be supervised carefully by a physician.

The first sign of influenza is usually a high fever of 101° F to 102° F, with peaks that can reach as high as 106° F. The fever is accompanied by chills, headache, muscle and joint pain, weakness, and malaise (feeling generally bad). In strain B, there may be severe gastrointestinal signs, with vomiting and diarrhea, but these are unusual in the more common types of flu. The patient's voice may become hoarse, and this may be followed by a dry throat, nasal obstruction, cough, and nosebleed. Children may develop swollen neck glands. Eyes may become watery, red, itchy, and the patient may find it uncomfortable or painful to look at light. In children, the illness may resemble croup, with harsh breathing and choking. In mild, uncomplicated cases, symptoms may last 3 to 5 days, and the patient is up and around—feeling tired for some time afterward—within a week. Sometimes, however, complications set in. The most common are bacterial infections, which invade the body with weakened defenses. (Also see Chapter 21 on Infectious Diseases, page 430.)

Pneumonia

Pneumonia is a general term for inflammation of the lung in which fluid and cells from the inflamed tissues fill the air spaces in the lungs, making it difficult to breathe. Although cases of pneumonia are generally classified as bacterial or nonbacterial, they can be caused by bacterial, viral, or fungal infection or by chemical damage from inhalation of certain poisonous gases. Legionnaires' Disease is now recognized as a type of pneumonia. Pneumonia can affect one or several lobes of the lung (lobar pneumonia), or be spread throughout the lung in a patchy fashion (bronchopneumonia).

The symptoms, treatment, and prognosis of pneumonia depend not only on its type, but also on the general health of the patient. In the vast majority of cases, especially since the advent of antibiotics, complete recovery is the expected outcome. But for the very young (under one year), the very old, or those already debilitated by a serious illness such as heart disease or cancer, pneumonia can be fatal. In addition to general debilitation, predisposing factors include acute viral respiratory infections ranging from the common cold to influenza, alcoholism, malnutrition, coma, foreign matter in the respiratory tract, and long-term therapy with immunosuppressive drugs.

Symptoms of pneumonia vary, as does the pattern of onset, but they generally include a cough that often produces blood-streaked phlegm. Fever may range from 101° F to 104° F and may be accompanied by chest pain, general muscle aches, chills, cyanosis (blueness), or intestinal symptoms. (For more information, see Chapter 21 on Infectious Diseases, page 435.)

Pleurisy and Pleural Effusion

In a small number of patients, the aftermath of pneumonia is pleurisy, an inflammation of the pleura—the two-ply membrane that encloses each lung and lines the chest cavity. Pleurisy can also be a complication of tuberculosis or a chest injury. With the universal use of antibiotics, it is a relatively rare condition in this country.

The layers of the pleura are joined at the edges so that the pleura might be compared to a closed balloon, completely empty of air and wrapped tightly around each of the lungs. Normally, only a thin lubricating layer of fluid lies between the inner pleural lining and the outer one, and the lungs move freely within the pleura during breathing.

If the pleura becomes inflamed or roughened by infection, the movement of the lung may be restricted, and breathing, especially deep breathing, will be painful. (See figure 22.5.) The condition may also be accompanied by a dry, painful cough; weakness; headache; and loss of appetite.

Sometimes excess fluid seeps into the pleural

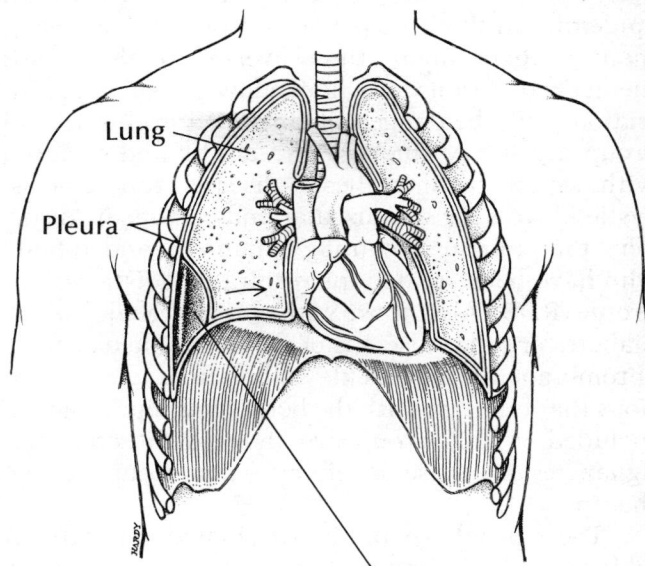

Buildup of fluid between the pleural layers

Figure 22.5. **Pleurisy is a painful disorder in which fluid builds up between the layers of the pleura, the 2-ply membrane surrounding the lung and lining the chest cavity. Inflammation of the pleura may occur; if bacteria or other microorganisms invade the pleura space, a serious infection may result.**

space, a condition known as pleural effusion. The pain may stop (and be replaced by breathlessness) because there is no longer any friction between the two layers, but pleural effusion is a serious matter that may reoccur if not promptly attended to. As with pleurisy, it is treated by treating the underlying condition, as well as by draining of the effusion.

Pneumothorax

A break in the seal of the pleural cavity may result in the entrance of air. In older children and adults (see Pneumothorax in Children, page 459), pneumothorax is most often due to trauma or injury to the chest, but it can occur spontaneously in otherwise healthy, vigorous individuals. (See figure 22.6.)

- *Open Pneumothorax*—Results when a penetrating chest wound enables air to rush in and causes the lungs to collapse.
- *Closed Pneumothorax*—The chest wall is punctured or air leaks from a ruptured bronchus or perforated esophagus and eventually ruptures into the pleural space.
- *Pulmonary Barotrauma*—A patient whose lung function is being maintained mechanically may have air forced into the lungs, which may rupture the pleural space.

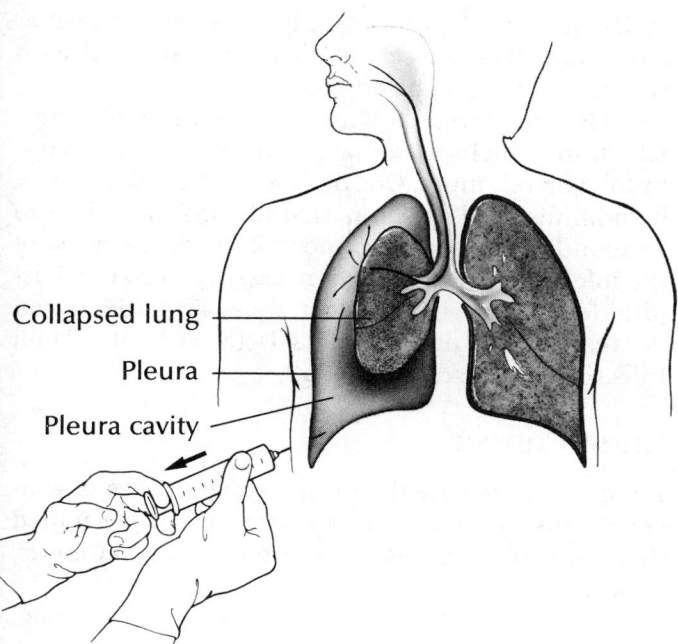

Collapsed lung
Pleura
Pleura cavity

Figure 22.6. **A pneumothorax, or collapsed lung, may result from an injury or a weakness causing a rupture of bronchus, or an air sac, that causes air to leak out of the lungs. If the collapse is extensive or seems to be progressing, air may be withdrawn from the surrounding pleural cavity to permit the lung to re-inflate.**

Pneumothorax may also occur spontaneously (mainly in men ages 20 to 40) when a symptomless weak point—a bubblelike structure—develops in the lung. Symptoms may vary but can include sharp chest pain, trouble in breathing, and a dry, hacking cough.

A small, spontaneous pneumothorax requires no treatment. But in major ruptures, where tension in the chest becomes unbalanced, the air must be removed by an emergency surgical procedure.

Pulmonary Alveolar Proteinosis

In healthy lungs, the alveoli, some 300 million small sacs with walls the thickness of bubbles, are the terminal spaces through which oxygen flows to the blood vessels in the lungs—and to the rest of the circulatory system. Pulmonary alveolar proteinosis is a condition in which these spaces fill with granular material consisting mostly of fat and protein from the blood.

Alveolar proteinosis occurs in previously healthy people, primarily men between the ages of 20 and 50. It may be localized in one of the lungs, or spread throughout one or both. It may progress, remain stable throughout the patient's life, or clear up

spontaneously. Indeed, there may be no symptoms. A patient may live his entire life with alveolar proteinosis. But it may also cause severe breathing difficulties during physical activity or when the patient coughs. Sometimes the disease can be diagnosed by x-ray, or by tests that show a reduction in breathing ability and the ability to use oxygen. In severe cases, bronchopulmonary lavage (surgical rinsing of the lungs) is performed under general anesthesia; however, most cases clear up without treatment.

Loeffler's Syndrome

A patient who has a cough, fever, and breathlessness may be x-rayed, and it will be found that there are transient shadows in the chest which, added to the evidence from a blood test, indicate Loeffler's syndrome. Most cases are due to worm infestation; a few follow the administration of drugs.

Goodpasture's Syndrome

An uncommon hypersensitivity disorder, Goodpasture's syndrome is believed to be an autoimmune process related to antibody (disease-fighting factor) formation in the body. It is characterized by lung hemorrhage and renal disease. Goodpasture's syndrome occurs most frequently in young adult males and can be rapidly fatal. Experimental drug and surgical treatment of the lungs and kidneys may be undertaken.

Atelectasis

In the normal respiratory process, gas passes through the terminal air spaces of the lungs (the alveoli) and into the bloodstream. If the respiration process is interrupted due to bronchial obstruction, pneumothorax or other conditions, or enlargement of structures adjacent to the lungs, the gas may be absent from a portion of the lungs. In this case, that portion of the lung may collapse, a condition known as atelectasis. It may cast a shadow on a chest x-ray that is very difficult to distinguish from pneumonia.

Tuberculosis

Although most people today are only vaguely familiar with tuberculosis (TB), at one time it was the leading killer in this country. Worldwide, it is still a major cause of death, taking 3 million lives per year. But in this country, it is no longer a major threat, even though it still occurs among the aged, the poor, and alcoholics who are malnourished. Some recent cases may be due to immigrant populations harboring the bacillus.

Tuberculosis is a contagious lung disease that is spread by close and direct contact with an infected person's sputum or droplets from sneezing or coughing. Sometimes it spreads to other parts of the body, particularly the kidneys and bones. According to the American Lung Association, most people who contract TB today probably have harbored the causative bacilli for years, usually without knowing it. Children who live under poor conditions in a household with an untreated TB patient also are in danger of contracting the disease.

Symptoms include a chronic cough, fatigue, weakness, unexplained weight loss, loss of appetite, and spitting up blood. These symptoms should be checked promptly by a doctor. A tuberculin skin test can determine whether a person has come in contact with the causative microorganism sometime in the past; a chest x-ray can detect an active infection or lung damage. When TB is found in a child, it is espe-

cially important to test family members and other close contacts to be certain there isn't an adult with severe, but unrecognized, disease.

TB is now treated with a combination of drugs, which may include isoniazid, streptomycin, ethambutol, and refampin. One or more of these drugs may be administered over a period of time, usually 6 to 18 months. By that time, most patients are cured of the infection. It is no longer necessary to go to a hospital for long periods; in fact, most TB patients can be treated on an outpatient basis. (See Chapter 21 on Infectious Diseases, page 436.)

Lung Cancer

Lung cancer is now the most frequent cause of cancer deaths in both men and women. For a detailed discussion of lung cancer, see Chapter 20 on Cancer, page 403.

AIR POLLUTION

EVERY DAY, in any American community, airborne contaminants that affect health are being released into the outdoor atmosphere. They come from combustion processes in industries, motor vehicles, and homes. Depending on weather conditions, they may:

- Be absorbed into the atmosphere, inactivated for the present.
- Create episodes of potentially dangerous air pollution in one or more areas of the city or town. Rural areas are not exempt from air pollution, but the more industrial activity, the more motor vehicles, the more potential for pollution.
- Be blown or carried by clouds hundreds of miles to another city, where they pollute that other community's atmosphere.

Motor vehicle emissions—a black cloud of smoke coming from an improperly tuned engine, or waves of vapor arising from a typical rush hour traffic jam—can contaminate the area around the road for hours. Industrial fumes, smoke, or chemicals can regularly pollute a neighborhood, or there may be an accident in which chemicals are inadvertently released in heavy concentrations.

Household products can be contaminants if they pervade a room or house and have the potential for affecting the occupants' health. So can the gases and chemicals from home heating and cooking.

There are several common types of pollutants:

- Sulfur oxide/small particle pollutants created as a result of burning sulfur-containing fuels, most particularly from fossil-fueled (oil and coal) power plants.

- Pollutants emitted by motor vehicle exhaust—carbon monoxide, oxides of nitrogen, ozone, and light-reactive compounds.
- Localized, hazardous pollutants such as arsenic, asbestos, beryllium, cadmium, hydrogen sulfide, lead, and mercury, which are emitted by local manufacturing plants, refineries, and smelters. The U.S. Environmental Protection Agency (EPA) has said that exposure to any amount of asbestos, beryllium, mercury, and vinyl chloride (common in plastics manufacture) is hazardous.
- Gases and outdoor pollutants that invade the home or which are created by home heating, cooking, or by household products. The recent increase in the use of wood-burning stoves has led to an increase in indoor pollution and represents a special hazard to those with sensitive lungs, e.g., asthmatics.
- Tobacco smoke.

Because these compounds are now so common in our atmosphere, and cannot be separated out from other possible causes of illness, researchers establish the case for their pollutant capabilities through several means: statistical evaluation of excessive ill health in populations exposed to pollutants, or epidemiology; animal studies; controlled human-exposure studies; and observations by physicians or their patients leading to the conclusion that a particular person's ill health is related to an air pollutant.

Air pollution results in:

- *Increased numbers of deaths among people with cardiac and respiratory disease.* There have been a number of acute air pollution episodes in this country and others in the years since World War II. A striking increase in the number of deaths in the affected communities was reported each time, particularly among those persons who already suffered from heart and chronic lung disease.

- *Increasing numbers of people becoming ill with chronic respiratory disease.* Ozone and nitrous oxide have been shown in experiments to induce changes in the lungs similar to those seen in emphysema. It is considered one of the factors responsible—along with cigarette smoking, recurrent infections, or occupational lung hazard exposure—for chronic bronchitis, emphysema, and other chronic lung disease.

- *Stepped up severity of asthma attacks.* Studies have shown that patients with asthma have more frequent and more severe asthma attacks when pollution levels are high. Other studies indicate that air pollutants make asthma patients more susceptible to other asthma-producing stimuli.

- *More acute bronchitis, pneumonia, and other chest illnesses* among adults who live in communities where fossil-fuel pollutant levels are high. They are a definite component in children's respiratory illnesses.

- *An association with temporary difficulty in breathing* in children and adults.

- *Cancer of the lung.* When combined with cigarette smoking, air pollution is seen as a probable contributor to lung cancer.

- *More deaths among people who are hospitalized with heart attacks* when there are increased concentrations of carbon monoxide in the air. One study indicated that angina patients developed pain more rapidly at these times.

- *Irritation of the eyes, nose, and throat and changes in behavior and heart function.* Ozone, the major component of smog, irritates the pharynx and trachea, causing a burning sensation in the upper part of the chest. Increased concentrations of carbon monoxide in the blood have been shown to reduce attention; inhalation of airborne lead in sizeable amounts can give rise to neurologic changes.

Indoor Pollutants

Some outdoor pollutants—such as ozone and carbon dioxide—may invade the indoors. Others may be generated indoors as well as outdoors: Carbon monoxide, for example, can be produced by heating devices in disrepair and can cause carbon monoxide poisoning. Nitrous oxide, produced by gas cooking, has been suggested as a likely cause of some respiratory problems. In addition, some building materials can contaminate the air. Formaldehyde, for example, used in binding agents for wallboards, may cause some sensitive people to have skin or respiratory irritations. Aerosol propellants have been thought to cause short-term respiratory or cardiac

effects in occupational settings. Misused—deliberately inhaled—they have caused sudden deaths from heart arrhythmias.

Tobacco smoke is a well-known source of annoyance as an indoor air pollutant. Studies have indicated that children from homes where the caretaking parent smokes do not develop lung function as well as children from homes where there is no smoking; they also have increased respiratory diseases in the first year of life. Other studies have indicated reduced lung function in middle-aged nonsmokers exposed to smoke at work.

National Standards for Air Quality

The federal Environmental Protection Agency (EPA) is charged with developing and maintaining standards of ambient (outdoor) air quality under the Clean Air Act of 1970, which protect the most sensitive individuals: those with allergic sensitivities, those for whom it has been determined pollutants are a health hazard, those whose bodies are still developing and whose lungs need defense.

The Department of Labor, through the Occupational Safety and Health Administration (OSHA) develops and maintains safe air-quality standards in the workplace. The pollutant levels permitted in the workplace, presumably among healthy workers, are generally higher than what is permissible in the general population.

Both agencies have offices in Washington and in major cities throughout the country and can provide more information. Other sources for information about air-quality standards are the National Clean Air Coalition in Washington and local affiliates of the American Lung Association.

What Can Be Done?

- Learn what air pollution control laws are in effect in the local community. Violators should be reported.

- Support regulation by participating in public hearings.

- Work with others for less-polluting solid waste disposal.

- Support public transportation; it can have a positive effect on auto pollution levels.

- Be sure that air pollution devices on the family car are working. Some states now require emissions inspections of all motor vehicles.

- Check heating systems in the home to be sure they are operating properly.

- Don't burn trash. Many communities have local laws against it.

- Keep house heat low; use electrical appliances as infrequently as possible. Use the car only when necessary.

- Use the appropriate type of gasoline for the car. Substituting leaded for unleaded fuel does not provide better performance and is a source of pollution.

- Use face masks carefully chosen to fit the individual's face and the contaminants for which they are intended.

- Choose the right type of room air purifier. The machines require the user to breathe just in front of them to obtain the maximum benefit. The room must be tightly closed, and the machine selected for its ability to clean the air in a room of a particular size. If room conditions are right, the most effective recirculating filters, according to the American Lung Association, are those that incorporate a chemical filter and a high-efficiency particulate filter. Regular maintenance—cleaning and filter replacement—is essential.

- Consider installing an air purifying device for a building equipped with central air-conditioning. An engineering study is recommended to decide on proper type and placement, particularly for large buildings.

OCCUPATIONAL LUNG DISEASES

EACH YEAR, about 65,000 Americans develop a respiratory disease related to their work environment, with an annual death toll of 25,000. Most people's lungs can withstand temporary or occasional exposure to hazardous substances. Some diseases develop when a worker's lungs are suddenly overwhelmed by fumes, smoke, or other substances. But most people who develop occupational lung disorders do so over a long period of time, with repeated exposure to a hazardous substance.

Sometimes these diseases may take 20 or more years to develop; by that time, the worker may have retired or changed jobs, making the original cause of the disease less apparent. There are 2 basic types of occupational lung disease: those caused by dust in the lungs (pneumoconioses) and those caused by hypersensitivity to substances at the worksite. In addition, some lung cancers are thought to be triggered by exposure to certain substances in the workplace, and there are some diseases, such as byssinosis, which afflicts cotton workers, that combine hypersensitivity and dust exposure.

Pneumoconioses

Over the years, this disease has had a number of names: grinder's rot, miners' phthisis, and miners' asthma are but a few. While the specific causes and manifestations may vary, all forms of pneumoconioses are caused by industrial dust that accumulates in the lungs and eventually interferes with lung function.

Silicosis. More than 1 million American workers are at risk for silicosis. Silica is the most common mineral on earth and is used in many industrial processes, including foundry work, pottery making, and the manufacture of glass, tiles, and bricks. Finely ground silica, especially dangerous when inhaled, is used in abrasive soaps, polishes, and filters. Stonemasons and sandblasters may also be affected by silicosis. So may miners, ore, sand, clay, and soil workers.

Chronic silicosis is seen in those workers who have inhaled relatively low concentrations of industrial dust for 10 to 20 years. The accumulated dust causes a tissue reaction which results in the formation of small, whorl-shaped nodules scattered throughout the lungs. They may remain in a worker's lungs throughout his entire life, having absolutely no effect. Or they may enlarge, increase in numbers, and come together. Breathlessness becomes a problem, and there may be a cough and sputum production.

Twenty to 30 percent of all chronic silicosis victims progress to complicated illness. At this stage, fibrous tissue replaces soft lung tissue, restricting the lungs' function and leading to breathlessness, weakness, chest pain, a cough, and sputum production. The victim becomes a respiratory cripple, likely to die of heart failure caused by the lung disease (cor pulmonale).

Acute Silicosis. Sometimes workers exposed to considerable silica dust over a short period of time, like sandblasters, tunnelers, and drillers, develop acute silicosis. It is rapidly progressive, as unremediable as lung cancer, disabling, and likely to claim its victim within 5 years. The disease is characterized by difficulty in breathing, loss of weight, fever, and coughing. The alveoli become inflamed and fibrosis—hardened tissues in the lungs—develops. Many victims of acute silicosis are young, active people. TB used to be a common complication of silicosis; now that TB has declined in the country as a whole, it is less common.

To prevent silicosis, dust control is necessary. This may mean wetting-down of mines and improved ventilation, or special suits and breathing apparatus. Experts disagree on whether the protection now given workers is adequate.

Coal Workers' Pneumoconiosis.

Coal workers' pneumoconiosis (CWP), commonly called black lung disease, is a potential danger for 250,000 coal miners in the United States. The simple form of the disease affects an estimated 10 to 30 percent of all coal miners. It is more prevalent in miners of anthracite or hard coal than in miners of bituminous or soft coal. Silica, kaolin, mica, beryllium, copper, basalt, cobalt, and other minerals have also been found in miners' lungs. When the condition becomes legally compensible, it is called black lung.

In black lung disease, industrial dust accumulates in the lungs and can be seen in x-rays. This dust may cause no difficulties for the worker. But in about 3 percent of miners with this dust accumulation, fibrosis develops. Each fibrotic area grows, then merges with others. Eventually, most of the lungs are filled with stiff tissue that prevents breathing. Black lung disease victims may die from respiratory failure, heart failure, or severe infection. Dust control is of great importance in coal mining.

Asbestos-Related Lung Disease

Asbestos may cause lung cancer and fibrosis both in those who work with it and others who are exposed to it. Among some groups of workers who are heavily exposed to asbestos, says the National Cancer Institute, as much as 20 to 25 percent of all deaths are from lung cancer. In the general population, the lung cancer death rate is about 5 percent of all deaths.

But asbestos exposure is not limited to workers. Asbestos, a virtually indestructible fiber, has been used broadly in construction, insulation, and other building materials for many years. Its much-prized durability may make it a hazard for those who live, work, or go to school in buildings which were built with asbestos products. Demolition workers and do-it-yourselfers who are renovating older buildings run the risk of extensive exposure to asbestos. Public buildings—schools in Wyoming and New Jersey, university buildings in Connecticut and California, for example—have been temporarily closed because asbestos was found to be flaking from the walls or ceilings.

Asbestos occurs in several different forms. The medically important ones are crocidolite and amosite.

Asbestosis.

This is fibrosis caused by asbestos and begins when asbestos fibers accumulate around the lungs' terminal bronchioles. The body attempts to deal with them by surrounding them with tissues which present a characteristic appearance. The tissues are called fibroids. Symptoms when these fibroids increase and begin to come together may include a cough, sputum, weight loss, and increasing breathlessness. Asbestosis victims usually die about 15 years from the onset of the disease.

Lung Cancer.

The asbestos worker who smokes is estimated to be 90 times as likely to get lung cancer as the smoker who has never worked with asbestos.

Mesothelioma.

A cancer of the pleura or chest lining surrounding the lungs, mesothelioma accounts for 7 to 10 percent of the deaths among asbestos workers. It is inoperable and always fatal. Most cases of mesothelioma occur when workers are exposed to crocidolite fibers, which are fine and straight. The disease has also been reported in those with very little exposure to crocidolite fibers, such as among spouses of asbestos workers and in people living near plants.

Other Cancers.

Asbestos workers have a higher-than-average rate of other cancers, particularly of the esophagus, stomach, and intestines. Asbestos-contaminated mucus, cleared from the lungs and swallowed, is thought to be the culprit. In recent years, the number of asbestos-related diseases has been increasing. Much tighter controls on all uses of asbestos are clearly needed, as well as the use of substitute materials wherever possible.

Many other dusts may accumulate in workers' lungs. Most are, at this point, regarded as not being disease-producing. But a number, such as aluminum, beryllium, carbon black, fiberglass, fuller's earth, kaolin, mica, talc, and tungsten carbide have recognized adverse effects on lung health.

Some workers may be exposed to a variety of dusts; their worksites may include a variety of dust-producing materials. Other workers change industries and inhale first one kind of dust, then another. Pneumoconiosis caused by a mixture of dusts can be difficult to diagnose. As a general rule, the amount of fibrosis present is dependent on how much silica has been inhaled.

Hypersensitivity Diseases

When a worker suffers an allergic reaction to substances in the work environment, he or she is seen to be experiencing an occupational lung disease. Depending on its severity, it can be an annoyance or a precursor of serious illness.

Hypersensitivity reactions can occur in the large airways (bronchi), in the smallest airways (bronchioles), or in the alveoli, the terminal respiratory sacs. In general, the finer the dust inhaled, the smaller the passages into which it will go to cause a reaction.

Occupational Asthma. About 10 percent of the population has a genetic tendency to develop allergies. These workers will be more likely to develop occupational asthma than would others.

Some substances are known to provoke allergic reactions if there is sensitivity: detergent enzymes, platinum salts, cereals and grains, certain wood dusts, isocyanite chemicals used in polyurethane paints, some printing industry chemicals, and some pesticides. In the presence of these and other agents, the victim's airways contract, and excess mucus makes respiration difficult. Once away from the source of distress, the occupational asthma patient finds the asthma has disappeared. The obvious solution is for such a patient to avoid employment that involves exposure to allergenic substances.

Allergic Alveolitis. "Farmer's lung" is the best known example of this hypersensitivity disease which is caused by fine organic dust inhaled into the alveoli, the lungs' smallest airways. The allergic reaction is caused by moldy hay, as well as by dusts from other organic substances, including moldy sugarcane, barley, maple bark, cork, animal hair, bird feathers and droppings, mushroom compost, coffee beans, and paprika. Isocyanite paint chemicals also have been shown to induce allergic alveolitis.

The allergic alveolitis reaction is characterized by a tired feeling, shortness of breath, dry cough, fever, and chills. The symptoms may last for 1 to 10 days. Sometimes emergency treatment and hospitalization are needed for acute attacks. Acute attacks may be treated with steroids and other drugs. Recovery from an episode can take up to 6 weeks, and there may be some lung damage. The farmer can consider changing occupations or merely changing storage techniques, since reaction is triggered by mold, and mold occurs when farm products are not properly dried and stored.

Byssinosis. This hypersensitivity reaction occurs in cotton workers and among those in the flax and hemp industries. Commonly known as "Monday fever" or "brown lung," byssinosis is caused by parts of the cotton plant which are found in bales of cotton brought to the work environment for initial processing. Those who open fresh bales of cotton or those who do the first cleaning are at greatest risk for byssinosis. The worker first experiences a feeling of tightness in the chest upon returning to work on Monday after a weekend away from the processing plant. (At no time, by the way, is there "fever" associated with Monday fever.) Eventually, it begins to persist into Tuesday, then into the rest of the workweek, and finally into weekends and other time off. If a worker leaves the industry, he or she generally recovers completely. Continued exposure, however, increases the risk of chronic bronchitis and emphysema. Some people never develop Monday fever. Others develop it soon after starting on the job. Others get it only after many years. Its progress, too, can vary from worker to worker.

Industrial Bronchitis. A controversial topic, industrial bronchitis is either an entity caused by substances in the workplace, or a misnomer for bronchitis produced by other irritants in various aspects of the worker's life, including cigarette smoking. The medical community does know that bronchitis is much more prevalent in industrialized areas and that occupational lung hazards do contribute to its development.

Occupational Lung Cancer. Cigarette smoking is acknowledged to be the single most important cause of lung cancer. But considerable evidence now suggests that workplace air pollutants are significant causes as well. Many cancers, including lung cancer, occur more frequently in industrialized areas than in rural areas. And lung cancer occurs more frequently among workers handling a variety of substances, including arsenic, bis-chloromethyl ether, coal tar and pitch volatiles, petroleum, mustard gas, coal carbonization products, chromates, asbestos, x-rays, radium uranium, nickel, and isopropyl oil. Chemists, painters, and printers also seem to have an increased risk of lung cancer.

Cigarette smoking, added to the effects of industrial cancer-inducing agents, greatly increases the incidence of lung cancer in workers. Lung cancer, although very seldom curable, is largely preventable. Cigarettes are the single most important factor in lung cancer, but occupational substances that produce cancer can be controlled or replaced.

Other causes of occupational lung disease include:

- FUMES. When solids such as metals are heated to become vapors, then cooled quickly and condensed into fine solid particles in the air, fumes may result. Fumes that cause lung disease may come from nickel, cadmium, chromium, and beryllium, among others. Breathed into the lungs, these particles can cause lung inflammation, bronchitis, metal fume fever, and lung cancer. Workers in industrial high heat operations like welding, smelting, furnace work, and pottery making are most often exposed.

● SMOKE AND GASES. Firefighters used to consider themselves "leather-lunged" and prided themselves on fighting fires without airpacks or masks. But no more: Few firefighters will enter the scene of a blaze today without self-contained breathing apparatus to protect lungs from poisonous gases, smoke, and to supply oxygen.

In a fire, polyvinyl chloride, of which furniture and decorations are often constructed, becomes a major menace to firefighters' lungs. A product of modern plastics, it releases hydrogen chloride, phosgene, and carbon monoxide on combustion, all injurious to the lungs. Phosgene is extremely poisonous and has been used in warfare. Modern climate-controlled buildings with airtight windows trap smoke, increasing toxic content. Exposure to these substances regularly can be a cause of emphysema, bronchitis, asthma, and shortness of breath.

On other workers' jobs, poisonous gases may be generated by chemical reactions and high heat operations like welding, brazing, smelting, oven drying, and furnace work. It is important that conditions in the workplace which are hazardous to lungs be prevented by changing ingredients, work practices, or machinery; by improving ventilation; by training workers.

Sometimes even the climate in an office building can be hazardous to health. Underground garages, buildings straddling highways, or environmentally sealed buildings may potentially present problems associated with high carbon monoxide levels. Woodburning stoves, currently used as an economical way to produce heat, are responsible for indoor pollution and have induced exacerbations of asthma.

SUMMING UP

THE HUMAN RESPIRATORY SYSTEM is responsible not only for providing each cell of the body with essential oxygen, but also with removing body wastes, filtering out infectious agents, and providing the air needed for speech. Although the lungs are built to last a lifetime and are amazingly rugged, considering the abuse to which they are subjected in the form of smoke and other pollutants, there are a number of disorders that impair lung function. Some of these disorders are temporary and relatively harmless; others may be life-threatening.

Any chronic breathing problem or other symptom such as blood in the sputum or a chronic cough should be checked promptly by a doctor. Not smoking and avoiding industrial and other pollutants that may be damaging or irritating to the lungs are other steps we all can take to ensure pulmonary health.

23 Diabetes and Other Endocrine Disorders

Donald A. Holub, M.D.

INTRODUCTION

THE ENDOCRINE SYSTEM is a complex network of glands or glandular tissue that secretes hormones. These hormones, which act as chemical messengers, control many vital functions and affect virtually every organ system and part of the body. For example, hormones control or regulate such diverse functions as reproduction and growth, metabolism, and maintenance of the body's fluid balance, among many others. Together with the nervous system, the various hormones enable us to react to changes in our environment, both internal and external.

Many facets of the endocrine system are not fully understood; every now and then, a previously unidentified hormone is discovered and important new facts about known hormones are constantly being accumulated. Tissues or glands known to secrete hormones are the pituitary, thyroid, adrenal, and parathyroid glands; the ovaries, testes, pancreatic islets of Langerhans, thymus, kidneys, hypothalamus, gastrointestinal mucosa, and pineal body.

In general, the hormones produced in these glands and tissues travel through the bloodstream and exert their action on organs and tissues away from their origin. There also are tissues that produce "local" hormones or hormonelike substances, such as prostaglandins, with specific, localized functions, many of which are unknown or poorly understood.

Since there are so many different types of hormones with a wide array of functions, it follows there are numerous ways of classifying these substances. One common classification lists them according to their chemical derivation: the steroid hormones, which are derived from cholesterol; and hormones derived from protein, peptides, or amino acids. Steroid hormones include the sex hormones (testosterone, estrogen, progesterone, adrenal androgens, etc.); mineralocorticoids, which regulate the body's fluid and salt balance; and glucocorticoids, which are important regulators of glucose metabolism and which include the only significant glucocorticoid, cortisol, a so-called "stress hormone." These hormones pass through their target cell membranes and act directly on the cell nuclei. In contrast, the peptide, protein, or amino acid hormones, which include insulin, growth hormone, epinephrine (adrenaline), and many others, do not actually enter the target cells. Instead, they attach themselves to specific receptor sites on the cell surface and work through other mediums—one of the most common is a substance called cyclic AMP—to perform their given functions.

The release of hormones may be triggered by nerve impulses, elaborate feedback systems involving other hormones or body substances, or a combination of the two. The various hormones circulate in very small quantities and have very specific target cells or receptors. All in all, the endocrine system is one of the body's most complex and finely tuned; so long as the delicate balance of the many different hormones is maintained, the person is not aware of just how many vital functions are being performed with amazing efficiency and interdependence. (See figure 23.1.) But when the system goes awry, usually because of too much or too little of one or more hor-

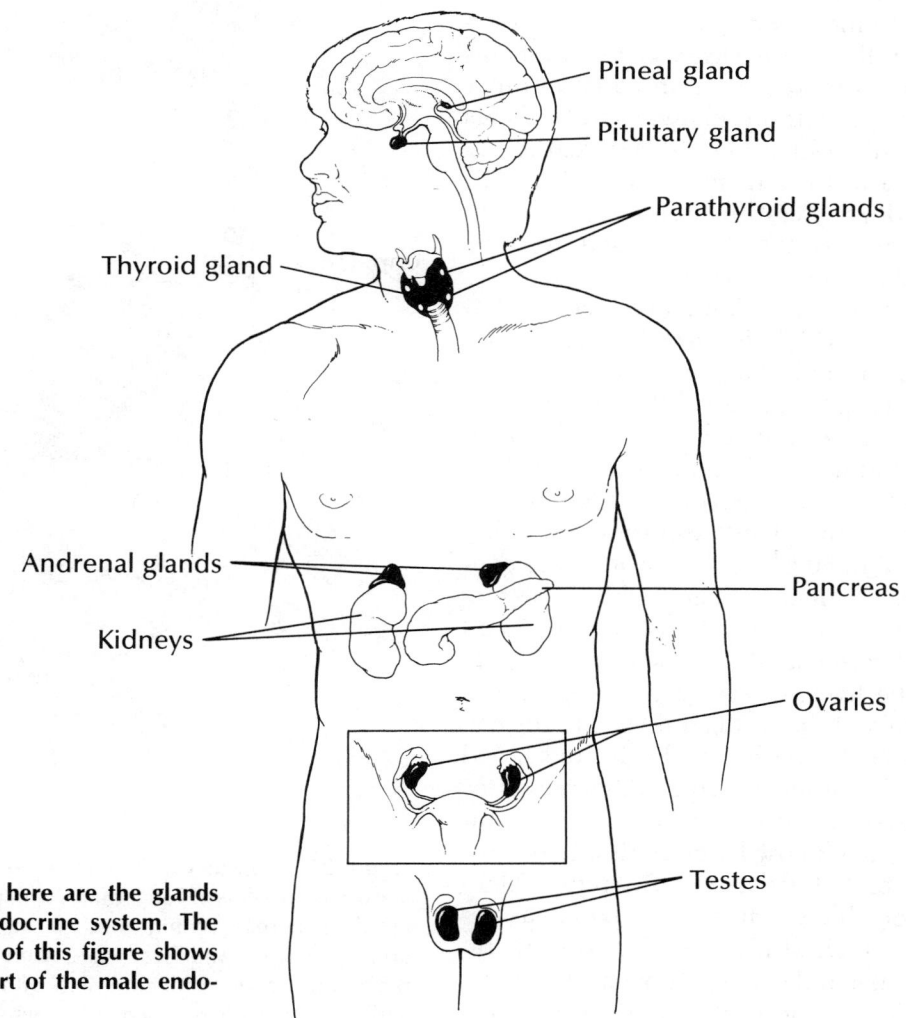

Figure 23.1. **Shown here are the glands that make up the endocrine system. The box in the abdomen of this figure shows the female counterpart of the male endocrine sex glands.**

mones, the resulting symptoms are often dramatic and even life-threatening. In recent decades, tremendous gains have been made in diagnosing and treating many of these endocrine disorders. The discovery of insulin for the treatment of diabetes, for example, has saved hundreds of thousands of people from an early death. Screening newborn infants for thyroid deficiency can now prevent cretinism, a particularly severe form of mental retardation. New tests capable of measuring even very minute hormone levels now make it possible to diagnose endocrine disorders more accurately and also to monitor treatment more effectively. In this chapter, the more common endocrine disorders will be described, along with summaries of their diagnosis and treatment.

DIABETES MELLITUS

DIABETES IS A CHRONIC DISEASE affecting many organs and body functions, especially those involved in metabolism. The disease is caused either by a lack of the hormone insulin or by the body's inability to use it. This hormone is particularly essential in carbohydrate metabolism, the process by which sugar and starches are broken down into glucose (blood sugar), the body's principal fuel. Although there is no cure for diabetes, most cases can now be controlled adequately enough for the patient to lead a relatively normal, productive life.

Diabetes is the most common endocrine disorder. About 10 million Americans have diabetes mellitus, and it is estimated that an equal number may have the disease without knowing it. Diabetes is directly responsible for about 40,000 deaths per year, but when deaths from its many complications, such as kidney failure or cardiovascular disease, are added, the figure rises to 300,000, making it the third leading cause of death in this country.

The specific endocrine gland involved in diabetes is the pancreas, which lies in the upper midabdomen. Scattered through the pancreas are clusters of hormone-producing tissue called the islets of Langerhans. These islets contain 2 types of cells: beta, which produce insulin, and alpha, which produce glucagon. Normally these 2 hormones regulate the amount of glucose in the blood. Almost all carbohydrate and about 50 to 60 percent of protein are converted into glucose, which is then "burned" as fuel by almost every type of body cell. (See figure 23.2.)

After a meal, almost all of the carbohydrate passes through the liver, where 55 to 60 percent is stored as glycogen and the rest is returned to the circulation as glucose for use by the brain, red blood cells, muscle, and fat tissue. When glucose rises after a meal, the pancreas secretes insulin, which increases the uptake of glucose by body tissues or promotes its conversion to fatty tissue. (See figure 23.3.) When the level of glucose drops, the pancreas releases glucagon, which stimulates the liver to release stored glycogen and convert it back to glucose. When insulin deficiency prevents the body from utilizing its glucose, the body starts to burn its own fat

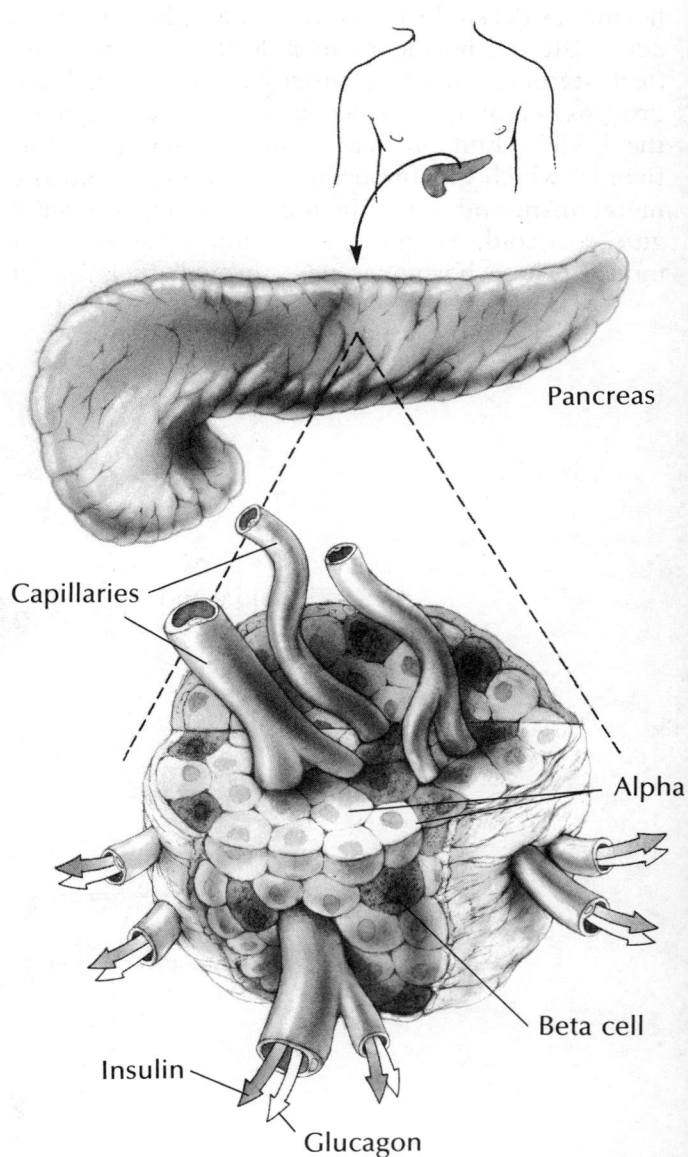

Figure 23.2. **Insulin is manufactured in tiny clusters of cells known as the islets of Langerhans, which are scattered throughout the pancreas. Within these islets are alpha cells, which secrete glucagon, and beta cells, which secrete insulin. This schematic drawing shows an islet, with the capillaries entering and insulin being released into these minute blood vessels, which carry it throughout the body.**

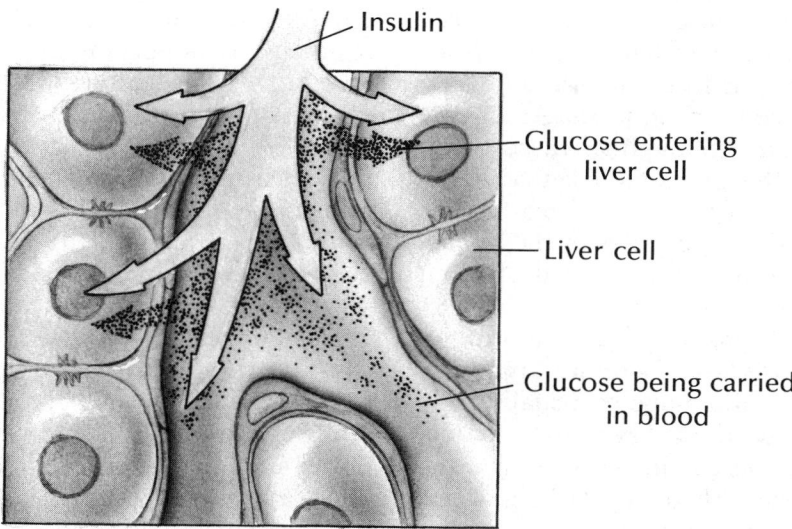

Insulin

Glucose entering liver cell

Liver cell

Glucose being carried in blood

Figure 23.3. **Schematic drawing showing the role of insulin in regulating blood sugar. In the presence of insulin, glucose is absorbed from the blood into the body cells, which require it for fuel.**

and muscle—a potentially dangerous situation because this can lead to an accumulation of ketones and other acidic by-products in the blood, a condition called ketoacidosis. If untreated, this can lead to coma and death.

There are 2 distinct types of diabetes mellitus: Type 1, in which the beta cells cease to produce insulin; and Type 2, in which the beta cells produce varying amounts of insulin, but the body is unable to use it effectively. Type 1, also referred to as juvenile diabetes, insulin-dependent diabetes, or ketosis-prone diabetes, usually begins in the first 3 decades of life, but there are exceptions; a small percentage develop the disease after the age of 30. It is the more serious form of diabetes; before the discovery of insulin in the early 1920s, most Type 1 diabetic patients died of ketoacidosis or other complications of the disease

within a few years of its onset. Today, the majority of Type 1 diabetic patients can lead reasonably normal lives by taking regular insulin injections. Fortunately, of the 2 types of diabetes, it is the more rare, making up about 10 percent of the total diabetic population.

Type 2 diabetes occurs most frequently during middle age or pregnancy, although again there are exceptions. It occurs most frequently in overweight people, and most cases can be controlled by weight loss, diet, and exercise. There also are drugs, called oral hypoglycemics, that help the body make more effective use of its own insulin. These may be prescribed, with or without supplementary insulin, for Type 2 diabetic patients whose disease is not controlled by diet and exercise.

SIGNS OF DIABETES

DIABETES IS AN ANCIENT DISEASE; it is described in the Egyptian Ebers Papyrus, which were written in about 1500 B.C. Early Greek physicians gave the disease its name based on its symptoms: diabetes means siphon or fountain, referring to the copious urination characteristic of the disease in its early, untreated state. These early doctors also observed that the urine had a sweet odor and taste; therefore the term "mellitus," which comes from the Latin word for honey. As glucose builds up in the blood,

some of it spills over into the urine and is excreted. The earliest tests for diabetes involved smelling and even tasting the urine for sweetness; even today, cases of unsuspected diabetes may be first discovered by finding sugar in a routine urine test.

Diabetes should be suspected in anyone who unexplainably begins experiencing excessive, almost insatiable thirst; frequent urination, hunger, and loss of weight. There also may be feelings of weakness, mood swings, an increased vulnerability to infection, such as slow-healing cuts or increased vaginal infections in women, fatigue, leg cramps or pins and needles sensations in the toes and fingers; impotence; blurred vision, or hemorrhages of tiny blood vessels in the retina. Sometimes these symptoms are ignored until the approach of ketoacidosis, which is marked by a fruity, sweetish breath odor, tremendous thirst, weakness, dryness of the tongue and skin, nausea, and vomiting. Untreated, this can progress to diabetic coma and death.

Many of these symptoms do not appear until an advanced stage of the disease; there are also large numbers of people with mild diabetes (usually Type 2) who do not have any noticeable symptoms. A doctor may be alerted to the condition when routine blood or urine tests show high levels of glucose. However, sugar in the urine (glycosuria) is not always a sign of diabetes; it may simply mean that the kidneys are unable to handle normal amounts of sugar and are excreting some of it in the urine. Conversely, there are people with diabetes who do not have glycosuria, or have it only erratically. Therefore, urine tests do not give a definitive diagnosis of diabetes; instead, this is determined by testing the blood for glucose.

Several measurements of blood sugar may be needed before diabetes is diagnosed or ruled out. In Type 1 diabetic patients, diagnosis is usally straightforward because the pancreas is producing little or no insulin. A morning blood sample is taken before any food has been consumed—a fasting blood glucose—and if 2 separate tests are positive (more than 140 milligrams of glucose per deciliter of blood [140 mg/dl]), a diagnosis of diabetes is established. In cases in which the fasting blood glucose is high, more than 105 mg/dl, but less than 140 mg/dl, additional testing may be necessary if there are symptoms that suggest diabetes. If there are no symptoms and no family history of the disease, further tests may not be performed at this point, but the patient will be asked to return for periodic blood sugar measurements. If the patient is overweight, he or she may be instructed to go on a weight-reduction diet and also to increase exercise.

If further tests are indicated, a glucose tolerance test will be included. This test is designed to measure the body's reaction to consumption of a large amount of sugar or glucose. To help ensure accurate results, it is important that patients undergoing a glucose tolerance follow specific instructions for several days before the test to prevent inaccurate results. For example, patients undergoing a glucose tolerance test should consume at least 100 to 150 grams of carbohydrate per day for the 3 preceding days. (See accompanying food tables for carbohydrate content of typical foods and portions.)

Lack of exercise also can skew the results of a glucose tolerance test. People who are sedentary—particularly those who are hospitalized or confined to bed—will have higher blood glucose than normally active people. Pregnancy alters glucose levels; therefore, different criteria are used to diagnose diabetes at this time. Liver disorders, previous gastrointestinal surgery, and certain other illnesses and a number of drugs also can alter the results of a glucose tolerance test. Before undergoing the test, ask your doctor if there are any special instructions you should follow; also be sure your doctor is aware of your medical history and any drugs you are taking.

In any event, a positive glucose tolerance test still does not always mean the patient has or will develop overt diabetes. Studies involving several hundred patients found that only 22.9 percent of the 401 patients who had positive results actually developed symptomatic diabetes over the next 5 years, and most of these patients were in the top range, with very high blood glucose (200 mg/dl) after 2 or 3 hours, or they had other risk factors, such as a family history of the disease, were over the age of 50, or were overweight. At one time, many of these borderline cases were labeled "prediabetic," a practice that is now discouraged because the majority never actually develop the disease, but may experience detrimental psychological and economic effects that go with such a label. For example, diabetic patients often cannot get insurance or they pay very high premiums. Some employers are reluctant to hire or promote diabetic patients, even though their work and attendance records may be superior to those of a nondiabetic peer. Although these borderline patients should undergo periodic testing and follow commonsense preventive measures, they should not think of themselves as being "sick."

CAUSES OF DIABETES

THE CAUSES OF both Type 1 and Type 2 diabetes are unknown. A number of precipitating factors have been identified, however. A family history of diabetes increases the risk for both types, indicating there may be a genetic predisposition. A number of researchers believe that a fault in the immune system may be a factor in Type 1 diabetes. One theory holds that in certain genetically susceptible people, an infection of the pancreas may prompt the immune system to, in effect, turn on itself and destroy the insulin-producing beta cells. This theory is bolstered by the frequent finding that the onset of diabetes comes on the heels of a viral infection, such as the flu, chickenpox, or bad cold. Unusual stress also seems to precipitate diabetes in some patients; in fact, there is a specific stress-induced form of diabetes that disappears once the stress is resolved. Again, this has led researchers to theorize that the immune system may be involved, since stress appears to influence this system.

Because the pancreas continues to produce at least some insulin in Type 2 diabetes, this form of the disease is considered more a disorder of insulin resistance, meaning the body is not using the hormone effectively, than one of insulin deficiency or pancreatic failure. Studies have found that some Type 2 patients actually produce normal or higher-than-normal amounts of insulin.

Pregnancy is another fairly common precipitating factor, particularly among overweight women over the age of 30 who have a family history of diabetes. Certain drugs, infection, and trauma are still other factors that have been linked to the onset of Type 2 diabetes in some patients.

COMPLICATIONS OF DIABETES

THE METABOLIC PROBLEMS associated with diabetes affect the entire body; similarly, the complications of the disease are wide-ranging and affect many different organ systems. The primary complications, which occur most commonly in Type 1 diabetes, may appear relatively rapidly and are directly related to the level of blood glucose. If the blood glucose is too high (hyperglycemia) and there is inadequate insulin to utilize it, the body will begin to break down fat and muscle tissue for fuel. Signs of hyperglycemia usually come on over a period of time and may go unnoticed until they progress to serious ketoacidosis. Warning signs of hyperglycemia and ketoacidosis include:

- Increased thirst and urination
- Nausea and vomiting
- Feeling of weakness or fatigue
- Large amounts of ketones in the urine
- Blood sugar measurement of more than 300 mg/dl
- Signs of dehydration, such as dry mouth, dry skin
- A fruity breath odor
- Heavy, labored breathing that is also rapid and deep
- Fixed, dilated pupils and difficulty in focusing
- Loss of consciousness

Regular monitoring of blood sugar and the urine for ketones, which will be discussed in the following section, can prevent severe hyperglycemia and ketoacidosis.

Low blood sugar (hypoglycemia) also can pose serious problems for the diabetic patient, especially one with Type 1 diabetes who takes insulin injections. Taking too much insulin may lead to rapid depletion of available blood glucose, resulting in an insulin reaction or shock. Warning signs of an insulin reaction include:

- A cold, clammy feeling
- Tingling sensation of the mouth, fingers, or other parts of the body
- Excessive sweating
- Paleness
- A feeling of weakness or faintness
- Headache
- Hunger
- Irritability and change in mood or personality
- Impaired vision
- Trembling
- A rapid heartbeat
- Sudden feeling of drowsiness
- Abdominal pain
- Sudden awakening from sleep accompanied by other symptoms, especially a cold sweat
- Loss of consciousness and coma
- Inability to waken diabetic patient

Countering an insulin reaction calls for taking a simple sugar, such as a glass of orange juice or soda (not sugar-free or diet), candy, fruit or, in cases of rapid deterioration or loss of consciousness, administration of an injection of glucagon, which almost immediately converts glycogen stored in the liver to glucose. If glucagon is not available, and the patient is unconscious, honey, sugar syrup, or other absorbable simple sugar can be placed under the tongue where it will be absorbed into the body. (Strategies for preventing and countering insulin reactions will be discussed in more detail in the following section on treatment.)

Long-term complications are varied, and usually do not become evident for several years or even decades after the onset of diabetes. A number of recent studies indicate that, for many patients, secondary complications may be minimized or even prevented by maintaining normal blood glucose. But there are enough exceptions to make development of complications highly unpredictable. Not all patients develop secondary complications; there are others in whom the type and severity of problems seem unrelated to either the duration of the diabetes or the degree of control.

As noted earlier, many different organ systems are affected by diabetes and the type of complications vary from patient to patient. Some of the more common complications are summarized below.

Infection

Infection is a special hazard for people with diabetes. Diabetic patients are not only more susceptible to infection, but their disease is also exacerbated by infection. Diabetes lowers the body's natural resistance in a number of ways. For example, it is thought that Type 1 diabetes may be caused by a defect in the immune system; this may carry over to other disease-fighting mechanisms. Poorly controlled diabetes appears to hinder the ability of white blood cells (leukocytes) to carry out their function of destroying invading microorganisms. This makes the diabetic patient more susceptible to infections, both from invading bacteria, fungi, and other foreign organisms, as well as from normally benign organisms that inhabit the body or environment without causing disease. Types of infections that are particularly common among diabetic patients include urinary tract infections; thrush, gum disease, and other mouth infections; both superficial and systemic fungal infections; vaginitis; and wound infections. Even a trivial cut or sore may prove difficult to heal and develop into a serious, even life-threatening problem.

In addition, infection markedly increases the need for insulin; in fact, blood sugar often rises even before there are any symptoms of infection. If the illness involves nausea, vomiting, or diarrhea, keeping blood sugar under control may prove doubly challenging because the patient is unable to eat normally. Some patients mistakenly think that because they are unable to eat, they do not need to take insulin while ill, a move that can lead to ketoacidosis. Even if no food is consumed, the body requires insulin for metabolism. Diabetic patients are advised to call their doctors at the first sign of even a trivial illness such as a common cold or upset stomach for guidance in managing both it and the diabetes.

Diabetic Complications Affecting the Eyes

Diabetes has an adverse effect on almost every part of the eye and it is now the leading cause of adult blindness in the United States. Although only a small percentage of diabetic patients lose their eyesight, most have some evidence of eye damage after 5 to 10 years. The most serious complications are those involving the retina and the lens, although other parts of the eye also may be damaged.

Diabetic retinopathy is potentially one of the more serious eye complications. The retina is the layer of light-sensitive cells that line the back three-quarters of the eyeball. More than 70 percent of diabetic patients have some degree of retinopathy after 10 years of having diabetes; fortunately, most do not suffer serious loss of vision. Retinopathy most commonly affects the tiny capillaries that nourish the retina. The walls of these blood vessels weaken and balloon out, forming tiny aneurysms. Sometimes these weakened blood vessels leak blood, resulting in dot or flame hemorrhages, which may reduce the sharpness of vision. Eventually, some of these weakened blood vessels die, and if the retina does not get enough oxygen and other nutrients, some of its tissue also dies. This dead tissue forms minute clumps called cotton wool exudates.

In some patients, there is an overgrowth of new blood vessels in the retina, a condition called proliferative retinopathy. These vessels are often very fragile and leak blood into the vitreous humor, the jellylike substance inside the eyeball. This blood can dim vision or cause temporary blindness, which disappears when the blood is reabsorbed. Permanent loss of vision may occur, however, if scar tissue forms and damages the retina.

Fortunately, there are a number of new treatments for diabetic retinopathy that can help prevent blindness or minimize loss of vision. Many of these treatments involve laser surgery, the use of concentrated light to destroy some of the excess or weakened blood vessels. In some cases, the laser beams may be used to destroy tiny portions of the retina, thinning out the tissue to increase the underlying blood flow. If there has been bleeding into the vitreous humor, it may be removed (vitrectomy) and replaced with an artificial substance to restore eyesight. Advances in microsurgery of the eye also are of great benefit to diabetic patients, enabling doctors to repair detached retinas and other abnormalities caused by progressive retinopathy.

When diabetes affects the eye lens, cataracts are

the common result. In many instances, these cataracts are similar to those that commonly occur in older people; however, in diabetic patients, the cataracts form earlier and develop more rapidly. Cataracts usually can be treated by removing the diseased lens and then wearing glasses, a contact lens, or implanted artificial lens to overcome the farsightedness that occurs when the natural lens is removed.

Although many diabetic patients encounter only relatively minor eye problems, it is very important that all people with the disease see an ophthalmologist regularly. Depending upon the individual circumstances, this may be as often as every 2 or 3 months, or every 6 months or year for patients with minimal or slowly progressing eye conditions. In addition, any symptoms such as blurring of vision, hemorrhages, or other changes should be checked promptly. In many instances, prompt treatment in an early stage can prevent further or permanent loss of vision.

Circulatory and Cardiovascular Complications

About three-fourths of the deaths among diabetic patients are caused by cardiovascular complications. People with diabetes have a much higher rate of heart disease and circulatory disorders than the general population. The specific problems range from an increased risk of heart attacks, strokes, and high blood pressure to impaired circulation involving both large and small blood vessels. Hardening of the arteries (arteriosclerosis) and a buildup of fatty deposits (atherosclerosis), both exceedingly common health problems for the entire population, appear at an earlier age and advance more rapidly in people with diabetes. High levels of blood cholesterol and triglycerides are common among both men and women with diabetes. Women, who ordinarily have lower blood lipid levels and a lower incidence of heart disease than men, often have very high levels of blood lipids when they have diabetes. High blood pressure, which increases the risk of strokes and heart attacks, also is very common among diabetic patients.

How diabetes promotes cardiovascular and circulatory abnormalities is unclear, but again, many researchers think the answer lies in the abnormally high blood glucose. Studies have found that high blood glucose affects several blood components, particularly red blood cells and perhaps the platelets, and these abnormalities may play a role in the development of arteriosclerosis. (See Chapter 19 on Heart and Blood Vessel Disease, page 389, for a more detailed discussion.) Insulin appears to increase lipid synthesis in the artery walls, which may help promote the buildup of fatty deposits. Since many Type 2 diabetics actually have high levels of insulin, even though their bodies do not effectively utilize it, some researchers think this may be a factor in the high degrees of atherosclerosis among these patients. In Type 1 diabetes, however, insulin therapy inhibits the atherosclerotic process by normalizing blood sugar.

Diabetes also has damaging effects on the capillaries, or microcirculation, which nourishes the individual body cells. In diabetes, there is a thickening of the basement membranes, the substances that separate the epithelial cells lining the various body surfaces and the underlying structures. When the capillary basement membranes become thickened, the vessels often are unable to carry adequate blood to the tissues they serve, resulting in poor circulation. The limbs are particularly vulnerable to these circulatory problems, partly explaining why diabetic patients have a high incidence of leg and foot problems. Poor circulation to the lower limbs is particularly common in diabetes, resulting in chronic skin ulcers; leg cramps or pain, especially when walking or climbing stairs; and, in some cases, gangrene and amputation can be prevented by early treatment of infections or other problems. (See section on Foot Care for a more detailed discussion, page 498.)

Nervous System Complications

Diabetes-related disorders of the nervous system (diabetic neuropathy) cause a variety of symptoms: slowed reflexes, sexual impotence, loss of sensation, intermittent episodes of pain, and exacerbation of circulatory disorders, among others. The early signs of diabetic neuropathy include tingling sensations in the fingers and toes, feelings of muscular weakness and, in a large percentage of men, impotence. The neuropathy also compounds other diabetes-related complications. For example, if there is a loss of sensation to the feet and legs, as well as diminished circulation of blood, the patient may not be aware of an injury or infection until it develops into a serious open ulcer.

Pain is a common feature of diabetic neuropathy. This may range from minor discomfort or tingling sensations to severe pain. The pain may take the form of sharp stabbing pains that come and go, deep aches that make sleep or normal activities difficult, or very sensitive skin that reacts to even a slight touch.

Although the symptoms of diabetic neuropathy may not become evident for years, new highly sensitive nerve function tests have found that nerve deterioration oftens begins in the early stages of both types of diabetes. Both sensory and motor nerves may be involved and the effects vary greatly from patient to patient. In some people, symptoms of neuropathy never develop, even though tests may show that some nerve fibers have been damaged. In others, the symptoms may appear early in the disease and progress rapidly. In many instances, the neuropathy becomes evident by its effects on other systems controlled by the autonomic nervous system. Sexual impotence, gastrointestinal problems, bladder disorders, irregular heartbeats, or blood pressure abnormalities are examples of disorders that may be traced to the autonomic nervous system.

The precise mechanisms whereby diabetes damages the nervous system are unknown, but there is evidence that high blood glucose and insulin deficiency are likely causes. There may also be other unidentified factors at work, especially in light of the fact that nerve damage sometimes occurs before there is marked elevation of blood glucose or other symptoms of diabetes.

Treatment of diabetic neuropathy centers on achieving good control of the underlying diabetes by normalizing blood glucose. In addition, specific symptoms often can be relieved by treatment. For example, painkilling drugs may be prescribed for the discomfort associated with neuropathy; loss of muscle control, such as foot drop or ankle weakness may be relieved by mechanical devices. The skin, particularly on the feet and lower legs, should be inspected regularly and any break, callus, or other potential problem, should be treated promptly and aggressively to prevent its worsening.

Impotence is a particularly worrisome complication for many men with diabetes. Very often they are embarrassed or reluctant to talk to their doctors about the problem. In recent years, implanted devices to help men with organic impotence achieve and maintain an erection have enabled many diabetic patients to regain the ability to have sexual intercourse. Information about these prostheses can be obtained from the primary physician treating the diabetes or from urologists experienced in treating sexual problems in diabetic men.

Complications Involving the Kidneys

Kidney failure is another serious potential complication of long-standing diabetes. The kidneys are complex, highly efficient organs that filter waste material from the blood for disposal from the body. Each kidney contains more than 1 million nephrons, which are minute filtering systems. Damage to the tiny blood vessels in the nephrons can eventually lead to progressive kidney failure, which is charac-

terized by the excretion of protein and other nutrients in the urine.

Diabetes also increases the kidney's vulnerability to infections. People with the disease should be particularly aware of any symptoms of kidney or urinary tract infections (flank pain, difficult or burning urination, urgency to urinate, passage of urine discolored by blood) and see a doctor promptly if they should occur.

Improved treatments of kidney failure, specifically hemodialysis using an artificial kidney and replacement of diseased kidneys with healthy transplants, have greatly improved the outlook for patients with advanced diabetic kidney disease (diabetic nephropathy). But these measures do not cure the underlying disease. Studies have found that kidneys transplanted in patients with poorly controlled diabetes will develop diabetic nephropathy within a few years. There is evidence, however, that bringing elevated blood glucose into the normal range can reduce kidney damage.

Psychological Effects of Diabetes

No discussion of diabetic complications is complete without at least a mention of the emotional problems that so often accompany the disease. Any chronic disease carries the potential for profound emotional effects on both the patient and those close to him or her. This is particularly true of diabetes which is not only a lifelong disease, but also one in which the patient has to pay particular attention to almost every aspect of day-to-day life. Anger, depression, anxiety, and feelings of deep frustration are common reactions. Poorly controlled diabetes, with its abnormal swings from high to low blood sugar, also produces mood changes and feelings of irritability, anxiety, depression, and euphoria.

The emotional stress can become a vicious cycle: Poorly controlled diabetes can produce negative psychological responses that in turn can further exacerbate the disease. It is well known that emotional stress or upset has a profound effect on blood glucose. For example, stress triggers the classic "fight or flight response," which is marked by increased heart rate and rises in both blood pressure and blood glucose and increases in epinephrine and adrenal hormones, such as cortisone. These automatic responses are intended to provide the extra energy to overcome a dangerous situation. A certain amount of stress is unavoidable and even desirable, but very often, people overreact to even trivial events as if they were a major stress. In the diabetic person, this may mean a constant roller coaster effect of hormonal changes that inhibit the action of insulin at a time when the body is releasing more blood glucose.

Obviously, achieving an equilibrium of emotional well-being is particularly important for the diabetic patient, even though many factors and circumstances may make this more difficult than for a non-diabetic.

Studies have found that many diabetic patients are helped in achieving enhanced well-being by maintaining better blood glucose control. Very often, diabetic patients feel they have no control over the disease or their lives. This has changed in recent years as improved techniques in self-monitoring have made it possible for patients to learn how to normalize blood glucose and also, how to better match insulin, food, and exercise to achieve more flexibility in their lives. (See The Role of Self-Monitoring, page 492.)

TREATMENT OF DIABETES

THE GOALS OF treating both Type 1 and Type 2 diabetes are essentially the same: to minimize both short- and long-term complications by normalizing levels of blood glucose. Normal blood glucose is defined as falling between a low of 50 mg/dl and a high of 150 mg/dl, although some doctors are not as rigid about the upper level, and will not be concerned over blood sugars hovering in the 200 mg/dl range. Studies have found, however, that complications are most likely to be minimized if blood glucose can be controlled in the 50 to 150 mg/dl range.

The specific treatments for the two types of diabetes are quite different. Type 1 diabetes requires insulin injections and matching insulin intake to diet and exercise to control blood glucose. In contrast, most people with Type 2 diabetes do not require insulin injections (although there are exceptions who do); instead, most can be treated by diet, exercise, and, if needed, drugs that increase the body's ability to utilize insulin. The basics of both approaches to treatment will be outlined in this section.

Treatment of Type 1 Diabetes

Before the discovery of insulin by 2 Canadian researchers in 1921, the only treatment for Type 1 diabetes was a rigorous diet low in calories and carbohydrate. This approach prolonged the lives of some diabetic patients, but without insulin, most died of the disease within a few months or years. While the discovery of insulin was a giant step forward, it is not a cure for the disease. Insulin must be injected regularly for a lifetime. Because insulin is a protein hormone that would be destroyed by the digestive processes if it were taken orally, it must be administered by injection. Most people with Type 1 diabetes take their insulin via injections into the subcutaneous tissue that lies just under the skin. In recent years, however, some patients have started wearing insulin pumps, portable computerized devices that are designed to administer constant small amounts of insulin (as well as larger amounts to cover meals and other circumstances) through an indwelling needle and catheter. These devices are still in an experimental stage and are not appropriate for certain types of patients, such as those whose diabetes is erratic (brittle). (Other methods of giving insulin, such as by inhalation or in an oral form, are under study, but are not yet available.)

There are 3 basic types of insulin: fast-acting (e.g., Regular or Semilente), which takes effect in 30 to 60 minutes and has a total duration of action lasting 4 to 6 hours; intermediate-acting (e.g., NPH or Lente), which takes effect in 3 to 4 hours and has a total duration of 20 to 24 hours; and long-acting (e.g., Ultralente or PZI), which takes effect in 6 to 8 hours and lasts 32 hours or longer. Some patients with mild diabetes can be controlled on a single daily dose combining a fast-acting and intermediate- or long-acting insulin. Increasingly, however, the trend is to multiple daily injections, frequently a combination of fast- and intermediate-acting insulin to avoid the highs and lows in blood glucose that are common with single-dose regimens and also to enable the patient to have more flexibility in lifestyle. In any event, it is important to understand the different types of insulins, to know when each will reach its peak of action (see table 23.1), and to know how to match insulin with food and exercise to maintain as normal a level of blood glucose as possible. Not all physicians agree on how best to achieve this, and there is no one regimen that works for all or even most patients. Each treatment schedule must be individualized to meet the needs and lifestyle of each patient; it also may need to be adjusted frequently as circumstances change. For example, insulin needs go up under periods of stress or infection and during the premenstrual week in women of child-bearing age. People who exercise a good deal need less insulin than even normally active people. Insulin requirements rise markedly during pregnancy, the adolescent growth spurt, or during a period of insulin resistance or acidosis. All of these many variables will be confusing and even dis-

Table 23.1 CHARACTERISTICS OF INSULINS

Insulin	Type	Onset (hr)	Peak action (hr)	Duration (hr)
Regular	Fast-acting	0.5–1	2–4	4–6
Semilente	Fast-acting	1–2	3–6	4–6
NPH	Intermediate	3–4	10–16	20–24
Lente	Intermediate	3–4	10–16	20–24
Ultralente	Long-acting	6–8	14–20	32 +
PZI	Long-acting	6–8	14–20	32 +

couraging to a newly diagnosed patient; most people, however, quickly learn how to adjust insulin, food, and exercise to control blood sugar, especially if they have been taught how to monitor their own blood glucose as well as test their urine periodically for sugar and ketones.

Diet is also an important factor in the overall management of Type 1 diabetes. The precise diet depends upon the individual patient and the physician and dietitian. Most regimens recommend that 50 to 60 percent of the total calories be from carbohydrates, with most coming from starches or complex carbohydrates, 20 to 25 percent from protein, and 20 to 30 percent from fats. In addition to counting calories and distributing them among the nutrient groups, it is also important to follow a regular meal/snack pattern or eating schedule. One frequent eating schedule calls for 3 small meals and 3 or 4 snacks consumed throughout the day. The eating schedule depends upon the types of insulins used and the needs of the patient. Once blood sugar is normalized, most patients find they can adopt a diet and meal pattern that fits their individual lifestyle and food preferences. But arriving at this point often requires careful planning with a dietitian, physician, or diabetes educator.

Calculating the Carbohydrate Content of Common Foods.

The following charts list the approximate carbohydrate content per serving for common foods. Since a substantial amount of protein is also converted to glucose during metabolism, the protein content is also indicated.

MILK AND MILK PRODUCTS

Skim Milk

8-oz. cup contains:
Carbohydrate: 12 grams
Protein: 8 grams
Calories: 80

Whole Milk

8-oz. cup contains:
Carbohydrate: 12 grams
Protein: 8 grams
Calories: 150 *(approximate)*

Consult nutritional labels for carbohydrate content of yogurt and other milk products.

NONSTARCHY VEGETABLES

Serving size: ½ cup cooked
Carbohydrate: 5 grams
Protein: 2 grams

Asparagus	Carrots	Beets	Spinach	Sauerkraut	Vegetable juice
Bean Sprouts	Cauliflower	Chards	Turnips	String beans	cocktail
Beets	Eggplant	Collards	Mushrooms	(green or yellow)	Zucchini
Broccoli	Green pepper	Dandelion	Okra	Summer squash	
Brussels sprouts	Green beans	Kale	Onions	Tomatoes	
Cabbage	Greens *(cooked)*	Mustard	Rutabaga	Tomato juice	

Serving size: 1 cup raw

Cabbage	Chinese cabbage	Endive	Lettuce	Spinach	Radishes
Celery	Cucumber	Escarole	Parsley	Tomatoes	Watercress

STARCHES: BREADS, CEREALS, GRAINS, AND STARCHY VEGETABLES

For more precise amounts, consult nutritional labels. Many items, particularly breads and cereals, vary greatly in carbohydrate content. If labels are not available, the following can be used to calculate approximate amounts.

Nonstarred items contain:
Carbohydrate: 16 grams per serving
Protein: 3 grams per serving

Starred items contain:
Carbohydrate: 20 grams per serving
Protein: 2 grams per serving

Item	Serving size
BREAD	
White, Italian, French	1 average slice
Wholewheat, rye	1 average slice
Pumpernickel, raisin	1 average slice
Pita bread	½ large or 1 small
Bagel, small	1 oz. (approx. ⅓)
English muffin	½
Plain roll, small	1 oz. size
Frankfurter roll	1 oz. (approx. 1)
Hamburger roll	1 oz. (approx. ½)
Tortilla, 6 in. diameter	1 oz. (approx. 1)
Biscuit, 2 in. diameter	1 oz.
Bread crumbs, dried	¼ cup
Bread sticks	¾ oz.
Bread stuffing*	½ cup
Cornbread stuffing	⅛ cup
Croutons	¾ oz.
Corn bread 2 in. x 2 in. x 1 in.	1½ oz. (approx. 1)
Corn or bran muffin	1 oz. (approx. ½)
Popover	2 oz.
Shake 'n' Bake	⅓ cup
CRACKERS	
Animal crackers	10
Arrowroot	2
Graham, 2½ in. square	3
Matzoah, 6 in. square	⅔
Melba toast, thin slice	5
Oyster	21
Ritz	7
Rye wafers 2 in. x 3¼ in.	3
Saltines	7
Soda, 2½ in. square	3

Item	Serving size
Triscuits	5
Uneeda Biscuits	4
Vanilla Wafers	5
Wheat Thins	12
Zweiback	3
CEREAL	
Bran flakes	½ cup
Other ready-to-eat, unsweetened	¾ cup
Puffed cereal	1 cup
Cooked cereal	½ cup
Grits, cooked*	⅓ cup
GRAINS	
Barley, cooked	½ cup
Rice, soaked*	½ cup
Pasta: Noodles, macaroni, spaghetti, etc.	
Cooked tender	½ cup
Cooked firm*	½ cup
Popcorn, popped (no fat added)	3 cups
Cornstarch, cornmeal, tapioca	2 Tbsp.
Flour, all-purpose	2½ Tbsp.
Wheat germ	3 Tbsp.
Pancake, cooked, 5 in. diameter	1½ oz.
Cous cous*	½ cup
STARCHY VEGETABLES	
Baked beans (with pork and tomato)	⅓ cup

Item	Serving size	Item	Serving size
Dried lentils, cooked	½ cup	Potato, white with skin (2¼ in. diameter)	3 oz.
Dried lentils, raw	⅛ cup		
Kidney beans, cooked	⅓ cup	Potato, mashed with milk	⅔ cup
Corn niblets, cooked	½ cup	Pumpkin, canned	¾ cup
Corn on the cob, 6 in. long ear	½ ear (2½ oz.)	Squash, acorn	¾ cup
		Hubbard	1 cup
Lima beans	⅔ cup	Butternut	½ cup
Mixed vegetables, cooked	⅔ cup	Winter	¾ cup
Parsnips, diced, cooked	⅔ cup	Yam or sweet potato, in skin	⅓ cup
Peas, green, cooked	¾ cup		
Plantain, green, 5 in. long	½ fruit		

MEATS AND PROTEIN FOODS

The following items do not contain carbohydrates, but are good sources of protein, fat, and calories. In calculating the amount of protein, calories, and fat, be particularly conscious of the fat. The nutritional breakdowns in this table are based on fat content.

LOW FAT

Serving size: 1 oz. unless otherwise indicated
Protein: 7 grams per serving *(approximate)*
Fat: 3 grams per serving *(approximate)*
Calories: 55 per serving *(approximate)*

Beef

Baby beef *(lean)*	Chipped beef
Chuck	Flank steak
Tenderloin	Plate ribs
Plate skirt steak	Round *(bottom or top)*
Rump	Tripe

Lamb

Leg *(trimmed)*	Rib *(trimmed)*
Shank	

Pork

Leg *(trimmed)*	Ham *(trimmed, center slices)*

Veal

All cuts, trimmed

Poultry

Chicken *(without skin)*	Turkey *(without skin)*
Cornish hen	Guinea hen
Pheasant	

Fish

Any fresh or frozen
Canned salmon, tuna, mackerel, crab, or lobster   ¼ cup
Clams, oysters, scallops, or shrimp   *5 pieces or 1 oz.*
Sardines *(drained, ¼ cup)*

Cheese

Low-fat *(less than 5% fat)*
Cottage cheese, dry, 2% butterfat   *¼ cup*

MEDIUM FAT

Serving size: 1 oz. unless otherwise indicated
Protein: 7 grams *(approximate)*
Fat: 5.5 grams *(approximate)*
Calories: 75–80 *(approximate)*

Beef

Ground *(15% fat)*	Corned beef *(canned)*
Rib eye	Round *(ground)*

Pork

Loin	Shoulder arm
Shoulder blade	Butt
Canadian bacon	Boiled ham

Organ meats *(all high in cholesterol)*

Liver
Kidney

Heart
Sweetbreads

Eggs

1 medium *(high in cholesterol)*

Cheese

Cottage cheese, creamed
(¼ cup; add 2 grams
carbohydrate)
Mozzarella

Farmer's cheese
Parmesan *(3 Tbsp.)*
Ricotta
Neufchatel

HIGH FAT

Serving size: 1 oz. unless otherwise indicated
Protein: 7 grams *(approximate)*
Fat: 8 grams *(approximate)*
Calories: 100 *(approximate)*

Beef

Brisket
Ground beef *(20% fat)*
Chuck *(ground)*
Steaks *(club, rib)*

Corned beef *(brisket)*
Hamburger *(commercial)*
Roasts *(rib)*

Lamb

Breast

Pork

Bacon
Spareribs
Ground pork

Deviled ham
Loin *(back ribs)*
Country style ham

Veal

Breast

Poultry

Capon
Goose

Duck

Cheese

Cheddar
Gruyere
Other hard cheeses

American
Cream

Processed meats

Cold cuts
Frankfurter *(1 small)*

Peanut butter

2 Tbsp. contain 5 grams carbohydrate, 9 grams protein, 16 grams fat, 200 calories

---

FRUITS, BERRIES, AND FRUIT JUICES

Carbohydrate: 20 grams

Item	Serving size	Item	Serving size
Apple (2¾ in. diameter)	1 medium (5 oz.)	Cider	⅔ cup = 5 oz.
Apple juice	⅔ cup = 5 oz.	Cranberries (unsweetened)	1 cup
Applesauce (unsweetened)	¾ cup	Dates, pitted, whole	3½ medium (1 oz.)
Apricots, fresh	4 medium (6½ oz.)	Figs, fresh (2¼ in. diameter)	2 medium (3 oz.)
Apricots, dried (1½ in. diameter)	6 halves (1 oz.)	Figs, dried	2 small (1 oz.)
Avocado (3½ in. diameter)	½ or ½ cup puree	Fruit cocktail, unsweetened	1 cup
Banana (7¾ in. x 1⅓ in. diameter)	1 small (4½ oz.) or ⅔ cup sliced	Grapefruit (3½ in. diameter)	1 whole (13 oz.)
Berries		Grapefruit juice	7 oz.
Blackberries	1 cup	Grapes, European	¾ cup or 22 medium (3 oz.)
Blueberries	1 cup		
Raspberries	1 cup	Grape juice	½ cup = 4 oz.
Strawberries	1½ cups (or 10 large)	Kumquats	6 medium
Cherries, whole (incl. pit, stems)	16 large or 1 cup	Lemon, raw, peeled	3 medium
		Mango	⅔ cup diced or sliced

Item	Serving size	Item	Serving size
Melon		Pineapple, diced	1 cup (raw)
Cantaloupe (5 in. long x 2 in. wide)	1 slice or 1½ cups diced	Pineapple chunks, frozen	1 cup unsweetened
Honeydew (6½ in. long x 4 in. wide)	1 slice or ½ cup	Pineapple juice	⅔ cup = 5 oz.
Watermelon	¾ cup	Pineapple, sliced, unsweetened (3½ in. x ¾ in., each slice)	2 slices
Nectarine (2½ in. diameter)	1	Plums, raw (2½ in. diameter)	2 medium = 5 oz.
Orange (3 in. diameter)	1 medium	Prunes (unsweetened)	4 medium
Orange juice	5 oz. or ¾ cup	Prune juice	3 oz.
Papaya (3½ in. diameter)	1 or ¾ cup mashed	Raisins	3 Tbsp. (1 oz.)
Peach (3½ in. diameter)	1 large (7 oz.)	Rhubarb, cooked	¼ cup, unsweetened
Pear (3 in. x 2½ in.)	1 medium	Tangerine	1 medium
Pears, canned, unsweetened	1 cup	Tangelo	1 medium
Persimmon, native	1 medium (3 oz.)		

At first, a newly diagnosed patient with Type 1 diabetes may feel that there is an almost overwhelming number of things and techniques to master. Many physicians feel that this is best accomplished in a hospital setting, where the diabetes can be brought under control under the supervision of health professionals and at the same time, the doctor, diabetes educator, dietitian, exercise physiologist, and other involved health professionals can spend the time needed to teach the basics and monitoring techniques that are so important in on-going treatment. Although close supervision of and rapport with the treating physician are vital elements in successful diabetes control, in the final analysis, day-to-day treatment is the responsibility of the individual patient. Even children as young as 7 or 8 years of age should be taught how to inject their own insulin and how to monitor their

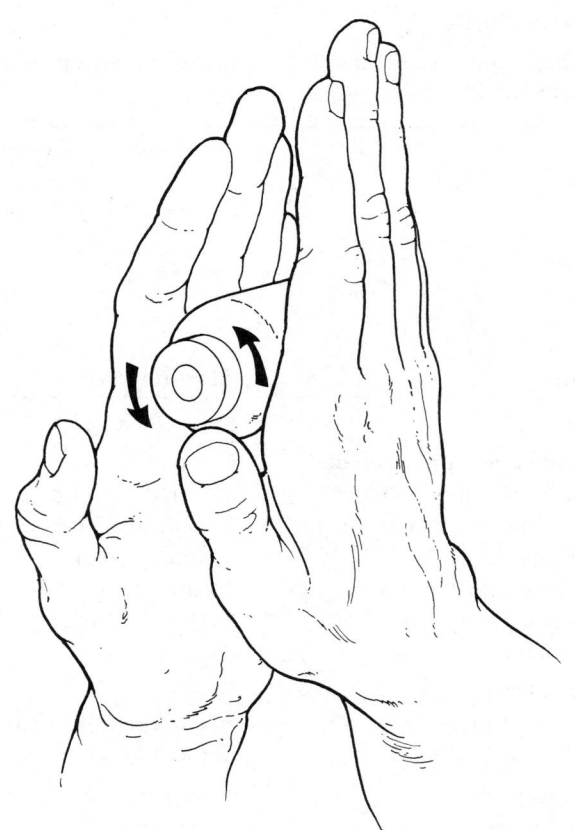

Figure 23.4. **To mix the insulin, gently roll the bottle, but do not shake—this will cause air bubbles to form.**

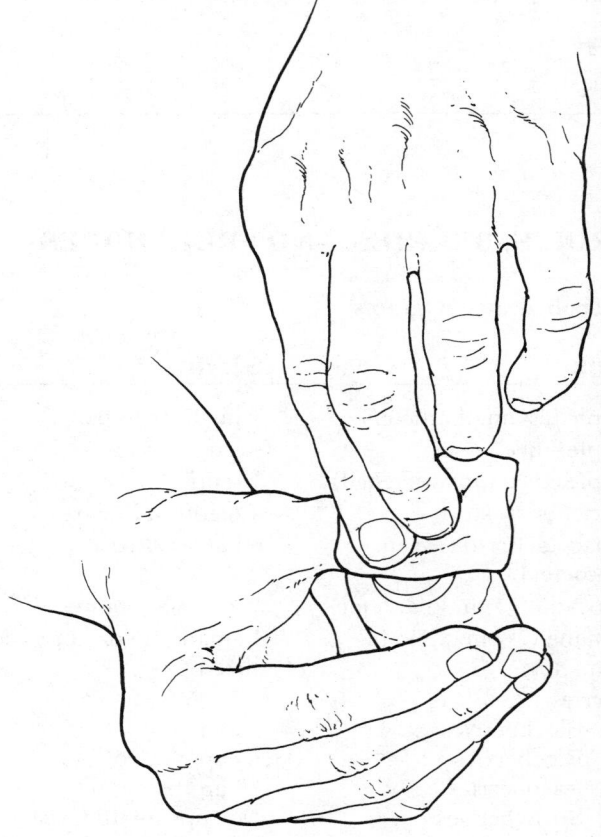

Figure 23.5. **Wipe the bottle top with an alcohol swab to minimize contamination and chance of infection.**

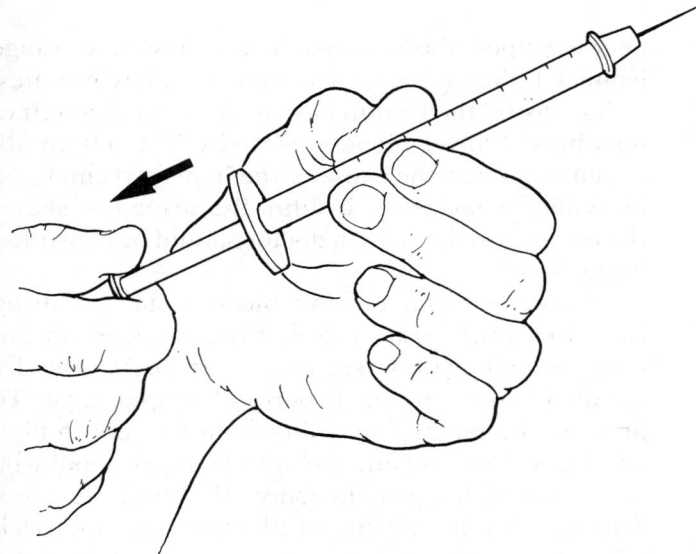

Figure 23.6. **After checking the syringe, withdraw the plunger to the needed dosage and draw air into the syringe.**

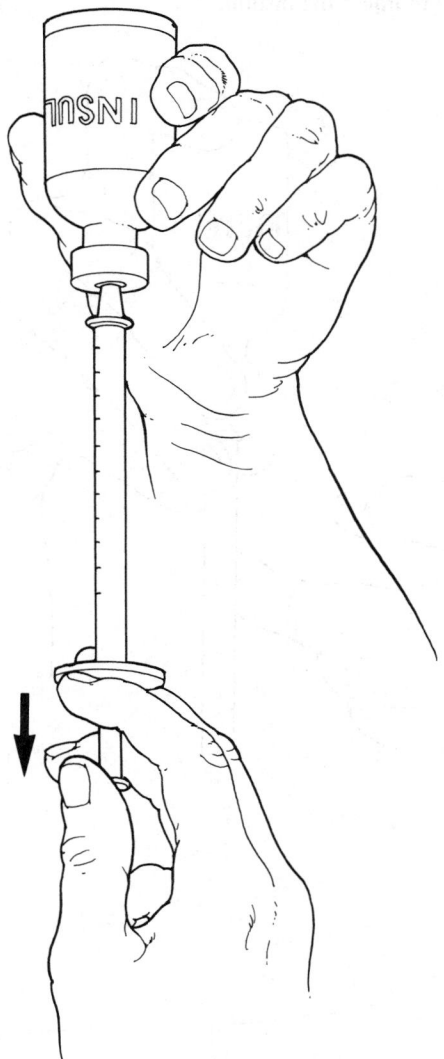

Figure 23.8. **With the bottle upside down, pull out plunger until it is about 5 units beyond the dosage.**

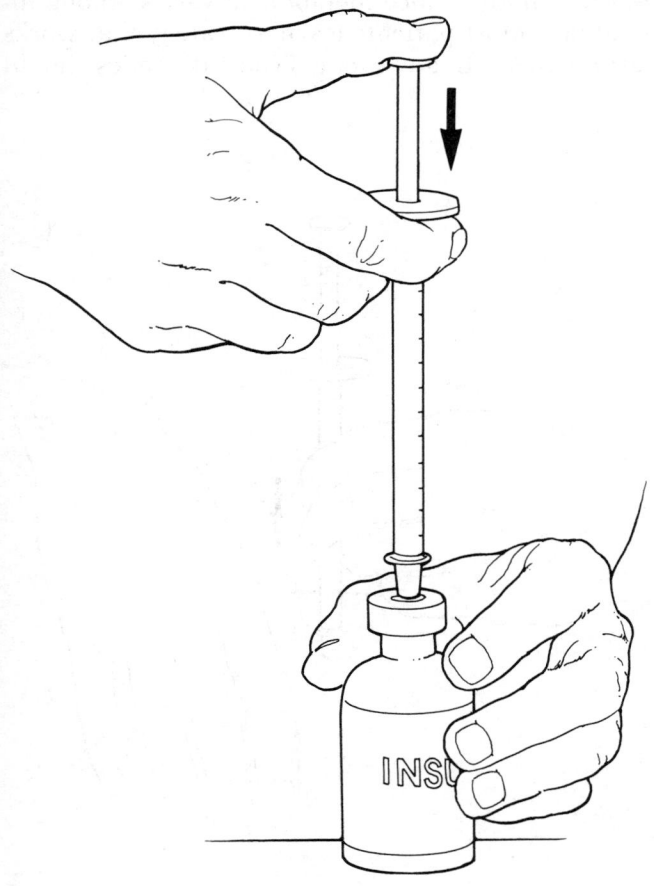

Figure 23.7. **Insert the syringe needle into the insulin bottle and push the plunger down to inject air into the bottle.**

blood and urine. Initially, many people are reluctant to inject themselves. Still, this is one of the first techniques that must be mastered. Most people find that once they learn how, the injections are relatively painless and become almost routine. (Figures 23.4–23.15 show how to mix and inject insulin.)

Even when diabetes is under good control, most patients will from time to time experience an episode of hyperglycemia or hypoglycemia. Knowing how to handle these episodes is yet another aspect of overall self-management. If blood sugar is too high, for example, steps should be taken to lower it. De-

Figure 23.9. **Carefully examine the syringe to make sure there are no air bubbles. If there are, gently tap the syringe until the bubbles move to the top. Now push the plunger back to the exact dosage and remove the syringe from the bottle. You are now ready to inject the insulin.**

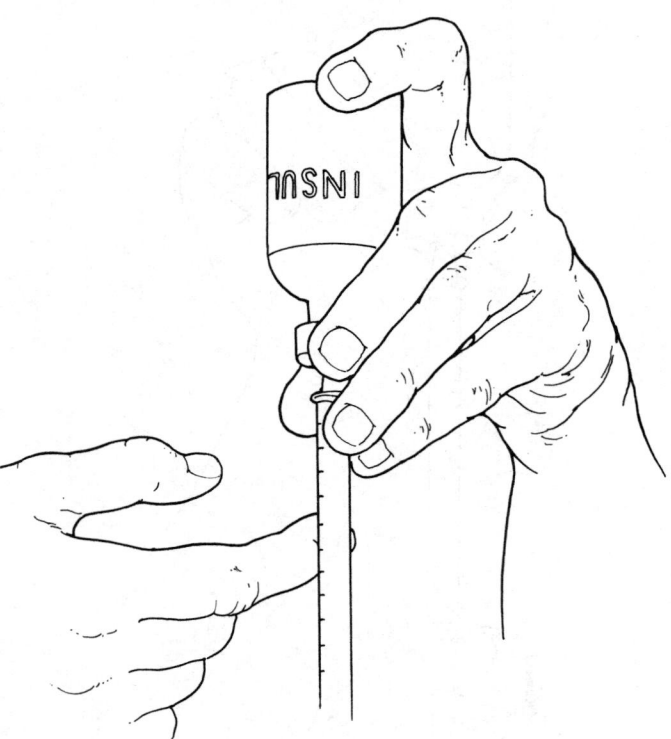

pending upon the circumstances, these may range from skipping a meal, exercising for a few minutes, or increasing the insulin dosage. In general, a unit of insulin will lower blood glucose by 20 to 60 mg/dl, depending upon the cause of the hyperglycemia and individual response to insulin. If a urine test shows the presence of ketones, a doctor should be consulted immediately.

Hypoglycemia, or low blood sugar resulting from too much insulin, a delayed meal, or an unusual amount of exercise, usually can be successfully handled by consuming a source of simple sugar. To prevent "bouncing," or going from too low to high and back down again, the simple sugar should be combined with a protein source that will provide a delayed, slower infusion of glucose. One approach might be to drink a few ounces of orange juice for a fast source of sugar, and to follow this with a glass of milk or a slice of bread and cheese, to provide a slower, more sustained release of glucose. Blood sugar should be measured 15 or 20 minutes after taking the food to make sure that it is having the desired effect. If blood glucose is still too low, additional juice or a second glass of milk may be needed. What works for one person may not necessarily be best for another since metabolism varies among individuals. Most patients learn a strategy that works best for them. In any event, Type 1 diabetics should

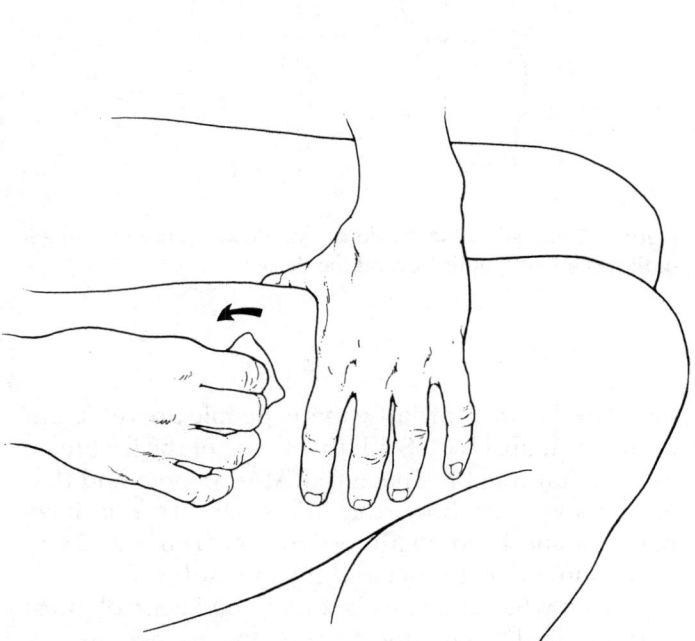

Figure 23.10. **Select a site that has not been used recently and carefully wash it with an alcohol swab.**

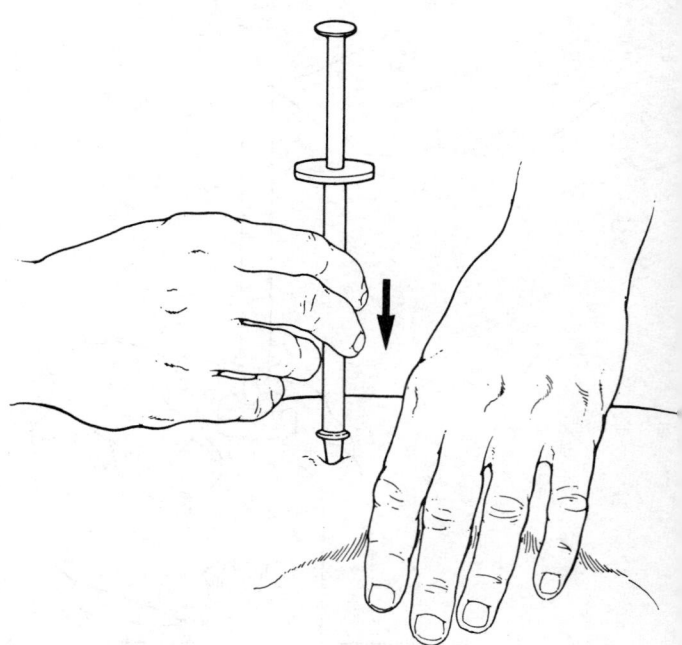

Figure 23.11. **Gather up a fold of skin and insert the needle at a 45° to 90° angle.**

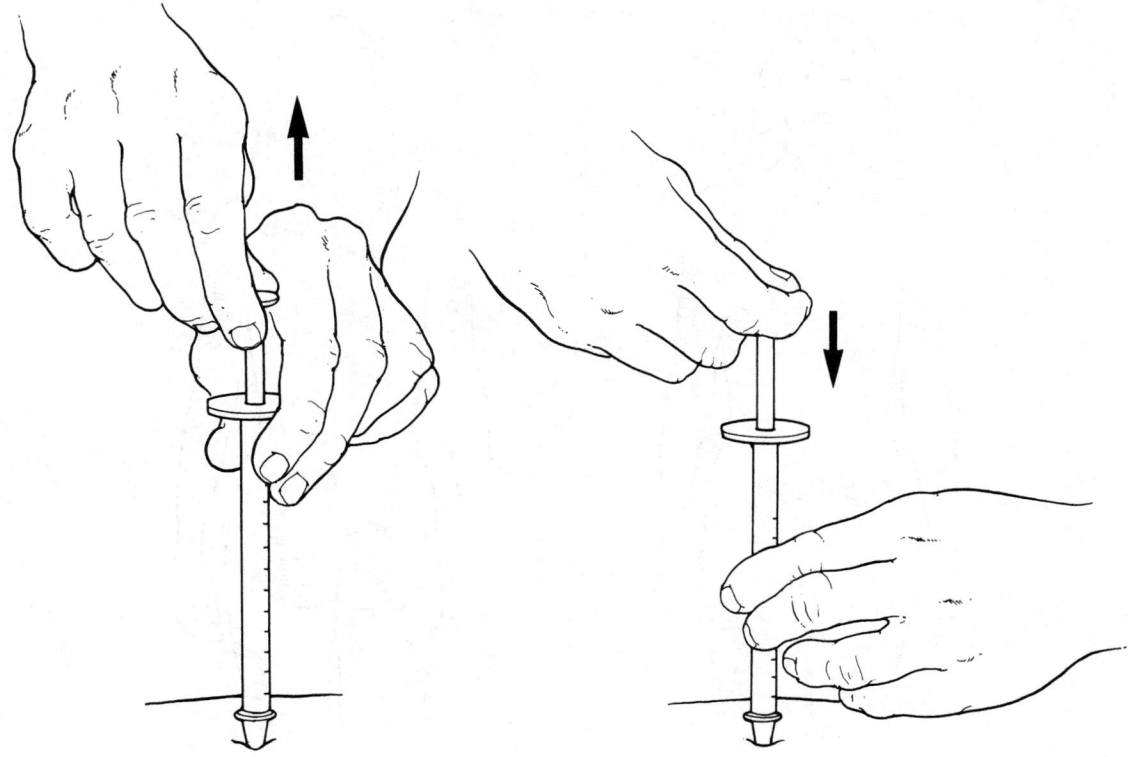

Figures 23.12 and 23.13. **Pull the plunger up slightly and then push it in to inject the insulin.**

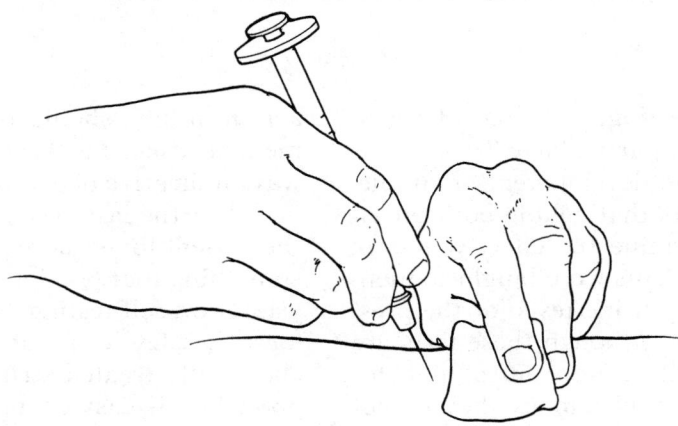

Figure 23.14. **Remove the needle and gently cleanse the site with an alcohol swab. Do not rub, however, as this may hasten insulin uptake.**

always have a convenient, quickly accessible source of simple sugar with them at all times. This may be sugar cubes, candy, orange juice, or similar foods. Bear in mind, however, that a simple sugar taken alone may result in an undesired yo-yo effect that can be avoided by combining the simple sugar with a protein and perhaps a complex carbohydrate, such as a slice of bread.

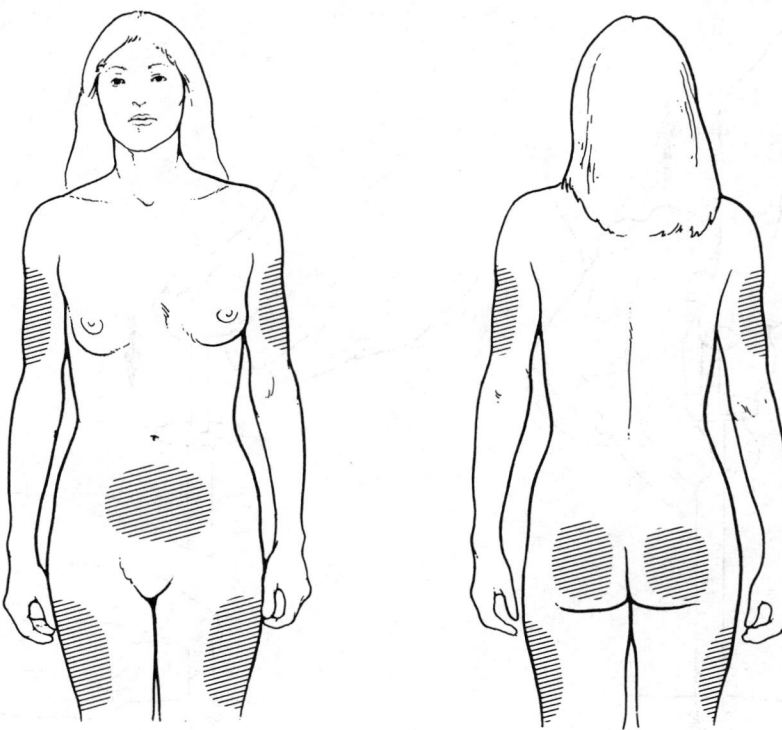

Figure 23.15. **Injection sites should be rotated to prevent damage to any particular area from too frequent shots. Insulin may be injected in any of the shaded areas indicated on the figures above. Most patients work out a rotation schedule (e.g., right forearm, left forearm, abdomen, right thigh front, left thigh front, and then a similar rotation for the back), altering it to avoid areas that may become lumpy or hard. Any signs of inflammation or infection at an injection site should be checked promptly by a doctor.**

The Role of Self-Monitoring. In recent years, the treatment of diabetes, particularly Type 1, has been revolutionized by the development of simple, relatively inexpensive tests that enable both physician and patient to determine the effectiveness of treatment. Heretofore, patients were taught to monitor their diabetes by daily urine tests for the presence of sugar and ketones. Although these tests are useful in detecting markedly out-of-control diabetes and in detecting the presence of ketones, they are not very meaningful in day-to-day management or in handling an episode of hypoglycemia, for example. Not all patients "spill" sugar into the urine, even though their blood glucose may be too high. Conversely, there are patients (e.g., pregnant diabetics) with altered kidney function who may have sugar in the urine even though the blood levels are in the normal range. Also by the time sugar appears in the urine, the blood levels may again be normal. In short, urine tests are not very helpful in indicating the present level of blood glucose and therefore are not useful in telling the patient or physician what

action, if any, should be taken at a particular moment in time. Furthermore, urine tests are not always indicative of overall long-term control.

Over the last decade, it has become possible for the patient to measure his or her own blood sugar—something that previously required laboratory analysis. Now, self-testing can be done in 2 or 3 minutes for just a few cents and a modest expenditure for chemically treated strips and a glucose meter. The procedure is easy enough for a child to master and can be carried out in most places and situations. Supplies needed for self-test are sterile needles or lancets, alcohol swabs, gauze pads or tissues, chemically treated reagent strips, and a portable glucose meter. The procedure involves pricking a finger, drawing a couple of drops of blood, and following the instructions for whatever testing system is being used. The tests can be used to determine whether blood sugar is too high or too low at any given moment so the patient can take appropriate corrective action. This may involve adjusting an insulin dosage, skipping a meal, eating something immediately, postponing an exercise session, or making any number of other adjustments to normalize blood sugar.

Just as important, however, is the role self-monitoring can play in long-term treatment. Patients who practice self-monitoring are encouraged to keep a daily diary in which they record blood glucose measurements, food intake, and other relevant facts. (See figure 23.16.) This diary forms a permanent record that enables both the patient and doctor to get an overall picture of the effectiveness of treatment and also of situations that are likely to pose problems. In this way, a patient can plan more effec-tively; if he or she knows that a certain event or situation is likely to raise or lower blood sugar, preventive measures can be taken in advance. In this way, a patient gains a true feeling of mastery over the disease, a far better situation than feeling that it is the disease that is in control.

So far as many physicians are concerned, an even more useful test has been developed that they can use to determine overall blood glucose control. This test is based on the knowledge that consistently high levels of blood glucose alter the red blood cells over a period of time. Glucose molecules become permanently attached to hemoglobin, the compo-

Figure 23.16. **All diabetic patients should learn to keep a careful diary, such as the model shown here. This will help both patient and physician spot patterns that are likely to cause problems and to take corrective action. From *Diabetes Record Book*, Squibb-Novo, Inc., Princeton, N.J. 08540.**

nent in the red blood cell that carries oxygen. When the glucose molecule binds to hemoglobin, the structure is changed and the resulting cell is called glycosylated hemoglobin. Normally, only a small percentage of hemoglobin is glycosylated. In poorly controlled diabetes, the level of glycosylated hemoglobin, expressed as hemoglobin Alc, will be much higher; perhaps 9 to 12 percent or more. A high reading indicates that blood glucose has been elevated over the previous month or 6 weeks; a reading in the normal range means that blood glucose has been normal during that period. Regular self-monitoring combined with periodic measurements of hemoglobin Alc are now invaluable in achieving overall control of diabetes.

Treatment of Type 2 Diabetes

As indicated earlier, people with Type 2 diabetes outnumber those with Type 1 about 9 to 1, and most of the estimated 10 million undiagnosed diabetics also fall into this category. The majority of Type 2 diabetics are middle-aged or older and overweight. Fat tissue is known to increase insulin resistance, and since Type 2 diabetes is primarily a disease of insulin resistance rather than insulin deficiency, there has been a tendency to attribute the cause to the obesity. However, this now appears to be an oversimplification and factors other than the obesity are also believed to be involved, although these have not been clearly identified. Insulin uptake by the cells is a complicated process that is not fully understood. Cells that require insulin to utilize glucose have specific insulin receptors; when insulin binds to these receptors, changes take place within the cell that enables it to burn glucose. Studies have found some patients with Type 2 diabetes have abnormal insulin receptors, but this is not a universal finding, indicating that there are still other factors involved. Also, some Type 2 patients produce progressively less insulin and, in time, may require insulin replacement.

Although Type 2 diabetes may not carry the same risk of death from ketoacidosis, it does involve many of the same risks of complications as Type 1 diabetes. Therefore, the treatment goal is to normalize blood glucose in an attempt to prevent or minimize these complications. Type 2 diabetics may have marked hyperglycemia, but most do not require insulin injections. In fact, 80 percent of all Type 2 diabetes patients can be treated with diet, exercise and, if needed, oral drugs to lower blood sugar (hypoglycemic agents).

Dietary treatment for Type 2 diabetes also differs markedly from the restrictions that apply to Type 1. Type 2 diabetics do not need to distribute their total calories over a specific number of meals and snacks, nor is it so important to distribute the calories among the 3 nutrient groups, although patients usually are advised to lower fat consumption and to increase intake of complex carbohydrates and fiber. Hypoglycemia is not a problem in Type 2 diabetes; therefore, patients do not need to eat extra food to prevent low blood sugar while exercising. The single major dietary restriction involves total calories. (An obvious exception is normal-weight Type 2 patients who do not need to lose weight; oral hypoglycemic drugs may be prescribed for these patients.) As anyone who has repeatedly tried to diet knows, it can be very difficult to adhere to a low-calorie diet, especially when it is for life. It is understandable, therefore, that a major difficulty in Type 2 diabetes is adhering to the prescribed diet. Various approaches have been tried—behavior modification, peer support groups, hypnosis, group therapy, intensive patient education. While any one of these approaches works for some patients, the overall success rate remains low.

Regular aerobic exercise, which decreases insulin resistance and also helps burn excessive glucose, is also an important element in treating both Type 1 and Type 2 diabetes. In addition, regular exercise may help lower blood lipids and may reduce some effects of stress—both important factors in treating diabetes and preventing complications.

Oral hypoglycemic drugs may be prescribed for normal-weight Type 2 diabetics or for those patients whose blood glucose is not controlled by diet and exercise. These drugs fall into 2 categories: sulfonylureal agents and diguanides (phenformin). The diguanides are rarely used in this country now because of their potential for serious side effects. In contrast, the sulfonylureal drugs are widely used and available under several different brand names with somewhat different formulations. As their name indicates, these drugs are closely related to the sulfa drugs, which were the major antibiotics before penicillin was discovered. Studies during World War II found that laboratory animals given sulfa drugs often died of severe hypoglycemia. In the 1950s, researchers capitalized on these findings and developed a line of drugs that lowered blood glucose. The drugs do not help Type 1 diabetics, but for patients who still produce some insulin, they can be quite effective. Initially, the drugs appear to stimulate the pancreas to produce more insulin; after a period of time, however, the insulin production returns to previous levels or may even be lower. The continued effectiveness of the drugs is then attributed to lowered insulin resistance, which enables the body to make better use of the insulin it produces.

The sulfonylureal drugs now available in this country are tolbutamide (Orinase), chlorpropamide (Diabinese), acetohexamide (Dymelor), tolazamide (Tolinase), glipizide (Glucotrol), and glyburide (Micronase or DiaBeta). The major differences among them involves their durations of action. Tolbutamide is a fast-acting drug with a short duration of action, meaning it should be taken 2 or 3 times per day. Acetohexamide also is fast-acting, but it has a longer duration of action and needs to be taken once or twice a day. Tolazamide takes about 7 hours to reach its peak, and it continues to work for 12 to 24 hours; it also is taken once or twice a day. Chlorpropamide may not start to act for several days, and it has a long duration of action—up to 60 hours—meaning it is taken only once a day. Glipizide and glyburide are newer drugs and sometimes referred to as second-generation sulfonylureals. Initial stud-

ies indicate that these drugs may prompt a somewhat different pattern of insulin response than the older drugs and they tend to have a more rapid onset of action. Since individuals respond differently to all of these drugs, it sometimes takes several weeks to arrive at the most effective dosage. The usual strategy is to start with a small dose and, depending upon effect on blood glucose, to increase the dosage and/or number of times it is taken each day until blood glucose is normalized. Table 23.2 summarizes the major features of the oral hypoglycemic drugs.

People taking these antidiabetes drugs should be cautious about taking other drugs that may interact with them to increase their lowering of blood sugar. Specific drugs that should be avoided include sulfa drugs used as antibiotics, chloramphenicol (e.g., Chloromycetin), bishydroxycoumarin (Dicumaril), phenylbutazone (e.g., Butazolidin), oxyphenbutazone (e.g., Tandearil), and clofibrate (Atromid-S).

Table 23.2 ORAL HYPOGLYCEMIC AGENTS

Generic name	Brand name	Times taken (per day)	Onset of action (hr)	Duration of action (hr)
Acetohexamide	Dymelor	1–2	1–2	12–24
Chlorpropamide	Diabinese	1	Several days	60
Glipizide	Glucotrol	1–3	30 min	Up to 24
Glyburide	Micronase or DiaBeta	1–2	30 min	12 or more
Tolazamide	Tolinase	1–2	3–4	12–24
Tolbutamide	Orinase	2–3	1	6–8

DIABETES AND PREGNANCY

BEFORE THE DISCOVERY of insulin, there is no record of any woman with Type 1 diabetes having a baby that survived. It was highly unlikely that a woman with diabetes would become pregnant and, if she did, the baby was virtually certain to die, usually before birth. In many instances, the woman also died.

This outcome began to change with the widespread use of insulin. Recent studies have found that much of the risk to both mother and baby can be minimized by a program of strict control aimed at maintaining blood glucose between 70 and 140 mg/dl, with a mean of 80 to 87 mg/dl throughout pregnancy. Ideally, the program begins before pregnancy is attempted; most experts agree that the woman should have normal blood sugar for at least

2 months before conception and any diabetes complications such as retinopathy, kidney problems, high blood pressure, or other cardiovascular disorders should be minimal and under control.

Carrying a diabetic pregnancy to a successful conclusion, namely, the birth of a full-term, healthy baby without serious problems for the mother, is a tremendous amount of work that should not be entered into lightly. It requires diligent monitoring by both the woman and her doctor and a full understanding of how to adjust insulin and food intake to maintain normal blood sugar. But the increasing number of diabetic women who succeed is proof that the effort pays off. Throughout the pregnancy, frequent self-testing of blood sugar—usually 6 or 7 times per day—is a must. In addition, urine should be checked at least once a day for ketone bodies.

Insulin dosages change throughout the course of pregnancy. As pregnancy progresses, the amount of insulin required by the mother rises. Glucose in the mother's blood passes freely to the fetus but insulin does not. Thus, if the fetal blood glucose is too high, the baby will begin producing insulin. Since insulin is also a growth hormone, an excess of it can make the baby grow too large. The extra insulin and high blood glucose tend to lower the fetus's potassium, resulting in flaccid muscles and even potentially fatal arrhythmias. As the pregnancy nears term, the baby is carefully monitored by both the mother and her physician. The mother will be asked to do daily fetal movement checks, or "kick counts." (A drop in movements may be a sign of fetal distress.) Since near-term fetal death is common in diabetic pregnancies, most doctors are anxious to deliver the baby as soon as it is clear that it is mature enough to do well. Thus, during the thirty-sixth or thirty-seventh weeks of pregnancy, the amniotic fluid may be tested to determine whether the fetal lungs are fully developed. During this time period, the fetal heart also may be tested. As soon as the lungs are mature enough to function on their own, most doctors prefer to deliver the baby as soon as possible, either by inducing labor or cesarean section. As more is learned about maintaining normal blood glucose throughout pregnancy and the outcome of natural labor and delivery, the number of cesareans among diabetic mothers is being reduced. Because managing a diabetic pregnancy is demanding for both mother and physician, it is advisable to seek an obstetrician who is experienced in this area, or perhaps one who works in collaboration with an endocrinologist or internist who specializes in diabetes. In addition, a neonatologist or pediatrician who specializes in high-risk babies also should be available to attend the baby. Although an increasing number of babies born to diabetic mothers are perfectly normal, there is still an increased risk of birth defects and other problems. The baby should be carefully examined shortly after birth, and then taken to a high-risk nursery for observation for 24 hours. If no problems develop in this time, chances are good that the baby can be returned to a regular nursery and his or her mother.

Gestational Diabetes

Gestational diabetes is defined as diabetes that appears during pregnancy and then disappears immediately following delivery. It sometimes goes unnoticed, especially if blood glucose is not checked periodically. Gestational diabetes is most common among women over the age of 35 who are overweight, who have already had a large (over 9 pounds) baby or were big babies themselves, and who have a family history of diabetes. Although gestational diabetes may be so mild that it produces no obvious symptoms in the mother, it poses many of the same hazards to the fetus as other types of preexisting diabetes. Therefore, the goal again is to protect both the mother and baby by maintaining normal blood glucose. Sometimes this can be done by diet alone; if this is not adequate, insulin injections will be needed. In either event, the woman should be taught self-testing of blood glucose and practice the same careful monitoring outlined above.

DIABETES IN CHILDHOOD AND ADOLESCENCE

TYPE 1 DIABETES very often appears during childhood or adolescence, creating special problems for the entire family. Before the discovery of insulin, very few diabetic children reached adulthood; today, the large majority not only survive, they also are able to participate in school and other normal childhood activities. But there are often many medical and emotional difficulties along the way. Designing an effective treatment program often involves counseling the entire family since the attitudes of parents, siblings, and even close friends are crucial in creating an environment for healthy development and also for treating a difficult disease that requires almost constant attention.

From the outset, it is vital that the child and parents establish good rapport with the physician who will oversee treatment. This may be a pediatrician experienced in treating diabetes, an endocrinologist, internist, or family physician who is experienced in treating diabetic children. Many doctors are attuned to treating diseases or medical crises that are short-term; diabetes, however, is a life-long disease that may involve occasional emergency situations, but is more likely to demand careful day-to-day attention, support, and patient education. In addition, childhood or adolescent diabetes carries special problems.

Insulin dosages are often difficult to gauge; things like frequent viral infections, growth spurts, emotional lability, and erratic exercise and eating patterns are typical of childhood but can have a profound effect on insulin requirements. The youngster should understand that diabetes is a serious disease, but it can be managed in such a way that he or she can participate in normal family, school, and social activities and responsibilities. Care also must be taken not to let the disease hamper normal development. The task is to find a middle ground that promotes a normal lifestyle, yet is in keeping with a treatment program.

The treatment program is often developed while the child is hospitalized; this gives doctors, dietitians, and other members of the treatment team a chance both to stabilize the disease and to teach the child and family the basics of its management. In a very young child, the burden of treatment rests with the parents. Very often, both child and parents must overcome fears of getting and giving injections. But in most instances, the injections quickly become a part of daily routine and cease to be a source of fear or anxiety. As soon as possible, children should be taught to administer their own injections; this usually can be accomplished by the time they are 7 or 8 years old, although parental supervision may still be needed. Children of this age also can be taught the basics of testing their own blood and urine.

Adolescence brings a new set of problems, both among patients who acquired diabetes at an earlier age and among those who are newly diagnosed. Adolescence is undoubtedly one of life's most turbulent periods. The hormonal changes, growth spurt, and emotional lability characteristic of this age may well trigger diabetes; in any event, they all make the disease more difficult to control. At this stage of life, young people need to declare their independence; a diabetic child who has managed very well up to this point may suddenly rebel and have the disease go out of control. Peer pressures and the need for peer acceptance become very important. Parents are understandably worried about the consequences of poorly controlled diabetes; at the same time, the adolescent has a compelling need to become independent of parental control.

Until recently, tight control of blood glucose was not the major objective in treating young diabetics; instead, the strategy was to get the patient through the difficult growing and adolescent years, and then to try to establish a better treatment program during young adulthood. The major fallacy to this approach was that by adulthood, the patient already may have developed serious kidney disease, eye problems, and other long-term complications. Today there is more emphasis on working with the child and family to normalize blood glucose as much as possible and still permit normal development. Again, self-monitoring has become an important part of this strategy. By learning what is involved in good diabetes control and having the tools to monitor progress, the child is more likely to assume the responsibility for self-treatment. Adolescent support groups also are very important in helping young people cope with their disease and the lability typical of their age.

IN CASE OF EMERGENCY

PEOPLE WITH DIABETES—or any hidden medical condition—should always carry an obvious form of identification that will alert doctors or others to the disorder. Medic Alert is one of the most widespread systems. The Medic Alert Foundation, a nonprofit organization founded by a California physician, provides identification emblems that members wear, as well as a wallet card and other identification material. A Medic Alert bracelet or other identification immediately indicates that the wearer has a medical problem that may require prompt treatment if the person is unable to convey this information. This can be lifesaving for the diabetic patient who lapses into unconsciousness or is injured in an accident and is unable to speak. The Medic Alert bracelet and card contain the wearer's identification number and a telephone number that can be called collect for specific medical information about the patient. A lifelong membership costs $15, which covers the cost of the Medic Alert bracelet or necklace, wallet card that is reissued annually, and the 24-hour emergency telephone service. The fee is tax-deductible. More information can be obtained by writing Medic Alert Foundation International, P.O. Box 1009, Turlock, California 95381.

SMOKING AND OTHER HEALTH HABITS

GOOD HEALTH HABITS described throughout this book apply to people with diabetes as well as the general population. But there are some areas that are particularly important for the diabetic patient. Smoking is at the top of the list. Cigarette use compounds many of the complications of diabetes: It hinders circulation, promotes heart disease, and damages numerous other body systems that already are increasingly vulnerable because of the diabetes itself. While no one should smoke, this is doubly true of the person with diabetes, particularly if there are signs of circulatory or cardiovascular complications.

A moderate lifestyle, which is increasingly advocated by physicians and other health professionals for the entire population, is yet another important aspect of living with diabetes. Even though diabetes is a disease that demands constant attention, people with it still can do almost anything in moderation. So many of the restrictions of the past have given way to new understanding of the disease and its control. There are numerous examples of people with diabetes who have risen to the top of their chosen careers—everything from professional athletes to world leaders. Foods that were once forbidden on most diabetic diets are now enjoyed in moderation. A diabetic patient may have to do more planning, but there are very few things or activities that are strictly "off limits." And the better the control of the disease, the more freedom that can be enjoyed.

THE BASICS OF FOOT CARE

PROPER FOOT CARE is of special importance to the diabetic patient. Ordinarily trivial things like corns, calluses, blisters, bunions, cuts or other injuries, and ingrown toenails all can become major medical problems for the person who has diabetes. Serious foot infections, gangrene, and amputation all are more common among diabetic patients; fortunately, many of these problems can be prevented by meticulous foot care.

Several diabetic complications conspire to make the feet particularly vulnerable. Diabetic patients are more susceptible to infection; since the feet are frequently injured just by wearing shoes or walking around, hard-to-heal foot infections are very common. The impaired circulation that is another common complication of diabetes is particularly pronounced in the feet and lower legs. This also slows the healing process and the poor delivery of oxygen makes the lower limbs more susceptible to certain microorganisms that thrive in an oxygen-poor environment. The nerve damage that is also a common complication of diabetes further compromises the feet by reducing sensitivity to pain and discomfort. Most people who develop corns, calluses, sores, and other foot problems are driven by the resulting discomfort to take corrective action. But the diabetic patient may not perceive any pain and not be aware of the problem until it develops into an infected ulcer or other major disorder. Damage to the motor nerves, which in turn promotes a weakening and shrinking of muscles, also may promote the development of certain foot deformities, such as hammertoes or clawfoot. These deformities also make the feet more vulnerable to infection.

Still another potential foot problem results from damage to the autonomic nerves, which control sweat glands. Patients with this complication often develop overly dry skin that develops tiny cracks where bacteria and fungi can thrive, leading to infection.

Regular preventive foot care involves both regular checks by a foot specialist and special attention to personal foot hygiene. Specific aspects of diabetic foot care include:

- *Shoes.* Make sure shoes are comfortable and properly fitted. Patients with foot deformities or other problems may be well advised to have custom-made shoes; in any event, shoes should be fitted by a knowledgeable salesperson and should be made of a soft, pliable material such as leather. Moleskin or lamb's wool may be used to prevent rubbing and relieve pressure and special shoe inserts may be advised. These, however, should be fitted by a specialist. Avoid walking barefoot, even at home, to reduce the risk of splinters and injuries. Sandals or open shoes also may not offer adequate foot protection.

- *Stockings.* Stockings also should fit properly and be made of absorbent, nonbinding material. Discard stockings with holes or rough spots.

- *Daily care.* Feet should be carefully inspected at least once a day for any sign of reddening or discoloration, blisters, or other irritations. Any skin problems, such as cracking or dryness, should be attended to promptly. Ingrown toenails, corns, and calluses should be dealt with by a foot specialist or other health professional; don't try to remove or pare corns yourself and avoid using chemical corn removers. Feet should be washed daily. A fine brush or pumice stone may be used to remove dead skin gently, but avoid excessive rubbing. Rinse and dry thoroughly; if skin is dry, apply a lubricating lotion.

- *Toenails.* Toenails should be groomed regularly with nail clippers, emery board, or file (not scissors). Trim the nails straight across and avoid cutting into the corners, which may promote ingrown toenails. Patients with failing eyesight or poor coordination should have someone else tend to regular foot grooming.

OTHER ENDOCRINE DISORDERS

MANY ESSENTIAL endocrine functions are controlled by the hypothalamus, which lies at the base of the lower brain, and the pituitary, a tiny gland that is connected to the hypothalamus and is located in a bony portion of the base of the skull. The hypothalamus serves as the link between the endocrine and nervous systems; functions that it controls include appetite, temperature, sleep, sexual function, and fluid balance. In many instances, the hypothalamus controls these functions by releasing hormones that are either sent to the pituitary for distribution to other parts of the body or which stimulate the pituitary to release other hormones. Specific hormones and their functions include:

- *Vasopressin.* This hormone is produced in the hypothalamus and released by the posterior lobe of the pituitary. It is sometimes referred to as the antidiuretic hormone or ADH; its major function is to prevent the kidneys from excreting too much water, thus helping to maintain the body's fluid balance, and to constrict, or narrow, the small blood vessels.

- *Oxytocin.* Also produced in the hypothalamus and released by the posterior lobe, oxytocin induces labor by causing the uterus to contract when pregnancy reaches full term. This hormone also promotes the production of milk and therefore plays an important role in breast-feeding.

- *Prolactin.* This hormone is produced in the anterior lobe of the pituitary and stimulates the breasts to produce milk at the end of pregnancy.

- *Growth hormone (somatotropin).* This hormone is also produced in the anterior lobe and it stimulates the growth of muscle and bone in children and adolescents.

The other pituitary hormones act as tropins, meaning they stimulate other endocrine glands to produce their respective hormones. These include:

- *ACTH (adrenocorticotropic hormone).* This hormone stimulates the adrenal glands to produce glucosteroid hormones (cortisol) and male-type hormones.

- *TSH (thyrotropin).* This hormone stimulates the thyroid to secrete thyroxine hormone.

- *LH (lutenizing hormone).* In men, LH stimulates the testes to secrete male hormones; in women, it stimulates the ovaries to produce estrogen.

- *FSH (follicle stimulating hormone).* In men, FSH stimulates the testicular tubules to produce sperm; in women it stimulates the ovarian follicles to produce a ripened ovum (egg).

- *MSH (melanocyte stimulating hormone).* MSH stimulates the production of pigment cells in the skin.

Disorders of the hypothalamus and pituitary are relatively rare and often involve tumors that either cause an over- or underproduction of hormones. If the pituitary gland ceases to produce its hormones (panhypopituitarism), the target glands are affected in sequence, beginning with the gonads, then the thyroid, and finally the adrenals. In addition to signs of underfunction of the various endocrine glands, there also may be headaches and visual symptoms. If the disorder is less generalized, affecting the secretion of some hormones but not total pituitary deficiency, the symptoms will be related to the specific hormone(s). Disorders resulting from hypothalamus or pituitary dysfunction include the following.

GROWTH ABNORMALITIES

AN OVERPRODUCTION of growth hormone can cause acromegaly, a disease characterized by excessively large hands, feet, and jaw. This disease occurs in adults whose long bones have fused, and therefore cannot grow. But the excessive growth hormone causes other bones to broaden or grow, leading to the distorted appearance. It is usually caused by a tumor of the anterior lobe of the pituitary, and can be treated by surgical removal of the tumor, radiation therapy directed to that area of the gland, or, rarely, by drugs to control the release of the hormone. Gigantism is a rare disorder of children caused by a pituitary tumor that secretes excessive growth hormone, causing excessive growth of long bones. The large majority of tall children do not have a hormonal disorder; they are simply genetically programmed to grow tall. In contrast, gigantism is characterized by growth far above the normal standards and very often by acromegaly as well.

Dwarfism, or restricted growth, may be caused by the failure of the pituitary to secrete adequate growth hormone, or by any number of other causes, including thyroid disorders, malnutrition, and other illnesses. Again, most cases of short stature are not dwarfism; instead, the child is following an inherited tendency toward shortness. If hormonal deficiency is causing a failure to grow, hormone therapy during the growing years usually can stimulate normal growth.

ABNORMALITIES OF SEXUAL DEVELOPMENT

SINCE THE PITUITARY secretes vital gonadotropic hormones that stimulate the testis and ovary to produce their respective sex hormones, many problems involving sexual development can be traced to pituitary dysfunction. Premature or precocious puberty, for example, often may be caused by premature release of gonadotropins (although it also may be caused by disorders involving other endocrine glands). Normally, the hypothalamus initiates puberty by stimulating the pituitary to release gonadotropins. If this occurs prematurely, a very young child may develop secondary sexual characteristics and proceed to sexual maturity. This can be suppressed by taking hormones known as progestogens until the appropriate time for the onset of puberty.

Failure to develop sexually, sometimes referred to as sexual infantilism, may be caused by lack of gonadotropins or by other endocrine disorders, such as failure of the testis or ovary to function. If a child reaches the age of 15 or 16 and shows no signs of puberty, a careful examination by an endocrinologist may be in order. Although these problems again are rare, many can be resolved by taking the appropriate hormones.

ABNORMALITIES INVOLVING MILK PRODUCTION

EXCESSIVE PRODUCTION of prolactin can cause milk production in a woman who is not nursing or even in a man. In a woman, excessive prolactin may result in a failure to menstruate and infertility. Since the excessive prolactin does not always cause milk production, hormone studies may be required to pinpoint prolactin excess as a cause of menstrual or fertility problems. The problem may be caused by the presence of a pituitary tumor or from certain drugs, such as tranquilizers or oral contraceptives.

DIABETES INSIPIDIS

THIS DISORDER IS CAUSED by lack of ADH, which results in the kidneys secreting excessive amounts of water. Excessive thirst and urination are the primary symptoms. (The disorder should not be confused with diabetes mellitus, which is caused by a lack of insulin and resultant metabolic abnormalities.) The disorder can be treated by taking ADH, either by injection or via a nasal spray. An opposite condition marked by an excess of ADH also occurs, in which too much ADH results in a diminished flow of urine and a dilution of the blood. It may be caused by a disorder of the hypothalamus or by some brain or lung diseases, in which ADH is produced in excess ("inappropriate ADH secretion"). Treatment involves identifying and correcting the underlying cause.

THYROID DISORDERS

THE THYROID is a small, butterfly-shaped gland that lies over the trachea (windpipe) just below the larynx. (See figure 23.17.) The thyroid differs from other endocrine glands in that it requires an outside substance, iodine, to produce its hormone, thyroxine. The process is initiated by TSH from the pituitary; in order to function properly, the thyroid requires a properly functioning pituitary, a small but steady supply of iodine, and, of course, normal pathways of hormone synthesis.

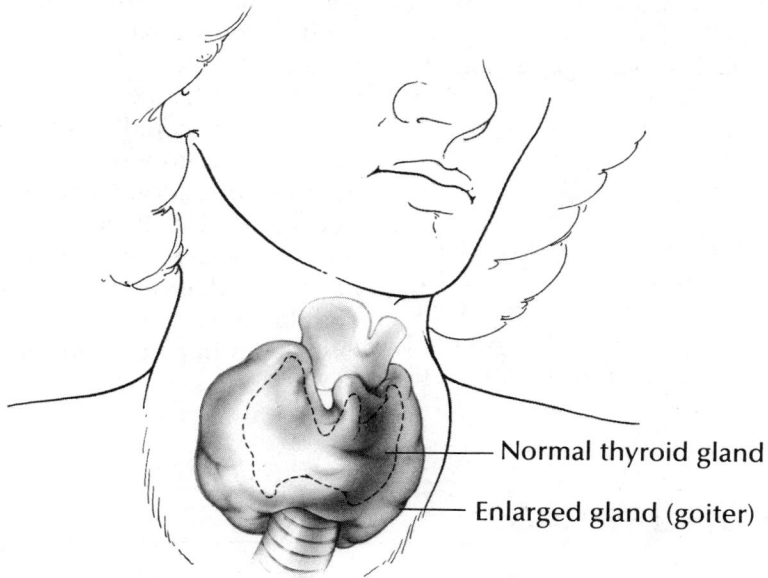

Normal thyroid gland

Enlarged gland (goiter)

Figure 23.17. **A normal thyroid gland and the enlargement typical of a goiter.**

Virtually all metabolic processes are affected by thyroid hormone. If there is too much thyroid hormone, metabolism is speeded up; if there is too little, everything slows down. In either instance, the disorder may be signaled by an enlargement of the thyroid gland itself, known as goiter. In the past, iodine deficiency was the most common cause of thyroid disease. Today, however, iodine is readily available, either from foods or in supplements added to salt in areas in which the soil and foods are deficient in this mineral.

Overactive Thyroid

An overactive thyroid, or hyperthyroidism, is caused by excessive production of thyroid hormone; the most common cause is a disorder known as Graves' disease. The cause of Graves' disease is not known for certain, but it may be related to genetic factors affecting the immune system. This condition is characterized by loss of weight from the speeded up metabolism; a rapid heart rate; muscle weakness; tremor; increased sensitivity to heat and a hot, flushed skin; and feelings of anxiety and nervousness. The eyes may bulge and take on a staring appearance and a goiter may develop. Hyperthyroidism is less commonly due to tumors of the pituitary, thyroid, or placenta.

Graves' disease may be treated by giving drugs that inhibit production of thyroid hormone, the use of radioactive iodine to destroy part of the thyroid gland and thereby reduce hormone production, or

by surgical removal of part of the gland. The choice of treatment depends upon the age and overall condition of the patient, the size of the thyroid itself, and the preference of the patient.

Underactive Thyroid

The most common cause of underactive thyroid, or hypothyroidism or myxedema, is an autoimmune disorder in which the gland is slowly destroyed by the body's immune system. Other causes include lack of TSH from the pituitary, or a congenital defect in which a baby is born with no thyroid or one that does not produce enough hormone. It is vital to detect this infantile hypothyroidism, because without adequate thyroid hormone, the brain does not develop properly, resulting in cretinism. These babies tend to be very lethargic and they fail to thrive or grow properly.

Hypothyroidism is characterized by a slowing down of all body processes. At first, the symptoms may be barely noticeable: a feeling of lethargy, aching muscles, growing intolerance to cold, or constipation are common signs that are often attributed to other causes. Weight gain, even with reduced food intake, occurs. As the disorder progresses, the face becomes puffy and the skin dry. The voice deepens. Feelings of depression and increasing lethargy also are common.

Treatment is relatively simple, i.e., taking replacement thyroid hormone for life. Detecting congenital hypothyroidism is particularly important to prevent the severe mental retardation and growth problems it causes. Screening for thyroid hormone in newborns can detect this disorder early enough to prevent some, if not most, of the problems caused by infantile thyroid deficiency.

Goiter

Goiter refers to any swelling or overgrowth of the thyroid gland. The most common causes are the development of benign nodules or chronic (Hashimito's) thyroiditis, an inflammation of the gland due to an autoimmune disease. Rarer causes of goiter include benign or malignant tumors, congenital thyroid enzyme deficiency, and iodine deficiency. Treatment of the goiter depends upon the cause. Nodular goiter, a condition occurring most commonly in middle-aged women who suddenly develop an overgrowth or swelling of part of the gland, may require surgical removal of the diseased portion, or administration of thyroid hormone to shrink the nodules. In such cases, careful evaluation is needed to determine whether the growth is due to nodular goiter or a tumor. (Thyroid cancer is discussed in Chapter 20 on cancer, pages 419.)

PARATHYROID DISORDERS

The parathyroid glands are located on the back and side of each thyroid lobe. They secrete a hormone that controls the level of calcium in the blood. If blood calcium falls, a rise in parathyroid hormone releases small amounts of this mineral, which is vital to proper muscle and circulatory function, from the bones. (Calcitonin, a hormone produced by special cells in the thyroid, may help regulate levels of blood calcium by promoting its storage in the bones.) Excessive parathyroid hormone, which usually results from benign tumors of the parathyroid glands, can cause kidney stones and other symptoms, such as headache, fatigue, increased urination, and thirst. The condition can be treated by removing the tumors surgically.

A deficiency in parathyroid hormone is a rare condition, usually associated with removal of the thyroid gland or with an autoimmune disorder affecting the parathyroids. Muscle contraction or spasms and convulsions caused by lack of calcium are the major symptoms. Treatment with calcium and vitamin D supplements, since parathyroid hormone is not available for therapy, is necessary for the rest of a patient's life.

DISORDERS RELATED TO GONADS

INFERTILITY, delayed or premature puberty, failure to menstruate, development of inappropriate gender characteristics, and numerous other disorders related to sexual development may be caused by an excess or deficiency of hormones produced by the gonads (testis or ovary) or the gonadotropins from the pituitary. Numerous chromosomal abnormalities also may cause these problems. These disorders are relatively rare, but some of the more common are briefly reviewed here.

Male Disorders

Failure to Develop Sexually. This may range from delayed puberty, which usually can be corrected by administration of the appropriate gonadotropin (see discussion under Pituitary Gland) to eunuchoidism, which may be caused by a lack of gonadotropins or by a failure of the testis to develop and produce male hormones. If this dates from childhood, the boy is likely to grow very tall, without development of the usual secondary sex characteristics, deepening of voice, and muscular development. There will also be infertility since the testes will not produce sperm, and a lack of sex drive. Administration of male sex hormones can correct most of the problems, but will not produce fertility. Treatment for infertility is available (human gonadotropin injections) when fertility is desired.

Undescended Testes. About 3 percent of newborn boys will have undescended testes; within the first year of life, the problem will correct itself in all but about one half of 1 percent. This may be corrected by injection of gonadotropin, but if the testis still does not descend to its proper position in the scrotum, surgery to reposition it may be required. The purpose of such surgery in childhood is to preserve future fertility and to prevent the later development of testicular tumors.

Infertility. There are many causes for male infertility, most of which are unrelated to hormonal imbalances. (See Chapter 10 on Sexual and Reproductive Health, page 151.) Klinefelter's syndrome, a rare chromosomal disorder, appears during puberty and is characterized by the development of small, hard testes lacking the tubules needed to manufacture sperm. The patients also may have abnormal breast development and a eunuchoid appearance with long arms and legs. Since this is a chromosomal disorder, in which the male has an extra X (female) sex chromosome, there is no treatment for infertility. However, male hormones usually help to restore sex drive and potency.

Female Disorders

Failure to Develop Sexually. As in males, this may be caused by a deficiency of gonadotropins from the pituitary or by a failure of the ovaries to produce female hormones. Again, most of these problems can be corrected by administering the appropriate hormones.

Failure to Menstruate. Amenorrhea may have a number of causes, including hormonal imbalance, structural abnormalities, malnutrition, emotional problems, chronic illness, excessive exercise, certain drugs including oral contraceptives, among others. Sometimes hormonal imbalances cause other symptoms in addition to the menstrual failure or irregularity. One example is a condition known as polycystic ovary or Stein-Leventhal syndrome. In this disorder, the ovaries secrete an excessive amount of male hormone. Despite normal female hormone secretion, the imbalance causes signs of virilism, including excessive body and facial hair, acne, weight gain, and failure to menstruate or extreme irregularity. The condition is thought to be caused by faulty pituitary gonadotropin regulation; treatment consists of taking female hormones for the hairiness and acne, and of "fertility" hormones if pregnancy proves to be impossible.

ADRENAL DISORDERS

THE ADRENAL GLANDS are triangular-shaped and rest atop each kidney. Each has 2 parts, the cortex, which produces the steroid hormones, such as aldosterone and cortisone; and the medulla, which secretes catecholamines, such as epinephrine (adrenaline) and norepinephrine. Since catecholamines are produced by many other body tissues, the adrenal medulla is not essential to maintain life. In contrast, the cortex, which makes up the outer layers of the gland, secretes hormones that are essential to a number of body functions. Aldosterone helps maintain fluid balance by retaining salt in the body; the sex steroids have actions similar to the hormones produced by the ovaries and testes; the glucocorticoids are involved in sugar and protein metabolism, maintenance of blood pressure, and responding to physical stress. They also are involved in an intricate feedback relationship that triggers the release of certain pituitary hormones. Specific disorders related to adrenal failure include the following.

Addison's Disease

This term applies to the gradual destruction of the adrenal glands, usually from an autoimmune disorder, but also due to other diseases, such as tuberculosis. Symptoms include increasing fatigue, loss of appetite, abdominal pains, nausea, dizziness or fainting, a darkening of the skin, and inability to cope with even minor physical stresses. One of the major dangers involves an inability to overcome even a minor infection, which may precipitate extreme weakness, shock, and death. Treatment involves replacement of the missing cortisol, either with cortisol or cortisone tablets and an aldosterone substitute, such as Florinet.

Cushing's Syndrome

This disorder is caused by excessive glucocorticoids, usually the result of an ACTH-producing tumor of the pituitary gland. Other causes are due to excessive ACTH from malignant tumors of various glands, or to tumors of the adrenal glands. The major symptoms are muscle wasting and weakness; accumulation of fat on the face, trunk, and neck (sometimes leading to a humped appearance); thinning of the skin, leading to bruising and stretch marks; and a reddening of the skin and excessive hair growth. As the disease progresses, there may be high blood pressure, increased susceptibility to infection, and diabetes mellitus.

Treatment depends upon determining the cause. If there is an adrenal tumor, its removal is imperative. If the problem lies in the pituitary, the pituitary tumor may be removed surgically, or radiation can be administered to the pituitary to stop its overproduction of ACTH. If the entire pituitary gland is removed, as is occasionally necessary, then replacement therapy for hypopituitarism (cortisol, thyroxine, sex hormones) is necessary.

Drug-Related Adrenal Insufficiency

The most common cause of adrenal insufficiency is due to steroid therapy for nonendocrine diseases, such as asthma or arthritis. Long-term steroid therapy causes atrophy (shrinking) of the adrenal glands and lowered ACTH secretion. Recovery of adrenal function may take 6 to 12 months following withdrawal of steroid therapy; during this time, patients are at high risk for shock during physical stresses (surgery, anesthesia, infections, etc.) because of their cortisol deficiency.

Hyperaldosteronism

This disorder, marked by overproduction of aldosterone, is usually caused by small hormone-producing tumors. Since aldosterone is the most powerful of the salt-retaining hormones, its excess leads to high blood pressure and a depletion of potassium, which is essential for proper muscle function and maintaining the body's biochemical balance. Symptoms of hyperaldosteronism, in addition to high blood pressure, include muscle weakness and cramps and sometimes excessive urination at night. Treatment involves removing the aldosterone-producing tumor. There are some cases that can be controlled by drugs, especially if both adrenals are secreting excessive aldosterone (primary hyperaldosteronism).

SUMMING UP

THE ENDOCRINE SYSTEM enables us to adapt and respond to our environment, both internal and external. It is a highly complex system, with intricate feedback networks and chemical or neural signals to keep the various hormones in proper balance. Diabetes is the most common endocrine disorder, and thyroid disease also occurs frequently. The others are relatively rare, but when they occur, they can cause a wide range of symptoms affecting all organ systems as well as psychological responses. Advances in measuring levels of the various hormones now makes it easier to diagnose accurately many endocrine disorders. Most can be treated either by replacing deficient hormones or curtailing the overproduction of others.

24 Disorders of the Digestive System

Lewis P. Schneider, M.D.

INTRODUCTION

As ITS NAME INDICATES, the major function of the digestive tract is to break down food into forms that can be absorbed and utilized by the body and to eliminate the waste. Digestion is a complex process that involves a number of finely coordinated chemical and mechanical functions. These are controlled by intricate feedback systems involving the nervous and endocrine systems.

In recent years, a number of new diagnostic procedures have been developed that enable physicians to visualize almost every part of the digestive tract. As a result, digestive disorders can now be diagnosed with far greater precision than in the past. In addition, new drugs, such as those for treating peptic ulcers, have made some of the more common digestive disorders easier to manage. Development of a vaccine against some forms of hepatitis also has far-reaching implications, including the prevention of liver cancer in high-risk groups. In this chapter, common disorders affecting the upper gastrointestinal tract and small intestine will be discussed. Disorders affecting the colon will be covered in the following chapter.

ANATOMY AND DIGESTIVE PROCESS

THE DIGESTIVE TRACT is often described as a hollow tube, beginning in the mouth and ending with the anus. Its 25- to 30-foot length is divided into a number of different sections, each with distinct functions, and branching off it are the digestive organs and glands, including the liver, gallbladder, and pancreas.

Digestion is both a mechanical and a chemical process. It begins in the mouth, where food is broken into smaller pieces by the jaws and teeth and mixed with saliva, produced by the 6 salivary glands, located in 3 pairs on each side of the face. (See figure 24.1.) The saliva contains amylase, the first of many digestive enzymes that break down food into its component parts as it moves through the digestive tract. Specifically, amylase begins to break complex carbohydrates, or starches, into simple sugars that are used by the body for fuel.

After the food is chewed, it is swallowed, an almost unconscious effort that actually involves a carefully coordinated closing of the larynx, to prevent food from going into the windpipe, as it moves into the pharynx, the funnel-shaped structure leading to the esophagus. The esophagus, sometimes referred to as the gullet, is a hollow muscular tube,

about 1 foot long, that carries the bolus of chewed food or liquids to the stomach. The esophagus passes through an opening (hiatus) in the diaphragm, the muscle wall that separates the chest and abdominal cavities. Below this is the juncture of the esophagus and stomach, with a valve mechanism (esophageal sphincter) dividing the two. As food approaches the sphincter, it relaxes, allowing the bolus to pass into the stomach. It then closes again to prevent a backflow or regurgitation of stomach contents into the esophagus. The bolus is moved through the esophagus (and entire digestive tract) by peristalsis, a coordinated series of wavelike muscular contractions, and, to a lesser extent, by gravity.

The stomach is a pear-shaped, muscular organ situated mostly on the left-hand side below the lower ribs. The upper, wider part is the fundus; the lower portion tapers into the pyloric canal, which pumps partially digested food from the stomach into the duodenum, the uppermost section of the small intestine. The stomach has 3 layers of muscle, running up and down, horizontally, and crosswise. Contractions of these muscles produce the churning action that mixes the food with digestive enzymes and hydrochloric acid—the gastric chemicals that further break down complex nutrients (carbohydrates, proteins, and fats) into their component parts. Hydrochloric acid is a potent chemical produced in cells located in the stomach wall. It is capable of burning skin and would eat through the stomach wall and other intestinal organs if they were not protected by a mucous coating. Most of the bacteria and other microorganisms in food are killed by the gastric acid; people with low acid production may be more susceptible to intestinal infection. The stomach also produces pepsin, the digestive enzyme that breaks down proteins into amino acids. Pepsin works in the presence of hydrochloric acid; when the partially digested food leaves the stomach, other digestive enzymes and chemicals complete the digestion of protein.

By the time the food leaves the stomach, it has been transformed into a thin liquid. Emptying of the stomach through the pyloric valve into the duodenum involves an intricate system of signals generated by stomach movement and pressure traveling to the brain via the vagus nerve and then back to the pyloric valve, which relaxes to permit an outflow of stomach contents. Only a small amount is released at a time, resulting in a steady outflow of about 1 percent of the stomach contents at each opening.

The small intestine in an adult is about 22 feet long and lies coiled in neat loops below the stomach

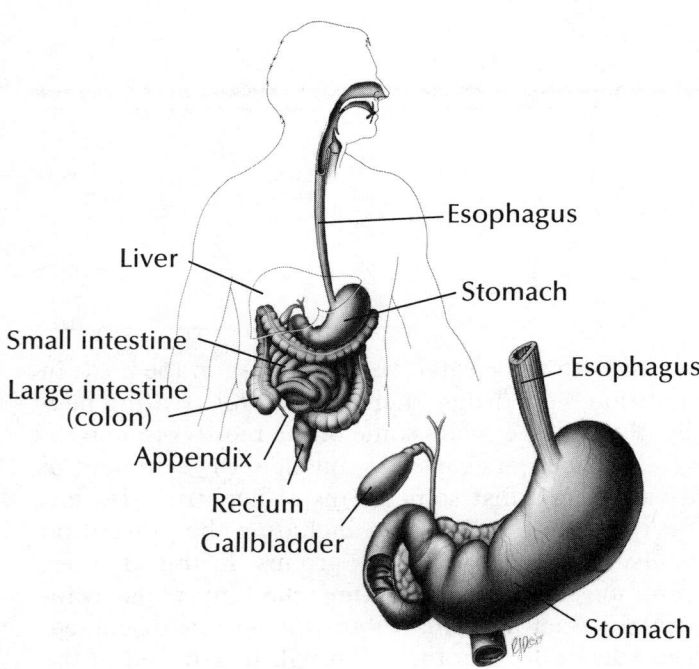

Esophagus

Liver

Stomach

Small intestine

Esophagus

Large intestine (colon)

Appendix

Rectum

Gallbladder

Stomach

Figure 24.1. **The normal gastrointestinal tract is shown here from its beginning in the mouth to its end in the anus.**

and surrounded by the colon or large intestine. It has 3 sections: the duodenum, jejunum, and ileum, but these are more anatomical designations than distinctive parts. The digestive process is completed in this organ and the nutrients to be utilized by the body are absorbed from it. Digestive juices from the pancreas and bile from the liver and gallbladder empty into the duodenum, giving it an alkaline environment. The flow of these digestive products is stimulated by hormones produced in the small intestine in response to the presence of food. The intestine walls are covered with millions of tiny fingerlike projections, the villi, through which the digested food passes into the capillaries or, in the case of most fats, into the lymph channels.

Undigested food, water, and other intestinal waste passes from the lowermost portion of the ilium into the cecum, the first portion of the large intestine, located in the lower righthand section of the abdominal cavity. (The veriform appendix, a small, finger-shaped tube, extends from the cecum.) The colon is also divided into 4 areas; the ascending colon moves up the right side from the lower abdomen; the transverse colon crosses the abdominal cavity from right to left under the stomach; and the descending colon goes down the left side, curving into the sigmoid colon, which empties into the rectum. Although the colon is much shorter than the small intestine (about 3 feet), it takes about 12 to 14 hours or more for the waste material to move its length for elimination through the rectum and anus. In the colon, much of the water is extracted from the contents and returned to the circulation; this transforms the liquid mass to the more solid feces. The colon also contains many different bacteria which break down some of the dietary fiber that is not digested by the stomach or small intestine.

Branching off the intestinal tract are the major digestive organs, the liver and pancreas, and the gallbladder, which stores bile produced in the liver for later release into the duodenum. The liver, which weighs 3½ to 4 pounds, is one of the body's largest organs and one of its most complex. The liver performs many biochemical functions, ranging from manufacturing bile, cholesterol, vitamin A, clotting factors, and complex proteins, to regulating the amount of glucose and protein that enters the bloodstream for distribution to body tissues and detoxifying alcohol and other potentially harmful chemicals. It also acts as a storage house for glycogen, which is readily transformed into glucose to provide fuel for body tissues; blood; iron and other minerals; and fat-soluble vitamins. The gallbladder is a small, saclike structure that is linked by ducts to both the liver and duodenum; its function is to concentrate and store bile, which is needed to digest fats.

The pancreas is about 8 inches long, with its broader end adjacent to the duodenum and its tail extending up under the stomach. The larger portion of the pancreas is devoted to the manufacture of digestive juice that contains enzymes needed to digest carbohydrate, proteins, and fats. Scattered throughout the organ are tiny clusters of cells, the islets of Langerhans. Two important hormones, insulin and glucagon, are produced in these islets and are essential for the metabolism of carbohydrates (and to a lesser extent, proteins and fats) and the regulation of blood sugar (glucose). (See Chapter 23 on Diabetes and Other Endocrine Disorders, page 474, for a more detailed discussion.)

Although each portion of the intestinal tract has its own distinct function, there is enough overlap and duplication that almost normal digestion can continue even if a large portion is removed because of disease or injury. For example, the entire stomach may be removed and the patient can still eat a reasonably normal diet and lead a normal life. Similarly, portions of the small intestine and all of the colon and the gallbladder can be removed if need be. In contrast, the liver is absolutely essential to maintain life. Although the pancreas produces essential hormones, these can be replaced by injection if the pancreas is no longer functioning or removed. In addition, the pancreatic enzymes required for metabolism of carbohydrates, proteins, and fats may be supplied as oral medication in nonfunctioning pancreatic states.

Still, human digestion is a wonderfully engineered and coordinated process. While the end products of digestion can, to a certain extent, be duplicated in a laboratory, the process is not nearly as efficient or fast as what takes place within the body.

DIGESTIVE DISORDERS

FROM TIME TO TIME, most people experience a mild digestive upset: heartburn, indigestion, diarrhea, among others. Most of these are self-limiting and often require only commonsense remedies, such as avoiding foods that seem invariably to produce discomfort, or modifying eating habits. If the symptoms are recurrent or become progressively worse, obviously a physician should be consulted. Following are some of the more common digestive disorders affecting the upper gastrointestinal tract and small intestine; problems involving the large intestine are covered in the following chapter.

NAUSEA AND VOMITING

NAUSEA AND VOMITING are not diseases as such, but symptoms of a large number of different disorders. At some point, almost everyone experiences the queasy feeling of nausea or the uncontrolled, forceful regurgitation of food that is characteristic of vomiting. The vomiting reflex is controlled at a site in the brain stem known as the "vomiting center." The sensation of nausea may be triggered in the middle ear, the gastrointestinal tract, or the brain. When these impulses are received by the vomiting center, a sequence of responses is set in motion. The esophageal sphincter relaxes, the diaphragm and abdominal muscles contract, the larynx (windpipe) closes, the lower (pyloric) part of the stomach contracts, and its contents are expelled through the esophagus and mouth.

The feeling of nausea and the vomiting reflex may be triggered by a wide range of stimuli or circumstances: motion sickness, food poisoning, viral or bacterial illness, many different kinds of drugs, certain foods, emotional distress, unpleasant odors, sights or sounds, among many others. Often, nausea and vomiting are symptoms of specific diseases: Heart attacks, kidney or liver disorders, some types of cancer, or infections are among the many examples. Nausea and vomiting are common in the first 3 months of pregnancy. (See Chapter 11 on Pregnancy and Birth, page 176.) Babies and young children also may be particularly susceptible to nausea and vomiting. This should not be confused with the common "spitting up" that occurs when a baby eats too much or has air bubbles. (See Chapter 12 on Infancy and the Early Years, page 210.)

In general, if the nausea and vomiting are short-lived and related to an identifiable cause—eating a food that caused an upset stomach, car sickness, or a viral illness—they probably are not cause for concern. If they are accompanied by other symptoms, such as a high fever, pain, diarrhea, profuse sweating, or are prolonged and recurrent, a doctor should be seen. Also, prolonged vomiting can lead to dehydration, especially in a young child or if it is accompanied by diarrhea. Vomiting associated with surgery, radiation therapy or drugs, such as anti-cancer drugs, alcohol, or morphine, often can be controlled by other drugs. There also are a number of drugs to prevent the nausea and vomiting associated with motion sickness and vertigo. If certain foods invariably seem to trigger nausea and vomiting, simply avoiding them usually will solve the problem. If the nausea and vomiting stem from other organic conditions, identifying and treating them usually will resolve the problem.

GASTROINTESTINAL PAIN

LIKE NAUSEA AND VOMITING, pain is not a disease, but a symptom associated with many disorders, both organic and psychogenic. Since pain is highly subjective and perceived differently by different people, it is often difficult to pinpoint its origin and cause. In general, there are 4 sources of gastrointestinal pain: visceral pain, which originates in the abdominal organs or viscera; somatic pain, which originates in the abdominal wall; referred pain, which originates in another area but is perceived as gastrointestinal; and psychogenic, which has a psychological origin but is felt in the abdominal area. Visceral pain is usually described as "deep," dull, or aching and is generalized without localization. Somatic pain tends to be more localized near its origin and is sharper than visceral pain. Visceral pain may progress to somatic pain. For example, pain associated with appendicitis begins as a generalized pain around the navel and only with progression of the inflammatory process is pain in the right lower quadrant experienced. Referred or psychogenic pains are often more difficult to pinpoint since they vary from person to person and according to the circumstances involved. Deep fear or an emotional upset may manifest itself as a "pain in the pit of the stomach"; pain referred from a surgical incision may be perceived as coming from within the gastrointestinal area; kidney, nervous, heart, or certain neuromuscular diseases all may produce pain referred to the gastrointestinal area.

Pain that does not go away in a few hours, that recurs, that is particularly persistent, or that is accompanied by other symptoms—fever, weakness, sweating, pallor, bleeding from the mouth or bowel, bloating, among others—should be promptly investigated. Severe pain that comes on suddenly also may indicate a serious problem that should be treated without delay. The intensity of pain itself is not necessarily an indication of seriousness, however. Many serious gastrointestinal disorders may produce little or no pain, while some trivial or self-limiting conditions may bring on excruciating pain.

HEARTBURN AND INDIGESTION

HEARTBURN, OR ACID INDIGESTION, is a burning sensation that arises behind the sternum (breastbone) and may spread to the throat, jaw, or mouth. (See figure 24.2.) It is not related to the heart, although people sometimes mistake the symptoms for those of heart disease. Instead, it is caused by a backflow, or reflux, of stomach acids into the esophagus, a condition called gastroesophageal reflux.

It may be promoted or worsened by lying down following a meal, but the underlying cause is likely to be a weakness or malfunctioning of the sphincter muscle between the esophagus and stomach. This sphincter functions as a valve, opening to admit food passing through the esophagus into the stomach, and then closing to prevent a backflow. Conditions and circumstances that may interfere with the func-

Figure 24.2. **Anatomy of heartburn. Heartburn is caused by a backflow of the stomach contents into the esophagus. This drawing shows the position of the esophagus and stomach; the inset illustrates an opening in the valve between the two, permitting a backflow from the stomach.**

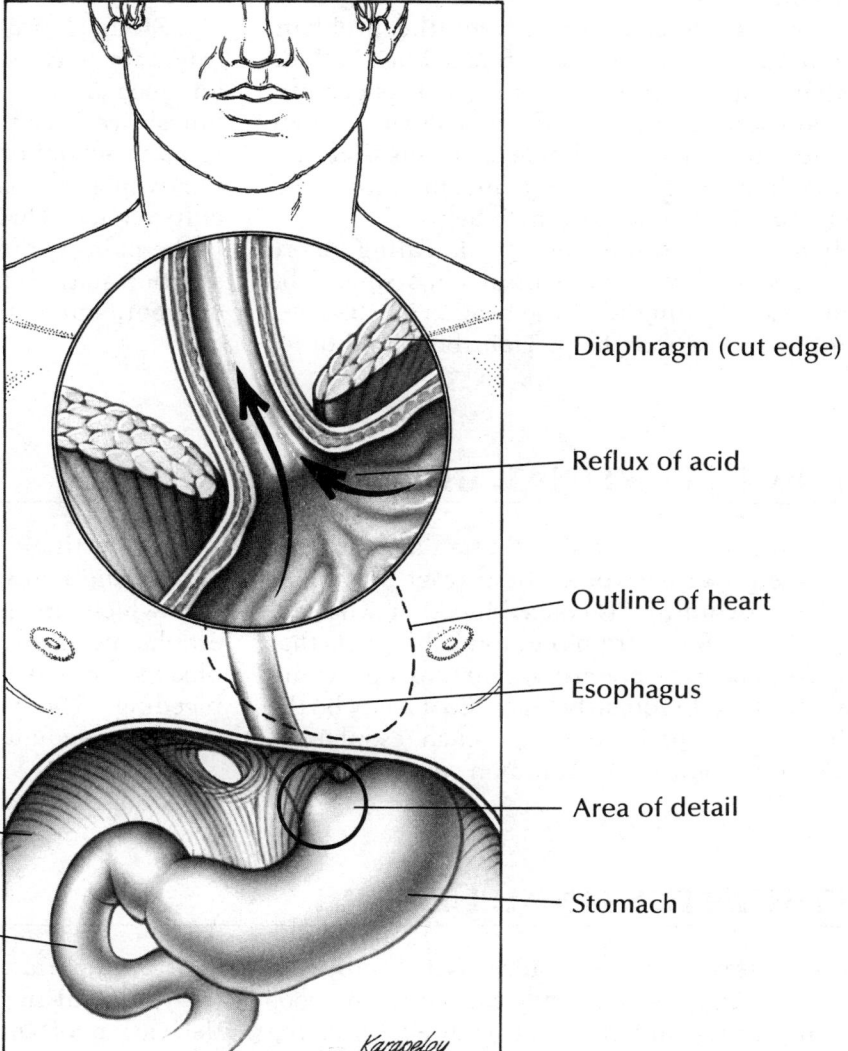

Diaphragm (cut edge)

Reflux of acid

Outline of heart

Esophagus

Area of detail

Stomach

Diaphragm

Small intestine

tioning of this sphincter include congenital malformation, stress or emotional upset affecting the nerves that control the muscle action, obesity, pregnancy, and excessive air swallowing or a buildup of intestinal gas. A structural problem, such as a hiatus hernia, which results in the upper portion of the stomach pushing through the opening in the diaphragm through which the esophagus passes, also may cause acid reflux and heartburn. (See section on Hiatal Hernia, page 513.)

Recurrent acid indigestion may damage the esophagus, causing inflammation (esophagitis), a narrowing of the organ, or ulcers. Therefore, repeated bouts of heartburn should be investigated by a physician, who may take x-rays or perform other tests to determine the cause. The use of antacids to neutralize the stomach contents usually will provide relief from simple heartburn. However, frequent use of these (or any other medications) should be checked with a doctor. Commonsense measures, such as avoiding stress, especially at mealtimes, and forgoing foods and drinks that seem to trigger attacks, often is sufficient to prevent the problem. Foods that are frequent causes of heartburn include those that contain caffeine (coffee, tea, chocolate, and certain soft drinks), alcohol, fats, citric or other acids, and foods such as cabbage or beans that produce intestinal gas. Eating frequent, small meals instead of 2 or 3 large ones also may help.

If lying down prompts an attack, eating before going to bed or taking after-meal naps should be avoided. Also, sleeping with the head of the bed elevated a few inches may help. Tight belts and other constrictive clothing also should be avoided.

Indigestion (dyspepsia) is mistaken for heartburn, but it usually involves other vague symptoms, such as abdominal pain, a bloated feeling, belching, nausea and vomiting, and sometimes diarrhea. Sometimes the digestive problems may have an identifiable cause, such as peptic ulcer, esophagitis, gallbladder or liver disease, bacterial or viral infections, or the use of certain medications, and such possible causes should be ruled out in investigating recurrent indigestion. Most often, however, there is no organic cause for the problem. Excessive air swallowing may contribute to feeling bloated and to excessive belching. A review of eating habits (chewing with the mouth open, talking while chewing, gulping down food) may reveal a tendency to swallow too much air. A response to stress or emotional unrest may manifest itself in abdominal pain and heartburn or indigestion. Certain foods, caffeine, alcohol, or carbonated beverages, may contribute to the discomfort. Keeping a food diary may help pinpoint specific offenders.

Stomach problems also may be of psychological origin, or may be an attention-getting device, albeit an unconscious one. Complaints of "my stomach hurts" are often heard from children who don't want to go to school or perform an unpleasant task; similar responses may occur in adults who have difficulty coping. This is not necessarily malingering nor is the pain imaginary, as is often assumed. But the solution may well rest in a reevaluation of lifestyle or emotional factors rather than medical treatment.

GASTROINTESTINAL BLEEDING

BLEEDING MAY BE the first sign that an abnormality exists in the upper gastrointestinal tract. It may be in the form of vomiting up of red blood or what appears to be fresh blood from the stomach. Stools that are black and tarry frequently signal upper gastrointestinal bleeding. Frequently black stools may be the only clue of bleeding from the stomach, esophagus, or duodenum. Some of the common causes of upper gastrointestinal bleeding include ulcers, gastritis, benign and malignant tumors, and esophageal varices, which are prominent veins that form in the esophagus as a result of liver disease. When varices bleed the blood loss may be profuse. Any evidence of bleeding, whether in the stool or in vomitus, requires immediate medical attention.

GASTROINTESTINAL ULCERS

A GASTROINTESTINAL or peptic ulcer is a chronic sore or crater extending through the protective mucous membrane lining and penetrating the underlying muscular tissue. An ulcer can form in any area exposed to gastric acid and pepsin, a digestive enzyme instrumental in the breakdown of protein and the derivation of the term "peptic ulcer." The areas most commonly affected are the upper part of the duodenum, the stomach itself (gastric ulcers), and, less commonly, the esophagus.

The precise cause of gastrointestinal ulcers is unknown. Although peptic ulcers occur only in the presence of gastric acids, they are not necessarily related to an overproduction of acid, as is commonly assumed. Some people who produce low levels of acid develop ulcers, while there are others who produce large amounts yet are ulcer-free. An imbalance in the production of acid versus protective mucus is suspected as a likely cause; without sufficient mucous membrane, even a small amount of acid can cause an ulcer. (See figure 24.3.) A number of factors can effect mucus production, but stress and the use of nonsteroidal anti-inflammatory drugs like aspirin are the most frequently encountered. Indeed, in the popular mind, ulcers are commonly associated with the stress-ridden rising executive. Still, this is by no means a universal finding. Many people subjected to enormous stress never develop ulcers and others who seemingly lead a calm, relatively stress-free life may develop them. Other precipitating causes include certain drugs, such as aspirin and other anti-inflammatory agents, and surgery. Cigarette smoking and alcohol use may exacerbate existing ulcers, but it has not been proved that they actually cause them. Also, contrary to popular belief, spicy foods do not appear to be a cause.

Ulcers may occur at any age. Abdominal pain is a common symptom, usually described as a gnawing ache or burning sensation that is relieved by milk or antacids. The location and type of pain also depends upon the type of ulcer. Typically, a duodenal ulcer produces recurring pain, usually 2 or 3 hours after eating, and the discomfort is relieved by eating. If the ulcer is located in the stomach, however, eating may provoke rather than relieve the pain. It should be noted that a large number of ulcer patients, perhaps as many as 50 percent, do not experience the characteristic abdominal pain, or are not aware of it until other symptoms such as gastrointestinal bleeding or obstruction occur. Also, the pain may be attributed to other causes, such as indigestion or an irritable bowel. Other possible symptoms of peptic ulcer include bloating, nausea, and vomiting; these are most likely to occur if the ulcer is in the pyloric channel—the lowermost part of the stomach where food passes through the pyloric sphincter into the duodenum. An esophageal ulcer is likely to cause discomfort when swallowing or lying down.

An ulcer may be diagnosed by x-ray studies using a barium swallow. This chalky substance provides the contrast needed to make the intestinal tract visible on an x-ray film. Endoscopy, in which a long, flexible tube with fiberoptic viewing devices is threaded through the mouth and into the intestinal tract, also may be used to establish a diagnosis. (See Chapter 4 on Diagnostic Tests and Procedures, page 50.) Since stomach and other gastrointestinal cancers sometimes carry symptoms similar to those of an ulcer, a microscopic examination of tissue samples or cells shed from the gastrointestinal tract may be indicated. These samples may be collected during endoscopy or from washing or brushing techniques.

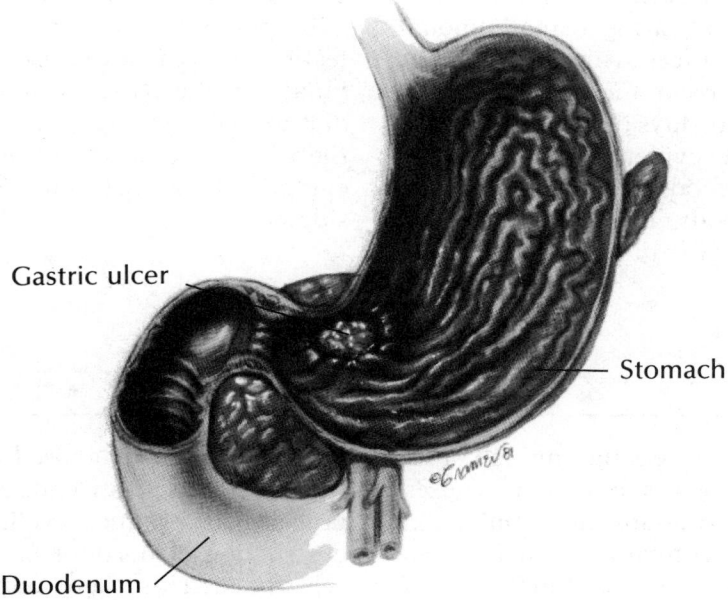

Gastric ulcer

Stomach

Duodenum

Figure 24.3.   **Cross section of the stomach showing a gastric ulcer in the lower portion.**

Still another possible test involves an analysis of gastric secretions to determine the amount of hydrochloric acid that is being secreted.

Gastrointestinal bleeding is a major and common complication of untreated peptic ulcers. In addition scarring and the formation of adhesions in the stomach or duodenum can lead to obstruction. In some patients, the ulcer may perforate through the intestinal wall, spilling the contents into the abdominal cavity. This is always a medical emergency, usually requiring surgery and intensive treatment to prevent peritonitis.

Some gastrointestinal ulcers heal by themselves without any special treatment. But to avoid possible complications, treatment aimed at healing the ulcer and then preventing a recurrence, is advised. Patients who smoke are strongly urged to quit; while there is no evidence that cigarette use per se causes ulcers, studies have found that they heal more quickly if smoking is discontinued. Alcohol and caffeine stimulate the production of gastric acid and should be avoided until the ulcer has healed. (Decaffeinated coffee and caffeine-free tea or soft drinks can be safely substituted.) Drugs, such as aspirin, that irritate the intestinal tract and which may in themselves cause ulcers, also should be avoided or used with caution. If stress is a factor, changes in lifestyle or the development of more effective coping techniques may be in order. (See Chapter 17 on The Effects of Stress on Health, page 336.)

Diet, long the major treatment for peptic ulcers is still important, but the emphasis has shifted considerably in recent years. At one time, the typical ulcer diet was made up of bland foods, with heavy emphasis on milk and milk products, and frequent, small meals. Since milk and eating a small amount of food provide relief from ulcer symptoms in many patients, these are still recommended. However, they are no longer the mainstays of ulcer treatment, nor is there any convincing evidence that it is necessary to avoid many of the foods once barred on most ulcer diets. If certain foods, for example, highly spiced dishes, fatty foods, or fruit juice, seem to pro-

voke ulcer symptoms, then obviously it is wise to avoid them. But foods that do not cause symptoms usually can be enjoyed in moderation.

Antacids, which neutralize or absorb gastric acid, are still useful in treating ulcers and preventing a recurrence. But the real revolution in ulcer treatment in recent years has been the introduction of new agents that lower the production of gastric acid by blocking the histamine H_2 receptors. Cimetidine was the first of the H_2 blocking agents introduced in this country; since then, other similar drugs such as ranitidine have been introduced. Although these drugs usually provide relief from ulcer symptoms in a week or so, healing may take 6 to 8 weeks or longer; also, small doses may be prescribed over a longer period to prevent recurrence. H_2 blocking agents also may be prescribed in conjunction with antacids or other drugs to increase their effectiveness.

Another new pharmacologic approach to treating ulcers involves giving sucralfate, a drug that forms a protective coating over the ulcer, thus allowing it to heal without disrupting the flow of gastric acid. The H_2 blockers and coating agents have helped reduce the rate of ulcer surgery in this country, but there are still instances in which an operation may be indicated. As noted earlier, a perforated ulcer almost always requires prompt surgery. In patients who cannot undergo surgery, other emergency treatments, such as suction of the spilled intestinal contents from the abdominal cavity and antibiotic therapy, will be administered.

Recurrent gastrointestinal bleeding also may be an indication for surgery. Intestinal obstruction that is not relieved by other treatments or which recurs is still another reason for operating. Any gastrointestinal malignancy is also an indication for surgery. Finally, some patients find that drug therapy and diet are not adequate to relieve their symptoms. If the ulcers are disabling or likely to cause further complications, their surgical removal may be considered.

GASTRITIS

GASTRITIS IS A TERM to describe inflammation of the stomach lining. Acute gastritis has many causes: drugs, ingestion of corrosive substances, infection, shock, surgery, an allergic response, alcohol, among others. Symptoms include loss of appetite, nausea, and vomiting; bleeding and pain similar to that of a gastric ulcer also may occur. Many patients, however, have no specific symptoms.

Gastritis is diagnosed by viewing the stomach interior through an endoscope. The inflammatory process will produce swelling, ulcerated areas, and destruction of portions of the lining. In some rare types of gastritis, there may be a shrinking of tissue, a condition called atrophic gastritis. In another rare type of gastritis, called hypertrophic gastritis, there is an overgrowth of stomach lining and glands.

Treatment depends upon the underlying cause of the gastritis. Often, identifying and remedying the cause is all that is needed. Since one of the major complications of acute gastritis is hemorrhage, treatment often involves steps to prevent bleeding. Antacids are the usual mainstay of treatment. H_2 blocking agents such as cimetidine or ranitidine are indicated in gastritis under certain circumstances.

DISORDERS OF THE ESOPHAGUS

Difficulty in Swallowing

Dysphagia, the medical term for difficulty in swallowing, may arise in the esophagus or the pharynx. Typically, the patient will complain that "food seems to get stuck" or takes too long going down. The dysphagia may be accompanied by pain or burning. In any event, any persistent difficulty in swallowing should be promptly investigated since this is a major symptom of esophageal cancer. Fortunately, esophageal cancer is relatively rare and the problem is likely to have other causes. But since this type of cancer is difficult to treat, especially in an advanced stage, its early diagnosis is particularly important. (See Chapter 20 on Cancer, page 412, for a more detailed discussion.)

Other possible causes of dysphagia include nervous or muscular disorders, such as myasthenia gravis, which may also affect adjacent organs. Muscular disorders, such as smooth muscle spasm, may interfere with normal muscular contractions and sphincter control that provide for the orderly movement of food through the esophagus. Esophageal ulcers, accompanied by scarring and adhesions, may narrow the passage enough to cause difficulty in swallowing solid foods, especially things like meat or bread. Infection, structural abnormalities, and reflux of stomach acid and contents are still other possible causes of difficult or painful swallowing.

In many instances, the symptoms point to a diagnosis. If further tests are needed, these may include x-ray studies, viewing the inside of the esophagus through a flexible tube equipped with fiberoptic devices, and an analysis of secretions in the esophagus. Tests of muscle and sphincter tone and function also may be performed.

Treatment of the esophageal symptoms will depend on the cause. If dysphagia is due to a benign stricture as a result of acid refluxing from the stomach to the esophagus, the stretching of the stricture is performed. This is accomplished by a method called bougienage, whereby metal or rubber tubes of increasing caliber are passed into the mouth and driven through the stricture until dilation is achieved.

If dysphagia and pain are caused by spasm in the esophagus, then medication which allows the muscle to relax is tried and frequently effective.

Chronic esophageal spasm, or achalasia, is a disorder characterized by an unusually high pressure in the gastroesophageal sphincter. The sphincter does not relax properly to allow the passage of food into the stomach. This can be treated with mechanical dilation. If this fails, surgery may be recommended.

Hiatal Hernia

The esophagus passes through an opening in the diaphragm—the muscular wall dividing the chest cavity and abdominal cavity—known as the hiatus. When this opening becomes weakened and stretched, allowing a portion of the stomach to bulge through into the chest cavity, the condition is referred to as a hiatal or esophageal hernia. (See figure 24.4.) This is actually a very common anomaly and, quite often does not cause any discomfort or unusual symptoms. If, however, the sphincter at the lower end of the esophagus becomes weakened, allowing some of the stomach acids and other contents to flow back into the esophagus, pain and a burning sensation may result. Persistent exposure of the esophageal tissue to gastric acid also can cause inflammation (esophagitis) and even ulcers.

A hiatal hernia can be diagnosed with x-ray studies following a barium swallow or through endoscopy. Since the symptoms of pain spreading from below the sternum (breastbone) to the neck, jaw, and perhaps arms are also typical of coronary heart disease, tests for heart disease also may be performed to rule out this possibility.

A number of common eating habits and practices can aggravate hiatal hernia. Eating a large meal at night and then lying down or going to bed early promotes the backflow of food and gastric acid from the stomach to the esophagus. Unconscious air swallowing—drinking carbonated beverages, talking while eating, chewing gum, chewing with the mouth open—can add to the discomfort. Pregnancy or obesity also may worsen symptoms of hiatal hernia. Stooping or bending over, especially after eating, may promote reflux; wearing constrictive clothing is yet another factor that may contribute to the symptoms.

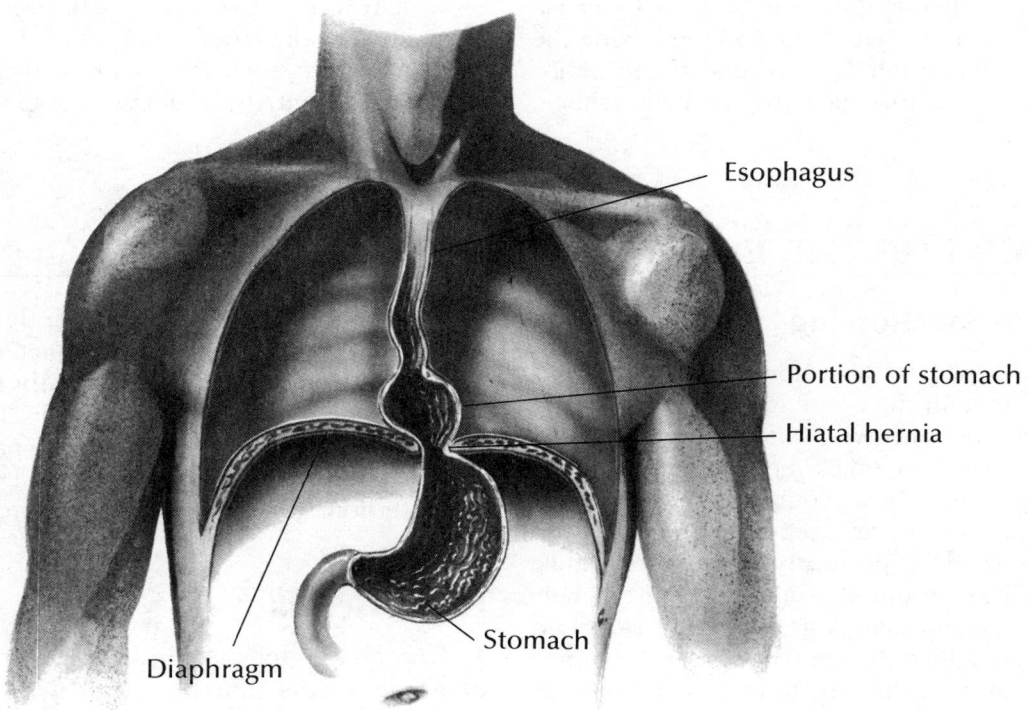

Figure 24.4. **View of a hiatal hernia, with a portion of the stomach squeezed above the opening in the diaphragm.**

Specific remedies include avoiding practices that seem to worsen the reflux. Eating frequent, small meals may help, as will avoiding lying down or going to bed after eating. Elevating the head of the bed a few inches also may help prevent reflux into the esophagus. Some doctors also advise taking an antacid 1 hour or so after eating to neutralize the stomach acids. Losing weight if obesity is a factor and not wearing tight belts, girdles, or other constrictive clothing also are advisable.

If these conservative measures fail, surgery to tighten the hiatal opening may be recommended. It is estimated, however, that only a small number of patients with hiatal hernia need surgery.

Esophageal Diverticula

This is a relatively rare condition in which weakened segments in the esophagus form small outpouches. (See figure 24.5.) These sometimes fill with food, which may then be regurgitated when lying down or bending over. If such regurgitation occurs at night and the material is drawn into the lungs, aspiration pneumonia—a potentially life-threatening condition—may result.

Esophageal diverticula are diagnosed by x-ray

studies taken following a barium swallow. Most cases do not require specific treatment unless the pouches are large enough to interfere with swal-

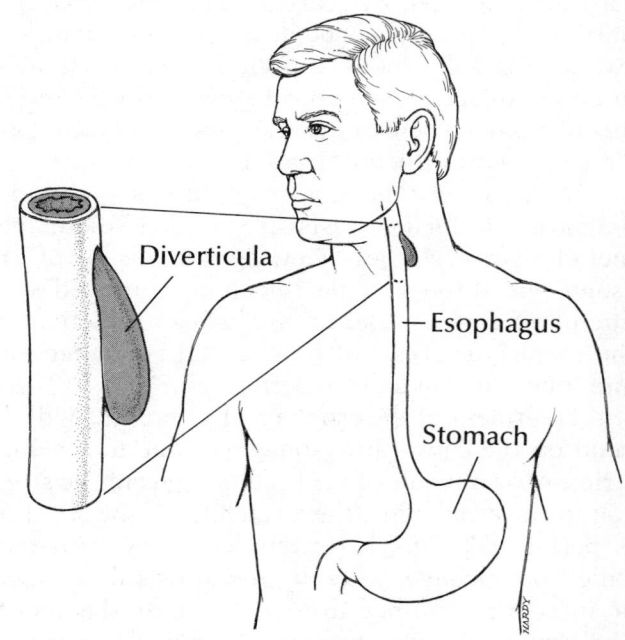

Figure 24.5. **Esophageal diverticula are outpouches that develop in weakened segments of the esophagus.**

lowing or there are other serious symptoms. In these unusual circumstances, surgical removal of the diverticula may be required.

Esophageal Rupture

Infrequently, the esophagus will become ruptured or torn, resulting in bleeding. Most esophageal ruptures occur in the lowermost portion and may be caused by retching or vomiting. The bleeding frequently will stop on its own; if not, the rupture will have to be sutured or ligated. Perforation or rupture of the upper esophagus is more serious and requires emergency surgery to repair the tear, and drainage of blood from the chest cavity.

Congenital Defects

Several congenital malformations of the esophagus occur in a small number of infants. One of the most serious is esophageal atresia, in which the esophagus ends in a self-contained pouch rather than the stomach. This condition requires surgery shortly after birth to link the esophagus and stomach and to permit the normal flow of food. Other possible congenital malformations include narrowing or strictures of the esophagus, which make it difficult for the infant to swallow, especially when solid foods are introduced. These often can be corrected by dilation.

DISORDERS OF THE SMALL INTESTINE

DIGESTION IS COMPLETED in the small intestine and the usable nutrients from food are absorbed into the circulation from this organ. Understandably, then, many of the disorders affecting it involve these processes; including such things as ulcers (discussed in an earlier section), intestinal obstruction, and the various malabsorption syndromes. Intestinal inflammatory disorders, such as ileitis and enteritis, also are relatively common.

Malabsorption Syndromes

Many different conditions and circumstances affect the ability of the small intestine to absorb nutrients adequately. Examples include a fault in the digestive process, such as a failure to produce enzymes needed to break down certain foods; structural defects or tumors in the intestine itself; inflammatory processes, intestinal infections, and other diseases; and congenital defects. Injury or surgical removal of portions of the small intestine also may result in absorption problems.

Symptoms vary according to the cause, but the most common are weight loss; abdominal discomfort, including cramps, gas, and bloating; diarrhea; abnormal stools; nutritional deficiencies; anemia; and in children, a failure to thrive or grow. Specific malabsorption disorders include the following.

Lactose Intolerance. This is a common disorder caused by a lack of lactase, an enzyme secreted in the walls of the small intestine that is needed to break down lactose, the sugar in cow's milk. It is most common among blacks and people of Asian origin, although it is estimated that up to 75 percent of all adults (excluding those of northern European extraction) may have some degree of lactose intolerance. If there is insufficient lactase, the milk sugar is not digested, resulting in diarrhea, cramps, abdominal gas, and rumbling sounds. In babies or young children who are fed mostly cow's milk, there also may be weight loss or failure to gain. Although lactase deficiency is the most common of the carbohydrate malabsorption syndromes, there also may be a lack of other enzymes needed to absorb different sugars (disaccharides), resulting in symptoms similar to those of lactose intolerance.

Lactose intolerance is suspected when the symptoms invariably occur after consuming milk or milk products. Diagnosis is confirmed by a lactose tolerance test, in which a lactose drink is given and then the patient monitored for gastrointestinal symptoms, such as diarrhea and cramps. There also will not be the usual rise in blood glucose (sugar) that follows consumption of lactose. Other tests may include an analysis of the stools for a high acid content.

Lactose intolerance is treated by avoiding cow's milk and other products that may contain lactose. Babies will be given a formula based on soy or other milk substitutes. There are also milk products in which the lactose is predigested. Also, yogurt and certain cheeses usually can be tolerated because the lactose already has been broken down.

Celiac Disease. Celiac disease is a hereditary disorder involving an intolerance to gluten, a protein found in wheat and rye flours. It usually appears in childhood, although there are cases in which it is not diagnosed until adulthood. Symptoms include a failure to grow in childhood, weight loss, abdominal bloating and discomfort, anemia, and the passage of fatty, foul-smelling stools that float to the top of the toilet water. The disorder often can be diagnosed on the basis of symptoms and confirmed by examining a small sample of intestinal tissue. As the disease progresses, the fingerlike villi that line the intestinal walls, and from which nutrients are absorbed into the bloodstream, will become flattened and smooth. This impairs the body's ability to absorb a variety of nutrients, explaining the weight loss and nutritional deficiencies that are common to celiac disease.

Treatment involves consuming a gluten-free diet. In addition to breads and other obvious sources of wheat or rye flours, gluten is added to a wide variety of foods, including things like soups, gravies, ice cream, and many other commercial products. Thus, food labels should be carefully examined for the addition of gluten or grain products. Patients with celiac disease often can benefit from nutritional counseling, especially since the disorder often results in a variety of nutritional deficiencies, including anemia, which require vitamin and mineral supplements. In some severe cases, steroid drugs may be prescribed for a period to help promote recovery of the intestine.

Tropical Sprue. This disorder is uncommon in the United States, although it is seen occasionally among people from the Caribbean, India, and Southeast Asia. The cause is unknown, although it is assumed to be related in some way to nutritional deficiency and environmental factors, including infection, intestinal parasites, or perhaps consumption of certain food toxins.

Tropical sprue causes varied symptoms, including anemia and other nutritional deficiencies, weight loss, and diarrhea. A sore tongue also is common, as are symptoms of other malabsorption syndromes, such as passage of fatty stools. Diagnosis is based on an analysis of intestinal tissue samples, showing deformities in the intestinal villi.

Treatment consists of folic acid and long-term antibiotics. Treatment may be continued for 6 months or longer, depending upon the severity of the disease.

Whipple's Disease. This is a relatively rare disorder, mostly affecting middle-aged men. Symptoms include severe malabsorption, nutritional deficiencies, chronic low-grade fever, diarrhea, joint pain, weight loss, and darkening of the skin pigmentation. Many other organs, including the brain, heart, lungs, and eyes, may be affected. The cause of Whipple's disease is unknown, although it is as-

sumed to be from some sort of bacteria. At one time, the disease was invariably fatal; now, however, most cases can be cured or effectively controlled with long-term use of antibiotics, such as tetracycline.

Miscellaneous Causes. In addition to specific intestinal abnormalities or deficiencies, a number of other disorders can hinder absorption. Congestive heart failure, scleroderma, intestinal lymphoma, liver disease, and bacterial overgrowth are among the numerous conditions that can hinder absorption from the small intestine. Intestinal damage from radiation therapy or certain drugs also may affect absorption. Whenever there is unexplained weight loss, abdominal discomfort or symptoms, and nutritional deficiencies, malabsorption should be suspected.

Intestinal Obstruction

Intestinal obstruction can result from either a mechanical blockage or from a type of intestinal paralysis (adynamic ileus) in which peristalsis (the coordinated muscular contractions that propel food through the gastrointestinal tract) ceases. Mechanical blockages may be caused by tumors, adhesions or scarring, congenital abnormalities, and strangulated hernia, among other factors. Paralytic ileus, more common in the colon than in the small intestine, may be caused by infection, surgery or other trauma, or certain metabolic disorders that affect muscle function; for example, potassium deficiency (hypokalemia).

The obstruction may be complete or partial; in either instance, symptoms are likely to include vomiting, bloating, and abdominal cramps. If the obstruction is high, the vomiting is likely to be more severe and may result in a biochemical imbalance and shock. If the obstruction is complete, the vomitus may resemble feces. Complete obstruction also results in constipation and severe bloating caused by a buildup of intestinal gas. These symptoms also may be present in a partial obstruction, but not to such a severe degree. Obstruction caused by a strangulated section of intestine, usually the result of a hernia, may lead to gangrene and perforation of the intestine—a life-threatening situation.

Diagnosis is based on symptoms and x-ray studies to locate the site of obstruction. Treatment involves surgical correction of the obstruction as soon as possible, especially if it involves a strangulated hernia or other condition likely to lead to tissue death. The intestinal contents are removed through an intestinal tube. Antibiotics may be given to prevent or treat infection.

Intestinal Gas

Excessive intestinal gas may be manifested in 3 ways: belching, abdominal bloating and pain, and the passage of rectal gas (flatus). Gas is a common symptom of many intestinal disorders. Very often, however, it is a result of diet or faulty habits. Chronic belching, for example, is often linked to excessive air swallowing or to a nervous habit. Some people, particularly mouth breathers, swallow a large gulp of air before each belch. The air travels partway down the esophagus and is then forced back up. Some of the air may enter the stomach, forming an air bubble that grows with each new addition of air. This may cause a bloated feeling and additional belching. A conscious effort to avoid belching often helps; although momentary relief may follow a belch, it is likely to worsen the problem by promoting further air swallowing.

Abdominal bloating and discomfort may be due to a number of disorders, or it may simply be that the individual perceives even a normal amount of intestinal gas as uncomfortable. Drinking carbonated beverages, eating foods that produce excessive gas (e.g., beans, cabbage, and other such vegetables; milk; bran; cereal grains; beer; alcoholic beverages) may worsen the problem. Symptoms may be relieved by avoiding foods that seem to produce gas and by exercising moderately following a meal. Exercise helps stimulate the movement of gas through the digestive tract.

Rectal gas is usually linked to diet, particularly the consumption of carbohydrates that are not completely broken down in the stomach and small intestine. These undigested foods move into the colon, where bacteria go to work. The resulting fermentation process produces gas. People with lactose intolerance and other malabsorption problems often produce excessive rectal gas; very often, however, the gas is not linked to any disease process or abnormality. Some people simply produce more gas than others. In these instances, the best treatment is avoiding foods, particularly those containing nonabsorbable carbohydrates, that produce gas.

Intestinal gas accompanied by other symptoms should be investigated by a doctor, as should gassiness that is not relieved by dietary changes and other conservative measures.

Diverticulosis

Diverticula are outpouchings that form in weakened segments of the intestines. The most common sites along the small intestine are the duodenum and jejunum, particularly near the junctures where arteries penetrate the intestinal tissue. There is also a congenital abnormality called Meckel's diverticulum, which forms in the lower part of the ileum.

Diverticulosis becomes increasingly common with age. Most diverticula do not cause any symptoms. In some people, however, they may cause bleeding; less commonly, they may become inflamed, resulting in pain, bleeding, and sometimes perforation of the intestinal wall.

Meckel's diverticulum, also usually asymptomatic, is found in 1 to 2 percent of the population. The pouch may be up to 2 inches long and sometimes it has an acid-producing lining, similar to that of the stomach. This type may lead to ulceration and pain. In some instances, the pouch also may be filled with intestinal contents and become inflamed, producing pain and symptoms similar to those of appendicitis. Treatment is surgical removal in an operation similar to an appendectomy.

Regional Ileitis (Crohn's Disease)

Regional ileitis is a chronic inflammatory disorder affecting the lower part of the small intestine, and sometimes the colon and other parts of the digestive tract. It usually appears during young adulthood, although there are instances in which it starts even earlier. Symptoms include chronic diarrhea, abdominal pain, fever, loss of appetite, and weight loss. The symptoms sometimes mimic those of appendicitis; the swelling and inflammation also cause varying degrees of intestinal obstruction in some patients.

The cause of Crohn's disease (named for an American, Dr. Burrill Crohn, who first described the disorder) is unknown. It appears to run in families and is somewhat more common among Jewish people. An autoimmune process is thought to be a causative factor. The disease often affects specific segments of the intestine, hence the term "regional" ileitis. It may be accompanied by other disorders, such as arthritis.

Crohn's disease is diagnosed by an analysis of symptoms and x-ray studies, involving both an upper and lower gastrointestinal series using barium. There is no specific treatment for the disorder, although a number of different therapies are used to relieve specific symptoms. Drugs may be prescribed to relieve the cramps and diarrhea; abscesses and infection are treated with antibiotics. Corticosteroid drugs are often prescribed to treat acute attacks. Some patients have been helped by drugs that suppress the immune system. Artificial feeding may be indicated during acute flareups to maintain nutrition.

In some cases, fistulas—abnormal connections between cavities or surfaces—may form, leading to pain, perforation, infection, weight loss, and other symptoms, including obstruction. Surgery to re-move the diseased portions of the intestine may be needed to relieve symptoms, but this does not cure the disease, which is likely to recur in other parts of the gastrointestinal tract.

LIVER DISORDERS

THE LIVER, in addition to being the body's largest solid organ, is also one of the most complex, carry-ing on many essential metabolic and chemical func-tions. The liver produces many important body chemicals or substances, including bile, digestive enzymes, urea, clotting components, cholesterol, and proteins. It is essential in the metabolism of fats, carbohydrates, proteins, and the various vitamins and minerals. It controls the level of blood sugar and lipids, and also metabolizes or detoxifies drugs and potentially harmful chemicals, including alcohol. It also acts as a storehouse for blood, vitamins and minerals, and glycogen, the stored form of glucose, the body's major fuel.

In view of the number and variety of functions performed by the liver, it is understandable that the organ is susceptible to a number of disorders. (See figure 24.6.) In fact, it is somewhat surprising that liver disease is not more common than it is, espe-cially in light of the fact that it is exposed to so many different and potentially dangerous substances and microorganisms. Part of the reason is the fact that the liver has an amazing ability to regenerate itself. Also, the liver is composed of large numbers of indi-vidual units called hepatic acini; the organ can un-dergo substantial injury and still be able to function because there are so many of these units. Sometimes extensive liver disease exists without producing ob-vious symptoms; more often, however, there are signs. These include the following:

- *Jaundice.* In jaundice, the skin, whites of the eye, and other tissues take on a yellowish hue. The urine also may be darker than normal. It is not a disease, per se, but a symptom caused by an excess of bile pigments (bilirubin) in the body. Bile pigments are produced by the liver during the breakdown of red blood cells. A liver inflammation (hepatitis), obstruction of the bile ducts, or an excessive breakdown of red blood cells all can result in jaundice. Treatment of jaundice depends upon identifying its cause and then resolving it.

- *An enlarged liver.* A number of disorders, including hep-atitis, biliary obstruction, cirrhosis, cancer, or a fatty

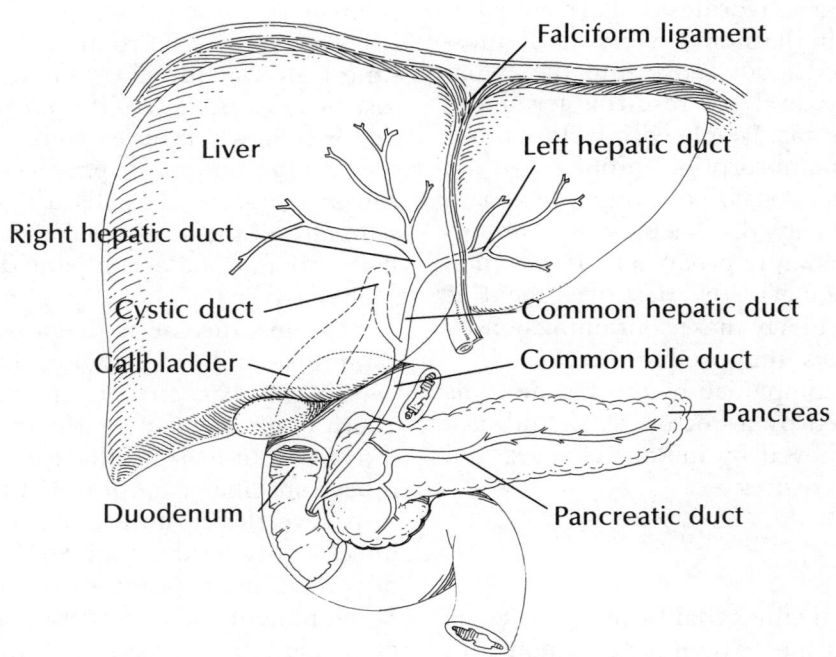

Figure 24.6. **The liver performs a number of vital functions, including many that are closely associated with adjacent digestive organs.**

liver, can result in liver enlargement (hepatomegaly). There also may be tenderness or pain, usually a deep aching sensation that is felt when the organ is palpated.

- *Accumulation of fluid.* This symptom, which is referred to as ascites, is marked by a buildup of fluid in the peritoneal cavity. The most common cause is cirrhosis, but it also may occur in chronic hepatitis and obstruction of the hepatic vein. Ascites also may develop from conditions that are not related to the liver, such as congestive heart failure, thyroid disorders, pancreatic and kidney diseases, or cancer which has started in or spread to the peritoneum. (The peritoneum is a thin layer of tissue covering the intestines.)

- *Miscellaneous symptoms.* Liver disease may cause a number of varied symptoms affecting different body systems. Many of these are rather vague and are characteristics of other diseases; thus diagnosing liver disease is often a matter of ruling out other possible causes of the symptoms. Loss of appetite, fever, general malaise, fatigue, anemia and other blood and circulatory disorders, changes in body chemistry, kidney failure, and coma are among the many symptoms that may be caused by liver disease. Diagnosis usually requires a number of laboratory tests and also may involve x-ray studies, radionuclide and CT scans, and liver biopsy. (See Chapter 4 on Diagnostic Tests and Procedures, page 47.)

Hepatitis

Hepatitis, an inflammatory disease that results in the destruction of patches of liver tissue, is one of the most common of all liver diseases. Most hepatitis is caused by viruses, but alcohol, drugs, and a variety of viral, bacterial, fungal, or parasitic infections also can cause liver inflammation.

Different viruses—A, B, and non-A, non-B—cause viral hepatitis. Hepatitis A virus is shed from the body through the intestinal tract and is spread mostly by consuming foods that have been contaminated with some sort of fecal contact. For example, an infected person may transmit the virus by handling food with unwashed hands. Epidemics of hepatitis A may occur by consumption of shellfish taken from polluted waters. The disease also may be contracted by direct physical contact with a person with an active infection. After being infected, a person produces antibodies against the disease, which are protective for life. Studies have found antibodies against hepatitis A in people who have not had clinical symptoms of the disease, indicating that many people have mild hepatitis A without knowing it.

Hepatitis B, sometimes referred to as serum hepatitis, is spread by direct blood contact. At one time, blood transfusions were the most common source of hepatitis B, but this has changed with the development of a screening test that can identify contaminated blood. Today the use of contaminated needles by drug abusers is a more common source of the disease. The disease may be spread by other direct contact; sexual contact, particularly among homosexuals, is a common example. Unlike hepatitis A, a person harboring the virus can spread it to others even when there is no active infection. In fact, it is thought that there is a large pool of asymptomatic carriers. Not as much is known about non-A, non-B hepatitis, although it is thought that it, too, is transmitted through direct blood contact, including asymptomatic carriers.

The incubation period for hepatitis A is about 2 to 6 weeks, and can vary from 4 to 25 weeks for B and non-A, non-B types. Symptoms may vary from mild, flulike symptoms to severe liver failure, coma, and death. Typically, the disease starts with loss of appetite, nausea and vomiting, fever, and, among smokers, a distaste for cigarettes. There may be itching hives and joint pain. After a few days, the urine may become dark and the skin and eye whites may become yellowish. Stools are a light yellow and may be looser than normal. In a physical examination, a doctor often finds that the liver is enlarged. A specific diagnosis is made by identifying the virus antigen in the blood, stool, or liver. Most cases of hepatitis A resolve themselves without specific treatment other than bed rest for 4 to 8 weeks. Family members and other people exposed to the disease may be given immune serum globulin as a preventive measure. This also may be advised for people traveling to areas where hepatitis A is endemic.

Hepatitis B is generally the more serious form of the disease. In some patients, it may follow a course similar to hepatitis A; in others, however, it may quickly evolve into liver failure. A large number of hepatitis B patients also develop a chronic, subacute form of the disease without obvious symptoms. In some people, this subacute hepatitis is relatively benign; in others, however, there is continuing liver damage that may progress to cirrhosis or liver cancer. In population groups where hepatitis B is endemic, liver cancer is common and is thought to be related to the disease. The recent development of an effective vaccine against hepatitis B promises to improve the long-term outlook against this disease. At present, its high cost has limited the widespread administration of the vaccine to people who are at high risk of developing the disease. Newer production techniques are now being introduced that should lower the cost of the vaccine and make it more widely available, especially in parts of the world where hepatitis B and liver cancer are now common.

Hepatitis patients should not consume alcohol

and certain drugs that are metabolized in the liver. Rest is also an important component of treatment; bed rest is advised during the symptomatic stage, and a reduced schedule may be recommended for several weeks or even months following recovery.

Cirrhosis

Cirrhosis is a term used to describe a number of different liver disorders marked by progressive destruction of liver tissue and development of scarring, fibrosis, and fatty deposits. Cirrhosis may result from chronic hepatitis and other conditions. In this country, however, the most common cause is alcoholism. Normally, the liver can detoxify moderate amounts of alcohol without problems. But consumption of large amounts, for example, a pint of whiskey per day for several years, invariably produces varying degrees of liver damage. Besides alcoholic hepatitis progressing to cirrhosis, viral hepatitis, specifically hepatitis B and non-A, non-B hepatitis, can evolve into cirrhosis.

Typically, men over the age of 45 have been the most common cirrhosis patients. With the increasing number of women alcoholics, this is changing. In its early stages, cirrhosis may not cause any obvious symptoms. As the disease progresses, symptoms may include a hard, small liver, enlarged spleen, loss of appetite, fatigue, weakness, accumulation of fluid, jaundice, a reddening of the palms, and development of spider naevi (networks of tiny, spiderlike blood vessels under the skin). Portal hypertension, high blood pressure involving the liver's circulatory system, is also common. Anemia and various metabolic abnormalities may develop.

There is no specific cure for cirrhosis and the prognosis depends upon its cause. Cirrhosis related to chronic viral hepatitis is difficult to arrest. In contrast, cirrhosis caused by alcoholism may have a more optimistic outcome if it is detected in an early stage and the patient abstains from all alcohol use. In addition, a nutritious diet with appropriate vitamin and mineral supplements should be consumed.

Other treatments depend upon specific symptoms. For example, if there is edema, salt consumption may be restricted and a diuretic prescribed. Anemia will be treated by dietary supplements, etc.

Biliary Cirrhosis

Biliary cirrhosis is a disorder of bile secretion from the liver. It may be secondary to obstructed bile ducts or it may be a primary disorder with no immediately apparent cause. Primary biliary cirrhosis occurs most frequently in middle-aged women. Symptoms include jaundice; darkened urine and pale, yellowish stools that contain fat; itching and a darkening of the skin. Cholesterol levels are usually high and there may be fatty deposits under the skin (xanthomas). Secondary biliary cirrhosis may follow long-standing gallbladder or bile duct disease.

Treatment depends upon the cause of the disease. Secondary biliary cirrhosis often can be cured by correcting any obstruction of the bile ducts. There is no specific treatment for primary biliary cirrhosis other than providing relief from the various symptoms and giving a nutritious diet with appropriate vitamin and mineral supplements.

Fatty Liver Disease

A buildup of fatty deposits in the liver can have many causes, including metabolic disorders, diabetes, Reye's syndrome, pregnancy, obesity, and a toxic response to certain drugs and chemicals, particularly carbon tetrachloride, alcohol, and corticosteroids. Very often, there are no obvious symptoms, but an enlarged liver may be noted during a physical examination. In some patients, there may be pain in the upper right-hand side of the abdomen, and/or jaundice. Diagnosis is made by obtaining a sample of liver tissue and noting the abnormal presence of fatty deposits. Treatment depends upon identifying and correcting the underlying cause.

GALLBLADDER DISEASE

THE FORMATION OF GALLSTONES (cholelithiasis) is the most common manifestation of gallbladder disease. The gallbladder, which is linked by small ducts to the liver and small intestine, acts as a storehouse for bile, the substance needed to digest fats. Bile is produced from cholesterol by the liver and some of it is concentrated and stored in the gallbladder for use in digesting a fatty meal.

About 10 percent of the population is thought to harbor gallstones. They are more common in women than men, and their incidence increases with age. Most gallstones are formed from cholesterol; being overweight and having a high level of blood cholesterol increase the risk of developing them. In most people, the gallstones are "silent," producing no symptoms. Others may complain of bloating, gassiness, abdominal discomforts, and other symptoms similar to those of indigestion. In a significant number, however, multiple stones develop, which can cause attacks of severe colicky pain, starting in the upper abdomen and often radiating through the right side up to the right shoulder blade. The attacks are often provoked by eating fatty foods or alcohol. Occasionally, a stone or stones will become lodged in the common bile duct, which is shared by the liver and gallbladder and which leads to the small intestine. (See figure 24.7.) This can produce severe pain and jaundice and may require prompt surgery.

Because the course of gallstones is highly unpredictable—many people have them for years with no problems and then suddenly develop jaundice and other serious symptoms—many doctors advocate removal of a diseased gallbladder as a precautionary measure. Others advise more conservative treatment, which includes weight loss if needed and a moderate, low-fat diet. Administration of a new drug made from a bile acid, chenodeoxycholic acid, is sometimes effective in dissolving small noncalcified cholesterol gallstones, but this may take several months and the drug does not dissolve other types of gallstone. Also, it may take 2 or 3 years of constant chenodeoxycholic therapy to dissolve the stones and it does not prevent their recurrence.

The gallbladder itself may become inflamed, a condition called cholecystitis, usually as a result of gallstones. Symptoms of chronic cholecystitis include frequent nausea, loss of appetite, gassiness, and abdominal pain, ranging from vague and mild to severe and colicky. The pain often occurs at night, especially after a heavy or fatty meal. Often the symptoms are mistaken for indigestion or hiatus hernia; a diagnosis can be confirmed, however, by ultrasound studies. Acute cholecystitis is marked by constant, often severe pain, especially at night. An attack may be provoked by a gallstone blocking the duct, infection, or irritation from digestive enzymes. Severe cholecystitis can progress to tissue death and gangrene of the organ, followed by perforation, but this is uncommon.

Surgical removal of the gallbladder usually is advised for chronic or acute cholecystitis, especially in view of the fact that a significant number of patients with gallbladder disease eventually develop cancer of the organ. Sometimes the operation will be delayed until an attack of acute cholecystitis subsides, but this depends upon individual circumstances. In general, gallbladder removal (cholecystectomy) is a relatively simple operation that produces dramatic relief from symptoms. The patient usually can leave the hospital in 2 or 3 days, with further recovery of a few weeks at home.

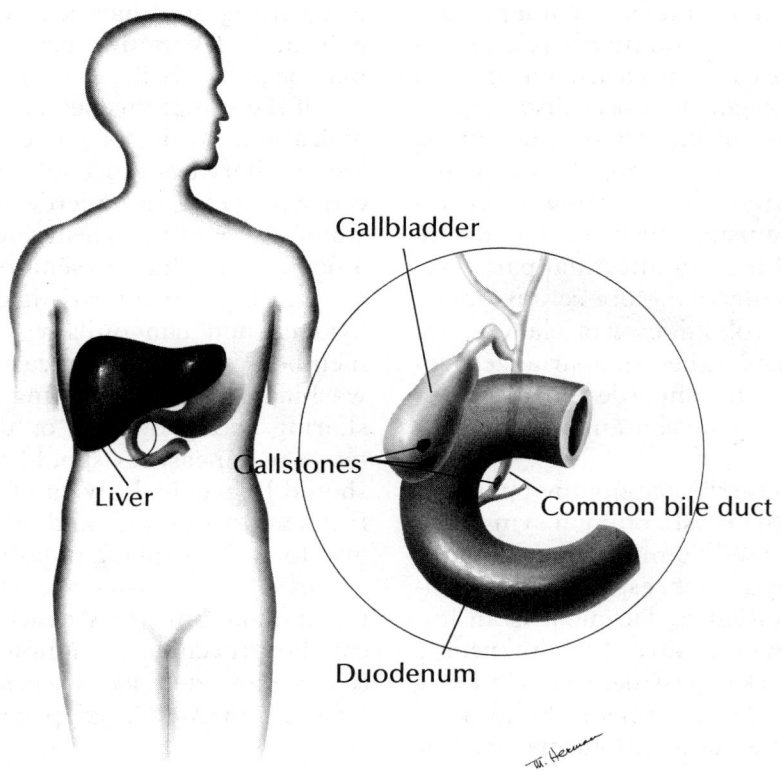

Figure 24.7. **A diseased gallbladder with a gallstone blocking the common bile duct that connects the liver, gallbladder, and duodenum of the small intestine.**

PANCREATITIS

THE PANCREAS has two important functions: In its exocrine portion, it produces many of the digestive enzymes needed to break down proteins and carbohydrates, and scattered throughout the organ are specialized endocrine cells that produce insulin and glucagon. The digestive enzymes flow directly into the duodenum; the pancreatic hormones are released into the blood. (See Chapter 23 on Diabetes and Other Endocrine Disorders, page 474.)

Pancreatitis is an inflammation of the organ caused by a buildup of digestive enzymes within it. An acute attack is often a result of gallstones, alcoholism, duodenal ulcer, or injury. An acute attack is characterized by the onset of severe, steady abdominal pain, nausea and vomiting, fever, a lowered blood pressure, fast heart rate and clammy skin. The disorder is diagnosed on the basis of symptoms and blood tests. In a large number of cases, the pancreatitis is caused by biliary tract disease; if this is suspected, ultrasonography or CT scans may be performed.

Chronic pancreatitis may develop over a period of time without the sudden, dramatic symptoms of an acute attack. Fat digestion is impaired, resulting in fatty stools. There may be recurrent abdominal pain and other symptoms; x-ray studies may find stones or areas of calcified tissue within the organ. If the problem is due to a partially obstructed pancreatic duct, it may be resolved by surgery.

During acute pancreatitis, the treatment strategy involves stopping the flow of pancreatic enzymes as much as possible. No food is given, although intravenous fluids usually are necessary to maintain the body's biochemical balance. If the attack is due to gallbladder disease, a cholecystectomy may be performed, but usually not until the pancreatitis subsides. Other treatments depend upon symptoms and complications.

INTESTINAL INFECTIONS

THERE ARE MANY different infections that affect the gastrointestinal tract. Many of these are lumped under the term gastroenteritis, commonly referred to as "stomach flu." Most cases of gastroenteritis are caused by viruses, although the upset also may be due to toxic substances, antibiotics or other drugs that alter the natural bacterial population of the lower gastrointestinal tract, or a reaction to certain foods. Other microorganisms, such as Salmonella bacteria, Shigella bacillus, and intestinal parasites, also may cause gastroenteritis. More serious infectious diseases, such as typhoid fever or cholera, are rare in this country and other industrialized societies, but still occur in underdeveloped areas where food and water may be contaminated by unsanitary conditions.

Nausea, vomiting, diarrhea, abdominal pains or cramps, and fever are the most common symptoms of gastroenteritis. Repeated vomiting and diarrhea can quickly lead to dehydration, especially in an infant or young child, so fluid replacement is an important part of treatment. Most healthy people recover from a mild attack of gastroenteritis in 1 or 2 days without any special treatment. Solid food should not be eaten while the symptoms persist, but extra fluids should be consumed, especially if there is vomiting and diarrhea. Antidiarrhea drugs may help and, if vomiting persists, an antiemetic drug may be prescribed.

If the symptoms persist or there are signs of dehydration, a doctor should be consulted. Also, bloody diarrhea, especially in a person who has recently traveled to underdeveloped countries or the tropics, should be investigated for the possibility of amebic or bacillary dysentery.

Since gastroenteritis is often the result of poor hygiene and can quickly spread to other family members, preventive measures such as carefully washing hands after going to the bathroom, not sharing eating utensils or dishes, and other commonsense measures should be practiced. Travelers should be particularly careful to avoid eating fresh fruits and vegetables and other uncooked foods and also to avoid drinking unbottled water or other beverages. The causes of traveler's diarrhea are not fully understood, but many experts feel that many cases can be prevented by following these precautions. (For a more detailed discussion, see the section on Diarrhea in Chapter 25, page 527.)

PERITONITIS

THE ABDOMINAL CAVITY is lined by a two-layered membrane, the peritoneum. Peritonitis is an inflammation of this membrane, almost always as the result of an injury or infection caused by a ruptured appendix, perforated ulcer, or diverticulitis, or as a result of abdominal surgery. In women, pelvic inflammatory disease involving the Fallopian tubes, which lie over the peritoneum, also may cause peritonitis.

Peritonitis is always a serious situation, calling for intensive antibiotic therapy and other treatment as indicated by the cause. Fortunately, it is now relatively rare in this country, thanks to advances in treating the underlying causes and the preventive use of antibiotics.

SUMMING UP

THE GASTROINTESTINAL TRACT is responsible for the digestion and absorption of food, which involves complex mechanical and chemical processes. The more common problems involving the gastrointestinal tract—occasional heartburn, indigestion, viral gastroenteritis—are usually short-lived and often related to eating indiscretions or temporary circumstances. More serious disorders, such as ul-cers, are now much easier to diagnose and treat. In this chapter, the more common disorders affecting the upper gastrointestinal tract and small intestine have been reviewed; disorders of the colon are discussed in the following chapter. The various gastrointestinal cancers are covered in Chapter 20 on Cancer.

25 Disorders of the Large Intestine

Peter J. Buchin, M.D.

INTRODUCTION

THE LARGE INTESTINE, also called the colon, is the site of the final phase of the digestive process that is described in the previous chapter. The colon is mainly involved in processes that solidify the waste products so that they may be excreted. It is subject to a number of disorders, which are often evaluated and treated by a gastroenterologist, a specialist who generally has had 3 years of training and board certification in internal medicine, followed by additional training in gastroenterology, and is qualified to treat digestive and liver diseases. Many gastroenterologists also have special training in technical procedures such as endoscopy, colonoscopy, and sigmoidoscopy. (For more information on specific diagnostic procedures, see Chapter 4 on Diagnostic Tests and Procedures, page 58.) The patient may also be referred to a general or colorectal surgeon if surgical treatment is being considered.

Anatomy

Three to 4 feet in length and wider in diameter than the small intestine, the large intestine is connected to the smaller one via the ileocecal valve. This valve permits passage of waste materials into the first part of the large intestine—the cecum—a pouchlike chamber that is located in the lower right part of the abdomen. Projecting out from the cecum is the appendix, a thin finger-shaped organ that appears to have no function in humans. (See figure 25.1.)

From the cecum, the colon extends upward into the upper right part of the abdomen, just below the liver, crosses to the left, turning downward again at the spleen, and descending into the lower left part of the abdomen. These sections are known, respectively, as the ascending colon, the transverse colon, and the descending colon. The turn at the liver is

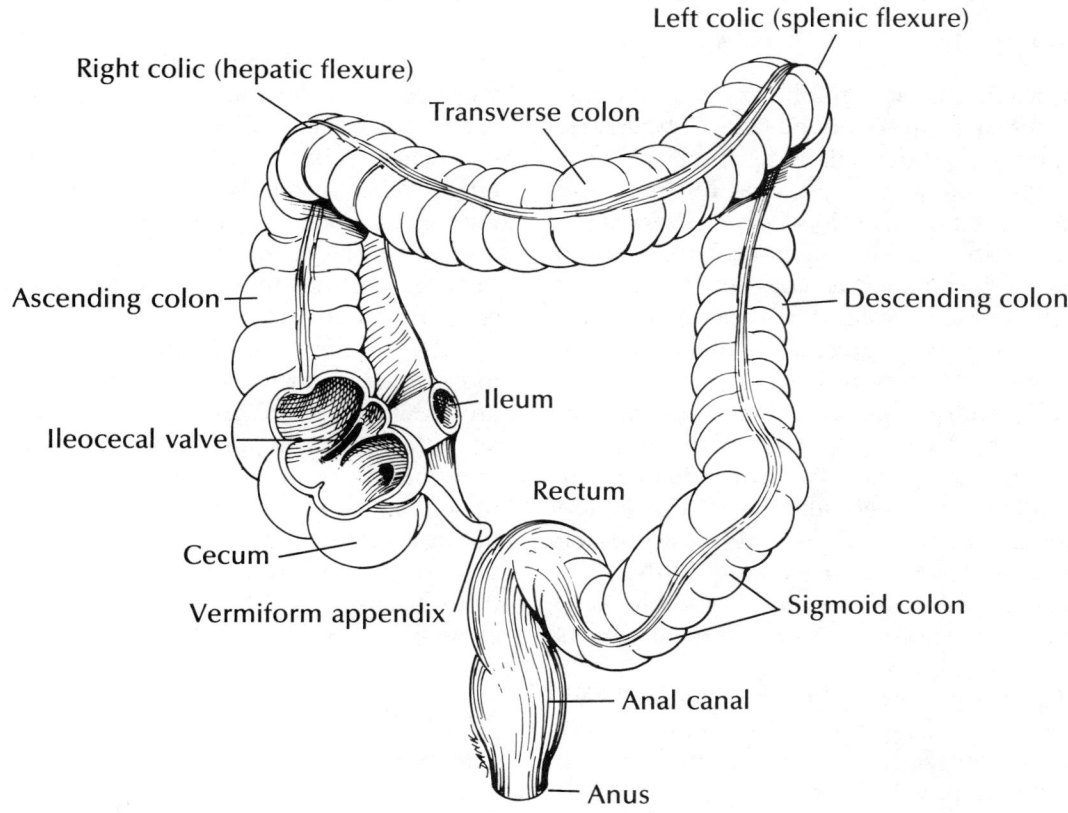

Figure 25.1. **The colon, or large intestine, begins on the lower right side and curves up, across, and then down the abdominal cavity, ending at the anus.**

called the hepatic flexure; the turn at the spleen is the splenic flexure. From the descending colon, the intestine makes an S-shaped curve into the middle part of the abdomen; this part is known as the sigmoid colon. Finally, there is a straight section, 6 inches in length, called the rectum.

During the digestive process, food passes from the small intestine through the ileocecal valve into the cecum. Unlike the small intestine, which is more involved in the absorption of nutrients, the large intestine serves mainly to absorb salt and water from the semi-liquid stool so that the stool will be solid in form.

If it were not for this process, the average person, instead of passing between 3½ and 9 ounces of solid stool per day, would have to evacuate more than 1 quart of liquid material several times daily—resulting not only in discomfort and dehydration, but also in depletion of important body salts such as sodium and potassium.

Instead, the water and salts are absorbed, by a complex mechanism, into the cells lining the intestine and eventually into the bloodstream. The colon

naturally contains large amounts of bacteria which help break down some dietary fibers and other waste products and nitrogenous wastes in the stool that are not digested by the stomach and small intestine. From these, it forms small amounts of hydrogen, and methane and nitrogen gas. As in the small intestine, the waste material is moved along by regular contractions. If these contractions are altered by intestinal infections such as viral gastroenteritis and dysentery, by spasm, or by other nondigestive diseases such as diabetes mellitus or thyroid disease, excessive liquid material will flow into the large intestine, overwhelming its ability to absorb salt and water and resulting in diarrhea.

Waste products can take anywhere from 3 to 18 hours to pass through the large intestine to the rectum. From there the stool passes through the anus, the opening at the lowermost end, from which it is finally excreted. At the bottom of the anus are 2 muscles, the internal sphincter and the external sphincter, which must be relaxed in order for stool to be evacuated.

SYMPTOMS

Abdominal Pain

Pain felt in the abdominal region may have its roots in the large intestine and may be caused by a stricture, polyp, or malignancy blocking the large intestine, which causes distention; a viral infection that results in decreased contractions; diverticulosis (see page 531); intestinal spasm (see page 530); or an inflammatory condition such as colitis. Occasionally, patients with arteriosclerosis may develop an injury to the intestine caused by decreased blood flow and known as a bowel infarction.

Because the large intestine winds throughout the abdomen, the location of the abdominal pain does not always correspond to a clearly defined part of the intestine. Nerve fibers also travel throughout the intestines, and pain originating from a problem in one area can sometimes be felt in another. The pain of a distended intestine, caused by a blockage, may be felt at the site of the distention itself, not the blockage.

Although many types of lower abdominal pain can be traced to conditions in the large intestine, the pain can also be caused by disorders of the gallbladder, liver, kidneys, pancreas, spleen, stomach, small intestine, and reproductive organs. Determining the origin of the pain often requires a thorough physical examination, blood tests, urine analysis, and in some cases, additional diagnostic procedures.

Pain can result when nutrients such as sugars are not properly absorbed by the intestine, but are fermented by bacteria, a process that generates excess gas. Lactose intolerance is an example of such a malabsorption problem. (See Chapter 24 on Disorders of the Digestive System, page 515.)

Severe injury to the intestine from causes such as circulatory disturbances of the blood vessels which lead to it can also cause pain, as can ischemic bowel disease, which is found occasionally with elderly patients with severe heart disease.

Tenesmus, a sensation describing rectal fullness and an inability to evacuate, which is relieved by flatus, defecation, or with an enema, is a fairly common complaint. It can be associated with disease in the rectum and is often found in diverticular disease and spastic colon.

Very specific information about when and where the pain, discomfort, or bleeding occurs and what may trigger it are extremely important to the physician in making the proper diagnosis. Patients may find it helpful to keep a diary of symptoms, food intake, and activities to help determine whether the symptoms occur after eating certain types of food or with certain types of exercise or activity, and whether symptoms are relieved with specific medications or food, or with movement of the bowels.

Digestive symptoms may be subjective. A tolerable level of discomfort to one person may be intolerable to another. A good relationship between doctor and patient is very helpful, so that by working together they may find the best treatment or program based on an accurate assessment of symptoms.

The patient should be particularly careful to look for the presence of blood in the stool or to report any new onset of abdominal or digestive symptoms or a change in the digestive pattern or a change in the stool pattern. In addition, weight loss or vomiting or the development of anemia should prompt the possible consideration of evaluation of intestinal diseases. In children, the first manifestation of intestinal disease may be painless, but may be failure to grow properly.

Constipation

Constipation can be defined as a decrease in the frequency of stool, or difficulty in formation or passage of the stool. Frequency of bowel movements may vary within populations, and from one country to another. Many Americans feel they need 1 stool daily, but there is no medical evidence to support this. Each person has his or her own bowel pattern, and what is "normal" may range from 3 bowel movements per day to only 3 per week. If this frequency becomes considerably less, if there is pain, or if the stools passed are very hard, an individual can be considered constipated.

The number of stools per day may be influenced by diet and activity. People who lead a sedentary life or are confined to bed will sometimes become constipated, possibly because of decreased contractions of the intestine and of decreased liquid intake, causing hard stool. Often a diet that is very low in fiber —one devoid of fruits and vegetables—will result in constipation. Other causes of constipation include:

- Abnormality in the contractions or motility of bowel muscles, which can be related to changes of pressure in the intestine and is thought by many doctors to be related to a disorder known as spastic colon, irritable colon, or irritable bowel syndrome. (See page 530.) Neurological and endocrine disorders, such as underactive thyroid gland or diabetes mellitus, can also influence contractions of the intestine and cause constipation.

- Medication, including analgesics such as codeine and

other narcoticlike drugs, and certain antacids, particularly those containing large amounts of aluminum.

- Blockage of the path of the intestines from a stricture (narrowed area), or by a malignant or benign tumor or polyp, or from diverticulosis (see page 531), which results in a tortuous path in the intestine.

- External causes, in which an organ or tissue mass presses on the intestine from the outside, which may occur with an enlarged prostate that presses on the rectum, or in endometriosis, a gynecologic condition that can result in compression of the large intestine.

Diarrhea

Diarrhea can be defined as an increase in the frequency, volume, or liquid content of the stool. This also can be arbitrary, and what some people call diarrhea may in fact simply be frequent movements of small amounts of solid material. For the average person in the western hemisphere, 100 to 250 grams (3½ to 9 ounces) of solid or semi-solid stool per day is a normal amount, with diarrhea being a significant increase in that amount.

Diarrhea can result from the inability of the intestine to absorb nutrients, salt, and water properly or from a number of conditions that cause the intestine to lose (secrete) fluid and salt. These include:

1. Infections of the gastrointestinal tract, either viral, bacterial, or parasitic (see page 522). Some in-

---

TREATMENT OF CONSTIPATION AND DIARRHEA

Constipation

A patient who has constipation, particularly if this represents a change in bowel habits, should see his physician for a checkup, including an abdominal and rectal examination to check for blood in the stool, and a blood count to check for anemia, hypothyroidism, and diabetes. In many cases, sigmoidoscopy, barium enema, and sometimes colonoscopy may be needed.

Treatment, if no reason for the constipation is found, may involve cautiously increasing the amount of fiber or bran in the diet. This is often done by beginning with increased amounts of canned fruits, and finally salad greens, fresh fruits, and vegetables, which have the most pulp or fiber. Patients who have diverticulosis should avoid popcorn or fruits and vegetables that contain seeds or pits.

Increased walking and other activity may increase bowel function. Sometimes, taking the time to eat slowly, rather than rushing through meals, may also help with constipation. Sometimes stool softeners (e.g., Colace), may be of value, and drinking adequate liquids is helpful. Some patients are helped by starting their morning with fruit such as prunes or apricots, or fruit juices, often in conjunction with bran (e.g., Metamucil, Konsyl, or Hydrocil).

Laxatives may be needed, particularly in elderly patients, or for people who are temporarily bedridden while recovering from an unrelated illness. In this case, magnesia-containing medications (Milk of Magnesia or Citrate of Magnesia), Senna, Dulcolax, castor oil, or enemas (such as Fleets Phospho-Soda) may be recommended. If the physician discovers an impacted stool in the anal area, as can occur especially in elderly or bedridden patients, enemas are often very important as the first step of treatment.

These remedies accomplish their jobs in many ways, but some, if used long-term, may present a potential problem of changes in the ability of the colon to contract normally and a resulting dependence if they are used regularly. Pregnant women should consult their doctors before taking any medication, including laxatives.

Diarrhea

Most bouts of diarrhea not associated with fever or intestinal bleeding are self-limited—that is, they will last a certain amount of time and then stop by themselves. In fact, it may be best not to treat mild diarrhea for the first few hours, since it may be the body's way of helping to purge itself of an intestinal infection. If the diarrhea persists, use of a kaolin-pectin preparation (such as Kaopectate) or bismuth (such as Pepto-Bismol) is often enough to relieve it. Temporarily avoiding high-fiber foods may also help until a self-limited infection is resolved.

If these medications don't relieve the diarrhea promptly, or if there is fever, vomiting, abdominal pain, or blood in the stool, the patient should consult a doctor for evaluation, which may include rectal examination to exclude occult blood in the stool, sigmoidoscopy, and culture of the stool for bacteria and parasites. The physician may prescribe more potent medications, such as Lomotil, Immodium, or Paregoric, which primarily serve to relieve the symptoms.

Diarrhea is sometimes caused by antibiotics and, in this case, the physician may want to discontinue them. Some physicians prescribe yogurt or lactobacillus as a way of restoring the normal ecological balance of the intestines by replacing intestinal bacteria destroyed by the antibiotics.

fections involve both the small and large intestines; others are limited to one or the other.

2. Inflammation of the large or small intestine, as with ileitis, or colitis (see page 529).

3. Benign or malignant tumors that can either damage the cells of the intestine and thus impair absorption of nutrients or salts and water, or cause the intestines to actively secrete increased amounts of salt and water, as with rare tumors found in carcinoid syndrome and Zollinger-Ellison syndrome.

4. Medications, such as antibiotics, quinine and quinidine, and certain diuretics, as well as alcohol, that change the contractions of the intestine or change the bowel's normal intestinal flora or bacterial "ecological milieu."

5. Cystic fibrosis, chronic pancreatitis, and other diseases of the pancreas, an organ responsible for making digestive enzymes, can cause a decrease in enzyme formation which can in turn lead to diarrhea and malnutrition.

6. Hyperthyroidism and in some cases diabetes mellitus (which may also cause constipation).

In general, patients with diarrhea resulting primarily from small intestinal disease will have more significant malnutrition initially and less in the way of watery diarrhea, whereas patients with primarily large intestine disease will initially have dehydration and water and salt depletion, although malnutrition may occur later. For some people, stress can play a large role in exacerbating or causing diarrhea or even constipation. (See Intestinal Spasm.)

Rectal Bleeding

Most blood passed through the anus originates in the rectum or large intestine. The bleeding can sometimes be caused by local irritation of the anal area or by hemorrhoids, which is usually a simple matter to treat. (See Hemorrhoids, page 533.) However, rectal bleeding can be from other, more serious conditions, and therefore, most patients with rectal bleeding will need an evaluation to exclude other abnormalities of the small and large intestines. Generally this includes a physical exam, including a digital-rectal exam; a Hemocult test to check for hidden traces of blood in the stool; a proctosigmoidoscopy (with either a rigid or flexible fiberoptic instrument), and x-rays of the colon (a barium enema).

If the barium enema does not explain the bleeding or if it shows an abnormality in the large intestine with inflammatory, polypoid, or possibly malignant characteristics, further examination with a fiberoptic colonoscope will usually be done. This allows the gastroenterologist or colorectal surgeon to visualize the abnormality further, to take a biopsy

sample through the colonoscope and, in some cases, to remove polyps nonsurgically with the same instrument.

In cases of severe or unexplained rectal bleeding, an angiogram (arteriogram) or a nuclear scan of the blood vessels leading to the intestine and stomach may be helpful in identifying the site of bleeding. (For more information, see Chapter 4 on Diagnostic Tests and Procedures, page 55.)

Occasionally, rapid and vigorous bleeding from the rectum is the result of disease above the colon. This is often the case when the stool is very dark or black, representing breakdown products of blood. In such a situation, bleeding may originate from an abnormality of the stomach, duodenum, or small intestine. In this situation, evaluation may include an upper endoscopy, visualization of the stomach and duodenum using an instrument similar to a colonoscope, but swallowed, as well as x-rays, such as a gastrointestinal series and small bowel x-rays. (See Digestive System Tests in Chapter 4 on Diagnostic Tests and Procedures, page 58.)

New, nonsurgical methods using a colonoscope to treat bleeding that results from blood vessel malformations are now being studied.

Blockage of the Intestine

Generally, a patient with a sudden blockage (obstruction) of the colon will have a distended abdomen and decreased bowel function, often with no stools and no flatus for days. The digital rectal examination may show no stool in the rectum, suggesting a blockage above it, and an abdominal x-ray may show dilation of part of the intestine above the blockage. The immediate treatment of this acute blockage is intravenous therapy, and then prompt evaluation of the colon by means of a careful barium enema and, in some cases, a colonoscopy.

The blockage may be caused by a tumor, a stricture or diverticulosis, or a volulus (twisting of the intestine). If surgery is needed, the abnormalities may be removed or resected immediately, or a two-stage procedure may be used, in which the distended intestine is initially compressed by means of a colostomy or ileostomy, and then the abnormalities are removed in a second procedure after the inflammation has subsided.

In some cases, a blockage results from compression on the outside of the colon. This may be the result of adhesions—matting, pressing or looping together of internal structures—from a previous operation, such as an appendectomy or hysterectomy. Infections, gallbladder disease, and rare neurological and muscular disorders of the intestine can occasionally create symptoms of a blockage when there is none, a condition known as ileus or pseudo-obstruction.

Abdominal Gas

It is normal to have some gas pass through the rectum, although the amount varies from one person to another. Excess gas or flatus can come from a number of causes, including:

1. A diet high in fiber (fruits and vegetables), which leaves large amounts of unabsorbable materials, such as pectin and cellulose (the cell walls of these foods) in the intestines. Certain fruits and vegetables, such as beans, cucumbers, and pickles, may especially increase the amount of abdominal gas.

2. Swallowing air, as a result of anxiety or certain lung diseases in which patients hyperventilate.

3. Lactose intolerance (see page 515).

4. Gastrointestinal infections, which may lead to increased gas as a by-product of the bacteria.

5. Drinking excess beer or carbonated beverages, which may result in excess gas from the swallowed air in carbonation.

6. Fermentation by bacteria of nitrogenous and other waste products in the intestine may result in production of more than normal amounts of methane, nitrogen, and carbon dioxide, which may escape through the rectum.

A patient with excessive abdominal gas should be examined to exclude such serious causes as lactose intolerance, intestinal infection, or malabsorptive diseases. If none of these is present, the condition may be treated by substituting a polished bran such as Metamucil or Konsyl for fiber, as it is more readily absorbed, and the patient put on an otherwise low-fiber diet. Simethicone, an ingredient in some over-the-counter remedies, may break up gas bubbles, although the method is not fully understood. Decreasing intake of carbonated beverages and avoiding drinking through a straw may help some patients.

Gradual reintroduction of progressive amounts of fiber in the diet might start with well-cooked canned vegetables or canned fruit cup (low-fiber content) and then, if the patient is able to tolerate it, cooked frozen vegetables or peeled fruits, such as bananas (moderate fiber content). Finally, if additional fiber is desired, fresh vegetables or salads and fresh fruits, including the skin, may be added (high fiber content).

DISORDERS OF THE COLON

Crohn's Colitis

Crohn's disease produces chronic inflammation that may involve any part of the digestive tract, although it generally involves the lower small intestine and parts of the large intestine. (By definition, ileitis means that the ileum or lower small intestine is involved; colitis means that the large intestine is involved.) The patient with Crohn's disease will generally experience diarrhea, weight loss, and often abdominal pain, fever, and nausea. There may be problems in absorbing nutrients, which may lead to deficiencies of calcium, vitamin B_{12} and folic acid.

Patients with Crohn's disease sometimes have a family history of ileitis or colitis. Stress may also play a part in the disease but this link is not fully understood. The disease often begins before age 30 and may involve only 1 or 2 attacks or may recur every few months to every few years throughout life. Children sometimes experience ileitis and ileocolitis and may have few symptoms other than malnutrition and general failure to grow and develop.

The inflammation of Crohn's disease can be either contiguous or can involve different parts of the intestine, often sparing certain intervening parts, called "skip areas." Some patients with Crohn's colitis may have associated nondigestive abnormalities, such as pinkeye (uveitis), arthritislike joint pains, the presence of kidney stones or gallstones, and certain rare types of skin rashes.

Certain blood tests, including sedimentation rate and white blood count, may be helpful in diagnosing Crohn's disease. Generally, however, tests such as sigmoidoscopy, barium enema, colonoscopy, and barium x-rays of the upper gastrointestinal tract and small intestine are needed to make the diagnosis. Biopsy of the intestine via the colonoscope or sigmoidoscope may help confirm the diagnosis.

Crohn's disease can be treated medically with a drug called sulfasalazine (Azulfidine)—a combination of a sulfa antibiotic and an aspirin derivative taken in pill form. Prednisone, a type of steroid or cortisone derivative, can also be used, although there may be side effects with the long-term use of cortisone, including lowered resistance to infection, elevated blood sugar, occasional thinning of bones and skin, cataracts, and stomach ulcers. Because bacteria sometimes grow in large number in the intestines of Crohn's patients, these patients are sometimes given antibiotics as well. Nutritional deficiencies may need to be treated with supplements of iron, folic acid, vitamin B_{12}, and calcium. New anti-inflammatory and immunosuppressive medications are currently being tested for use in some cases.

Most Crohn's patients can be treated as outpatients, but in some cases, hospitalization for diagnostic testing, nutritional support, and intravenous therapy may be needed. If the patient does not respond to medical treatment, surgical removal of part of the intestine may be necessary. Since the disease may recur even after surgical removal of the abnormality, medical treatment is used whenever possible before surgery is considered. (For additional information, see Chapter 24 on Disorders of the Digestive System, page 517.)

Ulcerative Colitis

This disease is similar in some ways to Crohn's colitis (see previous section); in fact, in some patients it is difficult to differentiate between the two in diagnosing the condition. As with Crohn's, there is often a family history of either ileitis or colitis, the disease appears to be correlated in some cases with stress, and certain skin rashes, abnormalities of the gallbladder, and kidney stones are sometimes found.

In general, the inflammation with ulcerative colitis is continuous from the anus to a specific level of the large intestine (the level varies with the patient), whereas Crohn's may begin farther up the colon and spare the lower rectum. Ulcerative colitis, however, is generally limited to the colon and involvement of the small intestine is usually much less than that of Crohn's disease. Patients with ulcerative colitis tend to have more rectal bleeding and watery diarrhea and dehydration, but less severe malnutrition than those with Crohn's. The patient may have fever, anemia, and an elevated white blood count. Sigmoidoscopy shows redness and inflammation in the rectum.

A biopsy of the rectum (obtained through a sigmoidoscope or a colonoscope) may be helpful in confirming inflammation and in excluding infection, which can mimic both ulcerative colitis and Crohn's disease, as a cause. Stool specimens for special smear and culture analysis may be needed to exclude bacterial dysentery and parasitic infections.

Treatment of ulcerative colitis is similar to that for Crohn's—sulfasalazine (Azulfidine) or prednisone. A limited, less serious type of ulcerative colitis, called ulcerative proctitis, which involves only the lower few inches of the rectum, may respond to the use of topical cortisone suppositories, cortisone foam, or so-called "cortisone enemas." Patients with ulcerative colitis and Crohn's disease are often able to relieve symptoms somewhat with a modified low-fiber diet, in which case vitamin supplements may be needed.

Medical treatment is used whenever possible, but those few patients who continue to have severe diarrhea, bleeding, and anemia may require surgery to remove the diseased section of the intestine. In some cases, an operation is performed to create a hole, or stoma, in the abdominal wall, to which a bag is attached to collect waste materials that can no longer be passed through the anus. This procedure is called an ileostomy if it involves the ileum (the bottom part of the small intestine) or a colostomy if it involves the large intestine. New procedures are being developed to allow the two cut ends of the colon to be stitched together so that food passage and defecation remain relatively normal. Potential recurrence of colitis in the lower rectum, however, remains a concern.

Patients who have had ulcerative colitis involving most of the large intestine for at least 10 years, and especially those afflicted for more than 20 years, appear to be at risk for developing malignant tumors of the colon. Many physicians feel that these patients should be periodically screened by colonoscopy in conjunction with barium enema and colon biopsy as a way of detecting these tumors early should they develop, although there is some disagreement about the frequency and characteristics of this screening. Nevertheless, patients who have had ulcerative colitis for a number of years require close medical attention to watch for development of narrowing and tumors of the colon.

Spastic Colon (Irritable Colon or Intestinal Spasm)

This abnormality can affect both the small and large intestines, although it more often involves the large intestine. Instead of the normal, rhythmic contractions of the intestines that propel food and waste along, the contractions are irregular. The symptoms include cramplike abdominal pain, which is often relieved by belching or moving the bowels, although the bowel movements themselves may be painful. There is often constipation or diarrhea and, in some cases, constipation on some days and diarrhea on other days. Some patients will also have ulcer-type symptoms such as heartburn or upper abdominal indigestion. People often suffer with this condition for many years without seeking medical treatment and generally do not have signs of anemia, rectal bleeding, or weight loss.

The exact mechanism of spastic colon is not fully understood. Actually, there may be several different abnormalities lumped together under this category. Stress may play a role in some cases, and there is sometimes a family history of this condition.

In middle-aged or older patients where other diseases may be likely, diagnostic tests will usually include routine blood tests, barium x-rays and sigmoidoscopy, and tests for lactose tolerance or a trial of a lactose-free diet. Barium x-rays may not be necessary in teenagers or younger patients who show no signs of malnutrition, anemia, or bleeding, and who respond quickly to symptomatic treatment. In either case, the patient should be asked for a specific history of what foods or activities trigger the symptoms.

Stress in one form or another appears to play a significant role in many patients with intestinal spasm. The specific mechanism is not yet defined, but so-called abnormal motility (too vigorous or impaired contractions of the intestine) appears to play a role, often in conjunction with upper gastrointestinal symptoms such as heartburn, and acid-related stomach pains. Reduction of stress, supervised exercise when the physician feels it is safe, and rest may be helpful. Overwork, emotional stress, financial or family problems, or such events as a new job may bring on a recurrence of symptoms.

Treatment may vary greatly from one patient to another and often requires close cooperation between the doctor and patient. It may include the use of brans such as polished psyllium (e.g., Metamucil, Konsyl, or Hydrocil) or a high-fiber diet and exercise (which may increase bowel function). For other patients, a low-fiber diet may be needed, particularly if the patient has primarily diarrhea. Medications such as antispasmodic drugs combined with mild sedatives and atropinelike substances may be helpful in decreasing the contractions of the intestine. These include Donnatal, Librax, Bentyl, and Combid.

Diverticulosis

Some patients, as they get older, develop diverticulosis—pouches of the colon that can occasionally become acutely inflamed (a condition known as diverticulitis), causing abdominal pain and accompanied by fever. (See figure 25.2.) In such patients, the acute attack may be improved by a low-fiber diet, a liquid diet, antibiotics, bed rest or hospitalization, or a combination of these. Long-term treatment of patients with noninflamed diverticulosis often involves a moderate increase in the consumption of bran or fiber, although nuts, popcorn, raisins, seeded grapes, and other foods with pits may need to be avoided, since they can lodge in the diverticular pouches and cause inflammation.

It appears that many patients with diverticulosis have associated spastic colon. The diagnosis is generally made by barium enema and sigmoidoscopy and, in some cases, colonoscopy. The majority of patients with diverticulosis do not require surgery, but a few with recurrent attacks of bleeding or severe inflammation may require removal of part of the intestine.

Appendicitis

The appendix is an extension of the cecum (the beginning of the large intestine) in the lower right side of the abdomen. No definite function has been found as yet for the appendix, which is composed of lym-

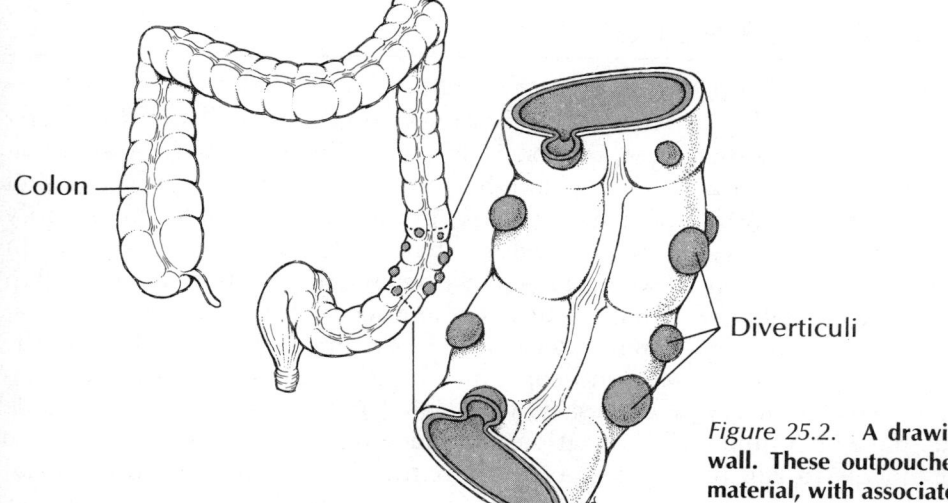

Colon

Diverticuli

Figure 25.2. **A drawing showing diverticuli along the colon wall. These outpouches sometimes become filled with fecal material, with associated infection (diverticulitis).**

phoid tissue and thus may be involved in making antibodies. For reasons not fully understood, the appendix sometimes becomes inflamed and fills with pus, resulting in appendicitis, which generally affects children, teenagers, or young adults. The initial symptom is pain, which generally starts in the upper abdomen and then moves to the lower right part of the abdomen. Other symptoms may include nausea and vomiting, constipation, and fever. There is often an elevated white blood count. Appendicitis may mimic various infections, gynecologic conditions such as a ruptured ovarian cyst or an infection of a Fallopian tube, or Crohn's colitis.

The standard treatment of appendicitis is prompt surgical removal, sometimes accompanied by antibiotics. If the appendix ruptures into the abdomen, peritonitis sets in and the operation may become an emergency procedure.

INTESTINAL INFECTIONS

PEOPLE WHO TRAVEL to areas where there is endemic infection or who contract intestinal infections from contaminated food may develop fever, diarrhea, and intestinal cramps. Many of these appear to be viruses that are self-limited and can be treated symptomatically with a low-fiber diet and such antidiarrheal medications as kaolin and pectin (Kaopectate), or bismuth (Pepto-Bismol).

In some cases, the doctor may order special tests, such as cultures of the stool, to check for bacterial dysentery or to exclude salmonella, shigella, and campylobacter. E. coli is a recently discovered bacterial infection that often causes "travelers' diarrhea." A patient may sometimes contract a diarrheal illness from a pet bird or dog. In some cases, antibiotics are needed to treat such infections. In addition, a patient who develops a type of dysentery may need to have people living in his or her household also see a physician to be tested for an infection.

Parasite infections, including giardiasis and amebiasis, are common and may cause a variety of digestive illnesses. These parasites may be passed by food handlers or through sexual or other close contact. They are usually diagnosed by testing the stool. In some cases, blood tests, such as an amoebic antibody test, may be helpful in diagnosing amebiasis. Aspiration of fluids from the small intestine may be needed to diagnose giardiasis. Since amoebic dysentery can sometimes mimic colitis, sigmoidoscopy and rectal biopsy may help distinguish amoebic dysentery from colitis. Treatment with special antibiotics may be necessary. Anyone planning a trip to an area where there may be contaminated water or disease should consult his or her physician first for guidelines on dietary treatment. In general, when traveling to an endemic area, it is best to avoid eating unwashed or uncooked fruits or vegetables and to use bottled water rather than local water. It may be wise to take along a bismuth medication, such as Pepto-Bismol, or antibiotics to use, but this should be discussed with the physician. Travelers may want to ask their family doctor for suggestions on doctors or hospitals in the areas they plan to visit. (Also see Chapter 21 on Infectious Diseases, page 440.)

GROWTHS OF THE LARGE INTESTINE

Polyps

These are small, mushroomlike abnormalities of the intestine that may have a stalk or be flat without a stalk and can vary from under 2 millimeters (less than $\frac{1}{10}$ of an inch) to over 2 inches in diameter. (See figure 25.3.) There are several different types of polyps, as well as pseudo-polyps—areas of inflammation associated with colitis.

Patients with polyps may have rectal bleeding or signs of blood in the stool when tested chemically (as with a Hemocult card), or may have abdominal pain. There is some tendency for polyps to run in families, and a patient who develops one colon polyp may be likely to develop colon polyps in the future.

Diagnosis is primarily made with a sigmoidoscopy and barium enema. With newer types of barium x-rays, physicians are able to identify smaller polyps than were identified years ago. In some cases, however, the diagnosis of a small polyp may require a colonoscopy. Many polyps can be removed with a tiny instrument threaded through the colonoscope, making more complicated surgery unnecessary. Occasional risks of colonoscopy include perforation and bleeding of the intestine, but these risks have been reduced with advances in technical design of the colonoscope. Some polyps, such as those that are very large or without a stalk, cannot be removed via a colonoscope. In these cases, the section of the colon containing the polyp may have to be surgically removed.

Generally, the larger the polyp, the greater the chance that it will be malignant. Very tiny polyps have a very small risk of malignancy. Recent research suggests, however, that all but the very smallest polyps should be removed, since some polyps will grow, develop malignant features, and bleed. Adenomatous and villous polyps appear more likely to be linked to malignancy than do hyperplastic polyps.

Patients with a history of colon polyps need regular close follow-up by a physician. There is some difference of opinion on how often this follow-up should be scheduled and what it should include, but

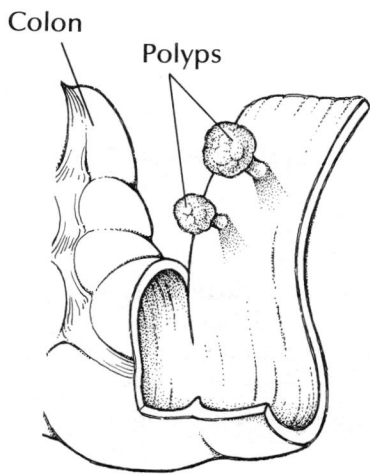

Figure 25.3. **Intestinal polyps are mushroomlike growths that form along the colon wall.**

many specialists recommend an annual digital rectal examination and test of the stool for blood (Hemocult), as well as periodic sigmoidoscopy and barium enema and, in some cases, colonoscopy. The patient's physician will usually base the decision about barium enema versus colonoscopy on the patient's age and overall health. Close relatives should also be seen on a regular basis and have rectal exams, stool tests for blood, and periodic sigmoidoscopy as well.

Cancer

Colorectal cancer is a major form of cancer in the United States. Many colon cancer patients who are diagnosed early (using the various screening tests mentioned previously) have a good prognosis. Symptoms that may first alert a physician to the possible diagnosis include history of prior colon cancer, occult blood in the stool, unexplained anemia, overt rectal bleeding, unexplained weight loss or abdominal pain, or a change in bowel habits, such as constipation or progressive thinness in the caliber (diameter) of stools. In general, colon cancer is treated by surgical removal of part of the large intestine, preceded by blood tests and diagnostic x-rays and scans to see if the tumor has spread (metastasized) beyond the colon. Additional treatment such as chemotherapy depends on the stage of the tumor (whether or not it has metastasized, or spread). Now under study are methods of removing very early (superficial) tumors of the colon through the colonoscope or sigmoidoscope, especially in elderly patients who might not tolerate major operations well. (For more information, see Chapter 20 on Cancer, page 409.)

DISORDERS OF THE RECTUM

Hemorrhoids

These are defined as the abnormal enlargement of what are otherwise normal veins in the anal area. (See figure 25.4.) They are often caused by increased pressure at the time of defecation, as is found in people with constipation or obesity or during pregnancy. Hemorrhoids are occasionally also found in patients with liver disease, such as cirrhosis, because of increased pressure in the veins of the intestine.

Hemorrhoids can cause bleeding, but often this appears as fresh, red blood on the toilet tissue when wiping, rather than as darker blood mixed with the stool. In most patients, because of the possibility of a more serious condition, rectal bleeding should not be ascribed to hemorrhoids without further investigation. The diagnosis may involve anoscopy, in which a small plastic or metal instrument called an anoscope is inserted into the lower few inches of the rectum to allow the doctor to detect the presence of hemorrhoids and associated local inflammation (cryptitis). Sigmoidoscopy and barium enema may be needed to look farther up to rule out other diseases that cause bleeding or rectal pain.

Medical treatment of hemorrhoids involves various methods to reduce the chances of flare-ups and

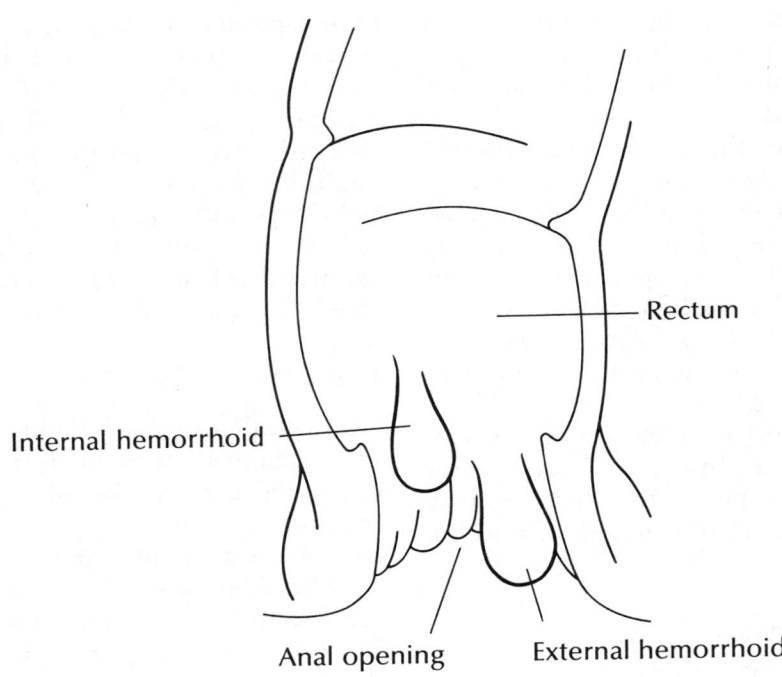

Figure 25.4. **A cross section of the lower rectum showing both internal and external hemorrhoids.**

to soothe inflammation and itching if flare-ups occur. These may include increasing the intake of liquids to prevent the stool from getting too hard or from getting impacted; the use of stool softeners, such as Colace, or bran (Metamucil); warm baths to soothe the anal area; weight loss to reduce straining at the stool; and local use of soothing creams and suppositories. Creams and suppositories containing cortisone may be used occasionally, but only under the supervision of a physician. Any medication used during pregnancy, when hemorrhoids may flare up, should be checked with the woman's physician first.

If the hemorrhoids don't respond to medical treatment, surgery by a gastrointestinal or colorectal surgeon may be required, although this is less common than many years ago. Surgical treatment may involve using rubber bands to ligate, or tie off, the hemorrhoid; injecting a chemical into a hemorrhoid to sclerose it (encourage the growth of fibrous tissue that keeps blood from flowing into it); or removing a clot from a hemorrhoid surgically. In rare cases, removal of the entire hemorrhoid (a hemorrhoidectomy) may be needed.

Anal Fissure

An anal fissure—a shallow, thin ulcer of the anal canal—can result from passage of large, hard stools or may be secondary to anal surgery, proctitis, or other diseases. Since the surface of the skin at the anus has been worn away, defecation irritates the fissure and may cause the sphincter muscles to go into spasm, resulting in intense pain. Fissures are often associated with constipation or stool that is inadequately emptied, and may be associated with stress or hemorrhoids.

The fissure can usually be seen by the physician on examination, although anoscopy may be used to confirm the findings. Treatment involves stool softeners, addition to the diet of brans such as Metamucil, warm baths, and topical creams. Surgery is generally not needed but is reserved for severe cases. After the fissure has healed, which may take 2 to 3 weeks, a sigmoidoscopy may be performed to exclude other conditions of the rectum.

Anal Fistula

A fistula is an abnormal opening to the skin, in this case generally from the intestine itself, through which watery pus drains, irritating the skin and causing itching and discomfort. It may occur after inflammation (as from Crohn's colitis), and occasionally in association with diverticulosis or rectal infection or abscess.

Sigmoidoscopy may be necessary to exclude inflammation or underlying rectal disease. Treatment is similar to that for hemorrhoids, and involves local hygiene (such as use of clean moist pads to wipe away stool at the time of defecation), as well as stool softeners, bran, warm baths, and topical creams. In some cases, topical or systemic antibiotics may be needed. Surgery is sometimes recommended and may be curative, but there can be recurrences, especially when the fistula has been caused by Crohn's disease.

SUMMING UP

THE LOWER INTESTINAL TRACT continues the digestive process that begins when food is chewed, swallowed, and then initially broken down in the stomach and small intestine. The large intestine solidifies the waste materials so that they can be eliminated from the body.

Maintaining the health of the lower digestive tract is largely dependent on eating a balanced diet with enough natural fiber to maintain regular elimination habits and on being vigilant about signs, such as rectal bleeding, or change in bowel habits, that may indicate the presence of anything from easily treated hemorrhoids to more complex disorders, such as diverticulosis, polyps, and colon cancer. More sophisticated diagnostic tools, such as the colonoscope, than were available in the past allow physicians to diagnose these disorders more easily and earlier, with the goal of better prognosis.

26 Blood Disorders

Arthur Bank, M.D.

INTRODUCTION

WHEN PATIENTS are told by physicians that they have abnormal blood tests, they usually envision leukemia or other serious diseases. With our ever-widening use of blood tests, there is an increased likelihood that any single test may be abnormal, but the odds are small that an unusual result is due to a serious disorder. More likely, it represents a value (result) a bit outside the normal range or reflects a relatively minor condition.

The most common blood abnormalities are not serious. They may be reactions of the body to infections or deficiencies, and they are treatable. There are diseases that are malignant, severe, and life-threatening, but even among these there are many that, if properly treated, can result in long survival and even cure.

THE BLOOD AND ITS COMPONENTS

TEN AND ONE-HALF PINTS of blood circulate constantly through the body of the average adult, bringing to each cell the oxygen, nutrients, and chemical substances necessary for its proper functioning and,

at the same time, removing waste products.

The blood consists of 2 basic parts: the formed cells, or corpuscles, and the fluid plasma in which they are carried. Blood cells are formed in the bone

536

marrow, found in cavities within many bones throughout the body, but primarily in the flat bones, such as the ribs and the breastbone, or sternum. On occasion, blood cells can be produced where no bone exists, such as in the liver, spleen, and lymph nodes. Blood production in these extramedullary sites is normal in fetal life, but distinctly abnormal after birth.

Most blood cells are red cells, or erythrocytes, and their major function is to carry oxygen from the lungs to other parts of the body. Their red color comes from the pigment hemoglobin, which combines with oxygen and carries it in the blood. Red cells are smaller than white cells and they live about 120 days.

The oxygen carried by hemoglobin and released to the cells of various tissues is used for the cells' energy-producing processes, vital to the continued function of the tissues and organs. For example, when the body exerts a large amount of energy, such as during running, it uses up oxygen rapidly and the muscle cells begin to accumulate acidic substances. To compensate, breathing becomes more rapid in order to increase oxygen intake and the heart beats faster to pump the blood throughout the body. The tissues receive more oxygen, and this reverses the buildup of the acidic substances.

For every 500 red cells in the circulating blood, there is a white cell, or leukocyte. The white blood cells, of which there are 5 different types, are the body's main defense against disease and a wide variety of foreign invaders. The major type of white cell used to fight infection is called the granulocyte, so named because it contains granules. The granulocytes are stored primarily in the bone marrow and released into the bloodstream rapidly and in large numbers in response to infection, foreign substances, trauma, or tissue damage. In contrast to the red blood cells, the granulocytes live a very short time in the circulating blood and are rapidly destroyed in the process of doing their work.

Another type of white blood cell is the lymphocyte, which forms antibodies and provides specific immunologic defenses against foreign antigens. Specialized lymphocytes are stored primarily in the lymph glands, part of the lymphatic system which drains wastes from the skin and other tissues of the body and provides protection of the body against foreign substances and bacteria. The swollen glands that sometimes accompany a sore throat are caused by a proliferation of lymphocytes and are an example of the response of the lymph node system to an infection. The lymphocytes produced and stored in the lymph nodes circulate in the blood, and then recirculate through the lymph nodes. Many of these cells are extremely long lived, and contain "biochemical memories" of exposure of the body to various foreign substances, allowing them to combat these substances rapidly if they return. (For more information, see Chapter 32 on Allergies, page 638.)

Smaller still than the red blood cells are the platelets, colorless disks that are actually not cells at all, but fragments of a type of cell called a megakaryocyte. Together with the blood vessel walls and substances in the plasma called coagulation factors, platelets form the body's blood-clotting mechanism. They are the major protection of the body against continued bleeding when a blood vessel is damaged or severed. Platelets disintegrate as part of the clotting process; otherwise, they live an average of 10 days.

Plasma is a yellowish fluid in which all of these cells are suspended. It also contains chemicals like salts, various proteins, antibodies, and blood-clotting factors.

DIAGNOSING BLOOD DISORDERS

EXAMINING THE BLOOD under a microscope reveals myriad conditions, not only possible blood disorders, but also diseases of various organs of the body. These conditions can be as diverse as a bacterial infection with a high granulocyte count or a cancer of the colon first suspected because of an iron deficiency anemia. Blood samples for diagnostic tests are collected from a vein in the arm in a procedure known as a venipuncture and can be used for a number of tests, the most common of which are the blood counts.

The routine blood counts include a measurement of the red blood cells—either their precise number, as in a red blood count (RBC), or their relative number, which is reflected in two ways. It can be given as the amount of blood cells per total volume of blood, which is known as the hematocrit (HCT), or the amount of hemoglobin present in a given amount of blood, which is known as the hemoglobin concentration (HGB). The RBC, HCT, and HGB all look at the same factor: the number of hemoglobin-carrying red blood cells present in a sample of blood. A significant decrease in the RBC (or the HCT or the HGB) is known as anemia, and

BLOOD TYPES

In each person's blood are a specific and inheritable set of antigens, or cell proteins, on the surface of each red blood cell and another set of antibodies in the plasma, or liquid portion of the blood. If samples of 2 incompatible types of blood are mixed, the antibodies of one will cause the red cells of the other to clump together, or agglutinate.

Blood types have been classified in several ways, but the best known system is the ABO blood group system, which divides blood into 4 types: A, B, AB, and O. In the United States, 45 percent of the population is type O; 40 percent is type A; 10 percent is type B; and 5 percent is type AB.

Individuals with type A blood have A antigens on their red cells and antibodies against type B antigens in their plasma, while those in type B have B antigens on their cells and antibodies against group A in their plasma. Those with AB have both A and B antigens on their cells but no antibodies in their plasma, so they can receive any type of blood, and are known as universal recipients. Those with type O have neither A nor B antigens on their cells, so their blood will not be agglutinated by any recipient's antibodies. Thus, they are known as universal donors. On the other hand, they have both A and B antibodies in their plasma and can receive only O type blood.

Another major classification system is the Rhesus system, which divides each of the ABO blood types into either Rh positive or Rh negative, depending on whether a so-called Rhesus antigen or factor is present in the red cells. Blood with the factor (Rh positive) is by far the more common, accounting for 85 percent of all blood. (For more information about the Rhesus factor, see Chapter 11 on Pregnancy and Birth, page 170.)

A person's blood type is not particularly important unless he or she needs a transfusion, in which case it is crucial that the transfused blood be of the same type. Mismatched blood can cause agglutination of the red cells and lead to serious complications.

can reflect a variety of diseases affecting the entire body, as well as those localized to the blood system.

The white blood count (WBC) is another routine test. Changes in the WBC reflect the presence of infection or, on occasion, the presence of diseases affecting the blood forming system or other systems of the body. Thus, the WBC can be a mirror of disease in one of many organs. Likewise, elevations or depressions of the platelet count can reflect diseases of the blood system per se, or disorders of other organs that result in abnormalities in the blood. Certain infections cause increases in the number of platelets, while others cause decreases.

The values obtained in the blood counts are often useful to physicians in determining whether a patient is sick, and they provide clues as to which particular system of the body is affected. A normal blood count is reassuring, since it indicates no significant defects in these cells and will rule out such disorders as leukemia, severe anemia, and coagulation abnormalities. On the other hand, many diseases, such as cancer, heart disease, high blood pressure, and degenerative disorders, may show no significant changes in the level of the blood counts.

Other blood tests record the time it takes a sample to clot, which may indicate deficiencies of the blood coagulation factors, and the rate at which red cells in a blood sample settle to the bottom of a glass tube (erythrocyte sedimentation rate), which may be useful in determining whether or not something is wrong with a patient, but not in diagnosing a particular condition. The remainder of the tests commonly performed on the blood are indications not of blood disorders but of other disease conditions. They measure the chemicals that circulate in the plasma, including electrolytes, such as sodium and potassium; other metal ions in the blood, such as calcium; and certain proteins that reflect diseases of the kidney, liver, and less often, other organs.

Bone Marrow Examination

The other major type of blood test is a bone marrow examination. The bone marrow is normally an intricately regulated organ system in which red blood cell production is balanced with normal needs, white blood cell production and release is tightly controlled, and the production of platelets is closely managed by the need for platelets for coagulation. Abnormalities in bone marrow function may be indicative of anemia or infection or of more serious diseases, including leukemia and other forms of cancer. For routine bone marrow examination, done under local anesthesia, a long, thin needle is inserted into the pelvis or sternum (breastbone) and a small amount of marrow fluid is withdrawn (aspirated) for microscopic examination. It is a simple procedure that can be performed in an office; in the hands of a skilled operator it is virtually painless.

Often, a bone marrow biopsy—removal of a small core of bone and marrow—is performed at the same time as bone marrow aspiration. The biopsy provides additional useful information regarding possible abnormalities in the bone marrow.

DISORDERS OF THE RED BLOOD CELLS

THE MOST COMMON DISORDER of the red blood cells is anemia, which can vary from mild to severe. Anemia results when the amount of hemoglobin in the blood is less than is needed to carry oxygen to all the cells of the body. There are several ways in which anemia can occur. Since iron is needed to create hemoglobin, an inadequate supply of it will lead to an underproduction of hemoglobin and thus to iron-deficiency anemia. Or the body may produce hemoglobin that is defective, which happens in such inherited disorders as sickle cell anemia. Since hemoglobin is transported in red blood cells, anemia may result from an underproduction of these cells. This can be caused by a lack of vitamin B_{12}, in which case the disorder is called pernicious anemia, or by a lack of folic acid. Underproduction of cells may also result from invasion of the bone marrow by cancer, leukemia, or lymphoma, or destruction of bone marrow cells by drugs or unknown elements.

Finally, the red blood cells may be produced at a normal rate, but broken down (hemolyzed) too quickly, a condition that leads to hemolytic anemia. Hemolytic anemias may be caused by the presence of antibodies in the blood resulting from infections, drugs, or a variety of inherited conditions, such as sickle cell anemia or thalassemia.

Regardless of the cause, the symptoms of anemia are usually the same: weakness and general fatigue, and in more severe instances, palpitations and shortness of breath—first on exertion and then at rest. Pallor or paleness of not only the skin, but also the gums, eyes, and nailbeds, is another common symptom. In hemolytic anemia, there may be jaundice of the skin and whites of the eyes. In severe cases, there may be actual heart failure or chest pain due to cardiac disease induced by the anemia. Most often, with mild to moderate anemias, weakness and fatigue are the major manifestations. Anemia is only a sign of disease and the underlying condition causing the anemia must be determined by other blood tests, as well as a physical examination and a detailed patient history.

Iron-Deficiency Anemia

Iron kept in reserve in the bone marrow, liver, and spleen is used by the body to manufacture hemoglobin. This iron is replenished when foods are eaten that contain large amounts of the mineral, and also when the red blood cells break down and the iron in them is recycled.

A lack of iron reserves, most commonly caused by bleeding, can lead to iron-deficiency anemia. This disorder occurs much more often in women than in men and is due primarily to menstrual bleeding, either normal or abnormal. Even normal menstruation can deplete the body of iron reserves over a period of months, but the problem is usually corrected easily with iron supplements. Routine use of iron supplements now prevents most cases of anemia during pregnancy, once a common problem. Iron deficiency anemia is not a disease per se, but instead a complex of symptoms. A specific cause for iron-deficiency anemia should be sought in all cases except for menstruating or pregnant women.

Blood loss also commonly occurs from the gastrointestinal tract. This bleeding can sometimes be detected by bowel movements that are black or tarry or that contain red blood, but it also can be occult (hidden) and asymptomatic. The blood loss may be from a peptic ulcer, polyp of the colon, or from cancer of the stomach or intestine. Occasionally, bleeding from hemorrhoids is severe enough to cause anemia. Significant blood loss from the urinary tract or from the respiratory tract is very unusual and not often the cause of a significant anemia. Blood loss from an injury rarely causes anemia. Treatment for the underlying causes of iron-deficiency anemia may be simple or complex, depending on the specific condition—an ulcer must be treated; a cancer removed. The resulting anemia usually can be treated simply with iron supplements taken orally for 12 months not only to correct the anemia, but to replenish the body's iron stores.

Inadequate iron reserves may, on rare occasion, be due to insufficient iron in the diet, but this occurs primarily in young children, and in the elderly, who may be on economically restricted diets. It can often be corrected by increasing the intake of such foods as meats and dark green leafy vegetables. (See Chapter 16 on the Fundamentals of Health, page 293.)

Pernicious Anemia

Pernicious anemia is caused by a deficiency of vitamin B_{12}, which is necessary for production of all cells in the body. Since B_{12} is readily available in meats and easily stored in the liver, most healthy people other than strict vegetarians have a 3- to 5-year reserve in their bodies. Thus, a deficiency is usually caused by a failure to absorb the vitamin through the digestive tract. People with this deficiency often lack a substance called intrinsic factor, normally secreted by the stomach. Alternatively, they may have had part of the stomach or intestine surgically removed, or a small segment of the intestine called the ileum may be diseased.

In addition to the usual symptoms of anemia, this condition often produces loss of appetite and weight, intermittent constipation and diarrhea, abdominal pain, and a swollen or burning tongue. There may be some neurologic involvement, evidenced by tingling sensations in the hands and feet, difficulty in balance, and lack of coordination. There may also be mild depression, irritability, and confusion.

Pernicious anemia can be treated by intramuscular injections of vitamin B_{12}, several times a week in the beginning and less often as reserves begin to build up in the liver. Eventually, a patient can receive injections once a month, but they must be continued throughout life. Although many of the symptoms will begin to disappear shortly after the injections are begun, neural improvement can take many months.

Anemia Due to Folic Acid Deficiency

Anemia caused by a deficiency of folic acid (a B vitamin) is almost always due to poor diet, and is usually seen in patients whose alcohol intake is high (since alcohol interferes with metabolism of the vitamin). It can, however, also occur in patients with cancer, celiac disease (a malabsorption problem), and other disorders. The deficiency can be corrected with a change in diet and folic acid supplements, either injected or given orally. Because anemia due to folic acid deficiency looks just like pernicious anemia but requires different treatment, careful diagnostic tests must be performed to distinguish between the two.

Hemolytic Anemia

If the red blood cells are broken down (hemolyzed) at a faster rate than normal, before they can be replaced, hemolytic anemia may result. Sometimes, this is due to a hereditary condition called spherocytosis, in which the red blood cells are small and round (spherocytic), but it may also be caused by the presence of antibodies in the blood which attack the red cells, drugs taken for other conditions, or a variety of inherited disorders, such as sickle cell anemia and thalassemia.

Hemolytic anemia has the same symptoms as other anemias and may also produce jaundice. This is because the breakdown of the red blood cells releases hemoglobin that is converted into the pigment bilirubin, which turns the tissues of the skin and whites of the eyes yellow. The spleen, which is where most red blood cells are normally destroyed,

may become enlarged from an overaccumulation of cells and can be detected on physical examination of the upper left part of the abdomen. Signs of heart failure and an enlarged liver may indicate that the anemia is severe. In some cases, particularly hereditary spherocytosis, removal of the spleen (splenectomy) may produce a cure. In others, the liver and other phagocytic cells may destroy the abnormal red cells after splenectomy.

Glucose-6-Phosphate Dehydrogenase Deficiency

This enzyme deficiency of the red blood cells, known as G6PD, is a sex-linked inherited disorder that, like hemolytic anemia, causes the premature breakdown of red blood cells. It affects about 10 percent of black males in this country, a smaller number of black females and, to a lesser degree, a variety of Caucasian ethnic groups. A number of drugs, from sulfa drugs to more exotic substances, such as antimalarials, as well as viral and bacterial infections, can precipitate a hemolytic process, resulting in anemia in individuals who have this deficiency. Since the hemolysis only affects older cells, the disease is relatively self-limiting, especially in blacks. Nevertheless, the offending drugs should be identified and avoided if possible. In Caucasians, the disease can be more serious.

Aplastic Anemia

Aplastic anemia is a relatively rare disease in which the marrow does not function normally and the production of all blood cells is drastically reduced. In primary aplastic anemia, the cause is unknown and it is difficult to treat. Secondary aplasia is more common, although still rare, and is generally caused by drugs or toxic substances. Chemical agents such as benzene and arsenic can cause the problem, as can exposure to radiation or many of the chemotherapeutic drugs used in cancer treatment.

Aplastic anemia generally develops slowly and its symptoms depend on which cells are affected. A decrease in red cell production brings on the usual symptoms of anemia, while a decrease in white cells results in susceptibility to infections, and a decrease in platelets increases the chances of spontaneous bruising and bleeding.

The most common treatment is transfusion of whole blood to sustain life until the marrow begins to function again. This is usually accompanied by antibiotics to combat infection. In patients under age 40, bone marrow transplantation is very useful if a compatible donor is available. If the aplasia is caused by a toxic agent, its removal may be enough to bring about a recovery. The prognosis varies, depending upon the underlying cause. Those of unknown origin (idiopathic) have a poorer prognosis, and about half of those patients with severe anemia succumb to bleeding or infection within a year.

Sickle Cell Anemia

Sickle cell anemia is an inherited hemoglobin disorder that affects blacks primarily. Children who inherit the sickle cell gene from one parent are said to have sickle cell trait, but will not develop the disease. In areas of the world where malaria is common, these children actually tend to survive better than those without the trait, leading geneticists to believe that sickle cell was an adaptational response to the tropical disease.

Children who inherit the sickle cell gene from both parents have predominantly sickle cell hemoglobin which causes the red cells to become deformed, actually taking on a sickle shape when they are deprived of oxygen. These children may suffer anemia ranging from mild to severe. In addition, they are prone to painful sickle cell crises, which happen during the normal passage of red blood cells through the smallest blood vessels in the body, the capillaries. Once they have given up the oxygen to the body's tissues, the red cells tend to sickle and then occlude the small blood vessels. This in turn prevents additional oxygen from reaching the tissue or organ, causing more sickling, damage, and pain. These crises tend to occur during infections, but they can also happen in the absence of other disease.

Although sickle cell anemia varies greatly in severity, it is a serious illness for which there is no cure. Death can occur during an acute crisis due to a severe infection or to damage to a vital organ. More often, crises are repetitive and patients have a shortened life span secondary to chronic organ damage. Blacks who are known to have sickle trait in their families are usually advised to seek genetic counseling before or early in pregnancy, since sickle cell anemia can be diagnosed prior to birth.

Thalassemia

The thalassemia syndromes are another group of anemias that are inherited. They are found most often in people of Mediterranean background, although there are cases in most areas of the world. Like sickle cell trait, thalassemia trait can be inherited from one parent (which is generally not serious) or both parents, when it is called thalassemia major. Statistically, the chances are 1 in 4 that a child will inherit the thalassemia gene from both parents if they are carriers.

There are 2 main types of thalassemia, known as alpha and beta. In rare cases, if the severe form of alpha trait is inherited from both parents, the result can be death of the fetus, a condition that is most prevalent in Southeast Asia. Blacks with alpha-thalassemia trait essentially never have the severe form.

If the beta trait is inherited from both parents, it usually results in a severe, eventually fatal condition called Cooley's anemia. Children with this condition need repeated blood transfusions, which leads to the buildup of iron in the body, resulting in damage to the liver, heart failure, and death in the teens or early twenties.

Fortunately, there have been many exciting advances in recent years in the understanding of the thalassemias, and several new approaches to therapy. These include the use of iron chelaters, chemical substances capable of binding the excess iron and removing it from the body. The chelating agent is most effectively administered by a mechanical pump that pumps the agent underneath the skin while the child is asleep. Still in the experimental stage are techniques such as bone marrow transplantation and transfer of genes into cells to actually correct the genetic defect.

Polycythemia Vera

Polycythemia vera is a blood disorder that usually results in an increase in all blood cells, with the red cells being the most severely affected. This increase makes the blood more viscous, meaning it will not flow through the blood vessels as easily, and this can lead to strokes or damage to a variety of tissues and organs.

In diagnosing polycythemia vera, the physician must distinguish it from other conditions in which the blood count is increased. For example, certain cardiopulmonary diseases can reduce the amount of oxygen that reaches the tissues. To compensate, the body increases the number of red blood cells that carry this oxygen. This also happens to people who live at high altitudes, where there is less oxygen in the air they breathe. Certain tumors, especially those of the cerebellum, the kidney, liver, and ovaries, can also cause an increased number of red cells, and this is known as erythremia or secondary polycythemia.

In polycythemia vera, there may be an increase in just the red cells, in both the red and white cells, or even in the red cells, white cells, and the platelets as well. An increase in the number of platelets due to any cause can result in clotting or, paradoxically, to increased bleeding. Physical signs of polycythemia vera include headaches, dizziness, shortness of breath, difficulty in concentration, night sweats, a flushed complexion, and itchy skin, especially after a hot bath. Usually the spleen becomes enlarged and there may be attacks of gout. Occasionally, there may be no symptoms at all.

Polycythemia vera can be treated in several ways. If only the red blood cells are affected, then removing blood (by venesection or phlebotomy) is the most common treatment. If the red blood cells, white cells, and platelets are increased, radioactive phosphorus treatments or chemotherapy may be used.

DISORDERS OF THE WHITE BLOOD CELLS

SINCE THE PRIMARY FUNCTION of white blood cells is to protect the body against disease, an increase in production of these cells can be a normal, benign response. Bacterial infections are the major cause of an increase in the number of granulocytes (specialized white cells). Burns, poisons, drug reactions, excessive strenuous exercise, and heart attacks are a few of the other conditions that can increase the number of granulocytes. The increase in the white blood count may also be accompanied by other symptoms of the underlying condition, such as fatigue, weakness, fever, sweating, weight loss, and lack of appetite. Unfortunately, these symptoms are also commonly seen with certain malignant disorders such as acute leukemia, chronic leukemia, lymphoma, and other forms of cancer, and it is a challenge for the hematologist and internist to distinguish between these and benign conditions.

Infectious Mononucleosis

One of the disorders occasionally confused with acute leukemia is a benign condition called infectious mononucleosis (a disease associated with the Epstein-Barr virus) which can present many of the same symptoms. "Mono," as it is sometimes called, occurs primarily in the young and its common symptoms include fatigue, weakness, sore throat, fever, weight loss, enlarged lymph nodes, and an enlarged spleen. To complicate things further, many of these symptoms are also present in cases of infectious hepatitis, another viral disorder.

In infectious mononucleosis, there is usually no anemia or decreased numbers of platelets, while in acute leukemia, these abnormalities are relatively common. Special antibody tests can differentiate between the two. Another distinguishing finding is the presence of characteristic atypical lymphocytes in the bloodstream in mononucleosis.

Leukemia

Normally, the number of white blood cells in the body remains constant, since the number of new ones produced equals the number that die. In leukemia, the white cells produced continually multiply, even though they are not needed, spreading through the body and interfering with body functions.

There are actually 2 types of leukemia: acute and chronic. In the former, a group of immature blood cells called blast cells is usually present in great numbers, and in the latter, mature cells are equally elevated. Leukemic cells can crowd out the normal bone marrow elements, often producing symptoms throughout the body. The red cells are decreased and anemia results; the number of normal white cells decreases and infection results; the megakaryocytes and platelets are decreased and bleeding occurs.

Acute leukemia, which accounts for about half of all leukemia cases, is diagnosed by a bone marrow aspiration (see page 54) that shows an increased number of blast cells. It progresses very rapidly and, without treatment, can result in death in 2 to 4 months, or even weeks. Even with treatment, the long-term prognosis, especially for adults, is not good. Some forms of childhood acute leukemia, however, can be successfully eradicated in close to 50 percent of cases.

Chronic leukemia usually develops more insidiously, over a period of years. It generally affects adults and its prognosis is better than that of acute leukemia; frequently patients with this type of leukemia live many years. In chronic leukemia, the cells in the circulating blood may be almost entirely normal, but the total number of white cells is high: often 100,000 to 200,000 or more per cubic millimeter of blood, instead of the normal number of about 5,000 to 10,000 per cubic millimeter.

Acute and chronic leukemias can be further classified according to whether they originate from granulocyte precursors, in which case they are called myeloid or myelogeneous, or from lymphocyte precursors, in which case they are called lymphocytic. Thus, the 2 most common types of acute leukemia are acute myeloid or myelocytic leukemia (AML), which occurs primarily in adults, and acute lymphocytic leukemia (ALL), which occurs primarily in children. The hematologist is able to distinguish between them by measuring levels of enzymes in the leukemic cells, and by using special stains that react differently to different cells.

Acute Myelogenic Leukemia (AML).

AML can be frightening in the rapidity of its onset, sometimes progressing in just a few weeks. In addition to severe anemia, with its typical symptoms, there is an increased tendency to bruising, bleeding, and infection.

If untreated, AML can be fatal within weeks. Various combinations of anticancer drugs can rid the bone marrow of the malignant cells, but also destroy many of the healthy cells in the marrow. Once the healthy cells begin to reproduce in significant numbers, usually in 2 to 3 weeks, the patient's condition can be expected to improve markedly, provided the leukemia cells have been eradicated. Treatment also includes blood transfusions to control the anemia, platelet transfusions to combat bleeding and bruising, and antibiotics to manage infection.

Acute Lymphocytic Leukemia (ALL).

ALL primarily affects children under age 5, who often show signs of anemia, fatigue, fever, and bleeding, indicating a depressed functioning of the bone marrow. Bone pain, swelling of the lymph glands, and enlargement of the kidneys suggest that the leukemia is infiltrating other organs. Without therapy, or if therapy is ineffective, ALL can be fatal in 2 to 4 months. Fortunately, therapy is often effective and the cure rate has now reached more than 50 percent. The goal of therapy in ALL is to achieve a state of remission, in which the leukemic cells in the bone marrow are no longer apparent and the bone marrow function returns to normal. The longer the state of remission, the better the chances for long-term survival.

The treatment of acute leukemia in children or adults is quite intensive and usually requires prolonged hospitalization. Because the drugs used further decrease the amount of normal bone marrow activity, platelet and whole blood transfusions are also needed, as well as antibiotics for infection. Severe infection and bleeding can occur both as a result of the disease and from chemotherapy. Leukemia is often accompanied by profound depression and anxiety as a result of the severe psychological trauma.

Treatment of Acute Leukemia.

Treatment of acute leukemia should only be undertaken at an institution experienced in treating large numbers of patients with this disorder. Most large medical centers have special hospital units in which patients with acute leukemia are cared for, and where nursing and hospital personnel as well as physicians are specially trained to deal with both the physical and psychological complications of these diseases.

Leukemia patients need the strong support of families, friends, physicians, and hospital personnel. This is why it is so important that they be cared for in an atmosphere in which there is both confidence and experience in the care of these illnesses. A successful outcome of treatment of acute leukemia usually leads to the appearance of a normal blood count and of a well patient, and this is worth fighting for.

New drugs are constantly being developed which have the ability to destroy leukemia cells, and during the past 10 years various drug combinations have resulted in significant improvements in the treatment of acute leukemia in both children and adults.

Adult acute leukemia is much less responsive to therapy than childhood ALL. Patients who do not respond to treatment live an average of 3 months from the time of diagnosis, while individuals who do respond live an average of 1 year or more, and a small number are long-term survivors. New techniques, such as bone marrow transplantation, may prolong life in the future.

Chronic Myelogenous Leukemia (CML).

Unlike acute leukemia, CML, which occurs primarily in men between 20 and 50, can develop gradually, almost insidiously. In CML, the number of granulocytes is markedly increased, as well as the number of immature cells in the peripheral blood and bone marrow, much more so than with a benign condition.

The symptoms of CML vary greatly. The individual may show none at all, and the disease may be discovered quite by accident through a routine blood test. Or there may be only anemia or general malaise. At the other extreme, there may be weight loss, night sweats, fatigue, and an enlarged spleen that may cause discomfort in the left side of the abdomen or be large enough to be felt by the patient.

A diagnosis of CML is verified by tests to detect the level of an enzyme called leukocyte alkaline phosphatase, which is markedly reduced in these patients, and the presence of a chromosomal abnormality called the Philadelphia chromosome (ph[1]), which occurs in 90 percent of CML patients.

CML cannot be cured, but chemotherapy can produce a remission and allow the patient to live a relatively normal life for a period of years. Unfortunately, many cases eventually progress to the acute stage and result in death, with half of the patients succumbing 3 to 4 years after their initial diagnosis.

Chronic Lymphocytic Leukemia (CLL).

The other form of chronic leukemia, CLL, generally affects people from 40 to 70, with most cases beginning after age 60. It results from defective white blood cells (lymphocytes) which proliferate. There is decreased antibody production, leaving the patient vulnerable to infections. In the more advanced stage, the abnormal lymphocytes invade the bone marrow and various organs. Bone marrow infiltration interferes with production of red cells, normal white cells, and platelets, which leads to anemia, infections, and increased bleeding. This process may take several years, during which time there may be no symptoms.

When CLL does produce symptoms, they may be similar to CML: increasing fatigue, loss of appetite and weight, and night sweats. In other cases, the first symptoms may be swelling of the lymph glands or spleen. Anemia and recurrent infections may be the first indication in still other cases.

Treatment may include steroids, chemotherapy, and radiotherapy. The prognosis for CLL is much better than for CML, with patients often surviving 5 to 10 years after the initial diagnosis, and 20 percent surviving 20 years.

Agnogenic Myeloid Metaplasia

Agnogenic (meaning of unknown origin) myeloid metaplasia is an abnormality in which the bone marrow becomes progressively fibrotic over a period of years. Red cells, white cells, and platelets are produced outside of the marrow, in extramedullary sites in the spleen and in the liver, either of which can become markedly enlarged. There can be a severe anemia, and the white blood cell and platelet counts may vary from the normal value. Treatment, which may relieve symptoms but does not produce a cure, includes radiotherapy, chemotherapy, and sometimes removal of the spleen. The prognosis of this condition is poor, and 50 percent of patients die within 5 years of diagnosis, often of AML.

Granulocytopenia

This condition, also known as agranulocytosis, is characterized by a decrease in the number of white cells known as granulocytes. It can be due either to a decreased production of granulocytes by the bone marrow or to the increased destruction of the cells. Certain types of drugs, especially those taken for thyroid problems and cancer, can markedly decrease white blood cell production. Infiltration of the bone marrow with cancer or leukemia cells and aplastic anemia can also lead to decreased granulocyte production. Increased destruction of granulocytes is usually due to either drugs or antibodies to granulocytes, or to increased destruction of cells by an enlarged or abnormal spleen. Whenever a patient is treated with a drug that is known to cause either bone marrow suppression or production of antibodies which can react with the granulocytes, the white blood count must be carefully monitored to ensure that this complication does not occur.

Granulocytopenia is very rare, affecting 1 person in every 100,000, and is usually mild. It often manifests itself as a series of infections, especially of the mouth and throat, or in pneumonia. If the condition is due to a drug reaction, it is usually reversible within a week to 10 days if the drug is stopped. Accompanying infections are treated with antibiotics.

DISORDERS OF LYMPHOCYTES

LYMPHOCYTES are a class of white blood cells that control the immune reactions of the body. The B lymphocytes produce antibodies which help fight off disease. The T lymphocytes interact with the B lymphocytes to help them produce antibodies, and they also attack infections directly by helping the body to recognize foreign substances. Both types of cells must function normally for the immune system to protect the body against serious disease and death. In certain viral conditions and other infections, there is a loss of T cell function.

Two types of T cells are known to exist—T helper cells and T suppressor cells. T helper cells increase the production of T cells and interact with B cells to produce antibodies. T suppressor cells, on the other hand, kill T helper cells, and reduce the T cell responsiveness. In infectious mononucleosis and other viral diseases, T suppressor cells increase in amount and make individuals suffering from these diseases susceptible to a variety of other infections as well.

There is a similar increase in T suppressor cells in acquired immune deficiency syndrome (AIDS), a disease on the rise during recent years and seen primarily in homosexuals and drug abusers. However, in AIDS, the resulting T helper cell suppression appears to be permanent, and patients with this syndrome are at great risk for certain so-called "opportunistic infections," such as pneumocystis carinii and toxoplasmosis, which ordinarily do not cause disease in otherwise healthy humans. A rare form of cancer, Kaposi's sarcoma, is also commonly seen in AIDS patients.

Lymphomas

Lymphomas are cancers of the lymphatic system, especially of the lymph nodes. Lymphomas can also occur without evidence of T cell suppression, and most are of unknown cause.

The lymph node is normally composed of T and B cells. A clone of either type of cell can become malignant, proliferate, and take over the entire node. In more advanced cases, the malignant lymphocytes can spread to other organs in the body. Thus, there are T cell lymphomas, B cell lymphomas, and mixed cell lymphomas composed of both. The B cell lymphomas are more easily treatable with chemotherapy, although not easily curable. The T cell lymphomas, many of which involve the skin, are rarer and more difficult to treat. (For more details, see the lymphoma section in Chapter 20 on Cancer, page 417.)

Hodgkin's Disease. Hodgkin's disease is a form of lymphoma diagnosed by the characteristic presence in the lymph nodes of a unique cell called the Reed-Sternberg cell. Hodgkin's disease represents a special class of lymphoma in that its spread is predictable and its response to treatment dramatic. The disease usually spreads from the lymph nodes in the neck, chest, and armpits to the spleen, and then the liver or nodes bordering the aorta.

Hodgkin's disease affects primarily those between 15 and 35 and over 50, and is more common in men than in women. The first sign is usually persistent swelling of the lymph nodes in the neck, chest, or armpits. If the disease has begun to spread, fever, night sweats, weight loss, and bone pain may also occur.

Caught early, before it has spread to other parts of the body, Hodgkin's disease has a 90 to 95 percent cure rate with radiotherapy. If it has spread, chemotherapy using a combination of drugs, or radiation with chemotherapy may also produce a cure, although not as often. In advanced cases, patients become resistant to chemotherapeutic drugs and eventually succumb to infection or other complications.

Non-Hodgkin's Lymphomas. In contrast to Hodgkin's disease, non-Hodgkin's lymphomas usually have spread by the time the initial diagnosis is made, making cure more difficult. Although relatively rare (7,000 to 8,000 new cases per year in the United States), these lymphomas are somewhat more common than Hodgkin's disease. They are divided into a number of different types, depending on the appearance of the biopsy material, and are usually treated by combination chemotherapy, since radiotherapy is not often successful.

Non-Hodgkin's lymphomas may start in the same way as Hodgkin's, with swelling of the lymph glands in the neck, armpits, or groin, but may also include an enlarged spleen, anemia, and general malaise. Weight loss, night sweats, and fever are indications that the disease has spread. Chemotherapy and steroids may result in remission in about 50 percent of cases, but the remission period is shorter than in Hodgkin's.

Multiple Myeloma

The plasma cells are a specialized type of lymphocyte that normally produces antibodies. In multiple myeloma, plasma cells begin to multiply in an uncontrolled fashion until they take over the marrow and spill out into other parts of the body. As they multiply inside the marrow cavities of bones, they disrupt production of normal blood cells and destroy the bone, causing severe pain.

While anemia and increased vulnerability to infection may be the first signs of this cancer, the most characteristic symptom is bone pain, with the eventual deterioration and easy fracturing of the bones, especially the vertebrae. Myeloma affects mainly those over 50 and is twice as likely to occur in men as in women.

Although there is no cure for myeloma, chemotherapy can prolong life for several years until the patient becomes resistant to treatment. Radiotherapy may be used to relieve the bone pain, while transfusions can be used to ameliorate the anemia.

(For more information on lymphocytic disorders, see Chapter 20 on Cancer, page 417.)

DISORDERS OF BLOOD COAGULATION

BLOOD COAGULATION, or blood clotting, is a complex process that involves platelets, coagulation factors that circulate in the blood, and blood vessels. The primary defense against bleeding is the response of the injured blood vessel and the formation of a platelet plug. When a large vessel is cut, it contracts to prevent bleeding and platelets rush to the site to form a plug. After this immediate response, coagulation begins. A number of enzymes in the blood plasma are activated and together form fibrin, a strong cross-linked protein, which becomes part of the physical clot. Significant abnormalities in the platelets, or in the coagulation factors that result in fibrin formation, or in the blood vessels themselves, can all lead to excessive bleeding.

Thrombocytopenia

Disorders of platelets are usually due to decreased numbers of them, a condition known as thrombocytopenia. The most common form of this condition is idiopathic (of unknown cause) thrombocytopenic purpura, most often due to an immune response in which the body actually develops antibodies against its own platelets so that they break down at an abnormal rate. This results in bleeding from small blood vessels, and the bleeding appears as pinpoints, called petechiae, in the skin and mucous membranes. Lymphoma and an unusual disorder called lupus erythematosus can also give rise to too few platelets, as can infections and administration of a number of drugs, such as quinine and quinidine. These drugs should be stopped immediately if thrombocytopenia and petechiae are found.

Alternatively, thrombocytopenia can be the result of decreased production of platelets by the bone marrow, either due to aplastic anemia or to invasion of the bone marrow by leukemia, lymphoma, or marrow fibrosis. The appearance of a few petechiae on the lower legs of young women is not uncommon and does not necessarily mean the disease is present; this can be easily confirmed with a simple platelet count.

Coagulation Factor Deficiencies

Coagulation factors are mainly proteins that are converted from inactive to active forms whenever a blood vessel wall is damaged. There are at least 12 of them, all identified by roman numerals. Coagulation factor disorders can be inherited, such as hemophilia, or acquired, such as a condition known as disseminated intravascular coagulation. Since many of the factors are made in the liver, diseases that affect the liver, like alcoholic cirrhosis and acute and chronic hepatitis, are associated with numerous clotting disorders.

When patients develop blood clots in their legs (deep vein thrombosis) or lungs (pulmonary embolus) normal blood coagulation is suppressed by the use of anticoagulant medications. These patients must be monitored carefully, as bleeding can be a side effect of this treatment. Substances that break down (or lyse) blood clots, such as streptokinase and tissue plasminogen activate (TPA), are useful in treating an acute coronary artery occlusion, a component of most heart attacks.

Congenital Hemophilia. The best known of the congenital disorders of coagulation are hemophilia A and B, associated with a decrease in the activity of Factor VIII or of Factor IX, respectively. Hemophilia is usually passed from mother to son. Women are carriers, but they don't manifest the disease themselves, although they may have a lower than normal level of Factor VIII in their blood. The disorder can be mild or severe, with the more severe cases manifesting themselves early in life. Children usually show easy bleeding in large joints, such as the knees, and marked defects in clot formation. In milder forms, the disease may not show up until later in life.

Treatment of hemophilia generally consists of transfusions of concentrates of blood products in which there is a large amount of Factor VIII or Factor IX, depending on the condition present in individual cases. While many hemophiliacs can lead a relatively normal life, extra precautions must be taken in engaging in sports and with surgery or dental care; some 10 percent of patients with hemophilia develop antibodies to Factor VIII and become more difficult to treat.

Disseminated Intravascular Coagulation. One special group of coagulation disorders associated with diffuse bleeding from many sites, as well as increased clotting, is called disseminated intravascular coagulation (DIC). In this syndrome, the coagulation system is overactive, causing increased clotting. On the other hand, there is an increase in the dissolution of clots because of an increased production of another enzyme, called plasmin, which normally degrades fibrin in the clot.

DIC usually occurs secondary to a number of other conditions, including overwhelming infection, certain forms of cancer, leukemia, certain obstetrical conditions, and shock. There is an increased consumption of coagulation factors with a marked decrease in platelets and in many of the coagulation factors, but the reasons for this are not understood. Bleeding ensues and can be fatal. The primary treatment of DIC is successful treatment of the underlying condition, whether it is shock, sepsis (blood infection), or cancer. Replacement of the missing coagulation factors is often necessary.

SUMMING UP

BLOOD DISORDERS can range from relatively benign to serious and can be acquired or inherited. Many can be treated simply with iron or vitamin supplements, or by attending the underlying causes, such as occult bleeding. Others are more severe, requiring hospitalization, drug therapy, and the care of a hematologist or oncologist. The prognosis for many of these diseases becomes increasingly better as various combinations of new drugs produce longer and longer survival rates. Relatively new treatments like bone marrow transplantation and iron chelation are showing promising results. As with any serious disease, prompt diagnosis and early treatment are important.

27 Disorders of the Musculoskeletal System

Harold M. Dick, M.D.

WE OFTEN TAKE for granted our ability to walk, run, swing our arms, or climb stairs. But if a bone or muscle disorder should suddenly prevent the continuation of such movements or a disease should make each movement a painful effort, we would find our daily lives severely compromised.

BONE DISORDERS

ORTHOPEDIC PROBLEMS (those affecting the human skeleton and its system of joints) surpass any other disease group in the frequency with which they disrupt the normal quality of life. More than 20 million Americans suffer from limited activity, disability, impairment, and handicapped movement as a result.

The human body contains 206 bones which constitute about one-tenth of total body weight. (See figure 27.1.) Together, the bones provide the sup-

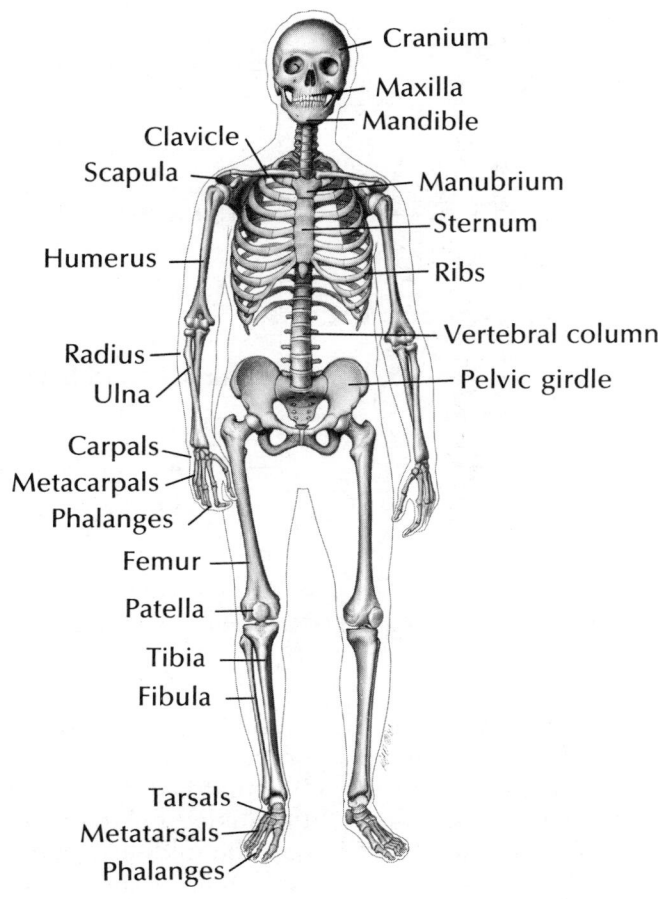

Cranium
Maxilla
Mandible
Clavicle
Scapula
Manubrium
Sternum
Humerus
Ribs
Vertebral column
Radius
Pelvic girdle
Ulna
Carpals
Metacarpals
Phalanges
Femur
Patella
Tibia
Fibula
Tarsals
Metatarsals
Phalanges

Figure 27.1. **An overview of the skeletal system.**

porting framework and protection for many vital organs. The skull protects delicate brain tissue. The spinal column encases the spinal cord, the main switchboard of nerves that carries messages between the body and the brain. The rib cage shields the heart, lungs, liver, and kidneys. Bones in the pelvic area anchor the spine and encircle the bladder. In women, the pelvis forms a protective ring around the reproductive organs and protects the embryo.

Because the bones are housed beneath the skin where they cannot be seen, many people have the misconception that the skeleton is one part of the body that does not change over time. In fact, cells in bone tissue work constantly to create, maintain, and dissolve old bone. This process of bone replacement continues during the entire life span.

LOW BACK PAIN

Anatomy of the Spine

The spine is the foundation of human movement and flexibility. It allows the body to remain in an upright position and helps support the body's weight. Its enormous strength and flexibility permit it to withstand the jarring and jolting physical demands of daily life.

Thirty-three bony blocks, or vertebrae arranged in 5 sections, make up the spine. (See figure 27.2.) To keep these vertebrae in their proper position, the spinal column depends on a complex system of ligaments, cartilage, and muscle. Working together, this system provides strength and ease of motion, and prevents the spinal column from collapsing. When the muscles become weak, however, the system loses stability, resulting in pain and a weakened spine.

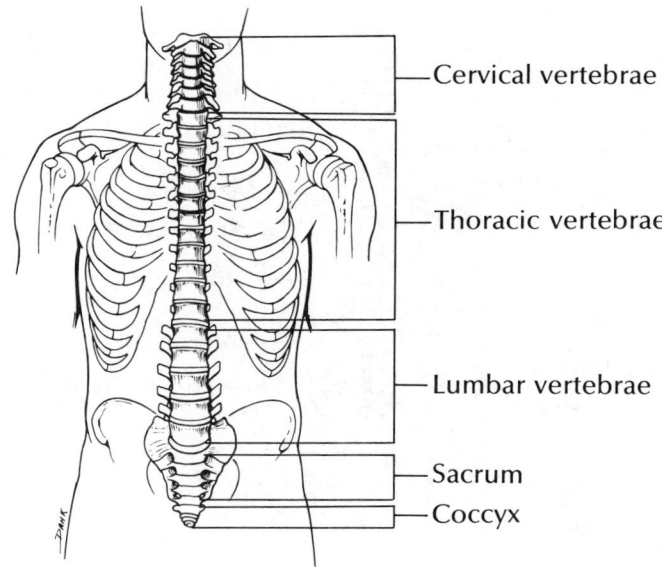

Cervical vertebrae

Thoracic vertebrae

Lumbar vertebrae

Sacrum

Coccyx

Figure 27.2. **The spinal column and its divisions.**

The spine's upper region (cervical) contains 7 vertebrae in the neck area, which support the head and protect the spinal cord. Below the cervical vertebrae are 12 thoracic vertebrae, each of which is joined to a rib. The lower back region, consisting of 5 lumbar vertebrae, is designed to bear most of the weight and stress of the upper body. At the base of the spine are 5 sacral vertebrae, fused into one bone, known as the sacrum. Below it are 4 coccygeal vertebrae (the tailbone). A close look at a vertebra shows a thick cylindrical bone with a hollow core from which 3 bony pieces thrust outward—one on each side and one toward the rear. These smaller bones join those of the adjacent vertebra at a joint called a facet, a source of pain if thrown out of alignment by arthritis or abnormal movement. When the vertebrae are aligned, a canal is formed through which the spinal cord passes. Spinal nerves that connect the cord to the body's network of nerves pass through openings between the vertebrae. These openings are susceptible to pressure or damage from fractures or protruding disks, one common cause of pinched nerves.

The lumbar region is the site of most back pain. Here, the vertebrae are large—both because of their weight-bearing function and because the central spinal canal is smaller than in the cervical region.

Poor Posture

Poor posture is the most common underlying cause of back pain. It can change the normal curvature of the spine and put abnormal stress on its supporting muscles and ligaments. The body's normal center of gravity allows a person to stand upright. Imagine a line that is dropped from ear level straight down to the ankle. It should cross the outer tip of the shoulder, the middle of the hip, the back of the kneecap, and finally hang in front of the ankle joint. If this center of gravity is too far forward, the imaginary model will lean to the front. If the line is too much to the rear, the model will lean backward. To try to accommodate to the proper center of gravity, a person with poor posture may have adopted rounded shoulders or a swayback.

In early fetal developments, the spine is C-shaped. After birth, a forward curve develops in the cervical spine. This is called normal cervical lordosis and is essential to keep the head in position over the spine. Meanwhile, the thoracic spine, where the ribs are attached, develops a backward curve known as a kyphosis. The posterior curve that forms in the lumbar region in the lower spine is called a lumbar lordosis. These curves are normal and necessary to help protect the spine in the event of injury. If these natural curves are altered too much, stress is placed on the vertebrae, and pain can follow.

When the body begins to develop rounded shoulders and a caved-in appearance around the chest, the condition is known as kyphosis. This can lead to a shortening of pectoral muscles in the chest as well as muscles lying between the ribs. Exercise programs can help correct mild forms of this condition. In some patients, braces also may be necessary.

When the normal forward curve (lordosis) of the cervical and lumbar spine is exaggerated, hyperlordosis results. This condition puts a great strain on the lumbar vertebrae and on the small joints between them. Lordosis, or swayback, allows the abdomen and buttocks to jut out and results in a vicious cycle—the more the abdomen protrudes, the more the buttocks stick out. At the same time, muscle tone gets weaker and back pain increases. If a program of weight loss and exercise is undertaken, the symptoms of hyperlordosis can be relieved. (See figure 27.3.)

Poor posture habits usually begin in childhood. Years of slouching, assuming round shoulders, or a swayback eventually produces a range of problems, from back pain to more complicated disorders, such as osteoarthritis or disk problems.

Potential back problems can be prevented by practicing good posture, whether standing, sitting, or sleeping. Practice makes perfect. If poor posture has been a longtime habit, the muscles that help a person to stand erect will have to be retrained to perform their intended job. It's essential to stand tall, holding the head straight and keeping the abdomen in. Do not allow the buttocks to protrude or the back to swoop inward in swayback fashion.

Trauma

Much back pain is caused by trauma, such as a fall down a staircase or a sudden strain while lifting a heavy object. While an acute lumbar strain occurs suddenly, another form of trauma—chronic lumbar strain—is the result of repeated strains. In chronic form, the strain can appear with the slightest provocation. (Strain injuries should not be confused with sprains. A strain is a small tear within the muscles, while a sprain is an injury to a ligament that holds bone to bone.)

Occasionally a fall on the buttocks or feet may produce a compression fracture, in which the vertebrae collapse into a wedge shape. Compression fractures usually occur in bones weakened by osteoporosis in people over 60. (See page 555.)

Herniated Disks

Joining each pair of vertebrae is a flat circle of cartilage and fibrous tissue that acts as a shock absorber. The tough, fibrous outer portion is called the annulus fibrosis. The gelatinous material inside is known as the nucleus pulposus. When the gelatinous

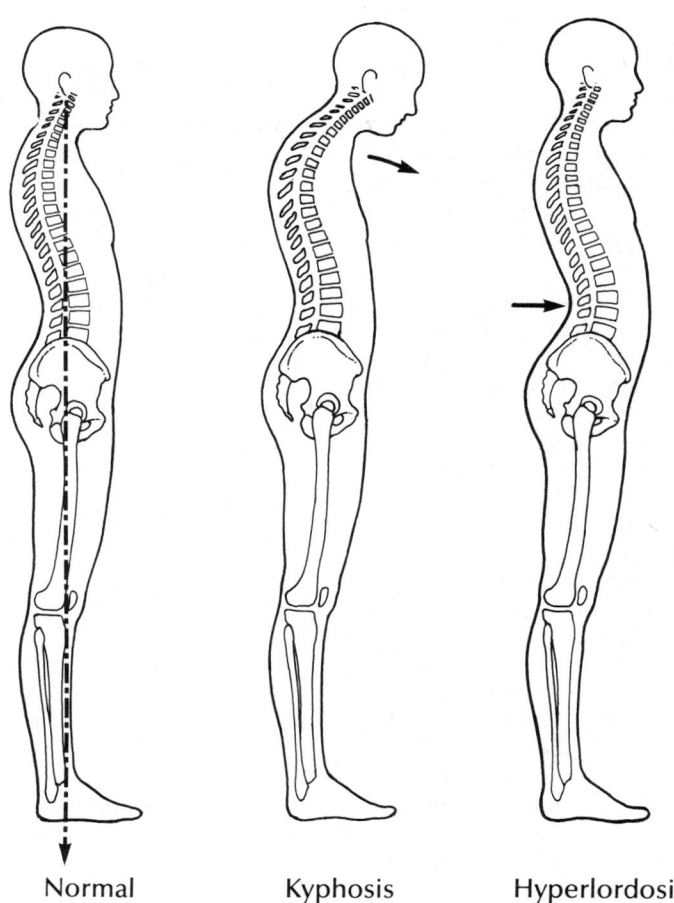

Normal   Kyphosis   Hyperlordosis

Figure 27.3. **Common postural defects.**

interior leaks though the fibrous portion, due to injury, repeated minor trauma, or the aging process, a hernia, commonly known as a slipped disk, may form in the area. The crippling pain of degenerative disk disease and disk herniation can affect children, although rarely, as well as adults. Though the popular misnomer for this condition is a slipped disk, there is, in fact, no slippage. Instead, the affected disk balloons out from between the bony parts of the vertebrae. If the bulging, or herniated area is large enough, it may press on a nerve, causing severe, and sometimes incapacitating, pain sometimes beginning immediately or a few hours after an injury. (See figures 27.4A and 27.4B.) Usually, the sciatic nerve, which begins in the lower spine and runs down the back of each leg, is affected. Sciatic pain—sciatica—is generally located in the lumbar region and can radiate over the buttock, rear thigh, and calf, and can even extend into the foot.

Herniation most frequently affects the fourth and fifth disks in the lumbar region although this problem can also occur in the uppermost vertebrae (cervical) around the neck, and cause the same kind of symptoms in the arms as it does in the legs when there is sciatic pain.

Pain from a herniated disk can be relieved with bed rest, muscle relaxants, and anti-inflammatory drugs. Traction and manipulation may be necessary in some cases. Surgery can also relieve pain in most patients.

An alternative to surgery, which involves the injection of the enzyme chymopapain into the damaged disk and causing it to shrink, is a treatment now available in some medical centers. Chymopapain, which is derived from the papaya tree, is an ingredient found in meat tenderizers to soften muscle fibers. It works by dissolving the inner vertebral disk without damaging nerve roots and surrounding structures. Although chymopapain has been approved by the Food and Drug Administration, its long-term effectiveness has not yet been proven clinically.

BACK CARE BASICS

For the body to enjoy good health and ease of movement, certain principles must be practiced to avoid strain on the muscles, joints, bones, and ligaments. Practice of these principles begins with proper posture, which simply means walking, sitting, standing, lying down, and working in a relaxed but correct position that can benefit the back and the body's internal organs.

Correct posture is a learned habit that can offer a lifetime of support and protection for the back. Regular practice of carrying the body properly can leave a person looking and feeling better as well as protecting the back by strengthening the muscles.

Here are some basic posture rules:

- *Lifting heavy objects.* Don't bend over from the waist. (This rule applies even if the object to be picked up is light, such as a piece of paper.) Instead, squat down by the object with the back straight and the knees bent. Then, slowly rise with the object and let the quadriceps muscles in the thighs do the work.

- *Standing.* Stand up straight with the shoulders back, the abdomen pulled in, the chin in, the small of the back flat, and the pelvis straight. If an imaginary line dropped from the ear does not pass directly across the outer tip of the shoulder, the middle of the hip, the back of the kneecap, and the front of the ankle bone, then the posture is out of alignment and needs to be corrected. When standing for long periods of time, move around frequently and shift the weight from one foot to another. High-heeled shoes can affect stance by tilting the pelvis in a forward position and thus straining the back.

- *Sitting.* Sitting can be quite stressful on the back if it is not done properly. A straight-back chair with good lumbar support is the best choice. Elevation of the feet can help relieve swayback. (A person who must stand in one position for a long period of time should elevate one foot slightly by placing it on a footrest. This helps to flatten the lumbar spine and reduce the muscle fatigue that accompanies swayback.) During long-distance travel, take regular stretch breaks. On car trips, place a small pillow behind the lower back.

- *Sleeping.* Lying down is the least stressful posture—if it is done properly. Use of a firm mattress or a bedboard under the mattress can provide the proper support. The fetal position (lying on the side with the knees bent at right angles to the body and the neck straight) is the most effective sleep posture. A pillow that is too high can strain the neck, arms, and shoulders. Avoid sleeping on the stomach because it increases swayback in the lower spine. Sleeping on the back can be restful when a small pillow is placed between the head and neck and another pillow under the knees.

Following recovery from a herniated disk, it is possible to resume an active lifestyle. Herniated disks often can be prevented by keeping body weight normal, maintaining a proper diet, and exercising to keep the muscles in good tone.

Unstable Vertebrae

Severe back pain may be due to unstable vertebrae. When a vertebrae is unstable in the lumbar area, it shifts forward and backward on the vertebra underneath, causing lower back pain. The problem usually arises from the third and fourth or fourth and fifth lumbar vertebrae. Spinal exercises and use of a special corset can produce marked improvement. Surgery rarely offers a cure for these patients because arthritis may have changed their entire spine. However, if the pain persists, surgical fusion to weld the unstable vertebra to the one above and the one below it can provide relief.

Managing Back Strains and Sprains

When acute lumbar strain incapacitates a patient, the following usually are recommended: absolute bed rest, warm tub baths and applications of heating pads, anti-inflammatory agents such as aspirin, and in some cases, massages and use of a corset until the discomfort is gone. Upon improvement, an exercise program can encourage weakened muscles to grow stronger.

Those suffering from chronic lumbar strain can benefit by undertaking a weight loss program if necessary, correcting posture deficiencies, using a firm mattress, and beginning a daily regimen of exercises to strengthen the lower back.

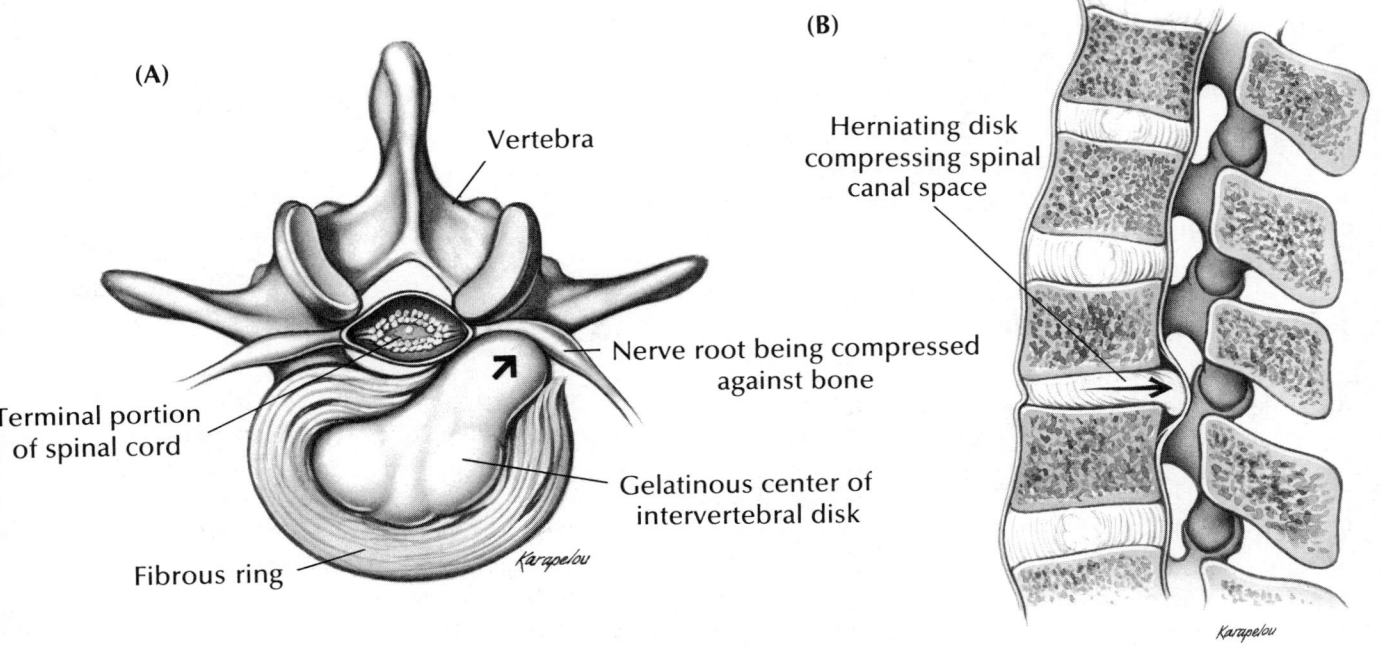

(A)

Vertebra

Terminal portion of spinal cord

Fibrous ring

Nerve root being compressed against bone

Gelatinous center of intervertebral disk

Karapelou

(B)

Herniating disk compressing spinal canal space

Karapelou

Figures 27.4A and 27.4B. **Herniated disk as viewed from a cross section of a lumbar vertebra as seen from above (27.4A) and a side view showing the herniated disk pressing into the spinal canal space (27.4B).**

FRACTURES

A FRACTURE is a break in a bone, whether it be a shaft or a joint. The physical force that produces the fracture can also injure soft tissue surrounding the affected bone.

While normal bones are strong and hard, they also are somewhat elastic. In young children, they are capable of bending much like the branch of a tree. Because of this elasticity, a young bone can crack without actually breaking. This is known as green-stick fracture. A variety of forces acting upon older bones, such as bending or twisting force that is greater than the bone can withstand, will break it crosswise or at an angle.

Types of Fractures

- A fracture may be *simple*, in which the bone is broken, with minimal damage to the surrounding skin and tissue.
- A *compound* fracture involves tissue damage and possibly bone protruding through the skin.
- A fracture *dislocation* may occur if the joint fragments that normally hold 2 bones together are torn apart and a bone breaks during the injury.
- A *comminuted* fracture is one in which bone is crushed into small pieces at the end of the fracture.
- *Compression* fractures result from crushing forces that jam one bone surface against another. Young children who suffer compression fractures also may experience what is called a buckle fracture because of the buckling effect it produces in the bone. A compression fracture may result from a fall on the buttocks or feet, which forces the vertebrae to collapse into a wedge shape. (See figure 27.5.)

A partial fracture is a hairline crack in a bone. Often, it is called a stress fracture. Such fractures may not be visible on an x-ray until several weeks after occurring. Rest is the best treatment for a stress fracture.

Recognizing a Fracture

Broken bones may occur on the ski slopes, in an automobile accident, in a person's home, etc. The usual symptoms include localized pain that is made worse by movement; an inability to use the affected area; the grating of bone ends; tenderness and swelling; deformity of the area; muscle spasm during slight movement. Some patients have reported hearing the bone break during the injury. (For emergency treatment of fractures, see that section in Chapter 7 on First-Aid Procedures, page 116.)

Treatment of Fractures

After a fracture has been diagnosed, treatment begins by realigning the affected bones in a procedure known as closed or open reduction, depending upon the severity of the break.

In closed reduction, surgery is not necessary; orthopedic surgeons use the sense of touch to feel the fracture, which has been locally anesthetized, and with the help of three-dimensional x-rays, realign the bone. Once the bone is back in position, the area is immobilized with a plaster cast.

Open reduction involves exposing the fracture site by surgery so that the bones can be realigned

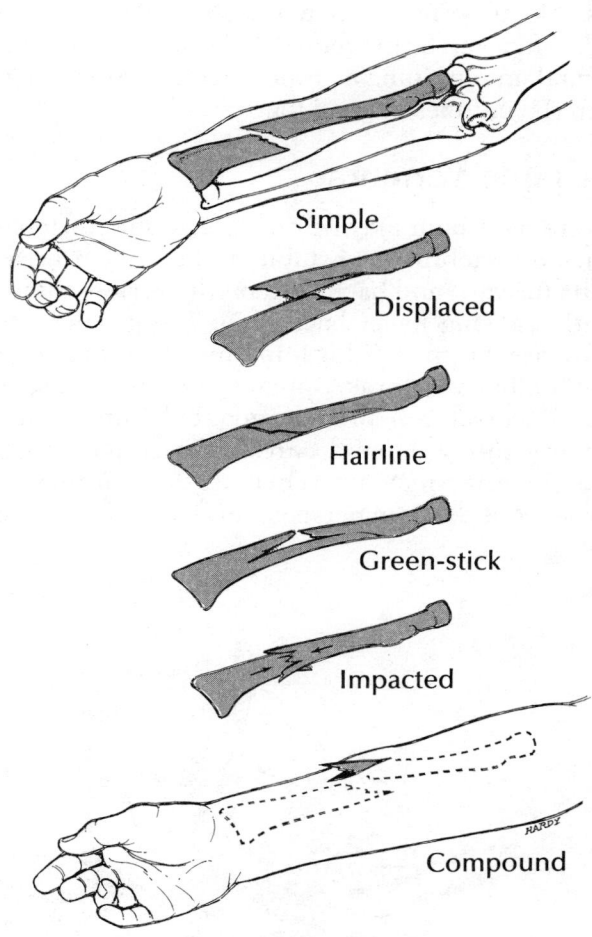

Figure 27.5. **Types of fractures.**

under direct vision. Care must be taken to protect the undamaged tissue in the area and the blood supply from the fragments of the fracture. When surgery is undertaken, an internal metallic device designed to maintain rigidity, such as a plate or pin, normally is installed. Some fractures of the hip and elbow may require replacement with a prosthesis. (See Total Joint Replacement, page 559.)

Some fractures that are not severely displaced can be treated by external splinting without manipulating the bones. Other fractures only may require a protective device, such as an arm sling.

Compound fractures require specialized emergency treatment to minimize the risk of infection. Affected bones may be repositioned by either the closed or open method, depending on the size of the wound. Once the bones are realigned, they must be immobilized until they have healed. This happens when the tissues produce a substance called callus, which binds the bony fragments together. Plaster of

Paris casts may be applied to some fractures, such as a broken arm. Traction may be necessary to immobilize a larger area, such as a fractured thigh bone. Some broken bones need internal devices, such as pins and plates, to keep the damaged bones in position.

One of the dangers of immobilization is that the surrounding muscles will atrophy. A physical therapist will know what exercises should be done to keep the muscles in as good condition as possible under the circumstances. Regaining use of the damaged area will be much faster if the exercises are done properly.

Healing of Fractures

The time required to heal a fracture varies with age, the location and type of fracture, and the amount of blood supply to the area. Fractures heal rapidly in children; an 8-year-old's, about 12 weeks. In adults, it may take up to 6 months for a fracture to heal fully.

A fractured bone surrounded by muscle tends to heal more rapidly than a fracture within a joint. A long and slanting fracture heals faster than one that runs directly across the bone, due to its larger surface area for healing.

OSTEOPOROSIS

BONES NEED CALCIUM to maintain their strength, hardness, and to stay healthy. Milk, the main source of calcium in the diet, is important for the growing skeletons of children and adolescents as well as the bone-forming cells of adults. Regular daily consumption of at least 1 cup of skim or low-fat milk is essential for adults who want to keep their bones strong and to help prevent osteoporosis, a disease in which the body's bone mass decreases and bones become thin and brittle. Bones weakened by osteoporosis, a disease common to postmenopausal women, are prone to fracture if a person falls.

When calcium enters the body, it is absorbed into the bloodstream. If there is any excess, it is deposited in the end of the bone shafts where it is stored until the body needs to tap this reserve. (Some is also excreted via the kidneys.) When the calcium supply is deficient, the blood must take it back from the bones. If calcium intake remains inadequate over a long period of time, the bones eventually become porous and weak.

It is not known why calcium loss occurs. That postmenopausal women tend to get osteoporosis points in the direction of a hormonal disorder as estrogen in women of this age falls off sharply. Estrogen therapy is one treatment but its ability to decrease calcium loss may last only several years. Increased calcium intake and exercise are other therapies. The links between lack of exercise and osteoporosis are becoming firmer as research into the causes of this disease progresses.

The disease most frequently affects the spinal column, causing backaches and rounded shoulders. In severe cases, the bone becomes as porous as a sponge and can collapse as a result. Collapsing vertebrae, which can cause sudden and sharp backaches, is one reason why elderly people tend to get shorter.

OSTEOMALACIA

THIS DISEASE, caused by a vitamin D deficiency, also results in weakened bones. Vitamin D is found in milk, eggs, and liver and it is activated by sunlight. It aids in the body's absorption of calcium. A lack of vitamin D thus prevents the bones from absorbing calcium; the symptoms of the disease are similar to those of osteoporosis. Though rare in the industrialized world, it is more common among pregnant women, who have a higher need of calcium.

PAGET'S DISEASE

BONE CELLS responsible for dissolving old bone and replacing it with new bone begin to work at an accelerated rate in Paget's disease. The diseased bone that is created is larger, weaker, and has more blood vessels than normal bone.

The primary bones affected by Paget's disease

are the shin bone (tibia), thigh bone (femur), hip bone (pelvis), the vertebrae, and the skull. The disease may be limited to one bone or it may spread into several bones. Normal bone has its own unique architecture. Bone affected by Paget's disease develops an irregular pattern inside its cellular structure.

Paget's disease affects a small percentage of people over 40. Mild forms of the disease have no symptoms. In severe cases, pain may be intense. As bones become enlarged, they may compress against adja-

cent nerves. As the disease progresses, the legs may become bent or bowed, the skull may grow larger, and the spine may bend slightly, making the person appear to be leaning to one side. Severe skull enlargement can compress the auditory nerve and cause a loss of hearing.

The cause of Paget's disease remains unknown. Current treatment includes administration of medications to reduce the abnormal bone turnover and to relieve the pain.

SCOLIOSIS

SCOLIOSIS is progressive lateral curvature of the spine occurring either in the thoracic region or in the lumbar spine. (See figure 27.6.) The onset of

scoliosis may occur during infancy, the juvenile years (age 4 to 9), or in the adolescent years. The infantile type more commonly affects males and, for

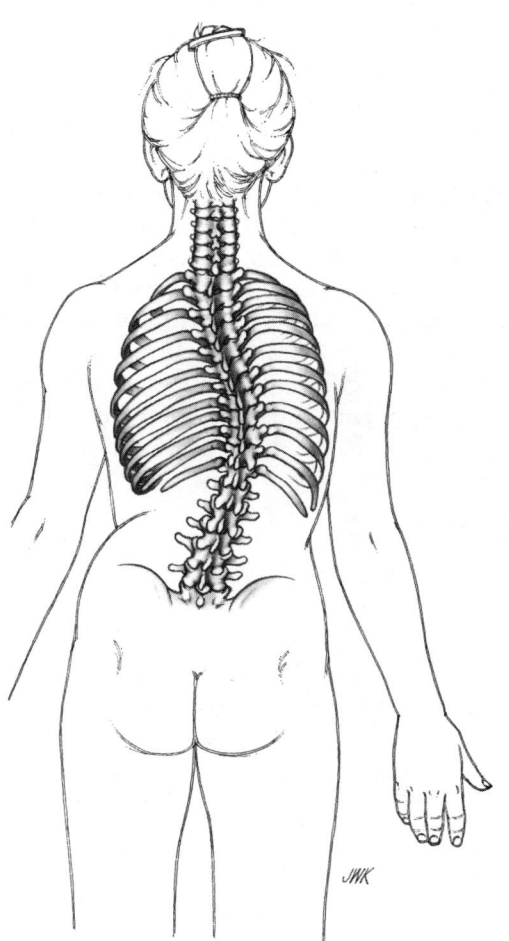

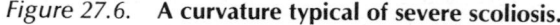

Figure 27.6.   A curvature typical of severe scoliosis.

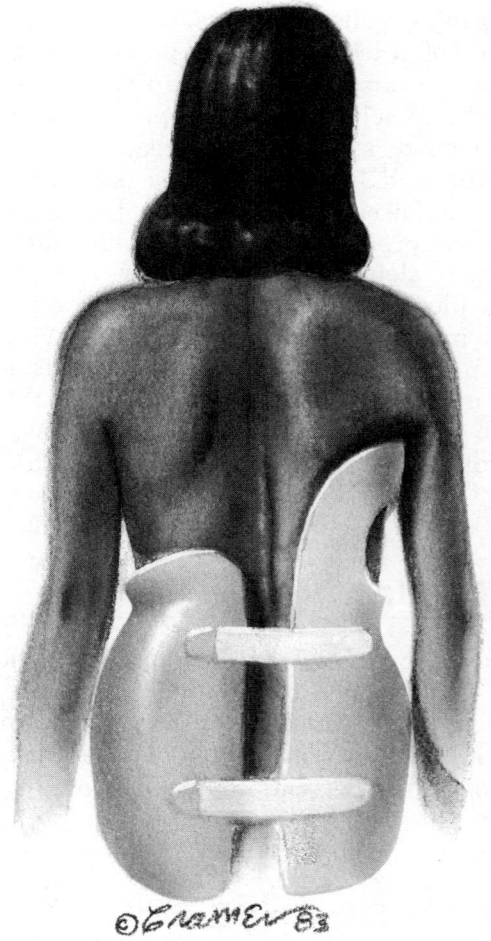

Figure 27.7.   The type of brace commonly used to treat scoliosis. These are molded to fit the body and are concealed by clothing.

some reason, it is not prevalent in the United States. Juvenile scoliosis may first appear by age 6 when a thoracic curve begins to form in both boys and girls who are affected. Some cases may not be noticeable until the child reaches adolescence. The curve becomes increasingly apparent as the skeleton grows to maturity.

As the disease progresses, the vertebrae rotate toward the concave part of the curve. This can cause the ribs to crowd together on one side while they are widely separated on the other. Kyphosis, with its rounded shoulders and sunken chest appearance, and lordosis (swayback) often accompany scoliosis. The curvature may force the spaces between the spinal disks to become narrow. Also, the vertebrae become thicker on the outer edge of the curve.

A small number of cases result from habitually poor posture or from a discrepancy that is produced by one leg being shorter than the other, usually because of a tilted pelvis. However, the majority of cases have an unknown cause and are considered to be genetic in origin. Females are more predisposed to adolescent scoliosis than males.

A spinal brace can halt the progression of the curvature in the majority of cases. (See figure 27.7.) If the curve begins to produce a deformity, it can be corrected by surgery. Specially designed hooks can be implanted above and below the curve and an instrument known as the Harrington rod attached to them. When the spine is maneuvered into a straight line, the area surrounding the rod is packed with small pieces of bone taken from the pelvis. As healing progresses, the rod and bone fragments fuse together into a single unit. A newer, still experimental treatment involves using electrical stimulation to strengthen the back muscles and correct the curvature.

Because scoliosis is a progressive disease, it can cause pain, disability, and deformity in severe cases. The disease does not stop upon passage into adulthood. Anyone with scoliosis should be examined at least once a year to monitor any progression of an untreated curve. If changes take place, immediate treatment is recommended. A progressing case of scoliosis can produce cardiac and lung problems in later years.

OSTEOMYELITIS

WHEN BACTERIA enter the bone tissue, an infection called osteomyelitis can cause serious inflammation in bones and joints throughout the body. The infection begins when bacteria from the environment enter exposed areas through broken skin. Compound fractures suffered in automobile accidents carry a high risk of osteomyelitis. In children, it is often caused by staphylococcus bacteria. The organism usually enters the body through an infection of the mucous membranes, such as a strep throat, or through an infected sore on the body.

If untreated, osteomyelitis rapidly spreads through the bloodstream, eventually damaging the bone. Symptoms include constant and severe, often excruciating, pain near the end of the bone, followed by swelling. Children with osteomyelitis require immediate hospitalization upon diagnosis. Early treatment can save the bone from destruction. Because bone is hard tissue, it is often resistant to antibodies and is difficult to treat. (See also the section on Osteomyelitis in Chapter 21 on Infectious Diseases, page 441.)

BONE TUMORS

WHEN A TUMOR grows in or around the spine, it is usually benign. Such an abnormal growth is rarely life-threatening. However, a tumor can cause pressure and pain if it presses against a nerve root or if it

grows larger and begins to interfere with the function of an organ in the surrounding area. Enlargement of a tumor in the thoracic or cervical spine can create pressure on the spinal cord, possibly causing muscle weakness and, in rare cases, paralysis.

Two common benign tumors are lipomas and osteoid ostomas. A lipoma, or a small, fatty tumor, frequently appears in areas of tissue between the skin and various muscle groups in the spine. It feels tender at times but need not be removed unless it continues to grow. An osteoid ostoma is a small tumor appearing in the vertebrae or a long bone, which can cause piercing pain but can be relieved by taking aspirin. Surgical removal of the tumor can eliminate the pain.

An indication that a tumor may be developing is if the pain is not relieved by lying down. Most back pain disappears when the pressure is taken off the vertebrae. Pain caused by a tumor is the exception.

The appearance of a tumor growing in a bone often indicates that cancer cells have migrated (metastasized) from a malignancy elsewhere in the body. Tumors rarely begin in bone. An exception is myeloma, a cancer of the blood cells that eventually damages the bone marrow. (For bone cancer, see this section in Chapter 20 on Cancer, page 417.)

SPONDYLOSIS

MANY PEOPLE OVER 40 may suffer from spondylosis, a degenerative disk condition that can decrease flexibility in the spinal column and cause pain in the lumbar region. Spondylosis is characterized by a narrowing of the disk that serves as a cushion between the vertebral bodies. In some cases, bony spurs may form. Usually, this condition has no symptoms. While spondylosis is relatively common in the lumbar region, it also may occur in the cervical spine.

ANKYLOSING SPONDYLITIS

ANKYLOSING SPONDYLITIS, also known as Marie-Strümpell disease, is a form of rheumatoid arthritis that attacks the tendons, ligaments, and fibrous joint capsules around the spine. As the disease progresses, these normally soft tissues in the sacroiliac and intervertebral joints ossify, or turn into bone. As the ossification progresses, the vertebral bodies fuse together, turning the spine into a rigid piece of bone. Sometimes, the hips are also affected. The stiffened spine may make it impossible for the patient to stand erect or to look straight ahead. An x-ray of an affected spine has the appearance of a bamboo pole; thus this condition often is described as "bamboo spine."

This disease mostly affects young men between the late teens and age 30. The condition begins with low back pain which is not relieved by rest. Morning stiffness also may be present. There may be tenderness around the heels. Joints between the rib cage and vertebrae become inflamed, causing pain and loss of motion. When the vertebrae become fused to the rib cage, breathing becomes difficult.

While treatment cannot halt the course of ankylosing spondylitis, specially prescribed exercise regimens can allow the patient to retain as much of an upright posture as possible. Nonsteroidal antiinflammatory drugs may provide some relief. Surgery may be helpful in selected cases. (Also see section on spondylitis in Chapter 28 on Arthritis, page 579.)

BUNIONS

A BUNION forms when the bursa (a sac of fluid at friction points between the tendons and bone in some areas and between bone and the skin in others) becomes inflamed along the edge of the joint at the base of the big toe. Long periods of pressure from a tight-fitting shoe can cause the inflammation and pain. This often happens if the big toe is forced into a position where it presses inward and overlaps the second toe. The base of the big toe then is pushed beyond normal alignment of the foot, resulting in the prominence typical of a bunion. (See figures 27.8A–27.8C.)

The pain can be alleviated by lessening pressure on the bunion, accomplished by enlarging the shoe or by cutting out a portion of leather around the point of pressure. High-heeled and pointed-toe shoes should be avoided. If a bunion persists, surgical removal may be necessary.

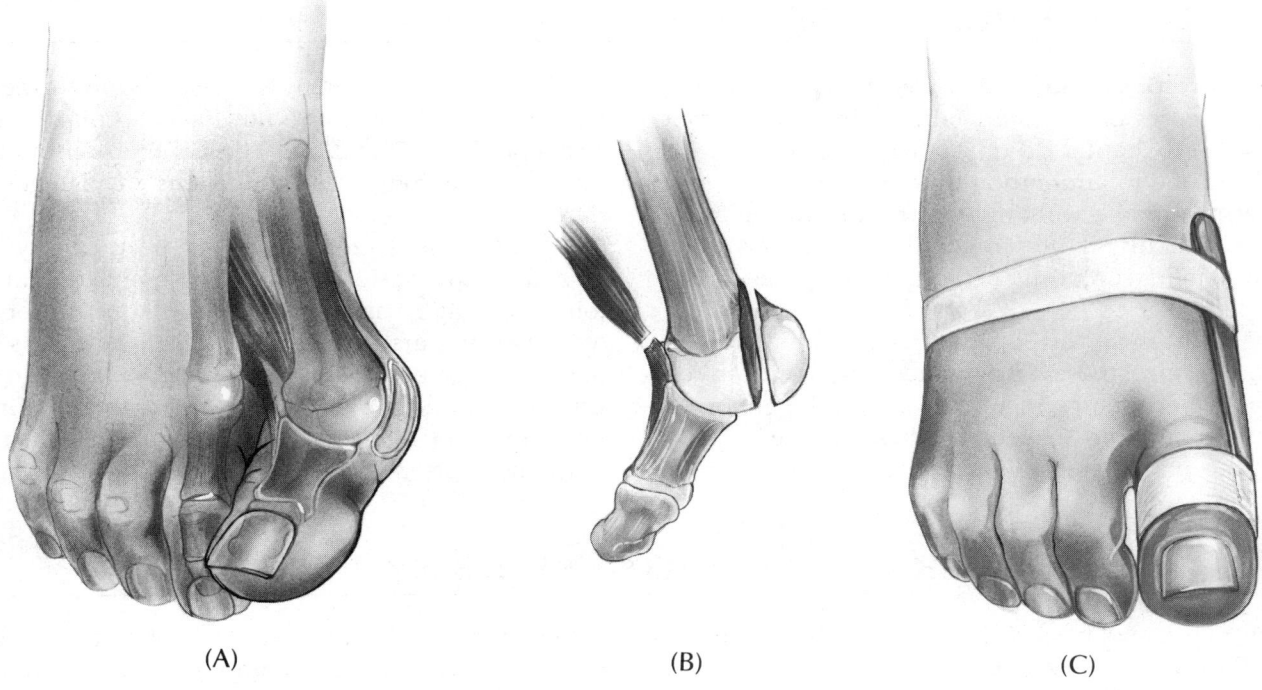

(A)　　　　　　　　　　(B)　　　　　　　　　　(C)

Figures 27.8A, 27.8B, and 27.8C. **In a bunion, the bursa of the big toe becomes inflamed, forcing the toe out of proper alignment (27.8A). Corrective measures include surgery (27.8B) to remove a portion of the toe joint or splinting (27.8C) to force the toe into proper position.**

HAMMERTOES

A HAMMERTOE IS A PAINFUL deformity that usually affects the second toe. The toe takes on a clawlike appearance, either because of a malalignment of the joint surfaces or a shortening and weakening of the toe and foot muscles. People with diabetes are prone to developing hammertoes because of the nerve and muscle damage that is a common complication of the disease. Wearing shoes that are too short also can cause a hammertoe. Special orthotic appliances to relieve and redistribute pressure often help. Pain may be relieved by injections of corticosteroids and local anesthetics. In severe cases, surgery to correct the deformity may be recommended.

BONE TRANSPLANT

WHEN CANCER or a congenital bone fracture in a limb resists healing, amputation may be necessary. However, partial transplant may be able to save the limb in some cases. The procedure, called a vascularized fibula transplant, frequently involves removing the diseased portion of the tibia (the thick bone in the lower leg) or a portion of the pelvis and replacing it with the fibula (the thin bone that extends from the knee joint to the ankle) from the normal leg. Blood vessels are reattached under an operating microscope to restore blood flow to the transplanted bone tissue and to promote its healing.

Removal of the fibula will not weaken the leg because the tibia, which remains in place, bears most of the weight that the body places on the leg. Though the fibula has a much smaller diameter than the tibia, the segment that has replaced the diseased part of the tibia increases its width over time to nearly the diameter of the tibia.

Cadaver bone may be used in some cases (an allograft), but it has a tendency to dissolve, shrink, and break after a few years. When transplanted bone comes from the patient (an autograft), the risk of rejection by the body's immune system is eliminated.

TOTAL JOINT REPLACEMENT

RHEUMATOID ARTHRITIS or osteoarthritis, degenerative diseases of the joints, affect millions of Americans. (See Chapter 28 on Arthritis, page 564.) The swelling and inflammation that typify these diseases sometimes make walking or arm and finger movements difficult, if not impossible. When crippling occurs, joint replacement surgery may be recommended.

Advances in orthopedic technology have resulted in prostheses to replace any joint in the body—whether hip, finger, knee, shoulder, elbow, or wrist. A ball-and-socket prosthesis made of polyethylene plastic and metal alloys that replaces the hip is the most common. It is usually preformed in patients over 60 who are not likely to place undue stress on the artificial hip. The same procedure may relieve some congenital conditions in younger patients.

Replacement of the hip has been highly successful. Many patients who have one artificial hip joint eventually may require replacement of the other because arthritis usually affects both hips. Replacement of knee joints can restore the ability to walk in a patient also hobbled by arthritis. Finger joints made of silicon create ease of motion with virtually no friction.

MUSCLE DISORDERS AND SPORTS INJURIES

OVER 600 MUSCLES drape the human skeleton and give the body its characteristic form. They enable us to walk down the street, dodge an obstacle and to stoop over, pick something up, and stand upright again. The muscles that we are most aware of are called skeletal or striated muscles, the ones that we see under the skin and that we can consciously flex and relax. They are connected to our bones by tough tissue called tendons. We are not conscious of the other two kinds of muscle in our bodies—of our internal organs such as stomach, intestines, uterus, and blood vessels. They are not attached to bone; they act slowly and they can stay contracted for long periods of time. Cardiac muscle is similar to smooth muscle in that its movements are not under our control; but it is, as its name implies, found only in the heart.

The great majority of muscle disorders are caused by exertion or strain that we are not accustomed to. Sports enthusiasts or those just beginning an exercise program are frequent victims, though muscle disorders are by no means restricted to those who exercise. A city dweller, forced into a sprint to cross a street against the light, could easily suffer the same muscle strain as someone just beginning to jog, as could a weekend gardener, housepainter, or carpenter. The injuries discussed in this section are thus common to anyone suddenly exerting himself. First, though, it is fitting to mention something about the value of staying in shape and about getting into shape.

Increasingly, Americans of all ages want to be physically fit. Exercise is important for maintaining healthy bones as well as for general fitness and well-being. Athletes, and those who regularly exercise, tend to have more muscle and more bone than those who are sedentary. But if exercise is to be of any value, it must be done regularly. Before plunging into any activity, using common sense is advised. People in the 40-and-over age group about to begin an exercise program and who live a sedentary lifestyle should have a routine medical examination.

Most sports injuries are the result of muscles that are out of condition. A person who works at a desk Monday through Friday and attempts several sets of tennis on a weekend without adequate conditioning is setting himself up for injury. If the chosen sport cannot be played daily, the sports enthusiast should at least work out by running or by doing calisthenics. Golfers, tennis players, racquetball players all can benefit from the same advice—develop a program that requires exercise at least 3 times per week. The proper conditioning can improve a person's body as well as his game.

Whatever the activity, it is important to prepare the body for exercise with a 10-minute warm-up session. Warm-ups start blood flow to the muscles and prepare them for the physical stress that will follow. A runner who fails to stretch before jogging increases the likelihood of developing a tear in a tight muscle. Another amateur athlete who enjoys golf may have weak abdominal muscles that cause low back pain after the first few holes. Weak or tight muscles practically invite injury. Special exercises to correct deficiencies in any area can eliminate most muscle pain if practiced regularly.

Those athletes who have suffered a muscle injury should wait until the pain disappears before using the muscle again. Otherwise, the injured area is more susceptible to further damage. Whether this is a sprain, strain, or fracture, make sure that the affected area has regained sufficient strength and flexibility to withstand repeated motions.

Someone who has been sidetracked by low back

pain should avoid contact sports which require sudden twisting, turning, and stopping. Football and soccer fall into this category. Bowling should be approached with caution because it requires bending and twisting, which can strain the back if the bowler is not careful. Softball can require sudden movement, such as running to catch a pop ball or sprinting to a base. This sudden call to action can damage weak or tight muscles.

Swimming is an excellent sport. The risk of injury is much less than that posed by running. This is because the swimmer is not using gravity-related muscles. Also, half of the swimmer's weight is suspended by the water in the pool.

Some injuries are very common. Among them are shin splints, runner's knee, pulled hamstrings, Achilles tendonitis, ankle sprain, arch sprain, Charley horse, muscle cramps, tennis elbow, and baseball finger in addition to fractures and bone bruises.

Shin Splints

This occurs when the tough, fibrous membrane that surrounds the bone and attaches it to the muscles along the tibia (the main bone in the calf) becomes inflamed and swollen. Shin splints can be caused by improper conditioning or by running on a hard surface. Rest and heat can relieve the pain they cause. They can be prevented by doing specific lower leg conditioning exercises.

Runner's Knee

A knee injury can result from sprains to the ligaments. A sprain, if mild, produces pain upon movement and local swelling. Swelling can be reduced by packing the area in ice and wrapping it with an elastic bandage. A severe sprain may produce tears in the cartilage which can cause a great deal of tenderness, swelling, and pain upon movement. This requires immediate medical attention.

Pulled Hamstrings

The hamstring muscle runs from the buttocks across the back of the thigh. Inadequate conditioning or a sudden stop or a sudden burst of activity can strain it.

Achilles Tendonitis

Tightness in the soleus muscle of the calf just above the heel can cause tendons in the area to become inflamed or to rupture during strenuous exercise. When the area suffers a strain, rest and anti-inflammatory medication are recommended. Torn Achilles tendons may require surgery to repair them. A lift may be inserted in the shoe heel of the affected leg to help relieve strain on the tendon.

Ankle Sprain

A sprain is a stretch or tear of the ligaments, the tissue that attaches one bone to another. (See figure 27.9.) If an ankle sprain is severe, it is accompanied by pain, swelling, tenderness, and an inability to move the area. Mild sprains can be treated with rest, ice, and elevation within the first 24 hours after injury to relieve the pain. If pain and swelling persist

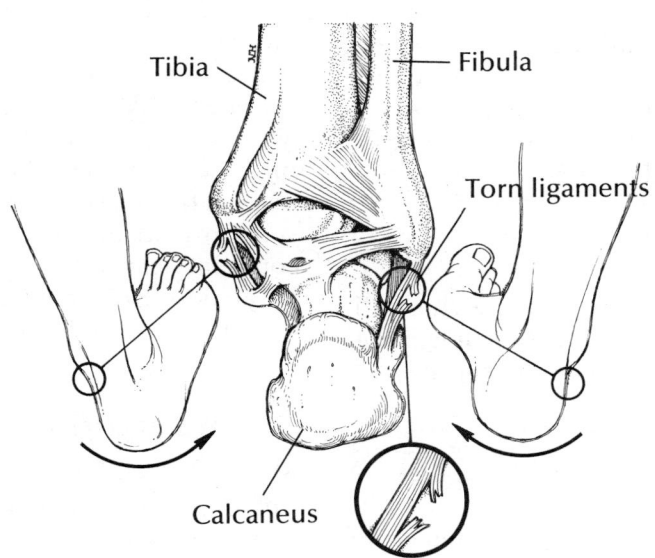

Figure 27.9. **This shows the tears in the ligaments of the ankle typical of a sprain.**

for more than 2 or 3 days, a doctor should be seen. Most sprains should heal within 2 weeks.

Arch Sprain

The main arch of the foot, called the longitudinal arch, may be subject to sprain. Injury usually is due to an overextension of the ligaments. Ice treatment and an elastic bandage are helpful for this type of sprain.

Charley Horse

When a ligament suffers an acute strain or sprain due to sudden stretching, the muscle fibers tear and blood may collect in a small area under the skin. Tenderness, pain, and local swelling usually are present. Resting the area and taping it with adhesive strapping can relieve pain.

Tennis Elbow

This syndrome common to tennis players affects people whose occupations call for frequent rotary motions of the forearm while the hand and wrist remain in the same position. Tennis elbow begins with an ache over the outer part of the elbow and then moves into the forearm. Constant grasping and twisting motions inflame the tendons on the outer side of the elbow as a result of chronic irritation of the area near the elbow joint. Resting the forearm by placing it in a splint and application of moist heat can relieve the symptoms.

Little Leaguer's Elbow

Youngsters whose bones are still growing can strain the elbow when throwing a ball. When there is pain, inflammation may be present. If unattended, the bone eventually could suffer a fracture. If the elbow sustains a strain injury, further pitching should be stopped until the area is fully healed.

Baseball Finger

When the end of a finger is hit by a fast-moving ball, the force can separate the first joint of the finger and the tendon from the bone. This condition may require a splint to immobilize the area.

Dislocation

Dislocations, especially of the shoulder, often occur in sports. A severe blow to the shoulder, a fall, or a twisting of the arm can cause joint ligaments to tear so that bones that should fit next to each other are suddenly separated. A dislocated joint is characterized by pain, swelling, rapid discoloration of surrounding tissue, and inability to move the area and a misshapen appearance. The joint must be immobilized and splinted to allow for healing.

Muscle Cramps

This sudden and sharp pain is generally associated with muscle spasms, which may result from an injury to the area, from stretching the muscle too much, or from an inadequate blood supply to the affected area. When cramps occur, gently but firmly rub the area—but do not attempt to stretch it too far.

Bursitis

A bursa is a tiny sac located where tendons pass over areas of bone around the joints. The bursae help minimize friction around instantly moving body parts. Trauma or overuse can cause the bursae to become inflamed. Bursitis can occur in the shoulder, knee, elbow, and in the hip. Splinting of the area, rest, and cortisone therapy, usually by injections into the inflamed area, are used to treat bursitis.

Myofascitis

Unaccustomed muscular exertion and unusual posture may result in inflammation and tenderness of the muscles and the sheaths that enclose them, the fascia. Myofascitis usually affects middle-aged people. Firm, but tender knots develop in the band of tissue on both sides of the spine, causing locally severe but ill-defined pain. Myofascitis is usually triggered by overuse of the affected muscles, especially in those with poor muscle tone who attempt strenuous activity. The pain may also begin after exposure to cold air or a draft. Medications, such as cortisone, can relieve pain. More lasting relief can be achieved by improving posture, reducing body weight, and exercising regularly.

Costochondritis

Also called Tietze's syndrome, costochondritis is an inflammation of the cartilage of one or more ribs, most commonly the second and third ribs. The condition may occur at any age, but it is more common in young adults. While the cause is unknown, onset may follow a severe blow to the chest. It may also be a part of generalized polyarthritis. The pain accompanying this disorder is usually intensified by actions that change the position of the ribs: bending, lying down, sneezing, coughing, and the like. The affected area of the chest is sensitive to the touch. Patients may believe that they are experiencing a heart attack; however, simple pressure on the chest wall will reproduce the symptoms.

This inflammatory disorder is usually of short duration. If treatment is required, it usually involves a short course of corticosteroid injections or anti-inflammatory drugs, coupled with reassurance of its benign nature.

Hernia

Our internal organs are sheathed and held in place by a wide band of muscle extending from the groin to the ribs. Without this, they would bulge out. As a result of a sudden strain, a weak point in the muscle wall may tear, allowing the internal organs, most often the intestine, to squeeze through the gap. This typically happens in 3 places—in the groin, either when internal organs force aside the weak abdominal muscles in the groin or because, in males, internal organs push their way down the inguinal canal, through which the testes descend shortly before or after birth; near the navel, where the abdominal muscles are weak; or somewhere in the line between the navel and the breastbone, where the muscle wall is thin. The symptoms are a sudden lump under the skin, a localized tenderness, and sometimes a heaviness in the region. The danger is that if the intestine has pushed through the muscle wall, its contents can be prevented from moving. This is called an obstructed hernia. The more severe danger is that the blood supply to the intestinal segment will be cut off and the tissue will die, resulting in gangrene. In both cases, surgery will probably be needed and medical attention should be sought as soon as the uncharacteristic bulging is noticed.

28 Arthritis

Israeli Jaffe, M.D.

INTRODUCTION

ARTHRITIS is the leading cause of physical disability in the United States. An estimated 30 million people suffer from one of its many forms and, each year, more than half of them seek professional help in dealing with it. Of this number, about 3 to 4 million have to restrict their normal activities in some way because of the disease. But, despite this, more and more arthritis patients are being helped with new medications and other approaches to treatment, as well as a greater understanding of the nature of the disease.

The term arthritis means "inflammation of the

joint." Together with the rheumatic diseases that affect the soft tissues, arthritis encompasses more than 100 different conditions. Of these, the most widespread is degenerative joint disease (sometimes referred to as osteoarthritis), which is most common among older people. With increasing life expectancy, the number of patients suffering from degenerative joint disease keeps growing. Rheumatoid arthritis, which may occur at any age, is one of the most destructive of the joint diseases. Gout is the one in which treatment has been most successful. There are many others, the most common of which will be discussed in subsequent sections of this chapter.

Arthritis is not restricted to any geographic location, climate, or age. It has been diagnosed in the skeletons of prehistoric man, and it is common among most warm-blooded animals. Even though the cause or causes of most forms of arthritis are still unknown, significant advances in diagnostic techniques, medications, and surgical procedures now enable most patients to live reasonably active, productive lives.

Arthritis may be found in a wide variety of circumstances: genetic predisposition, biochemical abnormalities, endocrine disorders, as a complication of other diseases, and most probably, a fundamental defect in the immune system. In some cases, it may be the direct or indirect result of infection, athletic injury, or surgery. The earlier the symptoms are recognized and treated, the better the outcome for the patient.

JOINT STRUCTURE

BEFORE DISCUSSING specific types of arthritis, it may be useful to begin with an overview of joint structure and function. A joint forms the connection between two bones. (See figure 28.1.) In order for a joint to move freely, the bone ends are covered with cartilage—a tough, slippery material that acts as a protective cushion. The bones are connected to each other by ligaments—tough bands of tissue that hold the joint in place and reinforce the joint capsules.

The muscles are attached to bones by tendons, bands of tissue that are longer than ligaments. Each joint is lined by a synovial membrane, a sac containing synovial fluid, which acts as a lubricant, enabling the joint surfaces to function in a smooth, friction-free way. Normally, the fluid is viscous, clear, and nearly colorless, and it provides nourishment for the cartilage, which contains no blood vessels.

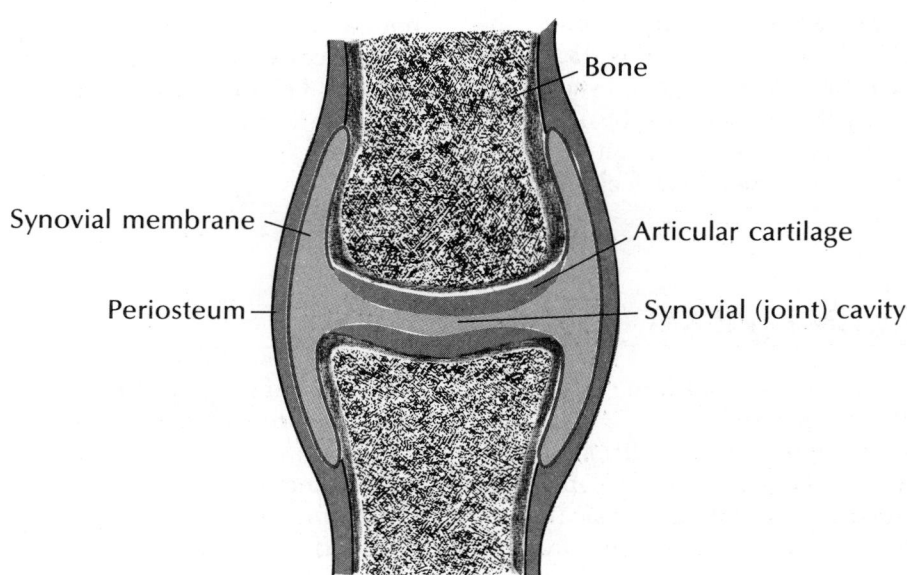

Figure 28.1. **Structure of a normal joint.**

WHEN TO CONSULT A PHYSICIAN

FROM TIME TO TIME, everyone has aches and pains that are similar to those of some kind of rheumatic or arthritic disorder. In most instances, these turn out to be temporary and do not require medical attention. In contrast, most forms of arthritis are chronic. While there may be long periods of symptom-free remission, there is usually no permanent cure. With proper diagnosis and treatment, most types of arthritis can be controlled. The earlier a diagnosis is established, the better; therefore, anyone experiencing symptoms or signs suggesting the possibility of arthritis should be seen promptly by a physician. These include:

- Persistent pains in the joints that interfere with normal activities.
- Persistent pain and stiffness on arising in the morning.
- Soreness and swelling in any joint or in a symmetrical (both sides of the body) pair of joints.
- Pains in the joints that interfere with sleep.
- Loss of weight, fatigue, and fever accompanied by joint pains.

HOW THE DIAGNOSIS IS ESTABLISHED

AN INTERNIST or family practitioner can usually make an initial diagnosis based upon medical history, physical examination, x-rays, and laboratory tests. Analysis of the synovial fluid may also be needed, especially if it is suspected that the arthritis may be caused by infection.

When the diagnosis is in doubt, or when rheumatoid arthritis, lupus, or other more serious and uncommon forms of the disease are suspected, the patient may be referred to a specialist for further evaluation. Since there are only about 3,000 rheumatologists in the United States, this may involve going to a major medical center or university hospital. However, many smaller communities and rural areas now have access to arthritis treatment centers that serve as clearinghouses for information about doctors, specialized clinics, and related services.

THE RIGHT DOCTOR

AS WITH ANY CHRONIC DISEASE, long-term management of arthritis requires establishing a good rapport and working relationship with the doctor in charge of overall treatment. The physician should be experienced in treating the particular type of arthritis; he or she should also be a person with whom both the patient and family members feel comfortable. There are still many unanswered questions about arthritis and living with a chronic disease can be physically and emotionally trying for everyone involved. Feelings of fear, anger, frustration, or depression are common, and should be recognized and dealt with.

THE TREATMENT TEAM

VERY OFTEN, care is a team effort with the patient as the most important member because he or she must follow the day-to-day regimen. In addition to the physician in charge, members of the treatment team may include other medical specialists, physical therapists to set up the right programs for maintaining joint and muscle function, visiting nurses or other home health aides, and orthopedic surgeons. Increasingly, occupational therapists are being consulted to help with the practical mechanics of getting through a day: dressing and undressing, coping in the kitchen, learning new ways of getting into and out of a car, performing job-related tasks, and maintaining mobility as much as possible.

A comparatively new specialist is a person who is trained in the fitting of splints, braces, and foot supports. Known as orthotics, this practice has been increasingly helpful to arthritis patients. Appliances of lightweight metal or plastic, which often are worn during sleep or for a few hours in the daytime, support joints in ways that can retard the development of permanent deformity.

Psychiatric social workers and family counselors are still other allied health professionals who may be helpful for arthritis patients and their families. Adults who feel guilty about their inability to care for their children or to perform competently at their jobs, and adolescents whose social, academic, and athletic lives have been disrupted are among the typical patients who may need supportive therapy in order to cope successfully with the emotional impact of their illness.

CLASSIFICATION OF ARTHRITIS

THERE ARE SEVERAL WAYS of classifying the various types of arthritis. In its latest *Primer on the Rheumatic Diseases*, the Arthritis Foundation lists 10 different categories of arthritis according to the pathology and mechanisms involved. Many physicians and patients, however, may prefer a simplified system that groups types of arthritis according to the structures that are most involved.

- *Arthritis involving inflammation of the joint membrane.* This type of arthritis is characterized by inflammation of the synovial membrane, which lines the joint. It is a major feature of rheumatoid arthritis and other inflammatory joint disorders.
- *Arthritis involving cartilage breakdown.* Degeneration of cartilage, the gristlelike material that covers the ends of bones, is a major characteristic of degenerative joint disease or osteoarthritis. It is usually associated with aging or "wear and tear," and is most common in middle-aged and older people.
- *Arthritis involving metabolic disorders.* Gout is the major form of arthritis in this category. In this disorder, tiny urate crystals are deposited in the joint space, leading to inflammation and, very often, extreme pain.
- *Arthritis resulting from infection.* A number of infectious agents can invade the joint space, resulting in inflammation. The most common types of infectious arthritis are caused by bacteria, particularly the gonococcus and staphylococcus, but viruses, fungi, and parasites also may cause arthritis.
- *Arthritis resulting from trauma.* Athletes and other people who place undue stress on certain joints are particularly susceptible to traumatic arthritis. Tennis elbow and runner's knees are common examples. The inflammation often involves tendons and muscles, and may be a temporary condition that disappears with rest and corrective measures.
- *Arthritis involving the spine.* The most serious form of spinal arthritis, ankylosing spondylitis, may occur by itself or as a component of other diseases, such as ulcerative colitis, psoriasis, or Reiter's syndrome. Stiffness is a major characteristic; in severe cases of ankylosing spondylitis, the spine may become quite rigid.
- *Arthritis associated with other diseases and miscellaneous causes.* Many diseases involve the joints and result in considerable pain and inflammation. Common examples include hemophilia, sickle cell anemia, diabetes, thyroid and other endocrine disorders, inflammatory bowel disease, hepatitis, and psoriasis, among others.

Psychological factors are sometimes associated with arthritislike symptoms. Psychological stress or tension also may produce generalized aching, which may be mistaken for arthritis.

AN OVERVIEW OF TREATMENT

TREATMENT FOR ARTHRITIS has several goals: relief of pain, reduction of stiffness, control of inflammation, maintenance of joint mobility, and prevention of deformity. Very often, a combination of therapies may be required. These may include drug therapy, a regimen of rest and exercise, the use of physical therapy and, if indicated, surgical correction of deformed joints or their replacement with artificial ones. An overweight patient may be advised to lose weight to relieve stress on weight-bearing joints. In some instances, a readjustment of responsibilities at home, on the job, or at school may be advised.

Other Approaches to Treatment

Rest and Exercise. A combined schedule of rest and exercise is an important component in treating rheumatoid and other forms of inflammatory arthritis. Long periods of bed rest are discouraged because this can increase muscle wasting and stiffening of the joints. Similarly, excessive or improper exercise can exacerbate the inflammatory process and increase joint damage. A careful regimen that combines rest with exercises to promote and maintain joint mobility without undue stress should be designed to meet individual patient needs.

Heat. Heat, administered in the form of warm baths or wet compresses, is one of the oldest methods of relieving chronic pain. Some people find that starting the day with a warm bath or shower helps relieve morning stiffness; others like to use heat both before and after exercise. Hot wax treatments, in which paraffin wax is melted and a painful hand placed in it, is an old remedy that many arthritis patients find helpful.

Cold. Cold may be very useful for acute pain, particularly after injury to a joint or its surrounding ligaments and tendons. A plastic bag filled with ice may be applied for short periods, directly to the inflamed area.

Surgery. In recent years, major advances have been made in developing artificial joints to replace those severely damaged by arthritis. Perhaps the most successful to date are the artificial hip joints and artificial knees. Although these operations have gained a good deal of public attention and are now performed widely throughout the industrialized world, it should be stressed that joint replacement is reserved for advanced disease. While the artificial joints are highly useful in restoring joint function, they do not work as well as natural ones, and there is a risk of infection and other complications. Therefore, joint replacement is generally considered a treatment of last resort. Nonetheless, the total hip replacement must be regarded as a major milestone in arthritis therapy, and many individuals are highly functional members of society today only because of this surgery.

Other operations are available to reduce deformity and restore function. These include synovectomy, which involves removal of the diseased synovial membrane, and orthopedic procedures to realign deformed toes or fingers.

Experimental Treatments

Research and experimental testing of new treatments for arthritis are constantly being undertaken to find more effective approaches to the disease. Current experimental treatments, in addition to new drugs, include plasmapheresis, a procedure in which the blood is circulated through a machine to filter out components thought to contribute to the inflammatory process, and total body irradiation, which is meant to kill the lymphoid cells that make anti-

bodies. These treatments are highly experimental and carried out on a very controlled basis at a few research centers.

Quackery

In sharp contrast to legitimate experimental treatments are a wide variety of unproven therapies, many of which are outright quackery with no real medical merit or benefit. Whenever we have a chronic disease with no satisfactory treatment or cure, we are likely to find unscrupulous individuals who prey upon its victims. While it is unfortunate that there are people who set out to profit from the misfortune of others, the fact remains that each year hundreds of millions of dollars are spent on worthless quack remedies by willing victims. Rheumatoid arthritis patients seem to be particularly susceptible to quackery, perhaps because it is a disease that may come and go spontaneously, and because conventional therapies are often so unsatisfactory. If a period of remission happens to coincide with a quack treatment, there is a natural tendency to credit the therapy, even if the improvement is totally unrelated.

Examples of arthritis quackery include things like copper bracelets, bee venom, flu shots, megavitamins, and a variety of diets, balms, or salves. None of these has any beneficial property aside from a possible placebo effect. People who resort to such obviously worthless remedies often defend their action by saying: "I've tried everything my doctor recommends and I still have arthritis. What do I have to lose?" Aside from the money, time, and energy that could be better spent, all too many people who have resorted to arthritis quackery have lost a good deal because not all of these worthless remedies are as harmless as copper bracelets. The arthritis pills and shots offered by clinics on the Mexican border, for example, often turn out to be large doses of steroids, which can have very serious side effects. DMSO, an industrial solvent that is absorbed through the skin, is widely available as an arthritis remedy, even though it has never received FDA approval. Animal studies have found that DMSO is potentially harmful and the FDA has rejected it for human use. (When DMSO is applied in a diluted solution on the skin, it is not harmful, but if it is taken internally, it may be highly toxic.) Nevertheless, faddist publications continue to promote it as a "miracle" drug that is being suppressed by the medical establishment in much the same way that Laetrile is being suppressed for cancer therapy. There is no evidence supporting claims that either DMSO or Laetrile is of any value, and people who resort to treatment with either are falling victim to a hoax.

COMMON TYPES OF ARTHRITIS

RHEUMATOID ARTHRITIS

RHEUMATOID ARTHRITIS is the most common form of crippling arthritis, with an estimated 5 to 8 million Americans affected by the disease. Rheumatoid arthritis may occur at any age from infancy to late adulthood but, for the most part, it tends to strike at the prime of life—in the thirties and forties. For reasons that are not fully understood, the disease is more common and severe in women than in men. The severity of rheumatoid arthritis varies, and many people have it in a very mild form. It tends to wax and wane, sometimes seeming to disappear almost entirely. Often though, the course tends to be progressive, with attacks occurring at more frequent intervals, with the periods of remission tending to become shorter.

Like many forms of arthritis, pain and stiffness are major symptoms; in rheumatoid arthritis, however, these symptoms are characteristically worse upon arising in the morning and tend to lessen as the day progresses. Pain and stiffness are symptoms of inflamed joints and inflammation is the hallmark of rheumatoid arthritis. Its early symptoms are usually redness, swelling, and warmth in the affected joint. There is probably no other disease in all of medicine where body tissues suffer such a prolonged and sustained inflammatory response.

The disease is characterized not only by inflammation of the joints themselves, but it is also a systemic disorder, affecting the entire body. Patients suffering from rheumatoid arthritis are truly sick. They very often experience symptoms of weakness and listlessness, and they tire easily and may have loss of appetite and weight. These symptoms represent the body's response to some of the toxic products resulting from the chronic, sustained inflammation. It is not uncommon for patients with this disease to feel exhausted by 3 or 4 o'clock in the afternoon, even on a day when very little work has been done. Furthermore, there are times when rheumatoid inflammation extends beyond the joints themselves, and may involve major organs of the body such as the eyes, heart, or lungs, and the membranes that cover them. The muscles also may be affected.

In rheumatoid arthritis, the inflammation initially is confined to the synovium, the delicate membrane that lines the joint. While synovitis is not unique to rheumatoid arthritis, the rheumatoid type of synovitis tends to be persistent and appears to have as its ultimate "purpose" the destruction of what is called the articular cartilage, which acts as a cushion or shock absorber between the opposing ends of bone that make up the joint.

The rheumatoid synovial membrane undergoes a large degree of swelling and enlargement, mostly due to an accumulation of cells devoted to sustaining the inflammation and producing various types of antibodies. This thickened and active synovial membrane begins to attack the articular cartilage, and until the articular cartilage in a given joint is completely destroyed, the rheumatoid synovitis never fully subsides. It seems plausible that there may be some as yet unidentified substance in the articular cartilage itself that incites this intense synovial inflammatory reaction. (See figure 28.2.)

In addition to inflammation of the synovial membrane, there is also an accumulation of fluid within the joint space itself. Both of these factors produce pain, and it is this swelling and distention of the joint that pulls on delicate nerve fibers and sends pain messages to the brain. Whenever intense inflammation exists, the body responds by attempting to immobilize or rest the inflamed area. In the case of an inflamed joint, this manifests itself as muscle spasm or muscle stiffness, and this stiffness makes motion about the joint even more difficult and painful for the rheumatoid patient. In arthritis, the stiffness is counterproductive; although the response is intended to splint or rest the joint, it actually makes use of the joint all the more difficult, and too much immobilization can result in loss of function.

As the articular cartilage becomes progressively destroyed—the process may take many years—the edges of bone meet each other. When this occurs, the inflammation tends to subside and the bones fuse together. When a rheumatoid joint has become completely fused, either naturally. or, in some cases surgically, then the process subsides in that particular area. But this is a great price for relief of pain—the complete loss of function in that joint.

The Disease Process

While it is not known what triggers the rheumatoid process or what continues to give it momentum as the disease evolves, we now understand something of the way in which inflammation destroys the joint structures. Rheumatoid factor, a substance found in the blood and joint fluid of about 80 percent of adult patients with rheumatoid arthritis, is a gamma-globulin, or an antibody. This antibody is of a par-

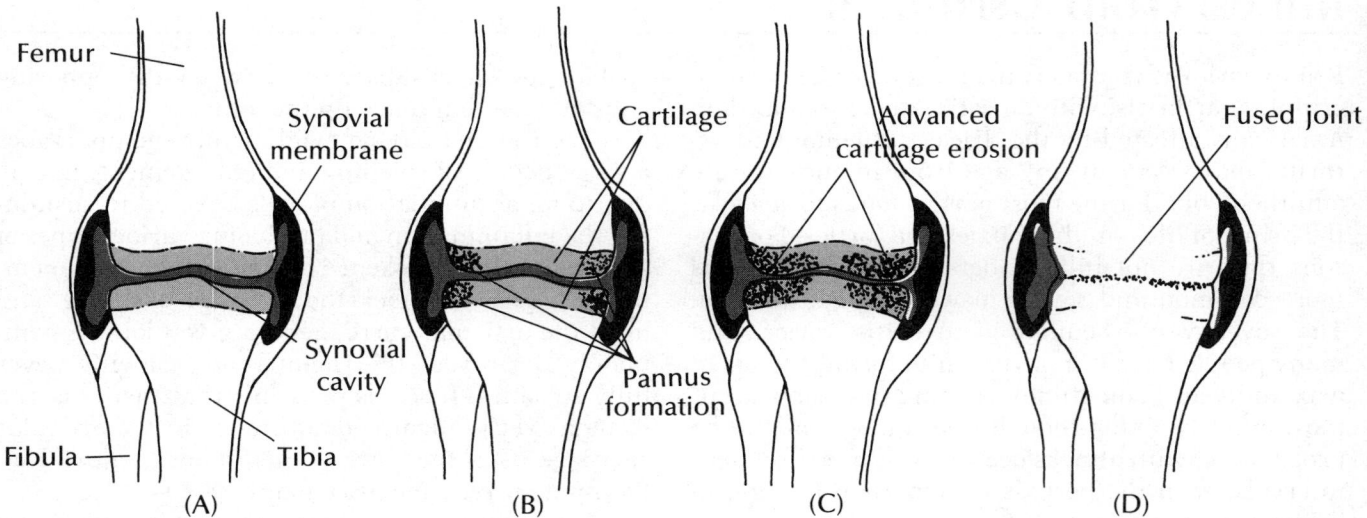

Figure 28.2. **Progression of rheumatoid arthritis. The process begins with inflammation of the synovial membrane (A) and progresses to pannus formation and erosion of cartilage (B). In the more advanced stages, pannus formation continues (C) and there is further erosion of cartilage. Finally, the joint cavity is destroyed and the articulating bones, in this drawing the knees, become fused (D).**

ticular class that is directed against the patient's normal gamma-globulin, and is therefore an autoantibody directed against a natural body constituent. The detection of rheumatoid factor in the joint fluid, synovial membrane, and blood of arthritis patients led researchers to theorize that it may play a role in inducing or sustaining the characteristic inflammation. In the patient with rheumatoid arthritis, the antibody is made directly by certain synovial cells, and is released directly into the joint space. There, it interacts with the patient's own gamma-globulin, forming an immune complex, which can itself cause inflammation. This occurs by invoking another body constituent called complement, which is a very complex substance composed of many, many fractions.

Complement attracts inflammatory cells to enter the joint space and engulf these immune complexes. These scavenger cells often break, and when they do, they liberate enzymes that can destroy joint tissue. Thus, in the body's effort to eliminate these immune complexes, inflammation results, and as a by-product of the inflammation, substances are produced that destroy tissue. By-products of these dying tissues cause more inflammation as the body attempts to clear away the debris. There appears to be a circular process in the rheumatoid joint which feeds upon itself and which has as its end result increasing destruction of tissue.

The synovial lining cells multiply rapidly and begin to resemble "factories" for antibody production—making more and more of the immune complexes. Furthermore, the synovial membrane itself then begins to attack the articular cartilage directly. The synovial membrane forms what is called a pannus, which begins to envelop the articular cartilage and grow around it. As the pannus derived from the rheumatoid synovial membrane comes into contact with the articular cartilage, the cells of the pannus make an enzyme called collagenase, which "opens the door" to the articular cartilage itself, thereby allowing tissue-destructive enzymes to enter and destroy the cartilage further.

As yet, we do not know what sets the process in motion or what is responsible for the formation of the rheumatoid factor and the immune complexes. Some researchers believe that a virus or other infective agent may be responsible. Others believe that there may be more than one inciting cause, and that it might be just a portion of a bacterium that has passed innocently through the body and joint tissues. This foreign substance could perhaps become lodged or hidden in the articular cartilage, and in the body's attempt to rid itself of this "antigen," the cartilage is destroyed.

Of course, there are patients who do not have rheumatoid factor detectable either in the blood or the synovial fluid. How can arthritis occur in these patients? So far, this question is unanswered. In some patients, it appears that there may be rheumatoid factors, different from the classical type, that are not detected by the usual tests. Of the 15 or 20 percent of the patients with rheumatoid arthritis who test negative for the rheumatoid factor in its usual form, a large percentage will have less readily detectable rheumatoid factors, which might conceivably play a similar role in the initiation and maintenance of rheumatoid joint inflammation.

Clinical Manifestations

Rheumatoid arthritis tends to involve joints in a symmetrical fashion; if finger joints on one hand are involved, for example, it is likely that the same joints on the other hand also will be affected, but not necessarily simultaneously.

In the affected joints, there will be pain and swelling and, as noted earlier, morning stiffness, which is perhaps the most sensitive measure of the degree of inflammation. Function becomes the key word as the disease progresses. For the parent who is unable to diaper the baby, the secretary who can no longer type, the individual who no longer can dress or take care of personal needs, the disease has begun to take its toll.

Steps in Diagnosis

Rheumatoid arthritis is diagnosed by analyzing the patient's medical history and from the results of physical examination. Usually, certain laboratory tests will confirm that there is inflammation in the body. One very useful test in this regard is the sedimentation rate, which measures the rate at which red blood cells fall in 1 hour within a specially calibrated tube. An elevated sedimentation rate does not necessarily lead to a diagnosis of rheumatoid arthritis, since the test measures inflammation in the body of whatever cause, but it does correlate well with the degree of the inflammatory process of rheumatoid arthritis. A fall in the sedimentation rate usually means a decrease in inflammation and an improvement in the disease and the converse is also true.

Patients with rheumatoid arthritis often show moderate anemia, which is largely due to a suppressive effect of the chronic inflammation on the blood-forming organs. This anemia is not materially helped by iron or vitamins, although there is often a superimposed iron deficiency due to hidden bleeding from the gastrointestinal tract caused by the anti-inflammatory drugs.

Treatment of Rheumatoid Arthritis

As in any chronic disease without an identified cause, effective treatment of rheumatoid arthritis tends to be difficult. While we have drugs to help relieve symptoms, control of the underlying process in an attempt to prevent joint destruction and deformity is only partially effective. Nevertheless, there is ground for optimism. As our understanding of the mechanism of the rheumatoid inflammation increases, the development of more drugs to interrupt this process can be expected.

Since a basic hallmark of the disease is inflammation, it follows that drugs whose major function is the suppression of inflammation clearly have a place in the treatment program of patients with rheumatoid arthritis. As noted in the introductory section of this chapter, aspirin is one of the oldest drugs available which can be used for this purpose. Aspirin is both a painkiller (analgesic) and an anti-inflammatory drug; the difference lies in the dosage. The maximum analgesic effects are achieved with 2 regular (5-grain) aspirin tablets taken every 4 hours or so. In contrast, a much higher dose—usually 16 to 24 5-grain tablets per day—is required to control joint inflammation.

Although high-dose aspirin is highly effective in controlling inflammation, it may produce undesirable side effects. Ringing in the ears, nausea, stomach or duodenal ulcers, gastrointestinal bleeding, and abdominal pain are among the most common side effects of aspirin therapy. Aspirin also reduces the blood's clotting ability, which may result in bleeding problems. These adverse reactions can often be minimized by reducing the dosage and by taking the aspirin with food (for example, milk and bread) or antacids, to help protect the stomach. Time-released, arthritis strength, and other "special" aspirin formulations are highly promoted for the treatment of arthritis, but many experts feel that these forms may be only slightly better or more protective than ordinary aspirin. Extra-strength aspirin simply contains more acetylsalicylic acid, the active ingredient in the drug. The same effect can be achieved by taking an equivalent amount of regular 5-grain or 325-milligram tablets. Some doctors recommend buffered aspirin, which contains an antacid, but again, the same effect can be achieved at a lower cost by using regular aspirin and an antacid or milk to protect the stomach.

Tylenol and other forms of acetaminophen, the major nonaspirin painkiller, are analgesic with only weak anti-inflammatory effects at very high dosages. Thus, they may relieve minor arthritis pain, but they are not as effective as high-dose aspirin in controlling inflammation.

The newer nonsteroidal anti-inflammatory drugs (NSAIDs) are as effective as, or more effective than, aspirin, and they have much less potential for gastrointestinal irritation and bleeding. These drugs interfere with the production of prostaglandins, hormonelike substances that are thought to play a role in the inflammatory process (among many other functions). Specific drugs in this category, listed alphabetically by generic name followed by brand names in parentheses, are: diflunisal (Dolobid); fenoprofen calcium (Nalfon); ibuprofen (Motrin, Rufen, or in an over-the-counter, nonprescription strength: Advil and Nupren); indomethacin (Indocin); meclofenamate sodium (Meclomen); naproxen (Naprosyn); phenylbutazone (Butazolidin); piroxicam (Feldene); sulindac (Clinoril); and tolmetin sodium (Tolectin). These drugs, when taken in their recommended doses, are at least as potent as large doses of aspirin in controlling inflammation, and often may not be as likely to cause gastric distress and bleeding. They may therefore be tolerated by patients who cannot take aspirin in the required dosage. Nevertheless, they may have adverse effects, which include gastrointestinal bleeding, nausea, heartburn, stomach ulcers, rash, itching, kidney irritation, sedation, headache, and mood changes. Side effects should be reported promptly to your doctor, who may change the dosage or the drug.

No one NSAID is distinctly superior to the others. Although all NSAIDs are believed to be similar in their mechanism of action, they are chemically different, and individual patients differ in their response to them. Thus, one drug may work better than others for a given patient at any given time, or be better tolerated. This is why the trial-and-error approach is often needed before arriving at the most effective drug and dosage. These drugs act fairly rapidly, and a physician can judge, usually within 7 to 10 days, which will be best for a particular patient. After prolonged use, they may lose their effectiveness and others may then be substituted. One of the oldest NSAIDs, phenylbutazone (Butazolidin), has very little place in the treatment of chronic rheumatoid arthritis because of its potential for serious toxic effects, particularly on the bone marrow.

Corticosteroids—powerful drugs that counter inflammation—also are used to treat rheumatoid arthritis, although they have failed to "cure" the disease, as was first thought when cortisone was introduced some 40 years ago. Steroids may produce dramatic initial relief of the pain, swelling, and inflammation of arthritis, but these effects tend to be temporary and their long-term use produces a host of serious adverse effects. These include lowered resistance to infection, a thinning of the bones (os-

teoporosis) and skin, gastrointestinal ulcers and intestinal bleeding, mental changes (nervousness, insomnia, depression, and psychosis), diabetes, and cataracts. The adrenal glands undergo a temporary loss of function during (and after) prolonged steroid therapy, and supplementary or additional steroids must be taken in the event of stressful situations, such as surgery, infection, or injury. Obviously, systemic steroids should be used cautiously and under careful medical supervision. An alternative approach is to inject a small amount of a steroid directly into the inflamed joint, thereby avoiding the problems of systemic administration. There is, however, a limit on how many injections may be administered to a particular joint within a given time period.

In the 1930s, it was discovered by chance that soluble salts of metallic gold helped patients with rheumatoid arthritis. Gold injections may cause a number of adverse reactions, including skin rashes and damage to the blood-forming organs and the kidneys. With a greater understanding of the proper method of dosage, most of these side effects have been greatly decreased and gold treatment has become an accepted standard treatment for severe rheumatoid arthritis. Unlike cortisone and nonsteroidal anti-inflammatory drugs, gold seems to suppress the disease process at a very fundamental level, although how this occurs is unknown. It must be given for a prolonged period of time—usually 3 or 4 months—before its beneficial effects become apparent—but even after the injections have been discontinued, these effects usually persist for many months. This is in sharp contrast to the anti-inflammatory drugs, which work within hours following their administration, only to have the effects disappear shortly after the last dose.

About 70 percent of all patients receiving gold will experience benefit and, in such patients, it is accepted practice to continue maintenance treatment with an injection every 3 or 4 weeks for an indefinite period in order to sustain the improvement. This is particularly important because a second or third course of gold is often less effective than the initial one, and the maintenance gold injections are usually associated with very little risk. A true remission induced by gold is very similar to that which occurs naturally in the evolution of the disease; unfortunately, this does not occur in all patients. Those who respond will experience a decrease in morning stiffness, an increase in strength and sense of well-being, and a decrease in signs of inflammation in the joints with less swelling and less limitation of motion. These patients can usually reduce their dosage of nonsteroidal drugs or corticosteroids. In time, the favorable effects of gold may be lost despite maintenance therapy. In addition, there are patients who are not helped by gold or who cannot tolerate it because of toxicity.

There is a new form of gold (auranoflin or Ridaura) that is taken by mouth, but as of this writing, it has not been approved for general use in this country. This oral gold produces fewer side effects, but it also is not quite as effective as the injections. For patients who cannot tolerate the injections, however, it may be a possible alternative.

Penicillamine is yet another of the slow-acting drugs which may be used for progressive arthritis that is not adequately controlled by other medications. This drug, which is taken by mouth, is a chelating agent normally used to remove excessive lead, copper, or other metals from the body or to treat cystinuria, a particular type of kidney stone disease.

Penicillamine was first studied in rheumatoid arthritis because it caused a disappearance of rheumatoid factor from the blood. Some of these patients went into a remission similar to that which could be induced by gold. Penicillamine has been under extensive clinical study for the last 15 years, and it has been found to be as effective as gold in producing improvement in rheumatoid arthritis. It has the advantage that it can be taken by mouth, thereby avoiding the discomfort of weekly injections, but it has many side effects, some of which are similar to those produced by gold. In some instances, it can be used as an alternative to gold when that drug can no longer be tolerated or has become ineffective.

Antimalarial agents, such as chloroquine and hydroxychloroquine (Plaquenil), are effective in controlling the inflammation of rheumatoid arthritis and a mild form of lupus, called discoid lupus. It is not known how the drugs work, but they are usually well tolerated. Their major potential side effect involves damage to the retina; arthritis patients taking antimalarial drugs are advised to see an ophthalmologist every 6 months for a careful eye examination. Since these drugs are also slow in onset of effectiveness, they, like gold and penicillamine, should be taken along with aspirin or an NSAID.

Other drugs that may be used to treat refractory rheumatoid arthritis include immunosuppressive drugs, which counter the immunologic processes responsible for the tissue destruction. Unfortunately, the overall results with the use of these agents has not been uniformly successful and their potential for toxicity is high.

Finally, a new class of compounds under study for possible use in rheumatoid arthritis is the immunoenhancing or immunoregulatory agents. Why would one want to stimulate the immune response when overactivity by immunological tissues is part of the destructive process? The explanation for this apparent contradiction is that if a hidden infective agent or antigen is responsible for inducing rheumatoid inflammation, then an augmentation of the immunological response rather than its suppression might eliminate it. More study is needed before we will know if this strategy works. Clinical research has shown, however, that the immunostimulant drug Levamisole produces remission in some patients, but with an unacceptably high incidence of side effects.

Nondrug Treatment of Rheumatoid Arthritis.

In addition to drug therapy, both physical therapy and orthopedic surgery play a major role in the treatment of rheumatoid arthritis. When applied during the acute phase of the disease, physical therapy, such as heat, rest, and gentle massage, is directed toward reducing inflammation. In addition, physical measures can help prevent deformity and restore function.

Physical therapy is most effective when drug therapy has been successful in suppressing the basic inflammatory process. Vigorous physical therapy designed to restore joint function cannot be applied until inflammation has been controlled, because it can aggravate the disease process. Even so, many physiotherapeutic measures can be done by the patient at home, and these greatly facilitate restoration of joint function and rehabilitation.

As noted earlier, orthopedic surgery is becoming increasingly important in the overall treatment of rheumatoid arthritis. Certainly the most exciting and revolutionary progress has been made in the area of total joint replacement. This technique was pioneered initially for the hip joint, which remains the most successful of the total joint replacement procedures. Replacement of the knee is a newer development, but while the results are somewhat less satisfactory, they are continually improving. Both of these operations involve the removal of the diseased joint, including as much of the synovium as possible. This explains why the results in the hip are so uniformly good, for there are no remnants of the aggressive, diseased synovial tissue left to continue their destructive process. (See figure 28.3.) In the total knee replacement, all synovium cannot be removed, and low-grade arthritis activity can continue around the prosthesis. In some patients, both hips and knees have been successfully replaced with a remarkable restoration of function. Recent results of total shoulder and elbow replacement give cause for optimism that these joints as well will be increasingly benefited by surgery.

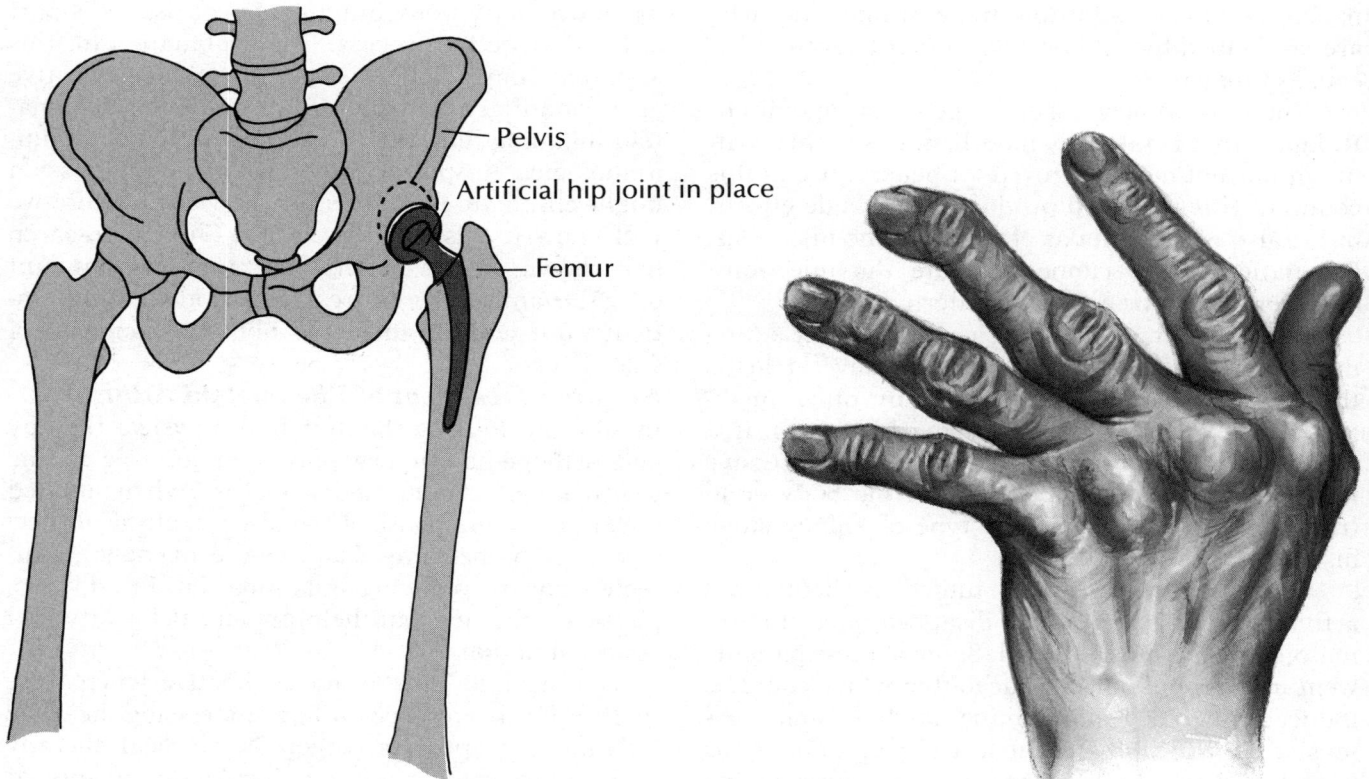

Figure 28.3. **Total hip joint replacement with prosthesis.**

Figure 28.4. **Hand deformed by rheumatoid arthritis.**

For other joints, particularly the wrist and hand, surgical treatment is directed mostly toward removing as much diseased synovium as possible, repair of ruptured tendons, and correction of deformities with plastic implants. (See figure 28.4.) Results are sometimes very good, but the success rate is not nearly as uniformly good as that found in the larger joints. Even though the orthopedic surgeon may achieve a very good cosmetic result in a rheumatoid hand—that is, it may look much less deformed—function is not always improved to a comparable degree. On balance, though, the increasing application of sophisticated orthopedic procedures to the patient with rheumatoid arthritis is a most promising development.

DEGENERATIVE JOINT DISEASE

DEGENERATIVE JOINT DISEASE, sometimes referred to as osteoarthritis, is by far the most common of all the arthritic disorders. More than half of the adult population over the age of 30 will have some features of this disease, either by symptoms or on x-ray examination. If one lives long enough, degenerative joint disease is bound to develop, but usually it is very mild, producing few if any symptoms.

The term degenerative joint disease is preferred by today's rheumatologists, reserving the term osteoarthritis for a less common inflammatory variety of the disease. This inflammation, or primary osteoarthritis, involves more pain, swelling, and redness than the more common degenerative joint disease.

As its name implies, degenerative joint disease results from a breakdown of tissue—in this instance, the articular cartilage between the two bony surfaces making up a joint. The primary defect appears to be in the cartilage itself and, as far as we know, it is due to various biochemical and mechanical factors that are poorly understood.

The disease will frequently occur in response to

repetitive trauma or injury to a given joint. For example, pneumatic hammer operators very often develop severe degenerative arthritis of the shoulder joint, but only on the side used to hold the hammer. Pianists or typists frequently develop degenerative joint disease of the fingers.

Degeneration of the articular cartilage is not simply a matter of age, physical abuse, or overusage. When the disease involves the hips, for example, it will frequently be predominantly or entirely on one side, even though both hips bear equal weight and stress.

When degenerative joint disease affects the weight-bearing joints, particularly the knees and hips, it can cause considerable pain and loss of function, sometimes requiring corrective surgery. But most instances of degenerative joint disease do not significantly interfere with activities of daily living, and this is the big difference between the long-term effect of this disease compared to rheumatoid and other types of chronic inflammatory arthritis.

Degenerative Joint Disease of the Hands

The small joints of the hands are probably the most common area affected by degenerative joint disease. In the fingers, the disease is largely restricted to the end joints. As the cartilage of these terminal joints degenerates and the bones begin to rub one against the other, new bone is produced as part of the reparative process, forming bony spurs called Heberden's nodes. (See figure 28.5.) This new bone growth usually occurs without symptoms, at least in the early stages, but sometimes Heberden's nodes can be very red and tender. With time, they gradually heal and remain as bony protrusions, somewhat unsightly in appearance, but producing no loss of function because the middle joints, which so frequently are involved in the rheumatoid process, are usually

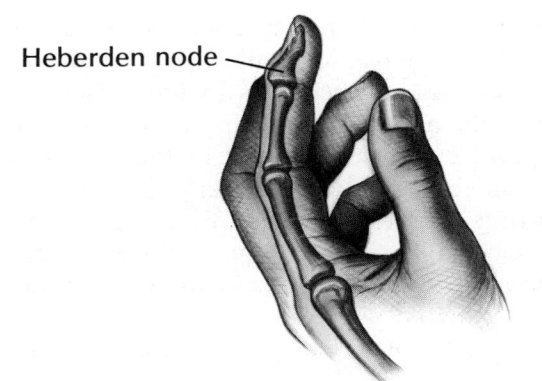

Heberden node

Figure 28.5. **A drawing showing the bony spurs of Heberden's nodes, which form on the terminal finger joints.**

not affected. In contrast, primary or inflammatory osteoarthritis may involve these middle joints, causing a much greater degree of disability because this type of degenerative joint disease is associated with considerable inflammation and may be sometimes confused with rheumatoid arthritis. Osteoarthritis almost always attacks the base of the thumb, a fact that may be helpful in diagnosis. Also, the bony growth associated with all forms of degenerative joint disease produces very hard nodules that are very different from the soft, spongy swelling found in the rheumatoid joint. Primary osteoarthritis also tends to run in families. X-ray studies, as well as certain laboratory tests, will differentiate this type of osteoarthritis from rheumatoid arthritis.

Degenerative Joint Disease of the Spine

Degenerative joint disease of the spine also involves cartilage degeneration and new bone formation, or spurs. In the spine, bony overgrowths narrow the openings (the exit foramina) through which the nerve roots emerge from the spinal canal. Even a very slight bony protrusion into this space can produce direct pressure on the sensitive nerve roots. Here, spinal degenerative joint disease can be very severe and almost totally incapacitating, not because of its local effect upon the spinal joints themselves but because of the direct pressure on the nerves. The symptoms are similar to those of a ruptured (herniated) disk. As nerve tissue is irritated by this pressure, it becomes swollen, further increasing the nerve compression.

When nerves in the cervical or neck area are compressed, bed rest and traction or other physical therapy measures may be required. As the symptoms subside, a cervical collar may be prescribed to help bear the weight of the head and to restrict neck motion.

Bony spurs in the lower spine may compress nerves to the lower trunk and legs, causing sciatica, a pain in the lower back, thigh, and leg. Muscle weakness and loss of reflexes may also occur. Treatment of degenerative joint disease of the lower back may require varying periods of complete bed rest and pelvic traction. If this does not work, surgery to remove the bony spur may be contemplated.

Degenerative Joint Disease of the Hip and Knee

Degenerative joint disease often involves the weight-bearing joint, particularly the hip. The process may take many years to produce symptoms, even though there may be x-ray evidence of joint degeneration.

Also, there may be long periods of remission during which the disease process is halted for reasons that are not yet fully understood. It usually appears predominantly if not entirely on one side, at least initially.

As the disease progresses, pain, stiffness, and resistance to motion due to mechanical factors become increasingly severe. While degenerative joint disease most commonly produces most of its symptoms at the end of the day (in contrast to rheumatoid arthritis which is invariably worse in the morning), in the advanced stages there is often morning stiffness as well.

If the disease becomes incapacitating, surgery to replace the hip joint may be indicated. This operation is remarkably successful and can be performed even on the elderly.

The knee is also commonly affected by degenerative joint disease. In advanced disease, surgical replacement with an artificial knee joint may be considered, but the results are not quite as successful as with the hip. More commonly, the surgeon may simply remove some of the loose fragments within the joint, using a device called an arthroscope.

When degenerative joint disease involves the foot and ankle, there is relatively little that the surgeon can do except to fuse the joint, so drugs remain the mainstay of treatment.

Drug Therapy for Degenerative Joint Disease

The goal of drug therapy in degenerative joint disease is suppression of inflammation and consequently, relief of pain. Pain and stiffness associated with degenerative joint disease usually can be relieved by analgesics, which simply blunt the pain impulses to the brain, and by anti-inflammatory drugs, which temporarily suppress inflammation. Again, aspirin, which combines both properties, is a mainstay of treatment. For those who cannot tolerate aspirin, NSAIDs may be prescribed. In many instances, they are superior to aspirin and are better tolerated. (See page 572.)

Among the many NSAIDs, indomethacin (Indocin) is unusually effective in degenerative joint disease involving the hip. Cortisone or other steroids should not be used except for those instances when they may be injected directly into the joint cavity to bring about temporary reduction of inflammation. This procedure is most often done to the knee joint and it cannot be repeated too often because the drug itself may damage the cartilage.

Promising Discovery

Researchers recently discovered that in certain cases of inflammatory degenerative joint disease, tiny crystals of a substance called hydroxyapatite are present in the joint fluid. These crystals are shed from the bone, presumably as the bone surfaces rub against each other, and they are capable of causing inflammation. Osteoarthritis patients who have these crystals can be greatly relieved by inserting a hollow needle into the joint space and withdrawing the fluid. This aspiration is followed by injection of a small amount of cortisone into the joint cavity.

GOUT

GOUTY ARTHRITIS is one of the rheumatic diseases that can be discussed with great optimism. While gout is not curable, there are highly effective drugs that are now used to treat acute attacks and also to prevent flare-ups.

Gout is caused by an excess of uric acid, a waste product derived from the metabolism of cell nuclei, in the blood. This excess of uric acid in the blood (hyperuricemia) may have more than one cause, but in primary gout, it is due to a metabolic fault resulting in overproduction, or a kidney impairment that prevents normal elimination. Some gout patients have a combination of both factors. Increasingly, we are seeing a type of secondary gout produced by certain drugs, most notably the diuretics used to treat high blood pressure and heart failure. These diuretics impair the kidney's ability to eliminate uric acid. Even aspirin, when taken regularly in low doses, may cause hyperuricemia and, sometimes, an incorrect diagnosis of gout. Other conditions that may lead to hyperuricemia include diseases of the blood cells and blood-forming organs, certain cancers, and even psoriasis. All of these disorders involve an abnormally rapid breakdown of cell nuclei, resulting in excess uric acid. Elevated uric acid levels do not always lead to gout; there are many instances of hyperuricemia without symptoms of gouty arthritis.

An acute attack of gout is caused by the precipitation, within the joint space, of sodium urate crystals. These crystals produce severe inflammation leading to excruciating pain. (See figures 28.6A

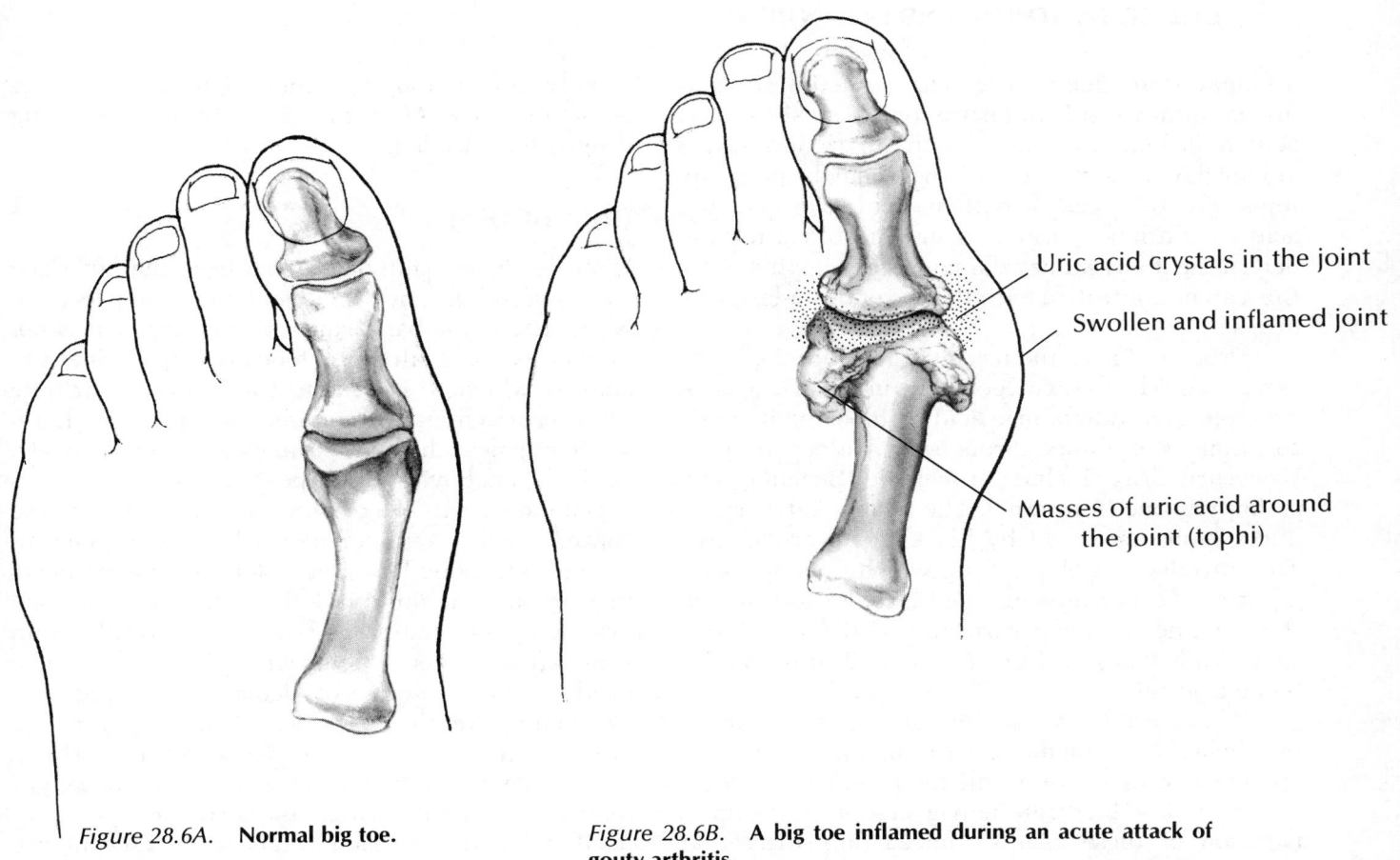

Uric acid crystals in the joint

Swollen and inflamed joint

Masses of uric acid around the joint (tophi)

Figure 28.6A. **Normal big toe.**

Figure 28.6B. **A big toe inflamed during an acute attack of gouty arthritis.**

and 28.6B.) As the urate crystals increase within the joint, more and more of the cells that respond to a "foreign invader" are drawn into the joint space in an effort to clear the fluid of the crystals. As the cells ingest these crystals, some become destroyed in the process and they release chemicals that further aggravate the inflammation. A true vicious circle is in operation.

There are a number of drugs that can successfully abort an acute gouty attack. The most specific one is colchicine, which has been known since the time of Hippocrates. In fact, colchicine is so specific for gout that if an acute attack of joint pain is dramatically relieved by colchicine, the diagnosis is almost surely gouty arthritis. During an acute attack, a tablet of colchicine is generally taken hourly until the pain is relieved or until nausea and/or diarrhea develop. These side effects can be very unpleasant, but often the colchicine must be taken until they occur in order for it to have its maximum beneficial effect. If the inflamed joint does not respond to colchicine, it often means that some disorder other than gout is responsible for the arthritis. After gout has been clearly diagnosed, acute attacks may be terminated by using any of the NSAIDs.

After the acute attack of gout has subsided, the treating physician should try to determine whether there are underlying, secondary causes for the hyperuricemia. For example, if a particular diuretic is causing the hyperuricemia, alternative drugs may be prescribed. If there are no secondary factors, the problem can be assumed to be primary gout, which occurs mostly in men who often have a family history of the disease. After the first acute attack, the best policy is observation. It is impossible to predict when, if ever, another attack will occur. If a patient experiences frequent, recurrent attacks, the next step is usually to prescribe colchicine as a preventive agent. This involves taking 1 or 2 colchicine tablets daily, indefinitely. This will often prevent acute attacks even though the colchicine has no effect on the blood uric acid level. Sometimes, colchicine will cause either nausea or diarrhea, even at these very low dosages, or the drug may be well tolerated but may not succeed in preventing acute flare-ups. In either of these situations, a drug to lower blood uric acid may be prescribed, although these are generally reserved for treatment of chronic gout.

Chronic gout is usually, but not always, characterized by frequent, recurrent attacks. There are some patients who have large deposits of uric acid in the tissues, called tophi, but who have never experienced an acute attack of gouty arthritis. In some cases, the initial manifestation is the development of a kidney stone due to uric acid. Sometimes hyperuricemia may result in microscopic deposits of uric acid in the kidney tubules, which can produce severe kidney damage, even though there may be no symptoms. For this reason, patients with elevated uric acid should have periodic urine and blood tests to determine if any kidney damage is developing. If so, this can be controlled with the use of urate-lowering drugs.

Drugs to lower the uric acid fall into 2 general categories. The first category, the uricosuric agents, promote excretion of uric acid by blocking its reabsorption as it filters through the kidney tubules. Uricosuric drugs include probenicid (Benemid) and sulfinpyrazone (Anturane). The second category reduces blood uric acid by blocking its production. The introduction of the drug which does this—allopurinol (Zyloprim)—marked a major advance in the treatment of hyperuricemia and gout. Sometimes both types of drugs are needed to normalize blood uric acid.

When urate-lowering therapy is first started, prophylactic colchicine or anti-inflammatory drugs must be continued for a time to prevent an acute attack of gout, which can be triggered by the administration of these agents. Indeed, any drug that rapidly lowers blood uric acid may paradoxically trigger an acute attack. After a normal uric acid level has been maintained for several months, colchicine or an anti-inflammatory prophylactic agent usually can be stopped without danger of inducing an acute attack. After that, only the urate-lowering drug will be needed.

Role of Diet

Historically, the gout patient has been characterized as an overweight, overindulgent, gluttonous person. Nonetheless, the basic cause of primary gout is *not* dietary excesses, although foods rich in purine substances, which give rise to uric acid, may contribute to hyperuricemia. The modification of the diet to restrict purine-rich foods—things like organ meats, sardines, anchovies, dried peas, and other legumes—is not necessary if a person is taking medication to control the uric acid. A noteworthy exception has to do with alcoholic beverages. Both wine and spirits may impair the ability of the kidney to eliminate uric acid from the blood, which may result in an acute attack. Thus, patients with gout must often be prudent with their use of alcohol and, if possible, eliminate it entirely, at least until appropriate urate-lowering drugs have had a chance to work.

If a person with gout is severely obese, weight reduction is in order. Often, the correction of obesity itself will bring about a normalization of serum uric acid, without resorting to drug treatment. Here again, weight reduction must be gradual, for a sudden, sharp deprivation in calories may result in secondary hyperuricemia and acute gouty attacks.

PSEUDOGOUT

PSEUDOGOUT, like true gout, is characterized by deposits of crystals in and around the joints. Instead of uric acid, these crystals are formed from calcium pyrophosphate dihydrate (CPPD), and the preferred medical term for the disorder is calcium pyrophosphate deposition disease. The disorder is differentiated from gout and other types of arthritis by the presence of CPPD crystals in the synovial fluid.

An acute attack of pseudogout may be quite painful and last for 2 or more days. In about half of these attacks, the knee is the target joint. Other joints commonly affected include the wrists, fingers, toes, hips, shoulders, elbows, and ankles. Attacks may be provoked by surgery or severe illness, such as a heart attack or stroke. Very often, however, the disease may progress without acute attacks and give rise to chronic inflammation and calcification of the joint cartilage (chondrocalcinosis) and symptoms that may resemble those of rheumatoid arthritis.

Pseudogout also may be mistaken for inflammatory osteoarthritis or may accompany degenerative joint disease. Some patients may have the disease with relatively few symptoms or signs other than calcification of cartilage, which can be detected by x-ray studies.

Pseudogout is more common in men, but it also occurs in women. The likelihood of having it increases with age; research has found that 6 percent of the population 70 years or older has some evidence of CPPD deposits.

The treatment of pseudogout is not as clear-cut as that of true gout. There are no drugs that prevent the buildup of CPPD crystals. NSAIDs are usually effective in controlling the joint inflammation. An attack may be treated with cortisone injected into the joint after aspiration of the fluid containing the crystals. Oral use of colchicine is not as effective as it is for true gout.

JUVENILE RHEUMATOID ARTHRITIS

JUVENILE RHEUMATOID ARTHRITIS (JRA) afflicts about 200,000 children in the United States, with girls more commonly affected than boys.

Morning stiffness, swelling and tenderness of the affected joints, and varying degrees of pain are common signs of JRA. Fever, a characteristic rash, weight loss, and fatigue are other symptoms pointing to possible JRA. Often, however, a child will not complain of symptoms until they seriously interfere with normal activities. The arthritis may affect many joints, usually in a symmetrical fashion, or be monarticular or pauciarticular, involving either of two joints.

There are no tests that specifically diagnose JRA, but the disease should be suspected in any child who has joint inflammation lasting more than 6 weeks. Since a number of other disorders produce symptoms similar to those of JRA, diagnosis often involves eliminating the possibility of these other diseases, which include congenital abnormalities, infection, childhood cancer, and trauma.

At least 75 percent of children with JRA eventually enter long remissions with little or no disability. Some may go on to develop adult rheumatoid arthritis or ankylosing spondylitis, but most do not. In some children, other organs, particularly the heart and eyes, may also be involved.

Treatment of JRA is similar to that for adult rheumatoid arthritis, with aspirin the basic therapy. Children who cannot tolerate aspirin may be given NSAIDs. If these drugs are inadequate to control the disease, gold therapy or penicillamine may be tried in some patients. In general, steroids are not recommended for children with JRA except for those with severe disease, because of the possibility of growth retardation when these drugs are given daily.

Proper exercise and rest also are important in treating JRA. Night splints may be used to prevent deformity. In any event, the child should be encouraged to be self-sufficient, attending regular schools and leading as normal a life as possible.

ANKYLOSING SPONDYLITIS

ANKYLOSING SPONDYLITIS differs from many of the other arthritic disorders in that it is far more common in men than women. The term ankylosing spondylitis refers to what is usually considered its most common feature, a spine with the vertebrae fused in a bent-over position. Although the disorder does involve mainly the spine, it may affect certain peripheral joints as well, especially hips, shoulders, and rarely, even the small joint of the hands and feet.

The most common target joint of spondylitis is the sacroiliac joint, which is at the base of the spine where the vertebral column joins the ileum, one of the pelvic bones. The sacroiliac is not a true joint since it has no motion; nonetheless, it can be the site of intense inflammation and pain. This disease is most common in young adults, but in some instances, it may occur in children, as a form of chronic juvenile polyarthritis, or start in middle age. Also, it is often associated with other disorders, such as Reiter's syndrome (see page 580) or the arthritis accompanying ulcerative colitis, regional enteritis, or psoriasis.

The predominant symptoms of ankylosing spondylitis—pain and stiffness—are similar to those of any other inflammatory arthritis, but they are usually localized to the back, especially the lower portion. Since these symptoms tend to worsen after periods of inactivity, morning stiffness is a common feature. The disease also may cause systemic symptoms, such as a low-grade fever, lassitude, and easy fatigue, but usually, patients with this disorder do not feel as generally ill as those with rheumatoid arthritis. Like so many arthritic disorders, spondylitis tends to wax and wane in severity, with long periods of remission followed by flare-ups with no evident cause.

There is a striking association between ankylosing spondylitis and the histocompatibility antigen HLA B27, which can be detected in the blood. About 95 percent of white patients who have spondylitis will be HLA B27 positive, while an otherwise healthy white population will have about a 10 percent incidence of HLA B27. The association is weaker in blacks, but it is still highly significant. This is perhaps the most dramatic evidence of the relationship of a genetic predisposition with the development of a rheumatic disease.

As ankylosing spondylitis progresses, the involved joints are gradually replaced by fibrous connective tissue and ultimately, new bone. This bony bridging results in immobility, and stooping and rigidity may result. Disability from ankylosing spondylitis is more likely to be due to the spinal deformities, rather than the pain and stiffness which can usually be relieved with anti-inflammatory drugs.

Treatment of Spondylitis

Physical therapy is very important in treating ankylosing spondylitis to prevent the characteristic stooped posture as the spine begins to fuse. In addition, the joints where the ribs and vertebrae join also may be involved. If the ribs and spine become fused, breathing may be impaired due to a stiffening of the chest wall. Normally, the ribs flare in and out as we inhale and exhale air. This bellows-like action, which helps fill the lungs with air, is gradually lost in spondylitis unless preventive measures, such as breathing exercises, are followed.

The pain and stiffness of spondylitis may be relieved by analgesics and NSAIDs. These drugs are important not only to relieve the symptoms but also to permit the patient to undergo appropriate physiotherapy. The exercises to help maintain a normal posture and breathing must be done daily—sometimes several times during the course of a day. This is why the physical therapist is an integral member of the treatment team in spondylitis.

REITER'S DISEASE OR REITER'S SYNDROME

REITER'S DISEASE, which is found mostly in young men, may be associated with sexual exposure, often without development of any known venereal disease, or with bacterial infections of the intestine. Following either of these, the classic symptoms of Reiter's may appear. These include joint inflammation, sometimes of the large joints or, alternatively, only the spine and sacroiliac joint; inflammation of the eyes (usually a conjunctivitis); urethritis, resulting in pain and burning upon urination; and skin eruptions involving the mouth, palms, soles of the feet, and sometimes the genitalia. Heel pain caused by inflammation of the Achilles tendon also is common. These symptoms usually evolve over time, thus the true clinical picture of Reiter's disease may not be immediately apparent.

Reiter's often coexists with spondylitis, and as in spondylitis, genetics appears to play a role. Many patients with both diseases carry the antigen HLA B27, which may make them react to certain common infections in an unusual manner, resulting in development of these diseases. This would explain why Reiter's classically follows an intestinal infection or sexual exposure.

PSORIATIC ARTHRITIS

PSORIATIC ARTHRITIS is another inflammatory joint disease characterized by the presence of the B27 antigen in a large number of patients. Rheumatoid arthritis and psoriasis are two separate diseases that may coexist. Psoriatic arthritis, however, is a different disease with its own identifiable characteristics.

Psoriatic arthritis most commonly affects the fingers and toes with typical involvement of the adjacent nails and skin. There may be considerable pain and disability. The disorder can lead to a sausagelike deformity of the fingers and distortion of the nails. Other joints may be involved symmetrically and in some patients who have the HLA B27 antigen, there also may be inflammation of the spine.

Treatment entails taking aspirin or other anti-inflammatory drugs. Steroid injections may offer temporary improvement. In the more severe cases, injectable gold is helpful and usually produces results as good as those achieved in rheumatoid arthritis. The immunosuppresive drug methotrexate may be used in very aggressive forms of psoriatic arthritis, but since it may damage the liver, its use requires careful monitoring.

ENTEROPATHIC ARTHRITIS

ENTEROPATHIC ARTHRITIS is associated with inflammatory bowel disease. The joint inflammation may occur with the intestinal disorder or develop afterward. Sometimes, especially in Crohn's disease, it may precede the bowel symptoms. In any event, the arthritis usually subsides as the underlying intestinal disorder is controlled, and development of joint deformities or other permanent damage is unusual. About 10 percent of patients with chronic inflammatory disease of the intestine also develop ankylosing spondylitis—an association that is believed to be genetically determined because of the frequent finding of the B27 antigen.

ARTHRITIS DUE TO INFECTION

ARTHRITIS caused by a readily identifiable bacteria or other infectious agents is the only kind of arthritis that truly may be cured. Typically, bacteria invade a joint, resulting in infection and inflammation which can be cured by identifying the organism and then eliminating it with the proper antibiotic.

Time is the pivotal factor, since the longer the infection persists, the greater the degree of joint damage. If the infection is not halted promptly, a secondary chronic arthritis that cannot be cured may result. In such circumstances, degeneration of the joint from the secondary condition may continue even after the infection has been eliminated.

Bacterial arthritis can be produced by a variety of bacteria, and is usually associated with infection elsewhere in the body. For example, staphylococcus aureus, or "staph," is a common cause of infection, especially of the skin. People whose resistance is lowered by other circumstances, for example, long-term use of steroid drugs or certain other chronic diseases, such as diabetes, have an increased risk of having a localized staph infection spread to other parts of the body via the blood, a condition called bacteremia. There are many possible sources of the infection: the kidneys, lungs, and gallbladder are common examples. When bacteremia occurs, the joint seems to act as a filter, trapping the blood-borne bacteria and resulting in a secondary joint infection.

People whose joints have been damaged by rheumatoid arthritis also may be vulnerable to bacterial arthritis. An infection should be suspected in a rheumatoid patient when there is a persistent flare-up in a single joint. In such circumstances, a sample of joint fluid should be removed for laboratory study to see if an infectious agent is present.

OTHER TYPES OF INFECTIOUS ARTHRITIS

Gonococcal Arthritis

This is caused by the same organism responsible for gonorrhea. It has become increasingly common in recent years due obviously to the rise in sexually transmitted diseases. In fact, gonococcal arthritis is one of the most serious complications of gonorrhea because it can lead to permanent joint destruction within only a few days following the first sign of joint pain. Sometimes a person may have gonorrhea without experiencing the characteristic symptoms of painful urination or discharge. In such cases, gonococcal arthritis may not be suspected until permanent damage has occurred. If gonorrhea is a possible cause of the joint inflammation, antibiotic treatment should be started immediately, even before the diagnosis is confirmed.

Tuberculous Arthritis

Arthritis caused by tuberculosis (TB) is now rare, but before the development of effective antibiotic treatments for TB, this was a common condition. TB attacks both the large joints, such as knees and hips, and the spine. It is diagnosed by removing some of the diseased joint tissue and examining it under the microscope and subjecting it to special culture. The arthritis can be cured by long-term use of the antibiotics used to treat TB of the lung.

Lyme Arthritis

This is the newest infectious type of arthritis to be recognized. It was first discovered in the area surrounding the town of Lyme, Connecticut; hence its name. The understanding of the cause, mode-of-transmittance, and the cure of this illness was achieved in a remarkably short time, thanks to the use of modern techniques of microbiology and epidemiology, applied by investigators from Yale University. The disease is caused by the bite of a particular tick, which introduces the invading germ, called a spirochete, into the skin of the victim. At the site of the tick bite, a characteristic rash called erythema chronicum migrans is found. This rash is unique to this disease, and has a red ring that increases in diameter with each passing day. Vague symptoms of low-grade fever and muscle aches may be associated. Treatment at this time with the antibiotic tetracycline results in a cure.

If the disease is not recognized and effectively treated at this stage, it may subsequently develop into a generalized arthritis which can progress to many joints and go on for months or even years. In addition, internal organs, including the heart and brain, may be attacked. In this case, large doses of intravenous penicillin may be successful in achieving a cure.

Lyme disease may be looked upon as a model of nature, in which a known infective agent can lead to a chronic polyarthritis due to the initiation of an immune response to the invading germ, because in the later and systemic phases, the inciting germ can no longer be found.

Osteomyelitis

This is an infection of the bones which is more common in children than adults. When osteomyelitis occurs, the neighboring joint should be carefully studied for possible infection. Similarly, bones should be examined for possible infection in cases of infectious arthritis.

Rheumatic Fever

This disease, which is usually a consequence of an untreated strep infection, is particularly damaging to the heart. Typically, it follows a strep throat. One of the first signs may be a painful inflamed knee or other large joint. Aspirin usually controls the arthritis and the disease almost never results in permanent damage to the joints. Antibiotic therapy should be undertaken promptly in the hope that irreversible heart damage will be prevented. Fortunately, rheumatic fever has been decreasing thanks to proper antibiotic treatment of strep throats and is not the threat that it once was.

Fungal Arthritis

This type of arthritis may be associated with regional or occupational fungal lung infections (see page 470) or of a generalized fungal infection. People who are most vulnerable are those with a chronic disease that lowers resistance or a history of alcoholism, drug addiction, long-term antibiotic or steroid therapy. In the United States, the most frequent fungal (mycotic) infections responsible for joint inflammation are coccidiomycosis, also called desert rheumatism or valley fever; sporotrichosis, which may be spread via the lymph system from a skin lesion or from inhaling the spores; blastomycosis, which may spread to the joints from the skin or lungs; and candidiasis. Diagnosis involves identifying the causative fungus followed by treatment with the appropriate antifungal drug.

Viral Infections

Arthritis is a common component of a number of viral infections, including infectious mononucleosis and rubella (German measles). The arthritis usually subsides with the primary disease, but there are instances in which the joint inflammation may continue intermittently. Aspirin or other anti-inflammatory drugs are usually sufficient.

COLLAGEN VASCULAR DISEASES

COLLAGEN VASCULAR DISEASES have many features in common with rheumatoid arthritis. They also share many of the immunological abnormalities found in other forms of arthritis. But in contrast to rheumatoid arthritis, these diseases often involve the skin and vital internal organs, such as the heart, kidney, and lungs, making them potentially more serious. The major disorders included among the collagen vascular diseases are systemic lupus erythematosus (SLE), scleroderma or progressive systemic sclerosis (PSS), dermatomyositis, and vasculitis.

The cause of the collagen vascular diseases is unknown, but it is generally believed that they are related. Many patients will have characteristic features of more than one of these diseases as their illness evolves with time. In recent years, more effective treatments for collagen vascular diseases have been developed, but we are still unable to overcome the basic factor or factors that initiate the disease process.

SYSTEMIC LUPUS ERYTHEMATOSUS

SYSTEMIC LUPUS ERYTHEMATOSUS, also referred to as SLE or simply lupus, is one of the most serious of all of the rheumatic diseases because it can involve the kidneys or other vital organs. Like rheumatoid arthritis, lupus occurs predominantly in women, but the reasons for this are not known. It may strike at any age, from childhood into the sixties and seventies, but most patients with lupus will develop it when they are young adults. The symptoms largely depend upon the organs involved, and as the disease runs its course, usually over a period of years, different target organs may be affected. The degree of disease activity varies from potentially life-threatening flare-ups to complete remissions.

The cause of SLE is not known, but certain facts have emerged as a result of years of intensive research. It appears that patients with SLE have a defect in their immune system, particularly with the regulation of the production of antibodies, the protein substances that normally help to defend against infections. In SLE, many of these antibodies are defective or ineffective for their intended purpose, and are directed against one or more of the body's normal tissues. Sometimes, this "autoantibody" formation leads to damage to a vital tissue. They may develop an antibody to a substance called cardiolipin, which gives rise to a false positive blood test for syphilis. Some patients are repeatedly treated with penicillin, in the erroneous belief that they have acquired the venereal disease.

Damage to vital organs may be from a *direct* effect of antibody on a specific tissue, such as occurs when red blood cells or blood platelets are destroyed by an antibody which specifically attacks them, or *indirectly* as may occur in the kidney. In lupus, there are antibodies directed against certain of the protein components of cell nuclei, such as DNA. In some patients, DNA and antibody to DNA can be found circulating in the blood as immune complexes—an antigen and its antibody—similar to the immune complexes in the joint fluid in rheumatoid arthritis. In SLE, however, the complexes circulate throughout the body in the bloodstream. As the blood passes through the kidney, these complexes may be trapped by the delicate filtration network that forms the basic structure of the kidney. Once caught, the complexes induce an inflammatory response in the kidney, ultimately leading to damage to the organ. A substance called complement is brought into the reaction, and it further contributes to the destructive inflammatory process, largely by attracting more inflammatory cells. In this sequence of events, there is no antibody directed against kidney tissue itself; instead, the organ is an "innocent bystander" which is injured simply as a result of performing its intended function, the filtration of the blood.

Immune complexes also may be found in the skin, central nervous system, and other vital organs, but only in the kidney is their relationship to the production of disease so well understood. We do not know the nature of the immunological defect that causes the body to make antibodies to its own DNA and other proteins, which leads to immune complex formation. Nevertheless, the principle of treatment is to try to limit the damage. This is done in 2 ways. The first is to reduce the inflammation that results from the presence of the complexes, by employing the most potent anti-inflammatory drugs, the corticosteroids. In addition, the amount of abnormal antibody produced is reduced to decrease the amount of immune complexes present. This is done with medicines called immunosuppressives and with higher doses of corticosteroids.

The basic triggering factor(s) that initiate the antibody abnormality are not known. Some believe that a virus or other infective agent is responsible, but the proof is still lacking. Other research suggests that there is a basic genetic defect in the control of immunological responsiveness, which must be present in order for some external factor—virus, chemical or drug, or ultraviolet light—to start the process. In some patients, for example, exposure to the ultraviolet rays found in sunlight can result in a flare-up of lupus, which is why they are advised to avoid any exposure to the sun. After even a mild sunburn, all of us may have an increase in free DNA from the injured skin, which is fed into the bloodstream and eliminated. In SLE, however, an antibody is produced against this DNA and gives rise, in some patients, to one type of circulating immune complex, which is trapped in the kidney. This is thought to be one possible mechanism by which ultraviolet light can cause a flare-up of the disease, or even induce the first attack. Other factors that seem to trigger flare-ups of lupus include overfatigue, emotional stress, childbirth, and infection, but they do not share the specific predictability of sun exposure.

SLE is a complicated disease affecting many organ systems. The term "lupus" means wolflike and refers to the characteristic "butterfly rash" that is seen over the cheekbones and gives the face a wolflike appearance. The rash is not always present, but when it is, it strongly suggests the likelihood of lupus. A variety of rashes almost anywhere on the body is another common finding in lupus. Many SLE patients also have Raynaud's syndrome, a blanching of the hands and feet on exposure to the cold, which disappears after warming.

Joint disease that in many ways is almost identical to that of rheumatoid arthritis is often found in SLE. There is usually a considerable degree of synovitis, swelling, and inflammation of the joint tissues, but SLE patients only rarely develop deformities. Arthritis symptoms may be present for years before involvement of the skin or other internal organs becomes evident. Some patients who are diagnosed as having uncomplicated rheumatoid arthritis ultimately are found to have SLE and, in retrospect, probably had it all along.

Course of the Disease

Since SLE may involve almost any vital organ, the various combinations of symptoms differ from patient to patient and from time to time during the evolution of the disease. Thus, a lupus patient may initially seek treatment for an emotional disturbance and, years later, develop arthritis and a characteristic rash. Or another may first consult a kidney specialist or a cardiologist. As indicated earlier, a positive blood test for syphilis may be detected during a premarital physical examination. It may be the first marker of lupus, preceding other manifestations by years. When there are symptoms and signs of possible lupus, a number of laboratory tests that may be of diagnostic help may be ordered.

Outlook in SLE

The outlook for survival in SLE has been greatly enhanced by the proper use of corticosteroid drugs. For example, many researchers believe that these agents in high doses are capable of arresting and even reversing lupus kidney disease. In some cases, steroid drugs also appear to help patients with central nervous system and other life-threatening manifestations of lupus. Steroid drugs suppress the inflammation and consequent damage to internal organs. In high doses, they are also immunosuppressive, decreasing the amount of antibody and immune complexes. Hence they attack the disease on two levels. The side effects of steroids, which may include puffing or rounding of the face, acne, an increase in facial hair and weight gain, diabetes, cataracts, osteoporosis, peptic ulcers, and psychosis make their prolonged use difficult. Nevertheless, it is important to realize that a severe attack of lupus often can be adequately suppressed by these drugs, preventing permanent damage to vital organs. Side effects sometimes can be reduced by giving the drugs on alternate days, but this is not always possible and treatment must be individualized.

Perhaps one of the most serious steroid-induced complications in lupus patients is increased susceptibility to infection. Lupus patients are already infection-prone because their antibodies are often ineffective and they may have a decreased number of white blood cells. The corticosteroid drugs further aggravate the problem, but these risks must be taken to control the disease.

Sometimes, other drugs that suppress or kill certain cells that cause lupus inflammation and abnormal antibody formation may be used. These drugs, referred to as cytotoxic or immunosuppressive agents, may reduce the steroid requirement in some patients. As with steroids, these cytotoxic drugs increase a person's susceptibility to infection, often from rare and unusual microorganisms.

Despite the problems in treating lupus, patients today have a much better outlook than ever before. Sophisticated laboratory tests aid both in diagnosis and in the proper use of powerful drugs to treat the disease. Finally, our increasing understanding of SLE itself has further improved the outlook for a normal, productive life despite the seriousness of the disease.

SCLERODERMA

SCLERODERMA (progressive systemic sclerosis) is a disorder characterized by excessive buildup of fibrous connective tissue. Initially scleroderma, which means thickening (sclero) of the skin (derma), was thought to involve only the skin. Recently, however, it has been recognized that vital internal organs also may be the targets of increased collagen deposits. Hence, the term progressive systemic sclerosis (PSS) is more accurate and will be used here except in situations involving only the skin, which will be referred to by the older term, scleroderma.

In PSS, there often is an associated arthritis even though the joints are not the main targets of the disease. In addition to mild joint inflammation, there are changes in the tissues around the joints due to deposition of excessive amounts of connective tissue, resulting in reduced mobility. With the progressive thickening and tightening of the skin about the fingers, motion becomes increasingly restricted. Larger joints, such as the elbows and knees, also may be involved.

Thickening of the skin may occur anywhere in

the body, especially in the face. Scleroderma is usually chronic and progresses over a period of many years; however, there may be periods when the disease seems to be static. Occasionally, it may go into remission, either in certain localized areas or throughout the body. When this occurs, the skin appears to be perfectly normal, as though it had never been attacked by scleroderma.

For reasons that are not understood, the basic disease seems to be confined to the fibroblasts, the cells that make fibrous connective tissue or collagen. The processes that regulate these cells appear to go out of control. The fibroblasts behave almost as though they were continually stimulated to produce collagen. For example, when we cut ourselves, the wound heals with new connective tissue and new overlying skin. Once the cut is healed, the reparative process stops and new collagen ceases to be produced. In contrast, in scleroderma or PSS, fibrous tissue is produced at an accelerated rate, even without the stimulus of a wound. As a result, increasing amounts of young or immature collagen are continuously being laid down in the involved tissues, replacing the normal cells with connective tissue, as though it were a scar. This makes the skin, for example, thick and tight as the normal elastic tissue is replaced by dense fibrous tissue. Hair growth and sweating generally stop as the hair follicles and sweat glands are destroyed. Often the patient may experience intense itching as normal skin structures are replaced by excessive collagen. The superficial layers of the skin atrophy or shrink as their blood supply is decreased due to the strangulating effect of the dense new collagen in the underlying layers. The blood vessels themselves become narrowed. If the hands are affected, as they often are, tightening of the skin over the fingers results in a similar physical narrowing of the tiny blood vessels vital to their nourishment, and skin ulceration may develop on the fingertips and over the joints and bony prominences. These ulcers, which are usually painful and often become infected, are very difficult to treat and greatly interfere with the use of the hand. With progressive loss of blood supply, more distant tissues such as the ends of the fingers are unable to obtain adequate oxygen via the circulation and may gradually become shortened.

When PSS attacks internal organs, the disease may be life-threatening. In the lung, for example, PSS may cause an increase in connective tissue in the delicate air sacs, a condition called pulmonary fibrosis. The normal process of oxygen transfer from the inhaled air to the blood is progressively blocked. As a result, blood is deprived of its normal oxygen content, leading to shortness of breath, which is often further aggravated by restriction in chest wall movement because of thickening of skin over the chest.

If the heart is affected, there may be a replacement of the pericardium, the membrane surrounding the heart, by increased fibrous tissue. This can encase the heart in a progressively tightening "shell" that restricts the normal pulsation and pumping of blood. More commonly, the actual heart muscle fibers themselves are replaced with ineffective scar tissue, leading to progressive heart failure.

In the gastrointestinal tract, PSS may cause difficulty in swallowing, malabsorption of digested food into the circulation, or severe constipation and possible intestinal obstruction, depending upon the structures that are affected. The kidney is still another vital organ where PSS may strike, sometimes leading to a very severe form of hypertension.

Other Manifestations of PSS. Raynaud's syndrome or Raynaud's disease, a condition in which there is blanching of the skin of the hands and sometimes of the feet upon exposure to the cold, may occur independently, or may be associated with PSS, lupus, rheumatoid arthritis, and other mixed forms of connective tissue disease. The walls of the small-to medium-size arteries in patients with Raynaud's are unduly sensitive to cold. When exposed to low temperatures, they become severely narrowed, which causes the blanching. Even so simple an act as reaching into the freezer chest in the supermarket can be a formidable task for people with Raynaud's, and many wear gloves even in warm weather to avoid attacks.

Because of the high incidence of Raynaud's syndrome and PSS, some researchers believe that the hypersensitivity of blood vessels to temperature change, and perhaps to other stimuli as well, may be responsible for causing some of the structural abnormalities in PSS.

DERMATOMYOSITIS AND POLYMYOSITIS

DERMATOMYOSITIS AND POLYMYOSITIS are connective tissue diseases in which arthritis is present, but plays only a minor role compared to involvement of the muscles. The two disorders are very similar except that dermatomyositis involves the skin as well as the muscle, while polymyositis involves only muscles. Both have some features in common with rheumatoid arthritis, lupus, and progressive systemic sclerosis.

The major manifestation of polymyositis is inflammation, leading to destruction of muscle and increasing muscular weakness. As the disease progresses, the muscle tissue is replaced by functionless scar tissue. Muscles of the shoulder, arms, pelvis, and thighs are the most frequent targets, but the reasons for this are unknown.

As the disease spreads, other muscles may become involved. For example, the diaphragm and chest wall muscles, which are needed for breathing, may be attacked. The pharyngeal muscles, which are needed for swallowing, can be weakened to the point where swallowing solid foods becomes impossible. Heart muscle is still another potential target. This is particularly noteworthy because of the many similarities between the heart muscle fibers and those of the voluntary muscles, which move the limbs. When heart muscle is involved, there may be disturbances in the heart rhythm, which require drug therapy.

When dermatomyositis attacks the skin, there is a characteristic purplish rash, found mostly on the face and upper chest, although it may occur anywhere on the body. Associated with this rash, patients will often have swelling around the eyes, especially upon arising in the morning. There also may be scaly, reddened eruptions over the small joints of the fingers, sometimes over the eyelids, and occasionally on the shoulders or upper back. These eruptions, which may be somewhat itchy, are so specific that they almost indicate the diagnosis.

Although the causes of dermatomyositis and polymyositis are unknown, it appears that abnormal immunological factors are responsible for at least part of the inflammatory attack against muscle tissue. The symptoms of muscular weakness usually wax and wane in severity, but in some instances, the disease may progress rapidly. Treatment may involve using a corticosteroid drug, although their effectiveness is less predictable in these disorders than in some other inflammatory diseases. As a result, many rheumatologists turn to one of the cytotoxic drugs to work in conjunction with the corticosteroids in attempting to suppress the muscle inflammation and to retard the destructive process. Usually, by combining the two classes of drugs, lower and safer doses of both can be used, thereby avoiding some of the more serious side effects that might be produced when either is used alone in higher doses.

Patients who are not helped by drugs may benefit from plasmapheresis, a new technique that is used experimentally to treat several connective tissue diseases. This technique involves removing large amounts of the patient's blood and putting it through a machine which separates it into its component parts. The red blood cells are returned to the body and the plasma and often the lymphocytes are discarded. These plasma exchanges are usually done 2 or 3 times per week for 3 to 4 weeks, and sometimes bring about a temporary but dramatic improvement in muscle strength. Sometimes, plasmapheresis will be so effective that the patients will respond to drugs that had previously failed to work.

Although plasmapheresis is still a research tool for this and the other autoimmune diseases, it is particularly appropriate to mention it here. Some researchers believe that there are substances circulating in the blood that contribute to the muscle weakness, and that these may be a by-product either of damaged muscle or of the immunological process that leads to the damage. The removal of these substances by plasmapheresis provides a new approach for this and other connective tissue diseases that fail to respond to conventional treatment.

VASCULITIS

VASCULITIS, as the name implies, is an inflammation of the blood vessels—both the arteries and the veins. Diseases in this category are relatively rare and comprise some of the most baffling and poorly understood disorders in medicine. Very often, the diagnosis remains unsuspected for long periods because of the variable way in which these disorders behave.

Inflammation of a blood vessel, particularly a small artery, can cause a narrowing of its lumen (internal diameter). If the vessel becomes completely closed, the tissue normally nourished by the diseased artery will die or be severely damaged.

Some forms of vasculitis are believed to result from an allergy or hypersensitivity, such as an adverse reaction to certain drugs. Sulfa drugs were very common causes of vasculitis, particularly in the early days of their use when the preparations were more crude and the dosages given were higher than today.

Patients with vasculitis, particularly when it involves widespread areas in the body, may be extremely ill with a generally poor prognosis. One particular type of vasculitis, which affects older people, involves inflammation of the cranial or temporal arteries, the vessels that serve a portion of the facial, jaw, and tongue muscles, the scalp, and most important, the retina. Cranial arteritis is the most common cause of sudden blindness in the elderly. Usually only one eye is involved but sometimes it occurs in both. This condition is successfully treated with corticosteroids, provided that treatment is started before there is significant loss of vision. It is often associated with a syndrome of severe muscle pain and stiffness called polymyalgia rheumatica. This illness is also largely confined to the elderly. It is almost always associated with a very high sedimentation rate, which measures the amount of inflammation, and it usually responds dramatically to cortisone-type drugs in low doses. Polymyalgia may occur without cranial arteritis, but because of the association, arteritis should be suspected in patients with polymyalgia.

Another form of vasculitis is called Wegener's granulomatosis. This is an extremely rare disorder which attacks the respiratory tract, the nasal sinuses, and the kidney in a progressively destructive process. Wegener's granulomatosis was once invariably fatal but now most patients can be treated successfully with cytotoxic or immunosuppressive drugs.

Patients with generalized or systemic vasculitis will often have paralysis of a foot or a wrist as a result of loss of blood supply to the peripheral nerve serving that limb. The blood vessels of the lung may also be affected, resulting in asthmalike symptoms.

The development of asthma relatively late in life is very unusual, and may signify vasculitis.

The skin is another common site for vasculitis of all types. It shows up as areas of hemorrhage and death of superficial skin tissue due to loss of circulation.

There is another type of vasculitis known as Takayasu's disease, which occurs almost exclusively in young women. The inflammation is largely restricted to the branches of the great artery which leaves the heart (the aorta). It has also been called "pulseless" disease, for the diseased arteries may be so narrowed that a pulse cannot even be detected at the wrist. Patients with this disease will very frequently have symptoms of dizziness, light-headedness, weakness, and difficulty in using the arms, due to muscle pain from even slight physical effort. This is a direct result of lack of oxygen to the muscles, as the narrowed arteries are unable to deliver the increased amount of blood required during muscular effort. Corticosteroid therapy may be effective against Takayasu's disease, but the disease may go into remission without treatment.

These diseases are a few examples of the very broad spectrum of disorders included in the category of vasculitis. They are often difficult to diagnose, for their onset and evolution may be vague and ill-defined. The more classic types are easier to identify, but because of their relative rarity they are often not suspected until late in the course of the illness. Biopsy of an involved organ such as the kidney, muscle, or liver may be required in order to establish that a vasculitic process is indeed present.

SUMMING UP

IN THIS CHAPTER the more common forms of arthritis have been reviewed. Each year brings new advances in the diagnosis and treatment of the various types of arthritis, and with these, greater hope for the future. Now most arthritis patients can expect to live useful, relatively pain-free lives thanks to greater understanding of the diseases involved and new developments in drug therapy, surgery, and the more effective employment of physical therapy and rehabilitation.

29 Brain, Nerve, and Muscle Disorders

Timothy A. Pedley, M.D.

INTRODUCTION

THOUGH MODERN MEDICINE has an enormous array of measuring instruments, computers, and laser technology at its disposal and has made vast strides toward eliminating many of the maladies that afflict the human body, it has come up with nothing to match the overwhelming complexity of the brain and nervous system. This intimidating mass of gray matter, white matter, and electrical impulses, combined with the sprawl of the peripheral nerves interacting with the muscular system, creates an awe-inspiring synthesis of thought, emotion, and action with no apparent limits.

Research has not unraveled all of the brain's complexities, but attempts to fathom the depths of such a complex mechanism have given rise to a foundation of understanding. To comprehend the disorders that can occur to this system, it is helpful to have an outline of how its pieces fit together and

what they do. The brain is part of the central nervous system (CNS), which also includes the spinal cord, both of which are encased in bone for protection: the brain within the skull, and the spinal cord within a canal that is surrounded by the vertebrae of the spine. The peripheral nervous system comprises the nerve roots and nerves that supply the muscles and various organ systems of the body. (See figure 29.1).

The sections of the spinal cord and the nerve roots that emerge from it are named according to their location at various levels of the spine. Thus, at the bottom of the spine are the sacral nerve roots; above these are the lumbar, thoracic, and cervical nerve roots. Nerve signals travel up and down the spinal cord, which links the brain to the rest of the body.

The spinal cord is connected to the brain by the

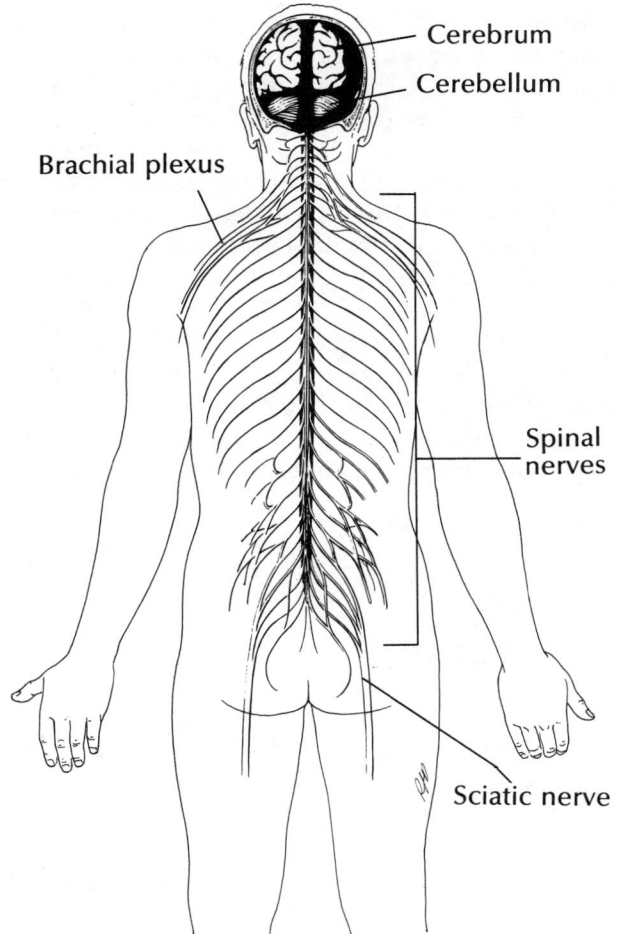

Cerebrum
Cerebellum
Brachial plexus
Spinal nerves
Sciatic nerve

Figure 29.1. **An overview of the central nervous system, showing the brain, spinal cord, and major nerve roots radiating from the spinal cord.**

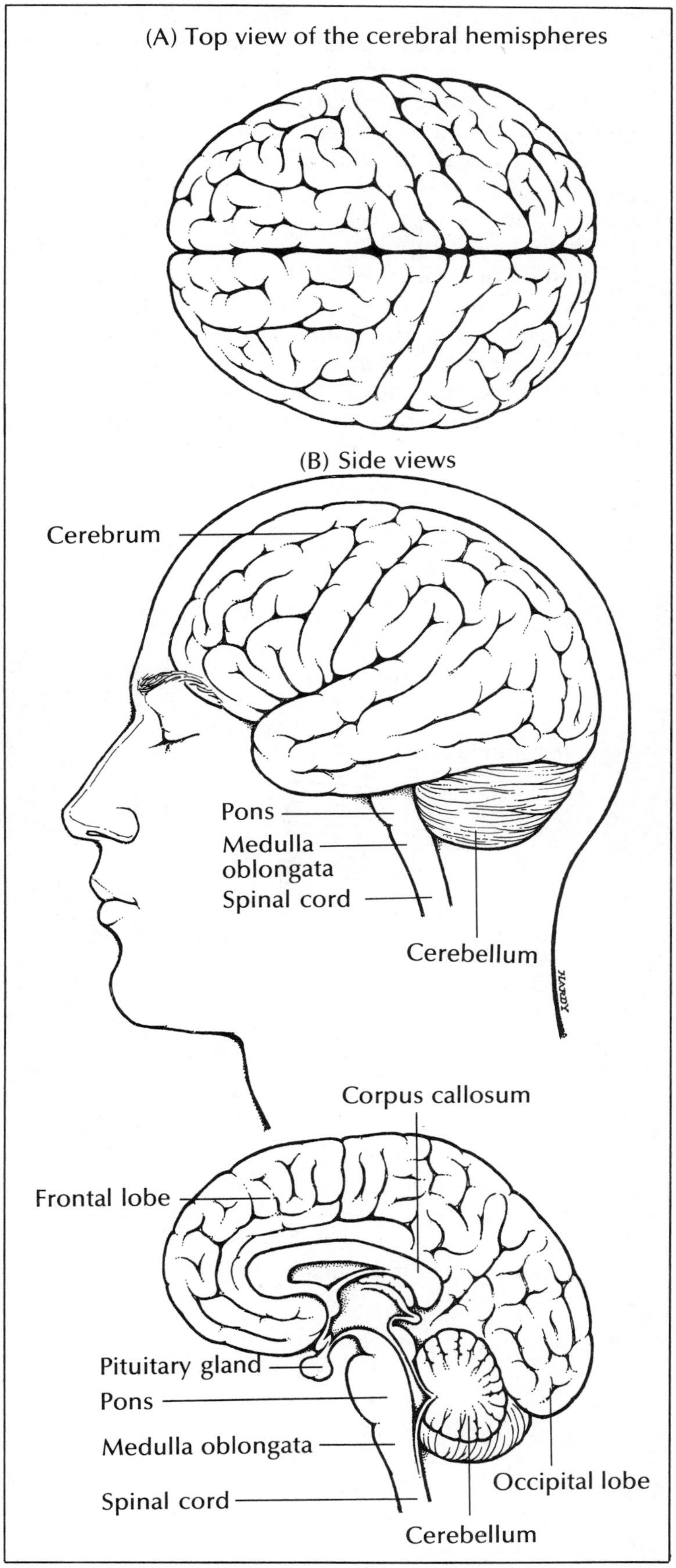

brainstem (comprising the medulla, the pons, and the midbrain), which maintains such vital bodily functions as breathing and circulation. Paired cranial nerves exit from the brainstem to control eye movements, muscles and sensation of the face, taste, swallowing, and tongue movements.

Above the brainstem are the largest components of the brain, the cerebrum and the cerebellum. (See figure 29.2.) The cerebrum is divided into left and right hemispheres which, in turn, are further divided into lobes. The cerebral hemispheres control such functions as speech, memory, and intelligence. Some of these functions, such as speech, are controlled by specific areas, while others, such as memory, seem to be controlled by the cerebral hemispheres in general. Under the cerebral hemispheres is the cerebellum, which controls certain subconscious activities, especially coordinating movement and maintaining balance.

Deep in the core of the brain, at the top of the brainstem, are other important structures: the hypothalamus, a major endocrine regulatory center influ-

(A) Top view of the cerebral hemispheres

(B) Side views

Cerebrum
Pons
Medulla oblongata
Spinal cord
Cerebellum

Corpus callosum
Frontal lobe
Pituitary gland
Pons
Medulla oblongata
Spinal cord
Occipital lobe
Cerebellum

Figure 29.2. **The brain, as seen from various views.**

encing sleep, appetite, and sexual desire; and the thalamus, a critical relay station that links the cerebral hemispheres to all other parts of the nervous system. Feeding the brain and its components with oxygen and nutrients are two main sets of blood vessels, the paired carotid and vertebral arteries. These then subdivide into smaller blood vessels which supply different regions of the brain. (See figure 29.3.) When blood supply to an area of brain is interrupted, or when a blood vessel hemorrhages, a stroke occurs.

The brain and spinal cord are covered with three layers of membranes called meninges and they float in cerebrospinal fluid, a waterlike bath that cushions the soft brain structures from injury against the encasing bones. Samples of cerebrospinal fluid can be obtained by penetrating the subarachnoid space (between the middle and the innermost membranes) with a needle placed in the lumbar section of the spine. This procedure, known as a lumbar puncture, provides important clues about diseases that impair CNS function. (For more information, see Chapter 4 on Diagnostic Tests and Procedures, page 64.)

Disorders of the brain and spinal cord are treated by neurologists and neurosurgeons, physicians and surgeons who have several years of specialized, advanced training beyond medical school. The disorders they treat range from the simple to the very complex.

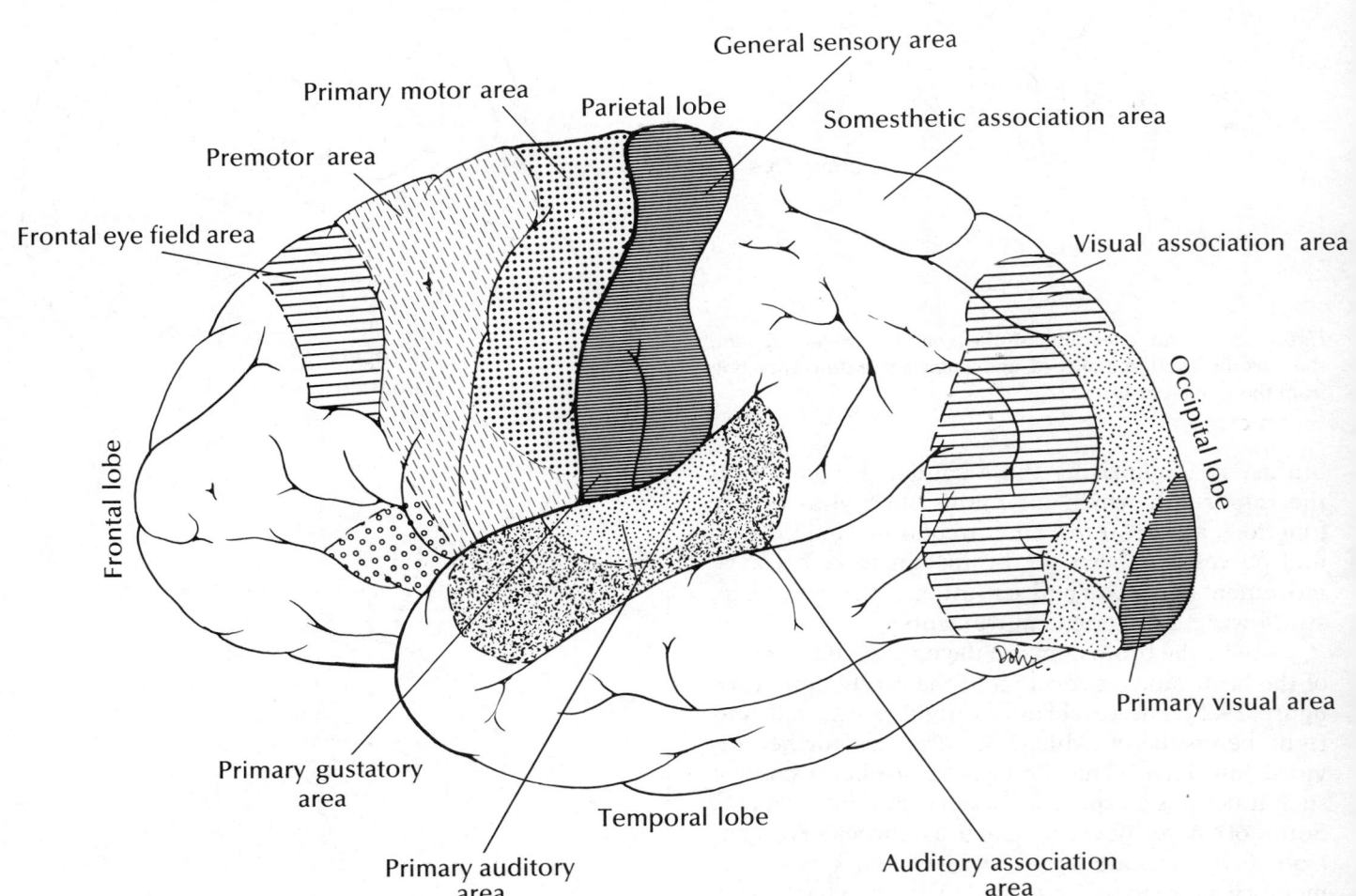

Figure 29.3. **A map of the brain showing the major functional areas.**

GENERAL SYMPTOMS

Headache

Headache is one of the most ubiquitous of symptoms, experienced at one time or another by virtually everyone. There are many causes of headache, but only a few are serious. The most common form is caused by painful contractions of muscles of the head and neck due to stress or other psychological factors (tension headache). Another frequent cause of headache is migraine, which results from abnormally dilated and painful blood vessels on the scalp, about the eye, or in the neck. Both these types may be aggravated by an individual's inability to adjust to the environment or to a change in lifestyle.

Headache can arise from structures outside the skull (scalp, external and middle ear, teeth, sinuses, blood vessels, and muscles of the face, head, and neck) or from intracranial sources (pain-sensitive structures located within the skull). These include the dura, which is the outermost layer of the membrane surrounding the brain and spinal cord, the large arteries at the base of the brain that serve the dura, the cranial nerves, and the upper cervical nerves.

Although the brain is necessary for perception of pain, the brain itself is not sensitive to pain. Extracranial headaches can be caused by muscular contraction, enlargement of the scalp arteries, and various inflammatory processes that affect sensitive areas of the head. Intracranial headaches result from dilation or contraction of intracranial arteries, inflammation or stretching of the meninges, or the effects of pressure caused by tumors or other mass lesions.

In young people, headaches are most often caused by migraine or tension. Persistent headaches that occur for the first time in an older person are less likely to result from these causes. Individuals over the age of 50 who begin to have unremitting headaches may have cranial arteritis (an inflammation of the blood vessels of the head), glaucoma, cerebrovascular disease, a brain tumor, or meningitis. When sudden, severe headache is accompanied by loss of consciousness or decreased vision, it is most likely due to a hemorrhage beneath the middle meningeal layer or within the substance of the brain.

Determining the exact nature of the pain is an important step in the diagnosis of headache. For example, if there is a throbbing quality, especially when the pain is located behind the eyes or on one side of the head, the pain probably arises from vascular structures. A throbbing, "sick" headache with nausea is characteristic of migraine. On the other hand, neuralgia—pain along the course of a nerve—is quite different; it is felt as a sharp, stabbing sensation. The pain of tension and muscular contraction headaches is a steady, nonthrobbing pressure that often feels like a tight band has been pulled around the head. The intensity of the pain does not necessarily indicate the seriousness of its cause: Headache may be severe with anxiety and mild with a brain tumor.

Another key to diagnosis is whether the headache is accompanied by other symptoms. For example, migraine, unlike muscular contraction headaches, often causes nausea and visual symptoms such as blind spots, sparkling points of light, or sensitivity to light.

Headaches can also be caused by psychological factors. As a rule, all physical possibilities for headache should be eliminated before the headache is linked directly to an emotional conflict or other psychiatric disorder. This can often be done solely on the basis of a careful history and physical examination, but laboratory tests are sometimes necessary as well.

Treatment of headache varies with the diagnosis. Nonaddictive analgesics are useful for pains of lesser intensity; headaches associated with stress or tension may respond to psychotherapy, tranquilizing drugs, biofeedback, or acupuncture. Migraine is best treated prophylactically by drugs that reduce the abnormal dilation response of blood vessels. These commonly include ergotamine and its derivatives (e.g., Cafergot) and propranolol (Inderal). In rare instances when headaches are caused by an allergy, removal of the allergy-causing element may be all that is necessary, while on the extreme end of the treatment scale, surgery for removal of an intracranial mass may be necessary.

Dizziness and Vertigo

Many systems within the body help to maintain a sense of equilibrium or balance. The sense of sight plays an obvious and important role, as does the vestibular system, the structures of the inner ear and their nerves that are concerned with balance. The auditory system senses position relative to direct or reflected sounds, while the limbs and muscles have sense organs which help to determine posture in relationship to the outside world. Even the sense of touch—expressed through pressure on the hands and feet and the feeling of weight that clothes produce—adds to the overall sensation. All these sensory inputs to the brain interact to communicate information about the body's position and movement. Disturbances in any of these may cause feelings of dizziness and sometimes vertigo as well.

Dizziness is a light-headed or woozy feeling of impending faint, or a feeling of unsteadiness in walking. Many healthy people experience occasional attacks of dizziness which, by themselves, do not signify serious disease. Dizziness is often associated with minor changes in blood flow to the brain. Thus, it is frequently related to syncope (fainting) which arises from momentary impairment of the delivery of blood, oxygen, or glucose to the brain. The individual feels faint, looks pale or ashen, and wants to sit down. Vision may darken or "gray out." Loss of consciousness may follow, but is usually regained within a minute or two if the patient lies down.

Rarely, mild epileptic seizures may cause symptoms that superficially suggest dizziness or vertigo but are actually due to disorientation, feelings of unreality, or brief lapses of memory. Conditions that cause loss of coordination of the legs, difficulty standing, and poor balance in walking may simulate dizziness, but are generally unrelated.

Vertigo is a type of dizziness felt as a shift in a person's relationship to the normal environment (a feeling that the room is spinning is common) or as a sense of movement in space. The victim may fear standing up and will usually minimize movement to avoid nausea and a feeling of rotation.

Intense vertigo with nausea is most often caused by a disorder of the semicircular canals and the vestibular system of the inner ear. This may come on abruptly and last days or weeks before subsiding. When self-limited and not associated with other neurological signs, the condition is termed labyrinthitis or vestibulitis. Although the cause is unknown, a viral inflammation is suspected in many cases. Because of the proximity of the balance and the hearing mechanisms, vertigo is sometimes accompanied by tinnitus, a buzzing or ringing sound caused by a disturbance in the cochlear portion of the auditory nerve—the nerve that is responsible for perception of sound. (For more information, see Chapter 34 on Diseases of the Ear, Nose, and Throat, page 673.)

Another condition is positional vertigo, which occurs only with a change in head position, such as leaning forward or backward, looking up or down, or turning quickly. Attacks are brief, lasting only a few seconds. Positional vertigo occurs most often in middle-aged patients for no apparent reason. Similar symptoms are common after head trauma or may accompany a stroke.

As with headache, accurate diagnosis requires establishing the exact type of feeling—dizziness or vertigo—as well as the conditions under which they are felt and any accompanying neurologic or audiologic symptoms.

Back Pain

Back pain, especially low back pain, can be a debilitating disorder and one of the most elusive to treat effectively. Low back pain commonly results from muscular imbalance due to misalignment of the spine. The underlying problem is often poor abdominal and back muscle tone, obesity, or degenerative changes in the vertebrae secondary to arthritis. Back pain of this type is often chronic, coming and going for months or years. Treatment includes muscle-strengthening exercises, improved posture, weight loss, and modification of furniture to provide better back support when the patient lies down or sits.

Another common cause of severe low back pain is a herniated disk. Typically, the pain is of sudden onset, often occurring after heavy lifting, twisting, or violent sneezing or coughing. The victim may be unable to stand, but the pain subsides promptly when the patient lies down. If the herniated disk pinches a nerve root, pain radiates into one or both buttocks or down the back of the leg to the knee or foot, a pattern known as sciatica. The distribution of pain gives a precise picture of the nerve root involved. Many ruptured disks can be treated with strict bed rest, but sometimes surgery is necessary to remove the portion of the disk that is pressing on the nerve. (For more information, see Chapter 27 on Disorders of the Musculoskeletal System, page 551.)

DISORDERS

Dementia

Dementia is the term used to describe a progressive and usually irreversible loss in intellectual function that eventually impairs an individual's ability to work and socialize. Some of the functions that are typically affected in dementia are memory, learning ability, judgment, rational thought, personality, and the capacity for abstract thought.

The most common cause of dementia is Alzheimer's disease, which affects nearly 1.5 million

Americans and is responsible for 20 percent of patients confined to nursing homes and other chronic care facilities. Alzheimer's disease is due to an unexplained degeneration of nerve cells. Recent research has linked this degeneration to a disturbance within nerve cell networks that utilize the neurotransmitter acetylcholine. The disease begins insidiously with mild forgetfulness and mood changes, often depression. The nature of the disease becomes clear, however, as mental abilities continue to deteriorate so that the patient becomes unable to work, loses the way in familiar surroundings, and repeats conversations endlessly. Apathy alternates with irrational behavior but the person cannot be reasoned with. Eventually, the victim becomes completely incapacitated, unable to be left alone. Speech fails so that even the most basic needs cannot be communicated. No treatment—including attempts to restore normal acetylcholine nerve cell function—has been effective to date. (For additional information, see Chapter 14 on The Middle Years and Aging, page 271.)

Another significant cause of dementia is cerebrovascular disease. Individuals who have suffered multiple strokes affecting large parts of both cerebral hemispheres become demented in a condition known as multi-infarct dementia. Brain tumors, severe or multiple head injuries (as with boxing), and several uncommon infectious diseases of the brain are less frequent causes of dementia.

Stroke

Stroke, sometimes called cerebrovascular accident (CVA), is a sudden neurological disorder due to interruption of the blood supply to part of the brain. Stroke occurs most often after the age of 65, and more men than women are affected. People with high blood pressure have a substantially higher incidence of stroke. Stroke also occurs more often in heavy smokers, diabetics, and persons who are obese or who have high blood levels of fat and cholesterol. Several different mechanisms may result in stroke: thrombus formation, embolus, and hemorrhage. It is important to determine which mechanism caused the stroke, because treatment and outcome differ with each type.

Thrombus formation, or thrombosis, is an obstruction within an artery achieved through the gradual buildup of material that has been likened to rust in a pipe. This most often results from arteriosclerosis in which deposits of fat and cholesterol form plaques along the arterial walls. Enlargement of these plaques may progress to occlude the artery, so that the flow of blood is severely restricted or blocked altogether. When this happens within arter-

ies supplying the brain, a stroke will occur if alternative routes, known as collateral circulation, are not available to deliver an adequate blood supply.

An embolus is an obstruction within an artery due to material that was formed elsewhere in the body (in the heart, for example) and floated free in the circulation until it finally lodged in an artery too small to permit its passage. The embolus then blocks blood flow, depriving the brain of nourishment beyond the blockage and producing a stroke. Emboli are usually composed of fragments of blood clots, or clumps of platelets, fibrin, and cholesterol.

The third major category of stroke is hemorrhage resulting from a rupture of an intracranial blood vessel. When this happens, blood erupts at high pressure into the soft brain tissue or spaces surrounding the brain. Normal brain cells may be destroyed, and the shock of the blood vessel rupture often results in severe headache and coma. When the blood ruptures primarily into the spaces around the brain, the stroke is termed a subarachnoid hemorrhage. Rupture into the brain substance itself is called an intracerebral, or intraparenchymal, hemorrhage.

A stroke is frequently preceded by an important warning sign—intermittent symptoms of neurological impairment called transient ischemic attacks (TIAs). (Ischemia is the term for insufficient blood circulation.) As the name implies, TIAs are only temporary (usually lasting from minutes to a few hours) and therapy must be started quickly to forestall a stroke with its more permanent disability.

The symptoms of a stroke depend on the artery involved and on the area of the brain affected by the interrupted blood supply. Strokes occurring in brain areas supplied by the carotid artery or its branches commonly affect vision and cause aphasia, the inability to use language properly; partial or complete paralysis of the face, arm, and leg (hemiparesis); and loss of sensation or ability to perceive the environment correctly. The hemiparesis and sensory disturbance occur on the side of the body opposite to the occluded cerebral blood vessel. Strokes that involve the vertebral circulation will produce some combination of double vision, slurred speech, incoordination, difficulty swallowing, and various patterns of weakness or sensory loss that involve parts of both sides of the body.

Treatment of stroke is largely preventive. Control of blood pressure, weight reduction, elimination of cigarette smoking, and proper diet and exercise all have salutary effects on reducing the incidence of stroke. Recognition and early treatment of TIAs may interrupt the progression to a full-blown stroke.

Treatment may require use of medications to reduce blood clots forming in narrowed blood vessels or the heart. Aspirin has been found to be a potent inhibitor of platelet aggregation. Warfarin (Coumadin), an anticoagulant that blocks some of the crucial steps in the clotting process, is also commonly used.

Surgery to remove the arteriosclerotic blockage in a blood vessel (usually the carotid artery), a procedure known as endarterectomy, is an alternative for carefully selected patients. Recently, a surgical technique has been developed to provide additional blood flow to the brain by connecting superficial arteries in the scalp directly to intracranial vessels. In cases of hemorrhage due to a weakness in the blood vessel wall, known as an aneurysm, surgery is necessary to repair the tear if rebleeding is to be prevented.

Once a stroke has occurred, physical, occupational, and speech therapies are important. During the rehabilitation phase of treatment, the medical program will also include recommendations designed to reduce the risk of further stroke. Although in general, disability that persists beyond two weeks without any improvement is likely to be permanent, some recovery of lost function almost always takes place, and full recovery is possible. (For more information, see Chapter 19 on Heart and Blood Vessel Diseases, page 385.)

Parkinson's Disease

Parkinson's disease, sometimes called shaking palsy, usually begins between 50 and 65 years of age. The disabling symptoms include muscular rigidity, slowness and poverty of movements, and tremor. Other signs of the disease may have been present, in retrospect, before the diagnosis is actually made. These include diminished blinking and reduced spontaneity of facial expression, stiff postures, loss of ease in changing positions (such as attempting to sit or stand), and a tendency to remain in a single position for unusually long periods of time. It is usually a shaking tremor of the hands, however, that finally brings the patient to a physician.

The disease results from a deficiency of dopamine, a chemical that is important in the transmission of nerve impulses in the basal ganglia of the brain. The basal ganglia are situated deep in the cerebral hemispheres and are important in regulation of smooth, rapid movements of the limbs and body. In the basal ganglia, there is normally a chemical balance between dopamine and acetylcholine, another so-called neurotransmitter that participates in the process of relaying messages from one nerve cell to another. With dopamine deficiency, as in Parkinson's disease, this balance is disturbed and there is a relative preponderance of acetylcholine activity. The main goal of treatment is to restore the chemical balance between dopamine and acetylcholine. Most patients are now given L-dopa (Sinemet), a compound that the body converts into dopamine, or other drugs that simulate the action of dopamine. Either alone or in combination with L-dopa, other agents may be used to counter the relative excess of acetylcholine. The most common of these are trihexyphenidyl (Artane) and benztropine mesylate (Cogentin).

Despite treatment, the disease is slowly progressive; the severity of symptoms at any time is directly related to the degree of dopamine deficiency. Nonetheless, dopamine replacement therapy has substantially improved the functional capacity and survival time of patients with this disorder.

Epilepsy

Contrary to popular belief, epilepsy refers not to a specific disease, but to a group of symptoms caused by a number of different conditions. What they all have in common is an excessive electrical excitability of the brain. This results in an intermittent electrical overload that is followed by sudden, recurrent, and transient changes of mental function or body movement. Common manifestations include partial or total loss of consciousness and muscle spasms or other involuntary movements.

What causes the neurons to discharge excessively is not known. In some patients, inheritance appears to be an important predisposing factor. In others, a head injury creates a scar on the brain that becomes a source of electrical irregularity. Brain tumors or strokes account for a small number of cases. In half the patients with chronic epilepsy, however, the cause is unknown. In these individuals, seizures typically begin early in life, usually before the age of 20, and continue for many years.

There are two principal categories of seizures: focal or partial seizures that begin locally in a part of the brain and generalized seizures that seem to involve all of the brain from the outset. Focal seizures sometimes spread to involve all of the brain, in which case they are called secondarily generalized seizures. These major groups are further subdivided into types based on the clinical pattern of attacks.

Absence, or petit mal, seizures are short, lasting only a few seconds. The only manifestations are brief lapses of consciousness during which the patient stares ahead. Sometimes the stare is accompanied by rhythmic twitching of the eyelids or face muscles. Absence seizures begin and end abruptly. Whatever activity or behavior is in progress when a seizure begins ceases during the attack but is resumed immediately when the seizure is over. These brief seizures may occur up to several hundred times daily. They are most common in children after the age of two, and rarely begin after age twenty.

Tonic-clonic or grand mal seizures are the most familiar form of convulsion. There is a sudden and complete loss of consciousness. The patient falls and the arms and legs stiffen, then begin a rhythmic jerking. There may also be a high-pitched cry at the outset of the fit as a result of air being forced over the vocal cords. Sometimes the patient may bite the tongue and be incontinent. This all occurs within two minutes, followed by a more relaxed state of unconsciousness for another minute or so. After this the patient will be confused, sleepy, and uncooperative for fifteen minutes to several hours before full recovery.

Complex partial seizures, or psychomotor attacks, usually arise from electrical discharges involving the temporal lobe of the brain and vary considerably in their manifestation. Often there is a warning, known as an aura, which may be anything from a subjective sense of fear to an unpleasant smell, abdominal sensation, or distortion in perception. The aura is followed by depressed consciousness and loss of speech, accompanied by automatisms—automatic movements such as chewing, repetitive swallowing, fidgeting of the hands, or purposeless moving from place to place. After the attack, the patient is momentarily confused and cannot remember details of the episode.

Simple partial seizures result from seizure discharges that involve parts of the motor or sensory areas of the brain. In "Jacksonian seizures" (named for John Hughlings Jackson, the great English neurologist who first described them), jerking occurs in the muscles of the hand and side of the face opposite the side of the brain showing the abnormal electrical activity. The muscles jerk on the opposite side because some of the nerve fibers cross to the other side in the brainstem.

Patients with epilepsy should receive a careful physical examination, including a detailed history, in the search for clues to an underlying brain disorder. An electroencephalogram (EEG), which measures the electrical activity of the brain, is done in every case to document and define the nature of the electrical disturbance. A computerized tomographic (CT) brain scan is often performed as well. (See the section on Brain Tumors, page 596.) Other laboratory tests, depending on individual circumstances, may include blood tests and a lumbar puncture to obtain cerebrospinal fluid for analysis.

For the vast majority of patients with epilepsy, treatment means taking anticonvulsant drugs. In general, carbamazepine (Tegretol), phenytoin (Dilantin), or phenobarbital is prescribed for focal and tonic-clonic seizures, while valproate (Depakote) or ethosuximide (Zarontin) is favored for absence attacks. Treatment needs to be individualized, however, and sometimes combinations of these medications or others not listed will be necessary. Additional important measures include making changes in lifestyle, as appropriate, to accommodate the chronic illness.

With medication, the vast majority of epileptics can live normal lives. Children, with only minimal restrictions, can participate in sports, but safety and supervision should be emphasized. Adults can continue working, although those with active seizures must avoid driving, working at exposed heights, and operating dangerous machinery. Driving restrictions are changed and sometimes removed after the patient demonstrates an extended period of seizure control through treatment. (Additional information about available services, education, and employment is available from The Epilepsy Foundation of America, listed in Part VII, Directory of Resources, page 801.)

Multiple Sclerosis

Multiple sclerosis is a disease that destroys myelin, an insulating material that covers nerve fibers and is necessary for the normal electrical function of the nervous system. As a result, an electrical short circuit develops, and normal electrical impulses cannot be carried by the nerves. The type of symptoms that result depends on where in the brain and spinal cord this process takes place, but usually, multiple sites are involved. Myelin has some ability to repair itself, but with repeated attacks of inflammation, scarring (sclerosis) takes place and permanent loss of function may result.

Because almost any area of the brain and spinal cord that contains myelin may be affected, the symptoms are extraordinarily diverse. The course is first one of appearance and then disappearance of disability. As the disease progresses, however, remission of symptoms between attacks becomes less and less complete.

It is not possible to provide a typical picture of multiple sclerosis. Some of the common symptoms, however, include loss of vision in one eye, double vision, loss of coordination and trembling of a hand, instability in walking, spasticity, loss of bladder control, and peculiar spontaneous sensations such as a pins-and-needles feeling over part of the body, called paresthesias. At first, the patient may have only intermittent symptoms. Since the physical examination at this stage may be completely normal, the patient's complaints may be dismissed initially as "psychosomatic" or "hysterical."

Although the cause of the disease is unknown, evidence suggests there may be an immunologic basis, since the body makes antibodies or activates lymphocytes against one of its own constituents, in this case myelin. Some researchers think a virus may trigger this type of pathological immune response. While there is no cure, the severity of attacks may sometimes be lessened by drugs that suppress inflammation (prednisone and ACTH) or blunt the immune response (cyclophosphamide). Physical therapy and rehabilitation are important in controlling symptoms and adapting to disability.

Brain Tumors

The two major categories of brain tumor are primary—those that develop only in the brain—and metastatic—those that originate elsewhere in the body but spread through the bloodstream to involve the brain secondarily. Each major category is represented by many different types of tumor, each with its own prognosis and, often, its own treatment. Almost nothing is known about the cause of brain tumors. While treatment results are often dismal, some tumors can be cured. Except in rare conditions, inheritance does not play a significant role.

Brain tumors can occur at any age and cause symptoms of great diversity. To a large extent, however, the symptoms are relatively independent of the exact tumor type. Many patients have symptoms of a cerebral disturbance that are referable to pressure effects on the brain caused by the tumor. These symptoms include headache, blurred vision, vomiting, and mental dulling. Localized signs of brain dysfunction occur when vital areas of the brain that regulate specific functions, such as language ability or motor control, are compromised or destroyed by the tumor.

To help determine the location, type, and extent of a brain tumor, laboratory tests are necessary. They are also essential because many symptoms of brain tumor can occur with other diseases such as stroke, subdural hematoma (a hemorrhage beneath the dura usually caused by head trauma), and infections. Without question, the most valuable laboratory aid is computerized tomography (CT), a special x-ray test in which a computer is used to reconstruct cross-sectional images of the brain on a screen. Normal and abnormal structures are clearly depicted. The value of CT is enhanced by injecting a contrast agent into the bloodstream which will concentrate in or outline some tumors. Other diagnostic tests include electroencephalography (EEG), which measures the electrical activity of the brain, and cerebral angiography, an x-ray examination of the cranial blood vessels.

Treatment of a tumor depends on the type, location, and extent and whether it is benign or malignant. Benign tumors can often be removed completely by a skilled neurosurgeon. In cases of malignant brain tumors, surgery is also required to relieve pressure by removing as much of the tumor as possible and is typically followed by radiation treatments. The role of chemotherapy in the treatment of malignant primary brain tumors is still experimental.

Encephalitis and Meningitis

Viral infections like the common cold are regularly encountered in everyday life, but far less often does one cause serious brain disease. Encephalitis is an inflammation that results from a viral infection of the brain, or from the spread to the brain of an existing systemic infection, such as measles or mumps. At other times, the brain may be involved without evidence of infection elsewhere in the body. Symptoms include fever, headache, epileptic seizures, confusion or delirium, and, when the infection is severe, paralysis and coma. Although mild cases recover completely, permanent neurologic abnormalities may result. How ill a patient becomes with encephalitis depends on the type of virus and the body's immune response.

A particularly serious form of encephalitis, and the one that is most often fatal, is caused by the herpes simplex virus. With herpes encephalitis, the onset of illness is abrupt, marked by seizures, mental changes, and rapid onset of coma. In recent years, the availability of antiviral drugs to treat herpes encephalitis has substantially decreased mortality.

Meningitis is an inflammation of the meninges, the membranes covering the brain and spinal cord, which is usually accompanied by fever, headache, and a stiff neck. It is often caused by viruses, but bacterial infection may also be the cause. In general, viral meningitis is a less serious illness than bacterial meningitis. Diagnosis is made by analyzing cerebrospinal fluid obtained by a lumbar puncture (spinal tap). Bacterial meningitis can be treated with antibiotics that are specific for the infective organism, but there is no comparable therapy for viral meningitis. Once a bacterial infection has been excluded, bed rest, fluids, and aspirin will suffice for most patients.

Cerebral Palsy and Mental Retardation

A child's brain is especially vulnerable to injury just before or during birth, and during the first few months of life. If an injury occurs at this time, resulting in a functional handicap that mainly affects motor performance, the child is said to have cerebral palsy. If the brain damage is more extensive and affects learning and reasoning functions, then mental retardation is the result. Since neither condition becomes worse, these disorders are said to be "static."

Mental retardation and cerebral palsy can result from a number of conditions, including inadequate blood or oxygen supply to the fetus, infection, marked prematurity with intracranial bleeding, and trauma during delivery. Breech delivery, difficult and prolonged labor, and multiple births have an increased incidence of cerebral palsy and retardation.

There are three types of cerebral palsy—spastic, dyskinetic, and ataxic—classified according to their major clinical signs. Two of these types, or even all three, may appear together. Although cerebral palsy is not progressive, the pattern of disability may change as the child grows, or in response to treatment.

Spastic cerebral palsy is characterized by hemiparesis (partial paralysis of the arm and leg on one side), tetraparesis (partial but relatively equal paralysis of all four limbs), or diparesis (partial paralysis of both legs with minimal or no apparent involvement of the arms). In addition to weakness, spastic limbs caused by a birth injury may be thinner and smaller than normal extremities.

Dyskinetic cerebral palsy is the term applied to cases with abnormal involuntary movements such as writhing, twisting, or twitching of the limbs. Ataxic cerebral palsy is uncommon and rarely the sole symptom of disability. Ataxia—the lack or loss of coordination or control over skilled voluntary movements—can result from a number of causes, and these must be ruled out before a diagnosis of ataxic cerebral palsy is made.

Treatment of cerebral palsy and mental retardation is difficult because the underlying birth injury is permanent and, at present, irreversible. Motor function can be improved, however, and the success rate is high if treatment begins early. There is, unfortunately, no consensus about the best treatment, but the goals of therapy are straightforward: to improve function, to control epileptic seizures if present, and to help parents determine the best place and kind of education in order to establish as normal a life as possible.

Physical and occupational therapy, speech therapy, and sometimes drugs to reduce spasticity, all play a role in treatment. Failure to treat a spastic child may result in fixed joint and limb deformities and even more severe functional disability. School placement is especially critical; the primary criterion should be the child's learning ability, not the physical handicap.

Attention Deficit Disorder

Another, possibly related, condition is the attention deficit disorder, sometimes called minimal brain dysfunction. This diagnosis applies to children who are not retarded but who have learning problems and impaired visual/spatial coordination. Children with this disorder usually have difficulty concentrating, are easily distracted and impulsive, and are often hyperactive. Paradoxically, treatment of these latter symptoms often involves drugs that are actually stimulants but, when used judiciously, are quite effective. These drugs, such as methylphenidate (Ritalin), pemoline (Cylert), and dextroamphetamine (Dexedrine), should only be used as part of a comprehensive treatment program that includes neurological assessment, family counseling, and proper school placement.

Bell's Palsy

Bell's palsy is the term used to describe paralysis of muscles on one side of the face. It occurs suddenly and is often first noticed when the patient wakes up. Normally there is no pain, but there may be a slight discomfort in the region of the jaw or behind the ear. The paralysis results from temporary damage to the facial nerve. Although the cause is unknown, a viral infection is suspected. The disorder occurs at all ages, but is more frequent between 30 and 60.

Features of the syndrome include sagging of the muscles of the lower half of the face on one side. In mild cases, the facial weakness is noted only when the patient smiles. Sometimes, the eye cannot be fully closed on the affected side and, when this is attempted, the eye tilts upward. Tearing may result because the lid loses its normal function in moving tears into the lacrimal ducts.

The severity of muscle paralysis depends on the extent of nerve damage. Fortunately, 90 percent of patients with Bell's palsy recover completely, or nearly completely, even without treatment. Some physicians prescribe prednisone (a cortisone substance) to reduce suspected inflammation in the area of nerve damage. Others believe this is usually unnecessary. If eyelid function is compromised, the eye must be covered to prevent inadvertent injury from foreign objects. (For more information, see Chapter 34 on Diseases of the Ear, Nose, and Throat, page 680.)

Trigeminal Neuralgia

Trigeminal neuralgia (tic douloureux) is the most frequent of all neuralgias and results from dysfunction of the fifth, or trigeminal, cranial nerve. The cause is unknown but the disorder occurs most frequently in middle or old age. The cardinal symptom is severe paroxysms of sharp, bulletlike pains that are felt in the gums, teeth, and lower face. In most instances, the pain is present for weeks or months and then ceases spontaneously for a variable period. As the patient grows older, these periods of remission tend to become shorter. Although attacks of trigeminal neuralgia may be incapacitating, the condition is not fatal, nor do other symptoms develop. Treatment with carbamazepine (Tegretol), a strong analgesic, is effective in many individuals, but in some intractable cases, surgery on the nerve is required for pain relief.

Muscular Dystrophy

Muscular dystrophy is an umbrella term used to indicate several inherited diseases of muscle that cause progressive weakness and disability. The most common types are Duchenne, fascioscapulohumeral, limb-girdle, and myotonic.

Duchenne dystrophy is the most severe and probably the best known. Symptoms usually appear before age three as difficulty in walking or climbing stairs. A waddling gait, muscle wasting, and curved posture become evident. As the disease progresses, the child becomes wheelchair bound, usually by the teen years. Duchenne dystrophy is an inherited disorder that is sex-linked and recessive, which means that although women are carriers, the actual disorder is confined to males. Since there is no effective treatment, genetic counseling is an important consideration for women whose brothers or maternal uncles were victims.

Fascioscapulohumeral dystrophy appears in adolescence with weakness of the face and arms. The illness progresses very slowly and, since the legs are only mildly affected, patients maintain the ability to walk. Limb-girdle dystrophy is probably not a distinct disease, but rather a group of different muscle diseases that have in common a weakness of the upper legs and arms.

Myotonic dystrophy, unlike the more common dystrophies, not only causes muscle weakness and wasting, but affects several other organ systems as well. These include the eyes (cataract formation),

the heart, and testes. The striking feature of this disorder is myotonia, or failure of muscles to relax normally after sudden, vigorous use.

Narcolepsy and Sleep Apnea

In the past 20 years, major medical advances have been made in the recognition, understanding, and treatment of sleep disorders. Indeed, an entire new field has emerged called chronobiology—the study of biological rhythms such as the waking-sleep cycle. One of the most common complaints indicating a possible sleep disorder is that of excessive daytime sleepiness. Afflicted patients complain of inability to stay awake during important activities such as driving a car or eating meals, a constant feeling of sleepiness throughout the day despite adequate nighttime sleep, serious disruption of work efficiency, and a reduction in leisure and family time. The two most frequently encountered medical disorders producing pathological somnolence are narcolepsy and sleep apnea.

Narcolepsy is a syndrome of unknown cause. It typically begins in adolescence or early adult years. The two major symptoms are recurring periods of excessive and uncontrollable daytime sleepiness, and cataplexy—an episode of abrupt, short-duration muscle weakness that occurs without loss of consciousness and is usually triggered by an emotional reaction such as laughing. Other characteristic symptoms which occur less frequently include vivid visual hallucinations, especially when falling asleep, sleep paralysis (inability to perform voluntary movement when falling asleep or on awakening), and automatic behavior which the patient later does not remember. Most of these daytime symptoms have been related to the abnormal intrusion of fragments of the phase of deep sleep known as REM (rapid eye movement) into the waking state. The diagnosis of narcolepsy can be confirmed by special EEG studies. Treatment includes use of stimulant drugs to maintain wakefulness, and compounds such as imipramine (Tofranil) or protriptyline (Vivactil) to prevent cataplexy.

Sleep apnea, sometimes called hypersomnia-sleep apnea syndrome, also causes excessive daytime sleepiness which is usually more pervasive and less episodic than the somnolence of narcolepsy. Additional nighttime symptoms are characteristic, including loud snoring that recurs in regular cycles, restless sleep with frequent and brief arousals, and unusual sleep postures. The syndrome is due to obstruction of the upper airway which produces the short episodes of breathing stoppage that characterize apnea. Less than complete obstruction results in loud snoring, and frequent arousals occur when the patient awakens in order to overcome the airway blockage.

Most patients are between the ages of 40 and 70, and men are affected 20 times more often than women. More than half the sufferers are obese, which further compromises the normal flow of air. Weight reduction, therefore, is an important part of therapy. A variety of drugs has been tried, but none with any consistent degree of success. More important are steps that reduce the airway obstruction. In severe cases, this may mean performing a tracheostomy to ensure adequate air exchange.

Motor Neuron Disease

Sometimes called Lou Gehrig's disease after one of its most famous victims, amyotrophic lateral sclerosis (ALS) is a disease of middle or late life that results from a progressive degeneration of nerve cells controlling voluntary motor functions. The first symptoms differ from patient to patient, but at some point there will be difficulty walking from leg weakness or stiffness, clumsiness of the hands, slurred speech, and an inability to swallow normally. The muscles of the arms and legs waste away, and as they do, rippling of muscle fibers—called fasciculations—may be observed under the skin. Eventually, walking is impossible and the hands become useless, although sensation is always normal. The cause is unknown and there is no treatment at present.

Peripheral Neuropathy

The peripheral nervous system—comprising the motor nerves and the sensory nerves—connects the central nervous system with the various organs and muscles of the body. In a sense, the peripheral nerves are the cables that allow the brain's commands to be conveyed to all parts of the body (motor nerves) and relay sensory information back to the brain (sensory nerves). Some diseases selectively damage the peripheral nervous system without affecting the brain and spinal cord. When this occurs, the patient is said to have a peripheral neuropathy, which may involve either a single nerve (mononeuropathy or mononeuritis) or many nerves and their terminal endings (polyneuropathy).

In the most common pattern of polyneuropathy, symptoms begin gradually, usually over months. The patient's feet and hands become numb (sometimes called a "stocking-glove distribution"), and the numbness is accompanied by a prickly pins-and-needles feeling called paresthesias. If the condition goes untreated, loss of sensation will become increasingly severe and will spread up along the legs and forearms. As the sensory impairment worsens, the muscles of the feet, ankles, fingers, and hands weaken. Sometimes the skin becomes so sensitive that the merest touch is painful.

Many diseases can produce peripheral neuropathy and, although there is no specific medical or surgical treatment, proper treatment of the underlying cause may lessen the progress of the disorder. Among the more common disorders causing peripheral neuropathy are diabetes, chronic alcoholism, and malnutrition. The disorder is also associated with cancer, and may result from prolonged exposure to various toxic chemicals, such as arsenic, mercury, and lead.

Carpal Tunnel Syndrome

One of the more common forms of mononeuropathy is the carpal tunnel syndrome. In this condition, a branch of the median nerve in the forearm is compressed at the wrist as it passes through the tunnel formed by the wrist bones, or carpals, and a ligament that lies just under the skin. The syndrome occurs most often in middle age and affects more women than men. It is usually due to arthritis or other disorders that affect bones and ligaments. Sometimes fluid accumulation (edema) or sudden weight gain such as occurs in pregnancy may also put pressure on the nerve in the carpal tunnel.

The symptoms are initially intermittent but then become constant. Numbness and tingling begin in the thumb and first two fingers; then the hand, and sometimes the whole arm, becomes painful. The pain may be quite severe and can awaken the patient from sleep. Gradual weakness and wasting of the thumb muscles occur if treatment is not instituted.

If symptoms are relatively mild, a wrist splint may be helpful. Weight loss, control of edema (usually with diuretics), and treatment of arthritis may help. If the symptoms progress despite these measures, and especially if weakness appears, a simple surgical procedure can be used to cut the ligament at the wrist and thus relieve pressure on the nerve.

Guillain-Barré Syndrome

The Guillain-Barré syndrome is an illness that usually occurs one to two weeks after a mild viral infection such as a sore throat, bronchitis, or flu. Symmetric weakness of the limbs develops over a few days, sometimes progressing to complete paralysis. The face muscles may be paralyzed as well, making it impossible to swallow normally. In severe cases, paralysis of respiratory muscles requires tracheostomy and artificial ventilation. With intensive medical treatment and support, the majority of patients recover, but about one-third are left with some residual weakness.

The illness results from inflammation and destruction of myelin similar to that seen in multiple sclerosis. The main difference, however, is that multiple sclerosis attacks the central nervous system, whereas in the Guillain-Barré syndrome it is the peripheral nerves that are affected. Another difference is that Guillain-Barré syndrome does not recur ex-

cept in rare instances. The nerve damage is thought to be the result of an abnormal immune reaction directed against the myelin of the peripheral nervous system. Diagnosis is made by the clinical features, characteristic changes in cerebrospinal fluid, and electrical studies of the peripheral nerves and muscles, a procedure known as electromyography (EMG).

HEAD AND SPINAL CORD TRAUMA

Head Injury

Head injury, especially from car and motorcycle accidents, is one of the most common causes of accidental injury and death in the United States. Although injuries may happen at any age, they are more common among young adults, especially men. Injuries from motor vehicle accidents are estimated at more than 3 million annually. Many could be prevented by observing speed limits and wearing seatbelts or motorcycle helmets.

Head injuries can be divided into three major categories: closed head injuries, depressed fracture of the skull, and compound fracture of the skull.

Even with closed head injuries, there can be damage to the brain, although it is usually less severe than when there are obvious skull fractures. Brain damage results from bruising or swelling of brain tissue, or internal hemorrhage.

The mildest form of closed head injuries is a concussion, in which there is brief loss of consciousness, but no permanent effects.

With depressed skull fractures, the outer skull remains intact, but small fragments of underlying bone are pushed down and may compress or lacerate the brain beneath. The degree of damage to the brain can vary.

Compound fractures are more serious and much more likely to result in brain damage. In these cases, the outer tissues are torn, the skull opened, and the brain tissue exposed.

The symptoms of a brain injury vary and are directly related to the severity of damage. Concussion may be followed by headache, dizziness, and amnesia about events immediately before or after the injury. More serious head injuries may cause difficulty in speech, bleeding from the nose or ears, muscular weakness, paralysis, and long periods of altered awareness or coma. Serious injury may also result in convulsive seizures. The effects of head injury may be completely reversible, but in some

cases, some neurological impairment may be permanent.

Anyone who loses consciousness following head injury should be seen by a doctor. Even slight bumps on the head that result in severe head or neck pain should be examined. More serious injuries that produce any of the symptoms described above should be viewed as medical emergencies and the patient taken to a hospital emergency service at once. (For more information, see Chapter 7, Directory of First-Aid Procedures, page 116.)

The extent of injury is usually diagnosed by x-rays of the skull and CT scans. Electroencephalograms (EEGs) may also be helpful in determining the patient's prognosis. (For more information, see Chapter 4, Directory of Tests and Procedures, page 50.)

Treatment depends on the extent of the injury. It may range from bedrest and observation for 24 to 48 hours to surgery and extended postoperative care including physical and occupational therapy.

Following immediate treatment, the patient must be observed for late complications which include subdural hematoma (a blood clot between the layers of the tissue surrounding the brain) which may develop even weeks or months later, and epilepsy.

In more than a third of cases, even those involving mild head injury, patients suffer from a collection of sometimes vague symptoms known as "post-traumatic" or "post-concussive" syndrome. These symptoms, which may persist for weeks or longer, include headache, dizziness, insomnia, and such psychological disturbances as irritability, restlessness, inability to concentrate, personality change, and depression. Reassurance and support by family members and medical personnel are important to recovery and psychological counseling may be necessary as well.

Spinal Cord Injury

Injury to the spinal cord almost always results in some amount of permanent neurological damage. An estimated 150,000 persons in the United States, two-thirds of them under age 35, are now living with the consequences of spinal cord injury. Motor vehicle and motorcycle accidents, falls, and injuries involving sports such as diving and tobogganing are the most frequent causes. These accidents result in immediate stretching, crushing, laceration, or frank severing of the spinal cord. Since further damage can occur if the victim is improperly moved, a patient with known or suspected neck injury should not be moved until the head and spinal column can be immobilized and supported in a neutral position by trained emergency personnel. (For more information, see Chapter 7, Directory of First-Aid Procedures, page 117.)

Damage and disability resulting from a spinal cord injury depend not only on its severity, but also on its location, since it is the area of the body below the injury site that is affected. Injuries to the lumbar or thoracic region affect the function of the legs, bladder, and bowels; damage to the cervical end produces impairment in the arms as well.

Injuries to the spinal cord usually result in only partial recovery of function; sometimes there is no improvement. Surgery may be necessary to stabilize the spine or remove bone fragments. Physical and occupational therapy can help retrain muscles in the arms and legs that are partially paralyzed. Rehabilitation may also be necessary to assist with control over bowel, bladder, and sexual function.

Because the care and rehabilitation of spine-injured patients is long and complex, a number of major medical centers have developed separate units where special equipment and teams of specially trained medical personnel are available.

SUMMING UP

THE BRAIN and other parts of the nervous system, controlling the body's most vital functions, are overwhelmingly complex. They are extremely delicate, yet they are often able to withstand such serious injury as stroke and even recover lost function completely. The nervous system is subject to a variety of disorders, including common, usually benign, everyday conditions like headache, as well as complex diseases like Parkinson's disease and multiple sclerosis. For some diseases, cause and treatment are clearly defined; others, despite major advances in diagnostic procedures, such as CT scans and drugs that perform such functions as inhibiting and controlling nerve function, are not yet well understood and cannot yet be cured.

30 Kidney Diseases

Jay I. Meltzer, M.D.

INTRODUCTION

As ANIMAL LIFE EVOLVED from the sea to the land, the kidneys played a crucial role. Indeed, they held the key to the metabolic power to regulate the body's internal fluids so that animals could continue to be nourished as they were by the sea, enabling them to walk on dry land and to stay alive without dehydrating or developing biochemical imbalances.

Among the hundreds of metabolic tasks the kidneys constantly perform, there are still some major ones concerned with the preservation of our sea heritage: control of water balance, maintenance of mild alkalinity of body fluids, and removal of waste products of metabolism. In the course of performing these complex and vital tasks, the kidneys are subject to numerous diseases. Kidney diseases affect 13 million Americans and are fatal to 78,000 each year. If hypertension is included, the numbers are even

greater. Even so, the importance of kidney disease far outweighs the statistics because of our present scientific capability to save the life of every patient dying of kidney disease.

The federal government recognizes the uniqueness of kidney disease by making it a special case under the Medicare/Social Security Law, providing complete care for anyone in end-stage renal failure, regardless of age, occupation, or socioeconomic status. It does so at enormous cost, now approaching $2 billion yearly, primarily used to support chronic hemodialysis (artificial kidney machines) and kidney transplantation. The high cost is paradoxically caused by the very success of these two miracle treatments: Each year the number of patients enlisted and funded grows because they stay alive.

The large amounts spent to treat the ravages of

kidney disease have increased efforts at prevention. With an understanding of how the kidney works and how diseases affect it, all of us can have a role in prevention.

ANATOMY

To PERFORM THEIR vital and exacting tasks, the kidneys receive more blood from the heart than any other organ of the body. Almost one-quarter of the volume of every heartbeat goes to the kidneys. Handling this massive flow of blood—1½ quarts every minute—in an organ measuring only 4 inches high by 2 inches wide by 1 inch thick and weighing only 5 to 6 ounces requires a complex blood circulation. In fact, the arrangement of blood vessels in the kidney is the most complex by far of any in the body, allowing the enormous force of the blood to be weakened and controlled to an exacting measure of pressure and flow before it reaches the delicately thin membrane that filters the body fluids, making urine. (See figure 30.1.) This mesangial membrane is so thin, it can only be seen clearly when it is magnified 25,000 times by an electron microscope. Yet it accepts the pressure of the circulating blood, the force that pushes the body fluids through this delicate membrane like a sieve, retaining the cells and large protein molecules, and passing all the smaller chemicals in solution. Having let through all these chemicals, both the useful and the wastes, the kidney must then get back most of what it already has passed into the urine.

To understand how this is done, it is necessary to look at the kidney's functioning unit—the nephron—of which there are about 1 million. Each nephron is a cuplike receptacle emptying into a long, thin tubule lined by special cells with varying functions. Each of these long tubular units finally empties into the center of the kidney, from where urine passes into the ureters and then to the bladder, and is finally expelled from the body through the urethra.

The receptacles of the nephrons, called glomeruli, receive about 4 ounces every minute from the urine's side of the filtering membrane surface, or about 20 percent of the water content of the blood that flows through the kidney. As this large volume of early urine flows down the tubules, the lining cells begin the important task of recovering most of the precious water, nutrients, and salts, leaving mainly waste chemicals behind in as much water as is necessary to keep the body fluids like the primeval sea. The nephrons usually reabsorb 99 percent of the water, salt, and vital nutrients initially filtered. Although this seems wasteful, it enables the nephrons to make an enormous number of individual adjustments to the many components of our internal sea, providing reserve power in times of exposure or lack of food or fluid.

Because of its intimate relationship with such a large portion of the blood circulation, the kidney plays the major role in the regulation of blood pressure. The kidney needs to be able to control large volumes of blood, reducing its flow to just the right pressure against the delicate membrane, lest it break and hemorrhage, clogging the urine.

The kidney's blood pressure control mechanism operates like this: In the center of the nephron, a group of specialized cells senses the level of incoming pressure and responds by releasing renin, which acts as a chemical messenger that circulates to the entire body. If the pressure is too low, the messenger causes the muscles in the walls of all the vessels in the body to contract ever so slightly, raising the pressure by narrowing the size of the blood compartment. (Renin causes the blood to generate a chemical so powerful that one part per trillion raises the blood pressure.) If the pressure is too high, the cells make less renin and the vascular compartment tends to relax.

Renin plays another vital role: It sends a separate message to the adrenal gland, an endocrine gland at the top of the kidney, to make the hormone

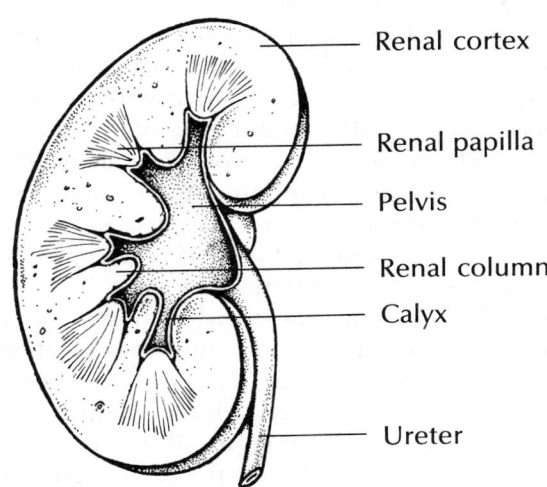

Figure 30.1. **Cross-sectional view of a normal kidney.**

Renal cortex

Renal papilla

Pelvis

Renal column

Calyx

Ureter

aldosterone, itself a chemical messenger. This second messenger circulates back to the kidney tubules, signaling the cells near the end to take back more salt and water from the urine. This retention of salt and water by the body raises the volume of plasma in the blood, filling the blood compartment more completely, and raising the blood pressure. This, in turn, reduces the release of the messages and sets a new equilibrium. It is easy, then, to see why diseases of the kidney affect blood pressure and blood pressure affects kidney function.

High blood pressure, or hypertension, can only develop when the kidney fails in its usual regulation of volume and tension. The "tension" in hypertension refers to the vascular tone of the smooth muscles in the walls of the arteries and arterioles, not to nervous tension, which does not cause high blood pressure. Nervous tension may *temporarily* cause the blood pressure to rise with exertion, heavy mental exercise (such as solving a math problem), or sexual arousal, but such rises cause no harm and are not to be feared.

HYPERTENSION

HYPERTENSION, or high blood pressure, is the most common and the most treatable of the diseases that affect the kidneys. In a small percentage of cases, another disease or condition—other kidney diseases, hormonal disorders, pregnancy, birth control pills, to name a few—can cause hypertension, in which case it is known as secondary hypertension. In the majority of cases, the cause is unknown, and the disease is referred to as essential hypertension. Except in very rare cases, called malignant hypertension, the blood pressure by itself does no immediate harm and, indeed, causes no symptoms. It takes perhaps 10 to 15 years for elevated pressure to cause symptoms. The damage comes only from the years of wear and tear on the walls of the blood vessels, mostly in the heart, brain, and kidneys. For this rea-

son, untreated hypertension greatly increases the risk of heart disease, kidney disease, and stroke.

Many people are able to control their blood pressure simply by restricting salt intake, getting regular exercise and, if necessary, losing excess weight. A number of drugs also are available to lower high blood pressure. However, drug treatment needs to be evaluated by both the doctor and the patient by weighing the pressure reductions achieved against the side effects, their severity, the present discomfort, and the future risk. Changing types of medication and dosage levels can sometimes control or eliminate unpleasant side effects. (For more information, see Chapter 19 on Heart and Blood Vessel Disease, page 372.)

INFLAMMATION OF THE KIDNEYS

KIDNEY INFLAMMATION, which can occur either in the glomeruli (the filtering cups) or in the tubules (the long segments leading into the central urinary stream), is the most common kidney disease condition. (For information on glomerular diseases, see page 607.)

The 2 major diseases that affect the tubules are bacterial pyelonephritis and nonbacterial tubulointerstitial disease, also called interstitial nephritis. Either disease can be acute or chronic, or both. The tubules are closely supported by a network of connective tissues and blood vessels, and the entire system is known as the tubulointerstitium.

Acute Bacterial Pyelonephritis

Doctors believe that the bacterial infection causing pyelonephritis may sometimes develop elsewhere in

the body and travel through the bloodstream to the tubulointerstitium. Far more commonly, however, the infection is a result of bacteria from outside the body traveling back up the urinary stream through the urethra to the bladder and eventually to the kidneys, in which case it is known as an ascending infection. This may explain why women, whose urethras are short and in close proximity to the anus, a potential source of bacteria, have 4 times as many cases of pyelonephritis as men.

The flow of urine backward is known as reflux and may be caused by an anatomical defect (often inherited) or by an obstruction. In the former case, instead of a tight valve between the bladder and the ureter, there is a wide opening. When the bladder contracts during urination, the urine goes both ways, out through the urethra and back up through the ureters. The defect is not easy to correct and those who have it are subject to repeat infections. Obstructions that cause reflux in women are commonly in the form of a stricture, or scar tissue, itself formed from infection or inflammation in the urethra. In young men, such strictures form less often and usually are a consequence of a venereal infection. In older men, the prostate is commonly responsible for obstruction to the flow of urine.

Despite such obstructions, reflux backup into the kidneys is rare. Most urinary infections remain confined to the bladder, where they are less serious. Even with severe obstruction by the prostate, kidney infection almost never happens unless reflux is encouraged by the insertion of catheters or instruments such as cystoscopes for diagnosis or treatment. The introduction of any foreign body into an area of obstruction is fraught with danger of infection which, because of obstruction, is doubly difficult to treat. Therefore, all such procedures must be given careful consideration.

Acute bacterial infection is somewhat common in pregnancy, occurring in perhaps 5 percent of cases. This may be because the ureters and other structures are dilated, just as they are in obstruction conditions, although there is no visible obstruction.

No matter what the underlying cause, the symptoms of acute bacterial pyelonephritis are the same. The first indication is usually a severe, shaking, teeth-chattering chill, accompanied by a high fever and pain in the joints and muscles. Attention may not be drawn to the kidneys at all. The situation may be especially confusing in children, when high temperature may suddenly bring on a seizure or a change in mental state, or in the aged, where any fever may bring on confusion or the infection may be masked by generalized aches and pains. Urinary frequency and discomfort with urination, so common in bladder infections, are unusual in kidney infections. It is necessary to feel the kidney manually to bring out the physical sign of tenderness which will indicate inflammation.

In acute infections, the symptoms develop rapidly, the fever noted first, followed by possible changes in the color of the urine, and then tenderness in the flank. As the kidney becomes more inflamed, pain, loss of appetite, headache, and all the general effects of infection develop. This type of kidney pain differs from the renal colic pain of kidney stones in that it is continuous and does not come in waves, stays in one spot, and is made worse by moving around.

The clinical diagnosis is strengthened by examination of the urine under the microscope for pus cells (white blood corpuscles) and active bacteria in large numbers. The diagnosis is confirmed by culturing the bacteria and identifying the particular species. While it is not always important to identify the species with a bladder infection, it is with kidney infections, which are deeper, with greater potential for bacterial invasion of the bloodstream. By isolating and identifying the species, it is possible to determine the type and dosage of antibiotic needed to kill the organism, thus assuring a complete cure. Complete cure of acute infections is always a major goal, because of the possibility the patient will develop chronic pyelonephritis.

Chronic Pyelonephritis

While patients with chronic pyelonephritis may have acute infections, sometimes there are no symptoms, or the symptoms are so mild that they go unnoticed. This carries the risk that the infectious inflammatory disease may slowly progress undetected over many years until there is enough deterioration to produce kidney failure. Thus, hypertension or anemia or symptoms related to renal insufficiency, such as fatigue and nocturia (awakening in the night to urinate), may be the first indication of trouble. Unfortunately, irreversible damage may already have taken place. Simple urinalysis and culture done routinely will detect silent pyelonephritis. If the test is positive, further checking, for curable obstructions, stones, or neurologic abnormalities, will help prevent chronic disease. Correction of all reversible conditions favoring infection and prompt, complete eradication of acute infections will prevent and minimize renal damage from pyelonephritis. Once chronic disease sets in, the patient is treated for renal failure. (See page 614.)

Nonbacterial Tubulointerstitial Disease

Like pyelonephritis, interstitial nephritis can be acute or chronic, or both. In this condition, inflammation develops in the area between the tubules. This is usually due to injury to the tubules themselves, which stimulates inflammatory cells locally and attracts others from the rich surrounding blood supply. The inflammation thus produced causes the kidney to swell and, if severe, may impair kidney function even to the extreme point of acute renal failure.

Acute Interstitial Nephritis and Drug Reactions. The most common cause of acute interstitial nephritis (AIN) is a drug reaction. There are many reasons for this distressing and increasingly common aspect of medical practice. Drugs are essentially foreign substances that the body naturally wants to expel.

Since the drug must dissolve in the body solutions in order to do its work, the only way out is through the urine, and thus, through the kidneys. Because the process of urine formation involves concentration of waste substances, the concentration of a drug in renal tissue may actually be many times higher than in other bodily fluids. This sets the stage for a toxic reaction.

There are also allergic reactions due to drug sensitivity. In these reactions, the significant factor is not the amount of the drug, but rather the nature of the body's immune system response. If the drug is marked as a foreign protein, usually by attaching to and altering some normal body protein, lymphocytes—the body's soldiers—will attack. Since the drug is often fixed to the tissues in the renal tubular cells by the act of excretion, the lymphocytes will attack there, causing interstitial nephritis.

The reaction may be confined to the kidneys, in which case the symptoms will depend on the severity of the reaction and whether it is acute or chronic. Or, the kidney involvement may be part of a general body reaction that includes fever, skin rash, and joint pains. A simple blood count will usually show a large number of specialized white blood cells called eosinophiles. The cells also enter the urine where they can be seen under the microscope if they are properly stained. Thus, it is necessary to be suspicious of a kidney reaction in order to diagnose interstitial nephritis properly, because routine urinalysis is not specific enough. This is even more important in the chronic type, where there may be no general body reaction. A chronic, low grade interstitial nephritis can proceed undetected for months, causing considerable, possibly irreversible, kidney damage.

While these problems usually occur only while a drug is being taken, they may continue afterward. This makes careful surveillance very important when taking drugs known to affect the kidney, especially for long time periods. Continuing to take a drug that has already begun to cause kidney damage is particularly dangerous, the more so because early removal of the offending drug may completely prevent permanent damage as well as acute renal failure.

It is not only the enormous number of drugs that leads to a high incidence of interstitial nephritis, but the many times drugs are given in combination. Drug combinations are particularly troublesome for the kidney. When drugs are tested for toxicity by the FDA, prior to release for public use, they are always tested singly. It is not possible to test every drug in combination with others, even a few others likely to be used with it. Consequently, knowledge of the toxicity of drug combinations comes only from clinical practice. The public at large becomes, in effect, the

testing ground, and this requires heightened surveillance on the part of both doctor and patient.

There are 2 types of drug interaction: The first when each drug is individually nephrotoxic (toxic to the kidney) and the combination is additive or multiplicative, and the second when something special about the effect of each drug adds up to a damage that would not be present with a single drug. Potentially serious drug interactions include:

- *Diuretics and prostaglandin inhibitors.* Both medications are widely used and often prescribed by different doctors, each unaware of the other prescription, so that neither is checking for a renal reaction. The chance for such interaction has increased greatly because prostaglandin inhibitors have been released for over-the-counter sale. The diuretics that can react are chlorothiazide, hydrochlorothiazide, chlorthalidone, and furosemide. The prostaglandin inhibitors are phenylbutazone, indomethicin, ibuprofen, sulindac, and piroxicam. The combination may produce acute renal failure and AIN. Prostaglandin inhibitors also tend to neutralize the antihypertensive effect of diuretics.

- *Diuretics and calcium supplements with or without vitamin D.* The diuretics that can cause hypercalcemia (too much calcium in the blood) are usually thiazides. Once again, a physician may be prescribing thiazides for hypertension not knowing the patient takes vitamin D supplements and calcium. Or calcium or vitamin D, or both, may be prescribed by a gynecologist or orthopedist for postmenopausal osteoporosis.

- *Analgesic (painkiller) combinations.* One of the first known toxic drug combinations was the aspirin-phenacetin combination (with small doses of codeine or acetaminophen) popularized by such drugs as the original Anacin, which has since been reformulated. Since these were available over-the-counter, some people used them regularly, perhaps daily, for years—even decades. A significant number of the daily users (and abusers) developed chronic renal failure from silent chronic interstitial nephritis. In fact, this disease could be so subtle as not to produce any indication of trouble, not even an abnormal urinalysis, until renal function began to deteriorate. Indeed, if far enough along, the disease could not be reversed by stopping. In Australia, the kidney disease is called "analgesic abuse," and is the most common cause of chronic renal failure requiring dialysis.

- *Chemotherapeutic agents.* A whole new group of agents has entered the nephrotoxicity picture—the strong cell toxins used to kill cancer cells which may cause damage to the kidney when they are excreted. Much has been learned about how to protect the kidney from damage by careful advance preparation, and much of this knowledge has been usefully applied to other drugs. Nevertheless, to the complications of advanced cancer, it is a medical tragedy to have to add kidney dialysis because of a drug-induced renal failure.

The problem of interaction is not confined to prescription drugs, but extends to clinical situations involving surgery, infection, and shock. The medications used—anesthetics, antibiotics, and antishock drugs—all have renal effects. The strain on the kidney from blood loss or dehydration significantly increases the chance of drug toxicity. In fact, interstitial nephritis and other drug toxicity usually occur in such a complex mixture of events that it is often impossible to tell which one factor was the cause. With more complex treatments, and treatment of patients who suffer from more than one disease and require multiple drug regimens, there will be even greater opportunity for drug-induced renal disease.

More and more, doctors are beginning to understand the multicausal nature of disease. Patients need to understand this as well and to accept a certain amount of medical uncertainty. They must begin to participate with their doctors in the decision to use drugs, knowing and accepting the possibility of side effects if they are outweighed by the positive effect of the drugs, but helping protect against them by continual monitoring. (For more information, see Chapter 40 on Proper Use of Drugs, page 772.)

There are other drug reactions that do not induce AIN but can cause a glomerulonephritis-like injury to the kidney. These are called specific immune-induced drug injuries, and the substances involved include gold (used for rheumatoid arthritis), penicillamine (for rheumatoid arthritis, Wilson's disease, and cysteinuria, a form of kidney stone disease), and captopril (for hypertension).

Glomerular Diseases

The glomeruli are the tiny filtering units of the kidneys, each one no more than 1 millimeter in diameter. Each glomerulus is one segment of a nephron, the basic functional unit of the kidney. To appreciate the size of these filters, consider that there are approximately 1 million nephrons in each kidney.

The glomerulus consists of a membrane with groups of capillaries on one side and nephron lining cells on the other. In the middle lie mesangial cells, which are part of the body's immune surveillance system. Specific kidney diseases affect the membrane and the cells in different ways. Although inflammation, scarring, or a decrease in membrane surface area will decrease the amount of glomerular filtration, the kidney is so effective at compensating that people rarely know their kidneys have lost function until only 20 percent remains. Signs such as high blood pressure and anemia develop with increasing frequency after loss of 30 percent, but develop so gradually that they are not felt.

Chronic inflammation of the glomeruli, or chronic nephritis, is usually discovered accidentally, either by a routine urinalysis or during the course of a doctor visit for another reason. In contrast, acute inflammation, or acute nephritis, comes with headache, swelling, and dark urine, the result of bleeding from the glomeruli. The individual who notices dark-colored urine should save a specimen to show the doctor.

Although glomerulonephritis is usually classified as either acute or chronic, some specific diseases have both acute and chronic phases.

Acute Postinfectious Glomerulonephritis. This is the general term for all cases of glomerulonephritis which follow an infection. Inflammation of the glomerulus is rarely caused directly by the infection, and thus, cannot be treated with antibiotics, as can pyelonephritis. But infection does play a role. Poststreptococcal glomerulonephritis, for example, is an acute inflammation of the kidney that occurs about 10 days after a streptococcal infection. With the control of strep infections by penicillin and other antibiotics, this type of nephritis has virtually disappeared from the United States, although it is still a major disease in tropical countries where hygiene is poor and skin infections are common and go untreated.

Many common viral infections, such as mumps, chickenpox, and measles, the virus of infectious hepatitis and mononucleosis, even malaria and syphilis, can cause postinfectious glomerulonephritis in essentially the same way as bacterial infections. In fact, the most common nephritis on earth is probably the one that follows malaria, because of the huge numbers of people who are infected with that disease. Glomerulonephritis is seen frequently in patients with acquired immune deficiency syndrome (AIDS).

In all these cases, treatment is directed first at curing the infection. The edema and elevated blood pressure that are caused by the fluid retention and decreased blood flow in the kidneys are treated first by restricting salt and water intake and then by diuretics, if necessary. Other antihypertensive drugs are rarely necessary. Once the infection is under control, treatment is directed at the complications of the disease. In extremely severe cases, dialysis may be needed for a period of time if there is near-complete renal failure. Bed rest does not seem to be necessary for the healing process. Almost all patients with acute postinfectious nephritis get better if the initiating disease is cured.

Chronic Glomerulonephritis. Up until the mid-1960s, chronic glomerulonephritis was the most common form of chronic renal failure. It was thought to be caused by unresolved acute glomerulonephritis, and no successful treatment was ever developed. Instead, the widespread use of antibiotics and improved health measures reduced the number of strep infections. This, rather than a solution to the immunologic injury problem, is the reason why there is less chronic glomerulonephritis today. When it occurs, there is still no way to treat the underlying disease.

Mesangial Glomerulonephritis.

Years ago, doctors were able to distinguish only 2 kidney diseases—acute nephritis and chronic nephritis. But there was a third nephritis, which resembled acute nephritis in that it followed infection (usually in 1 to 3 days) and resulted in bloody urine, but differed in that there was no swelling, hypertension, or kidney failure.

It was not until the development of renal biopsy, which allowed doctors to examine the renal tissue directly at the time of illness, that the third form was distinguishable from the other two. Eventually, it became clear that this form of nephritis damaged primarily the mesangium—the cells and matrix that hold up the glomerular capillary. The initial, and often the only, indication of disease in this area is blood in the urine. Since the capillary loop is not involved, there is no fluid retention or high blood pressure.

The most common form of mesangial glomerulonephritis is Berger's disease. It differs from acute postinfectious nephritis by the short interval between the infection and the bloody urine and by the absence, in the beginning, of proteinuria (protein in the urine), edema, hypertension, and renal failure. Although patients may have several attacks, fewer than 10 percent develop any significant scarring and thus, progression to renal failure is rare. Renal biopsy shows large deposits of antibodies in the inflamed areas and, although it is generally assumed these deposits cause the disease, researchers still don't know for sure. As with chronic glomerulonephritis, treatment is confined to control of complications and preservation of renal function. (For more information, see Chronic Renal Failure, page 615.)

Membranoproliferative Glomerulonephritis (MPGN).

Like mesangial disease, MPGN produces proteinuria, decreased filtration, and hypertension. But it also resembles Berger's disease in that it is often seen in children as an isolated abnormality of red cells in the urine. Unlike the other inflammatory diseases, it is commonly associated with a distinct abnormality in the immune system, easily detectable by a blood test. The course of this disease is highly variable, ranging from complete cure to progression to complete renal failure, and there is no proof that any specific therapy works. Immunosuppressive drugs like cortisone, cyclophosphamide, and azathioprine have been tried, but they sometimes have serious side effects.

Nephrotic Syndrome (Nephrosis).

The kidney's filtering membrane is constructed like a sieve that allows small molecules to pass through the blood, but retains the larger protein molecules. In nephrosis, the membrane is damaged by another illness, such as diabetes, or an injury, and large amounts of these proteins suddenly leak from the blood into the urine. Within a few days, the blood proteins are markedly depleted. The flow back to the blood of normal tissue fluid is also impaired, leading to tissue swelling all over the body. The kidney cannot properly excrete salt, and there is massive retention of salt and water, further aggravating the situation.

Nephrosis is most common in young children and, at its worst, can produce an almost grotesque bloating of the face (especially around the eyes), hands, feet, and abdomen. While this is extremely uncomfortable, in pure nephrosis, there is no loss of kidney function and no structural damage. Unless there is a complication such as infection or blood clots, it is not a life-threatening disease. Fortunately, it is one of the most treatable forms of nephritis. The great majority of cases are completely cured by treating with a corticosteroid drug such as prednisone and show no progression to renal failure. Even when there is a relapse, the patient usually responds well to the drug.

Unfortunately, nephrosis occurs in pure form in only about 20 percent of adult cases (although this number is about 85 percent in children). The rest of the time it occurs in association with various forms of nephritis or with diabetes. Consequently, when an adult patient has nephrosis, it is not always possible to determine the cause—and thus whether prednisone will be effective—without a renal biopsy. An alternative is to prescribe prednisone on a trial basis and test for a response. The reasons for and against each alternative depend on the case, and should be thoroughly discussed by the patient and physician before proceeding. For those patients who do not respond to prednisone, the control of fluid becomes a major problem, especially since some patients become resistant to diuretics. This may result in a serious metabolic imbalance. Dietary control of both salt and water can be very effective in chronic cases, but requires a great deal of discipline on the part of the patient.

Glomerulonephritis Associated with Other Diseases.

Because the kidney is a constant filter,

passing more than 2,100 quarts of blood daily, it is easy to see how abnormalities in the cells and in the blood serum may possibly injure it in passage. The mesangium—the central core supporting the kidney's filtering system—comprises cells closely allied to and communicating with the entire immune surveillance system of the body, so that it, too, is affected by other diseases that affect the body.

The most common example of this type of renal injury is that caused by the collagen disease systemic lupus erythematosus. Lupus is a disease of the immune system in which antibodies are formed to otherwise normal tissue, attacking protein in the body's cells and ultimately damaging the kidney. Lupus nephritis is one of the most treatable of renal diseases: The treatment, paradoxically, uses immunosuppressive drugs in a disease noted for suppression of normal immune response. Possibly because of their altered immune system, lupus patients tolerate kidney transplants better than others. In fact, active lupus rarely returns after transplantation, suggesting that the drugs used to control the effects of transplant may also control lupus.

KIDNEY DISEASE AND CANCER

A WHOLE HOST of kidney complications from cancer and its treatment are now being seen, mainly because of the great improvement in survival rates. As cancer patients live longer, the chance for renal complications increases, either from the antibodies caused by the development of the tumors, or because injurious proteins are produced, or because the chemotherapeutic agents themselves are nephrotoxic. Thus, a patient may survive a malignant cancer, only to develop renal failure and require dialysis.

KIDNEY STONES

FEW PAINS are as gripping as the pain caused by stones passing and blocking the kidney. This pain, called colic because it often comes in waves, is brought on by stretching of the ureters and kidney pelvis, the consequences of the stone blocking the normal flow of urine. The patient may find it agonizing to move, worse yet to stay still. Usually there are no other symptoms. In a significant minority of cases, however, there may be distention of the intestines, nausea, and vomiting. The stone may irritate the lining of the kidney and its tubes, resulting in blood in the urine that may only be seen microscopically or may occasionally be enough to color the urine visibly.

The most serious complication of a kidney stone is obstruction that leads to infection. (See figure 30.2.) In that case, there may be shaking chills with high fever—a situation that can be a real medical emergency. Since the bladder may not be affected there may be no other symptoms, such as frequency of or burning urination. Indeed, the urine itself may not look abnormal when held to the light because the infected kidney is blocked and the other kidney is making large volumes of normal urine. A microscopic examination is needed to identify the cause of the trouble.

Renal colic in the absence of complications is not a serious problem, if the pain can be managed. Most stones pass; procedures as surgery, cystoscopy, or reaching into the ureter with a basket to fetch the stone are rarely necessary. As long as there is no infection, the patient can safely wait weeks or even months to allow a small stone time to pass. In such cases, the colic will usually be intermittent, each episode nudging the stone along. As it does, the pain, which usually begins in the flank, may be perceived as moving around to the front and down toward the groin. When the stone reaches the lower ureter, the bladder may be irritated and there may be frequency of urination. Finally, once the stone moves into the bladder, the pain stops and the stone is usually quickly passed in the next urination.

Understanding this sequence will help in capturing the stone for chemical analysis, an important aid in diagnosis, treatment, and prevention. The final passage of the stone may seem like an anticlimax. It may break up into tiny pieces that resemble gravel or large grains of sand that vary in color depending on their chemical composition. If they seem small compared with the trouble they cause, it is because they are actually only part of the stone. The stones inside the body are composed of crystals held together in a matrix made of a sugar-protein substance that breaks up when the crystals are

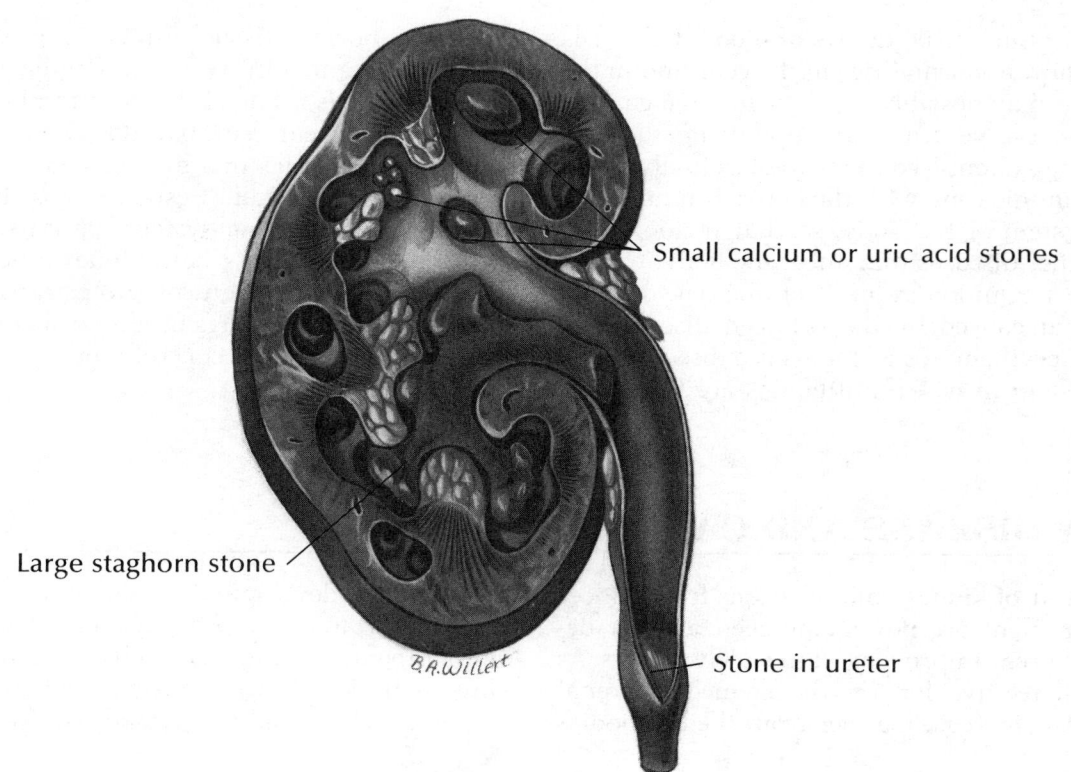

Figure 30.2.   **Kidney stones.**

passed. The crystals are so tiny that to catch them it is necessary to void into a receptacle and then filter the urine through a fine mesh.

Chemical analysis may determine which substances are present in the urine in such dense concentration that they form crystals. Sometimes, these chemicals, such as calcium, can then be reduced in the diet to help prevent further stone formation. An alternative, which is usually easier to achieve, is to increase urine output by increasing fluid intake. The amount of chemicals will remain the same, but the concentration will not be dense enough for them to form stones. Urine output must actually be measured and may have to be as high as 2 quarts or more.

A third method of preventing kidney stones, by using the body's own inhibitors, is currently under study. Under certain conditions when, for example, the body is dehydrated and the urine volume is very low, chemicals concentration may become so dense that crystals would begin to form were it not for naturally occurring substances in the urine that inhibit their formation. These natural inhibitors are also produced and excreted by the cells lining the bladder and urinary tract to protect them from becoming the site of stone formation if they are injured. Otherwise, the injury site would act as a focus for stone formation, much as an irritated oyster shell

becomes the site for pearl formation. If these natural inhibitors can be isolated and their role more fully understood, it may be possible to use them for prevention.

Causes of Kidney Stones

About 10 percent of kidney stones stem either from a problem of general metabolism affecting the entire body or from a structural or metabolic problem of the kidney itself. Structural problems (congenital defects as well as acquired defects, scars, and strictures) lead to poor drainage of the urine, stagnation, and bacterial infection. About 2 percent of patients who form stones have medullary cysts in the center of the kidney which disturb urine flow. These cysts and structural defects must be diagnosed by x-ray or ultrasound.

Metabolic problems include cystinuria, a birth defect that causes large amounts of the amino acid cystine to be excreted in the urine, and renal tubular acidosis, in which an alteration in acid-base chemistry leads to changes in the solubility of calcium and phosphorus, 2 chemicals that commonly form stones.

Diseases of general metabolism that cause kidney stones include gout, hyperparathyroidism, and excessive intestinal absorption. Many patients with gout have excessive amounts of uric acid in their urine. This may occur even when the amount of uric acid in the blood is normal, but is even more likely as the blood level rises. It is not unusual for uric acid stones to develop during certain treatments for gout unless precautions are taken to ensure that the uric acid does not clog the urine. Hyperparathyroidism is a fairly common endocrine disorder characterized by a high level of calcium in the blood and thus excessive calcium excretion in the urine. It is usually due to a small benign tumor in the parathyroid glands, behind the thyroid glands in the neck, and is easily cured by surgery.

Excessive intestinal absorption of oxalate usually occurs in patients with reduced intestinal surface area, either from disease or surgical procedures, such as bowel resections used to treat regional enteritis. Such patients cannot absorb fats normally and this causes binding of calcium in the intestinal fluids. Paradoxically, the binding of calcium permits the remaining intestine to absorb large amounts of oxalate, which crystalizes into stones. While it rarely happens today, excessive use of soda bicarbonate and milk for relief of excess stomach acidity can lead to so much calcium absorption that calcium stones will form.

Idiopathic Stone Disease

The remaining 90 percent of stone disease is idiopathic—of unknown origin—resulting from some sort of imbalance in the biochemical forces in the final urine itself. Idiopathic stone disease affects all ages and is a cause of considerable disability and, in the more serious cases, slowly progressive renal failure. Fortunately, stone disease is treatable, curable, and moreover, preventable. The percentage of serious cases is very low. Yet, because the total number of stone patients is high, a significant number of them will require either dialysis or transplantation each year, making stone disease an important public health issue.

Worldwide, the incidence of stone disease in a geographic area is roughly proportional to the protein level in the diet. Eskimos, whose diet is largely fat, and Amazon Indians, whose diet is totally vegetarian, rarely form stones. Although the relationship of protein to stone disease is not fully understood, protein does increase the acidity of urine, as well as increasing urinary excretion of uric acid, phosphorus, and calcium.

It would do stone patients no harm to decrease their protein intake and increase their urine flow by ingesting more fluid. Indeed, it is not clear that any additional treatment is necessary for the great ma-

jority of stone patients. The exact amount of protein restriction has not been determined, nor is the minimum daily requirement for protein intake known. But a safe, sufficient level would be 1 gram (0.035 ounce) for every kilogram (2.2 pounds) of body weight for an adult. This reduction will also tend to protect kidney function as well as to lower cholesterol.

The role of salt intake in stone disease has not been fully explored. There is a relationship between salt intake and calcium excretion: the more salt eaten, the more calcium excreted. Since the goal of most stone treatment is a reduction in calcium excretion, some salt restriction, or at least avoidance of high salt intake, is wise.

Idiopathic stone disease may begin with an attack of renal colic or may be inadvertently discovered in someone without symptoms by an x-ray or sonogram of the abdomen performed for some other reason. If the patient is alerted by the colic and is able to catch a stone as it passes and have it analyzed, testing can be done to determine its composition.

Hypercaluria and Hyperuricosuria

Hypercaluria—stone disease associated with too much calcium in the urine but a normal amount in the blood—may be the result of excessive absorption of dietary calcium or may be idiopathic. Tests involving a special diet and urinalysis are necessary to distinguish between the two types. Reduction of calcium in the diet is the standard treatment in the former case, while diuretics (usually thiazides) are used to dilute the concentration of calcium in the urine in idiopathic cases. Whether this medication will reduce stone formation any more than high fluid intake and diet remains to be proven. Given the benign nature of most stone disease and the extensive side effects of daily thiazide, many patients may choose diet over drug treatment.

Hyperuricosuria is a type of stone disease associated with too much uric acid in the urine, but a normal concentration in the blood and no gout. It has not been sufficiently explored, but there is reason to believe the level of uric acid excretion is related to protein intake. If the uric acid excretion rate is high, a low-protein diet may lower it. An alternative is daily doses of allopurinol, a drug used commonly for gout. Given the benign nature of most stone disease and the established value of high fluid intake and dietary treatment, patients may elect to forgo treatment with a drug they must take daily for years, perhaps decades.

Management of Stone Disease

Even with standard diet therapy, some patients will persist in passing many and painful stones and they must consider other measures. From a practical point of view, how many stones is enough to commit to drug treatment? This question is best answered by each patient individually. Some would prefer to have 1 stone every 3 or 4 years, provided there is no infection or complication, than to take medication daily and risk side effects. True, the stone attack may come at very inconvenient times and require medication itself, but many patients do not seem to suffer as a consequence of 3 or 4 stone episodes over a period of 10 to 15 years. The option to avoid drugs should be offered them. Others may have only 1 attack and be willing to put up with the inconvenience, expense, and risk of medication to avoid ever having a second one.

The key to sensible management is a careful assessment of stone activity. Inactive stone disease is common. It is not uncommon to pass one stone and never have one again, or have a second one 20 years later and then no more. Often, a patient will have a small stone in the kidney without symptoms for years, even decades. The size of the stone can easily be monitored. If it is not growing—or growing very slowly—no treatment may be necessary.

The major problem with kidney stones comes when they do not pass and the patient remains in pain or, more serious, the kidney stays blocked. Many stones will temporarily block the kidney for a day or two when they start to pass. With time, the body may adapt and the stone remain in the ureter without blocking. When the stone persists, threatening the kidney function and producing pain and disability, there are generally 3 options, depending on the stone's location. If the stone is low enough, near the bladder, it can be reached via a cystoscope with a basket-tipped catheter. The basket grasps the stone and pulls it out. While this works in the great majority of cases, it fails in a significant minority and the trauma of the procedure often requires follow-up surgery. Often, then, it is a judgment call as to whether to wait it out or go ahead with the procedure.

If the stone is high—in or near the pelvis—a tube may be inserted, under local anesthesia, through the skin and muscle into the kidney itself and the stone extracted. This requires wearing the tube for awhile and has a risk of infection and bleeding, but it is much safer than surgery.

If the stone is stuck in mid-ureter or in the kidney, the only option, until very recently, was surgery. But now there is a new treatment that promises to reduce the necessity for surgery to a very few cases. Underwater shock wave treatment, now rather expensive and confined to only a few institutions, is proving to be a very effective and safe, nonsurgical way to disintegrate stones by directing powerful shock waves at them while the patient is partially immersed in a special water tank. Experience shows that excellent technology encourages savings in the long run, and there is every reason to believe that this method will become lower in cost as it becomes more readily available. Soon doctors may be able to live up more fully to the Hippocratic oath, which pledges them "not to cut for the stone."

HEREDITARY KIDNEY DISEASES

RESEARCHERS have been able to identify a great and growing number of inherited kidney diseases, but most of them occur in only a few families. Hereditary kidney disease can usually be traced to one gene. If the gene is located on the X chromosome, it will be sex-linked; if located on one of the other 47, it is said to be autosomal. These genes can cause anatomic anomalies that are not necessarily associated with disease, have no proven inheritance pattern, and do not seem to affect life span, and they can also cause serious genetic diseases with specific inheritance patterns.

Solitary Kidney

Many people go through life never knowing they have only one kidney. It usually comes to light during some x-ray or ultrasonic examination of the kidneys undertaken because of symptoms or an abnormality found in the urine. People with one kidney are at special risk during pyelonephritis, trauma, with cancer, and with stone attacks, since any extra strain or blockage will sharply decrease overall kidney function. Yet, until recently it was assumed that life span was not affected. In the past few years, experimental data have questioned that assumption, an important factor in considering the safety of kidney transplant donation. The evidence is not conclusive, but certain cautions are now raised for people with one kidney, particularly concerning high protein intake, which may cause structural damage from increased demand in the remaining kidney.

Horseshoe Kidney

This genetic defect causes the lower half of both kidneys to remain fused, instead of separating as in normal development. This horseshoe shape may lead to excessive pooling of urine, making the person vulnerable to infection or stones. However, this happens rarely and the abnormality is generally benign, providing that unnecessary urologic procedures are avoided.

Anomalies of Renal Circulation

Usually there is only 1 renal artery, but occasionally an individual may have 2 or more, which may cause problems only if surgery is necessary. Aneurysms of the renal vessels are probably genetic in many cases, and can be detected by listening to the kidneys with a stethoscope. They may cause hypertension if they interfere with circulation, or rupture if they stretch beyond the size of about 1 inch in diameter. A rare inherited disorder, von Recklinghausen's disease, is often associated with aneurysms of the renal arteries.

Floating (Dropped) Kidney

Although this may not be genetic, it is a common (more so in women) and benign anomaly. The right kidney is not secure in the tissue space under the right twelfth rib, but "floats" in the abdomen in the region under the liver. Unfortunately, it is often mistaken for a tumor, leading to unnecessary and expensive testing and worry. Actually, the doctor should be able to diagnose it during a routine physical exam by carefully palpating with both hands.

Polycystic Kidneys

It is not unusual to have 1 or 2 cysts within kidney tissue. Although they may cause confusion and lead to unnecessary diagnostic procedures, they have no function and are harmless. In polycystic kidney (PCK) disease, the cysts are numerous, functional, and are formed by individual nephrons. In time, virtually all the nephrons of both kidneys either become cystic or are compressed, distorted, and rendered increasingly ineffective by the pressure of adjacent cysts. In the process, both kidneys enlarge to 3 or 4 times normal size while their function decreases. The patient is unaware of the disease unless some complication—hypertension, blood in the urine, pain caused by bleeding into the kidney, a stone, or infection—calls attention to the kidney, usually long before kidney failure has developed. Eventually, the kidneys become so large that it is

possible to feel them. Although some patients live a normal life span and a significant group live long enough to die of something else, until the advent of dialysis and transplantation, many patients with PCK eventually died of uremic poisoning.

Since nothing can be done about the cysts, the treatment is confined to that for complications such as infection, stones, bleeding, and hypertension. The general management of the disease is the same as for chronic renal failure. (See page 615.) In fact, it is important not to do any unnecessary procedures. Operations such as cyst puncture or removal designed to relieve pressure usually make the condition worse. Cystoscopy is of little value and only introduces the possibility of infection, which can be devastating to PCK patients.

Advances in the ability to control blood pressure safely, prevent stones, and cure infections have improved the prognosis for those with PCK. The new methods of managing chronic renal failure may do more, but in the last analysis, dialysis and transplantation are the treatments that have most dramatically altered prospects for PCK patients. Because they do not have disease outside the kidney (with rare exceptions involving the liver and brain), PCK patients are considered ideal candidates for dialysis and transplant, and indeed, they do better than those with other forms of kidney disease.

Although the gene for PCK is dominant, meaning there is a 50 percent chance that the children of those with the gene will inherit it, some do not develop enough cysts to matter until the fourth or fifth decade. Some live into their eighties, while others reach the point of renal failure in their forties, the average being around age 50. It is hard, then, to know what to advise people with PCK to do about having children, but genetic counseling is available to help with the decision.

Doctors are uncertain as to when diagnostic testing should be done for detection of the disease. The test—ultrasound—is a simple one, and if and when some means of preventing or limiting cyst formation is found, early detection may become very important.

Alport's Syndrome

Unlike most forms of glomerular disease where identifiable signs and symptoms make early diagnosis possible, Alport's syndrome is usually completely silent in its early stages. Some patients may show obvious signs of blood in the urine, but most do not realize they have the disease until the all-pervasive biochemical disturbances of uremia are present. The syndrome, which affects males much more seriously than females, is the result of a genetic defect in the construction of the glomerular basement membrane, making it thin and weak. While men usually develop renal failure by their twenties, women may have the gene and never develop any significant renal dysfunction. Thus, they may have children and pass on the gene without realizing it. Even so, the incidence of the gene is very low, affecting only a small percentage of families. For reasons not clearly understood, hearing loss is common; less frequently, there are problems with vision. There is no specific treatment for the disorder.

Cystinuria

Cystinuria is an unusual kidney disease caused by a metabolic defect in the enzymes needed to recover the amino acid cystine from the filtered urine. Cystine is one of the essential amino acids needed to make protein and maintain nitrogen balance. Normally, the renal tubules return most of the filtered cystine to the bloodstream. In cystinuria, huge amounts of cystine are lost in the urine. So high is the concentration that stones form and may block the kidney, causing renal colic. (See Kidney Stones, page 609.) Often, the stone production is so massive that the kidney becomes and remains obstructed, leading to renal failure. Attempts to dissolve the massive levels of cystine by increasing and alkalizing the flow of urine are not usually successful. The drug penicillamine can be used to make cystine dissolve more thoroughly, but is itself potentially toxic and needs to be given with care.

Renal Tubular Defects

Specific genetic defects can cause nephrogenic diabetes insipidus, vitamin D-resistant rickets, and renal tubular acidosis. Each of these defects in the renal tubules is caused by a different gene, but all show up early in life. Nephrogenic diabetes insipidus involves a lack of response of the kidney tubules to an antidiuretic hormone present in the blood. It usually presents itself with bed wetting, as the individual satisfies a pervasive thirst by drinking large quantities of liquids and producing a large volume of urine. The thirst, in a sense, provides the treatment, since most people will suffer no ill effects from the disorder if they drink sufficient quantities of water. But this solution is inconvenient and often difficult to achieve because of the high volumes involved. In these cases, salt restriction, thiazide diuretics, and prostaglandin inhibitors may be tried as well.

Vitamin D-resistant rickets shows up as a bone problem due to huge losses of phosphorus in the urine, again because of the inability of the tubules to reabsorb from the filtered urine. More common in males than in females, it can lead to various bone deformities if not treated with phosphate to improve the resorption of calcium in the intestine.

In renal tubular acidosis, an obvious early sign is a general failure to thrive. Unusual early stone formation within the body of the kidney is another sign, visible by simple x-ray. Since lack of treatment can lead to serious, even life-threatening, potassium depletion, it is important to diagnose this disease early, after which it can easily be treated with soda bicarbonate.

KIDNEY FAILURE

To UNDERSTAND KIDNEY DISEASE and how it is treated, it is also necessary to know about renal failure, which all kidney diseases have in common. Regardless of the type of kidney disease, if it causes renal failure, the major part of the symptoms and the treatment will be related to the renal failure, rather than the primary disease.

Fortunately, we have far more kidney functioning power than we need. This is why most patients do not develop symptoms until 90 percent of renal function is lost. If the loss is chronic and gradual, the body is able to adjust considerably to tolerate and compensate for the impaired function. When the loss

of function is rapid and acute, occurring in a matter of hours or a few days, the situation is entirely different. Thus, the distinction between acute renal failure and chronic renal failure is important. Regardless of the cause, all cases of acute failure will be treated in essentially the same way, all types of chronic failure in another.

When the kidneys fail to remove waste products from the blood, a condition known as uremia develops, and may eventually cut renal function to less than 5 to 10 percent of normal. Although the acute and chronic forms of uremia are somewhat different, the major symptoms are:

- Upset stomach, which may vary from simple loss of appetite to severe stomach pain, nausea, and vomiting (even vomiting of blood)
- Weakness, lack of energy, fatigue, and need for sleep
- Weight loss, not only of fat, but also of muscle
- Dry, often itchy, skin
- Peculiar odor to the breath, reminiscent of urine
- Pallor, due to anemia
- Shortness of breath, due to heart muscle weakness, hypertension, and fluid retention
- Edema, or swelling

In the very late stages, there may also be mental symptoms of agitation, twitching, stupor, coma, or seizures.

Acute Renal Failure

Because acute failure comes on suddenly and usually involves the entire kidney, the flow of urine is usually suppressed. Even when the urine flow is very low, however, it is surprising how few people notice it or realize the significance if they do. In those cases where a toxin such as carbon tetrachloride or a drug has caused the acute failure, the patient is often unaware of it until one or more of the symptoms of uremia develop. Since the loss of kidney function is acute and total, the body has little chance to compensate. Symptoms may develop within a few days, usually indicated by swelling of the feet, shortness of breath, or headache. All these symptoms relate to the acute retention of salt and water, sharply raising blood pressure, changing brain metabolism, and congesting heart and lungs.

The simplest way to detect this type of fluid retention is by weight. Each day, 2 or more pounds may be added. This is because the average urine flow is about 1 quart per day. When the water is not passed, it adds its weight (about 2 pounds) to the total body weight. Without treatment, the patient may develop more serious problems, including hyperkalemia, a buildup in the blood of the potassium that is usually excreted in the urine. Beyond a certain level, potassium is increasingly liable to cause an irregularity of heart rhythm or even heart stoppage of a kind not easy to reverse.

For these reasons, acute renal failure is a medical emergency, but one that is safely and completely treatable, if not by medications, then by dialysis. Rarely is it fatal. Since acute failure today is usually the result of disease—often very serious disease—elsewhere in the body, the outcome depends on the course of that disease.

The most common causes of acute failure are shock (usually from blood loss), infection, and drug reactions, often in combination. Most cases now occur in the hospital where the condition is easily and promptly diagnosed and acute kidney dialysis units are ready to begin treatment. When the underlying kidney insult has been corrected, most cases get better. Usually this takes only a few days, not enough to challenge the system seriously. If it takes longer, medicines are not enough and machine help may be needed. Thus, the artificial kidney is used to tide the patient over until the kidney damage has been repaired, a process that may take 2 weeks to 2 months. Those patients who do not respond to treatment have to be considered for chronic dialysis.

Chronic Renal Failure

Unlike acute renal failure, in chronic renal failure, the whole kidney does not go at once. As some nephrons become diseased, others compensate by enlarging and taking over some of the lost function. Since the body has time to adjust, the symptoms of chronic failure differ considerably from those of acute failure. In fact, the adjustments are so successful that symptoms rarely are perceived until 90 to 95 percent of kidney function is lost. (This is provided there is no intervening stress such as another illness, surgery, or a complication of hypertension.)

When symptoms do occur, they come on so slowly that patients make adjustments to them without thinking about it. Getting up at night to pass urine is an early sign of chronic renal failure, yet it seems natural enough when it happens, even to young people. Easy fatigue is adjusted gradually by doing less, perhaps sleeping more. Shortness of breath is obviated by avoiding stairs, hills, and lifting. Only when some minimum acceptable level of function is breached, or when some acute episode is precipitated by a complication like stroke, heart failure, inflamed stomach, colon, or heart sac, does the patient seek attention.

Treatment of Chronic Renal Failure. There have been several medical revolutions in the treatment of chronic renal failure in the past 25 years. The first, and most dramatic, was the extension of kidney dialysis from acute renal failure to chronic. Although this may not seem revolutionary today, it represented a radically new idea in therapeutics.

The artificial kidney filters the blood for 4 hours at a time, 3 times per week. Since it can only filter and cannot perform any of the kidney's many metabolic functions, restoration of true health is never achieved. What is remarkable is how well most patients manage to maintain varied and useful lives despite the chronic state of disease produced by maintenance hemodialysis. In addition to the rigid schedules dialysis patients must endure, their fluid intake and diet are restricted and regular medications are necessary, although the extent of these measures varies with the patient. Anemia, abnormal bone metabolism, chronic uremia, and diminished sexual function are only some of the conditions all dialysis patients live with. Many have to cope with high or low blood pressure, weakness, fatigue, cramps, weight loss, psychiatric disturbances, loss of nerve functions leading to muscle paralysis, and recurrent infections, not to mention all the other nonkidney diseases they bear. But knowing that the only alternative is certain death, the great majority are happy with the bargain.

No one predicted that the human body could adjust to the kidney machine so well. In fact, none of the kidney specialists anywhere in the world even remotely considered the possibility. From the time the artificial kidney was invented in 1946 until 1961, it was only used to tide over patients with acute renal failure who would eventually recover. Dr. Belding Scribner first used dialysis to keep patients alive and reasonably well while virtually the entire nephrology community considered it impossible, even immoral. Today, chronic dialysis is common, mainly because of government support, and the number of patients benefiting from it grows each year. Currently, about 60,000 people who would otherwise be dead are supported by kidney machines in hospitals, dialysis centers, or at home. The cost is about $30,000 in a hospital, $22,000 in a center, and $10,000 to $15,000 at home. The overall cost to the federal government is about $2 billion annually.

Dr. Scribner first solved the technical problem of having to connect the dialysis machine to the same place again and again by constructing an external blood shunt worn on the forearm. Today, an internal shunt is made with a small operation that allows the veins to become like arteries, a development that led to the rapid growth and facility of chronic dialysis, but also to a moral dilemma. Were it not for these simple technological advances, there would have been no agonizing over who should have kidney machines when they were in short supply or, now, when the supply is virtually unlimited, whether we should be spending these billions on a relative few when other diseases are in far more primitive states of conquest.

Kidney Transplantation

The kidney machine not only treats acute renal failure and chronic renal failure, but is vital to renal transplantation. Transplantation has always been the ultimate goal of treatment in chronic renal failure because it is the only treatment that restores reasonably normal human health. But transplant programs cannot exist without dialysis because most transplants do not function immediately, and the patient needs support during rejection episodes.

Transplants are of 2 types: with related donors and unrelated donors. The science of matching kidneys for transplantation is a direct outgrowth of the general science of immunology. Enormous progress has been made, but not all of the factors in a match have been fully identified. This may be the reason that transplants involving blood relatives are more successful, since more of the unknown factors may be matched. Although the success rate of the 2 groups is narrowing all the time, there is still a better survival rate and, on average, a much less complicated course with a well-matched related donor than with an unrelated one.

The value of a kidney from a related donor must be weighed against the pain and possible complications of kidney donation. Considering the personal benefits of contributing to, indeed giving, a new life to a loved one against the medical uncertainties of the situation should be a matter of informed consent and extended discussion between donor and physician. The general shortage of cadaver kidneys, the unrelated donors, and the difficulties of achieving a match in some patients puts great pressure on relatives, often to the point of requiring professional help.

Who should have dialysis and who should receive a transplant are difficult questions to answer and parallel the technical/moral dilemmas of the past. But transplantation, despite the newest medications, is inherently risky. The suppression and alteration of immunity creates its own set of problems and risks. There is no question that the first year of transplant has a greater mortality risk than dialysis. In fact, transplant is often considered for those who are doing poorly on dialysis because the risk/gain ratio then favors transplant. If the patient survives and the transplant is successful after 1 year, the risk goes way down.

The major early risk for transplant patients is infection, as technical complications from the surgery are now very rare. Infection can be serious and life-threatening because the body's normal immune response is suppressed by drugs given to lower the possibility of organ rejection. Since the doses of these immunosuppressant drugs are greatly decreased with time, this risk sharply decreases after the first year. However, another risk looms with the years—cancer. The very drugs used to treat cancer also cause it, so that the cancer rate in transplant patients is higher than normal. With time, recurrence of the original kidney disease is also possible in those with hypertension, nephritis, or diabetes, but is not usually significant.

The requirements for kidney donation are very strict—or should be. Thus, the number of end-stage kidney patients with willing, well-matched, healthy related donors is small, probably less than 1 in 10. The success of transplantation depends on regional networks or centers. The essential elements are rapid identification and typing of potential donors. Since these are usually accident cases or patients dying suddenly of other illness, special medical teams are needed to monitor the cases, protect the kidneys until they can be removed, and remove them after death. Such kidneys can be stored about 24 hours. On the other hand, patients waiting for kidneys need to be tissue-typed and tracked so they are ready to go within the 24-hour grace period. The larger the pool of donors, the more likely a specific kidney will be excellently matched. It is estimated that each potential kidney for transplant would need to be available to about 1,000 recipients to obtain maximum beneficial results. Practical matters of time and distance lower this ratio considerably. Considering the adverse conditions, the achievements of the transplantation networks are substantial, commendable, and gratifying.

The national average of related kidney donor graft survival for 1 year is now 75 percent; for cadaver kidney, it is 56 percent. The 5-year survivals are 65 percent and 40 percent, respectively. Patient survival rates are higher because most patients whose transplants fail are returned to dialysis. The new drug cyclosporine has improved 1-year cadaver graft survival to 75 percent.

Prevention of Chronic Renal Failure

The enormous financial burden of the dialysis-transplant treatment of end-stage renal failure has stimulated nephrologists to greater efforts at prevention and cure. It is disappointing to see how few cases of end-stage renal failure can be cured. This is because many of them are the consequences of improved life span of patients with other diseases. Better overall medical treatment has led to much longer survival—long enough for diseases in which the patient normally would have died of stroke, heart attack, or infection, now to survive and develop kidney disease. Diabetes and hypertension are now two large sources of patients with end-stage renal failure.

Although there have been a few spotty areas of success, the great amount of time and money invested in studying immunology for a possible way to alter the course of nephritis has produced very disappointing results. In the meantime, Dr. Barry Bren-

ner and his colleagues at Harvard Medical School have taken a completely different tack and come up with a very promising theory. Dr Brenner has determined that partial damage to a kidney as a result of disease causes a strain on the remaining nephrons, which must handle increased blood pressure and flow. The result is that they, too, begin a gradual but relentless progression toward total renal failure. But the strain is not inevitable; rather, it seems to be related to several factors, the most important of which is a high-protein diet. Preliminary tests in animals have shown that limiting protein intake can prevent further damage. It may take years before the results of this diet applied to humans are in and conclusive, but the risk/benefit ratio favors widespread application of the proposed dietary treatment, which is not harmful, although perhaps inconvenient and restrictive.

The diet requires that protein be limited to that level compatible with good nutrition, but not all authorities agree on what that level is. It is certainly not more than 1 gram per kilogram of body weight per day, and is probably less. It will be less for heavy people where most of the body mass is fat. In those with a high muscle-to-fat ratio, it may be advisable to reduce muscle mass. In any case, the level is probably not less than 25 to 35 grams daily and may also depend on the source of the protein—animal or plant.

There is evidence to suggest that reduction in phosphorus load provides additional benefits. This can be achieved with the use of binding agents in pill form, such as amphojel, which block absorption by the stomach. Salt restriction is often necessary, since impaired kidney function weakens the kidneys' ability to excrete salt, favoring development of hypertension.

Control of blood pressure is extremely important, and is usually accomplished with vasodilators or beta-blockers, since diuretics may interfere with glomerular filtration, renal blood flow, and uric acid excretion, which is already impaired. Patients with chronic renal failure are wise to take great precautions to avoid other diseases or infections that may lower their biologic reserve. Since, to varying degrees, their biologic functions may be already strained, a viral infection such as gastroenteritis with a fever, copious diarrhea, and fluid loss can be a major challenge to the system.

Finally, those with chronic renal failure and their physicians should be sure that the dosage of any medication taken for other conditions is adjusted for the degree of renal function and that drugs or drug combinations potentially toxic to the kidneys are avoided.

SUMMING UP

THE KIDNEYS play a crucial role in the body's circulatory and urinary systems by filtering waste products and toxins from the blood, while returning nutrients to the bloodstream and controlling blood pressure. Even though the kidneys are vital to survival, people can function with only one, which allows donation of a healthy kidney to a family member in need of one. Unfortunately, this also means that it is often not until they have very little function left that many people become aware that they have kidney disease.

Major kidney disorders include hypertension, kidney stones, inflammatory diseases of the neph-rons and the glomeruli, and the end result of many of these diseases if they remain untreated—kidney failure.

Fortunately, treatment has greatly improved with the development of new drugs, a better understanding of the role of diet (particularly the effects of restricting protein and sodium), and the complex therapeutic procedures of dialysis and transplant.

Patients can and should play a major role in their own therapy by monitoring their own blood pressure, monitoring the effects of drugs, deciding when to forgo drugs, and changing their diet.

31 Skin Diseases

Robert R. Walther, M.D.

INTRODUCTION

THE SKIN, the largest organ of the body, is extraordinarily complex in structure and function. The skin of the average man measures more than 2 square yards and weighs about 10 pounds. In just 1 square inch of skin there are approximately 30 million cells, 100 fat glands, 600 sweat glands, 20 small blood vessels, 65 hairs, numerous muscles, and thousands of nerve endings. The skin ranges in thickness from 1/2 millimeter in the eyelid to more than 2 millimeters in the palms and soles.

The functions of the skin are many and varied. It protects the rest of the body from chemicals, injuries, the sun and temperature extremes in the environment, and at the same time it keeps the inner environment stable and in place. It helps regulate heat, transmits sensation and, through its temperature, texture, clarity, and color, provides information about both physical and emotional states. Finally, because skin patterns are unique in each individual, fingerprints, palm prints, and sole prints provide a foolproof means of identification.

Since the skin is on public view, people of all

ages are concerned with its appearance. At least 10 percent of all patients seen by primary-care physicians are complaining of skin disorders. As the environment is increasingly polluted with toxic chemicals and irritants, there is the likelihood that skin sensitivity may increase. Though few skin disorders are life-threatening, they can be annoying, even debilitating. Chronic, unsightly disorders, however insignificant physiologically, can have a profound psychological effect, especially on the very young. It is important, then, to have a good grasp of how the skin works.

STRUCTURE OF THE SKIN

TO UNDERSTAND what can go wrong with the skin, a general knowledge is needed of its makeup, what it does, and how it does it. The skin is usually described as having 3 layers. The outer layer is called the epidermis, and the second is called the dermis. Underlying these is a layer of fat known as the subcutaneous tissue. (See figure 31.1.)

Epidermis

The epidermis, though paper-thin, is composed of many layers of cells. In the basal layer (the living epidermis), new cells are constantly being produced, pushing older cells to the surface. As they move upward and farther away from their source of nourishment they become flatter and smaller. They lose their nuclei, move out of the basal layer to the horny layer (the dead epidermis) and, after serving a brief protective function, are imperceptibly sloughed off. This process of changing living cells into a lifeless protein called keratin is referred to as keratinization and takes about 4 weeks. (See figure 31.2.)

These keratinocytes, which constitute about 95 percent of the epidermal cells, form the barrier—keeping harmful substances out and preventing water and essential substances from seeping out. The other 5 percent of epidermal cells are melanocytes which manufacture and distribute melanin, a dark protein pigment, the primary function of which is protection from ultraviolet rays. Skin color is determined by the amount of protein produced by these

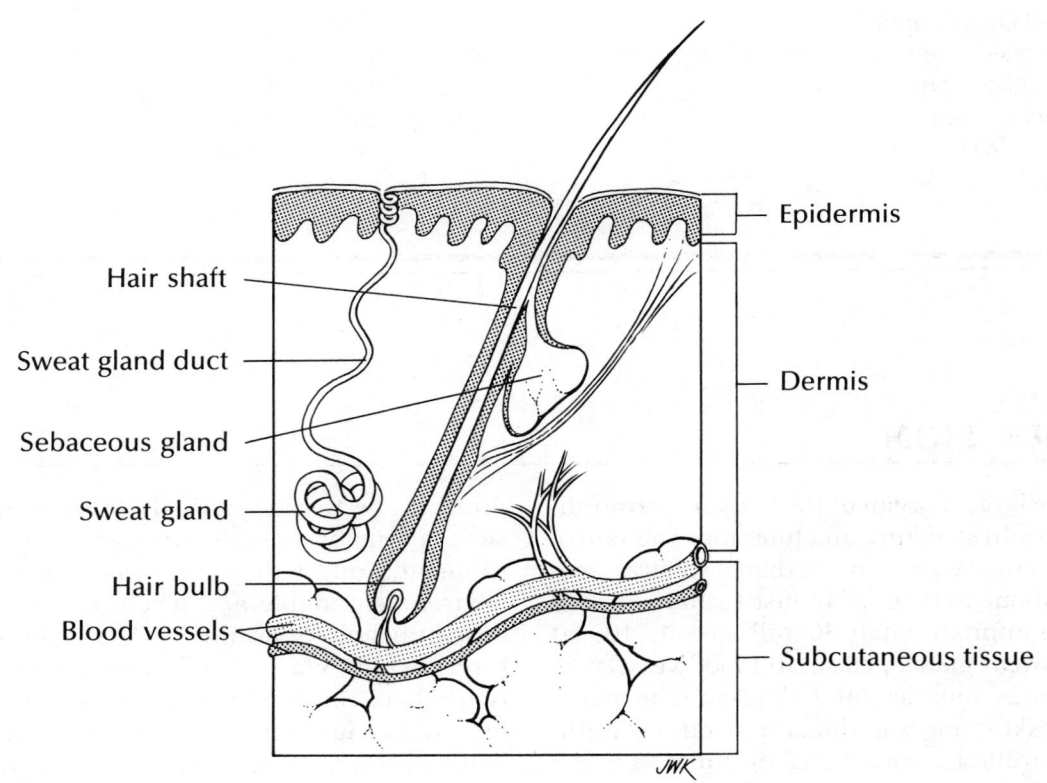

Figure 31.1. **Anatomy of the skin.**

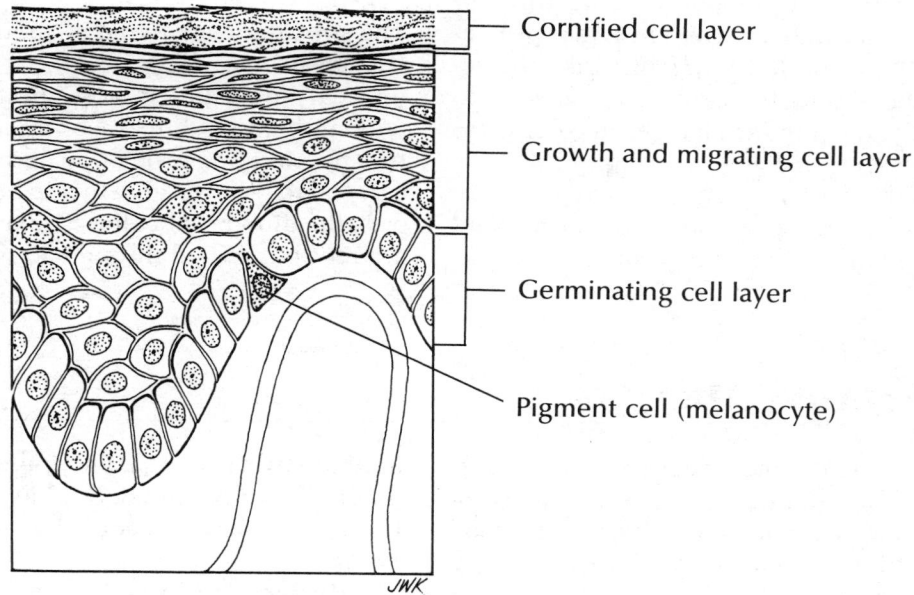

Figure 31.2. **Pattern of skin growth.**

cells, not by the number of cells, which is fairly constant in all races.

Hair and nails are specialized keratin structures and are considered part of the epidermis. These structures are largely cosmetic in the human being, having long since lost the functions of fur and claws as seen in other animals. The skin, however, is uniquely human, since it can betray emotion by blushing (shame), redness (anger), blanching (fear), sweating (tension), and goosebumps (terror).

Dermis

The dermis, or "true skin," is made up of water, gellike and elastic materials and collagen, of which collagen is primary. Embedded in this layer are systems and structures common to other organs such as lymph channels, blood vessels, nerve fibers, and muscle cells. But unique to the skin are hair follicles, sebaceous glands, and sweat glands.

Like the epidermis, the hair follicle manufactures a keratin structure, hair. These follicles are found everywhere on the body except for the palms and soles, though most of the hairs produced are fine, light hairs which, quite unlike the hair of the scalp, are scarcely visible to the naked eye.

The sebaceous glands are attached to hair follicles and through the follicle they secrete an oily substance, sebum, which both lubricates and protects.

Normally the sebum appears on the skin surface constantly and imperceptibly, but in areas richly endowed with large sebaceous glands such as the face, back, and chest, there are wide variations in individual formation of sebum.

There are 2 distinctive sweat-producing glands, the apocrine and the eccrine. The apocrine gland has no known physiological function and is apparently a holdover from times past. In the ear it forms a portion of what we see as ear wax. Otherwise, it is normally found only under the arms, around the nipples and navel, and in the anal–genital area. It is best known for its negative function—producing body odor.

The eccrine glands, on the other hand, are an advanced and extensive system of temperature control. Several million of the glands are distributed over the entire body, but the palms, soles, forehead, and underarms are more richly supplied.

Sweat (a dilute salt solution), the product of the eccrine glands, can be seen and felt. Its evaporation from the skin's surface causes cooling, and its absence because of excessive water loss without replacement can cause "heat stroke." Physical activity and hot environments are the chief causes of eccrine sweating, but emotional stress or eating hot, spicy foods can also produce considerable perspiration.

Another source of heat regulation in the skin is its vast network of tiny blood vessels. In hot weather these vessels dilate to lose heat, causing the skin to flush. In cold weather, they constrict to conserve heat, causing pallor. The blood coursing through these vessels supplies nutrients and provides protection for the cellular and fluid systems. Like the eccrine glands, these vessels are also responsive to emotional stress, effecting the changes in color mentioned previously.

We feel, rather than see, the function of the nerve endings. They sense pressure, heat, cold, and touch, providing both pain and pleasure.

Subcutaneous Tissue

The subcutaneous tissue is another layer of connective tissue specializing in the formation of fat. It is unevenly distributed over the body and there are wide individual differences in distribution. In addition to providing protection and insulation, it acts as a depository for reserve fuel to be drawn upon whenever the amount of calories taken in is less than the amount burned up through activity.

SKIN AND HAIR CARE

BECAUSE THE SKIN is the buffer zone for both internal and external environments, it is affected by internal activity and external conditions. Taking good care of the skin in its normal state is important both physiologically and cosmetically.

General good health, which results in part from a well-balanced diet and appropriate exercise, will go a long way toward assuring a healthy and attractive skin. Finding a way to manage stress is another fundamental of achieving "good skin." Just as other parts of the body may be adversely affected by prolonged, unrelieved stress, the skin also can be affected.

One of the most serious stresses to the skin is exposure to the sun. Dark or light, skin regularly exposed to long periods out of doors may become excessively "leathery," wrinkled, and prematurely aged. Daily moisturizing, protective clothing, sunscreens, umbrellas, and hats (especially for bald heads) are all important protective measures, but avoidance is probably the best. Fair-skinned people—those with a pale complexion (and perhaps freckles), blue eyes, and blond or red hair—are particularly at risk of serious damage from prolonged or too-rapid exposure. Even those with darker skin and eyes who normally tan more than burn need to be careful.

While mild sunburn heals readily and has no immediate serious effects, sun-induced skin damage is cumulative and irreversible. Although this damage is often equated with acute cases of sunburn, repetitive short exposures, even with no visible sunburn, can also lead to long-term skin damage. Cosmetic considerations aside, the most serious consequence of too much sun exposure is an increased risk of skin cancer, the most common form of cancer in the United States. (See Skin Cancers, page 630.)

The most serious sun damage is done by ultraviolet rays, and these rays are most intense in the hours between 10 A.M. and 2 P.M. (11 A.M. and 3 P.M. daylight savings time). Sunbathing and outdoor activities are best scheduled before and after these times.

Ultraviolet rays can be harmful even in the shade, where their intensity may be as much as 50 percent of that in bright sun, and on cloudy or hazy days, when 70 to 80 percent of ultraviolet rays reach the ground. Some conditions can even intensify ultraviolet exposure: sandy beaches by 25 percent and snow by 100 percent.

Even clothing is not certain protection against ultraviolet rays. More than 20 percent of the rays penetrate the type of looseknit fabrics often worn in warm weather, so that those particularly susceptible to burn may need to apply sunscreens to their upper bodies even when dressed.

There are 2 types of sun protection preparations: sun-blocking agents and sunscreens. Sun-blockers are usually thick, white, completely opaque ointments that may contain zinc oxide. They are especially useful in protecting areas like the nose and lips which burn easily. Whereas these preparations deflect ultraviolet rays, sunscreens absorb the shorter, most harmful ones and may also have some effect on the longer rays that are more prominent in the morning and late afternoon. The best sunscreens contain PABA (para-aminobenzoic acid) or its derivatives and are rated 10 or above.

Although the foregoing admonitions apply to all people, no matter what race or skin type, different skin types do require different regimens with respect to external care. There are 3 basic skin (and hair) types—normal, oily, and dry. For those with normal skin and hair, deodorant soaps, detergent-type shampoos, frequent baths, and shampoos are usually tolerated well. Astringents are not necessary and heavy oil-based creams are not advised, but since most cosmetics and soaps are formulated for "normal" skin, almost any choice will be all right.

A different approach must be taken for dry skin, which appears in many younger people, but affects all skins types with aging. Any bathing or showering removes from the skin the oil that traps water and keeps the skin moist. The best way to combat this is with baths that include a minimum of a 15-minute soak to hydrate (restore moisture to) the skin, followed by an all-over application of a moisturizing cream or lotion containing oils or 10 percent urea.

Products vary in the amount of oils or urea they contain, and the choice depends not only on how quickly an individual's skin absorbs the moisturizer but also on personal preference about the feel on the skin. What may be tolerable to one person may feel "greasy" to another. Experimentation may be necessary to find the right product and also to determine how often to use it. A minimum would be once a day after bathing.

Showers should be avoided if at all possible; those who don't feel clean without one should take a bath first and finish with a quick rinse under the spray. Mild soaps and nonalkaline shampoos are best; harsh soaps, such as those containing deodorant, should be avoided. In cosmetics, the heavier, oil-based formulations will be tolerated, but for those who prefer something lighter, a moisturizer containing urea may be used. Astringents should be avoided.

For oily skin, the more washing the better, at least 3 times per day for the face. If regular soaps don't degrease adequately or if acne is a problem, there are many good over-the-counter acne soaps. These should be introduced to the skin gradually. Astringents are recommended and should be used frequently. Washing the hair daily, even twice daily, with an alkaline shampoo, is a good idea. Cosmetics (water-based formulas only) should be used sparingly, if at all.

Dry and oily hair are treated much the same as dry and oily skin. If hair is oily, it cannot be washed too much. If it is dry, shampoos should be less frequent and followed by the application of acid rinses or oil-based conditioners. Regardless of hair type, the hottest settings of hair dryers, hot curlers, and curling irons should be avoided, not only to prevent damage to the hair, but to protect the skin from burning.

Guidelines for cosmetics use according to skin type are more difficult. Many cosmetics and cleansing products, even those designed to treat acne, contain irritants and blackhead-forming chemicals. In addition, people differ in their sensitivity to various ingredients. Trial and error is the best approach to finding those products suited to the individual.

ITCHING

Itching all over without any sign of rash can be caused by any number of illnesses, environmental conditions, or even psychological problems (nervous itch). The elderly and those with excessively dry skin often suffer from itching in the wintertime, when the air is very dry, and in excessively humid weather as well. The answer to this problem is frequent lubrication of the skin and a modification of the environment to regulate the excessive dryness or humidity. (See discussion on dry skin, above.)

Itching is also a symptom of kidney, liver, or thyroid disease and of internal cancer. On occasion, itching without rash can be a reaction to medication. Itching associated with allergies and the itch-scratch-itch syndrome are discussed on page 641.

If no physical cause for the itch can be found, then psychiatric evaluation is in order. Anxiety, severe depression, and other psychological factors can result in persistent itch, and the itch usually disappears when the psychiatric problem is under control.

DISEASES OF THE SKIN

SKIN DISORDERS occur throughout the population in all ages and social groups. Few are related to poor hygiene and few are contagious. Some respond quickly to treatment, others defy cure. Some are amenable to home treatment, some require professional help. (Skin problems that affect only infants or small children are dealt with in Chapter 12 on Infancy and the Early Years, page 194.)

Dermatitis

Dermatitis, also called eczema, has many causes, among which are allergic and toxic reactions, irritations, infections, and genetic predisposition. The skin changes that occur in all forms of dermatitis are essentially the same. First there is reddening (erythema) and swelling (edema). These will be followed by blistering (vesication) and oozing, and then crusting and scabbing. If the condition becomes chronic, it will lead to thickened, marked skin (lichenification), peeling or chafing (excoriation), and color change (either hypo- or hyperpigmentation). All these phases are accompanied by itching (pruritus).

There are many forms of dermatitis, each presenting a somewhat different pattern. Those most frequently seen by physicians are described below.

Atopic Dermatitis. Atopic dermatitis is an inherited condition that usually appears first in infancy and then at intervals into adult life. It is often seen in association with other atopic conditions, such as hayfever, asthma, or hives, but is not triggered by pollen or other airborne irritants.

The term atopic is derived from the Greek word *atopos* which means "away from the place." It describes a family of sensitivities to ordinary substances to which most people have no reaction. Hence, the sensitivity is out of place.

Symptoms can range from a red blistering rash to a thickening and discoloration of the skin. From puberty on, it usually appears as dry, itchy patches in the folds of the elbows and knees. It itches intensely, and many of the problems seen by doctors are a result of the itch-scratch-itch syndrome. At times, the itch precedes the rash.

Atopic dermatitis may be particularly harmful to emotional health. It is most severe in the critical developmental periods of infancy and adolescence and can interfere with the mother-child relationship and with development of a healthy self-image. Throughout life intermittent episodes may be triggered by emotional stress.

Episodes of atopic dermatitis may be set off by extreme temperatures, sweating, irritating medication, clothing (especially wool or silk), grease, oils, soap and detergents and, on occasion, by environmental allergens. It is not generally related to any food allergies.

Atopic dermatitis is usually accompanied by lowered resistance to wart infection and vaccinia viruses (used to inoculate against smallpox) and a lowered incidence of contact dermatitis. Sufferers are at risk of generalized infection if they have a herpes simplex eruption, for example, but they are 10 times less likely to be sensitive to poison ivy than the general population.

There is no cure for this disorder, but the symptoms can be relieved. The aims of therapy are to decrease trigger factors, reduce itching, suppress inflammation, lubricate the skin, and alleviate anxiety, all of which may be accomplished to a large extent by the patient himself. In addition to follow-ing the dry skin regimen discussed on page 623, the patient should take the following preventive measures:

1. Apply any prescribed emollients or medication immediately after bathing.

2. Keep temperatures as constant as possible and avoid excess humidity and, if possible, live, or vacation in a warm, dry climate.

3. Avoid irritating fabrics such as wool, silk, and rough synthetics; wear absorbent, nonirritating materials next to the skin.

4. Use mild laundry soap and make sure clothes are well-rinsed.

5. Treat any infection of the skin promptly.

6. Seek whatever help is necessary to maintain emotional stability.

If preventive measures are not adequate to control chronic atopic dermatitis, the doctor may prescribe one or more treatments. The most common is a corticosteroid ointment stronger than that available over the counter. This is sometimes prescribed in conjunction with other emollients. Tar compounds are often used for treatment of prolonged, chronic dermatitis. The doctor may suggest taking an antihistamine by mouth to control itching and allow sleep. As these often induce drowsiness, they should not be taken before driving. In extremely recalcitrant cases, photochemotherapy may be used along with tars or emollients.

Chronic Dermatitis. Chronic dermatitis comes in a variety of forms and appears in different age groups, but there are many similarities. All are of unknown origin, all are very itchy and may be prolonged or exacerbated by complications arising from the effects of the itch-scratch-itch cycle.

Chronic circumscribed dermatitis (lichen simplex), a very common disorder that is perpetuated by repeated scratching, is often found in patients with other atopic problems such as asthma or allergic rhinitis and with a family history of atopic disorders. It appears in areas that are easy to reach and scratch, such as the ankles or shins, the neck, the forearms, and sometimes the inner thighs and the anal–genital area.

Well-defined patches of skin, which are made thick and leathery from continual scratching, become even more sensitive and itchy as a result of repeated trauma. Scratching the itch becomes pleasurable and encourages a continuation of the cycle. The itching may be continuous, spasmodic, or sudden and violent, but the scratching becomes a fixed pattern. When the itching occurs in the groin area, scratching can be intensely pleasurable, almost erotic, so that the secondary pleasure may make it difficult for the patient to cooperate in therapy.

If the original cause of the itch can be discovered and removed, the condition may be quickly relieved. However, even if the cause is unknown, effective therapy can often bring about remission of the itching and the lichenification in several weeks.

A physician may choose to prescribe a corticosteroid cream or ointment, corticosteroid injections, or topical photochemotherapy. It may also be necessary to cover the affected areas for a period of time to preclude continuing trauma by scratching. An antihistamine or a tranquilizer before bed may be prescribed as well.

Nummular Dermatitis.

Nummular dermatitis is so named because the eczema appears in coin-shaped plaques. It is found most often in older people, in those with extremely dry skin, or in children with atopic dermatitis.

Itching is the primary symptom, and these round, red, weepy or crusty eruptions are usually found on the backs of the hands or the forearms, on the lower legs, or on the buttocks. The cause is often unknown, but sometimes a dry environment, other skin diseases, or emotional stress may trigger an outbreak. Nummular dermatitis is much more common in winter, with remission often occurring in summer. Treatment is similar to that for lichen simplex. If dryness is a factor, steps discussed in the dry skin regimen (page 623) should also be taken.

Contact Dermatitis—Irritant and Allergic.

Contact dermatitis may result from irritants or substances to which an individual has become allergic. Depending upon the source of irritation, the duration or frequency of exposure, and other variables, different uncomfortable changes in the skin occur.

Irritant contact dermatitis occurs when the skin is exposed to a mild irritant—such as detergents or solvents—repeatedly over a long period of time or to a strong irritant, such as acid or alkali, which can cause immediate damage to the skin.

This disorder is an "occupational hazard" for housewives, chemical workers, doctors and dentists, restaurant workers, and others whose work brings them into regular or prolonged contact with soaps, detergents, chemicals, and abrasives. These substances either erode the protective oily barrier of the skin or injure its surface.

Allergic dermatitis occurs when skin which has been sensitized to a specific substance comes in contact with that substance again. With the exception of poison ivy and poison oak, to which about 70 percent of people become sensitized after first contact, most contact allergies produce sensitivity in only a

few people. The most common of these allergies are nickel and other metals, rubber and elasticized garments, dyes, cosmetics (especially nail polish), and leather. But anyone can become sensitized to almost anything, so the search for the offending substance is often tedious and success is sometimes elusive.

In irritant dermatitis the skin becomes stiff, dry, and tight-feeling. It may crack, blister, or become ulcerated. Some itching may accompany mild inflammation, but the fissures and ulcers will be painful, not itchy. Mild irritants cause a progression from reddening and blistering to drying and cracking, while strong irritants cause blistering on contact and then erosion and ulcers.

Allergic dermatitis appears as reddening, followed by blistering and oozing. In severe cases there may be swelling of the face, eyes, and genital area. The rash will appear wherever the allergen has touched the skin, either directly or by transference from the hands. However, the palms, soles, and scalp seldom show any reaction. Fluid from the blisters will not spread the disease to other parts of the body or to other people.

There are no tests to determine the cause of irritant dermatitis. Finding the source may require persistent and creative detective work on the part of both doctor and patient. Patch tests can often determine or point the way to the allergens responsible for the reaction in allergic dermatitis. It may, however, take some sleuthing to find the specific product or products which contain the offending substance.

Preventive measures for irritant dermatitis are easy to define and difficult to carry out. The disease is usually the direct result of the working environment, and adequate protective measures are often impractical, if not impossible, to achieve. To the extent possible, then, it is recommended that the patient take the following precautions:

> 1. Wear cotton gloves under rubber gloves for all wet work. If gloves are impractical, use a barrier cream to protect the skin. Reapply the cream 2 or 3 times per day and after each handwashing.
> 2. Avoid or decrease exposure to workday irritants, such as harsh soaps, solvents, abrasives, and the like. Use the mildest soaps possible or waterless cleaners to clean the hands.
> 3. Use hand cream or lotion as frequently as possible.

The only preventive measure for allergic dermatitis is to wash exposed skin thoroughly as soon as possible after contact with the allergen. There appears to be little benefit from injection to desensitize the patient to poison oak or ivy, and there can be dangerous and unpleasant side effects.

The doctor's treatment of contact dermatitis will depend upon the type and severity of the disease. Chronic contact dermatitis will be treated with one or all of the treatments described for chronic circumscribed dermatitis (page 624). Since secondary bacterial infections are common, antibiotics may also be given. If an allergen is defined by patch testing, the dermatologist can provide a list of cross-reacting materials.

In the acute blistering or weeping stages of contact dermatitis, compresses, soaks, and lotions may be recommended. After scales begin to form, a corticosteroid cream or lotion may be used; if there is severe itching, antihistamines by mouth are indicated. If swelling and large blisters are present, systemic corticosteroids may be required. This will usually produce a marked improvement within 48 hours.

For acute irritant dermatitis the first measure is prolonged irrigation with water followed by treatment appropriate for burns. The exact nature of this treatment depends upon the nature of the irritant. For this reason, it is important that the doctor have the fullest possible information about the chemical composition of the irritant.

Hand Dermatitis. Hand dermatitis, popularly known as "dishpan hands" or "housewife's eczema," is a common chronic disorder that is difficult to diagnose precisely because it may be a manifestation of one or several causes or predisposing factors. Different conditions may be similar in appearance.

This disorder is most often seen as irritant contact dermatitis, but it may be any of the following as well:

1. A remnant of atopic or nummular dermatitis, appearing as described above; primarily on the backs of the hands and perpetuated by the itch-scratch-itch syndrome.
2. Allergic contact dermatitis, especially between the fingers and on the backs of the hands.
3. Dishydrotic eczema, little bubbles under the skin on the palms and between the fingers, often seen in association with nervous tension and excessive sweating.
4. Fungal infections or inflammation associated with fungal infections on the foot.
5. Viral infections, such as herpes simplex (popularly known as cold sores or fever blisters when it appears around the mouth), or warts.
6. Psoriasis, especially of the nails.
7. Drug reactions.

Symptoms will vary from a reddening and chapping (mild), to bubbles under the skin (moderate), to blisters, ulcers, hardening of the skin, and deep cracks or fissures. Treatment is the same as for contact dermatitis, except in the case of fungal infections.

Stasis Dermatitis. Stasis dermatitis is caused by poor circulation and is seen primarily in middle age, especially in women who have borne several children or in those who have a history of thrombophlebitis of the legs.

It usually first appears on the inside of the lower leg around the ankles as red, scaly patches that do not itch. Pruritus and secondary infection may follow. Stasis dermatitis is very easily sensitized to many topical preparations; contact dermatitis may occur. Complications must be diagnosed and treated appropriately to avoid development of severe ulcerations.

A common treatment for uncomplicated conditions is support stockings. Since this disorder is a result of a circulatory problem, the dermatologist may suggest consultation with a vascular specialist.

Intertrigo

Intertrigo is an eruption of the skin caused by the friction of two adjacent skin surfaces. The underarms, groin, inner thighs, breasts, and other skinfold areas in obese people are the areas involved. The rubbing together of these surfaces along with the heat and sweat retained in these generally covered areas, combine to provide a perfect environment for the growth of bacteria, fungi, and yeast. The presence of these organisms may then cause ulceration, and the ulcers may in turn be invaded by other organisms.

To treat this condition the opposing skin surface must be kept clean, free of friction, and open to the air to the extent possible. Absorbent powders should be applied to dry surfaces. A hair dryer on the cool setting is helpful in drying skin folds. Any infectious organisms must be eliminated by appropriate medication.

Acne

Acne is so common in teenagers that it is sometimes considered a normal part of development. As many as 4 out of 5 teenagers have acne—some for only a few weeks, some for a year or so, but most for about 10 years, into early adulthood. In rare cases it continues throughout life. In women, its first appearance in the mid-twenties or mid-thirties is not unusual.

Although just about everybody has it and almost nobody suffers dire physical effects, it can leave serious physical and emotional scars if it is ignored. At a time when cosmetic beauty is given primary value, acne comes along and causes otherwise happy, outgoing youngsters to become miserable social outcasts and, often as not, it is the source of continual parent-child discord.

Since the cause of acne is frequently misunderstood, the "victim" may be accused of being responsible for his or her condition. Parents often blame their youngsters for eating too much junk food, eating too little, eating too much, not washing properly, not getting enough sleep, sleeping too much, being obsessed with the opposite sex, having no interest in the opposite sex, ad infinitum. The truth is, none of these things has anything to do with acne, and if there is any "blame" attached to the disorder, it may well belong to the parents' genes.

Though no exact cause is known, factors that contribute to acne have been identified. First of all, heredity plays an important role. Children whose parents, either one or both, have had moderate or severe acne are far more likely to suffer from the disorder than children whose parents had either mild acne or none at all. Just how the tendency is passed along is not understood.

Oily skin is another contributing factor in acne. In particular, severe acne is most often found in those who have excessively oily skin. Since some people with oily skin do not have acne and some people with dry skin do, no absolute correlation can be made.

Androgens, male sex hormones produced by the testes or ovaries and adrenal glands in both sexes, regulate the size and activity of the oil glands. Acne results from the effects of androgens which are produced in increased amounts at puberty. These androgens cause the oil glands to produce a substance called sebum, which comes up through hair follicles to lubricate the skin. In acne, the passageway gets plugged up. The sebum may combine with keratin particles which are sloughed off in the hair follicles and sometimes with bacteria that normally reside there. The result is some form of inflammation. (See figure 31.3.)

Blackheads (open comedones), the mildest form of acne, result when sebum combines with skin pigments (not dirt) to plug the pores. If the pores become stuffed with sebum and scales below the surface of the skin, a whitehead (closed comedone) appears. In severe acne, pressure sometimes builds up in these closed pores and they rupture and spread under the skin. Bacteria in the injured area can lead to more widespread inflammation. These painful cysts can leave scars if unattended. The degree of scarring is also genetically determined.

Whether or not the acne sufferer need see a doctor depends more on the perception of the patient than the severity of the condition. Some young people are traumatized by even relatively mild erup-

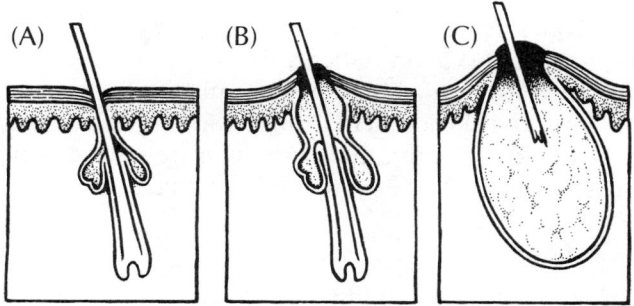

Figure 31.3. **Development of acne. (A) Normal sebaceous gland; (B) blackhead or small, open comedone; (C) cystic acne.**

tions and need the support and encouragement of a physician. Others will take mild acne in stride, follow a reasonable hygiene regime, and wait it out.

The main treatment for mild acne is thorough cleansing 2 or 3 times per day and shampooing frequently to keep greasy hair off the face. The object is to keep the affected areas as free of oil as possible. However, irritation from too vigorous scrubbing is to be avoided. If cleansing alone does not keep all the blackheads in check, the patient can try over-the-counter creams, lotions, and gels applied directly to the lesion for added help in drying. Over-the-counter benzoyl peroxide preparations are good for acne pimples, provided they are used as directed to avoid irritation. If cosmetics are used to cover the problem, they should be water-based products. Oil-based moisturing products only add to the problem. When these home measures fail, the doctor may prescribe a peeling agent, vitamin A acid, an antibiotic cream, or an oral antibiotic.

The antibiotic tetracycline has been extremely effective in preventing the development of scarring pustules. It is usually given in a normal dosage for a few weeks and then gradually reduced to a maintenance level dose of about one-quarter normal strength and may be taken for months or even years (with periodic interruptions to see if the acne has cleared up on its own). Fewer than 10 percent of patients treated with tetracycline have had any unwanted side effects, and for this group there are alternative antibiotics.

In severe, recalcitrant acne a recent therapy that is successful in suppressing acne is 13-*cis*-retinoic acid, which is similar to but less toxic than vitamin A. This treatment should be administered only by a dermatologist.

A caution to all acne sufferers: Blackheads should be removed only with a specially designed instrument by someone trained to use it correctly. Picking, prodding, or lancing should be strictly in the hands of the professional. Otherwise, severe scarring may result.

Some scarring may occur even with the best medical supervision. When this happens, dermabrasion (professional skin planing) can significantly improve the situation. This must wait until the acne has subsided. Individual scars can be raised using surgery or filled with silicone or collagen.

Rosacea

Some people tend to flush easily in the areas of the forehead, the nose, the cheekbones, and the chin. In a few individuals this becomes recurrent or permanent and rather marked. This condition is called rosacea.

It appears most often between the ages of 30 and 50. Women are affected 3 times as often as men, but men are far more likely to have the most severe form of rosacea. Fair-skinned people are more susceptible than those with dark skin.

The reddened skin may or may not show pimples or pustules. In more severe cases, pustules will form on the nose and can be extremely tender. There may also be a thickening of the affected skin, and in men there is sometimes a proliferation of reddish tumors on the nose, causing it to be grossly enlarged.

The cause of rosacea is unknown, but it is often triggered or worsened by ingesting hot liquids, spicy foods, or alcohol. Emotional stress, excessive heat or cold, or sunlight may also set off a reaction. Treatment is similar to that used for acne. Tetracycline is given to control pustule formation and topical medications are applied to active inflammation.

Seborrheic Dermatitis

Many people have dandruff, which is a moderate form of seborrheic dermatitis. This is characterized by scaling of the scalp and is controlled with frequent shampooing, either with regular shampoo or one of several special dandruff shampoos, the most effective of which is best determined by trial and error.

In more extensive seborrheic dermatitis, the scaling is found not only on the scalp but in the eyebrows, around the nose, behind the ears, in the underarm and anal–genital areas and, in obese people, in almost any body fold. The scales of seborrheic dermatitis are accompanied by redness and may crust and ooze.

The cause of seborrheic dermatitis is not known, but it appears to relate to a constitutional predisposition and is commonly exacerbated by physical or emotional stress. There is an increased incidence of this disorder in those with Parkinson's disease and other neurologic disorders.

A reddening and scaling of the eyelids and mild conjunctivitis often accompany seborrheic dermatitis, and sometimes this is the only manifestation of the condition.

Topical corticosteroid therapy is often the most effective treatment for seborrheic dermatitis. It may be prescribed as a lotion, cream, gel, or ointment, depending on the location of the lesions. For extensive cases, corticosteroid injections will be needed in conjunction with topical therapy. Milder cases often respond to over-the-counter steroids. When steroid ointments are used intermittently around the eyes, regular checks on intraocular pressure are required to ensure against glaucoma.

Sebaceous Cysts

Sebaceous cysts, often called wens, are saclike structures filled with a cheesy substance produced by the cells lining the sac. They develop as little swellings on the face, scalp, or back and at first can hardly be felt. Sometimes they remain very small, and since they are painless and benign, they are often left alone.

However, these cysts can sometimes grow to be quite large and unsightly, and they are prone to infection. Attention should be paid to any cyst that becomes red or tender, and steps should be taken to prevent the spread of infection.

The surgical removal of a sebaceous cyst is a simple, outpatient procedure whereby an incision is made in the skin lying over the cyst, the sac is removed, and the incision is stitched with nonabsorbable sutures which are removed about a week later. It is wise to have cysts removed if they are troublesome.

Psoriasis

Psoriasis has a well-earned reputation for being intractible. This common complaint affects more than 1 percent of the population, and in most cases it is chronic, erratic, and thoroughly unpredictable. It is true that there is no cure, but psoriasis is quite treatable and, with appropriate therapy, can be rendered minimally annoying in the vast majority of cases.

Its exact cause is unknown, but there seems to be a genetic predisposition in many patients, and it is somehow related to a defect in the production of the epidermal layer of the skin. Instead of taking the usual 26 to 28 days to form the epidermis, the process is speeded up to take only 3 to 4 days. This causes an abnormal outer layer of skin which we see as round or oval red patches of skin covered with silvery scales.

Typical places for the outbreaks to occur are the

scalp, elbows, knees, palms, and soles. But they can occur on the lower back and in the folds of the skin, especially in obese people. If psoriasis is present in a warm, damp skin-fold area, it will probably have no scales.

Occasionally, psoriasis will begin as a group of little pimples instead of scaly patches. This is especially common when the onset is triggered by a sore throat or a similar streptococcal infection. In severe cases the patches may spread and run together or the body may be virtually covered with a red bumpy rash.

Psoriasis generally first appears in early adulthood, but it can show up for the first time late in life. It frequently first appears after an injury to the skin or a generalized infection, and once it has appeared it can be precipitated or aggravated by emotional stress, drug reactions, or strep throat.

The nails are also involved in a psoriatic attack. The mildest form of psoriasis of the nails is a pitting on their surface. At other times, a dry, scaly material builds up under the nails and separates the nails from the nail bed.

About 5 percent of psoriasis patients develop an arthritis which is different from rheumatoid arthritis. It most commonly affects the hands, but in severe cases the back may be involved as well.

The unpredictable nature of psoriasis is perhaps the most difficult factor in its management. About two-thirds of patients treated have significant periods of remission. However, neither physician nor patient can be sure whether the remission will last a few weeks, a few months, a few years, or forever.

Treatment of psoriasis is usually topical (medication applied to the skin) rather than systemic (medication ingested or injected). Corticosteroid creams or ointments, coal tar preparations, and ultraviolet light are all used in therapy. Tar plus ultraviolet light treatment has been very beneficial to those with widespread psoriasis, and there are a variety of regimens of this nature designed for home and hospital use.

Other treatments may include acid gels or creams for the removal of scales, retinoids (derivatives of vitamin A and vitamin A acid), tar shampoos and steroid lotions for the scalp, and anti-inflammatory medication for arthritis pain.

A new approach to the treatment of psoriasis is called PUVA. A psoralen pill is taken prior to exposure to ultraviolet light which enhances the healing quality of the light. This is used primarily for severe psoriasis. It must be continuous to prevent relapse, and the possibility of serious side effects, including an increased risk of skin cancer, must be considered.

Some internal drugs used in treating cancer, such as methotrexate, are also effective in treating severe psoriasis. The side effects can be unpleasant and even seriously damaging, however, and care must be taken that the cure is not worse than the disease.

Urticaria and Drug Eruptions

Urticaria, commonly called hives, affects about 20 percent of Americans at some time in their lives. A hive is an itchy swelling that comes and goes in a short period of time. A single hive is usually a reaction to an outside irritant, such as an insect bite. Multiple hives, called urticaria, are usually an allergic reaction to some internal agent. Hives can be due to many causes: foods (especially shellfish, nuts, and berries); medications; heat, cold, or sunshine; infections; insect bites; and emotional stress. When the hives continue for an extended period of time (chronic urticaria), there are probably multiple trigger factors.

The first line of therapy is to find and eliminate the trigger factor or factors. For symptomatic treatment until the cause can be found, the doctor may suggest cool compresses, soaking baths, or lotions to alleviate itching. He or she will undoubtedly prescribe some type of antihistamine, and if lesions are acute or more severe, adrenaline injection.

Hives are a typical form of allergic drug reaction. They generally occur within an hour of administration of the offending drug. Sometimes there will also be swelling of the larynx as well. Late reactions appear more than 3 days after administration and may show up as a rash, hives, or as a fever or some abnormal reaction of one of the organ systems.

Rashes, the most common type of drug reaction, usually appear within a week, spread progressively from head to feet, and clear up in the same fashion, running a 2- to 3-week course. Therapy is the same as for urticaria.

The normal reaction to insect stings or bites is itching and pain with the formation of a wheal, all of which subside within a few hours.

Severe local reactions result in an unusual amount of swelling at the site of the sting. Toxic reactions occur when there are 10 or more simultaneous stings and may include nausea, dizziness, headache, and fever. Immediate systemic reactions, called anaphylaxis or anaphylactic shock, are life-threatening and require immediate attention. Within minutes after the sting the patient will exhibit hives, swelling of the larynx, and difficulty in breathing, cold sweats, abdominal cramps, and a sharp drop in blood pressure.

An injection of adrenaline is required immediately to raise the blood pressure and open up breathing passages. Antihistamine and corticosteroids are given after the immediate emergency has passed.

Those known to be sensitive to bee stings are at risk and should keep and know how to use an emergency first-aid kit for treating anaphylaxis. Anyone exhibiting a severe reaction to a bee sting should see an allergist and investigate the possibility of being desensitized, a controversial procedure.

Pityriasis Rosea

This skin rash of unknown origin appears primarily in adolescents and young adults. It starts on the trunk with 1 or 2 small red spots and spreads to cover all or part of the trunk and upper arms. The spots become red patches which may be itchy.

There is no danger attached to this rash and it goes away on its own, usually over a period of weeks. If the rash is somewhat itchy, calamine lotion will usually relieve the itch. However, if itching is severe, the doctor may prescribe antihistamine tablets or a steroid cream.

Since pityriasis rosea can be confused with secondary syphilis, a blood test should be done in all patients to rule this out.

Moles and Other Spots

Birthmarks and *moles* (pigmented nevi) are benign growths found in greater or lesser numbers on most people. The former, as would seem obvious, are present at birth; the latter begin to appear in early childhood. The great majority of birthmarks are dark brown and flat at birth and may become lighter and slightly raised as time passes. There are, however, strawberry marks which usually disappear, cherry-colored moles, port wine stains, and other colored lesions, most of which require no treatment unless they are unsightly or are located in an inconvenient spot. In rare cases an existing mole can become cancerous, and changes in color, size, or height should be checked by a dermatologist.

The sun and time are both the enemies of a flawless skin, as aging and exposure create a variety of spots and growths as well as the inevitable wrinkling. Heredity and environment largely determine how early these degenerative signs begin to appear.

Seborrheic keratoses are rough brown spots, either flat or slightly elevated, that grow on the back, chest, arms, and face, sometimes profusely. They are not dangerous, but too many can be a nuisance. They are easily removed, leaving no scars.

Actinic keratoses (also called solar keratoses) are flat, pink scaly spots that grow on sun-damaged skin. They are more frequent and more numerous in fair-skinned individuals, and they are a type of

growth that can become malignant. They should be removed individually or the whole area can be treated with a 5-fluoracil cream.

Liver spots (lentigines) are flat brown spots that are also associated with sun-damaged skin. Sometimes they are treated for cosmetic reasons, but they hold no risk.

Skin Cancers

Cancer of the skin is more common than all other types of malignancy combined. Most skin cancer is curable, particularly if caught in the early stages, which is why early detection and treatment are so important. Unfortunately skin cancer often looks just like benign skin conditions and vice versa, so self-diagnosis is not often possible. Most new growths and many changing conditions are harmless, but this is one time when it is better to be safe than sorry. Any skin lesion that changes in size, shape, or color, or frequently bleeds, even with apparent cause (such as a shaving nick), should be examined.

The 3 most common skin cancers are basal cell carcinoma, squamous cell carcinoma, and malignant melanoma. *Basal cell carcinoma* is the most frequently occurring skin cancer, and while it can appear at any time, it is more often seen in people over 40. Most of these tumors are formed on skin damaged by prolonged exposure to the sun. They rarely spread to other parts of the body, but if left untreated, they can invade other tissue.

Like basal cell cancer, *squamous cell carcinoma* is also associated frequently with sun-damaged skin and is found most frequently on the head, face, and hands. These lesions are also linked with exposure to chemicals and to long-standing infections and sites of x-ray therapy. Squamous cell cancer can be cured if treated early and though it can spread, it is not usually life-threatening.

Malignant melanoma is the leading cause of death from skin diseases and is a dangerous form of cancer indeed. Although it can arise from an existing mole, this is exceedingly rare. The vast majority of these cancers are new growths that are cancerous to begin with.

Malignant melanomas may differ in appearances, but characteristics that should be a signal to consult a doctor are these: irregular, speckled, mixed coloration of varying shades and hues; irregular shape; irregular surface; rapid change or growth.

Removal of basal and squamous cell carcinomas is localized, relatively easy, and may be accomplished by a variety of procedures. In malignant melanoma the growth, along with a large amount of the surrounding and underlying skin, will be removed to get any malignant cells that may have moved away from the original growth. (See also Chapter 20 on Cancer, page 420.)

INFECTIONS

Warts

Warts are a very common skin tumor caused by a viral infection. They can appear anywhere on the body, but hands and feet are the most common places. They occur most often in children and teenagers, older people having apparently developed an immunity to the virus. Warts are contagious, but tend to spread on the infected person rather than being passed to someone else.

Warts vary in appearance, and different types of warts tend to appear on different parts of the body. On the hands they are usually the horny nodule that most people associate with the name. When they grow on the soles of the feet, they look somewhat like small callouses because the pressure exerted by the body's weight causes them to grow beneath the skin surface, rather than being raised. They have a special name: plantar warts. On the neck and face, warts are apt to be smoother, more regularly shaped growths.

Except for plantar warts growing at pressure points on the heel or ball of the foot, warts are not painful or itchy. They may, however, interfere with work if they are inconveniently placed, and most people consider them unsightly.

It is important to remember that warts are benign and that treatment should also be benign. Fifty percent of all warts disappear within 2 years with no therapy at all. However, sometimes it is desirable to remove warts for comfort, convenience, or cosmetic reasons.

There are several ways to remove warts. The doctor will choose the method appropriate for the type of wart, its placement, the age of the patient, and other factors. All the following methods are used in one instance or another:

1. Home treatment with a commercial preparation, usually a salicylic acid–lactic acid paint.
2. Light electrodessication, a method whereby the growth is destroyed by burns of electric current. This method is not recommended for anyone wearing a pacemaker, and it has some potential for scarring.
3. Curettage, in which the growth is cut away with a curet, an instrument with a small loop-shaped cutting edge. Sometimes this is used in combination with electrodessication.

4. Cantharadin, a poison that causes blistering, breaking, and crusting. The preparation is painted on the wart and covered, and it gradually breaks down the growth, leaving no scarring.
5. Cytotoxic agents, which are "poison" to the cells. These are used especially for warts in the genital area.
6. Acids, which can be used at home and are slow but effective. These require repeated, persistent applications and have the potential for scarring.
7. Cryosurgery, freezing the growth with liquid nitrogen. This generally requires no anesthesia and is fairly quick therapy. Sometimes a small white spot remains where the freezing was done.

Mollusca

Mollusca are small viral growths which grow singly or in groups on the face, trunk, lower abdomen, pelvis, inner thighs, and penis. They are skin-colored or pearly white pimples with a small depression at the center. Mollusca were once found primarily on the face and trunk of children, but have recently become quite common in sexually active young adults. They may be treated by freezing, electrosurgery excision with a curet, or application of a blistering agent.

Fever Blisters and Cold Sores

At least 70 percent of the U.S. population has experienced fever blisters or cold sores by age 14. These infections are caused by herpes simplex Type I and are sometimes referred to as facial herpes. The sores generally, though not always, appear on or around the lips. The first infection may be very painful and disabling, but recurrent infections, involving up to 45 percent of the population, are more annoying than anything else.

Herpes is contagious. It appears 3 to 12 days after exposure and lasts 1 to 3 weeks, about 10 days for recurrent cases. The initial infection begins with a day or two of local tenderness. When the small blisters start to appear, there is more severe pain and the lymph nodes may be swollen and tender. There may also be a high fever and a malodorous oozing from the blisters, and it may be difficult to eat.

In recurrent infections, there is usually a burning or tingling sensation and the skin reddens slightly for several hours before the first blister appears. There is much less discomfort than with the first infection.

Recurrent herpes can be triggered by overexposure to sunlight, high fever or other infection in the body, trauma, menstruation, or emotional disturbance. It is often possible to discover why the infection has occurred, but it is not possible to prevent it at present unless the trigger factor can be completely removed or controlled.

A new antiviral compound, Acyclovir, is now available in oral and topical forms by prescription to treat or prevent recurrent herpes eruptions. Analgesics for pain and analgesic mouthwash to make it easier to eat may also be helpful.

Herpes simplex Type II (genital herpes) is discussed in Chapter 21 under Sexually Transmitted Diseases, page 443.

Shingles

Unlike herpes simplex, herpes zoster, more commonly called shingles, usually occurs only once in a lifetime. It is caused by the same virus responsible for chickenpox, which is thought to lie dormant in the body after recovery, until somehow it is triggered and reappears.

Shingles appears as a rash (clusters of blisters with a red base) on one side of the body or face in an area supplied by one particular spinal nerve. Sometimes the rash is preceded by several days of tingling or prickling sensations. Unfortunately, in a few cases, nerve pain (neuralgia) can persist for months or years.

As in herpes simplex, only the symptoms can be treated. The doctor may suggest anesthetic medications for the rash and aspirin or other analgesics for the nerve pain. Persistent neuralgia can often be treated with medications used for seizures or depression. By and large, time offers the only cure.

Bacterial Impetigo

Bacterial infections usually arise when there is a preexisting skin disease or a skin injury so that there is an entry point, or after treatment with antibiotics or steroids. The infection may be staphylococcal (staph) or streptococcal (strep), but in either case the pattern of symptoms is redness, blistering, and abscess.

These infections are most commonly seen in children, especially in warm and tropical climates, and more frequently where poor health, poor nutrition, and inadequate hygiene are present. Impetigo, the most common of the bacterial infections, may be caused by staph or strep or a mixture of both, but usually it is a staph infection. Little blisters appear, burst, and form a yellowish crust often about hairy areas. Generally the infection will go away by itself within 10 days, but it can spread and become more serious if not properly handled. If it is a strep infection it can cause kidney disease. In most cases there are no lasting effects and no scars.

Even though impetigo often disappears by itself, it is wise to treat it with a penicillin injection to prevent possible spread, to shorten the healing time, decrease the chance of recurrence and, in the case of strep infections, to reduce the level of contagion. The doctor might also recommend that the entire family bathe once a day with a special antibacterial preparation.

Folliculitis

Sometimes staph bacteria will enter the hair follicles and cause a superficial infection of the follicle called folliculitis. This problem often occurs in men as a result of the repeated trauma of shaving. It starts as a small pus-filled pimple with a red border and rapidly spreads to adjacent areas. It is usually superficial and can be treated successfully by the following hygiene measures:

1. The patient and family should bathe frequently and special attention should be paid to keep the nails short and clean.
2. Separate towels, washcloths, bed linens, and clothing should be used. These should be changed daily and laundered in boiling water.
3. Before shaving, the face should be washed with an appropriate antibacterial soap.
4. After shaving, alcohol should be applied and then an antibacterial cream should be rubbed into the infected areas.
5. Razors should be immersed in alcohol between shaves, and should not be shared by husband and wife.
6. The prescribed oral antibiotic should be taken for 10 to 14 days.

Furunculosis

Sometimes the deepest portion of the hair follicle becomes infected and the inflammation spreads to the surrounding skin, causing boils (furuncles) to form. These most often appear on the face, scalp, buttocks, or underarms and can be exquisitely painful. When they occur on the eyelid, they are called styes.

If the boils are not too large, they should be treated with moist heat only. However, if they are very large, the doctor may drain them by making a small incision after they come to a head. If the boils cause significant inflammation of surrounding areas, are accompanied by a fever, or appear on the upper lip, nose, cheeks, or forehead, they should be treated by a physician.

Carbuncles are staph abscesses that are larger and deeper than boils. They usually have several heads from which they drain, and are most often found on the neck, back, and thighs.

Cellulitis

Cellulitis is a skin infection that sometimes accompanies damage to the skin, poor circulation, or diabetes. The skin becomes red and swollen and is both warm and painful to the touch, and is sometimes accompanied by fever, malaise, chills, and headache. If antibiotics are not given, the condition may progress to abscesses and tissue damage.

One type of cellulitis is erysipelas, which usually starts with a headache, fever, and general distress, followed by small red patches which spread and swell so that the border is easy to see and feel. Erysipelas is a strep infection that can be fatal if not treated promptly with penicillin. Warm compresses and rest may also be recommended. (Also see Chapter 21 on Infectious Diseases, page 439.)

Fungal Infections

Yeast infections, caused by the candida species, are usually superficial infections on the skin and mucous membranes. Sores at the corners of the mouth, white patches on the inside of the cheek, redness and swelling around the fingernails, "cheesy" vaginal discharge, and moist red rashes on other parts of the body are common yeast infections.

This fungus normally lives in the intestine, vagina, and mouth where it is a benign organism. But through a process that is not clearly understood, it can change to a disease-causing agent under some circumstances. It is more likely to infect the obese, those already ill, diabetics, women taking antibiotics or birth control pills, and people who perspire profusely.

A number of preparations can be prescribed for topical use, depending on the location of the infection. In the case of repeated infection, a drug to destroy the fungus in the intestine may be given by mouth. Because prevention of recurrence is important, skin folds should be kept dry. (Specific fungal infections are discussed in Chapter 21 on Infectious Diseases, page 447.)

Tinea Versicolor

Tinea versicolor is a harmless infection that appears as flat, brown, or white scaly patches on the upper portion of the body. The infected areas lose their pigment and make the surrounding skin appear darker, especially after tanning. This is sometimes called "sun fungus." The scaling areas can be treated with a special shampoo solution, but in most cases the infection is recurrent. Weekly lathering with a zinc pyrathyone shampoo may be helpful.

INFESTATIONS

Pubic Lice

Pubic lice (pediculosis pubis), usually called crabs, are small, yellow-gray wingless insects that attach themselves to the skin in the pubic area and lay their eggs (nits) on the pubic hair. They cause itching and sometimes hives and are transmitted by sexual contact. They are eradicated by means of shampooing the infected area with one of several effective preparations available over the counter. Clothing and linen should be washed in very hot water and dried on the "hot" cycle.

Scabies

Scabies is caused by infestation with a mite. Like crabs, scabies is acquired primarily through intimate personal contact, but may also be transmitted through linen, towels, or clothing. The severe itching caused by infestation appears after 3 to 4 weeks and is at its worst just after going to bed.

An infestation of scabies will appear as little ridges on the skin or dotted lines ending in blisters. It is commonly found between the fingers, around the wrists, on the elbows, navel, nipples, lower abdomen, and in the genital area. Some people become sensitized to the mite and have hives, scaling, or other skin changes as well. It is not uncommon to see secondary bacterial infections and boils with scabies.

Treatment consists of using a pesticide-containing shampoo for pubic hair and a cream or lotion for other parts of the body. The whole body must be treated to get an effective cure. Clothing and linen should be washed, as with crabs.

The mite of canine scabies is also highly contagious and can be acquired through contact with a dog having mange. Canine scabies lesions are pimples or blisters without burrows and are found on the trunk, arms, and abdomen. One treatment with pesticide lotion is generally successful.

Head and Body Lice

Though they look much the same, head and body lice are different from pubic lice, discussed above. Head lice are transmitted through contact, clothing, or hairbrushes, while body lice are transmitted through bedding or clothing.

With head lice it is difficult to find adult lice in the hair, but nits can be found, especially around the ears and at the back of the head. They are extremely itchy, and sometimes they are accompanied by hives, generalized itching, or other conditions, such as impetigo or boils.

Body lice can rarely be found on the body, but rather in the seams of clothing and in bedding folds. On the body there may be scratch marks, hives, eczematous changes, and red pimples, especially on the back.

To treat head lice, a pesticide shampoo is left on the scalp for a few minutes, then rinsed, and the hair combed with a special comb to remove nits. For body lice, one need only wash with a pesticide preparation and wash all clothing and linen in very hot water, then dry on the hot cycle. Mattresses may be dusted with an appropriate powder.

Rare Diseases

Lymphogranuloma venereum and granuloma inguinale are relatively rare. The former is a systemic disease caused by a parasite. The first lesion, a little pimple or blister, which comes 1 to 3 weeks after infection, usually goes unnoticed. Two or 3 weeks after the appearance of the lesion, the lymph glands on one side of the groin become tender and swollen and the skin becomes tight and bluish-red. The swelling may fester. Antibiotics are usually prescribed, and the doctor may also aspirate the inflamed gland.

In granuloma inguinale there are painless but malodorous ulcers in the groin, and there may be some movable masses under the skin. Treatment is similar to that for lymphogranuloma venereum.

CORNS AND CALLOUSES

CORNS AND CALLOUSES appear where the foot or the hand has been subjected to repeated friction or pressure. Corns and callouses on the feet are usually caused by ill-fitting shoes; callouses on the hands are usually occupational marks: the laborer's calloused hands, the violinist's calloused fingers, the tennis player's calloused palm.

The only way to be rid of these uncomfortable annoyances is to remove the cause, which may mean referral to a podiatrist or an orthopedic surgeon. However, it is easy for the individual to allay the symptoms by following these procedures:

1. Apply a plaster (40 percent salicylic acid) just larger than the affected spot, then apply a felt pad to relieve pressure.

2. Leave the plaster and pad in place for 1 to 7 days, depending on the thickness of the corn or callous. Trial and error will show how long.

3. Remove the whitened, soft skin with a towel, pumice stone, or callous file.

4. Repeat until the lesion is gone completely. Continued protection with a felt pad may help prevent recurrence.

HAIR LOSS

HAIR, which for animals serves as a protective coat, has for humans primarily a cosmetic function. People can get along quite well without any hair at all, but for some reason, too much hair in the wrong place or too little hair in the right place is cause for great anguish.

There are roughly 100,000 hairs on the average head. Each hair is going through a growth cycle quite independent of every other hair. About 90 percent of scalp hairs will be in the first, or growing, stage at any one time, while 10 percent will be in the resting phase. The growth stage can last for as long as 4 to 5 years, but the resting stage lasts only a few months and ends when the hair falls out as a result of new growth underneath. The third stage is one of intense cellular activity in the hair follicles, which are responsible for the production of new hairs.

Perhaps 50 hairs per day fall out in the normal

process of combing, shampooing, and just sitting still. Abnormal hair loss is of several types and may be due to disorders of the metabolism, hair shafts, scalp, or psyche. Some kinds of balding (diffuse, nonscarring alopecia) are overcome naturally, some by therapy, and some not at all.

Male Pattern Baldness

Male pattern baldness may begin anytime after the mid-teens. First the hairline recedes at the temples, followed by some thinning on the top, with the crown becoming completely bald first. All the while the hairline between the temples has been gradually receding, and finally the receding hairlines meet, leaving a bald pate with a fringe around the sides and back.

Three factors are involved in male baldness: heredity, androgen hormones, and aging. Where there is a family pattern of baldness in the father or male members of the mother's family, there is a good chance of inheriting the tendency. Although the mechanism is not clearly understood, androgenic hormones interact with the hair follicles to cause hair loss, and aging causes the majority of men to be partially or completely bald by age 60.

This kind of hair loss is erratic and it is impossible to tell how quickly or how slowly the process will proceed. It is, however, inevitable. Women sometimes have male pattern baldness, but it is usually a mild form that appears late in life.

There is no known cure for male baldness, but there are several cosmetic or reconstructive measures which may be taken. No lotions or regimens have proved effective in restoring or slowing the balding process, but the problem can be disguised with no risk and relatively little expense using artificial hair pieces or hair weaving. Many men, however, want a more permanent solution, which at

MYTHS ABOUT SKIN

Myth: Shingles are caused by "nerves."

Truth: When shingles (herpes zoster) appears, it does inflame the skin in the area supplied by an individual nerve root, but the reason for its sudden appearance is unknown. It is not related to anxiety.

Myth: Diet is an important factor in acne.

Truth: The vast majority of people with acne can eat what they want without adverse effects to their skin.

Myth: Gradual tanning avoids the risk of skin cancer.

Truth: Although severe sunburns may be particularly damaging, most skin cancers are related to the total amount of sunlight absorbed.

Myth: Breaking the blisters of poison ivy will spread the rash.

Truth: The blister fluid does not contain allergens. When poison ivy appears as a line of blisters on the skin, it is because the plant has brushed the skin in that fashion, or the patient has gotten the oil on his hand and stroked the skin—not because the blister fluid has run on the skin.

Myth: Corticosteroid pills are very dangerous, even if taken for a few weeks.

Truth: This medication can be very beneficial in reducing acute inflammation and can be taken by most people for several weeks without side effects.

Myth: People with red noses and cheeks are drinkers.

Truth: Rosacea can cause an enlarged red nose even in a teetotaler.

Myth: Moisturizing creams prevent wrinkles.

Truth: The moisture that these creams provide hydrates the skin and may make wrinkles temporarily less noticeable. But since wrinkles are a factor of heredity, age, and sun exposure, only the sunscreens in these creams are helpful.

Myth: Baldness comes from the mother's side of the family.

Truth: A tendency to baldness is inherited from either side of the family. A maternal grandfather and uncles with thick heads of hair is no assurance against baldness.

Myth: Psoriasis is contagious.

Truth: While heredity is a factor in acquiring psoriasis, it is not a contagious disease.

Myth: Scabies and lice occur only in people with poor hygiene.

Truth: Head lice and scabies are commonly found in all socioeconomic groups where members are in close contact, from schools to prisons to cocktail parties.

Myth: Liver spots are an early sign of liver disease.

Truth: These dark, liver-colored spots, found in greatest concentration on the backs of the hands, are completely benign. They are related to age and sun exposure, but have no relation to the liver.

Myth: Atopic dermatitis is an allergy to certain foods.

Truth: Only rarely will a change in diet substantially improve this type of dermatitis.

present means undergoing hair transplants using the individual's own hair from other parts of the scalp. Artificial hair should never be used for transplants, as it will eventually be rejected and lead to infection and scarring.

Telogen Effluvium

Acute illness, surgery, stress, pregnancy, or cessation of birth control pills can cause a sudden temporary hair loss called telogen effluvium. These conditions or events cause hair shafts to stop growing and to enter the resting phase. The hair loss may not be noticed until 1 to 3 months after the inciting event. Patients are often alarmed when they see great amounts falling out, but by the time the hair loss occurs, the condition that caused it has already been corrected, so no treatment is needed.

Other Causes

When hair falls out in patches, it is called alopecia areata. When only a few spots become bald, the hair often grows back of its own accord. However, the earlier the onset of this disease or the wider the areas affected, the more disappointing the prognosis. In its most severe form (alopecia universalis) the individual loses all body hair including eyelashes, brows, and pubic hair. In moderate to severe cases, the only hope is that corticosteroids taken by mouth may arrest or decelerate hair loss.

Occasionally, hair is lost during the growing stage (anages effluvium). This is usually caused by the effects of drugs or other medical treatment, such as those used in conjunction with organ transplant or cancer therapy. The hair usually grows back when treatment is discontinued.

Hair shaft abnormalities can result from congenital disorders or from chemical or physical treatments. This causes the hair to break off easily and in severe cases causes diffuse thinning. Permanents or hair straightening treatments applied improperly or too frequently are common causes of this disorder.

Skin diseases that affect the scalp can cause hair loss, but it usually requires a very severe scalp problem to produce significant hair loss. Starvation, sudden weight loss through dieting, iron deficiency caused by blood loss, diabetes, thyroid disease, and other disorders can cause metabolic hair loss, which is usually diffuse.

32 Allergies

William J. Davis, M.D.

INTRODUCTION

To the body, the world is a hostile environment, teeming with bacteria, viruses, and other microbes bent on invasion. These vast legions of outsiders crave the body as an ideal place to live, grow, and multiply, and it is only by maintaining an ever-vigilant defense that the body avoids being overwhelmed. This defense is the immune system—a complex network of organs, glands, and cells that either blocks the entry of invaders, or, if it fails, seeks them out and destroys them.

For many people, though, the immune system can be too sensitive, responding to foreign substances that are inert and harmless—such as pollen, house dust, and animal dander—or ones that are even beneficial, such as foods and drugs. Instead of ignoring these substances, the immune system reacts to them, provoking inflammation, irritation, and many other forms of distress and discomfort in particularly sensitive sites—the skin, nose, eyes, throat, lungs, and digestive system. This overreaction or hypersensitivity to otherwise harmless substances is an allergy.

Allergy has plagued mankind almost from the beginning of recorded time. Documented allergic reactions occurred in ancient Egypt and in other early civilizations.

Today allergy is a leading cause of both acute and chronic disease among children and adults. Indeed, allergy causes children to miss more days of school than any other illness. Billions of dollars are spent each year on treating the estimated 40 million allergy sufferers in the United States.

The term *allergy* was coined in 1906 by Austrian pediatrician Clemens von Pirquet. Taken from the Greek *allos* ("change in the original state"), it referred to the fact that for some people an encounter with an otherwise harmless substance produced an altered sensitivity. Repeated contact led to a "hypersensitive" response and allergic disease.

Allergic disorders are for the most part "immunological" diseases, for they involve a very specific interaction of the foreign substance (called an allergen) with a specific protein made by the body, called an antibody. The symptoms and severity of allergies are extremely diverse, depending largely on the allergen. The inhaled or respiratory allergens—airborne pollen, mold spores, animal dander, and house dust—cause runny nose, sneezing, and itching eyes. (Seasonal reactions to pollens, which afflict 15 million Americans, are known as rose fever, hayfever, or allergic rhinitis.) The contact or skin allergens—poison ivy, poison oak, poison sumac, cosmetics, perfumes, chemicals, and metals—give rise to redness, itching, swelling, and blistering. Reactions to ingested and injected allergens—foods, drugs, and insect venom—can break out on or in almost any part of the body, and range from sneezing, itching, and hives to diarrhea, nausea, and vomiting. In rare cases, the airways become so constricted and the blood pressure so lowered that the victim falls into life-threatening unconsciousness or collapse, a reaction called anaphylactic shock.

Each year several hundred Americans suffer fatal anaphylactic reactions, mainly from wasp, yellow jacket, and honeybee stings and penicillin injections. For sensitive people, certain foods, especially nuts and shellfish, but occasionally milk and eggs, can also produce anaphylaxis. Rarely, an allergy treatment injection itself may produce a similar emergency. Asthma, often caused by allergic reactions is a major, chronic disease, affecting 10 million Americans and causing an estimated 3,000 deaths annually. Though asthmatic attacks can be brought on by exercise, aspirin, and viral infections of the respiratory tract, inhaled allergens are a major cause, particularly in children. Children with hay fever may be prone to later development of asthma. (For more information about asthma, see page 646 in this chapter and page 461 in Chapter 22.)

Allergies can develop at any age, but new ones rarely show up past age 40. Food allergies and asthma usually appear in childhood while reactions to drugs are most common among young and middle-aged adults. Allergic symptoms generally diminish gradually with age and sometimes will disappear completely.

The tendency to develop an allergy is inherited: Those with allergic conditions almost always have a close relative with some type of hypersensitivity. All that is inherited is a predisposition to develop an allergy, not sensitivity to the same allergens that trouble the parents or siblings. No one knows why specific allergies develop.

Several misconceptions have developed about allergies and allergic disease. Among them:

- *Moving to another part of the country will end the problem.* Though it might be possible to escape certain pollens and molds by relocating, allergies to the new region's molds and pollens can always develop. In Denver, for example, the ragweed pollen count is about 75 percent below that in Chicago, but Denver has sagebrush pollen, to which ragweed sufferers are usually sensitive. And hayfever patients fleeing to Arizona to escape ragweed will probably be sensitive to that state's cottonwood, ash, and olive trees. Finally, of course, allergies to foods, drugs, chemicals, house dust, and animals have nothing to do with geography.

- *Allergy is psychosomatic—more in the head than in the body.* Even though emotional distress can occasionally contribute to allergic or asthmatic problems, feelings do not cause the underlying sensitivity. Allergies now have a scientifically established physical basis, and the way they work in the body is being understood in greater detail all the time.

- *Even if a child is allergic to animal fur, he can safely keep a short-haired pet.* It's not the coat or fur that causes allergy but the dander, the small scales of dead skin constantly being shed. The only harmless pets for the dander-sensitive are fish and reptiles.

- *Allergies aren't serious; after all, no one ever dies from one.* True, hayfever won't kill you, but reactions to some injected or ingested allergens can lead to fatal shock. Severe asthma attacks can also be fatal.

THE ROLE OF THE IMMUNE SYSTEM: A BRIEF PRIMER

TO UNDERSTAND ALLERGIES, one must first understand the immune system, whose misdirected response causes allergic reactions. The job of the immune system is to search for, recognize, and destroy germs and other dangerous invaders of the body, known as antigens. It does this by producing antibodies or special molecules to match and counteract each antigen.

The key soldiers of the immune system are the lymphocytes, the white blood cells manufactured by the millions in the bone marrow. The lymphocytes produce antibodies specific to each unwanted antigen. Circulating in the bloodstream, the antibodies attack the antigen, or protect the body's cells from invasion by the antigen, or make the invader palatable to roaming scavenger cells called macrophages. Antibody-producing lymphocytes or plasma cells are called B cells. (See figure 32.1.)

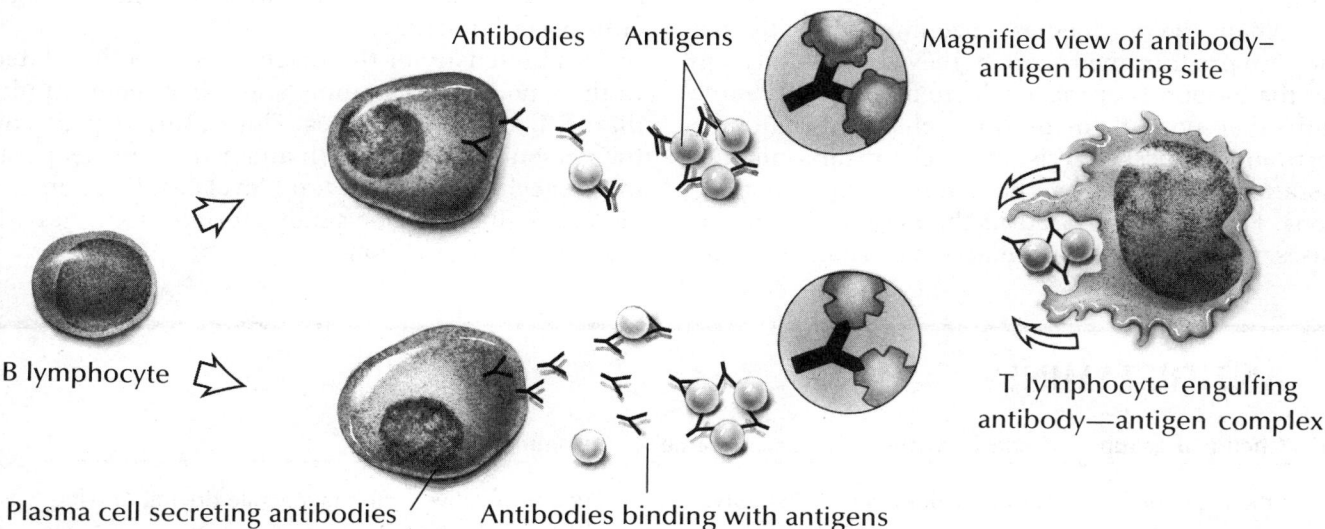

Figure 32.1. **What happens during an allergic reaction. When an allergen is present, the body responds by producing a B lymphocyte, which in turn stimulates the plasma cells to secrete an antibody against that particular antigen. These antibodies bind to the antigen, forming an antibody–antigen complex. This complex is then engulfed by a T lymphocyte.**

Scientists have discovered that some lymphocytes can attack antigens directly. These are processed by the thymus, a lymph gland in the chest, and are called T lymphocytes or T cells. T-cell immunity is called cell-mediated, while antibody immunity is known as humoral.

Whenever lymphocytes are activated, some of them become "memory" cells. Then the next time a person encounters that same antigen which earlier turned the lymphocytes on, the immune system "remembers" it and is primed to destroy it immediately. This is acquired immunity. (For a schematic illustration of the immune system, see page 428 in Chapter 21 on Infectious Diseases.)

Another way to acquire immunity is through immunization. Vaccines contain bits of an antigen that has been altered in some way so that it doesn't provoke a full-blown disease, but rather a weak immune response. This leaves a few memory cells standing guard to mount a quick, full-scale response should an invasion by the antigen occur.

The only natural immunity humans have lasts for a few months after birth. Babies are born with the same antibodies their mothers have, but these soon die out. A very small number of children are born not only lacking natural immunity but also the ability to acquire immunity. Some of these "immunodeficient" patients may live for years in germ-free rooms or "bubbles"; a few have been successfully treated with bone-marrow transplants.

Transient immune deficiencies can develop in the wake of diseases like leukemia and multiple myeloma, and even common viral infections. Certain drugs, radiation, stress, and malnutrition can also cause temporary, but nevertheless dangerously compromising, immunodeficiency.

Since we come into direct contact with so many substances every day, and ingest a wide variety of foods, drinks, and drugs, the immune system does not attack everything foreign to the body. Rather it selectively seeks out only those germs or other invaders that cause infection or that in some other way pose a potential hazard. Among people who inherit the potential for allergies, the immune system's selectivity breaks down, failing sometimes to distinguish between the benign and the dangerous, the good and the bad.

Antibodies charge down on harmless food, chemicals, pollen, or whatever else they misread and respond to it as an enemy. The immune system produces 5 main kinds of antibodies, but the principal one that participates in allergic reactions is immunoglobulin E, or IgE. Every individual has different IgE antibodies, and each allergic substance stimulates production of its own specific IgE. An IgE antibody made to respond to ragweed pollen, for example, will react only against ragweed and not oak tree or bluegrass or any other kind of pollen.

Among people with allergies, the IgE antibodies to their specific allergens exist by the millions, attached to either a type of circulating white blood cell (basophil) or to the so-called mast cells lining the respiratory tract, the gastrointestinal tract, and the skin.

When the antibodies encounter the allergen they are programmed against, they immediately signal the basophils or mast cells to unleash histamine and other potent "mediating" chemicals into the surrounding tissue. It is these chemicals—mainly histamine—that cause the familiar allergic reactions. Histamine released in the nose, eyes, and sinuses, for example, stimulates sneezing, a runny

nose, and itchy eyes; released in the lungs it causes narrowing and swelling of the lining of the airways and the secretion of thick mucus; in the skin, rashes and hives; and in the digestive system, stomach cramps and diarrhea.

The intensity of the reaction is directly related to the amount of histamine and other chemical mediators flooding the tissues. This in turn depends on the person's state of health and genetic makeup, or, more specifically, on his total level of IgE. Scientists believe a single major gene determines an individual's IgE concentrations.

ANTIHISTAMINES

Chemical group	Generic name	Brand name	Comments
Ethanolamine	Diphenhydramine	Benadryl	Potent sedative; don't take while driving or using heavy machinery
	Carbinoxamine	In Rondec	Less drowsiness than with Benadryl; also contains decongestent
	Clemastine	Tavist	Less drowsiness than with Benadryl
Ethylenediamine	Tripelenamine	Pyribenzamine	Drowsiness and possible gastrointestinal upset
Piprazine	Hydroxizine	Atarax	Used mainly for skin problems (itching, hives); causes drowsiness
Piperidine	Cyproheptadine	Periactin	Mainly for skin conditions
Phenothiazine	Promethazine	Phenergan	Heaviest sedative of any on this list, never drive after taking
	Methdilazine	Tacaryl	Somewhat less sedation than with Phenergan

The following are over-the-counter drugs that were formerly available only by prescription. They are relatively potent.

Chemical group	Generic name	Brand name	Comments
Alkylamine	Chlorpheniramine	Chlortrimeton	
	Brompheniramine	Dimetane	
	Triprolidine	In Actifed	Contains decongestant

EVALUATING ALLERGIES

SNEEZING, WHEEZING, scratching, itching, and a host of other annoying symptoms eventually bring the patient to the physician for evaluation. The physician will do 3 things—take a medical history, do a physical examination, and run various laboratory and allergy tests.

Interviewing the patient, or history-taking as physicians call it, is one of the most sophisticated and important investigation techniques in medicine today. It has no substitute. The patient must have

adequate time to explain all his or her symptoms and the doctor must take the time to ask probing questions so as to define the medical problem as specifically as possible. In an allergy evaluation, the questions asked and information obtained contribute roughly 80 percent to the solution. The questions will cover these areas:

● The chief complaint

● Any present illness

- Past medical problems
- Family medical history
- Environmental history (place of work, whether pets are kept at home, what trees are in the yard, etc.)
- Food history (everything eaten or drunk during snacks and meals)
- Social and emotional condition—now and in the past

The physical examination will include a close look at the skin, eyes, nose, ears, lungs, and abdomen. Diagnostic tests may include blood counts, nasal smears, x-rays, pulmonary function tests, and various cultures to test for the presence of infectious agents such as bacteria.

Specific allergy tests may include bronchial challenge (special breathing), lab tests such as the radioallergosorbent test (RAST), and skin tests. The latter are the basis for most diagnoses because they are more accurate and comprehensive than lab tests. However, a positive skin test is not proof that an allergy exists or that the allergen is clinically relevant, i.e., that it causes a significant reaction. Conversely, a negative skin test does not always mean the substance causes no allergic problem. So a skin test result must be interpreted cautiously and in conjunction with the patient's medical history. The most reliable skin tests are those for airborne substances such as dust, pollens, molds, etc. The results of food skin tests are the most equivocal.

PRINCIPLES OF TREATMENT

THE MOST COMMON THERAPY is allergy "shots." Injections in gradually increasing amounts of a patient's known allergens stimulates the production of a neutralizing antibody that blocks the troublesome IgE's interaction with the allergen and thereby prevents or curbs the release of histamine and other troublesome chemicals within the body. The injections, however, don't cure allergies; they simply make the patient less sensitive to them. There is no cure, although symptoms can be controlled to the point that they disappear, allowing a person with allergies to lead a normal life.

There are also medications that relieve the symptoms of allergy, the principal one being antihistamines. (The various drug therapies are discussed with each allergic condition.) Finally, there is environmental control: minimizing or eliminating the patient's contact with any substance that initiates or aggravates allergic reactions. The child allergic to down and feathers should use a pillow with synthetic stuffing, for example. The woman whose asthma is aggravated by dander should get rid of her cats, painful as it may be. To lessen indoor pollutants, the heating system may have to be changed and humidifiers added.

SKIN ALLERGIES

Atopic Dermatitis

Principally a disorder of infancy and childhood, atopic dermatitis (eczema) is characterized by extreme itching; persistent, frantic scratching; and thickening of the skin. Although the specific cause of eczema remains unknown, all patients have a highly sensitive skin susceptible to dermatitis. They also suffer from abnormal sweating, decreased skin-oil production, and a low itch threshold; things like heat, abrasions, and psychological tension can set them to scratching.

Up to 3 percent of infants develop eczema. Most come from families prone to allergy and suffer from other allergic disorders such as hayfever and asthma. Children usually outgrow the disorder by age 6, with delayed improvement setting in at puberty.

Successful treatment depends on breaking the itch-scratch-itch cycle. The skin should be kept moist and lubricated with creams and lotions. A pH-neutral soap such as Dove should be used for bathing, which should be done quickly about 3 times weekly. If there is still scratching, the physician will probably prescribe the vigorous use of antihistamines, especially hydroxizine (Atarax) and diphenhydramine (Benadryl).

When the skin is oozing, wet dressings may provide some relief. Coal-tar ointments are effective with thickened, chronic eczema (lichenification). The keystone of topical therapy is application of corticosteroid creams and ointments to the skin.

Contact Dermatitis

This is an inflammation of the skin caused by an irritant, such as a strong acid or alkali, or by an allergy. In contrast to respiratory allergy, contact dermatitis is a delayed-type hypersensitivity produced by the T cells and not by IgE antibody. Studies show that the 6 most common causes of the condition are (1) poison ivy, oak, and sumac; (2) paraphenylenediamine used in hair and fur dye, leather, rubber, and printing; (3) nickel compounds; (4) rubber compounds; (5) ethylenediamine—a preservative in creams and ophthalmic solutions; and (6) dichromates used in textile ink, paints, and leather processing. (Also see Chapter 31 on Skin Diseases, page 623.)

Plants. About half of all people are allergic to poison ivy, oak, and sumac, with reactions ranging from slight to severe. The offending agent in all 3 plants is an oily resin called urushiol that can be picked up either directly by accidental rubbing or indirectly by touching clothing or pets that have come in contact with it. It takes only a tiny amount to provoke a reaction. But urushiol must actually be touched to cause a problem; it's a myth that a rash can result from just being near poison ivy. Also contrary to popular belief, neither washing nor scratching the rash and blisters will spread the outbreak; there is no urushiol in the blister fluid.

It usually takes 1 or 2 days for the skin reaction to poison ivy to begin, but in the highly sensitive it may show up within only 4 hours. At first, the exposed skin becomes red and then bumps and blisters arise, usually accompanied by itching and swelling. The rash peaks at about 5 days and will disappear within 1 or 2 weeks even without treatment. Outbreaks rarely occur on the scalp, palms, or soles. Scratching the blisters risks introducing bacteria into the open sores, causing secondary infection.

The desert plant heliotrope, characterized by bluish-purple flowers on a stem that coils into the shape of a fiddle neck, can also cause contact dermatitis. Skin rashes are usually confined to the ankles and legs of persons walking through desert landscapes in the Southwest. The leaf and the pollen of the ragweed is another, though infrequent, cause of skin rashes; both contain a resin that dissolves in the natural oil of the skin. Other plants associated with skin rashes are sagebrush, wormwood, daisies, tulips, and chrysanthemums. A few people even have reactions to handling such foods as oranges, limes, celery, and potatoes.

If the offending oils from poison ivy and the other plants can be washed off within 5 minutes of contact, a reaction may well be prevented. Washing after that won't be protective but it at least will contain the area of involvement. Not only the exposed skin but also clothes should be washed with strong laundry soap and water as soon as possible. Avoid using rubbing alcohol; it tends to make the rash worse.

Itching can be relieved with calamine lotion, a poultice of baking soda or Epsom salts, or an over-the-counter ointment containing hydrocortisone. Severe cases, or outbreaks on the face or genitals, may require prescription cortisone ointments, antihistamines, and in some cases oral cortisone.

There is no practical way to desensitize the average person against poison ivy and its relatives, so avoidance is essential. Poison oak is more shrublike and its leaves are shaped somewhat like those of oak trees. It grows mainly on the West Coast and in the Southeast. Poison sumac, which favors swampy habitats, is a small 5-foot tree that produces telltale clusters of green berries. Harmless sumacs have red, upright berry clusters.

Cosmetics. Cosmetics in general are quite safe, and the proportion of users who develop allergic reactions is small. For susceptible people, the most common allergens are hair dye, eye shadow and eye makeup, lipstick, and nail polish. Less frequently, antiperspirants, perfumes, and colognes cause reactions.

Because the skin reaction—usually rash and inflammation—can be mistaken for other dermatologic conditions, many doctors will do patch tests. These involve applying suspected allergens to the skin, covering them, and waiting 2 days to see if a reaction occurs. Patch tests are the best single means of confirming a cosmetic as an allergen.

When allergy is suspected or confirmed, the use of cosmetics made with "hypoallergenic" ingredients is an alternative. A list of firms that make truly nonallergenic cosmetics is available without charge from the Asthma & Allergy Foundation of America in Bethesda, Maryland.

Chemicals and Metals. Formaldehyde, chlorine, phenol or carbolic acid, the various forms of alcohol, and other chemicals, and metals such as chrome, nickel, mercury, and beryllium can cause skin reactions among those who have developed a sensitivity to them after years of low-level exposure.

Most often, the rash—accompanied by itching and swelling—will break out within 24 to 48 hours of contacting the irritant material. It will then build in severity for up to a week and gradually go away. Certain allergens, such as film developers and rubber chemicals, can cause hives (or urticaria) instead of the classic red rash and blisters. Hives are itching, sometimes burning, wheals or blotches.

Most allergy-generating exposure to chemicals and metals occurs in certain industrial occupations, but because the substances are used in many household products—ranging from furniture to insecticides and antifreeze to nylon—sensitivity can build up in the home as well. Of all the offending chemicals, formaldehyde is by far the most ubiquitous. A highly active compound that exists in nature as a gas, it has little odor but can cause a burning sensation in the eyes and mucous membranes. It is found in foam insulation, particle board or wallboard (used in construction and in nearly all furniture), rugs, carpets, permanent-press clothing, waxes, dyes, polishes, plaster, and paper. A by-product of gasoline combustion, it also exists in the atmosphere as a pollutant.

Not surprisingly, specific chemical and metal allergens can be difficult or even impossible to pin down. The physician will have to ask detailed questions about work and leisure activities and do careful examinations of the rash so as not to mistake it for other skin disorders. The best means of confirming a suspected allergen is with a patch test. A tiny amount of the allergen is placed on the skin and left covered for 2 days to see if a reaction occurs.

The treatment for all types of contact dermatitis—essentially the same as that for poison ivy (see page 121)—can only somewhat alleviate the symptoms, so the best strategy is avoidance. In the case of formaldehyde, this may not be feasible, but at least protective steps can be taken. New permanent-press clothing should be washed several times before use; products made with particle board should be coated with a sealant, and homes insulated with formaldehyde foam should be avoided.

Drugs. Aspirin and ampicillin often cause skin rashes, but these are not usually true allergic reactions (see page 648). Agents that provoke actual contact dermatitis because of an allergic response are cocaine, novocaine, and other local anesthetics; penicillin; neomycin; streptomycin; and the sulfa drugs. Reactions are largely confined to surgeons, dentists, and workers who manufacture the drugs.

Urticaria and Angioedema

Urticaria, or hives, is an itchy eruption characterized by raised, reddened, swollen welts of various sizes which come and go. Welts may last for only a few minutes or for several days and typically recur in crops or bunches. Angioedema is a deeper swelling, especially of the face (eyes and lips), but often involving the hands and feet as well. More than 20 percent of us will have hives sometime during our lifetime.

Body chemicals released during an allergic reaction—mainly histamine—precipitate these conditions, but the cause of the reaction itself remains mysterious for most victims. The allergist and dermatologist frequently consult to try to pinpoint a culprit. The cause can be just about anything: foods, drugs, pollen and other inhalant allergens, physical agents, insect bites, infections, underlying illness, heredity, and even psychic factors.

Among foods, berries, fish, shellfish, nuts, eggs, and milk are usually incriminated. Penicillin and aspirin are the chief drug offenders while pollens and animal dander are the standard inhalant causes. Even heat, light, and cold can cause outbreaks.

In evaluating urticaria, a detailed history and a 2- to 4-week diary are crucial. Treatment can be with antihistamines, epinephrine, terbutaline, cimetidine, cromolyn, and rarely, oral cortisone.

A rare hereditary form of hives, called hereditary angioedema (HAE), exists as a disorder of a blood protein that is part of the immune system. It causes *nonitchy* swelling and often includes cramping abdominal pain and diarrhea. The condition can be dangerous if the throat swells (laryngeal edema). Treatment is with specialized hormones.

Physical Reactions

Some people are allergic to physical stimuli such as heat, cold, pressure, light, and sun rays. They break out in hives and suffer other reactions. Those susceptible to physical allergy often have unusually sensitive skin—just hand stroking will cause them to break out in hives. If a blunt object is rubbed on them, a swelling or "wheal" response begins within minutes; a game of tic-tac-toe is not out of the question on such "dermagraphic" skin.

Some examples of physical allergy are these: Pressure on the hands or feet can cause swelling; vigorous exercise, emotional stress, or even a hot shower can provoke tiny hives (called cholinergic urticaria); and cold urticaria can develop following rewarming of body parts exposed to cold air. The treatment of most physical allergies is a strong antihistamine.

There is no treatment, however, for sun-induced (solar) urticaria. Typically, this strikes people in their thirties and forties after about 30 minutes of exposure. Perfumes and even sunscreens themselves can sometimes precipitate the reaction, and so can a wide variety of drugs—antibiotics, antifungals, antihistamines, diuretics, hypoglycemics, and tranquilizers.

RESPIRATORY ALLERGIES

Allergic Rhinitis—Pollen

To reproduce by cross-pollination, plants make male germ cells called pollen. Those produced by flowers and taxied from one plant to another by bees are relatively large, waxy, and generally harmless to people. But the tiny, light, dry pollens thrown off in prodigious quantities by weeds, grasses, and trees—and carried on wind currents for up to 400 miles—are nasty pests to the estimated 20 million Americans with hayfever (as well as to most asthma victims). When these people breathe in airborne pollen, it provokes the IgE antibodies to release histamine (see page 638), which in turn causes inflammation and swelling of the fragile lining of the nose, sinuses, eyelids, and surface layer of the eyes (conjunctiva). The result: a watery nasal discharge, violent sneezing, runny eyes, nasal congestion, and an itching sensation in the nose and throat, and on the roof of the mouth. Some ultra-sensitive people sneeze 10 to 50 times in a row several times a day, becoming so exhausted they cannot work.

Pollen allergy is seasonal, following the cycles of nature according to local geography. Trees generally shed pollen in the spring, grasses in the early summer, and ragweed—the chief irritant east of the Rocky Mountains—in the late summer. In warm, southern states this means 8 or 9 months of pollen exposure a year.

After ragweed, the most significant sources of allergic weed pollen are sagebrush, redroot pigweed, careless weed, spiny amaranth, Russian thistle or tumbleweed, burning bush, and English plantain. Next to weeds in producing troublesome pollen are grasses, most notably timothy, redtop, Bermuda, orchard, sweet vernal, rye, and some bluegrasses. As for trees, almost every popular variety is a culprit, including elm, maple, oak, ash, birch, poplar, pecan, cottonwood, and mountain cedar.

Most airborne pollen is so small it's invisible—no bigger around than the width of a hair. It can enter houses through tiny cracks, screens, even window air-conditioners. One plant can generate a million pollen grains, and counts as low as 20 (grains per cubic meter of air) can provoke allergic reactions. Counts drop on rainy days and soar on hot, sunny, windy days.

Pollen counts announced on radio stations or printed in newspapers, while they may be accurate for the exact time and spot when they were taken, are practically meaningless. The amount of pollen in the air varies mile to mile and hour to hour, depending on local vegetation, wind direction and velocity, and other weather conditions. And different sampling methods produce different counts.

Other Inhalant Allergies

Molds. These simple microscopic fungi abound in the environment living in the soil and on food, plants, leather, dead leaves, and other organic matter. Though they can be destructive, causing food to spoil or clothes to mildew, they're also beneficial, speeding decay of garbage and fallen trees, helping to make cheese, and fertilizing gardens. One of the best known molds is in fact a lifesaver—penicillin, which grows on bread.

Molds reproduce by developing and shedding spores, or seeds, and these spores can cause hayfeverlike symptoms in susceptible people (strictly speaking, hayfever refers only to pollen allergy). Like pollen, mold spores are borne by the wind and predominate in the summer and early fall. But molds thrive year-round in warm climates, causing allergy at least 9 months per year in most of the South and Southwest. Indoors, they also shed spores year-round, living in damp cellars, mattresses, stuffed furniture, stuffed animals, fibers, wood, and even wallpaper. Generally speaking, though, it requires exposure to dry soil or composting plant debris and such activities as cutting grass, harvesting crops, or walking through tall vegetation to provoke an allergic reaction. Because of their occupations, however, some susceptible people—farmers, gardeners, botanists, grain-mill workers, furniture repairers, and handlers of fruit and vegetables—are plagued by repeat attacks.

Most mold allergy is caused by the spores of *Alternaria* and *Hormodendrum*, which flourish in the Midwest and grow least in dry regions. The usual indoor offenders are *Aspergillus*, *Penicillium*, *Mucor*, and *Rhizopus*.

It's impossible to avoid mold spores but exposure can be minimized. Old, moldy, or mildewed books, furniture, and bedding should be discarded, and damp basements should be dried with dehumidifiers. Visible mold growths on basement and bathroom walls should be attacked with disinfectant sprays or liquids. Mold-proof paint can be used in place of wallpaper, and synthetic materials should be used for furniture and bedding.

Animal Dander. Dander, or the scales shed from the skin, hair, and feathers of birds and animals, is a significant source of year-round allergy. In most cases, anyone allergic to pollen or molds is or will become sensitive to dander. This creates a wrenching dilemma for cat, dog, and bird lovers, because allergists say the only acceptable pets for the dander-sensitive are fish and reptiles. Unfortunately, bathing dogs frequently doesn't help enough to matter. Down-stuffed pillows, quilts, and coats should also be removed. For some dander-susceptible people, wool is also a problem; they should avoid clothing, bedding, or carpeting made with significant amounts of it.

Dust. Although house dust harbors pollen, mold spores, and animal dander, its principal allergen is thought to be mites, microscopic spiderlike insects found throughout the world. Mites live only during the warm months but reactions of those allergic to them are usually worse in winter. This may be because after summer the mites die and disintegrate into fragments, which can reach the respiratory tract more easily than intact mites.

Dust also contains disintegrated stuffing materials from pillows, mattresses, toys, and furniture, as well as bits of fibers from draperies, blankets, and carpets. The breakdown of these materials from prolonged use seems to make them irritants to people with allergic rhinitis, hayfever, and asthma.

Dust-proofing should start in the most frequently occupied room of the house, the bedroom. The room should be rather spartan, with no upholstered furniture, carpeting, Venetian blinds, bookshelves, or stuffed animals. Avoid bunk beds and canopy beds, and enclose mattresses, box springs, and pillows with allergen-proof coverings. Wet-dust the entire room daily.

In the rest of the house, frequent wet-dusting is also advised, along with weekly washing of scatter rugs and furniture covers. If the allergic person does the cleaning, he or she should wear a disposable surgical mask covering the mouth and nose.

Ideally, the house should have a centralized system that heats, humidifies, cools, and filters the air throughout. The level of dust can be further reduced by attaching various air purifiers to the central unit. There are also portable air-purifying machines that can be used in the bedroom, but allergy sufferers should beware of exaggerated claims for these appliances.

Miscellaneous Irritants. There are scores of other substances that exacerbate allergic reactions once they enter the respiratory tract. These include smoke, mists, and fumes from commercial and industrial activities; smoke from pipes, cigars, and cigarettes; cosmetic powder and baby powder; and some powdered laundry detergents. People allergic to pollen, mold spores, and dust will more than

likely be sensitive to one or more of these irritants, whereas people who have none of the major inhalant allergies are probably not bothered. No one with any inhalant allergy should smoke or spend much time in an environment contaminated with tobacco smoke.

Diagnosing Inhalant Allergies

Pinpointing specific allergies—sufferers usually have more than one—is no simple task. Allergists say that 2 of 10 allergies become sort of a "wastebasket diagnosis" in which diverse, vague symptoms are attributed to all kinds of allergies.

Careful notation of the time of an allergic reaction is the best starting point on the path to a correct diagnosis. For example, if a person has respiratory symptoms at the same time each year, then certain pollens or molds, depending upon geography, are suspect. Or if symptoms flare only when visiting certain people's homes, then an animal allergy could be at work. For these reasons, physicians may ask patients to keep a diary of their reactions.

The next step will probably be a skin test, in which tiny amounts of suspected allergens are applied to the skin and the reaction is observed. Usually 6 to 12 substances are tested at the same time, each injected separately into the uppermost layer of the upper arm skin. Within 10 to 20 minutes, if any of the substances are allergenic, they will cause a pale bump, like a hive or mosquito bite, surrounded by an angry red halo (erythema). The bigger and more ragged-edged the bump, the greater the degree of allergic reaction, but not always.

Unfortunately, skin tests are far from foolproof. Not all substances to which a person shows an allergic reaction on a test will actually produce symptoms in the course of natural exposure. (This "false positive" result plagues many medical tests.) And if too much of the allergen is injected, almost anyone will seem to be allergic to it. Moreover, a few people react to the very solvent used to prepare the test solution, or just to the injection itself.

Nor are skin tests always 100 percent safe. In rare cases, even the tiny amount of allergen being tested can trigger a systemic reaction by the entire body, rather than just a local reaction at the injection site. Unless a drug called epinephrine is administered promptly, the reaction may result in sneezing, hives, wheezing, and very rarely, even in shock.

Because of the problems of the skin test, scientists have been searching for an alternative, but nothing superior or even equal to it has turned up. The best new diagnostic technique is a simple blood test called radioallergosorbent test (RAST) that determines how much of a specific kind of IgE antibody the patient carries. But the blood sample must be sent off to a special laboratory and fewer allergenic substances can be tested than with skin challenges. RAST is also less sensitive, but it is safer. Research on it is continuing.

Treatment

No respiratory allergy can be cured but its miseries can be greatly lessened. The first line of attack is avoiding the allergen as much as possible; steps have already been outlined. If controlling the environment isn't feasible, antihistamines and decongestants might adequately lessen the symptoms. Antihistamines are more effective when given prophylactically or at the first sign of an attack; some are sold over the counter, but the more potent ones can be obtained only with a prescription. (See box on page 640.) The more effective they are, though, the greater their chances of causing drowsiness, dry mouth, and blurred vision. (Antihistamines should not be taken by persons with glaucoma.) There are also effective nasal sprays. Cromolyn (brand-named Nasalcrom) prevents the mast cells in the nose from releasing histamine. The nasal steroids—beclomethasone (Beconase and Vancenase) and flunisolide (Nasalide) are anti-inflammatories that reduce the mucosal damage caused by allergic reactions.

The next step up in drug therapy is the oral steroids, the powerful anti-inflammatory agents that chemically resemble hormones. These drugs can be dramatically effective but they cannot be used at high doses or for very long without creating a host of serious side effects.

For long-term alleviation, there are "allergy shots," a form of immunotherapy or desensitization that involves the periodic injection of small amounts of the confirmed allergens over the course of several years. Simply put, the injections make the immune system more tolerant of the allergen. Instead of producing the troublesome IgE antibodies, the body makes a protective blocking antibody which combines with the allergen to block the release of histamine and other bothersome chemicals.

Each offending allergen has its own preparation, but several allergens can be combined in one shot. Weekly dosages begin very small and are gradually increased, but not to the point where they actually provoke allergic symptoms. It can take anywhere from 12 weeks (in the case of ragweed allergy) to 2 or 3 years to attain a maximum dose of immunization. After that, maintenance shots are given every 2 to 6 weeks, sometimes for many years. Timing is important for seasonal pollen and mold allergies. Shots should be planned so that the maximum dosage will be reached by hayfever season.

Allergy shots work well for many people—6 million Americans alone get them—but they have several drawbacks. For one thing, they are inconvenient and expensive, requiring repeated visits to a physician over an indefinite period. The visits can be long since many doctors ask patients to remain in the office for up to 20 minutes after the shots to observe the reaction (in very rare instances, generalized reactions can occur). Another drawback is that for some people allergy shots simply don't work, or they don't work any better than fake injections or placebos.

ASTHMA

THE CAUSE OF ASTHMA in most children and many adults is allergy, particularly to pollen, mold spores, animal dander, and house dust. The condition, usually inherited and first manifested in childhood, is a chronic, noncontagious disease of the lungs in which breathing becomes difficult because of obstruction of air in the bronchial tubes. Air flowing through the narrowed tubes produces the classic symptom of wheezing. Another near-universal sign is the coughing up of excess mucus (sputum).

Nearly 10 million Americans have asthma, and it along with the other allergic disorders are the leading cause of chronic illness among children. A large proportion of youngsters outgrow the condition, but no one knows exactly how many.

As in other allergic diseases, allergens stimulate IgE antibodies to produce histamine and other powerful chemical mediators. (See page 638.) It is the site of the chemical reactions—in the lungs—that distinguishes asthma. The powerful chemicals released by the antibodies swell the lining and tighten the muscles of the airways, and step up the production of mucus.

Asthma can also be caused or exacerbated by respiratory infections, exercise, and aspirin and other anti-inflammatory drugs. Emotional distress has a much smaller role than originally thought.

In persons with allergic asthma, the treatment is similar to that for the other forms of allergy: avoidance of the allergen, desensitization with allergy shots, and in severe cases, occasional steroid therapy. In addition, expectorants and bronchodilators are often prescribed. There is one drug that can prevent some asthma attacks, but there is no cure for the disease. For a fuller discussion of asthma, see Chapter 22 on Respiratory Diseases and Lung Health (page 461).

FOOD ALLERGIES

PROBABLY MORE MISGUIDED apprehension and misinformation surround food allergies than any other type of allergic disease. The result is that many people who think they're sensitive to certain foods actually aren't.

One common source of confusion is that a bad reaction to food can be caused by factors other than allergy: contamination by a toxin-producing bacteria, irritable bowel syndrome, stress, an inability to digest a particular substance, such as lactose in milk or gluten in wheat (called food intolerance). Some people can even psychologically talk themselves into allergiclike reactions. Another cause of misdiagnosis: popular books that blame foods for conditions they couldn't cause—fatigue, nervousness, painful menstrual cramps, and bedwetting, to mention only some.

Food intolerance and food allergy are often confused but are quite distinct: those with intolerance lack certain enzymes needed for digestion, while those with allergy have an antibody response. The enzyme lactase helps digest one of the sugars in milk, and when it's absent the undigested milk fraction causes abdominal cramps and diarrhea—clearly not an allergic reaction. Most peoples of the world, except those from northern Europe or descended from northern Europeans, cannot tolerate milk or any product to which milk or milk solids have been added. (Many lactose-intolerant people can, however, consume hard cheeses and cultured dairy products like yogurt and sour cream, in which much of the lactose is predigested.) A blood test can confirm lactose intolerance.

Another common intolerance is for the glutamate in the food additive monosodium glutamate (MSG). Susceptible people experience dizziness, sweating, ringing in the ears, and a feeling of faintness shortly after eating MSG-laden foods. Because so many Chinese dishes call for MSG, the reaction is sometimes called Chinese restaurant syndrome.

Some people have mild intolerance to vegetables—especially peas and broccoli, which cause intestinal gas. Others experience indigestion and diarrhea when they consume mushrooms and certain wines.

A true food allergy produces a set of specific allergic symptoms, and this relationship can be repeatedly demonstrated. Classic symptoms are abdominal pain, diarrhea, nausea or vomiting, cramps, hives, eczema, swelling of the eyes, lips, face, and tongue, and occasionally, hayfeverlike reactions. Foods most often incriminated include milk, eggs, nuts, fish or shellfish, chocolate, wheat, corn, berries, peas, beans, and gum arabic, a thickener used in processed foods.

A few foods provoke a reaction almost as soon as they're put in the mouth and thus are easy to identify and eliminate from the diet. Most, though, are difficult to pinpoint, not only because of their delayed reaction but because some provoke reactions only at certain times or in certain quantities or with a certain frequency of consumption. Degree of cooking also modifies the allergic response, and additives—mainly vegetable gum thickeners and yellow food dye No. 5—can sometimes be the culprits instead of the food itself.

An accurate diagnosis of a food allergy can be a time-consuming matter but it's worth the trouble considering the consequences of a mistaken conclusion. Special diets are often expensive, inconvenient to obtain, and difficult to prepare, especially if the allergen is milk, eggs, or wheat, all common ingredients in prepared foods. The patient may have to stay on an exclusion diet for life.

One method of self-diagnosis is by a process of elimination. All but a few foods are avoided, and after a week or so the abandoned items are added back to the diet one by one. Or if certain foods are already strongly suspected, they are dropped for at least a week and then added back one at a time in excess quantity to see if a reaction occurs.

Physicians will usually begin their diagnostic sleuthing with a detailed questioning of the patient's diet and its relationship to the complaints. Some doctors will request that the patient keep a careful diary of the times, contents, and reactions to every meal, snack, and drink over a period of several weeks.

This history-taking will sometimes be supplemented with skin or blood tests, but these have limited value. Many people will have positive reactions but fail to show reactions when they actually consume the suspected food. In one study, 60 percent of children whose skin tests indicated certain food allergies turned out to be tolerant of the foods when clinically tested for allergic response. Conversely, because the extracts used in the skin tests tend to lose potency quickly, many people won't show test reactions to foods they are actually sensitive to.

One valuable but complicated way to confirm a food as an allergen is for the doctor to challenge the patient with that food in a "double-blind" fashion in which neither he nor the patient knows whether the suspect item has really been administered (a nurse or other third party keeps track of things). This is done by making a dried preparation of the food and enclosing it in opaque capsules. If the patient reacts to capsules with the test food but not to the blanks—

and does so more than once—this confirms the food is allergenic.

Once proved provocative, a food should be avoided in all forms for at least 6 months. A small amount may then be tried; if nothing happens, the food can be eaten, but only on occasion, because the allergy may reappear at any time. Young children found to have food allergies should be retested every 3 or 6 months since they often outgrow them.

Sometimes, despite the best efforts of both doctor and patient, the cause of a suspected food allergy can never be found. In such cases, the doctor may prescribe antihistamines and other drugs to relieve the symptoms. No drug is curative or preventive. Many food allergies, however, disappear as the patient grows older.

DRUG ALLERGIES

PRACTICALLY ANY MEDICINE can cause an allergic reaction, but penicillin—including relatives like ampicillin—is the major offender. Other medications people are sensitive to include the sulfa drugs, barbiturates, anticonvulsants, insulin, local anesthetics, and contrast dyes used in x-ray studies. The latter are injected into the blood vessels to help outline organs in the x-ray film. Among about 3 percent of patients, these dyes, which contain the allergen organic iodine, cause reactions such as hives, itching, asthmatic attacks, and even shock.

About 1 million Americans suffer reactions to aspirin that mimic allergic response but involve no truly immunologic mechanism. Nearly 1 out of 4 people with chronic hives, for example, see their condition worsen after taking aspirin. And a small percentage of asthmatics will suffer acute bronchospasm.

Ampicillin is another drug that produces a pseudoallergenic response. In a large number of people treated with the widely prescribed antibiotic, a nonallergic skin rash breaks out that may be mistaken for allergic dermatitis.

Ironically, skin rash is the most common truly allergic response to a drug. Hives is the second. The penicillins can stimulate both, as well as a reaction delayed for up to 3 weeks called serum sickness, which is characterized by fever, joint symptoms, skin eruption, and swelling of the lymph glands. In rare cases, penicillin, streptomycin, insulin, and tetracycline—like the injected contrast dyes—can cause shock.

Because these drugs are so important in modern medicine, people with known allergies are sometimes successfully induced to tolerate them. The drug is given in slowly increasing doses until therapeutic levels are reached. In some patients, the immune system comes to tolerate the drug permanently. Another strategy is to give antihistamines and steroids before and along with the drug, thereby attenuating the reaction.

In the case of penicillin, skin testing can predict sensitivity in nearly all patients. Skin testing can also forewarn of allergy to insulin and horse serum, which was formerly used in some vaccines. But for almost all other drugs, skin testing is ineffective or dangerous.

That leaves experience as the only means of uncovering sensitivity to most drugs. In this kind of discovery process, the doctor relies strongly on the patient's accurate and detailed recall about the drug taken—when, how much, the length of time before symptoms appeared, and what other medications were in use at the time. Too often patients fail to report use of laxatives, nose drops, tonics, cold remedies, vitamins, ointments, birth control pills, douches, suppositories, aspirin, antacids, and other products purchased off the drugstore shelf because they don't consider them "drugs." Once a person knows he has an allergy to a drug, he should always pass that information along to a new physician during the first visit. (For more information, see Chapter 40 on Proper Use of Drugs, page 772.)

INSECT ALLERGIES

FOR MOST PEOPLE, the bite or sting of a bee, wasp, ant, mosquito, or other angry insect causes momentary pain followed by redness, irritation, and itching around the wound for a few hours. For people allergic to insects, the results are a lot more discomforting, and sometimes even dangerous. Their skin breaks out in hives, the eyes itch, the chest and throat feel constricted, a dry cough comes on, and there's often nausea, abdominal pain, vomiting, and dizziness. In the highly sensitive, breathing becomes difficult, speech slurred, and a sense of confusion and impending disaster may take over. In a few, rare cases, the victim will turn blue, lose control of urination, and fall into life-threatening unconsciousness or shock within as little as 10 minutes.

Unfortunately, there's no way in advance to know which people will have the more worrisome allergic reactions. Allergy to insects exists as often among people who have no other allergies as among those who do. Even experience from past stings is no sure predictor: about half the victims of sting may have an entirely normal response on one occasion but suffer a serious allergic reaction the next time.

People are not allergic to insects per se—only to their venom. Toxic components of the venom cause the irritating local reactions that everyone gets. It's the venom's other chemicals, which provoke histamine release, that provoke allergic responses. In the United States, only a few stinging insects—honeybees, bumblebees, wasps, hornets, yellow jackets, ants—cause serious allergic reactions. Of these 6, reactions to the yellow jacket and the honeybee are the most common. Mild reactions can be caused by biting flies, mosquitoes, ticks, and a few spiders.

A nasty newcomer to the list of troublesome insects is the fire ant. Introduced accidentally many years ago in Alabama, it has spread to at least a dozen southern states and seems impossible to contain. The ant actually bites first, and then, hanging on like a bulldog, swivels about, stinging repeatedly. The potent venom is a very real hazard to those allergic to it, capable of causing severe systemic (throughout the body) reactions.

A reaction to an insect sting can be immediate or delayed. In most cases, the sooner the reaction starts the more severe it will be. Systemic responses usually begin in 10 to 20 minutes. Delayed reactions can occur several hours to several days later, producing a form of serum sickness—painful joints, fever, hives, and swollen lymph glands. Both immediate and delayed reactions can occur in the same person following a single sting.

Diagnosis

If the offending insect is not available, the doctor may be able to identify the culprit by asking about its appearance, mode of movement, and the time of day and the place where the sting occurred. Some insects leave telltale mouthparts or a stinger in the skin, and others, such as the fire ant, make characteristic patterns of multiple bites.

A diagnosis can often be confirmed with a skin test, but it can't be given until a few weeks after the sting, by which time the skin has replenished its supply of IgE antibodies used up during the allergic reaction. The arm is the usual site for the test because a tourniquet can be applied to impede absorption of the tiny venom sample if the patient reacts too strongly to it.

A relatively new diagnostic technique is the blood test called RAST. A blood sample is taken and sent to a lab where it is exposed to specially prepared venom from the suspected insect. The test reveals whether the patient produces an IgE antibody in response to the venom.

Treatment

The first goal is to keep the amount of venom in the blood as low as possible. Honeybees leave their stinger in the skin, so it should be removed immediately. If the sting is on the arm or leg, a tourniquet should be applied above it and loosened briefly every 10 minutes so that circulation isn't impaired. A cold pack will help reduce pain and swelling.

A serious response should be treated as an emergency. A double dose of antihistamine will decrease the severity of the reaction, but *the most effective treatment is an injection of adrenaline or epinephrine.* In acute shock or airway closure, intravenous fluids, oxygen, and a surgical opening in the windpipe (tracheotomy) may be necessary. Steroids, which act more slowly than adrenaline, may be given for persistent swelling and hives.

For people with a known serious insect allergy, physicians recommend 2 precautionary measures. First, they should wear a Medic Alert identification bracelet or tag or carry information on a wallet card stating the specific allergy. Second, they should carry an emergency kit (available only by prescription) containing epinephrine in a syringe ready for injection, antihistamine tablets, a tourniquet, and alcohol swabs. The kit is not intended to replace medical help, but to buy precious time to get the victim to an emergency room.

Prevention

Just as people can get allergy shots to build up tolerance to pollens and other respiratory allergens, those with known allergies to insects can obtain protection via periodic injections, too. Extracts of the offending insect's venom are used, and at first, the weekly shots are very feeble. Gradually the strength of the extract builds until the patient can tolerate what might be a normal exposure to a sting or bite. Once the maintenance dose is reached, it is given at 4- to 6-week intervals throughout the year. The maintenance shots must be continued indefinitely.

Avoidance

Susceptible people should make themselves as unattractive to insects as possible. To bees, brown or black clothing is provocative, whereas white is not. Scented soaps, perfumes, suntan lotions, and other cosmetics should not be used when out-of-doors.

Another preventive strategy is to avoid loose-fitting clothes so that the insect cannot get between the material and the skin. And as little skin should be bared as possible, despite the warm weather. Shoes are preferable to sandals.

Picnics are a bad idea because they attract yellow jackets and ants. Garbage cans should be kept clean, sprayed with an insecticide, and tightly closed. Trees laden with ripe fruit should be avoided.

Susceptible people should also keep car windows closed; let someone else mow the lawn, trim the hedges, and tend the flower garden; and avoid clover. If an attack seems imminent, they should not swat at the bee or flail the arms, but rather retreat slowly, keep calm, and make no sudden movement.

ANAPHYLAXIS

THE MOST FRIGHTENING AND SEVERE—but fortunately the most infrequent—allergic reaction is known as anaphylaxis. It starts within a few minutes after exposure to the allergic agent and progresses rapidly. The main reaction is a constriction or narrowing of the airways and the blood vessels, resulting in difficult breathing, rapid pulse, a fall in blood pressure, and even cardiovascular collapse and shock. Several hundred Americans die of anaphylactic shock each year.

Anaphylaxis can result from reactions to drugs like penicillin, insulin, aspirin, and contrast materials used in x-rays; horse serum (used in some vaccines); insect stings; and certain foods. Even everyday respiratory allergens like pollen can sometimes provoke reactions that suddenly escalate into anaphylaxis.

Anaphylactic shock is a critical medical emergency in which just a few minutes' delay in getting treatment can be fatal. The therapy is an immediate injection of epinephrine or adrenaline, which opens up the airways and blood vessels. Other medications may be used to aid breathing or increase the blood pressure; these include antihistamines, oxygen, steroids, and aminophylline. People known to have severe reactions to insect stings and other allergens should carry emergency kits containing epinephrine. (See page 649.)

33 The Eyes

Anthony Donn, M.D.

INTRODUCTION

THE EYE is the body's most sensitive tissue, and it has been estimated that four-fifths of our knowledge is acquired through sight. Yet many people are poorly informed about their eyes and how to protect them from injury or disease. Even simple misconceptions about whom to consult for professional eye care and when can lead to permanent loss of some aspects of vision, caused by conditions such as amblyopia ("lazy eye") or glaucoma.

The eyes are very sensitive not only to information but also to irritation. Fortunately, certain very painful conditions, such as damage to the cornea due to ultraviolet light or overuse of contact lenses, are actually trivial and will clear up in a few days with rest and painkilling drugs. Other conditions that are far more serious, however, may cause no symptoms at all in their early stages, because they involve less sensitive structures deep within the eye.

For millennia, human beings have been fascinated by each other's eyes. New techniques and inventions of the past few decades promise that many more of us can enjoy clear sight for most or all of our lives.

This chapter begins with a description of the structures within the eye, and how they convey a picture of the world. The different eye care specialists are listed, with the examinations they perform. The section on eye care covers safety measures — including sunglasses and protective goggles—and first aid after injuries. The variations in shape of the eyeball and the different kinds of lenses used to correct them are described next. The causes and treatments for 3 major "thieves of sight"—amblyopia, glaucoma, and cataract—are discussed, as are the many ailments, trivial and serious, that can cause painful, red eyes.

Eyelid problems and growths within the eyeball may also be major or minor, depending on the cause. Damage to the retina, at the back of the eye, is among the leading causes of blindness in the United States. Diseases that harm the retina are explained at the end of the chapter, along with the current treatments.

THE EYE AND HOW IT WORKS

THE EYE is often compared to an extraordinarily sensitive camera. By following the path of a ray of light, we can describe the structure and function of the cornea, iris, lens, and other parts of the eye. (See figures 33.1 and 33.2.)

The eyes are well protected by a circle of bone—the eyebrow, cheekbone, and the bridge of the nose. The bony housing, like the camera body, continues around the back of the eye; it is called the orbit.

The eyelids form the eye's second line of defense,

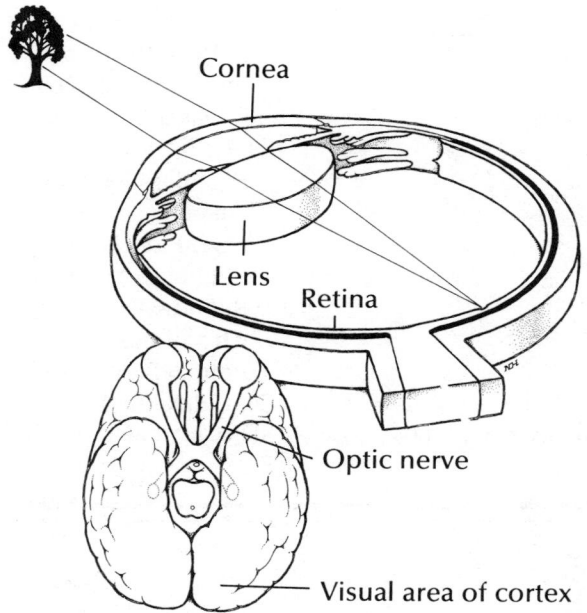

Figure 33.1. **How the eye sees. A ray of light enters the eye through the cornea and lens and is transmitted to the retina, where the light impulses are transmitted to the optic nerve and then to the visual cortex, the area in the brain where the signals are interpreted.**

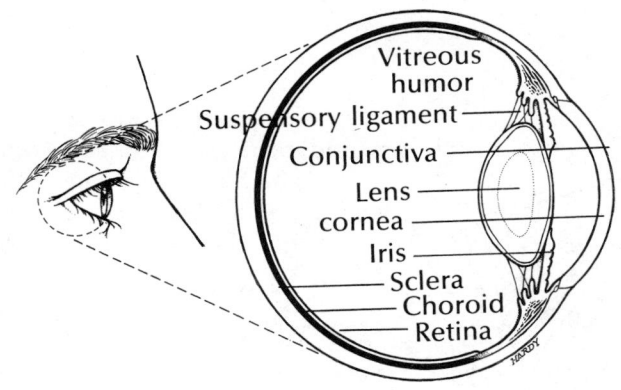

Figure 33.2. **Structures of the eye.**

protecting it from dust, intense light, and impact. From birth, a reflex reaction shuts the lid tightly at the sight of an oncoming object. New contact lens wearers often have considerable difficulty learning to insert their lenses because of this reflex.

Inside the upper lid are tear glands. By blinking, the eyelids push the tears across the eyes every few seconds while we are awake, like a windshield wiper, moistening and cleaning them. During sleep, the closed eyelid prevents harmful drying of the eye's surface. Tears usually collect in the lacrimal sac, connected to the nose. This is why nose-blowing always follows tears.

A single layer of tissue called the conjunctiva runs along the inside of the eyelid and then turns to meet the outside of the eyeball, the sclera, or white of the eye. In the center is the cornea, the transparent part of the eyeball, over the iris. The conjunctiva and sclera are filled with small blood vessels, and when these become enlarged or broken through irritation, infection, or injury, the eye becomes red.

Attached to the eyeball under the conjunctiva are 6 muscles that turn the eye in any direction. These muscles move thousands of times a day, without any conscious effort, to concentrate the attention of both eyes on external objects. They continue to work when the body is asleep, in the rapid eye movement associated with dreaming. The cornea is a thin, tough, transparent membrane in front of the eyeball. It provides about two-thirds of the focusing power of the eye, while the lens supplies about one-third. The lens focuses by altering its outer curvature and thus changing the angle at which the light passing through it is bent. This process is called refraction. Compared to the photographer's bulky zoom lenses, the cornea is a marvelous piece of equipment. It is exquisitely sensitive to pain: a tiny piece of grit on its surface can be disabling. Yet its outer layer regenerates very rapidly after injury,

usually without scars that might impair vision.

Inside the cornea is the anterior chamber filled with aqueous humor, a clear, watery liquid, which also cushions any impact to the eye. Normally, the aqueous humor flows from behind the iris (the colored part of the eye) through tiny ducts in the cornea. If this flow is blocked, the result is glaucoma, either acute or chronic, depending on the type of blockage.

The amount of pigment in the iris determines the color of a person's eyes: the more pigment, the browner and darker the eye. A more important function of the iris is its work as a shutter, controlling the amount of light that enters the eye, like the diaphragm of a camera.

The pupil corresponds to the camera's aperture. The size of the pupil—the opening in the iris—is controlled by involuntary muscles. By constricting to 1/25th of its maximum size, the pupil can adjust to a wide variation of light intensity. It also dilates in response to excitement and attractive sights, and many drugs can affect its size.

The lens, behind the iris, is shaped like the lentil seed that gives it its name. It is made up of long, highly elastic fibers that expand and contract to focus the light rays from objects outside the eye onto the retina at the back of the eye. Although it has neither blood vessels nor nerves, the lens continues to accumulate new fibers throughout life. The additional bulk makes the lens less elastic, so that eventually it cannot focus on near objects. This is why so many people who have never had vision problems find by late middle age that they need reading glasses.

The largest section of the eye is the vitreous chamber, the round space between the lens and the retina at the back. (See figure 33.3.) It is filled with vitreous humor, a clear, colorless, gelatinous fluid. Opaque bits of debris in the vitreous humor—called floaters—may cause occasional "spots before the eyes." They are usually leftover material from the prenatal growth of the eye. Hemorrhage or other events that cloud the vitreous humor can destroy vision. Fortunately, vitreous humor can sometimes be replaced, through a surgical procedure, with clear saline solution or aqueous humor.

Lining the back of the vitreous chamber is the retina, a pinkish net the thickness of onionskin. The retina corresponds to the film of the camera. Within its 10 layers are the rod cells that perceive light and the cone cells that perceive light and color. The rods outnumber the cones by 20 to 1 and need far less light to function. Because there are fewer cone cells and because they need more light, it is difficult to discern color when the light is dim.

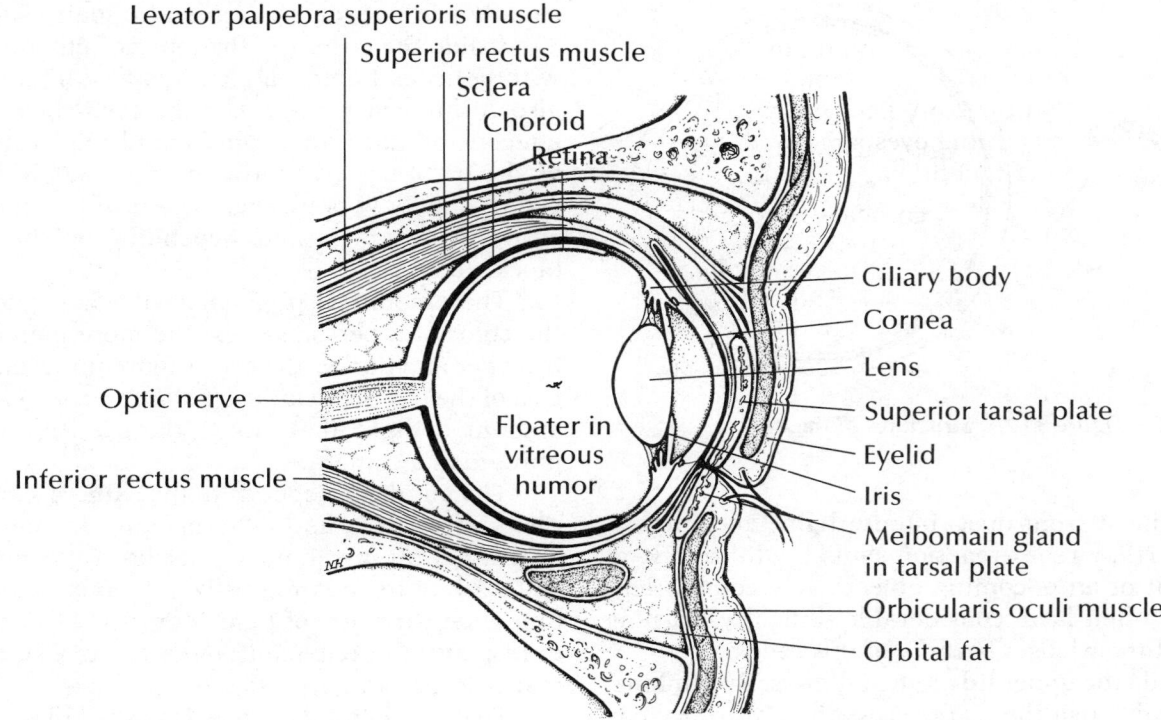

Levator palpebra superioris muscle
Superior rectus muscle
Sclera
Choroid
Retina

Optic nerve

Inferior rectus muscle

Floater in vitreous humor

Ciliary body
Cornea
Lens
Superior tarsal plate
Eyelid
Iris
Meibomain gland in tarsal plate
Orbicularis oculi muscle
Orbital fat

Figure 33.3. **Anatomy of the eye.**

Rod and cone cells convert the light that strikes them into electric impulses that are carried by the optic nerve to the visual cortex, a region at the back of the brain that interprets these signals to create a picture of the world outside. Sometimes interference with the visual cortex can result in a visual illusion, as when a blow on the head makes the recipient "see" stars.

Eye "Doctors"—Who They Are, What They Do

Professional eye care can be provided either by an ophthalmologist or by an optometrist. An ophthalmologist is a physician who specializes in diagnosis and treatment of eye diseases and conditions. Formally called an oculist, the ophthalmologist can also prescribe corrective lenses and perform surgery on the eyes. In some states, ophthalmologists may give more complete examinations than other specialists because the use of certain drops is restricted to them.

An optometrist is not a medical doctor, but a graduate of a school of optometry, with "O.D." or "D.O.S." after his or her name. Optometrists are trained to diagnose refractive errors and to pre-

scribe lenses to correct them. They can detect signs of disease in the eye—and diseases detectable through examination of the retina—but an ophthalmologist or other specialist must be consulted for a complete diagnosis and treatment.

Opticians are specialists in fulfilling the prescriptions of ophthalmologists and optometrists. They grind and dispense lenses, fitting them into frames, but do not examine the eyes for refractive errors or signs of disease.

Experts differ about how often routine eye examinations are necessary. Adults under the age of 40 should be examined only every 3 years—not annually, as many people believe. People who wear corrective lenses may be reexamined every 1½ years. Some experts maintain that young people without corrective lenses or symptoms can safely go 5 years between examinations. Of course, symptoms like a need to move the head to see distant or very close objects, blurring of vision, or any noticeable difference between the sight in the two eyes are good reasons for a checkup.

Ophthalmologists agree that children should have a first eye examination by the age of 3, and a second one on starting school. Children often don't know what they're supposed to see, so parents should be alert for signs of eye problems: frequent eye-rubbing, closing or covering one eye, inability to do close work, blinking or squinting or complaining about bright lights. These, as well as reddened, itchy, watery, or burning eyes, are good reasons for parents to consult an ophthalmologist. Nearsighted children will want to sit close to the blackboard, movie screen, or television. Obviously, any vision problem can interfere with education and possibly with social adjustment.

The National Society for the Prevention of Blindness has an eye test for preschoolers. Parents can use it at home to discover whether a child needs a professional evaluation. The test is available free, in English and Spanish, from the Society, at P.O. Box 426, New York, New York 10019.

The Eye Examination

There is no one set formula for examining eyes. The eye doctor starts with a few basic tests and then uses the results to select from a menu of additional investigational techniques.

The examination should begin with a general medical history and a history of the patient's vision. The patient should recount any medications being taken; any eye problems, either long-standing or recent; and occupational and recreational activities, all of which can affect the examination.

The doctor may begin the physical examination by testing the movements of the eye, both separately and together. Can both eyes focus on an object moving toward them? Do they move easily from side to side and up and down? How big are the pupils, and do they react quickly and adequately to changes in light?

Next, the doctor will use a slit-lamp microscope to obtain a magnified view of the outer layers of the eye, looking carefully for signs of injury or disease.

The hand-held device with a bright light used next is called an ophthalmoscope. With this, the examiner looks through the eye to the retina, checking the tiny blood vessels for damage due to high blood pressure or diabetes. Detachment of the retina from the back of the eyeball or blank spots on its surface will also be picked out by the ophthalmoscope.

The patient can read letters on a chart (called a Snellen Chart) or screen to test for refractive errors, but should also look through a phoropter, the black metal mask into which the examiner inserts different lenses. People sometimes worry about giving a "wrong" answer, but the examiner can obtain 95 percent of the data necessary to prescribe lenses by using different lenses to focus on the retina. The same lens that gives the examiner the clearest picture of the retina will give the patient the clearest view of the outside world. Answers from the eye merely confirm the physical information. If there is any contradiction, the doctor will repeat the question or use additional lenses until the issue is resolved.

Peripheral vision should be tested by using moving objects, and color vision by a series of colored cards.

Finally, for those over 35 or 40, every eye examination should include a test for glaucoma with a device called a tonometer, which uses a probe that touches the eyeball to determine the pressure. Drops are used to paralyze the blinking reflexes. Tonometers that use a fast puff of air and do not require drops are sometimes used to screen large groups of people for glaucoma, but they are not as accurate.

In the past, many eye examiners routinely used eyedrops to enlarge the pupil and look into the eye. This is no longer considered necessary in all cases. Enlarged pupils can temporarily disable the patient by making bright light uncomfortable. And the chemicals themselves may irritate the eye, besides making it difficult to determine the eye's normal functioning. Certain diseases—especially cataract and retinal disease—may make drops necessary. But the normal eye can be adequately examined without them.

Besides diseases of the eye, the eye examination may also reveal the effects of diseases elsewhere in the body. These include high blood pressure, diabetes, blood disorders, and tumors of the pituitary. Arthritis and other connective tissue disorders also affect the eye.

Color Vision

As explained previously, the cone cells in the retina are the units that "see" color. There are 3 types: red, blue, and green. Any of the 3 types may be defective, but most color-blind persons have trouble distinguishing reds from greens, especially in pastel shades. Difficulty in differentiating blues and yellows is another, much less common form of color-blindness. The extent of the defect can be determined by examining a series of cards marked with multicolored dots, which will show different words or numbers when read by color-blind persons and those with normal vision.

Color-blindness, which is almost never a significant handicap, is hereditary; the defect is carried on the X chromosome. Ten times as many men as women are affected: 6 percent and 0.6 percent of the population, respectively. Women may be carriers, transmitting the gene to their sons.

EVERYDAY EYE CARE

Safety

Approximately 35,000 Americans each year sustain eye injuries serious enough to warrant emergency-room treatment. Most of these accidents occur in the summer, when sports involving rackets, sticks, balls, bicycles, and pools alternate with gardening, sunbathing, and do-it-yourself projects.

The National Society to Prevent Blindness estimates that 90 percent of all these eye injuries could have been prevented, often by adhering to simple safety practices such as the use of inexpensive goggles. Although many eye injuries can be cured, it makes sense to avoid possible pain, hospitalization, and even partial loss of vision by observing a few precautions.

Sunburn

There are 2 types of eye injuries caused by the sun. Ultraviolet light from the sun reflected by snow, from a suntan lamp, or from welding equipment can damage the cornea. Often, the effect takes 12 to 24 hours to develop, and the victim awakens in the middle of the night with searing pain and a feeling of sand or grit in the eyes. An ophthalmologist can prescribe painkilling drugs, and the cornea usually regenerates after a few days under an eyepatch.

Sunglasses can prevent these problems. Many brands are labeled with light transmission factors denoting the percent of light that gets through. To protect the eyes from sun, the light transmission factor should be 30 percent or less; 10 to 15 percent is better for glare from sand, water, or snow. Effectiveness can also be tested by wearing the glasses in front of a mirror. Sunglasses should be dark enough to hide the eyes behind them.

For skiers and yachtsmen, polarized or mirrored lenses are the best protection against glare. Gradient density lenses—the kind that are darker at the top—can increase comfort on a sunny day. But phototropic lenses—the ones that darken in sunlight and become pale indoors—are not usually successful. They take up to 10 minutes to change color, may not become dark enough for really bright sun, and never fade completely, so they cannot be used as a combination of regular prescription glasses and prescription sunglasses.

For use under a sunlamp (a device most dermatologists discourage), special goggles are essential. That intense light can burn the cornea in just a few minutes, even through sunglasses *and* closed eyelids.

The best lens colors for sunglasses are gray, brown, or green, in that order. Prescription sunglasses are better than clip-on lenses. For active sports, sunglasses should have a strap going around the head or wires over the ears to avoid breakage and loss.

Eclipses or Solar Burns

People who stare directly at the sun during an eclipse can suffer infrared (heat) burns that damage the surface of the retina. The lens focuses rays on rod and cone cells, causing permanent loss of vision. Avoiding solar burn is simple. People should not look at the sun—during an eclipse or otherwise—through smoked glass, through exposed film, and especially not through optical instruments like telescopes that focus the sun's rays on the retina.

Impact Injury

Racket sports, bicycling, gardening, and home carpentry can all prove destructive to the unprotected eye. Even today's mandatory impact-resistant prescription lenses can be broken by a projectile from a machine tool, lawnmower, or squash racket. For this reason, industrial safety glasses or sports eye protectors are recommended by the National Society to Prevent Blindness. These cost from about $15 to about $40 for models without prescription lenses. They can be obtained through opticians, eye doctors, suppliers of safety equipment, and sporting goods stores.

Industrial-quality safety glasses should have plastic lenses and bear the code number Z87.1, 1979, to show that they conform to the National Standard Practice for Occupational and Educational Eye and Face Protection. They should be worn to trim shrubs, run a power lawnmower or carpentry tools, or spray pesticides or paint.

The best sports eye protectors are goggles molded from optical-quality polycarbonate lenses designed to withstand severe blows. They can be purchased in stylish, lightweight wraparound models with clear or sunglass-dark lenses.

Swimming is wonderful exercise, although it can cause eye problems. Chlorine in pools can make the eyes feel dry and scratchy, the result of a mild chemical burn on the cornea. Some people have very sensitive corneas and cannot swim in pools at all. Freshwater swimmers face the possibility of eye infections, especially when many others use the water.

The solution is a pair of swim goggles. They should be water-tight and cost under $5.00. Swimmers should use only their own towels to lessen the chance of contracting or spreading eye infections.

FIRST AID FOR EYES

ALTHOUGH PROTECTED in its circle of bone, the eye and surrounding areas may be injured by blows, foreign particles, cuts, burns, and chemical irritants. In these cases, the first few moments can be essential to future sight.

Foreign Bodies

This heading includes everything from the relatively harmless eyelash to the dangerous sliver of steel. An eyelash or speck of dust should first be located by looking in a mirror. If it is visible, it can usually be removed by wiping it toward a corner of the eye with a moistened tip of a clean handkerchief. A few sharp blinks may be necessary to move the object off the sensitive cornea. If this doesn't work, pulling the upper lid down over the lower lashes may wash the object out.

The lower lashes may also help to wipe the undersurface of the upper lid. If none of these works, a physician or hospital emergency room should be the next step.

More serious injuries are often due to small fragments of wood or metal that penetrate the eye during metalwork or carpentry. A splinter shot from a machine may enter the eyeball so quickly that it causes only mild pain and little external injury. However, a delayed reaction or infection may destroy vision even years later. This kind of injury should be covered with an eyepatch and referred to an ophthalmologist. Often a dangerous piece of metal can be removed easily by an expert with a magnet. (For further instructions see Chapter 7, A Directory of Common First-Aid Procedures, page 114.)

Cuts and Bruises

A black eye is a bruise of the cheek, eyelids, and eyebrow. Like other bruises, its spread may be lessened by a cold compress used immediately. An icebag is neater and cheaper than a steak, but neither will reduce a black eye once the color is fully developed.

A blow hard enough to produce a black eye may also have damaged the more sensitive eyeball and nerves, and warrants a complete evaluation by an ophthalmologist, especially if the patient has pain in the eye, or double or blurred vision. The same is true of cuts around the eye. External bleeding may be stopped by applying pressure, but bleeding behind the cornea may require hospitalization.

In either case, it is extremely important not to attempt to force open an eye that has swollen shut after an injury, or press on it in any way. Sometimes the eyelid is the only thing holding a perforated eyeball together. The ophthalmologist may be able to suture the eyeball together—but only if it arrives in the operating room intact.

After a serious eye injury, the ophthalmologist will perform a number of studies to evaluate the extent of the damage, using painkillers if necessary. Injuries to the outer layers of the eye usually heal without medical intervention. Even hemorrhages under the conjunctiva—blood-red patches in the white of the eye—will vanish on their own in a few weeks. Injuries to the cornea often heal in a few days, although wounds due to wood splinters often take longer. The doctor may prescribe an eyepatch, antibiotics, painkillers, or drops to prevent the eye from moving. Ice will limit pain and damage on the first day; heat will promote healing thereafter.

In cases of severe injury, the ophthalmologist and patient may be forced to contemplate removal of a lacerated, blinded eye to prevent a condition known as "sympathetic ophthalmia." In this situation, leaving the injured eye in place for more than 12 days precipitates the loss of vision in the uninjured eye, resulting eventually in total blindness. Luckily, the tragedy is rare and becoming rarer, occurring in only 0.1 percent of cases, down from 2 to 4 percent during World War I.

Chemical Burns

Water is the first aid for injuries due to chemicals. Use a spray nozzle from a kitchen sink to wash the irritant out of the eye. Position the head with the more injured eye lower. Using a gentle spray, rinse for at least 5 to 10 minutes Do not try to "counteract" the irritant with another chemical. Then take the injured person to an ophthalmologist or emergency room.

The ophthalmologist will evaluate the condition of the injured eye. If the damage is limited to the outer layer of the cornea, and the inner layers are still transparent, the injury, however painful, may heal after only a few days of rest. Antibiotics, analgesics, and drops to paralyze the eye muscles will promote healing. A patch may also help the injured eye.

In more severe cases, the damage penetrates the cornea, making it opaque and white. In this event, the injury is usually irreversible. Corneal transplants are necessary to restore sight, and even they are not always successful in the severely burned eye.

EYE CARE, EYE MYTHS

WE USE OUR EYES every minute that they are open, but when we speak of *overusing* them, we generally mean close work—reading, sewing, handicrafts—activities during which the eyes are focused at an object 12 to 18 inches away for long periods of time. For this kind of work the optimum light is a 100-watt bulb a few feet away, behind the shoulder, or on the side, so that there is no glare.

It is *not* true that reading in poor light, or without glasses, or for too long will injure the eyes. But these habits may cause eyestrain, a tired feeling in the eye muscles from holding the same position for too long. Sometimes eyestrain is accompanied by headache. Eyestrain may be avoided by resting the eyes every half hour—gazing off into the distance or just letting the eyes unfocus. Frequent eyestrain may indicate the need for new glasses, or a new prescription.

Over-the-counter eyedrops will not help eyestrain, but they may be soothing to eyes irritated by dust, smoke, or air pollution. The best way to use them is lying down. Squeeze a few drops into the corner of the eye and let them wash across the eyeball.

Many doctors feel these medications are overused. They may provoke allergic reactions and are easily contaminated by bacteria. As with other drugs, they should not be borrowed or lent, and they should be discarded when old. Their worst side effect, however, may be the delay in consulting a professional for a serious eye problem.

REFRACTIVE ERRORS

LIGHT STRIKING THE EYE is refracted (bent) by the lens and cornea so that the rays come to a sharp focus on the retina. For this to happen, the refractive powers of the lens and cornea, and the length of the eyeball must be exactly correlated. In many people, however, heredity or environment—no one knows which—have created an imbalance, so that the rays focus in front of or behind the retina at least some of the time. These people are nearsighted or farsighted, respectively. People with irregularities in their corneas, so that only some of the light rays focus on the retina, have astigmatism. In most cases, these conditions are correctable with lenses. (See figure 33.4.)

Refractive errors are described by numbers. The familiar "20/20" is normal vision, describing a person who sees at 20 feet what other people with normal vision see at the same distance. Farsighted people may have 20/10 vision, but be unable to read print at the usual reading distance. (See figure 33.5.)

In most states, corrected vision of 20/40 or better is required for a driver's license. A person whose vision is around 20/60 may function adequately in normal household activities, but most people whose vision is worse than this notice that something is wrong. Vision of 20/200 or worse that cannot be corrected with lenses constitutes legal blindness in most states. Almost 20,000 Americans are legally blind because of myopia. Many people with vision this poor can easily take care of themselves, although they may be limited in many activities, such as reading or driving.

Nearsightedness

Myopia or nearsightedness usually begins in the school years, from the early grades through the late teens. Both boys and girls have it in equal numbers, and it often runs in families. The growing eye becomes too long, so that rays of light from distant objects focus before the retina. The condition may develop rapidly in the teenage years, so that new glasses are needed every 6 months, but it often stabilizes in a person's twenties, necessitating little change in prescription until after age 40. Signs of myopia in children include squinting, holding books close to the face, and needing to sit at the front of the classroom or theater.

Corrective treatment for nearsightedness almost always involves the use of eyeglasses or contact

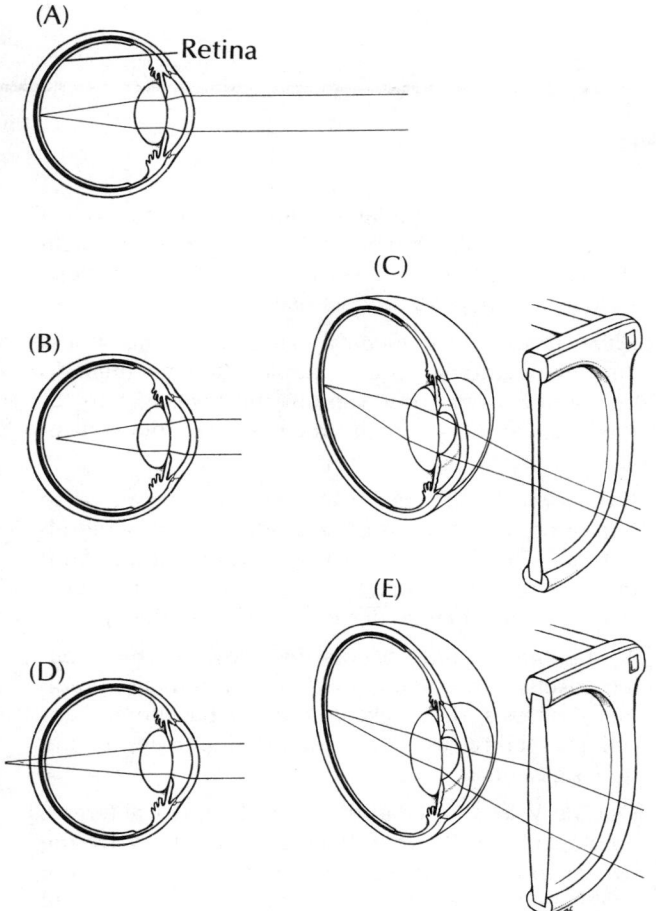

Figure 33.4. **Common visual disorders. (A) Normal (20/20) vision, in which light rays focus sharply on the retina; (B) myopia (nearsightedness), in which light rays from a distance come to sharp focus in front of the retina; (C) myopia corrected by eyeglasses with concave lenses; (D) hyperopia (farsightedness), in which light rays from close objects come to sharp focus behind the retina; (E) hyperopia corrected by eyeglasses with convex lenses.**

lenses. But public attention has recently been drawn to a new surgical procedure called radial keratotomy. This is an experimental operation in which the surgeon makes a series of cuts, arranged like spokes of a wheel, in the cornea, flattening its curvature and permanently correcting the myopia, if successful.

First developed in the Soviet Union, radial keratotomy has been performed in this country only in the last 5 years, so that the long-term results are still unknown. The short-term risks include infection, perforation of the cornea, and incomplete correction of the myopia. Only a few ophthalmologic surgeons are experienced in this operation, and they restrict it to highly motivated adult patients who absolutely cannot tolerate spectacles or contact lenses.

Farsightedness

There are 2 refractive conditions that interfere with near vision. One is hyperopia, a usually congenital condition in which the eye is too short so that rays of light cannot intersect on the retina. Most farsighted people with hyperopia do not need glasses until the age of 40 or so.

The other kind of farsightedness, presbyopia, affects almost all people in their fifties and sixties. As the lens accumulates more fibers, it becomes less able to accommodate to near vision. At first the person can adjust to this change, perhaps at the cost of eyestrain or headache. But eventually almost everyone will need reading glasses. (People who already have hyperopia will need them sooner than others.) Some myopic people with presbyopia are able to see distance by removing their glasses, but may require bifocals.

200 feet   **20 feet**

Figure 33.5. **Meaning of 20/20 vision. In normal 20/20 vision, a person can see the 85 on the sign at a distance of 200 feet. In contrast, a person with 20/200 vision must be 20 feet from the 85 to see it.**

COMMON EYE SIGNS AND SYMPTOMS

Hemorrhage. A red blob that appears suddenly in the white of the eye is called a subconjunctival hemorrhage. These usually develop after a small injury to the eye, or even a cough or a sneeze. Although they look alarming, they are almost always harmless. If they recur, however, they may indicate a blood disease or high blood pressure. The blood is usually absorbed within 2 weeks; there is no special therapy to hasten its disappearance.

Spots. "Spots before the eyes"—also called floaters—are usually trivial. Most are caused by bits of debris floating in the vitreous humor. Brown or red spots, however, are often signs of vitreous hemorrhage, leakage of blood from the retina into the vitreous chamber. These spots are danger signs: They may be followed by retinal detachment. Retinal detachment often begins with a shower of sparkling spots and the sensation of a curtain moving across the eyes. This is a medical emergency. (See Diseases of the Retina, page 669.)

A light spot or scintillating flash may also result from an abnormal stimulation of the visual system. These are called "positive scotomas," and are often part of a migraine.

Pain. Pain in the eye is always important. Unless the cause is obvious, like a foreign body or minor injury, it should be investigated by an ophthalmologist.

Pain due to bright light, however, is common, especially in fair-skinned persons. Dark glasses will usually ensure comfort. If sensitivity to light develops suddenly, it may indicate disease.

Blind Spots. The medical name for a blind spot is "negative scotoma." Many people who have them do not notice them. They warrant full investigation, as they may result from hemorrhage or optic nerve damage.

Protruding Eyes. An overactive thyroid can cause one or both eyes to protrude gradually, over a month or more. Tumors can also cause slow protrusion. Sudden protrusion of one eye usually means a hemorrhage or inflammation in the orbit behind the eye.

Nystagmus (Rolling or Jerking Eyes). This problem results from some form of brain dysfunction: multiple sclerosis, drugs like alcohol or barbiturates, or others. Medical treatment for the underlying condition is essential.

Double Vision. Double vision (the medical term is "diplopia") results when the brain cannot resolve the two pictures it receives from the two eyes. It is not simple blurred vision. It may result from injury or from stabismus (squint or cross-eyes) or from palsy of the eye muscles. Both strabismus and ocular muscle palsy can be caused by serious ocular or neurologic disease, such as diabetes or aneurysm.

Astigmatism

Sometimes the cornea is not symmetrical, but steeper or flatter in places. The blurred vision that results is astigmatism. Astigmatism may be combined with nearsightedness or farsightedness, and like them is correctable with lenses.

Corrective Lenses

Refractive errors cannot be corrected by eye exercises or diet. Curved lenses are necessary to compensate for the defect in the eye and make the light rays entering it focus on the retina. (See figure 33.1.)

Eyeglasses with handles or frames have been in use since the Middle Ages. But only since the Industrial Revolution have standardized, machine-ground lenses been available to most people. Convex lenses—thicker in the center—cause the light rays to converge, hitting the retina of the farsighted eye. Concave lenses—thicker around the edge—spread the light rays, moving the focus back toward the retina of the nearsighted eye. Cylindrical lenses—with the thickness distributed along one axis—correct astigmatism.

Bifocals, invented by Benjamin Franklin, combine 2 types of lenses: a prescription for reading at the bottom of the lens and another one for far vision at the top. They are usually worn by older people with presbyopia who prefer not to carry 2 pairs of glasses for near and far vision. Trifocals, with 3 prescriptions, for near, middle (1½ to 4 feet), and far distances, are also available for those who need them. Half-glasses can be useful for people who need only a reading prescription. "Invisible" bifocals—glasses that show no line where the 2 prescriptions join—are also available, but many people have trouble adjusting to them. All of these glasses may be colored or coated for use as sunglasses.

Contact Lenses

Entertainers, athletes, cataract patients, people whose occupations require good peripheral vision free from eyeglass fogging, and people who just don't like wearing glasses, all can choose among several types of contact lenses. Fourteen million Americans now wear little curved disks of plastic over their corneas, and most are delighted with the improvement in convenience, appearance, and in many cases, vision itself. But unless they are carefully fitted and handled, contact lenses can be anything from a waste of money to a threat to sight.

There are at least 4 types of contact lenses on the market now. Some types are more suitable than others for some people, and other people cannot wear them at all. Persons whose eyes are severely irritated by allergies or occupational exposure to dust or chemicals, individuals with overactive thyroids, uncontrolled diabetes, or severe arthritis of the hands, and those whose eyes are dry because of pregnancy, birth control pills, diuretics, antihistamines, or decongestants are less likely to find contact lens-wearing easy. Parents of adolescents with myopia may prefer to wait until their eyes stabilize before paying for contacts.

Buying Contact Lenses

The first consideration in purchasing contact lenses is the skill and professional training of the person who fits the lenses, and his or her readiness to spend time and effort on the patient. For this reason, the low-priced lenses advertised everywhere may not be a bargain. There may be hidden costs for appliances needed to clean the lenses or for visits after fitting. Or worse, cut-rate lenses may be so poorly fitted that they wind up in a drawer.

Contact lenses should be prescribed by an ophthalmologist or optometrist who specializes in them. The cost may range from $125 to $500, depending on the type of lens and type of doctor. The fee should include a complete examination of the eyes and checkups for up to a year after the contact lenses are fitted. Insurance is usually extra, and many people—especially hard-lens wearers—do without it.

Lenses to fit a given individual may be obtainable immediately, or they may have to be ordered or even custom-made. Discomfort or consciousness of new lenses is normal at first, but any actual pain during the break-in period should be referred to the eye doctor. Checkups of new lenses are recommended after 1 week, 2 weeks, 1 month, 6 months, and 1 year.

Hard Lenses. Hard contact lenses have been available since 1938 and are still the most popular type. They provide better visual correction than soft lenses, especially for people with severe astigmatism or irregular corneas. In addition, they are less expen-sive than other types and easier to clean. They can be polished and reground when scratched or outgrown, thus saving the expense of a new pair.

Bifocal hard lenses are available, with the reading prescription either as a ring around the outside, or weighted to sink to the bottom of the lens. Fitting these can be difficult, however, and many people never adjust to them.

Hard lenses are available with tints, either as sunglasses or for cosmetic reasons. They can even turn brown eyes blue.

The drawback of hard contact lenses is the initial discomfort. The break-in period takes at least 2 weeks to go from half an hour to a full day. If lens-wearing is interrupted for a few days, the slow adaptation must be repeated, so these lenses cannot be reserved for special occasions.

Other possible drawbacks include an increased sensitivity to light and foreign particles in the eye. For this reason, new hard-lens wearers should invest in sunglasses—a dark pair for sunny days, and a light pair to use as a windscreen. Many people find hard lenses more uncomfortable during colds and allergic attacks. Hard lenses are more easily dislodged from the cornea and the eye itself, although easier to find, than soft lenses. Also, many hard-lens wearers report blurred vision after they remove their lenses to put on spectacles.

Gas-Permeable Lenses. Unlike conventional hard lenses, these have openings to permit some of the oxygen and carbon dioxide in the air to reach the cornea, so that it can "breathe." For this reason, they are more comfortable—and more expensive—than ordinary hard lenses. They are often worn by people with severe astigmatism or irregular corneal surfaces who cannot tolerate other hard lenses.

Soft Lenses. The major advantage of soft contact lenses is their comfort. Made of a water-absorbent plastic, they mold to the cornea. The adjustment period is much shorter: They can be worn for a whole day within the first week. Foreign objects do not intrude beneath the lens, the eyes do not become more light-sensitive. They very rarely fall out and are easier to insert than hard lenses, and they are available in bifocal and tinted models. The disadvantages include greater expense, both initially and in the upkeep. Because they absorb water, soft lenses must be sterilized by heat or chemicals every night. They are more fragile than hard lenses, and proteins in tear fluid may cloud them after 2 years or so, necessitating replacement. If dropped, they fall silently, sticking to walls and floors, looking like a drop of water or scrap of cellophane, and often drying out irrevocably before they can be found.

In addition, soft lenses absorb chemicals from the air and cosmetics from the hands. And they may become uncomfortably dry under a hair dryer, in hot rooms, or in very windy or dry weather.

Extended-Wear Lenses.   Unlike other types of contact lenses, extended-wear lenses can remain in the eye during sleep. In fact, these special soft lenses can be left in for 2 weeks at a time. They have a higher water content than other lenses and permit more oxygen to reach the cornea. They do have to be cleaned and sterilized periodically. They are most useful for people who cannot manage daily cleaning because of arthritis or other reasons, and people who need clear vision immediately upon awakening.

CARE OF CONTACT LENSES

- Clean hands are essential for inserting or removing contact lenses.
- Lenses should not be worn while swimming. Soft lenses absorb chemicals from the water; hard lenses float out of the eyes.
- Except for extended-wear lenses, sleeping with lenses on will hurt the eyes by depriving the cornea of oxygen.
- Contact lenses should be inserted before makeup is applied, and removed before it is removed. Water-soluble makeup is best. "Lash-building" mascara may drop particles into the eyes, which is especially irritating with hard lenses. Eyeliner applied between the lashes and the eyes may discolor soft lenses permanently.
- Aerosol sprays and contact lenses don't mix.

Sprays should be used before lenses are inserted—if at all.
- Burning, redness, pain, unusual light sensitivity, and hazy vision all are danger signs that should be referred to an ophthalmologist.
- Putting hard contact lenses in the mouth to moisten or clean them is a sure route to infection.
- People who wear Medic Alert identification bracelets and others liable to lose consciousness should include the information that they wear contact lenses.
- An extra empty lens case and an extra pair of lenses (or glasses) may prevent a vacation or business trip from becoming a disaster.

STRABISMUS AND AMBLYOPIA

Newborn babies take a few months to learn to focus their eyes. Strabismus, a general term for various types of cross eye, wall eye, or squint, is usually outgrown when the baby reaches the age of 6 months or so. But if it is not, the child must have medical treatment—perhaps including surgery—or the sight of the wandering eye will be lost to a condition called amblyopia, or lazy-eye.

Amblyopia occurs because the brain abhors double vision. If one eye sends signals that are much weaker, distorted, or inappropriate, because of refractive errors or lack of alignment, the brain will reject them and rely solely on signals from the stronger eye to make up its picture of the world. If this rejection is continued by a young brain, eventually the brain will become unable to interpret images from the weaker eye. By the age of 6 or 7, when the problem is discovered in school, it is often too late to restore sight to the weaker eye. Binocular vision, and with it depth perception, is permanently lost.

Warning Signs

Parents should watch out for any signs of strabismus in a child over 6 months old, even if only slight or occasional. Some children have broad folds on the sides of their noses, making their pupils seem too close together. To differentiate these normal children and detect even slight strabismus, look at the reflection of a candle or penlight in the child's eye. In normal children, the spots of light may lie on either side of the pupil, but they will be symmetric. In a child with strabismus, one spot will be off-center, and lie over the iris, not the pupil. (See figure 33.6.)

Other signs of amblyopia include rubbing the

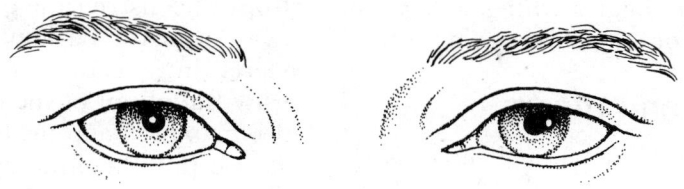

Figure 33.6. **Warning sign of strabismus. In this drawing, the light reflected from a penlight is asymmetrical, with the pinpoint centered in the pupil in one eye, but off-center over the iris in the other.**

eye, tilting the head to see, covering one eye, and difficulty with games that require estimation of distances for catching or throwing a ball. Even small babies can be tested by covering one eye at a time. The baby with amblyopia will fuss and cry when the good eye is covered. However, amblyopia may occur without easily detectable signs. This is why children should have a first eye examination before the age of 4.

Treatment

Amblyopia should be corrected as early as possible. If the amblyopic eye is weak because of a refractive error, the child will wear special glasses to correct it: one corrective lens and one blackened one to force

the brain to depend on the corrected weaker eye. Sometimes the child need only wear an eyepatch.

If the amblyopia is due to muscle weakness, however, special eyedrops may be prescribed to force the child to rely on the weaker eye. Exercises may also help strengthen the eye muscles. In other cases, surgery to tighten one muscle or loosen another may help the child gain control of the wandering eye.

Treatment of amblyopia should begin when the child is 3 or 4. The longer the condition lasts, the less chance there is of conquering it. Exercises may help children as old as 7 or 8. After this age, however, even though surgery may make a squint less noticeable, it will not restore binocular vision.

THE RED EYE

Conjunctivitis

"Pink eye" is caused by an allergy or an infection of the lining of the eyelid by bacteria or viruses. The eyes become red and irritated with a sandy or burning feeling. The disease may follow a cold or sore throat and is most common in children. Sometimes pus is visible in the eye or causes the eyelids to stick together. Pink eye is contagious and sometimes spreads through a whole grade school.

Conjunctivitis should be treated by a physician, who will prescribe antibiotics, usually in the form of drops or ointment. Oral antibiotics may be used if the disease is related to a sore throat.

Allergic conjunctivitis may be helped by steroid eyedrops, but this therapy has severe side effects so the prescription must be followed exactly. Where no infectious agent is found, soothing drops may be prescribed until the discomfort subsides.

To avoid the spread of pink eye, persons who have it should stay home, wash their hands frequently, and use separate towels and face cloths. Linens should also be washed thoroughly.

Old or borrowed eye makeup has also been implicated in the spread of conjunctivitis. Experts recommend not sharing eye pencils and discarding mascara after 4 to 6 months.

Corneal Injuries

A person with corneal injury may go to sleep normally, unaware of the problem, only to wake a few hours later with swollen, red, extremely painful eyes. There are 2 common causes: overuse of hard contact lenses and overexposure to ultraviolet light.

The treatment consists of an eyepatch, painkilling drugs, and reassurance, and the condition usually clears up in a few days. Prevention consists of wearing ultraviolet-proof goggles while sunbathing or welding, and limited contact lens wearing time.

Corneal Infections and Ulcers

An ulcer is an open sore. Infections, such as conjunctivitis, can lead to corneal ulcers, and corneal ulcers caused by injuries due to foreign particles in the eye often become infected. As with conjunctivitis, the infecting organisms may be bacteria or viruses.

Symptoms are much more obvious in bacterial than in viral infections. In either case, the sensitive cornea is very painful, the eyeball becomes pink or red, and vision is blurred behind the ulcer. Bacterial ulcers generate pus; viral ulcers do not. A bacterial ulcer may be seen in the mirror as a whitish abrasion on the cornea. Viral ulcers of the cornea are usually caused by herpes simplex virus. The herpes ulcer is shaped like a tree branch (hence its name, "dendritic ulcer"), and is usually only visible by coating the eye with a fluorescent dye.

Corneal ulcers demand prompt medical treatment. If neglected, they may permanently scar the cornea, or even cut through it, infecting the entire eyeball and mandating surgery to close the opening. The ophthalmologist will prescribe antibiotics in the form of drops, ointments, or oral medicine. In severe cases, antibiotics may be injected near the eye. Viral ulcers are treated with antiviral drops or ointments, as often as once an hour. This will control the current ulcer, but like other herpes infections, dendritic ulcers can recur. If the cornea is badly damaged, a corneal transplant may be necessary to restore sight.

Narrow-Angle or Congestive Glaucoma

Narrow- or closed-angle glaucoma occurs when the iris dilates and blocks the outflow of aqueous humor. It is much rarer than open-angle glaucoma (see below), amounting to only 5 to 10 percent of total glaucoma cases. Unlike open-angle glaucoma, it is impossible to ignore: Within days, the eye becomes red, rock-hard, and painful enough to cause nausea and vomiting. The cornea appears hazy, lights develop halos, and vision is poor. Closed-angle glaucoma is an obvious eye emergency.

The ophthalmologist will first administer eyedrops to constrict the pupil, hoping to move the iris away from the outflow ducts. Other drugs, administered intravenously or by mouth, will attempt to draw liquid out of the eye. Massage of the eye may also help break up the blockage.

Despite these measures, corrective surgery usually is necessary to prevent blindness and prevent recurrences. Using a scalpel or laser, the ophthalmologist makes a wider outflow duct through the iris for the aqueous humor. The operation requires a brief hospital stay. Laser surgery may be performed on outpatients, with eyedrops for anesthesia. The tendency to develop closed-angle glaucoma is inherited, and usually affects both eyes.

Uveitis

Uveitis is an inflammation of the rearmost globe of the eye, including the iris (iritis). The eye will become painful, light-shy, and red, but not hard as in closed-angle glaucoma. Vision is poor.

The treatment consists of atropine to dilate the pupil and prevent the iris from sticking to the lens, and steroids to reduce the inflammation. Uveitis should be treated by an ophthalmologist.

Hemorrhage

Sometimes one of the tiny blood vessels in the eye breaks, spilling blood beneath the white of the eye. This frightening-looking red patch is not serious unless accompanied by pain; usually it will clear up within 2 to 3 weeks without any treatment. Recurrent hemorrhages may signal the onset of a blood disorder or the overuse of anticoagulant drugs.

Scleritis and Episcleritis

These 2 conditions are inflammations of the outermost layers of the eye. Scleritis is often associated with rheumatoid arthritis or digestive diseases, and causes a dull pain. It is the more serious disease of the two, as the sclera may be perforated. Both conditions can be treated with anti-inflammatory drugs, taken either orally or as eyedrops. Episcleritis may clear up on its own.

GLAUCOMA

IT IS ESTIMATED that 1 out of every 25 Americans has glaucoma, but only half of these people are aware of the disease. More than 62,000 Americans are legally blind due to glaucoma with an additional 5,350 losing their sight each year. The disease can cause extensive damage before the symptoms are noticed.

The damage of glaucoma can be contained by simple medications, but first the disease must be detected. For this reason, persons over 40 should be tested regularly, as described in the section on Eye Examinations (page 665).

What Is Glaucoma?

In 90 to 95 percent of cases, glaucoma occurs when the outflow of aqueous humor is blocked. In open-angle glaucoma, the drainage is slowed, so that fluid and pressure build up slowly. (For more on closed-angle glaucoma, see the section on The Red Eye, page 665.) The increased pressure in the eyeball pinches in the blood vessels that supply the optic nerve. Starved, the nerve dies slowly. Peripheral vision decreases, or the victim may first notice halos around lights. Eventually, the eye can achieve only tunnel vision. If untreated, blindness results.

Usually glaucoma is inherited. Parents may be carriers without developing the disease, however, so family history is not a sure guide. Glaucoma usually occurs after the age of 40, but abnormal development of the eye may cause glaucoma in infants and toddlers. Injuries, cataracts, and bleeding in the eye may also precipitate glaucoma. Infants with congenital glaucoma will have an aversion to light, enlarged corneas, copious tearing, and big, cloudy-looking eyes. Surgery may be necessary to save the infant's sight.

Treatment

Glaucoma may be detected by an optometrist or ophthalmologist, but only the ophthalmologist is qualified to treat it. There are many forms of treatment, all aimed at reducing pressure in the eye.

Glaucoma is defined as an intraocular pressure of more than 21 millimeters of mercury. However, most doctors do not automatically begin treating every patient at this point. Different people have differing sensitivity to the pressure. The ophthalmologist must look into the eyes for signs of damage and test for loss of peripheral vision. Therapy should begin only when pressure is high enough to cause the individual damage. Patients with pressures above 21 but no visual loss should be retested every 6 to 8 months.

For most patients, therapy consists of eyedrops, every day for life. Timoptic (timolol maleate), taken once or twice a day, reduces fluid formation and increases outflow. Pilocarpine, another form of eyedrops, is taken 3 or 4 times per day to decrease the size of the pupil and thus increase outflow. Diamox (acetazolamide), an oral medication, reduces fluid formation for those who have difficulty administering eyedrops. These drugs may be taken singly or in combination. Marijuana also reduces intraocular pressure, but studies to determine the active ingredient and solve problems of drug tolerance are still not complete.

For the 10 percent of glaucoma patients who are not helped by medicine, surgery offers sight-saving alternatives. The traditional operation opens up drainage by removing a part of the iris; newer methods involve implantation of a tiny plastic valve to permit outflow of liquid.

Patients with glaucoma have an additional problem in that many medications may increase ocular pressure, exacerbating the disease. These drugs include many remedies for stomach and intestinal problems. Patients with glaucoma must be sure that any other physicians they may see know about their condition and are careful not to prescribe anything that might worsen it.

EYELIDS

EYELIDS USUALLY fall under the care of the ophthalmologist when something goes wrong. Most eyelid problems are related to infections and are not serious. However, eyelids are subject to skin cancers, so any bump or change in a mole or birthmark deserves professional attention.

Blepharitis

Blepharitis is an infection of the edges of the eyelids. They become red, sticky, and crusty, and sometimes the victim has to unstick them to see anything in the morning. The eyeball may also become red. Some-times the infection is associated with dandruff or a *Staphylococcus aureus* infection like a boil.

In most cases, treatment consists of antibiotic drops or ointments. Any associated condition must be cleared up also. More serious cases may require oral antibiotics for cure.

Styes

A stye is nothing more than a pimple on the edge of the eyelid. A warm compress (a very clean lint-free cloth soaked in warm water and wrung out) held against the eye for 10 minutes, 4 times per day, will hasten its disappearance. A physician can prescribe an antibiotic ointment to apply under the lid. The rare resistant stye may require lancing and drainage.

Chalazion

A smooth, round bump some distance from the edge of the eyelid is probably a chalazion. These painless lumps occur when a gland in the lid becomes blocked. Sometimes they disappear after a regimen of warm compresses and antibiotics like that used for styes. Unfortunately, they are more stubborn than styes. Although they do no harm if left in place, they can be removed surgically under local anesthesia in the ophthalmologist's office and require only the wearing of an eyepatch until the next morning.

Basal Cell Carcinoma

Any growth on the eyelid that does not vanish within a few days should be inspected by a physician, as it may be a basal cell carcinoma. This relatively common skin cancer often begins as a round, dimpled bump with a pearllike sheen. Basal cell carcinomas are relatively slow-growing and noninvasive, but should be removed as soon as possible. (See page 630.)

Xanthelasmae

These are soft, yellowish skin growths that sometimes appear on the eyelids of persons with high cholesterol (hyperlipidemia) or diabetes. They are harmless, but can easily be removed if the patient wishes, although they may eventually grow back. (It should be noted, however, that development of xanthelasmae may be a sign that blood cholesterol should be measured.)

Entropion and Ectropion

Sometimes the eyelid turns in, a condition called entropion. The eyelashes scratch the surface of the eye. A small piece of tape may be used to keep the eyelid in its proper position until an ophthalmologic surgeon can correct the condition.

The reverse problem, when the lower eyelid becomes loose, falling away from the eye and revealing the conjunctiva, is called ectropion. The condition is commonly seen in older people. If the eyelid is very loose, tears intended to moisten the eye may flow out of the center, rather than crossing to the tear duct by the nose. This can be annoying enough to warrant surgery to tighten the lid.

Drooping Upper Lids

Very few people are born completely symmetrical. Some children are born with an upper eyelid that droops over one eye, perhaps blocking the vision. This should be corrected early to avoid the development of amblyopia, or "lazy eye." The surgery involves shortening the muscles that hold the lid up.

In adults, drooping eyelids—the medical term is "ptosis"—is a sign of muscle weakness in the eyelid. Sometimes the weakness is the effect of old age. Ptosis may also result from nerve or muscle damage due to injury or a disease such as diabetes, myesthenia gravis, stroke, or aneurysm inside the skull. Obviously, a physician must be consulted to determine the true cause of ptosis.

Treatment of ptosis often depends on treatment of the underlying cause. If the eyelid sags because of an injury, surgery can strengthen the muscle by shortening it, or the eyelid can be supported by specially designed eyeglasses or contact lenses.

INFECTIONS OF THE TEAR GLANDS AND DUCTS

THE TEAR GLANDS over the outside corner of the eye and the ducts leading from the inside corner to the nose may also become infected. When redness and swelling affect the lower lid near the nose, the infection is "dacryocystitis": infection of the tear ducts. When the tear glands above the outside corner of the eye are infected, the medical term is "dacryoadenitis." (See figure 33.7.) Pressing on the tear sac under the inside corner of the eye may produce a backflow of pus into the corner. Treatment consists of warm soaks and antibiotics: in the form of eyedrops for inflammation of the tear ducts, but in oral form for infected glands. Oral antibiotics may be used for stubborn infection of the tear ducts. If the infection continues, surgery may be necessary to clear out the passage from the eye to the nose.

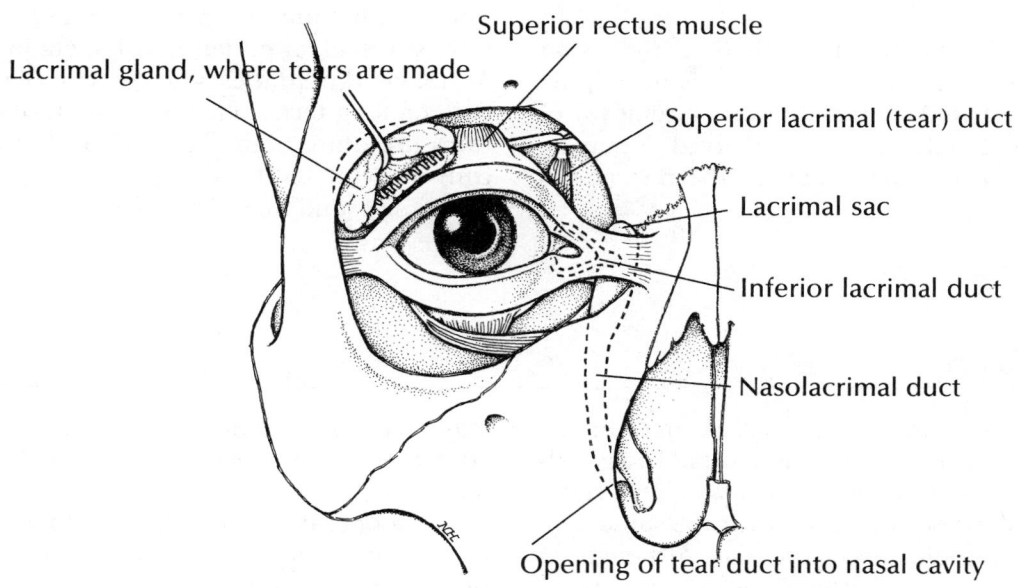

Superior rectus muscle

Lacrimal gland, where tears are made

Superior lacrimal (tear) duct

Lacrimal sac

Inferior lacrimal duct

Nasolacrimal duct

Opening of tear duct into nasal cavity

Figure 33.7. **Where tears come from.**

GROWTHS WITHIN THE EYEBALL

PINGUECULA is the name for one or more soft yellow patches growing on either side of the eyeball, usually in a person over 35. The condition is benign and no treatment is necessary.

A fleshy growth starting from either corner of the eye and moving toward the cornea is a pterygium. It is associated with exposure to wind and dust. It is also benign, but can be removed surgically for cosmetic reasons or if it impinges on the visual field.

Cancers

Retinoblastoma. Retinoblastoma, the second most common childhood cancer, is most often found in children under the age of 4. The family often notices the first sign when the tumor may be seen through the pupil as a white reflection, like that in a cat's eye. Later stages bring pain, redness, and visual loss. In at least 20 percent of cases, both eyes are affected and the disease is inherited—half the children of retinoblastoma patients develop retinoblastoma.

Over half the cases of retinoblastoma are curable through a combination of surgery and radiation. In fact, as the tumor grows, it may cut off its own blood supply and regress on its own. However, the chance that the retinoblastoma may spread along the optic nerve toward the brain makes firm intervention necessary.

Radiation therapy may be sufficient to destroy the cancer in its early stages without harming the eye, as retinoblastomas are very sensitive to radiation. Small "plaques" of radioactive material are sewn to the outside of the eyeball over the tumor for a few days and then removed. The lens may be damaged but vision is preserved in most early-stage cancers. Chemotherapy may also be used. Surgery involves removal of the eye and attachment of an artificial one. The surgery is followed by a week in the hospital, but no pain. A patch is worn for several weeks until a false eye can be attached to the eye muscles so that it will move naturally. If both eyes are affected, the eye with the more advanced tumor is removed and the other eye treated with radiation to preserve vision. Laser therapy is a new technique for precisely targeting retinoblastoma.

Melanoma. Most melanomas are skin cancers. However, they are also found inside the eye, sometimes causing a form of glaucoma. Melanoma is an extremely fast-growing cancer and the prognosis for a person with one so close to the brain is not good.

Sometimes a melanoma may appear as a dark spot in the white of the eye. If it lies on the back of the eye, it may cause no symptoms at all. If it is in the center, vision may become unclear or objects may seem distorted. Immediate treatment is necessary.

Surgical removal of the eyeball is the usual treatment. If one eye has already been removed, the other may be treated with radiation or removal of the tumor only. If only the iris is involved, it may be removed in an iridectomy, leaving the rest of the eye.

New forms of radiation using protons (hydrogen ions) and helium ions promise a higher rate of long-term survival for patients with melanoma of the eye. Although the studies are not complete (they lack data on long-term follow-up), the 18-month survival rates are quite high. Research is continuing at the University of California at San Francisco, Harvard University, and in Switzerland.

CATARACTS

THREE THOUSAND YEARS AGO, physicians in India described an operation to cure cataracts. Today, almost half a million Americans each year undergo a remote descendant of that surgery for the same condition—a growing opacity of the lens. Although 95 percent of patients see better after surgery, ignorance and fear still delay the operation, and some 5,000 people each year become blind because they refuse to have it. In 1978, an estimated 41,500 Americans were legally blind for this reason.

About three-quarters of cataracts are caused by age—so-called senile cataracts. The cataract may begin as a small cloudy spot in the lens that does not interfere with sight. As it grows, vision clouds. The world appears grayer and mistier, as if a series of veils is being drawn across it. Brighter lights and stronger lenses are required for reading and double vision may occur. Night driving becomes difficult as the glare from oncoming headlights is dispersed by the lens. After a while, new glasses no longer help.

Cataracts may also develop after an injury puncturing the eye or exposure to radiation, such as x-rays, microwaves, and infrared rays. Diseases such as uveitis or diabetes also may be responsible.

Congenital cataracts can often be prevented. German measles (rubella) in a pregnant woman may cause her baby to have congenital cataracts; this can be forestalled by ensuring that women who have not had rubella have a rubella vaccine before they become pregnant.

Galactosemia, a hereditary disease, causes cataracts to form in newborn infants. They can be prevented by a special diet that excludes galactose, a milk sugar.

Treatment

The only effective treatment is surgery, not diet, drugs, or exercises. Advances in surgical techniques have made it unnecessary to wait until the cataract is "ripe," or completely opaque. It should be removed as soon as it interferes with daily life—at 20/40 vision in a diamond cutter, but as late as 20/200 in a retired person who doesn't care for reading.

The operation should be performed by an ophthalmologic surgeon with extensive experience in removing cataracts. Since many different methods are in use today for anesthesia, hospitalization, and correction of vision after cataract surgery, as well as removal of the cataract itself, the patient should discuss all these areas thoroughly before choosing a surgeon.

General anesthesia may be used, but local anesthesia is safer and simpler, especially for elderly or ill patients. One injection paralyzes the lid to prevent blinking during the surgery; another prevents the eyeball from moving. The operation takes 1 hour and involves little or no pain.

In some cases of senile cataract, the entire lens and its capsule are removed, usually by inserting a freezing probe (a cryoprobe), which sticks to the lens and draws it out. Another common technique, phacoemulsification, involves an ultrafast vibrator to break up the lens, which is then vacuumed up (aspirated) through a hollow needle. Children have very soft lenses, which can be aspirated without previous ultravibration. The cornea is then sutured together.

These techniques may be used on an outpatient basis, but most physicians prefer to monitor their patients overnight, or longer. A 4- to 7-day hospital stay is not uncommon. Many patients find that they can return to normal activities soon after leaving the hospital.

Cataracts often appear in both eyes and may grow at different rates in the same person. In this case, the most severely affected eye is usually corrected first. Several months may pass to ensure complete healing without infection before the second cataract is removed.

Replacing the Lens

After surgery, the patient needs a new lens to replace

the one that was removed. In the past, glasses as thick as the bottoms of soda bottles were used. These have many drawbacks: They magnify the image of the world and restrict the field of view to straight ahead. When used on one eye, they make it difficult for the brain to reconcile the magnified and unmagnified images. For these reasons, most people prefer a lens that fits on or in the eyeball.

Intraocular lenses can be almost like having new eyes. They are implanted permanently into the eye during the same surgery that removes the cataract. The patient does not have to bother with the care of contact lenses, making this an especially helpful technique for elderly people with arthritis of the hands. Over the past few years there has been a marked increase in the use of intraocular lenses. They are now used to treat more than 75% of cases in this country.

After cataract surgery, many patients are troubled by bright sunlight, which can cause serious burns of the eye. (For more on protection, see the section on Sunburn, page 656.)

In about 50 percent of cases, especially if the patient is under age 50, contact lenses that rest on the cornea are the treatment of choice. (See the section on Contact Lenses, page 660, for a description of the different kinds.) They can be fitted about 6 weeks after surgery, but the wearer must be able to handle them properly and keep them clean.

DISEASES OF THE RETINA

THE ROD AND CONE CELLS of the retina are the organs that actually perceive light and color. Any damage or derangement involving the retina therefore constitutes a serious threat to vision. Among the most common causes of blindness are diseases that damage the retina and such inherited conditions as retinitis pigmentosa.

Macular Degeneration

The macula is the part of the retina with the sharpest sight. A dense concentration of rods and cones helps us see fine details at the center of the field of vision. In almost 8,000 Americans each year, mostly older people, the surface of the macula degenerates enough to cause legal blindness. Usually the immediate cause is poor blood flow to the retina, but a few cases are inherited. Gradually and painlessly, central vision becomes blurry in one or both eyes.

In the early stages of the disease, magnifying glasses may help the victim read. Laser treatments may help by sealing leaks under the retina and reattaching parts of it. In the later stages, sharp central vision is lost completely. But most of the 58,000 Americans who are legally blind due to macular degeneration can care for themselves and get around easily, because the outer field of vision remains undamaged.

Diabetes and the Retina

About 4,700 Americans each year lose their sight because of retinal damage due to diabetes. More than 32,000 Americans are legally blind because of diabetic retinopathy (the medical term). The danger increases with the duration of the disease: After 15 years, two-thirds of diabetics show signs of damage, rising to 90 percent after 30 or 40 years.

The ophthalmologist will first notice the widening of the tiny veins in the retina, which often swell to pinch the arteries where they cross each other. The disease weakens the walls of the veins, causing outgrowths and expansions that appear as tiny red dots. These break, causing little hemorrhages that may vanish or leave tiny white scars that mark areas where vision is lost.

As the disease progresses, new blood vessels grow over the retina and into the vitreous humor. These also swell and bleed, causing large hemorrhages that obscure sight. Sometimes they clear up without treatment, but there resorption can lead to retinal detachment (see below).

Medical care for this condition begins with good control of diabetes. In many patients, lasers can be used to coagulate the outgrowths and leaks in old blood vessels and stop the new blood vessels that threaten the retina. This procedure can be performed on outpatients under local anesthesia. Vision threatened by a blood-clouded vitreous humor can be restored by replacing the fluid with a clear saline solution, a surgical procedure called vitrectomy. (For more details, see Chapter 23 on Diabetes and Other Endocrine Disorders, page 480.)

High Blood Pressure

Hypertension or high blood pressure can also cause hemorrhages and patches of scar tissue in the retina. Depending on whether the damage is due to a sudden peak in the blood pressure or to a long, steady rise, the tiny arteries in the retina become thin and tortuous, or so thick-walled that the blood inside cannot be seen. "Floaters" (moving spots before the eyes) may appear in the vision, but often, sight is normal.

The chief significance is that these changes in the retina due to hypertension mirror more serious changes elsewhere in the body, especially the kidneys and heart. Treatment consists of lowering the blood pressure through diet or drugs, or both. This alone may correct the visual problems.

Retinal Detachment

The retina receives oxygen and nutrients from the blood vessels at the back of the eyeball. Occasionally—more often in an older person who is nearsighted—fluid leaks beneath the retina and it peels away from its backing like loose wallpaper. (See figure 33.8.) Sometimes detachment follows an injury to the eye. The victim sees dark spots or light flashes; a curtain may seem to blot out part of the field of vision, or the world may seem blurred or distorted.

This is a genuine ophthalmologic emergency. If the retina is not reattached to its source of nutrients within a short period of time, the rod and cone cells will die and vision loss will be permanent. The ophthalmologist will use general anesthesia and one or more of the following techniques: draining the fluid under the retina; using a very cold instrument (a cryoprobe) to make the back of the eyeball stickier; pushing the back of the eyeball toward the retina with special instruments; sealing holes in the retina with a laser. Surgery is successful in about 90 percent of cases. The hospital stay usually lasts about 1 week.

Retinitis Pigmentosa

Retinitis pigmentosa is an inherited disease in which the retina degenerates in tiny patches. It affects about 1 million people in the United States. The patient first notices poor night vision, then loses peripheral vision, although central vision may be as good as 20/50 until middle age. There is no known treatment and eventually tunnel vision results. About 23,000 Americans are legally blind due to retinitis pigmentosa. Newly developed glasses employ precision optics to provide a horizontal widening of the field of vision. These experimental devices are odd-looking, heavy, and expensive (about $2,000), but they enable some victims of retinitis pigmentosa to hold jobs and even drive.

Choroiditis

The choroid is the layer of blood vessels that underlies and nourishes the retina. An inflammation here can spread to the retina and the resultant scars may permanently impair vision. In many cases, the disease is due to infection with a microbe called *Toxoplasma gondii*, transmitted to children through contact with feces of dogs or—more rarely—cats. The infection can also be transmitted by a pregnant woman to her baby, causing more severe disease. In many cases, however, the cause cannot be determined.

The condition is painless but causes blurred vision. Children who have the disease in one eye may develop amblyopia. In adults, the severity of the disease depends on the location of scarring: the closer to the macula, the more likely the loss of clear vision in the center of the field of vision. The sooner medi-

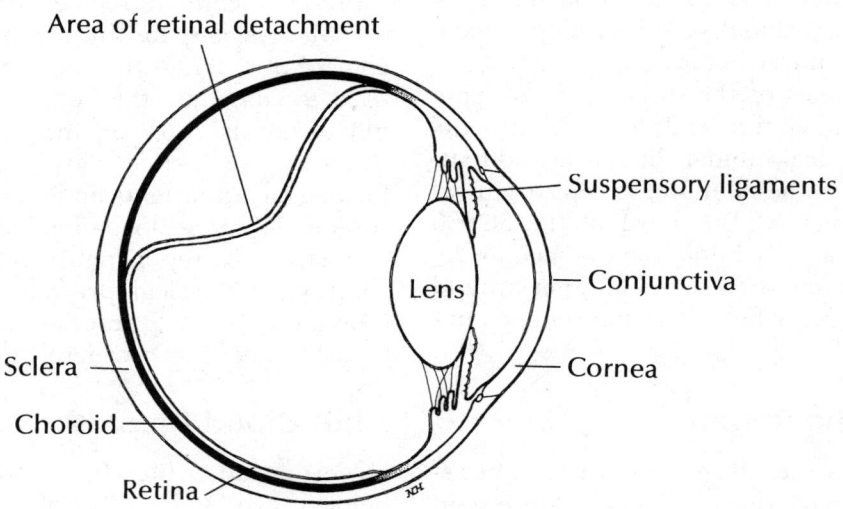

Figure 33.8. **Detached retina.**

cal therapy begins, the less likelihood of scarring. Therapy consists of steroids to control the inflammation. In congenital infections, drugs to suppress the immune system may be necessary.

Retinal Blood Vessels

The retina is nourished and cleansed by a set of tiny blood vessels, the retinal arteries and the retinal veins. Especially in older persons, these fine vessels sometimes become blocked with a blood clot (thrombosis) or fatty deposit (embolus).

The symptoms depend on which kind of vessel is blocked. If it is an artery, the retina it supplies stops functioning, causing blindness in part or all of one eye. Unlike retinal detachment, the loss often involves the upper or lower half of the field of vision. If the blocked blood vessel is a vein, it may rupture, spilling blood and fluid into the vitreous humor, blurring and clouding vision over a few hours.

Blockage of a retinal artery is an emergency, like retinal detachment. Without a blood supply, the rod and cone cells of the retina will die. Massage of the eyeball, drugs, or surgery may be necessary to dislodge the blockage. In many cases, vision can be only partially improved.

Retinal vein blockage is less dire. Especially in younger people, the spilled blood may be resorbed. There is no other treatment, although complications, such as overgrowth of new blood vessels, may be halted through coagulation with a laser. Because blockage of a retinal vein may be undetectable to the victim, regular eye examinations are essential so that treatment of underlying causes, like high blood pressure, can prevent further damage.

DISORDERS OF THE OPTIC NERVE

ATROPHY OF THE OPTIC NERVE is another common cause of blindness, responsible for about 2,000 new cases of legal blindness in the United States each year. A total of 34,500 Americans are legally blind because of optic nerve atrophy.

The most common cause is an increase in pressure inside the skull. This may be caused by a growth or by very high blood pressure. The increased pressure causes swelling of the optic disk—the area in the back of the eye where the blood vessels and the optic nerve pass through to the brain. The optic disk becomes swollen and presses on the nerve. The patient may or may not see white or dark spots. As the optic nerve atrophies from the pressure, vision becomes poor. Part of the visual field may be lost. The condition is called papilledema.

Treatment of papilledema is aimed at correcting the causes of the increased cranial pressure. Vision usually returns to normal within 2 months.

SUMMING UP

OUR EYES provide the most precious of our senses—vision—through which we learn about our world. Yet many people endanger their sight through ignorance or carelessness. Regular—although not necessarily yearly—eye checkups are essential to young and old alike. Simple eye protectors could prevent many eye injuries, with attendant pain and disability, including blindness.

A bewildering assortment of corrective lenses is available to compensate for nearsighted, farsighted, or astigmatic vision. Good professional attention will facilitate prescription and adjustment to contact lenses or glasses.

New techniques and devices are now used to treat cataracts, detached retinas, and the damage due to diabetes. Glaucoma, the "sneak thief of sight," can be arrested through careful use of medications.

With proper care, our eyes should last a lifetime, and may even outlive us to serve others.

34 Diseases of the Ear, Nose, and Throat

Malcolm H. Schvey, M.D.

INTRODUCTION

WITHIN THE RELATIVELY SMALL structure of the ears, nose, and throat are several very complex mechanisms that allow us not only to make sound, but to hear it; to keep our balance; to smell; to breathe in and filter air; and to swallow food and water. These mechanisms are interrelated and generally carry out their functions without our being aware of the processes at work. Although these structures are complex, they are in many ways not far removed from the more primitive form in which they once existed—first in aquatic animals and later in more primitive land species.

The doctor trained to diagnose and treat disorders of the ear, nose, and throat is the otolaryngologist, sometimes referred to as an ENT specialist, and the discipline is considered a subspecialty of surgery.

PART I: THE EAR

THE EAR is divided into 3 parts: the external ear, the middle ear, and the inner ear. (See figure 34.1.) The outer ear consists of the auricle or pinna—the cartilage and skin that we see on the outside of the skull—and the outer ear canal, which conducts sound to the middle ear. At the entrance to the middle ear is the eardrum, a thin membrane that is stretched across the end of the outer ear canal.

The middle ear is a cavity that contains 3 connected bones, collectively called the ossicles, and each named for the object it resembles: the malleus (hammer), the incus (anvil), and the stapes (stirrup). Leading from the bottom of the middle ear cavity to the back of the nose is a narrow channel called the Eustachian tube. When an individual swallows or yawns, the muscles attached to this tube pull on its edges and open it so that the air outside may replenish the air supply in the middle ear. The Eustachian tube thus serves to equalize the air pressure on the inside of the eardrum with that on the outside.

The middle ear opens into the inner ear via the oval window, which is covered by the footplate of the stapes bone. On the inner side of that plate, the stapes is bathed with the fluid of the vestibule, which is contiguous with the fluid of the cochlea. This structure, shaped something like a snail shell and lined with tiny hairs, is the major part of the hearing mechanism. The second part of the inner ear is the labyrinth, which is responsible for balance.

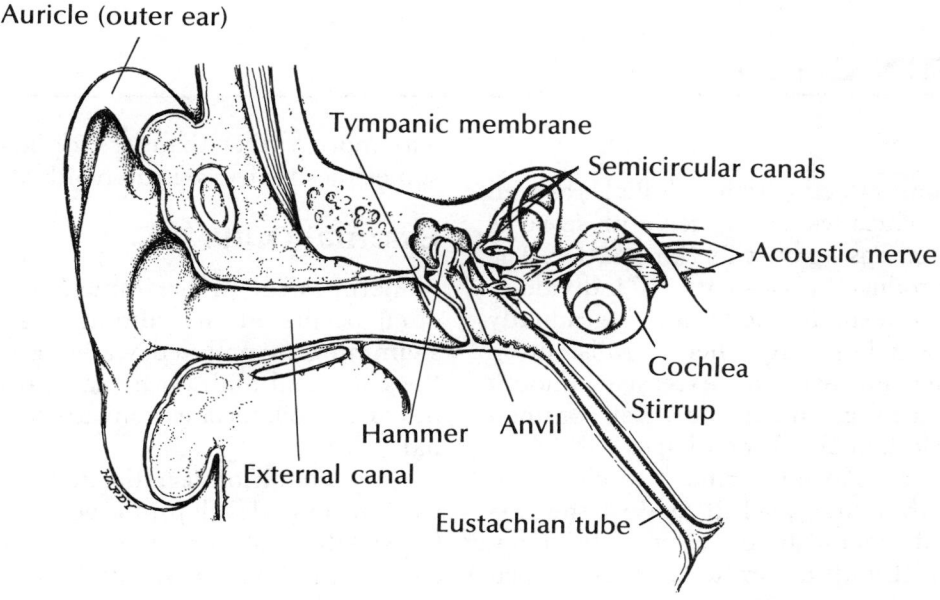

Figure 34.1. **Structures of the ear.**

HEARING

SOUND IS ESSENTIALLY VIBRATION. When the vibrations are very rapid and of a small amplitude, the sound is high pitched; when they are slow and of a large amplitude, the sound has a low pitch. The ability to perceive vibration existed in very early forms of life found in an aquatic environment. Even now, the inner part of the human ear is virtually the same as the entire ear structure of many aquatic creatures, such as sharks. The later formation of the middle and outer ear has allowed the vibrations to be augmented so that they can be perceived by humans and animals living in a gaseous environment, which does not carry vibrations as strongly as water does.

The vibrations, or sound waves, are funneled from the outer ear through the outer ear canal until they strike the eardrum, making it vibrate. These vibrations pass via the eardrum through the middle ear, which magnifies the sound and transfers it to the fluid of the inner ear cochlea. The tiny hairs lining the cochlea are stimulated by the waves and transmit these stimulations via the auditory nerve to the brain, which perceives the impulses as sounds.

The middle ear is basically designed for functioning on land, not for reentry into water. Consequently, one of the major sources of acquired ear disease is swimming. Nor was this part of the ear designed for rapid changes in pressure or altitude. Another important cause of middle ear disease in adults is a rapid change in pressure, like that experienced in flying or scuba diving.

BALANCE

THE SECOND PART of the inner ear is the labyrinth—2 connected chambers and 3 connected, fluid-filled semicircular canals at right angles to one another. When the head or body is tilted, or moved up and down or back and forth, the fluid in these canals and chambers is set into motion or, if already in motion, is set to rest. It is the changes in motion or rest of these fluids which produce the impulses that enable us to detect the movement, and provide information to the brain about the head's position. This information, along with sight and impulses from the muscles, helps determine what movements the body must make to maintain balance. Disorders or infections of the labyrinth often result in difficulties in balance and vertigo, which is a kind of dizziness that feels as if the individual or his surroundings are spinning.

THE EXTERNAL EAR

Earwax

The outer ear canal is lined with hair follicles as well as glands that produce wax, and they both serve as protective mechanisms against foreign matter. The amount of wax produced varies with the individual. In most people it is a small amount and it gradually moves to the external opening where it rolls out on its own. In some, however, an excessive amount forms, often hardening, and is the most common cause of hearing loss in people of all ages.

Cotton sticks should not be used to clean out earwax because they may pack it against the eardrum. Rather, this should be done by a physician, who may remove it with a curette (a scoop-shaped instrument) or wash it out. Occasionally, a suction device may be used. Softening agents may make the wax more, rather than less, difficult to remove, but sometimes their use is unavoidable.

External Otitis

Sometimes called "swimmer's ear," external otitis often occurs in the summertime, especially after swimming in polluted water. Eczema develops in the ear canal and, once the skin is broken, germs, fungus, or bacteria can invade the tissues of the canal.

The condition usually starts with itching of the ear and may develop into very severe pain, caused by swelling of the tissue in the canal pressing against the bone. There may also be foul-smelling, yellowish pus oozing from the ear, or blocking it and affecting hearing. (See figure 34.2.)

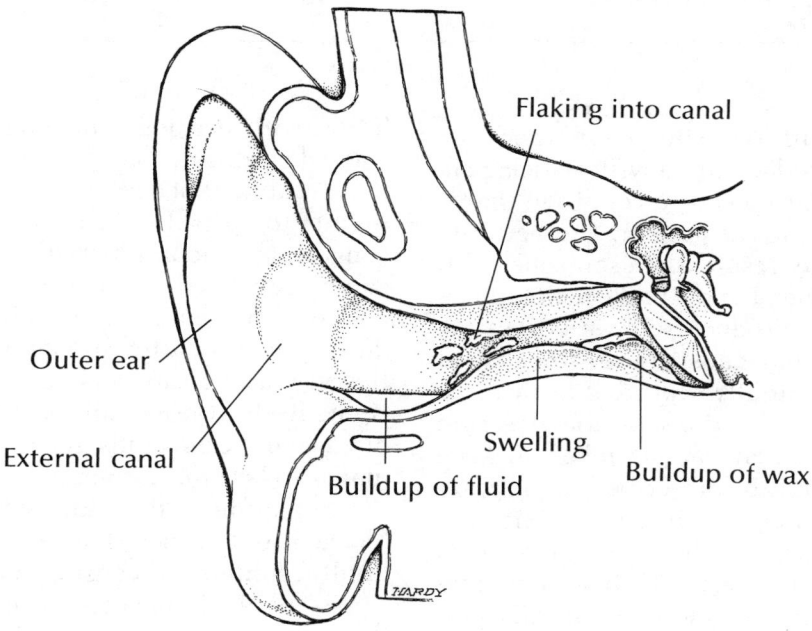

Figure 34.2. **External otitis, inflammation of the external ear.**

External otitis is usually treated with drops containing a steroid or cortisone derivative, along with a topical antibiotic to control the infection. Care must be taken not to get water in the ear while the infection is healing.

External otitis can be caused by substances other than water, such as hair spray or hair coloring dye. To help prevent this, balls of lambswool can be placed in the ears while these substances are being used. Unlike cotton balls, which absorb liquid, lambswool tends to repel it.

On rare occasions, external otitis is caused by a fungus, usually *Aspergillis niger*, which produces coal-black spores like those often seen on old bread. It may become so firmly entrenched that it remains even after the eczema is healed, but once identified by its characteristic color, it is easily treated with a dusting of sulfanilamide powder.

Furunculosis

Furunculosis, or recurring boils, is similar to external otitis, but is caused by an infection of a hair follicle in the ear canal. Like external otitis, it can result in painful swelling and is treated with systemic antibiotics as well as eardrops.

Benign Cysts and Tumors

Sebaceous cysts, which arise from skin glands and usually contain a medium thick fluid, often develop just behind the outer ear. Treatment is usually not necessary, but if they become large or are prone to recurrent infection, they may be removed surgically.

Exostoses are benign tumors of the ear canal resulting from an overgrowth of bone about two-thirds of the way in toward the eardrum. The growth may become large enough to block the ear canal, and only then will it have to be removed surgically. This is a tricky procedure which requires that the skin covering the exostoses be left intact, since it is more resistant to infection than the tissue that may grow to replace it if the original skin is lost. Exostoses grow extremely slowly and may never reach a size where they become a problem.

Foreign Bodies

Otolaryngologists see everything from bugs to seeds, pieces of plastic or paper, and even earplugs stuck in ears in such a way that the patient is unable to remove them. In fact, it is best for the patient not even to try. Removal is relatively easy with the right instrument, generally a special type of tiny forceps known as "alligator" forceps, but difficult and even potentially dangerous with the wrong instrument. Attempts by other than an experienced physician with the right instrument may drive the object farther into the ear. An insect in the ear is particularly annoying, and can sometimes be immobilized with drops of mineral oil until a physician can remove it.

THE EARDRUM

Trauma

Trauma to the eardrum (tympanic membrane) can be caused by accidental laceration with a stick, pencil, bobbypin, or similar object—a condition that is painful and frightening to the patient. Another form of external trauma may result when someone is hit over the ear with an open hand. Unlike a closed fist, an open hand usually produces an air pocket between it and the ear canal, causing pressure against the eardrum that can actually rupture it inward.

Most traumatic perforations of the eardrum heal spontaneously if great care is taken to keep them dry. Antibiotics may be prescribed as a precautionary measure. If water gets in and an infection occurs, however, the hole in the eardrum is much less likely to heal spontaneously. If this occurs and the hole remains, it must be closed surgically at a later date. Even when the laceration is very large, if no external material is placed in the ear and no infection occurs, it will generally heal on its own.

Bullous Myringitis (Infectious Myringitis)

In this condition little water blisters develop on the eardrum, causing inflammation and severe pain. The cause may be bacterial or viral and the disease is not fully understood. It is usually treated with systemic antibiotics or with eardrops containing steroids and antibiotics, or both, to prevent infection of the vesicles as they break open. The infection can be very painful, but is usually not very serious. In most cases the eardrum returns to normal in a week or so.

Retracted Eardrum

Many problems of the middle ear are caused by an obstruction of the Eustachian tube, which runs from the back of the nose to the middle ear. If this tube is blocked so that air cannot pass freely to and from the middle ear, the eardrum cannot function properly. If it is blocked completely, the air in the middle ear is gradually resorbed and a vacuum will form, pulling the eardrum inward, causing pain and interfering with hearing. This condition is called a retracted eardrum.

Treatment of a retracted eardrum consists of attempts to open the Eustachian tube with nasal decongestants and antihistamines so that the pressure can be equalized. If this is not successful, the physician may make a little slit in the eardrum, a procedure known as a myringotomy. This allows air in, the vacuum disappears, and often the condition rights itself. However, if there is underlying chronic disease in the adenoids, the problem in the eardrum may also become chronic.

Sometimes the Eustachian tube becomes blocked, but rather than a vacuum being formed, fluid accumulates, causing pain. Treatment is the same—nasal decongestants and antihistamines or, if necessary, a myringotomy.

Barotitis Media (Barometric Otitis, Baurotrauma)

When the eardrum is retracted by a change of atmospheric pressure while the Eustachian tube is blocked, which often happens to individuals who fly or scuba dive when they have a cold or stuffy nose, the condition is known as barotitis media. It is painful and usually reduces hearing temporarily, but it often responds easily to treatment and is seldom very serious. Generally the symptoms clear up spontaneously, but if not, treatment with antibiotics and decongestants, and possibly a myringotomy, may be necessary.

If the changes of air pressure are very great or if the Eustachian tube is extremely blocked, the pressure may cause bleeding of the little capillaries in the middle ear. The blood filling the middle ear acts as a sound barrier, and there may be a considerable hearing loss, as well as a peculiar feeling of being under water.

If air travel with a stuffy nose is unavoidable, nasal decongestants or antihistamines should be taken an hour before takeoff and again an hour before landing.

THE MIDDLE EAR

Acute Otitis Media

Although they go by various names, there are basically 3 types of acute otitis media. In the mildest form of this disorder—secretory otitis media—there is fluid in the ear, but no infection. In serous otitis media, there is fluid and infection. If serous otitis media is not treated, it may lead to the third type—acute purulent otitis media—in which pus forms

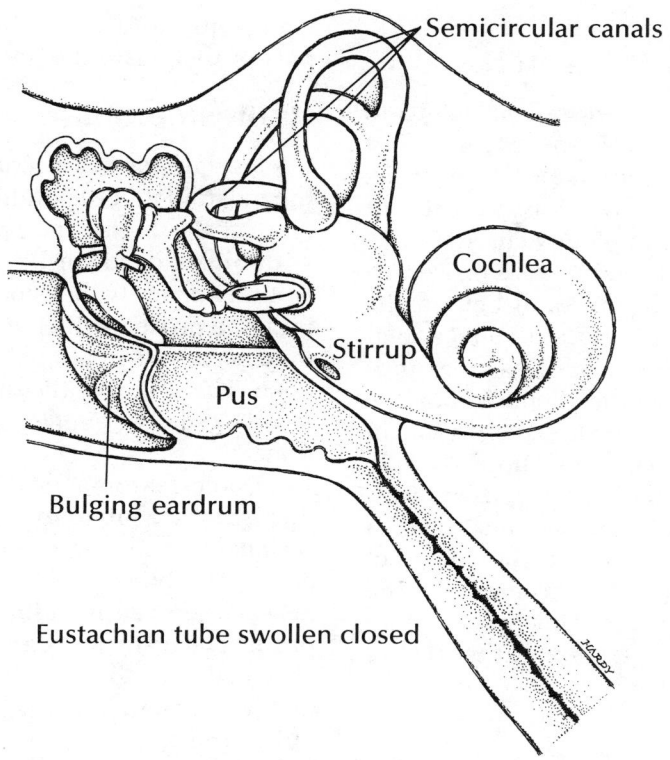

Figure 34.3. **Otitis media, inflammation of the middle ear.**

and fills the middle ear. (See figure 34.3.)

Secretory otitis media is usually caused by obstruction of the Eustachian tube or abnormal production of fluid in the middle ear and is treated with decongestants and, if necessary, by myringotomy (surgical incision of the eardrum).

Serous otitis media can also be caused by an obstruction of the Eustachian tube and is often secondary to some other upper respiratory infection or to enlarged adenoids, or both. It causes pain and some temporary hearing loss. If not treated, it can develop into acute purulent otitis media.

Acute purulent otitis media, or middle ear abscess, is common in infants and children, from 3 months to puberty. It produces a severe, persistent earache and may cause temporary hearing loss. If the eardrum ruptures, the discharge may be bloody at first and then become a thick pus. At the time of rupture, the pain is abruptly relieved.

Treatment requires heavy doses of antibiotics plus nasal decongestants and antihistamines. If it appears that the eardrum may rupture, the physician will probably perform a myringotomy rather than permit the eardrum to rupture on its own, since the surgical cut is clean and will almost always heal spontaneously, whereas the rupture may not. Myringotomy also relieves the pain and provides drainage,

which in itself is important in the treatment of the disease.

Chronic Secretory Otitis Media

Secretory otitis media may also be chronic, a condition most often found in children and frequently due to the presence of large amounts of adenoidal tissue. Sometimes it occurs in adults who have permanent or recurrent blockage of the Eustachian tube, or recurrent changes in the consistency of the liquid that is produced in the middle ear, or both.

The condition is usually treated with antihistamines and nasal decongestants. If these medications are ineffective, and the adenoids are enlarged, the best course is usually surgical removal, a simple procedure that usually ends the problem.

In lieu of an adenoidectomy, or in cases when this surgical procedure is not effective, the alternative is to place a small plastic tube through the patient's eardrum so that the ear is inflated artificially and the fluid can drain from the middle ear. The major disadvantage of this method is that no water must be allowed to get into the ear, meaning the patient must not swim and must be extremely careful when bathing, two difficult things to accomplish with young children over what may be a period of years.

Chronic Serous Otitis Media and Chronic Purulent Otitis Media

Both these conditions can progress from acute to chronic problems, and although the cause is not clear-cut, the adenoids may play a significant role. Sometimes the attacks are not really recurrent, but a single one which is never completely cured.

The infection spreads to the mastoid process, a honeycombed area of bone in the skull behind the ear which has few blood vessels. Because only a relatively small amount of blood reaches this area, antibiotics which travel through the bloodstream are less effective in fighting an infection there than in the middle ear itself, where the blood supply is rich. Therefore, a recurrent problem is often caused by insufficient antibiotic treatment, which results in a subclinical remnant of infection in the mastoid. When the antibiotics are stopped, the remnant in the mastoid reinfects the middle ear. This process may easily be mistaken for a new infection, rather than a reoccurrence.

Acute Mastoiditis

The mastoid process is a honeycombed section of bone located behind the outer ear and connected to the middle ear. When the middle ear becomes infected, the infection spreads to the mucous membrane covering the mastoid process and the walls of the bone itself. If the infection is severe enough, the bony honeycomb can be destroyed, and the result is referred to as acute mastoiditis. Until the early 1950s, acute mastoiditis was a major cause of death in children, but now that acute purulent otitis media can be treated with antibiotics, acute mastoiditis is relatively uncommon. Should antibiotic treatment prove ineffective and acute mastoiditis develop, a simple mastoidectomy—surgical removal of all or part of the mastoid bone—may be required.

Cholesteatoma

Cholesteatoma is a peculiar disorder that occurs in the mastoid and the middle ear. A cholesteatoma is a type of epithelial inclusion cyst—a cyst that fills with bits of dead surface skin cells (epithelium) that would normally be sloughed off. As the cyst enlarges, a process which is often rapid in children, but may be slower in adults, it destroys the surrounding bone. The origin of the disorder is not totally understood: It may be congenital or it may follow an infection.

Cholesteatomas are not malignant and do not metastasize (spread to other sites), but they can have serious consequences, possibly destroying the eardrum, the bones of the middle ear, and the facial nerve, and even invading the skull surrounding the brain. The disorder is an ongoing, chronic condition that can only be eradicated after time-consuming and very meticulous surgery. Treatment often requires repeat procedures, either because little pieces have been missed or because the cyst has grown back.

The surgery often involves rebuilding the bones of the middle ear with various plastic prostheses or with bits of the patient's cartilage. When it is successful (and this is more likely in adults than in children), normal hearing may be restored and the cavity closed off. Some patients have had 3 or 4 operations and finally have been totally cured, with hearing restored. Others get discouraged after 1 or 2, and the alternative is to perform a radical mastoidectomy, which leaves an open cavity, through which the physician can periodically clean out the debris that collects.

THE INNER EAR

Ménière's Disease

Although the exact cause of this relatively uncommon disease is not known, the effects can be disabling. The theoretical cause is an increase of fluid in the labyrinth, putting pressure on the membrane of the labyrinth wall and affecting both balance and hearing.

Historically, accountants, dentists, otolaryngologists, and watchmakers—people who do fine, meticulous work that requires great concentration and control of the hands for long periods of time—are more prone than others to develop this condition. In fact, it was originally called watchmaker's disease. This is not necessarily true now, and the condition seems to be more frequent in women than in men.

Symptoms are absent between flare-ups; the typical signs of the disease are threefold: There is a fluctuating sensorineural hearing loss, fluctuating vertigo, and recurring or fluctuating tinnitus (ringing or buzzing in the ear). The vertigo consists of dramatic and violent attacks, during which the patient feels that either he or the room is moving. These attacks may be so severe that the patient cannot stand and often has nausea, retching, and vomiting.

The condition may affect only one ear or, in 20 percent of cases, may grow to include both ears. The baseline hearing between attacks gradually gets lower and lower. The attacks vary considerably from one patient to another and within each case as well. One person may have weekly attacks lasting 4 hours; another may have attacks lasting 1 hour twice a year; a third may have 3 attacks a day; and a fourth, 1 attack in 6 years.

Diagnosis will usually consist of audiometry, a measurement of how well the patient hears sounds of various frequencies conducted both through the air and through the bones in the head.

The only proven, reliable treatment for Ménière's disease is surgery. Nonsurgical treatments that may work in some cases include a low-sodium diet, reduction of nicotine and caffeine, the use of diuretics to eliminate salt, and various types of anti-vertigenous drugs such as Dramamine or Antivert. A recent treatment has been the use of the drug scopolamine transdermally—through the skin—by attaching a small patch of it behind the ear where it gradually releases a small amount of the drug into the body. It is difficult to assess the results of drugs like scopolamine on a condition as variable as Ménière's: Did a 3-year remission happen as a result of a drug, or would it have happened anyway with no treatment?

Surgical treatment centers on selective destruction of the balance mechanism or the nerve of balance or a method by which the excess fluid which accumulates in the ear will drain off as the attack starts. If there is no hearing left and the only problem is dizziness, the physician may choose to destroy the entire inner ear via a safe and easy surgical procedure. Since there is no hearing, there is nothing to lose by this method, because the balance function will be handled by the other ear as well as by sight and muscle impulses. (See Balance, page 674.)

For patients with bilateral Ménière's disease, treatment is even more difficult. Sometimes surgical intervention on the worse side will stop the majority of attacks. In the past, streptomycin was sometimes used in exceptionally large doses, which had the effect of destroying the balance mechanism, while not affecting the hearing. Some patients are willing to endure having to use their tendon reflexes and their eyes to achieve balance (meaning they have no sense of balance in a completely dark room) in order to stop the attacks of vertigo.

Acoustic Neurinoma

A neurinoma is a tumor that arises from the cells of the thin sheath that covers a nerve. In the case of an acoustic neurinoma, the tumor arises on the vestibu-lar rather than the acoustic nerve, and grows very slowly, often taking many years to mature. It may present only mild, transient dizziness and unsteadiness, tinnitus (ringing in the ear), and eventually a gradual loss of hearing in the affected ear. The tumor is not malignant and radiation will have no effect on it, but if it is found while it is still small, it can often be removed surgically. Even if it is discovered when it has grown too large to remove completely, partial removal may still be possible.

Labyrinthitis

This disease involves the whole inner ear and may occur as a bacterial infection secondary to acute otitis media or to purulent meningitis, or may be a viral infection. In either case, it produces extreme vertigo—a feeling that the victim or his surroundings are spinning—and often nausea and vomiting. When the disease is bacterial, there is a total loss of hearing on the affected side, unless the infection is caused by tuberculosis or syphilis, in which case the hearing loss may be partial. Treatment consists of heavy doses of antibiotics.

The viral form is usually self-limiting and, indeed, there is some difference of opinion among physicians about the existence of a viral form; often, the symptoms are ascribed to another cause. To confuse matters further, the term labyrinthitis is often inappropriately used for any disease characterized by dizziness. The only treatment for the viral form of labyrinthitis is bed rest, tranquilizers, and a medication such as Antivert to combat the dizziness.

Vestibular Neuronitis

This disorder is characterized by a sudden loss of the balance mechanism in one ear. The victim is so violently dizzy that he or she usually cannot walk for several days or weeks, and may be unable to get up and move around at all. If the loss is total, the individual should be seen by a doctor at once.

Vestibular loss may be precipitated by a virus (viral neuronitis) or may be caused by a tiny blood clot in the arterial system that feeds the balance mechanism. These blood vessels are so small that they can be blocked by a microscopic clot of no more than 4 or 5 red cells clumped together.

Treatment, about which there is considerable difference of opinion, may depend on whether the loss of balance or hearing is total or partial, and on whether it is treated within the first 24 hours or later. Anticoagulants, to thin the blood and perhaps dissolve the clot, are sometimes used, at times in conjunction with vasodilators, to expand the blood vessels and allow the clot to pass. These seem to work best when used in the first 24 hours. Corticosteroids may be used when the condition is thought to be caused by a virus.

If the loss is only partial, the chance for spontaneous recovery is quite good. If the loss is total, the chance of spontaneous recovery is poor. With time, however, the balance mechanism of the other side will compensate and the symptoms will disappear. Continuing symptoms indicate that the damage to the vestibular system is still in flux, preventing compensation by the other side.

Bell's Palsy

Bell's palsy is not, strictly speaking, an ear disease. Rather, it is a type of muscle paralysis believed to result from a swelling of the nerve that controls all of the muscles of expression in the face. But since the facial nerve runs, for a large part of its peripheral course, through the middle ear and the mastoid, the disease is often treated surgically by an otologist (an otolaryngologist whose subspecialty is ear diseases).

The exact origin of Bell's palsy is uncertain, but it is believed to be caused by a virus. The facial nerve begins to swell and, because it (the section running through the ear and mastoid) is encased in a bony sheath, it has no room to expand. If the increased pressure on the nerve continues for a sufficient period, or if the pressure is severe enough, the facial nerve will destroy itself irreparably.

Fortunately, about 90 percent of patients recover spontaneously, without treatment. If the facial paralysis is not total, recovery will be complete. Those 10 percent who do not recover spontaneously will have permanent facial paralysis unless they are treated. The best method of treatment is still somewhat controversial and, at present, both steroids and surgical decompression of the peripheral nerve are used.

A series of tests has been developed to allow the otologist to determine the electrical activity of the nerve and to judge whether there will be permanent damage, in which case surgery may be warranted. The surgical procedure decompresses the facial nerve by removing the bony sheath and slitting the membrane beneath it to expose the nerve. A less drastic, but not always successful measure, is the use of prednisone, a corticosteroid, taken orally. In either case, it is important for the patient to receive prompt testing and evaluation first, so that if the medical treatment is tried and is not successful, the otologist will be able to evaluate the need for surgery. (For more information, see Chapter 29 on Nerve and Muscle Disorders, page 597.)

HEARING PROBLEMS AND HEARING LOSS

THERE ARE 2 BASIC TYPES of hearing loss: conductive and sensorineural (or perceptive) hearing loss.

Conductive Hearing Loss

In this case, the loss is due to an interference with the mechanism of conduction that carries the sound waves from the air to the fluid medium. The cause can be as simple as earwax, fluid in the ear, a torn eardrum, or an exostosis (see page 675) in the ear canal, or it may be due to a disorder known as otosclerosis. In most, if not all, cases, once the cause is found and removed or treated, hearing returns.

In *otosclerosis*, which often runs in families and which occurs more frequently in women than in men, the bone of the otic capsule (the bony wall of the inner ear) becomes disorganized. Some bone is resorbed and new bone is laid down. This sometimes results in a buildup of inappropriate bone around the stapes footplate, fixing this bone and preventing the vibration that is necessary to conduct the sound to the inner ear. The disease is treated by a surgical procedure called a stapedectomy, which replaces the stapes with a prosthesis.

Sensorineural (Perceptive) Hearing Loss

This type of hearing loss occurs in the inner ear, in the nerve from the inner ear to the brain, or in the brain. Sensorineural losses are easily detectable and differentiated from conductive hearing losses by hearing tests. Unlike conductive losses, they cannot be corrected surgically.

Gradual perceptive losses are a normal part of aging. When the condition is severe, it is known as *presbycusis*. In this case, the sensory neuroreceptor cells in the inner ear degenerate and there is a gradual loss of hearing. In some cases, there may be a loss of ability to discriminate sounds. That is, a person may be able to hear sounds, but may not be able to make words out of them.

Presbycusis generally begins to affect people between ages 55 and 65, but may not occur until much later. Men are affected more often and more severely than women.

Acoustic trauma is another common cause of perceptive hearing loss. It may come from trauma— a blow to the ear—or from excessive noise. The noise may come from environmental factors, such as living near an airport, or from occupational factors, working with or near heavy machinery, or from listening to excessively loud music.

"Rock and roll deafness" is an increasing community health problem causing hearing loss in some young people who attend concerts where the sound is overamplified or who listen to music with earphones at too high a volume. Teenagers should not use earphones with loud music, although their use with soft music is not a problem. And they should be taught that if the sound at concerts hurts their ears, it is loud enough to do permanent damage, and they should leave immediately.

Hyperacusia

This condition, excessive sensitivity to noise or to sound, is often a symptom in certain stages of Ménière's disease and may be a symptom of perceptive hearing loss when recruitment is found. Recruitment is a phenomenon whereby a patient is unable to hear sound at a soft level, but when the volume is raised, is able to hear it at the same level of loudness as someone who has normal hearing.

Tinnitus

Tinnitus, or the sensation of sound in the ear when there is no sound, is an annoying, extremely common symptom, which can be due to anything from wax in the ear to disease in the cortex of the brain. It may take the form of ringing, buzzing, whistling, or hissing, and it may be intermittent or continuous. It is usually associated with hearing loss, but its cause is not always clear. If it is caused by something as simple as earwax, removing the wax will relieve it. Treating the underlying disease may or may not stop the tinnitus. Tinnitus may be a symptom of an ear disorder, but it may also be a symptom of anything from cardiovascular disease to hyperthyroidism.

Some patients tolerate the condition better than others. Some may find that the tinnitus is easier to tolerate if they play music to mask the sound. In fact, there is a device called a tinnitus masker, worn like a hearing aid, which produces a neutral sound that acts in the same way as music.

Hearing Aids

Hearing aids are helpful in certain types of perceptive hearing losses, but not in others. They must be fitted by an audiologist, a professional trained in the technique of conducting tests that measure hearing and those that indicate the cause of a hearing loss, and in fitting hearing aids.

The ability to obtain comfortable hearing often depends on the individual patient and his pattern of perceptive hearing loss, as well as the skill of the audiologist.

If the perceptive hearing loss is rather flat, i.e., if it is at the same level throughout all frequencies, a hearing aid may function well, allowing the patient to have good hearing and discrimination with it. This is often the case in Ménière's disease.

Often in presbycusis the hearing loss is in the high frequencies. Special hearing aids are made that magnify the high frequencies only, but as the aid magnifies, the problem of hyperacusia sometimes develops, making the hearing aid almost useless. Recruitment (see above) also makes it very difficult to fit a hearing aid.

Sudden Hearing Loss

This condition is characterized by sudden, usually instantaneous, loss of hearing in one ear or, rarely, both. Like vestibular loss (see page 679), it may be precipitated by a virus or may be directly caused by a tiny blood clot in the arterial system that feeds the hearing mechanism.

As with vestibular loss, treatment may depend on whether the loss of hearing is total or partial, and on whether it is treated within the first 24 hours or later. Anticoagulants, to thin the blood and perhaps dissolve the clot, are often used, sometimes in conjunction with vasodilators, to expand the blood vessels and allow the clot to pass. Corticosteroids may be used when the condition is thought to be caused by a virus.

If the hearing loss is partial, the chance for spontaneous recovery is quite good. If the loss is total, however, the chance of hearing returning spontaneously is poor. Total loss is an acute emergency, and the individual should be examined by a doctor at once. A good test of whether a hearing loss affecting only one ear is total or partial is to hold a telephone receiver to that ear. If a dial tone can be heard, the loss is only partial.

PART II: THE NOSE AND THE PARANASAL SINUSES

THE NOSE

AIR BEGINS ITS JOURNEY to the respiratory system through the nose, which filters, warms, and moistens it before it passes through the pharynx, larynx, and trachea into the bronchi and the lungs. For this purpose, the external nose contains a septum (the wall dividing the 2 nostrils) composed of cartilage and bone covered by a layer of mucous membrane; and 6 or 8 turbinates. (See figure 34.4.)

The turbinates are thin curlicues of bone, also covered by thick mucous membranes, which curve from the outer part of the nose in toward the septum. Under the mucous membrane is erectile tissue which is sensitive to temperature and causes tissues of the area to swell with the influx of blood when there is an abundance of cold, dry, or contaminated air. This narrows the passages and thus slows up the incoming air, allowing the turbinates to warm and humidify it. When the turbinates become erect they give rise to large amounts of mucus, which is why noses are runny on cold days.

The sticky mucous lining of the nose and nasal passages acts as a filter, trapping bacteria and airborne dirt particles. The mucus is then moved by the action of hairlike cilia to the back of the nose and then into the throat and swallowed or moved to the front of the nose where it can be blown out.

The nose also contains the organ of smell, which in turn affects taste. Odors are detected by the very fine and sensitive hairlike ends of the olfactory nerve, which begins with the olfactory bulb in the brain and ends in the roof of the nose. The nerve endings pick up scents and transmit this information to the brain, which matches it against stored information from past experience, and thus perceives and identifies smells. Since 95 percent of the ability to taste relies on the ability to smell, a loss of sense of smell will greatly diminish taste, and thus enjoyment of food.

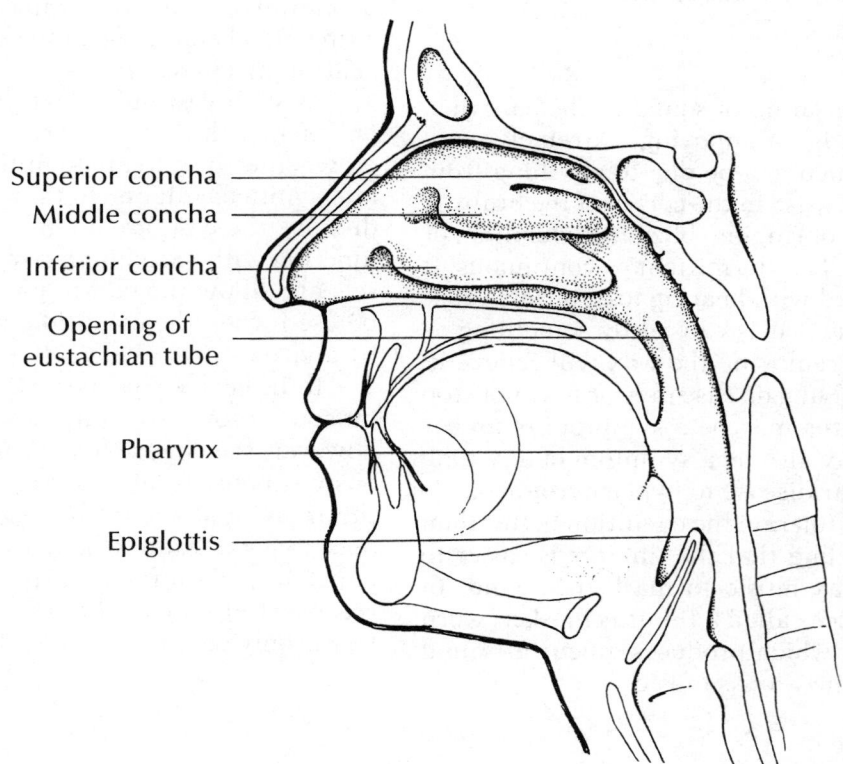

Superior concha
Middle concha
Inferior concha
Opening of eustachian tube
Pharynx
Epiglottis

Figure 34.4.   **Structure of the nose and nasal passages.**

Deviated Septum

No one has a nasal septum that is exactly in the midline, and every septum is deviated to some degree. But if the deviation is severe and there is a history of recurrent disease which can readily be correlated with the condition, the deviated septum can be corrected by surgery that is, in most cases, fairly simple. (See figure 34.5.) Sometimes the procedure is performed at the same time as rhinoplasty, a procedure to reshape the external nose (see below).

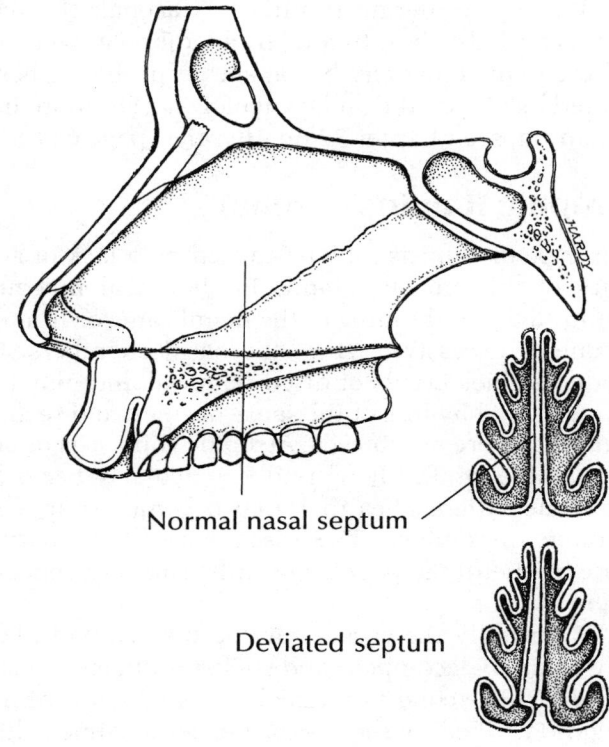

Normal nasal septum

Deviated septum

Figure 34.5. **Deviated septum.**

Anatomical Deformity

Rhinoplasty is a surgical procedure used to change the structure of the external nose, either to repair it after a fracture or simply to improve its appearance. The bones may be fractured and brought closer to the midline to give the upper part of the nose a thinner appearance. Then the cartilage below is trimmed so that it will be suited to the appearance of the newly shaped upper part. Sometimes, only the cartilage need be reshaped. Depending on the hospital and often the geographical area, the operation may be performed by an otolaryngologist, a plastic surgeon, or a general surgeon.

Rhinophyma

Sometimes the epithelium—the upper layer of skin on the external surface of the nose—thickens greatly and the nose assumes a large, bulbous appearance, a condition known as rhinophyma. Although the condition has often been associated with alcohol abuse and, indeed, may occur in people who are heavy drinkers, it also occurs in people who do not use alcohol at all. Treatment is a surgical procedure in which the excess epithelium is sliced off from the outside and the nose usually resumes its natural shape.

Epitaxis (Nosebleed)

Simple nosebleeds not obviously caused by a blow to the nose are often caused by picking it. Or they may result from continually breathing very dry air, which causes the nasal mucous membranes to dry out, crack, and bleed. Sometimes, they are caused by hypertension, when the blood pressure is high enough to rupture the wall of the thin vessels in the mucous membrane.

Nosebleeds are also commonly found in people who drink excessive amounts of alcohol, perhaps because alcohol has a tendency to dilate the blood vessels. Since the mucous membrane of the nose contains blood vessels that are relatively large and exposed to the external environment, spontaneous bleeding can easily take place if the membrane is disturbed or altered in any way.

In the overwhelming majority of cases nosebleeds are not serious and are easy for individuals to take care of themselves. The simplest way to handle a nosebleed is to have the person sit up, rather than lying down, so that gravity will slightly lower the blood pressure in the upper part of the body, and so that the blood will be more likely to run out the nose rather than to run back into the mouth to be swallowed.

The fleshy part of the nose should be grasped and pinched together for about 5 minutes, to give the blood a chance to clot. The use of ice and cold packs is questionable. Although cold does constrict the blood vessels somewhat, it probably will not have much effect on the nosebleed.

On rare occasions, a nosebleed is more serious and may not respond to simple pressure. It may be posterior, well behind the fleshy area, causing a lot of the blood to run down the back of the throat and be swallowed or spit out, even when the patient is sitting up. This is often a sign that the nosebleed will not stop on its own.

If the nosebleed does not stop easily or recurs frequently, the patient should see his or her doctor, who will sometimes pack the nose with petroleum jelly and gauze for a day or two, if the bleeding is in the anterior part of the nose. Posterior nosebleeds require more complicated and uncomfortable postnasal packing. Cauterizing the site of the bleeding with electrocautery or silver nitrate is another common treatment.

Chronic Rhinitis

Rhinitis is an inflammation of the membrane lining the nose and may result from a number of causes. Ordinary chronic rhinitis, of unknown origin, consists of inflamed nasal mucous membranes, red and enlarged turbinates, excess production of mucus, and sometimes, pus and a postnasal drip, all of which make the patient miserable.

Chronic rhinitis may be occupational, afflicting those who manufacture or work with chemicals, such as housepainters and photo developers; or it may be environmental, afflicting, for example, those who swim in a chlorinated indoor pool; or it may be neither.

Treatment consists of trying to eliminate the irritant and of local treatment on the inside of the nose, possibly with local injections of steroids.

In vasomotor rhinitis, there is some swelling of the mucous membranes but they do not become red or inflamed. The turbinates, however, are in a continual state of erection, resulting in a stuffy nose, a postnasal drip, and susceptibility to sinusitis.

Chronic allergic rhinitis results when the nose sets up a defense system to an inhaled substance to which the body is allergic. It produces a mucous discharge that is very thin and watery, and the turbinates enlarge and become very pale, almost blue-white. If the allergy-producing substances can be isolated—if, for example, the patient's problem begins and ends at a specific time of the year, suggesting a pollen allergy—the patient can be desensitized.

If the condition lasts throughout the year, the patient is probably allergic to a number of things and attempts at desensitization may be long, arduous, expensive, and often futile. A treatment that works for some people is the injection directly into the turbinates of small amounts of long-acting steroids. Antihistamines and nasal decongestant tablets are also used and, if they don't work, steroids may be prescribed.

When the allergic rhinitis is seasonal, the patient is probably best treated by an allergist; when it is perennial, however, he or she is probably best treated locally by the otolaryngologist. (For more information, see Chapter 32 on Allergies, page 644.)

Atrophic Rhinitis (Ozena)

This type of rhinitis may be caused by a lack of activity of the mucous glands in the nasal mucous membrane or a thinning of the membrane, or it may be due to excessive size of the nasal chambers. It produces thick crusts of dried material and may be accompanied by loss of the sense of smell and recurrent and severe nosebleeds. Atrophic rhinitis is often untreatable, and although not particularly hazardous to the patient's health, it may become a source of extreme discomfort. The disease seems to occur more frequently in people of southeastern European origin.

Eventually the crusts may become so bad that they begin to decompose and stick, producing a noxious odor. The condition may be treated with saline irrigation, whereby the doctor flushes a saline solution through the nasal cavities, or with local use of steroids, either injected or topical.

PARANASAL SINUSES

THE SINUSES—air-filled cavities in the bones surrounding the nose—are divided in 4 pairs: frontal, ethmoid, sphenoid, and maxillary. Like other parts of the nasal passages, they are lined with sticky mucus, and a bacterial infection that causes an inflammation of this lining is called sinusitis. The infection may partially or totally obstruct the flow of air and mucus into the nose, and may be accompanied by pus. (See figure 34.6.)

Acute Sinusitis

In true acute sinusitis, the bacterial infection may be accompanied by large amounts of pus, which may or may not be able to drain into the nose by itself. Even if the pus can drain by itself, the condition requires treatment by a physician with antibiotics and nasal decongestants. If the affected sinuses are blocked, the doctor may be able to facilitate drainage through irrigation: injecting fluid with a large needle through an area of the sinus that is easily accessible and then allowing the fluid to drain out through the nose.

A severely deviated nasal septum may predispose the patient to recurrent attacks of acute sinusitis, and surgical correction may be necessary in some cases.

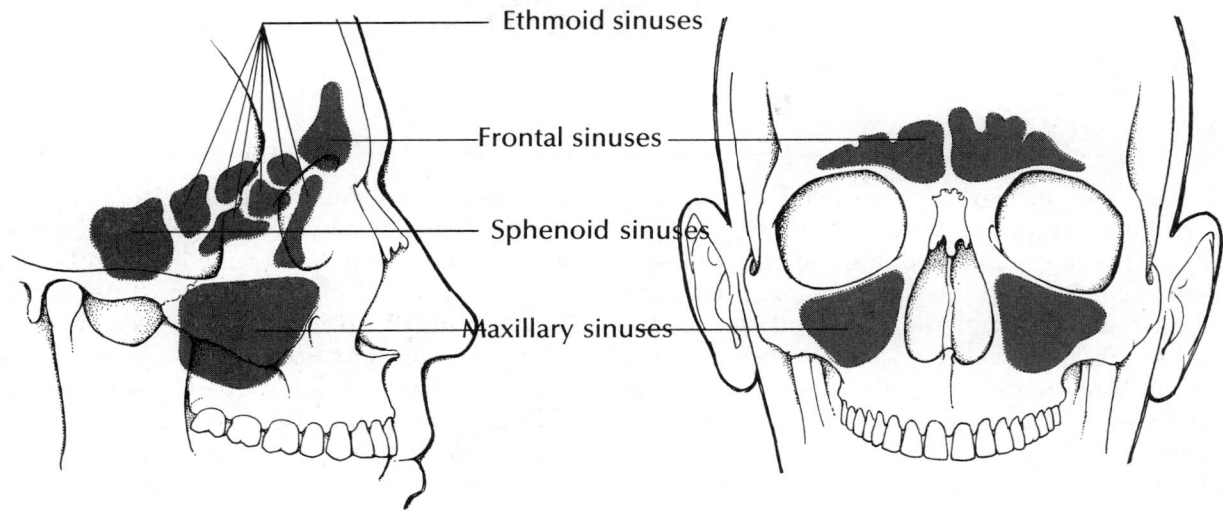

Figure 34.6. **Sinuses of the nasal passages.**

Chronic Sinusitis

Chronic sinusitis is usually secondary to an anatomical deformity which is either congenital or was produced during the course of multiple attacks of acute sinusitis. If the cause was anatomical malformation, it must be corrected. Often, after many attacks of acute sinusitis, the openings of the sinus into the nose become narrowed or closed completely, leaving no possibility of drainage from the sinus and making it necessary to create surgically a new route of drainage.

A deviated septum is often the cause of chronic frontal sinusitis, since drainage of the frontal sinuses depends almost entirely on gravity moving the contents of the sinuses down through a small opening which may be totally or partially blocked by the deviation.

Chronic sinusitis may also be caused by recurring cases of acute sinusitis that have not been treated vigorously or early enough, so that secondary scarring causes a gradual closure of the openings of the sinus into the nose. In those instances, the only rational treatment is surgery, either to reopen the natural openings of the sinuses, or to create an artificial opening through which the sinuses may drain. True chronic sinusitis is a relatively uncommon disease; more likely, when something is wrong, it is chronic rhinitis. (See above.)

Nasal Polyps

These are not true polyps in the sense that they do not result from growth of a new or abnormal type of tissue. They are really swollen sinus lining tissue that protrudes into the nasal cavity, and they can

follow allergy, vasomotor rhinitis, or other chronic disease. (See figure 34.7.)

Nasal polyps may appear singly or in clusters and look something like pearly grapes. Although they are benign, they may obstruct nasal passages, making breathing difficult, and may affect the sense of smell. They are usually removed under local anesthetic with a snare, a procedure that may have to be repeated as other polyps appear.

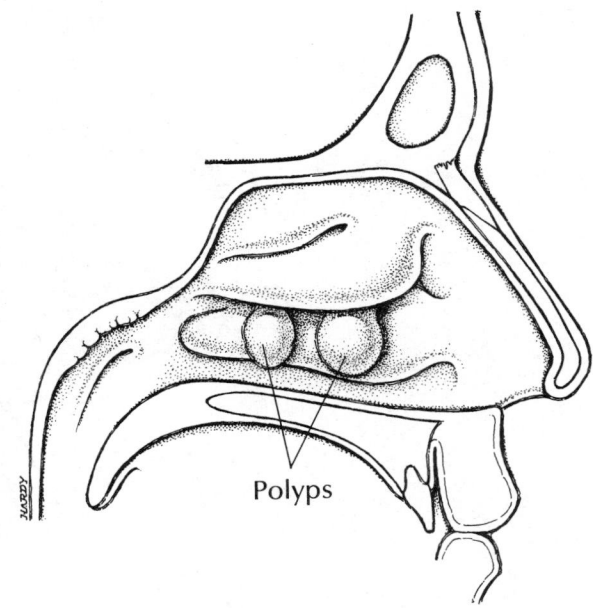

Figure 34.7. **Development of nasal polyps.**

PART III: THE THROAT

THE PHARYNX

THE THROAT, or pharynx, is ringed by muscle and cartilage and contains 2 important passageways—for air into the lungs and food into the digestive system—as well as the mechanism for producing sounds. Air travels from the nose and the mouth down through the trachea, or windpipe, into the bronchi and the lungs, while food and water travel from the mouth into the esophagus and then to the stomach.

Located in the pharynx between the mouth and the trachea are the tonsils and adenoids and the larynx (or voice box), which contains the vocal cords. The epiglottis, a lidlike structure at the top of the larynx, closes during swallowing to deflect food and water away from the windpipe and into the esophagus. (See figure 34.8.)

Pharyngitis

Pharyngitis, which may be acute or chronic, is simply a sore throat, which may be accompanied by fever and, if the throat is particularly inflamed, may cause difficulty in swallowing. It may be a symptom of an infection elsewhere or a chronic problem.

The acute forms of pharyngitis may be due to streptococcus, staphylococcus, or any of a number of other bacteria which, if treated promptly with antibiotics, are usually self-limiting. If not treated, the infection may lead to more serious conditions. (See Chapter 21 on Infectious Diseases, page 431.) Local irritation, from smoking or excessive consumption of liquor, can also cause pharyngitis, as can air pollutants. With either type (bacterial or irritant), rest and aspirin may help relieve the pain.

Tonsils and Adenoids

The tonsils, located in the folds of the throat between the tongue and the palate, are usually rather large in infants. Unlike adenoids, which normally shrink throughout childhood and virtually disappear by puberty, tonsils shrink to about the size of almonds in adults, but do not disappear.

Tonsils and adenoids begin as protective mechanisms, acting as sieves or filters to keep disease from entering the body, but they lose this function about the time the child is 3 years old. Sometimes, the tonsils are overwhelmed by the disease microorganisms

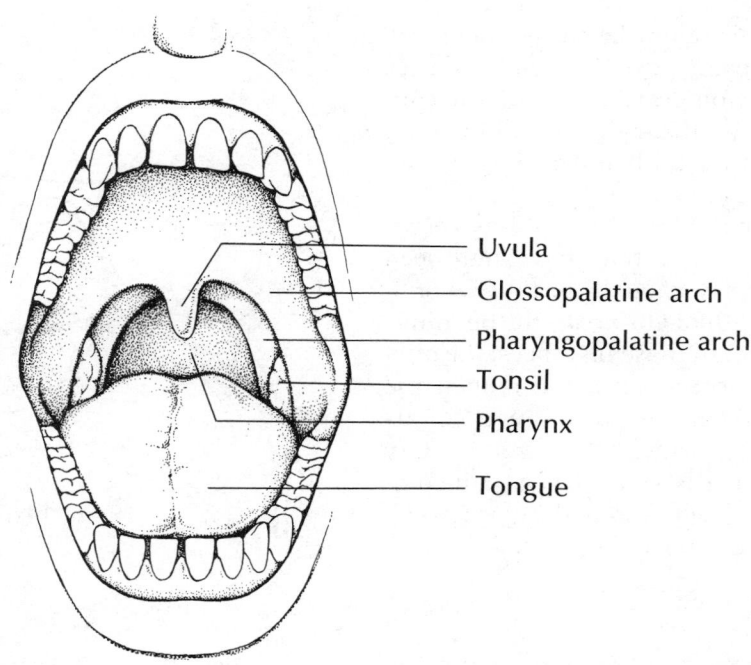

Figure 34.8. **Structures of the mouth and throat.**

they are trying to filter out and they become greatly enlarged.

Before the advent of penicillin and other antibiotics, infected tonsils were removed almost routinely. Tonsillectomies are now performed only when infected tonsils are an obvious source of difficulty for the child or adult. As a rule of thumb, if there are 3 or more attacks of tonsillitis with high fevers within a year, removal is warranted. Once removed, they do not grow back, although adenoids can never be removed completely, and regrowth in young children is not uncommon.

Occasionally, a child's tonsils and adenoids will become so enlarged that he or she is not able to breathe or even eat properly, or they will block the opening to the Eustachian tube and result in secondary middle ear disease, either an accumulation of fluid in the ear or acute otitis media.

Peritonsillar Abscess (Quinsy)

Another disease associated with tonsillitis is peritonsillar abscess, which is much more likely to be seen in young adults than in children. Here the tonsil becomes infected, but an abscess (a collection of pus) forms between the tonsil and the tissue of the soft palate. The infection may spread, before it abscesses, into a fairly large area of the soft palate, and when the abscess finally forms, it may include a good portion of that side of the soft palate.

The abscess may displace the tonsil, and cause pain, fever, and difficulty in swallowing. Spread of the infection to spaces in the neck and down into the chest can lead to a number of complications, including infection of the tissue between the lungs or the lining covering the heart. It may even be fatal if the resultant inflammation is severe enough to push the tongue upward and cause strangulation.

The abscess must be drained surgically and the infection treated promptly with antibiotics. Since the condition tends to recur, it is usually advisable, after the acute infection subsides, to remove the tonsils.

Juvenile Angiofibroma

This benign tumor of the nasopharynx region is seen almost exclusively in boys before puberty, and on rare occasion in girls at the same age. Although the tumor has a natural tendency to diminish after puberty, it can grow rapidly and invasively and, if untreated, may infiltrate the bones at the base of the skull. At this point, it may be so extensive that it is almost impossible to remove, and the result can be fatal. Even if treatment is instituted early, it is complicated by serious bleeding from the large number of blood vessels within the tumor.

Treatment may be by embolization or surgical excision, or both. With embolization, the doctor (using x-ray visualization) injects small pellets of plastic or gluelike material through a catheter into some of the blood vessels in order to block them off. Without the blood supply, the tumor has a tendency to shrink.

THE LARYNX

THE LARYNX, or voice box, contains 2 flaps of tissue called the vocal cords. The larynx is controlled by muscles that open and close it, allowing the passage of air and the tensing of the vocal cords. As air passes over the tensed cords, they vibrate, and these vibrations produce sounds that are then shaped by the mouth and tongue into words.

Hoarseness

When the vocal cords are irritated and become inflamed, or if the muscles of the larynx are affected, the sounds produced when air passes over them will be distorted, giving the characteristic hoarseness that is a symptom of laryngitis. Hoarseness may also be caused by anything from flu to overuse or misuse of the voice by excessive singing, yelling, or speaking. It is often the first sign of a tumor on the vocal cords, the overwhelming majority of which are benign.

Acute Laryngitis

Acute laryngitis is caused by an infection, often by a virus organism, and is generally self-limiting. Occasionally the laryngitis is caused by a bacterial infection that must be treated by antibiotics and can be more damaging to the larynx than the viral type. In either case, complete voice rest and warm fluids will also help.

Chronic Laryngitis

Chronic laryngitis is usually caused not by infection but by irritation. One of the most common causes is excess intake of alcohol, which is relatively toxic to the larynx. People who drink a great deal may develop a condition called pachydermia, in which the folds of the vocal cords take on the appearance of elephant skin. They become extremely hoarse, developing a voice which is often hardly understandable.

Other irritants can also cause chronic laryngitis: People who work in paint factories, with paint remover, or at any job involving heavy exposure to organic chemicals are prone to this condition. On rare occasion, chronic laryngitis precedes cancer of the larynx.

As with acute laryngitis, voice rest and warm liquids may help the irritation, but are only temporary. The underlying cause must be treated as well.

Polyps

People who abuse their voices through excessive improper use (such as screaming, shouting, or speaking in an unnaturally low frequency) sometimes develop polyps on their vocal cords. These polyps result from swelling of the loose connective tissue directly below the mucous membrane of the vocal cords. (See figure 34.9.) The bulge that is produced becomes larger and initially appears like a half moon on the edge of the cord. With continued use of the voice without treatment, the polyps will develop into globular structures connected to the vocal cord by thin stalks. They are easily removed by laryngoscopy, in which a metal tube with a light on the end is passed through the mouth and into the throat and a small, sharp, cup-shaped punch is threaded through the tube and used to clip off the polyp.

Nodules

Nodules, which are somewhat different from polyps, are seen in singers, speakers, and people who often abuse their voices. The nodules are composed of epithelium, the covering surface of skin or mucous membrane, and they could be compared to a corn on the toe. Although the nodules can easily be removed, they will return if the patient continues to use his or her voice improperly. Voice therapy is usually recommended and may begin before the surgery and continue afterward.

Contact Ulcers

Contact ulcers are sores that appear on the vocal cords where the two cartilages that act as an anchor for the muscle portion of the vocal cords touch each other. They are often difficult to get rid of, and will recur, even after surgical removal. Voice rest and retraining is usually the best treatment.

Juvenile Papillomas

Juvenile papillomas are warts, thought to be caused by a virus, that grow on the vocal cords of children (primarily males), often diminishing spontaneously at puberty. They are not malignant, but they are extremely difficult to remove completely without damaging the larynx, and the rate of recurrence is very high. Although the papillomas are benign (degenerating to cancer only very rarely), their excessive growth can obstruct breathing and make them potentially fatal if not treated. Recently, laser treatment has proved more satisfactory than traditional surgical methods.

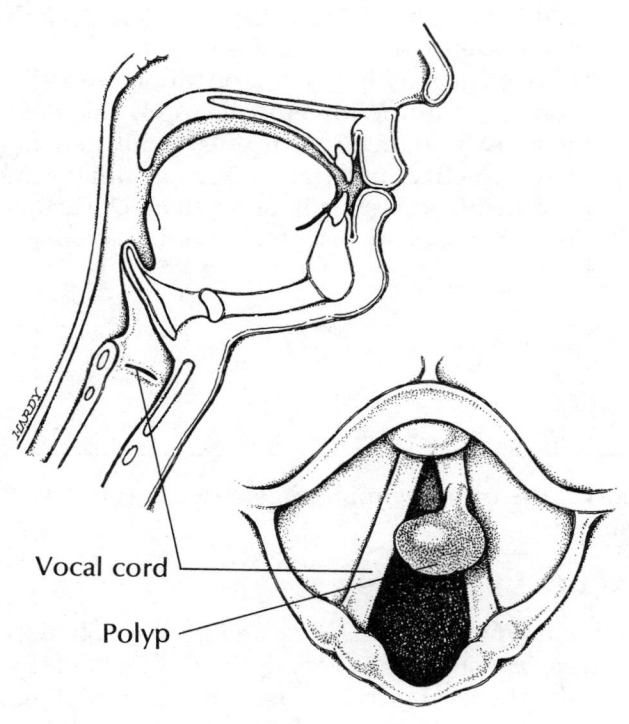

Vocal cord

Polyp

Figure 34.9. **Vocal polyps.**

35 Maintaining Oral Health

Irwin Mandel, D.D.S.

INTRODUCTION

AMERICANS are taking better care of their teeth. In the past decade, tooth decay has dropped by 32 percent in children aged 5 to 17 and the number of children with no cavities at all has risen by almost 10 percent. At the same time, the number of denture-wearers declined from 35 to 24 percent of the adult population. These encouraging changes are due to a number of factors. The fluoridation of municipal water supplies, which began in the 1950s, has grown to the point where now more than half of the U.S. population enjoys this important benefit. Increased use of fluoride toothpastes and mouthwashes (especially in school-based programs), as well as applications of fluoride directly onto the teeth, have made important contributions to the reduction of tooth decay. Educational campaigns in schools and clinics, and efforts on the part of private dentists, have resulted in greatly improved oral hygiene. Improved tools and materials for dental restorations have played their part, and increasing numbers of people are availing themselves of regular dental care. An appreciation of the role of diet in the maintenance of healthy teeth and the increased use of low- or nonfermentable sweeteners in candy, chewing gum, and soft drinks have made a significant contribution as well.

Reflecting an awareness of the importance of dental health, dental care insurance as an employment benefit is a rapidly growing trend. Some 90 million people are now covered by some form of prepaid dental coverage, mostly through group plans offered by unions or employers. Predictions are that, by 1990, more than 100 million will belong. Insurance policies favor prevention: Full coverage is usually provided for diagnostic services and preventive care, while other treatment is often only partially covered.

Nevertheless, the nation spends more than $25 billion annually on dental care. (The average family bill is now over $200.) In addition, dental disease is responsible for the loss of some 32 million working days per year. And these costs barely reflect the effect of dental disease on the quality of life—in pain, discomfort, tooth loss, poor self-image, and the psychological trauma associated with wearing dentures.

DEVELOPMENT OF THE TEETH AND JAWS

BY THE END of the third month of fetal life, the jaws are well formed and tooth development is well advanced. The primary (deciduous) teeth begin as groups of cells in the developing jaws, each group corresponding to the tooth. The first evidence of mineralization of the hard tissues of the teeth—the enamel and dentin—is found in about the fourth month of pregnancy.

Six or 7 months after birth, the first teeth start to emerge in the front of the mouth. There is a wide variation in time of appearance, but in general, the primary teeth in the lower jaw (the mandible) emerge before those in the upper (the maxilla), and the incisors emerge before the molars. By the time the child is 3 years old, the full set of primary teeth will usually be in place.

The permanent teeth develop in a similar way, but form somewhat later. The first permanent molars often mineralize before birth; most of the permanent canines and incisors mineralize in the early months of childhood.

The first permanent molars appear behind the primary teeth in the back of the mouth at about 6 years of age, often leading to the impression that they are part of the primary set of teeth. As the other permanent teeth emerge, the other primary teeth become loose and fall out painlessly. By the age of 14, all 28 permanent teeth have usually emerged, leaving only the last 4 third molars (the wisdom teeth) to complete their growth.

Tooth Structure and Type

Each tooth, whether primary or permanent, has a crown visible in the mouth above the level of the gum (gingiva) and a root which is embedded in a socket in the jaw. (See figure 35.1.) The incisors and canines normally have only 1 root; the premolars or bicuspids have 1 or 2 and the molars 2 or 3 (or, occasionally, 4). The roots of the primary teeth are thinner than those of the permanent teeth and are thus more liable to fracture. Both primary and secondary teeth are similar in structure, although the primary teeth have relatively larger pulp chambers, and relatively thinner enamel and dentin. Enamel, the hardest tissue in the body, is insensitive and incapable of self-repair. It acts as the protective covering for the tooth crown. Dentin makes up the bulk of the tooth structure. It comprises millions of tiny cells arranged in tubules, which extend from the pulp to the junction between the enamel and the dentin. It is sensitive, and though extremely hard, is softer than enamel. The pulp chamber, which occupies the space in the center of the crown, and the canal, which runs through the root, contain the living tissue of the tooth. This pulp contains nerves and blood vessels that supply the cells extending into the dentin. The nerves and blood vessels enter the tooth at the end of the root. The root itself is covered with cementum, a hard, bonelike tissue, in which fibers are embedded to attach the tooth to its bony socket.

Although similar in structure, teeth vary in shape according to their different functions. The incisors have sharp chisel-shaped crowns that cut food. The canines, with their single-pointed cusp, are used to tear. The premolars, located behind the canines, are used to crush and tear food, while the multi-cusped molars in the back of the mouth grind it. (See figures 35.2A and 35.2B.)

Supporting Structures

The gum surrounds the neck of the tooth. It is attached close to the area where the enamel and the cementum meet, and it forms a firm cuff around the crown. A shallow crevice (the gingival crevice) between the gum and tooth is barely evident when the gum is healthy. At the base of the crevice, the gum tissue merges into the periodontal ligament, a thin layer of tissue lying between the cementum and the jawbone (aveolus) and attached firmly to both. The fibers of the periodontal ligament support the tooth in its socket, hold neighboring teeth together, and bind the gum firmly against the tooth. Both the gums and the periodontal ligament have a rich supply of blood and nerves.

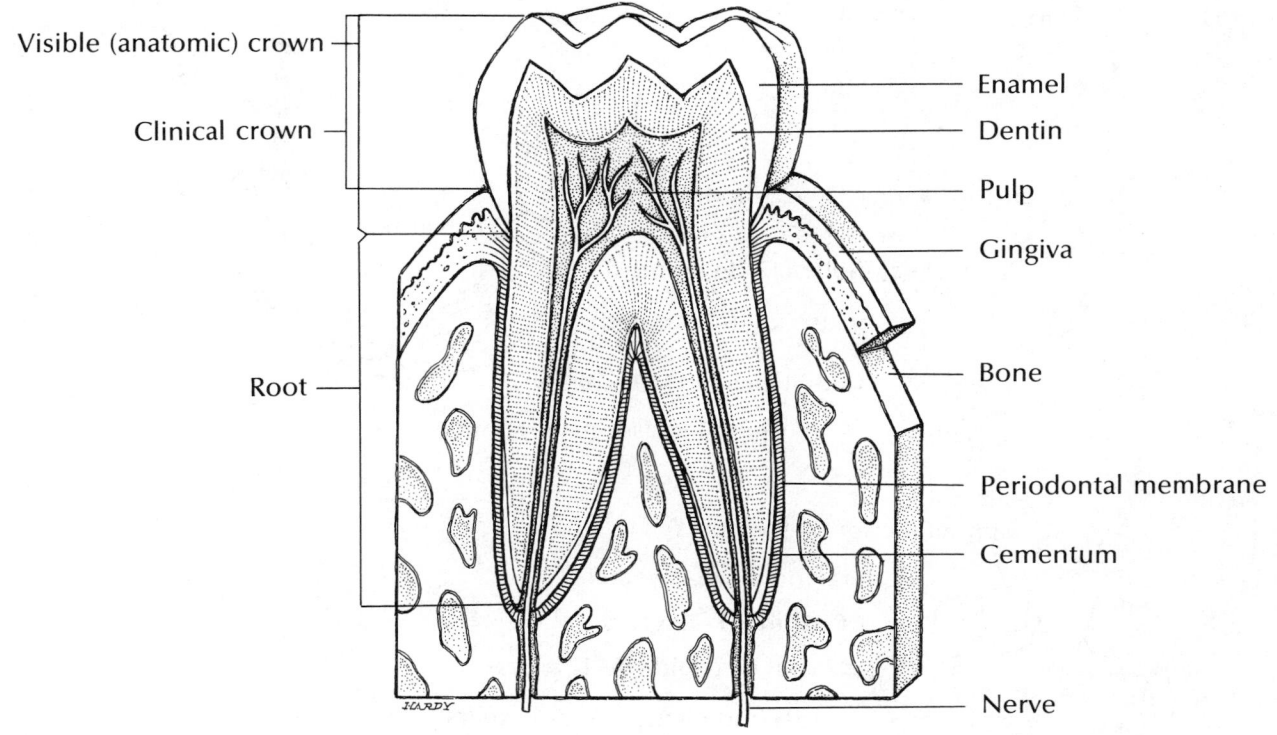

Figure 35.1. **Structure of a normal tooth.**

DEVELOPMENTAL ABNORMALITIES

Impacted Teeth

Modern man has a smaller jaw than his primitive ancestors, but teeth of a similar size. Children frequently develop teeth too large for their jaws, which, as they erupt, become rotated, tilted, or displaced. Sometimes they are blocked by teeth already in the jaw and mouth and remain completely or partially buried in the jaw. This most frequently affects the last molar, or wisdom tooth. An impacted wisdom tooth may lead to infection of the overlying soft tissues. It may also press on the periodontal ligament of the neighboring molar and damage it. Pain, recurrent infection, and actual or potential damage to the adjacent teeth are common reasons for extraction of wisdom teeth.

Malformed Teeth

The great majority of malformed teeth are the result of some infectious or febrile illness in infancy or early childhood. The 6-year molars and the 8 front teeth are most often involved, since these are the teeth developing during these years. The crowns of the teeth are pitted or grooved, and may have an unsightly brown color.

Structural abnormalities of the tooth enamel vary from common, small white blemishes to comparatively rare, gross abnormalities of the enamel or dentin, or both. These severe abnormalities require crowns for appearance's sake, and to protect against wear.

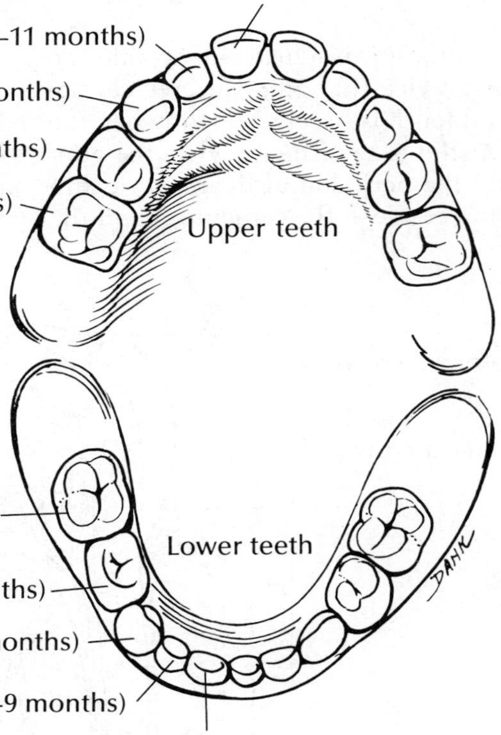

Central incisor (7–9 months)
Lateral incisor (9–11 months)
Cuspid (18–20 months)
First molar (14–16 months)
Second molar (24–26 months)

Upper teeth

Figure 35.2A. **The primary or "baby" teeth.**

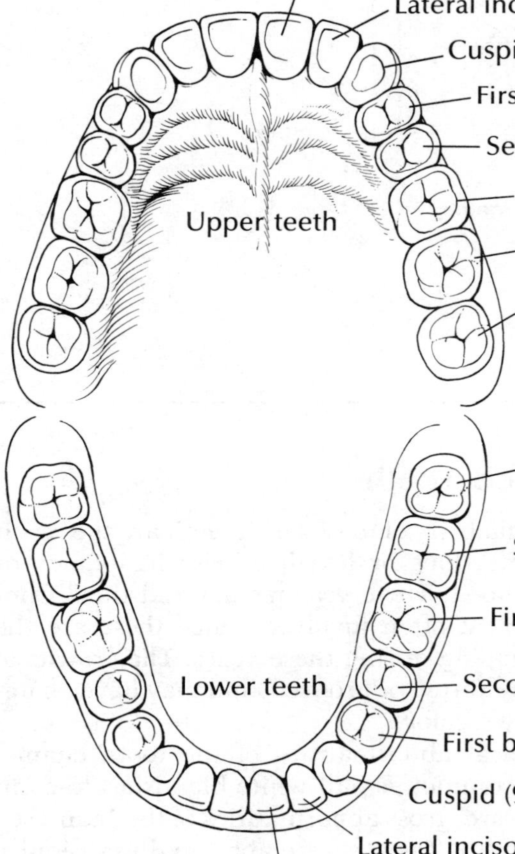

Second molar (20–22 months)

Lower teeth

First molar (12–14 months)
Cuspid (16–18 months)
Lateral incisor (7–9 months)
Central incisor (6–8 months)

Central incisor (7–8 years)
Lateral incisor (8–9 years)
Cuspid (11–12 years)
First bicuspid (10–12 years)
Second bicuspid (10–12 years)
First molar (6–7 years)
Second molar (12–13 years)
Third molar (17–21 years)

Upper teeth

Figure 35.2B. **The secondary or permanent teeth.**

Third molar (17–21 years)
Second molar (11–13 years)
First molar (6–7 years)
Second bicuspid (11–12 years)
First bicuspid (10–12 years)
Cuspid (9–10 years)
Lateral incisor (7–8 years)
Central incisor (6–7 years)

Lower teeth

Tetracycline Staining

Tetracycline antibiotics administered to women in late pregnancy or to children under 7 years of age are incorporated into the enamel and dentin of the forming teeth and may lead to discoloration. This discoloration varies from yellow to dark gray-brown, depending on the type of tetracycline used and the length of treatment. Tetracycline staining is less common now than formerly, since doctors are aware of this side effect and prescribe alternative antibiotics where possible during these periods.

Abnormal Jaw Relationships

Disproportion or malposition of the jaws rarely affects chewing ability, but often causes concern for esthetic reasons. Treatment can vary from simple orthodontics to extensive bone surgery, depending on the severity of the problem. Surgical treatment of severe abnormalities (orthognathic surgery) is becoming more commonplace.

Cleft Lip and Palate

Clefts of the lip and palate, which affect about 1 child in 1,000, occur when the embryo's facial folds fail to unite in the palate or upper lip region. They may involve the upper lip or the palate, or both. (See figure 35.3.) Although the causes are not well understood, it appears that most cases of cleft palate are due to a genetic predisposition combined with a specific agent such as rubella (German measles) during the first trimester of pregnancy, or drugs (for example, the antiepileptic drug Dilantin, or corticosteroids) taken during pregnancy.

If untreated, cleft lip and/or palate may cause disfigurement to a greater or lesser degree, swallowing problems, and speech difficulties. A cleft lip is usually repaired early in life by a simple surgical procedure. A cleft palate is usually repaired later in childhood. Exactly when the operation is done varies with the child and the rate of development. The timing of surgery is a very important aspect of the treatment. Prior to the surgery, a removable device is inserted to temporarily close the palate and ensure proper feeding and normal speech development until the operation is performed. In some situations, because of continuing growth, use of this device is alternated with surgery several times.

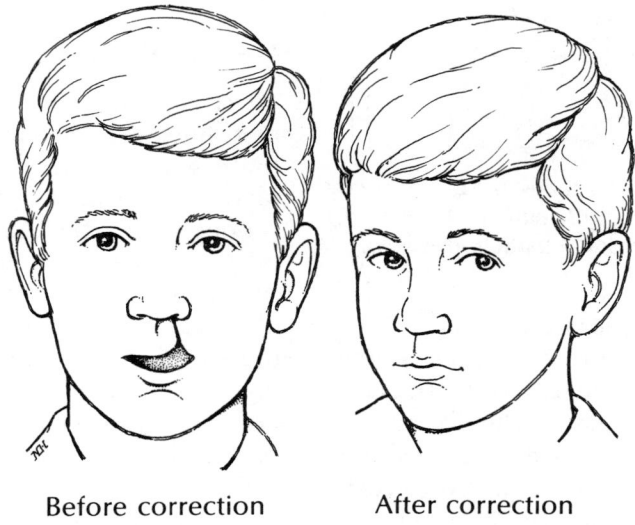

Before correction   After correction

Figure 35.3. **Cleft lip.**

DENTAL CARIES

Second to the common cold, tooth decay (caries) is the most prevalent disease in the United States and the principal cause of tooth loss before the age of 35. This progressively destructive disease primarily affects children and young adults, but continues as a problem throughout adult life. Recent studies, in fact, point to a marked increase in root caries among adults. As people keep their teeth longer, their gums recede, and the root surface becomes exposed. This surface, covered by cementum rather than enamel,

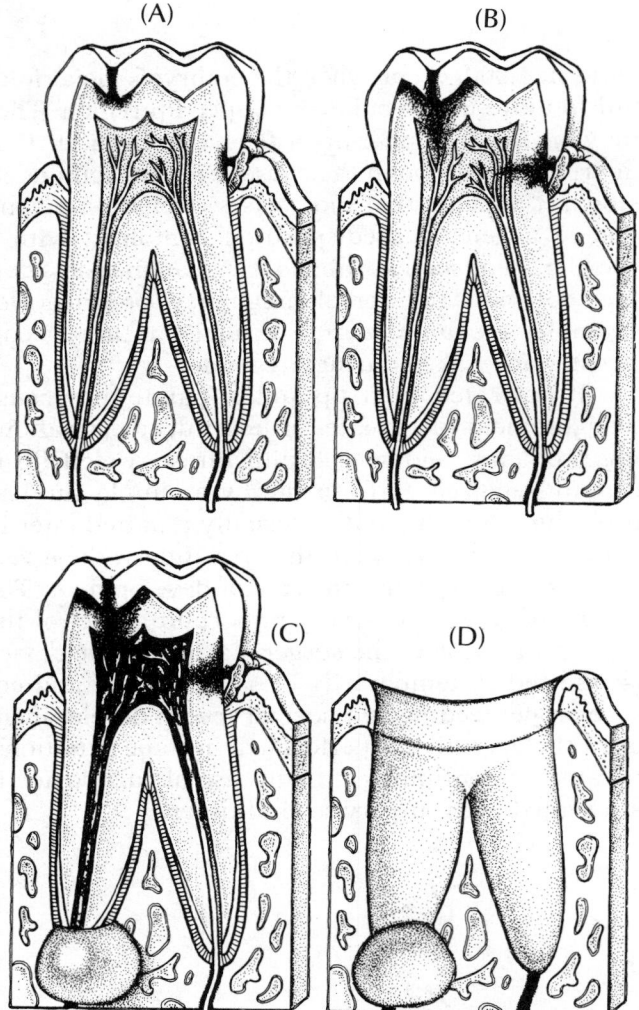

Figure 35.4. **Development of dental caries. (A) Decay breaks through enamel and attacks dentin; (B) pulp is attacked; (C) pulp is destroyed and abscess forms; (D) tooth is extracted.**

is very vulnerable to decay. (See figure 35.4.)

Despite recent advances in prevention, almost half of all American children have some tooth decay by the age of 4, and many by age 2. The average 12-year-old has 4 tooth surfaces that are decayed and filled, and 11 by the age of 17. As many as 70 percent of the children of low-income families may never go to a dentist, and up to 85 percent of their cavities will go unfilled. The proportion of decayed to filled teeth is much higher among nonwhite than among white children.

Caries is a bacterial disease. Studies have established that, in experimental animals at least, it is clearly transmissible. In humans, indirect evidence shows that it can be transmitted from parent to child through kissing or using infected utensils. However, because caries is so extraordinarily prevalent, and because it is not life-threatening, little attention is paid to the question of transmissibility.

Caries results from an interplay of forces: spe-cific bacteria, a predisposing dietary intake, and a susceptible tooth surface. The offending bacteria are a part of plaque, a gelatinlike mat that adheres to specific sites on the teeth—principally the depth of the pits and the fissures on the grinding surface of the molars and the premolars (the occlusal surfaces) and the area along the gum line, both on the outer surfaces and between the teeth. (Plaque also adheres to dental restorations of all kinds.) These are the areas not cleared by the action of the lips or cheeks, tongue movement, or through the flow of saliva.

The plaque bacteria use sugar as their main source of energy. In the course of metabolizing this energy, the bacteria liberate a variety of acids, some of them strong enough to dissolve the very substance of the tooth. In a sense, the teeth become victims of their own environmental pollution.

A number of different kinds of sugars (sucrose, glucose, fructose, maltose, lactose) can fill the energy needs of plaque bacteria and lead to the formation of plaque acids. In addition, starch—which is converted to maltose and glucose by enzymes in the mouth—can cause decay. But there are clear-cut differences in the amount of decay that the various sugars can cause. Sucrose is without a doubt the most conducive to dental decay.

Mechanisms

There is a tendency to equate caries with cavities. In fact, however, the cavity is a late manifestation of the disease. Each time that sugar is ingested, the plaque bacteria produce acid. The greatest damage is done within the first 20 minutes after the sugar is taken. Repeated cycles of acid generation will in time (usually within 1 to 2 years) cause the first visible signs of caries: an opaque white or brown spot on the surface of the enamel. At this stage, the outer layer is relatively intact, although the subsurface layer of enamel is partly demineralized. Later, the surface breaks down and becomes roughened and stained.

As soon as the bacteria have broken through the enamel, they invade the dentin that lies beneath it and spread into it, widely undermining the enamel. (It is because of this that a large cavity will appear quite small on the surface.) The undermined enamel chips or fractures, and the cavity, are now visible. As the bacteria and their products pass deep into the tooth through the tiny tubules in the dentin, pain is experienced—especially when sweet foods or hot or cold liquids are consumed.

Continuing deeper into the tooth, the bacteria and their irritant products inflame the pulp tissue, causing more pain. Blood vessels in the pulp dilate, but the pulp is unable to swell sufficiently to accommodate the increased fluid (as would be the case with a boil on the skin) because it is completely surrounded by the rigid tooth structure. Instead, the swelling blocks the tiny opening at the end of the root, impairing the blood supply to the pulp. Rampant infection and impaired blood supply combine to cause the pulp to die—unless the infection is treated quickly, in which case the pulp may recuperate.

The death of the pulp usually causes severe pain, although occasionally the pulp dies slowly and almost painlessly. After the death of the pulp, the pain disappears because of the death of the nerve tissue, and there will be no more perceived problems unless the "dead" tooth abscesses—which it is very prone to do—perhaps several years later.

An abscess forms when the bacteria and their products pass out of the end of the root canal into the surrounding bone and soft tissue. The blood vessels in these tissues become inflamed and infected. There is often persistent, throbbing pain. The tooth becomes extremely sensitive to pressure and touch.

Fortunately, the destructive scenario of tooth decay is not set in motion every time we ingest sugar. Protective components of the teeth and saliva are able in most instances to prevent the demineralization process. Moreover, this inherent resistance can be augmented by a number of preventive approaches.

Prevention

What we now know about how caries develops suggests a 3-part strategy for prevention: (1) combating the cariogenic bacteria; (2) modifying the diet; and (3) increasing the resistance of the tooth to dissolution.

Combating Bacteria. Because plaque with a high concentration of acid-producing bacteria (especially *Streptococcus mutans*) is necessary for caries to develop, a logical preventive approach is to combat these bacteria. Techniques include removing the plaque through good oral hygiene practices (see box on page 696 and figures 35.5A and 35.5B.), using antibacterial agents directed toward the microorganisms in the plaque, and preventing the bacteria from adhering to the teeth with the use of a vaccine. These latter techniques hold great promise, but are still largely in the experimental stage.

Toothbrushing on a regular basis is effective in removing plaque in those areas that the brush can reach. The use of dental floss can compensate for the inability of the toothbrush to remove plaque from between the teeth. Five to ten minutes' thorough brushing and flossing daily, supplemented by regular cleaning by a dentist or oral hygienist, can be very effective on all but the occlusal surfaces (the biting surfaces of the molars and premolars).

Plastic sealants placed on the occlusal surfaces after the teeth appear in the mouth (6 to 12 years) are effective in preventing plaque formation and breakdown of the enamel in this vulnerable area. Application of the sealant is a quick and simple procedure—usually all the molars can be sealed in less than 1 hour.

In a recent study, 95 percent of the teeth treated retained their sealants at the end of 3 years. In another study, conducted over a 6-year period, the sealant was completely or partially retained in 84 percent of the teeth treated. Research indicates that the use of sealants reduces decay by about 50 percent.

Modifying the Diet. Where caries is concerned, the form and frequency of sugar ingestion is more important than the amount of sugar consumed. A "sweet tooth" that is gratified by between-meal snacking on foods high in sucrose almost guarantees tooth decay. It is sensible to reduce the intake of sugar in general—and of sucrose in particular—and to limit the intake of sugar to mealtimes. (See box on recommended snacks, page 698.)

Some foods seem to have inherent protective qualities. Cocoa and rice hulls, for example, contain a still unidentified substance that is anticariogenic. Phosphates in foods have similar protective qualities. And cheddar cheese, eaten at the end of a meal, generates a protective response, neutralizing mouth acids.

Fibrous foods, such as fruits and vegetables, while they do not remove plaque or food particles, have value in preventing caries. They stimulate salivation, a natural mouth rinse. When salivation is suppressed, due to diseases of the salivary glands or as a side effect of certain drugs—or is low in volume, as during sleep—caries becomes more prevalent.

Increasing Resistance to Decay. One of the most important factors determining the resistance of a tooth to subsequent attack by plaque acids is a proper level of fluoride during tooth formation in the first few years of life. Fluoride is incorporated into the enamel of developing teeth, modifying their crystal structure and making them more decay-resistant. The recent drop in caries among children is credited largely to fluoride, since there is no apparent decrease in the prevalence of decay-producing bacteria, and no decrease in sugar consumption.

When fluoride is present in the drinking water, at the rate of 1 part per million, providing the proper level of fluoride is simple. Over half the population in the United States (123 million people) enjoy this

HOW TO BRUSH AND FLOSS YOUR TEETH

Although a number of toothbrushing methods are acceptable, the American Dental Association suggests the following for dental hygiene at home.

1. Place the head of the toothbrush against the teeth, with the bristle tips angled against the gum line at a 45° angle.

2. Moving the brush back and forth with a short (half a tooth wide) stroke in a gentle scrubbing motion, brush the outer surfaces of each tooth, upper and lower, keeping the bristles angled against the gum line.

3. Using the same motion, brush the inside surfaces of the teeth.

4. Scrub chewing surfaces of all teeth, using a light pressure, letting the bristles reach into the grooves of the teeth.

5. To clean the inside of the front teeth, tilt the brush vertically and make several gentle up and down strokes with the "toe" (the front part) of the brush over the teeth and gum tissue of the upper and lower jaws.

6. Brush the tongue to freshen the breath.

Only the tips of the bristles actually clean. It is important to use a light pressure so as not to bend the bristles. The position of the toothbrush should be changed frequently.

A note on brushes: In general, a brush with soft, end-rounded or polished bristles is less apt to injure gum tissues than one with hard bristles. The brush should be replaced often—every 3 or 4 months. Brushes come in children's and adults' sizes and should be chosen to fit comfortably in the mouth.

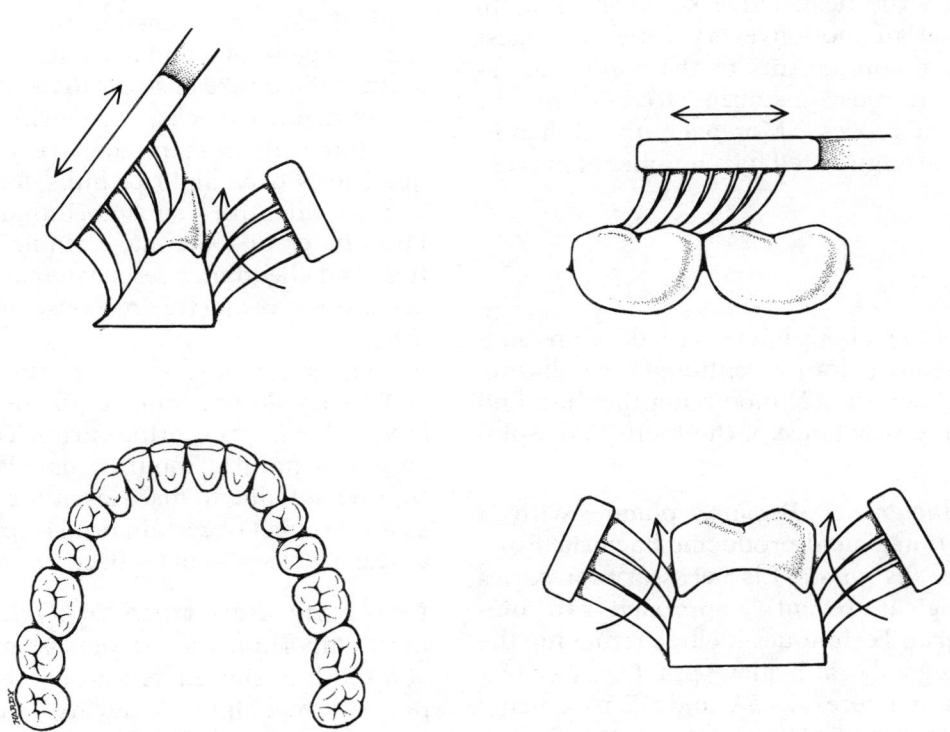

Figure 35.5A. **How to brush your teeth.**

A little practice is necessary to develop skill in flossing, but once learned, it takes only a few minutes.

1. Break off about 18 inches of floss and wind most of it around the middle finger of one hand. Wind the rest around the middle finger of the opposite hand, to take up the floss as it is used.

2. With the thumb of one hand and the forefingers of the other, guide an inch of floss between the teeth. Hold the floss tightly and use a gentle sawing motion.

3. When the floss reaches the gum line, curve it into a C-shape against one tooth and slice it into the space between the tooth and the gum until you feel resistance.

4. Holding the floss tightly against the tooth, move it away from the gum, scraping the side of the tooth.

5. Wind the floss around the middle finger, so that a fresh section is in position and repeat for all teeth. (It is helpful to think of the mouth as consisting of 4 sections and to floss one at a time.)

When you begin flossing daily, your gums may bleed and become slightly sore. As the plaque is broken up, however, the gums will heal and the bleeding will stop. If bleeding does not stop after 4 or 5 days, consult your dentist. Improper flossing can injure the gums.

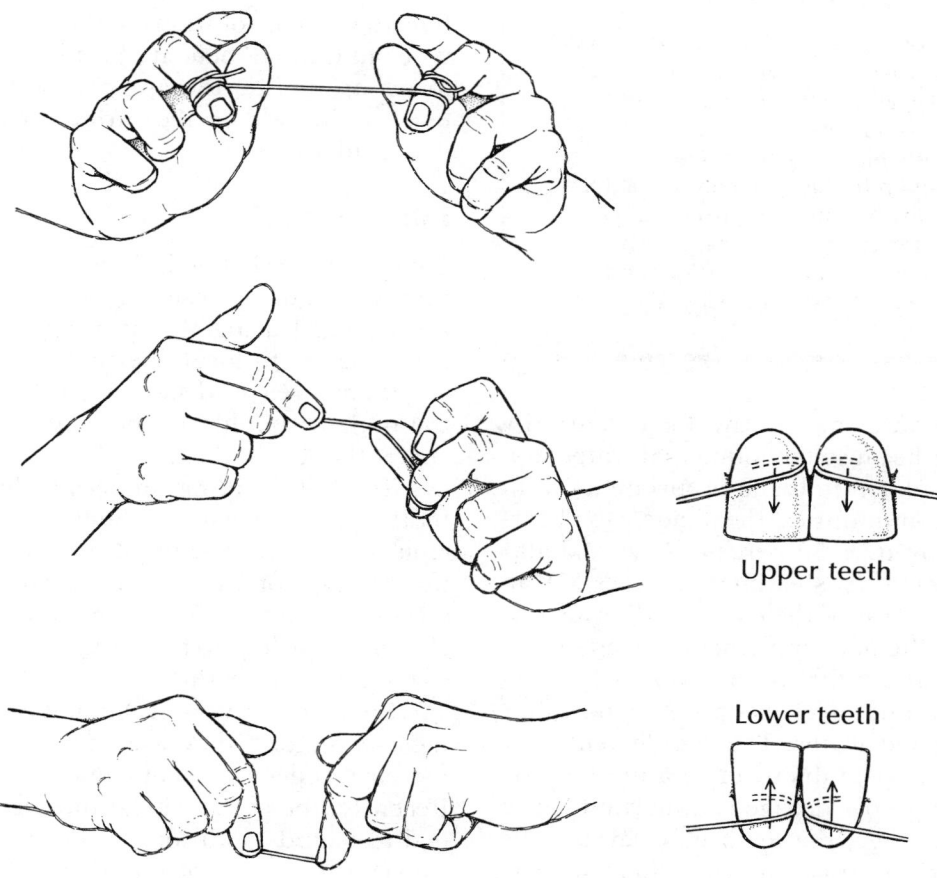

Upper teeth

Lower teeth

Figure 35.5B. **How to floss your teeth.**

SNACK FOODS THAT ARE NOT CARIOGENIC

FOOD GROUP	SNACKS
Bread and cereal	Popcorn (unsalted)
Fruits and vegetables	All raw fruits and vegetables Unsweetened juices
Meats and proteins	All meats Hard-boiled eggs Bean dips Nuts (unsalted)
Other	Sugarless gum Sugarless candy Sugarless soft drinks Coffee or tea without sugar

Milk is a good snack and also a good mealtime drink. Taken with sweetened foods, it can help wash sugar from the mouth.

Some fruits—oranges, pineapples, peaches—are very high in natural sugar. Therefore, although fruit is generally a healthier snack than a candy bar, frequent fruit snacks can be damaging to the teeth. Dried fruits such as raisins are not only sweet but also sticky and should be avoided as between-meal snacks.

benefit, either because the local water is naturally high in fluoride or because the municipal water supply has been fluoridated to the appropriate level. In such fluoridated communities, the incidences of caries has dropped by over 50 percent. (Every dollar spent on fluoridation, it is estimated, saves $50 in dental bills.) In the rest of the country, fluoride can be prescribed as a dietary supplement during the period of tooth formation (that is, until about 14 years of age) and will produce a level of protection similar to that of fluoridated water. The supplement may take the form of drops, tablets, or vitamin-fluoride combination. The proper dosage is important, since with too high a dosage, the teeth will develop the white spots or discolorations known as fluorosis. The dosage is 0.25 mg daily for children from birth to 2; 0.5 mg daily for children 2 to 3; and 1.0 mg/day for children 3 to 14, or until a year after all the permanent molars have appeared.

Fluoride has its greatest effect just before and just after the emergence of the teeth. This is why it is continued for a year after all the permanent teeth are in place. For the same reason there is no particular advantage in pregnant women taking fluoride supplements; it is in the months after childbirth, rather than before, that the fluoride is most beneficial.

There are no side effects to the proper use of fluoride and no effects other than dental fluorosis with elevated levels. More than 35 years of research in many countries attest to the safety and value of fluoridated water and fluoride supplements. There is no truth to the rumors that fluoride is responsible for cancer, birth defects, or any other condition. The only recognized concern is for patients on hemodialysis, who should use demineralized or distilled water, so as not to build up a high concentration of fluoride (and other ions) in their blood.

The regular use of fluoride toothpaste and mouthwashes *at any age* reduces decay yet further on a topical basis, i.e., in interaction with the tooth surface. And for children, the topical application of fluoride gels or solutions in the dental office can provide additional benefit. People who use multiple forms of fluoride therapy can build a high enough level of fluoride on the surface enamel virtually to defy acid attack.

Fillings

Before a tooth is filled, decay must be meticulously removed and the resulting cavity shaped to retain the filling. During this procedure, pain is usually controlled with local anesthetics. Since these anesthetics can react adversely with other medications, the patient should tell the dentist about any drugs currently being taken.

The ideal filling material should match the tooth tissue in wear-resistance, strength and, if possible, in color. It should also react as the tooth does to chewing forces and to changes of temperature within the mouth. Therefore, different materials are chosen according to the requirements and functions of the different teeth.

So-called silver, or amalgam, fillings are the most common. They are composed of an alloy of mercury and a variety of metals in addition to silver. Recently, the conventional mixture has been modified to include additional copper—this is markedly superior to earlier formulations.

Gold foil is occasionally used to fill small cavities in the front teeth. The most common use for gold, however, is in the form of a cast inlay. The material is strong and does not corrode or change its shape in the mouth. However, it is expensive and there is a higher risk of decay around the edges of such fillings than around amalgam fillings.

Plastic composite materials are used for fillings in the front teeth. They can be matched very closely in color to the tooth, are easy to use, and do not dissolve in the mouth fluids. Composites have not been strong enough in the past for use in the back teeth, which are subject to heavy biting forces. Clinical studies, however, now indicate that the addition of strontium particles and other materials to composites should enable them to serve as filling materials in molar and bicuspid teeth.

Root Canal and Extraction

Fillings are done on living teeth. When the caries is so extensive that it has caused the pulp of the tooth to die, the only feasible options are root canal therapy or extraction—whether the tooth has abscessed or not.

In root canal therapy—a multiphase procedure designed to save a badly diseased tooth—all traces of pulp tissue are removed from the pulp chamber and the canals. The canals are filed out, reamed, and sterilized; they are then closed with small gutta percha cones and cement. A perfect seal is imperative in order to avoid infection permanently.

When root canal therapy is not feasible, the dead tooth probably will be extracted. (Abscessed primary teeth are almost always extracted and, if the permanent tooth will not emerge for 6 months, space maintainers are put in place.) Local anesthetic is usually used. The extracted tooth will often be replaced with a fixed bridge or a partial denture. (See Replacing Missing Teeth, page 702.)

Crowns

It is sometimes necessary to cover the entire tooth surface above the gum line with a replacement crown or cap. (The terms are synonymous and interchangeable, although people usually use the term "cap" when referring to the front teeth.) This is nec-essary when a tooth has been severely damaged by decay or has been heavily filled, when it is necessary to protect thin sections of the tooth or back teeth that have had root canal treatment, or when front teeth are unsightly due to decay or injury.

A tooth is prepared for a crown by removing all the enamel, together with enough of the underlying dentin to provide for a sufficiently substantial crown. Impressions (molds) are then taken of the tooth stub, as well as of the neighboring and opposite teeth, to ensure a precise and functional fit. Gold is used for crowns on the back teeth where strength is required, often with plastic or porcelain facings. On the front teeth, a combination of gold and porcelain is widely used, since it is thus possible to make a crown that is both strong and attractive (the porcelain can match the tooth color almost exactly). Increasingly, porcelain alone is used as a crown for a single tooth, since the new materials are much stronger than those previously used.

Bonding

Bonding is an increasingly popular alternative to a crown for a tooth that is chipped, or has stains, cracks, or flaws in the enamel. First, the enamel is lightly etched with an acid solution to improve retention. This is followed by a paste made of plastic combined with finely ground quartz, glass, or silica—matched as closely as possible to the tooth color—applied in layers until the imperfection is repaired or the stain covered. The restoration is then set or "cured" by means of a chemical process that often uses ultraviolet or visible light.

In badly chipped or misshapen front teeth, for which the paste would not be adequate, thin acrylic shells or veneers can be bonded directly to the front surface of the teeth via acid etching. Unlike a crown, bonding and veneers are not permanent and the procedure may have to be repeated after several years of wear.

PERIODONTAL DISEASE

WHILE CARIES is the principal cause of tooth loss before age 35, periodontal disease is responsible for most loose teeth and 70 percent of the tooth loss after age 40. In fact, it has been estimated that 100 million Americans suffer from periodontal disease in some degree. It affects all who have their natural teeth (except the very young), whether a full set or only a few remaining ones. Sixty percent of those 45 and older suffer from its most severe form, i.e., peri-odontitis with pockets—and there is a steady increase in severity with increasing age. The cumulative effect of bacterial plaque on the periodontal tissue has been blamed for this, rather than degenerative tissue changes that occur as part of the aging process.

Periodontal disease occurs in the periodontium: the gums (gingivae), the periodontal ligament, and the alveolar bone that together make up the supporting structure of the teeth. There are several types of periodontal disease, but they have one thing in common: They all lead to destruction of the structures supporting the teeth. (See figure 35.6.) As with caries, bacterial plaque is an underlying cause of periodontal disease, although the kinds of bacteria and the destructive process are different.

Gingivitis is a superficial inflammation of the gum tissue, due to irritation by bacteria products in the plaque. It usually first manifests itself at puberty and then tends to exist at a chronic level throughout life, in differing degrees of severity. The first sign of gingivitis is red, swollen gums which bleed easily when subjected to pressure. This is especially noticeable with toothbrushing (the "pink toothbrush" is almost always the first symptom). Because gum inflammation may cause little discomfort and progresses slowly, gingivitis is often neglected until it is far advanced and the required treatment is extensive.

Unless reversed by successful treatment (see below), gingivitis usually progresses to periodontitis, which used to be called pyorrhea (from the Greek, "a flow of pus"). With long-standing gingivitis, the continuing formation of irritating bacterial products causes a pocket to form between the tooth surface and the gums. Plaque continually builds up in this pocket and cannot be reached with a toothbrush.

This leads to increased inflammation and in turn a deepening pocket—a vicious circle that can only be reversed through effective treatment. The progressive inflammation destroys the periodontal ligament. The margin of the gums detaches from the teeth and the pus oozes from the periodontal pockets. The adjacent bone becomes affected and progressive bone loss leads to loosening teeth, which may eventually fall out. In general, the younger the patient at the onset of bone loss, the poorer the chances of saving the teeth. Periodontitis is usually painless unless an acute infection is superimposed on the chronic condition, such as an abscess in one or more of the pockets.

Necrotizing ulcerative gingivitis, also called trench mouth or Vincent's infection, usually affects young adults, although it is seen in people of all ages. It may be mild or severe, acute or chronic. In this form of periodontal disease, the gums usually *are* painful and there is often profuse bleeding on the slightest provocation. The gum points (papillae) between the teeth are destroyed, leaving craters that collect food debris and plaque, and the affected area is covered with a whitish layer of decomposing gum tissue. There is a strong association between this infection and emotional stress.

Localized juvenile periodontitis (LJP), also known as periodontosis, is a particularly fulminat-

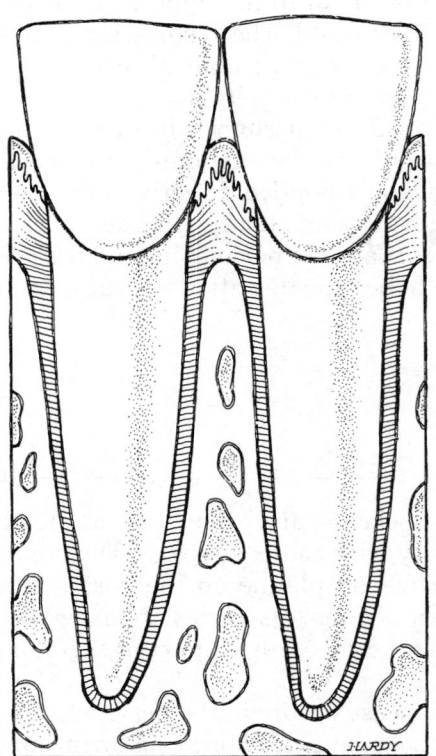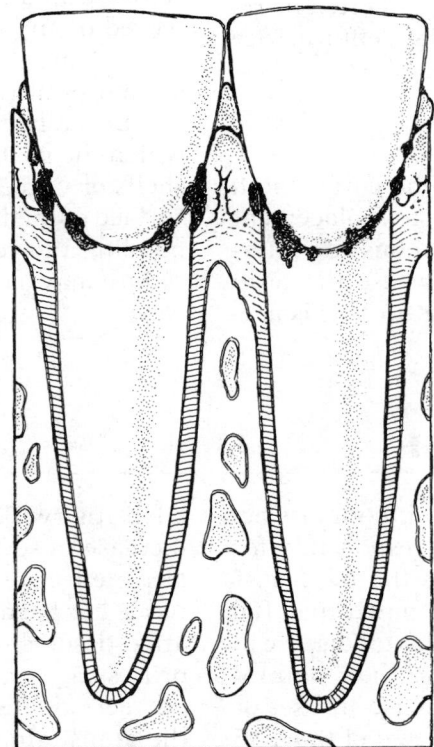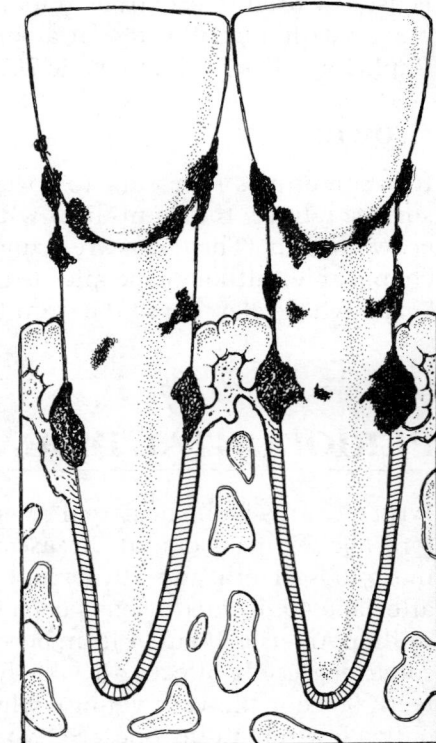

Figure 35.6. **Development of periodontal disease.**

ing form of periodontal disease that affects a small segment of the teenage and young adult population (1 to 3 percent). There is marked destruction of the bone around the front teeth and first molars.

Causes

The cause of gingivitis is bacterial plaque. The accumulation of plaque is usually heaviest near the gum margin and between teeth, the areas that are not self-cleaning. It causes inflammation of the gums, mainly as a result of the toxins and enzymes produced by the bacteria. Plaque can mineralize to form tartar, or calculus. Calculus most commonly forms in those parts of the mouth that are closest to the salivary glands—inside the lower front teeth and on the outer surface of the upper molars and in the periodontal pockets. If not adequately removed, the plaque and calculus build up in layers, increasing the bacteria in the mouth and leading to further inflammation of the gums.

Periodontal disease is the result of poor dental hygiene, but it can be aggravated by overhanging rough margins or fillings, which accumulate plaque, and by maloccluded teeth—teeth that don't come together correctly and may generate abnormal biting forces. The nervous habit of grinding or clenching the teeth during sleep, called bruxism, can also overload the periodontal structure and contribute to the breakdown of the supporting tissues. Smoking is a further aggravating factor, shown by the fact that smokers tend to have more periodontal problems than nonsmokers.

There are also systemic factors in periodontal disease. People with diabetes, thyroid disorders, and a variety of blood conditions may have a higher risk of developing advanced periodontal disease. Deficiencies of vitamin C and (possibly) folic acid also contribute to an increasing rate of periodontal breakdown. Gingivitis is often particularly marked during puberty and again during pregnancy, suggesting a hormonal factor. Plaque bacteria are able to utilize the increased hormonal levels available in the fluid adjacent to the gingiva. In pregnancy, noticeably swollen gums that bleed easily are common as early as the second month. After delivery, the gingiva usually return to the prepregnancy condition.

Prevention

Thorough brushing and flossing of teeth will help keep bacterial plaque and calculus formation to a minimum. For some patients, dentists also advise the use of special toothpicks, interproximal brushes, or an interdental stimulator. The rubber or plastic tip found on many toothbrushes is not basically a cleaning instrument (although it can be used as one); rather, it is designed to massage the gum tissue between the teeth. Irrigants, such as a WaterPik, can supplement cleaning techniques in areas difficult to reach with a toothbrush. Irrigation does not remove plaque; rather it flushes out plaque's toxic products. However, even the best oral hygiene will not completely prevent plaque formation, nor will it remove calculus that has already formed and is firmly attached to the teeth at the gum line and below. Calculus must be removed professionally by scaling the teeth with a sharp instrument or the more modern ultrasonic device which vibrates the calculus off the teeth. The combination of personal plaque control and appropriately scheduled office visits is the key to preventing periodontal disease.

Treatment

In the earlier stages of the disease, treatment usually involves regular prophylaxis, root planing, and curettage under the gum margins. This treatment removes calculus and plaque from the tooth surfaces, as well as inflamed tissue from the pockets around the teeth, by use of a curette, a spoon-shaped instrument. With the removal of the bacterial colonies and the mechanical and chemical irritants that cause inflammation, the gum will usually reattach itself to the tooth, or will constrict enough to eliminate the pocket. In most early cases, subgingival curettage and good oral hygiene are all that is required for satisfactory results.

In more advanced cases, pockets can be eliminated by a minor surgical procedure called gingivectomy. This is performed under local anesthetic and a dressing is placed to cover the wound for a week or so, while it heals. A similar procedure, the gingivoplasty, is used to remove excessive gum tissue and to provide a new and healthier shape for the gums, helping them to stay self-cleaning.

In many cases, flap procedures are required. During this treatment, the gum tissue is lifted away from the teeth, all the underlying infected tissue and calculus are removed, the bone is recontoured, and the gum is then replaced in its proper position, sutured, and allowed to heal. In advanced cases, osseous surgery may be performed to correct defects in the bone structure caused by the periodontal disease or by certain anatomic deformities.

Other treatments may be necessary, depending on the nature of the periodontal problem. One is occlusal adjustment, which is the reshaping of the chewing and biting surfaces of the teeth so that the pressures sustained by the teeth are distributed evenly. There are also cases of chronic gum conditions that can be helped by moving the teeth by orthodontic treatment. For habitual tooth grinders, appliances can be constructed to be worn at night to protect the teeth from excessive pressure.

A recently advocated nonsurgical treatment for periodontal disease—named for Dr. Paul Keyes, who developed it—involves, in addition to careful scaling and curettage in the dental office, assiduous daily home care using such antibacterial agents as salt, baking soda, and hydrogen peroxide to sup-press the infection. The results of this home care are monitored by microscopic examination of the bacterial debris under the gums. If necessary, antibiotic treatment is given. Keyes treatment, which has received much publicity, should not be seen as a substitute for conventional treatment, but as an alternative that may be appropriate at some stages of the disease for some people. The same meticulous removal of tooth deposits is required for this as for any other treatment, and once this has been done, the maintenance of periodontal tissues becomes in large degree the responsibility of the patient.

REPLACING MISSING TEETH (PROSTHODONTICS)

AFTER A PERMANENT TOOTH has been lost, the teeth on either side of the space gradually tilt toward the gap, and the teeth in the opposite jaw begin to slip vertically toward the space. Because repercussions are widespread and encourage further caries and periodontal disease, missing teeth should be replaced, if at all possible. There are several options open to those who need a false tooth or teeth.

A fixed bridge can be used if there is a firm tooth on each side of the space where the tooth (or teeth) has been lost. Crowns are prepared for these supporting teeth (often using porcelain or plastic facings to make the restoration more esthetic) and the replacement teeth are soldered onto the crowns. The whole is then cemented permanently onto the stubs of the supporting teeth. An advantage of a fixed bridge is that it acts as a splint to the supporting teeth, making them more stable. It is, however, an expensive and time-consuming procedure. Moreover, if additional teeth are lost, they cannot be added to the bridge. When teeth are missing in several areas in the same jaw, additional stability may be obtained by joining the bridges, or by splinting (joining loose and strong teeth together).

A removable partial denture is usually used to replace multiple missing teeth. It rests on the soft tissues of the lower jaw, or on the palate, and is held in place with clips (clasps) and supports. Partial dentures greatly increase the surface area in the mouth that is subject to plaque formation and must therefore be meticulously cleaned. Fortunately, this is quite easy. Over time, because of the tension produced by the retaining clips, a partial denture tends to loosen the supporting teeth. However, it is considerably less expensive than a fixed bridge and is more versatile because additional lost teeth can usually be added to it.

If all the teeth are missing in an arch, a full den-ture is made to restore both the teeth and the underlying, gradually shrinking bony support. An upper denture is almost always quite satisfactory; the ridge and the hard palate are completely covered and usually a seal can be formed which holds the denture in place. A lower denture is frequently troublesome. Because of the limited amount of bony surface available, there is a tendency for it to become dislodged while chewing, or even, on occasion, while speaking.

Some patients are candidates for immediate dentures. These appliances are prepared prior to the removal of the remaining natural teeth and are inserted into the mouth immediately following extraction. In this way, the patient is spared the potential embarrassment of temporary toothlessness. These dentures, however, must be refitted when the jaw heals. If healing results in extensive change, new dentures must be made.

Because of shrinkage of the bony base of the jaw, a denture will require regular relining to prevent movement that could encourage further shrinking of the tissues, the production of mouth ulcers, or excessive growth of the tissues adjacent to the dentures. Despite some inevitable loss in chewing ability, most people function well with dentures.

An overdenture is a variation of a full denture. Where possible, 2 to 4 teeth in the arch are saved and their crowns ground down to small stubs. Gold thimbles are cemented to these stubs and the denture is prepared to fit over these pegs and the bony ridge. Overdentures are particularly successful in the lower arch, where retention of full dentures is often a problem. Care must be taken, however, to protect the stubs with good oral hygiene and the use of fluorides if root surfaces become exposed.

Various inert materials have been inserted in the jaws in an attempt to replace missing teeth or to help stabilize full dentures by augmenting the natural ridges of the jawbones. Metallic implants are permanently inserted below the soft tissues to provide greater surface area, to help keep the dentures in place. The surfaces of the metal implants must be microscopically clean so that the implant is accepted by the host tissue. A new process called glow-discharge cleaning sterilizes these devices; it should markedly improve their maintenance in the mouth.

EMERGENCY TREATMENT FOR DISLODGED TEETH

A TOOTH that is dislodged in an accident, athletic or any other injury, can often be replaced in its socket. This applies to both children and adults. The tooth should not be cleaned but should be placed in water or milk or wrapped in a wet cloth and a dentist or dental clinic contacted immediately. If the tooth is replaced in its socket within 30 minutes, there is a good chance of successful reattachment.

PREGNANCY

IF TOOTH DECAY is associated with pregnancy, as the adage "a tooth is lost for every child" implies (this has never been shown to be true), it is probably because some women tend to neglect their teeth during pregnancy and in the months following delivery. Calcium is *not* absorbed from the mother's teeth for the benefit of the fetus, and pregnancy as such is not responsible for caries. The nutrients required for the proper formation of the primary teeth—calcium, phosphorus, protein, iron, vitamins A, C, and D—are provided by an average well-balanced diet. Sugar intake should be kept to a minimum for the sake of both mother and fetus.

In general, extensive dental treatment should be avoided during the first trimester of pregnancy, because of possible damage to the fetus. This is a particularly rapid period of fetal growth, and the time in which the majority of malformations develop. A history of miscarriage or other medical conditions may make it advisable to postpone any dental treatment until after delivery. During the last 2 or 3 months, a pregnant woman may find sitting or reclining in the dentist's chair uncomfortable, and may wish to avoid extensive treatment for that reason. Routine care, especially of the soft tissues, is important because gingivitis of pregnancy is a very common problem. Benign pregnancy tumors of the mouth may also occur (although only rarely) as a result of poor oral hygiene. If these are large and painful, they may have to be removed surgically.

Unless it is unavoidable, general anesthesia should never be given at any time during pregnancy, as it exposes the fetus to the danger of oxygen deficiency and increased stress. Any treatment involving drugs—even local anesthetics and aspirin—requires consultation between the dentist and the obstetrician. Valium, for example, which is frequently used in dentistry for sedation, is known to cause fetal damage. Dental x-rays should be kept to a minimum and a lead apron should be used to protect the fetus against harmful radiation.

INFANCY AND EARLY CHILDHOOD

Teething

The emergence of the primary teeth (see figure 35.2A) is frequently preceded by excessive salivation and a tendency to keep a hand or finger constantly in the mouth. In many children, some degree of gum inflammation and flushed cheeks accompany teething. There may also be general disturbances: loss of appetite, irritability, disturbed sleep, or a rash around the mouth. The symptoms of teething may be relieved by giving the baby a teething ring or a hard, unsweetened rusk to chew on.

Oral Hygiene

Even before the teeth appear, the gums should be cleaned with a piece of gauze or a clean cloth after each feeding, which will help the child become accustomed to having the mouth cleaned. Once the teeth have emerged, parents should clean them with a soft toothbrush. Children can begin to learn to brush their own teeth by the age of 2 or 3, but close supervision is necessary until the age of 6 to 8, to ensure an adequate performance and to prevent the child from swallowing the toothpaste. Flossing should be part of the child's regular oral hygiene routine from the age of 6 or 7, depending on the manual dexterity of the child.

Healthy primary teeth are necessary for proper chewing, clear speech, and an attractive appearance. Moreover, they reserve space for the permanent teeth, allowing them to grow into their appropriate spaces. To prevent neighboring teeth from drifting into the space left by a prematurely lost first or second molar, space maintainers (fixed metal bands) may be fitted.

Nursing Bottle Mouth

Severe tooth decay is sometimes seen in infants and young children. In extreme cases, only the roots of the front teeth in the upper jaw remain. This condition, known as nursing bottle mouth, is the result of giving children a bottle of sweetened water, juice, milk, or formula at bedtime or naptime. The long-term presence of sugar in the mouth, combined with lack of salivation during sleep and the tendency of liquid to pool around the front teeth, result in rampant dental decay. Plain water only should be given if a baby requires a bottle for comfort before falling asleep.

The First Dental Visit

The best time for a first dental checkup is when the child is 2 or 2½ years old, by which time all the primary teeth will have emerged. Parents should not delay dental care until a child develops a toothache or some other problem. Dental treatment following a night of toothache can be a frightening experience for a young child and may lead to an association—perhaps a permanent one—between dentistry and pain.

An essential part of preventive dentistry is the gradual education of the young child about the importance of oral health. The first visit to the dentist is a natural extension of the education already begun at home. Started early, preventive treatment—examination of the teeth, cleaning, polishing with a fluoride preparation—gives the child confidence in the dentist and a sense of familiarity with the equipment in the dental office. In this way, if caries develops, it can be treated without distress to the child, or the parent.

THE DISABLED

ALMOST 15 PERCENT of the American population (some 33 million people) have some sort of chronic physical, mental, or emotional condition that to some extent affects their ability to care for themselves. For the disabled, dental health is often neglected because of other pressing health problems. As a result, periodontal disease, untreated tooth decay, and missing teeth are particularly prevalent among this segment of the population.

Some disabilities are responsible for particular dental problems. Down's syndrome, for example, is associated with missing teeth, malocclusion (teeth that don't come together properly), and periodontal disease. Underdeveloped enamel that is pitted or irregular is seen in children with cerebral palsy. In both children and adults, oral health can be affected by medications. Radiation therapy, tranquilizers, and barbiturates result in lack of salivation. Dilantin, a drug that controls seizures, may cause abnormal gum growth which affects chewing.

Still, most of the oral problems of the disabled are caused by the diseases that affect the population generally: caries and periodontitis. Since the emphasis today is on caring for the disabled at home as much as possible, the responsibility for preventive care of the teeth and gums must often be assumed by parents and family members. Brushing and flossing techniques may have to be modified in light of the disability, and it may be necessary to see a pedodontist rather than a general dental practitioner. (See box on Dental Specialists, page 707.) However, with care and patience it should be possible to avoid serious dental problems.

MISCELLANEOUS DISORDERS

Canker Sores

Canker sores (apthous ulcers) occur singly or in groups inside the mouth—on the inside surface of the cheeks and lips, on the tongue and the soft palate, and at the base of the gums. These sores resemble craters and range in size from ⅛ inch to more than 1 inch in diameter. They can be both painful and disabling, especially when they are numerous and interfere with talking and eating. The ulcers may recur 2 or 3 times per year or, in a small number of cases, may be continuously present as an uninterrupted succession of lesions.

The cause of canker sores is not known, although some people seem to be especially susceptible to them, and an inherited predisposition may be involved. However, a number of triggering mechanisms have been identified, some of which are preventable. Recurrent canker sores are associated with injuries such as pricks or punctures within the oral cavity. In some people, they have also been linked to deficiencies of iron, folic acid, vitamin B_{12}, or a combination of these; many of these cases clear up with nutritional therapy. Physical and emotional stress are also factors—canker sores are common among students during examination periods. A fever or the onset of menstruation may also provide the trigger.

Canker sores form rapidly and usually heal rapidly, even when untreated. If they become infected, the antibiotic tetracycline may be prescribed or, in very severe cases, steroid drugs may be used to reduce inflammation.

Temperomandibular Joint Syndrome (TMJ)

Myofascial pain-dysfunction syndrome, of which TMJ is one manifestation, occurs when the muscles used in chewing and the joints of the jaw fail to work in conjunction. TMJ may have any number of causes, among them such habits as clenching or grinding the teeth (bruxism), malocclusion (poor bite) that puts muscles under stress and causes a spasm, accidents damaging the bones of the face or jaw or, occasionally, disease such as arthritis. The underlying predisposition, however, is often stress-related.

The classic symptoms of TMJ are pain and tenderness of the jaw muscles, clicking and grinding noises during movement of the jaw, and limited or irregular jaw movement.

The basic problem, aggravated by oral conditions, is often an emotional one. The development of symptoms seems to be caused by a combination of factors: a physiologic predisposition, psychological and physical stress, and the individual's inability to cope with stress. Stress management, together with supportive treatment with heat and muscle relaxants, can often have a profound effect. Any treatment involving appliances to improve the bite should be of reversible nature.

ORTHODONTICS

CROWDED TEETH, a bite that is out of alignment horizontally or vertically, gaps between the teeth, and prognathism (protrusion) of either jaw, may all pose problems for dental and general health, as well as affecting appearance. Maloccluded teeth are more difficult to clean and may be more susceptible to caries and periodontal disease. They can cause muscle tension, pain, and emotional problems. Moreover, if chewing is difficult, soft foods are likely to be chosen and nutrition may suffer as well. The correction of malocclusion is therefore always advisable. This is the province of the orthodontist.

Although it is estimated that 90 percent of all children aged 12 to 17 with correctible malocclu-

sions are not treated, some 400,000 new patients start orthodontic treatment each year. The majority are in their early teens, but some are younger and 15 to 20 percent are adults, a percentage that is steadily on the rise. Active orthodontic treatment takes an average of 2 years, followed by a similar, sometimes longer period of stabilization of the teeth in their new position. In adults, whose bone is more dense than that of adolescents, the treatment may take somewhat longer.

Many factors contribute to the irregularities and poor occlusion that require orthodontic treatment. Crowded teeth, wide spacing, and incorrect relationships of the jaws are inherited malocclusions that cannot be prevented. Thumb-sucking that persists after the permanent incisors have come in may open up lasting spaces. An abnormal swallowing reflex, in which the tongue is thrust violently against the teeth and the muscles around the mouth contract strongly, is responsible for many cases of malocclusion. Mouth breathing and lip biting may be associated with the condition, but probably don't cause it.

An orthodontist's choice of treatment for his patient is determined by both dental and cosmetic considerations. The health and stability of the teeth in their projected new positions must be considered and so must the facial contours that will result from repositioning the teeth. In some situations (cases with a marked overbite, for example) the method chosen may be extraction in conjunction with the use of a fixed appliance (braces). Four bicuspids are usually selected, one from each quadrant of the mouth, and extracted in a single session under either local or general anesthesia. Stainless steel bands are then fitted and cemented onto the teeth. Tubes in which the arch wires will be anchored are welded onto the bands on the terminal teeth, usually a molar in each quadrant; the other teeth receive brackets. Increasingly, transparent plastic is being used in place of steel, and frequently brackets and tubes are bonded directly to the teeth. Flexible wires are then inserted. By adjusting these arch wires, steady horizontal or vertical pressure can be maintained on the tooth surface and transmitted through the periodontal ligament to the bone. Gradually, the bone resorbs and the tooth drifts into the space thus created. On the tension side, meanwhile, new bone is built up. This alternation of resorption and deposit is the basic orthodontic process.

Give-and-take displacement of this kind is effective in straightening individual teeth. However, when all the teeth in one jaw—or even the jaw itself—must be moved, some other means of applying force must be found. Frequently, the necessary anchorage is found in the opposing jaw. Thus, if the upper teeth protrude, elastic bands are attached to link the front part of the appliance in the upper jaw with the back part of a similar appliance in the lower jaw. The upper teeth will be pulled back and the lower one will tend to come forward. In some cases, anchorage is needed outside the mouth—the elastic force of "night braces," for example, is anchored on the top of the head or the back of the neck.

Serial extraction is a preventive measure that is used in cases of severe overcrowding of the teeth. Selected primary teeth are extracted at intervals to allow the permanent teeth to emerge in their proper places in the dental arch. Those permanent teeth for which there is no room are extracted when (or before) they appear. Serial extraction is usually supplemented with mechanical orthodontic treatment.

In extreme cases where conventional orthodontic measures have failed or are considered inadequate, surgery may be performed. For example, protrusion of the lower jaw can be corrected by a procedure in which a section of the jaw is removed and the remaining portion is set back in the correct position. Surgery can also adjust open or closed bites that might never respond to orthodontic force. Such procedures are usually done from within the mouth, so there is no visible scarring.

After even the most successful orthodontic treatment, there is the possibility of a relapse—the return of the teeth to their original position. The retention phase of orthodontic treatment is as important as the movement phase. Various devices are used to forestall relapse: retainers (removable plates carrying wires that press on the front teeth), lingual arches (rigid bands between the lower bicuspids), and positioners (rubber mouthpieces, representing ideal models of the patient's tooth structure, worn 4 hours each day).

In both the movement and the retention phases of treatment, the patient's cooperation is essential. Adolescents, however, are often unreliable in their use of night braces, removable appliances, and rubber bands. It is for this reason, among others, that some orthodontists prefer to start treatment before adolescence, when children are generally more cooperative. With the increasing use of transparent plastic in place of steel, and of appliances worn on the inside of the teeth, compliance among adolescents may improve.

Oral Hygiene During Orthodontic Treatment

A well-cemented band or bonded bracket can protect the covered part of the tooth from caries. If, however, food and bacterial plaque remain around the band or bracket, some of the cement dissolves and the result is decalcification (white spots similar to those of early decay). Scrupulous oral hygiene is especially important when there are orthodontic appliances in the mouth. Similarly, fluoride treatment and attention to the diet should not be ignored. Brushing with a fluoride-containing toothpaste and rinsing with a fluoride mouthwash is especially important just before and during orthodontic treatment.

ANXIETY

FOR MANY DENTAL PATIENTS, the scheduled reexamination is a cause for anxiety, both in anticipation of and during the treatment itself. Tape-recorded relaxation instruction, hypnosis, and biofeedback training have been found to be effective in reducing anxiety during routine dental treatment (musical programming, on the other hand, has no significant effect). Biofeedback is the more effective method. In a short period of training—as little as 8 minutes—patients can learn to control muscle tension and greatly reduce anxiety by observing a display of their muscle activity on a TV-like screen.

DENTAL CHECKUPS

ALTHOUGH THE NUMBER of people who visit their dentists regularly—that is, at least once per year—has risen over the past 2 decades, about half the population still fails to visit a dentist in any given year. The reasons range from disability and fear to financial factors. A large number of people, however, simply do not understand the need for regular care and the importance of dental health for general well-being. They seek treatment only when driven to do so by pain or discomfort.

Dental checkups should begin in early childhood and continue throughout adult life. The frequency of the examination should be determined on an individual basis, based on such factors as the degree of decay activity, the amount of periodontal disease, and the presence of full dentures. In general, dentists recommend that the mouth should be reexamined according to the following schedule:

> *Every three months.* (1) For those of any age, if there is a high decay rate (6 or more cavities per year); (2) for adults whose oral home care is poor, even if the decay rate is low.

> *Every six months.* (1) For those with a low to moderate decay rate (1 or 2 cavities per year) and adequate oral hygiene; (2) for denture-wearers who use tobacco and alcohol; (3) for adults over 35 who use tobacco and alcohol.

> *Once a year.* (1) For adults experiencing no decay, whose oral home care is excellent and who do not use tobacco or alcohol; (2) for denture-wearers who are experiencing no problems and do not use tobacco or alcohol.

X-rays

X-rays are used in dentistry, as in other medical fields, to aid in the diagnosis of disease. The radiation dosage is extremely small, but as a precautionary measure, the lower abdomen should be protected with a lead apron. This is particularly important during pregnancy and for women during childbearing age in general. X-rays can reveal the

---

DIRECTORY OF DENTAL SPECIALISTS

About 80 percent of all dentists are general practitioners. In addition, there are the following specialists:

Endodontists deal with the diagnosis and treatment of diseases of the tooth pulp and injuries involving the pulp and supporting tissues.

Oral pathologists specialize in the interpretation and diagnosis of the changes caused by disease in the tissues of the oral cavity.

Oral and maxillofacial surgeons treat diseases, injuries, and defects of the jaw, mouth, and face, using surgery. They also perform extractions.

Orthodontists are concerned with the guidance and correction of the growing or mature dentofacial structure; they treat conditions that require moving the teeth or correcting malformations or poor relationships of teeth and jaws.

Pedodontists specialize in the dental problems of children from birth through adolescence; they also care for patients beyond adolescence who have special mental, emotional, or physical problems.

Periodontists specialize in treating disease of the tissues supporting and surrounding the teeth.

Prosthodontists are concerned with the design and fitting of dentures, bridges, and other replacements for missing teeth.

Although any licensed dentist can practice in any dental specialty even if he or she is not qualified to do so by training or experience, specialized work usually requires a specialist. A board-certified specialist has satisfied requirements of training and experience designed to assure competence. Each of the dental specialty programs requires 2 years of postgraduate training, with the exception of oral surgery, which requires 3 or 4 years.

HOW TO JUDGE A DENTIST

There are many sources for referrals to a good dental general practitioner: the family doctor, the local pharmacist, the local dental society, a hospital, or a university with a dental school. Especially good sources of recommendation are specialists—orthodontists, periodontists, or endodontists—who are keenly aware of the quality of work of the general practitioners in the area.

On the first visit, a good dentist should:

1. Take a complete medical and dental history, including information on drug allergies and such chronic illnesses as diabetes, bleeding problems, rheumatic or other heart valve disease.

2. Emphasize prevention and give appropriate advice on home oral health techniques.

3. Explain treatments and fees clearly and be willing to provide written estimates and itemized bills.

4. Give emergency care.

5. Discuss alternative treatments and possible complications.

extent of decay, cavities hidden between the teeth or under the gum line, bone damage from periodontal disease, tumors, fractures in the teeth or jawbone, impacted teeth, and abscesses. They are therefore an essential diagnostic tool in dentistry, but should be used for diagnostic purposes only—not as a routine. Any unnecessary radiation is excessive radiation. In the absence of conditions requiring more frequent x-rays, a full-mouth x-ray record should not be made more than once every 5 years.

RESEARCH—THE NEXT DECADE

Antibacterial Agents

There has been little success in developing agents to control all the potentially cariogenic bacteria in plaque. Scientists have therefore turned their attention to a search for agents that affect S. mutans, the major decay-producing bacteria. Preparations of antimicrobial agents in slow-release devices attached to the teeth offer an attractive possibility for delivering an antibacterial drug. However, thus far, the ideal agent has not emerged.

There are a number of antibacterial agents that may have an impact on the bacteria involved in gingivitis and periodontal disease. Chlorhexidine, widely used in Europe, should begin to appear in U.S. products over the next few years. Antiplaque mouthwashes for reducing gingivitis are under active study.

Anticaries Vaccine

Animal experiments with a vaccine directed against S. mutans have been effective in markedly reducing new decay. Work with humans is only beginning. In a recent study, human subjects ingested capsules of modified S. mutans over a 10-day period. They developed elevated levels of antibodies in their saliva and significantly fewer bacteria were able to establish themselves in the oral cavity. However, many problems, including the demonstration of the safety of this approach, remain to be solved.

Other Research Projects

Recent studies of the association of specific bacteria with some forms of periodontal disease open up the possibility of an eventual vaccine. Because of the involvement of the immune system in the progression of periodontal disease, this will be a complex undertaking.

Active research is also being undertaken in the development of biological materials to fill in defects in the jaw, to stimulate bone formation, and to act as a "glue" to support teeth and bone weakened by periodontal disease.

Researchers are learning that deficits in salivary flow, or the body's various defense systems, make some people more prone to tooth decay than others. For these caries-prone people, a slow-release fluoride implant, now under investigation, will be particularly beneficial. Attached to a molar, the tiny device will release fluoride continuously into the saliva, providing sustained fluoride protection.

36 Mental and Emotional Health

Donald S. Kornfeld, M.D., and Philip R. Muskin, M.D.

INTRODUCTION

IN THE PAST, the mentally ill were considered outcasts, put into the same class as paupers, the lame and blind, and people with leprosy and epilepsy. Mental illness was often viewed as a sign of possession by a devil, or at best, moral weakness. General reform of these attitudes and treatments began in the late eighteenth century, when the insane began to be seen as treatable. The concept of asylums was developed, not as a means to lock the mentally ill away but as a means to provide them with "asylum" or relief from the conditions they found troubling.

Beginning in the 1950s, the treatment of the mentally ill experienced a transformation because of the discovery of new drugs such as chlorpromazine

(Thorazine), which could relieve the symptoms of the major mental illness, schizophrenia, and imipramine (e.g., Tofranil) for the treatment of depression. This development had two important influences on psychiatry: It allowed many mentally ill people to find relief and a more normal life without resorting to institutions, and revised society's understanding of emotional illness. Research has also established biological abnormalities associated with psychiatric disorders. Mental illness has thus become more accurately perceived as similar to other medical afflictions.

However, unlike diseases such as smallpox or rheumatic fever, the basic prevalence of mental illness has not been reduced. It continues to affect about 2 percent of any society, whether primitive or industrialized—although the figures may vary depending on how a particular society defines and tolerates mental illness.

The mind is a composite of the higher actions of the nervous system. These patterns reflect both genetic and learned influences, and conscious and unconscious factors. The brain is also subject to the involuntary influences of the autonomic nervous system and endocrine gland system. (See figure 36.1.) These systems can affect mood as well as raise blood pressure, increase the heartbeat, and cause other physical reactions to stress. Mental disorders cannot be separated from the actions of the rest of the body, and in many cases mental and physical illness seem to be inextricably bound to each other.

For this reason, doctors take emotional factors into account in evaluating their patients' health. Some psychiatric disorders are readily apparent. Some disorders, however, are more difficult to detect directly. The role of emotional factors should therefore be carefully evaluated by the doctor when a medical history is taken. This means that information about the patient's life at home, at work, and at school are important to a complete understanding of the problem that prompts a person to seek medical care. In this chapter, the more common psychological problems will be discussed, as well as some of the basics in maintaining emotional health and well-being.

DEPRESSION
(Prepared in collaboration with Ralph N. Wharton, M.D.)

DEPRESSION is the most common serious psychiatric problem, affecting millions of people each year. In the public mind, it is often confused with unhappiness, grief, and other such emotions stemming from misfortune or a sad event, such as the death of a loved one. Such events are in the realm of almost every human being's experience, and unhappiness is a natural response to them. Indeed, the absence of unhappiness in a life would almost certainly be abnormal. Depression, on the other hand, is a true disease affecting both the mind and body. While not everyone who might feel "depressed" needs or even wants treatment, there are many people who have the clinical disease of depression who do not recognize or admit it. The tragic consequences include suicide (a leading cause of death in certain age groups) and the inability to function to one's full potential.

In recent decades, studies of the brain have established that clinical depression may be a biological disease based on a chemical disorder, not unlike many other organic diseases. While the specific biological basis of the illness remains unknown, research has suggested that the problem may lie in the complex neurotransmission system of the brain.

This is a system of about 10 to 15 chemicals that transfers signals from nerve cell to nerve cell. One theory, known as the "catecholamine hypothesis," suggests that the disorder in depression involves the chemical messengers that regulate the neurotransmission system. It is not clear whether, in a particular person, these chemicals are produced in insufficient quantity or are rendered ineffective by being broken down too quickly after they are released. However, most of the highly successful antidepressant drugs are aimed at correcting these chemical imbalances in the brain.

Causes of Depression

In many instances, depression has no identifiable cause. In others, it may be triggered by a sad event, such as a death or loss of a job. On rare occasions, certain medications may have depression as a side effect, particularly in people already prone to the problem. An illness, such as the flu or some other viral infection, may lead to a short-lived depression. Depression is surprisingly rare, however, in people with major disease such as cancer or heart disease. While this depression is often related to fears about

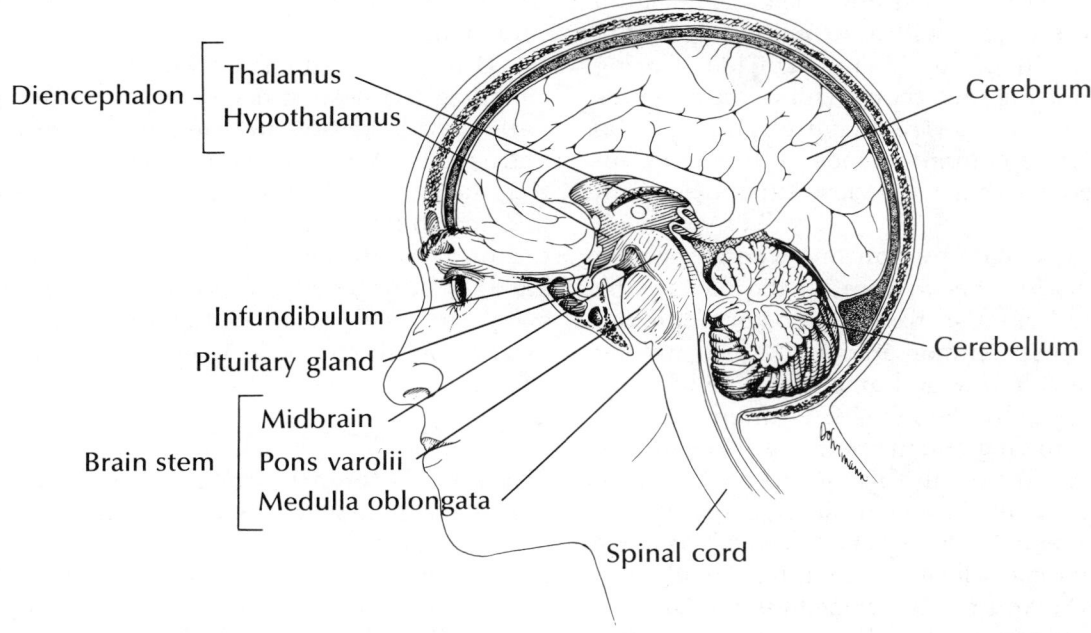

Figure 36.1. **The brain and its major structures.**

the condition, it can also be associated with other personal problems which are exacerbated by the occurrence of serious illness. Psychotherapy is often quite helpful in these situations.

Signs of Depression

There are several features that distinguish clinical depression from unhappiness. It is very common for depressed people to feel that nothing can ever make them better, a depressing thought itself. Persistent pessimism is a symptom of the disease. Questions that may be asked in evaluating depression include: How long have these feelings persisted? Can the mood be lifted under certain environmental circumstances or is it pervasive and constant? Is there a pervasive feeling of hopelessness? A lack of self-esteem? Trouble sleeping? A change in appetite? A loss of interest in sex and other pleasurable activities?

In depression, the worst time of day is in the morning with improvement in mood as the day goes on. Clinical depression is also accompanied by several physical symptoms that are distinct from simply feeling "blue." For example, insomnia is a common problem; the person often has no trouble falling asleep, but then awakens a few hours later and is unable to sleep again. The sad mood is also accompanied by disinterest in food, work, and sometimes sex, slowness of movement or speech, a tendency to look on the negative side of things and

sometimes, most important, thoughts of suicide. Thoughts of suicide are a warning sign to see a doctor, who should be told of such feelings because these will determine the way the depression is treated.

There are variations of these classic signs of depression. Some patients, for example, will not have insomnia but will sleep more. Instead of losing their appetite, they will eat more.

Still another form of the disease is manic depression, also called bipolar affective disorder. Typically, the patient has wide mood swings, going from the depths of depression to manic euphoria. Generally, the episodes of mania begin suddenly, worsen rapidly, and may last for weeks. The course of manic depression is often erratic: A person may have one attack at the age of 20 and be fine until the age of 70. Or attacks may follow quickly, one after another, increasing in frequency with age, leaving the person feeling as though he or she is on a constant emotional roller coaster. Mania occurs in some people without intervening episodes of depression.

The Danger of Suicide

Suicide is the most serious consequence of depression. Suicidal thoughts do not necessarily entail active planning to end life. Rather, they may reflect the feeling that life is not worth living. The doctor should be told of these thoughts since they are a measure of the patient's distress. The patient should not assume the doctor will ask; many doctors are mistakenly afraid of mentioning suicide, fearing they may be putting such thoughts into the patient's head by merely asking. Treatment of patients who are more likely to commit suicide will be more intensive, preferably under the close supervision of a psychiatrist.

The risk of suicide by someone who is severely depressed calls for special care on the part of the family as well as the treating doctor. Suicidal thoughts are most common among the aged, among men, among alcoholics, and among people who are not married and live alone. Increasingly, adolescents are committing suicide, making it one of the leading causes of death in this age group. A family history of suicide, or a previous suicide attempt always points to extra risk. Of course, thoughts of suicide do not inevitably lead to attempted suicide, but the risk is there and merits immediate and special care from the physician, family, or friends. It is important that the patient realize that others understand the anguish that has led to such thoughts and that they want to help alleviate this pain as quickly as possible. However, if someone has made clear plans to end his or her life, psychiatric care and perhaps hospitalization should be undertaken as quickly as possible. In any event, the ill person should not be left alone.

Treatment of Depression

Depression commonly ends spontaneously. However, an attack may last about 6 months or longer. Therefore, treatment should be instituted to alleviate suffering and impaired performance. Depression responds best to a combination of drug therapy, which may take several weeks to reach its full effectiveness, and psychotherapy.

Depression is often very well treated by the family doctor alone, and may never require a visit to a psychiatrist. A person being treated for depression can expect brief weekly visits to the doctor for 6 to 8 weeks, by which time most people will have had a significant benefit from the antidepressant drug.

There are several caveats about drug treatment that even many doctors do not fully understand. Most important, the tranquilizers such as chlordiazepoxide (Librium) or diazepam (Valium) are not effective in treating depression, and may even worsen the illness. Also, many doctors are understandably reluctant to prescribe what seem like high doses of the antidepressants, but these doses are often required to have the desired effect. Furthermore, the drugs alone are not sufficient; proper

treatment also includes psychological support of some kind.

Before prescribing an antidepressant drug or changing the dose, a doctor will need to check the patient's blood pressure and pulse both standing and sitting. A patient can expect to stay on drug treatment, once the effective drug and dose is identified, for up to a year or more. When the patient and doctor agree that it is time to stop the drug, it will have to be tapered off slowly. Any recurrence of symptoms, such as loss of appetite or early morning awakening, should be a signal to contact the doctor again.

TYPES OF ANTIDEPRESSANTS

Tricyclic Antidepressants. Drugs in this class, named for their 3-ring chemical structure, have been used for the treatment of depression since the late 1950s. Unlike amphetamines (sometimes referred to as "uppers"), tricyclic antidepressants do not produce a "high," but simply relieve depression. The drugs seem to have the effect of increasing either the amount or the activity of the catecholamine neurotransmitters.

The choice of drug depends on 2 factors: whether the patient needs to be calmed down or sedated, and which side effects will be least troublesome. For instance, amitryptiline (Elavil) and doxepin (Sinequan) are the most sedating drugs in this class, useful for people with depression who are agitated or who have trouble sleeping. In the latter case, the drug should be taken at bedtime. Imipramine (Tofranil) and desipramine (Norpramin) are less sedating, and more useful for patients who have little anxiety and loss of energy.

The most common side effects of these drugs are dry mouth, constipation, mild urinary problems, and temporary blurred vision. Most patients can learn to live with them by resorting to relatively simple solutions, such as taking laxatives for the constipation and sucking hard candies to relieve the dryness of mouth. Narrow-angle glaucoma (the rare form of this eye disease) can be worsened by some of these drugs. Memory loss and delirium can occur in the elderly. The tricyclics occasionally cause impotence, which can be alleviated by adjusting the time when the drug is taken in relation to sexual activity. When taken in large doses just before bedtime, some tricyclics may cause nightmares; if so, the dose should be reduced. They sometimes also cause a craving for sweets and subsequent weight gain.

A common problem with the tricyclic antidepressants is orthostatic hypotension, a sudden drop in blood pressure that occurs when standing up quickly, leading to dizziness or a feeling of faintness.

This usually can be overcome by learning to rise in 2 stages; for example, rising to a sitting position when getting up in the morning, and then sitting on the edge of the bed for a minute or so before standing. Standing in one position for too long also can cause orthostatic hypotension. Standing with the head thrown back can also bring on this problem; men taking these drugs should avoid standing in a head back posture while shaving.

Initially, there had been some concern regarding the use of these drugs in patients with heart diseases. Research has shown, however, that they may actually be helpful for patients with certain cardiac arrhythmias. But there are some conditions, such as conduction defect (a disruption of the electrical activity of the heart muscle), in which they can produce problems.

Both the effectiveness and side effects of tricyclic antidepressants can be influenced by other drugs the patient may be taking at the same time. For instance, when tricyclic antidepressants are taken along with diuretics (drugs used to treat high blood pressure or edema), the problem of orthostatic hypotension may be increased. Thus, a doctor should be made aware of any other drugs, including nonprescription medications and alcohol, that are being used.

There are great individual differences in the effects of these antidepressant drugs, and the effective dose varies widely from one patient to the next. Elderly people may be more sensitive to these drugs because their livers are not as efficient in metabolizing them, and therefore could need lower doses. The side effects, particularly dry mouth and blurred vision, often appear early in the treatment before the drug has begun to have any effect on the depression. These are not reasons to discontinue treatment, but rather signs that the drug is beginning to work.

There is a continuing effort to produce new antidepressants that are just as effective as the ones currently used but have fewer side effects. Many of these "new" medications offer no advantage over the ones we have now, in spite of their advertising claims. Some are advertised to work more quickly, others to have fewer side effects. There are several of these new drugs now on the market: maprotiline (Ludiomil), amoxapine (Asendin), trimipramine (Surmontil), and trazodone (Desyrel). Whether these medications are truly better than imipramine, desipramine, amitriptyline, or nortriptyline remains to be seen. While they are not yet available for general use in our country at this writing, nomifensine and buproprion are new drugs that may offer effective treatment with fewer side effects and be especially useful for elderly depressed patients.

Monoamine Oxidase (MAO) Inhibitors.
These drugs also have the effect of increasing the action of the catecholamine neurotransmitters, but in a different way: They disarm the body's enzymes that break down these neurotransmitters. Tranylcypromine (Parnate) and phenelzine (Nardil) are the most commonly prescribed drugs in this group. They tend to act more quickly than the tricyclics, but their side effects can be more dangerous. Therefore, MAO inhibitors are usually used if tricyclic antidepressants fail to show the desired effect. (A word of caution for patients taking MAO inhibitors: These drugs interact with certain foods, most notably aged cheeses and Chianti wines, and can produce a life-threatening hypertensive crisis. A doctor or pharmacist should provide a list of foods and drinks that should not be consumed while using these drugs.)

Lithium.
For the relatively rare disease of manic depression, lithium salts have proven a remarkably effective way to prevent mood swings. They are not effective promptly in treating an existing episode of mania, for which the doctor will probably prescribe an antipsychotic agent such as chlorpromazine. However, because lithium has a preventive action, it may be prudent to start both drugs at once. Because manic depression is more severe when it begins late in life, it is more common for lithium to be prescribed for people in their later years. For younger patients, it is probably wise to seek the help of a psychiatrist in addition to the family doctor before embarking on lithium treatments.

Lithium causes a wide range of side effects, some merely irritating but others potentially serious. These effects are usually related to the dose of the drug. Doctors, therefore, monitor the drug's concentration in the blood and adjust the drug dose accordingly. The minor side effects of lithium—transient nausea and slight tremors—usually disappear with time and can be alleviated by adjusting the dose. Thirstiness is another relatively trivial side effect. However, the drug can also cause severe nervous system side effects (although there is no evidence of permanent damage to the nervous system). These may include muscle twitching, vertigo, sleepiness, and seizures.

Before embarking on lithium treatment, it is also wise to have blood pressure measurements, thyroid studies, and a urine analysis. Lithium should be used with particular care in people with heart failure or liver disease, and probably should not be taken by people on diuretic drugs or a salt-restricted diet. Since lithium also can upset the body's electrolyte balance, it is important to drink at least 8 glasses of water per day.

ELECTROSHOCK TREATMENT/ ELECTRICAL-STIMULATING TREATMENT

Electroshock treatments (EST) are the subject of some continuing controversy, both among health professionals and the general public. Although electroshock therapy conjures up frightening images, modern EST is extremely safe and is the most rapid and effective treatment for major depressive disorders. In EST an electric current is passed through the brain. The only visible sign of the "shock" is a slight twitching of the eyelids. Because of the use of muscle relaxants and the hypnotic sodium pentathol, it is now never a painful treatment and the patient does not experience any type of "shock."

EST is used when rapid results are vital, such as with acutely suicidal patients or those in whom drug treatments have failed. Treatments are generally given 3 times per week for 2 weeks, and usually do not extend beyond 6 to 10 treatments. Although EST is usually given during hospitalization, it can be an outpatient procedure for an otherwise healthy patient in a situation where suitable medical staff and equipment are available in case of emergency.

The treatment is completely safe except for people who have recently had a heart attack. Although EST may cause temporary memory loss, a short course of 6 or 8 treatments does not produce any brain injury or permanent amnesia as some people fear. After the course of EST is finished, every patient should have a course of antidepressant medication and psychotherapy.

PSYCHOTHERAPY

Research suggests that optimal treatment for depression is a combination of drugs and psychotherapy. During the acute phase of depression, psychotherapy provides emotional support until the medication begins to take effect. The focus can then shift to an attempt to better understand the psychological factors that caused the depression to occur at this time. For example, an individual may have a low self-esteem, an attitude that increases vulnerability to depression. He or she may need to learn to express hostile and assertive feelings and may not fully understand the difference between reasoned, controlled expression of desires and an angry outburst. Thus, many depressed people are individuals who tend to trap their angry feelings inside themselves, producing a self-imposed passivity.

People with depression may gain substantial help from someone who simply listens attentively to their concerns; others need help thinking through the solutions to external problems that may contribute to their depression. Support groups and the understanding concern of family members are very helpful. Many depressed people benefit from making new contacts and developing new activities. Behavior therapy, or cognitive therapy, may be helpful in bringing about change, especially in milder cases.

ANXIETY

ANXIETY AND FEAR are normal emotions that occur as part of the "fight-or-flight" response in the face of danger or stress. This response is almost involuntary and marked by several physical reactions prompted by an increased flow of catecholamines, chemicals in the blood that include adrenaline or epinephrine and which stimulate the sympathetic nervous system. The physical reactions include a quickened heart rate, a rise in blood pressure, muscle tension, and increased awareness. All are designed to give a person the extra strength needed to escape from or overcome a dangerous situation. This "fight-or-flight" response was particularly important for primitive man, who was confronted by many environmental dangers. In a modern society, a certain amount of anxiety is unavoidable and still may prove beneficial. For example, a certain amount of anxiety before an examination or job interview may actually improve performance. However, there are many times when anxiety is inappropriate; when neither fighting nor fleeing will relieve the problem, and instead, may produce feelings of irrational fear or panic.

Fear and anxiety are often used to mean the same thing in everyday speech, but they have different meanings when used medically. Fear is a reaction to an understandable, identifiable current danger; anxiety is a conscious reaction to an unconscious stimulus, the sensation many people describe as "nervousness." What frightens one person may have no effect on another, an observation that is equally true for what makes someone anxious. People are "anxious" when they know, or think they know, what will happen, but they are "afraid" when they know, or think they know, what will happen and expect it to be unpleasant.

People who have a physical disease, or have reason to think they do, usually have to deal with anxiety. This can cause them to deny the existence of real problems, and delay seeking help, or it can interfere with the success of treatment. There are many other circumstances in which people suffer real fear or concern about problems they cannot immediately solve. This is a normal response, but if the anxiety reaches a point where it interferes with normal living, then it is a clinical illness. For example, a person may feel anxious about losing a job. If the job is, indeed, in danger and the anxiety prompts an effort to find a new job, then it is an appropriate reaction to a real threat. If, however, the job is not in jeopardy and the anxiety leads to paralyzing fear and inability to perform, professional help is needed.

Anxiety can also be the first noticeable sign of depression, or a full-blown psychosis. It is very important to understand when anxiety is normal, and when it requires treatment as a problem in itself.

Often anxiety is a temporary feeling that passes with time, for example, after an operation that has obviously been successful. Among people who have been ill, anxiety can cause serious problems of its own. After a heart attack, for example, fear of a second attack may prevent the individual from returning to a normal life. Anxiety that sex will cause a second heart attack can even lead to serious sexual problems. Many people, particularly patients in a hospital, are simply frightened to admit their own fears and anxieties—the first step necessary for relief. Many such feelings are normal, but are not part of the physical problem. They may require some form of psychotherapy so that someone who has recovered physically can return to a normal life.

Hyperventilation

Hyperventilation, or overbreathing, is one common manifestation of anxiety. The overbreathing causes a rapid loss of carbon dioxide from the blood. It causes faintness, numbness, visual disturbances, tingling in the arms, legs, and mouth, headaches, and even chest pain. All of these symptoms are the result of the imbalance of blood gases as a result of breathing too quickly or deeply. Very often, the person is unaware of the rapid breathing because the person is anxious. Far too often this problem is treated with tranquilizers. If these sensations are due to nothing more than anxiety, they can be relieved by simply holding your breath for a while or breathing into a paper bag so that the exhaled carbon dioxide is reinhaled until the proper balance of blood gases is restored.

Post-Trauma Anxiety

People who have survived a frightening trauma such as a serious accident or have been at the scene of a shooting may have long periods of increased anxiety, with understandable feelings of vulnerability. They may have trouble sleeping, frequent nightmares, may startle easily, and be irritable during the day. It's common for such a person to fear he is "going crazy," but this reaction is entirely normal. The opportunity to talk to someone about these feelings provides great reassurance and relief. In addition, tranquilizers or tricyclic antidepressant drugs can provide effective and safe relief for such "traumatic anxiety," provided there is no medical problem (such as head injury) which would make their use dangerous.

Phobias

Phobias are defined as unreasonable fears associated with a particular situation or object. Phobias usually represent a displacement of an unconscious fear onto an unrelated object. A person with a phobia does not feel anxiety unless presented with the situation around which the phobia centers.

Fear of flying, for instance, is one type of phobia. Many people feel some understandable nervousness at flying, but can calm themselves by remembering previous safe flights or recalling safety statistics. The person with a true flying phobia may know the same facts, but be unable to control his or her emotional response to the same situation. People with phobias are often aware of their "irrational" fear but are unable to do anything about it. They often conceal their fear or rationalize it with seemingly logical reasons. Many people treat their own phobias, such as fear of driving, quite effectively by simply avoiding the situation or thing they fear. In some circumstances, such as for an inner-city dweller who does not need to drive, a driving phobia is not really disabling. If the same person moves to a rural area the phobia may seriously restrict his or her life. Phobias can be treated quite effectively by behavior therapies such as desensitization therapy, in which someone with a phobia is trained to imagine elements of the frightening circumstance gradually, under very relaxed conditions in a therapist's office. Eventually they are no longer afraid of the feared object.

Agoraphobia, the fear of open spaces or crowds, is a common, often disabling phobia. A person with agoraphobia often becomes increasingly fearful of venturing out; going into a restaurant or store can produce controllable feelings of fear and panic. If the agoraphobia is allowed to progress, the person may become a virtual prisoner in his or her home. Agoraphobia does not respond as well as the other phobias to desensitization; treatment may involve drug therapy as well as a gradual moving out into places and situations that produce the fear and anxiety.

Panic Attacks

In some people, phobias such as agoraphobia are severe and result from what psychiatrists call Panic Disorder. The typical symptoms are palpitations, shortness of breath, dizziness, weakness, and sweating. Hyperventilation is a common component. These frightening physical symptoms are often accompanied by a fear of impending doom, such as going crazy or dying suddenly. Someone experiencing such a panic attack may think he or she is having a heart attack and may go to a hospital emergency room, only to be told "nothing is wrong." This is of comfort only until the next attack occurs.

Many people with panic disorder mistakenly relate the symptoms to whatever they were doing when the panic attack occurred, and thus restrict their activities ever more severely. They logically, but incorrectly, assume that the subway, elevator, crowded store, etc. caused the attack. As they continue to restrict their activities, in an attempt to control the attacks, they eventually may become agoraphobic, afraid to go out of the house at all. Doctors often misdiagnose the problem as hypoglycemia or ordinary anxiety and treat it with improper drugs, or else the person who has the attacks may seek comfort in alcohol—approaches that can be not only useless, but addictive.

The appropriate treatment for such panic attacks is with tricyclic antidepressants even though the individual is not depressed (see Depression, page 710), which can relieve the problem in 90 percent of cases—although a person with panic attacks may also need brief treatment with antianxiety drugs to treat the fear of the attacks. The dose and side effects of these drugs vary widely, and psychotherapy will probably also be necessary. Relaxation therapy (see below) and behavior therapy may also be useful for this purpose along with medication, although if the condition has persisted for years, it may take months or even years to get rid of it.

Antianxiety Drugs

Tranquilizers, or antianxiety drugs, can be useful in certain situations. But they also carry some potential for dependence and abuse. It is very important to be certain they are the most appropriate way to deal with anxiety before embarking on this kind of solution to the problem. Well-meaning doctors may prescribe these antianxiety drugs when they feel they cannot solve the problem by talking about what is troubling the patient.

The antianxiety drugs known as benzodiazepines, including alprazolam (Xanax), lorazepam (Ativan), diazepam (Valium), and chlordiazepoxide (Librium) are the third most commonly prescribed drugs in the United States. (The most commonly prescribed drugs are antibiotics and cardiac drugs.) They are the most effective drugs in the treatment of anxiety, but they can be troublesome drugs. While physiological dependence on them is not common at usual doses, anyone can become psychologically addicted to them. Thus, any treatment with these drugs should be directed specifically at anxiety and should be limited to a matter of days or weeks. If anxiety persists for more than about a month, the drug should be stopped over a period of days and psychiatric treatment pursued to understand the cause of the anxious feelings.

Although these drugs are not commonly addictive in the usual sense, there may be withdrawal symptoms when they are suddenly stopped after long use. Also, particularly in the elderly, they may cause "buildup" reactions such as sleepiness, delirium, and possibly even depression. The benzodiazepines also interact with other drugs, particularly with alcohol, which can be potentially fatal. People should not drink any alcohol at all while taking these drugs, nor should pregnant women take these drugs unless the anxiety itself is so severe as to endanger the continuation of the pregnancy.

Other drugs have been used in the past to treat anxiety. Meprobamate (Miltown), for example, was once very popular but is not as effective or as safe as the benzodiazepines. Barbiturates are often used to treat anxiety, but their primary action is to produce drowsiness, and the danger of addiction and death from intentional overdosage make them an unwise choice for treating anxiety. Neuroleptics, such as haloperidol (Haldol) and chlorpromazine (Thorazine), also cause drowsiness, and are usually used to calm violent, aggressive, and psychotic patients. Drugs intended for other purposes, such as beta-blockers (e.g. propranolol [Inderal]) have occasionally been used for anxiety, but they do not directly affect the psychological feeling of fear. Propranolol, however, may be useful in treating stage fright as long as that fear is not a symptom of panic disorder.

Relaxation Therapy

This commonsense method of anxiety relief is related to techniques, such as transcendental meditation, that have been in use for thousands of years. Relaxation therapy has helped many people learn to reduce their own anxiety or stress. Studies have shown that people who undergo relaxation therapy show the opposite of the instinctive "fight-or-flight" stress reactions; that is, their heartbeat slows and they breathe more slowly.

One of the best things about the relaxation response is that it allows you to control your anxiety by yourself (although it is often used in combination with psychotherapy). The basic method is quite simple:

1. Find a quiet place, and arrange not to be disturbed. Put yourself in a comfortable position sitting in a good chair or couch. Do not lie down; falling asleep is not part of the therapy.
2. Close your eyes and concentrate on your breathing. Each time you exhale, think of the number "one." (After training, many people switch to another calming word, or say a brief prayer with each breath.) When distracting thoughts occur, think "oh, well," and then go back to concentrating on breathing. These distracting thoughts will occur and are just to be ignored.

PSYCHOSIS
(Prepared in collaboration with Stuart Yudofsky, M.D.)

PSYCHOTIC is a term used often in ordinary speech, but it has a very precise meaning to psychiatrists. A person with psychosis has an impairment of thinking or mood in which his or her interpretation of reality and of daily events is severely abnormal. Psychosis is a symptom, like pain or fever; in no way does it point to a specific psychological or physical illness. While psychological factors undoubtedly contribute to psychosis, there is substantial evidence that there are chemical abnormalities in the brains of people with this problem. Put simply, psychosis is the ultimate result of a disordered brain.

Signs of Psychoses

Psychotic people, whatever the cause of their problem, exhibit one or more of the following characteristics:

- *Disordered thinking.* Most commonly, people with thought disorders suffer *delusions*, i.e., false beliefs that cannot be shaken by the application of a logical argument. Patients with delusions may be convinced that there is a world conspiracy to "get them" or that their body odor or appearance is offensive, but delusions may be more focused and simple. For example, a patient could suffer the deluded conviction that her neighbor had poisoned her dog 2 years previously.

- *Disorders of perception.* To misinterpret your senses—to mistake the moan of the wind for the sobs of a person, for example—is called an illusion, and is not necessarily the sign of psychiatric disorder. What is abnormal is hallucination, where there is no contribution from the senses to be misinterpreted, but rather the impression of something existing that is not actually there. Commonly it is a sound of buzzing or ringing, or hearing music when there is nothing happening to create such a sound. Auditory and visual hallucinations are usually a sign of psychosis, and

may be evidence of brain tumors or of a reaction to poison or drugs.

- *Language disorders.* All of us have encountered people, quite normal people, who don't seem to make sense or continually interject irrelevant topics into the conversation, who prattle on in boring detail, or who can't stay on the subject. This may be irritating, but it is not necessarily a sign of psychosis. However, when carried to the extreme, each of these characteristics can be part of psychosis. A psychotic person may be incapable of answering a question directly or sticking to one topic. Psychotic people may also stop talking in midsentence and abruptly fall silent, only to resume a few moments later, apparently unaware of the self-interruption. Another clue to psychosis is an excess of literal or concrete thinking, such as that shown in the patient who, upon being asked what was on his mind, replied "My skull."

- *Disturbance of affect.* Many people with psychosis (including many with obvious brain damage) show inappropriate or labile *affect*; that is, their apparent emotion is either not consistent with what they are thinking, or fluctuates much more rapidly than normal. Thus a psychotic person may laugh, cry, and show rage all within a few minutes. This may look like the person is "high" or "manic." True mania, which often alternates with depression (see Depression, page 710), is a state of unaccountable euphoria, agitation, and energy, most often accompanied by poor sleep and a lack of good judgment. Other psychotic people may be consistently apathetic and dull.

Types of Psychoses

Organic Brain Disorders.   Any of the aforementioned symptoms may be caused by a physical abnormality or disturbance in the brain. There is a wide variety of possible causes of brain damage,

among them tumors, infections, epilepsy, hemorrhage, and poisons. For psychosis to be explained by an organic problem, however, requires medical laboratory evidence, clues from physical examination, and sometimes a history of some known brain-damaging event such as a poisoning or a physical accident. The treatment of an organic brain syndrome, naturally, depends on its specific cause.

The term "dementia" is commonly used to refer to organic brain syndromes in the elderly which are believed to be irreversible. In some cases, this assumption of irreversibility is tragically mistaken (see Common Psychiatric Problems among Older People, page 731) and leads to a failure to treat the reversible condition.

One of the most common symptoms of organic brain disorders is delirium. Specifically, delirium involves disturbances of attention, memory, and orientation. A delirious person is usually disoriented in terms of time and space, and has incoherent thoughts and speech. The person may alternate between being sleepy or lethargic and being unable to sleep and being agitated. Other problems include impairments of normal movements and disturbances of perception. Visual hallucinations are more common in patients with deliria than in patients with psychosis from nonorganic causes.

Often, the delirious patients in an ordinary hospital are found in the intensive care unit (ICU), not because delirious people are taken to the ICU, but because (for a variety of reasons) people in an ICU seem particularly prone to delirium. Part of this is undoubtedly due to the variety of very serious illnesses treated in an ICU, but it has become obvious that the environment of an ICU itself can contribute to causing a delirium. It is a stressful, disorienting place, after all, with bright lights, constantly beeping medical equipment, the noise of respirators, and little to distinguish night from day. These factors compound a severe illness and often lead to delirium.

Antipsychotic drugs such as the phenothiazines and haloperidol are very useful in controlling delirium. If possible, a delirious patient should be put in a private well-lit room with a well-secured window, and efforts should be made to improve his or her sense of time and space. It is also good for the patient to have his or her own nurse, to reduce the disorientation of many new faces. Regular bedside visits from family and friends are extremely helpful. A large calendar helps to reduce time disorientation as well.

Psychosis Due to Drugs and Alcohol.
"Substance abuse" is one of the most common causes of organic brain syndromes. Combining alcohol and drugs such as the barbiturates is so dangerous that it can easily be fatal. Perhaps worse, it can cause brain damage so severe that the penalty is a permanent "vegetative" coma.

On a milder but still serious level, alcohol, marijuana, opiates, barbiturates, cocaine, and amphetamines and, on rare occasions, benzodiazepines such as diazepam (Valium) can all cause a delirium. In some cases, particularly after overdosing from cocaine or amphetamines, the results may not be easily distinguishable from a psychosis, such as schizophrenia; the only way to tell the difference is to detect the drugs with laboratory tests. These psychoactive drugs may provoke aggression, hostility, and violent behavior in usually calm, controlled individuals.

Problems are particularly common when someone habituated to such substances is, perhaps accidentally, prevented from taking them for a day or so. Withdrawal symptoms include tremors, weakness, and irritability, which progress to depression and confusion in the second day. Untreated withdrawal may cause delirium, seizures, terrifying hallucinations and, in rare instances, may be fatal. Withdrawal is treated with relatively small doses of similar drugs or with drugs that substitute for the addicting substance. Drugs like diazepam (Valium) are used to treat alcohol withdrawal but not barbiturate withdrawal. Withdrawal from barbiturates or from drugs like glutethimide (Doriden) or ethchlorvynol (Placidyl) must be treated with barbiturates.

Some of the most frightening and disorienting mental reactions can come from ingestion of the hallucinogenic drugs: lysergic acid diethylamide (LSD), mescaline, psilocybin, phencyclidine (PCP, also called angel dust), and occasionally marijuana or hashish. The consequences are unmistakable: panic, anxiety, and fear of "losing your mind," fearful disorientation, delusions, illusions, and hallucinations.

The best treatment for such a "bad trip" is isolation in a safe, quiet environment with someone in attendance to provide reassurance that the drug will wear off in time and will not cause insanity. In general, sedatives and tranquilizers should be avoided because they may be dangerous in combination with the hallucinogens. In some cases, if the psychotic symptoms persist, treatment with an antipsychotic drug such as haloperidol will be necessary.

Certain drugs used for medical reasons may also cause psychosislike behavior as an effect of overdose. These include many over-the-counter sleeping pills, antihistamines, antidepressants, and drugs used for Parkinson's disease. Psychosis may also be the result of protracted use of steroids. It may also occur with sudden withdrawal of steroids.

Mania. Sometimes, but not always, alternating with periods of depression, mania is an episode of mood elevation out of the bounds of reason. During a manic episode, a person will be excessively optimistic, may show increased energy, have excessive drug and alcohol use, have less of a need for sleep, may be excessively talkative, and show poor judgment or lack of common sense. The treatment of mania and manic depressive illness are discussed under Depression.

Schizophrenia. About 1 percent of the population has schizophrenia, which is a disease of disorganization of social and psychological function including social withdrawal and eccentric behavior. Schizophrenia occurs in men and women and in all cultures around the world. It appears to run in families.

It is quite likely that, in time, science of the brain will have divided the many forms of schizophrenia into an organized series of specific neurobiological defects. For the moment, the diagnostic pattern is still somewhat unclear, but there are 2 notable forms of the disease. One appears gradually in early life, becomes chronic, and is very unlikely to improve with time. The other form comes on abruptly much later in life, and is more amenable to treatment.

The first symptoms of chronic schizophrenia often appear just after puberty, when an adolescent begins to show less interest in social activity and increasingly idiosyncratic behavior, such as a lack of interest in personal hygiene and the usual social niceties. Eventually the language and behavioral abnormalities of chronic schizophrenia begin to appear: a blunted or dull outward attitude and bizarre or even magical patterns of thought. The schizophrenic often has an unusual way of speaking, making tangential statements or peculiar and sometimes very funny metaphors and connections between ideas. The individual is rarely aware, however, of the humor in their statements. People with chronic schizophrenia alternate between periods of very disordered behavior and stretches when they may seem relatively normal.

A second variety of schizophrenia often appears in the late twenties or early thirties without any preceding period of social withdrawal. The abnormalities of thought, speech, and behavior set in quickly, often associated with an obviously stressful precipitating event. Particularly in the case of what seems to be adult-onset schizophrenia, it is vitally important to rule out possible organic brain disorders. The drugs used to treat schizophrenia will mask the psychotic symptoms and the true cause will be missed. Such a patient should undergo an unusually vigorous examination, ideally in close consultation with a family doctor for information on how the patient has reacted to stress in the past. The doctor will also need to know about the patient's family history of mental illness, his or her own medical history, including mental and intellectual status, and extensive laboratory tests.

Not infrequently such patients need to be hospitalized for observation, particularly if they are judged to be dangerous to themselves or to others. It may be necessary, however distasteful, to use coercion or even enlist the help of the police in order to hospitalize such a person. The family and friends should remind themselves that diagnosing and treating the problem is in the patient's best interests, and once better a schizophrenic person will be grateful for the help given when he or she was ill.

Drugs to Treat Psychosis

The drugs used to treat psychosis are often referred to as major tranquilizers. Their principal action, however, is not to cause "tranquillity" or sedation, but to reduce or completely eliminate psychotic symptoms and behavior. These antipsychotic drugs appear to act by blocking the chemical receptors in the brain that normally link up via the chemical nerve messenger called dopamine. Researchers are now looking into the possible causative role of dopamine in psychosis.

People with acute organic brain disorders usually cannot tolerate high doses of the major tranquilizers, but schizophrenic patients can tolerate quite high doses, averaging about 600 milligrams in the case of chlorpromazine (Thorazine) or a similar antipsychotic medication. Haloperidol (Haldol) is much stronger, and doses of about 15 to 50 milligrams are usually adequate.

The antipsychotic drugs are very effective; they also cause a range of side effects. Nonetheless, most people take these drugs without any signs of systemic reaction. A dry mouth may be very common but diminishes with time. Constipation, loss of bladder control, blurred vision, and inhibition of ejaculation can also occur. The phenothiazine antipsychotics such as chlorpromazine (Thorazine) or thioridazine (Mellaril) can cause sensitization of the skin to sunlight. Thioridazine, in excessive doses, can cause harmful deposits of pigment on the retina of the eye. These drugs should be used with caution with other drugs since interactions are common.

Sometimes, the antipsychotic drugs may cause orthostatic hypotension, a feeling of faintness on rising quickly from a chair or bed. (Also see section on Treatment of Depression, page 712.) These drugs may cause tremors and other symptoms that are also common to Parkinson's disease: a frozen appearing face, stiffness of the body, and jerky agitation of the legs. These problems can be alleviated by either reducing the dose or using the same drugs used to treat Parkinson's disease itself.

The most troublesome side effect of the antipsychotic drugs is tardive dyskinesia, i.e., involuntary and abnormal facial movements such as grimacing, sticking out the tongue, and sucking motions. There is no solution to this unfortunate side effect, although it may disappear after several months if the drug is discontinued as soon as the involuntary movements begin. The risk of tardive dyskinesia makes it essential that schizophrenia is diagnosed with certainty, and that the benefit of antipsychotic drugs in improving the patient's life is weighed against the possibility of this potentially disfiguring side effect.

Management of Psychosis

For many people, acute psychotic episodes and even chronic schizophrenia with periods of normality are managed very well without ever entering a hospital.

Such people invariably feel embarrassed about their psychotic episodes; however, psychosis is a psychobiological reaction to stress, akin to and in fact no more shameful than ulcers, asthma, or colitis. It is a medical illness like any other medical illness, it just affects the brain.

Drug treatments for such patients seldom need to extend more than about 6 months after the symptoms begin to disappear. Meanwhile, there should be a concerted effort to address the patient's psychological problems, the origins of stress, and the emotional difficulties in dealing with it. This kind of therapy should be well under way by the time of the discontinuance of drug therapy.

Some chronic schizophrenics, however, become frantic and more psychotic at the prospect of curtailing drug treatment, and may need to use antipsychotic drugs for very long periods. Such people also often benefit from group therapy and sheltered workshops. Some of these patients may require drug therapy for many years, if not their whole lives, to remain symptom-free.

SEXUAL DISORDERS

OURS IS A LIBERATED TIME when information and discussions about sexual intercourse are not only freely available but sometimes tiresomely so. Nonetheless, people do not discuss their own sexuality easily, even with their own partners. Many physicians are not as informed as they might be about sexual matters, and thus the prevalence of sexual disorders is difficult to ascertain. These problems may persist longer than almost any other problem related to health as they are not brought up by patients nor recognized by physicians.

Pleasurable, fulfilling sexual intercourse in hu-

man beings is a complicated interaction of physical, psychological, and external factors. A disturbance of any of these factors may lead to unsatisfactory sex, either temporarily or for prolonged periods. In other cases, a lack of information about sex may lead to sexual dysfunction, often complicated by misplaced guilt about some aspect of sexuality. Therefore, the solution for sexual problems is highly variable, depending on the cause of the difficulty. (For a more detailed discussion of sexual problems and their solutions, see Chapter 10 on Sexual and Reproductive Health, page 155.)

SLEEP DISORDERS
(Prepared in collaboration with Neil Kavey, M.D., and Kenneth Attschuler, M.D.)

NORMAL SLEEP is not, as was once thought, a period of quiet, passive repose. It is a complex physiological period, which can even be stressful in itself, and may profoundly affect an existing disease or the way a person feels the following day.

There are 5 distinct phases of a night's sleep which flow into each other: awakefulness, drowsiness, moderate sleep, and deep sleep, alternating

with each other. The fifth stage of sleep, called rapid eye movement (REM) sleep (because of its recognizable characteristic eye movements), is the stage in which dreaming occurs and is characterized by breathing and heart patterns that are similar to those measured when awake.

Healthy people show a wide range of normal sleeping patterns; some people feel rested with only

5 or 6 hours of sleep while others absolutely require 9 or 10 hours. Thus insomnia is often a subjective diagnosis; it happens when someone is not getting enough sleep to feel comfortable and alert during the day. People with insomnia may have difficulty falling asleep, staying asleep, sleeping deeply enough, or sleeping long enough into the morning. Sometimes even sleeping too much can be a sleep disorder.

There are a large number of causes of sleep disorders, extending from medical or psychiatric problems to medications that have sleep disruption as a side effect. All-night sleep studies are often necessary to establish a diagnosis, especially when medical problems are suggested. In some cases, medical tests show no objective evidence of sleep abnormalities in someone who feels he or she has a sleep disorder. Many such people do not understand the necessity for good sleep habits or the normal changes of sleep with aging; in other cases, the inability of medical science to detect an abnormality reflects the relative ignorance that still exists in the science of sleep.

Insomnia

Due to Illness.
Disorder of the heart, lungs, kidney, liver, pancreas, and digestive systems, nutritional or endocrine problems, as well as infections are only a few of the medical problems associated with abnormal sleep patterns. People can be awakened by palpitations, indigestion, asthma, muscle aches, or any number of symptoms, or they may be wakeful for no apparent reason at all. Surgery almost always causes some temporary sleep disruptions. Treatment of a sleep disorder caused by an illness is almost always related to treatment of the illness itself, and someone who has an existing illness should immediately ask his or her doctor whether the illness could be responsible for the sleep problem. Sleeping tablets may be helpful, on a short-term basis, for this type of insomnia.

Due to Psychological Causes.
Many people have, at some time, been so excited about something that they could not sleep. Anxiety, tension, and anticipation can cause temporary sleep abnormalities in healthy people, but sleep disorders are also a feature of almost every major psychiatric disorder.

Temporary periods of sleep disruption are not harmful to a person's long-term well-being, but they can, under the wrong circumstances, evolve into a long-term problem. After several sleepless nights, an individual can become conditioned to regard bed as a place to toss and turn and fret, rather than sleep. This problem can be aggravated by attempts to solve it: taking daytime naps, using sleeping pills or alcohol, and getting to bed at irregular hours.

There are several ways to treat insomnia without seeing a doctor, if the sleeplessness is not caused by illness or by a serious psychiatric problem. A person should avoid lying in bed fretting if he or she does not fall asleep, but rather get up and do something restful, such as reading a good but unexciting book until drowsiness occurs. Television may be too stimulating for this purpose and should be avoided.

No matter how sleepy the individual feels the next day, he or she should not take a nap; any decrease in ability to function the next day will be due more to anxiety about sleeplessness than to the bad night itself. Exercise during the day or the early evening often helps increase sleepiness at bedtime, and limited use of sleeping pills may help to associate bed with sleep once more (although long-term use of sleeping pills can disrupt the sleep cycle). It also helps to be aware that sleep cycles normally change with age. Not only do elderly people have shallower and shorter periods of sleep, but by the age of 40 it is normal to have more difficulty falling asleep and to wake up more often during the night.

In people with major mental illness, sleep fluctuates enormously. People with schizophrenia often sleep less well than healthy people, and early morning awakening and other sleep disturbances are a common problem in depression. (See section on Depression, page 710.)

Due to Medications.
The effect of medications in altering sleep is all too often forgotten. Even the sleep medications themselves, while sometimes useful on a very short-term basis, lose their effectiveness after about 2 weeks. After that, many people who suspend taking such drugs ironically fall prey to *drug withdrawal insomnia*, which causes a feeling of agitation and, at times, frightening dreams. It may take several weeks for sleep to return to normal, as the drug is gradually withdrawn.

Most of the psychoactive drugs, such as the barbiturates and benzodiazepines, actively interfere with the sleep cycle. While alcohol may be helpful in inducing drowsiness, it can also seriously disrupt sleep patterns, particularly if it is used chronically.

Sleep Disorder Syndromes

Nocturnal Myoclonus and Restless Legs.
Some people experience involuntary jerking motions of the legs periodically throughout the night which either keep them awake or disturb their sleep without their awareness of being wakened. The myoclonus or muscle jerks may also cause hypersomnolence, that is, sleeping too much during the day.

Such people may be drowsy during the day, and may awaken with leg pains in the morning. This syndrome may be associated with the use of certain drugs that affect the nervous system. It may be helped by the use of benzodiazepines, but there is no known cure.

Nocturnal myoclonus may be accompanied by an aching, restless sensation in the legs, especially in the evening, or the *restless legs syndrome* may occur on its own. Getting out of bed and walking, or continually changing position, are ways patients can obtain relief until they are properly diagnosed and treated.

Disorders of the Sleep–Wake Cycle.

Like hibernating animals, all human beings have inborn "biological clocks" set in accord with the cues of nature. The basic biological rhythms of body temperature and hormone production cannot be altered with ease, and sleep will also be affected by attempts to shift the internal clock. Anyone who has taken a plane flight through several time zones knows the best modern example of this: jet lag. Similar sleep disruptions occur in people who work night shifts or do not keep to a regular sleep–wake schedule, who may, after a while, feel drowsy when awake and have difficulty working well. In a few rare cases, the internal clock is naturally set "incorrectly," and may need to be brought into line with the environment.

Some people, by diligently setting a schedule that conforms to the solar day, can reset their own biological clock. For others, including those people with an inborn disorder of the internal clock, it is necessary to get medical help to reset their clocks. They are put on a schedule of getting up later and later each day until they have gone around the clock and get sleepy at a normal bedtime. After that, it is essential that they adhere to the same waking hour each day and avoid naps.

Hypersomnolence

Hypersomnolence, the problem of being too sleepy and sleeping too much, while not as common as insomnia, is not rare. Daytime drowsiness may, in fact, be caused by an unrecognized sleep disturbance. Like insomnia, hypersomnolence may be caused by medical illness, psychological factors, or the use of medications. Most importantly, it may be caused by the use of sleeping pills themselves.

Sleep Apnea.

"Apnea" means lack of breathing, and that is the potentially fatal problem that characterizes this form of hypersomnolence. People with sleep apnea experience interruptions in breathing during sleep, from about 30 to several hundred times a night. Naturally, this cessation of air flow can be very damaging to the heart and lungs, yet the sleeper may not even be aware of the problem.

Sleep apnea is most common in adult males, but can affect children and may also be associated with sudden infant death. The problem may occur because of a disorder in the involuntary trigger for breathing, which is located in the medulla at the base of the brain, or it may be associated with physical abnormalities of the chest, neck, and back.

A person with sleep apnea may feel he has slept well, but is still drowsy in the daytime. Naps may not help at all. Morning headaches are common in sleep apnea. The diagnosis is made by watching the patient while asleep; it is often made by a spouse, particularly since the syndrome can cause loud snoring followed by periods of silence. Jerky, forceful breathing movements follow, concluded by a loud snort as the obstruction is overcome and normal breathing begins again. The period of apnea may or may not cause the person to awaken. The diagnosis is firmly established in a sleep lab, and more doctors are becoming aware of the syndrome.

Where sleep apnea is caused by a physical abnormality, the treatment is direct. In some cases, the treatment of sleep apnea is simply to pin a tennis ball to the back of the pajamas, to prevent the sufferer from sleeping on his or her back. In seriously obese patients, the syndrome may disappear after weight loss. Surgical treatment is commonly used. For example, extra folds of tissue that block the airway during sleep can be removed in a simple operation. Treatment of sleep apnea due to an abnormality of the breathing trigger in the medulla is more difficult; medroxyprogesterone (Provera) may stimulate breathing, or it may be necessary, in extreme cases, to implant a pacemaker in the diaphragm.

Narcolepsy.

This sleep syndrome, more than all the others, can effectively prevent normal life. A narcoleptic is overcome with irresistible drowsiness during the day, and recurrent brief "attacks" of involuntary sleep occur. After a 10- or 15-minute sleep attack the person feels rested only briefly, and then returns to the sensation of sleepiness that pervades life. The sleep attacks may be accompanied by cataplexy (sudden loss of muscle tone) and by hallucinations or a brief total body paralysis (called sleep paralysis) as the person is falling asleep or awakening. A narcoleptic will always fall asleep when in an environment that is dark and quiet, but he will also suffer sleep attacks at the most unlikely times: while talking, working, or even driving.

In a narcoleptic, bursts of emotion, such as sadness, surprise, or anger, may bring cataplexy on. The patient may remain conscious but apparently paralyzed during such an attack which can be, naturally, very frightening.

Narcolepsy usually begins after the age of 15 and persists for life. The cause of the disease is unknown. On occasion, it follows brain infections or head trauma. The illness can be seen as a disorder in which the brain's resources for stimulating alertness are insufficient to suppress sleep. In most cases, there are no evident medical abnormalities. The diagnosis may be fairly obvious from the symptoms. The doctor may send a suspected narcoleptic to a sleep laboratory for a test to see how quickly he falls asleep given an opportunity to nap several times during an 8-hour day.

Treatment of narcolepsy is difficult. Amphetamines and other stimulants may be successful in keeping the patient awake during the day, but they have little or no effect on the cataplexy, sleep paralysis, or the hallucinations. These symptoms may be helped by adding other types of medications.

Problems During Sleep

Sleepwalking. A sleepwalker may simply move around in bed, or he or she may arise and leave the house while asleep. The episodes usually last only a few minutes, and the sleepwalker often returns to bed by himself or is easily led there. Sleepwalkers stare ahead, apparently seeing, and are difficult to arouse. Characteristically, they do not remember their excursions.

Sleepwalking, or *somnambulism*, is not rare in children. It is not seen as abnormal or a sign of psychological distress, and most children outgrow it.

Adults with somnambulism are a different story. While a normal person under unusual stress may have an isolated episode of sleepwalking, repeated somnambulism is often a sign of a serious problem. It may result from epilepsy or a side effect of psychoactive drugs.

There is no known cure for sleepwalking, and time solves the problem for most children. For adults, reduction of the doses of drugs that may cause it is a good idea. Benzodiazepines or antiepileptic drugs may help to reduce the frequency of episodes in adults. In either case, care must be taken that sleepwalkers don't hurt themselves. They should sleep on the first floor and dangerous objects should be kept out of the area where they sleep. Doors and windows should be locked at night.

Nightmares and Night Terrors. These are 2 related and frightening interruptions to a good night's sleep. A nightmare, as almost everyone has experienced it, is a frightening "bad dream" with a memorable plot, from which a sleeper awakens, frightened but alert. Night terrors, on the other hand, are sudden attacks of panic that often cause a sleeper to bolt up suddenly, screaming in terror. He or she may remain terrified and confused for many minutes, and remember nothing other than a single vivid, terrifying image.

It appears that night terrors can occur in infancy and they are not uncommon in childhood. It may be agonizing for parents to watch a child endure such episodes repeatedly, but, as with sleepwalking, they usually disappear as a child grows up.

In adults, nightmares or night terrors are more likely to be related to a significant problem. Grownups, or children with longstanding nightmares and night terrors, should probably seek help from a sleep disorder center. Benzodiazepines such as diazepam (Valium) taken at bedtime may relieve the problem, probably by interfering with the stage of sleep in which the night terror occurs.

Sleep Rocking or Head Banging. The technical name for this problem, which usually begins at about 6 months of age and disappears later in childhood, is jactatio capitis nocturna. The cause is not at all clear, although it tends to run in families. Taking the antidepressant imipramine (Tofranil) at bedtime is occasionally helpful.

Bruxism. The dentist is the usual person to inform someone that, unwittingly, he or she has been grinding their teeth at night. Spouses are often aware of this behavior, but not the person doing it. The episodes last 10 or 15 seconds and occur throughout the night. Psychological factors may contribute, and psychotherapy may help.

PSYCHOLOGICAL PROBLEMS OF CHILDREN
(Prepared in collaboration with Richard A. Gardner, M.D.)

AS ANY PARENT KNOWS, it is almost impossible to define what constitutes a "normal" child. Any child's behavior can, at times, seem not only abnormal but irritating and even utterly inexplicable to an adult.

The most helpful person to a disturbed child may be the family doctor, who knows the child and the family well, and whom the child may have grown to trust. Particularly if a child has a fairly good relationship with the pediatrician or family doctor, it is an excellent idea to seek assistance from that source first. In addition, the family doctor is probably the best person to decide when more expert psychiatric care is needed.

Some of the best judges of whether a child is abnormal are his or her schoolmates. If a child fails to seek friends or be sought as a friend among other children the same age, there is reason for concern.

Another astute judge of when a child may need outside help is, obviously, his or her teacher. Both classroom behavior and grades are important for the teacher to assess. Often the teacher has had contact with children of a particular age for many years, and can therefore identify a troubled child. In general, school officials are reluctant to refer a child for psychiatric counseling; if they do, it is almost invariably a sign that the child truly needs such help. Another clue is grades: Grading is a well-established system for determining where a child stands in relation to his or her peers, and poor grades are good reason to inquire into a child's emotional state.

However, one cannot assume that a teacher can diagnose a child's problems psychiatrically. If parents are concerned about a child's behavior at school, they should not ask the teacher for absolute judgment, but rather for comparison with "the average" or with other children in the class.

There are exceptions, of course, but in general a child who generally functions well at home, in the neighborhood, and at school, is unlikely to be suffering psychological problems. Any normal child will have transient problems in any one of these areas; but parents should watch for problems that persist. Only if a particular behavior problem persists is it warranted to seek professional help for it.

Learning Disabilities

It is rarely obvious at the outset why a child is not learning well; the problem may be physical, psychological, or both. One possibility is the existence of minimal brain dysfunction (MBD).

In general, MBD is thought to be a mild neurological problem. The disorders described under MBD are due to any of a wide variety of problems a child may have in dealing with the world, including vision and hearing disorders, an inability to be attentive, and even mild problems with physical coordination which may interfere, as an example, with the ability to hold a pencil.

The cardinal symptom of MBD is *hyperactivity*, a fairly loose term in itself. Hyperactivity may be a sign of anxiety or tension in a child, rather than a telltale clue of MBD. A parent should beware of taking the description "hyperactive" too seriously without having the child carefully evaluated by an expert professional.

An examination for MBD should include testing for a wide variety of hearing and vision defects that may contribute to learning disabilities, as well as a careful look for signs of coordination problems or mild speech disorders, and intellectual deficits.

If a child proves to have a deficit in any of these areas, further tests will be necessary. The drugs used to treat MBD are dextroamphetamine sulfate (Dexedrine) or methylphenidate hydrochloride (Ritalin), which act to reduce the child's activity level and improve concentration.

About 1 in 4 children with signs of MBD do not benefit from drugs, and may become even more agitated. In these cases, special tutoring by someone trained to teach children with MBD may be needed. Some very useful books about MBD are:

1. *MBD: The Family Book about Minimal Brain Dysfunction*, by R. A. Gardner. Jason Aronson, New York, 1973.
2. *A Word or Two about Learning Disability*, by Doreen Kronick. Academic Therapy Publications, San Rafael, California, 1973.
3. *What about Me? The LD Adolescent*, by Doreen Kronick. Academic Therapy Publications, San Rafael, California, 1975.

Learning disabilities may also be due to many other factors. Obviously, if parents do not place much emphasis on education, a child is unlikely to try very hard at school. However, parents who push too hard, expecting perfection, may create children who fear failure and therefore are unable to perform at all. Poor performance may also be an expression of a child's hostility toward his or her parents. In such cases, where the origins of learning disability are psychological, it is likely that the best treatment is psychotherapy that involves the entire family to varying degrees.

School Phobia

This term is probably a misnomer. The more accurate name is separation anxiety disorder, since what the child fears is separation from his or her parent, not school per se.

Not infrequently, "school phobia" sets in after a period in which the child went to school without any obvious problems. It may be brought on by a traumatic event (divorce, an illness for which a parent had to be hospitalized, a death) or the birth of a younger sibling. Suddenly the child begins to find any number of excuses not to go to school, and often not to get out of bed. For each excuse that is explained away another will appear. Some children with "school phobia" scream in the most frightening way when forced to go to school.

Often, the parent in such a situation has been overprotective, refusing to allow the child to go outside alone, to ride a bicycle in the street, or play without supervision. The obvious message to the child is that the outside world is a dangerous place. Such a parent may also allow the child to stay home from school with every minor physical complaint.

Hidden behind separation anxiety disorder, often, is a complex set of unconscious and subconscious reactions. The disorder may actually be a way of dealing with the hostility to the parent who has prevented the child from having a normal relationship with peers and normal independence for his or her age. For the parent, in turn, these actions may express hidden hostility against the child and a desire to be free of him or her. By envisioning dangers to the child—and then preventing them—the parent has found a socially acceptable way to resolve his or her hostility. The child does the same in reverse; in separation from the parent at school he or she cannot be sure that the things secretly wished for have not actually happened to the parent.

While the pediatrician or family doctor may be able to treat mild cases of separation anxiety disorder, the more severe cases require the help of a child psychiatrist. The physicians and family must make it clear that unless there is bona fide evidence for significant physical illness, the child must go to school each day. A child who returns home at midday with an "illness" must not be allowed to play or watch television, but should be returned to school for the remainder of the day.

Such a treatment may seem cruel, and even some professionals think so. In the long run, however, it is undoubtedly less cruel than allowing the child to continue to miss school and failing to resolve the fear of separation. Often, the parent will express a willingness to comply with these measures but will not do so; school officials may also become fed up and may not be overeager to cooperate. It is essential, however, that a child with any extended history of school phobia—and the parent—have psychotherapy to resolve the problems in their relationship. Only by regularly attending school will the child gain the measure of independence from his or her parent that is vital to normal maturation.

The same problem may occur in adolescence, without the screaming and hysteria, in which case it is referred to as *school refusal.* Its origins are usually the same, but it comes on more slowly and the outlook is not as good. Without psychotherapy, the youngster may well drop out of school.

Enuresis or Bed-Wetting

One difficulty in defining and treating enuresis is the lack of consensus as to when the "normal" child should gain control of his or her bladder. This tends to happen earlier in girls than in boys, but most doctors would not become concerned about a child of 4 or even 5 who still wets the bed. In fact, the problem is common enough in children over 6 not to be considered a disease per se. By puberty most enuretic children no longer wet at night, but the problem persists in an unknown number of adults.

No one knows for certain whether most bed-wetting is a physical or psychological problem. From about 1930 to 1960 it was taken for granted that the disorder was psychological, but as organic explanations for psychological problems have come to hold sway, ever more people believe that in many cases there is a neurophysiological component to enuresis.

Many children with wetting problems have little or no evidence of other psychological troubles. Some psychological theories trace bed-wetting to repressed hostility or sexual problems, but in many cases this does not seem to fit the evidence. It seems at least equally plausible that enuresis is due to a lag in development of the nervous system controls on elimination in combination with a susceptibility of bladder controls to the influence of stress. In any event, a consultation with a urologist may be advisable to rule out a physiologic cause of the problem.

Even where bed-wetting is not psychological in origin, it can cause emotional problems. The situation is undeniably embarrassing and uncomfortable. It may either prevent a child from enjoying such peer activities as a pajama party, or cause him or her to be the subject of ridicule from friends.

A fairly simple home remedy for bed-wetting, for a start, seems to reduce the problem in about a third of cases. This is to restrict the child's liquid intake after supper while providing salty snacks such as potato chips or pretzels to retain water in the body. This treatment is not a cure, and its effect may be more psychological (giving the child a feeling he or she is doing something about the problem) than physical.

There are also electronic devices that sound an alarm at the passage of the first drops of urine to the bed. For a small percentage of users, this method succeeds in solving the problem in a few weeks, either through the power of suggestion (as with the salty snacks) or because of negative conditioning (children grow to associate urination with the unpleasant alarm, and subconsciously or unconsciously control themselves). However, it has drawbacks: Many bed wetters are heavy sleepers, and the rest of the family may respond to the shrill alarm to find the child sound asleep in a pool of urine.

If neither of these treatments works or is acceptable, a brief course of the drug imipramine (Tofranil) sometimes resolves the problem by contracting the urethral sphincter. If nothing works—which is still the case in a significant proportion of cases—and if there is indeed no evidence of psychological problems, the child should be encouraged to believe that he or she will outgrow the problem. This is most often the truth.

Encopresis

Improper control of the bowels, or encopresis, is another disorder that is hard to pin down because the limits of normality are not clearly defined. However, children over the age of 4 or 5 who are not bowel-trained need professional help. Children with significant encopresis should see a child psychiatrist for treatment of their underlying disorder.

Bed wetters tend to lose control when they are sleeping at night; children with encopresis also pass feces during the day, so it is usually difficult to determine whether or not the behavior is truly involuntary. Therefore, while organic disease is still not out of the question, it is far more likely that a case of encopresis has psychological origins. Many children with the problem have been abused, neglected, or otherwise mistreated, and it is difficult to avoid the conclusion that encopresis is their way of expressing anger and hostility. In fact, what more effective way is there to disgust parents and other adults than by filling a room with the odor of a bowel movement?

However, encopresis is sometimes a by-product of the attention deficit that occurs in children with MBD. They may not associate the stimulus of a full bowel with the need to go to the bathroom as soon as possible.

Obesity

Serious obesity in children almost always has at least some of its origins in emotional problems. There are many emotional sources of obesity. For everyone, food is at least in part a symbol of mother love, and a child's obesity is often a sign of an overprotective mother. The child may also use food as a substitute for attention. A tendency to obesity can be aggravated by mothers who coax their children into eating, and use external clues rather than the child's own hunger to decide when and how much the child should eat.

In some families, large size is viewed as a sign of strength and power, and children make themselves large so as not to be seen as weaklings. Food is also pleasurable and can be in a sense addicting, since like many adults, children may overeat in order to compensate for an inner unhappiness.

Obviously, if serious obesity has its origins in emotional problems, simply putting the child on a strict diet will not resolve it. Crash diets are always to be avoided, and even the strict diet gives a child the subliminal message that afterwards he or she can go back to overeating. If the obesity is a family problem, family counseling is advisable to help change eating habits. If it has its origins in some unhappiness experienced by the child, counseling may address and relieve the problems that are leading to the obesity in the first place.

Problems Caused by Divorce

Most parents fear that divorce will be psychologically damaging to a child. What is true for the parents is true to a degree for the children: Divorce may in the long run be preferable to daily life in a situation of total conflict. Or it may not. We are talking about 2 alternatives, both of which are undesirable.

The main determinant of whether children will suffer psychologically from divorce is how their parents relate to them, before the event and after. If the divorce is relatively civilized and the children are not brought between the parents in the conflict, the adverse effects on the child are minimized. Another important factor is the involvement of the absent parent after the separation: Maintaining a reliable, affectionate contact with the children will also help reduce the negative effects of the divorce. Parents who are separating tend to have a variety of concerns about the children. Some of the most common are:

1. *How old should the children be before being told?* All the children should be told, regardless of age, at the same time. Leaving any of them out as "too young to understand" will undoubtedly lead to resentment. There are things they may not understand, indeed, but what matters is the impression of candor and openness.
2. *When should the children be told?* To tell younger children a few months in advance of a divorce is not very meaningful; the child may not appreciate such a time span and may begin to deny the fact. Denial can even happen in older children. However, it is a mistake to wait until the bags are packed. The optimum time is probably a few weeks before the separation, allowing time to adjust to the situation.
3. *Who should tell the children?* Ideally, both parents *together* should tell the children, so that both establish a reputation as the providers of information and as sources for future discussion. Such ongoing dis-

cussions are invaluable in preventing a host of untoward reactions in the children.

4. *What should the children be told?* They should be told, as honestly as possible, the reasons for the separation. The reasons should impart new information: not "Mommy and Daddy don't love each other any more" (which is no more meaningful than saying "They buried Granddaddy because he was dead"). Instead, the children should be given more specific reasons as the parents perceive them. Evasion will contribute to the very natural and common assumption on the part of the children that the divorce was really their fault.

Two common and misguided bits of advice relate to how the single parent should talk about the absent parent. "Never criticize the other parent behind his or her back," divorced people are often told, and "Always tell the children that the other parent loves them." The first counsel may lead the child to idolize the absent parent, and it is far more worthwhile for a child to realize that parents are imperfect than to carry around an example he or she cannot ever hope to emulate. As to the second bit of advice, it is most unwise when obviously untrue, in the case of abandonment, and will lead the child to think that the remaining parent is a liar. If the absent parent is unreliable about visits, the child needs to know that the parent has difficulty providing love and the child should be encouraged to seek other loving relationships to fill the gulf.

Many children have been helped by reading *The Boys and Girls Book About Divorce*, by R. A. Gardner (Bantam, New York, 1971) and their parents can benefit from *The Parent's Book about Divorce*, by the same author (Bantam Books, New York, 1979).

Death of a Parent

This is one of the most severe traumas a child can undergo, and how well he or she emerges from the shock depends greatly on how other family members, including the dying parent, handle the situation. There are 3 reactions common to grief in adults, which also occur in children: denial, anger, and repression of sad feelings. The way in which children are allowed to resolve these emotional reactions to death will determine how badly scarred they will be by the experience.

Denial is a normal reaction, particularly in the case of a parent who is still alive but dying. It is far more likely to become a serious problem in children whose parent is actively denying his or her own impending death. In such a case, it well behooves another close relative to be sure that the child has support in adjusting to the death. Perhaps even more damaging than active denial is a well-meaning conspiracy to prevent the child from learning the truth. Older children in particular may suspect a "cover-up" and come to distrust their loved ones at the worst possible time—an emotion that will remain permanently unresolved in the case of the dying parent.

Anger at a beloved parent who has "abandoned" a child by dying is a common reaction that needs to be expressed in order to prevent repression and guilt later on. Therefore, it is wise to draw the child of a dead or dying parent into discussions about the death, and to encourage expression of feelings, so that they can be identified as normal.

However, it is particularly important not to encourage feelings of guilt in children by coaxing them to be "brave" or making casual remarks about their behavior such as "How can you laugh and play at a time like this?" Laughter and play are, for children, as necessary as tears to the resolution of grief, and games that may seem ghoulish to adults are the normal child's way of coming to terms with the ultimately unacceptable reality of death.

Attending a funeral can be, for a child as for anyone else, a very useful way of confronting denial and sorrow. The presence of the coffin or urn provides a concrete way for the child to accept the subsequent absence of the parent. Furthermore, seeing others mourn will help the child to find it acceptable to express his or her own grief.

ADOLESCENCE
(Prepared in collaboration with Richard A. Gardner, M.D., and Richard Wortman, M.D.)

AN ADOLESCENT is part child, part adult; a person deeply involved in discovering an independent identity. Some adolescent problems have their roots in childhood and are an extension of the emotional problems of a child. Others, such as depression and suicide attempts, may appear to be very similar in character to the emotional problems of an adult. However, these disorders may take on a special coloration that reflects the problems of adolescence. Many other kinds of behavior that may be viewed as "crazy" by adults are a normal part of adolescence and adolescent rebellion.

Adolescents are deeply concerned with establishing personalities different from those of their parents, or from those which their parents may expect them to have. A healthy adolescent may do this by excelling at a sport or at school. Another apparently healthy way to do this is to reject parental values of religion, dress, and the like. It is the adolescent who shows deviant behavior in establishing this independence who is the one who probably has emotional problems. Here we are defining "deviant" in terms of his or her general age group, not of parents' value systems.

What does "deviant" mean when applied to a young teen? As with children, there are several realms in which adolescents' behavior can be examined for clues to their psychological health: home, friends, school, and leisure activities. But there is a qualitative difference between normal and abnormal behavior.

The normal adolescent has the freedom and opportunity to initiate hobbies and other activities outside regular schoolwork. The lack of any interests other than "hanging out" may be a sign of trouble. Poor grades are also a red flag, although they may be a sign of a rebellion against overeager parents and may improve as the adolescent matures.

As the child approaches the early teens, he or she normally becomes more of a "groupie," highly conformist with peers and interested in group activities. Also, earlier for girls than for boys, there are the beginnings of interest in the opposite sex. Even more than in childhood, the opinion of peers is a good way to judge whether an adolescent is functioning well in his or her society. If everyone is wearing hair purple this year, that is a sign of normality in an adolescent's terms; however, if the peer group repeatedly refers to someone derogatorily as different, as a "slut," a "bully," or a "creep," it is a good sign of emotional problems in that person. In the late teen years group identity begins to give way to closer individual friendships, and it is common for someone that age to prefer a few friends to a crowd.

Depression

Unhappiness is inevitable during the confusing time of adolescence, but it is dangerous for adults to take episodes of depression too lightly in teenagers. Teenage suicide in stable, affluent communities has become disturbingly common. In fact, suicide is the third leading cause of death among adolescents. It behooves the parents of a frequently unhappy or listless teenager to familiarize themselves with the warning signs of clinical depression. (See the section on Depression, page 710.) This problem in adolescents is treated much as it is among adults, with antidepressants and with psychotherapy.

Problems with Body Image

Many young adolescents suddenly find themselves in the body of an adult although they continue to feel like children. Body image, therefore, becomes particularly important and often troublesome at this stage of life. Boys who are underdeveloped sexually, and girls who develop breasts and pubic hair quite early, require support and understanding, if not special counseling. Acne is a common problem which may seriously impair a child's self-image and social life through no fault of his or her own. There are medical treatments for acne, and teenagers with severe acne cases should see a dermatologist for the sake of their psychological health.

Adolescents who are physically normal but obsessed with looking better should be reminded that people come in a wide range of body shapes. They need to know that this variation is normal and even attractive, and that attractiveness depends most on the ability to make the best of one's own physical assets rather than trying to look like what one is not. Requests for cosmetic surgery such as a "nose job" or breast reduction on the part of a teenager who looks fine should generally be met with reassurances regarding the reality of their appearance. If the requests persist, the youngster should definitely see a psychiatrist to talk about his or her body image problems.

Anorexia Nervosa

Most teenage girls diet, and it is rare for a teenage girl not to be on a diet at some time. In most cases, except where the girl stays too long on a fad or crash diet, this should be tolerated without concern. However, in the case of some girls (and rarely in boys), excessive dieting is a sign of anorexia nervosa, a serious and potentially fatal eating disorder.

The problem usually begins at that time when a girl becomes concerned about her sexual maturation. She becomes convinced that she is "too fat" and restricts her eating to the stage of thinness and, in the worst cases, to emaciation. Arguments that she is not fat but thin are ignored. Home life becomes a power struggle to coerce the girl to eat, which she will almost invariably refuse to do. Untreated, someone with this disorder may well starve herself to death in front of her horrified parents.

Several emotional factors seem to contribute to

anorexia nervosa. The girl fears sexual development and can delay it by starving herself. But she also fears growing up in general. She may also be expressing hostility against her parents, especially if she manipulates them by asking for a particularly exotic or complicated dish and then refusing to eat it. These individuals can use eating as a means of controlling their parents. Finally, a girl with anorexia nervosa may be unwilling to admit that she cannot completely control how her adult body will look, and starving herself is a way of trying to do so.

Like most diseases, anorexia nervosa can range from mild to severe, and the mild is far more common. Mild cases may be treated by the family doctor, but severe cases should have the care of a child psychiatrist who specializes in this disease. Meanwhile, parents should avoid dieting themselves or trying to coax their daughter to eat. They should not do anything abnormal by way of providing her with food, but should do what they can to help her gain a healthy attitude toward sex, growth, and adulthood.

Drug Abuse

It is normal for some teenagers to experiment with drugs, particularly with tobacco, alcohol, and marijuana, which they may not classify as drugs. Speaking psychologically, this is a fairly normal expression of adolescent rebellion and independence; the danger, of course, is that they will harm themselves permanently. Probably the best thing parents can do to encourage their youngsters not to smoke or drink excessively is not to do so themselves, and to portray such behavior as undesirable.

PCP ("angel dust") presents a special danger in that it can cause aggressive violence, convulsions, and coma as well as psychosis. Teenagers should be aware of this danger. The consequence of drug use that tends to distress an adolescent most is addiction, the risk of needing increasingly higher doses, of needing to steal in order to afford drugs, and of the anguish of withdrawal. While they may not become physically dependent on the drug, regular use of marijuana or small doses of barbiturates or benzodiazepines may lead to psychological addiction to the drug. They feel that in order to enjoy music, a walk in the park, or a party with friends they must be "high." If they can be made to see that their zest for life is hostage to the drug, they may come to accept counseling, withdrawal, and a drug-free life.

Violence

Adolescents often have bodies as large as their parents, but lack an adult's control over their consider-

able tension and confusion. Thus they may lash out occasionally with violence that probably surprises and frightens them as much as it does their parents. This is distressing, but is usually not a sign of mental illness, unless someone is physically hurt or the episodes occur regularly.

Violence may, however, be the effect of a psychosis or of a psychogenic drug. In such cases, hospitalization and medication are required, and it may take assistance from the police to obtain help. If the violence is a part of a pattern of progressive intimidation and delinquency, with little sign of regret on the part of the teenager, medications and even psychiatry may have little to offer.

Treatment of Adolescent Problems

Parents who are themselves in therapy tend to overestimate their adolescent children's needs for psychiatric care. As with children, the family doctor is an excellent first source of counsel about the emotional problems of adolescence.

If psychiatric help is needed, a consultation will determine which type is most effective in a given situation. For example, group therapy can be more helpful than individual counseling for certain adolescents. Some teens mistrust adults, function much better in groups than alone, and may value the chance to speak up only when they feel like it. Often the problems of adolescence involve the whole family, and family therapy may be advisable.

Where the problems of adjustment are very serious, the courts may become involved and may recommend or at least allude to the possibility of transferring an adolescent to a group residential center to remove him or her from the troubling home environment. In most cases, the purpose of such suggestions is to startle the adolescent into confronting his or her problems. In such a case, the adolescent will need a good lawyer, but it should be evident that the lawyer is not trying to "get the kid off" but to request fair treatment from the judge, no more and no less. The usual sentence for a mild adolescent legal offense is probation in custody of the parents.

The appropriate drug treatment for the psychiatric problems of an adolescent is often the same as for an adult, but there are a few caveats. Adolescents may have great difficulty staying with a preventive drug regimen that has side effects, and they may need very close supervision and support in this matter. They are also more prone than adults to abusing the drugs used for psychiatric problems. Except in the rare case of a very well-adjusted teen undergoing a particularly traumatic but short-lived period of stress (such as the death of a parent, for instance), it is extremely unwise to allow adolescents to take antianxiety drugs, which can be habit-forming. (For more discussion, see Chapter 13 on Adolescence and Sexual Maturity, page 254.)

FAMILY AND MARITAL PROBLEMS
(Prepared in collaboration with Michael Milano, M.D.)

IN MANY CASES of individual emotional or psychiatric difficulties, the patient's emotional environment—his or her family—is an integral part of the problem. Many problems may stem more from the interaction of family members than from any one individual. Even if family members are not the cause of the problem, they soon become participants in the problem. Many family therapists will dispense with deciphering the cause of the problem and concentrate on the response to the problem. This idea reflects the fact that many "individual" psychological difficulties will not be solved until the entire family becomes part of the treatment.

Family therapy can reveal the ways in which the feelings of each family member are interdependent. In many cases, family therapy reveals that a psychiatric problem resides not only within the individual, but also within family relationships. Family members may feel "trapped" in a limited pattern of responses to a problem. The more rigid and predictable the behavior pattern, the more troubled the family. Only by observing and treating the entire family can a therapist untangle these relationships and help to free the individuals from rigid patterns of response to one another.

Marital Problems

Within a marriage, the content of problems commonly relates to money, sex, lack of communication, and interference from the outside world, such as relatives, affairs, drinking, gambling, and other such factors. However, most relationships are buffeted by some of these factors without floundering. Therefore, the therapist will begin by focusing on the structure of interactions between the partners rather than on the more obvious problems.

A successful marriage is a combination of complementarity and symmetry. Complementarity is based on the principle that opposites attract and may enrich each other. In the happy marriage, the partners will refer to "helping each other out," each contributing unique talents, both in the practical and emotional sense, and pursuing his or her own interests and hobbies. On the other hand, there will be a measure of symmetry, areas in which both partners are equally competent and will share roles and tasks, and find pleasure in doing the same things together or individually.

When either the complementary or symmetrical quality of a relationship goes awry, the sense of a common goal and cohesive interaction disappears. Complementarity may turn into competition, and the marriage may begin to be characterized by bickering and even ridicule. A partner may project feared weaknesses onto the spouse and attack him or her to keep these "defects" at a distance. Such relationships may seem doomed to an outsider, and yet may be quite stable in their conflict, for each partner may need some of the complementary weaknesses each has disavowed with such passion. The counselor may lead each partner to see that if he or she is not perfect, then the spouse should not be expected to be perfect. Each partner may then begin to adopt the feared traits and thus become more complete within and more tolerant and accepting of the other.

Marriages also can be oversymmetrical and become "stale." The most frequent area of the problems is likely to be sexual, because each partner tries too hard to please the other and worries about performance. Such partners need to learn the value of self-gratification in sex (see Chapter 10 on Sexual and Reproductive Health, page 155) and may need permission to express their differentness in sexual and other areas.

Marriage counseling commonly involves seeing both partners, usually at the same time. A good marriage counselor will avoid taking sides in any dispute and will aim to open new lines of communication between the spouses by making them aware of the patterns their relationship has established, and their needs to grow as individuals.

Family Problems

Families seldom seek family counseling on their own account, but it should be considered when several family members have serious emotional problems, when an adolescent is showing severe signs of rebelliousness, when family members cannot agree on what to do or when they constantly blame one another for the problem.

The family unit may be divided into subsidiary relationships in understanding its interactions. The marital unit is one subsystem of interaction, which should properly have its own set of rules and its own boundaries from the rest of the family. Sibling interactions are another subunit, and may vary tremendously in nature. There are a wide variety of problems that can occur inside the family system.

- Some parents fear the risks of maturation and independence for their children, and never allow the boundary between parent and child to develop normally.

- Other parents, overworked, inexperienced, or overwhelmed by life, provide little guidance and their children become dominated by the culture of peers on the street. Little sense of family develops and interactions are haphazard and undisciplined.

- Some family members establish such strong relationships and commitments outside the home that the integrity of the family unit is threatened.

- Families affected by serious mental illness or other reasons for feeling "special" may isolate themselves from the outside world, limiting the children's ability to establish normal friendships.

- Triangles often form, in which two family members "gang up" on a third. This may lead the excluded to establish an alliance with another family member, and complex balanced systems of rivalry and hostility may develop.

In any of the above situations, only one family member may seem to suffer, but change will be impossible without undergoing counseling as a group. The family members must discover their role in the problem to solve the individual's original problem. Therefore, family therapy involves both "healthy" family members and those with recognizable problems. The therapist may request change on the part of all family members. For example, members may be asked to break down rigid barriers such as the gap between the "black sheep" and the well-behaved children. A good family counselor will initially contact most family members directly before initiating therapy, and will resist taking sides throughout.

The therapist will probably not focus on the complaints of individual family members, but will isolate specific problems in communication for the family to work on at home. The counselor may direct the ogre or the workaholic to put the children to bed before talking to his or her spouse. He or she may give the irresponsible child some simple jobs to do, for the fun of knowing it is possible. The counselor will almost certainly focus on communication problems inside the family, so that the family can solve its own problems, rather than trying to impose a solution from the outside.

Most family therapists initially settle upon limited and specific goals. Family therapy may take several months, but a good program will be successful in a limited period of time. If therapy is successful, individual family members may decide afterward to continue in individual counseling.

COMMON PSYCHIATRIC PROBLEMS AMONG OLDER PEOPLE
(Prepared in collaboration with Richard J. Glavin, M.D., and Paul F. Califano, M.D.)

ALTHOUGH EVERY AGE seems to bring its own set of problems, older people may be especially afflicted. As we grow older, we not only become increasingly prone to serious physical disorders, but we also are faced with major life changes, including retirement and the loss of loved ones. Unfortunately, there is often a tendency to ignore or neglect psychological problems among the aged, accepting them as inevitable or untreatable. In reality, neither physical nor mental decline are inevitable concomitants of aging, as evidenced by the ever increasing number of people achieving active and healthy older years. Also important is the fact that most psychiatric problems among older people are treatable, especially if they are properly diagnosed in their early stages. This was aptly noted by a British psychoanalyst more than 30 years ago: "It is the age of the neurosis, not the age of the patient, which determines how amenable it is to treatment."

Most of the mental and emotional problems discussed elsewhere in this chapter—depression, anxiety, psychosis, sexual dysfunction, and others—may occur at any age, including the later years. In general, their treatment in the aged is the same as in younger people with one important exception: Drug dosages often have to be lowered to compensate for the liver's reduced ability to metabolize certain chemicals. Although many people tend to associate psychotherapy with younger age groups, in some instances it can be even more effective among older people. Often, younger people still have a need to "do things their way"; in contrast, older people may be more willing to explore alternatives if they recognize that their way is not working.

In assessing mental or emotional problems in an older person, it is usually necessary to look into a number of factors. For example, in dealing with changes in behavior, such as excessive drinking, eating disorders, or failure to take needed medicine, the problem is often dismissed as "senility" or perhaps suicidal desires. Upon investigation, however, the problem may be traced to any of a number of causes: anxiety, depression, organic brain disease, a physical illness, malnutrition, or drug interactions, to name but a few.

Older people also are prone to hypochondriasis—the preoccupation with physical symptoms and fear of serious illness, despite reassurance to the contrary by a physician. Since serious illnesses become increasingly common with age, it is understandable that many older people may become preoccupied with symptoms and illness. While it may be tempting after a while for family members and others to dismiss such a person's symptoms as being "imaginary," it is still important to rule out organic illness, depression, and anxiety. And even if no organic basis for the complaints can be found, one should recognize that the symptoms and anxiety are very real to the patient, and should not be lightly dismissed. Such people need to be reassured that "there is nothing to worry about," as opposed to "there's nothing wrong." Going from doctor to doctor or seeking more and more tests are common traps in dealing with hypochondriasis; it's far better to try to reassure the person that the condition is benign and must be adjusted to, and that regularly scheduled visits to his or her doctor for treatment of symptoms, reassurace, and emotional support are all that is needed. Although listening to constant complaints may be frustrating to family members and physician alike, a sympathetic, caring attitude often will help resolve the problem or at least make it more bearable.

Depression in the Aged

Depression, a very common disorder among older people, is frequently ignored or misdiagnosed. Many of us assume that depression is an inevitable part of aging, and understandably so. Feelings of sadness, anger, or unhappiness are natural responses to the loss of loved ones and diminished physical abilities. The unhappy person nevertheless retains the capacity for enjoyment should some positive event occur. The depressed patient, on the other hand, is incapable of pleasure and also has such symptoms as loss of appetite and insomnia. As emphasized in the section on depression, this is a medical disorder, even though it shares many of the features of normal responses to sad or disheartening life events.

In treating depression in the elderly, several factors that may not be so important among younger people should be taken into consideration. Older people generally take more drugs, and a number of drugs (e.g., beta-blockers or tranquilizers) may contribute to depression. Also, a person may be conscious of early signs of organic brain disease, such as inability to concentrate or loss of memory, leading to feelings of depression. When someone begins to give away cherished or important items in an apparent anticipation of death, depression and thoughts of suicide may be present. Since suicide is a very real danger of depression, such signs always should be taken seriously and psychiatric help sought. It does no good to lecture the depressed person or urge him or her to "pull yourself together" or "keep a stiff upper lip." Depression is an illness and requires medical care. Drugs and, in some cases, electroshock therapy can successfully treat this condition.

In treating depression in the elderly, physicians use smaller drug doses than for younger adults. Experts on antidepressant therapy in the elderly therefore urge "start low and go slow." If drugs prove ineffective in overcoming the depression or if the threat of suicide is great, electroshock therapy may be considered. Since the temporary memory loss that accompanies EST can be very disturbing to an older person, who may already have memory problems, the treatments usually are spaced further apart than in a younger patient. Also, fewer treatments may be administered.

Sleep Problems of the Elderly

Many older people complain that they have difficulty sleeping. Sleep patterns do change as we grow older: There is often increased difficulty falling asleep; there is some loss of the deep-sleep stages 3 and 4 and therefore sleep may become lighter and more easily interrupted. If the older person is reasonably alert during the day, he or she is probably getting enough nighttime sleep. The body merely requires less sleep now.

Of course, true insomnia may develop in the elderly in association with other problems. For example, depression is associated with early-morning awakening. Successful treatment of the depression will alleviate the sleeping difficulty. For the person who has fallen into the habit of daytime napping, providing more interesting daytime activities may help. In any event, it is wise to avoid taking sleeping pills. These drugs often create new problems, especially when taken for long periods. If drugs are considered necessary, they should be used for only a short time and the person should be watched closely for adverse side effects.

Paranoid Reactions

Many older people develop paranoid reactions, which range from mild suspicions to more serious delusions. Sometimes these reactions are related to other factors in aging, such as diminished eyesight or hearing, which reduce a person's ability to discriminate and cope with stress. In other cases, they may be a sign of organic brain disease or some other illness. In any event, the hallmark of paranoia is the denial of any personal deficiency or responsibility; instead, the problems lie with others or the environment. An older woman may forget where she put her purse or a piece of jewelry, but instead of blaming herself, she will immediately conclude that she has been robbed. Or a man may have difficulty hearing what is said, but instead of attributing his problem to failing ears, he may accuse everyone of whispering or trying to hide things from him. Such people may become fearful of all sorts of plots against them. Simply denying that anyone means them harm or that the delusions are false seldom does much permanent good. In some cases, mild doses of an antipsychotic drug may be helpful, but again, special care must be taken to guard against adverse side effects and drug interactions.

Dementia

As noted earlier, dementia is a deterioration of mental capability due to organic brain disease. Many people still mistakenly consider dementia, or "senility," as inevitable with age and a hopeless, untreatable condition. Both assumptions are false; most people do not suffer dementia as they grow older, and there are many types of dementia that can be reversed or halted with proper treatment. Thus, when dementia is suspected, it is vital that every attempt be made to determine whether it is, indeed, true dementia, and if so, its cause. There are many possible causes of reversible dementia; these range from brain injuries to nutritional deficiencies, adverse drug effects, infections, systemic illnesses, toxic substances (including alcohol), or hormone disorders.

Evaluation of dementia should include a mental status examination and other tests of mental functions as well as a careful physical examination and a number of laboratory tests. The examining physician should also determine what drugs are being taken, including nonprescription medications and alcohol. Since malnutrition and vitamin deficiencies can cause dementia, eating habits should be reviewed. Many older people are malnourished for a variety of reasons, including economic factors, difficulty in chewing, loss of appetite, inability to shop or cook, and metabolic disorders. Depression may be misdiagnosed as dementia, as may thyroid disorders and other organic illnesses.

Alzheimer's Disease

Alzheimer's disease, or senile dementia, is a progressive, irreversible form of dementia that has gained considerable public attention in recent years. Its cause is unknown. Researchers have begun to identify subtypes of the disease and are searching for effective methods of treatment. The major distinguishing signs of Alzheimer's are degeneration of the cerebral neurons, and ultimately, atrophy (shrinking) of areas of the brain, which can be detected by CT scans. Obviously, before Alzheimer's is diagnosed, other possible causes of dementia should be ruled out, and CT scans and other appropriate tests should be performed.

Although there is currently no effective treatment of Alzheimer's disease, steps can be taken to minimize or delay its effects for both the victim and family. These include:

- Treating other conditions that may contribute to the mental deterioration. Inadequate nutrition, loss of hearing or failing eyesight, and advancing cardiovascular disease are among the treatable conditions that may increase the severity of dementia.

- Making the most of remaining capabilities while reducing the need for lost function. People with failing memories should be encouraged to make lists. Alarm clocks can be set as reminders to take medicine. Daily medications can be laid out each morning so that the patient will know if each dose has been taken.

- Treating behavioral symptoms, such as agitation and paranoia. Drugs such as haloperidol or chlorpromazine can minimize or control some of these symptoms, but will not improve memory.

- Helping family members cope. Understandably, Alzheimer's is a particularly difficult disease for family members. A spouse, children, or grandchildren often are devastated to watch a loved one gradually succumb to Alzheimer's. There are now a number of services and agencies to help family members cope with caring for an Alzheimer's patient. These range from visiting homemakers to skilled nursing services. Eventually it may become impossible to provide the needed care at home and placement in a nursing home or other residential facility may be necessary. (See Chapter 2 on The American Health-Care System and How to Use It, page 34, and Chapter 3 on Meeting the Needs of the Aged, page 43.) This is always a difficult move for everyone concerned, but sometimes it is the best alternative. But before such placement is made, the facility should be carefully investigated by family members and, if possible, the family's physician. Since it is such a traumatic time for everyone involved, special family counseling may be advisable.

37 Disorders Common to Women

W. Duane Todd, M.D.

INTRODUCTION

MANY OF THE MOST COMMON medical problems experienced by women are related to their reproductive functions. From menarche through childbirth to menopause and beyond, a number of minor complaints and annoyances, as well as serious disorders, arise in the female reproductive system. In addition to being aware of possible warning signs that should prompt a woman to see a gynecologist, women also should practice a number of preventive measures, such as contraception and breast self-examination, and have regular Pap smears.

CHOOSING AN OBSTETRICIAN/GYNECOLOGIST

AN OBSTETRICIAN/GYNECOLOGIST (OB/GYN) is a physician who specializes in treating the diseases affecting women, especially diseases of the sexual organs. A gynecologist should be able to act as a resource to help a woman get answers to her questions on health, sexuality, and fertility. It is important that a woman establish a good patient-physician relationship with an obstetrician/gynecologist who can help her make decisions about her gynecological health. A woman may locate an obstetrician/gynecologist through recommendations from friends, other health professionals, a local medical society, or personnel at the local hospital who work regularly with obstetrician/gynecologists. She may want to meet with several before making a choice.

An important credential for a gynecologist to possess is certification by a gynecological specialty board. A young gynecologist, who has completed specialty training and passed a written examination, but who has been in practice for less than the required 2 years prior to submitting case records to the certification committee and taking an oral examination, is called "board eligible."

Board certification is not a guarantee of special competence, but it does indicate that the doctor's technical skill and experience have been tested by his or her peers.

It is also useful to inquire:

- About the doctor's places of internship and residency: A university-affiliated teaching hospital offers the intern or resident especially good instruction and a wide variety of cases with which to polish professional skills.
- With which hospitals the doctor is affiliated: Doctors are granted the privilege of practicing at various hospitals. Hospitals connected to medical schools, those with more than 200 beds, those accredited by the Joint Committee on Hospital Accreditation, are considered to be the best-equipped.
- The professional societies to which the doctor belongs: Gynecology is a fast-changing field and membership in professional societies, such as the American College of Obstetricians and Gynecologists (ACOG) which offer continuing education conferences and meetings, indicate that the physician is interested in keeping abreast of medical advances. A physician who is a fellow of ACOG has been accorded special recognition by colleagues.

In the final analysis, however, the patient's level of comfort with her doctor's personal style is probably key. The average woman will visit her gynecologist dozens of times even if she is never sick a day in her life, and will discuss with her gynecologist some of the most intimate questions of life. The patient owes it to herself to feel comfortable with that physician, and to experience an atmosphere of mutual respect.

THE GYNECOLOGICAL EXAM

AFTER TAKING a patient history that includes familial disease history, personal health, and information about menstruation, pregnancy, childbirth, and contraception, the gynecologist will perform a physical examination with emphasis on examination of the breasts, abdominal and pelvic organs. The physician or a staff member will also take the patient's blood pressure, weight, and possibly a blood or a urine sample for analysis. The patient commonly sits up while her breasts are examined by the gynecologist. The first step is visual inspection for depressions, bulges, unusual-appearing moles, dark or reddened areas, swelling, sores, or areas of the skin with rough appearance. The second step is palpation, performed while the patient is lying down. The physician skillfully checks for lumps, thickenings in the breasts, or enlargements in the lymph nodes (part of the body's disease-fighting system) in the armpits and other sites.

The gynecologist next palpates the patient's abdomen to check for unusual formations in the abdominal cavity, which includes the internal reproductive organs. Then the gynecologist will perform an examination of the patient's external genitalia for sores, reddened or crusted areas or other abnormalities, followed by a pelvic examination.

The pelvic examination is performed by sliding an instrument called a speculum into the vagina. This should not cause discomfort; if it does, the woman should tell the physician. When the speculum is opened, the patient's lower internal reproductive organs can be seen with appropriate lighting and can be reached with the gynecologist's gloved fingers. The physician will examine the vagina, cervix, and uterus for growths and discolored or hard-

ened spots, will press on the patient's abdomen with one hand while locating the ovaries internally, and will feel for unusual conditions. The physician may also rub a small wooden spatula over the cervix to obtain a smear of secretions which will be studied for abnormal cells. The smear may be used for one of several tests, but the most common is the Papanicolaou or "Pap" test, an important screening tool for cervical cancers.

Finally, the physician will insert a lubricated gloved finger into the patient's rectum, at the same time pressing with the fingers in the vagina to feel for unusual conditions that might have been missed before. If a woman needs to be fitted for a diaphragm or other contraceptive device, the physician or a staff member will probably do so at this time.

The physician should report findings to the patient as the examination progresses or immediately afterward in the privacy of his or her office. There should always be an opportunity for the patient to ask questions.

ANATOMY OF THE BREASTS

AMERICAN CULTURE places importance on the size of the female breast, but size has little to do with the function of this organ.

In the center of each breast is the nipple, which is surrounded by a pigmented circular area known as the areola. (See figure 37.1.) The color of the nipple varies from individual to individual, from a light pink to a deep brown or almost black. Generally, the color deepens during pregnancy. The base of the nipple is ringed with tiny oil-producing montgomery glands that help keep the nipple supple. Some women have hairs around the areola.

The nipple is made of erectile tissue and, in some women, the nipple is constantly erect. In others, the nipple only becomes erect when stimulated by cold, physical contact, or sexual activity. Most women's nipples protrude beyond the areola, but some are inverted. This in itself is not a problem, but changes in the condition are a warning sign requiring further attention from a doctor.

The interior of the breast is divided into several sections called lobes, which are further subdivided into lobules. Each lobule contains milk-secreting glands cushioned by fat and fibrous connective tissue. An intricate system of tiny ducts arranged like tree branches carries the milk produced by the glands to the ampulla, a collecting chamber imme-

diately below the nipple. The entire breast is richly supplied with blood vessels.

The connective fibrous tissue attaches the breast to the muscles of the chest wall—the pectoral muscles. The breast itself contains no muscle tissue, and bust-increasing exercises can only increase pectoral muscle size so the breasts protrude more. No amount of exercise, creams, or other activity will make the breasts themselves larger.

The pectorals extend into the armpit or axillary area, which contains lymph nodes. Lymph is a transparent body fluid found in tissue spaces throughout the body. Like blood, it circulates throughout the body in its own system. It plays a major part in the body's disease-fighting efforts. Lymph passageways are punctuated by clusters of lymphatic tissue, called lymph nodes, which act as filters for bacteria, thrown-off cells, and other substances from the lymph fluid.

The breast also contains sensory nerves that are exceptionally sensitive. This is why an infant's sucking stimulates its mother's nerves and causes breast milk to be produced, and why some women's breasts are sexually sensitive.

Breast milk production is complex. Thousands of cells in the milk glands absorb basic substances—like water, salts, sugar, fats, and small nitrogen-

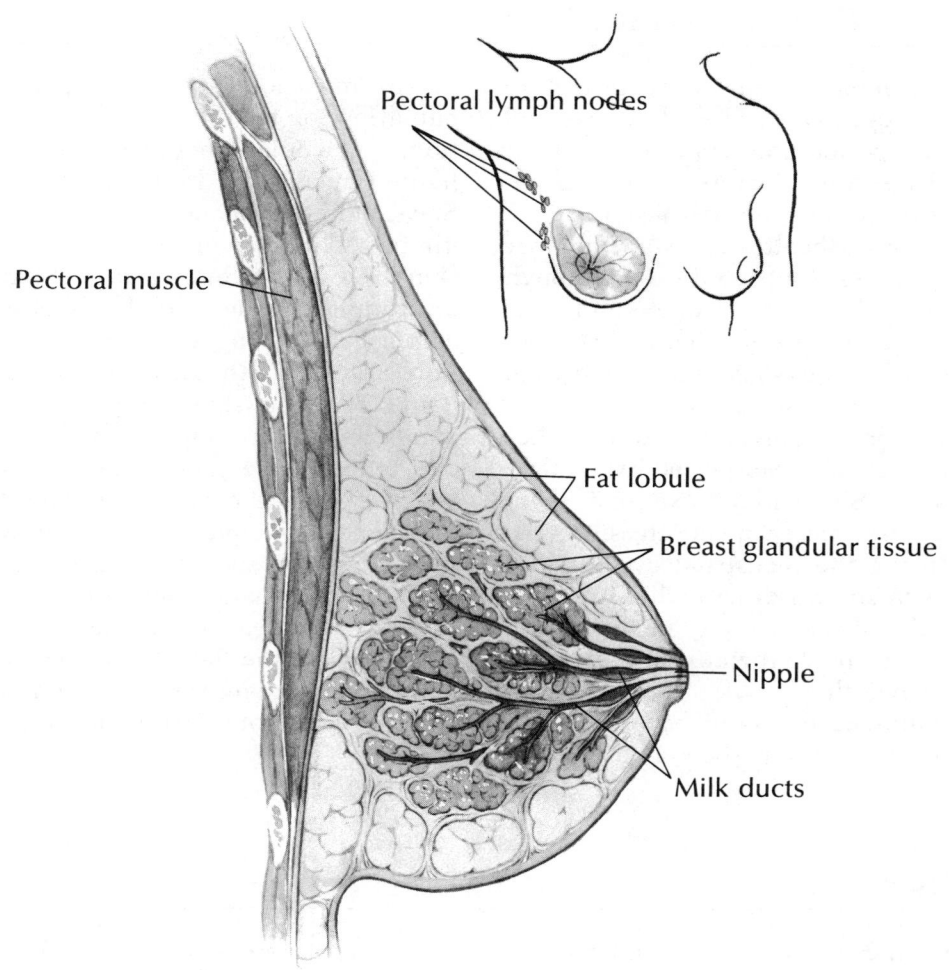

Pectoral lymph nodes

Pectoral muscle

Fat lobule

Breast glandular tissue

Nipple

Milk ducts

Figure 37.1. **Normal breast anatomy.**

containing molecules—from the bloodstream, and use them to compound milk. Although breast milk is not normally produced until the infant begins sucking, a woman's body anticipates the possibility of pregnancy every month and begins to prepare for it in response to normal monthly changes in hormone balance.

During the first half of the menstrual cycle, the hormone estrogen is produced by the ovaries in increasing quantities and stimulates the growth of new cells in the glands, ducts, and fibrous tissue of the breast. This increase in cell activity is accompanied by an increase in blood flow to the breast, which may be experienced as fullness, warmth and, sometimes, tenderness. At about the middle of the monthly cycle, a ripe egg (ovum) is released from the ovary, and as a result, the second ovarian hormone, progesterone, is released into the bloodstream. The secreting process then begins in the gland cells.

There may be an increased sensation of warmth, fullness, or tenderness in the breasts.

If pregnancy does not occur, the hormone levels shift again. The changes that the hormones stimulated in the breast are reversed: New cell growth slows and blood supply to the area is diminished. Secretions and cells are reabsorbed by the body to make room for the next cycle's cells and secretions. Breast swelling diminishes and breast tissue softens. If pregnancy does occur, the buildup of duct, gland, and fibrous tissue continues. After the pregnancy is over, another hormone, prolactin (produced by the pituitary gland at the base of the brain), is released and this triggers the actual production of breast milk. As a baby sucks, more prolactin and, therefore, more milk, is produced. As the baby is weaned, the prolactin levels fall, and the production of breast milk tapers off.

BREAST SELF-EXAMINATION

MANY DOCTORS recommend that women start to practice breast self-examination after they have had their first menstrual period and continue the habit throughout their lives. Most doctors want their patients to learn the technique and will take the time to teach it, or will ask a health-care staff member (nurse or physician's assistant) to do so. Although breast cancer is extremely rare in women under 30, it is useful for a woman to examine her breasts consistently throughout her life, since there are benign conditions that can occur at any age.

The best time for a woman to examine her breasts is about a week after her period, when they are least congested. She should examine them monthly, at the same time each month, since the breasts change during the menstrual cycle. Older postmenopausal women and others whose periods are irregular, should choose one day in the month for breast examination and do their examinations on the same day every month.

Breast self-examination should be done when the patient is relaxed and not rushed or distracted.

The examination consists of 2 parts: inspection and palpation, or feeling. To begin the inspection portion, the woman should stand in front of a well-lighted mirror and let her arms hang at her sides. She should note shape, depressions or bulges, moles, dimples, dark or reddened areas, swellings, sores, or skin with a rough or orange peel-like texture as well as prominent veins. She should observe nipples and areola color changes, scaling, dimpling, or retraction, as well as the direction in which the nipples point. Then she should repeat the inspection with hands pressing on hips (to make the pectoral muscles bulge in the chest) and with hands raised, elbows flexed, and placed behind her head.

Next the woman should lie down on a couch or bed. Each arm should be raised and the breast felt with the other hand, then examined with the arm at the side. The breast should be felt gently and systematically with the flat of the fingers of the opposite hand. (For more information about breast self-examination see Chapter 20 on Cancer, page 405.)

THE PELVIS

A WOMAN has both external genitals and internal reproductive organs which are with her from birth, but which change as she matures, from the time of menstruation until after menopause and into old age. Diagrams can convey a sense of the various organs, but there are many variations on the normal. (See figure 37.2.)

The external genitalia are categorized as the *vulva*. The vulva include:

- *Mons veneris* or "Mount of Venus"—pad of fatty tissue covering the pubic bone. At puberty an increased output of 2 hormones, estrogen from the ovaries and androgen from the adrenals, stimulate growth of pubic hair to cover this area. After menopause, when hormonal levels tend to decrease, the hair may thin out, become straighter, or turn gray.

- *Labia majora*—These 2 folds of fatty tissue touch to protect the urinary and reproductive openings that lie between them. These outer lips change in size during a woman's life and also vary in size (and color) from individual to individual. Childbirth, too, changes their position slightly so that they may normally be open a little. The skin on the insides of the labia majora has tiny bumps—glands that keep the area moist.

- *Labia minora*—The inner lips, which usually protrude less than the outer lips, come together at the intersec-

tion of the mons veneris. The fused portion, or prepuce, covers the clitoris.

- *Clitoris*—The clitoris is made of erectile tissue, which fills with blood and swells during sexual arousal. The visible portion is about the size of a pencil eraser. The rest of the clitoris is hidden underneath the surface of the skin, and is connected to veins throughout the pelvis which also become congested with blood during sexual arousal. The clitoris is involved directly or indirectly in all female orgasms.

- *Vestibule*—Between the labia minora are the urethral meatus, through which a woman urinates, and the opening to the reproductive tract, the vaginal introitus. Two small Bartholin's glands, which keep the opening of the vagina moist, are also located here.

- *Hymen*—In some women, the hymen is a semicircular strip of mucous membrane that fringes the lower edge of the vaginal opening. In others, it circles the vaginal opening. There may be several openings in it, or one large opening. Some women are born without one. In some rare cases it may block the vaginal opening and it may then become necessary for a doctor to open it to allow for the passage of menstrual blood. The membrane can be stretched by exercise, masturbation, a tampon, or intercourse.

- *Vaginal opening*—This is the channel through which sexual intercourse takes place, through which men-

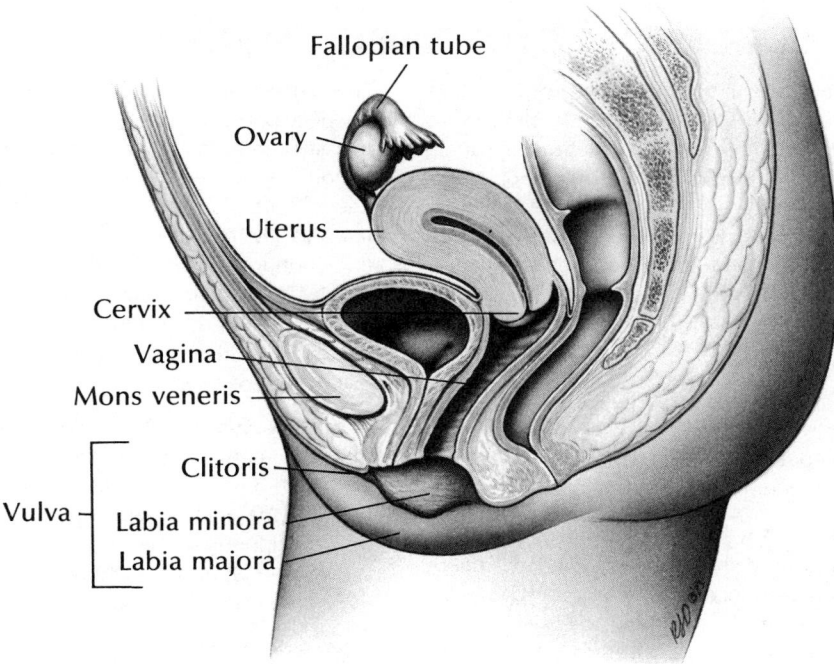

Figure 37.2. **The female reproductive organs.**

strual fluid passes, and through which babies are born.

• *Vagina*—A woman's vagina is actually a tube, about 5 inches long, with walls that expand during intercourse and expand even more during childbirth. (In their normal state, the walls of the vagina gently touch each other.) The vagina produces continuous secretions that help keep it clean and maintain the acidity of its walls to prevent an infection from starting.

The first third of the vagina is sensitive; the other two-thirds has fewer nerve endings. The bladder lies close to the vagina, and pressure on the vaginal walls may be felt in the bladder as well. The rectum, too, is located on the underside of the vagina. The vagina is a closed system; tampons cannot "get lost." Above the vagina is the cervix, or neck of the womb.

• *Cervix*—The cervix, or cervical os, is the opening to the uterus. Tampons and other objects cannot pass through the os into the uterus. Sperm, however, can, and it is also through the opening that the menstrual blood passes from the uterus.

• *Uterus*—About the size and shape of an inverted pear, the uterus is a hollow organ lined with a special layer—endometrial tissue—that thickens and is shed each month during the menstrual period. It is here that a fertilized ovum or embryo implants itself to develop. In most women, the uterus is tilted forward, almost forming a right angle to the vagina and resting on the bladder. In nearly a third of women, however, the uterus tilts backward, which is not abnormal.

• *Fallopian tubes and ovaries*—Extending from the upper portion of the uterus on either side are the Fallopian tubes, two 4- to 5-inch tubes with tiny fingerlike projections. Nearby are two small oval organs on their own supportive bands of ligament, the ovaries. The ovaries produce substances that cause the uterine lining to thicken each month and they produce a ripe egg (usually one, but sometimes more) most commonly every 28 to 32 days. The egg is reached for by the Fallopian tube's projections and drawn into the tube. If a man's sperm meets and fertilizes the egg in the Fallopian tube, pregnancy begins.

MENSTRUATION

Puberty and the Beginning of Menstruation (Menarche)

Every normal baby girl is born with the potential to reproduce, with 2 million or so primitive ova or eggs already in her ovaries. By age 7, about 300,000 remain—the others have been resorbed by the body. Puberty is the time in a young girl's life when her

SYMPTOMS SUGGESTING GYNECOLOGICAL DISORDERS

Vaginal Discharge (Leukorrhea). Any previously unnoticed vaginal discharge should be investigated. When associated with itching, burning, or irritation, it usually suggests some type of vaginitis. In the absence of associated symptoms, it may indicate a minor disorder related to the cervix, such as polyps. When blood is present in the discharge, it may indicate a more serious problem, including cancer, and should be promptly evaluated.

Irritation (Itching or Pruritis). Itching, burning, or irritation of the external genitalia usually indicates some local infection of the vagina, or external genitalia, commonly yeast, trichomonas, or a nonspecific vaginitis. Occasionally it may be related to local skin conditions, particularly in women beyond menopause.

Abnormal Bleeding. Any bleeding outside of the normal menstrual cycle and flow should be checked. A general guideline is that unusual bleeding superimposed on a normal cycle may indicate a developing disorder such as polyps or leiomyomata (fibroids), but rarely more serious conditions such as cancer. Unusual bleeding in which the normal cycle suddenly changes is most commonly related to minor hormonal changes, such as menstrual cycles without ovulation.

These are common in the first few years of menses and as a woman approaches menopause. When pregnancy is possible, some abnormality of pregnancy (e.g., threatened abortion or ectopic pregnancy) must be considered. Any bleeding after a woman has ceased menstruating for 1 year requires prompt attention. Although most commonly related to benign conditions, it also may indicate a cancer of the uterine lining (endometrium).

Amenorrhea (absence of menses). During the reproductive years in sexually active women, the first consideration should be the possibility of a pregnancy. Other conditions that may be related to amenorrhea are birth control pill use, active breast-feeding and, not infrequently, minor hormonal disturbances such as anovulation (lack of ovulation). Occasionally it may indicate a more serious problem related to the pituitary gland (hyperprolactinemia and adenomas), anorexia nervosa, pelvic tuberculosis, endocrine disturbances arising from the ovary, adrenal gland, or thyroid, and some forms of systemic illness.

External Genitalia Pain. The development of pain in the external genitalia most commonly is related to infection. The most common types are an infected sebaceous gland, Bartholin's gland, or a herpes infection.

Lower Abdominal Pain. Pain in the lower abdomen is not necessarily of gynecological origin. It often is related to the gastrointestinal tract or urinary system. Gynecological conditions that may result in abdominal pain are threatened abortions, ectopic pregnancies, complications related to leiomyomata (fibroids), ovarian cysts, salpingitis (infection in the Fallopian tubes), adenomyosis, and endometriosis. The pain in these conditions is usually moderate to severe. Pain related to the physiology of the menstrual cycle, i.e., mittelschmerz and primary dysmenorrhea, are usually of less severity.

Low Back Pain and Pelvic Pressure. Low back pain is most commonly related to the back and not of gynecological origin. Low back pain (more a discomfort) and pelvic pressure may be related to problems of relaxation of the pelvic supports; cystocele, and uterine prolapse. The symptoms commonly increase as the day progresses while the woman is in the upright position.

Abdominal Swelling. Any noticed growth within the abdomen requires prompt attention. The most common gynecological conditions are leiomyomata (fibroids) and ovarian cysts. Occasionally there may be a progressive enlargement of the entire abdomen, usually related to fluid within the abdominal cavity (ascites). This is not necessarily of gynecological origin, but often is related to ovarian tumors.

Vaginal Protrusion. The sudden or gradual protrusion or bulge at the vaginal opening is usually related to a weakening of the supports to the pelvic structures, and is most often seen in women beyond menopause. It usually represents a cystocele or uterine prolapse.

Urinary Incontinence. Involuntary loss of urine is generally one of two types. Loss of urine because of the sudden urge to urinate is called urgency incontinence, and is usually caused by intrinsic bladder problems, commonly a low-grade infection. Loss of urine during sudden strain, (i.e., coughing, laughing, sneezing) is called stress incontinence and this form is usually related to the gynecological condition called cystocele or urethrocele. It is most common in postmenopausal women.

Painful Intercourse (Dyspareunia). Painful intercourse may occur at any time during a woman's sexual life. It is most common in postmenopausal women due to decreased hormonal effects on the vagina. In menstruating women it is usually related to a vaginal infection. Occasionally it may be due to involuntary contraction of the muscles of the vaginal outlet (vaginismus).

reproductive organs mature and what has been an invisible process becomes visible. Menarche is the term given to the time when a girl has her first menstrual period—usually sometime between the ages of 10 and 16—and is considered physically capable of becoming pregnant.

Before menstruation begins, many developmental changes, visible and invisible, will already have taken place. The hypothalamus, which controls the body's production of hormones, has been sending substances to the pituitary gland, located at the base of the brain. The hormones produced by the pituitary gland stimulate the ovaries, and they begin secreting estrogen, which helps the eggs mature. By the time a girl is 8, she will typically be producing small amounts of estrogen. This hormone, along with others, is responsible for a sudden growth spurt, change in body proportions, the growth of pubic hair, development of breasts, and the appearance of underarm hair. In addition, the girl's external genitalia begin to look more like a woman's and the internal organs grow and change so they can accommodate reproduction.

When a certain level of estrogen production is reached, an egg is released from the ovaries, and the follicle or egg container within the ovary begins to secrete another hormone, progesterone. The progesterone and estrogen combination causes the lining of the uterus to thicken in preparation for nourishing and sustaining a fertilized egg. If pregnancy does not occur, the follicle dies. The progesterone level drops, the uterine lining breaks down and is shed, and the girl has her first menstrual period.

Menstrual cycles tend to be irregular during the first years, and this probably has something to do with the body's need to establish its hormone level patterns. Most researchers say that young girls do not release an egg every month, and that the bleeding is not due to the lowering of the progesterone levels, but to the thickness of the uterine lining from which parts eventually break off and are shed. However, it is wise to assume that if a young girl has begun to menstruate she is ovulating and is able to become pregnant.

It is important for a young girl to have an adult who can ease her transition into womanhood with information and understanding. A girl's reactions to menstruation tend to follow the patterns she observes in her immediate environment. If her mother or the other people in her life consider the process of menstruation to be a "curse" or an "illness," she is likely to develop the same attitude. If they let her know that menstruation is part of the process of growing up and achieving adulthood, along with the capacity for childbearing, she may have a much more positive attitude.

Menstruation in the Mature Woman

Menstrual flow usually amounts to 4 to 6 tablespoons of vaginal and cervical secretions, tissue, and blood. Some women pass clumps of menstrual tissue that look like blood clots, particularly after they have been lying down and the fluid has had a chance to pool in the upper vagina and become somewhat clotted. Menstrual fluid has no odor until it comes in contact with air and vaginal bacteria.

Menstruation in a mature woman usually occurs regularly; cycles anywhere from 20 to 40 days are considered within the normal range. Some women have longer or shorter cycles than these, and they are considered normal, too, as long as there is not excessive bleeding and the cycles are fairly regular. Both physical and emotional stress can cause menstrual irregularities. The menstrual cycle is divided into 4 phases:

1. The bleeding phase, or time of the actual menstrual flow.

2. The proliferative phase, when the body is preparing itself for pregnancy. (There is a slight vaginal discharge at this time.)

3. The ovulation phase, when the ripe egg is released from the ovary. (Vaginal discharge increases and the mucus is thicker.)

4. The secretory phase, which usually lasts for 14 days, after which the menstrual flow starts and the cycle begins again.

Women who have light flows may use as few as 1 or 2 menstrual tampons or sanitary pads per day. Women with heavier flows might require 8 to 10 tampons or pads per day. Menstrual sponges, which can be rinsed out and reused, are also available in drug stores. The size of a tampon or a pad refers to its absorption ability; a menstruating woman of any age may use any size tampon as long as it can be inserted comfortably, and any size pad that can be worn comfortably. Some tampon manufacturers produce slim sizes in several absorbencies for young women.

Tampons and Toxic Shock Syndrome

Toxic shock syndrome (TSS) is a newly defined and relatively rare disease about which there are still unanswered questions. TSS usually affects menstruating women under the age of 30, but men and children, as well as nonmenstruating and old women, have been affected.

TSS is caused by a bacterium that is often found in the nose and mouth. Some women also have this organism in their vaginas. The bacterium produces a toxin and, if there are sufficient bacteria present, the toxin may be released into the bloodstream, possibly with fatal consequences.

The majority of TSS victims have been tampon users, but medical researchers are not sure what that role is. TSS was first identified in association with a brand of super-absorbent tampons, since withdrawn from the market. But most tampons now contain some type of super-absorbent fiber. One current theory is that tampons trap the bacteria and provide a breeding ground for them. If a woman leaves a tampon in place for some time as is the practice with the super-absorbent types, the opportunity for the bacteria to grow and produce toxins is increased. Another theory is that the super-absorbent fibers cause microscopic lacerations in the vagina that make possible transmission of the bacteria or toxin.

TSS is characterized by sudden onset of fever, vomiting, and diarrhea, sometimes accompanied by headache, sore throat, and aching muscles. There may be a dramatic drop in blood pressure within a day or two. The woman may go into shock, become disoriented, and suffer kidney failure. At the same time, a red, peeling rash may develop, particularly on the palms and soles of the feet. In mild cases, only one of the symptoms may be evident. The disease tends to recur and can be fatal. A woman wearing a tampon who begins to experience symptoms should remove it and seek immediate medical advice. Antibiotics, medication to stabilize blood pressure, and fluids may be given.

A woman who chooses to use tampons should change them frequently and alternate between the use of tampons and pads. One who has had TSS should not use tampons at all.

Menopause

Like menarche, which is just one sign of a growing girl's reproductive maturity, menopause—the cessation of menstrual periods—is one part of the "climacteric" phase of an older woman's life.

During menopause, the ovaries stop producing eggs, so the high levels of estrogen and progesterone in the body drop. The hormones produced by the pituitary change, too.

Typically, menopause is a process of gearing down: an irregular menstrual pattern, with the periods eventually stopping altogether. The age at which this happens has been getting later and later. It is not unusual for women to be menstruating in their mid-fifties. Women whose mothers had later menopause will probably do so themselves.

Climacteric women are also more susceptible to vaginal and urinary infection, since both types of tissues tend to thin; to osteoporosis, or loss of bone density, which may make a person more susceptible to bone fractures; and to hot flashes, short episodes of profuse sweating characterized by a feeling of intense heat. Although most women experience hot flashes, menopause seems to have become less of a

problem than it once was. Consultation with a physician is important should a woman experience severe symptoms.

Conditions Related to Menstruation

Premenstrual Syndrome (PMS). PMS includes changes in a woman's body as her hormone levels prepare her for pregnancy each month. Some of the changes—such as increased energy, sexual desire, or feelings of well-being—can be positive. The symptoms which come to the gynecologist's attention, however, are the troublesome ones. The way an individual woman experiences them is due to her own body chemistry.

PMS usually starts in the week before a woman's menstrual period begins. Symptoms can include swelling in the joints, abdomen, breasts, and genitals; nausea, vomiting, diarrhea, constipation, headaches, depression, lethargy, fatigue, anger, anxiety, dull aches, skin problems, respiratory problems, and weight gain. There may be changes in sleeping or eating patterns. In all, more than 150 different symptoms have been associated with PMS.

The cause of PMS is unknown, although most experts feel that it is related to hormonal changes that occur during the latter part of the menstrual cycle. Limited research indicates that the hormone progesterone, which is produced during the second half of the period, may be responsible for the changes. But other factors also may be involved.

So far, there is no single treatment that relieves all the various symptoms of PMS. For some women, hormone therapy is helpful. Women who are troubled by depression and other mental changes may benefit from antidepressant drugs. Vitamin E supplements and caffeine restriction relieve breast symptoms for some women. Many women are comforted to realize that their problems have an organic basis and are shared by millions of other women. If they recognize that their symptoms are cyclic, they can plan their schedules accordingly. In the meantime, research is going forward at a number of centers that may provide more definitive answers regarding the causes and treatment of PMS.

Menstrual Cramps. Most women experience menstrual cramps (dysmenorrhea) at some time. Primary dysmenorrhea—menstrual cramps of uncertain cause—may appear in the early teens and become less severe after a woman reaches her middle twenties or gives birth. Secondary dysmenorrhea—often associated with some underlying disorder—may appear at any time, but begins most frequently when a woman is in her thirties or forties.

Some women—young teenagers who have just

begun menstruating and women taking birth control pills—tend not to have cramps. This has been attributed to the fact that cramps are associated with ovulation, and young girls may not yet be ovulating, while the effect of birth control pills is to suppress ovulation.

Primary dysmenorrhea may be mild or severe, and the cramps may differ from month to month or year to year. Some women have dysmenorrhea all their reproductive lives; most find they no longer have it after they have given birth.

If the dysmenorrhea is secondary, the symptoms may be related to an underlying condition. There may be changes in the menstrual flow to a gushing, flooding type, or premenstrual staining as well as pain on intercourse, and the pain may tend to get worse with every period. With secondary dysmenorrhea, there may be pain on both sides, or the pain may be relieved as the period progresses.

While secondary dysmenorrhea may be caused by disorders of the reproductive system, no one is quite sure why women have primary dysmenorrhea. Recent research has centered on the possible role of prostaglandins, hormonelike substances that are produced throughout the body. Research is being done in this area; until the time that a source of primary dysmenorrhea is isolated, the woman and her physician should decide what type of relief to seek. The first step is to determine through a thorough medical and menstrual history, followed by a pelvic examination, and possibly other tests as well, whether there is a secondary cause for the cramps. If the cause is a disorder of the reproductive system, its treatment may relieve the cramps.

The treatment of primary dysmenorrhea depends on the severity of symptoms. Heat, exercises, deep breathing, and sexual activity have all been found to relieve cramps in some women. Other women are helped by analgesics such as aspirin, nonaspirin pain relievers, over-the-counter drugs especially prepared for the relief of menstrual cramps, prescription painkillers, and the use of birth control pills. In recent years, nonsteroidal anti-inflammatory drugs, such as those used to treat arthritis, have been found effective in relieving menstrual cramps in up to 80 percent of women. These drugs act by blocking prostaglandin production.

Mittelschmerz. Middle pain is a sharp, cramplike pain which some women experience at the time of ovulation, in the middle of the menstrual cycle. Some women also experience midcycle bleeding, which is the result of a rapid drop in estrogen levels. If the bleeding is more than occasional, and if it persists for more than a day, the woman should seek medical advice: It could be a symptom of a more serious problem. (See also Premenstrual Tenderness and Swelling of the Breasts below.)

CONDITIONS OF THE BREASTS

Premenstrual Tenderness and Swelling

The most common breast condition many women deal with once their menstrual cycles are established is monthly swelling and sometimes painful tenderness (mastodynia) that may precede a period.

Wearing a bra, or switching to a stretchier one, can help. So can avoidance of excess salt, sugar, coffee, tea, and alcohol, any or all of which may help reduce the overall feeling of premenstrual tightness and puffiness.

Usually, once the period is over, the patient may not think of it again, until it recurs, but chronic swelling in the breast becomes significant as a woman gets older. Sometimes, after the period is over, the lumpiness of the breasts may remain; in fact, a certain amount of lumpiness in breasts is normal.

If a woman is not in the habit of doing breast self-examination monthly—or even if she is—she may one day find a lump that wasn't there before. Panicky anxiety is a normal reaction. Most women promptly go to their doctors, some may live silently with the lumps, afraid to go to a doctor and have the diagnosis be cancer. However, four out of five lumps turn out to be benign.

Fibrocystic Disease

Fibrocystic disease results when the normal changes that take place every month as a mature woman's breasts prepare for milk production during pregnancy become exaggerated. During the first half of the menstrual cycle, the cells of the milk-secreting glands—the ducts that carry the milk and the supporting fibrous tissue—multiply. After ovulation occurs, other hormone levels rise and the milk-producing process continues. If pregnancy does not occur, the process stops and the fluid is reabsorbed by the breast tissues.

After many cycles, as a woman gets older. it is

more difficult for the lymph system to absorb the fluid completely after every cycle, and more difficult for the breast tissue to be reabsorbed. As a result, fluids may be trapped and form cysts. These cysts may persist, or disappear permanently after 1 or 2 menstrual periods, or disappear, only to return years later.

There are 2 types of fibrocystic disease. One is characterized by lumpiness and tenderness in both breasts, which is most pronounced in the week before the onset of menstruation. Afterward, the lumpiness and pain lessen. The other type typically occurs in one breast, and is usually characterized by several quite distinct, rounded lumps that move freely within the breast tissue. The lumps feel either soft or firm.

For some women, the pain associated with fibrocystic disease can be quite intense. With larger cysts, removal or aspiration can alleviate the pain. But pain is also associated with the more diffuse form of the disease. One of the biggest concerns about fibrocystic disease is its relationship to cancer. Women with fibrocystic diseases are 4 times more likely to develop breast cancer than women who do not have these conditions. Some doctors think that women who develop the disease before they are 20 are at higher risk for cancer than those who develop fibrocystic disease later on.

The first step in diagnosing fibrocystic disease is needle aspiration, a simple office procedure. A needle is used to remove fluid from the cyst, and this may cause it to collapse. If this happens, the doctor may advise the woman to wait and see, and return in a month or two for reexamination. Occasionally, the fluid removed from the cyst is sent to a laboratory for analysis. Mammography, an x-ray study of the breast, is also sometimes done. The lump can also be removed and examined microscopically. Approaches to treatment include caffeine restriction, vitamin E, and, if indicated, hormone therapy.

Fibroadenomas

Fibroadenomas are benign tumors of the breast that are usually composed of fibrous and glandular tissue. They occur during a woman's reproductive years, most often in women 20 to 40. Usually felt as round, firm tumors, with a somewhat rubbery texture, fibroadenomas are freely movable and not attached to the skin. Usually they occur singly and are found around the nipple or in the upper sides of the breasts. They tend to be small, and without tenderness or other symptoms.

There is a less common "juvenile" fibroadenoma that affects teenage girls and accounts for a small percentage of the cases. This juvenile type looks and behaves differently from the adult type (which can also occur in young girls). The surface of the fibroadenomas tends to be covered with dilated veins and the skin over the tumor may be tense, although the tumor is not fixed to it. The juvenile tumor is generally larger and grows much faster, so that it is sometimes mistaken for cancer, but it is a benign condition.

The fibroadenoma is not related to cancer or considered precancerous in any sense. In adolescents, there are few other conditions it may be confused with; however, in older women, it may be confused with other, possible precancerous conditions such as fibrocystic disease. Certain types of cancer that occur almost exclusively in older women may also imitate the appearance of a fibroadenoma.

In more than 80 percent of all cases, 1 of these 2 benign conditions causes the "lumps" which make a woman think she may have cancer. Both fibroadenomas and cysts should be confirmed by the physician.

In older women, the doctor will want to do the usual diagnostic tests for evaluating any breast lump to eliminate the possibility of cancer. Treatment of this condition in older women includes removal of the tumor, along with a margin of surrounding tissue, since there are a few cases in which cancer has arisen there. In young girls, treatment is usually delayed so that the breast can develop normally.

Mastitis

Infections of the breast are not uncommon in women who are nursing a child. The source of the infection is usually bacteria that enter through a crack, or fissure, in a nipple. Because the breast has a great deal of fatty tissue and a widely dispersed blood system, the infection does not spread rapidly, but tends to remain localized in one area of the breast. The patient notices swelling, redness, a sensation of heat in the affected area, and pain or tenderness. The overlying skin may be red, and if the process continues for a long time, the infected area may become hardened. The infection may be mild, producing only an area of tenderness and a slight redness in the overlying skin, or it may be more serious, triggering a defense mechanism in the surrounding tissue. In such cases, special cells in the neighboring tissue pour out secretions that harden and wall off the infected area, thus protecting the healthy tissue. This walled-off area, full of pus and infection, is called an abscess.

In nursing women, diagnosis is fairly simple. It is complicated in non-nursing women by the fact that the symptoms may be produced by a rare form of cancer as well. If a woman is breast-feeding, treatment with proper antibiotics (which will have no effect on either nursing or the baby) is given for a week. In women who fail to respond to treatment or who don't have a recent history of breast-feeding, a needle biopsy may be done: The fluid aspirated through a needle is studied microscopically and will usually reveal signs of infection indicating that the condition is a breast abscess, not a cancerous process. A mammogram (special breast x-ray) or excisional biopsy (removal of the lump for microscopic study) may be necessary.

Because the internal structure of the breast is compartmentalized with fatty tissue, it may be difficult for the antibiotics to reach the site of the infection. In such cases, the infected areas may need to be drained. If this does not clear up the infection, additional surgery may be necessary. This procedure is generally not damaging and heals with minimal scarring.

Intraductal Papillomas

Overgrowths of the lining of the duct system of the breasts, simple papillomas are entirely benign. Duct papillomatosis, however, is a form of cystic disease thought by many experts to be a precancerous condition. The chief symptom is a bloody discharge from the nipple, but this symptom is not always present. Lumps or thickening in the breast may also appear. Diagnosis is by any of the procedures used in the diagnosis of breast lumps. If a definite mass can be felt, treatment of simple papillomas is surgical removal. In older women with duct papillomatosis and other risk factors for breast cancer, a subcutaneous mastectomy may be recommended. (See Chapter 20 on Cancer, page 405.) If no lump can be found, the doctor may recommend careful follow-up, including biannual mammograms.

CONDITIONS OF THE EXTERNAL GENITALIA

MOST DISEASES affecting the vulva are skin conditions. The vulva is particularly susceptible to irritation because the area is naturally warm and moist. Underwear and pantyhose without a cotton crotch discourage air circulation and provide a warm, moist climate. Bacteria can therefore breed on the skin surface, and irritations develop.

Vulvitis

This term describes a range of irritations characterized by itching, redness, and swelling. Sometimes the woman scratches and further irritates the skin, which may begin oozing, scaling, crusting, or forming fluid-filled blisters called vesicles. The scratching may also thicken the skin and give it a whitish appearance, which can be confused with *vulvar dystrophy* (see below).

Allergic vulvitis is the result of the vulvar skin's allergic reaction to a substance. When the substance comes in direct contact with the skin, the condition may be called "contact dermatitis." Substances causing allergic reactions can include perfumed soaps, laundry detergents used to wash underwear, vaginal sprays and deodorants, and powders. Menstrual blood, feces, and other normal body secretions can also cause contact dermatitis, as can medications taken by mouth or injection or applied to the vulva. Reaction to a substance usually takes place within a few days, and may range from mild redness to severe swelling. Itching is almost always present.

Yeast vulvitis is generally a secondary infection to a vaginal infection.

Vulvar Dystrophies

These are a group of diseases that cause abnormal changes in the skin of the vulva. Unattended, they have the potential to become malignant. Vulvar dystrophies typically appear in postmenopausal women, but at times they can appear in younger women or even young girls.

These dystrophies may first appear as dry, thick, reddened areas of the skin, but as the disease progresses, the red areas will turn opaque white. Raised blisters may form white patches on the skin, and the layer of fat under the vulvar lips may flatten out. The skin tends to assume a dry, papery appearance. At a later stage it may become shiny, the clitoris may shrink, and the vaginal opening may become constricted. Not all women have these symptoms, but the whitish areas tend to develop tiny cracks, which results in more itching, scratching, and irritation, and sometimes additional infection.

A vulvar biopsy is done to permit diagnosis, either in the doctor's office using local anesthetic or under general anesthetic in a hospital. If the biopsy reveals abnormal cells, an operation to remove the vulvar skin may be performed. But, eliminating the conditions that may have caused the vulvar dystrophy is usually the treatment of choice. Contributing factors may include a vaginal infection, tight clothing which does not allow air circulation, synthetic garments that contain irritating chemicals, powders, deodorants, and perfumes. The symptoms are treated with cold soaks and cortisone creams or lotion.

Bartholin's Gland Abscess

The Bartholin's glands, which secrete a fluid that keeps the vagina moist, lie right inside the vaginal opening on either side. Normally, they are not noticeable, but they may become infected with gonococcus, the bacterium that causes gonorrhea, or with other bacteria. When this happens, the skin around the glands may become red and swollen and the opening of the gland may be obstructed. The gland may ooze pus or, if obstructed, may swell with pus to form a Bartholin's abscess, which is usually hot and tender.

Bed rest, painkillers, ice packs or hot sitz baths, and antibiotics are used to treat the condition. If an abscess has formed, the doctor may decide to open and drain it. Often after a Bartholin's gland infection a cyst, called a Bartholin's cyst, may form. If the cysts are large enough to be bothersome, they will require treatment, usually surgical removal or creating a permanent new opening called marsupialization.

Sebaceous Cysts

Sebaceous cysts are formed when the oil-producing glands in the skin of the vulvar area are blocked. The cysts, filled with an oily material, are prone to infection and abscesses (collections of pus surrounded by inflamed tissue). If they are large and bothersome, they should be removed surgically, but usually no therapy is necessary.

Pubic Lice (Crabs)

Crabs, or *Phthirus pubis*, are body lice that live in pubic hair and sometimes in the hair on other parts of the body, by attaching themselves with crablike claws. They are about the size of a pinhead and, since they are a whitish-gray color, are just barely visible to the naked eye on light-skinned people. They live off their human hosts by sucking blood from the tiny blood vessels in the area.

Lice have a life span of about 1 month and they reproduce rapidly. The female attaches the eggs, called nits, to the side of a pubic hair, and they hatch in a week. At the age of 17 days, the lice can reproduce themselves.

Pubic lice can be spread by sexual contact with an infected person or by contact with clothing, bedding, toilet seats, or anything else that is infested with lice or their eggs. Although it is possible to have crabs without any symptoms, many people develop severe itching that scratching only intensifies. There may also be a mild rash of small blue dots, the result of bleeding in the tiny blood vessels beneath the skin.

Lice and their eggs can be eradicated with a prescription medication, which is available as a shampoo or lotion. Usually repeated applications following the physician's directions can rid the body of lice promptly. Additional treatment requires laundering or dry cleaning any materials—clothing, linen, mattresses—which may be lice-infested, or leaving everything without human contact for 2 weeks. In that time, the eggs will hatch and the lice will die because they can only survive for about 24 hours without a human to whom to attach themselves. Sexual partners should be treated also.

DISORDERS OF THE VAGINA

Warts

Genital or venereal warts (condyloma acuminatum) are very common. They are caused by the papilloma virus, and are usually transmitted by direct sexual contact. The warts, which are not painful, appear 1 to 2 months after exposure, usually on the bottom part of the vaginal opening. They may also be found on the vaginal lips, inside the vagina, on the cervix, and around the anus. They may appear as small, dark bumps, or grow to assume a cauliflowerlike appearance.

Small warts can be dried by applications of a chemical, which must be done by a doctor or trained health professional. Warts can also be removed by "freezing" (cryotherapy), or by laser surgery. They can recur if all warts are not removed, and a woman may catch them again from a sexual partner. Regular Pap smears are important for women who have had genital warts since they are associated with an increased risk of cervical cancer.

Vaginitis

Every woman normally has a slight discharge from the vagina. This discharge is made up of cells and secretions from the vaginal walls as well as cells shed from the uterus and cervix. The amount, consistency, and color of the discharge changes over the course of a woman's menstrual cycle and over the course of her lifetime. The discharge is usually a clear or milky color, and somewhat slippery; moderate in quantity, thin or watery, and with a mild odor. It may dry a slightly yellowish color on the underclothes. There is an acid/alkaline balance in the vagina, maintained by bacteria which are present in the vagina of every healthy woman. If this balance becomes upset, yeast, fungi, and other harmful organisms normally present may grow in large amounts, irritate the vaginal walls, and cause infection. At such times, there may be an abnormal discharge, mild or severe itching and burning of the vulva and chafing of the thighs and, occasionally, frequent urination.

Vaginal infections develop as a result of generally lowered resistance from lack of sleep; poor diet; infection elsewhere in the body; douching that has upset the acid/alkaline balance; birth control pills; pregnancy; hormonal changes including those resulting from birth control pills, pregnancy, and certain illnesses; antibiotics; diabetes or a prediabetic condition; or cuts, abrasions, or other irritations in the vagina.

There are a number of precautions a woman can take to avoid vaginal infections. She should:

- Keep the external genitalia clean, and dry carefully after bathing. This prevents odor more safely and effectively than douching.
- Avoid irritating sprays and soaps.
- Wear cotton underwear. Nylon underwear and tight pantyhose retain moisture and heat and aid in the growth of harmful bacteria.
- Avoid pants that are tight in the crotch and thighs.
- Wipe the anus after defecation from front to back to prevent bacteria from the anus from entering the vagina.
- Change tampons frequently; some doctors advise their patients to douche after the menstrual period is over to remove any fibers from tampons which may remain in the vagina.
- A woman who has a history of yeast infections and is taking antibiotics may want to ask her doctor to prescribe prophylactic medication to take with the antibiotics.
- Make sure that sexual partners are clean; use of a condom can provide added protection. Birth control jellies have been found to slow the growth of bacteria that cause certain forms of vaginitis.

Yeast Infections

When the acid/alkaline balance in a woman's vagina is disrupted, yeastlike organisms (such as candida or monilia) may grow in great numbers and cause a thick, white vaginal discharge. Treatment consists of local therapy, usually in the form of vaginal suppositories, creams, or powders.

Women susceptible to yeast infections may want to eat yogurt, which contains harmless bacteria that may restore the acid/alkaline balance, or ask the physician to prescribe yeast medication.

Trichomoniasis

Trichomonas is a one-celled parasite that is found in both men and women. The majority of women who have this organism in their vaginas are without symptoms. They may develop a thin, foamy vaginal discharge that is yellowish-green or gray and has a foul odor. Trichomonas can also cause urinary infection. It is most often contracted through intercourse, but can also be passed on by moist objects such as towels, bathing suits, underwear, washcloths, toilet seats, and benches in locker rooms.

Metronidazole, which causes adverse reactions in some people, is the most commonly used prescription treatment. The doctor should explain possible side effects to the patient, and the patient should report them at once if they occur. Few other drugs are available. Some doctors also advise their patients to use an acidic douche. In addition, the physician will recommend abstaining from intercourse until the infection is cured, use of a condom, or treatment of the woman's partner.

Chlamydial Infections

Chlamydia are cellular parasites that are not true bacteria and that have many of the characteristics of viruses. They cause inflammation of the urethra, the tube that conducts urine from the bladder to the outside of the body (nongonococcal urethritis) which is characterized by discharge and pain on urination. Chlamydial infection is quite common in men, and often, when a man is diagnosed as suffering from chlamydia, his sexual partner is advised to receive treatment. Similarly, persistent gonorrhealike symptoms in women may be the result of chlamydial infection. The result of chlamydial infection in women is not fully known. It may clear up spontaneously, remain in a latent state, or it may lead to pelvic inflammatory disease (PID) and even infertility. There are new tests that make chlamydia easier to diagnose than in the past; treatment involves two weeks of antibiotic therapy and then retesting to make sure the organism has been eliminated.

Nonspecific Vaginitis

Vaginal infections other than those listed above are called nonspecific (hemophilus or Gardnerella). Discharge can be white or yellow and possibly streaked with blood. Hemophilus infections seem to occur primarily during the reproductive years and are commonly transmitted through sexual intercourse. About three-quarters of women with hemophilus will be without symptoms at first, but many will develop an odorous discharge, which typically looks like a thin, grayish flour paste. Diagnosis is made by microscopic study of a smear or culture of the discharge, and treatment is usually with vaginal suppositories containing antibiotics. Sexual intercourse is usually not recommended until the infection has cleared up.

Postmenopausal Vaginitis

After menopause, when the tissues of the vagina are not being stimulated by estrogen from the ovaries, the walls of the vagina become smooth, drier, and less elastic. There is less lubrication and the entire vaginal canal shrinks. Tiny sores may appear in the vaginal wall, causing a blood-tinged discharge. There may be burning or itching and intercourse may feel uncomfortable. The dried-out skin may be easily injured, and minute cracks, prone to infection, may occur and cause nonspecific (atrophic) vaginitis. A number of treatments are used successfully, ranging from improved diet and vinegar douches to estrogen replacement therapy. Regular sexual intercourse stimulates blood flow in the area and keeps tissues supple.

Vaginal Cysts

A number of benign or noncancerous swellings can affect the vagina. The 2 most common are inclusion cysts and Gartner duct cysts.

Inclusion Cysts. Found at the lower end of the vagina, they are caused by the inclusion of little tags of skin beneath the surface of the skin, usually as the result of imperfect healing of surgical scars, tears, or lacerations acquired during childbirth or through injury. Occasionally, they occur near the top of the vagina as a hysterectomy scar. Small, with rather cheeselike contents, they may cause no problems. If they do, they may be removed surgically.

Gartner Duct Cysts. These cysts are the most common form of vaginal tumor and arise from the remnants of an embryonic organ called the Gartner duct. They may remain small and trouble-free, or they may become so large as to bulge from the vaginal opening. They are treated the same way as inclusion cysts.

DES-Induced Changes

Beginning in 1940, the synthetic hormone DES was given to probably millions of pregnant women in the United States to help prevent miscarriage, premature birth, and other pregnancy problems. Although it has since been shown that the drugs were of no real value in preventing these problems, the result of their use was that a small number of the daughters of these women developed a rare form of vaginal cancer, clear cell adenocarcinoma (see Chapter 20 on Cancer, page 412), while others developed less serious cervical, uterine, and vaginal abnormalities, including vaginal adenosis. We are now learning that there may be some pregnancy-related problems in some of these young women.

Vaginal Adenosis. This is a condition in which the glandular tissue that normally lies in the cervical canal is found in the vaginal cavity. It is due to a birth defect apparently engendered by the mothers of these daughters having taken DES during their pregnancies. Between 30 and 90 percent of DES daughters have this disorder. It tends to occur in young women, and the discharge caused by the disease may be mistaken for an irregularly established menstrual period. The ultimate effect on the fertility of these women is not yet known, but studies suggest that these women have more than average difficulty in becoming pregnant and carrying a pregnancy to term. The greatest concern about vaginal adenosis is what its relationship may be to cancer.

Loss of Pelvic Support

Fallen or prolapsed bladder (cystocele), and fallen or prolapsed urethra (urethrocele) indicate that these organs have dropped down from their normal positions and bulged into the vagina. These conditions may be due to a defect in the supportive tissue or to an injury connected with childbirth, and they occur most frequently in older women or those who have borne a number of children.

A woman with these conditions may have no symptoms, or she may experience a feeling of pelvic fullness or discomfort when bearing down. She may feel a bulge in the vaginal wall nearest the bladder and urethra, or may actually see a bulge at the vaginal opening. The symptoms are aggravated by standing for a long time. If the bladder or urethra extends far down, it may be uncomfortable to sit or walk, and sometimes the exposed tissues may become inflamed. There may be difficulty emptying the bladder and a woman may frequently feel the need to urinate. The urine that stays in the bladder provides a breeding ground for bacteria, and infections may develop. It also may become difficult to control the flow of urine, and sudden movements like coughs or sneezes may result in leaking.

The condition is not usually difficult to diagnose, and if there are no repeated urinary infections, and no particular discomfort, there may be no rush to treat it. Surgical repair is best done after a woman has had all of the children she wants. Sometimes special exercise can help make the repair and avoid surgery altogether.

Rectocele and Enterocele

Prolapse of the rectum, when the lower rectum bulges into the back wall of the vagina, and prolapse of the small intestine, when part of it may bulge into the upper part of the vagina, are a result of weakness in the tissues that support the organs and hold them in place. The weakness may be due to labor and delivery, aging, or sometimes congenital (inherited) weakness of that area. Often the conditions occur together. Rectoceles usually do not require surgical

correction, although it may be recommended for larger ones. The enterocele is somewhat more serious, since a loop of intestine may get caught in the bulge that protrudes into the vagina and interfere with proper blood supply to the intestines.

Prolapse of the Vagina, Uterus, and Cervix

Prolapses, or displacements of these organs from their normal position, caused by injuries to the supporting tissues (usually during childbirth), may not cause symptoms at all. (See figures 37.3 and 37.4.) Some women, however, will experience a heavy, bearing down sensation in their vaginas, and the sensation is aggravated when they have been standing all day. Treatment is either surgical repair or prescription of a device known as a vaginal pessary that may help alleviate the symptoms. The pessary fits around the cervix at the top of the vagina and helps prop up the prolapsed organs. It must be sized properly and kept clean.

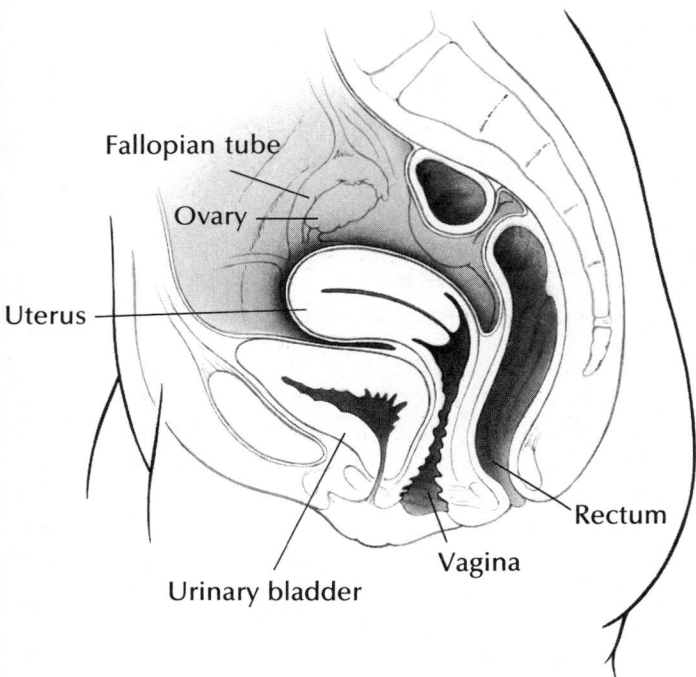

Figure 37.3. **Normal position of the uterus.**

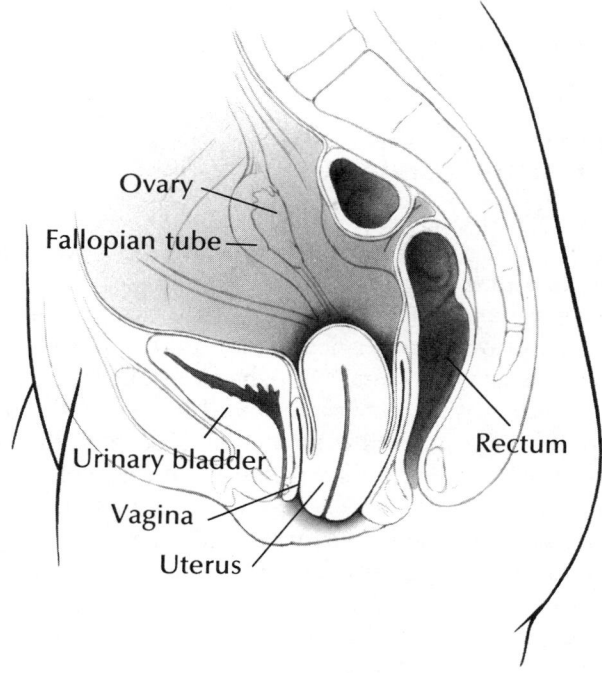

Figure 37.4. **Prolapsed, or tipped, uterus.**

DISORDERS OF THE CERVIX

THERE ARE 2 types of tissues in the cervix, each of which normally has its own place, and the 2 nor-

mally meet at 1 point. Sometimes these 2 types of tissues are displaced, or fail to meet each other, or become infected, or torn. When any of these occur, cervical disorders develop.

Cervicitis

This is a general term for inflammations of the cervix, which may be chronic or may result from a number of causes. Most of the time, cervicitis is associated with conditions of the vaginal cavity or other female organs. Some researchers say that many cases of cervicitis are due to infections caused by tears or lacerations to the cervix sustained during childbirth. With acute cervicitis, there is noticeable pus-filled discharge that may be clear, grayish, or yellow. If other organs are involved in the infection, there may be urinary frequency, urgency and pain, or burning and itching of the external genitalia. Cervicitis due to a tear or laceration will have less discharge. Since the condition can be caused by a number of organisms, the physician will try to identify it and will treat it with an appropriate antibiotic or sulfa drug. Care must be taken to keep the area clean. Sexual intercourse should be avoided until the condition clears up.

Cervical Erosion and Cervical Eversion

In cervical erosion, some of the cells on the surface of the cervical opening (os) have been worn away and the glandular surface of the cervix exposed—similar to what happens when skin on the outside of the body is grazed. In cervical eversion, the tissue that lines the cervical canal is pushed to the outer, vaginal portion of the cervix, and will protrude slightly into the vagina. Some women are born with this condition; many others will have some cervical erosion during their lives. Since its cause has not been precisely identified, treatment will vary, depending on what the doctor thinks is the cause. Some physicians treat erosions and eversions with drugs; others will destroy the eroded, everted tissue with electric cautery or by freezing the tissue off with cryosurgery. Others do tests to determine whether the erosion has abnormal cells, and if it does not, they leave it alone.

Cervical Polyps

Polyps are small protrusions that grow from a mucous membrane and tend to recur. In the cervix, polyps are tear-shaped growths with stems that grow from the mucous membranes of the cervical canal. Only rarely are they cancerous. Polyps may be caused as part of the body's effort to heal itself after the cervix has been injured, or they may be formed by hormonal secretions during pregnancy. Small polyps generally don't cause symptoms; larger ones do because they can be irritated by douching, intercourse, pelvic examinations, or straining when going to the bathroom. They may cause bleeding between periods or heavier periods, and they may block the passage of sperm, or be associated with infection, making it difficult for a woman to conceive. Polyps are treated by surgical removal, which may be done in a doctor's office. If there are a great many polyps, or they are very thick, hospitalization may be required.

Nabothian Cysts

When the glandular tissue in the cervix is trapped under regrowth of new tissue, cysts can develop. The new tissue may result from overgrowth of the tissue that lines the inside of the cervix onto the tissue that covers the outer portion of the cervix. Cysts may also be formed in older women, whose cervical tissue thins out and traps natural secretions. The cysts generally do not become infected unless the entire cervix is infected. They rarely require treatment, although some physicians choose to remove them through cauterization or cryosurgery.

Cervical Dysplasia (and Carcinoma *in situ*)

This condition results from abnormal development of the cells of the cervix. Most authorities consider cervical dysplasia and carcinoma *in situ* conditions conducive to the development of cervical cancer, the first step in a continuing process of abnormal cell changes that continue to progress over the years. Cervical dysplasia and carcinoma *in situ* is most frequently found in women aged 25 to 35, but it can also occur in women in their teen years or early twenties, and in older women as well. A Pap smear will reveal abnormal cell growth.

After one abnormal Pap smear, the smear will be repeated. If the results reveal abnormalities, the patient will undergo an office procedure called colposcopy and a tissue sample (biopsy) is taken for microscopic study. If the biopsy is negative, the woman should still be closely followed and another smear done in 6 months. Dysplasia may be treated by removal of the affected tissue (cone biopsy), cryosurgery, laser surgery, or occasionally hysterectomy. Follow-up after these procedures is important, lest the dysplasia recur or progress. (For more information, see Chapter 20 on Cancer, page 412.)

DISORDERS OF THE UTERUS AND FALLOPIAN TUBES

SEVERAL TYPES OF DISORDERS can affect the uterus and Fallopian tubes: infections that include the uterus and other organs in the pelvic cavity, conditions related to the lining of the uterus, distortions of the normal anatomy, either from birth or as a condition that develops when the woman is grown; and abnormal growths, which may be noncancerous or malignant.

Endometriosis

The endometrium is a special tissue that grows in the lining of the uterus each month to nourish a fertilized egg. If no egg is implanted, the endometrium is sloughed off (through menstruation). Endometriosis occurs when endometrial tissue grows somewhere besides the lining of the uterus, usually somewhere else in the genital tract, although the condition has been known to occur in other parts of the body. (See figure 37.5.)

Endometriosis most frequently occurs in women of childbearing age, and pelvic pain during menstruation is its most common initial symptom. Women who have had relatively pain-free periods in the past begin to develop steady, dull discomfort during their periods. Sometimes there is lower abdominal pain which starts just before the menstrual period.

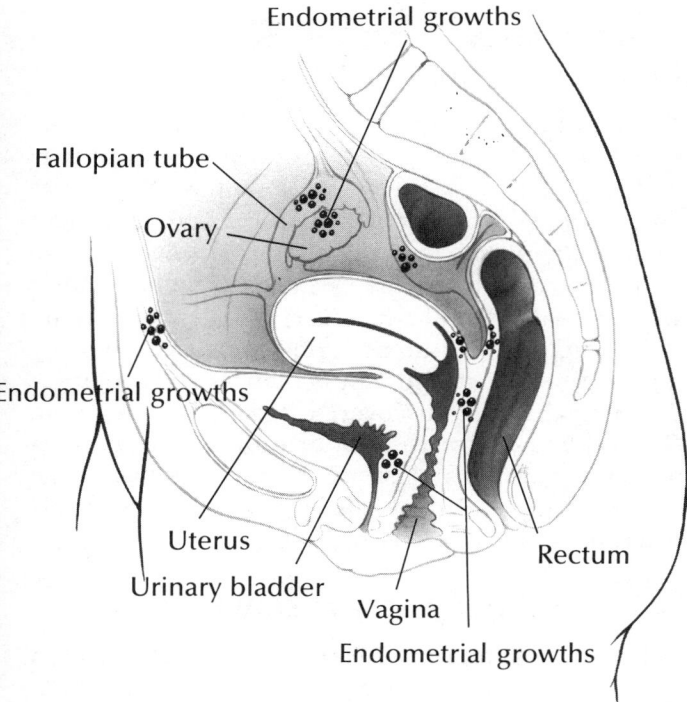

Endometrial growths

Fallopian tube

Ovary

Endometrial growths

Uterus

Urinary bladder

Vagina

Endometrial growths

Rectum

Figure 37.5. **Endometriosis, in which tissue that normally grows inside the uterus grows in other parts of the pelvic cavity or internal structures.**

Women who have endometriosis frequently have abnormal menstrual bleeding, and infertility is also common. When endometrial tissue is present in other parts of the pelvis, the body may respond by developing self-protective cysts over the misplaced tissue. Over time, responding to hormones, the endometrial tissue sloughs off. Eventually the cysts may burst and there may be abnormal bleeding of dark brown blood which has been collected over a period of time, causing severe pain. Swelling of the cysts is also responsible for much of the pain associated with endometriosis.

In response to irritation from the misplaced tissue and the cysts, the body may also form bands of fibrous material that seal over the ruptured cyst. Building of fibrous material can cause adhesions that literally stick the organs together. Endometriosis can affect individual reproductive organs or all of them and the rectum and intestines as well. Single nodules of endometrial tissue may be found in scars from operations and childbirth. Rarely, endometrial tissue migrates to the lungs or other parts of the body.

Diagnosis of endrometriosis is difficult to make without a visual examination of the pelvic organs. This is done by the physician who makes a small abdominal incision and inserts a lighted viewing instrument called a laparoscope.

Endometriosis treatment depends on many factors, including age and health of the patient, the severity of symptoms, and location and extent of the endometriosis. It is treated conservatively, especially in older women, since menopause and the reduction of estrogen production affects remission of the symptoms. Treatment with hormones and surgical removal of the endometrial material or the organs themselves is also done.

Adenomyosis

This is a condition in which the endometrial tissue, which usually sloughs off every month during the menstrual period, is instead found growing into the inner muscle wall of the uterus. It is most often found in women in their later childbearing years who have already had children. A woman may have adenomyosis and be symptom-free, with the condition being noted only when the uterus is removed for other reasons. Among those who have symptoms, the chief ones are abnormal menstrual bleeding and menstrual pain.

Diagnosis is usually based on uterine enlargement and cramplike uterine pain that persists throughout the period, becoming worse as the woman gets older. The disease is related to hormone production and is relieved once menopause takes place. Painkillers and patience are the most conservative treatment. If the pain is extreme and menopause far away, surgery may be indicated to remove the uterus and possibly the Fallopian tubes and ovaries.

Endometrial Polyps

Polyps or soft outgrowths in the endometrial tissue within the uterus are generally small, and may grow singly or in clusters. Most common in women of menopausal age, endometrial polyps may cause no symptoms and may only be found in the course of another operation. Or they may cause abnormal bleeding between periods, or occasionally protrude through the cervical opening and be seen by the gynecologist during an examination. Polyps that grow this way may produce cramping because they are expanding the cervical opening. Polyps that protrude may be injured and bleed, or may be twisted and lose their blood supply. Infection can result, and there may be a foul-smelling discharge. These protruding polyps are generally removed with dilation of the cervix and curettage (scraping with a blunt instrument).

Infertility may occasionally be traced to polyps that block the passage of sperm. Cancerous polyps are extremely rare.

Fibroids

As noncancerous tumors of the uterus, fibroids (Leiomyomata) grow in the thick muscular uterine wall. They are thought to be very common in women over the age of 30, and less common in young women. They usually shrink after menopause. In pregnant women and those on birth control pills, the rate of fibroid growth may be accelerated, as fibroids appear to be related to hormonal activity. Black women are somewhat more susceptible to fibroids at an earlier age.

Fibroids may have no symptoms and may only be discovered by the gynecologist during a pelvic examination. Symptoms depend on where in the uterus the fibroids are growing. There may be disturbances in urination, severe menstrual pain, excessive menstrual bleeding, and sometimes infertility.

Most fibroids do not require treatment, particularly if a woman is near menopause. But all fibroids should be carefully followed up with regular checkups. If a fibroid continues to grow, or is sufficiently symptomatic, it will require treatment. A malignant fibroid is rare.

Surgical treatment of uterine fibroids is either removal of the fibroids (myomectomy) or removal of the uterus (hysterectomy), depending on the woman's age, condition, and whether her family is complete.

Endometrial Hyperplasia

An abnormal condition in which the endometrial lining has grown too thick, endometrial hyperplasia usually occurs at the beginning or end of a woman's reproductive years. The predominant form, cystic hyperplasia, is benign. If laboratory examination of a sample of endometrial tissue reveals this type of hyperplasia, a few months on birth control pills may make the menstrual cycle more regular and take care of the problem. Dilatation and curettage (D&C) may be performed on an older woman, and no further treatment will be necessary. But if the laboratory report indicates *adenomatous hyperplasia*, more treatment is necessary. This type of hyperplasia is associated with endometrial cancer. Hysterectomy is the usual method of treatment, possibly accompanied by removal of the ovaries and Fallopian tubes. Sometimes hormone therapy is used instead, with the understanding that this places the woman at risk of having undetected cancer develop. (For more information, see Chapter 20 on Cancer, page 412.)

Congenital Abnormalities of the Uterus or Fallopian Tubes

The reproductive organs, like any other organ system, are sometimes affected by congenital abnormalities. There may be duplications or partial duplications of internal structures, or structures such as the uterus may be missing or misshapen so that they cannot support pregnancy. No one knows why these abnormalities occur; those that cause no symptoms and that do not interfere with pregnancy may not be discovered unless there is an autopsy at death or they are discovered during an operation. Generally, a doctor will not operate to correct uterine abnormalities unless all other causes have been ruled out and a woman is having problems with fertility, pregnancy, or giving birth.

Pelvic Inflammatory Disease (PID)

In Pelvic Inflammatory Disease, a bacterial infection enters the uterus and may spread to the Fallopian tubes, ovaries, and other tissues in the pelvic region.

The infection may be sexually transmitted and is usually secondary to gonorrhea, chlamydia, or use of an IUD, but it may also develop without obvious cause.

The patient may experience pain in one or both sides of the lower abdomen, pain during intercourse, fever, irregularities in the menstrual period, and possibly a heavy and odorous discharge. Untreated, PID can result in blocking of the Fallopian tubes, causing possible infertility and ectopic pregnancies. In rare cases, the bacteria may enter the bloodstream and cause blood poisoning (septicemia), peritonitis, and inflammation of the joints.

Antibiotics are the usual treatment for PID, along with pain relief, bed rest, and short hospitalization. The complications may require surgery.

DISORDERS OF THE OVARIES

Polycystic Ovaries (Stein-Leventhal Syndrome)

Under normal circumstances, follicles deep within the ovaries are stimulated to grow, mature, and rise to the surface of the ovary, where they burst and release an egg to the Fallopian tube, a process controlled by pituitary hormones. The remnants of the burst follicle then begin to produce progesterone, which stimulates the lining of the uterus (the endometrium) to grow thicker in case it needs to support a fertilized egg. The effect on the pituitary of an increase in progesterone production is to signal it to stop stimulating the development of eggs.

In polycystic disease, the follicles never erupt from the ovaries. They grow just under the ovaries' surface, and are produced again and again because the pituitary has not been signaled to shut off. Both ovaries become filled with tiny cysts and can become enlarged. A thickened capsule also grows to encase the ovary.

Polycystic disease is most common in women under 30. Symptoms include irregular menstrual periods, infertility (because there is no ovulation), abnormal hair growth, and excessive weight gain. The doctor will probably be able to feel enlarged ovaries, as well. Hormone assessment tests may be done, since patients with polycystic disease have characteristic hormone patterns. Treatment may be with hormones, the effect of which will be to stimulate the development of a normal menstrual cycle, as well as with fertility drugs. Although rare, surgery to reduce the bulk of the ovaries may be undertaken.

Benign Cysts and Tumors

Ovarian tumors may not produce symptoms at all. Some women may experience pain on intercourse and, as the tumor grows, feel pressure or fullness in the abdomen or pelvis. If there is pressure from the tumor on the bladder or bowels, irregularities in their function may be noticed. They can also block blood or lymph channels and cause varicose veins, hemorrhoids, and swelling of the legs or vulva. If they grow large enough, they can displace the uterus.

Ovarian tumors can cause irregularities in the menstrual cycle, and some of them produce hormones that give the patient increased female hormones or masculinizing characteristics. Occasionally an ovarian tumor may twist on its pedicle, resulting in pain, and the possibility that the blood supply to the tumor will be cut off. When this happens, the areas of the tumor that die will give rise to infection, swelling, and pain.

Cysts may also rupture during intercourse, a fall, childbirth, or surgery. The body may produce self-protective bands of tissue (adhesions) where the tumor's irritating contents have accumulated. If there is bleeding into the pelvic cavity from a ruptured cyst, the consequences may be very serious. This is not, however, a common occurrence.

Ovarian tumors are sometimes difficult to diagnose. It is not always clear whether the mass that the physician feels on examination is attached to the ovary, to some other organ, or is, perhaps, merely a full bladder. (Women should urinate before a pelvic examination as a matter of course.) It is also difficult to determine whether an ovarian tumor is benign or malignant without operating on it. A pathologist may need to examine the tissue removed, while the surgeon examines the rest of the woman's internal organs for any signs of malignancy. In young women who want children, the surgeon will make every effort to save the ovary. In older women, it is usually removed. If this is a concern, the woman and her doctor should discuss this before surgery takes place.

Physiologic Cysts (Functional Cysts)

Two types of cysts can develop which are exaggerations of the normal ovarian process in women during their reproductive years:

Follicle cysts occur when the chosen follicle within the ovary fails to release its ovum and continues to swell into a self-contained collection of fluid within the ovary or on its surface.

Corpus luteum cysts result from an irregularity in the hormone-producing corpus luteum, the burst follicle on the surface of the ovary which contained the ovum.

Normally, when pregnancy does not take place, the corpus luteum disintegrates. Instead, in this case, it swells with fluid and remains on the surface of the ovary as a cyst. Sometimes the small amount of bleeding that occurs when the corpus luteum bursts during its normal process is greater than usual and the cyst becomes filled with blood, called corpus luteum hematoma.

These cysts are small, so symptoms may not be as clear as with ovarian cysts. But they may also burst, causing pain. When this happens, laparoscopic examination of the ovaries is often the only way to differentiate between a burst physiologic cyst and a ruptured ectopic pregnancy.

Functioning Cysts (Hormone-Producing Tumors)

This type of ovarian tumor produces hormones that exhibit masculinizing or feminizing symptoms, or simulate the characteristic body changes of pregnancy. The more rare are the *masculinizing ovarian tumors* which induce absence of menstrual periods, decrease in the size of the breasts, loss of rounded contours of the figure, facial, and chest hair, deepening of the voice, and increase in the size of the clitoris. Once the tumor is removed, symptoms disappear.

There are a number of types of *feminizing tumors*. They may cause precocious (very early) puberty in young girls, abnormal uterine bleeding, or irregular periods. A large number of women with feminizing tumors also have endometrial hyperplasia. *Dysgerminomas* produce hormones associated with pregnancy and may result in an enlarged uterus and an absence of menstrual periods.

DISORDERS OF THE URINARY TRACT

Cystitis

Cystitis, or urinary tract infection (UTI), is so common that 1 in 5 women has it at least once and some women have repeated bouts of the annoying disorder. Cystitis results from bacteria entering the urinary tract opening just outside the vagina, and traveling to the bladder. Its symptoms include the frequent, urgent need to urinate; burning on urination, sometimes accompanied by a gnawing pain above the pubic bone; and, occasionally, blood in the urine.

The frequency of cystitis in women is the result of several factors: Women's lower urinary tracts (urethras) are short—not more than a few inches— and bacteria can be easily introduced into the bladder. (Men's urinary tracts tend to be considerably longer, giving the bacteria a considerably greater distance to travel.) The urinary opening is located at the site of intercourse, and bacteria may be introduced by the partner's penis; the anus is nearby and fecal bacteria may be introduced into the vagina and then into the urinary tract. If a woman does not urinate frequently or does not completely empty the bladder, the natural contents of urine provide an excellent breeding ground for bacteria.

Other common causes of cystitis include an improperly fitted diaphragm which causes irritation and infection, congenital abnormalities, foreign bodies—such as a catheter—in the bladder, and lowered resistance from illness, stress, fatigue, medication, or other medical procedures. In addition, pregnancy, labor, and delivery provide conditions for development of cystitis: pressure on the bladder from the pregnant uterus, incomplete urination, introduction of bacteria. Some women, during pregnancy, have asymptomatic cystitis which becomes apparent only by a culture.

Cystitis is readily diagnosed through urinalysis and culture, with the patient following special procedures to ensure the cleanliness of the specimen. The condition is ordinarily not serious and responds to a short course of antibiotic treatment. Most physicians prescribe drugs to be taken over 5 to 14 days.

During a bout with cystitis, the patient should avoid food and drinks that may irritate the bladder. These include coffee, tea, juices with high citric acid content, cola, alcoholic beverages, chocolate, and spices. She should drink 6 to 8 glasses of water per day to cleanse the bladder and urinary tract.

Some women drink cranberry juice or take vitamin C to prevent or help relieve cystitis. Both are excellent acidifiers of the urine and are useful for this reason. However, making the urine acidic can interfere with the action of the medication and cranberry juice has considerable sugar content, and vitamin C should be taken only in recommended amounts. It may be more healthful and less expensive just to drink double the usual amount of water.

If cystitis has not cleared up within a week, the physician may change the medication, or if a woman has recurrent episodes, the doctor may recommend that she be treated by a urologist.

To help prevent cystitis, a woman should:

1. Keep the vaginal area clean, including wiping from the front to the back after a bowel movement to prevent contamination of the urinary tract.

2. Use tampons, changed every 3 to 4 hours, instead of sanitary pads. (The pads can act as a culture medium for fecal bacteria, which may then be rubbed against the urinary outlet and invade the bladder.)

3. Wear cotton undergarments, which allow air circulation and discourage the warm, moist environment that is needed for bacteria growth. Nylon pantyhose should have a cotton crotch.

4. Avoid tight clothes in the genital area, such as controltop pantyhose and skin-tight jeans, as well as extended wearing of a wet bathing suit.

5. Urinate before and after intercourse and make sure her partner's hands and penis are clean.

6. Drink plenty of fluids and urinate as frequently as the need arises.

Stress Incontinence

Women have a sheet of muscles at the base of the abdomen known as the pelvic floor muscles. These muscles support the bladder and close at the top of the urethra, the short tube through which urine passes. Some degree of weakening of these muscles can easily occur due to childbirth or aging.

When a woman with weakened pelvic-floor muscles puts stress on them from laughing, coughing, or lifting, for example, she may urinate a little. If the annoying condition persists or becomes troublesome, she should consult her doctor. There will be tests to determine whether infection is present. If not, the condition is usually treated with exercises to strengthen the pelvic-floor muscles. Surgery to repair them is commonly necessary. Pessaries will rarely improve stress incontinence.

Irritable Bladder

Sometimes a woman's bladder contracts uncontrollably, giving her the urge to urinate. She may do so before she reaches the bathroom, or may have to get up frequently at night to urinate. The cause of this urge incontinence is most commonly related to a chronic inflammation of the bladder and may occur in connection with stress incontinence, prolapse of the uterus, or an infection of the urinary tract. (See Cystitis, above.)

After the patient consults her physician and it is determined that the condition is not due to infection, irritable bladder is usually treated with exercises to strengthen the bladder muscles. Drugs are also sometimes used to reduce the bladder spasms.

38 Disorders Common to Men

Harris M. Nagler, M.D., and Carl A. Olsson, M.D.

INTRODUCTION

IN MEN, even more so than in women, the organs of urine excretion and the organs of reproduction are intricately interrelated and are commonly referred to as the genitourinary system. The organs of the urinary system include the kidneys, the ureters, the bladder, and the urethra, and their main function is the production and excretion of urine in order to rid the body of waste products. The organs of the male genital system include the prostate, the seminal vesicles, the penis and, contained in the scrotum, the testicles, epididymides, and vasa deferentia.

Urology is the branch of medicine dedicated to the study and treatment of maladies of both systems. Urologists, who have postgraduate training in surgery, have been referred to as "gynecologists for men," because both specialties deal with the organs of procreation in their respective patients. However, the urologist also deals with diseases of the urinary tract and, indeed, many diseases of the genitourinary system occur in women. In fact, with alterations in social habits and mores, certain urologic diseases are occurring more frequently in women than in the past. For instance, the increased rate of smoking in women has led to an increased incidence of bladder cancer in women. Therefore, it is appropriate to consider the urologist as a physician dealing with the diseases of the urinary tract in both males and females and, in addition, with disorders of the male reproductive and sexual organs.

ORGANS OF THE URINARY TRACT

URINE FORMATION begins in the kidneys, a pair of organs located behind the abdominal cavity and beneath the rib cage on either side of the spine. As the body's cells break down the food we eat and release energy from it, they also produce chemical by-products, which collect in the bloodstream. The kidneys cleanse the blood of these waste products and excess water, forming urine, which is then transported to the bladder. (Because the kidneys are complex and subject to a number of disorders, they are covered more completely in Chapter 30 on Kidney Diseases, page 602.)

The ureters, 2 thin, muscular tubes leading from the center of each kidney, transport the urine formed in the kidney to the bladder by means of active waves of contractions (peristalsis). The urine is emptied into the bladder, a muscular pouch that temporarily stores and then excretes it from the body. Because the walls of the bladder are elastic, the bladder can expand as it fills with urine and contract forcefully as it empties itself of the stored urine.

Although infants empty their bladders involuntarily, without control of the brain, urination (or voiding) becomes a voluntary function as the brain and nervous system develop. Continence, or bladder control, is a complex event that requires bladder relaxation as well as proper functioning of the sphincter that controls its opening and closing. These functions are coordinated, and loss of control of either component may result in incontinence.

From the bladder, urine is carried out of the body by a thin tube called the urethra. In the female, the urethra is about 1 inch long and is situated in front of the vaginal wall, ending in the vulvar area. Because the urethra is so short and located so close to the vagina and the anus, women are more susceptible than men to contamination of the urinary tract with bacteria, and thus to urinary infections. The male urethra is much longer, traveling through the prostate gland and then through the undersurface of the penis to an opening in the tip of the glans (or head of the penis). This opening is called the urethral meatus.

THE MALE GENITAL SYSTEM

THE MALE GENITAL SYSTEM comprises the prostate, the seminal vesicles, the penis, and the scrotum with its contents, the testicles. (See figure 38.1.) Although the prostate serves no purpose in the urinary system, the normal growth of this gland may interfere with the passage of urine. The prostate does secrete various fluids that contribute to the formation of se-men—the fluid in which sperm is ejaculated during orgasm. The prostate is also the source of an enzyme called prostatic acid phosphatase. Measurements of this enzyme have been widely touted as the "male Pap test" for cancer of the prostate. Although the test can be useful in monitoring the course of prostate cancer, it has no value as a screening test and

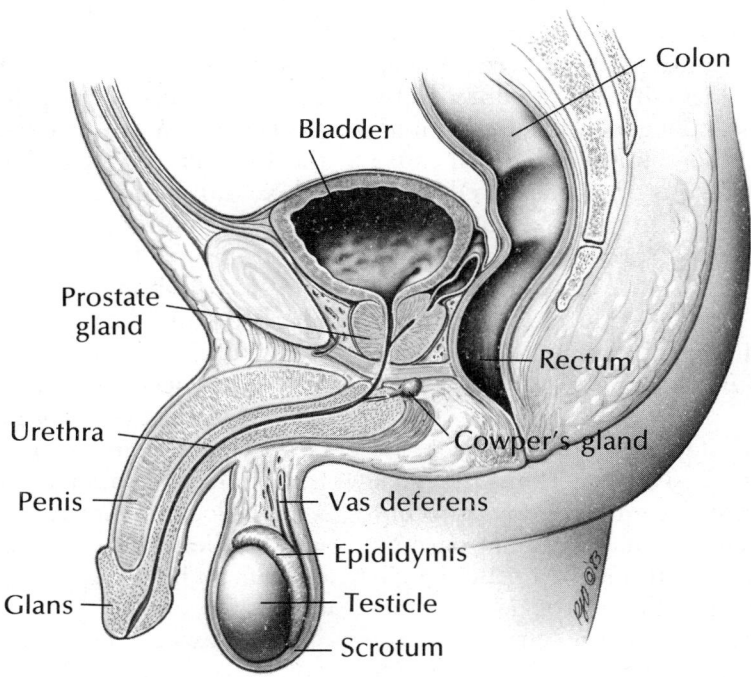

Figure 38.1. **The male genitourinary organs.**

does not supplant the need for annual examination of the prostate in men over the age of 40. The prostate normally enlarges (hypertrophies) with age and may eventually interfere with the flow of urine through the urethra.

The penis has 2 major functions—as an organ to transport urine and as a sexual organ—and specialized structures within it aid in these functions. The urethra, which travels within a cylindrical structure on the undersurface of the penis, transports urine and semen. Two other cylindrical struc-

tures forming the bulk of the penis aid in sexual function by filling with blood (engorging) during sexual arousal. (For more detail, see Chapter 10 on Sexual and Reproductive Health, page 136.)

Behind the base of the penis is the scrotum, a pendulous sac containing testicles, which produce both sperm and the male hormone, testosterone. Each testicle is suspended from a cordlike structure containing blood vessels and a muscular tube called the vas deferens, which carries the sperm from the testicles to the urethra.

SYMPTOMS OF URINARY PROBLEMS

CHANGES IN URINE COLOR, as well as difficulty or pain in passing it, are often among the first signs of a urinary infection or other disorder of the urinary tract. Urine is normally crystal clear and yellow, although the intensity of the color may vary from colorless to dark amber. These variations may be entirely normal and are usually dependent on the amount of fluid consumed and on environmental factors such as extreme heat, which tends to cause dehydration. Normally, the more fluid an individual drinks, the more diluted and lighter the urine becomes. Conversely, the less fluid the individual drinks or the more that is lost through perspiration, the more concentrated and darker the color.

Variations in color should not be a source of alarm. Extreme darkening of the urine, however, may indicate a more serious problem. Hepatitis or liver inflammation can cause urine to become deep orange in color, and will usually be accompanied by pale bowel movements and a general feeling of malaise. Small amounts of blood in the urine will cause the urine to become tea-colored. Tea-colored urine always represents the possibility of a serious disease in the urinary tract, and should never be disregarded by the individual. For example, the development of tea-colored urine soon after a sore throat or upper respiratory illness may indicate a kidney problem that requires an immediate evaluation by a kidney specialist.

The cardinal manifestation of urologic disease is bloody urine, or *hematuria*. This is perhaps the most alarming sign to the patient, and requires prompt diagnosis and treatment. Hematuria may or may not be associated with pain. It may be initial, i.e., in the first portion of the urination, or in the last (terminal) portion, or throughout the entire stream (total). Information from the patient about the pattern of hematuria may help the physician to make an appropriate diagnosis.

Pneumaturia, or air bubbles in the urine, is another sign of trouble. The air bubbles may actually be seen or may be noted by the sensation of air passing through the urethra. They may be the result of an infection caused by a gas-producing bacteria or of an abnormal connection between the bowel and the bladder. *Cloudy urine* may be another sign of a urinary tract infection.

Difficulties associated with the process of urination are also indications of urinary disease. In healthy adults, the bladder stores and expels urine voluntarily and without pain. *Pain* associated with urination (strangury) may indicate an abnormal blockage within the bladder or urethra; *burning* on urination (dysuria) generally indicates a urinary tract infection.

When the bladder is filled, the urge to urinate is perceived. Normally, adults are able to suppress the desire to urinate until they encounter an appropriate setting. When urination is voluntarily initiated, the bladder contracts forcefully and the sphincter relaxes, allowing forceful expulsion of the urine.

The *frequency* of urination is dictated by the consumption of fluids as well as by the production of fluid by the body. Normally, the bladder can hold nearly a pint of urine. The full content of the bladder is expelled with each act of urination. Frequency refers to the need to urinate more often than usual. It may be a sign of incomplete emptying of the bladder (see Urinary Retention), a bladder infection, a direct irritation of the bladder (such as a bladder stone), or a neurologic abnormality. Occasionally frequency will be the result of an abnormally high production of urine, which may be due to a kidney problem or diabetes.

Even when the desire to urinate frequently cannot be controlled, the individual acts of urination are usually controlled. The inability to store urine and to void voluntarily is called *incontinence* and may be the result of a urinary tract infection such as cystitis, of neurologic abnormalities (multiple sclerosis, spinal cord trauma, birth defects), of anatomic abnormalities, or of surgical procedures.

Urinary *retention*, the inability to empty the bladder of its stored urine, is a more urgent problem. Oftentimes, urinary retention is excruciatingly painful. Relief is obtained by allowing the urine to drain through a catheter (a rubber or silicon tube) inserted into the bladder via the urethra. Men are afflicted with urinary retention more often than women, most commonly because of an enlarged prostate. However, urethral stenosis or strictures—areas of narrowing or scarring—are other frequently encountered causes, and may be found in both sexes.

Sometimes urinary retention is insidious, with progressively larger volumes of urine being retained within the bladder (chronic urinary retention). Ironically, what often brings the patient to the doctor in this case is incontinence: The bladder capacity is overwhelmed and small amounts of urine will continuously leak, a condition known as *overflow incontinence*.

Bladder stones (vesical calculi) are most often found in conjunction with chronic urinary retention. If they are small, they may be easily passed during urination. Larger ones may cause pain (strangury) and sometimes blood on urination (hematuria), or an abruptly interrupted urinary stream. The underlying cause of bladder stone formation, such as outlet obstruction due to growth of the prostate, must be dealt with to prevent recurrence.

In addition to a physical examination to evaluate the cause of urinary incontinence or retention, the urologist may also perform special diagnostic procedures, such as a cystoscopy and urodynamic studies. During cystoscopy a telescopelike instrument called a cystoscope is inserted through the urethra, allowing the urologist to visualize the lower urinary tract. Urodynamic studies involve filling the bladder with specific amounts of fluid or carbon dioxide to determine if the bladder responds normally. (For more information, see Chapter 4 on Diagnostic Tests and Procedures, page 71.)

DISORDERS OF THE GENITOURINARY TRACT

EVERY PART of the genitourinary tract is susceptible to infection. Factors predisposing to recurrent infections vary according to age, sex, and environment, but most involve abnormal drainage of the urine from parts of the urinary system. In children, this may be due to congenital areas of narrowing which prevent the urine from draining from the kidney (congenital ureteropelvic obstruction) or to abnormal backflow of urine from the bladder to the kidney (ureterovesical reflux). In older men, an enlarged prostate results in failure of the bladder to empty, which may predispose to infection. Kidney stones may also prevent proper drainage from the kidney and may lead to infection.

Urologists attempt to differentiate between upper and lower urinary tract infections, which tend to have very different long-term outcomes. Infections of the lower urinary tract, though sometimes frustratingly difficult to treat, rarely cause long-term difficulties. The symptoms are generally more localized than those of upper urinary tract infections. Most commonly they are manifested by frequency (the need to urinate immediately after urination), burning or painful urination, bloody urine, and, occasionally, an uncontrollable urge to urinate (urgency incontinence). Rarely do patients with simple lower urinary tract infections have fever and chills.

An upper urinary tract infection (specifically a kidney infection), on the other hand, is usually accompanied by fever, chills, flank or back pain, and malaise. Patients with these infections generally look quite ill and debilitated. (Kidney infections, known as pyelonephritis, are discussed in Chapter 30 on Kidney Diseases, page 604.)

Bladder and Urethra

Cystitis. Because the bladder is located completely within the body, it normally is not subject to external bacterial infection. In fact, the bladder lining is resistant to the development of infections and the urine is normally sterile. However, the bladder drains externally via the urethra and the site where the urethra opens (especially in women) is a breeding ground for bacteria which, under certain circumstances, can work their way up to the bladder.

Women are especially prone to cystitis because the female urethra is shorter and bacteria haven't as far to travel. In fact, bacteria around the female urethral meatus may be inoculated into the urethra (and, thence, gain access to the bladder) during normal activities such as wiping, or sexual intercourse, because of the female urethra's location within the vulvar region. (For more information, see Chapter 37 on Disorders Common to Women, page 754.)

Cystitis in men is quite different from the disease in women. Unlike women, who can develop infections with no anatomic abnormality, infections in men are most often secondary to some other abnormality, such as prostate enlargement, stone disease, or the retention of large amounts of residual urine in the bladder after urination. Symptoms include frequency of urination and dysuria; the urine may be cloudy, foul-smelling and, occasionally, bloody. There may be associated lower abdominal pain and slight fever. Although antibiotics will usually take care of the bacterial infection, it is apt to recur if the underlying cause is not diagnosed and treated.

Urethritis. Urethritis is an inflammation of the urethra generally associated with a urethral discharge, ranging in color and consistency from thin and clear to thick and creamy yellow. The major symptoms are urinary frequency and pain on urination or ejaculation. Urethritis may be due to infection or nonspecific irritants. Specific, identified causes of urethritis include venereally transmitted diseases such as gonorrhea and chlamydia. Gonorrhea organisms are relatively easily identified by culture techniques. Chlamydia is an organism that is difficult to identify and is the most likely cause of nongonococcal urethritis.

The treatment for urethritis is antibiotic therapy, and generally the symptoms disappear promptly. Since urethritis can be sexually transmitted, the patient's sex partner may require treatment as well. Occasionally, urethritis will be persistent and troublesome to treat, and may lead to urethral scarring and stricture.

Urethral Stricture. Injury or chronic urethritis may result in scar tissue which can narrow or, in extreme cases, obstruct the urethra, making urination increasingly difficult and painful. Stricture may be treated by dilation (or stretching), in which the urologist inserts a thin, flexible instrument into the urethra to stretch it. The frequency of the treatments varies from patient to patient; however, most strictures do indeed recur. The area of stricture may also be sharply incised using a cystoscope in an attempt to reduce the blockage. This approach is less traumatic and may result in less frequent recurrence of the narrowing. Sometimes the strictures are so extensive or so unresponsive to dilation or incisional therapy that formal reconstructive surgery is required.

Stone Disease. The urine produced by the kidneys is a highly complex solution. Among its components are various inorganic minerals which, under certain conditions, can precipitate and form urinary tract stones.

Most commonly, a patient becomes aware of a urinary tract stone with the sudden onset of excruciating pain. This pain may be the result of the stone passing from the kidney to the bladder or from the bladder through the urethra. If the stone is in the kidney or ureter, the pain may begin in the flank region and move along the urinary tract to the anterior lower abdomen or, in men, to the tip of the penis. The pain is described as sharp, colicky, and coming in waves. It is often associated with profuse sweating, nausea, and vomiting, and sometimes with blood in the urine. Fever does not usually accompany the passage of a stone unless there is a concurrent urinary tract infection.

There are many reasons why stones occur. In some cases, anatomical abnormalities will lead to the stasis (or pooling) of urine, causing the precipitation of various organic and inorganic compounds, forming stones. Urinary tract infections, which change the acidity or alkalinity (pH) of the urine, and various metabolic abnormalities, can also lead to stone formation. Quite often, no cause of the stone formation can be identified.

The medical evaluation for urinary tract stones depends on the age of the patient and the size and number of stones. Passage of a stone during childhood or early adulthood, a family history of stone disease, or previous history of a stone passage will lead to a thorough anatomic, as well as metabolic, evaluation. Anatomic evaluation should include at least an intravenous pyelogram; metabolic evaluation should include blood chemistry analysis, 24-hour urine collection studies, and perhaps special test diets.

If the stones are large, causing total obstruction of the urinary collecting system, surgery will be required to prevent permanent damage to the kidney. Small stones may not cause total obstruction and may be monitored without surgery to see if they will pass through the tract spontaneously. If a stone is too large to pass, is growing, or is causing significant kidney obstruction and damage, treatment is necessary.

Traditionally, stones in the upper urinary tract (i.e., the kidney and upper ureter) have been removed via various surgical approaches. A recently developed procedure enables urologists to remove upper tract stones through tubes placed through the flank into the urinary tract (percutaneous stone removal). This new technique avoids large surgical scars, significantly decreases surgical risk, decreases kidney damage, and decreases postoperative pain and hospitalization. Not all stones, however, can be removed with this technique.

Stones of the lower urinary tract and the bladder can be removed through traditional surgical techniques, as well as through a technique known as stone basketing. In this case, an instrument, either a cystoscope or a ureteroscope, is passed into the bladder or through the bladder into the ureter and a snarelike basket is used to engage and extract the stone.

The objective of the treatment of urinary stones is the prevention of further stone formation. Treatment may include alteration of diet or specific medications, but the mainstay of any treatment is the maintenance of a high output of dilute urine, and this is best accomplished by daily consumption of large quantities of water.

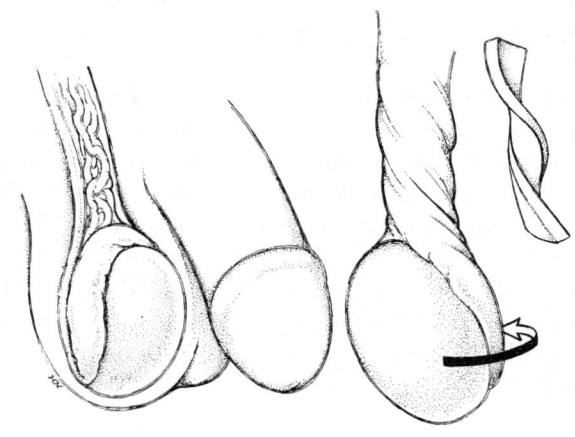

Figure 38.2. **Testicular torsion.**

Testicles and Scrotum

Epididymitis. The long, tightly coiled tube that is located behind each testicle and carries sperm from the testicle to the vas deferens is the epididymis. Inflammation of this structure, usually as a result of a bacterial or chlamydial infection that travels from the urinary tract to the sperm duct, is called epididymitis. It causes fever and pain, developing progressively over several hours, in the back portion of the testicles.

Epididymitis is treated primarily with antibiotics. Analgesics, bed rest, ice packs, and elevation of the scrotum may be prescribed for relief of the pain. Since some types of epididymitis can result from sexually transmitted bacteria, the patient's sex partner may also require treatment with antibiotics. Occasionally an episode of epididymitis is precipitated by extreme straining, which results in urine backing up the reproductive tract to the epididymis.

Testicular Torsion. Testicular torsion is the twisting of the testicle on the spermatic cord—the structure that suspends the testicle within the scrotum, and which contains its blood vessels. (See figure 38.2.) Torsion, although more common in adolescence, can happen anytime, at any age, either spontaneously (even during sleep) or following strenuous activity. It results in strangulation of the blood supply to the testicle and permanent damage if diagnosis and treatment are not immediate.

The major symptom is sudden pain, often sufficiently severe to cause nausea and vomiting. Swelling, redness, and tenderness of the scrotum ensue rapidly. Although occasionally the testicle may untwist itself as spontaneously as the torsion occurred, providing immediate relief, the patient should seek immediate medical attention. Diagnosis requires

medical expertise, since the symptoms of testicular torsion are often similar to those of epididymitis. Even if the physician is able, by gentle manipulation, to return the testicle to its normal position, surgery is usually done within a few hours to anchor it permanently in place.

Even if torsion involves only one testicle, the other one may also be at risk for twisting, because faulty "anchoring" of the testes is a congenital condition, often manifested on both sides. Therefore, surgery is necessary to anchor both testicles—a way of buying insurance for the uninvolved testicle. A testicle whose blood supply has become twisted may be literally strangulated, necessitating its removal. Sudden testicular pain always requires prompt medical attention in order to prevent the unnecessary loss of a testicle.

Orchitis. Orchitis is an infection of the testicle which most commonly occurs in conjunction with epididymitis that has not been properly treated. In this case orchitis is a bacterial infection and is treated with antibiotics. Occasionally orchitis is seen as a viral infection in conjunction with mumps (mumps orchitis). Although mumps orchitis is a rare phenomenon with the virtual eradication of mumps in this country, when it does occur, it may result in irreversible damage to the testes and infertility.

Any acute swelling or pain in the scrotum requires evaluation by a urologist to differentiate among orchitis, epididymitis, testicular torsion, and other conditions that require immediate attention.

Scrotal Masses. Although a lump in the scrotum can be caused by a number of conditions, including the painful ones listed above, the patient should always be wary that it is a testicular tumor, until a physician has determined otherwise. Any newly formed mass in the scrotum requires evaluation by a urologist to ensure that cancer is not present. (For more information, see Chapter 20 on Cancer, page 416.)

More than likely, the lump is benign, and may be a cyst or other inflammation of the epididymis. Cysts of the epididymis are quite common, especially in men over 40. Spermatoceles are cysts of the epididymis which can usually be felt as a swelling in the upper portion of the structure, above the testicle. Unless they grow large enough to cause discomfort, they should be left alone. Surgical removal may result in blockage of the epididymis and may impair fertility.

HYDROCELE. The most common scrotal mass is the hydrocele—an overaccumulation of the fluid that is normally found between the 2 layers of membrane that envelop the testicle. (See figure 38.3.) The excess may result from an overproduction or underabsorp-

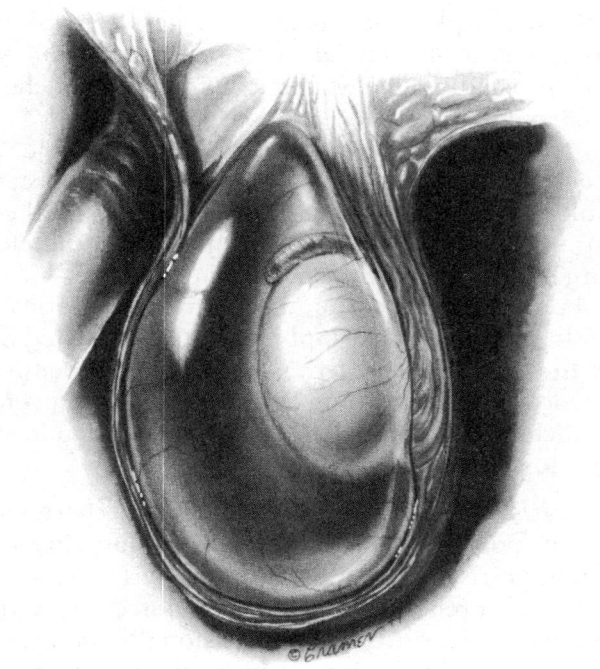

Figure 38.3. **Hydrocele, a fluid-filled mass in the scrotum.**

tion of the fluid; the specific cause is often not apparent. Occasionally, the hydrocele is the result of injury. Like cysts, hydroceles rarely require treatment. If the mass becomes so large that it is uncomfortable, surgery is the only effective approach to cure the problem permanently.

VARICOCELE. Another cause of a mass in the scrotum is a varicocele—an abnormally distended vein, like a varicose vein, in this case leading from the testicle.

Generally these veins are "one-way streets," allowing blood to drain from the testicle, but not to return. With a varicocele, the blood can remain static within the testicle, causing alterations in sperm production.

Although varicoceles are common and generally benign, they are also the most frequent cause of correctable male infertility. What the condition does to sperm production is not clear, but it may affect the testicle by increasing its temperature. Approximately 20 percent of fertile men have a varicocele, but twice as many infertile men have them. (For more information on infertility, see Chapter 10 on Sexual and Reproductive Health, page 148.)

If the varicocele is large or unsightly, it can be removed surgically. The more common reason for surgery for varicocele is impaired fertility; rarely will a varicocele be of such a size that symptoms arise which require intervention. The procedure is a relatively simple one, which can be done on an outpatient basis or with short hospital stay. The urologist makes an incision similar to that employed for hernia in the groin, and ties off the abnormal veins, preventing the blood from returning via this route. Since other veins take over the drainage function, the testicle is not damaged.

Newer techniques are available to block the varicocele by plugging it with either balloons or coils, thus preventing the abnormal blood flow. This technique is not widely available and seems to offer no particular benefit over the surgical approach. Its major disadvantage is the possibility that these devices may migrate elsewhere within the body and cause difficulty wherever they finally lodge.

Penis

Penile (Venereal) Warts. Penile warts (condylomata accuminata) look like warts found anywhere else on the body, except perhaps that they are more luxuriant in their growth. Like all warts, they are caused by a viral infection and therefore they are contagious. Since they are usually sexually transmitted, they require treatment of both partners. Many warts are treated by applying a topical medication, or "paint," but extensive warts may require removal by freezing with liquid nitrogen, vaporizing by laser therapy, or surgery.

The warts are generally found on the external genitalia, including the shaft and head of the penis, but occasionally, they will involve the part of the urethra that travels through the penis. In this case, the urologist may want to investigate the urethra and bladder by cystoscopy. Venereal warts are harmless if treated, but if they are allowed to proliferate, they can become infected and lead to complications. Most important, they are contagious and sexual abstinence is recommended until they are eradicated. Condoms may provide adequate protection if they are used carefully.

Priapism. Priapism is a rare and painful condition that produces a prolonged erection unaccompanied by any sexual desire. It may be caused by certain drugs, as well as by blood abnormalities such as leukemia and sickle cell disease. The result is that blood becomes trapped in the penis and causes its engorgement. Priapism is a serious condition, requiring immediate attention, lest the blockage cause permanent injury to the penis and impair the patient's ability to have a normal erection. Depending on the apparent cause of the priapism, treatment may be spinal or caudal anesthesia, surgery to establish new passageways for the blood to escape the penis, anticoagulants to thin the blood, or antihypertensive drugs to lower the blood pressure, as well as blood transfusions to remove damaged blood cells (sickle cells).

Balanoposthitis (Balanitis). In balanoposthitis, the glans (tip) of the penis become irritated and inflamed as a result of bacterial or fungal infection, irritation from chemicals in clothing, or an unknown cause. In men who have been circumcised, such inflammations are less common and limited to the glans penis (balanitis). Those with diabetes mellitus are particularly susceptible to this condition and those who develop these inflammations should be evaluated for diabetes.

Treatment consists of administering antibiotics for any infection, carefully cleaning the glans, and applying topical ointment to relieve the irritation.

Paraphimosis. In uncircumcised men, the foreskin occasionally becomes retracted behind the head of the penis and cannot be brought forward, resulting in severe swelling. This is a urologic emergency requiring immediate attention. An emergency circumcision or partial circumcision (called a dorsal slit) may be required.

Prostate

Because it is the organ most often affected by benign or malignant growth processes, the prostate is the organ most often associated with the urologist. Growth of the prostate leads to progressive obstruction of the flow of urine from the bladder, often the first symptom that draws attention to the growth. Routine yearly examinations of the prostate should be carried out in men over the age of 40, to make possible early diagnosis of possible cancerous

changes. A normal prostate is soft and smooth. If it is irregular, hard, and nodular, prostate cancer should be suspected and a tissue biopsy performed. As with all other tumors, the earlier the diagnosis is made, the better the chance for a cure. (For a detailed discussion of cancer of the prostate and other male genital-urinary tract organs, see Chapter 20 on Cancer, page 415.)

At puberty there is a spurt of growth of the prostate tissue, which then remains basically stable in size until approximately age 50, when there is a second growth spurt. The cause of this growth is not entirely clear, but the male hormone testosterone seems the most probable answer. (See figures 38.4A and 38.4B.) As the prostate grows—whether benignly or malignantly—the urethra that runs through it becomes progressively blocked, preventing the bladder from adequately emptying itself. This leads to the classic symptoms of prostate disease: hesitancy or difficulty initiating the stream of urine; frequency, the feeling of incomplete emptying of the bladder; nocturia, or awakening during the night to urinate; and dribbling at the end of urination.

Eventually, if these symptoms are allowed to progress, the patient may find himself entirely unable to urinate (urinary retention). When this occurs, a catheter (or hollow tube) is passed via the urethra into the bladder to obtain relief. Occasionally, due to the inability of the bladder to empty itself, pressure is transmitted back via the ureters to the kidney, and kidney damage ensues.

Generally the indication for a prostatectomy—surgical removal of the gland—comes from the patient: He is not sleeping well, he has great difficulty voiding in the daytime, he is generally unhappy with his voiding habits and he wants something done to improve the situation. Other indications are urinary retention or the inability to empty the bladder, or renal damage due to back pressure caused by the large amount of urine that remains in the bladder in the face of prostatic obstruction. Patients with prostatic obstruction are also more likely to develop a urinary tract infection and may originally seek medical treatment for cystitis.

Benign prostatic growths causing urethral blockage are treated surgically. The most common procedure is the transurethral resection of the prostate (TURP), in which an instrument called a resectoscope is passed via the urethra through the penis into the bladder. Using an electrified loop at the end of the resectoscope, the surgeon carves away the prostate from within to its outermost margins. This leaves a hollowed out shell that will gradually shrink down to form a channel for urine flow from

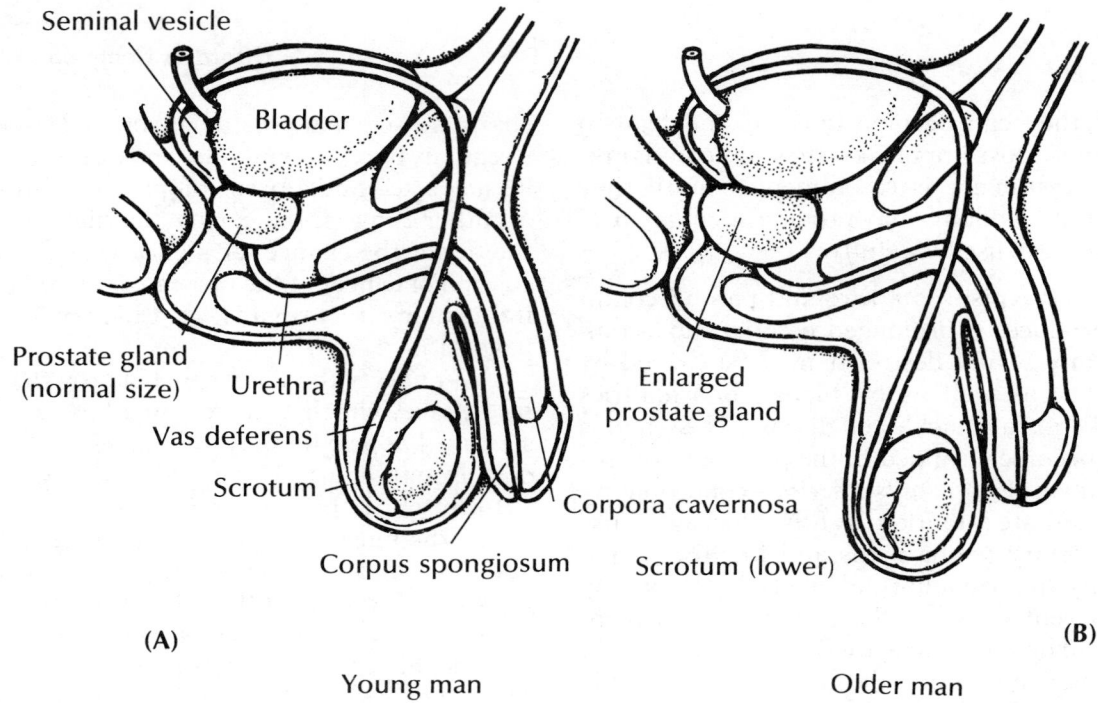

Seminal vesicle

Bladder

Prostate gland (normal size)

Urethra

Vas deferens

Scrotum

Corpus spongiosum

Corpora cavernosa

Enlarged prostate gland

Scrotum (lower)

(A)

(B)

Young man

Older man

Figures 38.4A and 38.4B. **Prostate gland in a young man and an enlarged prostate in an older man.**

the bladder to the urethra. After the surgery the patient has a catheter in place for 3 to 5 days and is usually discharged from the hospital within a week.

If the urologist feels the prostate is too large to be removed via the transurethral approach, an open prostatectomy may be carried out. In the open technique, an incision is made in the lower abdomen and the prostate is removed through an incision made into the bladder or into the prostate itself. (The particular approach used depends on the personal preference of the surgeon.) These procedures involve hospitalization of a week to 10 days. The recuperative process at home is generally longer for the open prostatectomy than for the transurethral prostatectomy, and this is the major advantage of the transurethral approach.

Acute Prostatitis. Acute prostatitis is often heralded by symptoms that are very similar to those of cystitis: frequent, painful urination and nocturia (awakening from sleep to urinate). There may also be a discharge from the urethra. Prostatitis may also be accompanied by fever, chills, and pain in the per-

ineal region behind the scrotum, the lower back, or the suprapubic region. The prostate itself will be very tender, which will be evident on physical examination.

Prostatitis is treated with antibiotics, given orally or intravenously, depending on the severity of the infection. Untreated prostatitis may result in an abscess and, although the symptoms may be the same, the condition becomes more resistant to antibiotic therapy and may require surgical drainage.

Chronic Prostatitis. The relationship between chronic prostatitis and acute prostatitis is not clear, but the chronic form may follow an episode of the acute. Chronic prostatitis is usually identified with persistent urgency, frequency, and painful urination, but not with a urinary tract infection. Its symptoms often include a feeling of heaviness or pressure behind the scrotum, in the lower abdomen just above the pubic hair, or in the lower back. Treatment usually consists of long courses of the same antibiotics used for the acute variety. Sitz baths may be recommended to relieve symptoms.

CAUSES OF MALE INFERTILITY

APPROXIMATELY 10 to 15 percent of all married couples suffer from infertility. Most couples assume that at the appropriate time they will be able to have children as desired. When they meet with the inability to achieve what is almost taken as an inalienable right, much anger, frustration, and depression often

ensue. Previously, couples who met with this frustration were able without much difficulty to adopt children and were thus less inclined to pursue their own fertility status. With current social mores and readily available contraception and abortion, this outlet has diminished greatly, and people are going to much greater extents to determine the cause of their infertility.

It is difficult to discuss male infertility as an entity separate from female infertility. Indeed, both male and female need to be functioning properly in order to achieve a pregnancy.

Problems with male infertility can be broken into 3 major categories: (1) failure, due to hormonal abnormalities, to produce an adequate number of sperm; (2) failure, due to testicular abnormalities, to produce an adequate number of functioning sperm; and (3) production of normal sperm which cannot be deposited in the female genital tract because of ductal obstruction or abnormal sexual function (such as premature ejaculation). (These problems are discussed in more detail in Chapter 10 on Sexual and Reproductive Health, page 148.)

MALE SEXUAL DYSFUNCTION

Erectile Abnormalities

Erection is a complex event dependent upon the normal functioning of several systems. It is induced by the rapid influx of blood into the spongy tissue that makes up most of the penis. The volume of blood in the erect penis is approximately 11 times that of the blood in the flaccid penis. This increased volume within the confined space of the tissues leads to the increased size and turgidity of the penis.

The neurologic and vascular systems appear to be necessary for the regulation of the blood flow into the penis. Hormones are also necessary for normal sexual development and, generally speaking, a normal testosterone level is necessary to preserve sexual desire as well as capability of the penis to become erect. However, it is important to note that no specific level of testosterone concentration is associated with an alteration of sexual activity. There appears to be a delicate interrelationship among the hormonal, neurologic, and vascular systems, but this is not yet totally understood.

The mind obviously has a great influence on sexual function. Even those who have no serious psychological problems and are involved in truly loving relationships may, in times of anxiety or stress, lose the ability to sustain an erection.

It is important that both the physician and the patient have a clear understanding of exactly the problem of concern to the patient. Once this has been determined, a complete history and physical examination will be used to attempt to identify possible causes for the dysfunction. Abnormalities may exist in the vascular, neurologic, or endocrine system.

Each of the systems can be assessed by physical examination and laboratory tests. Adequacy of blood supply to the penis can be ascertained by blood flow or pressure measurements within the penis. Neurologic adequacy is assessed by specialized nerve conduction studies, and endocrine abnormalities can be assessed by blood assays.

Other important causes of sexual dysfunction are medications, especially various antihypertensive drugs (used to control blood pressure). Mood altering substances such as alcohol, stimulants, and sedating agents can also affect sexual function. Finally, certain kinds of surgery, including repair of abdominal aortic aneurysms and radical surgery for either prostate or colon cancer, may result in impotence.

A unified and comprehensive diagnostic approach to impotence will often include nocturnal tumescence monitoring studies. These measure the ability to attain or maintain an erection by measuring episodes of erection that occur normally during sleep. Men of all ages will have erections that occur spontaneously during sleep. The measurement of the absence or presence of these erections may be helpful in diagnosis.

A sex therapist will often be consulted to help determine the cause of the dysfunction as well as to evaluate the appropriateness of various therapy alternatives.

The therapies available for the treatment of impotence range from behavioral (psychological) therapy to implantation of sophisticated devices to create an erection. The mainstay of treatment for organic impotence (impotence unrelated to medication or psychological problems) is implantation within the shaft of the penis of one of the various penile prostheses.

There are many designs of penile prostheses, ranging from very simple devices which are semirigid and which produce a permanent erection to a more complex system with inflatable cylinders that can be pumped up or deflated on demand. The semirigid prostheses are the simplest and most inexpensive. They have the disadvantage, however, of producing a constant erection, which at times can be cumbersome or embarrassing. Most modern semirigid prostheses are quite flexible, yet are still simple in design and nonmechanical. They can be manipulated, when not being used, into an unobtrusive position not apparent to the casual observer. The erection created is almost indistinguishable from a conventional one: wires embedded in a silicone rubber sheath allow flexibility and stability.

Inflatable prostheses are more sophisticated devices which, in the nonfunctional or flaccid state, are indistinguishable from the normal penis. When inflated, this type produces an excellent erection, essentially duplicating the normal erection. These prostheses consist of a pump that manually transfers fluid from a reservoir into cylindrical balloons implanted within the penis. The major disadvantage of these devices is the possibility of problems resulting from the more complicated surgical implantation process as well as to mechanical failures. The technology of penile prostheses is still developing and the more recent models have rectified many of the earlier mechanical difficulties these devices experienced. For some patients, these prostheses are extremely satisfactory.

Vascular surgery for impotence due to abnormal blood flow to the penis is a promising new treatment, but not well enough established to be totally reliable at this point.

Ejaculatory Abnormalities

Hematospermia.   Blood in the ejaculate is a frightening urologic symptom. Usually it gives the semen only a slight pink tinge or brownish tinge. At times, however, the ejaculate may be bright red. This is most often a self-limited process that may be secondary to inflammation due to either viruses or bacteria and, in general, no treatment is necessary. If the ejaculate continues to be bloody, the individual should consult a urologist.

Retrograde Ejaculation.   Retrograde ejaculation is a process whereby, with orgasm, the ejaculate is propelled back into the bladder rather than through the urethra and out the tip of the penis. Retrograde ejaculation occurs most often in males with diabetes and may be the first manifestation of abnormal sexual function associated with this disease. Additionally, certain medications, especially those prescribed for mood alteration, may cause ejaculatory abnormalities. Retrograde ejaculation in itself is a harmless phenomenon. If fertility is desired, however, this symptom may present a problem.

Premature Ejaculation.   Premature ejaculation is the inability to control ejaculation to the degree that it interferes with sexual functioning and satisfaction of oneself and one's partner. This is not associated with organic or physical abnormalities; it is a problem that can be dealt with relatively simply by using basic sexual therapy techniques.

When a man first experiences the problem of premature ejaculation his reaction may be to isolate himself from the sexual act in an attempt to delay ejaculation. This technique is detrimental to gaining better control because he becomes less aware of the imminent ejaculation. Rather, he should become more involved with sexual activity so that he can perceive the feeling of inevitability. When he feels this sensation, he should withdraw his penis from his partner's vagina (or discontinue stimulation if this occurs during foreplay) and he or his partner should apply gentle pressure to the head of the penis with the index finger and thumb. This will depress the inevitable climax and sexual activity can recommence.

With patience, the "squeeze" technique will generally result in better ejaculatory control. If, however, this cannot be attained without professional counseling, sex therapy is generally very successful in dealing with the problem. The important thing to remember is that premature ejaculation rarely represents a physical malfunction.

SUMMING UP

THE GENITOURINARY SYSTEM is a complex network of organs with specific functions and interrelationships: the kidneys, ureters, bladder, and urethra in both men and women are necessary for the normal production, storage, and evacuation of urine. Any change in urination should be a warning signal of potential problems and should be brought to the attention of a physician.

The male reproductive system is also a complex network, dependent upon the proper working of all its components for sexual and reproductive function. The treatment of male infertility and male erectile dysfunction has recently become much more enlightened and sophisticated. Since specialists are now much better equipped to deal with problems of male reproductive and sexual function, individuals with these maladies should not hesitate to seek professional help.

Part Six

DRUGS AND THEIR USE

39 The Home Medicine Chest

Hamilton Southworth, M.D.

INTRODUCTION

IT HAS BEEN ESTIMATED that about 90 percent of the symptoms—aches, pains, bruises, and other signs of discomfort or disease—felt by otherwise healthy adults are simply shrugged off and never reported to anyone. Most times, these discomforts cause little anxiety and are easily tolerated; their origin is readily understood and they subside relatively quickly. Often some quick remedy is used, like 2 aspirins for a headache. At least half of the remaining 10 percent of symptoms are discussed with family and friends and handled without professional advice. In only 2 to 5 percent of cases is medical consultation ever sought.

What often makes this all possible is the home medicine chest. It saves needless and costly trips to the doctor or clinic and may also prevent late night trips in search of an open pharmacy. Even if the individual has contacted a doctor (and assuming there is no serious emergency that should be dealt with immediately), the doctor is apt to suggest some interim home remedy until the patient can be seen later that day or the next.

PRECAUTIONS

IN STOCKING a home medicine chest there are a number of things to consider besides which individual items should be included: cost, bulk, shelf life, need for refrigeration, and the composition of the household, especially if there are children.

Are there small children who like to test things by mouth as well as by sight? Even if small children come only on a rare visit, the following precautions are advisable:

1. Medications should be out of reach of small hands and no handy chair should make them accessible.
2. Any medication that could be toxic in an overdose should be either locked up or in child-resistant bottles. (If the box is locked, the location of the key should be known to all adults.) The kind of bottle in which 2 arrows must be lined up may be difficult for adults with poor vision or arthritic fingers. Those that have to be pressed down firmly as they are unscrewed may be more satisfactory.
3. Medications should never be described to small children as "candy" to make their ingestion more acceptable. Sugared ones are unwise. If a reward seems necessary, it is better to follow the tablets or liquid with a spoon of syrup.
4. Small children should be taught never to take medicine unless it is given to them by an adult.

STORAGE

MUCH HAS BEEN WRITTEN about the value of having the medicine chest somewhere other than the bathroom because dampness and heat may shorten the shelf life of some medications. Often this is not practical, and simpler items are automatically put into the medicine cabinet over the sink. Nevertheless, potentially toxic medications should go in a box on a top closet shelf, and a fishing tackle box serves very well. Those drugs that would not keep well in the bathroom might be kept in the kitchen away from the stove, in a hall closet, or in another convenient place. If they are kept in the bedroom, care should be taken that they are never used in the dark when one could be mistaken for another.

Those medications that break down in heat, such as insulin or vaccines for allergy, must go in the refrigerator, but they are usually nontoxic on ingestion. If storage space permits, there is some value in separating medications for external use from those for internal use.

The shelf life of medications varies and often there are telltale signs when a medicine is past its prime: aspirin takes on a characteristic vinegar smell when it is no longer fresh; overage ointments harden or separate; the alcohol evaporates from tinctures; and liquids may change color, become cloudy, or separate, forming a solid mass at the bottom of the bottle. Antibiotics should probably not be kept more than 1 year. Simpler compounds, such as acetaminophen (Tylenol, etc.) or codeine in the form of white tablets, should be flushed down the toilet if they start to brown or crumble, as should any capsules that melt or stick together. Medications whose labels have been lost should be discarded immediately.

Fortunately, prescription drugs must now show an expiration date on the label, after which time they begin to lose potency. But it is a good idea with over-the-counter preparations to record both the date of purchase and the date first opened. The pharmacist may be able to assist you in determining how long to keep a medication. Buying the appropriate size or quantity is an important consideration. Aspirin by the hundreds may be a bargain for the office first-aid cabinet, but not for a small family who takes it only occasionally.

If a family member requires medication by injection, as much attention should be given to the directions for storage of the materials as to those for its administration. Nowadays, sterile, disposable needles are commonly used; they should be broken or snipped off with shears before discarding.

It may be practical, after an acute illness, to save remaining supplies of any prescription medication. The same medical condition may recur in the future and require the same remedy. However, since drugs can deteriorate and since similar disorders may be mistaken for each other, it is best to check with the physician before taking the drug again. Under no circumstance should it be given to anyone else without instructions from the doctor.

Keeping a list of contents attached to the inside of the cover or the door of the medicine cabinet or box will make checking and replacement easier. The name and phone number of the family physician, as well as the police and ambulance service, and the local poison control center (see Appendix A: Directory of Poison Control Centers, page 838) can also be recorded here.

HOME REMEDIES

THE PANTRY should not be overlooked as a source of remedies for common complaints. Traditional home remedies can play a role, either real or perceived. Most are harmless, some are helpful, and all have the advantage of making the patient feel he or she is "doing something" when more specific medication is not available. If taken with conviction, they may also have a definite placebo effect.

Baking soda (sodium bicarbonate), for example, may be the ultimate home remedy. Plain, it can be used as an underarm deodorant. Or sprinkled liberally into a tepid bath, it makes a soothing soak for sunburned skin. Mixed into a thin paste and applied

to the skin, it can also soothe poison ivy or insect bites. The same paste can be used to brush the teeth. Mixed with a small quantity of water, baking soda can be used as a mouthwash that will take some of the pain out of a canker sore. The same mixture swallowed can often relieve heartburn or an upset stomach.

White vinegar, too, is a versatile substance. It is often mixed with water for douching when an acid douche is required. It can also be used as a protection against "swimmer's ear" by adding 2 cc (30 drops) to an ounce of boiling water. When the mixture has cooled, 2 drops are used in each ear after swimming. The acid helps kill the bacteria that may be present in water trapped in the ear.

Chicken soup not only, as the old joke goes, "couldn't hurt," but it may actually help. It has the advantages of being nutritious, bland, hot, and easy to swallow, and it may be acceptable to those who otherwise have no appetite. It supplies fluids and soothes sore throats.

Regular tea contains tannic acid, which soothes mild burning or itching, and may relieve minor sunburn or similar mild irritations. A compress can be soaked in cool tea and applied to the skin, or wet teabags can be applied directly.

Herbal teas supply pleasantly hot, tasty, and perhaps sweetened fluids which may also help soothe a cold, although they haven't the nutritional value of chicken soup. Herbal teas have been touted for everything from constipation to premenstrual cramps to headaches, and many of them may in fact provide some relief for minor conditions. But taken in quantity they can produce diarrhea, vomiting, and kidney and urinary tract irritation, so it is best to limit their use to an occasional cup and it is essential to avoid any containing strong medicinals.

SUPPLIES

THE FOLLOWING CHARTS list first-aid and medical supplies for a family of adults, with additions for children.

FIRST-AID SUPPLIES

Band-Aids	One box of assorteds or at least six 1-inch and six 1½ inch
Tape	1-inch wide roll, either paper or cloth
Sterile gauze pads	Individually packaged, three 2-inch squares and three 4-inch squares
Cotton balls	One small bag
Ace bandage	One, 3 inches wide
Cotton tip applicators	One small package
Scissors	One pair, preferably blunt-tipped for removing dressings
Safety pins	Two or three large
Antiseptic	One small bottle of rubbing alcohol (70 percent solution) or a substitute
Eyewash (Collyrium)	One bottle with eye cup
Antibiotic cream	A 5-gram "ophthalmic" tube containing bacitracin or polymyxin or both (examples: Mycitracin, Neosporin). Antibiotic creams are generally effective for diaper rash
Anti-inflammatory/ anesthetic ointment	A 1-ounce or ½-ounce tube containing 0.5 percent hydrocortisone cream (example: Cortaid)
Antipruritic	An anti-itch lotion or spray containing calamine with phenol, for poison ivy, insect bites, etc. (examples: Caladryl, Rhulispray)

Petroleum jelly

Ice bag

Hot water bottle or heating pad

Tweezers and fine sewing needle—for splinters

Teaspoon (perhaps plastic) **or small calibrated plastic cup** (better for young children)

First-aid manual—perhaps the American Red Cross "Standard First Aid and Personal Safety"

Flashlight—to identify medications in case of blackout or disaster

SAMPLE MEDICATIONS

Antipyretics (to reduce fever) and mild analgesics (pain killers): 1 bottle of 5-grain acetaminophen (examples: Tylenol, Datril) or 5-grain aspirin tablets

Analgesics (stronger), such as acetaminophen with 30 milligrams of codeine (requires prescription)

Antacids, such as those containing aluminum hydroxide and magesium hydroxide (examples: Maalox, Mylanta)

Antihistamine/decongestant—to relieve cold or allergy symptoms (example: Chlor-Trimeton)

Cough syrup with expectorant (example: Robitussin DM)

Mild laxative (example: Milk of Magnesia)

Antidiarrheal medication with pectin or bismuth salicylate (examples: Kaopectate, Pepto-Bismol). The family's physician may want to prescribe something stronger, such as Lomotil.

Oral thermometer

SUPPLIES FOR CHILDREN

If there are young children in the family, the following should be added:

Pediatric acetaminophen

To use as an antipyretic and mild analgesic, in 75- to 90-milligram tablets for older children, elixir for younger children, and drops for infants (example: Tylenol). Aspirin is not recommended due to possible risk of Reye's syndrome.

Syrup of ipecac

Oral decongestant

Rectal thermometer

As an emetic in case of ingestion of excess medications or other toxic substances

(examples: Triaminic syrup, Dimetane decongestant elixir)

40 Proper Use of Drugs

Norman Kahn, D.D.S., Ph.D.

INTRODUCTION

AMERICAN DOCTORS currently write over 105 billion prescriptions per year, according to the U. S. Department of Commerce. That comes to almost 7 prescriptions per person. In addition, Americans annually spend about $50 each on nonprescription medications—so-called over-the-counter (OTC) drugs.

There are more than 7,000 prescription and nonprescription drugs listed in the *Physicians' Desk Ref-* *erence*, a standard guide to medicines. The list grows constantly, with about 5 prescription drugs added every month. The over-the-counter drugs comprise half a million products, from medicated shampoos to corn plasters for the feet. Besides the prescription drugs they take after professional diagnosis of a disease, people treat themselves for myriad ailments: insomnia, drowsiness, cold and flu symptoms, constipation, diarrhea, headaches, stomachaches, and skin problems. And many people seem unaware that some of their favorite beverages also contain drugs—alcohol and caffeine.

The ways to misuse drugs seem almost as numerous as the drugs themselves. All drugs—even aspirin—can have unpleasant side effects in some people. The chances of unwanted side effects can multiply when 2 or more drugs are combined in 1 patient. Drugs sometimes interact with foods and drinks: the combination may intensify a drug's effect or neutralize it. Or the combination may cause new, unforeseen side effects, not predictable from the action of each drug considered separately.

Ignorance deprives many people of the benefits of drugs. Taken improperly, medicines may lose their effect, lead to relapse, or cause adverse reactions. Nor are doctors immune to error. They can prescribe unnecessary drugs, or the wrong drugs, exposing the patient to side effects without the possibility of benefit.

Just as drug sales are big business—almost $5 billion for prescription drugs per year, and $5.5 billion in over-the-counter remedies—misuse of medicines and adverse reactions to medicines are a major part of health-care costs. Approximately 300,000 Americans each year are hospitalized because of adverse reactions to drugs; 18,000 hospitalized patients die from unforeseen side effects. To avoid these ill effects, people need to know as much as possible about the drugs they are taking—and why.

Information and the Doctor: A Two-Way Exchange

In every field of life, correct decision making depends on information. Yet decisions about medications are sometimes made without proper information, in a lack of communication involving both patient and doctor. To dispel this ignorance, both need to ask a barrage of questions, on everything from other medications to lifestyle of the patient, to effects and interactions of the proposed therapy. Only then can the optimum treatment, in the optimum amounts, be prescribed. And this information is necessary not only in dealing with the physician, but for dentists, podiatrists, nutritionists, and fitness counselors.

What to Tell the Doctor.   Among the facts the doctor needs to know:

- What other drugs is each patient taking? (This includes any over-the-counter medications, vitamins, minerals, etc.)
- Has the patient had any bad reactions to drugs?
- Is the patient pregnant? Or breast-feeding? Many

drugs can pass into the fetus or the mother's milk glands.

- Is the patient suffering from any chronic illnesses, such as high blood pressure or kidney disease? Some drugs worsen high blood pressure; kidney dialysis removes others from the blood. Hepatitis may change the body's reaction to drugs, some of which are disposed of via the liver.
- What are the patient's dietary habits, even reasonable ones? The person who likes to drink a lot of milk, for example, will have to avoid it for at least an hour after taking tetracycline.
- Does the patient use alcohol, tobacco, or caffeine? The patient may have to give a realistic assessment of his or her ability to give them up for the duration of the illness.

What to Ask the Doctor.   According to a 1983 CBS television network poll, less than 30 percent of the general population considers itself "well-informed" about prescription drugs. About 80 percent wanted more information on safety and efficacy. Other important areas of information were "proper home use, general health issues, misuse and dependency, and cost and value."

The problem of doctor–patient miscommunication is nothing new. In 1982, the American Medical Association began distributing patient information sheets about disease and treatments. Drug manufacturers, medical publishers, insurance companies, and individual doctors themselves prepare information kits for patients and the general public. Obviously, many people still feel that they are not receiving the kind of information they require to become full partners in their own medical care. Two surveys commissioned by the Food and Drug Administration pinpointed the source of the problem:

- Very few patients—only 2 to 4 percent—questioned their doctors or pharmacists about their prescriptions.
- Doctors interpreted the patients' silence to mean satisfaction with the information received.
- Most doctors and almost all pharmacists said that they provided written materials—anything from an illustrated brochure to a typed prescription label for the medicine bottle.
- But only 6 percent of patients said they received written information at the doctor's office; 15 percent said they had received written materials at the pharmacy.

Many factors inhibit patients from asking questions. They don't know what questions to ask. They are in awe of the doctor, or feel that questions may be taken as mistrust of the doctor's ability. They don't want to seem impudent, or to take up the doctor's valuable time. Or they may be too stunned and confused by the diagnosis to comprehend what the doctor is saying. They may even feel that it is somehow "wrong" for them to know more than the doctor has told them. None of these is a good reason. Ultimately, each patient will have to live with the effects of anything taken—or not taken—into his or her body.

Below is a list of questions each person should ask the doctor about any medicines prescribed. A pencil and paper will help keep the answers straight, especially if the patient requires more than one drug.

- What is the name of the drug? Many drugs have 2 names, the brand name and the generic name. It helps to know both.

- What is it supposed to do? When should this effect become noticeable? What should the patient do if no effect is seen? How will the effect change the course of the disease?

- How and when should it be taken? For how long?

- Can the drug be prescribed in a generic form, instead of under a more expensive brand name? Many new drugs are not available in generic form, and the doctor may prefer a particular brand for good reason (see below for further information).

- What are the most common side effects? Which should be reported immediately if they occur, and which are trivial? Some drugs, for example, turn the urine startling colors. Knowing this in advance can spare the patient unnecessary consternation. The patient should be well enough informed to be able to recognize the first symptoms of any serious reactions. However, many doctors fear that patients may develop symptoms by power of suggestion.

- What foods, drugs, drinks, or activities should the patient avoid while taking the drug? Many drugs can be inactivated or have their onsets-of-action delayed by food in the stomach; others must be taken with food to avoid irritating the stomach. A number of drugs make people drowsy and should not be taken before driving. Some drugs may have their effects multiplied by alcohol or other drugs.

- Is there any written information about the drug? If this material is available, it will reinforce the doctor's oral instructions and the patient's notes. Books, pamphlets, even magazine articles can be most helpful.

- Are there any alternatives to the use of drugs? Mild hypertension (high blood pressure), for example, can sometimes be relieved by weight loss, exercise, or the reduction of salt in the diet, or a combination of these measures. A determined person might want to try modifying his or her lifestyle before embarking on an endless course of antihypertensive drugs.

All this information is also available to the pharmacist. In filling a prescription, the patient should ask that exact instructions for use of the drug be typed on the label, along with the name of the drug. "Take as directed" could mean anything after the doctor's words have faded from memory.

The pharmacist will type all instructions from the prescription form onto the label. Problems may arise if the physician does not write them on the prescription. In this case, the patient can ask the pharmacist to call the physician for more precise instructions.

An FDA study concluded that the only way for doctor–patient and pharmacist–patient communications to improve was for the patient to ask more questions. Patients should feel free to call the doctor's office or pharmacy if additional questions come to mind after the office or pharmacy visit. If the health-care professional seems too busy to inform the patient adequately, the patient should consider finding another one who is not.

DRUG CLASSIFICATIONS

DRUGS can be classified in many different ways: over-the-counter vs. prescription vs. controlled drugs; by chemical structure; by the dosage form, i.e., oral medications vs. injectable products vs. drugs applied to the skin or body surface. In this section, prescription medications will be discussed by therapeutic classes—with descriptions of what the drugs are intended to accomplish inside the body. Many of these classes also contain nonprescription drugs.

Drugs to Treat Infections

In 1981, more drugs were prescribed to combat infections than for any other reason—182 million prescriptions, or over 13 percent of all prescription drugs, according to a study reported in the *Journal of the American Medical Association*. These include antibiotics, such as the penicillins, erythromycin, the tetracyclines, cephalosporins, and aminoglycosides, which operate against bacteria and some fungi.

Antibiotics, however, have no effect against certain forms of infections. To treat some parasitic infections such as those caused by amoebae, there are synthetic compounds available. Viruses are very resistant to available antibiotics. There are drugs that may help prevent some viral infections (amantadine for some forms of influenza) or may amelioriate the severity of an infection. The agents used in the treatment of genital herpes, for instance, do not cure the underlying disease, but they are helpful in controlling individual infections.

Other drugs in this class are used against tuberculosis, malaria, leprosy, and parasitic infections such as hookworm and roundworm.

Cardiovascular Drugs

The second most frequently prescribed category of drugs is the medications that affect the heart and blood vessels. If diuretics (used to promote the excretion of sodium and water and often prescribed for hypertension and heart failure) were included, it would be the largest category.

Cardiovascular drugs are those used to treat congestive heart failure, irregular heartbeat, angina pectoris, and hypertension. Digitalis, in one of its many forms, is the most important drug used against congestive heart failure, but this condition may also be treated with a vasodilator—a drug to dilate blood vessels. Digitalis may also be used to slow a too-rapid heartbeat. Other drugs used to regulate irregular heartbeat include beta-blockers (drugs that prevent excitation of the sympathetic nervous system), various forms of quinidine (a quinine derivative), and many other medications.

Beta-adrenergic blocking agents are also used to prevent angina. The most widely prescribed class of drugs for the treatment of an attack of angina is the nitrates: nitroglycerin placed under the tongue, rubbed into the skin, worn in an impregnated bandage, or even tucked into the cheek. Long-acting forms of nitrates are also used to prevent attacks. The third line of defense against angina is the calcium-channel blockers, a group of chemically unrelated medications that act by preventing spasms of the smooth muscle around the blood vessels supplying the heart.

Hypertension, or high blood pressure, is also treated with beta-blockers, calcium blockers, diuretics (discussed later in this section), and other drugs. These include alpha-adrenergic blockers, drugs that act somewhat like beta-blockers, but on a different aspect of the sympathetic nervous system; vasodilators, described above; and a number of drugs that decrease activity of the sympathetic nervous system.

Psychotherapeutic Drugs

In this classification are medications used to treat psychoses such as schizophrenia and other severe personality disorders; mood disorders such as de-

pression; and forms of substance abuse, including alcoholism. This group also includes antianxiety drugs (commonly referred to as tranquilizers), drugs used as adjuncts to anesthesia, and drugs used to treat attention-deficit disorder (also called hyperactivity).

Antianxiety drugs constitute a major portion of the drugs taken in this country, with diazepam (Valium), one of the group of drugs called benzodiazepines, being a longtime best-selling drug. These compounds are often used to suppress anxiety and produce sleep. By themselves, they are relatively safe, but can be extremely dangerous when combined with alcohol or other central nervous system depressants.

Antipsychotic or neuroleptic drugs are used to control the symptoms of acute psychoses: hallucinations, failure of logical reasoning, severe excitement, aggression, and delusions. These symptoms may be the result of acute mania, schizophrenia, paranoia, or other psychotic disorders.

Drugs Used in Affective Disorders. Affective disorders are the imbalances of mood more commonly known as manic or depressive illnesses. Unless treated with drugs or electroconvulsive therapy, severe affective disease may persist for at least 6 to 18 months or longer. Tricyclic antidepressants are the drugs most often used against depression. If for some reason they are ineffective or cause intolerable side effects, monoamine oxidase inhibitors are the second choice.

The use of monoamine oxidase inhibitors is complicated by the need for rigid control of diet and other drugs, especially stimulants, dextromethorphan, beer, wine, and caffeine. (For more specific information, see the section on Drug Interactions, page 779.) Lithium is most often used against mania patients with manic-depressive disorders. It has also been used in the treatment of some forms of depression.

Other Mental Disorders. An adjunct in the treatment of alcoholism is a drug called disulfiram, or Antabuse. If this drug is followed by the ingestion of alcohol, the disulfiram reaction will occur—flushing, difficulty in breathing, nausea, thirst, chest pains, palpitation, and vertigo are common. Great caution must be observed in the use of this drug and it should be used only in the broader context of a therapeutic program.

Attention-deficit disorder is a childhood syndrome of inattentiveness and impulsiveness, often with hyperactivity and learning problems. Paradoxically, this condition can be treated with stimulants. The most often used drugs are methylphenidate (Ritalin) and dextroamphetamine (Dexedrine).

Strong Analgesics

These are prescription painkillers, classified by their major ingredients.

Opiates and Opioids.

Opiates are derived from natural substances; opioids are synthetic substances with similar pharmacological properties, including the relief of pain.

Morphine is the prototype of the opiates and is used for moderate to severe pain, especially if short-lived, as in surgery, myocardial infarction, and biliary or renal colic. As morphine is constipating, it has been used in paregoric, to treat diarrhea. Opiates not only relieve pain, they allay fear and anxiety about it. Examples of the opiates and opioids are codeine, meperidine (Demerol), and methadone (Dolophine).

There are analgesics that share some opioid properties, but not others. Pentazocine (Talwin) and nalbuphine (Nubain) are drugs providing strong analgesia, but with a lessened capacity to cause severe respiratory depression in large doses. Propoxyphene (Darvon) is a relatively weak analgesic suitable for treatment of mild to moderate pain.

In effective doses, these drugs usually cause some sedation. Constipation may also become a problem, necessitating use of a laxative in long-term use. The most troubling problems, however, are tolerance and dependence. Tolerance—the need for increasing dosages to obtain a constant effect—may obscure the worsening of pain. Physical dependence is very rare when these drugs are used briefly, for acute pain, even when high doses are needed. It may develop after extended use; for example, several doses each day for 20 days.

Under the Controlled Substances Act of 1970, these drugs and others with the potential for abuse are classified into 5 "schedules," as follows:

Schedule I: Substances with a high abuse potential and no proven medical use. Examples: heroin and LSD. These are not legally available in the United States.

Schedule II: Drugs with a high potential for severe dependence and abuses but with accepted medical uses. Examples: morphine and its derivatives, short-acting barbiturates, amphetamines, and cocaine. Prescriptions for these drugs may not be renewed, nor can they be prescribed by phone except in an emergency.

Schedule III: Drugs with less potential for dependence and abuse than those of Schedule II and with medical usefulness. Examples: longer-acting barbiturates, some nonamphetamine stimulants, combinations containing small amounts of opioids. Prescriptions for drugs in Schedules III and IV may be renewed for a limited number of times over a 6-month period, if the physician authorizes it.

Schedule IV: Drugs with a low potential for abuse, limited dependence, and accepted medical usefulness. Examples: antianxiety drugs such as diazepam (Valium), phenobarbital, and other sedatives.

Schedule V: Drugs with a low abuse potential, limited dependence, and accepted medical usefulness, such as analgesic mixtures containing small amounts of opioids with other, nonopioid active ingredients. Prescriptions of Schedule V drugs may be redispensed only if the physician specifically says so on the prescription.

In addition to these federal regulations, many states have specific rules for handling prescriptions of certain drugs.

Nonopioid Analgesics.

This classification covers all the pain-relieving drugs that are not opiates or opioids. Many of these products, including aspirin and other derivatives of salicylic acid, are obtainable without a prescription. Aspirin is one of the two most widely used medications for treating mild pain— headaches, muscle and joint pains, for example. It also reduces fever and, in large doses, inflammation. The other widely used drug is acetaminophen (Tylenol, Datril, and many combinations), which is as effective as aspirin as a pain-reliever, with similar effects against fever. It is especially useful for those who cannot tolerate aspirin, but is not useful in the treatment of the arthritis diseases.

Recently, several new prescription pain-relievers with properties like those of aspirin have become available, and one—ibuprofen (Nuprin or Advil) is now available without prescription. These drugs are most often prescribed for mild-to-moderate pain, like that of osteoarthritis and postoperative dental pain, but can also relieve menstrual cramps much more effectively than aspirin.

Cough and Cold Medications

Americans spend an estimated $700 million each year on over-the-counter remedies for the all-too-common cold. In addition, doctors write almost 98 million prescriptions for cough and cold medications. Unfortunately, none of these has been proved to cure, prevent, or even shorten the course of a cold. Some of these products do relieve symptoms; others do little or nothing.

Diuretics

Diuretics are drugs that increase the output of salt and water in the urine, thereby preventing or relieving edema, the retention of water in tissues. They are prescribed for patients with congestive heart failure, hypertension, diseases of the liver and kidneys, and other conditions.

The most widely prescribed diuretics are thiazides, oral medications often used in the treatment of mild hypertension. They should not be taken by patients with severely impaired kidney function, and they may tend to deplete the body's potassium stores, necessitating supplements either in the form of potassium-rich foods (bananas, dried apricots, oranges, and other citrus fruits) or in prescription medications. Loop diuretics like furosemide (Lasix) are even more potent than thiazides, and are especially effective when given intravenously for rapid results in emergencies like acute pulmonary edema or hypertensive crisis. They have no advantage over the thiazides for the chronic treatment of essential hypertension, and cost much more. Potassium-sparing diuretics can be used with thiazides for a combined effect, especially in patients taking digitalis.

Hormones

When the body's endocrine glands produce insufficient amounts of a hormone, natural or synthetic replacements are used to correct the imbalance. Female sex hormones can become part of therapy for menstrual and menopausal disorders if physician and patient decide that the discomfort of menopause and the decreased risk of osteoporosis outweigh the increased chance of endometrial cancer. Male sex hormones compensate for pituitary or testicular inadequacies. Corticosteroids are useful as immunosuppressive agents and as anti-inflammatory agents in arthritis or asthma.

Antiarthritis Drugs

Many pain-relieving drugs are also effective against arthritis when taken at higher doses. These include high-dose aspirin and other salicylate-derived, nonsteroidal anti-arthritis agents. However, a wide range of newer nonsteroidal anti-inflammatory drugs tend to cause less gastric irritation than aspirin. Among these widely used drugs are ibuprofen (Motrin, Advil, and Nuprin), indomethacin (Indocin), sulindac (Clinoril), naproxen (Naprosyn), piroxacam (Feldene), fenoprofen (Nalfon), and diflunisal (Dolobid). When these fail to control arthritis, gold compounds, penicillamine, or chloroquine may be used. Allopurinol (Zyloprim), which prevents the formation of uric acid, or probenecid (Benemid), which increases the excretion of urates, are 2 drugs used for the treatment of acute gout.

Contraceptives

In this category are condoms and intrauterine devices, oral contraceptive drugs, postcoital or "morn-ing after" agents, and experimental products like long-lasting injectable contraceptives.

Antispasmodics

These drugs reduce the painful bowel spasms of irritable colon or diverticular disease. In combination with antacids, they can also be used to treat peptic ulcers.

Bronchial Therapy

Bronchodilators improve the breathing of asthmatics and patients with other lung diseases by widening air passages that have been constricted by muscle spasms. Theophylline is the most frequently used bronchodilator. Drugs that stimulate beta-adrenergic receptors, such as metaproterenol (Alupent), terbutaline (Brethine), and albuterol (Proventil), are also effective. Cromolyn (Intal) and corticosteroids can be used to prevent bronchoconstriction.

Dermatologicals

Under this heading come all drugs intended to improve the skin: skin abrasives; acne medications; antibiotics applied to the skin; medications for itches, rashes, psoriasis, fungal infections, warts, and seborrhea; shampoos, soaps, detergents, and other cleansers; skin softeners; steroid creams, and wound dressings.

Sedatives

Like antianxiety drugs, barbiturates can also be used to relieve insomnia and produce sleep. Barbiturates such as sodium thiopental can also be used to induce general anesthesia. Because these drugs have a greater abuse potential, however, and are lethal in larger doses, the benzodiazepines have replaced them as the pharmacologic mainstay for the treatment of insomnia. There are also many sedatives that are not barbiturates; however, most have similar potential for abuse or dangerous overdosage.

Nutrients and Supplements

Included in this category are solutions given intravenously to rectify imbalances in body chemistry and products used to maintain patients who cannot eat normal foods. The latter range from liquefied conventional food the patient can take through a straw to solutions that will sustain the patient completely when infused into a vein.

Diabetes Therapy

Depending on the nature of the disease, diabetics

may be treated with insulin or with oral hypoglycemic drugs. Insulin may be prepared from pork and beef pancreases or be created by recombinant DNA techniques in a form identical to human insulin. Oral hypoglycemics are used in less severe late-onset diabetes that cannot be controlled by diet alone.

Ophthalmic Preparations

These are drugs used to treat diseases of the eye, including glaucoma and infections, and eyedrops to dilate the pupil or paralyze the eye muscles. Also included under this heading are drugs either to facilitate diagnosis or surgery on the eye.

Vitamins

Prescription vitamins are used for patients who cannot obtain sufficient nutrients from their diets, either because of inborn metabolic problems or because of diseases such as cirrhosis of the liver that interfere with vitamin storage, function, or uptake. Most people, however, can obtain enough vitamins from a balanced diet.

Many people take over-the-counter vitamins in great quantities, in the mistaken belief that vitamins will give them energy, that more vitamins are intrinsically better, that conventional foods have had their natural vitamins processed away, or even that "natural" or "organic" vitamins are superior to synthetic ones.

Thyroid Therapy

Growth, development, and metabolism are profoundly affected by thyroid hormones. Insufficiency of natural thyroid hormones mandates lifelong replacement in most cases; in other patients, a natural surplus of thyroid hormone must be counteracted by radiation, surgery, or thyroid-blocking drugs.

SIDE EFFECTS AND DRUG ALLERGIES

SIDE EFFECTS are adverse reactions to drugs taken properly; i.e., at normal doses and without other complicating factors such as use of other drugs. Before drugs appear on the market, the FDA usually mandates testing in normal people and people suffering from the disorder to be treated. Then the benefits of the drug are compared with the risks, and guidelines for its use are drawn up. However, this testing may not reveal side effects that occur in less than 1 out of 1,000 cases, or only in special cases (e.g., thalidomide in pregnant women), or only after long use of the drug or as a delayed reaction.

Adverse reactions to drugs can range from a change in laboratory results, noticeable only with sensitive testing, to life-threatening allergic reactions. They can affect any organ or organ system, and often, confusingly, mimic new or exacerbated symptoms of the disease they were prescribed to cure.

There are several forms of adverse reactions to drugs. Physicians distinguish among intolerance, idiosyncrasy, and allergy to any given drug. "Intolerance" occurs when a patient shows undesirable effects like those of overdosage at normal therapeutic dosage levels. "Idiosyncrasy" occurs when a patient's metabolism handles a drug in an unusual, unpredictable way. These 2 forms of adverse reaction do not depend on previous exposure to the drug.

In drug allergy, which does depend on previous exposure (see Chapter 32 on Allergies, page 648), the reaction may be immediate—especially if the drug is taken intravenously—or the reaction may take a week to develop. Common allergic reactions to drugs such as insulin, penicillin, and barbiturates include low fever, itchy rashes, and hives. Treatment consists of discontinuing the medication.

Probably the most drastic drug reaction is anaphylaxis, a violent form of drug allergy. The first symptoms are all-over itchiness, especially on the soles of the feet and the palms. The skin of the face and ears may swell, mimicking a bad sunburn. The bronchial muscle—the muscle in the airway leading to the lungs—constricts, and the patient struggles for breath. The blood vessels dilate, blood pressure drops, and the patient faints. Deprived of oxygen, the brain and nervous system cannot narrow the blood vessels again, and the body cannot recover without immediate medical aid. Treatment consists of epinephrine, a drug that constricts blood vessels, and dilates bronchioles to open the airway. Steroid drugs may be given for a few days to aid recovery.

Other signals of allergy or serious adverse reactions to drugs include bleeding, wheezing, vomiting, impaired sight or hearing, and muscle weakness. Hives (itchy red lumps on the skin), headache, rashes, nausea, and drowsiness are less serious side effects. A physician should be consulted when side effects occur. Often another drug can be substituted; sometimes the patient must learn to tolerate the unpleasantness.

A person who has experienced an allergic reaction to a drug should carry a wallet card—or even wear an ID necklace or bracelet, with the information—even if the initial reaction was slight. Subsequent exposure to the drug may provoke more severe reactions.

DRUG INTERACTIONS

IN THE HUMAN BODY, 2 plus 2 does not always make 4. When drugs are taken together, they usually have an additive effect, but other results are possible. When the combined effects are greater than one would expect from adding the 2 drugs, the result is said to be synergistic. For example, trimethoprim and sulfamethoxazole, 2 antibiotics, interact synergistically and are commonly combined in 1 pill.

Some drug interactions are not beneficial. Drugs may counteract each other, canceling or diminishing any benefits, or the combination may produce too strong an effect, as when alcohol is combined with a sedative. Table 40.1 lists some important drug interactions involving prescription and nonprescription drugs.

Table 40.1 DRUG INTERACTIONS

This:	Plus:	May result in:
Alcohol	Central nervous system depressants: painkillers, antidepressants, antianxiety drugs, antipsychotics	An additive effect—oversedation: driving, operating machinery may be dangerous. Overdoses could be life-threatening.
Alcohol	Aspirin, other salicylates	Stomach irritation, especially for patients with ulcers. Acetaminophen should be used instead.
Aminoglycoside antibiotics, gentamicin (Garamycin), tobramycin (Nebcin)	Ethacrynic acid (Edecrin), a diuretic	Deafness.
Antacids	More antacids	Phosphate depletion, vitamin D deficiency. Consult physician for source of gastric upset.
Anticholinergics (drugs that block the parasympathetic nervous system)	Antispasmodic agents, antiparkinsonism drugs, antihistamines, antipsychotic agents, tricyclic antidepressants	Additive effects: dryness of mouth, blurred vision, acute glaucoma, constipation. Psychosis possible, especially in young and elderly.
Anticoagulants, oral	Aspirin and other salicylates, cimetidine (Tagamet), metronidazole (Flagyl), sulfonamides, trimethoprim sulfamethoxazole (Bactrim, Septra)	Added anticoagulant effect may cause hemorrhage.
Anticoagulants, oral	Barbiturates, carbamazepine (Tegretol)	Drugs in second column decrease anticoagulants in body and reduce effect.
Anticoagulants	Liver, leafy green vegetables, vitamin K	Loss of anticoagulant effect.
Carbamazepine (Tegretol)	Propoxyphene (Darvon)	Carbamazepine not excreted properly; dosage reduction needed.
Contraceptives, oral	Ampicillin, barbiturates, carbamazepine (Tegretol), phenytoin (Dilantin), tetracycline	Increased breakdown of estrogen, breakthrough bleeding, possible pregnancy.
Contraceptives oral	Smoking	Increased risk of heart attack, stroke.
Contraceptives, oral	Junk food diet	Deficiency of vitamin B and folic acid (source of B vitamins). Eat leafy green vegetables to avoid.

Table 40.1 DRUG INTERACTIONS (continued)

This:	Plus:	May result in:
Clonidine (Catapres)	Propranolol (Inderal)	Worsening of hypertension if clonidine is stopped.
Digoxin and other digitalis glycosides	Antacids, cholestyramine resin (Questran)	Loss of digoxin effect may be avoided by spacing out drug consumption.
	Corticosteroids, furosemide (Lasix), thiazide diuretics	Potassium depletion, with possible adverse effects on the heart. Potassium supplements may help avoid.
Furosemide (Lasix), thiazide diuretics	Indomethacin (Indocin), ibuprofen (Motrin), naproxen (Naprosyn, Anaprox)	Loss of diuretic effect.
Griseofulvin (Fulvicin, Grifulvin, Grisactin)	Fatty foods	Increased blood levels of the drug.
Guanethidine (Esimil, Ismelin)	Chlorpromazine (Thorazine), tricyclic antidepressants, dextroamphetamine (Dexedrine)	Loss of antihypertensive effect.
Heparin	Aspirin	Increased anticoagulant effect; acetaminophen should be used instead.
Hypoglycemics, oral	Alcohol, dicumarol, phenylbutazone; thiazide diuretics	Increased hypoglycemic effect. Reduced hypoglycemic effect.
Iron supplements	Citrus fruits and juices, vitamin C	Quicker absorption of iron.
Levodopa (Larodopa, Sinemet)	Pyridoxine (vitamin B_6)	Loss of anti-Parkinsonian effect.
Methotrexate (Mexate)	Aspirin and other salicylates	Increased concentration of methotrexate.
Monoamine oxidase (MAO) inhibitors (Eutron, Nardil, Parnate)	Amphetamines, ephedrine, phenylephrine, phenylpropanolamine, pseudoephedrine (last four in cold and allergy remedies; phenylpropanolamine, in diet pills) READ THE LABEL CAREFULLY TO AVOID	Hypertension; can be life-threatening; tyramine (in some cheese, red wine, etc.) should be avoided as well.
Monoamine oxidase (MAO) inhibitors	Aged cheese, Chianti, liver, pickled herring, fermented sausages (salami, pepperoni), yogurt, sour cream, broad beans, bananas, avocados, soy sauce, active yeast preparations, beer, sherry, large quantities of any wine	Very high blood pressure; can be life-threatening.
Pentazocine (Talwin)	Smoking	Faster metabolism. Higher doses needed.
Probenecid (Benemid), sulfinpyrazone (Anturane)	Aspirin, other salicylates	Loss of effect of probenecid, sulfinpyrazone. Acetaminophen should be used instead.
Tetracycline	Antacids, dairy products containing calcium, magnesium compounds, iron (in mineral supplements)	Loss of antibiotic effect. Intake should be separated by at least 3 hours.
Theophylline	Smoking	Faster metabolism. Higher doses needed.
Thyroid hormone	Soybeans, rutabagas, Brussels sprouts, turnips, cabbage, and kale	Loss of effect of hormone.

Drugs, the Sun, and Heat

Medication can greatly alter the body's response to heat and ultraviolet rays from the sun. Certain drugs increase the body's sensitivity, so that an ambient temperature that would normally provoke perspiration causes heat stroke instead; or the sunbathing time that usually provides a delicate tan inflicts painful sunburn, swelling, or even blistering. (See table 40.2.)

Patients should be careful to learn about these effects before risking sun and heat exposure. Although not everyone who takes the drugs suffers ill effects from sun and heat, knowledgeable patients can protect themselves with air conditioning, sun hats, long sleeves, and sunscreens.

Table 40.2 **COMMON DRUGS THAT PRODUCE REACTIONS TO SUN AND HEAT**

Drug	Category	Reaction	Drug	Category	Reaction
Amitriptyline (*Elavil*)	Antidepressant	Risk of sunburn	**Oral contraceptives** (*estrogen, progestin*)	Hormones	Sunburn
Atropine	Antispasmodic, anticholinergic	Risk of heat stroke	**Promethazine** (*Phenergan*)	Antinausea	Sunburn
Diazepam (*Valium*)	Antianxiety	Excessive sweating may cause overdose	**Sulfamethoxazole** (*Bactrim, Gantanol, Septra*)	Antibiotic	Sunburn
			Tetracycline	Antibiotic	Sunburn
Furosemide (*Lasix*)	Diuretic	Sunburn, heat stroke	**Triamterene** (*Dyrenium*)	Diuretic	Sunburn
Hydrochlorothiazide (*Esidrix and others*)	Diuretic	Sunburn, some loss of water and salt			

Drugs and Driving

Everybody knows that people who drink shouldn't drive, but not everyone realizes that many drugs make driving an unwise activity, by causing drowsiness, poor coordination, dizziness, blurred vision, or lightheadedness. These hazards occur in both prescription and over-the-counter drugs. The effects are even greater when the drugs are mixed with alcohol. A few examples include:

- Cough and cold remedies containing antihistamines, codeine, and sometimes alcohol, as well as scopolamine and dimenhydrinate (Dramamine), taken for motion sickness
- Pain relievers: propoxyphene (Darvon), meperidine (Demerol)
- Antianxiety: diazepam (Valium), chloridiazepoxide (Librium)
- Antipsychotic: phenothiazines (Chlorpromazine, Compazine, and Stelazine), haloperidol (Haldol)

FILLING THE PRESCRIPTION

Besides their notorious handwriting, doctors use a traditional set of Latin abbreviations to convey information to the pharmacist, and thence to the drug consumer. Most of these concern dosing and are listed in the box on page 782.

Usually, the name of the drug is the first word on the prescription. Next is form—tablets, capsules, liquid—and the strength, expressed by weight (250 milligrams, for example). The quantity covered by the prescription follows: 20 capsules, or 10 fluid ounces, for instance. Last come the directions for use, usually in Latin abbreviations. The prescription will also contain instructions on whether and how often it can be refilled.

The patient should read over the prescription in the doctor's office, and ask questions about anything not readily understood.

A LIST OF ABBREVIATIONS

aa	Equal amounts of each
aq	Water *(aqua)*
b.i.d.	Twice a day
coch or cochl	Spoonful
ea	Each
g	gram
gr	grain
gt	drop (plural: gtt)
l.a.s.	Label as such, i.e., label with the name of the drug. The AMA recommends this practice unless there is a reason to leave the patient in ignorance.
p.r.n.	As needed
q.2 h.	Every 2 hours; similarly, q. 3 h., etc.
q.d.	Every day
q.i.d.	Four times a day
t.i.d.	Three times a day
ut dict	As directed. The AMA counsels against this abbreviation on prescriptions, and recommends that instructions for taking medicine be written on the label.

Choosing a Pharmacy

Many factors determine which pharmacy a patient should use. They include:

- *Nearness and convenience.* A pharmacy around the corner may be best for patients who don't drive, parents scrambling to fill a prescription to combat a child's high fever, anyone who needs a pain reliever in a hurry. Sometimes the 24-hour, open-on-Sundays pharmacy is the only one in town. Home delivery may also be essential to get the drugs to the patient.

- *Cost.* Comparison-shopping may result in substantial savings. On the other hand, lower prices may mean fewer services. (See the section on Saving Money on Drugs, below, for other suggestions.)

- *Record-keeping.* Many pharmacies keep notes of all prescriptions made out to an individual customer or family. In this way, the pharmacist might notice drugs or drug combinations that might lead to failure of therapy.

- *Personal considerations.* Pharmacists can clarify many questions about medications, recommend nonprescription drugs, help evaluate symptoms—but only if the customer feels comfortable discussing medical problems. The pharmacist should ask the kinds of questions a physician should before recommending a medication or course of action.

Labels and Package Inserts

The following information should be on the label of every container of prescription medicine:

- Name, address, and phone number of the pharmacy
- Prescription number
- Patient's name
- How often and when to take the drug
- How much to take in each dose
- Any special instructions on storage or preparation
- Name of the physician
- Date the prescription was filled
- Name of the drug (if the doctor or state law indicates it should be written on the label)

The patient should check to make sure all these are clearly written on the label and ask any questions of the pharmacist before leaving the drug store. Certain drugs, especially oral contraceptives and estrogens, come with an FDA-mandated leaflet describing the risks and benefits of these products. These contain helpful information and warrant careful reading. Once again, any question should be referred to the doctor or pharmacist.

Saving Money on Drugs

The cost of medicines makes up a substantial part of the cost of medical care. There are several methods for the consumer to reduce the expense of drugs, both prescription and over-the-counter forms. They include:

- Buying generic, rather than proprietary, drugs, if possible. Newly developed drugs are usually marketed by one company exclusively, under a "proprietary" or brand name. After 17 years, the patent expires, and other companies may manufacture and sell the drug, under its "generic" name, the name assigned to it in the early stages of its development, or under other names. For example, chlordiazepoxide hydrochloride, the generic name for Librium, is now available under its own name or under such brand names as Clipoxide or SK-Lygen.

Most generic drugs are less expensive than proprietary versions, and they're just as effective. In a few cases, however, generic drugs are not "bioequivalent." This means that the body handles them differently from the proprietary product. Different filler, coating, or manufacturing processes may be responsible. In these cases, substitution may be unwise. In some states, pharmacists may substitute a generic drug for the proprietary form unless the physician specifies otherwise. In any case, the cost-conscious patient can ask the doctor if generic forms of prescribed drugs are available.

- Shopping around. Different pharmacies charge different prices for the same products. In many states, pharmacies can now advertise their prices on prescription as well as nonprescription drugs. Some will cite prices over the telephone.

- Buying in bulk. Buying a year's supply of a drug taken regularly—for instance, an oral contraceptive—may save money. But the patient should consult with the doctor or pharmacist first. Many drugs do not maintain their potency with time, but deteriorate—or decompose—within weeks. All drugs now carry an expiration date. A patient who will use the medication up before the expiration date should consider buying a larger quantity.

- Some medical insurance plans pay all or part of drug costs. Check your policy. Also, some employers—chiefly hospitals and universities—have a pharmacy where employees may buy drugs at cost. These may provide considerable savings to the customer.

TAKING MEDICATION

Forms of Medication

Drugs come in many shapes and sizes, according to properties of the chemicals themselves, the area of the body they are intended to act upon, the speed with which they are needed, and the convenience of patient and medical personnel.

A fast way to get drugs to permeate the body is by injecting them in liquid form into the veins. Injection into a muscle is also relatively quick, but more time passes as the drug finds its way into the bloodstream. Injection is necessary to administer drugs that cannot pass through the skin or that do not build up levels in the blood after oral ingestion. Liquids can also be taken by mouth, and this form is easier for those who cannot swallow pills. Drugs such as antacids, that are available both as liquids and as chewable tablets, will work more quickly in liquid form.

Some liquid medicines will not stay dissolved but will separate, like salad dressing. These suspensions, as they are called, need shaking before they are poured.

Technically, a "pill" is a round mass of medicine. A flatter disk is a tablet. Pills and tablets may be coated with a thin, protective layer, often meant to protect the patient's stomach from the drug (as in some forms of aspirin) or to protect the drug from the strong acids of the stomach. A capsule is a torpedo-shaped covering, usually made of gelatin, which encloses a powder within.

Some drugs can be absorbed into the blood through the skin or mucous membranes. Nitroglycerin ointment, for example, is rubbed into the chest to relieve chest pain. It can also be absorbed very rapidly through the mucous membrane in the mouth by placing it under the tongue. If it is swallowed, it is destroyed in the liver before it can work on the heart. A new drug form is the transdermal patch, a medicine-impregnated adhesive bandage from which the drug is gradually absorbed through the skin. This may be useful for short-term ailments such as air sickness, where the patient can remove the patch behind the ear while waiting for the seatbelt sign to go off. It is also useful for continuous administration of short-lived drugs such as nitroglycerin.

The Dosing Schedule

When a drug should be taken depends on how long it takes to reach the bloodstream, how long it remains in the blood in an active form, whether a constant level of the drug is essential, and how the drug interacts with food or the stomach, or both.

Drugs that might make the patient queasy or even nauseated because of irritation they cause on an empty stomach are often taken "with meals." The large volume of food diminishes the unpleasant side effects. On the other hand, some drugs may be inactivated by foods, or have their absorption slowed by a mass of food in the stomach. These may have to be taken before meals or between meals.

The body metabolizes different drugs in different ways. Some are absorbed almost immediately; others must pass through the stomach to the small intestine. Similarly, drugs persist in the bloodstream for differing lengths of time. The briefer this time period, the more often the drug must be taken. However, drug companies are now using new manufacturing techniques to produce many drugs in long-acting forms, as research shows that the fewer doses a person must take, the more likely it is that he or she will take all of them correctly.

Drugs that make the patient drowsy, either intentionally or as a side effect, can most easily be taken at bedtime, to minimize this sometimes hazardous side effect.

"Take 4 times per day" is one instruction the patient should always question. Only the doctor or pharmacist can say whether this means "At meals and bedtime" or "Every 6 hours, on the dot." In some cases, the need for a constant level of medication in the bloodstream is greater than the need for an uninterrupted night's sleep. The same question applies to less frequent dosing—"3 times per day" can mean "at meals" or "every 8 hours."

Another common problem is the missed dose. Sooner or later, almost everyone forgets to take medicine, and the greater the number of drugs a person takes, the more likely this is to occur. A person who has a complicated medication schedule, or who expects to need the medication for a long time, should ask the physician what to do if a dose is omitted. For some drugs, the answer is to take the missed dose as soon as it is remembered; for others, this might provide a dangerously high concentration of the drug when the next dose is taken.

In some cases, special measures must be taken to avoid a poor result of therapy. For example, a woman who forgets to take 1 oral contraceptive pill must take 2 pills on the next day. If she misses 2 pills in a row, she should take 2 pills on each of the next 2 days and use a barrier method of contraception in addition to the pills for the rest of the cycle.

In any case, it is essential to continue the medication until the physician approves its termination. The disappearance of symptoms is not enough to ensure that the drug has done its work. For instance, antibiotics may diminish the number of bacteria sufficiently to relieve disease symptoms. Discontinuing the antibiotic prematurely in this case may allow the remaining, usually more resistant, microorganisms to proliferate and reestablish the clinical problem.

It is not reasonable to discontinue a drug because it doesn't seem to work immediately. Some medications need a day or more to achieve a concentration high enough to relieve symptoms.

Side effects should be discussed with a physician before deciding to discontinue a drug. In the first place, they can be difficult to distinguish from new signs of disease. Second, many side effects are most intense at the very beginning of therapy, and may diminish thereafter. Third, the doctor must be consulted for a substitute therapy in any case; diseases don't disappear just because therapy is unpleasant.

Dosage Amounts

Generally, doctors try to prescribe the least amount of medication required to counteract the disease. If the disease does not respond, the dosage may be increased, the interval between doses decreased, or additional types of medications added. Thus, a major criterion in determining dosage amounts is the seriousness of the disease.

Age is another important factor. Elderly people often metabolize drugs more slowly. Since the drugs remain in the body longer, less is needed in each dose. Or the usual dose may be taken less frequently. The proportions of muscle and fat change in older bodies, changing metabolism of fat-soluble and water-soluble drugs. The same principles hold for younger people with a damaged liver or kidneys, the 2 organs responsible for the elimination of most drugs.

Elderly people often take several medications for different long-term conditions. Drug dosages and scheduling—and even the medications used—may need adjustment to prevent interactions between the drugs. Elderly people should be especially careful to inform each physician they consult about every medicine they take—including over-the-counter remedies and vitamins—and be sure to follow the precautions listed under Drug Safety, below.

Dosages and scheduling also differ for children. The most obvious factor is that children are smaller, and so generally need smaller doses. Dosages for children are usually based on the child's weight. Some drugs have paradoxical effects in children. For example, stimulants can be used to "calm down" hyperactivity in grade-schoolers. Many drugs affect the developing body, and should not be given at all to young children.

Weight is another factor that influences dosage. In some cases, a 250-pound football player needs more medication than a 90-pound gymnast—but less than the 250-pound diet dropout. This is because fatty tissue absorbs certain medications differently from lean muscle—faster for some drugs, slower for others. Elaborate formulas exist for determining the optimum dosage of some drugs according to body weight. This is another reason why doctors cannot prescribe over the phone.

DRUG SAFETY

DRUG SAFETY begins before the drugs arrive in the patient's home. Patients should look for over-the-counter drugs with safety seals, distant expiration dates, full instructions on the outside of the package, and childproof caps. When opening medications, they should be on the alert for broken or off-color tablets, capsules, or solutions, abnormal odor or taste, smeared or illegible labels, sediments or floating matter in solutions (unless they are designed to be shaken into a suspension), and foreign materials like metal, insects, or hair.

Defects of this sort should be reported to the pharmacist, who will make out a Drug Product Problem Report as part of a reporting program of the Food and Drug Administration. The report will be noted during FDA inspections of the drug manufacturing plants, and may occasion a recall of a batch of the drug.

Unless otherwise directed, drugs should be stored in a cool, dry place (which the bathroom is not). (See Chapter 39 on The Home Medicine Chest, page 769.) An important exception is nitroglycerin, which should be kept in the refrigerator to minimize evaporation. Drugs should be kept in their original containers to avoid confusion about which is which. In addition, certain drugs can be absorbed by improper containers and so lose potency.

In general, prescription drugs not currently in use should be discarded. An apparent recurrence of a long-ago disease may actually be due to a different cause and thus require different treatment; the same is true of a similar-seeming disease in another person. Drugs can become stale—or even harmful—with age. So there is no good reason to save unused medications or those that have passed their expiration dates. Flushing them down the toilet is a better method of disposal than throwing them out in the trash, where they might be found by someone's child or pet.

Childproof containers are safer in households where children live—or visit. However, if the patient cannot open childproof lids, the pharmacist can provide a simple-to-open container, which can be kept in a childproof place.

Managing the Complicated Drug Schedule

For most people, it's easy to remember to take a drug once a day, at bedtime. Problems arise when medications must be taken more often, on different schedules. These problems are compounded if the patient is elderly, busy, forgetful, or travels a lot.

One aid to memory is the drug schedule, a written checklist enumerating each dose by the hour, like a page in an appointment calendar. The list should be updated as necessary, with the name of each drug, the doctor, the date, the dose, and perhaps a brief description. It also provides a useful record of what drugs are in use.

Another method to ensure that the prescription is followed is to lay out each day's drugs in the hollows of an egg carton, one dose per section, with the time for taking it written on the side with a felt-tip pen. A flat plastic box with sections and a snap-tight lid, available in the notions department of a five-and-ten-cent store, may be more convenient for people on the go.

Safety with Children

Accidental poisonings of children by medicines have become much less frequent since childproof caps came into general use, but they still occur. Bright children can figure out ways to open the bottle, and children of all ages get at medicines when they're not safely locked away. Below are a few safety tips for people who live with children or expect to have young visitors.

- Lock all medicines away. Putting them on a high shelf will not protect toddlers who can stand on chairs. A cabinet with a childproof lock can hold medicines and poisonous household chemicals.

- Remember that "childproof" containers are not intrinsically impossible for children to open—they're just difficult. Given enough time, children figure them out, just like any other puzzle.

- Don't leave medicines alone with children. Possible danger times include the drive home from the drugstore, while the shopping bags are being unpacked, and while the medicine is being taken—especially if the doorbell or phone rings. In this case, take the medicine to the door or phone rather than leave it behind.

- Don't refer to medicines as candy. Many pediatricians express concern about sweet-tasting over-the-counter pills, fearing they may lead children to eat a handful. Rather than promising a child that the medicine will be delicious, offer a spoonful of something that really does taste good afterward. Have the treat available immediately, to wipe out the aftertaste.

- Don't take medicines in front of children: They love to imitate grown-ups.

TRAVELING WITH DRUGS

UNFORTUNATELY, travelers cannot leave their illnesses behind. The following tips may help people who must take medication while they travel.

- Don't forget to pack the medicine. Bring enough to cover the whole trip, plus extra in case of delay or loss.

- Carry at least 3 days' worth in the cabin with you

DOS AND DON'TS OF DRUG SAFETY

Do

- Use a memory aid as described under Managing the Complicated Drug Schedule, page 785.
- Pour liquid drugs with the label uppermost, to prevent obliterating instructions.
- Have drug containers clearly marked, with large type, if necessary.
- Inform each physician of all medications, including vitamins and over-the-counter drugs.
- Leave drugs in their original containers, and follow the directions on the label.
- Ask questions of physician and pharmacist if there is any doubt about how to take a drug.
- Take pills and capsules with about a cup of water, standing up, to help them go down more easily.

Don't

- Take drugs in the dark, or without reading the label.
- Accumulate drugs unless they are used at least occasionally.
- Take a drug prescribed for anyone else or offer prescription drugs to another person, no matter how similar the 2 complaints seem.
- Mix 2 different drugs in the same pillbox.
- Take up a long-abandoned drug again without consulting a doctor.
- Keep different drugs in very similar containers. Ask the pharmacist for a different bottle, if necessary.
- Transfer medicines from the original container to an unmarked (or incorrectly marked) container.
- Leave medicines on a bedside table, if you are able to get out of bed to take them. (This is to prevent overdosage caused by drowsy forgetfulness of the last dose.)

---

when you travel by plane. Otherwise a lost suitcase could be a disaster.

- Carry the drugs in their original containers, and keep a copy of the prescription for emergency refills, if needed.

- For a large amount of drugs or any controlled sub-

stance, federal authorities recommend that the patient carry a letter from the doctor explaining why and how the drugs are used.

- For foreign travel, have your physician write out the drug's generic name and trade names in the countries you will visit. Foreign trade names are available in the Merck Index (10th edition, 1983).

OVER-THE-COUNTER DRUGS

THERE ARE more than 300,000 different nonprescription remedies and they are taken for a myriad of ills, from the serious to the nonexistent. Almost everyone uses them. Over-the-counter drugs are currently being reviewed by special panels of the Food and Drug Administration, but the FDA cannot protect the consumer from taking the wrong pill, or the right pill improperly. Only the consumer can do that.

The first step to becoming an intelligent user of over-the-counter medications is to read the label *before* buying. The label must state all directions for use: what symptoms the drug treats, the dosage, who should *not* use the drug, the list of ingredients,

possible side effects, and precautions. All these will directly help the consumer decide whether the drug is suitable.

Follow the directions on the label. These drugs are real medicines. Overdosage, side effects, and drug interactions are just as likely as with prescription drugs.

Consult a doctor if symptoms persist after a reasonable period of time. The label will state how long is "reasonable." The symptoms may not be trivial, but signs of a serious underlying disease.

Don't mix drugs, or use alcohol in addition to drugs, unless a physician or pharmacist approves the mixture. Also, don't buy more than you can use.

These drugs can become stale too and should be discarded.

Pain and Fever Medications

Aspirin. At 200 billion tablets per year, aspirin is America's most widely used drug. Found in medicine chests, desk drawers, kitchen cabinets, handbags, aspirin is both overused—taken in too-large doses for inappropriate ailments—and underused—slighted in favor of less-effective narcotics for pain relief.

Aspirin—technically, acetylsalicylic acid—is a very effective pain reliever. For example, it is more effective than propoxyphene (Darvon) or codeine against pain of inoperable cancer or postoperative dental pain. It is best for mild to moderate pains, such as muscle aches, backache, toothache, and headache. It should be used for short periods only: chronic or recurrent pains should be referred to a physician. Frequent headaches due to stress or tension, so often depicted in television commercials, will respond better to avoidance of stressful situations, or better handling of them, than to painkillers.

Aspirin's second most important effect is its ability to lower fever. It also has an important anti-inflammatory effect, making it a major drug for the treatment of arthritis and rheumatic fever. Both these conditions should be monitored by a physician, however; doses of aspirin sufficient to control arthritis pain do not prevent the inflammatory progress of the disease. Aspirin, by acting on platelets, also reduces the formation of blood clots: for this reason it has been suggested as a preventive measure against heart attacks and stroke.

The antiplatelet activity of aspirin is an important side effect. People taking anticoagulants, and those with liver disease, vitamin K deficiency, or hemophilia should avoid aspirin, as should patients expecting surgery, and pregnant women.

The most common side effect of aspirin is gastrointestinal irritation. For this reason, people with ulcers should not take aspirin. Taking aspirin after a meal may lessen stomach irritation. A full glass of water or milk afterward also helps, but buffering the acid with antacids has not been conclusively proved to reduce injury to the stomach lining. Enteric coatings—thin outer layers that delay absorption of aspirin until it reaches the intestines—seem the best hope for those whose stomachs are irritated by regular aspirin.

Aspirin is a "real" drug: Overdoses can be fatal, especially to young children, and some people are allergic to it. It has been suggested that aspirin has been associated with Reye's syndrome, a rare but dangerous illness that occurs in children under the age of 16 who have taken aspirin for relieving the symptoms of viral diseases. This question is still under investigation.

Acetaminophen. Acetaminophen is very similar to aspirin in its effects against pain and fever. It has little effect on rheumatoid arthritis or blood clotting. It has fewer side effects: no stomach irritation and very few allergic reactions. However, massive overdoses can cause fatal liver damage; heavy use for several weeks can also injure the liver. For this reason, people with liver disease and heavy users of alcohol should not use acetaminophen.

Combinations and Extra-Strength Pain-Relievers. The active ingredient in a cup of coffee seems to boost the painkilling power of aspirin or acetaminophen, and for this reason caffeine is added to some brands. However, many people cannot tolerate caffeine, especially in the evening, and should look for another means to enhance the effect of the analgesic drugs.

Advertising tries to convince us that if we don't need a maximum-strength combination pain capsule for our headaches, we're just malingering. This isn't true. As with any other medicine, the minimum that works is the right amount to take. The standard aspirin tablet is 325 milligrams; "extra-strength" is 500 milligrams—the equivalent of 1½ regular tablets. But extra-strength products may cost far more than twice as much. If they seem more effective to some people, it may be due to the expectations raised by all those advertisements. On the other hand, 1,000 milligrams of either aspirin or acetaminophen may give greater pain relief than the traditional 2 tablets (600–650 milligrams), although not everyone can tolerate the larger doses of aspirin.

Cold and Cough Remedies, Allergy Medications

"The common cold lasts 7 days, but with modern medical care, this time can be reduced to a week." It's still true, unfortunately. Over-the-counter drugs can only relieve symptoms—and even antibiotics are useless against viral infections like cold and flu. Physicians recommend resting at home, breathing moist air from a vaporizer, and drinking plenty of fluids. A person who wants relief from symptoms should decide which are most troublesome and find a specific remedy, rather than using a "shotgun approach" with an all-in-one capsule.

Cough Suppressants. Coughing can be useful if it brings up mucus and secretion from the lungs. Asthmatics and people with emphysema or other lung diseases may need to cough for this reason. For others with a dry, "nonproductive" cough, effective cough-suppressing ingredients include codeine (a narcotic) and dextromethorphan.

Expectorants. These are supposed to thin out phlegm, mucus, and sputum so that they can be coughed away. Unfortunately, FDA panels have found none that are both effective and safe.

Nasal Decongestants. The kind applied directly to the nose are quite effective at clearing up stuffiness, but too-long use—more than about 4 days—can lead to a rebound effect, in which the nasal blood vessels enlarge tremendously as the previous dose wears off. Effective ingredients include oxymetazoline, ephedrine, phenylephrine, and racephedrine. Phenylpropanolamine and pseudoephedrine are 2 oral agents with similar effects.

Anticholinergics. These are drugs, found in some cold remedies, which dry up runny nose and eyes. However, they are extremely potent drugs, and none have been approved by the FDA for use in colds. They produce dry mouth, gluelike phlegm, rapid heart rate, and psychological changes. Names to avoid are atropine and belladonna alkaloids.

Antihistamines. These drugs block the release of histamine, a natural body substance that stimulates among other things the fluid-producing cells of nose, eyes, lungs, and skin. Antihistamines are used not only against allergic reactions and colds, but ulcers and skin irritations. Their action on the inner ear makes some of them useful against motion sickness and vertigo as well. However, they have a major side effect: drowsiness, which makes it unwise to operate machinery or drive after taking these drugs. Another annoying side effect is dry mouth. Different antihistamines have different potentials for causing drowsiness, however, and the amount differs from person to person. The drowsiness effect can be aggravated by alcohol.

The antihistamines below are safe and effective for use against some allergy and cold symptoms. Their relative risks of drowsiness are:

- Low: brompheniramine maleate, chlorpheniramine maleate, pheniramine maleate.
- Moderate: pyrilamine maleate.
- High: diphenhydramine hydrochloride, doxylamine succinate.

For information on over-the-counter drugs for constipation, diarrhea, and hemorrhoids, see Chapter 25 on Disorders of the Large Intestine, page 527.)

DRUGS OF THE FUTURE

THE FDA SUPERVISES the development and marketing of all drugs sold in the United States, both prescription and nonprescription. Development of most new drugs begins in the laboratories of pharmaceutical companies, but chemical companies, medical schools, universities, and the National Institutes of Health may all play a part in bringing drugs to market.

Animal studies determine the biological effects and dangers of the new chemical. The FDA requires that these studies show that the drug is safe enough to test in humans, and might provide some benefit. The FDA must approve reports of the animal tests and the company's plans to test the drug in humans. At this stage, the drug is an investigational new drug (IND).

The first stage of IND testing is determination of dosage, metabolism, and possible effectiveness in 20 to 80 persons, usually healthy volunteers. Sometimes patients who have the disease under study are used: All participants in the test must be properly informed so that they understand the risks of this experimental drug and can give "informed consent."

In phase II of testing, the safety, efficacy, and possible side effects of the drug are observed in perhaps 200 carefully monitored patients at risk of, or suffering from the disease that the drug is intended to prevent or cure. Additional animal tests may also be performed at this time.

In phase III, the most extensive tests of the drug's safety, efficacy, and optimum dosages take place in a large number of patients. Special attention is paid to reports of side effects. The drug is also compared with others and with placebo drugs— dummy medications—to ensure that the effects seen are not due to chance or hopeful expectations. When the drug sponsor believes these tests prove the drug is safe and effective against designated conditions, it applies for a New Drug Application (NDA) for approval to market the drug.

The NDA includes the drug's chemical structure, samples, reports of human and animal testing, proposed labeling, and an explanation of how the drug works. An FDA committee of physicians, pharmacists, chemists, and other professionals reviews the NDA, weighing the risks and benefits of the drug against each other. Serious side effects might be tolerated in a revolutionary new medication for a serious disease, but not for a drug that mimics others already on the market against the common cold.

If the drug is approved, the FDA then specifies the wording of the package insert, which contains a detailed explanation for physicians about the drug, its uses, its actions in the body, its adverse reactions, and how, when, and how much to prescribe. The FDA can also specify additional tests.

After the drug is released, the FDA mandates reports from the manufacturer at 3, 6, 9, 12, 18, and 24 months, and every year thereafter. Mistakes in manufacturing, contamination, or severe adverse reactions must be reported immediately. The FDA can obtain a court order for withdrawal of the drug, if necessary. In addition, the FDA reviews all the advertising and promotional materials on the drug to be sure that the claims are truthful, fairly balanced, and fully informative. Violations can be penalized by seizures of the drugs, remedial "Dear Doctor" letters, or corrective advertisements.

Nonprescription Drugs

Over-the-counter medications are currently being reviewed by special FDA panels, a huge job that began with amendments to the Federal Food, Drug, and Cosmetic Act in 1962. The FDA panels began reviewing drugs in 1972 and more than 10 years later have not yet finished. The 300,000 nonprescription drugs were analyzed by their active ingredients (surprisingly, there were only about 750), and these active ingredients were divided into 17 therapeutic classes. When the FDA panels are finished, all over-the counter drugs will contain ingredients proved safe and effective, and will be properly labeled. Already potentially dangerous drugs have been taken off the market: One example is phenacetin, a kidney-

damaging pain-reliever, once an ingredient in many combination analgesics.

More Information about Drugs

This chapter contains only a very brief overview of most often used medications. The standard reference book for prescription drugs, available in many libraries, is the *Physician's Desk Reference* (PDR), published yearly by Medical Economics Company. This tome contains a variety of useful facts: the names, addresses, and emergency phone numbers of most major drug manufacturers; listings of product names, both generic and proprietary; a photographic section with life-size color portraits of many drugs and drug containers; and addresses and phone numbers of poison control centers. By far the largest section is reprints or digests of the package inserts of more than 2,500 medications. Since the PDR is written for physicians and other medical professionals, the lay person may need a medical dictionary to decipher it.

A companion volume, although not as complete, is the PDR to Nonprescription Drugs. Other guides include *The Physicians' Drug Manual* (Biomedical Information Corporation), *The Handbook of Nonprescription Drugs* of the American Pharmaceutical Association, and the *AMA Drug Evaluations*, prepared by the American Medical Association Division of Drugs and covering both prescription and nonprescription drugs.

Of course, the patient's doctor is the best source for information specific to his or her condition. The pharmacist can also be consulted about prescription and nonprescription drugs. Only an expert with full knowledge of the patient can determine the best course of treatment for disease.

SUMMING UP

WITH DOZENS of new medications being developed each year, drugs are a mainstay of treatment in many important areas of medicine. In the case of infectious diseases and some forms of cancer, they can produce a cure. More often, they are used to modify the course of disease, to improve the quality of life, and sometimes to extend life.

Even when taken properly, some drugs can produce unforeseen adverse reactions or predictable side effects. Sometimes, these side effects must be weighed against the benefits of the therapy. In other cases, a substitute drug or a modified medication schedule will eliminate the problem.

More commonly, problems result from the improper use of drugs, whether inadvertent or not. Overdependency, failure to follow instructions, mixing drugs with alcohol, and failure of the patient to inform the physician about drugs already being taken are among the reasons.

To get the most benefit from drugs, and to use them safely, it is essential that consumers be thoroughly informed about the medications being prescribed for them. Patients must be sure that each physician they see has information about their medical history as it relates to drugs and the names of any other medications being taken.

Part Seven

DIRECTORY OF RESOURCES

41 Health Organizations and Resources for the Disabled

Ann Breuer, M.D.

INTRODUCTION

PHYSICALLY AND DEVELOPMENTALLY disabled people comprise the largest and least recognized minority in the world. Since 1 in 10 people worldwide (an estimated 36 million in the United States) is disabled, it is inevitable that each of us is or will be personally concerned with the welfare of at least 1 disabled friend or family member. The disability may be the result of illness, accident, injury, age, or congenital anomaly. It may be single or multiple, and include loss or impairment of manual dexterity, mobility, vision, hearing, mental or emotional function.

In a sense, everyone is disabled at one time or another in being unable to perform a task because of physical limitations or environmental barriers. When this happens, people try to minimize the limitation, modify the environment, or both. For example, to take a job on the one-hundredth floor of a building requires either sufficient physical stamina to make the climb each day or the use of an adaptive piece of equipment—an elevator. If the elevator is undependable and stamina is inadequate for the climb, the individual having to work in such a location would be handicapped.

People are always compensating for their disabilities by altering or removing "handicaps." The inconvenience and fatigue of walking from suburb to city is modified by using a car or a bus. A bridge or a boat makes it possible to cross a river or a bay without having to swim.

Resources for the disabled are a means of helping individuals modify their environment so that they are no longer handicapped in doing what they want to do. Elevators, cars, and bridges are taken for granted as necessary for the public good. For those who have additional limitations, it is merely a matter of more modifications—such as Braille signs and curb cuts—to make it possible to live without being handicapped by the environment.

People with physical and developmental disabilities are a vast and diverse group who should not be lumped together, although they often are. The one factor they do have in common is a need for some modification of the environment in order to achieve maximum potential and the highest possible degree of independence. This need presents a challenge for the disabled, their families, and for society as a whole.

Until early in the century it was not unusual for those with disabilities to be hidden away and cared for within the home or segregated in institutions. Advances in medicine and technology and the exigencies and ravages of 4 wars have changed the picture and the possibilities entirely, but unfortunately, the old attitudes sometimes linger.

Today there is an entire field of medicine devoted to the development or restoration of function. Called Physical Medicine at its inception at the turn of the century, it is now known as Rehabilitation Medicine. The doctors who specialize in this field are called physiatrists. They are first thoroughly trained in general medicine where they master the diagnostic and therapeutic skills of physical medicine. Then they specialize in the comprehensive management of patients with impairment and disability arising from neuromuscular, musculoskeletal, and vascular disorders, including the psychological and social aspects of various conditions. Unlike other areas of medicine which are aimed primarily at amelioration of disease or injury, rehabilitation medicine is concerned with restoration of the individual to a place in society.

Technological advances, particularly the miniaturization resulting from space research, have made possible many sophisticated aids that promise enormous strides in providing the means of greater communication, mobility, and independence for people with various disabilities. Systems are now available which operate with a touch of the chin or a finger, allowing people with minimal body mobility to control their wheelchairs, lights, heating systems, telephones, etc. In the near future, voice-activated systems should be perfected, further expanding the horizons of those with restricted movement.

There are advances, too, in attitude, both in society as a whole and among persons with disabilities. The government finally recognized the civil rights of disabled persons in the 1973 Rehabilitation Act (Public Law 93-112). Section 504 of the Act states that: No otherwise qualified handicapped individual in the United States shall, solely on the basis of his handicap, be excluded from participating in, be denied the benefits of, or be subjected to discrimination under any program or activity receiving federal assistance.

Because the Department of Health and Human Services (HHS) administers most programs serving disabled people, the Secretary of HHS (then called Health, Education and Welfare) was charged with writing the regulation pertaining to Section 504. It took 4 years and massive sit-ins by the disabled in Washington and HHS regional offices to get those regulations written and signed, but on April 28, 1977, it was at last accomplished and the civil rights of the disabled became protected by the law of the land.

There are still unanswered questions regarding the extent to which the government is responsible for absorbing the cost concomitant with disability. There are varying ideas about how the needs and desires of disabled citizens can best be met. But at last this diverse group for whom others have been speaking and making decisions has begun to organize into both specialized and general activist groups who are speaking for themselves and their loved ones.

Whether children or adults, the disabled themselves and those who care for them require a great deal of special information and perhaps aids of varying cost and complexity to compensate for the impaired function. Finding the correct information or the most appropriate aid can be a monumental task and an ongoing one. Where, then, does one turn for help? What are the resources available?

THE PRIMARY RESOURCE

THE CHALLENGE OF DISABILITY is different for each person and each family involved. In the care of a physically disabled adult, who else can know his precise needs as well as he does? With this knowledge, the disabled adult is necessarily his or her own best resource. It may be necessary to engage the support and assistance of family members or other care givers, but no one else has as much reason or motivation to secure the best possible life as the affected person. In the case of small children, parents must step in, but sooner than many would think, even a child is a very good judge of what is needed and what is possible.

Very often the necessary services come through

a variety of channels, and if one is not associated with a rehabilitation center, finding out which services are best and how they may be obtained can require persistence and detective skills of a high order. This is particularly true for people in rural areas at great distances from large medical centers.

There are 2 general sources of print information recommended as splendid starting points for almost any search. *Access* by Lilly Bruck (Random House, 1978) is a comprehensive guide for the disabled explaining the legislation affecting the disabled and detailing how to obtain the information, goods, and services necessary to life as a first-class citizen.

The Source Book for the Disabled, edited by Glorya Hale (Inprint Books Limited, London, 1979; printed in the United States by the Saunders Press, Philadelphia), is an illustrated guide to independent living for the physically disabled, with an extensive guide to agencies and organizations, literature, aids, communication, housing, sex, parenting, education, employment, and other topics.

Perhaps the most comprehensive sources of information on services and equipment for the dis-abled are the computer memory banks. There are presently 2 such data banks for the disabled: Accent on Information and Abledata.

Accent on Information is a service of *Accent on Living* magazine, a quarterly publication for disabled people. This service will search for specific equipment through the data banks at Illinois State University. Information on use and cost of service is available from Accent on Information, P.O. Box 700, Bloomington, IL 61701 (309-378-2961).

Abledata, a service of the National Rehabilitation Information Center at Catholic University in Washington, D.C., has information on approximately 7,500 items covering the needs of all types of disabilities. An information search from this service can provide a list and description of all makes of a desired product including prices and suppliers. Information on this service may be obtained through the Systems Manager, The Abledata System, National Rehabilitation Information Center, 4407 Eighth Street N.E., Washington, DC 20017 (202-635-6090 or TDD teletype 202-635-5884).

MEDICAL RESOURCES

MANY FACTORS impinge upon securing the best available medical care. The nature of the medical problem, the geographic location of the patient, and the family circumstances all dictate to some degree what kind of medical help is appropriate, beneficial, and practical.

For most physical disabilities, a rehabilitation center or the rehabilitation department in a medical center will offer the most comprehensive help. A physiatrist will oversee and coordinate the services of a whole battery of health-care specialists who may be helpful—depending on specific needs. The physiatrist will first work with any medical specialists who may be involved with primary care, such as a neurologist, a rheumatologist, a cardiovascular specialist, an orthopedist, or any other physician involved in the treatment of the disease or injury. With information on the underlying cause of the disability and the prognosis from the primary physicians, the physiatrist may then call on biomedical engineers, physical therapists, speech therapists, occupational therapists, or others specially trained to measure various physical abilities and design ways to improve or enhance them.

If the disability is sudden and causes severe psychological problems, a psychiatrist, a psychologist, or a social worker may be recommended for the dis-abled person or family members who need help. The social worker may be called upon to assist in the transition from hospital to home by finding appropriate community services such as homemakers, medical and social service agencies, etc., which may be needed.

If the disability is not one ordinarily requiring the help of a rehabilitation center, or if traveling to such a center is impractical, every local avenue of assistance should be investigated. The family physician is the first person to see. He may be able to make referrals or inquiries that would be difficult for the patient to achieve.

Other local or county resources include the visiting nurse service, the Social Work Department of the nearest hospital, and any clinics that deal with the specific disability. Indeed, the visiting nurse services are one of the best sources of help and information available in many local communities.

In the case of developmental disability, especially in the case of those capable of independent or moderately supervised living, the required services may fall more heavily into the areas of special education or occupational training rather than medical assistance.

Though developmental disabilities are organically based, they affect mental function to a greater or lesser degree and the most seriously affected require assistance in decision making as well as daily living.

The quality of service and information varies widely from hospital to hospital, agency to agency, and so forth. Some are fortunate in finding a treasure trove in one place. Others must search diligently and still feel they are not adequately served.

The search should not stop until the quality and quantity of service meets most of the needs of the disabled person and his family.

There is no single list of all rehabilitation facilities. The department of rehabilitation medicine at a university-based hospital will usually know what is available in the surrounding area.

AT HOME

THE AVERAGE DWELLING is not designed with the needs of the disabled in mind. Even the able-bodied who vary from the norm can find it uncomfortable to manage with cabinets or shower heads too high or too low, steps too narrow or too steep, windows too difficult to adjust, insufficient light, etc. To make a home both safe and comfortable for a disabled person may require only a few inexpensive modifications of existing furnishings or it may require costly architectural changes.

Since the cost can be significant and mistakes expensive, it is advisable to research the matter well. The help of a physical or an occupational therapist or a rehabilitation engineer may be invaluable. These specialists may be able to suggest specific devices or simple modifications that are perfectly suited to the problem. (Assistance from such specialists is best obtained through a primary-care physician or a physiatrist.)

For those without access to such professionals, there are other resources to tap. First try the nearest local or state chapter of the foundation or society that serves people with such a disability. Most of these associations have information and referral services which can recommend equipment and suppliers, and sometimes they can supply the names of others who have successfully dealt with the problem under consideration.

The public library or a good bookstore may have books or articles of help. New sources appear every year. Currently available are:

- *Catalogs of Aids for the Disabled*, Nancy and Jack Kreisler (McGraw-Hill; 1982).

- *Technology for Independent Living Resource Guide*, edited by Sandi Enders for the Rehabilitation Engineering Society of North America, available for $20 prepaid from RESNA, Suite 402, 4405 East-West Highway, Bethesda, MD 20814.

- *Access*, Lilly Bruck (Random House, 1978), lists information resources for all types of disabled, particularly

useful information on telephone, television, teletypewriter systems, and other communications aids for the blind and hearing impaired, as well as sources of possible financial assistance.

- "Housing and Handicapped People," Marie M. Thompson, containing information on home modification, is available free from The President's Committee on Employment of the Handicapped, Washington, DC 20036.

- *Housing and Home Services for the Disabled*, Gini Laurie (Lippincott, 1977).

Once the home environment has been modified as necessary to accommodate a physical disability, there still remain the issues of personal mobility and activities of daily living. A physical therapist is a specialist in mobility issues and is trained to evaluate and improve mobility through wheelchair training, gait training with assistive devices, and recommendation of special accommodations such as wheelchair lifts, bathroom aids, etc. Physiatrists and primary-care physicians may request a periodic consultation with a physical or an occupational therapist to evaluate mobility and to suggest any modification in equipment or method that change in condition or environment might warrant. An occupational therapist, an expert in upper extremity function and activities of daily living can, by evaluation, help a disabled individual gain better control over his or her body and become more self-reliant.

Working under the aegis of a physician, both the physical and occupational therapist can not only prescribe appropriate aids, but can often help in securing them from reliable sources. Since they keep abreast of new developments in their fields, they can often bring helpful information to their patients long before they would discover it on their own.

For information on a host of other helpful publications about self-help devices there is an annotated bibliography available from the National

Easter Seal Society, 2023 West Ogden Avenue, Chicago, IL 60612.

"Services for Special Needs" is a free booklet provided by local Bell Telephone offices describing devices available for those who have special communication needs.

OUTSIDE THE HOME

IT HAS NOT YET BEEN a decade since the regulations that affect barrier-free access to public buildings and transport and nondiscrimination in employment were put into effect. Changes are appearing everywhere, but it will be years before all the older buildings and systems can be modified to accommodate the disabled.

In the meantime, it is useful to find out exactly what the rights of the disabled are, where changes have been made, and how to employ available services to make it possible to enjoy the benefits of public transport, regular employment, cultural and educational opportunities, shopping, travel, and recreation.

First it is important to get *local* information. Depending on the size of the community there may be local "Access" booklets. The mayor's office is a good place to start when inquiring about local information.

In cities with large public transport systems, the transport authority will have information on barrier-free or alternative transit services. In smaller areas, the organizations dealing directly with specific disabilities usually know what kind of transportation is available.

Travel for business or pleasure requires particularly careful planning. There is a wealth of information available from the suppliers of services such as airlines, railways, buses, hotels, tourism offices, etc. *Access* by Lilly Bruck, mentioned at the beginning of the chapter, has a splendid section covering every aspect of travel, from sources of information to how to handle problems and how to complain effectively.

Mainstream, 1200 15th Street, N.W., Washington, DC 20005, is concerned with employment issues. This organization maintains an information center and has a telephone hotline from 9 to 5 weekdays (202-833-1163).

CENTERS FOR INDEPENDENT LIVING

IN 1972 A HANDFUL of disabled citizens in Berkeley, California, started an organization called the Center for Independent Living which rapidly grew into a large multipurpose community organization offering a wide array of services. Supported by federal, state, and private grants, the Berkeley Center for Independent Living has become the prototype for similar groups across the nation, and these centers are revolutionizing self-help and group mental health for large disabled populations.

The centers, largely staffed by disabled people, offer such services as counseling, education, housing, job placement, health care, wheelchair repair, transportation, attendant referral, financial advocacy, legal assistance, and sex counseling. The centers stress a holistic approach to living and health. They provide peers as role models and involve disabled individuals completely in deciding on and working toward a suitable, achievable, and gratifying goal. Centers for Independent Living also provide a peer support system, as well as education and counseling for families and the professional community.

Information about the location of approximately 200 centers throughout the country may be obtained from The National Council of Independent Living Programs, 4397 Laclede Avenue, St. Louis, MO 63108 (314-531-3050).

GENERAL PUBLICATIONS

IN ADDITION TO the publications of organizations concerned with specific disabilities, there are publications of general interest to people with a variety of disabilities. These include:

- *Accent on Living*
  P.O. Box 700
  Bloomington, IL 61701
  A pocket-size quarterly full of practical information

on transportation, housing, and other aspects of disabled living.

- *Rehabilitation Gazette*
  4502 Maryland Avenue
  St. Louis, MO 63108
  An international journal and information service for disabled people published annually. Contains a comprehensive list of U.S. periodicals and newsletters for persons with disabilities.

- Institute of Rehabilitation Medicine
  400 East 34th Street
  New York, NY 10016
  This institution also has a number of publications of interest.

ADVOCACY GROUPS

ADVOCACY GROUPS are springing up everywhere. Many are formed to agitate for local compliance with existing laws or regulations. Local newspapers and television programs frequently give information on the activities of such groups. All the Centers for Independent Living have advocacy groups, as do the Paralyzed Veterans of America. Another group, national in scope, is the American Coalition of Citizens with Disabilities, 1201 15th Street, N.W., Suite 201, Washington, DC 20005.

There are several consumer advocacy groups around the country to help individuals obtain greater freedom and rights. Included among these are the various Centers for Independent Living, Paralyzed Veterans of America, and the American Coalition of Citizens with Disabilities (see page 805 for complete list).

The federal Office for Handicapped Individuals (OHI), Department of Health and Human Services, 200 Independence Avenue, S.W., Room 338D, Washington, DC 20201 (202-245-1961), has a Clearinghouse on the Handicapped which can provide information on more than 200 federal programs serving disabled people. Call or write for specific information or a list of publications. The 10 regional OHI offices are listed on page 806.

The nearest office of the Social Security Administration is another important source of information. For those who encounter difficulties in dealing with this or other federal offices, help can often be found through senatorial or congressional offices.

Every state has a federally mandated Office of Vocational Rehabilitation, though designation will differ from state to state. It may be under the auspices of Labor, Education, or Social Services. County and local hospital social work offices have information on the services provided through Vocational Rehabilitation. These include free vocational counseling and referral to training programs or job placement services. For some, tuition and transportation costs may be paid.

There are a variety of educational services for the homebound, blind, or deaf, including closed-circuit television and telephone hook-up to various institutions such as public schools and community colleges. The National Library Service for the Blind and Physically Handicapped of the Library of Congress provides free cassette players and cassettes. There are a number of other organizations, such as The National Association for the Visually Handicapped, which supply complimentary services or additional types of equipment.

ORGANIZATIONS FOR PEOPLE WITH SPECIFIC DISABILITIES

THERE ARE numerous organizations that seek to serve the needs of those with a specific disability. Many are national in scope, with state or local chapters; others are local, having been created through the generosity and concern of some family or group. All of them provide useful public education materials, some have regular publications, and a few offer direct financial aid, equipment, or personal advice.

The Directory at the end of this chapter lists the national offices of specific disability groups. They should be able to make referrals to appropriate local affiliates as well as to other agencies which might be more helpful in a particular locale.

This list in the Directory is not exhaustive. There are many other sources of assistance and information, and each of the resources can point to others as well. The trick is to find the best source or combination of sources. With luck it can happen immediately, with persistence and patience it does happen eventually.

Any resource guide is apt to be out-of-date soon after it appears in print. Organizations, both public and private, frequently change names and addresses. Groups will merge, leases will not be renewed, or growth will dictate new headquarters. If the names and addresses given in the Directory of Resources appear to have changed, the information can be quickly updated by the nearest reference librarian. The *Encyclopedia of Associations* is published annually and lists virtually every nongovernmental organization in the United States. When names change or groups merge, the old names are carried in the index for a few years. In addition, the information given on the individual organizations in the directory will include former names. Federal organizations are similarly listed in the U.S. Government Manual.

DIRECTORY OF HEALTH ORGANIZATIONS AND RESOURCES

THE FOLLOWING LISTING includes major organizations and agencies that provide health information and other services. Most are national organizations and many have local chapters, which are not included in this directory. Check in your telephone white pages for possible listings. Telephone numbers have been supplied for those organizations able to handle phone inquiries. The others would prefer that inquiries be made by mail. Since organizations frequently move, all addresses are subject to change.

Aging

American Geriatric Society
10 Columbus Circle
New York, NY 10019
(212) 582-1333

Association for Alzheimer's and Related Diseases
360 North Michigan Avenue
Chicago, IL 60601
(800) 621-0379

The Gerontological Society of America
1835 K Street, N.W.
Washington, DC 20006
(202) 466-6750

National Clearinghouse on Aging
330 Independence Avenue, S.W.
Washington, DC 20201
(202) 245-2158

National Council of Senior Citizens, Incorporated
925 15th Street, N.W.
Washington, DC 20005
(202) 347-8800

National Council on the Aging
Suite 504, 1828 L Street, N.W.
Washington, DC 20036
(202) 223-6250

Alcoholism

Al-Anon Family Group Headquarters
P.O. Box 182, Madison Square Station
New York, NY 10159
(212) 481-6565

Alcoholics Anonymous, Inc.
175 Fifth Avenue
New York, NY 10010
(212) 473-6200

National Clearing House for Alcoholism Information
P.O. Box 2345
Rockville, MD 20852
(301) 468-2600

National Council on Alcoholism, Inc.
733 Third Avenue
New York, NY 10017
(212) 986-4433

Anorexia Nervosa

National Association of Anorexia Nervosa and Associated Disorders
Box 271
Highland Park, IL 60035
(312) 831-3438

Arthritis

The Arthritis Foundation
3400 Peachtree Road, N.E.
Atlanta, GA 30326
(404) 266-0795

Asthma and Allergy

American Lung Association
1740 Broadway
New York, NY 10019
(212) 889-3370

Asthma and Allergy Foundation of America
1707 North Street, N.W.
Washington, DC 20036
(202) 293-1260

Autism

National Society for Autistic Children
1234 Massachusetts Avenue, N.W.
Suite 1017
Washington, DC 20005
(202) 783-0125

Birth Defects

American Genetic Association
1028 Connecticut Avenue, N.W.
Washington, DC 20036
(202) 659-2096

March of Dimes/Birth Defects Foundation
1275 Mamaroneck Avenue
White Plains, NY 10605
(914) 428-7100

Blindness and Vision Problems

American Association of Workers for the Blind, Inc.,
AAWB/AEVH Alliance
206 North Washington Street
Alexandria, VA 22314
(703) 548-1884

American Council of the Blind
1211 Connecticut Avenue, N.W.
Washington DC 20036
(800) 424-8666

American Foundation for the Blind
15 West 16th Street
New York, NY 10011
(212) 620-2000

American Printing House for the Blind
1839 Frankfort Avenue
Louisville, KY 40206
(502) 895-2405

Associated Blind, Inc.
135 West 23rd Street
New York, NY 10011
(212) 255-1122

Better Vision Institute, Inc.
230 Park Avenue
New York, NY 10017
(212) 687-1731

Fight for Sight
139 East 57th Street
New York, NY 10022
(212) 751-1118

Guiding Eyes for the Blind, Inc.
611 Granite Springs Road
Yorktown Heights, NY 10598
(914) 245-4024
(information on guide dogs)

National Association for Visually Handicapped (Partially
  Seeing)
3201 Balboa Street
San Francisco, CA 94121
(415) 221-3201

National Library Service for the Blind and Physically
  Handicapped
The Library of Congress
1291 Taylor Street, N.W.
Washington, DC 20542
(202) 287-5100

National Society to Prevent Blindness
79 Madison Avenue
New York, NY 10016
(212) 684-3505

Recording for the Blind, Inc.
20 Roszel Road
Princeton, NJ 08540
(609) 452-0606

The Seeing Eye, Inc.
P.O. Box 375
Morristown, NJ 07960
(201) 539-4425

Blood Diseases

Leukemia Society of America, Inc.
800 Second Avenue
New York, NY 10017
(212) 573-8484

National Hemophilia Foundation
19 West 34th Street
New York, NY 10001
(212) 563-0211

National Sickle Cell Disease Program
  Division of Blood Diseases and Resources
National Heart, Lung and Blood Institute
National Institutes of Health
Room 504, Federal Building
7550 Wisconsin Avenue
Bethesda, MD 20205
(301) 496-6931

Cancer

American Cancer Society, Inc.
National Headquarters
90 Park Avenue
New York, NY 10016
(212) 599-8200

Cancer Counseling and Research Center
Suite 140
6060 North Central Expressway
Dallas, TX 75206
(214) 692-6311

Damon Runyon–Walter Winchell Cancer Fund
33 West 56th Street
New York, NY 10019
(212) 582-5400

Living with Cancer, Inc.
P.O. Box 3060
Long Island City, NY 11101
(718) 241-4100

National Cancer Institute
Cancer Information Clearinghouse
Office of Cancer Communications
Building 31, Room 10A18
9000 Rockville Pike
Bethesda, MD 20205
(301) 496-4070

Cardiovascular Disease

American Heart Association
7320 Greenville Avenue
Dallas, TX 75231
(214) 750-5300

Mended Hearts Club
7320 Greenville Avenue
Dallas, TX 75231
(for those who have had open-heart surgery)

National Stroke Association
1565 Clarkson Street
Denver, CO 80218
(303) 839-1992

The Sister Kenny Institute
800 East 28th Street
Minneapolis, MN 55407

Cerebral Palsy

United Cerebral Palsy Associations, Inc.
66 East 34th Street
New York, NY 10016
(212) 481-6300

Child Abuse and Neglect

American Humane Association
9725 East Hampden
Denver, CO 80231
(303) 695-0811

CALM, Child Abuse Listening Mediation, Inc.
P.O. Box 718
Santa Barbara, CA 93102
(805) 682-1366
(805) 963-1115 (hot line)

Clearinghouse on Child Abuse and Neglect Information
P.O. Box 1182
Washington, DC 20013
(202) 245-2856

Childbirth/Maternity Care

International Childbirth Education Association, Inc.
P.O. Box 20048
Minneapolis, MN 55420
(612) 854-8660

Maternity Center Association
48 East 92nd Street
New York, NY 10028
(212) 369-7300

Childhood Life-Threatening Illnesses

The Candlelighters Foundation
2025 Eye Street, N.W.
Washington, DC 20006
(202) 659-5136

The Compassionate Friends, Inc.
National Headquarters
P.O. Box 1347
Oak Brook, IL 60521
(312) 323-5010

National Sudden Infant Death Syndrome Foundation
310 South Michigan Avenue
Chicago, IL 60604
(312) 663-0650

New York City Program for Sudden Infant Death
520 First Avenue
New York, NY 10016
(212) 686-8854

Sudden Infant Death Syndrome (SIDS) Clearinghouse
Suite 600
1555 Wilson Boulevard
Rosslyn, VA 22209
(703) 522-0870

Cystic Fibrosis

Cystic Fibrosis Foundation
Suite 558
3384 Peachtree Road, N.E.
Atlanta, GA 30326
(404) 233-2195

Diabetes

American Diabetes Association, Inc.
Two Park Avenue
New York, NY 10016
(212) 683-7444

Joslin Diabetes Center
One Joslin Place
Boston, MA 02215
(617) 732-2400

The Juvenile Diabetes Foundation
23 East 26th Street
New York, NY 10010
(212) 889-7575

National Diabetes Information Clearinghouse
Box NDIC
Bethesda, MD 20205
(301) 652-5524

Digestive Diseases

American Digestive Disease Society
Suite 217
7720 Wisconsin Avenue
Bethesda, MD 20014
(301) 652-5524

National Digestive Diseases Education and Information
  Clearinghouse
Suite 600
1555 Wilson Boulevard
Rosslyn, VA 22209
(703) 522-0870

National Foundation for Ileitis and Colitis, Inc.
295 Madison Avenue
New York, NY 10017
(212) 685-3440

Drug Abuse and Narcotic Addiction

Cocaine Abuse Hotline
(800) COCAINE

Do It Now Foundation
P.O. Box 5115
Phoenix, AZ 85010-5115
(602) 257-0797

Drug Crisis Hotline
(800) 522-5353

Drug Abuse Clearinghouse
Room 10A53
5600 Fisher's Lane
Rockville, MD 20857
(301) 443-6500

Narcotics Education, Inc.
6830 Laurel Street, N.W.
Washington, DC 20012
(202) 722-6740

Epilepsy

Epilepsy Foundation of America
Suite 406
4351 Garden City Drive
Landover, MD 20785
(301) 459-3700

Epilepsy Institute
Suite 308
225 Park Avenue South
New York, NY 10003
(212) 667-8550

Family Planning/Sex Information

The Alan Guttmacher Institute
360 Park Avenue South
New York, NY 10010
(212) 685-5858

Association for Voluntary Sterilization
Suite 2300
703 Third Avenue
New York, NY 10017
(212) 986-3880

Emory University-Grady Memorial Hospital
Family Planning Program
80 Butler Street, S.E.
Atlanta, GA 90303
(404) 588-3680

Human Life and Natural Family Planning Foundation
1151 K Street, N.W.
Washington, DC 20005
(202) 393-1380

National Clearinghouse for Family Planning Information
P.O. Box 2225
Rockville, MD 20852
(301) 881-9400

Planned Parenthood Federation of America, Inc.
810 Seventh Avenue
New York, NY 10017
(212) 541-7800

Population Council, Inc.
One Dag Hammarskjold Plaza
New York, NY 10017
(212) 644-1300

Sex Information and Educational Council of the United
  States
Suite 801
80 Fifth Avenue
New York, NY 10011
(212) 929-2300

Fertility

American Fertility Society
Suite 101
1608 13th Avenue South
Birmingham, AL 35256
(205) 933-7222

Resolve, Inc.
P.O. Box 474
Belmont MA 02178
(617) 484-2424

Friederich's Ataxia

Friederich's Ataxia Group in America, Inc.
Box 1116
Oakland, CA 94611

Genetic Diseases

March of Dimes/Birth Defects Foundation
1275 Mamaroneck Avenue
White Plains, NY 10605
(914) 428-7100

National Clearinghouse for Human Genetic Diseases
Suite 500
805 15th Street
Washington, DC 20005
(202) 842-7617

National Genetics Foundation
555 West 57th Street
New York, NY 10019
(212) 586-5800

National Tay-Sachs and Allied Diseases Association, Inc.
122 East 42nd Street
New York, NY 10168
(212) 661-2780

Growth Disorders

Human Growth Foundation
4930 West 77th Street
Minneapolis, MN 55435
(612) 831-2780

Health Information

American Red Cross (ARC)
17th and D Streets, N.W.
Washington, DC 20006
(202) 737-8300

National Health Information Clearinghouse (NHIC)
P.O. Box 1133
Washington, DC 20013
(800) 336-4797
In Virginia: (703) 522-2590 (collect)

Hearing and Speech Disorders

Alexander Graham Bell Association for the Deaf
3417 Volta, N.W.
Washington, DC 20007
(202) 337-5220

American Humane Association
P.O. Box 1266
Denver, CO 80201
(Trains hearing dogs)

American Speech-Language-Hearing Association
10801 Rockville Pike
Rockville, MD 20852
(301) 897-5700

The Better Hearing Institute
1430 K Street, N., Suite 600
Washington, DC 20005
(202) 638-7577

Deafness Research Foundation
55 East 34th Street
New York, NY 10016
(212) 684-6556

National Association of the Deaf
814 Thayer Avenue
Silver Spring, MD 20910
(301) 587-1788

National Association for Hearing and Speech Action
10801 Rockville Pike
Rockville, MD 20852
(301) 897-8682 (in Maryland)
(800) 638-8255

National Association for Hearing and Speech Action
Suite 1000
6110 Executive Boulevard
Rockville, MD 20852
(301) 897-8682

Kidney Disease

National Association of Patients on Hemodialysis & Transplantation, Inc.
156 William Street
New York, NY 10038
(212) 619-2727

National Kidney Foundation, Inc.
Two Park Avenue
New York, NY 10016
(212) 889-2210

Learning Disabilities

American Association on Mental Deficiency
5101 Wisconsin Avenue, N.W.
Washington, DC 20016
(202) 686-5400

Association for Children with Learning Disabilities
4156 Library Road
Pittsburgh, PA 15234
(412) 341-1515

Federation for Children with Special Needs
Suite 338
120 Boylston Street
Boston, MA 02116
(617) 482-2915

Lupus Erythematosus

National Lupus Erythematosus Foundation
5430 Van Nuys Boulevard, Suite 206
Van Nuys, CA 91401
(213) 88-LUPUS

Medical Alert

Medic Alert Foundation International
P.O. Box 1009
Turlock, CA 95380
(209) 668-3333

Mental Health/Retardation

American Mental Health Foundation
Two East 86th Street
New York, NY 10028
(212) 737-9027

Association for Retarded Citizens
National Headquarters
2501 Avenue L
Arlington, TX 76011
(817) 640-0204

Kennedy Child Study Center
151 East 67th Street
New York, NY 10021
(212) 988-9500

National Association for Mental Health
1800 North Kent Street
Arlington, VA 20006
(703) 528-6408

National Clearinghouse for Mental Health Information
Public Inquiries Section
Room 11A-21
5600 Fishers Lane
Rockville, MD 20857
(301) 443-4513

Neurotics Anonymous International Liaison, Inc.
P.O. Box 4866
Cleveland Park Station
Washington, DC 20008
(202) 628-4379

Multiple Sclerosis

National Multiple Sclerosis Society
205 East 42nd Street
New York, NY 10010
(212) 986-3240

Muscular Dystrophy

Muscular Dystrophy Associations of America, Inc.
810 Seventh Avenue
New York, NY 10019
(212) 586-0808

Myasthenia Gravis

Myasthenia Gravis Foundation, Inc.
15 East 26th Street
New York, NY 10016
(212) 889-8157

Parkinson's Disease

American Parkinson's Disease Association
116 John Street
New York, NY 10038
(212) 732-9550

Parkinson's Disease Foundation
New York Neurological Institute
650 West 168th Street
New York, NY 10032
(212) 923-4700

United Parkinson Foundation
220 South State Street
Chicago, IL 60604
(312) 922-9734

Psoriasis

The National Psoriasis Foundation
Suite 200
6415 SW Canyon Court
Portland, OR 97221
(503) 297-1545

Respiratory Diseases

American Lung Association
1740 Broadway
New York, NY 10019
(212) 889-3370

Sexually Transmitted Diseases

AIDS National Hotline
(800) 342-AIDS

American Social Health Association
260 Sheridan Avenue
Palo Alto, CA 94306
(415) 327-6465

VD National Hotline
(800) 227-8922
in California: (800) 982-5883

Spina Bifida

Spina Bifida Association of America
343 South Dearborn Street
Chicago, IL 60604
(312) 663-1562

United Cerebral Palsy Association
66 East 34th Street
New York, NY 10016
(212) 481-6347

REHABILITATION ORGANIZATIONS

Amputees

Amputees' Service Association
Suite 1504, 529 North Michigan Avenue
Chicago, IL 60611
(312) 274-2044

The National Amputation Foundation, Inc.
12-45 150th Street
Whitestone, NY 11357
(718) 767-8400

General Rehabilitation

American Coalition of Citizens with Disabilities, Inc.
Suite 201
1200 15th Street, N.W.
Washington, DC 20005
(202) 785-4265

American Physical Therapy Association
200 South Service Road
Roslyn Heights, NY 11577
(516) 484-0095

Closer Look
P.O. Box 1492
Washington, DC 20013
(202) 833-4160

Disabled American Veterans
  National Headquarters
P.O. Box 14301
Cincinnati, OH 45214
(606) 441-7300

Federation of the Handicapped
211 West 14th Street
New York, NY 10011
(212) 242-9050

Goodwill Industries of America, Inc.
9200 Wisconsin Avenue, N.W.
Washington, DC 20014
(301) 530-6500

Human Resources Center
Willets Road
Albertson, NY 11507
(516) 747-5400

The National Easter Seal Society
2023 West Ogden Avenue
Chicago, IL 60612
(312) 243-8400

National Information Center for Handicapped Children
  and Youth
P.O. Box 1492
Washington, DC 20013
(202) 833-4160

National Paraplegia Foundation
333 North Michigan Avenue
Chicago, IL 60601
(312) 436-4776, 321-1629
(night line)

National Rehabilitation Association
1522 K Street, N.W.
Washington, DC 20005

National Rehabilitation Information Center
Catholic University of America
4407 8th Street, N.E.
Washington, DC 20017
(202) 635-5822

National Spinal Cord Injury Association
369 Elliot Street
Newton Upper Falls, MA 02164
(617) 964-0521

National Study Center for Emergency Medical Systems
22 South Green Street
Baltimore, MD 21201
(301) 328-3052
Spinal cord injury hotline: (800) 526-3456

Paralyzed Veterans of America
7315 Wisconsin Avenue, N.W.
Washington, DC 20014
(202) 429-9592

People-to-People-Committee for the Handicapped
Vanguard Building, 6th Floor
1111 20th Street, N.W.
Washington, DC 20210
(202) 653-5024

President's Committee on Employment of the Handicapped
1111 20th Street, N.W.
Washington, DC 20036
(202) 653-5044

Rehabilitation International
The International Society for Rehabilitation of the
  Disabled
432 Park Avenue South
New York, NY 10016
(212) 420-1500

Rehabilitation International, U.S.A.
1123 Broadway
New York, NY 10010
(212) 620-4040

Sister Kenny Institute
Chicago Avenue at 27th Street
Minneapolis, MN 55407

Advocacy Organizations

American Coalition of Citizens with Disabilities
1201 15th Street, N.W., Suite 201
Washington, DC 20005

Center for Concerned Engineering
1707 Q Street, N.W.
Washington, DC 20009

Centers for Independent Living
National Council on Independent Living Programs
4397 Laciede Avenue
St. Louis, MO 63108
(314) 531-3055

The Disability Rights Education and Defense Fund, Inc.
  Center
1346 Connecticut Avenue, N.W., Suite 1124
Washington, DC 20036
(202) 659-4684

National Center for Law and the Deaf
Gallaudet College
7th Street and Florida Avenue, N.E.
Washington, DC 20002

National Center for Law and the Handicapped, Inc.
1235 North Eddy Street
South Bend, IN 46617

Paralyzed Veterans of America
7315 Wisconsin Avenue, N.W.
Washington, DC 20014
(202) 429-9592

LEISURE ACTIVITIES FOR THE HANDICAPPED

Art, Dance, and Music

Arts
Box 2040
Grand Central Station
New York, NY 10017

Colorado Wheelers (Squaredance)
525 Meadlowlark Drive
Lakewood, CO 80226
($3 for 30-minute instruction cassette)

Music Services Unit
The Library of Congress
Division for the Blind and Physically Handicapped
Washington, DC 20542

Nature Study

The National Audubon Society
950 Third Avenue
New York, NY 10022
(212) 832-3200

Photography

Volunteer Service for Photographers, Inc.
111 West 57th Street
New York, NY 10019

Sports

American Association for Health, Physical Education and
  Recreation
Program for the Handicapped
1201 16th Street, N.W.
Washington, DC 20036

National Amputee Skiers Association
863 United Nations Plaza
New York, NY 10017

National Wheelchair Athletic Association
40-24 62nd Street
Woodside, NY 11377

National Wheelchair Basketball Association
University of Illinois
Rehabilitation-Education Center
Oak Street and Stadium Drive
Champaign, IL 61820

North American Riding for the Handicapped Association
Box 100
Ashburn, VA 22011

SOURCES OF EQUIPMENT AND AIDS FOR THE HANDICAPPED

Suppliers

Accurate Medical Service
8004 West Chester Pike
Upper Darby, PA 19082

E.F. Brewer Company
13282 West Carmen Avenue
P.O. Box 711
Butler, WI 53007

S.H. Camp and Company
P.O. Box 89
Jackson, MI 49204

Fashion-Able
Rocky Hill, NJ 08553

Ted Hoyler and Co., Inc.
2222 Minnesota Street
Oshkosh, WI 54901

Maddakk, Inc.
Paquannock, NJ 07440

G.E. Miller, Inc.
484 South Broadway
Yonkers, NY 10705

Nelson Medical Products
5690 Sarah Avenue
Sarasota, FL 33581

J.T. Posey Company
39 South Santa Anita Avenue
Pasadena, CA 91107

J.A. Preston Corporation
71 Fifth Avenue
New York, NY 10003

Rehabilitation Equipment Inc.
1556 Third Avenue
New York, NY 10028

Rehabilitation Equipment and Supply
1823 West Moss Avenue
Peoria, IL 61606

Fred Sammons, Inc.
P.O. Box 32
Brookfield, IL 60513

Self-Help Equipment Firms
Cleo Living Aids
3957 Mayfield
Cleveland, OH 44121

GOVERNMENT ASSISTANCE FOR THE HANDICAPPED

Federal Office for Handicapped Individuals
Department of Health and Human Services
200 Independence Avenue, S.W., Room 338D
Washington, DC 20201

REGIONAL OFFICES

Region/States	Address	Region/States	Address
Connecticut, Maine, Vermont, Massachusetts, Rhode Island, New Hampshire	John F. Kennedy Federal Building Government Center Boston, MA 02203 (617) 223-6820	Arkansas, Texas, Oklahoma, New Mexico, Louisiana	1507 Pacific Avenue Dallas, TX 75202 (214) 749-3574
Virgin Islands, New York, Puerto Rico, New Jersey	Federal Building 26 Federal Plaza New York, NY 10007 (212) 264-5763	Iowa, Kansas, Missouri, Nebraska	601 East 12th Street Kansas City, MO 64106 (816) 374-3667
District of Columbia, Maryland, Virginia, Delaware, West Virginia, Pennsylvania	P.O. Box 13716 Philadelphia, PA 19101 (215) 596-1224	Colorado, Montana, Utah, Wyoming, North Dakota, South Dakota	Federal Office Building 1961 Stout Street Denver, CO 80202 (303) 837-4106
Alabama, Florida, Georgia, Mississippi, Tennessee, South Carolina, Kentucky	50 Seventh Street Atlanta, GA 30323 (404) 526-3966	Arizona, California, Hawaii, Nevada, Pacific Territories (Guam and American Samoa)	Federal Office Building 50 Fulton Street San Francisco, CA 94102 (415) 556-0251
Illinois, Indiana, Ohio, Minnesota, Michigan, Wisconsin	300 S. Wacker Drive 15th Floor, Chicago, IL 60606 (312) 353-5194	Alaska, Idaho, Oregon, Washington	Dexter Horton Building 710 Second Avenue Seattle, WA 98101 (206) 442-5331

Federal Information Centers in 77 major cities will direct you to the correct federal, state, or local agency you need. Look in your telephone directory under U.S. GOVERNMENT, FEDERAL INFORMA-TION CENTER or write to General Services Administration, Washington, DC 20405 for the leaflet "Federal Information Centers."

Part Eight

MEDICAL TERMS AND THEIR MEANINGS

42 Understanding the Language of Medicine

Rita Charon, M.D.

INTRODUCTION

THE WORK OF MEDICINE is intimately connected to its language. Although the technology of health care gets more and more sophisticated, it is clear that the center of medicine is still the dialogue between the health-care provider and the patient. Medical interviews are complex conversations in which uncertainties, fears, hopes, and information are shared. The success of this conversation is crucial for both doctor and patient.

One thread of the conversation is a narration of the patient's life. During the dialogue between a doctor and a patient, which may take place over years or decades, the story of a life unfolds. Patients talk about their childhoods, their families, their activities, their plans. Many aspects of patients' lives enter into caring for their health.

A more specific level of the conversation is the reporting of symptoms. Patients must put their physical sensations into words, a task that challenges the most literate of us. Doctors must learn to understand the difference between a "pushing" pain and a "pressing" pain, or a "cramp" and a "stitch." The quality of the symptom can help to diagnose its cause; this is why patients are often urged to describe their sensations in detail. "Is the pain sharp or dull? Is it there all the time or does it come and go? Does it move around or does it stay in one place?" are all questions that most patients have been asked by their doctors.

The major part of the medical interview is the sharing of information. Patients tell about past hospitalizations, allergies, medications they take, and current medical problems. Doctors tell about what the symptoms may signify, what the diagnoses mean, what further tests need to be done, and what treatment can be offered. They give instructions about medicine, referrals to other health-care providers, diet, and exercise.

Interwoven into this dialogue is a thread of feelings. Because of the intimacy and the meaning of the topics discussed, many emotions are involved. Patients may be fearful or concerned. Doctors must deal with the uncertainty they face, for so much is not known and not understood in medicine even now. The feelings themselves may have brought the patient to seek medical attention, for a high proportion of visits to medical doctors are said to be prompted by anxiety, depression, or worries. Patients often talk with their doctors about troubles with families, with work, with money, or at home.

During the medical conversation, feelings between doctor and patient get expressed. They might be supportive, open, and helpful or they can be distant, hostile, and abrupt. The doctor may be able to empathize with the patient in distress, or might be perceived as ignoring the concerns brought by the patient.

Finally, there is a shape to the conversation between doctor and patient. Who does most of the talking? Who interrupts whom? Are the topics chosen by one person most of the time? Do they reach agreement on what to focus on? Who decides when the conversation is over? All these features reveal facts about the control of the doctor–patient relationship. It seems sometimes that there are two different conversations going on at the same time, one about the patient's world and one about the world of medicine.

The medical conversation, then, is a dynamic and complicated event. When all these levels are working well, the interview is smooth and effective. Patients and doctors learn about each other on a personal level. The health problems are described clearly, and the medical information is offered coherently. Emotional problems are openly addressed, and a supportive relationship is established. In this case, the doctor and the patient are talking the same language with mutual understanding and shared control.

When the conversation goes badly, the opposite occurs. Patients may not be clear in presenting their problems, doctors may not listen. Information may be given in scientific terms with no explanation. The real reason for the visit may not be expressed at all. One person may do most of the talking and prevent dialogue altogether. In this case, neither participant in the conversation feels heard. The work of medicine can't progress.

Studies are showing that the nature of the conversation between doctor and patient can have drastic effects on health care. Patients are more likely to follow advice and to keep return appointments when they feel that their doctors listen to them, understand their concerns, and convey interest in them. Even more importantly, we now think that good communication can improve the actual health condition of the patient. In some studies, patients who were allowed to ask questions and to clarify their understanding of their problems reached better control of their medical diseases.

We don't know how successful most doctors and patients are in talking with each other. There is active research in this field among medical doctors and social scientists who study language. We are learning that problems are widespread and that both doctors and patients are very troubled by the gaps in communication.

Fortunately, there is much that can be done to improve medical conversations by both doctors and patients. Medical schools have realized how important it is to teach their students how to talk with patients. Schools offer courses in medical interviewing skills, stressing the importance of listening to patients, recognizing the emotional issues raised, and responding in supportive and helpful ways. Because doctors spend so much time talking to each other, they have to be reminded how to speak in ordinary language about bodies and medical topics.

Patients are learning more and more about the language of medicine. Many health centers and doctors' offices have active programs in health education where patients can learn about diseases, treatments, and preventive health care. Patient self-help groups have been formed to share information about specific health problems. These groups, like the "Reach to Recovery" group for women who have had breast surgery, can make a big impact on the ability of a patient to deal with a disease and the changes it brings to his or her life. Health reporting on television and in the press has become quite sophisticated, giving medical news in ways that help people understand their own bodies. There is a growing library of books offered to the general audience about health and medicine topics.

This chapter gives you a glossary of medical terms to add to your knowledge of medical language. The dictionary is arranged to teach you about specific words and also to teach you how to interpret words by understanding smaller parts of them. You will see a list of prefixes and suffixes which will enable you to decode what many more complex words mean.

At Columbia University's College of Physicians & Surgeons, we believe that informed patients can be healthier patients. We offer this textbook to help patients be better informed, with this chapter as a road map.

Together, doctors and patients can improve their communication with each other. Patients will be empowered through education and sharing of control of health events. Doctors will grow in their ability truly to listen to patients, and to be not only diagnosticians and interveners, but also supportive presences in their patients' lives. We hope that doctors and patients are approaching a common language.

PREFIXES

a-, an-, Without, absent, deficient, not. Example: anaerobic (without oxygen).

ad-, Near, toward. Example: adrenal glands (glands located on top of the kidneys).

ambi-, Both. Example: ambidextrous (having equal dexterity in both hands).

anti-, Against. Example: antitoxin (substance that acts against a poison).

bi-, Two. Example: bicuspid (having 2 points or protrusions).

brady-, Slow. Example: bradycardia (slow heartbeat).

co-, con-, Together, in contact. Example: conjunctiva (the membrane that connects the eyeball to the eyelid).

con-, contra-, Against. Example: contraception (methods to prevent conception).

cyan-, cyano-, Blue. Example: cyanosis (the dark blue color of deoxygenated blood).

de-, Away, without, down from, out of. Example: dementia (madness, state of being "out of one's mind").

dia-, Through, completely, across. Example: dialysis (separation of particles from liquid through a straining device).

dys-, Difficult, bad. Example: dyspepsia (indigestion).

ect-, ecto-, Outside. Example: ectopic (displaced).

en-, endo-, Inside, within, inner. Example: endoscopy (internal examination).

epi-, On, over, next to. Example: epidermis (the outer layer of skin).

erythro-, Red. Example: erythrocyte (red blood cell).

eu-, Goodly, well. Example: euphoria (extreme elation).

ex-, Out of, away from. Example: exanthem (the appearance of lesions on the skin).

hemi-, Half. Example: hemiplegia (paralysis of one side of the body).

hetero-, Different. Example: heterogeneous (made up of differing components).

homo-, Alike, similar, the same. Example: homograft (transplant of tissue from one organism to another of the same species).

hyper-, Excessive, increased. Example: hypertension (high blood pressure).

hypo-, Insufficient, below. Example: hypotension (low blood pressure).

inter-, Between. Example: intertrigo (chafing between 2 skin surfaces).

intra-, Within. Example: intrauterine (inside the uterus).

leuk-, leuko-, White. Example: leukocyte (white blood cell).

lig-, Binding. Example: ligament (band of tissue that connects bones).

macro-, Large. Example: macrocyte (a large cell).

mega-, Large. Example: megacolon (an enlarged large intestine) or cardiomegaly (an enlarged heart).

melan-, melano-, Black, dark. Example: melanin (dark pigment).

met-, meta-, Change in, between, after. Example: metabolism (the total of all the chemical changes in the body).

micro-, Small. Example: microbe (very small living organism).

mono-, One. Example: monosaccharide (simple sugar).

myc-, myco-, mycet-, Fungal, relating to fungus. Example: mycotic infection (disease caused by a fungus).

ne-, neo-, New. Example: neoplasm (new growth, tumor).

olig-, oligo-, Scanty, little. Example: oliguria (deficient urine secretion).

ortho-, Erect, straight. Example: orthodontics (straightening of teeth).

osteo-, Bone. Example. Osteomalacia (softness of the bones).

pachy-, Thick. Example: pachyderm (thick skin).

pan-, Whole, entire. Example: pandemic (epidemic affecting entire area).

para-, Alongside of. Example: parasite (organism that lives on or in another organism).

patho-, Disease. Example: pathology (study of disease).

peri-, Around, surrounding. Example: pericardium (the membrane surrounding the heart).

phlebo-, Vein. Example: phlebitis (inflammation of a vein).

pneumo-, Air, lung. Example: pneumonia.

poly-, Many, more than normal. Example: polydactyl (having more than the usual number of fingers).

post-, After. Example: postmortem (after death).

pre-, Before. Example: prenatal (before birth).

procto-, Pertaining to the anus or rectum. Example: proctoscope (instrument to examine the anus and rectum).

proto-, First, earliest. Example: prototype.

re-, retro-, Again, back, behind. Example: repression (pressing back feelings into the subconscious).

retro-, Behind, past. Example: retroversion (turning back of).

rhino-, Nose. Example: rhinoplasty (plastic surgery of the nose).

schisto-, schizo-, Split. Example: schizophrenia ("split personality").

sclera-, Tough, hard. Example: scleroderma (hardening of the skin and connective tissue).

sub-, Under, less than. Example: subacute (less than acute).

super-, supra-, Above. Example: suprapubic (above the pubis).

syn-, syl-, sym-, Together. Example: syndrome (occurring together).

tachy-, Abnormally fast. Example: tachycardia (very fast heartbeat).

trichi-, tricho-, Hairy, hairlike. Example: trichiasis (ingrown hair).

tri-, Three, third. Example: trimester (one-third of pregnancy).

ultra-, Beyond. Example: ultrasound (sound waves out of the range of human hearing).

xanth-, Yellow. Example: xanthoma (yellow patch on the skin).

xero-, Dryness. Example: xeroderm (dry skin).

ROOTS

aden-, adeno-, Pertaining to a gland. Example: adenitis (inflammation of a gland).

andro-, andros-, Male. Example: android (resembling a male).

angi-, angio-, Vessel, usually a blood or lymph vessel. Example: angiography (x-ray study of blood vessels or lymphatic system).

arthr-, Pertaining to a joint. Example: arthritis (inflammation of a joint).

bleph-, Pertaining to the eyelid. Example: blepharitis (inflammation of the eyelids).

bronch-, broncho-, Pertaining to the windpipe. Example: bronchitis (inflammation of the windpipe).

cardio-, Pertaining to the heart. Example: cardiovascular.

cephal-, Pertaining to the head. Example: encephal- (inside the head, brain).

cerebr-, cerebri-, Pertaining to the brain. Example: cerebral.

chol-, chole-, Pertaining to bile. Example: cholecystectomy (removal of the gallbladder, where bile is stored).

cyst-, Pertaining to a bladder or sac. Example: cystoscopy (examination of the interior of the bladder).

cyt-, cyto-, Pertaining to cells. Example: cytology (cell biology).

dent-, dont-, Pertaining to teeth, or to a tooth.

derm-, derma-, dermo-, Pertaining to the skin. Example: dermatology.

enter-, entero-, Pertaining to the intestines.

gastr-, gastro-, Pertaining to the stomach. Example: gastroenteritis (inflammation of the stomach and intestines).

glossa-, Pertaining to the tongue. Example: glossoplegia (paralysis of the tongue).

gnatho-, Pertaining to the jaw. Example: gnathalgia (pain in the jaw).

gyn-, gyne-, Pertaining to women. Example: gynecology.

hema-, hemo-, Pertaining to blood. Example: hematoma (a blood-filled swelling).

hepar-, hepat-, Pertaining to the liver. Example: hepatoma (tumor of the liver).

hyster-, Pertaining to the uterus. Example: hysterectomy (surgical removal of the uterus).

iatro-, Pertaining to a physician, doctor. Example: iatrogenic (caused by a doctor).

idio-, Peculiar to a specific individual. Example: idiosyncrasy.

lipo-, Fat, fatty. Example: lipid (fatty substance).

lith-, Stone, sandy calcification. Example: lithiasis (formation of gallstones or kidney stones).

mamma-, mast-, Pertaining to the breast. Example: mammary gland (milk-secreting gland of the breast).

men-, meno- Pertaining to menstruation (monthly cycle).

metr-, metro-, Pertaining to the uterus. Example: metrorrhagia (bleeding from the uterus other than normal menstrual flow).

my-, myo-, Pertaining to the muscles. Example: myopathy (a disease of the muscles).

myelo-, Pertaining to the marrow. Example: myeloma (tumor of the bone marrow).

necro-, Pertaining to death. Example: necropsy (autopsy).

nephro-, Pertaining to the kidneys. Example: nephrolith (kidney stone).

neuro-, Pertaining to nerves. Example: neuralgia (pain along the course of a nerve).

ocul-, oculo-, Pertaining to the eyes.

odont-, odonto-, Pertaining to the teeth.

orchi-, Pertaining to the testes. Example: orchitis (inflammation of the testicles).

oro-, os-, Pertaining to the mouth or an opening.

ortho-, Straight, upright. Example: orthopnea (a condition in which one is able to breathe only when standing erect).

os-, oste-, osteo-, Pertaining to bones. Example: ossification (the process of becoming bone).

ot-, oto-, Pertaining to the ear. Example: otitis (inflammation of the ear).

path-, patho-, pathy-, Suffering or disease.

ped-, (1) Pertaining to the foot or feet. (2) Pertaining to children (pediatrics).

phag-, Pertaining to eating or swallowing. Capable of consuming. Example: phagocytes (cell capable of engulfing bacteria or debris).

phleb-, Pertaining to a vein. Example: phlebitis (inflammation of a vein).

plast-, Formation or reconstruction. Example: plastic surgery.

plegia-, Paralysis. Example: quadriplegia (paralysis of both arms and both legs).

pnea-, Pertaining to breathing. Example: dyspnea (difficulty breathing).

pneumo-, Pertaining to the lungs. Example: pneumonia (infection of the lungs).

presby-, Pertaining to old age, the aging process. Example: presbyopia (the progressive degeneration of the eyes associated with getting older).

psych-, psycho-, Pertaining to the mind. Example: psychogenic (originating in the mind).

pur-, pus-, pyo-, Pertaining to pus. Example: purulent (containing pus).

pyelo-, Pertaining to the pelvis (urine-collecting basin) of the kidney.

pyr-, pyret-, Indicating fever. Example: pyrexia (fever).

ren-, Pertaining to the kidneys. Example: renin (an enzyme produced in the kidneys).

rhin-, rhino-, Pertaining to the nose. Example: rhinoplasty (plastic surgery of the nose).

scler-, sclero-, Hard, stiff. Example: sclerosis (abnormal stiffening of a tissue).

sicca-, Dry, dryness.

somat-, somato-, Pertaining to the body.

stom-, stomato-, Pertaining to the mouth.

thor-, Pertaining to the chest.

thromb-, Pertaining to a blood clot. Example: thrombosis (formation of a blood clot in the blood vessels).

tract-, tracto-, Pertaining to pulling or extending. Example: traction (continuous pulling of a body part using weights and pulleys).

ur-, uro-, Pertaining to urine.
veni, veno-, Pertaining to veins.

SUFFIXES

-alg, -algia, Pain. Example: myalgia (pain in the muscles).

-cele, Swelling. Example: varicocele (swollen vein in the spermatic cord).

-cide, Capable of killing. Example: spermicide (agent capable of killing sperm).

-ectomy, Surgical removal. Example: splenectomy (surgical removal of the spleen).

-gen, -genic, Producing, indicating origin. Example: allergen (substance capable of producing an allergic reaction).

-gram, -graph, -graphy, Record, recording device, recording process. Examples: cardiogram, cardiography.

-ia, -iasis, Indicating diseased condition.

-itis, Inflammation. Example: tonsillitis (inflammation of the tonsils).

-lysis, Breaking down. Example: hydrolysis (breakdown of a substance by the addition of water).

-oid, Resembling, similar to. Example: adenoid (organ similar to a gland).

-ology, The science or study of; **-ologist,** one who studies, specialist in a particular branch of medicine.

-oma, Tumor, not necessarily malignant.

-osis, Diseased condition.

-ostomy, Surgical creation of an opening.

-otomy, Incision.

-penia, Scarcity, deficiency.

-plasia, -plasm, Formation, growth. Example: neoplasm (tumor).

-poiesis, Production.

-rhag, -rhagra, Excessive discharge. Example: hemorrhage.

-rrea, Flow. Example: leukorrhea (whitish discharge of mucus from the vagina).

-scope, Instrument for viewing. Example: cytoscope (instrument for viewing the interior of the bladder).

GLOSSARY OF MEDICAL TERMS

Abortion The interruption of pregnancy through expulsion of the fetus before it can survive outside the uterus (generally before the twentieth week of pregnancy). Abortion may be either induced (also called therapeutic) or spontaneous.

Abscess A localized buildup of pus due to the breakdown of tissue by bacteria.

Acidosis A disrupted acid/alkaline balance due to a depletion of the body's alkali supplies or a production of acid. The condition is linked with several disorders, such as diabetes.

Acne The inflammation of the sebaceous (oil) glands due to a buildup of sebum, a fatty substance discharged through the pores to lubricate the skin. The condition is associated with the hormonal changes of adolescence, but may occur at any age.

Addiction Physical and emotional dependence on a drug due to the body's adaptation to its presence.

Addison's anemia *See* Pernicious Anemia.

Addison's disease A disorder caused by insufficient secretion of aldosterone and cortisol from the adrenal glands, resulting in a variety of serious symptoms.

Adhesion The abnormal union of body surfaces caused by fibrous scars formed when tissues heal.

Adolescence The stage of development between puberty and full maturity.

Adrenal glands Endocrine glands that are situated just above the kidneys and which secrete important hormones. Among the hormones secreted are epinephrine (adrenaline) which affects heart rate and blood circulation and is instrumental in the body's response to physical stress, and cortisone, a natural anti-inflammatory. *See also* Epinephrine, Cortisone.

Adrenaline *See* Epinephrine.

Adrenocorticotrophic hormone (ACTH) A hormone produced by the pituitary gland in order to induce the secretion of corticoids from the adrenal glands.

Afterbirth The collection of special tissues which are associated with fetal development and which are expelled after the delivery of the body. *See also* Placenta.

Agalactia The inability to produce milk after childbirth.

AIDS (Acquired Immune Deficiency Syndrome) A sexually transmitted, incurable disease that attacks and weakens the body's immune system, leaving the patient open to "opportunistic" infections and disorders that are normally warded off.

Albumin A protein found in animals, plants, and egg whites; the presence of albumin in the urine could indicate kidney disease.

Alcoholism Dependence on or addiction to alcohol. A poisoning of the body with alcohol. Physical damage can occur in the liver, heart, and kidneys as a result of alcohol poisoning. It can also lead to decreased resistance to infections.

Allergen Any agent that produces an allergic reaction. Common allergens include animal fur, pollen, dust, and certain foods. *See also* Allergy.

Allergy A hypersensitive or exaggerated reaction to exposure to certain substances (*see also* Allergen) or conditions (such as sun rays). Manifestations of allergies include rashes, coldlike symptoms, headaches, gastrointestinal symptoms, and asthma.

Alkali Opposite and neutralizer of acid. Bicarbonate is the body's chief alkali.

Alveoli The microscopic air sacs in the lungs through which oxygen and carbon dioxide are exchanged.

Amenorrhea The failure to menstruate. Amenorrhea is a symptom of many diseases and conditions.

Amino acid The nitrogen-containing components of protein used by the body to build muscle and other tissue. Some essential amino acids must be supplied by eating high-protein foods while others are synthesized in the body.

Amnesia Memory loss.

Amniocentesis The extraction and examination of a small amount of the amniotic fluid in order to determine genetic and other disorders in the fetus. *See also* Amniotic fluid.

Amnion The bag of waters in which the fetus and the amniotic fluid are contained during pregnancy.

Amniotic fluid The fluid surrounding the fetus.

Amphetamine A drug that stimulates the central nervous system.

Analgesic Any substance that gives temporary relief from pain.

Androgen Hormones, such as testosterone and androsterone, which are produced in the testes and are responsible for male characteristics. They are also produced normally in small amounts in females.

Androsterone One of the male sex hormones.

Anemia A deficiency in the hemoglobin, the number of red blood cells, or in the amount of blood. Anemia is usually a symptom of an underlying disorder.

Anesthesia Loss of sensation or feeling. General anesthesia involves the whole body while local anesthesia involves only a particular area.

Anesthesiology The branch of medicine dealing with anesthesia and the application of anesthetic agents in surgery and pain relief.

Aneurysm A sac filled with blood which forms as a result of an abnormal widening of a vein or artery.

Angina Intense pain that produces a feeling of suffocation. The term is commonly used to refer to chest pains (angina pectoris) that are usually a result of an interruption of the oxygen supply to the heart muscle.

Angiography Examination of the interior blood vessels by injecting radiopaque substances so that any disorder or abnormality shows up on x-ray film. The record of pictures is called an angiogram.

Anoxia Oxygen deficiency.

Antacid An acid-neutralizing substance.

Antibiotic An antibacterial substance derived from bacteria, molds, and other substances. Penicillin is a common antibiotic.

Antibody The components of the immune system which eliminate or counteract foreign substances (antigens) in the body.

Anticoagulant An agent that retards the blood clotting process.

Antidote An agent that counteracts the effects of a poison.

Antigen A substance, usually a protein found in germs or foreign tissue, which stimulates the production of antibodies.

Antihistamine A drug that blocks histamine action. Since histamines are often produced in large amounts in response to allergens, they cause many of the symptoms associated with allergies; antihistamines are often used to relieve allergic reactions, such as hayfever or hives. Antihistamines also may be prescribed to counter nausea.

Antihypertensive Any drug that lowers blood pressure.

Antiseptic Any substance that prevents or slows the proliferation of germs or bacteria.

Antitoxin An antibody produced by or introduced into the body to counteract a poison.

Anus The opening at the end of the rectum (the last segment of the large intestine) through which fecal waste passes.

Anvil One of the tiny bones in the middle ear (also called the incus).

Anxiety Feelings of apprehension and undue uneasiness. Appropriate anxiety may occur in the face of identifiable danger. In contrast, clinical anxiety is the feeling of apprehension or fear, even in the face of no identifiable hazards.

Aorta The body's largest artery, it carries blood from the left ventricle of the heart and distributes it to all parts of the body.

Aphasia Loss of the ability to speak or to understand speech due to brain damage. The organs of speech may be unimpaired.

Apnea The absence of breathing.

Appendicitis An inflammation of the appendix which results in severe pain on the lower right side, fever, and nausea or vomiting. Appendicitis calls for immediate medical attention, usually requiring removal of the appendix.

Aqueous humor The fluid in the anterior part of the eyeball.

Areola A round pigmented area around a raised center, such as the nipple of a breast.

Arrhythmia Any deviation from the regular heartbeat rhythm.

Arteriole A tiny artery that joins another artery to the capillaries.

Arteriosclerosis Also called hardening of the arteries, this condition involves a thickening of the walls of the arteries resulting in a loss of elasticity. *See also* Atherosclerosis.

Artery A blood vessel that transports oxygenated blood away from the heart to the rest of the body.

Arthritis Inflammation of a joint.

Ascorbic acid Vitamin C.

Asphyxia Suffocation due to lack of oxygen or overabundance of carbon dioxide.

Aspiration The removal of fluids from the lungs or other body cavities. A suction or siphoning implement is used.

Aspirin   Acetylsalicylic acid. A drug used to relieve pain and lower fever. It is also an anti-inflammatory drug and anticoagulant.

Astigmatism   A defect in one of the eye's surfaces which leads to an inability to focus the eye correctly.

Asthma   A disorder of the respiratory system due to bronchial spasm that results in breathing difficulties.

Atherosclerosis   A form of arteriosclerosis in which, in addition to the thickening and reduced elasticity of the arteries, a fatty substance (plaque) forms on the inner walls of the arteries, causing obstruction to the flow of blood.

Athlete's foot   *See* Tinea pedia.

Atrophy   Wasting; degeneration of a body part through lack of activity or nourishment.

Auscultation   A method of examining the body by listening, usually using a stethoscope.

Autoimmune disease   Any disease in which the body manufactures antibodies against itself. The body regards its own tissue as a foreign body and acts accordingly to eliminate it.

Bacilli   Rod-shaped bacteria.

Bacteria   One-celled microscopic organisms. Some cause disease, others are harmless, and some are beneficial.

Bag of waters   *See* Amnion.

Barbiturate   A drug that produces a sedation, hypnosis, anesthesia, or sleep.

Barium tests   Diagnostic tests using barium, a metallic element which does not permit x-rays to pass through and therefore makes internal organs visible on x-ray films. Common barium tests are the barium swallow (upper GI series) and the barium enema (lower GI series).

B cell   A specialized type of white cell (lymphocyte) that works as part of the immune system by providing antibodies that attack foreign agents, such as bacteria or viruses.

Bedsore   Decubitus ulcer, an ulcerlike sore on the skin as a result of the pressure of the bed against the body.

Bell's palsy   A paralysis of the face muscles due to the inflammation of the facial nerve.

Benign   Harmless or innocent. Term is used to describe a nonmalignant tumor which will not spread or grow back after removal.

Bile   The bitter alkaline fluid secreted by the liver to aid in digestion. Bile is greenish-yellow until it is stored in the gallbladder where it becomes darker.

Biofeedback   A behavior modification therapy by which a patient is taught to control involuntary body functions such as blood pressure.

Biopsy   The examination of a small sample of tissue, taken from a patient's body, usually used to determine if a growth is cancerous.

Birth control   *See* Contraception.

Birthmark   A colored patch or skin blemish which is present at birth.

Blackhead   An open comedo, in which a follicle is clogged by fatty substances secreted by the sebaceous glands. Its black coloration is caused by exposure to air, not dirt as is commonly assumed.

Bladder   A sac that contains fluid or gas.

Bladder infection   *See* Cystitis.

Blastomycosis   A fungal disease usually affecting the lungs but sometimes the whole system.

Blind spot   The spot where the optic nerve and the retina connect. It is not light sensitive.

Blister   An accumulation of fluid causing a raised sac under the surface of the skin.

Blood   The body fluid circulated by the heart through a network of arteries, veins, and capillaries to provide oxygen and nutrients to all body cells and to remove carbon dioxide and wastes from them.

Blood clotting   The process of blood coagulation in which blood platelets and proteins join together to close up a break in the circulatory system.

Blood corpuscle   Either a red blood cell (erythrocyte) or a white blood cell (leukocyte).

Blood count   The amount of red and white blood cells in the blood.

Blood plasma   The part of the blood composed mostly of water (over 90 percent). The other constituents include electrolytes, nutrients, wastes, clotting agents, antibodies, and hormones.

Blood pressure   The force exerted by the blood against the arterial walls. A sphygmomanometer measures both the systolic pressure (when the heart is at maximum contraction) and diastolic pressure (when the heart is relaxed between beats).

Blood serum   The liquid that separates from the blood when it clots. It is the plasma without the clotting agents and is yellowish in color.

Blood sugar   The glucose that is circulated in the blood. It is the end product of carbohydrate metabolism (although protein and some fat also may be converted to glucose) and is the body's major fuel.

Blood transfusion   The intravenous replacement or replenishment of a patient's blood with healthy, compatible blood from an outside source.

Blood type   Grouping of hereditary factors in the blood. The 4 major groupings are O, A, B, and AB. It is essential to determine if the donor's and recipient's blood types are compatible before a transfusion is administered.

Blood vessel   A vein or artery.

Boil   A round, painful, pus-filled bacterial infection of a hair follicle, usually caused by staphylococci (also called furuncle).

Bone   The hard tissue of the skeleton.

Bone graft   Transplantation of bone from one person to another or from one part of the body to another.

Boric acid   A mild antiseptic powder which is poisonous if swallowed. It was once considered a useful household first-aid item, but it is no longer recommended because of its limited effectiveness and potential toxicity.

Botulism   A dangerous form of food poisoning caused by the toxin produced by botulinus bacteria. The toxin attacks the nervous system causing headache, weakness, constipation, and paralysis. The causative bacterium grows in anaerobic (without oxygen) conditions and therefore is found in improperly canned or improperly refrigerated fresh foods.

Bowel   Intestine, gut.

Brain   The central organ of the nervous system consisting of the cerebrum, cerebellum, pons varolii, midbrain, and medulla.

Breast   The mammary (milk-producing) gland and the fat and connective tissue around it.

Breech delivery (or presentation)   Delivery of a baby with either the feet or buttocks, instead of the head, emerging first.

Bright's disease   A term formerly used to describe nephrosis, a disease affecting the kidney's filtering units (nephrons).

Bromides   A group of drugs once used as anticonvulsants because of their sedative effects on the central nervous system. They have been replaced by newer, more effective drugs that do not have as high a risk of adverse reactions.

Bronchi   The 2 tubes branching off at the lower part of the trachea (singular: bronchus).

Bronchiole   Subdivision of a bronchus which leads to the alveoli in the lungs.

Bronchitis   Inflammation of the bronchi.

Bronchopneumonia   Bacterial infection that results in the inflammation of the bronchioles.

Bruise   Damage to the subcutaneous blood vessels resulting in the escape of blood into the other tissues. Characteristic features are pain, swelling, and discoloration of the skin. A bruise in which the outer layer of skin is not broken is called a contusion. An abrasion or laceration is a bruise in which the skin is broken.

Bulimia   Excessive appetite. Also refers to the binge–purge syndrome in which deliberate overeating is compensated for through self-induced vomiting, laxative use, excessive exercise, or starvation.

Bunion   A deformity of the big toe resulting from an inflammation of the joint that connects the toe to the foot.

Bursa   A fibrous, fluid-filled sac in the joints which aids movement by decreasing friction.

Bursitis   A painful condition involving inflammation of the bursa, a fluid-filled sac in a joint.

Caffeine   A substance that stimulates the central nervous system. It is present in coffee, tea, chocolate, and certain soft drinks.

Calamine lotion   A compound containing zinc oxide used to treat skin rashes, irritations, and other skin disorders.

Calcium   An essential mineral. Calcium is the main material in teeth and bones and vital to proper function of the heart, other muscles, and other body tissues.

Calculus   Abnormal stone formation in certain parts of the body such as the gallbladder or kidneys. Calculi are composed of minerals, cholesterol, bile pigments, or other substances, depending upon their location (plural: calculi).

Callus   (1) An area where the skin has become thick in order to protect itself against repeated friction. (2) The

partly calcified tissue that forms around a broken bone in the healing process.

Calorie   Measure of energy (heat) used in physics and in nutrition.

Cancer   A general term referring to the abnormal reproduction of cells in the body. The term covers many malignant tumors affecting many parts of the body.

Candidiasis   A yeast infection caused by the candida fungus. Also called moniliasis or thrush.

Canker sore   An ulcerlike sore on the mucous membrane of the mouth or lips.

Capillary   Minute thin-walled blood vessel, in a network which facilitates the exchange of substances between the surrounding tissues and the blood.

Carbohydrates   Organic compounds of carbon, hydrogen, and oxygen. They include starches, cellulose, and sugars and are divided into 3 groups: monosaccharides (simple sugars), disaccharides (containing 2 different sugars), and polysaccharides (complex sugars).

Carcinogen   Any agent that is capable of causing cancer.

Carcinoma   The type of cancer which originates in the epithelial cells located in glands, skin, and mucous membranes.

Cardiac   Pertaining to the heart.

Cardiograph   A device for tracing the movements of the heart. The record produced is called a cardiogram or electrocardiogram.

Cardiopulmonary   Pertaining to the heart and lungs.

Cardiovascular   Pertaining to the heart and blood vessels.

Carditis   Inflammation of the heart.

Caries   Tooth or bone decay.

Cartilage   The white, elastic tissue located in joints, the nose, and the outer ear.

Castration   The removal of ovaries or testes.

Cast   Fibrous material that has collected in body cavities and hardens to the shape of them.

Castor oil   An oil derived from a poisonous bean plant and which acts as a purgative or cathartic.

Cataract   An opacity or clouding of the eye lens, which can eventually lead to loss of vision as progressively less light is filtered through the lens to the retina.

Cathartic   Any substance that stimulates rapid intestinal activity resulting in bowel evacuation (also called purgative).

Catheterization   Any procedure in which a small flexible tube is inserted into the body for the purpose of withdrawing or introducing substances.

Caustic   Having the ability to destroy or corrode organic tissue.

Cauterization   The application of caustic chemicals or electrically heated devices for the purpose of eliminating infected, unwanted, or dead tissue.

Cavities   (1) Dental caries. (2) Hollow spaces.

Cell   A minute mass of protoplasm containing a nucleus; the structural unit of body tissue.

Cellulose   A polysaccharide carbohydrate (starch) found in plant cells. It is indigestible by humans but aids in the overall digestive process by providing roughage.

Cerebellum   The movement-coordinating part of the brain.

Cerebral cortex The convoluted outer surface of the brain.

Cerebrum The largest part of the brain, containing 2 hemispheres and the cerebral cortex, which controls thinking, feeling, and voluntary activities.

Cervix The neck, or the narrow part of the uterus.

Cesarean section Delivery of a baby through the abdominal wall by means of a surgical procedure.

Chancre The highly infectious ulcerated sore that is the first sign of syphilis.

Chemotherapy The use of chemicals to treat disease with minimal damage to the patient. Use in the treatment of cancer is widespread and has increased life expectancy of patients.

Chilblains Painful and itchy swelling of skin due to exposure to the cold.

Cholera An epidemic disease characterized by diarrhea, vomiting, thirst, and cramps. It is spread through polluted water.

Cholesterol A crystalline fatlike substance found in the brain, nerves, liver, blood, and bile. It is synthesized in the liver and is essential in the production of sex hormones, nerve function, and a number of other vital processes. Excessive consumption of dietary cholesterol (found only in animal products, such as fat, red meat, whole milk, and egg yolks) is thought to contribute to heart disease.

Chorea A disease of the nervous system manifested by spasmodic movements of the body.

Chromosome Any one of the rod-shaped bodies in the nucleus of a cell which carry hereditary factors.

Cirrhosis Chronic inflammation and hardening of an organ, usually the liver but occasionally the heart or kidneys are involved.

Cleft palate Congenital defect of the mouth in which the palate bones fail to fuse and result in a groove in the roof of the mouth. Harelip is often associated with cleft palate.

Climacteric Menopause.

Clitoris A small organ situated at the front of the vulva that is one source of the female orgasm. It contains erectile tissue and is the female counterpart of the male penis.

Colic Spasmodic pain in the abdomen.

Colitis Inflammation of the colon (large intestine), characterized by bowel spasms, diarrhea, and constipation. Ulcerative colitis is a more serious form of the disease, and is characterized by open sores in the lining of the colon and the passage of diarrhea streaked with blood and mucus.

Colon Large intestine extending from the small intestine to the rectum. Undigested food that is not absorbed by the body passes from the small intestine into the colon; water is extracted from the waste and it is eventually eliminated from the body in the form of a bowel movement.

Colostomy Surgical procedure to create an artificial anus in the abdominal wall.

Colostrum The pale yellow "first milk" secreted by women in the late stages of pregnancy and just after delivery.

Colposcope A magnifying device used to examine the cervix and vagina.

Coma State of unconsciousness from which one cannot be awakened.

Communicable disease Transmissable to other persons. Contagious.

Conception Impregnation of the ovum by the sperm.

Concussion Injury resulting from a severe blow or shock to the head.

Congenital Existing at birth or before.

Congestive heart failure A condition in which weakened heart muscles are unable to pump strongly enough to maintain normal blood circulation. As a result, blood backs up in the lungs and veins leading to the heart. Often accompanied by accumulation of fluid in various parts of the body.

Conjunctiva The transparent membrane lining the front of the eyeball and eyelid.

Conjunctivitis Inflammation of the conjunctiva.

Constipation A condition of infrequent and difficult bowel movements.

Contraception Prevention of conception. Birth control.

Contraceptive An agent used in preventing conception.

Contusion A bruise; bleeding under the skin.

Convulsions Involuntary spasms due to abnormal cerebral stimulation.

Cornea The transparent membrane that protects the outer surface of the eye.

Corns A patch of thickened skin (callus) usually occurring around the toes and caused by friction or pressure.

Coronary Related to the coronary arteries, the blood vessels that supply the heart muscle with blood.

Coronary artery disease Progressive narrowing of the coronary arteries, usually due to a buildup of fatty plaques (atheromas) along the vessel walls. The most common cause of angina pectoris and heart attacks. *See also* Heart attack.

Coronary thrombosis The blockage of a coronary artery with a clot (thrombus), a common cause of heart attacks.

Corpuscle A small mass of protoplasm. Red corpuscles are called erythrocytes and white corpuscles are called leukocytes.

Cortisol A principal hormone produced by the adrenal gland.

Cortisone Hormone preparation closely related to cortisol which acts as an anti-inflammatory agent and is used in treating various diseases. Corticosteroids.

Coryza Acute upper respiratory infection lasting only a short while. Head cold.

Cowpox A viral disease of cattle used to vaccinate against smallpox in humans. Since the worldwide elimination of smallpox, vaccination against this disease is no longer necessary.

Cranium The section of the skull that encases the brain.

Curettage A scraping out of tissue from an organ (particularly the uterus) for diagnostic purposes with a forklike instrument called a curette.

Cuspid Canine tooth; tooth having only 1 point.

Cuticle The epidermis (outer layer of skin); dead skin, especially that which surrounds finger- and toenails.

Cyanosis A condition in which tissue takes on a bluish tinge due to lack of oxygen.

Cyst An abnormal cavity or sac enclosing a fluid, gas or semi-solid substance.

Cystitis A bladder infection that is more common in women, but which also occurs in men.

Cystic fibrosis A hereditary respiratory disease occurring in early childhood. It is characterized by the buildup of mucus in the lungs and other abnormalities affecting the exocrine system (glands that secrete directly into their target organs, such as the sweat glands).

Cystoscopy A diagnostic procedure involving examination of the bladder with a cystoscope inserted through the urethra.

Cytology The study of the origins, structures, and functions of cells.

Dandruff A common condition in which white scales and flakes of dead skin appear on the scalp.

Debility Lessened ability; weakness.

Decubitus ulcer Bedsore.

Defibrillation Cessation of fibrillation (tremor or twitching of cardiac muscle) and resumption of normal heart rate through electric shock (defibrillator) or drugs.

Deficiency disease Disorder resulting from a nutritionally deprived diet or inability of the body to absorb needed nutrients.

Degenerative disease A group of diseases characterized by deterioration of body part(s) and resulting in progressive disability.

Dehydration Inadequate amount of fluids in the body caused by removal, abnormal loss, or failure to ingest fluids.

Delirium Mental disorder characterized by delusions or hallucinations. May be caused by disease, high fever, or drug use.

Delirium tremens Delirium suffered by chronic alcoholics as a result of withdrawal. Characterized by vivid hallucinations, uncontrollable trembling of hands, confusion, and nausea.

Delusion A false belief that persists even in the presentation of contrary evidence.

Dementia Deterioration of mental faculties due to irreversible organic causes.

Dementia praecox Schizophrenia.

Dendrite One of the threadlike branches of the nerve cell that transmits an impulse to the cell body.

Dentin The calcified tissue that encloses the tooth's pulp cavity.

Deoxyribonucleic acid (DNA) The fundamental component of all living matter, which controls and transmits the hereditary genetic code.

Depilatory An agent that removes hair.

Depressant An agent that produces a calming, sedative effect, slowing down body functions.

Depression An organic disease characterized by profound feelings of sadness, discouragement, and worthlessness unexplained by life's events. Depression is often recurring and interrupted by feelings of extreme euphoria, a condition referred to as bipolar depression or manic-depressive state.

Derma or dermis The skin.

Dermatitis Inflammation of the skin.

Desensitization (Immunotherapy) Neutralization of allergies by periodic exposure to progressively larger doses of the allergen.

Dextrose A form of glucose, a simple sugar.

Diabetes mellitus A chronic condition characterized by an overabundance of blood sugar due to insufficient insulin production in the pancreas or inability of the body to utilize insulin.

Dialysis A technique for separation of waste products or toxins from the bloodstream. Used in cases of kidney failure and overdose.

Diaphragm (1) The large muscle between the chest and the abdomen. (2) A dome-shaped rubber cap inserted vaginally to cover the cervix in order to prevent conception.

Diastole The interval between contractions of the heart (heartbeat) in which the heart relaxes. The diastolic reading obtained in blood pressure measurement is the lower number.

Diethylstilbestrol (DES) Synthetic estrogen hormone once used to prevent miscarriage. Its use is believed to have resulted in a higher incidence of vaginal and reproductive abnormalities, including difficulty in achieving or maintaining a pregnancy, among daughters born to women who took it. Sons may also suffer reproductive abnormalities. DES is also used to prevent conception if given promptly after unprotected intercourse (the so-called morning-after pill). Since it causes severe nausea and vomiting and other adverse effects, its use is limited primarily to rape victims.

Digestion The process by which food is transformed into absorbable nutrients.

Digit Finger or toe.

Dilation Enlargement or expansion of an organ, a passageway (e.g., blood vessel, or the pupil of the eye). May be artificially induced for therapeutic or diagnostic purposes.

Diplopia Double vision.

Disk (vertebral) The cartilage cushions between the vertebrae.

Dislocation The displacement of a bone from its normal position in a joint.

Diuretic Any substance that increases the flow of urine and excretion of body fluid.

Diverticulitis Inflammation of diverticula.

Diverticulosis A disorder in which diverticula, pouchlike sacs protruding from the wall of an organ, develop. Most commonly seen in the intestinal tract.

Dominant A term used in genetics to describe the stronger of 2 hereditary traits.

Dorsal Pertaining to the back.

Down's syndrome A congenital condition that may include mental retardation and physical malformations caused by abnormal chromosomal distribution. Also called Trisomy 21. Formerly called mongolism.

Dropsy *See* Edema.

Duodenum The portion of the small intestine closest to the stomach.

Dura mater The outermost layer of fibrous membrane

covering the brain and spinal cord. One of 3 types of meninges.

Dysentery Infectious inflammation of the bowel characterized by diarrhea with passage of blood and mucus and severe abdominal cramps.

Dyslexia Learning disability characterized by impaired reading ability and tendency to reverse characters.

Dysmenorrhea Painful menstruation or cramps.

Dyspareunia Painful sexual intercourse.

Dyspepsia Indigestion.

Dysphagia Difficulty in swallowing.

Dyspnea Difficulty in breathing.

Dystrophy Wasting, usually due to defective metabolism or nutrition.

Dysuria Painful urination.

Echography The use of ultrasound waves in detecting and diagnosing abnormalities. The results are called an echogram.

Eclampsia A sudden convulsive attack caused by toxemia during pregnancy.

Ectopic pregnancy Pregnancy in which the fertilized egg begins to develop outside the uterus, usually in the Fallopian tubes.

Eczema Skin rash characterized by itching and scaling.

Edema Swelling of body tissue caused by a buildup of fluid.

Effusion An accumulation of fluid between body tissues or in body cavities.

Ejaculation Emission of semen from the penis during the male orgasm.

Electrocardiography A diagnostic procedure in which metal plates (electrodes) are placed on body surfaces for the purpose of detecting and tracing electrical impulses from the heart. The resulting graph is called an electrocardiogram (EKG or ECG).

Electroencephalography A diagnostic procedure in which the electrical impulses from the brain are traced and recorded through metal plates (electrodes) attached to the head. The resulting graph is called an electroencephalogram (EEG).

Electrolysis Decomposition or destruction by means of electricity.

Elephantiasis Enlargement and swelling of body parts as a symptom of a tropical disease caused by a parasitic worm in the lymphatic system.

Electroshock therapy (EST) The use of a controlled amount of electric current in treatment of severe depression. The electric shock is administered through electrodes placed on the head. It is not used as often today as in the past, but in selected patients, it is still considered the most effective and fastest treatment for certain forms of depression.

Embolism Obstruction of a blood vessel by a solid body, called an embolus. Common emboli include blood clots, fat globule, or air bubble.

Embryo The term used to refer to the fetus in the first 8 weeks after conception.

Emetic Agent that induces vomiting.

Emission Discharge of fluid.

Emphysema A respiratory disease characterized by progressive loss of elasticity of lung tissue, making it difficult to exhale stale air fully. Most commonly caused by smoking.

Empyema Accumulation of pus in a body cavity, usually the lungs.

Encephalitis Inflammation of the brain due to virus infection, or lead poisoning, or other causes.

Endocrine system The physiological network of ductless glands which secrete hormones into the bloodstream to control the digestive and reproductive systems, growth, metabolism, and other processes.

Endometriosis A gynecological disease in which tissue normally found in the uterus grows in other areas.

Endometrium The lining of the uterus in which the fertilized ovum is implanted and which is shed during menstruation if conception has not taken place.

Endoscopy Diagnostic procedure using an illuminating optical instrument to examine a body cavity or internal organ.

Enema Fluid injected through the rectum to the lower bowel. Used to induce bowel movement or diagnose bowel disorders (barium enema).

Enteritis Inflammation of the intestine.

Enuresis Inability to control urination while sleeping. Bed-wetting.

Enzyme A substance, usually protein, which causes a chemical reaction. A catalyst.

Ephedrine Chemical used to dilate breathing passages and shrink mucous membranes. It also increases blood pressure and heart rate and should therefore be administered to heart patients only with discretion.

Epidermis Outermost layer of skin.

Epiglottis The flap of cartilage which covers the larynx in the act of swallowing and aids in directing food to the esophagus.

Epilepsy A disease of the nervous system characterized by convulsive seizures as a result of an imbalance in the electrical activity of the brain.

Epinephrine (also called adrenaline) The hormone produced by the medulla (inner core) of the adrenal glands. It is secreted in stressful situations in order to increase the body's capacity to respond or to speed up bodily processes.

Episiotomy An incision made in the final stages of childbirth from the vagina downward toward the anus.

Erection The stiffening or swelling of the penis or other erectile tissue as it becomes filled with blood.

Erysipelas A severe infectious skin disease caused by a streptococcal organism and characterized by swelling and redness.

Erythema Reddening of the skin due to dilation of the capillaries under the skin.

Erythroblastosis fetalis The anemic condition in infants due to Rh incompatibility between mother and child. The condition is seen in Rh-positive babies born to Rh-negative women. The mother builds antibodies against the baby's blood, destroying the red blood cells. It is seen only rarely in first babies because the mother usually is not exposed to the baby's blood until delivery. The condition can now be prevented by giving the mother a shot of Rh immune globulin shortly after the birth of an Rh-incompatible baby. Some doctors also administer the shot to an Rh-negative woman during the last trimester of pregnancy if there is a chance that the baby may be Rh positive, e.g., if the father has Rh-positive blood.

Erythrocyte   Red blood corpuscle.

Esophagus   Tube that transports food from the mouth to the stomach.

Estrogen   A primarily female sex hormone produced by the ovary, adrenal gland, and placenta. In women, it controls development of secondary sex characteristics, menstruation, and pregnancy. A small amount of estrogen is produced in the testes of the man, and also in fat tissue.

Eustachian tube   The tube that connects the middle ear to the pharynx.

Exophthalmos   Protruding eyeballs, sometimes due to diseases of the thyroid gland.

Expectorant   A drug that promotes the coughing of sputum.

Faint   Brief loss of consciousness due to insufficient blood in the brain.

Fallopian tubes   The 2 tubes extending one from each side of the uterus through which an egg must pass after release from the ovary. Also called oviducts.

Farsightedness   Also called hyperopia. A disorder of the eyes which causes difficulty in focusing on objects close up.

Fascia   Thin connective tissues that join the skin to underlying tissues.

Fat   An essential nutrient of animal or plant origin. May be saturated or unsaturated.

Fauces   The opening from the throat to the pharynx.

Feces   The waste matter discharged from the bowels.

Femur   Thigh bone.

Fertility   The ability to conceive.

Fertilization   Impregnation of ovum by sperm cell.

Fetus   An unborn baby after the eighth week of pregnancy.

Fever   Abnormally high body temperature. Generally above 98.6° F or 37° C.

Fiber   (1) Body tissue composed mainly of fibrils, tiny threadlike structures. (2) The plant cell components that are indigestible by humans. Dietary fiber. Roughage.

Fibrillation   Uncoordinated tremors or twitching of cardiac muscle resulting in an irregular pulse.

Fibrin   Protein formed in blood during clotting process.

Fibroid   A benign tumor of fibromuscular tissue, usually occurring in the uterus.

Fibula   The long, thin bone found in the lower leg.

Fission   Splitting.

Fistula   An abnormal connection between 2 body cavities.

Flat foot   A congenital or acquired deformity in which there is only a slight, or no, arch between the toes and the heel of the foot.

Flatulence   An overabundance of gas in the stomach or intestines.

Fluorine   A chemical that in small amounts prevents tooth decay.

Fluoroscope   A special x-ray that projects images on a screen. Used to observe the organs or bones while in motion.

Folic acid   A B-complex vitamin, used to promote blood regeneration in cases of folate deficiency. Occurs naturally in liver, kidney, green vegetables, and yeast.

Follicle   A small sac or tubular gland.

Fontanel   A membranous spot on a baby's head where skull bones have not yet come together.

Foramen   An opening. Usually used in reference to the opening in a bone through which blood vessels or nerves pass.

Forceps   Surgical instrument used to grasp or compress tissues.

Fracture   A crack or break in a bone.

Frontal   Pertaining to the front of a structure.

Frostbite   Freezing of the skin as a result of exposure to extreme cold. Affected area may become red and inflamed.

Fulminating   Developing quickly and with great severity.

Fungicide   Any substance that eliminates fungi.

Fungus   A low form of vegetable life including some which can cause disease. Fungal infections.

Furuncle (Boil)   A round, painful, pus-filled bacterial infection of a hair follicle.

Gallbladder   A membranous sac that is situated below the liver and condenses and stores the bile drained from the liver.

Gallstones   Stonelike masses that form in the gallbladder. May be composed of calcium, bile pigment, and/or cholesterol.

Gammaglobulin   The type of blood protein that contains antibodies to fight infection. Gammaglobulin can be separated from the other constituents in the blood and used to prevent or treat infections.

Ganglion   (1) A mass of nerve tissue, a nerve center. (2) A cystic tumor in a tendon sheath.

Gangrene   Death of body tissue usually due to loss of blood supply. Affected area becomes shrunken and black.

Gastrectomy   Surgical removal of a part or all of the stomach.

Gastric   Pertaining to the stomach.

Gastric juice   Acidic secretion of the stomach containing enzymes and hydrochloric acid to aid in digestion.

Gastric ulcer   A peptic ulcer that forms in the stomach.

Gastritis   Inflammation of the stomach.

Gastroenteritis   Inflammation of the mucous membranes of the stomach and intestines.

Gastroenterology   Study of the stomach and intestines and the diseases affecting them.

Gastrostomy Surgically formed fistula between the stomach and abdominal wall.

Gene A part of the chromosome which determines hereditary characteristics.

Genetics The study of heredity.

Genitals, genitalia Reproductive organs.

Geriatrics The branch of medical science devoted to diseases of the aged.

Germ Microorganism usually associated with causing disease.

Germicide Germ-killing agent.

Gerontology The study of aging and the diseases associated with it.

Gestation Pregnancy.

Gingivitis Inflammation of the gums.

Gland Any organ that produces and secretes a chemical substance used by another part of the body. Ductless, or endocrine, glands secrete into the bloodstream. Exocrine glands transport the secretion directly to a particular location.

Glandular fever Infectious mononucleosis.

Glans penis The head of the penis.

Glaucoma A disease of the eye in which increased pressure within the eye damages the retina and optic nerve. Leads to impaired sight and sometimes blindness.

Globulin The portion of blood protein in which antibodies are formed.

Globus hystericus The feeling of "a lump in the throat" due to hysteria, anxiety, or depression. Sometimes accompanied by difficulty in swallowing.

Glomerulus (glomeruli) A small tuft of blood capillaries in the kidney, responsible for filtering out waste products.

Glucose (dextrose or blood sugar) The most common monosaccharide (simple sugar) and the main source of energy for humans. It is stored as glycogen in the liver and can be quickly converted back into glucose.

Glucose tolerance test Test to determine body's response to a glucose challenge. Used to detect hypoglycemia or diabetes.

Glycogen Animal starch. The form in which glucose is stored in the liver. Glycogen is easily converted into glucose for body use as energy.

Glycosuria Sugar in the urine.

Goiter Enlargement of the thyroid gland which causes swelling on the front of the neck.

Gonad Primary sex gland. Ovary in the female; testes in the male.

Gonococci Kidney-shaped gonorrhea-causing bacteria.

Gonorrhea A common venereal disease caused by the gonococcus bacterium and characterized by inflammation of the urethra, difficulty in urination (in males), and inflammation of the cervix (in females).

Gout A metabolic disorder in which an overabundance of uric acid causes urate crystals to form in the joints and sometimes elsewhere.

Graafian follicles Tiny vesicles in the ovaries which contain ova before release (ovulation).

Graft Transplantation of tissue or skin from one part of the body to another.

Gram-negative or gram-positive Method of classifying bacteria according to how they are affected when stained with alcohol.

Grand mal A severe epileptic attack in which convulsions are accompanied by loss of consciousness.

Granulation The new skin tissue containing capillaries, blood vessels, and reparative cells that forms in a wound's healing process.

Granulocytes White blood cells (leukocytes) containing granules. They are manufactured in the bone marrow to digest and destroy bacteria.

Granuloma A tumor or growth containing granulation tissue.

Granuloma inguinale A contagious venereal disease characterized by ulcers on the genitals.

Gravel Fine, sandlike particles composed of the same substance as kidney stones but usually passed in the urine without notice.

Grave's disease One form of hyperthyroidism or an overactive thyroid gland, usually accompanied by abnormalities of the eyes and skin.

Gravid Pregnant.

Greenstick fracture Incomplete fracture due to the pliability of the bone. Usually occurs in children whose bones are still growing.

Grippe Influenza.

Gristle *See* Cartilage.

Groin The lower abdominal area where the trunk and thigh join. Also called the inguinal area.

Gumma A fibrous tumor filled with a rubberlike substance which occurs in the brain, liver, or heart in the late stages of syphilis.

Gynecology The branch of medical science that deals with the normal functioning and diseases of women's reproductive organs.

Gynecomastia Abnormal enlargement of the male mammary glands (breasts).

Halitosis Technical term for bad breath.

Hallucination A false perception believed to be real but actually having no basis in fact.

Hallucinogen Agent capable of producing hallucinations. Psychedelic drug.

Hallus valgus *See* Bunion.

Hallux The big toe.

Hammer toe A permanent hyperextension of the toe which cannot be flattened out.

Hamstring Group of tendons at the back of the knee.

Hangnail A piece of skin partly detached from the side of a nail which becomes irritated and inflamed.

Hansen's disease Leprosy.

Harelip Congenital defect of the lip due to a failure of bones to unite and causing a split from the margin of the lip to the nostril.

Hayfever An allergic reaction to pollen in which mucous membranes of the eyes, nose, and throat become inflamed.

Hearing aid Device used to amplify sounds for those with hearing difficulties.

Heart The muscular organ that pumps blood through the body. It is situated between the 2 lungs and behind the sternum.

Heart attack Myocardial infarction. Damage to part of the heart muscle caused by interruption of the blood circulation in the coronary arteries.

Heart block A condition of varying degree in which an abnormality in the tissues connecting the auricles and ventricles interferes with the normal transmission of electrical impulses and may lead to disturbances in the heart's rhythm or pumping action.

Heartburn Burning sensations in the upper abdomen or behind the sternum. Usually caused by the regurgitation of gastric juices into the esophagus.

Heart failure *See* Congestive heart failure.

Heart murmur Any of various sounds heard in addition to the regular heartbeat. Often associated with a diseased heart valve, but may also have a benign or harmless cause.

Heart–lung machine An apparatus that takes over for the heart during open heart surgery. The blood bypasses the heart and is oxygenated in the machine and pumped back into the body.

Heat exhaustion Collapse, with or without loss of consciousness, due to extreme heat conditions and loss of salt through sweating. In attempts to cool down the body surface, blood accumulates close to the skin, thus depriving the vital organs of full blood supply.

Heat stroke An emergency condition in which the sweating mechanism of the body fails, resulting in an extremely high body temperature.

Hemangioma A malformation of blood vessels which appears as red, often elevated mark on the skin. It may be present at birth and may require treatment if it fails to disappear on its own.

Hematemesis Vomiting of blood.

Hematology The scientific study of blood.

Hematoma A blood-filled swelling resulting from blood vessels injured or ruptured by a blow.

Hematuria The presence of blood in the urine.

Hemiplegia Paralysis affecting one side of the body.

Hemochromatosis (bronzed diabetes) Abnormal accumulation of iron deposits in the body as a result of a metabolic disturbance. Symptoms include a bronzing of the skin, diabetes, and cirrhosis of the liver.

Hemodialysis Removal of waste materials from the blood. The artificial kidney performs this function.

Hemoglobin The red pigment contained in red blood cells and combining the iron-containing heme with the protein-containing globin. Hemoglobin is responsible for transporting oxygen to body tissue and removing carbon dioxide from body tissue.

Hemolysis Breaking down of red blood cells.

Hemophilia An inherited blood disorder in which the blood is unable to clot causing severe bleeding from even minor wounds. The disease only affects males but is passed on by female carriers.

Hemoptysis Spitting up blood.

Hemorrhage Abnormal bleeding due to rupture of a blood vessel.

Hemorrhoids (piles) Varicose veins in and around the rectal opening. Hemorrhoid symptoms include pain, bleeding, and itching.

Hemostat An instrument that prevents bleeding by clamping a blood vessel.

Heparin Anticoagulant substance that is found in the liver and other tissues. It is sometimes administered to prevent blood clots. It also may be used to treat a threatened stroke, thrombophlebitis, and various clotting diseases.

Hepatitis Inflammation of the liver, usually due to a viral infection but can also be the result of alcoholism and other conditions. Hepatitis B is transmitted through blood contact (e.g., contaminated hypodermic needles or transfused blood from a hepatitis B carrier). Hepatitis A is transmitted through fecal contact, usually contaminated food. A third type, non-A, non-B, is not as well understood as the other two.

Hepatoma Tumor of the liver.

Heredity The transmission of traits from parents to offspring. Genetic information is carried by the chromosomes.

Hermaphrodite An individual possessing both the male and female sex organs.

Hernia The abnormal protrusion of part or all of an organ through surrounding tissues.

Heroin An additive narcotic drug derived from opium and a form of morphine (diamorphine).

Herpes simplex Recurring infection caused by herpes virus. Type 1 involves blisterlike sores usually around the mouth and referred to as "cold sores" or "fever blisters." Type 2 usually affects the mucous membranes of the genitalia and can be spread by sexual contact. In unusual circumstances, either type can cause damage to other parts of the body, such as the eyes or brain. Also, the distinctions between Type 1 and Type 2 herpes is not as clear as once thought; either virus can cause genital or oral sores.

Herpes zoster (shingles) A painful viral infection resulting in inflammation and blisters following the path of a nerve. It is caused by the same virus that causes chickenpox, which remains in the body in a latent form and may erupt many years later in an attack of shingles.

Hiatal hernia A disorder in which a portion of the stomach protrudes through the esophageal opening of the diaphragm and which may cause symptoms of indigestion, heartburn, or regurgitation of food.

Hiccups (hiccoughs) An involuntary spasm of the diaphragm followed by the sudden closing of the glottis which coincides with the intake of a breath.

High blood pressure *See* Hypertension.

Histamine A chemical found in body tissue and released to stimulate production of gastric juices for digestion. In an allergic reaction, excessive amounts of histamine are produced and cause surrounding tissue to become inflamed. Antihistamines are thus prescribed for relief from allergic attacks.

Hives (urticaria) Itchy red and white swellings that appear on the skin usually in an allergic reaction.

Hodgkin's disease A serious disorder of the lymphatic system in which the lymph nodes enlarge. Type of cancer.

Homograft Tissue or organ transplantation from one individual to another of the same species.

Homosexuality Sexual desire for those of one's own sex.

Hormone Secretion from an endocrine gland transported by the bloodstream to various organs in order to regulate vital functions and processes.

Hyaline A glasslike substance that occurs in cartilage or the eyeball.

Hyaline membrane disease (respiratory distress syndrome) A condition affecting newborn premature infants in which the air sacs in the lungs are immature and clogged with hyaline, a crystalline material that makes effective breathing difficult or impossible.

Hydrocele An abnormal accumulation of fluid, usually in the sac of the membrane that covers the testicle.

Hydrocephalus ("water on the brain") An abnormal increase in cerebral fluid resulting in an enlarged head.

Hydrochloric acid An acid, composed of hydrogen and chlorine, secreted by the stomach in the process of digestion.

Hydrolysis Division into simple substance(s) by the addition of water.

Hydrophobia *See* Rabies.

Hydrotherapy Treatment of disease or injury by use of baths or wet compresses.

Hymen The membrane partially covering the entrance to the vagina.

Hypercholesterolemia Excessive amounts of cholesterol in the blood, due to a metabolic disorder in which the body manufactures too much cholesterol or cannot process it correctly.

Hyperchlorhydria Excessive amounts of hydrochloric acid in the gastric juice.

Hyperemesis Excessive vomiting.

Hyperemesis gravidarum Excessive vomiting during pregnancy, commonly referred to as morning sickness.

Hyperglycemia Excessive amounts of sugar in the blood. One of the indications of diabetes.

Hyperhidrosis Excessive sweating.

Hyperinsulinism A condition in which excessive amounts of insulin cause abnormally low blood sugar. Similar to insulin shock.

Hyperkinesis Hyperactivity. Excessive movement or activity.

Hyperopia Farsightedness.

Hyperplasia Overgrowth of an organ caused by an increase in number of normal cells.

Hypertension High blood pressure. A condition in which the arterioles constrict and cause the heart to pump harder in order to distribute the blood to the body thus elevating the blood pressure.

Hyperthyroidism Overactivity of the thyroid gland. Symptoms include weight loss, restlessness, and sometimes goiters.

Hypertrophy Increased size of a body tissue or organ usually in response to increased activity.

Hypnosis A trancelike state in which a person's consciousness is altered to make him/her susceptible to suggestion.

Hypnotic A drug that induces sleep.

Hypochondria Excessive anxiety about and preoccupation with illness and supposed ill health.

Hypoglycemia Low blood sugar. Hypoglycemic shock due to insulin overdose is another term for insulin shock.

Hypophysis The pituitary gland.

Hypospadias A congenital malformation of the urethra.

Hypotension Low blood pressure.

Hypothalamus The part of the brain just above the pituitary gland. It has a part in controlling basic functions such as appetite, procreation, sleep, and body temperature and may be affected by the emotions.

Hypothyroidism Abnormal inactivity or decrease in activity of the thyroid.

Hysterectomy Surgical removal of the uterus.

Hysteria A neurosis, usually due to mental conflict and repression, in which there is uncontrollable excitability or anxiety.

Iatrogenic disease Any disorder or disease caused as an unintentional side effect of a physician's prescribed treatment.

Ichthyosis A congenital disorder in which the skin is dry and scaly.

Icterus Jaundice.

Idiopathic Peculiar to an individual or originating from unknown causes.

Ileitis Inflammation of the ileum (lower portion of the small intestine). Crohn's disease.

Ileum The lower portion of the small intestine.

Ilium Broad upper part of the hipbone.

Immobilization Making a bone or joint immovable in order to aid in correct healing.

Immunity State of resistance to a disease. Active immunity is acquired by vaccination against it or by previous infection. Passive immunity is acquired from antibodies either from the mother through the placenta during gestation or from injection of serum from an animal that has active immunities.

Immunization The procedure by which specific antibodies are induced in the body tissue.

Impacted Wedged in tightly and abnormally immovable.

Imperforate Without normal opening.

Impetigo Highly contagious inflammatory pustular skin disease caused by staphylococci or streptococci.

Impotence Inability of the male to achieve penile erection and engage in sexual intercourse.

Incisors The 8 sharp cutting teeth, 4 in each jaw.

Incontinence Inability to control release of urine or feces.

Incubation period The interval of time between contact with disease organisms and first appearance of the symptoms.

Incubator A temperature- and atmosphere-controlled container in which premature or delicate babies can be cared for. Also a container in which bacteria or other organisms are grown for cultures.

Incus The small bone of the middle ear which conducts sounds to the inner ear.

Indigestion An abnormality in the digestive process. Dyspepsia.

Induration Hardening of tissue.

Infarct An area of dead tissue as a result of a total blockage of the blood supply.

Infertility Inability to reproduce.

Inflammation The reaction of tissue to injury, infection, or irritation. Affected area may become painful, swollen, red, and hot.

Influenza ("flu") A contagious viral infection that occurs in epidemics.

Inguinal Pertaining to the groin.

Inoculation The intentional introduction of a disease agent to the body in order to induce immunity by causing a mild form of the disease.

Inoperable Not treatable by surgery.

Insemination Introduction of semen into the vagina either through sexual intercourse or artificially.

Insomnia Inability to sleep. Can be chronic or occasional.

Insulin The hormone produced and secreted by the beta-cells of the pancreas gland. Insulin is needed for proper metabolism, particularly of carbohydrates, and the uptake of sugar (glucose) by certain body tissues. A deficiency of insulin or the inability of the body to use insulin.

Insulin shock Loss of consciousness caused by an overdose of insulin.

Integument The skin.

Intention tremor Involuntary trembling triggered or intensified when movement is attempted.

Interferon A complex natural protein that causes cells to become resistant to infection.

Intertrigo (chafing) Superficial inflammation of opposing skin surfaces that rub together.

Intestines The section of the digestive tract extending from the stomach to the anus.

Intima The innermost lining of an artery.

Intracutaneous test Introduction of allergens into the skin in order to test sensitivity to particular substances.

Intrauterine contraceptive device (IUD) Device made of stainless steel, silkworm gut, or plastic which is inserted by a physician into the uterus to prevent pregnancy.

Intravenous Into or within a vein.

Intravenous feeding Nourishment through glucose solution and other nutrients injected directly into a vein.

Involution of uterus Shrinking of the uterus to normal size after childbirth.

Iris The round, colored portion of the eye that surrounds the pupil.

Iritis Inflammation of the iris.

Iron The essential mineral micronutrient of hemoglobin.

Iron lung A respirator. A machine that artificially expands and contracts to facilitate breathing for patients with paralyzed respiratory muscles.

Irreducible Incapable of being replaced to normal position. Applied to fractured bones or to hernia.

Ischemia Localized blood deficiency, usually as a result of a circulatory problem. For example, cardiac ischemia results when a coronary artery is so occluded that it cannot deliver sufficient blood to the heart muscle.

Islets of Langerhans The groups of cells (alpha and beta) in the pancreas that secrete endocrine hormones; the alpha-cells produce glucagon and the beta-cells produce insulin.

Isotope A chemical element similar in structure and properties but differing in radioactivity or atomic weight.

Jaundice Yellow discoloration of the skin and eyes caused by excessive amounts of bile pigments in the bloodstream.

Jejunum Part of the small intestine situated between the duodenum and the ileum.

Jigger Sand flea that burrows into skin in order to lay eggs causing itching and inflammation (also called chigger).

Jock itch *See* Tinea cruris.

Joint The point where 2 or more bones connect.

Jugular veins The 2 veins on the sides of the neck which carry blood from the head to the heart.

Kala azar A chronic infection transmitted by sandflies that occurs mainly in the tropics and Asia. Symptoms include anemia, fever, and emaciation.

Keloid An overgrowth of scar tissue after injury or surgery.

Keratin Substance that is the chief constituent of the horny tissues, such as the outer layer of skin, nails, and hair.

Keratitis Inflammation of the cornea.

Ketogenic diet A diet that results in the excessive burning of fat, which can lead to ketosis.

Ketosis The buildup of ketone bodies, highly acidic substances, in the body. This condition is often associated with diabetes and can lead to a fatal coma.

Kidneys The 2 bean-shaped glands that regulate the salt, volume, and composition of body fluids by filtering the blood and eliminating wastes through production and secretion of urine.

Kinesthesia Perception of movement, position, and weight. Muscle sense.

Klinefelter's syndrome Chromosomal abnormality in which an individual has 2 X and 1 Y sex chromosomes. As a result, the individual appears to be male but has oversized breasts, underdeveloped testes, and is sterile.

Kneecap Patella.

Knee jerk Reflex reaction in which the foot kicks forward in response to a tap on the ligament below the kneecap.

Kwashiorkor A disease caused by protein deficiency due to malnutrition. It occurs most often in underdeveloped countries where children do not receive enough protein (through milk or meat) in their diets. Symptoms include growth retardation, apathy, anemia, and abnormal distension of the abdomen.

Kyphosis A rounding of the shoulders or hunchback caused by poor posture or disease, such as osteoporosis.

Labia Liplike organs. Labia majora: 2 folds of skin and fatty tissue that encircle the vulva. Labia minora: the smaller folds inside the labia majora that protect the clitoris.

Labor (parturition) The rhythmic muscle contraction in the uterus in the process of childbirth.

Laceration A wound caused by the tearing of tissue.

Lacrimal ducts (lacrimal, or tear glands) The gland at the inner corner of the eye which secretes tears.

Lactation Production and secretion of milk by the breasts.

Lactic acid Acid produced by the fermentation of lactose; a waste product from the muscles.

Lactose A sugar contained in milk.

Lactovegetarian Vegetarian who eats dairy products.

Lancet Small double-edged knife used in surgery.

Lanolin Fat derived from wool and used as an ointment or lotion base.

Laryngitis Inflammation of the larynx characterized by hoarseness or complete loss of voice.

Larynx Voicebox. A cartilaginous structure containing the apparata of voice production: the vocal cords and the muscles and ligaments which move the cords.

Laser *Light Amplification by Stimulated Emission of Radiation.*

Laser beam A beam of intense controlled light which can sever, eliminate, or fuse body tissue.

Laxative Any agent that encourages bowel activity by loosening the contents.

Lead poisoning Intoxication from ingestion of lead.

Lecithin A waxy, fatty compound found in cell protoplasm.

Lens The transparent tissue of the eye which focuses rays of light in order to form an image on the retina.

Leprosy An infectious skin disease caused by bacteria and affecting the nerves and skin with ulcers.

Leptospirosis (infectious jaundice) An infectious disease spread to humans by urine of infected animals. Symptoms include jaundice.

Lesion Any breakdown of tissue, i.e., wound, sore, abscess, or tumor.

Leukemia A group of diseases of the blood-forming organs in which a proliferation of bone marrow and lymphoid tissue produces an overabundance of white blood cells (leukocytes) and disrupts normal production of red blood cells. A form of cancer.

Leukocytes White blood cells instrumental in fighting infection.

Leukocytosis Abnormal increase in the amount of white blood cells in the body, often due to the physiological response to infection.

Leukopenia Abnormal deficiency of white blood cells.

Leukorrhea Vaginal discharge of mucus. When discharge is heavy, it may be a sign of infection or disease.

Libido Term used by Freud for the desire for sensual satisfaction. Commonly used to mean sexual desire.

Ligament The tough, fibrous band of tissue that connects bones.

Ligature A thread of silk or catgut on wire used to tie off blood vessels to prevent bleeding during surgery.

Lipid Fat or fatlike substance such as cholesterol or triglycerides.

Lipoma A benign tumor composed of fat cells.

Lithiasis Formation of gallstones or kidney stones (calculi).

Litholapaxy Method of crushing a stone and removal of fragments from the urinary bladder through a catheter.

Lithotomy Removal of stone by cutting into the bladder.

Lithuresis Elimination of gravel in the urine.

Liver The largest internal organ of the body. Among its many functions are secreting bile and digestive enzymes, storing glycogen, neutralizing poisons, synthesizing proteins and producing several blood components, storing certain vitamins and minerals.

Lobotomy Surgical disconnection of nerve fibers between the frontal lobe and the rest of the brain. Once commonly used to calm uncontrollable mental patients.

Lochia Vaginal discharge of blood, mucus, and tissue after childbirth.

Lockjaw *See* Tetanus.

Lordosis Swayback. Condition in which the inward curve of the lumbar spine is exaggerated.

Low blood sugar Hypoglycemia.

Lues Syphilis.

Lumbago Lower back pain.

Lumbar Lower back between the pelvis and the ribs.

Lungs Two organs of spongelike tissue which surround the bronchial tree to form the lower respiratory system. Are vital to oxygenation of blood and expulsion of gaseous waste from the body.

Lupus erythematosus An inflammatory autoimmune disease. Systemic lupus erythematosus involves deterioration of the body's connective tissues.

Lymph Transparent yellowish fluid containing lymphocytes and found in lymphatic vessels. Lymphatic fluid.

Lymph nodes Oval-shaped organs located throughout the body that manufacture lymphocytes and filter germs and foreign bodies from the lymph.

Lymphocytes A disease-fighting type of leukocyte manufactured in the lymph nodes and distributed in the lymphatic fluid and blood.

Lymphogranuloma venereum A sexually transmitted viral disease that causes sores around genitals and swollen lymph nodes in the male groin.

Lymphosarcoma Malignant tumor of lymphatic tissue.

Maceration The softening of tissue in contact with fluid.

Macula Spot of discolored skin.

Macula lutea The small, yellow round spot on the retina. Center of color perception and clearest vision.

Madura foot Mycetoma. Fungus infection of the foot characterized by swelling and development of cystlike nodules. Occurs mostly in India and the tropics.

Malabsorption Defective absorption of nutrients in the small intestine. Malabsorption syndrome is characterized by steatorrhea (loose fatty stool) or diarrhea, weight loss, weakness, and anemia. May be caused by lesions on the intestine, metabolic deficiencies, or surgery.

Malacia Softening of a part.

Malaise A general feeling of illness and discomfort. Tiredness, irritability, and listlessness.

Malaria A tropical parasitic disease spread by mosquitoes. Symptoms include chills, fever, and sweating.

Mal de mer Seasickness.

Malignant Harmful, life-threatening. Used mostly in reference to a cancerous tumor.

Malingering Deliberate feigning of illness.

Malleus The largest of the 3 bones in the inner ear.

Malnutrition Insufficient nourishment due to poor diet or defect in body's assimilation.

Malocclusion Failure of the upper teeth to mesh properly with lower teeth.

Malpresentation Any abnormal position of the fetus in the birth canal.

Mammary gland Milk-secreting gland of the breast.

Mammography Diagnostic x-ray examination of the breasts.

Mandible Lower jawbone.

Mania Mood of undue elation and excitability often accompanied by hallucinations and increased activity.

Manic-depressive psychosis A mental illness characterized by alternating periods of depression and mania.

Manubrium The handle-shaped upper part of the breastbone.

Marijuana The hemp or cannabis plant. A hallucinogenic drug.

Marrow The soft substance present in bone cavities. Red marrow is responsible for red blood cell production. Yellow marrow is marrow which is no longer involved in making blood cells.

Massage Rubbing, kneading, and pressing the parts of the body for therapeutic purposes. Massage can stimulate circulation, reduce tension, relax muscles, and reduce pain.

Mastectomy Surgical removal of breast tissue.

Mastication Chewing.

Mastitis Inflammation of the breast.

Mastoid cells Hollow areas (air cells) located in the middle ear.

Mastoiditis Inflammation of the mastoid cells usually as a consequence of an untreated ear infection.

Masturbation Manipulation of the genitals for the purpose of deriving sexual pleasure.

Materia medica The study of the origin, preparation, and use of medicinal substances.

Maxilla Upper jaw.

Measles An acute infectious disease characterized by fever, rash, and inflammation of mucous membranes. It is caused by a virus.

Meatus Passage or opening.

Meconium The greenish pasty discharge from the bowels of a newborn baby.

Mediastinum The space that separates the 2 lungs and contains the heart, thymus, esophagus, and trachea.

Medicine (1) Science of healing. (2) A therapeutic substance.

Medulla The center of an organ, gland, or bone.

Medulla oblongata The brain part connected to the spine.

Megalomania Delusions of grandeur. Symptom of insanity characterized by an exaggerated self image.

Melanin Dark pigment found in hair, skin, and choroid of the eye.

Melanoma Tumor composed of cells containing melanin. Mostly benign but malignant melanoma is a rare and serious form of skin cancer.

Membrane A thin layer of lining of tissue.

Menarche Commencement of first menstrual period.

Meninges Membrane covering the brain and spinal cord.

Meningitis Inflammation of the meninges.

Menopause The period of time in which menstruation decreases and finally stops. The change of life after which a woman is no longer able to reproduce.

Menorrhagia Unusually heavy menstrual bleeding.

Menstruation The discharge of blood and tissue from the uterus every 28 days and lasting 4 or 5 days.

Mescaline A hallucinogen.

Mesencephalon The midbrain. The region between the cerebrum and the cerebellum.

Mesentery The folds in the abdominal lining between the intestine and the abdominal wall. They support the abdominal organs and supply them with blood and nerves.

Metabolism The combination of chemical and physical changes in the body essential for maintaining life processes. Basal metabolism is the minimum amount of energy required to sustain life while resting.

Metastasis The spread of disease from one body part to another usually by transfer of cells or germs through the blood or lymph.

Methadone An addictive synthetic narcotic used instead of morphine and administered in drug treatment centers to heroin addicts. Also may be used as a painkiller under some circumstances.

Metritis Inflammation of the uterus.

Metrorrhagia Bleeding from the uterus between menstrual periods.

Microtome A surgical instrument for cutting thin slices of body tissue for study.

Micturition Urination.

Migraine Periodic severe headaches usually affecting only one side of the head and often accompanied by nausea or vomiting, inability to look at light, and fluid retention. Also referred to as vascular headaches.

Miliaria Prickly heat, heat rash. Sweat trapped under skin because of gland obstruction. Produces itching, prickling pimples on the skin.

Miosis Contraction of the pupil of the eye.

Miscarriage *See* Abortion.

Mitosis Cell division.

Mitral valve The valve that allows oxygenated blood into the left ventricle from the left atrium.

Molar teeth The grinding teeth at the back of both jaws.

Mongolism *See* Down's syndrome.

Moniliasis Yeast infection usually caused by *candida albicans* and affecting the mucous membranes such as the lining of the vagina, mouth, and gastrointestinal tract; skin and nails.

Monocyte The largest type of white blood cell.

Mononucleosis, infectious A communicable disease in which the number of monocytes in the bloodstream increases. Symptoms include fever, swollen lymph nodes, and general malaise.

Mons veneris (or mons pubis) The pad of fatty tissue that covers the pubic bone of the female.

Morning sickness Nausea during the early stages of pregnancy.

Morphine A pain-relieving narcotic derived from the opium plant.

Motor Pertaining to movement, action.

Mountain sickness A temporary onset of symptoms of difficult breathing, headache, thirst, and nausea brought on by decreased oxygen in air at high altitudes.

Mucous Pertaining to mucus.

Mucous colitis Usually a functional disorder of the bowel characterized by mucus in the stool.

Mucous membrane Thin layers of tissue containing mucus-secreting glands.

Mucus The viscid secretion of mucous glands which moistens body linings.

Multiple sclerosis A degenerative disease affecting the central nervous system and brain, characterized by increasing disability.

Mumps A contagious disease affecting mostly children. Symptoms include painful swollen glands.

Muscle Body tissue that has the ability to contract.

Muscular dystrophy A disease appearing in childhood and characterized by a wasting of the muscles.

Myalgia Pain in the muscles.

Myasthenia Muscle fatigue or weakness. Myasthenia gravis is a chronic, progressive disease characterized by weakness of the voluntary muscles, especially those of the eyelids.

Mycetoma *See* Madura foot.

Mydriasis Abnormal dilation of the pupil.

Myelin The white fatty substance that covers most nerves like a sheath.

Myelitis Inflammation of the spinal cord or bone marrow.

Myeloma Malignant tumor of the cells derived from the bone marrow.

Myocardial infarction *See* Heart attack.

Myoma A tumor of muscle tissue.

Myopathy Any disease of the muscle.

Myopia Nearsightedness.

Myringitis Inflammation of the eardrum.

Myxedema Thyroid deficiency characterized by a slowdown in metabolism and body function. *See* Hypothyroidism.

Myxoma A tumor of the connective tissue containing mucoid cells.

Narcolepsy Neurological disorder characterized by an irresistible tendency to sleep.

Narcosis Unconsciousness and insensibility to pain brought on by a drug (narcotic).

Narcosynthesis A method for treating psychoneurosis in which a hypnotic drug is injected into the patient for the purpose of reviving suppressed memories.

Nares Nostrils.

Nasopharynx The part of the pharynx situated over the roof of the mouth.

Nausea A feeling of sickness in the stomach. Sometimes followed by vomiting.

Navel Umbilicus.

Nearsightedness (myopia) A defect of the eye in which the eyeball is too convex. This causes light rays to focus in front of the retina resulting in an inability to see objects clearly at a distance.

Necropsy Autopsy. Examination after death.

Necrosis Death and deterioration of tissue surrounded by living healthy tissue.

Neonatal Pertaining to the newborn (up to 1 month old).

Neoplasm A new and abnormal growth.

Nephrectomy Surgical removal of a kidney.

Nephritis Inflammation of a kidney.

Nephrolith Kidney stone.

Nephron The unit of the kidney in which waste is removed from the blood and urine is formed.

Nephrosis Kidney degeneration without inflammation.

Nerve A bundle of fibers which carries impulses between the nerve center (the brain and spinal cord) and the other parts of the body. There are 5 kinds of nerves: cranial, mixed, motor, sensory, and spinal.

Neuralgia Sharp, stabbing pain in a nerve or along its course. The pain is short-lived but recurring.

Neurasthenia A nervous condition in which one suffers from fatigue and loss of initiative. Usually accompanied by oversensitivity, restlessness, and uncalled-for irritability.

Neuritis Inflammation of a nerve.

Neurofibroma Tumor of nervous and connective tissues.

Neurofibromatosis A condition in which multiple tumors (neurofibroma) form under the skin or along the course of a nerve.

Neurology The branch of medicine dealing with the nerves and the central nervous system.

Neuron A nerve cell.

Neurosis A nervous disorder, usually related to anxiety, in which there is no functional degeneration of tissue.

Nevus A congenital pigment or elevated portion of skin. Birthmark.

Nictation (or nictitation) Wink. Rapid blinking of eyelid.

Nightblindness (nyctalopia) Reduced ability to see at night.

Nitrous oxide Laughing gas; an inhalant that induces euphoria and dulls the sensation of pain. Often used in dentistry.

Nocturia Urination at night.

Node A small protuberance or swelling. A knoblike structure. Nodule.

Nucleus The center part of any cell that is essential for cell growth, nourishment, and reproduction. Except for red blood cells, all human body cells have nuclei.

Nutrient A substance that provides materials the body needs, provides nourishment.

Nutrition The combination of processes by which the body or organism receives and uses materials essential for growth and maintenance.

Nystagmus Involuntary and repetitive oscillation of the eyeballs.

Obesity Excessive weight; body weight more than 20 percent above the average for one's age, height, and bone structure.

Obstetrics The branch of medical science dealing with pregnancy, childbirth, and neonatal care.

Occipital Pertaining to the back of the head.

Occlusion Used in reference to a closure of ducts and blood vessels. In dentistry, it refers to the fitting together of the upper and lower teeth.

Occult Undetectable by the naked eye.

Ocular Pertaining to the eye.

Olfactory Pertaining to the sense of smell.

Oligomenorrhea Infrequent or scanty menstrual flow.

Oligospermia Abnormally deficient spermatazoa in the semen.

Oliguria Deficient urine production.

Omentum A fold of the peritoneum (membrane lining of the abdomen) that covers and connects the abdominal organs.

Omphalitis Inflammation of the navel.

Oncology The scientific study of tumors.

Onychia Inflammation of the nail matrix, the tissue from which the nail grows.

Onychopagy Nail-biting.

Ophthalmitis Inflammation of the eye.

Ophthalmology The branch of medical science dealing with the eyes and their care.

Ophthalmoplegia Paralysis of eye muscles.

Ophthalmoscope An instrument for examining the interior of the eye.

Opiate Narcotic containing opium. Opiate drugs are used as painkillers, sedatives, or to slow gastric motility.

Optic nerve The fiber that transmits optic impulses from the retina to the brain.

Orbit Eye socket.

Orchiectomy (or orchectomy) Surgical removal of the testicles.

Orchitis Inflammation of the testicles.

Orgasm Climax of sexual intercourse.

Orthodontics The branch of dental science dealing with prevention and correction of teeth irregularities and malocclusions.

Orthopedics The branch of surgery dealing with diseases, disorders, and injuries to the locomotor system.

Orthopnea Condition in which breathing can only be facilitated when sitting or standing up.

Orthostatic Exacerbated by standing erect.

Osmosis The transfer of substance from one solution to another through a porous membrane that separates them.

Osseous Composed of or resembling bone tissue.

Ossicle A tiny bone. The 3 bones in the inner ear are ossicles.

Ossification The process of becoming bone or the change of cartilage to bone.

Osteitis Inflammation of bone.

Osteochondritis Inflammation of bone and cartilage.

Osteoma Tumor of bone tissue.

Osteomalacia A condition in which bones become soft, brittle, flexible, and painful due to a lack of calcium and vitamin D. Similar to childhood rickets.

Osteomyelitis Inflammation of the bone and marrow resulting from infection.

Osteopathy A system of treating disease that emphasizes massage and bone manipulation.

Osteoporosis A condition in which bones become porous resulting in increased fragility. Associated with the aging process.

Otitis Inflammation of the ear.

Otorhinolaryngology Branch of medical science that deals with the ear, nose, and throat.

Ovariectomy Surgical removal of ovary or ovaries.

Ovary The female reproductive glands whose function is to produce the eggs (ova) and the sex hormones estrogen and progesterone.

Oviduct *See* Fallopian tube.

Ovum The egg cell. The female sex cell which, when fertilized by the male sperm, grows into a fetus. The egg contains 23 chromosomes that pair off with 23 chromosomes in the sperm to make a complete set needed to start a new life.

Oxyhemoglobin Oxygen-carrying hemoglobin.

Oxygen The colorless, odorless gas that is essential for life. Oxygen makes up about 20 percent of the air.

Oxygenation The saturation of a substance with oxygen.

Oxytocin A pituitary hormone that is secreted during childbirth for the stimulation of uterine contractions and milk secretion. A synthetic form of oxytocin is administered sometimes to induce or hasten labor.

Ozone A form of oxygen that is used as a disinfectant.

Pacemaker (sino-atrial node) A small knot of tissue (node) in the right atrium of the heart from which the contraction of the heart originates. Artificial or electronic pacemakers are small, battery-operated devices that can substitute for a damaged pacemaker.

Pachydermia Abnormal thickening of the skin.

Paget's disease (1) A type of breast cancer in which the nipple becomes sore and ulcerated. (2) Osteitis deformans. A chronic bone disease in which rates of bone production and bone loss are increased, leading to thickened and softened bones.

Palate The roof of the mouth.

Palliative Any agent that relieves pain and symptoms of disease but does not actually cure it.

Palpate Examine by feeling with the hand.

Palpitation Rapid, throbbing heartbeat.

Palsy Paralysis.

Pancarditis Inflammation of all the structures of the heart.

Pancreas The gland situated behind the stomach. It secretes pancreatic juice containing enzymes to aid in food digestion, and also contains groups of specialized cells (islets of Langerhans) that secrete insulin and glucagon to regulate blood sugar levels.

Pancreatitis Inflammation of the pancreas.

Pantothenic acid One constituent of the vitamin B complex.

Papanicolaou smear (Pap test) The microscopic examination of cells shed from body surfaces; used routinely to screen for cancer of the cervix or uterus.

Papilla A small conical or nipple-shaped elevation.

Papilloma A tumor, usually benign, of the skin or mucous membrane.

Papule Small abnormal solid elevation on the skin.

Paraplegia Paralysis affecting both legs, usually due to disease of the spinal cord or injury.

Paralysis Loss of nervous function or muscle power due to injury or disease of the nervous system.

Paranoia A mental illness characterized by delusions of being persecuted or conspired against.

Parasite An organism that lives in or on another organism (host).

Parathyroid glands Four small glands embedded in the thyroid gland. The hormones secreted by the parathyroids control the body's calcium and phosphorus levels.

Paratyphoid fever An infectious disease whose symptoms resemble those of typhoid fever but are less severe.

Paregoric An opium compound that slows gastric action, thereby relieving cramps or diarrhea.

Parenchyma The parts of an organ that are directly related to the function of the organ (as opposed to supporting or connective tissues).

Parenteral A substance administered by injection or directly in the bloodstream rather than orally.

Paresis Slight paralysis.

Parkinson's disease (Parkinsonism) A disorder in which the patient suffers from tremors, stiffness, and slowness of movement.

Paronychia Infection of the tissues surrounding a nail.

Parotid gland One of the salivary glands located near the ear.

Parotitis Mumps. A viral disease characterized by the swelling of the parotid glands.

Paroxysm A sudden but temporary attack of disease or symptoms.

Parrot fever *See* Psittacosis.

Parturition Childbirth.

Pasteurization A process in which disease-causing bacteria in milk or other liquids are destroyed by heat.

Patch test A diagnostic procedure in which a suspected allergen is injected (in a diluted form) into the skin.

Patella Kneecap.

Pathogen Any disease-causing agent.

Pathology The science dealing with disease, its nature, and causes.

Pectoral Pertaining to the chest.

Pediatrics The branch of medical science dealing with children and the diseases affecting them.

Pedicle Stem of a tumor.

Pediculosis Lice infestation.

Pellagra A disease due to a lack of vitamin B_2 (nicotinic acid). Symptoms include skin rashes, weakness, and mental confusion.

Pelvis (1) A basin-shaped cavity, such as that of the kidney. (2) The bony basin-shaped cavity formed by the hip bone and the lower bones of the back.

Pemphigus A serious skin disease in which groups of large blisters on the skin rupture.

Penis The external male sex organ through which urine is passed and semen is ejaculated.

Pepsin A protein-digesting enzyme secreted by the stomach in gastric juices.

Peptic Pertaining to pepsin.

Peptic ulcer Ulcer in the stomach, duodenum, or esophagus that is related to pepsin.

Percussion A method of physical diagnosis by tapping or thumping a body part to produce sounds that indicate the size, density, and position of organs.

Perforation A hole or puncture. Usually made by injury or infection (as of the eardrum) or by an ulcer.

Pericarditis Inflammation of the pericardium.

Pericardium The 2-layer membranous tissue covering the heart. The layer closest to the heart is called the visceral layer. The other is the parietal layer.

Perineum The area between the anus and the genitals.

Periodontal membrane The tissue around the teeth covering the roots and connecting them to the jaw.

Periodontitis Inflammation of the periodontal membrane.

Periosteum The tough, fibrous membrane covering nearly all bone surfaces.

Peristalsis A wave of muscular contractions which push materials along the digestive tract.

Peritoneum The serous membrane that lines the abdominal organs.

Peritonitis Inflammation of the peritoneum.

Perleche A condition in which the corners of the mouth become cracked, raw, and thickened due to vitamin deficiency, bacterial infection, or other causes.

Pernicious Deadly, life-threatening.

Pernicious anemia Anemia caused by a deficiency of vitamin B_{12} or an inability of the body to absorb vitamin B_{12}.

Perspiration Sweat; the secretion of the sweat gland through the pores of the skin.

Pertussis Whooping cough.

Pessary (1) A device placed in the vagina to support the uterus or correct uterine displacements. (2) A vaginal suppository.

Petechiae Small hemorrhages under the skin.

Petit mal A form of epilepsy or seizure in which the person does not lose consciousness.

Phagocyte A cell that is capable of engulfing bacteria and debris.

Phalanx One of the bones in the finger or toe.

Phallus Penis.

Pharyngitis Sore throat. Inflammation of the pharynx.

Pharynx The mucous membrane-lined cavity at the back of the mouth. It extends to the esophagus.

Phimosis A condition in which the foreskin tightens so it prevents retraction over the head of the penis.

Phlebectomy Surgical removal of a vein.

Phlebitis Inflammation of a vein.

Phlegm Mucus, sputum.

Phobia An abnormally excessive and irrational fear. Some common phobias are acrophobia, fear of high places; agoraphobia, fear of open places; algophobia, fear of pain; claustrophobia, fear of closed places; ocholophobia, fear of crowds; triskaidekaphobia, fear of the number 13; and xenophobia, fear of strangers.

Physiology The study of cells, tissues, and organs, their functions and activities.

Pia or pia mater The innermost layer of the meninges

which covers the brain and spinal cord.

Pica   The craving or consumption of unusual substances that ordinarily are not food, such as dirt, chalk, or paint chips.

Pigment   Any coloring matter.

Piles   *See* Hemorrhoids.

Pimple   Common term for a pustule or papule.

Pineal body   A small gland, conical in structure, located on the back of the midbrain. Its function is not fully understood but it may be concerned with regulation of growth or of the sex glands.

Pink-eye   Contagious conjunctivitis.

Pituitary gland   The pea-sized gland located at the base of the brain. It is controlled by the hypothalamus and it, in turn, controls the hormone productions in many other endocrine glands.

Pityriasis   A skin disease in which patches of skin become red and scaly.

Placebo   A substance without medicinal properties which is administered for psychological benefit or as part of a clinical research study.

Placenta   The structure developed on the uterine wall about the third month of pregnancy. Through the placenta, the fetus receives nourishment and oxygen and eliminates waste products. It is expelled from the mother after childbirth. The afterbirth.

Plague   Any deadly contagious epidemic disease.

Plantar   Pertaining to the sole of the foot.

Plaque   Patch or film of organic substance on tissues, such as teeth or in arteries.

Plasma   The fluid part of blood. *See* Blood plasma.

Platelet (thrombocyte)   The colorless bodies in the blood instrumental in blood clotting.

Pleura   The membrane lining the chest cavity and covering the lungs.

Pleurisy   Inflammation of the pleura.

Plumbism   Lead poisoning.

Pneumonia   Infection of the lungs.

Pneumococcus   The oval-shaped bacterium responsible for diseases such as pneumonia, meningitis, and otitis media.

Pneumonitis   Inflammation of lung tissue.

Pneumothorax   Lung collapse due to air or gas in the chest cavity.

Pollinosis   An allergic reaction to plant pollens inhaled with the air.

Polyarteritis   Inflammation of a number of arteries.

Polycythemia   An overabundance of red blood cells in the blood.

Polydipsia   Excessive thirst, such as that which occurs in untreated diabetes.

Polyopia   Seeing multiple images of a single object.

Polyp   A nodular tumor, usually benign, that grows on a mucous membrane.

Polyphagia   Excessive eating.

Postpartum   After childbirth.

Pre-eclampsia   A toxic condition of pregnancy characterized by high blood pressure, edema, and kidney malfunction.

Premenstrual syndrome (PMS)   A variety of symptoms, both physical and emotional, associated with the menstrual cycle.

Prepuce   The foreskin of the penis.

Presbycusis   The normal decrease in hearing ability as one gets older.

Presbyopia   Increasing inability to see objects close up. Normal condition of midlife and getting older.

Prickly heat (miliaria)   Skin irritation or rash caused by perspiration.

Proctitis   Inflammation of the membranes of the rectum.

Proctoscope   A tubular instrument for examination of the interior of the rectum.

Progesterone   The female sex hormone which causes the thickening of the uterine lining and the other body changes before conception.

Prognosis   Prediction or forecast of the probable course and/or results of a disease.

Prolactin   Hormone secreted by the pituitary that stimulates the breasts to produce milk.

Prolapse   Downward displacement of an organ from its usual position.

Prophylaxis   Prevention of disease or its spread.

Prostaglandins   Hormonelike substances, secreted by a wide range of body tissues, that perform varying functions in the body. They are instrumental in stimulating uterine contractions during labor and birth and are also important in muscle function.

Prostatectomy   Surgical removal of all or part of the prostate gland.

Prostate gland   The male sex gland located at the base of the bladder.

Prosthesis   An artificial replacement for a missing body part.

Proteins   Complex nitrogen compounds made up of amino acids. Most of the tissues of body, especially the muscles, are composed primarily of protein.

Prothrombin   A substance in the blood which forms thrombin, an enzyme essential to blood coagulation.

Protoplasm   "The stuff of life" in cells. The essential jellylike substance in all living cells.

Protozoa   One-celled organisms, the smallest type of animal life. Amoeba and paramecia are protozoa. Some protozoa can cause disease.

Prurigo   A chronic skin disease characterized by small papules and intense itching.

Pruritis   Itching.

Psittacosis (parrot fever)   A disease similar to pneumonia and transmitted to humans by birds, such as pigeons.

Psoriasis   A chronic skin disease characterized by an overgrowth of the epidermis in which scaly lesions appear on various parts of the body.

Psychiatry   The branch of medical study dealing with mental health.

Psychoanalysis   A method developed by Sigmund Freud for the diagnosis and treatment of mental illness. The patient recalls past, perhaps forgotten, events in order to gain insight into the unconscious mind.

Psychogenic   Originating from the mind.

Psychology   The study of the mind and behavior.

Psychomotor   Voluntary movement.

Psychoneurosis   A mild emotional or mental disturbance, usually a defensive overreaction to unresolved conflicts.

Psychopathy Any disease of the mind.

Psychosis A mental illness originating in the mind itself rather than from environmental factors.

Psychosomatic Any condition either caused or exacerbated by emotional factors.

Psychotherapy Treatment of mental disorders based on verbal communication with the patient.

Ptomaine A poisonous substance produced by the decay of protein.

Ptosis A drooping, especially of the eyelid.

Ptyalin An enzyme contained in the saliva which initiates the breakdown of starch.

Puberty The age at which secondary sex characteristics develop and reproductive organs become functionally active. In girls, puberty is marked by the onset of menstruation and in boys by the discharge of semen and the change of voice.

Puerperium The period of time directly after childbirth until the time when the uterus has returned to its normal state.

Pulmonary Pertaining to the lungs.

Pulse The expansion and contraction of an artery as response to the expansion and contraction of the heart.

Pupil The opening in the middle of the iris of the eye which allows the passage of light to the retina.

Purgative A drug inducing evacuation of the bowels. A cathartic or strong laxative.

Purpura A disorder in which hemorrhages of tiny blood vessels cause purple patches to appear on the skin and mucous membranes.

Purulent Containing pus.

Pus A thick, yellowish fluid containing bacteria and white blood cells. Formed in some types of infection.

Pyelitis Inflammation of the kidney pelvis.

Pyorrhea The discharge of pus, usually from the teeth sockets.

Pyrexia Fever.

Pyrosis Heartburn.

Pyuria Pus in the urine.

Q fever A mild infectious disease caused by a rickettsia germ. It is usually transmitted from cows and sheep to humans by contaminated milk, tick bites, or contaminated food products.

Quarantine The isolation of persons who might be sick with or have come in contact with a communicable disease.

Quadriplegia Paralysis of the arms and legs.

Quickening The stage of pregnancy in which the first fetal movements are felt by the mother, usually around the eighteenth week of pregnancy.

Quinsy Acute inflammation of the tonsils accompanied by abscess.

Rabbit fever *See* Tularemia.

Rabies Hydrophobia. A deadly disease of the central nervous system caused by the rabies virus and spread by the bite of an infected (rabid) dog or other animal.

Radiation sickness Nausea and diarrhea caused by exposure to moderate radiation. Exposure to massive doses is extremely serious and perhaps fatal.

Radioactive Giving off penetrating energy waves to produce electrical or chemical effects.

Radium A highly radioactive metal used to treat cancer.

Radioisotope An element whose atomic number is the same as another but whose atomic weight differs. Radioisotopes can be injected into the body and traced with monitors for diagnostic purposes.

Rales Abnormal sounds from the lungs or bronchi.

Rash Eruption on the skin.

Rat-bite fever An infectious disease caused by bacteria spread to humans by rat bites.

Raynaud's disease A disease in which blood vessels of the fingers and toes constrict on exposure to cold, causing numbness and pallor. Blood vessels then expand causing area to tingle and become red or purple as the blood returns.

Recessive A term used in genetics to describe the weaker of two hereditary traits.

Rectum The portion of the large intestine closest to the anal opening. It consists of the rectal canal and the anal canal.

Reflex An unconscious, automatic response to a stimulus.

Refractory Not reacting to treatment.

Regeneration Repair or renewal of tissue.

Regurgitation Backflow.

Relapsing fever Recurrent fever as a symptom of infection caused by bacteria carried by lice and ticks.

Remission An easing of the symptoms or disease.

Renal Pertaining to the kidneys.

Renin An enzyme found in the kidney and capable of raising blood pressure.

Rennin The enzyme contained in the gastric juice that digests milk.

Repression The refusal of the conscious mind to acknowledge unacceptable or conflicting thoughts, feelings, or ideas.

Resection Removal of a part of an organ or tissue by means of surgery.

Respiratory distress syndrome *See* Hyaline membrane disease.

Respiration Breathing.

Resuscitation Restoration of breathing or heartbeat to one who is apparently dead or threatened with death.

Reticuloendothelial system A network of tissues containing cells (phagocytes) capable of taking up bacteria and foreign bodies in the bloodstream.

Retina The layered lining of the eye which contains light-sensitive receptors (the rods and cones) and conveys images to the brain.

Retinoblastoma A malignant tumor of the retina occurring in infants and children only.

Retinopathy An injury or disease of the retina, particularly common in insulin-dependent diabetes.

Retractors Devices used to pull back the edges of a wound.

Rh factor A group of antigens in the blood. Some people lack the Rh factor and are therefore designated as Rh negative. Complications can occur if an Rh-negative mother conceives and has an Rh-positive baby. *See* Erythroblastosis fetalis.

Rheumatoid factor Abnormal protein in the blood of most people afflicted with rheumatoid arthritis or other autoimmune diseases.

Rhinitis Inflammation of the mucous membrane of the nose; usually as a symptom of the common cold or allergies.

Rhinoplasty Plastic surgery of the nose.

Rhinovirus Any of the more than 100 viruses which cause the common cold.

Rhodopsin The visual purple in the rods of the retina. It becomes bleached when exposed to light and requires vitamin A for regeneration.

Riboflavin Vitamin B_2.

Rickets A childhood disease caused by a deficiency of vitamin D. Symptoms include improper development of bones and teeth because of a calcium/phosphorus imbalance.

Rickettsia Disease-causing microorganisms, smaller than bacteria but larger than viruses. Usually transmitted to humans by the bites of fleas, lice, and ticks.

Rickettsial pox A rickettsial disease spread by the bites of mites. Symptoms include a poxlike rash, headache, and fever.

Ringworm A fungal infection affecting the tissues of the skin, hair, nails, and scalp. Dermatophytosis is the general medical name and examples of ringworm infections are tinea pedis (athlete's foot) and tinea capitis of the scalp.

Rocky Mountain spotted fever A rickettsial disease spread by ticks. Symptoms include fever, headache, muscle pain, and rash.

Rods Cylindrical nerve structures in the retina. They contain rhodopsin and, together with the cones, they perceive the images of light, dark, and color which are transmitted to the brain.

Roentgen rays X-rays.

Rose fever An allergic reaction to roses; term often used to describe pollen and/or mold allergies that occur during the spring as opposed to hayfever, which is in the fall.

Roseola Any pink eruption on the skin.

Root canal The nerve-containing passageway through the root of the tooth.

Roughage Indigestible matter (such as fiber).

Roundworms Parasites found in contaminated feces. In humans, roundworms cause ascariasis, a condition whose symptoms include disruption of the digestive system and abdominal pain.

Rubella German measles.

Rubeola Measles.

Rupture A tearing or bursting of a part. Also, a hernia.

Saccharin A sugar substitute derived from coal tar.

Sacroiliac The joint connecting the base of the spine to the upper part of the hip bone.

Sacrum The triangular bone just above the coccyx, near the lower end of the spine. It is composed of 5 vertebrae that have fused together. Together with the bones of the pelvis it forms the sacroiliac joint.

St. Anthony's fire *See* Erysipelas.

St. Vitus' dance *See* Chorea.

Saline Salty.

Saliva The secretion of the salivary glands. Lubricates the mouth and throat and initiates the digestion of food with enzymes.

Salivary glands The 3 glands on each side of the face. The sublingual gland and submaxillary gland secrete saliva onto the floor of the mouth. The parotids are situated near the ears and secrete saliva through passageways in the back of the mouth.

Salmonella A group of bacteria primarily responsible for the gastrointestinal disturbances of food poisoning.

Salpingectomy Surgical removal of the Fallopian tubes. Tubal ligation. A method of sterilization.

Salpingitis Inflammation of the Fallopian tubes.

Sarcoma A malignant tumor from connective tissue.

Scabies Infestation of the skin by parasites (scabies mites) that burrow under the skin surface to lay their eggs. "The itch."

Scapula The shoulder blade.

Schick test A skin test for immunity to diphtheria.

Schizophrenia Dementia praecox. A group of mental illnesses classified as psychotic (rather than neurotic). Patient's thought patterns become disturbed and disorganized and hallucinations or delusions are common symptoms.

Sciatica Pain extending along the path of the sciatic nerve. Can be caused by a slipped disk or by a muscle spasm.

Sciatic nerve The largest nerve in the body. It branches out from the base of the spinal cord (where it is attached) to form the motor and sensory nerves of the legs and feet.

Sclera The fibrous outer coat of the eye.

Sclerosis Abnormal hardening or thickening of a tissue.

Scoliosis Curvature of the spine.

Scorbutus Scurvy.

Scotoma Any (normal or abnormal) blind spot in the field of vision.

Scrofula Tuberculosis of the lymph nodes in the neck.

Scrotum The pouch that holds the testicles in the male.

Scurvy A disease caused by a deficiency of vitamin C. Symptoms include anemia, weakness, and bleeding gums.

Sebaceous glands The oil glands that secrete sebum, a fatty substance to lubricate the skin.

Seborrhea Overactivity of the sebaceous glands resulting in a greasiness of the skin.

Sebum The fatty substance secreted by the sebaceous glands.

Secretion Any substance formed or emitted by glands or tissue. Various secretions perform various functions for the body.

Sedative An agent that calms and reduces excitability.

Semen The thick, whitish secretion produced by the male testes and sex glands and containing the male reproductive cells, the spermazoa.

Semicircular canals The 3 membranous canals of the inner ear that control the sense of balance.

Seminal vesicles The 2 glands that store the spermazoa.

Senescence The process of aging, growing old.

Senility Abnormal deterioration of mental function associated with increasing age. Many physical diseases, such as arteriosclerosis, may be associated with senility.

Sepsis The state of being infected by germs in the blood or tissues.

Septicemia Blood poisoning. The presence of living bacteria in the bloodstream.

Septum A dividing wall between 2 compartments or cavities.

Serum The fluid formed in the clotting of blood. Contains antibodies and is injected in vaccines to build up immunities to specific diseases.

Serum sickness An allergic reaction (usually hives and fever) to the injection or administration of serum.

Shingles (Herpes zoster) A virus infection of nerve endings characterized by pain and blisters along the course of the nerve. Caused by latent form of the same virus that causes chickenpox, usually years after that disease.

Shock A condition in which the body processes slow down in response to injury or extreme emotion. Symptoms include rapid pulse, low blood pressure, paleness, and cold, clammy skin.

Sickle cell anemia A hereditary type of anemia caused by malformed (crescent-shaped) red blood cells.

Siderosis Chronic inflammation of the lungs caused by inhaling iron particles. An excess of iron in the circulating blood.

Silicosis Inflammation and damage of the lung caused by silicon dioxide. It is an occupational disease associated with sand blasting and stone cutting.

Sinus A cavity, hollow space, especially of the nasal passages.

Sinusitis Inflammation of a sinus.

Smegma Thick sebaceous secretion that accumulates beneath the prepuce and clitoris.

Solar plexus A network of nerves in the abdomen.

Somnambulism Sleepwalking.

Somniloquy Talking in sleep.

Spasm Sudden and severe involuntary contraction of a muscle.

Speculum An instrument used to dilate a body passage in order to examine the interior, such as the examination of the vagina and cervix during a pelvic examination.

Spermatocele Enlargement of the scrotum due to the development of a fluid-filled sac (cystic dilation) of the tubules.

Spermatozoa Male reproductive cell. *See* Ovum.

Spermicide An agent that kills spermatozoa.

Sphincter A ring of muscle which encircles and controls opening of an orifice.

Sphygmomanometer An instrument used to measure blood pressure.

Spina bifida A congenital defect in which some of the vertebrae fail to close and therefore expose the contents of the spinal canal.

Spinal canal The central hollow formed by the arches of the vertebrae which contains the spinal cord.

Spinal column The structure formed from the 33 vertebrae (spinal bones). The backbone.

Spinal cord The cord or column of nerve tissue extending from the brain, enclosed in the spinal canal.

Spinal nerves 31 pairs of nerves that pass out of the spinal cord and carry impulses to and from all parts of the body.

Spinal tap The withdrawal of cerebrospinal fluid for the purpose of diagnosis or relief of pressure on the brain. Lumbar puncture.

Spirochete Spiral-shaped bacterium. Syphilis is caused by a spirochete.

Spleen A large lymphoid organ behind the stomach on the lower left side of the rib cage. Its function includes cleansing the blood of parasites and manufacturing lymphocytes. It is, however, not an essential organ to life since these functions can be performed elsewhere in the body.

Spondylitis Inflammation of spine.

Spore A life stage in the cycle of certain microorganisms in which it becomes inactive and highly resistant to destruction. A spore can become active again.

Sprain Injury to the soft tissue around a joint.

Sprue A chronic malabsorption disorder in which the body cannot absorb fats. Symptoms include diarrhea, indigestion, weight loss, and soreness in the mouth.

Sputum Discharge from the lungs and throat composed of mucus and saliva.

Stapes A tiny stirrup-shaped bone in the inner ear.

Staphylococci Spherical bacteria occurring in clusters. Responsible for food poisoning and skin infections, staph infections.

Steapsin Fat-digesting enzyme produced in the pancreas.

Steatorrhea Pale, bulky stools containing undigested fats.

Stenosis A narrowing of a body passage, tube or opening.

Sterile (1) Germ-free. (2) Unable to reproduce.

Sternum The breastbone. The bone in the middle of the chest.

Steroids (corticosteroids, cortisone) Natural hormones or synthetic drugs that have many different effects. Some steroids are anti-inflammatory and are used to treat arthritis, asthma, and a number of other disorders.

Stethoscope An instrument that amplifies bodily sounds.

Stillborn Term used to describe a baby born dead after the twentieth week of pregnancy.

Stomach The pouchlike organ into which the food flows from the esophagus. Digestion takes place here by means of enzymes and hydrochloric acid and also the churning action of the stomach muscles.

Stomatitis Inflammation of the soft tissues of the mouth.

Stool Feces. Evacuation of the bowels.

Strabismus An eye disorder in which both eyes are unable to focus simultaneously. Cross-eyedness.

Strain Injury caused by misuse or overuse of a muscle.

Strawberry tongue A bright red tongue with enlarged papillae. Associated with scarlet fever.

Streptococci Spherical bacteria that grow in chains. They are responsible for infections like scarlet fever and strep throat.

Striae Stripes, narrow bands. Stretch marks are a common example.

Stroke An interruption of the blood flow to the brain causing damage to the brain. Depending on the severity and location of the stroke, it may result in partial or complete paralysis or loss of some bodily function, or death.

Stroma The supporting tissue of an organ as opposed to the functioning part. *See* Parenchyma.

Stupor A state of impaired but not complete loss of consciousness and responsiveness.

Sty Infection of one of the sebaceous glands of the eye.

Subconscious The contents of the mind not in the range of consciousness.

Subcutaneous Under the skin.

Sulfonamides Sulfa drugs. A group of medicines that were the first antibiotic drugs.

Sunstroke Failure of the body's temperature control system as a result of overexposure to high heat and humidity. Body temperature rises to very high degree, leading to coma and death. *See* Heatstroke.

Suppository Medicated substance in solid form for insertion into a body opening, usually the vagina or rectum. They melt inside the body to release the medicine.

Suppuration Pus formation.

Suprarenal glands *See* adrenal glands.

Surgery The branch of medical science dealing with disease, deformity, or injury by means of operation or manipulation.

Suture (1) To join 2 surfaces by stitching. (2) The thread-like substance used to join 2 surfaces.

Sympathectomy Surgical removal of part of the sympathetic nervous system.

Sympathetic nervous system Part of the autonomic nervous system. A chain of spinal nerves whose functions include contraction of blood vessels, increase of heart rate, and regulation of glandular secretions.

Synapse The point of communication between nerve endings.

Syncope Fainting.

Syndrome A group of symptoms that occur together, presumably originating from the same cause.

Synovia The viscid fluid that lubricates joints.

Systole The contraction of the heart muscle. Systolic pressure is the greater of the two blood pressure readings (the other is diastolic).

Systolic murmur An abnormal sound heard during the contraction of the heart.

Tachycardia Excessively rapid heartbeat.

Talipes (clubfoot) Congenital deformity in which the foot is twisted out of the normal position.

Tampon A plug of cotton or other absorbent material that is inserted into a body cavity in order to soak up discharge, such as vaginal tampons to absorb menstrual flow.

Tartar Calcified deposits on the teeth that are from a buildup of plaque.

Tay-Sachs disease A congenital disease affecting the fat metabolism and the brain and characterized by progressive weakness, disability and blindness, and finally death. Also known as Amaurotic familial idiocy.

T cells A specialized type of white blood cell (lymphocyte) that works as part of the immune system by attaching itself directly to an invading organism, such as a parasite or fungus, and destroying it. *See* B cells.

Temple The portion of the head between the eye and the ear.

Tendinitis Inflammation of a tendon.

Tendon A white fibrous band that connects muscle to bone.

Tenesmus Urgent desire to evacuate the bowel or bladder with painful and ineffectual straining to urinate or to move the bowels.

Tensor A muscle that stretches or tenses.

Testicles, testes The pair of primary male sex glands enclosed in the scrotum. They produce the male sex hormone testosterone and the spermatozoa.

Testosterone The male sex hormone which induces the secondary sex characteristics.

Tetanus (lockjaw) A serious and acute infection caused by the invasion of toxic microorganisms into an open wound.

Tetany Muscular spasms and cramps due to muscular hypersensitivity. Causes include gastrointestinal disorders or calcium deficiency.

Thalamus An egg-shaped mass of gray matter at the base of the cerebrum.

Thermometer Instrument used to measure temperature.

Thiamine (vitamin B$_1$) One of the B-complex vitamins.

Thoracic Pertaining to the chest.

Thorax The chest.

Thrombin An enzyme that converts fibrinogen into fibrin which is necessary in order for blood to clot.

Thrombocyte Blood platelet, necessary for the process of blood clotting.

Thrombosis The formation of a blood clot that partially or completely blocks the blood vessel.

Thrombus A blood clot formed in a blood vessel.

Thrush A fungal infection (Candidiasis) of the mouth, often occurring in infancy, but also in immunocompromised people whose resistance to disease is lowered.

Thymus A gland active in childhood and located behind the breastbone. It plays a part in defending the body against infection.

Thyroid gland The ductless gland located in the neck. The secretions of the thyroid gland control the rate of metabolism, among other functions.

Thyroidectomy Surgical removal of the thyroid.

Thyroxin The primary hormone secretion of the thyroid gland.

Tibia The shin bone. The larger (inner) of the two bones of the lower leg.

Tic Involuntary spasmodic movements or twitching.

Tick A blood-sucking parasite that is associated with the spread of disease.

Tincture A medicinal mixture of alcohol and a drug.

Tinea (ringworm) Fungus infection of the skin, and depending upon the location, the cause of barber's itch, jock itch, scalp ringworm, or ringworm of the foot.

Tinea pedia (athlete's foot) A fungal infection of the foot characterized by itching, small sores, and cracks on the skin.

Tinnitus Ringing, buzzing, or other perceived noises that originate inside the head rather than from outside stimuli.

Tissue A group of cells or fibers which perform similar functions and together form a body structure.

Tonsils The 2 masses of lymphoid tissue covered by mucous membrane that are located one on each side of the back of the throat.

Tonsillectomy Surgical removal of the tonsils.

Tonsillitis Inflammation of the tonsils.

Topical Local.

Torticollis (wry neck) A condition in which the (sternocleidomastoid) muscle on one side of the neck contracts and pulls the head into an abnormal position.

Toxemia (blood poisoning) A condition in which poisonous compounds (toxins) are present in the bloodstream. Toxemia of pregnancy is another term for eclampsia.

Toxic Poisonous.

Toxic shock syndrome (TSS) An acute form of blood poisoning caused by the *Staphylococcus aureus* bacteria. It is associated with the use of superabsorbent tampons during menstruation but has been identified in children and men as well.

Toxin A poisonous substance produced by bacteria that may have serious effects in humans. Examples include toxic shock syndrome or botulism.

Toxoid A toxin that has been altered so that it is no longer poisonous but still stimulates antibody production. Used in vaccinations.

Toxoplasmosis A disease transmitted from animals (especially cats) to humans by parasite-infected feces or by eating undercooked meat containing the parasite. Infection during pregnancy can cause birth defects or fetal death.

Trachea The windpipe. The tube that extends from the larynx to the bronchi.

Tracheitis Inflammation of the trachea.

Tracheobronchitis Inflammation of the trachea and the bronchi.

Tracheotomy A surgical operation in which an artificial slit is made in the trachea in order to bypass an obstruction and allow air into the lungs.

Trachoma A contagious virus disease of the eye in which the conjunctiva and other mucous membranes become infected. May lead to blindness.

Traction Continuous pulling of a body part using weights and pulleys. Used in treatment of dislocations, deformity, and severe muscle spasm.

Tranquilizers A category of drugs used to relieve anxiety or calm disturbed behavior. "Minor" tranquilizers (such as Valium) are used to alleviate anxiety in stressful situations. "Major" tranquilizers (such as Thorazine) are used to reduce symptoms of mental illness (abnormal thought patterns, hallucinations) and make the patient more receptive to psychiatric treatment.

Transfusion The injection of fluids (usually blood or its components) into the circulatory system.

Transplantation The transference of an organ or tissue from one part of the body to another or from one individual to another.

Trauma Injury to the body or emotional shock.

Tremor Involuntary quivering or trembling. May have nervous, congenital, or organic origin or may result from certain drugs.

Triceps The muscle that extends the forearm.

Trichinosis A disease caused by ingestion of parasites often found in raw or insufficiently cooked pork.

Trichomoniasis Inflammation, usually of the vagina but also may affect the urethra in males, caused by a protozoan (single-celled) parasite, Trichomonas vaginalis.

Tricuspid valve The heart valve through which blood passes from the right atrium to the right ventricle.

Trigeminal nerve The fifth cranial nerve. Its 3 branches serve the face, the tongue, and the teeth.

Triglycerides The most common lipid found in fatty tissue. A high level of triglycerides may increase the risk of blood vessel or heart disease.

Truss A device used to hold a hernia or organ in place.

Trypsin An enzyme produced in the pancreas to digest proteins.

Tsutsugamushi disease A rickettsial disease found in Asia. Scrub typhus.

Tubal ligation (salpingectomy) Method of sterilization in which the Fallopian tubes are tied or cut so that the sperm is unable to meet the ovum.

Tubal pregnancy The most common form of ectopic pregnancy in which the fertilized egg starts to develop in the Fallopian tubes rather than in the uterus.

Tubercle (1) A nodule on a bone. (2) The lesion characteristic of tuberculosis.

Tuberculosis An infectious disease affecting the lungs most often but also other parts of the body. It is caused by the tubercle bacillus and symptoms include cough, chest pains, fatigue, sweating, and weight loss. Commonly referred to as TB.

Tuberculin test A skin test used to detect tuberculosis or tuberculosis sensitivity. An extract of tubercle bacilli is injected into the skin and a positive reaction indicates possible tuberculosis or a previous exposure to the disease.

Tubule A small tube.

Tularemia Rabbit fever. A disease of small animals that is spread to humans by direct contact (e.g., handling the meat of an infected animal) or by the bite of a vector, such as a tick or flea. Symptoms include chills, fever, and swollen lymph nodes.

Tumefaction Swelling.

Tumor An abnormal growth of tissue similar to normal tissue but without function. May be benign (harmless) or malignant (cancerous).

Tympanic membrane The eardrum.

Tympanum The middle ear.

Typhoid fever A bacterial infection spread through contaminated water, milk, or food, especially shellfish. Symptoms include fever and diarrhea and disease may cause fatal dehydration.

Typhus A rickettsial disease transmitted by lice to humans. Symptoms include headache, chills, pain, and fever.

Ulcer An open sore on the skin or in a body cavity. Term commonly refers to intestinal or peptic ulcers, which form in the digestive tract.

Ulcerative colitis An inflammation of the colon and rectum in which ulcers in the digestive tract cause bloody stool.

Ulna The larger bone of the forearm.

Ultrasound Sound waves of very high frequency used for diagnostic purposes. The echoes of the ultrasound are registered with devices that construct pictures showing internal organs.

Umbilical cord The tube that connects the fetus to the placenta and through which the fetus is nourished and wastes are disposed.

Umbilicus The navel. The round scar in the middle of the abdomen left by the cutting of the umbilical cord after birth.

Undulant fever (brucellosis, or malta fever) A disease transmitted from animals to humans through contaminated, unpasteurized milk products. Symptoms include fatigue, chills, joint pains, and a fever that undulates between near normal and extremely high (104° F).

Urea The nitrogen-containing waste product of protein breakdown that is excreted as the main component of urine.

Uremia A condition in which toxic substances remain in the blood due to the failure of the kidneys to filter out and excrete them.

Ureter One of the 2 tubes connecting the kidneys to the bladder and through which urine passes (by means of muscle contractions) into the bladder.

Urethra The tube through which the urine passes from the bladder to the outside. In the female, it is about 1½ inches long; in the male, it is 8 to 9 inches long.

Urethritis Inflammation of the urethra.

Uric acid An acid that is the waste product of metabolism. It is usually excreted in the urine and a buildup of it is characteristic of gout.

Urinalysis Examination and analysis of the urine for diagnostic purposes.

Urination (micturition) The discharge of liquid waste through the urethra.

Urine The amber-colored liquid produced in the kidneys from waste products filtered out of the blood. It is released through the ureters to the bladder where it is stored temporarily before excretion. The urine is discharged from the bladder through the urethra during urination.

Urogenital Pertaining to the urinary and genital organs.

Urology The branch of medical science that deals with disorders of the urinary tract of the female and the urogenital system of the male.

Urticaria (hives) An allergic reaction in which itchy elevations (wheals or welts) appear on the skin. May be due to a food allergy, drugs, or other substances. Antihistamines may be prescribed in serious or recurring cases, but most hives disappear in a few days with no treatment.

Uterus (womb) The hollow, pear-shaped muscular organ where the fertilized ovum develops during pregnancy. It normally weighs about 2 ounces but enlarges to 30 ounces in pregnancy.

Uvea The pigmented parts of the eye.

Uvula The small tag of tissue which hangs from the center of the soft palate at the back of the throat.

Vaccination Inoculation of an antigenic substance in order to stimulate immunity to disease.

Vaccine Dead or weakened microorganisms that prevent disease by stimulating artificial immunity.

Vaccinia Cowpox.

Vagina The muscular canal lined with mucous membrane which extends from the vulva to the uterus. Sometimes referred to as the birth canal.

Vaginismus Painful contractions of the muscles of the vagina; often responsible for painful intercourse.

Vaginitis Inflammation of the vagina, accompanied by discharge and discomfort.

Vagus The tenth cranial nerve that extends from the brain to serve the stomach, intestines, esophagus, larynx, lungs, and heart.

Varicella Chickenpox.

Varicocele Varicose or swollen veins in the spermatic cord.

Varicose veins Abnormally swollen, dilated veins in which the valves are weakened and therefore allow the backflow of blood. Areas most commonly affected are the lower legs and the rectum. *See also* Hemorrhoids.

Variola Smallpox.

Vas deferens The duct of the testes through which the spermatozoa must pass in ejaculation.

Vascular Pertaining to, or supplied with, vessels, usually blood vessels.

Vasectomy A method of sterilization of the male. The passageway of the vas deferens is cut off so that the spermatozoa cannot enter the semen.

Vasoconstrictor Any agent that causes the blood vessels to narrow or to contract.

Vasodilator Any agent that causes the blood vessels to widen or enlarge.

Vasomotor Having the ability to contract or enlarge the blood vessels.

Vector An animal, insect, or person that carries disease.

Vein The vessels that carry deoxygenated blood from all parts of the body back to the heart.

Venereal diseases Diseases transmitted through sexual contact.

Venesection (bloodletting) Cutting a vein for the withdrawal of blood.

Venipuncture Puncturing a vein for the withdrawal of blood.

Venous   Pertaining to the veins.

Ventral   Pertaining to the front of the body, the abdomen.

Ventricle   A small cavity, especially the 2 lower muscular chambers of the heart and the 4 cavities of the brain.

Venule   A small vein that serves as a link between the arterial and venous systems.

Verruca   A wart.

Vertebra   One of the 33 flat, roundish bones that make up the spinal column.

Vertigo   Dizziness.

Vesicle   A small sac or bladder.

Viable   Capable of survival.

Vibrios   Hooklike bacteria.

Villus   A microscopic finger-shaped projection such as those found in the mucous lining of the stomach walls.

Viral   Pertaining to a virus.

Virulent   Poisonous, disease-producing.

Virus   A submicroscopic organism that causes disease and is capable of reproduction only within the living cells of another organism (such as a plant, animal, or human). Viruses cause many diseases of humans ranging from mild ailments (such as the common cold) to serious, even fatal, diseases.

Viscera   The internal organs (viscus—An internal organ).

Visual purple   *See* Rhodopsin.

Vitreous humor   The jellylike substance that is found between the lens and the retina and that supports the interior parts of the eye.

Vocal cords   Two ligaments in the larynx, the vibrations of which produce the sounds of the human voice.

Volvulus   A twist or knot in the intestine that blocks passage.

Vomit   Ejection of matter from the stomach through the mouth.

Vulva   The external genitalia of the female including the clitoris and vaginal lips.

Vulvovaginitis   Bacteria-caused inflammation of the vulva and the vagina.

Walleye   An eye condition in which the cornea is whitish and opaque instead of clear; term also used to describe a form of divergent strabismus (crossed eyes) in which the images are slanted in different directions instead of merging into one.

Wart   Small, harmless growths on the skin caused by a virus.

Wasserman test   A blood test used to detect syphilis.

Wen   A sebaceous cyst caused by the obstruction of an oil gland of the skin.

Wheal   A temporary skin elevation usually a result of an allergic reaction.

White blood cell   *See* Leukocyte.

Widal test   A blood test used to detect typhoid fever.

Windpipe   *See* Trachea.

Womb   *See* Uterus.

Xanthoma   An accumulation or nodule of cholesterol that forms under the skin and appears as an elevated yellow patch.

Xeroderm   Dry skin.

Xerophthalmia   A dryness of the membranes of the eyelids and eye, associated with vitamin A deficiency.

Xerosis   Abnormal dryness.

Xiphoid   The sword-shaped piece of cartilage at the lower edge of the breastbone.

X-rays   Electromagnetic radiation waves of very short length that are capable of penetrating some substances and producing shadow pictures showing structures of differing densities.

Yaws (frambesia)   A tropical disease very similar to syphilis and caused by a spirochete resembling syphilis organisms.

Yellow fever   An acute disease caused by a virus spread by insect bites. Usually seen in South America and Africa.

Zoonoses   Any disease transmitted by an animal to humans.

Zoster   *See* Herpes zoster, Shingles.

Zygote   The fertilized egg before division.

APPENDIXES

Appendix A: Directory of Poison Control Centers

ALABAMA

State Coordinator
Department of Public Health
Montgomery, AL 36117
205-832-3194
    832-3935

Birmingham
The Children's Hospital of
    Birmingham
1601 6th Ave., S.
Birmingham, AL 35233
205-933-4050
800-292-6678
(Statewide)

Tuscaloosa
The Alabama Poison Control Center
Druid City Hospital
809 University Blvd., E.
Tuscaloosa, AL 34501
205-345-0600
800-462-0800
(Statewide)

ALASKA

State Coordinator
Department of Health and
    Social Services
Juneau, AK 99811
907-465-3100

Anchorage
Anchorage Poison Center
Providence Hospital
3200 Providence Dr.
Anchorage, AK 99504
907-274-6535

Fairbanks
Fairbanks Poison Center
Fairbanks Memorial Hospital
1650 Cowles
Fairbanks, AK 99701
907-456-7182

ARIZONA

State Coordinator
Arizona Poison Control System
College of Pharmacy
University of Arizona
Tucson, AZ 85724
602-626-6016
800-362-0101
(Statewide)

Flagstaff
Flagstaff Hospital and Medical
    Center of N. Arizona
1215 N. Beaver St.
Flagstaff, AZ 86001
602-779-0555

Phoenix
St. Lukes Hospital and
    Medical Center
525 N. 18th St.
Phoenix, AZ 85006
602-253-3334

Tucson
Arizona Poison and Drug
    Information Center
Arizona Health Sciences Center
University of Arizona
Tucson, AZ 85724
602-626-6016
800-362-0101
(Statewide)

ARKANSAS

State Coordinator
Division of Environmental
    Health Protection
Arkansas Department of Health
Little Rock, AR 72201
501-661-2301

El Dorado
Warner Brown Hospital
Emergency Room
460 W. Oak St.
El Dorado, AR 71730
501-863-2266

Fort Smith
St. Edward Mercy Medical Center
Emergency Room
7301 Rogers Ave.
Fort Smith, AR 72903
501-452-5100
Ext. 2401

Sparks Regional Medical Center
Emergency Room
1311 S. "I" St.
Fort Smith, AR 72901
501-441-5011

Harrison
Boone County Hospital
Emergency Room
620 N. Willow St.
Harrison, AR 72601
501-741-6141
Ext. 275

Helena
Helena Hospital
Emergency Room
Hospital Drive
Helena, AR 72342
501-338-6411
Ext. 340

Little Rock
University of Arkansas
    Medical Center
Emergency Room
4301 W. Markham St.
Little Rock, AR 72201
501-661-6161

Osceola
Osceola Memorial Hospital
Emergency Room
611 Lee Ave., W.
Osceola, AR 72370
501-563-7180

Pine Bluff
Jefferson Regional Medical Center
Emergency Department
1515 W. 42nd Ave.
Pine Bluff, AR 71601
501-541-7111

CALIFORNIA

State Coordinator
Emergency Medical Services
    Authority
1600 Ninth St., Room 460
Sacramento, CA 95814
916-322-4336

Fresno
Central Valley Regional
    Poison Control Center
Fresno Community Hospital
Fresno & R Sts.
Fresno, CA 93715
209-445-1222

Los Angeles
Los Angeles County Medical
    Association
Regional Poison Information
    Center
1925 Wilshire Blvd.
Los Angeles, CA 90057
213-484-5151

Oakland
Children's Hospital Medical
    Center of N. California
51st & Grove Sts.
.Oakland, CA 94609
415-428-3248

Orange
University of California
Irvine Medical Center
101 City Dr., Route 32
Orange, CA 92688
714-634-5988

Sacramento
Sacramento Medical Center
University of California at Davis
Poison Control Center
2315 Stockton Blvd.
Sacramento, CA 95817
916-453-3692
800-852-7221
(N. CA)

San Diego
San Diego Regional Poison
    Center
University of California at San Diego
    Medical Center
225 W. Dickinson St.
San Diego, CA 92103
619-294-6000

San Francisco
San Francisco Bay Area
Regional Poison Control Center
Room 1E 86
San Francisco General Hospital
1001 Potrero Ave.
San Francisco, CA 94110
415-666-2845
800-792-0720
(N. CA)

San Jose
Central-Coast Counties
Regional Poison Control Center
Santa Clara Valley Medical Center
751 S. Bascom Ave.
San Jose, CA 95128
408-279-5112
800-662-9886
(Statewide)

COLORADO

State Coordinator
Department of Health
Emergency Medical Services
    Division
4210 E. 11th Ave.
Denver, CO 08220
303-320-8476

Denver
Rocky Mountain Poison Center
Denver General Hospital
W. 8th Ave. & Cherokee Sts.
Denver, CO 80204
303-629-1123
800-332-3073

CONNECTICUT

State Coordinator
University of Connecticut
    Health Center
Farmington, CT 06032
203-674-3456

Bridgeport
Bridgeport Hospital
267 Grant St.
Bridgeport, CT 06602
203-384-3566

St. Vincent's Medical Center
2800 Main St.
Bridgeport, CT 06606
203-576-5178

Danbury
Danbury Hospital
95 Locust Ave.
Danbury, CT 06810
203-797-7300

Farmington
Connecticut Poison Control
   Center
University of Connecticut
   Health Center
Farmington, CT 06032
203-674-3456

Middletown
Middlesex Memorial Hospital
28 Crescent St.
Middletown, CT 06457
203-344-6684

New Haven
The Hospital of St. Raphael
1450 Chapel St.
New Haven, CT 06511
203-789-3464

Yale-New Haven Hospital
Department of Pediatrics
Pediatric Emergency Room
20 York St.
New Haven, CT 06504
203-785-2222

Norwalk
Department of Emergency
   Medicine
Norwalk Hospital
Maple St.
Norwalk, CT 06856
203-852-2160

Waterbury
St. Mary's Hospital
Emergency Room
56 Franklin St.
Waterbury, CT 06702
203-574-6011

DELAWARE

State Coordinator
Wilmington Medical Center
Delaware Division
Wilmington, DE 19801
302-655-3389

Wilmington
Wilmington Medical Center
Delaware Division
501 W. 14th St.
Wilmington, DE 19899
302-655-3389

DISTRICT OF COLUMBIA

State Coordinator
Department of Human Services
Washington, DC 20009
202-673-6741
673-6736

Washington
National Capital Poison Center
Georgetown University Hospital
3800 Reservoir Rd.
Washington, DC 20007
202-625-3333

FLORIDA

State Coordinator
Department of Health and
   Rehabilitative Services
Office of Emergency Medical
   Services
Tallahassee, FL 32301
904-487-1566

Bradenton
Manatee Memorial Hospital
206 Second St., E.
Bradenton, FL 33505
813-748-2121

Daytona Beach
Halifax Hospital
Emergency Department
P.O. Box 1990
Daytona Beach, FL 32014
904-258-1513

Fort Lauderdale
Broward General Medical Center
Poison Control Center
1600 S. Andrews Ave.
Fort Lauderdale, FL 33316
305-463-3131
Ext. 1955/6

Fort Myers
Lee Memorial Hospital
2776 Cleveland Ave.
P.O. Drawer 2218
Fort Myers, FL 33902
813-334-5287

Fort Walton Beach
General Hospital of
   Ft. Walton Beach
1000 Mar-Walt Dr.
Fort Walton Beach, FL 32548
904-862-1111
Ext. 106

Gainesville
Shands Teaching Hospital
   and Clinics
University of Florida
Gainesville, FL 32610
904-392-3389

Inverness
Citrus Memorial Hospital
502 Highland Blvd.
Inverness, FL 32650
904-726-2800

Jacksonville
St. Vincent's Medical Center
P.O. Box 2982
Jacksonville, FL 32203
904-387-7500
387-7499
(TTY)

Lakeland
Lakeland Regional Medical Center
Lakeland General Hospital
Lakeland Hills Hospital
Lakeland, FL 33802
813-687-1137

Leesburg
Leesburg Regional Medical
   Center
600 E. Dixie
Leesburg, FL 32748
904-787-9900

Melbourne
James E. Holmes Regional
   Medical Center
Emergency Department
1350 S. Hickory St.
Melbourne, FL 32901
305-727-7000
Ext. 675

Naples
Naples Community Hospital
350 7th St., N.
Naples, FL 33940
813-262-3131

Ocala
Munroe Regional Medical Center
131 S.W. 15th St.
Ocala, FL 32670
904-351-7607

Orlando
Orlando Regional Medical Center
Orange Memorial Division
1414 S. Kuhl Ave.
Orlando, FL 32806
305-841-5222

Pensacola
Gulf Regional Poison Center
Baptist Hospital
P.O. Box 17500
Pensacola, FL 32522
904-434-4611
800-874-1555
(Out of State)
800-342-3222
(Statewide)

Punta Gorda
Medical Center Hospital
809 E. Marion Ave.
Punta Gorda, FL 33950
813-637-2529

Rockledge
Wuesthoff Memorial Hospital
110 Longwood Ave.
Rockledge, FL 32955
305-636-4357

St. Petersburg
Bay Front Medical Center, Inc.
701 6th St., S.
St. Petersburg, FL 33701
800-282-3171
(Statewide)

Sarasota
Memorial Hospital
1901 Arlington St.
Sarasota, FL 33579
813-953-1332

Tallahassee
Tallahassee Memorial Regional
   Medical Center
1300 Miccosukee Rd.
Tallahassee, FL 32304
904-681-5411

Tampa
Tampa Bay Regional Poison
   Control Center
Tampa General Hospital
Davis Island
Tampa, FL 33606
813-251-6995
800-282-3171
(Statewide)

Titusville
Jess Parrish Memorial Hospital
951 N. Washington Ave.
P.O. Drawer W
Titusville, FL 32780
305-268-6260

West Palm Beach
Good Samaritan Hospital
Palm Beach Lakes Blvd.
West Palm Beach, FL 33402
305-655-5511
Ext. 4250

Winter Haven
Poison Control Center
Winter Haven Hospital, Inc.
200 Avenue F., N.E.
Winter Haven, FL 33880
813-299-9701

GEORGIA

State Coordinator
Department of Human Resources
Emergency Health Section
Atlanta, GA 30303
404-894-5170

Albany
Phoebe Putney Memorial
   Hospital
417 Third Ave.
Albany, GA 31705
912-888-4150

Athens
Athens General Hospital
1199 Prince Ave.
Athens, GA 30613
404-543-5215

Atlanta
Georgia Poison Control Center
Grady Memorial Hospital
Box 26066
80 Butler St., S.E.
Atlanta, GA 30305
404-588-4400
800-282-5846
(Statewide)
404-525-3323
(TTY)

Augusta
University Hospital
1350 Walton Way
Augusta, GA 30902
404-724-5050

Columbus
The Medical Center
710 Center St.
Columbus, GA 31902
404-571-1080

Macon
Medical Center of Central
   Georgia
Regional Poison Control Center
777 Hemlock St.
Macon, GA 31201
912-744-1427

Rome
Floyd Hospital
Turner McCall Blvd.
Rome, GA 31061
404-295-5500

Savannah
Savannah Regional EMS
  Poison Center
Department of Emergency Medicine
Memorial Medical Center
P.O. Box 23089
Savannah, GA 31403
912-355-5228

Thomasville
John D. Archbold Memorial
  Hospital
900 Gordon Ave.
Thomasville, GA 31792
912-226-4121
Ext. 169

Valdosta
South Georgia Medical Center
P.O. Box 1727
Valdosta, GA 31603
912-333-1110

Waycross
Memorial Hospital
410 Darling Ave.
Waycross, GA 31501
912-283-3030

GUAM

Coordinator
Guam Memorial Hospital
P.O. Box AX
Agana, Guam 96910
671-646-5801

Agana
Pharmacy Service, Box 7667
U.S. Naval Regional Medical
  Center (Guam)
FPO San Francisco, CA 96630
671-344-9265
    344-9354

HAWAII

State Coordinator
Department of Health
Honolulu, HI 96801
808-531-7776

Honolulu
Kapiolani-Children's Medical
  Center
1319 Punahou St.
Honolulu, HI 96826
808-941-4411
808-362-3585

IDAHO

State Coordinator
Department of Health & Welfare
Boise, ID 83720
208-334-4245

Boise
Idaho Emergency Medical
  Poison Center
1055 N. Curtis Rd.
Boise, ID 83706
208-334-2241
800-632-8000
(Statewide)

Idaho Falls
Consolidated Hospitals
Emergency Department
900 Memorial Dr.
Idaho Falls, ID 83401
208-522-3600

Pocatello
Idaho Drug Information Service
  and Poison Control Center
Pocatello Regional Medical Center
777 Hospital Way
Pocatello, ID 83202
208-234-0777
Ext. 2019
800-632-9490
(Statewide)

ILLINOIS

State Coordinator
Division of Emergency Medical
  Services and Highway Safety
Springfield, IL 62761
217-785-2080

Chicago
Rush Presbyterian-St. Luke's
  Poison Center
Rush Presbyterian-St. Luke's
  Medical Center
1753 W. Congress Pkwy.
Chicago, IL 60612
312-942-5969
800-942-5969
(Chicago and
N.E. Illinois)

Peoria
Peoria Poison Center
St. Francis Hospital
  and Medical Center
530 N.E. Glen Oak Ave.
Peoria, IL 61637
309-672-2334
800-322-5330
(Northern and
Central Illinois)

Springfield
Central & Southern Illinois
  Poison Resource Center
St. John's Hospital
800 E. Carpenter
Springfield, IL 62769
217-753-3330
800-252-2022
(Statewide)

INDIANA

State Coordinator
Indiana State Board of Health
Hazardous Products Section
  and Division of Drug Control
P.O. Box 1964
Indianapolis, IN 46206
317-633-0332

Anderson
Community Hospital
1515 N. Madison Ave.
Anderson, IN 46012
317-646-5143

St. John's Hickey Memorial
  Hospital
2015 Jackson St.
Anderson, IN 46014
317-646-8222

Angola
Cameron Memorial Hospital, Inc.
416 E. Maumee St.
Angola, IN 46703
219-665-2141
Ext. 146

Crown Point
St. Anthony Medical Center
Main at Franciscan Rd.
Crown Point, IN 46307
219-738-2100
Ext. 1311

Evansville
Poison Control Center
Deaconess Hospital, Inc.
600 Mary St.
Evansville, IN 47710
812-426-3333

Welborn Memorial Baptist
  Hospital
401 S.W. 6th St.
Evansville, IN 47713
812-426-8336

Fort Wayne
Emergency Department
Lutheran Hospital
3024 Fairfield Ave.
Fort Wayne, IN 46807
219-458-2211

Parkview Memorial Hospital
2200 Randalia Dr.
Fort Wayne, IN 46805
219-484-9711

St. Joseph's Hospital
700 Broadway
Fort Wayne, IN 46802
219-426-8280

Gary
Methodist Hospital of
  Gary, Inc.
600 Grant St.
Gary, IN 46402
219-886-4710

Hammond
Poison Control Center
St. Margaret's Hospital
25 Douglas St.
Hammond, IN 46320
219-931-4477

Indianapolis
Indiana Poison Center
1001 W. Tenth St.
Indianapolis, IN 46202
317-630-7351
800-382-9097

Kokomo
Howard Community Hospital
3500 S. LaFountain St.
Kokomo, IN 46901
317-453-8444

Lafayette
Lafayette Home Hospital
2400 South St.
Lafayette, IN 47902
317-447-6811

Poison Control Center
St. Elizabeth Hospital
1501 Hartford St.
Lafayette, IN 47904
317-423-6699

Lebanon
Witham Memorial Hospital
1124 N. Lebanon St.
Lebanon, IN 46052
317-482-2700
Ext. 241

Madison
King's Daughter's Hospital
112 Presbyterian Ave.
Madison, IN 47250
812-265-5211
Ext. 131

Marion
Marion General Hospital
Wabash and Euclid Aves.
Marion, IN 46952
317-662-4693

Muncie
Ball Memorial Hospital
2401 University Ave.
Muncie, IN 47303
317-747-4321

Richmond
Reid Memorial Hospital
1401 Chester Blvd.
Richmond, IN 47374
317-983-3148

Shelbyville
William S. Major Hospital
150 W. Washington St.
Shelbyville, IN 46176
317-392-3211
Ext. 252

South Bend
St. Joseph's Medical Center
811 E. Madison St.
South Bend, IN 46622
219-237-7264

Terre Haute
Union Hospital, Inc.
1606 N. Seventh St.
Terre Haute, IN 47804
812-238-7000
Ext. 7523

Valparaiso
Porter Memorial Hospital
814 LaPorte Ave.
Valparaiso, IN 46383
219-464-8611
Ext. 301

Vincennes
The Good Samaritan Hospital
520 S. 7th St.
Vincennes, IN 47591
812-885-3348

IOWA

State Coordinator
Department of Health
Des Moines, IA 50319
515-281-4964

Des Moines
Variety Club Poison and
  Drug Information Center
Iowa Methodist Medical Center
1200 Pleasant St.
Des Moines, IA 50308
515-283-6254
800-362-2327
(Statewide)

Dubuque
Mercy Health Center
Mercy Dr.
Dubuque, IA 52001
319-589-9099

Fort Dodge
Trinity Regional Hospital
Kenyon Rd.
Fort Dodge, IA 50501
515-573-3101

Iowa City
University of Iowa Hospitals
and Clinics
Poison Control Center
Iowa City, IA 52242
319-356-2922
800-272-6477
(Statewide)

Waterloo
Allen Memorial Hospital
Emergency Department
1825 Logan Ave.
Waterloo, IA 50703
319-235-3893

KANSAS

State Coordinator
Kansas Department of Health
and Environment
Bureau of Food and Drug
Forbes Field
Topeka, KS 66620
913-862-9360
Ext. 541

Atchison
Atchison Hospital
1301 N. 2nd St.
Atchison, KS 66002
913-367-2131
Ext. 111

Dodge City
Dodge City Regional Hospital
Ross & Ave. "A"
Dodge City, KS 67801
316-225-9050
Ext. 381

Emporia
Newman Memorial Hospital
12th and Chestnut Sts.
Emporia, KS 66801
316-343-6800
Ext. 545

Fort Riley
Irwin Army Hospital
Emergency Room
Fort Riley, KS 66442
913-239-7776

Fort Scott
Mercy Hospital
821 Burke St.
Fort Scott, KS 66701
316-223-2200
Ext. 136

Great Bend
Central Kansas Medical Center
3515 Broadway
Great Bend, KS 67530
316-792-2511
Ext. 115

Hays
Hadley Regional Medical Center
201 E. 7th St.
Hays, KS 67601
913-628-8251
Ext. 145

Kansas City
Mid-America Poison Center
University of Kansas
39th and Rainbow Blvd.
Kansas City, KS 66103
913-588-6633
800-332-6633
(Statewide)

Lawrence
Lawrence Memorial Hospital
325 Maine St.
Lawrence, KS 66044
913-843-3680
Ext. 162

Salina
St. John's Hospital
139 N. Penn St.
Salina, KS 67401
913-827-3187

Topeka
Stormont-Vail Regional
Medical Center
10th & Washburn Sts.
Topeka, KS 66606
913-354-6100

Northeast Kansas Poison Center
St. Francis Hospital and
Medical Center
1700 W. 7th St.
Topeka, KS 66606
913-295-8094

Wichita
Wesley Medical Center
550 N. Hillside Ave.
Wichita, KS 67214
316-688-2277

KENTUCKY

State Coordinator
Department for Human Resources
Frankfort, KY 40601
502-564-3970

Fort Thomas
St. Lukes Hospital
85 N. Grand Ave.
Fort Thomas, KY 41075
606-572-3215
800-352-9900
(Statewide)

Lexington
Central Baptist Hospital
1740 S. Limestone St.
Lexington, KY 40503
606-278-3411
Ext. 363

Drug Information Center
University of Kentucky
Medical Center
Lexington, KY 40536
606-233-5320

Louisville
Kentucky Regional Poison Center
of Kosair-Children's Hospital
NKC, INC.
P.O. Box 35070
Louisville, KY 40232
502-589-8222
800-722-5725
(Statewide)

Murray
Murray-Calloway County Hospital
803 Popular
Murray, KY 42071
502-753-7588

Owensboro
Owensboro-Daviess County
Hospital
811 Hospital Ct.
Owensboro, KY 42301
502-926-3030
Ext. 180

Paducah
Western Baptist Hospital
2501 Kentucky Ave.
Paducah, KY 42001
502-444-5180

Prestonburg
Poison Control Center
Highlands Regional Medical
Center
Prestonburg, KY 41653
606-886-5511
Ext. 132

LOUISIANA

State Coordinator
LSU Poison Control and Drug
Abuse Information Center
Louisiana State University
P.O. Box 33932
Shreveport, LA 71130
318-425-1524

Alexandria
Rapides General Hospital
Poison Control Center
P.O. Box 7146
Alexandria, LA 71301
318-445-4665

Lafayette
Our Lady of Lourdes Hospital
611 St. Landry St.
Lafayette, LA 70501
318-234-7381

Lake Charles
Lake Charles Memorial Hospital
P.O. Drawer M
Lake Charles, LA 70601
318-478-6800

Monroe
School of Pharmacy
Northeast Louisiana University
700 University Ave.
Monroe, LA 71209
318-342-3008

St. Francis Hospital
P.O. Box 1901
Monroe, LA 71301
318-325-6454

New Orleans
Charity Hospital
1532 Tulane Ave.
New Orleans, LA 70140
504-568-5222

Shreveport
Louisiana State University
Poison Control and Drug
Abuse Information Center
LSU Medical Center
P.O. Box 33932
Shreveport, LA 71130
318-425-1524

MAINE

State Coordinator
Maine Poison Control Center
Portland, ME 04102
207-871-2950

Portland
Maine Medical Center
Emergency Division
22 Bramhall St.
Portland, ME 04102
207-871-2381
800-442-6305
(Statewide)

MARYLAND

State Coordinator
Maryland Poison Center
University of Maryland
School of Pharmacy
Baltimore, MD 21201
301-528-7604
(Statewide)

Baltimore
Maryland Poison Center
University of Maryland
School of Pharmacy
636 W. Lombard St.
Baltimore, MD 21201
301-528-7701
800-492-2414
(Statewide)

Cumberland
Tri-State Poison Center
Sacred Heart Hospital
900 Seton Dr.
Cumberland, MD 21502
301-722-6677

MASSACHUSETTS

State Coordinator
Department of Public Health
Boston, MA 02111
617-727-2700

Boston
Massachusetts Poison Control
System
300 Longwood Ave.
Boston, MA 02115
617-232-2120
800-682-9211
(Statewide)
617-277-3323
TTY (MA Only)

MICHIGAN

State Coordinator
Department of Public Health
Emergency Medical Services
Lansing, MI 48909
517-373-1406

Adrian
Poison Control Center
Emma L. Bixby Hospital
818 Riverside Ave.
Adrian, MI 49221
517-263-2412

Ann Arbor
Poison Control Center
University Hospital
1405 E. Ann St.
Ann Arbor, MI 48104
313-764-7667

Battle Creek
Community Hospital
Pharmacy Department
183 West St.
Battle Creek, MI 49016
616-963-5521

Bay City
Bay Medical Center
1900 Columbus Ave.
Bay City, MI 48706
517-894-3131

Coldwater
Community Health Center
of Branch County
274 E. Chicago St.
Coldwater, MI 49036
517-278-7361

Detroit
S.E. Regional Poison Center
Children's Hospital of Michigan
3901 Beaubien
Detroit, MI 48201
313-494-5711
800-572-1655
(Statewide)

Flint
Poison Information Center
Hurley Medical Center
One Hurley Plaza
Flint, MI 48502
313-257-9111
800-572-5396
(Statewide)

Grand Rapids
Western Michigan Regional
Poison Center
1840 Wealthy, S.E.
Grand Rapids, MI 49506
616-774-7854
800-632-2727
(Statewide)

Jackson
Poison Control Center
W.A. Foote Memorial
Hospital
205 N. East St.
Jackson, MI 49201
517-788-4816

Kalamazoo
Midwest Poison Center
Borgess Medical Center
1521 Gull Rd.
Kalamazoo, MI 49001
616-383-7104
800-632-4177
(Statewide)

Great Lakes Poison Center
Bronson Methodist Hospital
252 E. Lovell St.
Kalamazoo, MI 49006
616-383-6409
800-442-4112
(Statewide)

Lansing
St. Lawrence Hospital
1210 W. Saginaw St.
Lansing, MI 48914
517-372-5112

Marquette
Upper Peninsula Regional
Poison Center
Marquette General Hospital
420 W. Magnetic Dr.
Marquette, MI 49855
906-228-9440
800-562-9781
(N. MI only)

Midland
Midland Hospital
Poison Control Center
4005 Orchard Dr.
Midland, MI 48640
517-631-8100

Pontiac
Poison Information Center
St. Joseph Mercy Hospital
900 S. Woodward Ave.
Pontiac, MI 48053
313-858-7373

Port Huron
Port Huron Hospital
Poison Control Center
1001 Kearney St.
Port Huron, MI 48060
313-987-5555

Saginaw
Saginaw Region Poison Center
Saginaw General Hospital
1447 N. Harrison
Saginaw, MI 48602
517-755-1111

Westland
Wayne County General Hospital
2345 Merriman Rd.
Westland, MI 48185
313-722-3748

MINNESOTA

State Coordinator
EMS Section
Minnesota Department of Health
717 S.E. Delaware St.
Minneapolis, MN 55404
612-623-5284

Duluth
St. Luke's Hospital
Poison Control Center
915 E. First St.
Duluth, MN 55805
218-726-5466

St. Mary's Hospital
407 E. 3rd St.
Duluth, MN 55805
218-726-4500

Fridley
Unity Medical Center
550 Osborne Rd.
Fridley, MN 55432
612-786-2200
Ext. 6844

Mankato
Immanuel-St. Joseph's Hospital
Poison Control Center
325 Garden Blvd.
Mankato, MN 56001
507-625-4031
Ext. 2760

Minneapolis
Hennepin Poison Center
Hennepin County Medical Center
701 Park Ave.
Minneapolis, MN 55415
612-347-3141

Morris
Stevens County Memorial
Hospital
Morris, MN 56267
612-589-1313
Ext. 231

Rochester
Southeastern Minnesota
Poison Control Center
St. Mary's Hospital
1216 Second St., S.W.
Rochester, MN 55901
507-285-5123

St. Cloud
St. Cloud Hospital
1406 6th Ave., N.
St. Cloud, MN 56301
612-255-5617

St. Paul
St. John's Hospital
403 Maria Ave.
St. Paul, MN 55106
612-228-3132

United and Children's
Hospital
333 N. Smith
St. Paul, MN 55102
612-298-8402

Minnesota Poison Information
Center
St. Paul-Ramsey Medical Center
640 Jackson St.
St. Paul, MN 55101
612-221-2113

Willmar
Rice Memorial Hospital
301 Becker Ave., S.W.
Willmar, MN 56201
612-235-4543
Ext. 560

Worthington
Worthington Regional Hospital
1016 6th Ave.
Worthington, MN 56187
507-372-2941
Ext. 109

MISSISSIPPI

State Coordinator
State Board of Health
Jackson, MS 39205
601-354-7660

Biloxi
Gulf Coast Community Hospital
4642 W. Beach Blvd.
Biloxi, MS 39531
601-388-1919

USAF Hospital Keesler
Keesler Air Force Base
Biloxi, MS 39534
601-377-6555

Brandon
Rankin General Hospital
Emergency Department
350 Crossgates Blvd.
Brandon, MS 39042
601-825-2811
Ext. 405

Columbia
Marion County General Hospital
Sumrall Rd.
Brandon, MS 39429
601-736-6303
Ext. 1020

Greenwood
Greenwood-Leflore Hospital
River Rd.
Greenwood, MS 38930
601-459-2790

Hattiesburg
Forrest County General
Hospital
400 S. 28th Ave.
Hattiesburg, MS 39401
601-264-4235

Jackson
St. Dominic-Jackson
Memorial Hospital
969 Lakeland Dr.
Jackson, MS 39216
601-982-0121
Ext. 2345

University Medical Center
2500 N. State St.
Jackson, MS 39216
601-354-7660

Laurel
Jones County Community
Hospital
Jefferson St. at 13th Ave.
Laurel, MS 39440
601-649-4000
Ext. 630

Meridian
Meridian Regional Hospital
Highway 39, N.
Meridian, MS 39301
601-483-6211
Ext. 440

Pascagoula
Singing River Hospital
Emergency Department
2609 Denny Ave.
Pascagoula, MS 39567
601-938-5162

University
University of Mississippi
School of Pharmacy
Poison Information Center
University, MS 38677
601-234-1522

MISSOURI

State Coordinator
Bureau of EMS
Missouri Division of Health
Jefferson City, MO 65102
314-751-2713

Cape Girardeau
St. Francis Medical Center
St. Francis Dr.
Cape Girardeau, MO 63701
314-651-6235

Columbia
University of Missouri
Hospital and Clinics
807 Stadium Rd.
Columbia, MO 65212
314-882-8091

Hannibal
St. Elizabeth's Hospital
109 Virginia St.
Hannibal, MO 63401
314-221-0414
Ext. 264

Jefferson City
Charles E. Still Osteopathic
Hospital
1125 Madison
Jefferson City, MO 65101
314-635-7141
Ext. 215

Joplin
St. John's Medical Center
2727 McClelland Blvd.
Joplin, MO 64801
417-781-2727
Ext. 2305

Kansas City
Children's Mercy Hospital
24th at Gillham Rd.
Kansas City, MO 64108
816-234-3000

Kirksville
Kirksville Osteopathic
Health Center
#1 Osteopathy Ave.
Kirksville, MO 63501
816-626-2266

Poplar Bluff
Lucy Lee Hospital
2620 N. Westwood Blvd.
Poplar Bluff, MO 63901
314-785-7721
Ext. 264

Rolla
Phelps County Regional
Medical Center
1000 W. 10th St.
Rolla, MO 65401
314-364-3100
Ext. 287

St. Joseph
Methodist Medical Center
Seventh to Ninth on Faron St.
St. Joseph, MO 64501
816-271-7580
232-8481

St. Louis
St. Louis Regional Poison Center
Cardinal Glennon Memorial
Hospital for Children
1465 S. Grand Ave.
St. Louis, MO 63104
314-772-5200

St. Louis Children's Hospital
500 S. Kingshighway
St. Louis, MO 63110
314-454-6099

Springfield
Ozark Poison Center
Lester E. Cox Medical Center
1423 N. Jefferson St.
Springfield, MO 65802
417-831-9746

West Plains
West Plains Memorial Hospital
1103 Alaska Ave.
West Plains, MO 65775
417-256-9111
Ext. 258

MONTANA

State Coordinator
Department of Health and
Environmental Sciences
Helena, MT 59620
406-449-3895

Helena
Montana Poison Control System
Cogswell Bldg.
Helena, MT 59620
406-442-2480
800-525-5042

NEBRASKA

State Coordinator
Department of Health
Lincoln, NE 68502
402-471-2122

Omaha
Mid-Plains Regional Poison Center
Children's Memorial Hospital
8301 Dodge
Omaha, NE 68114
402-390-5400
800-642-9999
(Statewide)
800-228-9515
(Surrounding states)

NEVADA

State Coordinator
Department of Human Resources
Carson City, NV 89710
702-885-4750

Las Vegas
Southern Nevada Memorial
Hospital
1800 W. Charleston Blvd.
Las Vegas, NV 89102
702-385-1277

Sunrise Hospital Medical
Center
3186 S. Maryland Pkwy.
Las Vegas, NV 89109
702-732-4989

Reno
St. Mary's Hospital
235 W. 6th
Reno, NV 89520
702-789-3013

Washoe Medical Center
77 Pringle Way
Reno, NV 89520
702-785-4129

NEW HAMPSHIRE

State Coordinator
New Hampshire Poison Center
NH-Dartmouth Hitchcock
Medical Center
2 Maynard St.
Hanover, NH 03756
603-646-5000
800-562-8236
(Statewide)

Hanover
New Hampshire Poison Center
Mary Hitchcock Hospital
2 Maynard St.
Hanover, NH 03756
603-646-5000
800-562-8236
(Statewide)

NEW JERSEY

State Coordinator
Department of Health
Accident Prevention and
Poison Control Program
Trenton, NJ 08625
609-292-5666

Atlantic City
Atlantic City Medical Center
1925 Pacific Ave.
Atlantic City, NJ 08401
609-344-4081
Ext. 2359

Belleville
Clara Maass Medical Center
1A Franklin Ave.
Belleville, NJ 07109
201-450-2000
Ext. 781

Berlin
West Jersey Hospital
South Division
Berlin, NJ 08009
609-768-6666

Boonton
Riverside Hospital
Powerville Rd.
Boonton, NJ 07055
201-334-5000
Ext. 186

Bridgeton
Bridgeton Hospital
Irving Ave.
Bridgeton, NJ 08302
609-451-6600
Ext. 251

Denville
St. Clare's Hospital
Pocono Rd.
Denville, NJ 07834
201-625-6065
Ext. 6063

East Orange
East Orange General Hospital
300 Central Ave.
E. Orange, NJ 07019
201-672-8400
Ext. 223

Elizabeth
St. Elizabeth's Hospital
225 Williams St.
Elizabeth, NJ 07207
201-527-5059

Englewood
Englewood Hospital
350 Engle St.
Englewood, NJ 07631
201-894-3262

Flemington
Hunterdon Medical Center
Route 31
Flemington, NJ 08822
201-782-2121
Ext. 369

Livingston
St. Barnabas Medical Center
Old Short Hills Rd.
Livingston, NJ 07039
201-992-5161

Long Branch
Monmouth Medical Center
Emergency Department
Dunbar and 2nd Ave.
Long Branch, NJ 07740
201-222-2210

Montclair
Mountainside Hospital
Bay and Highland Aves.
Montclair, NJ 07042
201-429-6202

Mount Holly
Burlington County Memorial
Hospital
175 Madison Ave.
Mt. Holly, NJ 08060
609-267-7877

Neptune
Jersey Shore Medical Center
Fitkin Hospital
1945 Corlies Ave.
Neptune, NJ 07753
201-775-5500
800-822-9761
(Statewide)

Newark
Newark Beth Israel Medical
Center
201 Lyons Ave.
Newark, NJ 07112
201-926-7240

New Brunswick
Middlesex General Hospital
180 Somerset St.
New Brunswick, NJ 08903
201-937-8583

St. Peter's Medical Center
245 Easton Ave.
New Brunswick, NJ 08903
201-745-8527

Newton
Newton Memorial Hospital
175 High St.
Newton, NJ 07860
201-383-2121
Ext. 270

Orange
Hospital Center at Orange
Emergency Department
188 S. Essex Ave.
Orange, NJ 07051
201-266-2120

Passaic
St. Mary's Hospital
211 Pennington Ave.
Passaic, NJ 07055
201-473-1000
Ext. 441

Perth Amboy
Perth Amboy General Hospital
530 New Brunswick Ave.
Perth Amboy, NJ 08861
201-442-3700
Ext. 2501

Phillipsburg
Warren Hospital
185 Roseberry St.
Phillipsburg, NJ 08865
201-859-1500
Ext. 222

Point Pleasant
Point Pleasant Hospital
Osborn Ave. & River Front
Point Pleasant, NJ 08742
201-892-1100
Ext. 383

Princeton
The Medical Center
at Princeton
253 Witherspoon St.
Princeton, NJ 08540
609-734-4554

Saddle Brook
Saddle Brook General
Hospital
300 Market St.
Saddle Brook, NJ 07662
201-368-6025

Somers Point
Shore Memorial Hospital
Brighton & Sunny Aves.
Somers Point, NJ 08244
609-653-3515

Somerville
Somerset Medical Center
Rehill Ave.
Somerville, NJ 08876
201-725-4000
Ext. 436

Summit
Overlook Hospital
193 Morris Ave.
Summit, NJ 07901
201-522-2232

Teaneck
Holy Name Hospital
718 Teaneck Rd.
Teaneck, NJ 07666
201-833-3242

Trenton
Helene Fuld Medical Center
750 Brunswick Ave.
Trenton, NJ 08638
609-396-1077

Union
Memorial General Hospital
1000 Galloping Hill Rd.
Union, NJ 07083
201-687-1900
Ext. 3710

Wayne
Greater Paterson General
    Hospital
224 Hamburg Turnpike
Wayne, NJ 07470
201-942-6900
Ext. 224

NEW MEXICO

State Coordinator
New Mexico Poison Drug
    Information & Medical Center
University of New Mexico
Albuquerque, NM 87131
505-843-2551
800-432-6866
(Statewide)

NEW YORK

State Coordinator
Department of Health
Albany, NY 12237
518-474-3785

Binghamton
Southern Tier Poison Center
United Health Services
Binghamton General Hospital
Binghamton, NY 13903
607-723-8929

Our Lady of Lourdes Memorial
    Hospital
169 Riverside Dr.
Binghamton, NY 13905
607-798-5231

Buffalo
Western New York Poison
    Control Center
Children's Hospital of Buffalo
219 Bryant St.
Buffalo, NY 14222
716-878-6754

Dunkirk
Brooks Memorial Hospital
10 W. 6th St.
Dunkirk, NY 14048
716-366-1111
Ext. 414

East Meadow
Long Island Regional Poison
    Control Center
Nassau County Medical Center
2201 Hempstead Turnpike
East Meadow, NY 11554
516-542-2324
516-542-2323
(TTY)

Elmira
Arnot Ogden Memorial Hospital
Roe Ave. & Grove St.
Elmira, NY 14901
607-737-4194

St. Joseph's Hospital
    Health Center
555 E. Market St.
Elmira, NY 14901
607-734-2662

Endicott
Ideal Hospital
600 High Ave.
Endicott, NY 13760
607-754-7171

Glens Falls
Glens Falls Hospital
100 Park St.
Glens Falls, NY 12801
518-761-5261

Jamestown
W.C.A. Hospital
207 Foote Ave.
Jamestown, NY 14701
716-484-8648

Johnson City
Wilson Memorial Hospital
33 Harrison St.
Johnson City, NY 13790
607-773-6611

Kingston
Kingston Hospital
396 Broadway
Kingston, NY 12401
914-331-3313

New York City
New York City Poison Center
Department of Health
Bureau of Laboratories
455 First Ave.
New York City, NY 10016
212-340-4494
        764-7667

Nyack
Hudson Valley Poison Center
Nyack Hospital
N. Midland Ave.
Nyack, NY 10960
914-353-1000

Rochester
Finger Lakes Poison Center
LIFELINE
University of Rochester
    Medical Center
Rochester, NY 14642
716-275-5151
        275-2700
(TTY)

Schenectady
Ellis Hospital
Poison Control
1101 Nott St.
Schenectady, NY 12308
518-382-4039
        382-4121

Syracuse
Syracuse Poison Information
    Center
750 E. Adams St.
Syracuse, NY 13210
315-476-7529

Troy
St. Mary's Hospital
Poison Control Center
1300 Massachusetts Ave.
Troy, NY 12180
518-272-5792

Utica
St. Lukes Memorial Hospital
    Center
P.O. Box 479
Utica, NY 13502
315-798-6200

Watertown
House of the Good Samaritan
    Hospital
Washington & Pratt Sts.
Watertown, NY 13602
315-788-8700

NORTH CAROLINA

State Coordinator
Duke University Medical Center
Durham, NC 27710
919-684-8111
800-672-1697
(Statewide)

Asheville
Western North Carolina
    Poison Control Center
Memorial Mission Hospital
509 Biltmore Ave.
Asheville, NC 28801
704-255-4490

Charlotte
Mercy Hospital
2001 Vail Ave.
Charlotte, NC 28207
704-379-5827

Durham
Duke University Medical Center
Poison Control Center
P.O. Box 3007
Durham, NC 27710
919-684-8111

Greensboro
Triad Poison Center
Moses H. Cone Memorial
    Hospital
1200 N. Elm St.
Greensboro, NC 27401
919-379-4105

Hendersonville
Margaret R. Pardee
    Memorial Hospital
Fleming St.
Hendersonville, NC 28739
704-693-6522
Ext. 555

Hickory
Catawba Memorial Hospital
Fairgrove-Church Rd.
Hickory, NC 28601
704-322-6649

Jacksonville
Onslow Memorial Hospital
Western Blvd.
Jacksonville, NC 28540
919-577-2555

Wilmington
New Hanover Memorial Hospital
2131 S. 17th St.
Wilmington, NC 28401
919-343-7046

NORTH DAKOTA

State Coordinator
Department of Health
Bismarck, ND 58505
701-224-2388

Bismarck
Bismarck Hospital
Emergency Department
300 N. 7th St.
Bismarck, ND 58501
701-223-4357

Fargo
St. Luke's Poison Center
St. Luke's Hospitals
Fifth St. at Mills Ave.
Fargo, ND 58122
701-280-5575

Grand Forks
United Hospital
1200 S. Columbia Rd.
Grand Forks, ND 58201
701-780-5282

Minot
St. Joseph's Hospital
Third St. & Fourth Ave., S.E.
Minot, ND 58701
701-857-2553

Williston
Mercy Hospital
1301 15th Ave., W.
Williston, ND 58801
701-572-7661

OHIO

State Coordinator
Department of Health
Columbus, OH 43216
614-466-5190

Akron
Children's Hospital Medical
    Center of Akron
281 Locust St.
Akron, OH 44308
216-379-8562
800-362-9922
(Statewide)

Canton
Aultman Hospital
Emergency Room
2600 Sixth St., S.W.
Canton, OH 44710
216-438-6203
452-9911

Cincinnati
Drug & Poison Information Center
Bridge Medical Science Bldg.
Room 7701
231 Bethesda Ave.
Cincinnati, OH 45267
513-872-5111

Cleveland
Greater Cleveland Poison
    Control Center
2119 Abington Rd.
Cleveland, OH 44106
216-231-4455

Columbus
Central Ohio Poison Center
Children's Hospital of Ohio
700 Children's Dr.
Columbus, OH 43205
614-228-1323

Dayton
Children's Medical Center
One Children's Plaza
Dayton, OH 45404
513-222-2227
800-762-0727
(Statewide)

Lorain
Lorain Community Hospital
3700 Kolbe Rd.
Lorain, OH 44053
216-282-2220

Mansfield
Mansfield General Hospital
335 Glessner Ave.
Mansfield, OH 44903
419-522-3411
Ext. 2545

Springfield
Community Hospital
2615 E. High St.
Springfield, OH 44505
513-325-1255

Toledo
Poison Information Center
Medical College Hospital
P.O. Box 6190
Toledo, OH 43679
419-381-3897

Youngstown
Mahoning Valley Poison Center
St. Elizabeth Hospital
Medical Center
1044 Belmont Ave.
Youngstown, OH 44501
216-746-2222
216-746-5510
(TTY)

Zanesville
Bethesda Poison Control Center
Bethesda Hospital
2951 Maple Ave.
Zanesville, OH 43701
614-454-4221

OKLAHOMA

State Coordinator
Oklahoma Poison Control Center
Oklahoma Children's Memorial
Hospital
P.O. Box 26307
Oklahoma City, OK 73126
405-271-5454
800-522-4611
(Statewide)

Ada
Valley View Hospital
1300 E. 6th St.
Ada, OK 74820
405-332-2323
Ext. 200

Lawton
Comanche County Memorial
Hospital
3401 Gore Blvd.
Lawton, OK 73501
405-355-8620
Ext. 296

McAlester
McAlester General
Hospital Inc., W.
P.O. Box 669
McAlester, OK 74501
918-426-1800
Ext. 240

Oklahoma City
Oklahoma Poison Control Center
Oklahoma Children's Memorial
Center
P.O. Box 26307
Oklahoma City, OK 73126
405-271-5454
800-522-4611
(Statewide)

Ponca City
St. Joseph Medical Center
14th and Hartford
Ponca City, OK 74601
405-765-0584

Tulsa
Hillcrest Medical Center
1120 S. Utica
Tulsa, OK 74104
918-560-5755

OREGON

State Coordinator
Oregon Poison Control and
Drug Information Center
University of Oregon Health
Sciences Center
Portland, OR 97201
503-225-8968
800-452-7165
(Statewide)

PANAMA

Ancon
U.S.A. MEDDAC Panama
Gorgas U.S. Army Hospital
Ancon, Panama
APO Miami 34004
252-7500

PENNSYLVANIA

State Coordinator
Director, Division of Drugs,
Devices and Cosmetics
Department of Health
P.O. Box 90
Harrisburg, PA 17108
717-787-2307

Allentown
Lehigh Valley Poison Center
Allentown General Hospital
17th and Chew Sts.
Allentown, PA 18102
215-433-2311

Altoona
Keystone Region Poison Center
Mercy Hospital
2500 Seventh Ave.
Altoona, PA 16603
814-946-3711

Bloomsburg
The Bloomsburg Hospital
549 E. Fair St.
Bloomsburg, PA 17815
717-784-4241

Chester
Sacred Heart General Hospital
Ninth and Wilson Sts.
Chester, PA 19013
215-494-4400

Danville
Susquehanna Poison Center
Geisinger Medical Center
N. Academy Ave.
Danville, PA 17821
717-275-6116

Erie
Doctors Osteopathic Hospital
252 W. 11th St.
Erie, PA 16502
814-454-2120

Millcreek Community Hospital
5515 Peach St.
Erie, PA 16509
814-864-4031

Hamot Medical Center
201 State St.
Erie, PA 16550
814-452-4242

Saint Vincent's Health Center
232 W. 25th St.
Erie, PA 16544
814-452-3232

Gettysburg
Annie M. Warner Hospital
S. Washington St.
Gettysburg, PA 17325
717-334-9155

Hanover
Hanover General Hospital
300 Highland Ave.
Hanover, PA 17331
717-637-3711

Hershey
Capital Area Poison Center
The Milton S. Hershey
Medical Center
University Dr.
Hershey, PA 17033
717-534-6111
(Treatment)

Jersey Shore
Jersey Shore Hospital
ER-Poison Center
Thompson St.
Jersey Shore, PA 17740
717-398-0100

Johnstown
Conemaugh Valley Memorial
Hospital
Poison Control Center
1086 Franklin St.
Johnstown, PA 15905
814-535-5351

Laurel Highlands Poison Center
320 Main St.
Johnstown, PA 15901
814-535-8255

Mercy Hospital
Poison Control Center
1020 Franklin St.
Johnstown, PA 15905
814-535-5353

Lancaster
Lancaster General Hospital
ER-Poison Control Center
555 N. Duke St.
Lancaster, PA 17604
717-295-8322

St. Joseph's Hospital
Poison Control Center
250 College Ave.
Lancaster, PA 17604
717-299-4546

Lehighton
Gnaden-Huetten Memorial
Hospital
11th & Hamilton Sts.
Lehighton, PA 18235
215-377-1300

Lewistown
Lewistown Hospital
Poison Control Center
Highland Ave.
Lewistown, PA 17044
717-248-5411

Nanticoke
Nanticoke State Hospital
N. Washington St.
Nanticoke, PA 18634
717-735-5000

Paoli
Paoli Memorial Hospital
Emergency Room
Paoli, PA 19301
215-648-1043

Philadelphia
Philadelphia Poison Information
321 University Ave.
Philadelphia, PA 19104
215-922-5523
922-5524

Philipsburg
Philipsburg State General
Hospital
Loch Lomond Rd.
Philipsburg, PA 16866
814-342-3320

Pittsburgh
Pittsburgh Poison Center
Children's Hospital
125 DeSoto St.
Pittsburgh, PA 15214
412-681-6669
647-5600

Reading
Community General Hospital
145 N. 6th St.
Reading, PA 19601
215-375-9115

Sayre
The Robert Packer Hospital
Guthrie Square
Sayre, PA 18840
717-888-6666

Sellersville
Grandview Hospital
Lawn Ave.
Sellersville, PA 18960
215-257-3611

State College
Centre Community Hospital
Orchard Rd.
State College, PA 16801
814-238-4351

York
Memorial Osteopathic Hospital
325 S. Belmont St.
York, PA 17403
717-843-8623
Ext. 123

York Hospital
1001 S. George St.
York, PA 17405
717-771-2311

PUERTO RICO

State Coordinator
University of Puerto Rico
Rio Piedras, PR
809-765-4880
      765-0615

Arecibo
District Hospital of Arecibo
Arecibo, PR 00613
809-878-3535
Ext. 707
809-878-8212

Fajardo
District Hospital of Fajardo
Fajardo, PR 00649
809-863-0505

Mayaguez
Mayaguez Medical Center
Department of Health
P.O. Box 1868
Mayaguez, PR 00709
809-832-8686
Ext. 1816
      1514

Ponce
District Hospital of Ponce
Ponce, PR 00731
809-842-2550

Rio Piedras
Childrens Hospital Center
of Puerto Rico
Rio Piedras, PR 00936
809-754-8535

San Juan
Pharmacy School
Medical Sciences Campus
San Juan, PR 00936
809-753-4849

RHODE ISLAND

State Coordinator
Rhode Island Poison Center
Rhode Island Hospital
593 Eddy St.
Providence, RI 02902
401-277-5727

Providence
Rhode Island Poison Center
Rhode Island Hospital
Annex Bldg. 422
593 Eddy St.
Providence, RI 02902
401-277-5727

SOUTH CAROLINA

State Coordinator
Department of Health and
Environmental Control
Columbia, SC 29201
803-758-5654

Charleston
National Pesticide Tele-
communications Network
Medical University of
South Carolina
171 Ashley Ave.
Charleston, SC 29403
803-792-4201
800-845-7633
(Outside SC)

Columbia
Palmetto Poison Center
University of South Carolina
College of Pharmacy
Columbia, SC 29208
803-765-7359
800-922-1117

SOUTH DAKOTA

State Coordinator
Department of Health
Pierre, SC 57501
605-773-3361

Aberdeen
The Dakota Midland Poison
Control Center
Dakota Midland Hospital
1400 15th Ave., N.W.
Aberdeen, SD 57401
605-225-1880
800-592-1889

Rapid City
Rapid City Regional Poison
Control Center
353 Fairmont Blvd.
P.O. Box 6000
Rapid City, SD 57709
605-341-3333
800-742-8925

Sioux Falls
McKennan Poison Center
McKennan Hospital
800 E. 21st St.
Sioux Falls, SD 57101
605-336-3894
800-952-0123
(Statewide)
800-843-0505
(NE, MN, IA)

TENNESSEE

State Coordinator
Department of Public Health
Division of Emergency Services
Nashville, TN 37216
615-741-2407

Chattanooga
T.C. Thompson Children's
Hospital
910 Blackford St.
Chattanooga, TN 37403
615-755-6100

Columbia
Maury County Hospital
1224 Trotwood Ave.
Columbia, TN 38401
615-381-4500
Ext. 110

Cookeville
Cookeville General Hospital
142 W. 5th St.
Cookeville, TN 38501
615-526-4818

Jackson
Madison General Hospital
708 W. Forest
Jackson, TN 38301
901-424-0424
Ext. 525

Johnson City
Johnson City Medical
Center Hospital
Emergency Department
400 State of Franklin Rd.
Johnson City, TN 37601
615-461-6572

Knoxville
Memorial Research Center
Hospital
1924 Alcoa Hwy.
Knoxville, TN 37920
615-971-3261

Memphis
Southern Poison Center
LeBonheur Children's
Medical Center
848 Adams Ave.
Memphis, TN 38103
901-528-6048

Nashville
Vanderbilt University Hospital
21st and Garland
Nashville, TN 37232
615-322-6435

TEXAS

State Coordinator
Texas Department of Health
Division of Occupational Health
Austin, TX 78756
512-458-7254

Abilene
Hendrick Hospital
19th & Hickory Sts.
Abilene, TX 79601
915-677-7762

Amarillo
Amarillo Emergency Receiving
Center
Amarillo Hospital District
P.O. Box 1110
1501 Coulter Dr.
Amarillo, TX 79175
806-376-4292

Austin
Brackenridge Hospital
14th & Sabine Sts.
Austin, TX 78701
512-478-4490

Beaumont
Baptist Hospital of Southeast
Texas
P.O. Box 1591
College & 11th St.
Beaumont, TX 77701
713-833-7409

Corpus Christi
Memorial Medical Center
P.O. Box 5280
2606 Hospital Blvd.
Corpus Christi, TX 78405
512-881-4559

El Paso
El Paso Poison Control Center
R.E. Thomason General Hospital
4815 Alameda Ave.
El Paso, TX 79905
915-533-1244

Fort Worth
W. I. Cook Children's Hospital
Cook Poison Center-Fort Worth
1212 W. Lancaster St.
Fort Worth, TX 76102
817-336-6611

Galveston
Southeast Texas Poison Center
The University of Texas
Medical Branch
Eighth & Mechanic Sts.
Galveston, TX 77550
713-765-1420

Harlingen
Valley Baptist Hospital
P.O. Box 2588
2101 S. Commerce St.
Harlingen, TX 78550
512-421-1859

Houston
Southeast Texas Poison
Control Center
Eighth & Mechanic Sts.
Galveston, TX 77550
713-654-1701

Laredo
Mercy Hospital
1515 Logan St.
Laredo, TX 78040
512-724-6247

Lubbock
Methodist Hospital
3615 19th St.
Lubbock, TX 79410
806-793-4366

Odessa
Medical Center Hospital
Poison Control Center
P.O. Box 7239
Odessa, TX 79760
915-333-1231

Plainview
Central Plains Regional
Hospital
2601 Dimmitt Rd.
Plainview, TX 79072
806-296-9601

San Angelo
Shannon West Texas
Memorial Hospital
120 E. Harris
San Angelo, TX 76901
915-653-6741
Ext. 318

San Antonio
Department of Pediatrics
University of Texas Health
Science Center at San Antonio
7703 Floyd Curl Dr.
San Antonio, TX 78284
512-223-6361
Ext. 473

Tyler
Medical Center Hospital
1000 S. Becham St.
Tyler, TX 75701
214-597-0351

Waco
Hillcrest Baptist Hospital
3000 Herring Ave.
Waco, TX 76708
817-753-1412

Wichita Falls
Wichita General Hospital
1600 8th St.
Wichita Falls, TX 76301
817-322-6771

UTAH

State Coordinator
Utah Department of Health
Division of Family Health
Services
Salt Lake City, UT 84113
801-533-6161

Salt Lake City
Intermountain Regional Poison
Control Center
50 N. Medical Dr.
Salt Lake City, UT 84132
801-581-2151

VERMONT

State Coordinator
Department of Health
Burlington, VT 05401
802-862-5701

Burlington
Vermont Poison Center
Medical Center Hospital
of Vermont
Burlington, VT 05401
802-658-3456

VIRGINIA

State Coordinator
Division of Emergency Medical
Services
Room 1102
109 Governor St.
Richmond, VA 23219
804-786-5188

Alexandria
Alexandria Hospital
4320 Seminary Rd.
Alexandria, VA 22314
703-379-3070

Arlington
Arlington Hospital
5129 N. 16th St.
Arlington, VA 22205
703-558-6161

Blacksburg
Montgomery County Community
Hospital
Rt. 460, S.
Blacksburg, VA 24060
703-951-1111
Ext. 140

Charlottesville
Blue Ridge Poison Center
University of Virginia
Hospital
Charlottesville, VA 22903
804-924-5543
800-446-9876
(TTY)
(Out-of-state)
800-552-3723
(TTY)
(Statewide)

Falls Church
Fairfax Hospital
3300 Gallows Rd.
Falls Church, VA 22046
703-698-3600

Hampton
Hampton General Hospital
3120 Victoria Blvd.
Hampton, VA 23661
804-722-1131

Harrisonburg
Rockingham Memorial Hospital
738 S. Mason St.
Harrisonburg, VA 22801
703-433-9706

Lexington
Stonewall Jackson Hospital
Lexington, VA 22043
703-463-9141
Ext. 219

Lynchburg
Lynchburg General Marshall
Lodge Hospital, Inc.
Tate Springs Rd.
Lynchburg, VA 24504
804-528-2066

Nassawadox
Northampton-Accomack Memorial
Hospital
Nassawadox, VA 23413
804-442-8700

Newport News
Riverside Hospital
500 J. Clyde Morris Blvd.
Newport News, VA 23601
804-599-2050

Norfolk
DePaul Hospital
Granby St. at Kingsley La.
Norfolk, VA 23505
804-489-5288

Petersburg
Petersburg General Hospital
Mt. Erin & Adams St.
Petersburg, VA 23803
804-861-2992

Portsmouth
U.S. Naval Hospital
804-398-5898
Portsmouth, VA 23708

Richmond
Central Virginia Poison Center
Medical College of Virginia
Virginia Commonwealth University
P.O. Box 522, MCV Station
Richmond, VA 23298
804-786-9123

Roanoke
Southwest Virginia Poison Center
Roanoke Memorial Hospital
Belleview at Jefferson St.
P.O. Box 13367
Roanoke, VA 24033
703-981-7336

Staunton
King's Daughter's Hospital
P.O. Box 3000
Staunton, VA 24401
703-885-6848

Waynesboro
Waynesboro Community Hospital
501 Oak Ave.
Waynesboro, VA 22980
703-942-4096

Williamsburg
Williamsburg Community Hospital
1238 Mt. Vernon Ave.
P.O. Drawer H
Williamsburg, VA 23185
804-253-6005

VIRGIN ISLANDS

Coordinator
Department of Health
St. Thomas, VI 00801
809-774-6097
    774-0117

St. Croix
Charles Harwood Memorial
Hospital
Christiansted
St. Croix, VI 00820
809-773-8331

St. John
Morris F. DeCastro Clinic
Cruz Bay
St. John, VI 00830
809-776-6252

St. Thomas
Knud-Hansen Memorial Hospital
St. Thomas, VI 00801
809-774-9000
Ext. 224/5
809-774-1212

WASHINGTON

State Coordinator
Department of Social and
Health Services
Seattle, WA 98115
206-522-7478

Seattle
Seattle Poison Center
Children's Orthopedic
Hospital and Medical Center
4800 Sand Point Way, N.E.
Seattle, WA 98105
206-634-5252
800-732-6985

Spokane
Spokane Poison Center
Deaconess Hospital
W. 800 5th Ave.
Spokane, WA 99210
509-747-1077
800-572-5842
(Statewide)
509-747-1077
(TTY)

Tacoma
Mary Bridge Poison
Information Center
Mary Bridge Children's Hospital
South L St.
Tacoma, WA 98405
206-272-1281

Yakima
Central Washington Poison Center
Yakima Valley Memorial
Hospital
2811 Tieton Dr.
Yakima, WA 98902
509-248-4400
800-572-9176
(Statewide)

WEST VIRGINIA

State Coordinator
The West Virginia Poison System
West Virginia University
School of Pharmacy
3110 MacCorkle Ave., S.E.
Charleston, WV 25304
304-348-4211
800-642-3625
(Statewide)

WISCONSIN

State Coordinator
Department of Health and
Social Services
Division of Health
Madison, WI 53701
608-267-7174

Eau Claire
Eau Claire Poison Center
Luther Hospital
1225 Whipple
Eau Claire, WI 54701
715-835-1515

Green Bay
Green Bay Poison Center
St. Vincent Hospital
835 S. Van Buren St.
Green Bay, WI 54305
414-433-8100

LaCrosse
St. Francis Medical Center
700 West Ave., N.
LaCrosse, WI 54601
608-784-3971

Madison
Madison Area Poison Center
University Hospital & Clinic
600 Highland Ave.
Madison, WI 53792
608-262-3702

Milwaukee
Milwaukee Poison Center
Milwaukee Children's Hospital
1700 W. Wisconsin Ave.
Milwaukee, WI 53233
414-931-4114

WYOMING

State Coordinator
Office of Emergency Medical
Services
Department of Health and
Social Services
Cheyenne, WY 82002
307-777-7955

Cheyenne
Wyoming Poison Center
DePaul Hospital
2600 E. 18th St.
Cheyenne, WY 82001
307-635-9256
800-442-2704

Appendix B:
Keeping Your
Medical Records

IN TIMES PAST, most people had a family doctor who cared for them from cradle to grave. This physician was likely to know a patient's entire medical history, as well as that of parents, brothers and sisters, even grandparents and neighbors. Of course, this has all changed; today we still may have a primary-care physician, but our medical care is likely to come from a number of sources: specialists, hospitals, clinics or out-patient departments, and so forth. Also, in our highly mobile society, we may move every few years and have to seek out a new health-care team. As a result, our individual medical records are likely to be widely scattered. This is why it is increasingly important that each individual assume the responsibility for keeping his or her own medical records.

On the following pages, you will find samples of the kinds of charts and records that each person should keep. By having a comprehensive medical history that includes such things as laboratory test results, x-ray examinations, medications, and a complete record of physician or hospital visits, you can often avoid unnecessary duplication of tests and treatments. Most of us keep such records of our automobile maintenance; keeping a personal medical history can be even more valuable and important.

The charts on the following pages are designed to get you started in keeping your own health records. They are adapted from the Personal Health Profile, a complete medical records system developed by Stanley Stevens, a hospital administrator and graduate of the Columbia University School of Public Health. The complete 104-page guide is designed for either individual or family use. For information on obtaining the complete guide, write: Personal Health Profile, Inc., 59 Harrington Avenue, Closter, NJ 07624; (201) 768-1463.

Form 1 **FAMILY TREE**

Name _____   Soc. Sec. No. _____

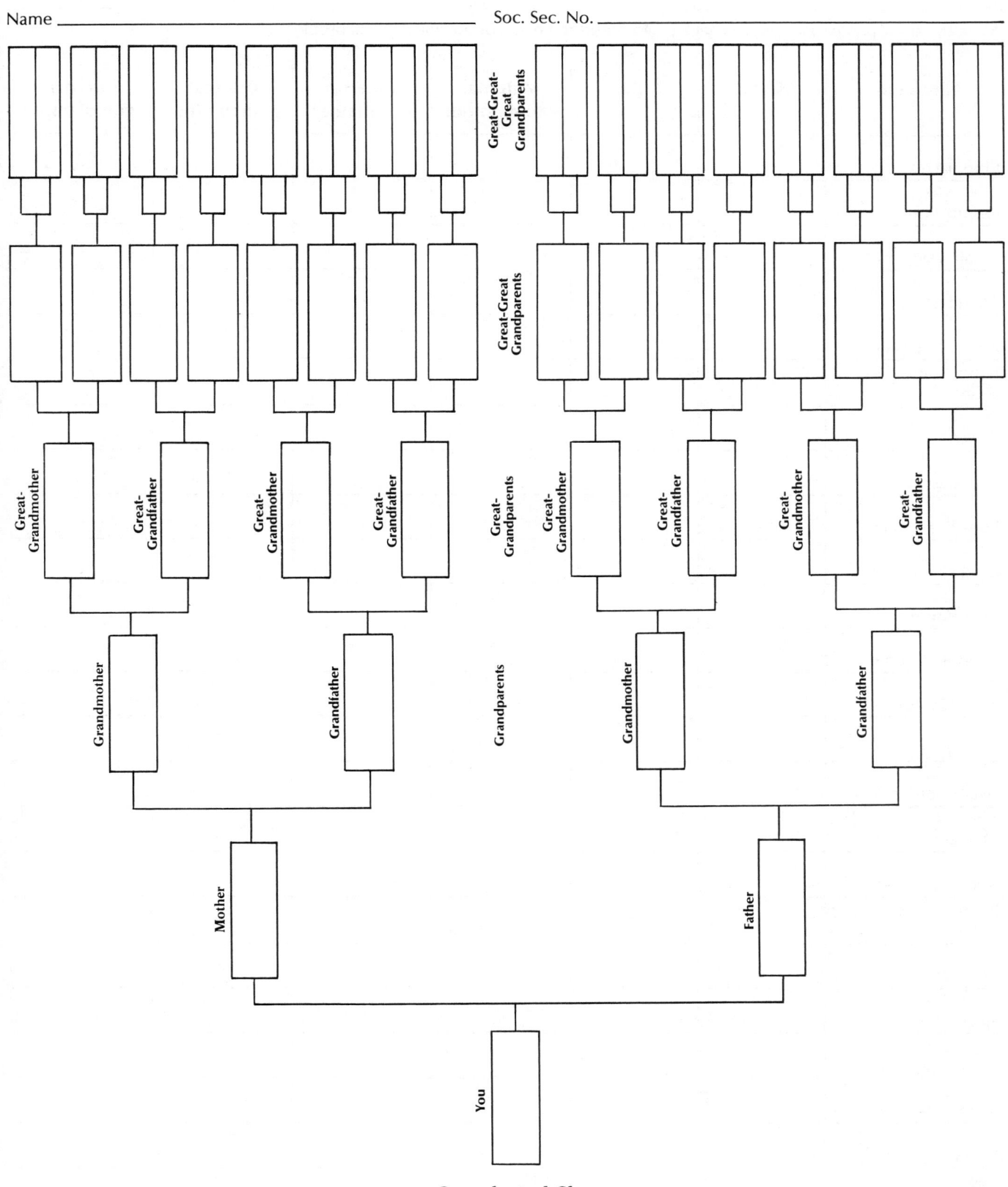

Genealogical Chart

Form 2 **FAMILY MEDICAL HISTORY**

Name _____ Soc. Sec. No. _____

Mark the appropriate space with a check ( ) or insert the name of specific medical problem.

Problem	Mother	Father	Maternal grandmother	Maternal grandfather	Paternal grandmother	Paternal grandfather
Birthplace						
Occupation						
Alcoholism						
Allergies						
Blood/Circulation						
Bones/Joints (where)						
Cancer						
Diabetes						
Digestive system						
Drug sensitivities						
Eye disorder						
Hearing disorder						
Heart disorder						
Kidney disorder						
Liver disorder						
Mental disorder						
Nerves/Muscles						
Reproductive system						
Respiratory system						
Stroke						
Urinary problem						
Major surgery						
Other						
Age/ Cause of death						

© *Personal Health Profile, Inc.*

Form 3 **RECORD of MAJOR MEDICAL PROBLEMS**

Name _____ Soc. Sec. No. _____

For quick review, major medical problems are separated from minor ones. Major problems are those that caused hospitalization, surgery, or an emergency. In the third column, summarize treatment and also refer to other pertinent charts (e.g., medications or x-rays)

Date	Major medical problem	Treatment, other forms

Form 4 **RECORD of MINOR MEDICAL PROBLEMS**

Name _____ Soc. Sec. No. _____

Minor medical problem—any accident or medical problem requiring treatment.

Date	Minor medical problem	Treatment, other forms

Form 5 **YOUR INFANT PROFILE**

Name _____ Male _____ Female _____

Date of birth _____ Day of week _____ Time _____

Place of birth _____ Birth certif. no. _____
City   County   State

Hospital _____ Address _____

Obstetrician _____ Address _____

Pediatrician _____ Address _____

Weight at birth _____ Length _____ Blood type _____ Rh factor _____

Color of eyes _____ Color of hair _____

Mother's maiden name _____

Mother's birthplace _____

Father's name _____

Father's birthplace _____

Birth defects, if any _____

_____

_____

Other information _____

_____

_____

_____

_____

_____

_____

_____

_____

Form 6 **RECORD of IMMUNIZATIONS and INFECTIOUS DISEASES**

Name _____ Soc. Sec. No. _____

A. Record of Immunizations

Immunization for	Age	Date	Booster Age	Date	Booster Age	Date	Booster Age	Date
Diphtheria								
Pertussis								
Tetanus								
Polio								
Smallpox								
Typhoid								
Rubella (Ger. measles)								
Mumps								
Measles								
TB								
Other								

B. Record of Infectious Diseases

Disease	Age	Date	Remarks
Chicken pox			
Measles			
Rubella (Ger. measles)			
Hepatitis			
Mumps			
Polio			
Pneumonia			
Pertussis			
Scarlet fever			
Other			

© *Personal Health Profile, Inc.*

Form 7 **RECORD of DOCTORS' VISITS**

Name _____ Soc. Sec. No. _____

Date _____ Age _____ Cost of visit _____

Doctor's name _____ Specialty _____

Reason for visit _____

Treatment prescribed _____

Comments _____

_____

Form 8 **RECORD of PRESCRIPTIONS and MEDICATIONS**

Name _____ Soc. Sec. No. _____

Date	Medicine prescribed	Rx No.	Pharmacy	Doctor	Cost

Form 9 **RECORD of HOSPITAL ADMISSIONS**

Name _____ Soc. Sec. No. _____

Date admitted _____ Date discharged _____ Age_____

Hospital _____ Tel. _____

Address _____

Hospital chart no. _____ Length of stay _____ Cost _____

Reason for admission _____

Doctor's name _____ Tel. _____

Discharge Plan _____

© *Personal Health Profile, Inc.*

Form 10 RECORD of EYE EXAMINATIONS

Name _____ Soc. Sec. No. _____

Date _____ Age _____ Eye problem _____

Vision: R.E. (OD) _____ L.E. (OS) _____ Color vision _____

Corrected: R.E. (OD) _____ L.E. (OS) _____

Prescription for eye glasses: R.E. (o.d.) _____

                                                        L.E. (o.s.) _____

Intra ocular tension (Glaucoma) _____

Other _____

Doctor _____ Cost _____

Form 11 RECORD of DENTAL CARE

Name _____ Soc. Sec. No. _____

Date	Tooth no.	Procedure	Dentist	Cost

Art Credits

The editors and publishers would like to thank the following individuals and organizations that provided the illustrations for this book:

American Cancer Society, New York, NY, figures 20.11 A & 20.11 B, page 416. American Heart Association, Dallas, TX, figures 6.1–6.25, pages 89–98. Douglas L. Cramer, figure 22.1, page 454; figure 22.2, page 454; figure 24.3, page 511; figure 27.7, page 556; figure 28.4, page 574; figure 38.3, page 762. Leonard Dank, figure 24.6, page 518; figure 25.2, page 525; figure 27.2, page 550; figures 35.2A & 35.2B, page 696. Robert Demarest, An Atlas of the Major Organ Systems, follows page 146; figure 10.1, page 137; figure 10.2, page 138; figure 10.3, page 141; figure 10.4, page 145; figure 10.5, page 145; figure 11.1, page 165; figures 11.2 & 11.3, page 180; figure 11.4, page 180; figure 11.5, page 182; figure 11.6, page 183; figure 11.7, page 183; figure 11.8, page 185; figure 11.9, page 187; figure 11.10, page 187; figure 11.11, page 188; figure 11.12, page 189; figure 11.13, page 191; figure 24.1, page 506; figure 27.1, page 549; figure 28.5, page 575; figure 29.1, page 589; figure 37.2, page 739; figure 38.1, page 757. Glenna Deutsch, figure 4.1, page 50; figure 4.2, page 54; figures 4.3A & 4.3B, page 55; figure 4.4, page 59; figure 4.5, page 60; figure 4.6, page 64; figures 4.7A & 4.7B, page 65; figure 4.8, page 66; figure 4.9, page 67; figure 4.10, page 70; figures 4.11A & 4.11B, page 72. Marsha Dohrmann, figures 19.1A & 19.1B, page 363; figure 19.2, page 371; figures 19.3A–19.3E, pages 375–377; figures 19.4A–19.4D, pages 378–379; figure 19.5, page 382; figure 19.6, page 383; figure 19.7, page 386; figure 19.8, page 387; figure 19.9, page 388; figure 19.10, page 390; figure 19.11, page 392; figure 19.12, page 393; figure 29.3, page 590; figure 36.1, page 711. Carol Donner, figures 27.8A–27.8C, page 559. Douglas Dunn, figure 21.1, page 428; figure 21.2, page 428; figure 21.3, page 429; figure 21.4, page 429; figures 22.4A & 22.4B, page 462; figure 25.4, page 534; figure 28.1, page 565; figure 28.2, page 570; figure 28.3, page 574. Neil Hardy, figure 5.1, page 78; figure 5.2, page 84; figure 6.26, page 100; figure 6.27, page 102; figure 7.1, page 109; figure 7.2, page 115; figure 7.3, page 117; figures 7.4A & 7.4B, page 118; figure 7.5, page 122; figure 22.3, page 457; figure 22.5, page 466; figure 24.5, page 514; figure 25.2, page 531; figure 25.3, page 533; figure 27.5, page 554; figure 27.9, page 561; figure 29.2, page 589; figure 30.1, page 603; figure 31.3, page 627; figure 33.1, page 652; figure 33.2, page 653; figure 33.3, page 654; figure 33.4, page 659; figure 33.5, page 659; figure 33.6, page 663; figure 33.7, page 667; figure 33.8, page 670; figure 34.1, page 673; figure 34.2, page 675; figure 34.3, page 677; figure 34.4, page 682; figure 34.5, page 683; figure 34.6, page 685; figure 34.7, page 686; figure 34.8, page 686; figure 34.9, page 688; figure 35.1, page 691; figure 35.3, page 693; figure 35.4, page 694; figures 35.5A & 35.5B, page 696; figure 35.6, page 700; figure 38.2, page 761; figures 38.4A & 38.4B, page 764. Kittie Herman, figure 24.7, page 521. John Karapelou, figure 6.28, page 103; figure 10.8, page 152; figure 10.9, page 153; figure 20.10, page 410; figure 24.5, page 509; figure 24.4, page 514; figures 27.8A & 27.8B, page 553; figure 27.6, page 556; figure 31.1, page 620; figure 31.2, page 621; Lauren Keswick, figure 13.1, page 237; figure 13.2, page 238; figures 14.1–14.3, page 268; figures 14.4–14.6, page 269; figures 20.1–20.4A & 20.4B, pages 405–407; figure 20.5, page 408; figure 20.6, page 408; figure 20.7, page 408; figure 20.8, page 409; figure 20.9, page 409; figure 21.5, page 436; figure 21.6, page 447; figure 21.7, page 449; figure 22.6, page 467; figure 23.1, page 475; figure 23.2, page 476; figure 23.3, page 477; figures 23.4–23.14, pages 488–491; figures 23.15 & 23.16, page 492; figure 23.18, page 501; figure 27.3, page 551; figures 28.6A & 28.6B, page 577; figure 32.1, page 639; figure 37.1, page 737; figure 37.3, page 749; figure 37.4, page 749; figure 37.5, page 751. Serono Laboratories, Boston, MA, figure 10.7, page 150. Squibb-Novo, Inc., Princeton, NJ, figure 23.17, page 493. Beth Willert, figure 30.2, page 610.

Figures 31.1 and 31.2 adapted from *Skintelligence*, by R. Walzer, Appleton-Century Crofts, 1980. Reprinted by permission of the author.

Figures 33.2 and 33.5 adapted from *Cataracts: The Complete Guide from Diagnosis to Recovery for Patients and Families*, by Julius Schulman, M.D., Simon & Schuster, 1984. Reprinted by permission of the publisher.

Index

in elderly, and dementia, 733
exercise after intake of, 308
and eye problems, 660
and fatty liver disease, 520
in gout management, 578
in hepatitis, 248, 519–520
and indigestion, 510
in influenza, 431
and intestinal gas, 517
with laryngitis, 432
lifestyle changes, benefits of, 288
liver metabolism of, 134
in myocarditis, 389
and nosebleeds, 683
and peptic ulcers, 512
in pregnancy, 173, 182, 348–349
and psychoses, 718
and rosacea, 628
safety considerations
automobile, 84
swimming and boating, 85
winter activities, 87
and vomiting, 508
Alcoholics Anonymous, 351, 352
Alcoholism, 716
acetaminophen and, 787
blood tests, 53
cirrhosis, 520
diagnosis of, 350–351
directory of health organizations and resources, 798
effects of alcohol, 346–348
fetal alcohol syndrome, 348–349
hepatitis, alcoholic, 347, 520
and infertility, 152
and living sober, 352
and magnesium deficiency, 298
nose deformities in, 683
and pancreatitis, 522
and peripheral neuropathy, 599
prevention of, 352
profile of, 349–350
treatment of, 351–352
tuberculosis in, 437, 467
withdrawal syndromes, 113, 348–350
Aldosterone, 179, 504
in Addison's disease, 503–504
adrenal gland production of, 503
in pregnancy, 179
renin and, 604
Alkaline phosphatase, 53
Alkalinity. *See* pH
Alkalis, poisoning by, 125
Alkylamine, 640
Allergic alveolitis, 472
Allergic rhinitis, 644, 684
Allergy, 15
in adolescents, 247
anaphylaxis, 650
asthma, 221–222, 463, 646–647
common misconceptions about, 638
defined, 634
dermatitis with, 624–625
directory of health organizations and resources, 798–799
drug, 648, 778–779. *See also* Drugs and medications, allergy to
informing doctor, 773
and kidney inflammation, 606
evaluating, 640–641
to eyedrops, 658
eye symptoms, conjunctivitis, 663
first-aid kit contents, 79
first-aid procedures, 105–106

and flu vaccine, 465
food, 647–648
in infant, 199, 204, 210
in infant, breast feeding and, 197
genetic inheritance of, 146
and headache, 591
immune system role in, 638–640, *639*
immunizations, 325
insect, 649–650
avoidance, 650
bee sting, 107
diagnosis, 649
prevention, 650
treatment, 649
and itching, 623
to jellyfish stings, 108
and nasal polyps, 685
occupational exposures, 318
occupational lung disease, 471–473
poison ivy, 121–122
principles of treatment, 641
respiratory, 644–646
alveolitis, 472
diagnosing, 646
other inhalant allergies, 644–645
rhinitis, 644, 684
treatment, 646
skin, 624–625, 641–643
atopic dermatitis, 641
contact dermatitis, 625, 641–643
physical reactions, 643
urticaria and angioedema, 643
vulvar, 745
skin reactions
in drug allergy, 648
itching, 623
Allergy medications
drug interactions, 780
home medicine cabinet supplies, 770
Allergy shots, 646
Allopurinol (Zyloprim), 578, 611, 777
Alopecia, 636
Alpha-1-antitrypsin, 455
Alpha-adrenergic blockers, 775
Alpha cells, of pancreas, *476*
Alpha-fetoprotein, in amniotic fluid, 169
Alprazolam (Xanax), 716
Alternaria, allergy to, 644
Alternative health care philosophies, 34–35
Aluminum hydroxide antacids. *See* Antacids
Alupent (metaproterenol), 777
Alveolar proteinosis, 467
Alveoli, 453, 454
allergic alveolitis, 472
in asthma, 462, *462*
Alzheimer's disease, 271, 592–593, 733
Amalgam fillings, 698
Amantadine, 431, 465
Amblyopia, 652, 662–663, *663*
choroiditis and, 670–671
Ambulance, in emergencies, 77
Ambulatory-care nurse specialists, 11
Ambulatory surgical centers, 20
Amebiasis, 450, 532
Amenorrhea, 249, 740
Amino acid metabolism
biotin and, 296
hereditary metabolic disorders, 65
Amino acids, 134, 293, 298
4-Aminobiphenyl, 316
Aminoglycosides, 261, 774, 779
Aminophylline, 650
Amitryptiline (Elavil), 712, 781
Ammonia, in jellyfish stings, 108

Amnesia, 116, 349
Amniocentesis, 65, 148, 169, 496
Amniotic fluid, assessment of fetal maturity, 190
Amoxapine (Asendin), 713
Amoxicillin, 223, 442
Amphetamines
abuse of, 354
adolescent use of, 253
delirium with, 718
drug interactions, 780
Amphojel, in kidney failure, 617
Amphotericin B, 447
Ampicillin
allergy to, 648
in arthritis, infectious, 441
birth control pills and, 139
drug interactions, 139, 779
rashes with, 643
Amputation
in diabetes, 481
first-aid procedures, 106
in peripheral vascular diseases, 390, 391
rehabilitation after, 804
Amyl nitrate, use as drug, 357
Amyotrophic lateral sclerosis (ALS), 599
Anacin, 606
Anal fissure, 534
Anal fistula, 534–535
Analgesics. *See also* Acetaminophen; Aspirin;
Nonsteroidal anti-inflammatory drugs;
specific drugs
in ankylosing spondylitis, 580
in arthritis, rheumatoid, 571
for cancer pain, 422
and constipation, 526
drug interactions, 606, 779
in headache, 591
home medicine cabinet supplies, 770
kidney toxicity of, 606
for menstrual cramps, 743
prescription, 776
strong, 776
in trigeminal neuralgia, 598
Anaphylaxis, 638, 650
after bee sting, 107
in drug allergy, 629, 778
first-aid procedures, 105–106
Anaprox. *See* Naproxen
Androgens, 777. *See also* Sex hormones, male
and acne, 246, 627
adolescent use of, 253
adrenal, 475
and external genitalia, female, 738
Anemia
in adolescence, 246
aplastic, 540–541
in arthritis, rheumatoid, 571
and behavioral changes in elderly, 265
bone marrow aspiration, 54
breathing difficulties in, 453
and constipation, 527
folacin and, 296
folic acid deficiency, 540
hemolytic, 540
in intestinal disease, 526
colon cancer, 410
hookworm, 450
malabsorption syndromes, 515, 516
ulcerative colitis, 530
iron deficiency, 246, 298, 539
in kidney disease, 607, 615
in liver disease, 519
cancer, 412
cirrhosis, 520

oral hypoglycemics and, 495
in vaginitis, 446
and vasculitis, 586
Sulfamethoxazole (Bactrim, Gantanol, Septra), 781
Sulfasalazine, 529, 530
Sulfinpyrazone (Anturane), 578, 780
Sulfonylurea oral hypoglycemics, 494, 495
Sulfur, 297–298
Sulfur oxide, 468
Sulindac (Clinoril), 572, 606, 777
Sunburn
  eye, 656
  first-aid procedures, 111
Sun exposure
  aging and, 264
  birth control pills and, 140
  after chemosurgery, 266
  drugs affecting sensitivity to, 140, 781
  emergencies, sunstroke, 121
  eye injuries, 663–664
  and hives, 629
  and keratoses, 630
  myths about, 635
  and rosacea, 628
  skin barriers to, 620
  and skin cancer, 420, 424
  and skin damage, 622
  in systemic lupus erythematosis, 582
Sunscreens, and hives, 643
Sun stroke, 121
Superior vena cava, 363
Superoxide dimutase, 258–259
Support groups
  in alcoholism, 351
  for diabetic adolescent, 497
  in Type 2 diabetes, 494
Suppositories, 534, 648
Suppressor T cells, 428, 429
Supraventricular tachycardia, 374
Surfactant, 459
Surgeon, choosing, 18
Surgery, 9, 15
  for adrenal insufficiency, 504
  and anal fissure, 534
  for anal fistula, 535
  for aneurysms, 391–392
  for appendicitis, 221, 532
  for arthritis, 568
  for blood vessel disease, 390–391
  for Buerger's disease, 391
  for cancer, 398, 399, 400
  cataract, 668–669
  and cerebrovascular disease, 386
  for cholesteatoma, 678
  coronary artery bypass, 381–382, 382, 381–382
  cosmetic, 266
  elective, 26–28
    admission, 27
    operating room, 27–28
    preoperative, 27
    recovery, 28
  with endocarditis, 388, 437
  eyelid, 666
  family practitioner's training in, 12
  for gallbladder disease, 521
  for glaucoma, 664
  and glucose levels, 478
  for goiter, 502
  and hair loss, 636
  for hemorrhoids, 534
  for hiatal hernia, 514
  and impotence, 765
  for impotence, 766

and infertility, 150
for intestinal blockage, 528
and intestinal obstruction, 516
joint replacement, 576
for kidney stones, 612
laser. See Laser surgery
for liver cancer, 412
and lung embolism, 456
for malocclusions, 706
for Meniere's disease, 679
nose, 683
and osteomyelitis, 442
ovarian cyst rupture during, 753
for paraphimosis, 763
for peptic ulcer management, 512
for pericarditis, 388
for periodontal disease, 701
for prostate disorders, 763–764
for Raynaud's phenomenon, 391
for retinal detachment, 670
for rheumatoid arthritis, 573–574
second opinion, 17
for sinusitis, 434
with spinal cord injury, 601
for trigeminal neuralgia, 598
for ulcerative colitis, 530
for urinary incontinence, 755
and urinary tract stones, 611
for urinary tract stones, 760–761
for uterine fibroids, 752
and vaginal inclusion cysts, 748
vascular, endarterectomy, 594
for venereal warts, 762
vertebral fusion, 552
and vomiting, 508
for weight loss, 306
Surgicenters, 20
Surmontil (trimipramine), 713
Suspensory ligament, 653
Swallowing
  in dermatomyositis, 586
  dysphagia (difficulty with), 412, 513
  in esophageal cancer, 412
  eustachian tube in, 673
  in Guillain-Barré syndrome, 599
  in scleroderma, 585
  in stroke, 593
Swallowing disorders, and malocclusion, 706
Swayback, 550, 551, 551, 555
Sweating
  in drug withdrawal, 113
  and fungal skin infections, 633
  with gastrointestinal pain, 509
  in heart attacks, 119
  in insulin reactions, 112, 479
  in shock, 104
  with vomiting, 508
Sweat-producing glands, 621
Swelling. See also Edema
  abdominal, in females, 740
  in drug allergies, 648
  in food allergy, 647
  in hypovolemic shock, 103
Swimmer's ear, 223, 432, 674, 711
Swimming
  eye protection, 656
  with otitis media, 677
  safety considerations, 85
Sympathetic nervous system
  in Buerger's disease, 391
  drugs acting on, 775
  heartbeat regulation, 373
  in high blood pressure, 373
Sympathetic ophthalmia, 657

Syncope, 113, 375, 592
Syphilis, 444–445
  in infertility, 151
  in pregnancy, 168, 176–177
    and miscarriage, 182
    and premature labor, 184
Syphilis blood test, systemic lupus erythematosis and, 584
Systemic herpes infections, 445
Systemic lupus erythematosus. See Lupus erythematosus
Systemic vasculitis, 587
Systems review, 16
Systolic pressure, 365, 366

T
Tablets, 783
Tacaryl (methdilazine), 640
Tachycardia, 373
  smoking and, 310
  ventricular, 374
Takayasu's disease, 587
Talc, and lung disease, 471
Talwin (pentazocine), 776, 780
Tampons, 237, 738, 739
  in cystitis, 755
  and toxic shock syndrome, 438, 741–742
Tandearil, 495
Tannic acid, as home remedy, 771
Tanning, myths about, 635
Tantrums, 208, 214–215
Tar ointments, 629, 641
Tardive dyskinesia, 720
Taste sense, 133
Tavist (clemastine), 640
Tay-Sachs disease, 65, 147
T-cell lymphomas, 545
T cells, 428, 429, 639, 639
  in contact dermatitis, 642
  types of, 544
Tea, as home remedy, 771
Teaching hospitals, 9, 24
Tear glands, 653, 666, 667
Technetium pyrophosphate, 56
Technology
  advances, 3–4
  misuse and overuse, 6–7
Technology for Independent Living Resource Guide, 795
Teeth. See also Dental health
  in bulimia, 252
  calcium and, 297
  in children, 212
  development, 690–692, 691
  and headache, 591
  impacted, 691
  phosphorus and, 298
  vitamin A and, 295
  vitamin D and, 295
Teething, 203, 205, 703
Tegretol (carbamazepine), 595, 598, 779
  drug interactions, 779
  in epilepsy, 595
  in trigeminal neuralgia, 598
Telephone numbers, in emergencies, 77
Telescoped intestine, 61, 528
Telogen effluvium, 636
Temperature
  heat exhaustion, 121
  hypothermia, 120–121
Temperature, body. See also Fever
  in infertility, 151
  ovulation and, 166
Temporal arteritis, 587